MIKRA

To the memory of my teacher and friend, Martin J. Mulder, who died in 1994 some years after the first publication of the *Mikra* volume. Martin Mulder combined patient and meticulous scholarship in the field of Hebrew and Old Testament studies with a fine sense for the mutually enriching cooperation of Jewish and Christian scholars in the exploration of their common heritage, the Hebrew Bible. The aim of the Compendia series, to offer a comprehensive presentation of the world of ancient Judaism and early Christianity, was very near to his heart. His death was a great loss to all who knew him.

Harry Sysling
January 2004

Bible Codex, Oriental Square Script of the Latter Prophets, Hosea 1:1-2:6, 10th-11th c. (JTS 232, ENA 346a, f. 97b).
Courtesy of the Library of the Jewish Theological Seminary, New York (Elkan Nathan Adler Collection).

MIKRA

Text, Translation, Reading & Interpretation
of the Hebrew Bible
in Ancient Judaism & Early Christianity

MARTIN JAN MULDER, EDITOR
HARRY SYSLING, EXECUTIVE EDITOR

© 2004 Hendrickson Publishers, Inc.
P. O. Box 3473
Peabody, Massachusetts 01961-3473

ISBN 1-56563-255-9

Printed in the United States of America

First Printing — August 2004

Originally published in 1988 by Van Gorcum, Assen, The Netherlands as part of the series *Compendia Rerum Iudaicarum ad Novum Testamentum*. Copyright © 1988 Stichting Compendia Rerum Iudaicarum ad Novum Testamentum.

Library of Congress Cataloging-in-Publication Data

Mikra : text, translation, reading, and interpretation of the Hebrew Bible in
    ancient Judaism and early Christianity / Martin Jan Mulder, editor ;
    Harry Sysling, executive editor
        p. cm.
    Originally published: Assen : Van Gorcum ; Philadelphia : Fortress, 1988.
    Includes bibliographical references and index.
    ISBN 1-56563-255-9 (pbk. : alk. paper)
    1. Bible. O.T.—Criticism, interpretation, etc., Jewish—History. 2. Bible.
O.T.—Evidences, authority, etc.—History of doctrines. 3. Bible. O.T.—
Versions. 4. Bible. O.T.—Criticism, interpretation, etc.—History—Early
church, ca. 30–600. 5. Judaism—History—Post-exilic period, 586 B.C.–210
A.D. I. Mulder, M. J.

    BS1186.M535 2004
    221'.09'01—dc22
                                                    2004047447

Preface

In June 1987, the first part of Volume Three in Section Two was presented to the public. Thereby a further step was made towards the realization of the ambitious project which is now well-known in scholarly and interested circles under its long Latin title *Compendia Rerum Iudaicarum ad Novum Testamentum*. In the Foreword to that volume, we expressed the hope that the next book would be published in the first half of 1988. We are only a few months later than we expected.

Although it is the last to appear, the present volume was planned as Volume One in Section Two. For good reasons we have maintained the original numbering of the volumes. This volume is devoted to *Mikra* – Scripture. It describes the origins of the Hebrew Bible, the history of its composition, its acceptance by various groups and its earliest translations. Its 'authoritative' interpretation by the Qumran Covenanteers, by Hellenistic Jewish authors and by the early Church Fathers is discussed. The exegesis of Mikra in Rabbinic Writings, in Samaritan and Gnostic circles is dealt with and much attention is paid to the use of the Hebrew Bible in the New Testament Church.

The Board of the Compendia Foundation feels deeply obliged to Professor Dr. M.J. Mulder of the University of Leyden who has been the inspiring editor of this volume right from the beginning. It is largely thanks to him that so many scholars of international repute have contributed to this volume. To all these distinghuished authors we are most grateful. We feel sure this publication will take its place in the scholarly literature on the subject and we confidently hope that it will be welcomed by scholars and interested laymen alike as a great help better to understand the complicated connections between ancient Judaism and early Christianity.

Books like the present one cannot be published without the dedicated assistance of an Executive Editor. The Board wishes to express its deep gratitude to drs. H. Sysling who with great expertise and painstaking exactitude bore all the vicissitudes that seem of necessity to accompany the production of a volume like the present one.

This publication was made possible through grants from a number of institutions to all of which we express our indebtedness. Of these we wish to mention specifically the Prins Bernard Fonds of Amsterdam and the Anne Frank Fonds of Basle.

The Board deeply regrets the untimely death of Professor Dr. H. Kremers of the University of Duisburg. Heinz Kremers took a keen and active interest in the aims of the Compendia from the very beginning. Even before the present Foundation had been set up, he took part in the deliberations of what was then called the 'Working group'. The learned world has lost an eminent scholar, those involved in the Jewish-Christian dialogue are bereaved of a courageous pioneer, and the Foundation mourns the loss of a dedicated friend.

R.A. Levisson

NOTE ON TRANSLITERATION

For the transliteration of Hebrew and Aramaic words the system of the *Encyclopaedia Judaica* (1971, vol. 1, p. 90) has generally been followed. This includes differentiation between a general and a more scientific rendering. Exceptions are the use of *ts* to represent *tsade* in the general system, and the use of the diacritical sign which is restricted to the more refined system. The same rules are adopted for titles of rabbinic works and names of Sages. Biblical names are given in their traditional forms.

ACKNOWLEDGEMENTS

The chapter on Transmission of the Biblical Text and the Introduction by M.J. Mulder were translated from the Dutch by P.J. Booij. The article of Ch. Perrot (Reading of the Bible in the Ancient Synagogue) was translated from the French by K. Smyth, and the contribution of R. Kasher on Rabbinic Literature was translated from the Hebrew by J. Feldman. Stylistic revisions of the articles by D. Dimant and R. Kasher were made by K. Smyth and H.S. Lake. A quantity of stylistic improvements were introduced throughout by P.J. Booij. The Accumulative Bibliography was typed out by N. de Wilde. Indices were prepared by M. Bezemer.

Quotations of biblical passages are usually from the Revised Standard Version, translations of Philo and Josephus from the Loeb editions. The Mishna citations follow the translation of H. Danby. In certain cases, however, a free rendering is given where a particular interpretation requires so.

The editors gratefully acknowledge permission to reproduce manuscript passages from the following libraries: Biblioteca Ambrosiana, Milano; Bodleian Library, Oxford; Cambridge University Library, Cambridge; Jewish Theological Seminary, New York; Hebrew Union College Library, Cincinatti, Ohio.

List of Illustrations

Contents

XV

Introduction

Notwithstanding its already considerable size, this volume of Section Two of the *Compendia Rerum Iudaicarum ad Novum Testamentum* should not lack a brief introduction. It is the first of the three volumes planned for this section (*The Literature of the Jewish People in the Period of the Second Temple and the Talmud*), in spite of the fact that the second and part of the third volume have already been published (*Jewish Writings of the Second Temple Period, ed.* M.E. Stone, 1984; *The Literature of the Sages, ed.* S. Safrai, 1987). In the case of a lasting work such as this it is not so much the chronological order in which the separate volumes appear that matters, but rather the creation of a thematic and logical coherence in the survey of the unique literature of the Jewish people of the period of the Second Temple and of that which immediately followed it.

The first volume is concerned with the wording of the time-honoured tradition which was laid down in the *Mikra*[1] and has subsequently grown from it. Despite the existing variety of interpretations, *Mikra* primarily denotes the correct reading of the sacred words, as they have been handed down to us through the activities of numerous writers and copyists in the text of Tenakh, usually called 'the Old Testament' by Christians. *Mikra* (מקרא) further means the way in which the sacred text has always been and ought to be recited ('to recite' is one of the meanings קרא has in Tenakh) and understood by those who have been closely connected with the texts. The emphasis of this volume, as expressed by the title, is on the biblical text and its translations, especially in the period of the Second Temple and the talmudic era. This cannot, however, be separated from the way in which the texts were read and interpreted. Indeed, the text does not exist without its interpretation. This is what distinguishes this volume from the two which follow it. Its general theme is: how did the biblical books develop into *Mikra*, and how could this unique text give rise to such a wealth of interpretations? One may also approach the problem by asking how people looked at the Bible and used it during the periods in question. What factors contributed to the authority of the 'canonical' writings over the various religious groups in the period of the Second Temple? This regards not only the

---

[1] In this volume, terms like *Mikra*, Bible, 'Holy Scripture(s)', etc. are used indiscriminately.

authority of the 'sacred' text itself, but also the authority assigned to its legitimate interpreters. And how did one establish the hermeneutical rules ('modes of interpretation'), which were created to legitimize one's own community? Can one discover any common traditions of interpretation here?

It virtually goes without saying that the reader is informed about Jewish traditions which belong to Judaism and Christianity alike or contribute to one's understanding of these. Accordingly, while the general principle which underlies each volume of this second section is maintained, the same authors or literary genres are sometimes dealt with in different chapters from different perspectives. Thus, in vol. 2 one finds articles about the works of Flavius Josephus and Philo of Alexandria as historians, written by H.W. Attridge and P. Borgen respectively. In our volume, these classical Jewish authors are discussed in the articles by L.H. Feldman and Y. Amir, this time from the point of view of the subject of this volume: 'Use, Authority and Exegesis of *Mikra*'. These contributions are complementary, as the different approaches and the specific knowledge of their authors widen the variety of the information given about the writers in question.

The material of the present volume has been spread over three sections, in which two lines may be discerned throughout. In the first section, attention is given to the text of the Hebrew Bible. The problem of its genesis is dealt with after a discussion of the forms of writing in ancient Israel and in in the early post-biblical period. For this, it was necessary to go back to the period *before* the Second Temple. The chapter about the growth of the Hebrew Bible and the long process during which the books which ultimately gained authority within a specific community were accepted is followed by a discussion of the complex process of transmission of the biblical text, of which several details remain obscure. Here again, the limits set by the period of the Second Temple and the talmudic era appeared too narrow and had to be extended up to our own days, so that even the editions of the Hebrew Bible which are in common use today have been included.

In the second section, attention is focused on the translations. Essentially, translations are also interpretations of the original text; and the interpretation of a given text 'in one's own words' is really a kind of translation, too. This section opens with an article about the function of the Bible, *viz*. the reading of the Bible in the ancient Synagogue. This is followed by a number of chapters about the origins of several ancient translations. The earliest of these and the first to be treated is the Septuagint. In the case of the Peshitta it was necessary to discuss the fascinating question whether we have here a Christian, a Jewish-Christian or perhaps even an originally Jewish translation. The fact that during the period of the Second Temple Judaism was not restricted to a single current, not even with respect to the use and interpretation of *Mikra*, is also evident from the diversity of interpretations, *e.g.* from the use made of the Bible by the Qumran sect, and further from apocryphal and pseudepigraphical literature, from the Greek works written by Philo of Alexandria and Flavius Josephus and from the smaller works by other Hellenistic Jewish writers. This is the starting point of the third section of this volume, which continues with a chapter about the interpretation of the Bible in rabbinic literature. Here we are introduced to what has justly been considered the main current of Judaism. Until today, the Samaritan tradition has constituted a side current, while in between Judaism and Christianity, to be distinguished but never entirely to be separated from them, the 'third component of the European tradition of culture'[2] may be discerned: the *gnosis*. At this point, we turn our attention to the Christian Church, in which Tenakh was accepted as canonical under the name of 'the Old Testament', as is apparent from almost every page of the New Testament and from the writings of the Church Fathers. Here the specific problems concerning the biblical canon in the Early Church are discussed, with reference to what has been said in the chapter about the growth of the Hebrew Bible. This serves as an introduction to the interpretation of the 'Old Testament' in the 'New Testament' and in patristic literature.

Here we may again refer to the title of the entire work of which this volume forms a part: *Compendia Rerum Iudaicarum ad Novum Testamentum*. The title reflects the two themes which again become visible in the present volume: 'Jewish matters' and 'the New Testament', *viz.* Judaism and Christianity and their relationship to the sacred texts, to *Mikra*. In the first two sections it is obviously the first theme that receives our main attention: *Mikra* is preeminently a 'Jewish matter', even if Christians have sometimes been deeply involved in the making of the biblical text (*e.g.* in the Hebrew editions of the Bible) and the translations (such as the Septuagint and the Peshitta, and of course the Vulgate). The third section contains a discussion of the New Testament and Jewish traditions in the Early Christian Church. It may be repeated here, perhaps superfluously, that it would be wrong to assume that the New Testament ought to or is meant to be the point of departure or the focus of attention of the contributions appearing in *Compendia*[3]. Special attention will be given to the relationship of the New Testament and of Early Christianity to Jewish traditions in the following section of the *Compendia*.

I should like to conclude this introduction by expressing my sincere appreciation to all the contributors, whose expert articles in some cases were written years ago. Thanks are also due to the translators of those contributions which were not originally written in English. Above all, I want to thank drs. Harry Sysling, whose name will remain permanently linked to this volume as 'executive editor'. Without his great expertise, perseverance, accuracy and dedication, this volume would never have acquired its present form. The reader should praise him for its qualities, and blame any imperfections on me.

---

[2] For this characterization, see: G. Quispel (ed.), *Gnosis. De derde component van de Europese cultuurtraditie*, Utrecht 1988.

[3] *Pace* G. Vermes, 'Jewish Literature and New Testament Exegesis: Reflections on Methodology', in: *JJS* 33 (1982), 374.

I should like to repeat here in a slightly modified form the words with which M.E. Stone concluded the 'Introduction' to the volume he edited: 'It is our aspiration that this volume will exemplify a way of looking at *Res Iudaicae ad Novum Testamentum* that is organic, coherent and open.'

Martin Jan Mulder
March 1988

Chapter One

Writing in Ancient Israel and Early Judaism

Aaron Demsky and *Meir Bar-Ilan*

General Introduction

The biblical world view encompasses the full breadth of man's existence from his very beginning in the then known world. In its attempt to explain the fundamental questions of man's being, to wit creation, man's purpose, his relation to God and to nature, the Bible focuses on the history of Israel, which was a late arrival on the Ancient Near Eastern stage. Thus the Bible and later Judaism find expression within the parameters of the ancient world, shaped by the great civilizations of Mesopotamia, Egypt, Canaan and later Greece and interacting with them for over 2000 years in the political, social and cultural spheres. In the first section* of this chapter, we will explore one aspect of that interaction, namely *the art of writing*, its adoption and its diffusion in the biblical period, and how it impinged on education and shaped religious beliefs and institutions in ancient Israel. The second half of the chapter will illuminate the social status, literary activity and realia of *the Jewish scribes*, the bearers of the biblical tradition in late antiquity i.e. from the Hellenistic age until the end of the rabbinic period.

---

* Each section represents the independent views of its respective author and reflects their sometimes different emphasis and interpretation of the sources.

1

Part One:
The Biblical Period (A. Demsky)

The Various Systems of Writing Prevalent in the Ancient Near East

It has long been realized that the beginning of history is inherently bound up with the invention of writing. It enabled ancient man to communicate his mundane needs as well as his intellectual and religious reflections in explicit terms for both contemporary and future generations. This milestone in the story of mankind was achieved toward the end of the fourth millennium B.C.E. in ancient Mesopotamia.

The earliest written documents were found in Uruk (biblical Erech) dating from ca. 3100 B.C.E.[1] About eighty-five percent of the archaic texts from Uruk are economic in nature (receipts, lists of expenses and commodities). It is generally assumed that the need to control an expanding economy associated with temple properties and income was the main factor in the invention of writing. The remaining fifteen percent of these early tablets are lexical, i.e. lists of items organized according to different categories indicated by signs that act as determinatives e.g. *GIŠ* 'wood', *KI* 'place' etc. The latter have been deciphered for the most part on the basis of almost exact copies in a more developed script found in Fara, some 50 km north of Uruk and dating about 600 years later! They would indicate that almost at the inception of writing professional scribes began producing helpful lists of terms that would conventionalize the technique, reducing the subjectivity that might ensue with the spread of writing. The great similarity between the Uruk and Fara collections over a 600 year period further illustrates the conservative nature of the profession and particularly of the educative process.

During this period the Mesopotamian script changed from an earlier pictographic system to a signary of wedge-shaped signs commonly called cuneiform. Along with these external changes in form, the signs were given additional values that went beyond the original logogram representing a concrete word, or idea i.e. a picture of a FOOT read not only 'foot' but also 'go, walk'. Now signs could represent homophonous syllables producing a fully phonetic system. For example the sign representing the logogram *AN* 'god', could be written as well

---

[1] See Nissen, 'Archaic Texts', *passim.*

for the syllable *an*. The end result was a mixed writing system of hundreds of signs representing logograms (including class determinatives) and syllabograms (including phonetic complements).[2]

A parallel development can be noted for writing in Egypt, the other great civilization of the ancient Near East.[3] The earliest known writing is associated with the beginning of the Dynastic period (ca. 3000 B.C.E.), thus suggesting the adoption of the idea of writing from an earlier Mesopotamian model. Both scripts are similar in principle in that they employ a mixed logographic-syllabographic signary. However, the Egyptian syllabary closely reflected the local language. The syllabograms were reduced to the consonantal root without vowels producing a system with one, two or three consonantal signs. Similarly, the form of the pictographic hieroglyphs were indigenous inventions which did not change much in the course of 2000 years. Alongside this monumental script, two local cursive scripts developed: The hieratic which was a linear counterpart of the pictorial hieroglyphs and better suited for writing with pen and ink on papyrus, and the later demotic script which appears in the seventh century B.C.E.

During the second millennium B.C.E., we find a plethora of scripts in the Levant besides the above two dominant systems of writing. Several were influenced by the above two (Hittite hieroglyphics, Linear A and B, Cyprohieroglyphics). Others reflect local experimentation and still defy decipherment (Byblian 'Pseudo-hieroglyphics', the Deir 'Alla tablets and the Phaistos disk).[4]

THE INVENTION OF THE ALPHABET

The most significant development in writing since its inception and phonetization was the invention of the alphabet which occurred in Canaan in the first half of the second millennium. It then evolved over a five hundred year period from an almost completely pictographic script to a standardized linear signary conventionally written from right to left in the early Iron Age.[5]

The 'alphabetic revolution' was the ability to radically reduce writing from hundreds of logograms and syllabograms to approximately thirty signs. This breakthrough was based on a sophisticated analysis of the phonemic system of Canaanite, giving each phoneme an appropriate sign. Sir Alan Gardiner, assuming that the names of the letters of the alphabet in Hebrew and Aramaic represented original pictographs, proposed the acrophonic principle.[6] He suggested that the alphabetic sign was chosen because it represented a word which

---

[2] See Gelb, *Study of Writing*, chs. 3, 6; Hawkins, 'Origin and Dissemination', pp. 133-43.
[3] Hawkins, pp. 143-48.
[4] Hawkins, pp. 148-57; Hawkins, 'Writing in Anatolia', pp. 363-75.
[5] See Driver, *Semitic Writing*, chs 2 and 3; Naveh, *Early History*, pp. 23ff.
[6] Gardiner, 'Egyptian Origin', pp. 1-16. On the proto-Sinaitic script, cf. Albright's decipherment (*Proto-Sinaitic Inscriptions*) and especially Sass' dissertation *(The Genesis of the Alphabet)*, ch. 3.

began with that particular phoneme. For example the bucranium or 'ox (head)' is called *'alf* 'ox' in Canaanite and represents the initial phoneme *'a*, similarly *bēt* 'house' represents the phonemic value *b*. Gardiner demonstrated this principle in his deciphering of the proto-Sinaitic script, found in the turquoise mines of Serabit el Khadem in southern Sinai. In particular he interpreted four recurrent signs as *b'lt* 'lady', a plausible Canaanite epithet for the Egyptian goddess Hathor, 'the lady of turquoise', worshipped at that site. The acrophonic principle suggests that not only the letter forms but their names (and perhaps their basic order) are intrinsic aspects of the invention of this script. In fact, an abecedary found at Ugarit from the fourteenth century B.C.E. listing Babylonian syllabic equivalents indicates that the alphabetic letter names are at least that old.[7]

In his study of the history and evolution of writing systems, I.J. Gelb has identified the 'Semitic alphabet' as actually being a syllabary of consonant plus vowel and therefore closer to an Egyptian model.[8] He maintains that only with the Greek innovation of the consistent use of vowel signs does the script become a true alphabet.

While Gelb's suggestion is convincing in terms of the development of writing and the dependence of different systems upon each other, it still raises some questions. For one, the fact that the Canaanite signary had only thirty signs at the most, immediately sets it off from other syllabic-only systems, which produced a signary of at least three times that number. Furthermore, not only can the letter be read as consonant plus any vowel, but also as just consonant. This versatility, probably a result of the nature of the Canaanite language, where all words begin with a consonant (cf. the above mentioned acrophonic principle), was a source of ambiguity, though probably less so for the ancient native speaker than for the modern reader of the unpointed text. In any case, the Ugaritic scribes meeting their multilingual administrative needs began experimenting with graphemes indicating different vowel sounds at least for the *'alf* ('a, 'i, 'u). They also began to use the so called weak consonants (*w, y*) to write long vowels. This method of indicating long vowels by *scriptio plena* is documented already in ninth century B.C.E. alphabetic inscriptions (e.g. Tel Fekheryeh, Mesha Stele). So if the system is not a 'true alphabet' in Gelb's terms it is certainly much closer to its Greek offshoot than to any syllabary, in number of signs, letter forms, order, names and even in its irregularities of vowel indication ultimately corrected in a consistent fashion in the Greek alphabet.[9]

On the basis of the evidence at hand, it must be assumed that the alphabet was conceived in Canaanite scribal circles in the first half of the second millenni-

---

[7] Cross and Lambdin, 'Ugaritic Abecedary'. But see Hallo, 'Isaiah', who argues that the letter names are secondary.

[8] Gelb, *Study of Writing*, pp. 122ff.

[9] See Naveh *Early History*, p. 11; Millard, 'Infancy', p. 395.

um B.C.E. The originator was probably familiar with several systems of writing, the Egyptian one having the greatest influence upon him regarding the consonantal values of the signs and some of the hieroglyphic forms which he adopted.

The invention of the alphabet compares with the greatest intellectual achievements of mankind, for it seems to be the result of deliberate reflective thought about how to improve upon an existing technique. It was not a chance discovery of an innovative scribe but rather 'required thorough analysis of the phonemic stock of his language, an analysis perhaps facilitated by the common practice of listing words as part of school training.'[10] The leap of genius was the theory that one could now reproduce written speech by some twenty-five to thirty graphemes instead of hundreds of logograms and syllabograms. We may assume that the idea was given immediate form when the scribe applied the acrophonic principle deriving the letter form from pictographs or geometric shapes as well as giving each one its own name. It is plausible that a set order of the letters was established which followed a mnemonic song thereby facilitating the learning process and the dissemination of this new invention.

This revolutionary idea is all the more amazing for the fact that it was produced by and for a very conservative body of professionals, heirs to a 1500 year tradition of writing. We have no way of knowing what motivated the invention of the alphabet, whether it was the result of pure reflective thought for its own sake, or encouraged as an expression of local needs and cultural pride in forming an indigenous system of writing, or whether it was the outcome of social and economic drives to create 'a speed course' for scribes who were needed to fill a professional gap.

Whatever the case, the alphabetic idea, after undergoing half a millennium of refinement and experimentation, would finally become the official medium of writing in the emerging societies of the early Iron Age. After another five hundred years, it would become the dominant script in the whole ancient Near East and literate Mediterranean areas. The social and cultural consequences of the spread of the alphabet were manifold, ultimately leading to widespread literacy and the democratization of higher culture, as well as innovative conceptions of worship and social institutions.

THE EVOLUTION OF THE EARLY ALPHABET

The alphabet went through various stages before it became a widespread medium of communication in early antiquity. The development of the various alphabetic scripts can be described in the form of a family genealogy.[11]

The relatively long formative period of some five hundred years in the development of the proto-Canaanite script was probably caused by the cultural and socio-political factors bearing upon writing in Canaan during the Middle

---

[10] Millard, 'Infancy', p. 394.
[11] See Naveh, *Early History*, p. 10.

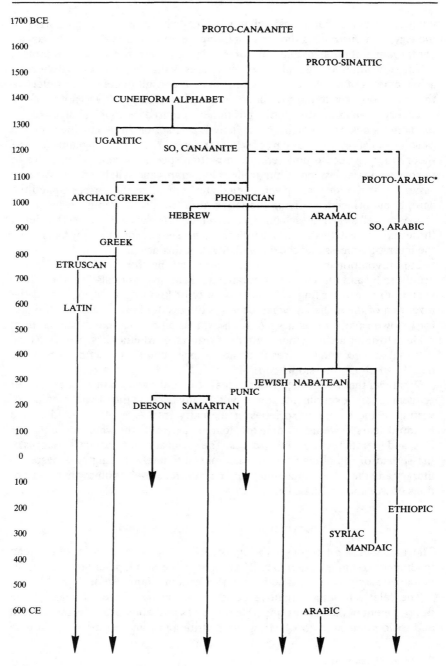

* Undocumented

6

Bronze IIB – Late Bronze periods.[12] The Canaanite city states were small administrative units, dominated politically and culturally by the great civilizations of Egypt and Mesopotamia and their northern neighbours, particularly the Hittites. The dependence of the conservative Canaanite scribal class upon the imperial writing systems further inhibited the development of the alphabet. However, during this period there was some local experimentation which produced some yet undeciphered scripts (Byblian pseudo-hieroglyph, Balu'ah inscription and the Deir 'Alla tablets). The Canaanite alphabet, radically different in conception and facility, became the most widespread and tenacious of the local scripts among the northwest Semites of the second millennium. The earliest of these alphabetic inscriptions is probably the pictographic *klb* from Gezer dated between 1700-1600 B.C.E.

In addition, the small corpus of less than forty inscriptions from Serabit el Khadm and its environs in south Sinai provides us with a full signary of some thirty letters. This system of writing was recognized as alphabetic writing of a Canaanite dialect and has been termed proto-Sinaitic.[13] There has been some discussion as to its date and position in the history of the alphabet. While most scholars accept a date around 1500 B.C.E. (Eighteenth Dynasty) others have argued for an earlier *ca.* 1800 B.C.E. date during the Twelfth Dynasty.[14] Since the south Sinai turquoise mines were worked over a long period of time, archaeological evidence can be brought in support of both dates. However, an earlier date would assume an unsupported theory that the alphabet was already invented in the Middle Bronze I period. The use of a highly pictographic alphabet in south Sinai has yet to be properly explained. It cannot be assumed that these mines were the source of inspiration of the alphabetic idea, i.e. the missing link with Egyptian script, nor can it be that this script was the invention of a supposed Canaanite slave labour force at this site. It is more than likely that the Semites writing Proto-Sinaitic were freemen, probably Canaanite merchants residing there.[15] It is quite plausible therefore that the so-called proto-Sinaitic alphabet was current in certain areas of southern Canaan like the Shephelah (Gezer, Lachish) or perhaps those cities bordering the Negeb from Gaza in the west to Hormah in the east.

One of the most interesting early developments was the application of the alphabetic principle to a cuneiform script written with stylus on clay tablets. This is no doubt the work of Canaanite scribes who perceived the advantages of the alphabetic principle combined with the status of cuneiform, studied in all the major centers of the ancient Near East. It is therefore not surprising that the main corpus of the cuneiform alphabet has been found at Ugarit and its

---

[12] Cross, 'Origins'; Millard, 'Infancy', see now the latest reassessment of the material by Puech, 'Origine', where he produces new drawings and some new readings for the mostly fragmentary linear inscriptions.

[13] Albright, *Proto-Sinaitic Inscriptions*.

[14] This problem has been discussed recently by Sass, *Genesis of the Alphabet*, pp. 161-69.

[15] *Ibid.*, p. 173. Cf. the inscribed Gezer jars dated to ca. 1600 B.C.E., Seger, 'Gezer Jar Signs'.

environs, where there were intense demands on writing in five known languages.[16] The Ugaritic alphabet, made up of thirty characters was used to write letters, administrative documents and especially Canaanite poetry and mythology.

This alphabet followed the basic letter order known from the later Phoenician alphabet, plus some five graphemes reflecting the full Semitic phonemic system (cf. classical Arabic). The scribes added another three letters to meet their needs for further precision. A variation on this system was already found in the Ugaritic archives, where a reduced cuneiform alphabet, written right to left represented a south Canaanite dialect. Other examples of the cuneiform alphabet have been found at such Canaanite sites as Beth-Shemesh, Taanach, Mt. Tabor and Sarepta, north of Tyre, as well as at Kamid el Loz in the Beqa'a. We may assume that alphabetic cuneiform was widespread among Canaanite scribes who used it for local administrative and literary needs. It disappeared with the destruction of Ugarit ca. 1200 B.C.E. and a bit later in the south, a victim of the new order which wiped away the direct Mesopotamian and Egyptian political and cultural domination.

During the thirteenth-twelfth centuries, we find more inscriptions in proto-Canaanite, though generally in fragmentary form. However, some are probably votive in nature like the Lachish ewer deciphered by Cross: *mtn: šy [lrb]ty 'alt*[17] i.e. 'Mattan. An offering to my Lady 'Elat', as well as the Lachish bowl and bowl from Qubur el Walaydah, near Tel el Far'ah in the Negeb.[18] Other inscriptions might be of an administrative nature, like the Beth-Shemesh ostracon and the Radana handle. The ostracon from 'Izbet Sartah near Tel Aphek was a writing exercise containing the earliest example of the twenty-two letter linear alphabet. It is noteworthy that it was incised from left to right and reflects a local tradition which transposed the letter order to *hēt-zayin* and *pe-'ayin*.[19]

To sum up, the major characteristics of proto-Canaanite are:

(1) The alphabet was invented ca. seventeenth century B.C.E., by Canaanites who had some knowledge of Egyptian writing.

(2) It was based on an acrophonic principle producing some 27 graphemes.

(3) For the most part, the letter forms were originally pictographic.

(4) The names and basic order of the letters were part of the original conception.

(5) The direction of writing was not set but rather dextrograde, sinistrograde, boustrophedon and vertical.

(6) The stance of most of the letters was often rotated ninety or one-hundred and eighty degrees.

(7) There were local traditions regarding the order of some of the letters.

[16] See Rainey, 'The Scribe at Ugarit'.
[17] Cross, 'Origin', p. 16.
[18] Cross, 'Newly Found Inscriptions', pp. 2-4.
[19] Demsky, 'Proto-Canaanite Abecedary'; *idem*, ''Izbet Sartah Ostracton'.

(8) The script is lapidary, though a more developed hand might have been used for writing on papyrus or skin, for which we have no examples.

THE NATIONAL SCRIPTS

During the first half of the first millennium B.C.E, three national scripts developed in Syria-Palestine from Proto-Canaanite: Phoenician, Hebrew and Aramaic.[20] The former script was used by the Phoenicians on their mercantile ventures around the Mediterranean as early as the eleventh century, as evidenced by inscriptions from Nora and Crete. By the ninth century it received the distinction, along with the Tyrian dialect, of becoming the medium of monumental inscriptions of local rulers (Kilamuwa of Samal [Zengirli] and Azitawada in Cilicia). With some minor variation it was later found in the western colonies, principally in Carthage, and is termed the Punic script.

The Hebrew script, first documented in the ninth century, was more restricted to the two Israelite Kingdoms and their periphery (Mesha Stele). During the period of the First Commonwealth it did not change much. It continued to be used in Second Temple times, but by the late third century B.C.E. it was superseded by the Jewish script (i.e. the so-called 'square' or 'Assyrian' script), which developed from the Aramean signary.

The Aramaic script had a greater circulation and was the least conservative in its development, especially once this script along with the spoken language (cf. 2 Kgs 18:26), became the international means of communication adopted by the neo-Assyrian empire. While the known Aramaic inscriptions of the ninth century are clearly local adaptions of the Phoenician script, the recently found contemporary Tel Fekheryeh inscription uses archaic signs sometimes closer to the 'Izbet Sartah ostracon of the twelfth century B.C.E.[21], indicating a more direct link with proto-Canaanite. Only in the Hellenistic period, when Aramaic was no longer the official language of the government, do we begin to note the more rapid evolution and diversification of the script into national styles.[22]

The Jewish exiles who returned to Zion from Babylon had adopted customs prevalent in the gentile environment where they had lived. They used the Babylonian month names (e.g. Nisan, Tishri, Kislev), and assumed foreign names (e.g. Mordecai, Esther, Zerubbabel). Alongside the Hebrew language and script, they began to use the Aramaic script and language. Some of the letter names were given Aramaic equivalents (e.g. *zayin*, *resh*).

By the third century B.C.E., a local Jewish script with its own characteristics developed out of the standard Aramaic.[23] It is documented in some early biblical manuscripts from the Dead Sea Scrolls. The Rabbis, attributing this

---

[20] Naveh, *Early History*, ch. 4.
[21] Abu-Assaf et al. *La Statue de Tell Fekherye*; But cf. Naveh 'Fekheryeh Inscription', who dates the script to the eleventh century B.C.E.
[22] Naveh, *Early History*, ch. 5.
[23] Cross, 'Jewish Scripts'.

square script to Ezra, called it *k'tav ashûrī* meaning either 'the Assyrian script', noting the historic circumstances of its foreign derivation, or the apologetic 'authorized script' *(me'ushar)*. It ultimately supplanted the Old Hebrew script termed by the Rabbis pejoratively as *k'tav ra'aṣ*, alternately *k'tav da'aṣ* (*Deeson* by the Church Fathers), or *k'tav lebona'ah*. By the end of the Second Temple period, the Jewish script was widely used for monumental and burial inscriptions and in biblical manuscripts, as well as for sundry graffiti.[24] In Judah, however, coins from the late Persian period were struck with Hebrew letters. Naveh has suggested that this is the case when the language is clearly Hebrew, whereas when the legend is Aramaic, the script follows suit.[25] Similarly, the Hasmonean kings (135-37 B.C.E.), the leaders of the First Revolt (66-70 C.E.) as well as Shimon Bar Kokhba (132-135 C.E.) struck coins in the Hebrew script. Indeed this phenomenon may be an expression of nationalistic tendencies. The Hebrew script is found in some of the Dead Sea Scrolls from Qumran where they denote sanctity. Such is the case where Hebrew characters are written for divine names such as the Tetragrammaton *(YHWH)* in scrolls using the Jewish script.

Fragmentary inscriptions with Hebrew letters have been found in Jerusalem as well as in Masada. Noteworthy is a seven-line epitaph found intact in a Jerusalem burial cave dating from the Herodian period. The text is Aramaic and is probably that of a heterodox sectarian or political separatist.[26] Diringer has suggested, quite plausibly, that the Old Hebrew script was widely employed by the Sadducees.[27] Judging from the Qumran material, it would seem that it had more currency among non-Pharisaic elements in the late Second Temple and early Roman periods. Indeed, normative Judaism expressed a strong negative attitude towards its use (*B.T. Sanhedrin* 21b-22a, *T. Sanhedrin* 4:5; *P.T. Megilla* 71 b-c). Rabbi Yehuda the Patriarch went so far as to claim that the square Jewish script was the original signary of the Tora only to be changed to Hebrew as a sign of the sin of the Golden Calf, and ultimately restored by Ezra. The Samaritan community has maintained this script down to the present.[28]

The Spread of Literacy in Ancient Israel

In the centuries of the second and first millennia B.C.E. (ca. 1700-330 B.C.E.) which form the chronological framework of biblical narrative during which almost all of Old Testament literature was composed, two basic patterns of literacy existed in the ancient Near East. The predominant form was the limited literacy of the highly trained professional scribes in the main cultural centers of Mesopotamia and Egypt and their peripheral offshoots. The second form

---

[24] Avigad, 'Palaeography of the Dead Sea Scrolls'.
[25] Naveh, *Early History*, pp. 114ff.
[26] *Ibid.*, pp. 123f.
[27] Diringer, 'Early Hebrew Script'.
[28] See Crown, 'Studies in Samaritan Scribal Practices'.

existed in the emerging literate societies, where writing skills could be found among various levels of society.[29]

The former pattern was determined for the most part by the complicated system of writing of hundreds of logo-syllabic signs that were mastered over a long period of in-training. The end result of this education was the control of virtually all the imperial, municipal, temple and civilian administration by a relatively small corps of professional scribes. Though there were times of expanded uses of writing, such as the Old Babylonian period (18-16th centuries B.C.E.), the number of literati probably never exceeded 2-5% of the population at any given time in ancient Mesopotamia and Egypt.[30]

The restricted 'scribal culture' is noteworthy for the formal educative process which not only trained the initiate in the technique of writing but also in the rudiments of such various subjects as mathematics, astronomy and engineering; it also fostered a professional *esprit* and the highest regard for being literate.

On the other hand, the simplified alphabet opened new vistas for the spread of higher culture. Its facility and obvious utility, in addition to new historical and social dynamics which characterized the Early Iron Age in Syria and Palestine, hastened the standardization of this local script. In particular, ancient Israel, having adopted the Canaanite alphabet early in its history and having left the most detailed record of its culture in the Bible, is the best subject for the study of an ancient literate society.[31]

The two main bearers of the Israelite literary culture were the priesthood, whose beginnings predate the Conquest and Settlement (late 13th century B.C.E.) and the royal bureaucracy established by King David (early 10th century B.C.E.). These groups were the link to the higher culture of the ancient Near East and through them the Canaanite literary legacy was reshaped to Israel's outlook. During the period of the First Commonwealth, others, like the prophets, craftsmen and farmers, adopted the medium of writing for their specific needs.

FORMAL EDUCATION

Formal scribal education,[32] which in its most elementary stage was probably widespread, can best be understood in the light of the biblical text and old Hebrew inscriptions. The key to literacy is obviously learning the alphabet. Early in its development, if not at its very conception, the order of the letters was established, which with minor changes has been maintained for 3500 years! The earliest abecedaria were found in Ugarit (14th century B.C.E.) in the alphabetic cuneiform. They represent a full northwest Semitic phonemic sys-

---

[29] Demsky, 'Extent of Literacy', p. 350.
[30] Oppenheim, *Ancient Mesopotamia*, esp. ch. 5; Baines, 'Literacy and Ancient Egyptian Society'; Baines and Eyre, 'Four Notes on Literacy'.
[31] Demsky, 'Extent of Literacy', *(passim)*.
[32] See Demsky, 'Education'; Lemaire, *Écoles*.

tem of twenty seven signs plus three additional signs added by local scribes for clarity in writing other languages. The placing of the additional letters at the end indicates that the main body and order was established before this date. Another text found at Ugarit gives the initial signs of their names, written in Babylonian syllabic script, proving the antiquity of the letter names.[33] Learning the established order was probably facilitated by a mnemonic song. Minor fluctuations of the letter sequence have been noted in the earliest linear abecedary found in 'Izbet Sartah (ca. 1200 B.C.E.), where the usual *zayin-hēt* and *'ayin-pe* have been reversed.[34] The latter reversal became standard among some scribal circles in Judah (e.g. Lamentations 2, 3, 4 and the Kuntilat 'Agrud abecedaries). Elementary exercises like combining different letters were developed, preferably by dividing the alphabet into equal halves and writing the first and twenty second (last) letter, second and twenty-first, third and twentieth and so on. This sequence is called *'at-bš (atbash)*. It was so common a learning practice procedure in the late Monarchy that the prophet Jeremiah inserted it into his prophecies, sure that it would be understood by his urban audience (Jer 25:26; 51:1, 41).[35]

By the late seventh century B.C.E., the letter order became a literary device for forming alphabetic acrostics of prophecy (Nah 1:2-11), religious song (e.g. Pss. 9-10, 34, 119, 145; Lam 1-4) and wisdom tracts (Prov 31:10-31; Sir 51). The letter sequence was also recognized as a memory aid for ordering information (Zech 8:14, cf. Isa 3:20).[36]

Learning the alphabet during the biblical period might have been more commonplace than is usually accepted and we might have to assume that the sundry abecedaria that have been discovered at Lachish, Kadesh Barnea and at Kuntilat 'Agrud as well as the late Second Temple examples from Gezer and Muhmas were the graffiti of non-professionals passing the time. In any case, knowledge of the alphabet created a passive literacy in the Israelite society. It should be mentioned in this context that the two ancient Hebrew references to literacy (i.e. Isa 29:11-12 and *Lachish letters* 3:8-9) specifically refer to the knowledge of reading *(yedi'at qr'o)* and not to the active aspect of writing and composition.

For those who learned to write, a frequent exercise was to practice the writing of their own name which they may have inscribed on pottery or other household items in order to indicate possession. Of course the need to prepare lists for administrative purposes was essential to a scribal education (cf. Judg 8:14).

Along with continued exercises in penmanship, the young scribe was introduced to encyclopaedic lists of objects and concepts from the world around him. Such was the case in the great centers of scribal culture in Mesopotamia

[33] Cross and Lambdin, 'Ugaritic Abecedary'.
[34] Demsky, 'Proto-Canaanite Abecedary'.
[35] Demsky, 'Sheshakh'.
[36] Demsky, "Izbet Sartah Ostracon', p. 143 and Puech, 'Abécédaire'.

and Egypt. These lists brought together like items (e.g. gods, geographical terms, titles, liquids, wooden and metal utensils, etc.) written with the same determinatives in the logo-syllabic scripts. No doubt they played an important practical part in scribal training. While these lists were probably learned by rote, the better student began to develop a more analytic perception of the world about him, which forms the basis of true knowledge. An elementary text of this general type might be the Gezer calendar, dividing up the year into agricultural seasons. As Albright noted, the text is set to metre and while a writing exercise, it was also learned by heart and recited orally.[37] Encyclopaedic lists are ascribed to King Solomon, 'the wisest of all men', who composed a list of flora 'from the cedar in Lebanon to the hyssop that grows out of the wall' (1 Kgs 5:13). Furthermore, he discoursed about the four genera of fauna: beasts, birds, creeping things and fishes in descending order of complexity. In the priestly schools, these categories were subdivided empirically i.e. on the basis of external characteristics, into pure and impure species (Lev 11; Deut 14:3-21). Similarly, the races of mankind (Gen 10) were determined by ethnic, linguistic and geographical considerations, though not by pigmentation. In fact, it has been suggested that Job 38-39 is actually based on a quiz of a teacher on the order of nature,[38] a subject familiar to the more advanced student of both the wisdom and priestly schools.

The scrivener then went on to learn the practical skills of writing contracts and letter formulae. There is a growing number of letters that have been uncovered written with ink on potsherd. These documents are called ostraca; the main collections from the biblical period have been found at Tel Arad and at Tel Lachish, dating for the most part to the beginning of the 6th century.[39] Registration of taxation at Samaria (early 8th century) and a judicial plea from Mesad Hashavyahu (late 7th century) should also be mentioned. There is evidence that most official documentation was written on papyrus imported from Egypt.[40] In order to carry out his duties, the young scribe at least learned how to prepare ink *(deyo)*, draw his lines and columns *(delet)* and cut the scroll *(megilla)*, for which he carried his utensils in a special case called a *qeset*, an Egyptian loan word (see Jer 36:18, 23; Ezek 9:2).

Upon entering government service in the royal courts of Jerusalem and Samaria, the more advanced scribe was called upon to specialize in various areas which moderns might term diplomacy and the exact sciences. Of course as we learn from the Egyptian scribal model,[41] his Israelite colleague probably mastered disciplines in both categories in addition to developing an efficiency in administration as well as a knowledge of the wisdom literature.

---

[37] Albright, 'Gezer Calendar'; *ANET*, p. 320.
[38] Von Rad, 'Hiob'.
[39] Pardee, *Handbook*, chs. 1-5.
[40] Haran, 'Scribal Workmanship'.
[41] Williams, 'Scribal Training'.

Uppermost for this level of education was the knowledge of foreign languages, primarily the *lingua franca*. Up until the rise of the Assyrian empire in the latter half of the eighth century, Phoenician was probably the most needed for international trade conducted by the court as well as for area diplomacy in Syria and Palestine.[42] For the latter period of the monarchy Aramaic became the medium for diplomatic exchange with the world empires (2 Kgs 18:26f.).[43]

The advanced scribe had to be familiar with international trade agreements (e.g. 2 Chr 2:2-25) and drawing up parity and vassal treaties as well as fealty oaths. The scribe had to know diplomatic etiquette, which no doubt included some knowledge of foreign literature, a fact that might explain the recognition of the works and lives of non-Israelite wisemen (Job, Agur bin Jakeh and Lemuel, king of Massa) in Wisdom books cultivated by the courts (cf. Prov 25:1).[44]

The court scribe was called upon to supervise the building of cities, fortifications and storehouses (1 Kgs 9:15, 2 Chr 8:3-6; 26:15) as well as other engineering feats (see 2 Kgs 20:20; 2 Chr 32:1-4, 30) that demanded the knowledge of higher mathematics and the preparation and reading of building and city plans as well as cartography (Josh 18:1-10; Ezek 4:1-2; 1 Chr 28:19).[45] Other functions connected with intercalation of the lunar and solar calendar assumed some knowledge of astronomy (Job 38:31-33). All in all, we must assume that there existed a school at the royal capitals for the training of the king's scribes. Adjunct to this program must have been one for the courtiers as well as for the royal entourage, seeing that the ideal king was to be literate (Deut 17:18-19; 2 Kgs 23:2; see also 1 Chr 27:32).

It was probably at these schools that the scribal ethic was conveyed and embellished and where the high standards demanded for government service, celebrated in the Book of Proverbs (e.g. Prov 8:15ff.),[46] as well as for copying texts were set.[47] Furthermore, these wisemen produced the court literature including the official records and texts for royal inscriptions in addition to hymns for special occasions in the life of the Israelite king composed by the court singers, inspired by David, the first and foremost member of this guild (1 Sam 16:16-23; 2 Sam 1:17-27; 22; 23:1-7; Amos 6:5).

---

[42] Mazar, 'The Philistines'.

[43] Mazar, 'The Aramean Kingdom'.

[44] The connection between Prov 22:17-24:22 and the Egyptian Sayings of Amenemope has long been recognized, see Eissfeldt, *Old Testament*, pp. 474f.; *ANET*, p. 421-25 (tr. J.A. Wilson).

[45] For a review of an Egyptian scribe's studies in these fields see 'A Satirical Letter', *ANET*, pp. 475-79 (tr. J.A. Wilson).

[46] See the illuminating Egyptian compositions 'In Praise of Learned Scribes' and 'The Satire on the Trades', *ANET*, pp. 431ff. (tr. J.A. Wilson).

[47] Millard, 'In Praise of Ancient Scribes'.

POPULAR LITERACY

Opinions have differed widely regarding the extent of popular literacy during the monarchy. While some scholars, particularly those of the Uppsala school,[48] have denied the widespread use of writing prior to the Exile, there is a renewed consensus especially among epigraphists that writing was common in ancient Israelite society.[49] The problem of determining the extent of popular literacy is basically methodological since there are no direct, absolute or objective criteria for measuring literacy.[50] In order to overcome this difficulty, we choose to speak in terms of a 'literate society', that is where writing was familiar to and employed by laymen in all walks of life.[51] We propose five criteria for determining the extent of popular literacy. After examining the existent Old Hebrew inscriptions and biblical sources according to these criteria, it will be shown that at least during the last two hundred years of the monarchy (750-586 B.C.E.), ancient Israel can be termed a literate society.

For one, there is an increasing sum of inscribed Hebrew personal seals reaching into the hundreds from this period.[52] A relatively high number have no iconographic motif. It has been suggested that this was due to the Josianic reform and ban on graven images. However, if we assume that the seal served a basically administrative function, noting ownership or supervision, and that aesthetic considerations were secondary, then the first criterion for wider literacy would be *the choice of a written word in place of a symbol or picture* for self-identification.[53]

A second indicator would be the *relative ubiquity of a vulgar script* on seals, jar-handles and graffiti. Various gradations of expertise in writing have been discerned on Old Hebrew inscriptions,[54] the more prominent being a formal professional hand and a free cursive used by the intelligentsia. The vulgar form would suggest that the common folk were writing simple notations.

Thirdly, the Hebrew epigrapha present an array of *inscriptions that were written by and for craftsmen and farmers* clearly not of the scribal and priestly classes. This material reflects the adoption of writing by potters, ivory joiners and builders and also includes a number of inscriptions concerning viticulture.[55]

The fourth criterion is drawn from the classical or so called Writing Prophets who lived between the late eighth to early fifth centuries B.C.E. Moved by the

---

[48] See Nielsen, *Oral Tradition*; Engnell, *A Rigid Scrutiny*, but compare the important work of Widengren, *Literary and Psychological Aspects* where he convincingly argues for both the oral and written aspects of literary composition and publication in antiquity.

[49] Naveh, 'Palaeographic Note'; Millard, 'Practice of Writing'; *idem*, 'Assessment'.

[50] Schofield, 'Measurement of Literacy'.

[51] Demsky, 'Extent of Literacy'.

[52] Avigad, 'Seal, Seals'.

[53] However, several seals from this period have iconographic motifs which easily reflect the owner's name, a sort of a personal symbol or emblem, a fact that might indicate the bearer's illiteracy. For example, see Avigad, 'Hebrew Seal'.

[54] See Naveh, 'Palaeographic Note'; Cross, 'Epigraphic Notes II' and 'Epigraphic Notes III'.

[55] See Demsky, 'The Genealogy of Gibeon', *idem*, 'Dark Wine'.

imperative to write down their prophesies, they clearly saw the potential in writing to illustrate and popularize their message.[56] In essence the prophetic presentation (e.g. Isa 8:1, Ezek 37:16; Hab 2:2) is a striking example of *the bridging process between a literate group and a lay audience.*

Lastly, we note that in societies where literacy was limited, as in Mesopotamia and Egypt, we find only paeons to the scribe and praise for his profession. Paradoxically, in the literate societies that emerged in Israel and later in Greece, we find *a critique of writing* pointing out its limitations particularly in the educative process as well as in its exploitation for deceitful purposes by professional scribes (Isa 10:1-2; Jer 8:8).

The Centrality of the Book in Israelite Religion and Early Judaism

As we have noted above, the Israelite priesthood was literate. The priests underwent a long period of formal education and apprenticeship necessary for the performance of their more advanced and varied ritual duties, which included expertise in sacrificial offerings, calendrical calculations, animal anatomy and medical knowledge.[57] In addition, priestly scribes were responsible to the king for the proper maintenance of the temple administration (2 Kgs 12:5ff.; 22:4ff.; 2 Chr 24:6). The Jerusalem priesthood and Levitical families loyal to the Davidic monarchy were also employed in the government service (1 Chr 26:29-32). Though we have no direct literary evidence for a school, we must assume that the priests received a formal education within such a framework in order to fulfill their sundry duties.

The term 'school' is used here to indicate a formal institution of learning which we assume to have existed at least in Jerusalem. However, the term, especially in 'the Priestly School' as used in biblical scholarship, denotes and identifies a theological or literary trend reflected in the composition of the biblical text. I would say that this latter 'school' characterizes the upper echelons of the former and should therefore be treated together. The priesthood was responsible for the crystallization, safekeeping and dissemination of the great body of priestly literature that contained the cultic duties of priest and laity as well as the historic reflections and religious beliefs of ancient Israel. (Similarly, I would argue that the 'Wisdom school', with its humanistic ethic, open to gentile influence, as reflected especially in the Book of Proverbs, was the intellectual vanguard of the scribal class.)[58]

It seems that the institution of the priesthood necessitated its own school in which the full gamut of studies was taught, from the mundane elementary program of reading, writing and basic arithmetic to that of the religious reflections preserved in the Bible. Toward the end of the monarchy, several of its

---

[56] See Kaufmann, *The Religion of Israel*, pp. 359-62.
[57] See Haran, *Temples*, chs. 4, 5, 11.
[58] But see Whybray, *Intellectual Tradition*.

more prominent students emerged from anonymity, such as the prophets Jeremiah and Ezekiel. The school obviously thrived during the Babylonian exile, where the cohesiveness of Tora study in communities of Priests and Levites (cf. Ezra 8: 16-19), buoyed by hopes of return, produced new cadres of teachers and tradents called *m'vinim*. Within this framework, older traditions like that of the classical prophets and the historiographic Book of Kings received their finishing touches (cf. the date in 2 Kings 25:27-30). By the early Second Temple Period there already existed a canon of Tora, prophetic literature and cultic song. Emerging from these priestly ranks were the prophets Zechariah (cf. Neh 12:16) and possibly Malachi as well as the innovative Ezra the Scribe whose mission would mark the beginning of a new era, characterized by midrashic exegesis and public worship centered around Tora readings.[59]

PRIESTLY INSCRIPTIONS

In recent years, various inscriptions have been discovered which can be classed as belonging to the cultic sphere. They include such items as the personal seal of Zechario the priest of Dor,[60] votive inscriptions on pottery bearing the word *qdš* i.e. 'consecrated'[61] or the inscribed ivory pomegranate *qdš khnim*.[62] The inscriptions of a pagan or heterodox religious nature found written with ink on plaster at Kuntilat Agrud in northern Sinai and at Deir 'Alla ('The Balaam Inscription') in Transjordan[63] may be hierologoi describing the sanctity of the site. They illuminate the Deuteronomic commandment 'to set up large stones, coat them with plaster and inscribe upon them all the words of this Teaching' at Shechem (Deut 27:2-4; Josh 8:32). Indeed, this practice of writing might have been more widespread in ancient Israel, thus explaining the paucity of monumental inscriptions chiseled in stone.

The recently discovered amuletic priestly blessing in Jerusalem,[64] incised on silver, would indicate the wider applications afforded by writing by freeing the power of the oral blessing from the limitations of time and place of the cultic setting and making it the personal and constant possession of the owner of the amulet. In fact, it might even be a literal concretization of the commandment 'to place My name upon the children of Israel, and I will bless them' (Num 6:22-27). Seen together, these various inscriptions seem to represent the work of a literate priesthood.

---

[59] Demsky, 'Ezra and Nehemiah', pp. 48-50, 58-65.
[60] Avigad, 'Priest of Dor'.
[61] See Aharoni, *Arad Inscription* 116ff. See now Cross 'Two Offering Dishes' (lit. cited). Note also the inscribed names of various priestly and Levitical families that resided in Arad, pp. 82-88.
[62] Lemaire, 'Une inscription'.
[63] Meshel, *Kuntilat 'Agrud*; Levine, 'Balaam Inscription' (literature cited) and especially Rofe's response on pp. 365-66.
[64] Barkai, *Ketef Hinnom*, pp. 34-37.

THEOLOGICAL IMPLICATIONS

We discern three main stages in the development and history of Israelite religion, namely the *preliterate* patriarchal period, the *literate* Mosaic faith and the post-Exilic *Book centered* reforms of Ezra.[65] The first two phases are described in the Pentateuch and represent the beliefs held by priestly circles of First Temple times. Without entering into the debates of the various schools of modern biblical criticism regarding the date, makeup and transmission of this literature and its components, we must emphasize that in the view of the biblical authors the nascency of the people of Israel and of the established forms of its religion as going back to the Exodus and Sinai is inherently connected with writing (e.g. Exod 17:14; 24:4, 7, 12; 32:15-16; 34: 1, 27-28; Deut 4:13, 5:19, 9:10, 10:1ff.).

This biblical viewpoint is in keeping with the technical developments in alphabetic writing during the 13th-11th centuries as described above, as well as with the theological changes accompanying the appearance of the national religions which typified the beginning of the Iron Age in Canaan and Syria.[66] The biblical distinction between Mosaic literacy and an earlier preliterate patriarchal period is difficult to prove or reject by objective criteria. However, it is not impossible that an appreciation of writing developed in Israel at a formative stage when that society, unrestricted by patterns of limited literacy, adopted the alphabet and its national institutions were taking shape at the same time. Certainly later, during the period of the monarchy with the institutionalization of the Temple and its cult and with the crystallization of an official theology, ancient Israel regarded the medium of writing as an integral part of its religious expression.

At the heart of biblical theology is the idea of a divinely revealed covenant at Sinai, physically represented by the Ten Commandments engraved on two tablets of stone. This written document expressed the unique relationship between God and the people of Israel and thus became the focus of the cultic appurtenances, the manifestation of the divine presence. The adoption of the neutral medium of writing thereby opened new vistas in religious experience.

The notion of divine reliance on writing is not unique to Israel. The scribes of the Ancient Near East regarded writing, like other arts, as an invention of the gods. Books of wisdom and esoteric divination were attributed to various deities. The motif of a heavenly Book of Life, in which the fate of all mankind was inscribed, was widely believed and adopted by Israel as well.[67] These beliefs, cultivated by the self-serving scribes of Mesopotamia and Egypt, reflect the thinking of a restricted group of literati preserving a divine gift, i.e. the art of writing. In contrast, in Israel there appeared the demythologized idea of God revealing His will by means of a document written first of all by Him (Exod

---

[65] See Demsky, 'Ezra and Nehemiah', 49f., 60ff.
[66] Cf. Albright, *Gods of Canaan*, passim and Mazar, 'Philistines', p. 170.
[67] Paul, 'Heavenly Tablets'.

24:12, 32:15-16 and 34:27-28) and whose message, albeit to be taught orally, is intended not only for a class of wisemen or priests but rather for all the people. The potential of writing, i.e. the alphabet, for the democratization of religion was becoming a reality.

The medium of writing found expression in the written covenant. It is clear that the Sinai covenant and its renewal ceremonies in biblical times (Josh 8:30-35; 24:2ff.; 2 Kings 17:35ff., 23:1-3; Neh 9-10) are an adoption of the written political treaties of both the parity and vassal types current in the ancient Near East during the second and first millennia B.C.E. Particularly, the vassal type with its demand for exclusive loyalty aptly suited the belief in one God. Thus the Sinai Covenant and its fuller exposition in the Tora scroll (see Deut 31:24-26) became central to Israel's faith.[68]

The idea of a revealed written document is so closely associated with the essence of historic monotheism that Christianity and Islam were able to compete with the authority of the Mosaic Tora only by replacing it with another authoritative book.It is no wonder then to find the precise definition of earlier believers in one God in the Kuranic term 'ahl al-kitāb, i.e. 'the people of the Book'.

The reciprocal influence of writing and monotheism can be seen in the biblical rejection of the plastic representation of the deity, a commonplace in all contemporary pagan religions: 'You shall not make for yourself a sculptured image, or any likeness of what is in the heaven above, or on the earth below, or in the waters under the earth' (Exod 20:4). It is most instructive that this opposition to an iconographic object of veneration is expressed in the written tablets of the covenant, which themselves became the new sacred symbol and tangible sign of His presence. Stored in the Ark, the footstool of the divine throne, the tablets were the focal point of cultic service in the Tabernacle and Temple and their later synagogal copies formed the centre of Jewish worship. By attributing the tablets of the covenant to divine authorship, the mundane treaty model was transformed and infused with a non-mythological holiness and became the means of comprehending God. The medium of writing therefore provided the solution of the problem how to represent physically an invisible and transcendent deity. Henceforth, not only the content of the covenant, but also the medium of writing became an influential factor in Israelite religion and in later Judaism.

A written Tora had another distinct advantage in establishing an authoritative version of the religious experience subsequently leading to the canonization of a text to which nothing may be added and from which nothing may be omitted (Deut 4:2, 13:1). While publicized orally, either at festive occasions or within family circles, it was the written form which provided the valid version.[69] It is not surprising then that we often find a reference to both an oral and a

[68] Weinfeld, 'Covenant' (literature cited).
[69] See Leiman, *Canonization*, 16ff.

written medium of composition, transmisson or publication of a literary passage (Exod 17:14; Deut 6:7-9; 31:19; 2 Sam 1:18 etc.).

If the written Tora was imbued with holiness, reading it could also be a religious experience. The king is commanded not only to have a copy of the Tora written for him by the priests, but 'Let it remain with him and let him read in it all his life, so that he may learn to revere the Lord his God, to observe faithfully every word of this Teaching as well as these laws.' (Deut 17:18-19). Periodic public readings (a reflex of the political treaty model) at the end of the sabbatical cycle were instituted in order to fulfill the imperative to teach the Tora to the masses (Deut 31:10-13). From the point of view of the religious establishment, the written word was meant to become an integral part of the religious consciousness of Israel. It was in Second Temple times that Judaism succeeded in inculcating the widespread influence of the Tora through new religious institutions. On the one hand, in the synagogue, the model for the later church and mosque, the Tora was read, translated and expounded on a weekly basis for the community at large. On the other hand, the house of study elevated learning the Tora to a religious experience and its teachers to an honoured status. In this communal institution, minors would be enrolled in the 'House of the Book' *(beit sefer)* for the study of the Bible. At the same time in the *beit talmud (P. T. Megilla* 3:1,73d), or *beit midrash* (Ben Sira 51:23), the mature student would listen to discourses on the biblical text, expounded and made relevant according to accepted methods of textual exegesis forming a substantial part of the Oral Tora of later rabbinic literature.[70]

Reviewing the period of more than fifteen hundred years from the end of the second millennium B.C.E. to the early centuries of the common era, we have found an inextricable connection between the medium of writing and the ancient history of Israel. The fortuitous coincidence of the standardization of the Canaanite alphabet adopted by Israel in its formative period set into motion momentous social and religious processes. For one, it made possible the formation of Israel as a literate society and the democratization of higher culture guarded until that time by the scribes of the ancient Near East. Furthermore, the association between writing and monotheism brought innovative literary expression of religious beliefs and duties, affecting not only the Jewish people but ultimately influencing Christianity and Islam down to our own times.

---

[70] Cf. Safrai, 'Education', 945ff.

Part Two:
Scribes and Books in the Late Second Commonwealth and Rabbinic Period
(M. Bar-Ilan)

The Scribes

STATUS, SOCIAL CLASS, TRAINING

Though the modern Jewish scribe *(sôfēr stam)* is known for his skill in traditional calligraphy, the scribe in antiquity was simply the man who could write in the social-religious sphere, where most people were illiterate or lacked expertise. Some of the scribes were employed as officials in government service, and their social status depended on their official administrative work. Other scribes, apparently with the same training and social background, did not work as civil servants but helped individuals by writing for religious and everyday purposes as well. The scribes provided all sorts of religious texts such as copies of the Bible, *tefillin* (Phylacteries) and *mezuzot*, as well as amulets in addition to writs and prosaic letters. Most of their work was copying from books before them, but some of them were independently creative, as is evident from the literary works of that time. When not engaged in writing or preparing the necessary utensils, they used to teach reading and, later, writing skills. Hence the close and ancient connection between official service and preserving the continuity of the profession.

So it is not surprising that in a traditional society, where the scribe represented religious and ritual tradition, his social status was highly respected (Sir 38:26ff.). Biblical figures such as Enoch, Moses and Elijah were considered great scribes of Israel (*B.T. Sota* 13b; *Seder Olam Rabba* 17).[71] Furthermore, traditions about literate heavenly angels (2 Enoch 8:5; 3 Enoch; *B.T. Rosh ha-Shana* 16b) indicate the high regard in which the scribal profession was held, achieving almost a divine status. Scribes in the past were considered as the teachers of the people, and a number of decrees were related to them (*M.*

---

[71] Harrington, 'Wisdom of the Scribe'; Krauss, 'Moses the Great Scribe'.

Yevamot 2:4). But despite this appreciation, the laity sometimes found their arrogant behaviour repulsive, and they made various accusations against the scribes, which in part arose from social conflicts between the laity and the elite scribes (Mark 12:38; *P.T. Sanhedrin* 10:1, 27d).

Most of the scribes of the end of the Second Temple period whose genealogy is known were priests: Yosef (*T. Shabbat* 13:11), Yohanan (*P.T. Maaser Sheni* 5:4, 56c), Beit Kadros (*T. Menahot* 13:19), Josephus and others. It is clear that during the time of the Temple, priests, some of whom were scribes, used to manage the Temple property, contributions and gifts in addition to annual tithes (Neh 13:13; *T. Shekalim* 2:14-15; Josephus, *War* 6:387-91). The Temple as the official cultural-religious center was also the center of the knowledge of reading and writing, and because of that the priests in charge of the Temple were evidently responsible for the preservation of the Tora, its copying in general and the scribal profession in particular.

The scribe began his studies at a comparatively late age, i.e. when his family was prepared to forgo his potential income, so that only rich people could afford such an investment and training. The rabbis said that ordinary priests were rich, so it is evident that in the days of the Second Temple scribes came almost exclusively from rich and distinguished families, most of whom, were priests or levites. But with the spread of Hellenism in the land of Israel, a process of secularization and diminishing status overtook the scribal profession, and among the people many scribes arose without any connection to an official position, the priesthood or the Temple. Apparently, together with the loss of status came economic decline as well, since the sages comment that no one who deals with books will become rich from his profession (*B.T. Pesahim* 50b).[72]

Children were taught to read from the Bible, but not necessarily to write (*Avot de-Rabbi Natan*, A6, p. 29). In antiquity specialization in writing involved the complicated techniques of preparing all the writing accessories: the parchment, the stylus and the ink, and therefore it was impossible to teach advanced writing skills to young children (as nowadays), so this level of teaching had to be postponed till the age of 14-15 after the elementary stage (Jub 11:16; *P.T. Ketubbot* 8:11, 32c). That is to say that even among those who knew how to read, many or, more accurately, most did not know how to write. In general, women were excluded from all formal studies, but occasionally they were also taught, and some of them were capable of writing their own bill of divorce (*M. Nedarim* 4:3; *M. Gittin* 2:5).[73] In rabbinic times, when a child reached puberty and a certain technical ability, he began to learn how to write in the scribe's home (*T. Sota* 6:2), and this included related skills such as preparing the skin, smoothing it for writing, cutting, sewing and pasting it, sharpening the knife, preparing the stylus, mixing the ink, and marking lines with a ruler. The exercises of the trainee included writing all sorts of writs as a preparation for his

---

[72] Sperber (ed.), *Massekhet Derekh Erets Zutta*, 158
[73] Ebner, *Elementary Education*; Aberbach, *Jewish Education*.

future profession (*M. Gittin* 3:1). It seems that the students were apprentices to their teachers, as was common in other professions in antiquity when skills were transmitted this way. When the student reached majority at the age of 18-20, he could practice independently as a scribe.

THE SCRIBES AS TEACHERS, THEIR CONNECTION TO THE TEMPLE

Some of the scribes were town scribes, as was the case for such communities as Ephesus in Asia Minor or Tarbant in the Galilee (Acts 19:35; *P.T. Megilla* 4:5, 75b).[74] The scribe made his living by writing on request as well as writing without a specific order, such as writing the Tora, and as a teacher as well (*T. Sukka* 2:6). For teaching, the scribe needed to provide his students with 'teaching material' and he did so by writing them little scrolls that contained small passages from the Bible: from Genesis, Leviticus, the 'Hallel' (Pss 113-118), or 'the Shema' (Deut 6:4-9, Deut 11:13-21 and [only later] Num 15:37-41). So it is evident that one person acted as both teacher and scribe. However, in the course of years the status of the scribe declined and he became subject to the local Sage (*P.T. Taanit* 2:13, 66a; *Midrash Psalms* 91).

It seems that the books of the Bible were preserved in the Second Temple in Jerusalem (*Sifre Deut* 356, p. 423), as the Tables of the Testimony were deposited in the tabernacle in early times, and part of the priests' duties was to copy and preserve them.[74a] The proofreaders in Jerusalem were paid by the Temple treasury (*B.T. Ketubbot* 106a), but it seems that this tradition arose only after control of the Temple was transferred from the priests to the Sages towards the end of the days of the Second Temple.[75] Among the members of the Sanhedrin were scribes, that is to say Sages (priests) who were scribes as well, who administered the legal system which required the writing of protocols, decrees and records (Mark 14:1; Luke 22:2; *M. Sanhedrin* 4:3). According to the orders of the Sages, scribes wrote the Temple letters to the Jews in the land of Israel and the Diaspora, in which they laid down guiding rules that expressed the connection and the authority of the Sages of the land of Israel over the Jews in the Diaspora (*T. Sanhedrin* 2:6).[76]

Books of the Tora, *tefillin* and *mezuzot* that were written by a proselyte Jew, 'Min' (sectarian Jew), Samaritan, gentile, apostate, slave, woman, deaf and dumb person, a fool or by one who did not know how to read, were considered as faulty and had to be put in a Geniza or to be burnt (*B.T. Gittin* 45b; *B.T. Menahot* 42b; *Massekhet Soferim* 1:13-14). Evidently, the Sages were displeased that so many people practiced writing sacred texts. Some of the Tan-

---

[74]   Klein, 'R. Shim'on the Scribe of Tarbant'.
[74a] Cf. Beckwith, below, pp. 40-45.
[75]   Kaufmann, *History*, 4, 563-68; Büchler, *Die Priester und der Cultus*.
[76]   Alexander, 'Epistolary Literature'.

naim were scribes, of whom the best-known was R. Meir, the pupil of R. Akiva, but even among the Sages not everybody knew how to write (*B. T. Hullin* 9b).

The Books

SCROLLS AND CODICES

The books of the Tora were written on skins of ritually pure cattle, although the Sages, as opposed to the Boethusians, also allowed skins of cattle which had not been slaughtered according to the law (*B. T. Shabbat* 108a). The skins were tanned for the Tora (*B. T. Gittin* 45b) with acidiferous liquids to remove the fat, and later smoothed, whitened with lime and cut to a convenient size. Three to eight 'pages' were prepared in every sheet (*Soferim* 2:10). After that lines were drawn with a ruler and a sharp instrument, so the scribe could 'hang' the letters on the lines. It seems that only in a comparatively late period did the scribes began to mark on each page 42 lines (corresponding to the number of letters in one of the names of God), though earlier they used to write on fewer lines on each page. The sheets were sewed together by the scribe with sinew from ritually pure animals, or with linen, till a complete book was prepared: a scroll which was 20-30 centimetres in width and 5-44 meters in length.[77] The sheets of the Tora were attached horizontally, but other writs were sometimes made up of sheets that were attached vertically, so the lines of the letters were parallel to the seam between the sheets (*B. T. Bava Metsia* 20b). Precious books were put in a sheath (sometimes even folded), and there was a wooden stick (later called *ets hayim*), to prevent over-folding and to speed the unrolling of the book as well (*T. Kelim, Bava Batra* 6:10). However, most of the books were wrapped in a cotton mantle and had no inside rod. Some of the books found in Qumran were preserved in big clay jars that had been manufactured especially for that purpose (cf. already Jer 32:14).

In the first century C.E., the codex was invented, the precursor of the modern book, in which both sides of the page were written on and each page was held in place by the binding. The transition from scroll to codex was rather slow and only in the fourth century were codices the majority among the written books. The congregations of Christians in Egypt were the first to adopt this form as a permanent way of writing and it seems that in Christianity, as a new religion without a scribal tradition, there was no objection to the change in form. The advantages of the codex are clear: convenience in storing, handling, reading or referring to a passage in it. It was not only lighter but, above all, cheaper because of the use of fewer skins than in the scroll (but its final price was not more than 10% lower than that of the scroll). It seems that Jewish scribes moved on to writing on codices as a result of foreign influence on the Jewish

---

[77] Cf. Kenyon, *Books and Readers*.

scribes, evident from the many Greek loan words that entered mishnaic Hebrew in the scribal profession (more than twenty, for example: *duchsustus, diphtera, deitheke, kolmos, kolan*, etc.). The ritual reading continued to be done from scrolls, but codices were in use for teaching and studying, though occasionally ritual reading from them was also permitted.[78] Despite the development of the codex, scribes continued to write scrolls even hundreds of years later, not necessarily Tora scrolls.[79]

TEFILLIN, MEZUZOT AND OTHER WRITTEN DOCUMENTS

The scribes wrote and prepared *tefillin* and *mezuzot*, articles whose connection to magic was well known in antiquity.[80] The *tefillin* (lit. 'prayers') were little boxes made of tanned skin painted black, in which little scrolls were put containing those paragraphs of the Tora related to this ritual (Exod 13:1-10; Exod 13:11-16; Deut 6:4-9; Deut 11:13-21). One *tefilla* was tied to the arm and the other to the head, and they were a kind of amulet. There were many customs in the fulfillment of this ritual, identifying those who were obliged to observe it as well as the internal order of the passages mentioned above.[81] It is possible that some of the laws describing exactly how these objects should be made were attributed to Moses in order to prevail over separatism. In the *tefillin* for the head from Qumran (*1OQPhyl* 1-4) more sections from the Tora were found, including *inter alia* the Ten Commandments in Deut 5.[82] It seems that before the crystallization of the halakha by the Sages, *tefillin* were opened daily before prayer and, after the scrolls in them had been read, were tied on the hand and on the head.

In the *mezuza* (lit. 'doorpost [inscription]'), a parchment that was attached to the doorpost, only two sections from the Tora mentioning this commandment were written (Deut 6:4-9; Deut 11:13-21), but sometimes there were also other sections and even names of angels for protection. The Samaritans observed this ritual by engraving the 'Shema' section or part of it on a stone placed at the doorway, either on the lintel or near the doorpost.[83] Besides Tora scrolls and other holy writs, the scribes used to write all sorts of documents including genealogical records *(k'tav yuhassin)*, personal letters, charms (*qamē'a*), promissory notes, deeds of sale or gifts, wills, bills of marriage and divorce, writs of manumission, *prosbuls* (a bill that enables the demand for repayment of a loan in spite of the laws of the sabbatical year [Deut 15:91]), decrees of court.

The scribes had a stock of forms for some of the bills (*M. Gittin* 3:2). Bills and letters were sealed with a bulla, a little lump of clay that was attached to the

---

[78] Aloni, 'The Scroll of the Tora'.
[79] Bregman, 'An Early Fragment'.
[80] Bar-Ilan, 'Writing Tora Scrolls'.
[81] Cowley, *Aramaic Papyri*, No. 81, 1. 30 תפלה זי כסף, '*tefilla* of silver' (and see below).
[82] Yadin, *Tefillin from Qumran*.
[83] Luria, *From Yanai to Herod*, 252ff.

string that tied up the bill, as was common in the ancient tradition of the scribes
(*M. Shabbat* 8:5, *M. Ahilut* 17:5). However, from the rare archeological findings of seals from the first centuries C.E. in comparison with the more than five
hundred seals that are known from earlier periods, it seems that seals were less
common, although ornamented signatures were not unknown (*B.T. Gittin*
36a). Samples of some of the bills common in the second century C.E., such as a
deed of sale, a bill of rent and others, can be seen in the findings from
Bar-Kokhba.[84]

WRITING MATERIALS

For other purposes all sorts of surfaces were used for writing: a plate of gold (the
section of the Sota [Num 5:11-31], *T. Sota* 2:1), silver (the blessing of the priests
[Num 6:22-27], from the recent archeological findings in Jerusalem from the
sixth century B.C.E.), copper (the so-called *Copper Scroll* from Qumran). From
the magic literature as well as from archeological findings, we know that not
only the above-mentioned metals were used and that there were even more:
iron, tin, lead, and bronze (*T. Kelim Bava Metsia* 1:11).[85] It is reasonable to
believe, therefore, that actually all the metals known at that time were in use for
writing. The metals were flattened into a minimal thickness measured in tenths
of a millimeter. To these comparatively expensive examples one may add
engravings on stone walls or lintels of monumental graves such as the graves of
the sons of Hezir, coffins or tombstones, such as the tombstone of King Uzziah,
on marble like in the Greek sign-board prohibiting the entrance of gentiles to
the Temple, and so on.[86] Writing in mosaic, such as known from the synagogues
of Ein-Gedi, Beit-Alpha, Rehov and other synagogues, is not known before the
fifth century C.E., and it was done not by a scribe but by an artisan, who might
even be gentile.[87]

For daily writing the scribes used parchments of different levels of tanning.[88]
The best and the most expensive parchment was considered to be that of deer
leather (thin, delicate and absorbing the ink well). After it in importance came
parchments from the hide of cattle, sheep, goats and cows (the upper side of the
leather, close to the hair); next came the *'gevil'* (the hide before it is split). The
Sages forbade writing on *diphtera* (δίφθηρα), the leather which was only
roughly tanned, on cotton or paper *(niar)*, i.e. papyrus, because of their inferior
quality (*B.T. Shabbat* 79b; *Soferim* 1:5). For daily purposes people used other
means of writing: on notebooks (πίναξ, two plates of wood put together and
waxed), painting on wooden boards (one of the Bar-Kokhba letters is a good

[84] Benoit-Milik-De Vaux, *Les Grottes de Murabaat*.
[85] Margalioth (ed.), *Sefer HaRazim*, 3, 74, 84, 87 and passim. Naveh, 'A Good Subduing' 367ff. For
the earlier period see Demsky, 'Writing and Writing Materials'.
[86] Cassuto-Salzman, 'Hebrew Inscriptions'; Ben-Dov, 'Hebrew Inscriptions Carved on Stone'.
[87] Naveh, *On Stone and Mosaic*.
[88] Herchberg, 'Tanning of Leather'.

example of that), writing on paper, trees or vegetables leaves, ostraca, egg shells and on other materials (*T.Shabbat* 11:8).[89] Because tattooing is forbidden in Lev 19:28, some Jews marked on themselves, for apotropaic purposes, a letter or a word with ink *(sphragis)*, showing that they were God's slaves. This custom is rooted in the Bible and it continued for hundreds of years in rabbinic as well as mystic circles and among Jewish-Christians (Ezek 9:4ff.; Rev 7:3, 9:4; *'Ma'aseh Merkavah'*).[90]

For ordinary writing with ink, the scribe used a *kolmus* (κάλαμος), which was made of a piece of reed cut to the width of the required letter, and sharpened at its edge. For writing on wax the scribe used a stylus made of metal, sharpened at one end and wide at the other end for erasing (*M. Kelim* 13:2; *T. Kelim Bava Metsia* 3:4). A twig was an inferior writing tool. Other 'pencils' made of metal, such as an 'iron stylus' (Jer 17:1), were better for stone or engraving on metal and were not in a common use. In a legendary tradition the divine stylus is described as made of gold (*Test. Abr.* Recension B 10).[90a]

The ink was made by the scribes out of a mixture of ground black soot, called 'the dust of the scribes' (*M. Shabbat* 12:5), together with fat and glueing agents so that the ink would adhere to the parchment.[91] Actually there were various recipes for ink, but olive oil with balsam resin, together with soot (and maybe with other materials), was thought to be the best (*B.T. Shabbat* 23a). It seems that Ben-Kamtsar, the scribe who refused to teach writing, was a priest who did not want to reveal the secret of the ink used by the priests, just as the priests avoided divulging the recipe of the shew-bread in the Temple, and like craftsmen that guard their craftsmanship as a professional secret (*M. Yoma* 3:7).[92] The addition of gall-nut or mineral mixtures to the ink, such as 'kankantom' (κάλκανθος), later known as vitriol (oxidized sulphate of copper), reinforced the colour, and this diminished the possibility of its being erased or forged (*B.T. Gittin* 19b) and improved the final product. Adding the powder of fragrant plants caused the books to have a pleasant odor (2 Enoch 10:3; *Sefer HaRazim*, pp. 1ff.). Inferior inks were made from all kinds of material such as fruit juices, congealed milk or blood, and others (*M. Gittin* 2:3; *T. Shabbat* 13:12).[93] However, ink or parchment substitutes that were, of course, cheaper were considered to be unsuitable for Tora writing (*M. Megilla* 2:2). Rich people could afford books written in gold, using powdered gold as the basic paint (*Ep. Arist.* 176). There were people who wrote only the name of God in gold (as the

---

[89] Schäfer (ed.), *Synopse zur Hekhalot-Literatur. (Ma'ase Merkava)* pars. 574-78. For magic writings, see Gaster, *Sword of Moses*.

[90] Schäfer, *Synopse*, 566; Bar-Ilan, 'Magic Seals on the Body'.

[90a] Cf. Charlesworth, *OTP* 2, p. 900.

[91] Carvalho, *Forty Centuries of Ink*.

[92] The traditional explanation that is given in *B.T. Yoma* 38b which ascribes jugglery writing to Ben-Kamtsar seems to be nothing more than a legend. Cf. Weinfeld, 'The Secret of the En-Gedi Community'.

[93] Herchberg, *Cultural Life*, 251ff.; Feliks, 'The Oak and its Products'.

Muslim calligraphy did later), similar to the custom of some of the scribes in Qumran of writing the name of God in paleo-Hebrew, though this practice was prohibited by the Sages (*Soferim* 1:8).[94]

Ink was in the form of a lump or cake of black fat that was put into a clay inkstand or an ink container *(bēt hadio)*, a vessel with a metal lid, apparently to preserve the ink for a longer time (*T. Kelim Bava Metsia* 4:11). Before it could be used, the ink had to be moistened (*M. Shabbat* 1:5). Wetting the script caused the erasing of the ink because of its water base (*T. Shabbat* 11:18; 13:4).

Writing

THE CHANGING OF THE SCRIPT

Among the Sages there was an opinion that writing was invented during the six days of creation (*M. Avot* 5:6), reminiscent of the mythic concept associated with writing among the neighbouring peoples. Writing was recognized as a religious command, though actually only scribes did it (just as circumcision was performed by professionals only). The collection of laws concerning scribes is called *Massekhet Soferim* (Tractate for Scribes) and though its final formulation is comparatively late, from the seventh or eighth centuries C.E., most of its statutes are from the first centuries C.E., if not earlier. There is no other profession to which so much religious attention was given (unless the order of *Zeraim* is viewed as a set of rules for farmers). A considerable part of tractate *Gittin* consists of exact rules for scribes in writing a bill of divorce. However, only writing the Bible was recognized as a religious duty and writing down oral traditions was prohibited (*B.T. Gittin* 60a). The source of this prohibition might be considered as a reflection of a society which respects oral tradition, which is anxious about books in general or is in fear of sects publishing their opinions in books in particular.[95] Accordingly, writing down prayers and benedictions was prohibited, though it was done, and the severity of the prohibition of writing prayers may be grasped from the fact that the Sages compared it to putting the Tora into a fire (*T. Shabbat* 13:4). It seems that committing the oral traditions, legends and prayers to writing did not begin before the third century C.E., if not later.

Some of the Sages of the talmudic period thought, like modern scholars, that the script had changed over the generations, though there were Sages who believed that no changes in the script ever occurred and the Tora was given to Israel in their script, i.e. the 'Assyrian script', later to be known as the 'square' script (*T. Sanhedrin* 4:7-8). However, while modern scholarship sees the change as a gradual process in the course of years (based on collected data and a

---

[94] Siegal, 'Alexandrians in Jerusalem'; *idem*, 'Employment of Palaeo-Hebrew Characters'.
[95] Cf. Ginzberg, *An Unknown Jewish Sect*, 106 n. 4.

diachronic typological comparison), the Sages thought that Hebrew script was changed at one specific time by a decree of Ezra the scribe from the 'old Hebrew', known as *da'ats (Deeson)*, to the 'Assyrian' script.[96] It seems that in these traditions the Sages expressed their criticism of sectarian scribes who kept to the ancient ways of writings, such as those at Qumran and particularly the Samaritan scribes. That is to say, the Tora books preserved by the Sages did not have letters in the old Hebrew script (*M. Megilla* 1:8).

The number of different writs and their various forms known from talmudic literature is much larger than the precedents known from the Bible. This fact, together with the changing of the script among the Jews that held firmly to the oral tradition, reflects the increasing spread of reading and writing in society. This increase diminished the value of writing and led to secularization of the scribal profession and to the scribes' loss of status.

Writing and erasing were prohibited on the Shabbat (*M. Shabbat* 7:11), and writing and proofreading were prohibited in the intermediate days of festivals (*M. Moed Katan* 3:4). The use of invisible ink was known, though rare (*P.T. Gittin* 2:3, 44b), and cryptic script, though basically different, can be found in Qumran manuscripts (*4QCry*). For the latter, the scribe changed the order of the letters from left to right, some letters he wrote in old Hebrew, or in Greek letters as well. Other cypherings were done by interchanging the letters in *'at-bš* (the first letter *Alef* for *Taw*, the last one in the alphabet, *Bēt* for *Shin*, and so on), and it seems that in doing so the scribes continued an ancient practice (*Sheshakh* = Babel, Jer 25:26).[97] It is possible that the comparatively late Samaritan custom according to which the scribe wrote his name in the Tora without changing the text by emphasizing certain letters in the text is rooted in practices of the first centuries c.e.[98]

Numbers were written in various froms: (1) the full word as in the Bible (e.g. 'three'), (2) one Hebrew letter only according to its position in the alphabet ('c'), (3) a Greek letter ('gamma', *M. Shekalim* 3:2), (4) or by special characters, such as in the *Copper Scroll* from Qumran or on ossuaries from the days of the Second Temple. Sometimes the scribes shortened the words for the sake of convenience, indicating it by means of a little mark like the letter *yod*. When later scribes deciphered the abbreviations, from time to time unsatisfactory interpretations caused the insertion of all kinds of misreadings into the text, as is known from biblical as well as talmudic and other rabbinic literature.[99] The scribe wrote faster than is common today. Speed in writing is considered

---

[96] Tur-Sinai, *Halashon Wehasefer*, 123ff.; Naveh, *Development of the Aramaic Script*.
[97] Cf. Demsky 'Sheshakh'.
[98] Ben-Zvi, *Book of the Samaritans*, 227ff.
[99] Driver, 'Once Again Abbreviations'; Lieberman, *About the Palestinian Talmud*, 9ff.; Epstein, *Mavo*, 1209ff.; Margalioth, 'Abbreviations and Shortenings'; Ashkenazi, 'Scribes' Errors'.

reprehensible nowadays, but Ezra the scribe was praised with the title *Sofer Mahir* i.e. 'a fast or accomplished scribe' (Ezra 7:6) and this was customary even hundreds of years later. The Sages demanded that the scribe copied the Tora from another scroll in front of him, though it seems that sometimes the scribes wrote from dictation or from memory (*T. Megilla* 2:5), e.g. the Sages permitted writing *tefillin* and *mezuzot* from memory (*B.T. Megilla* 18b). The name of God was spelled out by the scribe *(azkarot)* in order to avoid a mistake in his writing, and he made an effort to concentrate on his tedious copying, at least while writing the ineffable name.

If the scribe found that he had made a mistake by omitting a letter, he 'hung' it above the script (*Soferim* 8:2). A letter that had been written mistakenly was erased by scraping it off with a knife or a stone, except in the case of misspelling the name of God. Because of the holiness of the book, there were scribes who did not dare to erase, so they indicated the error by dotting the letters above (and beneath) the script or wrote their version, the correct one in their opinion, in the margins of the page. After the books were written, they were proofread once (or even more) and the Tora that the king of Israel was obliged to write (Deut 17:18) had to be proofread thrice in the presence of a court of priests, a court of levites and a court of distinguished Israelites (*T. Sanhedrin* 4:7).[100] The Sages prohibited the preservation of a book which had not been proofread, so no pupil might make a mistake and think that he knew the right text when he did not (*B.T. Ketubbot* 19b; *B.T. Pesahim* 112a). However, the Sages knew that there were variant types of traditional texts, though they did not permit them. The Sages knew that even the texts of the books of the Tora were not uniform (*Sifrei Deut* 356, p. 423); they were aware that people from Jersualem wrote slightly differently than usual (*P.T. Megilla* 1:11, 71d), or that in the Tora of R. Meir and in the *Severus scroll* the text deviated in more than thirty places (*Bereshit Rabbati*, pp. 209-10).[101] For that reason, perhaps, the more lenient Sages considered one, or even three, mistakes on a page tolerable (*P.T. Megilla* 1:11, 71c; *Soferim* 3:10). However, the Samaritan text of the Tora was considered by the Sages to be a forgery (*Sifrei Deut* 56, p. 123-24).[102] A verse from the Bible that was written in a letter, was to be written only after the line was marked with a ruler (*B.T. Gittin* 6b). To avoid the ruling and maybe for other reasons as well, the scribes wrote distorted verses in letters, and therefore there are many verses in talmudic literature that are cited incorrectly compared to the masoretic text.[103] However, the scribe knew that certain words had one spelling in the Bible and another in talmudic literature, especially in adding vowel letters (*B.T. Avoda Zara* 9a).

[100] Cf. Friedman, 'Wekhatav lo – 'Osse lo ketav'.
[101] Lieberman, 'Ktoveth Uzziahu'; Siegal, *Severus Scroll*.
[102] Weiss, *Mishut BaMikra*, 317ff.; cf. Bóid, below, pp. 608-10.
[103] Maori, 'Biblical citations'.

The scribes were ordered by the Sages to distinguish carefully between the different letters, especially those that look similar. Accordingly, they had to take care not to interchange the final and the middle letters and not to add or omit one (*B.T. Shabbat* 103b-104a; *B.T. Sota* 20a). However, there are places in the Bible where the scribes preserved the tradition of the text in front of them, in which regular letters appeared at the end of a word or a final letter stood in the middle (Isa 9:6; Neh 2:13). The scribes also wrote special letters that had an irregular form: smaller or larger than usual, twisted or distorted, 'hung', reversed, with crownlets, and so on.[104] It is possible that in doing so, scribes preserved accidental mistakes of an imprecise scribe, or hints that an ancient scribe wrote down for himself and for his pupils. It seems that Hebrew punctuation, as well as the accenting system and the stabilization of the 'Masora' (an organized method of listing all the peculiarities in the masoretic text), developed in the land of Israel not before the beginning of the seventh century C.E., and this may have been inspired by early Islamic culture.[105] From time to time, however, scribes would add all kinds of marks on their books, as is known from the books of Qumran, but they did not develop the marks into a unified and coherent system and only hundreds of years later did the scribes arrive at the punctuation of the phonetic vowels.

TYPOGRAPHY

The insistence on the typography of the text, the form in which the words should be written, was not known to the scribes except in a few cases. Special orders for the format in which the poetic text should be written were given regarding the 'Song of the Sea' (Exod 15:1-19), the 'Song of Moses' (Deut 32:1-43), and for the 'Song of Deborah' (Judg 5:1-31), the lists of the 'Kings of Canaan' (Josh 12:9-24), and the 'Sons of Haman' (Esth 9:7-9), but elsewhere the Sages did not give any instructions about how the text was to be written (*B.T. Megilla* 16b; *P.T. Megilla* 3:8, 74b). Usually poems were written like bricks 'blank space over print and print over blank space'. Nonetheless, because the poetic biblical structure has no uniformity, e.g. two, three or even more stanzas, the present typography reflects the mechanical writing of the scribes more than the inner structure of the text (such as in Deut 32:14-15). However, the lists of the 'Kings of Canaan' and the 'Sons of Haman' were written 'blank over blank and print over print', in list-form. Because the scribes did not insist on the typography of the text, the original character of the text got lost, for example the litany in Ps 136 and the alphabetic order of different chapters in the Bible (Pss 9-10, 145). The scribes of Qumran sometimes were strict in dividing the verses of the Psalms into stanzas according to the real structure, but they were not always consistent *(11QPs^a)*.

---

[104] Kasher, *Torah Shelema* 29 (1978).
[105] Aloni, 'Books and the Production of books'; cf. Mulder, below, pp. 109-11.

LANGUAGES

The languages commonly written in the land of Israel were: 'Old' and 'Square' Hebrew, Aramaic, Greek, Nabatean, Syriac, Tadmorite and Mandaic. It was forbidden to write the Tora in any language but Hebrew in the 'Assyrian' (square) script, although there were Sages who permitted the Tora, and even *tefillin* and *mezuzot* to be written in Greek, which were nevertheless considered holy (*M. Megilla* 1:8; *B.T. Megilla* 9a). Sometimes one document was written in two languages (*M. Gittin* 9:8), and it seems that there were scribes proficient in both Hebrew and Greek at least. For magical purposes the Hieratic script was also used, and special magical marks were used as well (*Sefer HaRazim*, p. 1ff.).

The writing was done while the scroll was on a desk or on the scribe's lap, but it seems there were scribes who could write letters while walking (*B.T. Shabbat* 80a).

The Maintenance of Books

READING IN THE SYNAGOGUE

The reading of the Bible in the synagogue on Saturdays, Mondays and Thursdays was done ritually, from a raised platform (or perhaps also from the Cathedra of Moses).[106] In the course of the centuries all sorts of laws were developed defining the exact way this should be done: how many persons should participate in the reading, how the passage was to be divided.[107] It was read only in the daytime, only if ten adult males were present, and a blessing was said before and after the reading (Neh 9:3-5; *B.T. Megilla* 21b; *P.T. Megilla* 3:7, 74b). At least ten verses were to be read each time and the reading of the whole Tora (Pentateuch) in the land of Israel was completed once in three years or a little more, depending on the different customs. In the synagogue, the Tora and the Prophets were read but the third part of the Bible *(Ketuvim)* was almost never read for liturgical purposes. The Scroll of Esther was read on the day of Purim (the reading at night was introduced only later) and the Scroll of Lamentations was read on the Ninth of Av. On festivals and on the first day of each month as well, the Hallel (Pss 113-118) was read; this reading was not done like ritual reading but rather as a form of responsive reading by the cantor and the public. In some congregations other books were read, such as Ruth during Pentecost and even *'The scroll of Antiochus'* on the Hannuka Sabbath.[108] The reading of this rabbinic work, based on the books of Maccabees, was unusual since only books of the Bible were read in the synagogue. In non-rabbinic congregations, as is evident from the New Testament, the Pseudepigrapha or non-Jewish tracts were read as well *(Syriac Apoc. Bar. 86)*.

[106] Bar-Ilan, 'A Rock, a Stone and a Seat', 15-23 (esp. n. 1).
[107] Elbogen, *Der Jüdische Gottesdienst*, 155f.
[108] Fried, 'Megilat Antiochus'.

The men that came up to the platform usually read the Tora themselves, but the illiterate needed a (professional) reader, as is known from the Temple (*M. Bikkurim* 3:7, *M. Yoma* 1:6) on the one hand and from the development of later Jewish law (according to which the reader was an expert in the cantilation) on the other. The Sages permitted bastards and others of disqualified origin to read from the Tora, which apparently reflects the social changes that took place earlier in the world of the Sages, thus providing a certain equality for all social classes in the eyes of the law. On the other hand, women and children were not allowed to read in public because it was thought to be disrespectful towards the congregation (*T. Megilla* 3:11; 1 Cor 14:34-35). The readers used only scrolls that contained the complete Tora because the Sages forbade reading from a *Humash*, a scroll of only one of the books (of the Pentateuch). The reading itself became the basis of a public sermon by a Sage or a Rabbi, in which he explained and taught statutes mentioned in the reading, laws and legends, as well as showing the relevancy of the Bible passage through verses from the whole Bible.[109]

The reading from the Tora was accompanied by an Aramaic translation because the laity did not understand Hebrew well enough. Some of the translators translated word for word (as in the greater part of the translation named after Onkelos), while others inclined to expansions in the areas of legend and law (as in the translation named after Yonatan, son of Uzziel). The Sages gave general instructions to the translators on how and what to translate (*M. Megilla* 4:9-10), but different places in the translations show that these orders were not always followed.[110] In some congregations the Tora was read in the Egyptian language, in Elamite, in the language of the Medes, or in Greek, and there were different opinions among the Sages concerning these readings (*M. Megilla* 2:1, *B.T. Megilla* 18b). Nevertheless, the Sages permitted reading the 'Shema' in Greek (*P.T. Sota* 7:1, 21b), a reading that actually was an oral recitation, necessary even in the land of Israel where there were Greek-speaking congregations.

Apart from the ritual reading, the Sages prohibited reading during the sabbath, not because of the reading itself, but rather because of the apprehension that the sabbath might be violated by accompanying acts such as repairing the candle (in order to increase its light), or leaving the house of study (of Oral Tora, *T. Shabbat* 1:11; *M. Shabbat* 16:1). They may have been afraid also that the book might be moved from private to public domain (*B.T. Megilla* 4b; *B.T. Gittin* 60a; *M. Eruvin* 10:3), or because the listeners might transgress the sabbath limits of the town.

A high percentage of the population did not know how to read and it seems evident that in rural areas and in small towns only one man could read from the Tora. We might conclude that in such settlements there was more than 90%

---

[109] Heinemann, *Public Sermons*.
[110] Shinan, *Aggadah in the Aramaic Targums*; Alexander, below, pp. 240-41, 249.

illiteracy (*T. Megilla* 3:12). According to R. Akiva, the Pseudepigrapha were not allowed to be read (*M. Sanhedrin* 10:1), but the historical reality was not in accordance with his strict opinion, and it is evident from talmudic literature that the Sages were acquainted with the Pseudepigrapha, partly at least (these forbidden books may have been the so-called 'books of Minim', i.e. heretical books), and other books such as Homer, books of medicine, of magic or of interpretations of dreams.[111] The Tora was a regular *vade-mecum*, taken on journeys and to the Temple as well (*M. Yevamot* 16:7; *P.T. Sota* 41a).

PRESERVATION OF BOOKS

To preserve the books (that is: scrolls), they had to be read from or rolled out at least once every thirty days to prevent their becoming mouldy (*M. Bava Metsia* 2:8; *T. Bava Metsia* 2:21). The Sages prohibited cutting or dividing the books of the Bible (*M. Bava Batra* 1:6), because they saw in it a denigration of their status, or out of fear that the books might get lost more easily. The books were kept in bookcases which were divided accordingly into small sections and apparently the order of the books in them (in the Temple) led to the traditional order of the books of the Bible.[112] A chest functioned as a movable bookcase (*M. Megilla* 3:1). Books of the Bible were specially honoured, and the congregation stood when they were brought in for reading and during the reading itself.[113] These were not the only customs: it was for example forbidden to put a book of the Tora on a bed, to throw it or to handle it while naked (*P.T. Megilla* 4:1, 74d; *Soferim* 3:12). People did not sit on a bench upon which a Tora had been placed, and intercourse was forbidden in an apartment where there was a Tora scroll (*P.T. Berakhot* 3:5, 6d).

THE GENIZA

Books and other holy objects that were so worn-out that a mistake might be made in reading from them were concealed. These books were not esteemed and even if they were found later, as actually happened, the finders did not attach any importance to their discovery. Books that were disqualified for religious reasons were hidden, that is to say, purposely concealed in a wall or placed in a burial chamber (in a *geniza*), so that they would not be used. The *geniza* reflected the honour Sages had for books, whatever their contents, but common folk burned books when they found defects in them (Acts 19:19). However, there were Sages who held the opinion that a Tora written by a sectarian Jew or by a Gentile should be burned, but not everybody shared that opinion concerning a Tora scroll written by a Gentile, and there were rabbis

---

[111] Karmeli-Weinberger, *Sefer Wesayif*, 1-11; Katz, 'Separation of Judaism and Christianity'.
[112] Sarna, 'Order of the Books'.
[113] Margalioth, *Ha-hilukim*, 173-74.

who even permitted reading from it (*T. Gittin* 45b). A reason for concealing a book might be a heterodox opinion and fears that its appearance in a book might give it authority. Accordingly, there were Sages who wanted to remove books from the Bible, such as Ezekiel, Proverbs, Song of Songs and Ecclesiastes (*Avot de – Rabbi Natan* A1, p. 2ff.). There were doubts even about the holiness of the books of Ruth, Esther and the Aramaic parts in Ezra and Daniel (*B.T. Megilla* 7a; *M. Yadayim* 4:5), but eventually interpreters were found among the Sages who could deal with the difficulties and surprises raised by these books and consequently they were 'canonized'. However, the book of Ben Sira was concealed, though there were Sages that cited from it many years later as if it were one of the books of the Bible (*B.T. Hagiga* 13a; *B.T. Bava Kamma* 92b; *Gen. Rabba* 73:12, p. 857).[114]

In a period when it was forbidden to write down oral traditions, including Aramaic translations of the Tora, the Sages ordered books that had not been written in accordance with their view to be concealed (*T. Shabbat* 13:2). The only book that the Sages of the Mishna esteemed, quoted from and acted according to, was '*Megillat Taanit*', The Scroll of Fasts (*M. Taanit* 2:8). This book, which apparently originated in the Temple, consists of a list of days in the year when fasts and laments are forbidden, but by the third and fourth centuries c.e. it lost its high position and was abandoned.[115] Therefore the only book that was kept in Jewish houses in late antiquity was the Bible (*Eccl. Rabba* 12:13), and the title 'the people of the book' (the people who admire and keep one book only, the Bible), which is first known from the Koran, apparently reflects an older reality.[116]

LIBRARIES

In the first centuries c.e., the synagogue functioned as a kind of library and the inhabitants of a town could force one another to buy holy scrolls of the Bible (*T. Bava Metsia* 11:23). And indeed, from literary sources (*P.T. Yoma* 7:1, 44b), iconographic motifs and archeological findings, it seems that in holy arks in the synagogues there were generally two to nine books and sometimes even twenty one![117] In contrast to this public form of storage, there were other books that were esoteric ('*Megillot Setarim*', scrolls of secrets), such as some of the books of the Essenes (Jos. *War* 2:137-42; 1 Enoch 68:1), and secrets of the priests (*T. Yoma* 2:7). Also the first Christians kept some of their writings secret, a phenomenon which has no parallel in the literature of the Sages. It seems that the remnants of the Qumran library, which housed hundreds of books, sometimes with several copies of a book, do not reflect the common

---

[114] Cf. Beckwith, below, pp. 67, 72-73.
[115] Bar-Ilan, 'Significance'.
[116] Leshem, *Shabbat and Jewish Festivals* 2, 511ff.
[117] Goodenough, *Jewish Symbols* 3, figs. 706, 707, 710, 964-74; Zussman, *Ornamental Clay-Candles*, 39ff., 62.

practice. The familiarity of Qumran's inhabitants with writing and books and keeping their books and beliefs in secrecy as well, was unusual. It seems that the lacunae in talmudic texts, to wit the ends of the Palestinian tractates of *Shabbat*, *Makkot* and *Nidda*, show that there were very few copies of some books.

SELLING AND LENDING OF BOOKS

Keeping books in a private house was considered an obligation, as is demonstrated by a law according to which a guardian should even sell houses and fields from orphans' property in order to purchase a Bible (*T. Terumot* 1:10). From this rule and from others, such as when worn-out books were considered as part of the *Ketubba* (*B.T. Gittin* 35a), it is obvious that books of the Tora and other writs were not considered cheap. A book of the Tora could have cost from 80 to 120 zuz, that is between 80 and 120 gold dinari (*Semahot* 6:11; *B.T. Bava Kamma* 115a). The Sages saw in lending books a fullfilment of charity 'at all times' (*Midr. Pss.* 106, ed. Buber, p. 454; *B.T. Ketubbot* 50a), though the loan was meant for reading or copying and not for study (*Soferim* 8:18). It was said about one who sells his books that he would never enjoy any blessing from the money of the sale (*T. Bikkurim* 2:15), though there were other Sages that permitted selling a Tora just for learning Tora or taking a wife (*B.T. Megilla* 27a). Books of the Tora, *tefillin* or *mezuzot* that became the property of gentiles were considered as captives that should be ransomed, but it was forbidden to pay more than their real value, so as to discourage stealing books (*M. Gittin* 4:6). The Sages of the Talmud forbade taking holy books out of the land of Israel, but even in their times this prohibition lost its relevance (*P.T. Sanhedrin* 3:10, 21d).

DEFILEMENT OF THE HANDS

All holy books, except the Tora in the Temple (*M. Kelim* 15:6), were considered to defile the hands, and therefore food that touched a book was considered unclean (*M. Zavim* 5:12). The handling of holy books, like putting on the *tefillin*, was considered to defile the hands, but not the whole body. This was a two-fold innovation: the uncleanness itself, the reason of which is not clear, and its being only partial (*M. Yadayim* 3:2).[118] The Sadducees opposed the Pharisees and believed that books do not defile hands (*M. Yadayim* 4:6), and it seems that they did not accept the innovation of the Sages. The traditional explanation according to which the uncleanness of books had been decreed to keep books away from food is not convincing (*B.T. Shabbat* 14a), and it is possible that attributing uncleanness to written books was meant to increase their reverence or perhaps the idea of uncleanness reflects the reaction of a society which venerated the Oral Tora and shrank from too-close a connection

---

[118] See Leiman, *Canonization*, 102ff.

with the Written Tora. Eighty-five letters were considered the minimum length for a book, as in the section that begins 'when the Ark was to set out' (Num 10:35-36), a passage enclosed between two signs in the form of the letter *nun* reversed, and considered to be a book in itself.[119]

CONCLUSION

In conclusion, in the hellenistic and Roman periods the book and the written letter reached all Jewish classes. Beyond the precincts of the Temple and the administrative courts the book, the stylus and the ink became commonplace means of communication. The daily encounter with script as in *tefillin* and *mezuzot* and especially the religious obligation to read the tora and the scroll of Esther in every congregation widened the literacy of the people so that eventually even the oral traditions gave way to this medium, as is evident from the writing down of the Mishna and other rabbinic literature. Thus, writing in general and reading the Tora in particular became central in the intellectual and practical world of the Sages. Rabbinic and sectarian views reflected in the inter-testamental literature only emphasize the continuity of the importance of the book in the life of the heirs of biblical Israel.

Selected Bibliography

The main tractate that deals with the rules and laws for the Jewish scribe is *Massekhet Soferim*, see the edition of HIGGER (1937).

A description of the scribes from the historical point of view is given by MANTEL, 'The Soferim' (1977). For the socio-historical background of the scribes and the development of the laws concerning literacy and illiteracy, see BAR-ILAN, *The Polemics between Sages and Priests* (1982).

The main classical works on Jewish books are: BLAU, *Studien zum Althebräischen Buchwesen* (1902), and KRAUSS, *Talmudische Archaeologie* 3 (1912), 300-36. For studies on scribal techniques in biblical times and their relationship to the scribes of Qumran (and later), see: HARAN, 'Scribal Workmanship' (1980-81); HARAN, 'Book-Scrolls' (1983) and HARAN 'Bible Scrolls in Eastern and Western Lands' (1985). Realia and all sorts of techniques of the scribes of Qumran are discussed in MARTIN, *The Scribal Character* (1958) and in SIEGAL, *Scribes of Qumran* (1975).

The development of the codex in the Roman world and among the Jews as well is described in ROBERTS-SKEAT, *Birth of the Codex* (1983); See also LIEBERMAN, *Hellenism in Jewish Palestine* (1962), pp. 20ff.

---

[119] Cf. Reynolds-Wilson, *Scribes and Scholars*. On the Hebrew book in later periods, see Steinschneider, *Vorlesungen*.

On Jewish books and scribes in the Middle Ages and their connections to ancient times, see HABERMAN, *The Hebrew Book* (1968); LESHEM, *Shabbat and Jewish Festivals* 3 (1969) pp. 171-212.

Chapter Two

Formation of the Hebrew Bible

Roger T. Beckwith

The Terminology Denoting Scripture

In rabbinic literature, a number of terms are used to denote the Scriptures. המקרא 'what is read', הכתוב 'what is written, Scripture', כתובים 'the Writings, Scriptures', כתבי הקדש 'the Holy Writings, Holy Scriptures', הספרים 'the books', עשרים וארבעה ספרים 'the 24 books', הספר 'the book', תורה 'the Law' are among these terms, though 'the Law' is more frequently used for the Pentateuch alone and 'the Writings, Scriptures' for the Hagiographa alone. Titles which subdivide the Scriptures into sections also occur. תורה ונביאים 'the Law and the Prophets' and תורה וקבלה 'the Law and Tradition' (probable meaning) simply distinguish the Pentateuch from the rest of Scripture, while תורה ונביאים וכתובים 'the Law, the Prophets and the (other) Scriptures' and תורה ונביאים וחכמה 'the Law, the Prophets and Wisdom' name the three sections individually.[1]

Because of the well-known problem about dating rabbinic material, we cannot be sure how old these titles are, but 'what is read' is doubtless derived from Neh 8:8 and 'the books' from Dan 9:2, so these two may well be pre-Christian. We are on surer ground with the titles that occur also in Greek.[2] 'What is written, Scripture' occurs as ἡ γραφή in John 20:9; Gal 3:22; 1 Pet 2:6; 2 Pet 1:20; *1 Clem.* 34:6; 42:5. 'The Writings, Scriptures' occurs frequently in the NT, and also in Philo, *On Abraham* 236, as αἱ γραφαί. 'The Holy Writings, Holy Scriptures' occurs in three different translations. As τὰ ἱερὰ γράμματα it occurs frequently in Philo and Josephus, and also in 2 Tim 3:15. As αἱ ἱεραὶ γραφαί it occurs often in Philo, and also in *1 Clem.* 53:1. As γραφαὶ ἅγιαι it occurs in Rom 1:2. 'The Law', embracing books outside the Pentateuch, occurs as ὁ νόμος or ἡ νομοθεσία in *Test. Naphtali* 8:7-8; 1 Cor 14:21; Philo, *On the Contemplative Life* 78, and is reflected elsewhere. All these titles therefore go back to the first century C.E. 'The Law and the Prophets', however, is at least a

---

[1] For these Hebrew titles, see Blau, *Zur Einleitung*, 1-20; Strack-Billerbeck, *Kommentar* 4, 415; Bacher, *Die älteste Terminologie*.

[2] Detailed information on Greek terms denoting Scripture can be found in Ellis, below, pp. 653ff.

century older, since it occurs (as ὁ νόμος καὶ οἱ προφῆται) not only in the NT and 4 Macc 18:10, but also in 2 Macc 15:9.

There are also many other Greek titles, from the first century C.E. or earlier, for which we possess no Semitic equivalent. 'The Holy Records', 'the Most Holy Oracles', 'the Oracles of God', 'the Oracles', 'the Holy Word', 'Moses and the Prophets', all occur more than once, in Philo, the NT or elsewhere. 'The Holy Books' occurs in three forms, two of which are pre-Christian. As τὰ βιβλία τὰ ἅγια it is found in 1 Macc 12:9 and as αἱ ἱεραὶ βίβλοι in an extract from Alexander Polyhistor preserved by Eusebius (*Preparation for the Gospel* 9:24).[3] Earliest attested of all are the three titles or descriptions used by the Greek translator of Ben Sira in his prologue (c. 130 B.C.E.). These distinguish the three sections of the canon, calling the first two 'the Law and the Prophets (or Prophecies)', but using a different phrase for the Hagiographa each time, thus indicating that this section did not yet have an agreed title.

Many of the titles occur in broadly Pharisaic sources, but to what extent they were used by the other Jewish schools of thought we have no direct means of knowing. For the Essenes, it may be significant that Philo uses 'the Law' and 'the Holy Scriptures' with reference to the Therapeutae (*On the Contemplative Life* 28, 75, 78), and the Qumran literature seems to reflect the titles 'the Law and the Prophets', 'Moses and the Prophets' (*1QS* 1:2-3; 8:15-16; *CD* 7:15-17). The Mishna represents the Sadducees as using the title 'the Holy Scriptures' (*Yadayim* 4:6). That many of the titles were in common use is suggested by the number that are adopted by Christians and employed in the NT.[4]

The Significance of the Temple Archive

In view of the divine origin which was attributed to the Scriptures, it is not at all surprising to find them described in the literature of the intertestamental and NT periods as 'holy'. The description is a very common one. Two of the early titles of the Pentateuch are 'the Holy Law' (*Letter of Aristeas*, Philo and Josephus) and 'the Holy Laws' (Philo).[5] Similarly, the OT in general is given the titles 'the Holy Scriptures' (Philo, NT, Josephus, *1 Clement*, rabbinic equivalent), 'the Holy Books' (1 Maccabees, Alexander Polyhistor, Philo, Josephus), 'the Holy Records' (Philo), 'the Most Holy Oracles' (Philo) and 'the Holy Word' (Philo, Josephus, *1 Clement*).[6] It will be seen from this that the expression 'the Holy Law' goes back to the second century B.C.E. *(Letter of Aristeas)*, and 'the Holy

---

[3] On Polyhistor, who is clearly echoing the usage of the Jewish writers from whom he is presenting extracts, see Attridge, 'Historiography', 160-61; Van der Horst, below, pp. 519-20.

[4] For a fuller account of the titles in use by the end of the first century C.E., including those attested only once, see my *Old Testament Canon*, ch. 3. Much of the material in this essay is drawn from that book, with the goodwill of the publishers, and reference can be made to it for further information on most matters with which the essay deals.

[5] *Ep. Arist.* 45; Philo, *QG* 2:14; *Abr.* 1; *Hyp.* 7:13; Josephus, *War* 2:229.

[6] For these titles see the foregoing.

Books' to the first century B.C.E. (1 Maccabees, Alexander Polyhistor); that the names are used by Palestinian writers and teachers (author of 1 Maccabees, NT writers, Josephus, rabbis) as well as by writers of the Diaspora; and that though the majority of these writers and teachers are of Pharisaic tendency, there are also Christians among them. Moreover, there is reason to think that the title 'the Holy Scriptures', either in its Greek or in its Semitic form, may have been used by the Essenes and the Sadducees, as well as by the Pharisees and the Christians.[7]

One of the corollaries of the holiness of the Scriptures was that they were especially suitable to be kept and used in holy places. This was recognized by the Therapeutae, whose affinities were Essene, in that they took into their 'sanctuary' (ἱερόν) none of the general necessities of life but only the Scriptures and other edifying books,[8] and it was recognized by the Pharisees and Sadducees, in that they admitted no books but the Scriptures and items like the priestly and Levitical genealogies into the Jerusalem Temple. Though there were also synagogues in use, the Temple, while it stood, was the holiest place of the nation's religious life, and the proper home for books publicly recognized as holy.[9]

The laying-up of books and writings in a holy place, and, in some cases, the writing of them there, are practices very early attested in the history of Israel, and parallelled among other neighbouring peoples. The earliest Israelite examples are those concerning the tables of the Ten Commandments and the Book of Deuteronomy, laid up, respectively, in and beside the ark of the covenant in the Tabernacle (Exod 25:16, 21; 40:20; Deut 10:1-5; 31:24-6); the record of Joshua's covenant with the people, written in the copy of the Book of the Law at the sanctuary of Shechem (Josh 24:26); and Samuel's account of the manner of the kingdom, laid up before the Lord, apparently at the sanctuary of Mizpah (1 Sam 10:25). The transference of the ark, still containing its tables, to Solomon's Temple, when the building was dedicated (1 Kgs 8:6-9; 2 Chr 5:7-10), and the finding of the Book of the Law in the Temple in the reign of Josiah (2 Kgs 22:8; 23:2, 24; 2 Chr 34:15, 30), indicate that the custom of keeping sacred writings in the sanctuary continued in the First Temple; and the Second Temple would have been the natural location for the library of the nation's religious records said to have been gathered together after the Exile by Nehemiah, and for that more certainly assembled after the Antiochene persecution by Judas Maccabaeus (2 Macc 2:13-15). In the first century C.E., when the Second Temple was coming to the end of its history, we have evidence, at which we shall be looking, both from Josephus and from rabbinic literature, that the Scriptures were laid

---

[7] See the first section of this chapter.

[8] See Philo, *Cont.* 25.

[9] The Scriptures were also kept in synagogues (Josephus, *Ant.* 16:164), in the 'ark of the Law', which was reckoned the holiest part of the building (*M. Megilla* 3:1).

up there, and also that the priestly and Levitical genealogies were compiled and kept there.

The writings laid up in the Temple and in the earlier Israelite sanctuaries were sacred either by reason of their origin or by reason of their subject-matter, or both. The tables of the Decalogue and the writings of prophets were of sacred origin. On the other hand, the 'letters of kings about sacred gifts' in Nehemiah's library (2 Macc 2:13), though later embodied in the Book of Ezra (Ezra 6:3-12; 7:12-26), were evidently included there in the first place because of their subject-matter; and, in the same way, it was doubtless because of subject-matter that the Temple was reckoned the right place for the priestly and Levitical genealogies to be kept. Josephus does not, indeed, say that these genealogies were kept in the Temple, only that they were kept at Jerusalem; but they evidently *were* kept in the Temple, since it was there, in the Chamber of Hewn Stone, that the Sanhedrin used them to test claims to priestly ancestry;[10] and this would explain why Josephus relates these genealogies so closely – and at first sight so confusingly – to the twenty-two canonical books, likewise kept in the Temple (*Ag. Ap.* 1:29-41).

The laying-up of something in the Temple had the effect of dedicating it to God, and so gave it an additional sanctity. The Greek verb ἀνάκειμαι which Josephus, in two passages quoted below, uses of the Scriptures 'laid up' in the Temple, is borrowed from pagan usage, and means 'to be laid up as a votive offering in a shrine', 'to be dedicated'. Once a book had been laid up in the Temple, it was available for use, as appropriate, by the officers of the Temple, the priests and Levites. The public reading of the Pentateuch in the Temple by the priests still continued in the first century, at least to some extent, and so did the singing of the Psalms there by the Levites; but even in the Temple the work of teaching seems to have been largely taken over by the lay rabbis, who taught there at festivals, as they did in the synagogue on sabbaths; and the presence of the Scriptures in the Temple must consequently have become, predominantly, a sign of their sacred status, and not an accessory to their liturgical use.

The statements in the *Antiquities* are these:

> A (or: the) scripture laid up in the Temple (ἐν τῷ ἱερῷ ἀνακειμένη γραφή) declares that God foretold to Moses that water would thus spring forth from the rock (*Ant.* 3:38, referring to Exod 17:6).
>
> Such, then, is the constitution that Moses left; he also handed over the laws written forty years before . . . Then he recited to them a poem in hexameter verse, which he has also left behind him in a (the) book kept in the Temple (ἐν βίβλῳ ἐν τῷ ἱερῷ), containing a prediction of future events . . . These books, therefore, he handed over to the priests (*Ant.* 4:302-4, concluding a summary of the laws of Deuteronomy, and referring especially to Deut 31:24-32:43).

---

[10] *T. Hagiga* 2:9; *T. Sanhedrin* 7:1; *Sifrei Num.* 116, p. 133-34 on Num 18:7.

That the length of the day increased on that occasion and exceeded the customary measure is made clear through the Scriptures laid up in the Temple (διὰ τῶν ἀνακειμένων ἐν τῷ ἱερῷ γραμμάτων, *Ant.* 5:61, referring to Josh 10:12-14).

These passages show clearly that the Temple Scriptures included Exodus, Deuteronomy and Joshua, and disprove the idea that they included only the Pentateuch. That they did include the Pentateuch is shown by the references in the Mishna to the liturgical reading of Leviticus, Numbers and Deuteronomy in the Temple (*Yoma* 7:1; *Sota* 7:7-8), and by the statement in *Sifrei Deut.* 356 (p. 423) and elsewhere that there were three copies of the Law in the Temple, each taking its name from a small textual variant which it contained, one of the variants being in Exodus and another in Deuteronomy. Moreover, both the Mishna (*Moed Katan* 3:4, variant text) and the Tosefta (*Kelim Bava Metsia* 5:8) speak of a copy of the Pentateuch in the Temple called 'the Book of Ezra'. This was probably the oldest and most revered copy of all, traditionally believed to have been written by Ezra the scribe.

Since the Temple Scriptures included Joshua, it may well be that they included others of the books which, in the Hebrew Bible, are assigned to the Prophets; and the above-mentioned passage from the Tosefta states that they did:

> The Book of Ezra, if it comes out (viz. of the Temple), makes the hands unclean; and not the Book of Ezra alone, but the Prophets and the Fifths. But another book makes the hands unclean if it is brought in there (*T. Kelim Bava Metsia* 5:8).

It will be seen that this passage also mentions 'the Fifths', and here 'the Fifths' probably means not 'the books of the Pentateuch' but 'the Psalms' (these also being in five books), used as a title not for the Psalter alone but for the third section of the Hebrew Bible, the Hagiographa, to which the Psalter belongs. Whether the Prophets were needed in the Temple (as in the synagogue) for public reading, we do not know; but we have noted that the primary reason for laying up books in the Temple was not their liturgical usefulness but their sanctity. Consequently, although only two of the Hagiographa (Psalms and Esther) were publicly read, even in the synagogue, we find that numbers of the Hagiographa were present in the Temple. For the Mishna and other Tannaic writings record that the high priest spent the night before the Day of Atonement in the Temple, where he was entertained and kept awake (so that he might not become ceremonially unclean through a nocturnal emission) by the reading of Psalms, Job, Proverbs, Daniel, Ezra or Chronicles.[11]

The passage from the Tosefta quoted above is also interesting for another reason. Clearly, it reflects the remarkable Pharisaic regulation that the Scrip-

---

[11] *M. Yoma* 1:6-7; *T. Yoma* 1:9; baraita in *P. T. Yoma* 1:6.

tures make the hands unclean. However, such a regulation obviously could not be extended to the Temple copies of the Scriptures, since the Temple was a holy place, from which all uncleanness had to be scrupulously removed (*M. Eruvin* 10:15; *M. Hagiga* 3:7-8; cp. 2 Chr 29:3-19; 1 Macc 4:36-46). Consequently, the Mishna rules that

> All books (viz. of Scripture) make the hands unclean, except the book of the Temple court (*Kelim* 15:6).

To this, the passage from the Tosefta adds the natural corollary that, if the Temple Scriptures were taken outside, they would lose their special prerogative and would make the hands unclean, like any other copy of the Scriptures. Then it goes on,

> But another book makes the hands unclean if it is brought in there.

Now, does this refer to uncanonical books, or to other copies of the Scriptures? Certainly, uncanonical books would not normally be brought into the Temple, which was the place for laying up holy books. On the other hand, the Pharisees did not hold that uncanonical books were liable to make the hands unclean; it was one of the great complaints of the Sadducees against the Pharisees that the latter said,

> "The Holy Scriptures make the hands unclean" but "the writings of Hamiram (Homer?) do not make the hands unclean" (*M. Yadayim* 4:6).

Moreover, the reasons why the Pharisees held that the Scriptures make the hands unclean[12] could not apply to ordinary books. So apparently the Tosefta is referring to canonical books, and is saying that other copies of the Scriptures must not be brought into the Temple, since these make the hands unclean wherever they are. It follows that, even if (as is likely) the Temple copies of the Scriptures had originally been brought in from outside, by the end of the Temple period this event (or, rather, these events) lay so far in the past that nothing of the kind was permitted any more. If the Temple copies of the canonical books needed to be renewed or increased in number, it could only be done within the Temple itself by the Temple scribes.

All this has important consequences for the history of the canon. As Moses Stuart pointed out, while the Temple stood, the main test of the canonical reception of a book must have been whether or not it was one of those laid up in the Temple.[13] The introduction of a book into the Temple collection would have been an occasion of great deliberation and solemnity, and an event which could hardly be either anticipated or reversed. If, as the Tannaic literature maintains, not just the Pentateuch and the Prophets but also the Hagiographa belonged to the Temple collection, and by the end of the Temple period had belonged to it

---

[12] See below (Terminology and Grounds of the Rabbinic Disputes).
[13] Stuart, *Critical History*, sect. 8.

for such a long time that it was no longer permitted even to bring in fresh copies of the books, let alone copies of fresh books, how can this be reconciled with the current belief that the Hagiographa were not formally recognized as canonical (or, if some of them were, others were still periodically being added) until the 'Council' of Yavne (Jamnia), held after the Temple had been destroyed? The truth must rather be that, even if it became possible, after the destruction of the Temple, to add certain *disputed* books to the canon (which is conceivable), the *undisputed* books, in all three sections of the canon, must have been canonical before the Temple was destroyed, and not just for a little while before, but for a very long while.

The Agreed Nucleus of the Scriptural Canon

BOOKS QUOTED WITH CONVENTIONAL FORMULAS

Which, then, were the undisputed books? To answer this question, we will now investigate which books were quoted with conventional formulas for citing canonical books, looking also at other references which indicate equally clearly that a canonical book is in view. Of course, writers of the intertestamental and NT period were aware of many books (for example, their own) which did not belong to the Jewish canon, and on occasion they made reference to such books. Though they would have known the canonical books, it is very rash to suppose that every book they knew was canonical. We will, therefore, confine ourselves to references where, either by the use of a conventional formula or in some other way, it is clearly indicated that the book the writer is referring to is one of the Scriptures.

References of this kind to the Pentateuch are especially common. To cite only the most striking, it is worthy of note that twice in the Apocrypha the book of the Law of Moses is effectively identified with the personified Wisdom of God (Sir 24:23; Bar 4:1); moreover, Genesis, Numbers and Deuteronomy are cited as parts of 'the Law and the Prophets', i.e. Scripture (4 Macc 18:10-19). Also, Deuteronomy or the whole Pentateuch is described as ἡ ἱερὰ βίβλος, 'the holy book' (2 Macc 8:23; cp. Deut 20:2-8), an expression twice echoed, in regard to Exodus or the whole Pentateuch, by Alexander Polyhistor (extract in Eusebius, *Praep. Evang.* 9:29). In the Pseudepigrapha, *Ep. Arist.* 177 describes the Pentateuch, brought to Egypt for translation into Greek, as God's 'oracles' (λόγια); *Jub.* 30:12 refers to Genesis as something which God has written; and *Ass. Mos.* 3:11-12 describes the warnings of Leviticus and Deuteronomy as 'that which Moses declared to us in prophecies'. In the Dead Sea Scrolls, the Books of Exodus, Leviticus, Numbers and Deuteronomy are all quoted with conventional formulas for quoting Scripture (*1QS* 5:15; *CD* 5:1-2; 7:6, 8-9, 19-20; 16:6-7, 10; 9:2; 10:16-17; 11:18). Quotations from all five books of the Pentateuch by Philo, both with conventional formulas for quoting Scripture and with significant formulas of his own, are too numerous to list. In the NT Jesus quotes Deuteronomy with conventional formulas (Luke 4:4, 8, 12 etc.), as Paul does Genesis (Rom 4:17; 1 Cor 15:45), Exodus (Acts 23:5; 1 Cor 10:7; 2 Cor 8:15) and Deuteronomy (Rom 12:19; 15:10; Gal 3:10, 13), and as Peter does Leviticus (1 Pet 1:16); moreover, Jesus quotes Genesis as the words of God (Matt 19:5), Luke quotes Exodus and Leviticus as from 'the Law of the Lord' (Luke 2:23-24), and, as Scripture (ἡ γραφή), John quotes Exodus (John 19:36) and Paul quotes Genesis (Rom 4:3; Gal 3:8; 4:30) and Exodus (Rom 9:17). Finally, Josephus says that five of the twenty-two inspired books immemorially accepted by the Jews are those of Moses (*Ag. Ap.* 1:37-43).

Of books outside the Pentateuch, Tobit cites predictions of Amos and Nahum by name, as being prophets (Tob 2:6; 14:4), and in Tob 14:4-7 it refers generally to the predictions of 'the prophets of Israel', among whom one can probably identify Isaiah, Jeremiah, Ezekiel and Daniel. The prediction of the Exile (v. 4) suggests Jeremiah particularly, the prediction of the return (v. 5) Isaiah particularly, the prediction of judgement on Babylon (v. 4) one or other of the two, the prediction of the rebuilding of the Temple (v. 5) Ezekiel, and the fulfilling of times and seasons (v. 5) Daniel.

Ecclesiasticus, in chapters 44-50, contains the great catalogue of 'famous men', who are arranged in chronological, rather than biblical, order, extending from the patriarchal period onwards, and who end with a non-biblical figure, the high priest Shimon the Just. Nevertheless, the catalogue is summed up after Zerubbabel, Jeshua and Nehemiah, in the last three verses of chapter 49, by returning to the very beginning of history, before introducing Shimon the Just in chapter 50; and this strongly suggests that the previous names have been biblical names, whereas the remaining one will not be. Certainly, all the books on which the author has drawn in chapters 44-49 are books which were later to stand in the Jewish canon, and which therefore in all probability already did. They unmistakably include Genesis (Sir 44:16-23; 49:14-16), Exodus and Leviticus (Sir 45:1-15), Numbers (Sir 45:15-24; 46:7), Joshua (Sir 46:1-10), Judges (Sir 46:11-12), Samuel (Sir 45:25; 46:13-47:8; 47:11), Kings (Sir 47:12-48:9; 48:11-23; 49:1-6), Isaiah (Sir 48:24-25), Jeremiah (Sir 49:6-7), Ezekiel (Sir 49:8-9), the Twelve Minor Prophets (Sir 49:10), Haggai (Sir 49:11), Malachi (Sir 48:10), Psalms and Proverbs (Sir 44:4-5 Heb; cp. 47:8, 14-17), Ezra-Nehemiah (Sir 49:11-13) and Chronicles (Sir 47:9-10). One should probably add that Ben Sira's interesting statement that Ezekiel 'made mention of Job' (Sir 49:9 Heb; cp. Ezek 14:14, 20) suggests that the Book of Job was also canonical. It is noteworthy too that these chapters dwell on the succession of the prophets – Moses, Joshua, Samuel, Nathan, Elijah, Elisha (Sir 46:1; 47:1; 48:1, 12) – and that the description of Joshua as 'the successor of Moses in *prophecies*' (Sir 46:1),[14] the accounts of the *revelations* in the books of Isaiah, Jeremiah and Ezekiel (Sir 48:24-25; 49:6-9), the mention of 'the *Twelve* [Minor] *Prophets*'

---

[14] This is the intelligent paraphrase of the Greek version.

(Sir 49:10) and the quotation of a 'written' prediction by Malachi (Sir 48:10; cp. Mal 4:5-6) all seem clearly to underline the fact that the books in question are prophetic and canonical.

Other evidence from the Apocrypha is that Baruch quotes a collection of predictions from Jeremiah with the phrase 'as Thou hast spoken by the hand of thy servants the prophets . . . thy words that Thou spakest by the hand of thy servants the prophets' (Bar 2:20-6); that 1 Maccabees quotes Psalms as predictive (1 Macc 7:16-17); that 4 Maccabees explicitly includes among 'the Law and the Prophets' Isaiah, Ezekiel, Psalms, Proverbs and Daniel (4 Macc 18:10-18); and that *2 Esdras (4 Ezra)* refers to the twenty-four inspired books which Ezra published openly, i.e. the books of the canon (*2 Esdr* 14:23-6, 38-47).

In the Pseudepigrapha, the *Martyrdom of Isaiah* refers to Isa 1:10; 6:1, as the words of a true prophet, falsely accused (*Mart. Isa.* 3:8-10); the Testaments of the Twelve Patriarchs refer to Ecclesiastes as part of 'the Law' (*Test. Naphtali* 8:7-10); and the apocalyptic pseudepigrapha, from *1 Enoch* onwards, display a general dependence upon Daniel, and ascribe their revelations to men presumably already known as 'prophets' from canonical sources, such as the various patriarchs, Moses, Ezekiel, Daniel and Ezra.

In the Dead Sea Scrolls, conventional formulas for quoting Scripture are used in the cases of the books Samuel, Isaiah, Hosea, Amos, Micah, Nahum and Proverbs (*1QS* 5:17; 8:14; *CD* 1:13-14; 4:20; 7:14-16; 8:3; 20:16; 16:15; 9:5, 8-9; 11:20-21; 13:23-14:1; *4QFlor* 1:7, 12; *11QMelch* 23). In addition, Isaiah, Ezekiel, Zechariah, Malachi and Daniel are quoted as divine or prophetic writings (*CD* 3:20-4:4; 4:13-14; 6:13-14; 7:10-12; 7:20-21, MS. B; *4QFlor* 1:14-17; 2:3-4). The Qumran Pesharim are often continuous commentaries on books (Isaiah, Hosea, Micah, Nahum, Habakkuk, Zephaniah and Psalms), and such books were, more likely than not, already canonical. Finally, the fact that the Qumran texts on the priestly courses maintain the twenty-four courses of 1 Chr 24, whereas twenty-six courses would have fitted much better into their calendar of exactly fifty-two weeks, suggests that the sect regarded Chronicles as canonical.[15]

Of the ancient Bible translations, the Septuagint refers to passages in Job with the formula 'it is written' (Job 42:17 LXX, alluding to Job 14:14-15; 19:25-6 LXX). It also attributes Lamentations, in a head-note, to the prophet Jeremiah.

In Philo, Joshua is referred to as part of 'the Holy Records' (*Hypothetica* 6:5); Judges and Samuel are quoted with a conventional formula for citing Scripture (*On the Confusion of Tongues* 128-32; *On the Migration of Abraham* 196-7); Samuel is quoted with the phrase 'as the Holy Word says' (*On Drunkenness* 143-52); Kings is referred to with 'the things revealed in the Books of Reigns' (*On the Confusion of Tongues* 149); Isaiah is quoted as a 'prophet', a 'friend of Moses', 'inspired', uttering 'oracles' (*On the Change of Names* 169; *On Dreams*

---

[15]   As is pointed out by Eybers, 'Some Light', 29-30.

2:172-3; *On Rewards and Punishments* 158-61; *Questions and Answers on Genesis* 2:26, 43; *De Deo* 6); and, with the same and similar expressions to those used for Isaiah, quotations are made from Jeremiah (*On the Cherubim* 49; *On the Confusion of Tongues* 44-51; *On Flight and Finding* 197-8), Hosea (*On Noah's Work as a Planter* 138; *On the Change of Names* 139-40; *Questions and Answers on Exodus* 2:76) and Zechariah (*On the Confusion of Tongues* 62). Philo often quotes Psalms, as by a 'prophet', an 'oracular man', a 'companion of Moses' or in other ways (*On Husbandry* 50-4; *On Noah's Work as a Planter* 29, 39; *Who is the Heir* 290, etc.). He also quotes Job, linked with a passage of Genesis, as part of a biblical syllogism (*On the Change of Names* 47-51), and he quotes Proverbs as by 'one of the divine choir' (*On Drunkenness* 31).

In the NT, Jesus quotes Isaiah (Mark 7:6-7; 11:17; Luke 22:37), Zechariah (Mark 14:27) and Malachi (Luke 7:27) with conventional formulas for citing Scripture; Paul does the same repeatedly with Isaiah[16] and Psalms,[17] and also with Habakkuk (Rom 1:17), Malachi (Rom 9:13), Job (1 Cor 3:19) and Proverbs (Rom 12:19-20); while other NT writers do so with Jeremiah (Heb 8:8-12), Zechariah (John 12:14-15), Psalms (Luke 4:10-11; John 2:17; 6:31) and Proverbs (Jas 4:6). Moreover, Jesus quotes Isaiah as by a prophet (Matt 13:14-15; John 6:45), Psalms as inspired (Mark 12:36) and Isaiah and Psalms as 'Scripture' (Mark 12:10-11; Luke 4:17-21; John 13:18); and in one or other of these ways the rest of the NT quotes Kings (Rom 11:2-4), Isaiah (in many places),[18] Jeremiah (Matt 2:17-18), Hosea (Matt 2:15), Joel (Acts 2:16-21), Amos (Acts 7:42-3; 15:15-18), Micah (Matt 2:5-6), Habakkuk (Acts 13:40-1), Zechariah (John 19:37) and Psalms (Matt 13:35; John 19:24; Acts 2:25-31; 4:25-6; Heb 3:7-11; 4:7). Jesus refers to the history of the prophet Jonah as a predictive sign or type (Matt 12:39-40). The Book of Revelation endorses various revelations and predictions of Ezekiel, notably the Gog and Magog prophecy (Rev 20:7-10; cp. Ezek 38-39). The Book of Revelation is likewise deeply indebted to the prophecies of Daniel, which also underlie much of the teaching of Jesus; and in Matt 24:15 Daniel is mentioned explicitly as a 'prophet', in relation to his prediction of the abomination of desolation (Dan 9:27 etc.), while in 1 Pet 1:10-12 'the prophets' seem to refer particularly to Daniel, with his messianic predictions (Dan 2, 7 and 9) and his concern about times and seasons (Dan 7:25; 8:13-14; 9:24-27; 12:6-13).

Looking back over all this evidence (nearly the whole of which dates from before the 'Council' of Yavne [Jamnia], where the Jewish canon is usually supposed to have been closed), one notes that, with the exception of the three short books Ruth, Song of Songs and Esther, the canonicity of every book of the Hebrew Bible is attested, most of them several times over. Obadiah is not

---

[16] Rom 2:24; 3:10-17; 9:33; 10:15; 11:8, 26-27; 14:11; 15:21; 1 Cor 1:19; 2:9; 15:54; 2 Cor 6:2; Gal 4:27.
[17] Rom 3:4, 10-18; 8:36; 15:3, 9-11; 1 Cor 3:19-20; 2 Cor 4:13; 9:9; Eph 4:8.
[18] Matt 1:22-23; 3:3; 4:14-16; 8:17; 12:17-21; John 12:38-41; Acts 7:48-50; 8:30-35; 13:34; 28:25-27; Rom 10:11; 1 Pet 2:6.

separately attested, but since the 'Twelve (Minor) Prophets' as a body are attested in Ecclesiasticus, this covers Obadiah as well. One cannot, it is true, just assume that all these writers accepted all these canonical books, when none of them actually mentions more than a proportion; but, on the other hand, since their silences can be easily explained by the fact that they simply referred to such books as were relevant to what they were writing, it is very striking that, over a period ranging from the second century B.C.E. (at latest) to the first century C.E., so many writers, of so many classes (Semitic, Hellenistic, Pharisaic, Essene, Christian), show such agreement about the canon, agreement both with each other and with the present Hebrew Bible. Ecclesiasticus, one of the earliest of these witnesses, is also one of the fullest; and since few, if any, of the witnesses are concerned with *asserting* the canonicity of the books they mention, and not rather with asserting something else on the basis of the *admitted* canonicity of the books, it is clear that they do not speak simply for themselves but at least for their own school of thought among the Jews, if not for Jewry as a whole. And if one takes the Septuagint and Philo as speaking for Hellenistic Judaism, the Dead Sea Scrolls as speaking for Essenism, the NT as speaking for Christianity and most of the other literature as speaking for Pharisaism, it is clear that in each group many of the books in all three sections of the Hebrew canon – Pentateuch, Prophets and Hagiographa alike – were accepted as canonical.

THE EVIDENCE OF JOSEPHUS

We have not yet considered the evidence of Josephus, except with regard to the Pentateuch, and his evidence on the canon is the fullest of all. This is not so much because he was writing his voluminous *Antiquities* and treatise *Against Apion* in the last decade of the first century, as because a large part of his *Antiquities* covers the same ground as the narratives of the OT, and because *Against Apion* is an apologetic work directed to Gentiles, who needed to have the Scriptures identified for them in a way that the Jews probably did not. In his *Antiquities* Josephus cites Joshua as included in 'the Scriptures laid up in the Temple' (5:61), Kings as included in 'the Holy Books' (9:28, 46; cp. also *War* 6:103-5, 'the Holy Word'), Isaiah as a 'book of prophecy' (*Ant.* 11:4-6; cp. also 10:35; 13:64, 68; *War* 7:432), Jeremiah and Ezekiel as books of prophetic predictions (*Ant.* 10:79-80; cp. also 10:104-7; 10:141-2; 11:1-2; *War* 5:391), the Twelve (Minor) Prophets as likewise books of prophetic predictions (*Ant.* 10:35),[19] Nahum as predictive (9:239-42), Lamentations as a book of prophetic authorship (10:78), and Daniel as included in 'the Holy Scriptures' (10:210; cp.

---

[19]   Josephus is sometimes thought to be referring in this passage to twelve of the thirteen prophetic histories of which he speaks in the passage of *Against Apion* discussed below. But he is speaking here of predictive rather than of historical books, and of books written by a single author (unlike the Book of the Twelve Prophets, which is counted as only one of the thirteen in the other passage).

also 10:266-81; 11:337; 12:322). Moreover, in certain passages of his *War*, he refers to the fulfilment of three ΟΤ predictions, which, although the books in question are not named, are probably from Ezekiel, Zechariah and Daniel.[20]

In *Ag. Ap.* 1:37-43, Josephus goes on to give his Gentile readers an account of the Jewish canon as a whole. He states that the inspired books are of prophetic authorship and are 'only twenty-two' in number. 'Five of these are the books of Moses', containing the Law and the history of the period from the creation of man to Moses's own death. 'From the death of Moses until Artaxerxes, the king of Persia succeeding Xerxes, the prophets after Moses recorded the events of their own times in thirteen books. The remaining four books contain hymns to God and precepts for human life'. With the reign of Artaxerxes, 'the exact succession of the prophets' ceased, so later books are not reckoned equally reliable. But these twenty-two books have been immemorially regarded by all Jews, from the time of their birth, as the 'teachings of God'.

Even if one allows for a little exaggeration, it is obvious that the canon of which Josephus speaks was not any recent construction. He concentrates on its historical content, because in this treatise *Against Apion* he is defending his *Antiquities*, a history largely based on the canonical books (*Ag. Ap.* 1:1-5), but he mentions that it includes also the Law of Moses and four books of a lyrical or proverbial character, so it is quite natural to find in it books of prophetic oracles as well. From the *Antiquities*, we already have the names of seven of his thirteen prophetical books (Joshua, Kings, Isaiah, Jeremiah-Lamentations, Ezekiel, the Minor Prophets, Daniel), or eight if Lamentations is reckoned separately from Jeremiah; and to carry the history in 'exact succession' (ἀϰριβὴς δια-δοχή) from the death of Moses to the beginning of the Book of Kings requires the inclusion of Judges and Samuel also. The history certainly continues after Kings, for 'Artaxerxes, the king of Persia succeeding Xerxes', is for Josephus the husband of Esther, and according to his account Ezra and Nehemiah laboured during the reign of Xerxes, this Artaxerxes's father (*Ant.* 11:120-3, 135, 159, 168, 179, 183; 11:184-5 etc.). It follows that Ezra-Nehemiah[21] and Esther must also belong to the 'thirteen books'. This leaves not more than two places among the thirteen to fill, and there are four books undisputed among the Pharisees (and Josephus was himself a Pharisee) still to be assigned. These books are Ruth, Psalms, Job and Chronicles. Psalms clearly belongs to the section of four books containing 'hymns to God and precepts for human life', and Ruth is a little book easily appended to Judges or prefixed to Psalms,[22] so

---

[20] *War* 6:310-12 (cf. Ezek 40:47; 42:20; 45:2); *War* 4:386-88; 6:109-10 (cf. Zech 12:2; 14:2, 14); *War* 6:310-15 (cf. Dan 7:13-14).

[21] Usually, but not always, in the narrative of his *Antiquities* Josephus follows 1 Esdras rather than Ezra. The explanation, as in the case of the Fathers of the first four centuries, whose practice is similar, is probably that 1 Esdras was regarded as an alternative Greek translation of Ezra and not as a rival book. See also Feldman, below, pp. 464-65.

[22] As beginning 'And it came to pass in the days when the Judges judged . . .' and as ending with the genealogy of the Psalmist David. There is direct or indirect evidence of the Jews treating Ruth in both these ways. See my *Old Testament Canon*, 120, 158, 185.

the remaining two prophetical books are probably the lengthy books Job and Chronicles.

The description of the final four-book section as comprising 'hymns to God and precepts for human life' is clearly suggested primarily by Psalms and Proverbs, and since Josephus's canon now contains three of the five books disputed by some of the rabbis (Ezekiel, Esther and Proverbs), the other two lyrical or proverbial books are probably the remaining two disputed books, the Song of Songs and Ecclesiastes. Alternatively, if Lamentations is reckoned separately from Jeremiah, this may be included here with one or other of the two disputed books. Ecclesiasticus would also suit the description of the four books, but its mention of Shimon the Just, whom Josephus dates long after Artaxerxes (*Ant.* 12:43), rules it out, and, as we shall see, Ecclesiasticus made a much weaker bid for a place in the Pharisaic canon than the Song of Songs or Ecclesiastes, while the remaining books of the Apocrypha made virtually no bid at all. At most, then, Josephus's canon differs from the contents of the Hebrew Bible by one book, in that it possibly omits Ecclesiastes or the Song of Songs.[23]

The Threefold Structure of the Canon

The Books of the Hebrew Bible are arranged in three sections: the Law, the Prophets and the Hagiographa. This mode of arrangement is frequently mentioned in the Talmud, but goes back to a much earlier period. There is evidence from well before the Christian era that the canonical books were already grouped in three distinct categories. The grandson of Jesus ben Sira, who translated his grandfather's book Ecclesiasticus out of Hebrew into Greek for the Greek-speaking Jews of Egypt, prefixed to the translation a prologue of his own, in which he thrice makes reference to the three parts of the canon. This prologue can hardly have been written later than about 130 B.C.E.[24] The relevant passages of the prologue (if given a literal rendering, based on the Revised Version) run as follows:

> Whereas many and great things have been delivered unto us by the Law and the Prophets and the others that have followed in their steps (διὰ τοῦ νόμου καὶ τῶν προφητῶν καὶ τῶν ἄλλων τῶν κατ' αὐτοὺς ἠκολουθη-κότων) . . . my grandfather Jesus, having much given himself to the reading of the Law and the Prophets and the other Books of the fathers (τοῦ νόμου καὶ τῶν προφητῶν καὶ τῶν ἄλλων πατρίων βιβλίων) and having gained great familiarity therein, was drawn on also himself to

[23] On the supposed evidence against the canonicity of some of the Hagiographa which certain writers have adduced from intertestamental sources, see my *Old Testament Canon*, 77-78, and the literature there cited. The eccentric *Psalms scrolls* of Qumran, to take the most topical example, are probably liturgical rather than biblical texts.

[24] The translator says that he had 'come into Egypt in the thirty-eighth year of Euergetes the King', i.e. in 132 B.C.E., and after 'continuing there some time' had made his translation. If the 'some time' had been long, he would presumably have dated his translation in a different way.

write somewhat pertaining to instruction and wisdom; in order that those who love learning, and are addicted to these things, might make progress much more by living according to the Law. Ye are entreated therefore to read with favour and attention, and to pardon us, if in any parts of what we have laboured to interpret, we may seem to fail in some of the phrases. For things originally spoken in Hebrew have not the same force in them when they are translated into another tongue: and not only these things, but also the Law itself and the Prophecies and the rest of the Books (αὐτὸς ὁ νόμος καὶ αἱ προφητεῖαι καὶ τὰ λοιπὰ τῶν βιβλίων) have no small difference when they are spoken in their original language.

The translator ends his prologue by saying that he has set forth his version of Ecclesiasticus for those

> who in the land of their sojournings are desirous to learn, fashioning their manners beforehand, so as to live according to the Law.

It appears, then, that for this writer there are three groups of books which have a unique authority, and that his grandfather wrote only after gaining great familiarity with them, as their expositor not as their rival. The translator explicitly distinguishes 'these things' (i.e. Ecclesiasticus, or uncanonical Hebrew compositions such as Ecclesiasticus) from 'the Law itself and the Prophecies and the rest of the Books'. Moreover, he regards even the Hagiographa as 'ancestral' (πατρίων) books, long enough esteemed to have been translated into Greek, and their number as complete ('*the* others that have followed in their steps', '*the* other Books of the fathers', '*the rest* of the Books'). And not only does he state that in his own day there was this threefold canon, distinguished from all other writings, in which even the Hagiographa formed a closed collection of old books, but he implies that such was the case in his grandfather's time also.

Passing on from the second century B.C.E. to the first century C.E., from Alexandria to Palestine, and from Jewish writings to Christian, the threefold structure of the OT canon is clearly reflected in a post-resurrection saying of Jesus's, recorded by Luke. Strictly speaking, the evidence supplied by Jesus's older contemporary Philo may be earlier than his own, but since Jesus's words will make Philo's easier to understand, we will look at his first. He addresses his disciples as follows:

> These are my words which I spoke to you, while I was still with you, that everything written about me in the Law of Moses and the Prophets and the Psalms must be fulfilled (Luke 24:44).

This saying suggests that 'the Law of Moses', 'the Prophets' and '(the) Psalms' are now established names for the three parts of the canon. 'The Prophets' has already occurred in the prologue to Ecclesiasticus, and 'the Law of Moses'

52

elsewhere,[25] but 'the Psalms' (ψαλμοί) is a novelty; hence some commentators suppose that the whole Hagiographa cannot be meant, but only the Psalter. However, the omission of the rest of the Hagiographa would be surprising in view of Jesus's regular use of the Book of Daniel in the gospels. In the prologue to Ecclesiasticus, the third group of books seems to have no title, since it is described rather than named, and in different words on each occasion; more-over, in later times the normal Jewish name for the third group is not 'Psalms' but *Ketuvim*, 'Scriptures' (Greek ἁγιόγραφα, 'Holy Writings', 'Hagiographa'); nevertheless, there appears to be sufficient evidence to show that at one period the title 'Psalms' was also in use, having been suggested, no doubt, by the fact that the Psalter was among the most important books which the third group contained, and was especially important in the liturgy; and by the further fact that, according to the traditional order, it was effectively the first book in the third group, Ruth serving simply as its introduction. In Philo, as we shall see, the third group is also named or described as 'Psalms' (ὕμνοι), and the name was evidently still in use in the tenth century, when the Arabian writer al-Masudi, in the course of a well-informed account of contemporary Judaism, speaks of 'the Law, the Prophets and the Psalms, which are the 24 books'.[26]

This statement increases the probability that certain passages in the Tosefta, the Palestinian Talmud and the Minor Tractates of the Talmud ought to be interpreted in the same way. In each of the passages the word חומשים 'Fifths', is used, and Jastrow in his Dictionary shows that this word can mean either the five individual books of the Pentateuch (as is more common) or the five individual books of the Psalter. In the quotations that follow, however, 'the Fifths' appears to be used absolutely, to mean the Psalter as a whole, and the Psalter appears to stand for the third group of the canonical books. The passages run thus:

> The Book of Ezra, if it comes out (of the Temple), makes the hands unclean; and not the Book of Ezra alone, but the Prophets and the Fifths. But another book makes the hands unclean if it is brought in there (*T. Kelim, Bava Metsia* 5:8).[27]

> If it (viz. the Book of Esther) is written (in a copy of) the Fifths, they do not read publicly in it (*P.T. Megilla* 2:3).

> In a scroll of the Law, the space of two finger-breadths must be left (between columns), but in scrolls of the Prophets and in scrolls of the Fifths the space of one thumb-breadth. In the lower margin of a scroll of the Law the space of a hand-breadth is left, and in the upper margin

[25] 1 Kgs 2:3; Dan 9:13; Ezra 7:6; 2 Chr 23:18; 1 Esdr 8:3; 9:39; Bar 2:2.

[26] See Kahle, *The Cairo Geniza*, 88-89. The '24 books' are the customary Jewish count for the complete canon.

[27] This is the passage quoted earlier with regard to the Temple archive, when it was noted that the 'Book of Ezra' in question was a Temple scroll of the Pentateuch.

two-thirds of a hand-breadth, but in scrolls of the Prophets and the Fifths three finger-breadths in the lower margin and two finger-breadths in the upper (*Sefer Tora* 2:3-4. Also *Soferim* 2:4, which gives the same rules almost *verbatim*).

The passages from the Tosefta and the Minor Tractates are alike in that they mention the Law and the Prophets as well as the Fifths, whereas that from the Jerusalem Talmud mentions the Fifths alone. The evidence that the Jerusalem Talmud has the Hagiographa in view lies in the simple fact that a scroll containing the Pentateuch or a scroll containing the Psalter without the rest of the Hagiographa could not in the nature of the case be used for the reading of Esther, whereas a scroll containing the Psalter together with the rest of the Hagiographa could. Such a scroll, says Rav (the teacher quoted), must not be used publicly for the reading of Esther at Purim; only the sort of scroll customary at the festival, containing Esther alone, is suitable. The evidence that the other passages refer to the Hagiographa is less direct but appears to the present writer adequate.[28]

A second saying of Jesus's makes further allusion to the three groups of canonical books.[29] His utterance about all the righteous blood of prophets from the blood of Abel to the blood of Zechariah, which is found in Matt 23:35 and Luke 11:51, in all probability implies that for Jesus and his hearers the canon began with Genesis and ended with Chronicles, seeing that the murder of Abel is recorded near the beginning of the former book (Gen 4:3-15) and the murder of Zechariah near the end of the latter book (2 Chr 24:19-22). This appears to reflect the traditional Jewish arrangement of the books, whereby Chronicles is not placed with Samuel and Kings, in the second group of books, but is put in the third and last group, as its concluding item.

Reverting to Alexandria and to Jewish writings, we must now consider the testimony of *On the Contemplative Life*, a little work which (following the manuscripts and the Fathers) has traditionally been attributed to Philo, and no doubt rightly. It describes a Jewish community whom he calls Therapeutae.

Now, *On the Contemplative Life* gives a significant account of the things which each of the Therapeutae takes with him into his oratory. He takes none of the common things of life, but

> (the) Laws, and (the) Oracles given by inspiration through (the) Prophets, and (the) Psalms, and the other books whereby knowledge and piety are increased and completed (νόμους καὶ λόγια θεσπισθέντα διὰ προφητῶν καὶ ὕμνους καὶ τὰ ἄλλα οἷς ἐπιστήμη καὶ εὐσέβεια συναύξονται καὶ τελειοῦνται), *Cont.* 25

---

[28] For a full statement of this evidence, see my *Old Testament Canon*, 113-15 and Appendix 1.

[29] Cf. *Old Testament Canon*, 212ff.

The first three groups of books here listed (without the article, as is common in titles) seem to correspond closely to those referred to by the grandson of Ben Sira and especially by Jesus, in Luke 24. Ὕμνοι, as Conybeare remarks,[30] is Philo's regular name for the Psalms; and that here again it refers not simply to the Psalter but to the Hagiographa in general is suggested by Philo's appeals to Job and Proverbs as Scripture, and by the Qumran community's appeals to Proverbs and Daniel as Scripture, which are noted above. The Therapeutae, with their monasticism, their calendrical peculiarities and their sectarian books and hymns, were clearly akin to the Qumran community, and Philo's statement may indicate that not only he, with his Pharisaic leanings,[31] but also the Therapeutae, with their Essene leanings, were accustomed to divide the canon into three sections. The only problem is what is meant by 'the other books (or things) whereby knowledge and piety are increased and completed'. These also are evidently books, both because of the context and because they 'increase knowledge', and the most likely explanation is that they are books outside the canon to which the Therapeutae nevertheless ascribe almost equal authority. (Philo does not necessarily share their view himself, any more than on some other points on which he records the Therapeutae's distinctive views.) The community at Qumran cherished pseudonymous apocalypses and prophecies such as *Enoch* and *Jubilees*, yet there is reason to believe that they recognized these to be outside the canon, as will be seen in a later section. The Qumran attitude was probably comparable to that of the apocalyptist who wrote *2 Esdras (4 Ezra)*, for whom there are ninety-four inspired books, twenty-four of them openly published (i.e. the books of the canon), and the other seventy reserved for the specially privileged (*2 Esdr* 14). The attitude of the Therapeutae was very likely similar, in which case 'the other books whereby knowledge and piety are increased and completed' refers to apocalypses and such which they greatly respected but which they grouped separately because they knew them to be no part of the canon.

It is thus a well-attested fact that, by the first century C.E., the division of the canon into three groups of books was widespread in the Jewish world, and that it was familiar to Jesus.[32]

THE ORIGIN OF THE THREE SECTIONS

According to the conventional theory, championed by Ryle,[33] the Pentateuch

---

[30] Conybeare, *Philo*, 312.
[31] See Belkin, *Philo and the Oral Law*; Borgen, 'Philo of Alexandria'.
[32] On the identification of the books in the three groups, see Ellis, below, pp. 655-79; the evidence of Josephus, Jerome and the baraita in *B.T. Bava Batra* 14b is presented also in my *Old Testament Canon*, 118-27, where the talmudic arrangement is shown to be probably the oldest, as is assumed in what follows.
[33] Ryle, *Canon*.

and the other two divisions of the canon were recognized one at a time, each as a complete whole, at three different eras. He bases this on the supposed facts that the Samaritan schism became complete in the fifth century B.C.E., and that the division of books between the Prophets and Hagiographa has no rhyme or reason. He supposes that the Samaritans took with them, when they separated, what was then the complete Jewish canon, the Pentateuch, and that this must therefore have been canonical by the fifth century B.C.E.. The Prophets must have become canonical after this, but before the books of Daniel and Chronicles had been written, or at least recognized (otherwise they ought to have been put in the Prophets, to judge by their character), and he therefore dates the canonization of the Prophets in the third century B.C.E. The Hagiographa, including Daniel, Chronicles and the disputed books, were not canonized until the 'Council' of Yavne (Jamnia), about 90 C.E.

We shall see in the last section of this chapter that Ryle's date for the completion of the Samaritan schism is probably much too early, and in what follows in this section that a rational principle is discernible in the distribution of books between the Prophets and Hagiographa, so both the linchpins of his theory give way. There is, in fact, no reason why an open collection of non-Mosaic Scriptures should not have been recognized alongside the Pentateuch, at least from the time that the editing of the Pentateuch was complete, since the continuity between the Pentateuch and the Book of Joshua is so strong; and if the editing of the Pentateuch overlapped with the period of the writing Prophets, as is usually believed, *several* of these may have been recognized alongside it, from that time on. Then, when the collection of non-Mosaic Scriptures was judged to be complete, it may have been organized and divided into the familiar Prophets and Hagiographa.

Eight arguments, in all, have been used to show that the Hagiographa must have been canonized later than the Prophets, but they all break down when tested. The argument from Chronicles and Daniel overlooks the facts that narrative books are not confined to the Prophets but are found in all three divisions of the canon; that those in the Pentateuch deal with an earlier period than those in the Prophets, and that those in the Hagiographa, even Chronicles, extend to a later period (that of the Exile and Return); that the first half of Daniel is also narrative; and that though the visionary books are mostly in the Prophets, the Wisdom books are all in the Hagiographa, and Daniel could alternatively be regarded as a Wisdom book.[34]

The most important of the other arguments are that the Hagiographa tend to be later works than the Prophets (true, but *only* a tendency); that the canonicity of four of the Hagiographa was disputed by certain rabbis (true, but so was the canonicity of Ezekiel, one of the Prophets); that the Hagiographa were not included in the Jewish lectionary (true in general, but Psalms and Esther *were*

---

[34] Daniel was 'chief governor over all the wise men of Babylon', and the words 'wise' and 'wisdom' occur in the book 26 times.

included, and the Prophets as a whole were not included either, only the whole of the Pentateuch); that in the Septuagint the Hagiographa are more freely rendered than the Prophets (true in general, but not in every case, and probably due to the aim of private rather than liturgical reading); that the rabbis attributed different degrees of holiness to the different divisions of the canon (true, but significantly they attributed a higher degree of holiness to the Pentateuch, and the same degree of holiness to the Prophets and Hagiographa); and that the Hagiographa cannot long have existed as a division of the canon when the prologue to Ecclesiasticus was written, since they had not yet acquired a definite title (true, but the prologue views them as a closed collection of old books, so the books they contained may have long been canonical, and only their separation from the Prophets something recent).[35] To pursue this last point, since the title 'the Law and the Prophets' for the whole canon is old (2 Macc 15:9), it may go back to a date before the subdivision was made, in which case there would have been a title ready to hand for one of the subdivisions but not for the other. Since the prologue to Ecclesiasticus was written about 130 B.C.E., and since the third division of the canon cannot have had a separate existence without a title for a very long period before that, the subdivision may have been made in 164 B.C.E., when one of the great crises in the history of the canon was overcome, through the gathering together of the scattered Scriptures by Judas Maccabaeus (2 Macc 2:14-15), after Antiochus Epiphanes had tried to destroy them (1 Macc 1:56-7).

How (by what physical means) Judas made presumably his classified collection of books is worth considering. He did not do it by putting the Prophets or the Hagiographa together in a single scroll, for the scrolls of the second century B.C.E. (as we know from the Dead Sea Scrolls and other evidence) were not nearly capacious enough. He must have done it primarily by compiling a list. In listing the books, he would not only have grouped them in their separate sections: he must also have arranged them in some order or other within those sections. And the order which he chose would have been one consonant with the principles on which he was grouping the books.

The separation of the first section of the canon from other sacred writings (or vice versa) must, whenever it took place, have been a deliberate and rational act, prompted by a consciousness of the unique significance of the life and work of Moses the lawgiver, seen as the culmination of all that led up to it in the previous history of the world. A formal decision to subdivide the miscellaneous non-Mosaic Scriptures would again have been a deliberate and rational act. If the act was performed by compiling a list, the list could be expected to reflect, in some degree at least, the rational considerations on which it was drawn up.

It is noteworthy that all three divisions of the canon include narrative books, covering successive periods of history. Those in the Law cover the period from the creation to the death of Moses, those in the Prophets (Joshua, Judges,

---

[35] For a full consideration of the eight arguments, see my *Old Testament Canon*, 138-49.

Samuel, Kings) cover the period from the entry into the promised land to Babylonian exile, and those in the Hagiographa (Daniel, Esther, Ezra-Nehemiah and Chronicles) cover the period of the Exile and Return. There is one other narrative book in the Hagiographa, relating to a different period of history, namely Ruth, but it is separated from the others and prefixed to the Psalms, evidently because it ends with the genealogy of the psalmist David. So its function is different. The order of the narrative books is evidently intended to be chronological, as is particularly clear in the Law and the Prophets. In the Prophets the narrative books come first, presumably because of the close link between the Pentateuch and Joshua. In the Hagiographa they come last, presumably so that Chronicles can sum up the whole sacred literature, beginning as it does with Adam and ending with the Return from the Exile.

Each of the divisions of the canon contains a second kind of literature also. In the Law it is of course legal, and is closely integrated with the narrative literature there; in the Prophets it is of course oracular, and is more distinct from the narrative books, the oracular books following them, in the order Jeremiah, Ezekiel, Isaiah, the Twelve Prophets; in the Hagiographa it is lyrical and sapiential, and is again distinct from the narrative books, the lyrical and sapiential books preceding them, in the order Psalms, Job, Proverbs, Ecclesiastes, Song of Songs, Lamentations. It is clear that the order of the non-narrative books in the Prophets and Hagiographa is not chronological, and they are in fact arranged in descending order of size,[36] with the single and trivial exception that the Song of Songs is put before Lamentations, so as to keep the three books associated with Solomon together.

But if Judas and his companions organized the books in this way, on a recognizible and rational principle, it implies that the identity of the books was known, and that the canon was closed. Nothing depends on Judas being the one who did it, but what is of real significance is that it had happened by the time the prologue to Ecclesiasticus was written, about 130 B.C.E.

The Date of the Closing of the Canon

It was suggested above that the threefold organization of the canon took place about 164 B.C.E. But if the canon was closed at that time, what are we to say to the common hypothesis that it was closed about 90 C.E., with the canonization of the Hagiographa by the 'Council' of Yavne (Jamnia), and was kept open until then by the disputes among some of the rabbis about five books – Ezekiel, Proverbs, Ecclesiastes, the Song of Songs and Esther? We are to say that there are too many weighty objections to this hypothesis for it to be maintained any longer. Thus,

---

[36] This was pointed out by H.L. Strack and L. Blau, taking a hint from A. Geiger's demonstration ('Plan und Anordnung der Mischnah') that the same was true of the tractates of the Mishna. Cf. Goldberg, 'The Mishna', 233 n. 55.

(1) One of the five disputed books, Ezekiel, belongs not to the Hagiographa but to the Prophets, which are usually held to have been closed centuries earlier.

(2) The Hagiographa in general had certainly become canonical long before 90 C.E. We have seen that the existence of the third section of the canon is acknowledged as early as the prologue to Ecclesiasticus, in the second century B.C.E. We have seen that some at least of the Hagiographa were canonical among the Essenes, and presumably had been so since before the beginning of their intense rivalry against the other two great schools, from the second century B.C.E. onwards. The section on 'The Agreed Nucleus of the Scriptural Canon' showed that four of the Hagiographa – Psalms, Job, Proverbs and Daniel – are among the OT books which, individually, have the fullest attestation to their canonicity in the literature of the last few centuries B.C.E. and the first century C.E.

(3) The decision at Yavne dealt only with Ecclesiastes and the Song of Songs – or, according to Rabbi Akiva, with Ecclesiastes alone (*M. Yadayim* 3:5). How, then, can it have decided the canonicity of books which, so far as we know, the assembly there did not even discuss?

(4) About 100 C.E. *2 Esdr* 14:44-48 says that the 24 inspired books of the national canon were (re)published by Ezra. How could such an assertion be made if five of the 24 books were known to have been added to the canon about 90 C.E., only ten or so years earlier?

(5) Much of the rabbinic evidence on the disputed books dates from well after 90 C.E. Many of the rabbis named in *M. Yadayim* 3:5; *T. Yadayim* 2:14; *B.T. Megilla* 7a as denying or questioning the canonicity of Ecclesiastes – Rabbi Yehuda bar Ilai, Rabbi Yose, Rabbi Meir, Rabbi Shimon ben Menasia – belong to the latter half of the second century C.E.; and R. Yose and R. Meir question the canonicity of the Song of Songs also. All the rabbis named in *B.T. Megilla* 7a and *Sanhedrin* 100a as denying the canonicity of Esther – Shmuel, Rav Yehuda, Levi bar Shmuel, Rav Huna bar Hiyya – belong to the third century C.E.. So either this evidence shows that the canon was still open long after 90 C.E. (incredibly long afterwards!), or it does not show that the canon was open at all.

What, then, is meant by a closed canon? If it means a situation where such unanimity about the identity of the canonical books has been achieved that no individual ever again questions the right of any of them to its place in the Bible, the canon of neither Testament has ever been closed, either among Jews or among Christians. The possibility of doubts about particular books arising in individual minds, and finding expression, can never be excluded. If, however, it means that such general agreement has been reached, both among the leaders of the community and in the body of the faithful, that any contrary voices raised, however eminent, have no significant effect upon religious belief or practice, then the canon may well have been closed before the rabbinic disputes about the five books even began. A parallel may be drawn with the history of the NT canon. Doubts about its exact limits had been laid to rest everywhere except in Syria by about the end of the fourth century. Yet as late as the sixteenth century, Luther revived the doubts that had once been entertained about four of its books (Hebrews, James, Jude, Revelation). What is equally significant, however, is that (for all Luther's eminence) his doubts had no permanent influence, even among Lutherans. Only his closest followers echoed his opinions on the matter, and the four books continued to be regarded and treated as inspired Scripture, on a par with all the rest. Why should it be thought any different with the rabbinic disputes? Is it not possible that the disputes were about books long acknowledged as canonical; so that two of them (Ezekiel and Esther) were already used in the public reading of Scripture, and all of them privately studied as Scripture, before and during the period of the disputes, no less than afterwards?

The theory that an open canon was closed at the 'Council' of Yavne about 90 C.E. goes back to Heinrich Graetz in 1871, who proposed (rather more cautiously than has since been the custom) that the 'Council' of Yavne *led to* the closing of the canon.[37] Though others have lately expressed hesitations about the theory, its complete refutation has been the work of J.P. Lewis[38] and S.Z. Leiman.[39] The combined result of their investigations is as follows:

(a) The term 'synod' or 'council' is inappropriate. The academy at Yavne, established by Rabbi Yohanan ben Zakkai shortly before the fall of Jersualem in 70 C.E., was both a college and a legislative body, and the occasion in question was a session of the elders there.

(b) The date of the session may have been as early as 75 C.E. or as late as 117 C.E.

(c) As regards the disputed books, the discussion was confined to the question whether Ecclesiastes and the Song of Songs (or possibly Ecclesiastes alone) make the hands unclean, i.e. are divinely inspired.

(d) The decision reached was not regarded as authoritative, since contrary opinions continued to be expressed throughout the second century.

The assumption that the canon was closed at Yavne about 90 C.E. has been elaborated by different writers in various ways. Some have seen it as part of the reorganization of Judaism after the fall of Jerusalem;[40] some, as part of the polemic against Christianity;[41] and some, as of a piece with the standardization of the masoretic text.[42] If, however, the canon was not closed about 90 C.E. but a long time before, all these corollaries lose the premiss on which they depend. Similarly, any inference that the canon was decided by councils must be abandoned. The session at Yavne was not a council, and the decision it made was not

[37] Graetz, *Kohelet*, 147-73.
[38] Lewis, 'What Do We Mean'.
[39] Leiman, *Canonization*, 120-24.
[40] Thus J.A. Sanders, *Torah and Canon*.
[41] Thus G.F. Moore, 'Definition'.
[42] Thus Meyer, 'Bemerkungen'.

regarded as authoritative: and, in so far as there *is* a parallel with ecclesiastical councils, it should be noted that the earliest important Christian council to deal with the canon was the Council of Hippo, as late as 393 c.e. The role of councils, therefore, was not so much to decide the canon as to confirm decisions about the canon already reached in other ways.

The Status of Particular Groups of Books

THE TERMINOLOGY AND GROUNDS OF THE RABBINIC DISPUTES

The accounts of the disputes about the five books, found in rabbinic literature, usually turn upon one or other of two curious expressions, 'make the hands unclean' and 'store away' *(ganaz)*.[43] The rabbis who were most troubled about any one of the five books were accustomed either to deny that it made the hands unclean (as the rest of the Scriptures did), or to urge that it be stored away (like a biblical scroll which was worn out). Both expressions relate primarily to the physical manuscripts of the five books. To make the hands unclean, the scrolls had of course to be touched, and to be stored away they had either to be buried or put in a geniza (store-room) and left to decay there. The approved method of storing away worn-out biblical scrolls is explained in the two Minor Tractates of the Talmud dealing with scrolls as follows:

> They should not be deposited in an unclean place but in a deserted spot where they decay of their own accord (*Sefer Tora* 5:14; *Soferim* 5:14-15).

The conditions under which a scroll made the hands unclean were two: first, that the text it contained was 'spoken in the Holy Spirit', i.e. divinely inspired (*T. Yadayim* 2:14; *B.T. Megilla* 7a), and secondly that this text was written in the scroll in the original Hebrew or Aramaic language, in the square script, on parchment and in ink (*M. Yadayim* 4:5). The latter condition could, of course, be fulfilled in the case of any Hebrew or Aramaic composition, so to deny that a particular composition made the hands unclean was to say that, *even when the latter condition was fulfilled*, the scrolls containing that composition did not make the hands unclean, owing to its lack of divine inspiration. In the records of three of the disputes, those about Ecclesiastes, the Song of Songs and Esther, it is stated by the opposing rabbis that the book in question does not make the hands unclean (*M. Eduyot* 5:3; *M. Yadayim* 3:5; *T. Yadayim* 2:14; *B.T. Megilla* 7a, *Sanhedrin* 100a), so this is equivalent to saying that it is not inspired Scripture. According to the rabbis mentioned, it is in the same position as Ecclesiasticus, of which the received view, not just the opinion of individuals, was that it did not make the hands unclean (*T. Yadayim* 2:13). It might be a

---

[43] On these expressions, see esp. Leiman, *Canonization*, ch. 2.

respected text – and Leiman[44] has cogently argued that even rabbis who denied that Ecclesiastes, the Song of Songs or Esther made the hands unclean conceded this about it – but it was not inspired.

Why contact with holy books was held to make the hands unclean rather than holy is a question to which no certain answer can be given. The most probable reason is that given by the Mishna and Tosefta themselves, where Rabbi Yohanan ben Zakkai answers the Sadducean objection to the teaching that the Scriptures make the hands unclean but the writings of Homer do not, by explaining that 'as is their preciousness, so is their uncleanness' (*M. Yadayim* 4:6), and continuing, 'so that they may not be made into spreads for beasts' (*T. Yadayim* 2:19). By declaring that the Scriptures made the hands unclean, the rabbis protected them from careless and irreverent treatment, since it is obvious that no one would be so apt to handle them heedlessly if he were every time obliged to wash his hands afterwards. The rule is therefore all of a piece with the custom of wrapping scrolls in a mantle (*M. Megilla* 3:1; *T. Megilla* 4:20), which both protected the scrolls from harm and the hands from defilement. The model on which the rule was based, according to Rabbi Yohanan ben Zakkai, was that of human bones (which are unclean), compared with the bones of animals (which are not): the uncleanness of human bones corresponds to their preciousness, he says, and preserves them from irreverent treatment.[45]

To return now to the other expression, 'store away' *(ganaz)*, this is what certain rabbis wished to see done, some with Ezekiel, some with Proverbs, and some with Ecclesiastes (*B.T. Shabbat* 13b, 30b, *Hagiga* 13a, *Menahot* 45a; *Pesikta de-R. Kahana* 68b; *Lev. Rabba* 28:1, pp. 358-59), and what actually was done, according to a variant reading in *B.T. Sanhedrin* 100b, with Ecclesiasticus. Indeed, a story in one of the Minor Tractates of the Talmud states that it was also done in ancient times with Proverbs, Ecclesiastes and the Song of Songs, until the men of Hezekiah, or, according to another recension, the men of the Great Synagogue or Great Assembly (prior to 200 B.C.E.), came and interpreted them (*Avot de-R. Natan* A1, p. 2). It is interesting that books could be expected to survive such treatment, for, unless the word is being used metaphorically (of which there is no indication), it means that all copies which could be found were buried, or left to decay in a geniza. Presumably, it was recognized that not all copies of books which were so widely known and respected *would* be found. To store away copies which were to hand was therefore to indicate disapproval of their use, but not to bring that use to an end. It was, nonetheless, a very drastic step to take. Though it did not imply that a book was uninspired (for worn-out scrolls of the Pentateuch were stored away, and they still defiled the hands if 85 letters were legible),[46] yet to do it to a book which was not worn out expressed the intention that the book should perish.

---

[44] Leiman, *Canonization*, 112-15.
[45] For analogous regulations and alternative explanations, see my *Old Testament Canon*, 279-81.
[46] *T. Yadayim* 2:10; baraita in *B.T. Shabbat* 116a.

Objects which were stored away were, at least usually, holy – such things as one was not permitted to throw away (baraita in *B.T. Megilla* 26b) or to destroy, and could even break the sabbath-rest to rescue from a fire, like texts and translations of the Scriptures (*M. Shabbat* 16:1; *T. Shabbat* 13:2). The reason for storing them away was that, though they might be holy, they were defective, or obsolete, or problematical in some other way. Worn-out biblical scrolls were stored away (see above) because they were *defective*, like scrolls containing too many corrections (baraita in *B.T. Menahot* 29b) or not properly written (*T. Shabbat* 13:4; *Sefer Tora* 1:10, 13; *Soferim* 1:9, 14). The Tabernacle, so we are told, was stored away under the Temple when Solomon's Temple was built, doubtless because it was now *obsolete* (*T. Sota* 13:1; *M. Shekalim* 6:1-2; cp. 2 Chr 5:5). A good example of the storing away of what was *problematical* is the proposal to store away all the silver and gold in the world, after the plundering of the Temple (*B.T. Avoda Zara* 52b); for no one could tell which silver or gold was holy, though some of it certainly was. The storing away of the Scriptures and Second Tithe from a city devoted to destruction (*M. Sanhedrin* 10:6) would also be due to their problematical character, for, being holy, they had to be exempted from the general destruction, yet they clearly could not be used. And it seems likely that all the remaining books which are known to have been stored away were stored away because they were problematical. In the case of Ecclesiasticus (*B.T. Sanhedrin* 100b, variant reading), the main problem is indicated by the Tosefta, namely, that its early date, not long after the era of the cessation of prophecy, created a danger that it would be regarded as inspired.[47] And in the cases of Ezekiel, Proverbs, Ecclesiastes and the Song of Songs, which are considered for the same treatment, the problem is clearly indicated, as we shall find, by those who called for them to be stored away. They must have been respected books, for there was no question of burning them, like the Gospels and the books of the heretics (*T. Shabbat* 13:5); but whether they belonged to the biblical canon or not cannot be decided by the use of the word 'store away', which was used both of books which belonged to it and of books which did not.[48]

The two expressions used of the five disputed books by those who disputed them are not, therefore, of exactly the same significance. To say that any of these 'did not make the hands unclean' was explicit and outspoken – it meant that the book was not inspired. To say that it should be 'stored away' was less precise and more guarded – it meant that the book was a respected one, whether inspired or not, but that it caused such grave problems that it would be better for it to perish. Nevertheless, the second statement was also an extremely serious

---

[47] *T. Yadayim* 2:13. See below.
[48] Among uncanonical books, not only Ecclesiasticus but also the (lost) *Book of Remedies* and the (lost) *Book of Genealogies* are said to have been 'stored away' (*M. Pesahim* 4:9, variant reading; *B.T. Berakhot* 10b, *Pesahim* 56a, 62b).

one to make, and, though more guarded than the first, it did not exclude the first, which could easily have been in the speaker's mind.

This conclusion is supported by the overlap between the two expressions. 'Store away' is used of Ezekiel and Proverbs, and 'does not make the hands unclean' is used of Esther, but of the other two books (Ecclesiastes and the Song of Songs) both expressions are used, the former in *B.T. Shabbat* 30b; *Avot de-R. Natan* A1, p. 2, and the latter in *M. Eduyot* 5:3; *M. Yadayim* 3:5; *T. Yadayim* 2:14. Similarly, both expressions are used of Ecclesiasticus, the former in *B.T. Sanhedrin* 100b (variant reading) and the latter in *T. Yadayim* 2:13.

Our conclusion is also supported by the first of the various grounds of the rabbinic disputes, to which we must now turn.

One of the two main grounds of the rabbinic disputes is that the book in question, whichever of the five it is, seems to be of secular character – that its outlook appears to be merely human and not divine. It may well be that this charge was brought against all the disputed books except Ezekiel. We cannot actually prove that it was brought against Esther, curiously – the only book in which the name of God does not appear – but there is evidence that this difficulty was felt about Esther as early as the Septuagint translation, where the prayers of Mordecai and Esther, and Mordecai's pious interpretation of his dream (Add Esth 10:4-13; 13:8-15:1; additions C, D and F), are presumably introduced to meet the problem. In the case of the books of Solomon, however, rabbinic literature itself makes the point. Not only are we told that some people ventured to quote the Song of Songs jestingly at banquets, or to sing verses of it to secular airs (*T. Sanhedrin* 12:10 and baraita in *B.T. Sanhedrin* 101a), but *Avot de-R. Natan* A1, p. 2 says of all the Solomonic books that the ancients 'stored them away' 'because they spoke [mere] parables and did not belong to the Scriptures', and goes on to illustrate its point by quoting passages of an erotic or hedonistic appearance from each of the three books (Prov 7:7, 10-20; Eccl 11:9; Cant 7:10,11-12). In the Tosefta similarly, though this time in regard only to Ecclesiastes, Rabbi Shimon ben Menasia is quoted as using the same argument:

> The Song of Songs makes the hands unclean because it was spoken in the Holy Spirit. Ecclesiastes does not make the hands unclean because it is [merely] Solomon's wisdom (*T. Yadayim* 2:14).

It is to be noted that the same objection is used in the previous passage as grounds for 'storing away'; and in the present passage as grounds for declaring that the book 'does not make the hands unclean'. This again shows that the two expressions, although not identical in meaning, are not far apart.

The other main ground of the rabbinic disputes lies in contradictions. The storing away of Ezekiel was proposed 'because its words contradicted the words of the Law' (*B.T. Shabbat* 13b), i.e. because the ceremonial law of Ezek 40-48 is hard to reconcile with that of the Pentateuch. The storing away of Ecclesiastes was proposed 'because its words are self-contradictory', and that of Proverbs for the same reason (*B.T. Shabbat* 30b). The Talmud goes on to instance the conflict between Eccl 7:3 and Eccl 2:2, Eccl 8:15 and Eccl 2:2, Prov 26:4 and Prov 26:5.

The accounts of these apparent contradictions, which some rabbis found it impossible to harmonize, have a rich and significant background. Harmonization of apparently contradictory passages of Scripture is a major preoccupation of the rabbinic literature, though it can be traced back to earlier times also. If Scripture is all true, or all authoritative, this necessarily implies that its apparent contradictions cannot be real, whether or not one knows how to reconcile them. The effort actually to do so may first have arisen out of practical necessity. Since the great ideal of post-exilic Judaism was obedience to the Mosaic Law, it must rapidly have become obvious that ways had to be found of coping with obscurities and seeming inconsistencies in the legislation. The law of the Second Tithe, which appears as early as Tob 1:7-8 and occupies a whole tractate (*Maaser Sheni*) of the Mishna, is a method of harmonizing the striking differences between the tithing law of Num 18 and that of Deut 14 and 26. Another example, which may also be ancient, is the method used in the Mishna to harmonize the law of the sin offering in Lev 4 with that in Num 15 (*Horayot* 2:6). Since no method of explaining such obscurities and reconciling such discrepancies was self-evidently right, it is natural that different schools of thought arose, and this was doubtless one of the chief reasons for the eventual emergence in the second century B.C.E. of the three great rival schools of the Pharisees, Sadducees and Essenes, which had among their distinguishing features many differences in the interpretation of the Pentateuchal legislation.

With Josephus, we find harmonization extended to the *narratives* and *prophecies* of Scripture,[49] and when we reach rabbinic literature, harmonizations of seemingly inconsistent statements of Scripture on any subject become legion. The rabbis do not hesitate to point out apparent contradictions within or between the books of the Pentateuch itself, in order to reconcile them. In addition to the examples from the Mishna noted above, one may cite the following: *M. Sota* 5:3 (statements in Numbers); *Mekhilta, Bahodesh* 7, p. 229; (a series of conflicting statements from the Pentateuch 'spoken at one utterance');[50] *Sifra, Wayikra* 1 (3b) (statements in Exodus and Numbers); *Sifrei Num.* 42 (p. 45); (statements in Numbers and Deuteronomy); *Sifrei Num.* 58 (p. 56); (statements in Exodus and Leviticus); *Sifrei Num.* 84 (p. 80); (statements in Numbers); *Sifrei Deut.* 134 (p. 191); (statements in Exodus and Deuteronomy); *Sifrei Zuta* on Num 6:26 (p. 248f.) (various Pentateuchal statements); the two Talmuds, passim.[51] In just the same way, the rabbis point

---

[49] *Ant.* 4:107; 8:406-08, 417-20; 10:105-07, 141-42. Cf. Philo, *Mos.* 1:268.

[50] I.e. to be understood in relation to one another, not independently.

[51] For examples, as also of the five categories of harmonizations which follow, see my *Old Testament Canon*, 285 and notes.

out and reconcile apparent contradictions within or between the books of the Prophets, within or between the books of the Hagiographa, between the books of the Pentateuch and the books of the Prophets, between the books of the Pentateuch and the books of the Hagiographa and between the books of the Prophets and the books of the Hagiographa. But where the rabbis found the most intractable contradictions was in Ecclesiastes and Proverbs (self-contradictions in each case) and in Ezekiel (contradictions of the Pentateuch). Faced with the unmanageable difficulties presented by those three books, some rabbis were prepared to postpone the problems to be solved by Elijah at his promised return (Mal 4:5-6); this is the attitude of Rabbi Yehuda bar Ilai and Rabbi Yohanan in regard to two of the passages where Ezekiel appears to contradict the Pentateuch (*B.T. Menahot* 45a, and baraita there cited). Others, as we have seen, wanted the three books to be 'stored away'. While others again undertook to harmonize even these formidable contradictions (*B.T. Shabbat* 13b, 30b, *Menahot* 45a).

In the light of the foregoing evidence, it will be seen that to suppose the canonicity of Ezekiel, Proverbs or Ecclesiastes doubtful simply because the rabbis pointed out contradictions in them would be a complete mistake. On these grounds, one would have to suppose the canonicity of virtually every book of the OT doubtful, and certainly that of all five books of the Pentateuch. The conclusion to be drawn is really the opposite. Since the rabbis pointed out apparent contradictions wherever they discovered them in the canonical books, there is every reason to suppose that they are doing the same in the cases of Ezekiel, Proverbs and Ecclesiastes. The only difference is that in these three cases they found the contradictions exceptionally difficult to harmonize. If the books had not been canonical, why should the rabbis have bothered to point out contradictions in them, since in uninspired books such contradictions were not surprising? It was only when a book was inspired that its apparent contradictions caused a problem, and these were the discrepancies to which the rabbis called attention and which they attempted to harmonize.

Secularity and contradictions were not the only grounds of the rabbinic disputes, but they were the only grounds alleged against more than a single book. Further objections, however, were brought against Ecclesiastes and Esther, and the objection brought against Ecclesiasticus, to justify its actual exclusion from the canon, was different again.

Ecclesiastes, which (as we have seen) was charged both with being secular and with containing contradictions, was also charged with containing passages of heretical tendency:

> The Sages sought to store away the Book of Ecclesiastes, because they found words in it which tended to heresy (*Pesikta de-R. Kahana* 68b; *Lev. Rabba* 28:1 pp. 358-59).

The objection about passages tending to heresy is not very different from the objection about contradictions. Passages tending to heresy contradicted the approved interpretation of the Scriptures, embodied in the Pharisaic tradition. However, a tendency to heresy did not contradict one particular passage of Scripture, as in the other case, but contradicted the general tenor of Scripture. It was here that the difference lay.

The ground of disputing, or rather rejecting, *Ecclesiasticus*, was the date at which it was written, after the cessation of prophecy:

> The books of Ben Sira and all the books which were written from then on do not make the hands unclean (*T. Yadayim* 2:13),

the explanation being that

> With the death of Haggai, Zechariah and Malachi the latter prophets, the Holy Spirit ceased out of Israel (*T. Sota* 13:2).

Here was an objection which could not be brought against any of the five disputed books, since none of them bore upon its face, as Ecclesiasticus did, evidence of having been written after the time of a figure as late in history as Shimon the Just (cp. Sir 50:1-3, where the famous high priest Shimon the son of Yohanan, or Onias, is named, and spoken of as already dead). For Ecclesiasticus, however, this statement showed that it had been written well after prophecy had ceased.

The grounds on which *Esther* was disputed were different again. We have seen, indeed, that it may have been objected to on the grounds of secularity, since some of the Septuagintal additions seem to have been designed to meet this difficulty. It may also have been objected to on the grounds of Esther's marriage to a pagan foreigner, which the book records without criticism, since one of the Septuagintal additions addresses itself to this point too, and makes Esther say that she abhors her marriage-bed and her crown, which she did not choose (Add Esth 14:15-16, addition C). There must have been a reason for such a strong statement; and it is, of course, true that Esther had no choice about being taken into the king's harem (Esth 2:8), in which situation she cannot be blamed for aspiring to be queen.

Neither of these objections, however, is explicit in rabbinic literature. The two which are explicit occur together in the Palestinian Talmud, where they are reported under the name of third and fourth-century rabbis who state that when Mordecai and Esther wrote to the Jews to enjoin the feast of Purim upon them, there was at first widespread resistance on the twin grounds that so nationalistic a feast would make them hated by foreigners, and that one should not make additions to the Mosaic Law (*P. T. Megilla* 1:4). Here, as with the report in *Avot de-R. Natan* A1, p. 2 about the books of Solomon, noted above, the dispute is retrojected into the distant past; but presumably these are the actual objections which led Shmuel and Rav Yehuda in the third century to deny that Esther made the hands unclean, and led Levi bar Shmuel and Rav Huna bar Hiyya at the end of the same century to think that, as a consequence, it did not need a scroll-mantle (*B. T. Megilla* 7a, *Sanhedrin* 100a). If Rabbi Yehoshua also disputed the canonicity of Esther at the turn of the first and second centuries, as apparently he did (*B. T. Megilla* 7a), then these were probably his reasons also.

The former reason is clearly the less important, for it would not show that the feast was not divinely instituted, or that the book which enjoined it was not divinely inspired. The latter objection, however, is more serious, for if it was an established principle that not only must the Prophets and Hagiographa not contradict the Pentateuch, but they must also add nothing to the substance of the Pentateuch, then Esther was clearly a problem, for it added a new holy day to those listed in Lev 23 and Num 28-9. Non-biblical holy days, of which there were many, did not raise this problem, since they were clearly part of tradition and not of Scripture. The problem was caused by holy days mentioned in the Bible, such as the new-year feast of Ezek 45:18-20, the four fasts of Zech 7:2-7; 8:19, the wood-offering days of Neh 10:34, and, most prominent of all, the feast of Purim, since these were at once biblical and non-Pentateuchal.

That the objection to such holy days was a new one, and did not mean that Esther was still outside the canon in the time of Rabbi Yehoshua, is suggested by six facts; which cannot, however, be detailed here.[52]

THE FIVE DISPUTED BOOKS AND BEN SIRA IN PHARISAISM

As we saw above, *Avot de-R. Natan*, A1 (p. 2) states that in ancient times (before the men of Hezekiah, or before the men of the Great Synagogue) the books of Solomon were actually stored away, and *P. T. Megilla* 1:4 says that there was widespread resistance to the feast of Purim when Mordecai and Esther first instituted it. It is commonly supposed that these traditions really apply to much later times, and tell us that in the period of the rabbinic disputes, or only just before it, the disputed books had been outside the canon and had generally been regarded as uninspired – a situation which would not have been changed but for the teaching of certain influential individuals, or the effect of external causes such as the rise of Christianity or the destruction of Jerusalem.

It is true that the grounds on which the ancients are stated to have stored away the Solomonic books or resisted the feast instituted in Esther were probably the very grounds on which certain rabbis disputed those books. But this at once gives rise to the alternative possibility that the rabbis who disputed them also devised the stories of ancient disputes about them, based upon the same grounds. And if they did devise the stories, their action would reflect a situation in which the sanctity of the books was in fact well-established, and any individual who questioned it was an innovator who needed to defend himself by such means for his temerity, against the widespread criticism which, in a traditional movement like Pharisaism, he would be bound to provoke by his novel view.

That this alternative hypothesis is the more probable is shown by the following indications of the limited extent of the disputes:

---

[52] They are detailed in my *Old Testament Canon*, 290-91.

(1) Except in the case of Esther, the disputes were, as far as we know, confined to the Pharisaic party.

(2) Even among the Pharisees, the only book which became an issue between major bodies of opinion was Ecclesiastes, which the school of Hillel declared to make the hands unclean, while the school of Shammai said that it did not (*M. Eduyot* 5:3; *M. Yadayim* 3:5). Those who said that the Song of Songs did not make the hands unclean, seem to have been a fairly small minority, so much so that Rabbi Akiva (*M. Yadayim* 3:5) and his pupil Rabbi Shimon ben Yohai (*B.T. Megilla* 7a) could deny their very existence. According to the explicit statement of Rabbi Shimon ben Yohai (2nd century c.e.), the schools of Hillel and Shammai both agreed that not only the Song of Songs but also Esther made the hands unclean. About 316 disagreements between the two schools are recorded in rabbinic literature, but only one of them relates to the canonicity of a biblical book – Ecclesiastes.

(3) Although we are told that, because of various difficulties, the Sages sought to store away, or would have stored away, Ezekiel, Proverbs and Ecclesiastes, there was evidently a presumption in favour of all three books, because as soon as a possible solution to the difficulties was put forward, the Sages abandoned their intention (*B.T. Shabbat* 13b, 30b; *Pesikta de-R. Kahana* 68b, etc.). The very fact that the disputed books are in the Hebrew Bible today, and are appealed to as authoritative throughout the rabbinic literature, indicates where the balance of opinion lay.

(4) There is very little evidence that influential individuals changed the opinion of the majority in favour of the canonicity of the disputed books. The only individual named as filling any such role is the first-century Shammaite teacher Hananya ben Hizkia ben Garon, who, according to Rav (3rd century c.e.), harmonized the contradictions between Ezekiel and the Pentateuch, and thus saved Ezekiel from being stored away (*B.T. Shabbat* 13b, *Hagiga* 13a, *Menahot* 45a). However, we saw in the previous section that in rabbinic literature harmonizations of contradictions are always within the bounds of canonical Scripture and not between books which are canonical and books which are not, so this presumably applies to Ezekiel as well. It follows that the only serious question at issue can have been whether to remove Ezekiel from the canon, not whether to add it as a fresh canonical book.

(5) If the rise of Christianity or the calamity of 70 c.e. caused the Pharisees to consolidate their position on the canon and to suppress divergent minorities, the outcome shows that the minorities must have been those who disputed the five books, not those who accepted them.

It is usually assumed that the rabbinic disputes were aroused by the proposal to add the five books to the canon, so that they reach as far back as the date when such action was first contemplated, and only die out after the step has irrevocably been taken. There is, however, no actual evidence for this assumption: the only evidence that there is, informs us what objections were brought against what books, and by whom, but whether with a view to preventing them

69

being added to the canon, or in the hope of having them removed from the canon, we are nowhere told. The only other thing we are told is that the objections were answered, with the result that the five books are in the Hebrew Bible today.

The earliest indication of a problem is the incompatibility of the Book of Esther with the Essene calendar (see below). The Essene calendar is first propounded in the *Astronomical Book* (i.e. chs. 72-82) of *1 Enoch*, very likely prior to the second century B.C.E. If the Essenes did not use Esther, they probably would not have taken it with them at the time of their separation from other Jews, which seems to have occurred about 152 B.C.E. Hence the absence of the book at Qumran. The Essenes, who were so opposed to mixed marriages, may also have been the first to raise the problem of Esther's marriage.

The fact that all the other books of the Hebrew Bible have been found at Qumran suggests that Esther may have been the last book (certainly, one of the last books) to be received into the Jewish canon. Indeed, if there had previously been doubt about the suitability of Esther for inclusion in the canon, the Antiochene persecution and the deliverance effected by Judas would be the events most likely to resolve it, since the book is concerned with an earlier persecution and an earlier deliverance. It may, therefore, be that 164 B.C.E., when Judas gathered together the Scriptures, was the very date when Esther was first added to the Temple library as definitely canonical (despite Essene reservations). The absence of Mordecai and Esther from Ben Sira's list of biblical worthies (Sir 44-49), probably written not later than about 180 B.C.E., would agree with this conclusion.

Any other book added so late would presumably be a book which the Essenes had supported, not opposed, in the earlier debate about it, since all the other books of the Hebrew canon have been found at Qumran. Certainly, the Essenes had no anxieties whatever about the Book of Daniel, which influenced them so much, though it too seems to be absent from Ben Sira's list.

If Esther was not added to the canon till so late a date, and without the full agreement of the Essenes, this might have led to greater sensitivity about the book, even among those who were not Essenes and did not accept the Essene calendar. When the Septuagint translation of Esther was produced, probably in 78-77 B.C.E.,[53] and ostensibly at least in Palestine (Add Esth 11:1, addition F), the translator expanded the text with aggadic additions, calculated to offset objections not only to Esther's marriage, but also to the secular appearance of the book. The latter objection may have been only hypothetical, but the strength of language in Add Esth 14:15-18 (addition C) suggests that the former objection was real; and it may have come from Essene quarters. The late date of the Septuagint version of Esther would be more natural if Esther was one of the last books added to the canon, and if the Essenes continued to treat it with reserve.

---

[53]   See Bickerman, 'Colophon'.

The difficulty that Purim excited the hostility of Gentiles may have arisen soon afterwards, since it is reported in the Palestinian Talmud (*P.T. Megilla* 1:4), and Palestine became a Roman protectorate in 63 B.C.E.

Anxiety having been felt among Hellenistic Jews about the secular character of Esther, it is not surprising that the same feature should have been raised by some as an objection against the books of Solomon, especially Ecclesiastes and the Song of Songs. This had presumably happened (though in rather different circles) by the first century C.E., since we know that in that century Ecclesiastes became an issue between the school of Hillel and the school of Shammai, and that around the end of the century a favourable vote was taken on both books at Yavne (*M. Yadayim* 3:5). It is not to be wondered at if the down-to-earth outlook of Ecclesiastes was more congenial to the lenient Beit Hillel than to the stringent Beit Shammai (though it may be only the pressures of controversy that made it a party issue);[54] while the Song of Songs naturally seemed erotic on a literal interpretation.

When the rabbis devoted themselves in earnest to the harmonization of all the apparent contradictions in Scripture, the many discrepancies between Ezekiel and the Mosaic Law must soon have attracted attention. Hananya ben Hizkia ben Garon, who is credited with solving these, belongs to the first century C.E. The proposal to store away books in which harmonization proved impossible, shows the seriousness with which the rabbis now engaged in this exegetical exercise, but it does not follow that they had always been ready to store away books on these grounds. Previously they may have been willing, as Rabbi Yehuda bar Ilai still was in the second century C.E., to believe that a harmonization was possible even when they could not find it, and to defer the problem till the return of the prophet Elijah (*B.T. Menahot* 45a). This was an old method of dealing with intractable problems (cp. 1 Macc 4:44-6; 14:41).

Ecclesiastes, being a disputed book for other reasons, was naturally combed for contradictions too, and attention was drawn not only to specific contradictions which were found, but also to a certain disharmony between some of its sayings and the general tenor of rabbinic exegesis and teaching. The objections of secularity and contradictions were raised also against Proverbs, but only briefly, it seems, and not before the objections to Ecclesiastes were on the way to being solved, i.e. not earlier than the last few decades of the first century C.E.

With the decline of Beit Shammai between 70 and 135 C.E. the dispute about Ecclesiastes died down, and so did that about the Song of Songs at the same period, though this had never been a party issue or nearly so widespread. Neither dispute is heard of as a live issue after the second century C.E. The prevalence of the mystical interpretation of the Song of Songs in rabbinic thinking must have contributed much to the silencing of objections to the

---

[54] On the idea that Ecclesiastes was not included in the LXX, but that Aquila's Greek translation was the earliest, see my *Old Testament Canon*, 302-04 and Appendix 4.

eroticism of the book, and its prevalence from the outset in the writings of the Christian Fathers suggests that it goes back to the first century C.E.

The difficulties about Esther which caused concern to Hellenists in the early first century B.C.E. (the secular character of the book and Esther's marriage) do not seem to have caused concern for long, since they are not mentioned in the rabbinic literature. All in all, the canonical position of Esther seems to have been very secure in the first century C.E. It was one of the 22 canonical books of Josephus, and presumably one of the 24 of 2 Esdras (4 Ezra), and Rabbi Shimon ben Yohai, as cited in the Talmud, denies that anybody at this date questioned it.[55] However, around the end of the first century or the beginning of the second, what seems to have been a new difficulty about the book was brought forward, probably by Rabbi Yehoshua ben Hananya. This was that the feast of Purim was more or less unique in Scripture, as being an addition to the institutions of the Pentateuch. Rabbi Yehoshua was distinguished for the independence of his exegesis, which brought him into continual controversy with his conservatively minded colleague Rabbi Eliezer ben Hyrcanus, and he also had many controversies with Rabbi Elazar of Modiim, of which this appears to have been one. The dispute probably became known to Palestinian Christians in the second century C.E., which would explain why Melito, who drew his canon from Palestine, omits Esther. A good many later eastern Fathers followed suit, but not western Fathers. Meanwhile, the dispute went on among the Jews until the end of the third century, later than any other, but eventually this dispute also was settled in favour of the book disputed.[56]

The case of Ben Sira is altogether different. In this case, as was seen in the last section, it was not just the opinion of certain rabbis but the general opinion that it did not make the hands unclean (*T. Yadayim* 2:13); similarly, it was not just a proposal of certain rabbis that it be stored away, but it actually was (*B.T. Sanhedrin* 100b, variant reading). No controversy on the matter is recorded. The main evidence to the contrary is the formula used by the fourth-century teacher Rabba bar Mari, 'written in the Hagiographa' or 'taught in the Hagiographa', with which he cites two related proverbs from Ecclesiasticus in *B.T. Bava Kamma* 92b. However, since there is no other evidence that Ecclesiasticus ever had a place in the Hagiographa, and since it is hard to believe that there was any uncertainty about the identity of the canonical books by the fourth century C.E., the most likely explanation is that Rabba bar Mari supposed himself to be quoting the Book of Proverbs. As both books contain so many proverbial statements, confusion between them has been apt to occur at all periods in history, and it would be particularly easy for this to happen in the age before the invention of concordances. The old canon of 24 (or 22) books was

---

[55] On the supposed evidence against the canonicity of Esther which has been drawn from the *Megillat Taanit* and from the absence of the Hallel at Purim, see my *Old Testament Canon*, 294-95.
[56] For a summary of the positive evidence in favour of the canonicity of the five disputed books, see my *Old Testament Canon*, 318-23.

complete without Ecclesiasticus, and prophecy was believed already to have ceased when it was composed (*T. Sota* 13:2),[57] so the main reason for mentioning it in the same connection as the disputed books was probably precautionary. Since it was a respected work, and was the earliest datable book in Hebrew after the cessation of prophecy, its inspiration needed to be denied, not because anybody had affirmed it, but in case they should make the mistake of doing so.

As L. Blau points out, the absence of disputes about the Apocrypha (or, for that matter, the Pseudepigrapha) in rabbinic literature is an eloquent fact.[58] Although arguments from silence are usually precarious, some silences are so strange as to provide telling evidence. If (as is commonly supposed) rabbinic tradition did not forget the unsuccessful disputes against five books which ultimately became canonical, one would even less expect it to forget the successful disputes against books which failed to become canonical; and if (as we have found to be the more likely interpretation of what happened) rabbinic tradition remembered the unsuccessful attempts to remove five books from the canon, one would expect it even more surely to remember successful attempts to remove books, which would probably have involved much longer and more heated controversies. Those writers like F.C. Movers who contend that the Apocrypha recognized by the Council of Trent were, at the beginning of the Christian era, in the standard Jewish canon, have to assume that the Jews afterwards removed them; and some, such as T. Mullen and S.M. Zarb, boldly affirm that they did so.[59] Yet not a trace of such events has been left in all the voluminous records of rabbinic tradition, and it is hard to resist the inference that no such events can possibly have occurred.

THE STATUS OF THE PROPHETS AND HAGIOGRAPHA IN SADDUCEEISM

The following arguments have been used to show that the Sadducees, unlike the Pharisees, Essenes and early Christians, agreed with the Samaritans in accepting only the Pentateuch as canonical, not the Prophets or Hagiographa.

(1) The Sadducees rejected belief in the resurrection, which is clearly taught or implied in the Prophets and Hagiographa (notably in Isa 26:19, Ezek 37:1-4 and Dan 12:2), so their canon must have consisted of the Pentateuch alone. However, Hippolytus tells us that they explained references to the resurrection in a non-literal manner, as referring to the children whom one leaves behind when one dies (*Refutation* 9:29), so the conclusion does not follow. It could equally well be argued that, since the Sadducees rejected belief in angels (which

---

[57] On the cessation of prophecy, see my *Old Testament Canon*, 369-76. On the 'outside books', with which Ben Sira is ranked by the two Talmuds, and on the other probable criteria for identifying them, see my *Old Testament Canon*, 366-69, and S.Z. Leiman there cited.

[58] Blau, 'Bible Canon'.

[59] Movers, *Loci Quidam*, 21-26; Mullen, *Canon*, 86, 142-43; Zarb, *De Historia Canonis*, 71-78, 95-102, 109.

appear in Gen 19:1, 15; 28:12; 32:1 etc.), the Pentateuch cannot have been in their canon either.

(2) When Jesus is in controversy with the Sadducees, he answers their argument against the resurrection by referring to the Pentateuch (Mark 12:18-27 etc.), though he could much more readily have answered it from the other sections of the canon, had the Sadducees accepted these. However, the Pentateuch was the *basic* section of the canon, and as the Sadducees had drawn their argument against the resurrection from the Pentateuch, Jesus draws his counter-argument from the same source (verses 19, 26). N.R.M. de Lange remarks that the rabbis also normally use the Pentateuch, not the Prophets or Hagiographa, to prove the resurrection.[60]

(3) According to Josephus (*Ant.* 18:16), the Sadducees 'own no observance of any sort apart from the Laws', i.e. the Pentateuch. However, as the following words hint, and as the more or less parallel account of the Sadducees in *Ant.* 13:297 explicitly states, the contrast is not between the Laws of Moses and the other books of the canon but between the Laws of Moses and oral tradition. Josephus elsewhere states that 'all Jews', presumably including the Sadducees, accept the 22 books of the canon (*Ag. Ap.* 1:39-43).

(4) Many of the Fathers, the earliest among them being Hippolytus (*Refutation* 9:29) and Origen (*Against Celsus* 1:49; *Commentary on Matthew* 17:35-6), definitely affirm that the Sadducean canon consisted simply of the Pentateuch. Since Hippolytus and Origen are two of the Fathers most distinguished for knowledge of Judaism, and wrote not long after the Sadducees disappeared from Jewish history, their statements should not be lightly rejected, as due simply to an ignorant confusion between the Sadducees and the Samaritans or some similar cause. This final argument, therefore, does seem to have considerable force.

However, before drawing conclusions from what these Fathers say, we must consider the evidence on the other side, which is as follows:

(a) The Sadducees did not have the same motives as the Samaritans for rejecting the Prophets and Hagiographa. According to one view, the Samaritans accepted the Pentateuch alone because, at the early period when they had separated from the Jews, the Jewish canon had likewise contained nothing but the Pentateuch: we have seen that there probably never was such a period, but even if there had been, it would not have affected the Sadducees, who had *not* separated from the other Jews, like the Samaritans. The more probable view is that the Samaritans accepted only the Pentateuch because the Prophets and Hagiographa support the Jerusalem Temple and denounce the sins of Ephraim: but such considerations would rather have recommended these books to the Sadducees.

(b) Josephus's works list the distinguishing tenets of the three great Jewish schools, and rabbinic literature mentions a great many of the points at issue

---

[60] De Lange, *Origen and the Jews*, 46, 173.

between the Pharisees and Sadducees, but neither source ever suggests that the Sadducees rejected the Prophets and Hagiographa. On the contrary, as Jean Le Moyne points out,[61] one of the later midrashim, the 'printed Tanhuma', seems to imply the opposite, stating that

> The Sadducees deny the resurrection and say, "As the cloud disperses and passes away, so he who descends to Sheol shall not come up any more" (Job 7:9).

(c) Most of the high priests after John Hyrcanus were Sadducees, and this is certainly true of those of the family of Boethus, who were high priests during the latter part of Herod the Great's reign (if it was they who gave the Sadducees their alternative name of Boethusians); and it is also true of Caiaphas, as is indicated by Acts 4:6; 5:17. The same is the case with the majority of the leading priests who surrounded the high priest.[62] Yet, when speaking of Herod's last years, one of the gospels represents the chief priests, together with the scribes, as expecting the 'Christ' (anointed one) or 'Son of David', who is foretold under the former title in Isa 61:1; Ps 2:2; Dan 9:25, and under the latter in 2 Sam 7:8-16; Pss 89:3-4, 28-37; 132:10-12, 17; 1 Chr 17:7-14, but not in the Pentateuch under either; it further represents them as quoting Mic 5:2 to show where the Christ would be born; and then, in the time of Caiaphas, it depicts them as resenting the application of the title 'Son of David' to Jesus (Matt 2:4-6; 21:15-16). Even more strikingly, the first two gospels both represent the high priest Caiaphas as adjuring Jesus to say whether he is the 'Christ', and as accusing him of blasphemy as soon as he admits it (Matt 26:63-6; Mark 14:61-4). How could this be, if the Sadducees rejected the Prophets and Hagiographa?

(d) The Sadducees had possession of the Temple, yet we saw earlier that the Scriptures laid up in the Temple included more than the Pentateuch. It is true that in their public actions the Sadducees usually had to fall in with Pharisaic views, because of the pressure of public opinion, but this hardly means that the chief priests would have had to let the Pharisees lay up new Scriptures in the Temple, and still less that the high priest would have had to let them read these Scriptures to him throughout the night preceding the Day of Atonement! Such attempts would probably have resulted in open disputes, and the memory of them would have been one of the constant grievances of the high-priestly families. It seems more probable that the Scriptures in question were already in the Temple before the Sadducees gained control of it in the late second century B.C.E., and, if they were already there so early, that they were part of the agreed common inheritance of both schools of thought.

Supposing, however, that the Sadducees accepted the Prophets and Hagiographa, as these four arguments suggest, why do Hippolytus and Origen say that they did not? No certain answer can be given, but the likeliest seems to be

[61] Le Moyne, *Les Sadducéens*, 173.
[62] See Jeremias, *Jerusalem*, 194, 229-30, 377-78.

that the Sadducees had joined up with the Samaritans in the second or early third century C.E., not long before the time of Hippolytus and Origen, and as a result had adopted, or had had attributed to them, Samaritan tenets which they had not previously held. The two groups had long held certain tenets in common, suggesting influence from one side or the other at a formative period in the past, so, when the Sadducees lost their only centre of influence among the Jews through the destruction of the Jerusalem Temple, it was reasonable that they should seek a home among the Samaritans. In rabbinic literature, indications of Sadducean activity die out in the mid second century, so the merger would have taken place between then and the writing of Hippolytus's *Refutation*, a few decades into the third century. Actual evidence for this hypothesis is not entirely lacking. For Hippolytus does not stop short at attributing Samaritan beliefs to the Sadducees – he completely identifies the two groups, giving no separate account of the Samaritans, and stating that the Sadducees live mainly round Samaria (*Refutation* 9:29). Similarly, pseudo-Tertullian's third-century appendix to Tertullian's *De Praescriptione* 45 describes the Sadducees as an offshoot of the Dositheans, the main divergent sect among the Samaritans, perhaps indicating that by his time they were a Samaritan rather than a Jewish group; and other Fathers, such as Epiphanius, repeat this. Nor is Samaritan testimony wanting on the matter, for in the Samaritan *Chronicle* written in Arabic in the fourteenth century by Abu 'l-Fath it is stated that the subdivisions of the Dositheans included some who pretended to be Sadducees, and also an elder named Zadok (the name from which the title 'Sadducee' is usually derived).[63]

ESTHER AND THE PSEUDEPIGRAPHA IN ESSENISM AND THE DEAD SEA COMMUNITY

As is well known, texts of all the books of the Hebrew Bible have been found at Qumran, with the exception of Esther. This would not be surprising, seeing that the manuscripts are only fragmentary and Esther only a small book, except that we know some Jews to have had problems with Esther, and that the book was needed for the festival of Purim, which would have caused copies to be multiplied. A comparison between the scrolls from Qumran and those from the Cairo Geniza yields the significant result that in the former case no fragment of Esther has been found, while in the latter case fragments of Esther are much more numerous than those of any other book outside the Pentateuch. This strongly suggests that the Qumran community were among those Jews who had problems with Esther, and that they did not observe Purim.

Of the difficulties which Esther posed for other Jews, the one that weighed most with the Essenes may have been Esther's marriage. *Jubilees* is extremely concerned about marriages with pagan gentiles, which must have become more frequent during the Hellenizing movement of the second century B.C.E., the

---

[63] See Isser, *Dositheans*, 80-84, 103-06. See also Bóid, below, pp. 625-28, 630-32.

century when the Essenes emerged as a distinct group; but the Book of Ruth raised much the same difficulty, and Ruth *has* been found at Qumran, so it is doubtful whether the Essenes would have regarded this problem with Esther as insuperable.

Much more difficult to handle, however, and unique to the Essenes, was the problem that Esther conflicted, so it seems, with their calendar. The Essenes had a fixed solar year of 364 days, in which, since it was exactly divisible into weeks, any particular day of the month always fell, year by year, on the same day of the week. The first day of the first month was always a Wednesday, and the fourteenth day of the twelfth month was always a Saturday, i.e. a sabbath. However, in the Book of Esther the fourteenth day of the twelfth month Adar is the second of the two days on which the Jews assemble to slay their enemies and the first of the two days on which it is appointed to keep the feast of Purim (Esth 9:15-22). Now, the Essenes were the strictest of the Jews in regard to the sabbath rest,[64] and one of the principles on which they drew up their calendar seems to have been that no dated event in the Bible must fall on a sabbath, lest it should be construed as work; and that holy days must not fall on sabbaths (except for the week-long festivals, where this could hardly be avoided), because extra sacrifices were offered on holy days, and the offering of unnecessary sacrifices on sabbaths was forbidden work (*Jub.* 50:10-11; *CD* 11:17-18). By beginning their year not on Sunday but on Wednesday, the Essenes skilfully avoided allowing any dated event or holy day in the Bible to coincide with any of the 52 dated sabbaths of their calendar.[65] However, this assumes that the Bible does not include Esther or the Apocrypha. In Tobit, Anna is doing her daily work on Dystrus 7, an Essene sabbath.[66] In 1 Maccabees, Simon ceremonially enters the liberated citadel of Jerusalem on the 23rd day of the second month, and appoints it as an annual festival (1 Macc 13:51-2). This again was an Essene sabbath. In 2 Maccabees, Nicanor attacks the Jews on the sabbath and dies in battle, whereupon the day in question, Adar 13, is appointed as an annual festival (2 Macc 15:1-5, 36). Adar 13 was not in fact an Essene sabbath, but to the author of the book, and perhaps to the Maccabees themselves, it clearly was one on that occasion. None of these three books, therefore, can have been in the Bible on which the Essene based their calendar, and the same applies to Esther, which describes 'work' taking place and a festival being instituted on another Essene sabbath, Adar 14.

Some time after the drawing up of the Essene calendar (which has been supposed very old, and must surely go back to the third century B.C.E.), Esther was received into the canon, and was probably included in the collection of Scriptures gathered together by Judas Maccabaeus after the Antiochene perse-

---

[64] See Josephus, *War* 2:147.
[65] See 'The Earliest Enoch Literature', by the author, 378-81, and J.M. Baumgarten there cited.
[66] Tob 2:12 (Codex Sinaiticus, the better text). Dystrus was a Macedonian lunar month, corresponding to Adar.

cution. This would have caused problems to the Essenes which it did not cause to Judas's other supporters, because Esther conflicted with their sacred calendar. In deference to Judas, they perhaps refrained from repudiating Esther, but they would not have used it, because of the embarrassment it caused them. It may in theory have been one of the 22 books of Greek Jubilees, but would not have been treated as such in practice. Then, when the Essenes broke with the Maccabees, which probably happened at the assumption of the high priesthood by Jonathan Maccabaeus in 152 B.C.E., and began to live a separate life, they would have taken with them into their separation all the canonical books which they both recognized and used; and this could explain the appearance at Qumran of all the books of the Hebrew Bible except Esther.

So much for the question whether the Essene canon included Esther or not. Did it, however, perhaps also include sectarian books, especially those Pseudepigrapha which both share the Essene outlook and claim prophetic authority, notably *1 Enoch*, the *Testament of Levi*, *Jubilees* and the *Temple Scroll*, all found at Qumran?

New light has been thrown on this question by the Qumran discoveries. It is probably no coincidence that the revelations to which the Qumran community laid claim were revelations of the *true meaning* of the Mosaic Law. The initiate, we are told,

> shall undertake by a binding oath to return with all his heart and soul to every commandment of the Law of Moses *in accordance with all that has been revealed of it to the sons of Zadok*, the Keepers of the Covenant and Seekers of His will, and to the multitude of the men of their Covenant (*1QS* 5:8-9).

Again,

> But with the remnant which held fast to the commandments of God, God established his Covenant with Israel for ever, *by revealing to them the hidden things in which all Israel had gone astray. His holy Sabbaths and his glorious appointed times*, the testimonies of his righteousness and the ways of his truth, and the desires of his will, 'which man shall do and live thereby' (Lev 18:5), *he laid open before them* (*CD* 3:12-16, Vermes's translation, conflated with Rabin's).

The people referred to under these characteristic names are the Essenes and proto-Essenes, and what is said to have been 'revealed' (גלה) to them, or 'laid open' (פתח) before them, is the true interpretation of the commandments of the Mosaic Law, such as the commandments about sabbaths and holy days. The interpretation of the Pentateuch embodied in the *Astronomical Book*, the *Testament of Levi*, *Jubilees* and the *Temple Scroll* was thus believed to be a newly revealed interpretation, which implies that it was different from the traditional interpretation, as it evidently was.

Since the Essenes regarded themselves as the elect of God (*1 Enoch* 93:10; *1QS* 8:6 etc.), there is no reason to doubt that they did believe their interpretation of the Mosaic Law to have been revealed to them, even though we may be unable to share their belief and may often find Pharisaic exegesis of particular laws more plausible than Essene. The Pharisees, of course, since they were rivals of the Essenes, would hardly have viewed Essene exegesis with even this degree of sympathy: indeed, on their traditionalist principles, they could have been expected to charge the Essene interpretation with being false because new. If, however, the Essene interpretation was revealed, it was not only the true interpretation but also the original interpretation. What harm, therefore, would there be (the Essenes may have asked themselves) in devising books which would 'prove' to such sceptics that it was the original interpretation, by being written in the names of the Lawgiver Moses himself and his patriarchal predecessors? In reality, of course, God does not need men's lies to support his truth, but, human nature being what it is, the issue is not always seen that way, even by men as strict in their general ethical principles as the Essenes were. And they may have comforted themselves that, since the Pharisees claimed that their *tradition* went right back to the age of revelation, to produce writings ostensibly dating from that age was not in principle anything different.

The Essenes, however, were not only concerned with the meaning of the Law but with the hidden truths of nature, the unseen world and the future, and some of them had a reputation for foretelling things to come. The methods by which the Essenes foretold the future have been discussed by the present writer elsewhere, in the light of their eschatological writings and the examples of oral predictions recorded by Josephus.[67] The conclusion reached in that discussion is that the three methods they used were the interpretation of the prophecies of the OT, the calculation of significant dates in history, and the casting of horoscopes.

If this is true, it means that the Essenes were not really intending to add to OT prophecy, any more than to OT law. As regards the Pentateuch, what their pseudonymous legal writings offered was an interpretation of it – a revealed interpretation, certainly, but not more than an interpretation. As regards OT prophecy, what their pseudonymous apocalyptic writings offered was again an interpretation of it – supplemented perhaps, but only from natural sources, like arithmetic and astrology, not from super-natural. This interpretation, too, was evidently held to be a revealed interpretation, but an interpretation was all that it aimed to be. If it seems sometimes an arbitrary interpretation, the extraordinary liberties taken in the Qumran biblical commentaries, or *pesharim*, in order to apply the Scriptures directly to themselves, help to show why.

Here again, we are not merely dependent on inference, but have explicit evidence in the Qumran texts. For in the Habakkuk Commentary (*1QpHab*

---

[67] See 'Significance', by the author, 199-202.

7:4-5), speaking of the interpretation of Habakkuk's prophecies, the commentator refers to the founder of the Qumran community as

> the Teacher of Righteousness, to whom God made known all the mysteries of the words of his servants the prophets.

The same thing is implied by an earlier passage of the work, where we read of those

> who will not believe when they hear all that is going to come upon the last generation from the mouth of the priest into whose heart God put understanding to interpret (פשר) all the words of his servants the prophets by whose hand God enumerated all that is going to come upon his people and upon his congregation (*1QpHab* 2:6-10, Horgan's translation).

For the Prophets also, therefore, the Teacher of Righteousness, and similarly gifted successors, had a newly revealed interpretation.

Since, however, it was only a revealed interpretation of Scripture, and not new Scripture, which the Essenes claimed to have received, it is not surprising that they put the books embodying it on a lower level than Scripture itself. The evidence that they did this is as follows:

(a) Though the Qumran literature (like other Jewish literature of its period) quotes the canonical Scriptures with great frequency, and uses conventional formulas for the purpose, it only rarely quotes the Essene pseudepigrapha, never using such formulas or giving any other clear indication that the works quoted were of prophetic or canonical authority. The only two quotations or references to Essene pseudepigrapha which are at all certain are the quotation from the Aramaic *Testament of Levi* in *CD* 4:15-19, introduced by the words 'about which Levi the son of Jacob said', and the reference to the 'Book of the Divisions of the Times into their Jubilees and Weeks' in *CD* 16:2-4, which is mentioned as containing 'the exact statement of the epochs of Israel's blindness to all these' (viz. to the commandments of the Law of Moses, rightly interpreted).[68] Such language does not imply canonicity.

(b) Columns 54 and 61 of the *Temple Scroll* reproduce without hesitation the Pentateuchal laws against false prophets. This lack of embarrassment makes it hard to think that the author really aimed to put himself or his compeers on a

---

[68] One might also mention (if only to dismiss it as irrelevant) the quotation from Joshua which follows three from the Pentateuch in *4QTest*, embedded in an interpretation which also accompanies the quotation in the Qumran *Psalms of Joshua*. The reason it appears in this form is doubtless that the connection of the quotation with those preceding it would be quite unintelligible otherwise. As Eybers says, it would be rash to suppose that it is the Qumran work which is being put side by side with the Pentateuch, rather than the canonical Joshua ('Some Light', 34).

par with Moses, or meant to provide, under his Mosaic disguise, more than just the true interpretation of Moses's Law.[69]

(c) As was seen earlier, Philo gives a significant account of the things which each member of the quasi-Essene Therapeutae took with him into his oratory. He took with him none of the common things of life but the books of the three sections of the canon 'and the other books whereby knowledge and piety are increased and completed' (*On the Contemplative Life* 25). These other books are doubtless identical with, or at least included in, the 'writings by men of antiquity, the founders of their school of thought', to which Philo later refers,[70] and are probably Essene pseudepigrapha which they greatly esteemed, as containing the revealed interpretation of the canonical books, but which (in this respect like the author of *2 Esdr* 14:44-48) they grouped separately as a sort of private appendix to the canon, out of a consciousness that such books were not really part of it.

(d) The fragmentary Greek translation of *Jubilees* (which, like the original, was more probably than not the work of an Essene) numbers the biblical books as 22 – a standard count for the books of the Hebrew Bible, leaving no room for any pseudepigrapha.

THE STATUS OF THE APOCRYPHA IN HELLENISTIC JUDAISM

Although the claim that the Apocrypha were once in the Palestinian canon breaks down completely as soon as the real Palestinian evidence is examined, one must still consider the possibility that the Hellenistic canon was wider than the Palestinian, and so was able to embrace them. This, of course, is the old theory of the Alexandrian canon, current since the eighteenth century. It is this theory which A.C. Sundberg's book[71] is devoted to demolishing, and although Sundberg's alternative theory (that there was complete vagueness about the canon, both in Palestine and in Alexandria, at the beginning of the Christian era) is equally vulnerable, the negative part of his thesis is very effectively established.

The original grounds for the Alexandrian canon hypothesis were the comprehensive manuscripts of the Septuagint. The Septuagint is a pre-Christian Jewish translation, and the larger manuscripts of it include various of the Apocrypha. Grabe's edition of the Septuagint, where the theory was first propounded, was based upon the fifth-century Codex Alexandrinus. However, as we now know, manuscripts of anything like the capacity of Codex Alexandrinus were not used

---

[69] The attempt of Yadin and others to put the *Temple Scroll* in a class by itself is fallacious. As Vermes points out in a private communication, the script it uses for the divine name is found at Qumran in non-biblical MSS as well as biblical. The *Temple Scroll* is like *Jubilees* in being a pseudonymous work attributed to Moses, and like both *Jubilees* and *I Enoch* in introducing God speaking in the first person (though doing this regularly rather than occasionally).

[70] Philo, *Cont.* 29.

[71] Sundberg, *Old Testament*.

in the first centuries of the Christian era,[72] and since, in the second century C.E., the Jews seem largely to have discarded the Septuagint in favour of revisions or translations more usable in their controversy with the church (notably Aquila's translation), there can be no real doubt that the comprehensive codices of the Septuagint, which start appearing in the fourth century, are all of Christian origin. An indication of this is that in many Septuagint manuscripts the Psalms are followed by a collection of Odes or liturgical canticles, including Christian ones from the NT. Also, the order of the books in the great fourth and fifth-century Septuagint codices is Christian, not adhering to the three divisions of the Hebrew canon; nor is there agreement between the codices which of the Apocrypha to include. Codex Vaticanus, Codex Sinaiticus and Codex Alexandrinus all include Tobit, Judith, Wisdom and Ecclesiasticus, and integrate them into the body of the OT rather than appending them at the end; but Codex Vaticanus, unlike the other two, totally excludes the Books of Maccabees. Moreover, all three codices, according to Kenyon, were produced in Egypt,[73] yet the contemporary Christian lists of the biblical books drawn up in Egypt by Athanasius and (very likely) pseudo-Athanasius are much more critical, excluding all apocryphal books from the canon, and putting them in a separate appendix. It seems, therefore, that the codices, with their less strict approach, do not reflect a definite canon so much as variable reading-habits; and the reading-habits would in the nature of the case be those of fourth and fifth-century Christians, which might not agree with those of first-century Jews. To bridge the gap between the fourth or fifth century and the first, one is thrown back on the records left by the Jewish and Christian writers who used the Septuagint during that period, and these records do not by any means show that the canon had a simple and unvarying history throughout it.

In support of the concept of the Hellenistic canon, it is often contended that the Hellenistic Jews (especially Philo) did not share the Palestinian idea of the cessation of prophecy, but regarded all philosophical sages as prophets. Thus, Rudolf Meyer asserts that, in Philo's view, all edifying literature is inspired, and Ecclesiasticus is on the same level as Proverbs.[74] Such a contention really proves too much, for if this were so there would be no bounds at all to the Hellenistic canon. True, Philo does show a proper recognition of the kinship between the prophet and those who learn from him, and in this sense speaks of conversion as a prophetic experience, the beginning of inspiration, and he speaks of the power to interpret Scripture in the same way. Yet this is a fashion in which Josephus too can speak, and even the rabbis: it is no peculiarity of Alexandrian Hellenism. What *is* peculiar to Philo's Hellenism is its great respect for the Greek philosophers, which leads him to read their ideas into the OT books which

---

[72] See Roberts, 'Codex', 186, 191-92. As regards scrolls, by the early centuries C.E. the Pentateuch was frequently written in a single scroll, but larger scrolls were still controversial (*P.T. Megilla* 3:1; *B.T. Bava Batra* 13b-14a).

[73] Kenyon, *Text of the Greek Bible*, 81, 84, 86.

[74] Meyer, 'Kanonisch und apokryph', 981.

he expounds. But even so, it is significant that he does not use the language of prophecy in relation to the Greek philosophers themselves: it is only when their ideas have been read into the OT text that they, so to speak, *become* prophetic. And though, as we have said, he recognizes a kinship between the OT writers and their modern disciples, he certainly recognizes a profound difference as well. The modern disciple can in no way dispense with the OT books, for the prophetic experience he enjoys is a purely dependent one. This is shown not only by the extreme veneration which Philo constantly expresses for the OT writers, but also by the remarkable fact that he never once quotes an uncanonical Jewish book. Ryle, who lists the resemblances in Philo to passages of the Apocrypha, remarks that 'there is no appearance, in any one of them, of definite quotation'; and Hornemann, who also makes such a list, speaks of 'the profound silence of Philo about all the apocryphal books', and points out that he quotes far more distinctly from the Greek philosophers than from any of the Apocrypha.[75]

Turning to arguments *against* the Alexandrian canon hypothesis, one must first note, with A.C. Sundberg, that it proceeded upon two assumptions which are now discounted. The first assumption was that Hellenistic Judaism was largely independent of Palestinian. This was far from being the case. The second assumption was that the Apocrypha (with the exception of Ecclesiasticus and 1 Maccabees, for which we have ancient testimony to the contrary) were mostly composed in Egypt and in Greek. This again is contrary to the prevailing view of modern scholars, according to which many of the Apocrypha are translations from Palestinian originals, in Hebrew or Aramaic, the important exceptions being 2-4 Maccabees and part at least of Wisdom. But if Alexandria looked to Palestine for guidance, how can it have added the Apocrypha to the Palestinian canon? And if not more than half the Apocrypha are of Alexandrian origin, why should it have wanted to do so?

A third consideration, with special reference to the cessation of prophecy, is that one would expect the Greek translation of 1 Maccabees to have given this idea currency in Hellenistic circles. Since the Hellenistic Jews shared the idea that all the biblical books were prophetic,[76] there is certainly something anomalous in the idea of the Hellenistic canon including a book which repeatedly asserts that prophecy had ceased long before it was written (1 Macc 4:46; 9:27; 14:41).

A fourth consideration is that (as we have seen) the prologue to Ecclesiasticus, which explicitly says that it was written in Egypt, makes no less than three references to the three divisions of the Jewish canon. Later, Philo also refers to them (*On the Contemplative Life* 25). Now, apart from the anomalous fourth-century reference to Ecclesiasticus in *B.T. Bava Kamma* 92b there is no evidence whatever that any of the Apocrypha ever had a place in any of the

---

[75] Ryle, *Philo and Holy Scripture*, xxxiii-v; Hornemann, *Observationes*, 28-33.
[76] See Wis 7:27 (re Proverbs), 11:1 (re the Law of Moses), and the writings of Philo, *passim*.

three divisions of the canon, and the passage of Philo puts esteemed uncanonical books in a separate fourth category.

A fifth consideration is the evidence of Philo's quotations. It was seen earlier that though Philo quotes all the books of the Pentateuch, most of the books of the Prophets and several of the books of the Hagiographa, often with formulas recognizing their divine authority, he never once quotes a book of the Apocrypha. But any hypothesis about Alexandrian Jewry to which the writings of Philo lend absolutely no support, can hardly be regarded as tenable.

One must therefore conclude that, on the canon as on other matters, the Hellenistic Jewry of the Diaspora took its lead mainly from Palestine. Such limited differences on the canon as existed in Palestine between the Pharisees and the Essenes may also have been reflected in Egypt, but Egypt did not create any tradition of its own on the matter. It certainly valued various uncanonical books in their Greek form, just as Palestine valued some of the same books and some other books in their Semitic form, but the idea that it added them to the canon has no significant evidence in its favour and considerable evidence against it.

All in all, then, it seems that for as long as the Temple stood there was no essential disagreement among the different Jewish schools and groups about the public canon. And if that was so, the very rivalry between some of those schools must have been one of the main factors responsible. The rivalry between Pharisees, Sadducees and Essenes had first become important around the time of the high-priesthood of Jonathan Maccabaeus (152-142 B.C.E), as a statement to that effect by Josephus (*Ant.* 13:171-3) and other evidence indicates.[77] From then onwards it is likely, in view of the intensity of the rivalry, that the canon was left untouched until after the suppression of the first Jewish revolt and the destruction of the Temple in 70 C.E., as a result of which events the Essenes and Sadducees lost most of their influence, and the Temple Scriptures were dispersed. Any literature, consequently, which is referred to as canonical by Pharisaic or Essene writers, or both, during the period of just over two centuries preceding the destruction, was probably canonical throughout the period for all three schools; and though, when the period had ended, it would have been possible for the triumphant Pharisees to have added further books to the canon, they would hardly have thought such action appropriate after the canon had remained unchanged for so long. Both their traditionalism and their continuing veneration for the Temple would probably have restrained them.[78]

---

[77] See Milik, *Ten Years of Discovery*, ch. 3.
[78] See Stuart, *Critical History*, sect. 10. On the question of the early Christian canon, and whether it included additional books, see Ellis, below, pp. 658ff., and my *Old Testament Canon*, 386-405.

The Samaritan Canon

The Samaritans, who regard themselves as the heirs of the northern kingdom of Israel, but have been regarded by their Jewish opponents as the heirs of the syncretistic alien settlers brought in by the Assyrians after carrying Israel into captivity, have a canon of their own, consisting simply of the Pentateuch. This canon, as we have seen, was regarded by Ryle as the original Jewish canon, which became fossilized among the Samaritans owing to the schism between the Samaritans and the Jews in the fifth century B.C.E.

It is true that, from that time on, the Jews seem to have fairly consistently refused to treat the Samaritans as adherents of the same religion, but, according to Josephus, the attitude of the Samaritans was less consistent until a much later stage. When they saw the Jews in prosperity they claimed to be Jews, but when they saw them in adversity they denied it. During this period, assimilation and influx of personnel would have been possible, and it is to this that Josephus attributes the building of the Samaritan temple on Mount Gerizim, modelled on that at Jerusalem, and the origin of many of the Samaritan priests, including their high-priestly family (*Ant.* 9:291; 11:306-12, 322-4, 340-1, 346-7; 12:257; 13:256; *War* 1:63).

Great hostility, however, arose in the second century B.C.E., culminating in the successful campaign waged against the Samaritans about 120 B.C.E. by John Hyrcanus, who destroyed Samaria and laid waste the Samaritan temple. Since it takes two sides to make a schism, it is probably the settled hostility of the Samaritans from that era on which should be regarded as the real beginning of the Samaritan schism, and important confirmatory evidence has now been provided by the Dead Sea Scrolls. For J.D. Purvis has cogently argued that the script, spelling and textual tradition of the Samaritan Pentateuch (apart from recognizably sectarian deviations) are all parallelled at Qumran, and thus were in use among Jews as well; and that the Qumran evidence enables us to date them as belonging to the Hasmonean period (mid-second to mid-first century B.C.E.) and to that period alone. This, therefore, was the era at which the literary and textual traditions of Jews and Samaritans diverged, and it is then that the promulgation of the distinctive Samaritan edition of the Pentateuch and the Samaritan repudiation of the other Jewish Scriptures is to be dated.[79]

Since 120 B.C.E. is well after the period assigned by Ryle's theory to the canonization of the Prophets (third century B.C.E.), and is even after the references to the three parts of the canon in the prologue to Ecclesiasticus, it is clear that, far from never having known the other Jewish Scriptures, the Samaritans must have deliberately repudiated them; and the likely reason for this would be the recognition that these other books give to the sanctuary at Jerusalem, and the denunciations that they contain of the sins of Ephraim. Though this is not true of every single book, yet, once it had been decided to make a selection of the canonical writings, what was simpler than to accept the

---

[79] Purvis, *Samaritan Pentateuch*, p. vii and ch. 1.

Law alone, since the Law was the oldest and most basic of the three devisions of the canon, and had been the earliest to reach its completed form?

The rejection of the Prophets and Hagiographa would have left the Samaritans without any account of the history of their forebears between the death of Moses and recent times. In due time they made good this lack by producing chronicles, which drew upon the Jewish Scriptures and upon traditions of their own which gave them a more distinguished past. The so-called *Samaritan Book of Joshua* is one of the earlier of these chronicles.[80]

Bibliography

Modern discussion of the OT canon really began in the sixteenth century, when Renaissance and Reformation scholars, echoing Jerome, attempted to recall the church to the canon of the Hebrew Bible. A new departure was made in 1719, when LEE propounded the hypothesis of a distinct Alexandrian Jewish canon, represented by the Septuagint manuscripts, and taken over by the Christian church; and another was made in 1842, when MOVERS argued that the canon taken over by the church did not yet contain the five biblical books disputed by certain rabbis. Then in 1871 GRAETZ put forward the theory that it was the 'Council' of Yavne (Jamnia), c. 90 C.E., that led to the closing of the Jewish canon.

Contrary to this trend, HORNEMANN in 1776 demonstrated that Philo of Alexandria makes no use of the Septuagint Apocrypha, and STUART in 1849 argued that the Temple archive and the rivalry between the Pharisees, Sadducees and Essenes must have made any addition to the canon after the second century B.C.E. very difficult.

RYLE in 1892 put forward the now standard view that the three divisions of the Hebrew Bible were canonized at three different eras, the Pentateuch in the fifth century B.C.E. (taken with them into schism, in the same century, by the Samaritans), the Prophets in the third century B.C.E., and the Hagiographa about 90 C.E.

In the last quarter of a century, SUNDBERG has refuted the Alexandrian canon hypothesis, LEWIS and LEIMAN have refuted the Yavne hypothesis, and PURVIS, on the basis of the Qumran discoveries, has shown that the Samaritan schism and canon are probably to be dated not before but well after the era assigned to the canonization of the Prophets. The scene is therefore set for a complete revision of the standard view, such as is sketched out in this chapter.

[80] See Crown, 'New Light'.

Decorated Page from the *First Kennicott-Bible* (1476) with Highly Stylized Implements of the Temple (MS. Kennicott 1, fol. 120 *verso*).

The manuscript was copied by Moses Jacob ibn Zabara in the Spanish town of Corunna, the illumination was done by Joseph ibn Hayyim. See Narkiss, *Hebrew Illuminated Manuscripts,* 74

Chapter Three

The Transmission of the Biblical Text

Martin Jan Mulder

Introduction

Before acquiring its present form, the Bible has passed through several stages. A first stage was that of 'oral' transmission. During a second stage, the various current sayings, stories, sagas and legends, and also letters, archival notes and other documents were collected and subsequently committed to writing in various scrolls. Thirdly, one may distinguish the stage of the canonization of the various books into what is now called the 'Bible'. At this point, the religious aspect of the written fixation of the text becomes obvious: it is *this* text in *this specific* form, which is looked upon as authoritative. Meanwhile, however, the process of multiplication and transmission of the text through copying has begun. In this stage of the development of the biblical text, the Ancient Versions are beginning to exert their influence. Text-forms come into being which differ from the present canonical text in many details, and sometimes also in major points. These can even give rise to the question whether our canonical text presents the correct text, and if not, which other text should be regarded as such.

In this article, however, we shall not discuss the first two of the above-mentioned stages, nor the process of the canonization of the Bible. The main subject of this article is the process of the transmission of the biblical text as we now know it, and its standardization. For many centuries Jews and Christians, briefly all those who for whatever reasons occupy themselves with the Old Testament or study it, have had at their disposal a virtually fixed *textus receptus* of the Hebrew Bible. In this century, for many people (especially Christians), it has acquired its standardized form in the reproduction of the *codex Leningradensis* in R. Kittel's *Biblia Hebraica*,[1] and recently for Jewish and Christian scholars also in the reproduction of that part of the *Aleppo codex* which is being edited in Jerusalem in the 'Hebrew University Bible Project' (= HUBP) by a

---

[1] Rud. Kittel, *Biblia Hebraica*³ (= BHK³), Stuttgart 1937 (and later reprints); since 1967, this has become the *Biblia Hebraica Stuttgartensia* (= BHS), edited by K. Elliger and W. Rudolph, in association with a number of other scholars. In this edition, H.P. Rüger was responsible for the masoretic text (= MT), and G.E. Weil for the *masora*. See below, pp. 128-30.

team led by M. Goshen-Gottstein.[2] One look at both editions and their critical apparatuses clearly shows that the above use of the terms 'standardized' and 'fixed' needs some further justification. Not only has the road from the *autographa*, assuming that in the distant past these did exist in every case, to the form they have today taken in our printed editions of the Hebrew Bible been long and winding, but the tradition itself – the actual *masora* – is also extremely complicated at many points, and has accordingly resulted in different forms, which have been reproduced in the above-mentioned editions more or less in their entirety, even if there are quite a few variants between them. The four critical apparatuses in the HUBP – edition show something of the history of the biblical text.[3] In the first place one finds here the variant readings that can be reconstructed on the basis of the 'ancient versions'– LXX, Peshitta, Vulgate, Aquila, Symmachus *et al.*. Secondly, one is given the variants which are to be found at Qumran and in rabbinic sources. In the third place, the medieval Hebrew manuscripts are adduced, including the above-mentioned *codex Leningradensis B 19*[A], on which BHK[3] and BHS are based, and also the *Cairo Codex*, which contains only the 'Prophets', the *Codex Reuchlinianus, et al.*. Fourthly, the masoretic peculiarities, which are mainly found in medieval Hebrew manuscripts, are brought to our attention.

In this article, we shall mainly deal with the demonstrable causes and factors which have contributed to the transmission of the biblical text in this specific form, which has been settled for many centuries both in its outlines and in many details. In the course of the ages, the Bible has passed through a period in which it was moving in the direction of the present MT. This age-long process can be divided roughly into: A. a pre-masoretic period; B. the period of the activities of the Masoretes; C. the period of the stabilization of the masoretic text. There is no need to deny the existence of 'oral transmission' of the biblical text or at least parts of it, not only before it was committed to writing – e.g. in the exilic period –, but also after that, concerning matters of pronunciation, faithful transcription, etc.[4] There is evidence of this in rabbinic literature, too.[5] We shall, however, have to base our findings on written data.

The Pre-Masoretic Period

If, within the scope of our article, we define the *masora* as the system of certain critical notes, accents and vowel signs accompanying the outward form of the

---

[2] Goshen-Gottstein, *The Book of Isaiah*. So far, only Isa 1-44 have been published, in two volumes (1975; 1981). Considering the set-up and scope of this work, it will take several decades for this valuable edition to be completed. Cf. also below, pp. 115 and 130f.

[3] Goshen-Gottstein, *The Book of Isaiah*, 11-20.

[4] Cf. Engnell, *Critical Essays*, 6: 'However, for an advocate of the traditio-historical method, it appears incontrovertible that, to a large extent, Old Testament literature ... has the character of an oral literature which was written down only at a relatively late period'.

[5] Cf. e.g. *B.T. Nedarim* 37b.

received text of the Bible,[6] we regard as the 'pre-masoretic period' the time at which this systematization is not yet – or at least not yet distinctly – found in the available texts. In itself, this does not necessarily imply that the work of those who are currently referred to as 'the Masoretes' has not yet begun. Caspar Levias, from whom we have partly borrowed the above definition of the concept of 'masora', even thinks that the beginnings of the activities of the 'Masoretes' should probably be placed in pre-Maccabaean times, and that the end coincides with the first printing of a MT in 1425. It is certainly true – and this will not escape our attention – that before the beginning of the actual work of *the* Masoretes, activities have been undertaken in or in conjunction with the transmitted biblical text with the intention of fixing the text and preserving it for posterity in a definite form. However, so as to prevent any misunderstandings, these activities had better be classified as 'pre-masoretic'.

A first point to be discussed in this connexion, is the fact that during the transmission *(traditio)* of the biblical text, that which was to be transmitted *(traditum)* was apt to suffer in due course the inevitable adaptations, alterations, revisions and the like.[7] After all, one of the characteristic elements of *traditio* in Israel has on the whole been the need, felt from one generation to another, to give fresh relevance to the old traditions for one's own generation. On the one hand, there is the reverential respect for what happened there and then in history; on the other, the need to apply this 'existentially' – here and now – to one's own age and situation. In later Jewish literature – in Targumim, Talmudim and Midrashim – time and again one comes across examples of adaptation and reinterpretation, founded on the biblical text, which are arranged around certain 'value concepts'.[8]

But what about the biblical text itself? Have such alterations continued to be made in it during the process of 'transmission', also after its written fixation? Such scholars as Nyberg[9] and especially Engnell[10] have very much emphasized the 'fixity' of the written Hebrew text of the Bible. This 'fixity' already existed on the level of oral tradition. It was not affected by the fact that this tradition was not committed to writing until post-exilic times. As for textual criticism, Engnell even stated that any attempt to go back behind the MT in order to get to the 'original text' was virtually tantamount to 'wishful dreaming'.[11] Other scholars from the 'Scandinavian school' did not go as far as Engnell. His successor at the University of Uppsala for instance, Ringgren, comparing the variant readings to be found in the rendition of two parallel fragments in the tradition of the biblical text, adopted the method of internal investigation. As is well-known, the MT contains several fragments whose text is identical or almost

---

[6] See e.g. the definition given in Levias, 'Masorah', 365.
[7] See for the words 'traditio' and 'traditum': Knight, *Rediscovering*, 5-20.
[8] See e.g. Kadushin, *The Rabbinic Mind*.
[9] Nyberg, *Studien zum Hoseabuche*.
[10] See for Ivan Engnell's works the bibliography in: Knight, *Rediscovering*, 406f., and the index.
[11] Knight, *Rediscovering*, 264.

identical, such as Ps 18 and 2 Sam 22; Ps 14 and Ps 53; Ps 40:14-18 and Ps 70; Pss 57, 60 and 108, etc.[12] In comparing Ps. 18 and 2 Sam 22, Ringgren found four types of variants:

1. orthographical variants, which had come into being in the course of the copying process;
2. different vocalizations of identical consonants, which may have originated in oral tradition, with a view to the correct reading of the text;
3. grammatical and stylistic variants, which may point to deliberate revisions of the text or to dialectical differences in Hebrew;
4. a small number of variants which may be indicative of forgetfulness in the process of oral tradition, e.g. in Ps 18:7 אשוע and in 2 Sam 22:7 אקרא.

From this, Ringgren inferred that, although there are undoubtedly many orthographical variants in these and comparable texts, a large number of mistakes must have been made during oral transmission. Each book of the Bible, however, should be studied separately. It is, moreover, extremely difficult to determine when any text was first committed to parchment or paper. Also, some texts may have been handed down orally for a very long time, despite their having been fixed in writing.

THE ACTIVITIES OF THE SOFERIM

It will be obvious that in the transition from oral to written tradition, the scribes played an important part. Many orally transmitted stories, songs, laws, etc. had in due course already acquired an almost canonical position as a result of their integration into the cult at the sanctuary (or: sanctuaries). Besides, the scribes of this *traditum* were not 'neutral' clerks, but the inheritors of a long and complex Israelite scribal tradition. The word 'scribe' (ספר) already occurs in the description of the royal chanceries when David and Solomon held the royal office (2 Sam 8:16-18; 1 Kgs 4:1-6, etc.), and later accompanies the 'administration' of other kings (Joash: 2 Chr 24:11f.; Hezekiah: 2 Kgs 18:18, 37). In many ways, the meaning of this word corresponds with what we find about 'scribes' in the international court vocabulary of that epoch. At least in Mesopotamia and Egypt, to say nothing of Sumer or Ugarit, the distinguished office of 'scribe' is found at an early stage. The term does not merely denote a regional scribe, it also indicates someone who is in the possession of wisdom and gives counsel – virtues that may surpass regional or even national needs. The great teacher of Israel's post-exilic age, Ezra the priest, is called a 'ready scribe' (Ezra 7:6), not least because of his supra-national significance and contacts. In addition to this, it is Ezra's priestly office that should be emphasized. A commitment to religion or an office at the sanctuary often went together with the scribal office, not only in the case of Ezra, but also in that of the *soferim* who succeeded him. This fact should be kept in mind in considering the transmission of the

---

[12] Ringgren, 'Oral and Written Transmission', 34-59.

biblical text. In a very creditable book, Fishbane has pointed out its consequences for biblical interpretations in ancient Israel.[13] According to him, ancient Israelite scribes had a thorough knowledge of technical details concerning
orthography, grammatical and syntactical peculiarities of the 'sacred texts', and
were in addition to that experts on matters like 'cultic purities or impurities', or
specialists in diagnosing contagious diseases, etc. 'The inevitable alliance between these priests and scribes who were (also) the custodians of the *traditum*
would have stimulated a cross-fertilization leading to true exegesis. . .'[14] Fishbane makes a detailed attempt to show the 'inner-biblical evidence' of this
exegesis, and to corroborate it by numerous examples. Their exact knowledge
of the letter of the Bible and their precise textual observations have not only
resulted in 'inner-biblical' exegetical notes and indications by the scribes of the
sacred text, but they have also influenced the exegetical techniques of the later
rabbinic Sages, 'a distinct class which began to interpret Scripture with an eagle
eye for its scribal minutiae'.[15]

One is tempted to enter at length into all the scribal 'inner-biblical' interpretations and corrections Fishbane adduces in his book. He illustrates the
extended and multiple scribal activities in Israel with abundant examples.[16]
Thus there are examples of the use of deictic elements such as the formulas הוא
and היא in geographical information (Josh 18:13; Gen 14:17, etc.), or in a case
of the removal of a textual obscurity like that in Ezek 31:18. Likewise, the
particle את can in certain cases be seen as an explicatory comment made by the
scribes (Hag 2:5a), just as זה, and there are even a number of scribal comments
to be noted in which no deictic element is used at all. In this connexion,
Fishbane points to the substitution of more or less obscure words in the books of
Samuel and Kings by clearer ones in Chronicles (ענותו in 2 Sam 7:10 by בלתו
in 1 Chr 17:9; חפצך in 1 Kgs 5:22 by צרכך in 2 Chr 2:15; and מופז in 1 Kgs 10:18
by טהור in 2 Chr 9:17).

Now of course, the examples quoted above do not constitute conclusive
evidence of the scribes' hermeneutical and exegetical activities. Many modern
scholars tend to look upon these glosses found in the biblical text as marginal
notes by former (arbitrary) readers, which had found their way into the biblical
text at an early stage, often before the LXX had produced its translation.[17] Yet

---

[13] Fishbane, *Biblical Interpretation*; for *sofēr* in Israel and its surroundings, cf. also Niehr, entry
sofēr, ThWAT, vol. 5, 921-29.
[14] Fishbane, *Biblical Interpretation*, 83.
[15] Fishbane, *Biblical Interpretation*, 84.
[16] See esp. Fishbane, *Biblical Interpretation*, 23-88. One of the examples of very ancient interpretation is also the rabbinic denotation of a dubious construction, the so-called הכרע (Gen 4:7;
49:6-7; Exod 17:9; 35:34; Deut 31:16), in which a word may be connected with either the foregoing or
the following, giving rise to entirely different interpretations; for this, see Jansma, 'Vijf teksten',
161-79.
[17] See Driver, 'Glosses'. Fishbane himself is also aware of the narrow margins on which his
arguments rest: 'It should be obvious, of course, that designating the above changes as scribal
comments is a loose characterization' (Fishbane, *Biblical Interpretation*, 57).

one may wonder who else these 'readers' and 'users' will or may have been but precisely those who were professionally occupied with the sacred texts or were *'hic et nunc'* to give fresh relevance to the traditional text. It is a fact that rabbinic tradition, too, knows about activities of the scribes *(soferim)*. Thus *B.T. Nedarim* 37b mentions five verses (Gen 18:5, 24:55; Num 12:14; Ps 68:26 with respect to the word אחר; and ps 36:7 with respect to the wordמשפטך) in which the scribes have omitted the *waw*-conjunctive (עטורי הסופרים), so as to restore readings which were apparently considered authoritative, as opposed to other readings.[18] In the same fragment a number of words are listed besides, which are to be read without being written, or the other way round (פרת [Euphrates] in 2 Sam 8:3; 'a man' in 2 Sam 16:23; 'come' in Jer 31:38, etc.; the opposite: נא must be omitted in 2 Kgs 5:18;ידרך in Jer 51:3 etc.). However, this list is not exhaustive. It is nevertheless remarkable that the readings of the *soferim*, their additions and omissions, are ascribed to a tradition of Moses from the Sinai, i.e. to a very early period, in which no signs were yet used in the biblical text, and in which it was not permitted to insert them into it. In the following we shall see, however, that many of the above-mentioned cases are also enumerated in the *masora magna* and *parva* of the Tiberian Masoretes. Other activities ascribed to the *soferim* are the 'scribal emendations', תקוני הספרים,[19] also designated by the word כנה *(pi'el)*, 'to use a substitute', 'to express oneself euphemistically'.[20] These 'emendations' are mentioned both by Alexandrian grammarians and in rabbinic sources, although their number differs according to the various sources and the reliability of this tradition is sometimes denied.[21] The *Mekhilta de-R.Yishmael* to Exod 15:7, for instance, *(Shirata* 6, pp. 135ff.) enumerates eleven cases of 'scribal emendations', but óther midrashim vary between seven and thirteen, while some masoretic notes go up to eighteen. A good deal of these emendations try to avoid anthropomorphisms felt as such. In 1 Sam 3:13, where God announces judgment on Eli and his sons, the Hebrew text says that Eli's sons brought a curse down 'on themselves' (להם). A *dativus ethicus* in a reflexive sentence is highly unusual from a syntactic point of view, and in addition the context shows that there is no relation with the preceding, in which, for instance, Eli's sons are reported not to know YHWH. One should therefore read אלהים ('god') instead of להם (cf. also LXX). So as not to associate the name of God with a curse, however, the text was altered.

---

[18] See for this and the following also, at great length, Ginsburg, *Introduction*, 307-468; cf. furthermore Dotan, 'Masorah', 1410; Fishbane, *Biblical Interpretation*, 82 n. 10.
[19] Lieberman, *Hellenism*, 28-37; Roberts, *The Old Testament Text*, 34-36; Barthélemy, 'Les Tiqquné Sopherim'; Tournay, 'Quelques Relectures', 405-536; McKane, 'Observations', 53-77; McCarthy, *Tiqqune Sopherim*; id. 'Emendations of the Scribes', 263f.; Fishbane, *Biblical Interpretation*, 66-74.
[20] See e.g. McCarthy, *Tiqqune Sopherim*, 18f.
[21] See e.g. the bibliographies in Lieberman, *Hellenism*; in Fishbane, *Biblical Interpretation*, 66, and in McKane, 'Observations', 53ff.

In order to avoid direct coincidence of terms denoting contempt, maledic-
tion, etc. of the divine name with the divine name itself, words were sometimes
interpolated in the text by way of 'euphemism'. Thus e.g. in 2 Sam 12:14, the
word for 'enemies': 'By this deed thou hast blasphemed (the enemies of)
YHWH'.[22] There are more such 'textual emendations' to be found in the books of
Samuel, which aim at safeguarding God, and also David, against collocations
reeking of blasphemy (cf. 1 Sam 20:16; 25:22). In addition, we want to draw
attention to the substitution of the theophoric element בעל in proper names in
the parallel passages in Chronicles by בשת or אל in Samuel; e.g. Eshbaal (1 Chr
8:33; 9:39) by Ishbosheth (2 Sam 2:8, 10, 12, 15, etc.); Beeliada (1 Chr 14:7) by
Eliada (2 Sam 5:16), etc.[23] Another example of the tendency to eliminate ideas
felt as 'pagan' from the received text is Deut 32:8, which says that YHWH 'fixed
the bounds of the peoples according to the number of "the children of Israel" '
(בני ישראל). The LXX and a fragment from the Qumran caves, however,
clearly indicate what Ibn Ezra had already suspected in the Middle Ages,
namely that the original wording must have been (בני אל(ים, 'sons of El [or:
gods]' – who might possibly be interpreted as 'angels'.[24] In all probability, in this
and similar cases we already meet a 'theologically motivated scribal correction',
even if it is not enumerated in any of the rabbinic lists.[25]

Besides the above-mentioned activities in the *traditio* of the Bible in the
pre-masoretic period, a number of other peculiarities may be mentioned which
must go back to ancient traditions. In fifteen places in the Bible there are dots
over and sometimes also below the words. In *Sifrei Num* 69 (pp. 64-65) to Num
9:10, a list is given of the places in the Pentateuch where these *puncta extraordinaria* can be found. Of those there are ten: Gen 16:5; 18:9; 19:33; 33:4; 37:12;
Num 3:39; 9:10; 21:30; 29:15 and Deut 29:28. There are four more places in the
Prophets: 2 Sam 19:20; Isa 44:9; Ezek 41:20 and 46:22, and one in the Hagiographa: Ps 27:13. Although many theories on the significance of these dots
have been put forward, their exact meaning is not clear.[26] They are not part of a
system of vocalization. They do, however, occur in Tora-scrolls which are
suitable for public recitation. In these dots, we probably already meet critical
notes on the text by the scribes.

'Isolated letters' (אותיות מנוזרות) are the nine signs which appear twice
at (before and after) Num 10:35-36 and seven times in Ps 107:21-26, 40. Their
shape and their exact position or number are not fixed, and the scribes were free
in their manner of noting them. In the various manuscripts, the signs gradually
developed a shape that resembled a reversed letter *nun*, and they were sometimes called that *(nun inversum)*. The aim of these signs before and after Num
10:35-36 is supposed to be to separate these verses: 'And whenever the ark set

[22] See Mulder, 'Un euphémisme'.
[23] See for other examples: Mulder, 'Un euphémisme', 113f.
[24] See e.g. the note in BHS ad loc.
[25] See Fishbane, *Biblical Interpretation*, 69f.
[26] Ginsburg, *Introduction*, 318-334; Dotan, 'Masorah', 1407f. (bibl.).

out. . .', etc. from the rest, as if this fragment were itself a book.[27] But here as well as in the case of Ps 107, scholarly opinion is divided about their true meaning.

Four times we find in the Hebrew Bible 'suspended' letters: the *nun* of Manasseh in Judg 18:30; and the *ayins* of the words מיער in Ps 80:14 and רשעים in Job 38:13, 15. In Judg 18:30, it obviously sounds almost blasphemous to make the 'idolatrous' priest of Dan a descendant of Moses. Such an annotation as this, too, may have been a pre-masoretic scribal activity.[28]

The custom of copying a number of letters in deviating shapes has in fact never been strictly settled. In one of the 'Minor Tractates' of the Babylonian Talmud, *Massekhet Soferim*, one finds a number of rules which aim at indicating which letters are to be written larger or smaller than the others.[29] Thus the *waw* in the word גחון, 'belly', is written large in Lev 11:42, because it is the middle letter of the Pentateuch. The famous שמע ישראל in Deut 6:4 must be written at the beginning of a line, and the letters of these words must be enlarged, while אחד must come at the end of the same line. According to the (later) Masora, only the *ayin* of שמע and the *dalet* of the last word are enlarged. From this slight inconsistency with the later Masora, one may conclude that these rules might be pre-masoretic, and might point to the age-long transmission of a (fixed) text. Concerning other letters that are also shaped differently, there is no certainty as to whether the tradition dates back to such an early period.[30]

Another activity which possibly goes back to before the beginnings of the work of the Masoretes, is the order and the division of the books of the Bible. The oldest division into 24 books is found *int. al.* in *B.T. Bava Batra* 14b and will be further discussed in the chapters dealing with the canon. In Palestine, the reading of the Pentateuch was completed in a three-year cycle, and the Pentateuch was thus divided into 154 (according to others 167) weekly sections *(sedarim)*. In Babylonia on the other hand, this reading took only one year, so that the Pentateuch was divided into 54 sections *(parashiyyot)*. The Babylonian liturgical division has superseded that of Palestine. Apart from this liturgical division of the Pentateuch, there existed a time-honoured division of the text into pericopes. This was related to the copying of the biblical books. This division is twofold: 1. the 'open' *parasha*, which always starts at the beginning of a (new) line (the preceding line thus remaining wholly or partially blank); 2. the 'closed' *parasha*, which may start at any other point than the beginning of the (new) line, provided that there remains a blank space of approximately nine letters on the line between it and the preceding *parasha*. The 'open' *parasha*

[27] Dotan, 'Masorah', 1408.
[28] Ginsburg, *Introduction*, 334-41.
[29] Slotki, *Masseketh Soferim*, 211-324, esp. ch. 9 (252-55).
[30] See Dotan, 'Masorah', 1409.

(פרשה פתוחה) is in some printed editions (e.g. BHS) represented by the Hebrew letter *pe*, the 'closed' *parasha* (פרשה סתומה) by the Hebrew letter *samekh*.[31]

In describing the transmission of the biblical text in the pre-masoretic period, we have at our disposal, besides the above-mentioned material, other data which we can compare with the MT, in the form of texts and textual fragments equally written in Hebrew. We have in mind the Samaritan Pentateuch (Sam-Pent) and the fragments that have been unearthed near Qumran and in other places near the Dead Sea and in the Judaean Desert.

This is not the place to deal with the origins and the antiquity of the Samaritans. Especially since the 'rediscovery' of the Samaritans, a good deal has been written about their religious life, about their use and interpretation of the Bible. Already in the previous century, Samaritan texts and traditions were being studied and compared with those of other (especially Jewish) sects.[32] It is, however, clear that the schism between Samaritans and Jews must have taken place before the beginning of the Common Era (according to the Samaritans, even at the time of Eli's unauthorized establishment of a sanctuary at Siloh). It has moreover exerted its influence on the tradition of the biblical text which Jews and Samaritans must once have had in common. This is especially the Pentateuch, which was held in high esteem by both groups. Between the Pentateuchal text of the MT and that of the Samaritan tradition – which was also written and handed down in a Hebrew script – approximately 6000 differences have been recorded, mostly superficial and often merely of an orthographical nature. There are, however, a number of variants of a more fundamental kind, which may point to editorial alteration as a result of the conflict between Jews and Samaritans, which is also referred to in the NT (e.g. John 4:4-42). Thus, after the last verse of the Decalogue (Exod 20:17; Deut 5:21), the SamPent inserts fragments from Deut 11:29f. and 27:2-7 which stress the sacred nature of Mount Gerizim (near Sichem), on which one finds the Samaritan sanctuary. In Deut 27:4, the MT reads: 'And when you have passed over the Jordan, you shall set up these stones, concerning which I command you on this day, *on Mount Ebal. . .*'. Instead of the latter words, the SamPent has the reading: 'on Mount Gerizim', and in this it is even supported by the Vetus Latina. In Gen 33:18 according to the MT, Jacob arrives שלם at the town of Sichem. In the SamPent, one finds instead the reading שלום.[33] This and similar examples do not prove that the Samaritans enriched themselves by 'sacred texts' at the expense of the

---

[31] See for further details: Oesch, *Petucha und Setuma*; also Ginsburg, *Introduction*, 9-65; and the article by Perrot in this volume.

[32] Cf. *int. al.* Montgomery, *The Samaritans*, 1-12, 46ff.; Lowy, *Principles*, 5-74; also Mayer, *Bibliography*; Bowman, *Samaritanische Probleme*; Mor, 'More bibliography'; Crown, *A Bibliography*; and the articles by Tal and Bóid in this volume.

[33] See for more examples *int. al.* Pfeiffer, *Introduction*, 101ff.

Jewish reading of the MT, nor is the opposite true. They do, however, prove that in a fairly constant text, alterations may have been made in the Hebrew by either party, in corroboration of its own, theologically biased, position and detracting from that of the opposite side. The Samaritan text furthermore shows – and in this it resembles the biblical fragments discovered near the Dead Sea – the much more frequent occurrence of e.g. vowel letters and *matres lectionis* than in the MT, so that this text-form may have been later than the MT. As a matter of fact, there are other resemblances to be noted between the SamPent and the Qumran finds, such as the textual agreement with *4Qpale-oEx*[m],[34] or that between SamPent and *4QNum*[b].[35]

The manuscripts of the SamPent date from the Middle Ages, just like almost all manuscripts of the MT.[36] In 1616, Pietro della Valle bought a manuscript from the French envoy in Constantinople, which was later printed in the Parisian Polyglot by Joh. Morinus. Since then, several other Samaritan manuscripts have become known, which were – only partially, however – published between 1914 and 1918 by A. von Gall in a critical edition.[37] Subsequently, the famous Abisha-scroll from the Samaritan sanctuary at Nablus and other manuscripts which may be used for a new edition of the SamPent, became available.[38] All the important work that has been done on the SamPent and on its comparison with the MT, underlines the fact that there are differences to be observed between the pre-masoretic SamPent and the MT, even if they are often not all that fundamental. In other words: about the beginning of the Common Era, there were several text-types (or, alternatively, texts) in which the OT had been handed down.

THE CONTRIBUTION OF THE DEAD SEA FINDS

The conclusion formulated in the last lines of the preceding paragraph, is merely confirmed by the discoveries near the Dead Sea which have already been referred to, among which are the biblical books and fragments which were found in the Qumran caves. As is well-known, from 1947 onwards, a number of scrolls were discovered by Bedouin about 7 miles south of Jericho, which have not only acquired great fame but were also followed by the discoveries of other biblical fragments in the Judaean Desert.[39] Although unfortunately many of

---

[34] Skehan, 'Exodus', 182-87.

[35] Cross, *The Ancient Library*, 186; cf. also Tov, 'The Text', 171.

[36] See Roberts, *The Old Testament Text*, 194, n. 5, who refers to E. Robertson, *Catalogue of the Samaritan Manuscripts in the John Rylands Library, Manchester*, Manchester 1938. The oldest manuscript dates from 1211, but the Abisha scroll (below, n. 38) is assumed to be considerably earlier.

[37] Von Gall, *Der hebräische Pentateuch*.

[38] See Kahle, *The Cairo Geniza*, 154; Tov, 'The Text', 169.

[39] For a bibliography, one may consult: Burchard, *Bibliographie*; Jongeling, *A Classified Bibliography*; besides: Fitzmyer, *The Dead Sea Scrolls*; Tov, 'The Text', 166-68; cf. also Grözinger *et al.*, *Qumran*, 2f.

these scrolls and fragments still have not been published, it is nonetheless possible to get a fair idea of the significance of these manuscripts for the pre-masoretic Bible. The complete scroll of the book of Isaiah from cave 1 (*1QIsa*ª), for instance, is hundreds of years older than its text in the earliest extant Hebrew manuscripts. The Qumran community, which must have possessed a substantial library,[40] not only had at its disposal – as far as we can gather – scrolls of the biblical text familiar to us (only of the book of Esther no fragments have been found so far), but they also read Hebrew and Aramaic books which are commonly counted as apocryphal or pseudepigraphic literature. It is doubtful whether at Qumran people held the same views as we about the canon and about the canonicity of those books which now constitute our Bible. Thus in a Psalms-scroll, alongside psalms we know from our Bible, one finds so-called apocryphal psalms and even 'songs of David' which so far had not been known elsewhere. Of certain biblical books, many copies must have been available. In 1965, Skehan presented a brief survey of the discoveries of the manuscripts from the Qumran caves 1 up to 11 known at the time. Of such biblical books as Genesis, Exodus or Deuteronomy, there appeared to have been well over 10 manuscripts, of Deuteronomy even over 20.[41] There were more than one or two copies of many other biblical books as well.

The importance of these (fragments of) manuscripts, dating from roughly 150 B.C.E. to 68 C.E. and originating from a community which – according to its 'Rules' – wanted to live close to the precepts of the Pentateuch, for the research done on the pre-masoretic appearance of the Hebrew Bible will easily be understood. The same is true of the scrolls and fragments of scrolls which were found in other places in the Judaean deserts and are of slightly later date. The finds in the wadi Murabba'at, Naḥal Ḥever and Naḥal Tse'elim,, for instance, date from about 130 C.E., those from Masada from about 70 C.E. On the whole, it can be said that these later scrolls offer a biblical text which is virtually identical with the MT as we know it. But this is also true of most of the scrolls from the Qumran caves. The variant readings one meets are mainly of an orthographic nature. Even if certain scrolls (e.g. the Psalms-scroll from cave 11: *11QPs*ª) deviate somewhat further from our MT, one can still discern the MT-tradition. The virtually complete Isaiah scroll from cave 1, on the other hand, does contain a number of readings which smooth out grammatical or contextual difficulties in the text. There are even scrolls which bear a close resemblance to other non-masoretical witnesses. We have already mentioned the resemblance of *4QpaleoEx*ᵐ to the SamPent. Besides, *4QJer*ᵇ is closely related to the LXX-version of Jeremiah. The latter is actually shorter than the MT by a seventh part and furthermore shows a different arrangement of chapters, pericopes and verses than the MT. The fragment of Jeremiah which has emerged at Qumran resembles the rendering of the LXX in both respects. It appears that

---

[40] See Fishbane's article in this volume.
[41] Skehan, 'The Biblical Scrolls', 87ff.

at some time a Hebrew text was current which differed from the one we have in our MT to a considerable degree. On the other hand, other texts have been discovered at Qumran which agree with the MT against other textual witnesses (e.g. *11QpaleoLev*), or which agree sometimes with the SamPent, sometimes with the LXX. Sometimes again, one meets readings at Qumran which are not found anywhere else, and may therefore be called unique.

Tov[42] has pointed out that in analysing the scrolls from the Judaean desert several aspects should be kept in mind:

1. the Qumran scrolls show a multiplicity of texts which was characteristic of the last centuries before the Common Era;

2. the scrolls originating from other places in the Judaean desert almost exclusively reflect the MT. Because these texts are younger than those of Qumran, it is thought possible that in that period a text identical with the MT had already superseded the other textual traditions. Moreover it should not be excluded that the nature of the scrolls may be dependent on the kind of people who left these scrolls in the desert. A sociological factor plays a part here, too.

3. Thus, according to Tov, the MT did not develop during the first two centuries of the Common Era, but already existed in the last two centuries before that beginning. And it is precisely certain finds of pre-masoretic texts from that period which will corroborate this assumption.

THE CONTRIBUTION OF THE ANCIENT VERSIONS

Because, as has been stated before, the LXX and the other ancient versions will be discussed at length elsewhere in this volume, we need not enter here into the – often intricate – history of these translations. The LXX in particular has a complex history. But of all translations, it is also the LXX which is one of the most important indirect textual witnesses for our Hebrew Bible. As is well-known, it must have come into being in Alexandria in Egypt as early as the third century before the beginning of the Common Era, at least as far as the Pentateuch and perhaps a number of other books are concerned. For the moment, it will be left undecided whether one should agree with Lagarde and speak of an 'Urtext' of the LXX, or – with Kahle – of a variety of translations which were eventually superseded by an 'official' translation. It is a fact that even after deducting a number of variants which are the result of exegetical interpretations or paraphrasing etc., there remain enough variants to suggest that the *Vorlage* of the LXX was not identical with the MT. In the case of the Peshitta and other ancient versions, the demonstrable differences are fewer, because their renditions kept closer to the MT. But from this diversity, sometimes of a modest nature, sometimes more important, it may be safely concluded that in the third century B.C.E and for several centuries after that, there must have been *different*

---

[42]   Tov, 'The Text', 183ff.

forms of the text of the Hebrew Bible. One might, for instance, think of the so-called pre-Lucian elements in the books of Samuel and Kings of LXX^Luc. Of special importance are those sections in which the LXX reflects a *Vorlage* of a Hebrew Bible of which the recension or text differs from the MT. Here, the LXX might reflect a stage in the development of a biblical book preceding the stage which has been fixed in the MT.[43]

SOME THEORIES ABOUT THE ORIGINS OF THE MASORETIC TEXT

Having arrived at this point in our discussion, we shall not enter at length into the history of the investigation of the text of the MT.[44] We shall however, deal with some of its moments, because they have some relevance to the history of the transmission of the biblical text. At the end of the 18th century, the large collections of variants compiled by B. Kennicott[45] and J.B. de Rossi[46] became available. These collections gave rise to debates, often motivated by theological concerns, about the 'fixed and immutable' Hebrew text. Most scholars, however, did not fail to perceive that the hundreds of variants which could be observed in the manuscripts, were often of a secondary nature. Rosenmüller[47] virtually summed up the criticisms of the collections of variants in writing after a discussion of Kennicott's work: 'Dieser ganze, mit so vielem Aufwande von Zeit und Kosten zusammengeführte Varianten-Wust giebt übrigens das einfache Resultat: dass alle noch vorhandne Codices im Verhältnisse zu den Originalen sehr jung sind . . ., dass sie sehr reich an Schreibfehlern sind, aber äusserst arm an wichtigen und brauchbaren Lesearten sind, dass sie sämtlich im Ganzen *eine* Recension darstellen, aus einer Quelle geflossen sind und dass folglich aus ihnen für die etwa verdorbenen Stellen des hebräischen Textes wenig oder gar keine Hülfe zu erwarten ist'. At that time the word 'recension' was still often used in the wider sense of 'family'.[48] Rosenmüller's *one-recen-*

---

[43] See Tov, 'The Text', 177. In this connexion, the reader is referred to the Hebrew Old Testament Project of Barthélemy and others, instigated by the United Bible Society, in which besides the methods of textual and literary criticism used in the BHK and BHS and the purely informative textual criticism as reproduced in the HUBP, a form of textual criticism based on the history of interpretation is applied. The text which was regarded as 'sacred scripture' during the period in which the OT canon came into being, is thought to be attainable in its original form. This period lasted from approximately the fourth to the first century B.C.E. Cf. also Schenker, 'Who steht die heutige Textkritik'.

[44] For this, see besides the reference books also Tov, 'The Text', 182-86; Goshen-Gottstein, 'Hebrew Biblical Manuscripts'.

[45] Kennicott, *Vetus Testamentum*. To the second volume of this work, he attached *Dissertatio generalis*, in which, among other things, he endeavoured to justify his work and classified the (694) codices he had consulted.

[46] De Rossi, *Variae lectiones*.

[47] Rosenmüller, *Handbuch*, vol. 1, 247. Cf. vol. 2, 48-53; in response to De Rossi's work, with abundant quotations from Eichhorn and Döderlein.

[48] See e.g. Metzger, *The Text of the New Testament*, 115 n. 2. J.S. Semler was the first to apply the term 'recension' to groups of NT witnesses.

sion-theory went unnoticed for a long time. This was changed by the studies of Paul de Lagarde. In a book of which he was the author, published in 1863,[49] he claimed, for instance, that the *puncta extraordinaria* and the *pesiq* or *paseq* – the vertical stroke between certain words in the Hebrew Bible[50] – prove that the copyists had made writing errors which were unavoidable as a result of their slavish fidelity and had accordingly furnished copies of the same original throughout. Or, in Lagarde's own words and his own style and spelling: 'es ergiebt sich also, dass unsere hebräischen handschriften des alten testaments auf ein einziges exemplar zurückgehn, dem sie sogar die korrektur seiner schreibfehler als korrektur treu nachgeahmt und dessen zufällige unvollkommenheiten sie herübergenommen haben. über diesen archetypus des masoretischen textes würden wir nur durch conjectur hinausgelangen können, wenn uns nicht die griechische version des alten testaments die möglichkeit verschaffte, wenigstens eine schlechte übersetzung eines einer andren familie angehörenden manuscripts zu benutzen'. Lagarde assumes an analogous development of the Hebrew and the Greek text, and he thinks that one may go back to the archetypes ('ein einziges exemplar') in both cases. The 'single copy' of the Hebrew text was sometimes regarded by him as the 'Palestinian recension', which was itself distinct from the 'single copy' of the LXX, which was called 'the Egyptian recension'. The text from which either of these copies was supposed to be descended (the 'Urtext') was thought to be attainable along eclectic lines. Although this has not always been done in modern scholarly literature, one should distinguish between Rosenmüller's *one-recension-theory* and Lagarde's *archetype theory*.[51] In the previous century, Lagarde's theory was accepted by many prominent scholars, whether or not with the necessary modifications, if they had not already developed similar ideas of their own.[52] Nevertheless, other prominent scholars dissociated themselves from Lagarde's point of view. As an example of this we mention Strack,[53] who attributed the striking similarities in the Hebrew manuscripts to the influence of the work of the Masoretes, and could not, therefore, share the opinion that all Hebrew manuscripts went back to a 'Mustercodex'. In the Netherlands, Abr. Kuenen criticized certain ideas of Lagarde's at an early stage, although two things were, according to him, beyond dispute: 1. the extant codices contain one and the same text ('. . . al onze codices vormen te zamen ééne familie'); 2. in the 6th and following centuries,

---

[49]   Lagarde, *Anmerkungen*, 1ff.

[50]   See Kennedy, *The Note-line*; Fuchs, *Pesîq*; Fishbane, *Biblical Interpretation*, 40. The precise meaning of this (multifunctional) stroke is not (yet) quite clear.

[51]   See Goshen-Gottstein, 'Hebrew Biblical Manuscripts', 256-63.

[52]   See e.g. Olshausen, *Lehrbuch*, 52 (§31ᵃ): 'Wenn in einigen Stellen des Alten Testamentes die Finalform eines Buchstaben in der Mitte des Worts oder umgekehrt die gewöhnliche Form am Ende gefunden wird, so ist der Grund davon darin zu suchen, dass in dem Exemplare der heiligen Schriften, welches die diplomatische Grundlage der heutigen Textesrecension bildete, der Schreiber entweder mit Absicht oder durch Versehen eine andre Wortabtheilung statuirte, als die jetzige'.

[53]   Strack, *Einleitung*, 196.

the MT was not 'made' or 'produced' by the Masoretes, but 'discovered' and 'fenced off'.[54]

The sharpest criticism, however, was made in our own century by Kahle, who dealt with the text of the Hebrew Bible and its history in a large number of studies.[55]

Kahle was moved to his criticism by studying the finds of biblical fragments in a *geniza* (= storage-room) of a synagogue in Cairo, which had been built in 882 C.E., and was rebuilt in 1890. This led to the discovery of the 'hidden treasures'. From the geniza appeared numerous manuscripts of the Bible, and also of other religious and liturgical books. Some of the biblical manuscripts, which can be dated in or even before the ninth century, occasionally show considerable textual divergencies from our present MT. In rabbinic literature, too, deviations from the MT occur in biblical quotations, just as in the Ancient Versions.[56] According to Kahle, there was not at first a single text of the Hebrew Bible, but there existed several *Vulgärtexte*. Kahle modelled his hypothesis on the (Aramaic) targumim, which had also circulated in different forms. He claims that during the first centuries of the Common Era, one of the said *Vulgärtexte* was rewritten in such a way that an official text could grow out of it. Some aspects of Kahle's theory were elaborated by other scholars, e.g. bij Gerleman, who investigated the nature of the *Vulgärtexte*;[57] by Sperber ('two traditions theory'), who reduced the number of witnesses to the text of the OT to two (Judah and North Israel);[58] by Lieberman ('three manuscript types'), who made a qualitative distinction between three kinds of manuscripts: the 'bad copies'; the 'received' text; and the 'accurate (temple-)copies'; and a number of other investigators.[59]

In the nineteen-fifties, the Qumran discoveries made Cross[60] formulate the theory of the 'local texts'. In the Pentateuch, he distinguished three text-forms:
1. the 'Palestinian' form, which indicates a textual type characterized by additions both in the text itself and in the orthography, and occurs especially in the Qumran texts and the SamPent;
2. the 'Egyptian' form, occurring mainly in the LXX-*Vorlage*, distinct from the Qumran texts, yet closer to these than to the MT;
3. the 'Babylonian' form, which makes a very conservative impression, and is represented in the MT.

Outside the Pentateuch, Cross also discovered these three text-forms in other books, e.g. in the text of Samuel. Its fragments in 4Q represent the Palestinian

---

[54] See Kuenen, 'De stamboom'. The quoted texts are to be found on p. 290.
[55] See for a list of Paul Kahle's writings: *Opera Minora*, XI-XVIII; further his *Cairo Geniza*.
[56] See Aptowitzer, *Das Schriftwort*, vols. 1-5.
[57] Gerleman, *Synoptic Studies*.
[58] See Sperber, *Septuagintaprobleme*, for an early criticism of Rahlfs' and Lagarde's position concerning an 'Urtext'.
[59] See Tov, 'The Text', 183.
[60] Cross, *The Ancient Library*, 161-94; Barthélemy, 'Text', 878-84.

text; the *Vorlage* of the LXX is stated to be from Egypt, and the origins of the pre-masoretic text probably lie in Babylonia. For Jeremiah, however, only two text-forms can be discerned, because in this case the Palestinian and the pre-masoretic forms coincide: there being a longer (4QJer[a]) and a shorter form (4QJer[b] and the LXX *Vorlage*) of the text. The latter is supposed to be of Egyptian origin. For Isaiah, the situation is different again.

Cross's theories, already put forward by, among others, Albright[61] and supported by Skehan,[62] also met with the vigorous opposition of Goshen-Gottstein, Talmon,[63] Barthélemy *et al.* Thus it could be argued against Cross that virtually nothing is known about the activities of Babylonian Jewry during the period from Ezra to Hillel. Nor do we know anything about the literary competence of the Egyptian Jews in the field of Hebrew. Moreover, we cannot automatically qualify as Egyptian every Hebrew *Vorlage* of the LXX. The decision whether or not two Hebrew manuscripts belong to two different textual types is often subjective. A weighty objection against Cross's 'local texts' theory is the fact that in the Qumran library, which was destroyed in 68 C.E., two textual traditions must have existed side by side for about two centuries, even though they were essentially different (e.g. those of Jeremiah). The pre-masoretic tradition of the text of Jeremiah is represented by a manuscript which must have been transcribed in the Hasmonaean period. Does Cross give an adequate answer to this problem by supposing that this manuscript must have been transcribed in Egypt and later taken to Qumran?[64]

Barthélemy has argued that the above-mentioned problems are not merely a matter of different text-forms, but also of different redactional traditions. In the case of the text of Jeremiah, for instance, the discrepancies between the MT and the LXX of Jeremiah are greater than might be expected of different text-types. Firstly, they differ in the order of the material. Secondly, the MT contains many deuteronomistic additions both in the prose and in the poetical parts. We have here obvious differences in the redaction of the material. In the 'pre-canonical' period, there was a 'redactional fluidity', which permitted the use of e.g. two forms of the book of Jeremiah at Qumran. A similar situation is found in the MT, in which parallel but divergent stories occur in Samuel and Kings on the one hand, and in Chronicles on the other. Besides, we should beware of ascribing our canonical conceptions concerning the Bible to the Qumran community. Still, there have probably been various degrees of canonicity at Qumran: the Pentateuch had already been clearly established, just as had certain prophetic writings, even if there were two 'recensions' of Jeremiah. Besides the psalms which are, for us, 'canonical', there were a good deal of other collections of psalms. In addition to the single copies of Ezra and Chronicles, eleven copies of

[61] Albright, 'New Light'.
[62] See above, note 41.
[63] See Talmon, 'The Old Testament Text', 195, for a diagram of the history of the biblical text before Origenes, on the basis of the 'local recensions theory'.
[64] See for these arguments: Barthélemy, 'Text', 879.

the book of Jubilees and ten of the book of Henoch came to light. From these examples, it might appear that at Qumran the list of 'sacred books' had not yet been closed. Viewed in this light, 'the theory of local texts appears much too narrow'.[65]

In the whole process of crystallization of the OT, Barthélemy distinguishes four subsequent stages:

1. the conviction that a certain book ought to be 'sacred scripture';
2. the literary crystallization of this book into one or several traditions in which no arbitrary redactional additions were permissible;
3. the transmission of the book by copyists 'of varying calibre', during which the book was to a certain extent subject to changes as a result of errors, conjectural emendations, harmonizations, etc.;
4. the community that accepts a text of this kind will try to prevent corruption of the text by taking certain measures:
   a. the fixation of the consonantal text;
   b. the preservation of the correct pronunciation and reading by means of the introduction of signs and other symbols.

SUMMARY

At the conclusion of this first section, in which the pre-masoretic transmission of the Bible has been discussed, it is clear that our view of the history of this transmission should be determined chiefly by the finds of the Qumran library. For if different text-forms are found within the community of Qumran, one may assume that comparable situations may have existed outside that community in the centuries before and in the century after the beginning of the Common Era. The variety of *text-forms* may even point in the direction of a variety of *texts*.[66] It is a remarkable fact that the biblical texts originating from other places in the Judaean desert, which are for the most part younger than the writings of Qumran, almost exclusively reflect – as has been said above – the tradition of the MT. These pre-masoretic texts demonstrate that the MT as we now know it was already developing in the last centuries before the beginning of the Common Era. An 'Urtext' of the biblical books has never existed. Many books have acquired their present form in the course of a process such as has been suggested by Barthélemy. Textual criticism can therefore never aim at reconstructing an 'Urtext'. Its highest achievable end is the reconstruction of the biblical text in the form in which it was current during a certain period. During every period there have been text-forms which differed from each other qualitatively. The Qumran finds demonstrate this for a crucial period of the history of the transmission of the biblical text. *Per analogiam*, the same must have been true in other places and at other times. The text which we now call the MT is

[65] Barthélemy, 'Text', 880.
[66] Tov, 'The Text', 184.

undoubtedly – in Tov's words[67] – 'the best Hebrew representative of *one* of the texts that was current in the fourth-third century B.C.'. Another representative of a similar text is the LXX. 'These texts can be considered "accurate" in the sense that after a certain point in time (4th-3rd century B.C.?) relatively few changes were introduced. By contrast, such changes were made in less accurately transmitted traditions that were open to changes, such as the Samaritan Pentateuch, several Qumran scrolls . . ., and the *Severus Scroll* . . .'. Such changes could for instance consist in a spelling with *matres lectionis* or in small grammatical alterations. Thus Tov considers the MT, the SamPent and the LXX not merely as *types* of texts but as *texts*. According to him – and this is an approach of the problem which is remarkable in view of the history of the investigation of the transmission of the biblical text – there were at Qumran not only the text-forms of the LXX, the SamPent and the MT, but at least one and perhaps as many as three others. The relation between these four (or six?) texts is characteristic of the relation between all *early* textual witnesses. In other words: the Qumran finds can no longer be reduced to the triple relationship of MT, SamPent and LXX either, even although many (Western) scholars are inclined to do so.

What we now call the 'masoretic text' appears to have been a Hebrew text which was authoritative in many respects and whose transmission was surrounded with great care in the Jewish world, even in sectarian groups, several centuries before the beginning of the Common Era, and thus also several centuries before the beginning of the activities of the 'actual' Masoretes, which will be discussed in the next section. In addition to it, other texts have existed, sometimes diverging greatly from the MT, which must have been authoritative in certain circles or in certain places, even alongside the 'official' versions (Qumran). Some ancient versions, e.g. the LXX, will have used such divergent texts as the *Vorlage* of their translation. The process of transmission of the biblical text, which is also dependent to a high degree on the period during which some of the biblical books were canonized (e.g. the Pentateuch at an early date, the 'Prophets', however, later, and the 'Writings' later again), was consolidated and standardized by the Masoretes.

The Masoretic Period

THE MEANING OF THE TERM MASORA

Rabbi Akiva, who lived from *c.* 50 C.E. to 135, is reputed to have said, according to one of his statements preserved in *Avot* 3:14: מסרת סיג לתורה, 'tradition is a fence around the Law'. The word 'tradition', *masora*, is characteristic of Akiva and of the history of the biblical text which continues after him in more

---

[67] Tov, 'The Text', 184f.

than one respect. Akiva himself is known as the rabbi who was able to derive many interpretations of Scripture even from the crownlets (תגין) on certain letters of the Tora. But after his martyrdom and the suppression of the Bar Kokhba Revolt, the Jewish community of Palestine suffered badly. Part of them fled to Babylonia, where a centre of Judaism was already in existence, which had perhaps succeeded in preserving a strict form of Judaism since long (think, for instance, of Ezra and Nehemiah, but also of the school of Hillel).[68] The Jews who remained behind in Palestine and those who emigrated to Babylonia founded 'schools' of Masoretes (בעלי המסורה), sometimes denoted by the terms 'Western' (ma'arba'e) and 'Eastern' (madinha'e), who differed from each other in the order of some of the biblical books, and also in the accentuation and punctuation of the manuscripts and in the orthography of certain words in the biblical text.[69] In the Eastern schools, a further distinction can be made between certain centres, of which Nehardea and Sura (and later Pumbedita) are the most famous. In Palestine, too, 'schools' were distinguished, of which later chiefly those of two 'families' of Masoretes became famous: the families of Ben Asher and Ben Naphtali.[70] Kahle demonstrated in 1902 that the Babylonian Masoretes differed from the Palestinian ones in the way they provided the biblical text with masora.[71] But what does masora mean in this connexion?

Admittedly, there is no complete agreement among scholars about both the orthography and the meaning of the word masora. Some prefer the spelling with double 's' to that with a single 's',[72] but this spelling difference is often connected with a difference in understanding of the derivation of the word. In the OT, the word מסרת only occurs in Ezek 20:37, in a difficult context and in a rather disputed sense.[73] It is often assumed that the word may derive from אסר 'to bind'. The post-biblical מסר 'to turn down, to hand over' is considered by others to be the root of masora, but this is late. It is also possible that the word מסרת has been formed on the analogy of כפרת, but there are no early witnesses for this, either, nor for the spelling massora. Kahle prefers the spelling masora,[74] just as does e.g. H.L. Strack,[75] but others, such as Levy[76] and Berg-

---

[68] Roberts, 'Text, OT', 585; cf. about the demographic and economic conditions after the Bar Kokhba Revolt: Avi-Yonah, *Geschichte der Juden*, 16-25; about the emigration to Babylonia: *id.*, 26ff. See on the school of Hillel, Gafni, 'Historical Background' 10-12; Safrai 'Halakha' 185ff.

[69] See Yeivin, 'Masora', esp. 153.

[70] Roberts, *Old Testament Text*, 43.

[71] Kahle, *Der masoretische Text*; cf. his study *Masoreten des Ostens*, xx-xxx; and also *Cairo Geniza*, 57-66.

[72] See also Weil, 'La Massorah', 11f.

[73] See Koehler-Baumgartner, *Hebräisches und Aramäisches Lexikon*, 575, *s.v.* מסרת. We may also mention Levine, 'From the Aramaic Enoch Fragments', who assumes a 'root-meaning' 'to separate, divide' for the verb מסר and pays attention to our word as well.

[74] Kahle, in: Bauer – Leander, *Historische Grammatik*, 71ff.

[75] Strack, 'Masora', 394; cf. also Bacher, *Die exegetische Terminologie*, vol. 1, 107ff.; 2, 115.

[76] Levy, *Neuhebräisches und Chaldäisches Wörterbuch*, vol. 3, 178ff.

strässer,[77] prefer the spelling with double 's'. There is a slight preference,[78] also in practice, for the former spelling, which is therefore followed in this article. Of more importance is the content denoted by the word: the transmission of the biblical text.

A good masora can only be achieved by a close guarding of the biblical text (the 'fence') and by protecting it from all alterations. This implies that the masora has both a restrictive and an interpretative aspect. In the course of the centuries, the rabbinic scholars, copyists and editors of the biblical text, who were called בעלי המסרת, and to whom we refer as 'Masoretes', collected or recorded in compilations numerous annotations in and with reference to the biblical text. By the 'masoretic' text of the Bible we mean therefore both the consonantal text which was handed down by the Masoretes and the punctuation, accentuation and further masora with which they provided this text. We have already noted that though aiming at stability and uniformity this masora varies nonetheless as one studies a Palestinian or a Babylonian text. We have mentioned moreover that in Palestine various 'families' were engaged in masoretic activities. We shall further see that various systems existed in that region, of which the 'Tiberian' system has eventually been stabilized as the standard system in our printed Bibles.

THE SOFERIM AND THE FIRST MASORETES

It is difficult to indicate exactly when the masoretic period begins. We have seen how already in the pre-masoretic period *soferim* were securing the biblical text in a definite form. These *soferim* must have had at their disposal certain norms and standards to achieve the set purpose. It is not known who these scribes were. The Talmud, however, does mention several rabbis who were known for their special interest in the biblical text, like R. Meir (*P.T. Taanit* 1:1, 64a; *Megilla* 4:1, 74d, etc.); R. Hananel (*P.T. Megilla* 1:11, 71c,d, etc.) and R. Shmuel ben Shilat (*P.T. Megilla* 71c,d, etc.). In the course of time the term *sofer* lost its association with 'book' (ספר) and was sometimes connected with the verb 'to count'. Thus it is said in *B.T. Kiddushin* 30a that the ancients were called *soferim*, because they counted all the letters of the Tora.[79] The Babylonian Talmud refers to temple officials who were appointed to revise the manuscripts of the Bible and restore any mistakes therein [*B.T. Ketubbot* 106a]. Thus once a year all the scrolls of the Pentateuch had to be taken to the temple for 'revision' (*B.T. Moed Katan* 18b Rashi). The 'standard model', which was kept in the Temple, originated in three manuscripts, each of which had its own peculiarities (*P.T. Taanit* 4:2).[80] Yet readings divergent from the MT kept being

---

[77] Bergsträsser, *Hebräische Grammatik*, vol. 1, 15f. (§ 3d).
[78] See Roberts, *Old Testament Text*, 49ff.; cf. also Dotan, 'Masorah, 1418f.; Yeivin 'Masora', 130f;
Z. Ben-Hayyim, 'Masora and Masoret', who connects this work with the 'counting' of the letters.
[79] See Dotan, 'Masorah', 1405.
[80] Weil, *Initiation*, 29f.; Ginsburg, *Introduction*, 408f.

found outside Qumran and other places in Palestine for a long time, as appears not only from biblical quotations in e.g. talmudic literature, but is also mentioned in the midrash.[81] Josephus, *Life* 418, mentions a gift of 'sacred books' which he received from the Temple through the Emperor Titus after the conquest of 70 C.E. In a midrash which was composed before 1280 and is ascribed to R. Moses ha-Darshan of Narbonne, a list is given of 32 variant readings in the Pentateuch, which are said to originate from a manuscript the Romans had supposedly taken to Rome after the fall of Jerusalem. In 220 C.E. the Roman Emperor Severus is reported to have presented the Jewish community of Rome with this manuscript. The manuscript has been lost, just as has, incidentally, the Severus Synagogue in Rome.[82] Other 'standard codices', though of later date, were the *codex Mugah*,[83] the *codex Hilleli*,[84] the *codex Zambuki*,[85] the *codex Jerushalmi*,[86] to name but these. The number of variant readings in these manuscripts basically concerns details, which can hardly suggest non-masoretic influence. As could be observed in the previous chapter, the masoretic text-form was fairly fixed. The manuscripts constituted a clearly coherent group, and most of the discrepancies and variants are thus often to be ascribed to copyists' errors. However, Goshen-Gottstein and Tov have rightly pointed out that for the text-critical analysis of these variants, it is important to remember 'that they should not be regarded as one source. Every individual manuscript must be compared separately with non-Massoretic sources'.[87] The (minor) variants both in the consonantal text and, later, in the vocalization demonstrate that the final stabilization of the biblical text has not yet been achieved, despite the work of the 'real' Masoretes, who wanted to secure the text with their vocalization and accentuation systems and their compilations of data.

The activities of the Masoretes in the narrow sense of the word are situated in the period between 500 and 1000 C.E., i.e. in the (early) Middle Ages. At that time, the masora was committed to writing in the codices, after undoubtedly having been handed down orally for a long time. Such scrolls as had been in use before the introduction and use of codices are indeed hardly suitable for annotations. Codices definitely became current with the Romans in the fourth century of the Common Era. In Hebrew, מצחף has become the usual word to denote a manuscript in book form since the eighth century.[88] Because the use of a codex was not permitted for the reading of the Tora in public worship, it could be used so much the better for annotations in the text and in the margins. But

---

[81] See Aptowitzer, *Das Schriftwort*.
[82] Ginsburg, *Introduction*, 410f.; Siegel, 'The Severus Scroll'.
[83] Ginsburg, *Introduction*, 429ff.
[84] Ginsburg, *Introduction*, 431ff.
[85] Ginsburg, *Introduction*, 432f.
[86] Ginsburg, *Introduction*, 433.
[87] Tov, 'The Text', 159.
[88] Dotan, 'Masorah', 1416.

also scrolls which had become unfit for use in public services could be provided with annotations. Such scrolls have been found in the above-mentioned Cairo Geniza. With, *int. al.*, Dotan, it may be assumed that the vocalization and accentuation signs were introduced into the text in the course of a period of two centuries, though not before the sixth century and not after the seventh.[89] As we know, Pinhas Rosh ha-Yeshivah is one of the Masoretes whose work is known in the masora. He lived in the first half of the ninth century. Asher ben Nehemiah, Aaron ben Asher's grandfather, probably lived at the same time as Pinhas. The former's grandfather was called the 'great elder', the founder of the dynasty of famous Masoretes who concerned themselves with the masora, the vocalization and accentuation of the biblical text. This Asher the Elder must have lived approximately in the second half of the eighth century. Besides, in the very beginning of the ninth century, when the punctuation and accentuation of the Bible had already been widely accepted, there was no memory left of the inventors of the system, so that it must have had its origins in the seventh century at the latest.

The Ben Asher family belonged to the so-called 'Tiberian Masoretes', whose work on the masora, punctuation and accentuation of the biblical text eventually gained final authority. Another family located there is that of Ben Naphtali. The Ben Asher family consisted of five generations who engaged in masoretic activities.[90] Some members of this family belonged (e.g. according to Kahle) to the community of the Karaites. Anan ben David, who in the beginning of the eighth century founded this sect which did not recognize the authority of oral law and accepted the Bible only in its written form, is supposed to have incited the family to serious study of the Bible, leaving aside oral tradition as recorded in talmudim and midrashim. Kahle's positive statements[91] about the membership of various members of the Ben Asher family of the Karaite community are not accepted by all investigators,[92] but we may take it for granted that the punctuation and accentuation as we now know it in our Hebrew Bible originated with the Ben Asher family. This was already claimed by Abraham ibn Ezra and R. Elijah Levita.[93] Besides the above-mentioned families, there have been several other Jewish scholars who concerned themselves with the masora and the punctuation system.[94]

---

[89] Dotan, *ibidem*, who indicates that for instance Jerome expressly states that the Jews do not use signs to denote the vowels.

[90] For further details about this family, see e.g. Kahle, *Cairo Geniza*, 75-82. Kahle dates these five generations between *c.* 780 and 930. *Masoreten des Westens*, vol. 1, 39.

[91] See his *Cairo Geniza*, 80-90, in which he puts forward several arguments in favour of his position.

[92] See Reiner, 'Masoretes, Rabbis and Karaites'.

[93] Dotan, 'Masorah', 1417f.

[94] Dotan, 'Masorah', 1471f.

THE SYSTEM OF VOCALIZATION AND ACCENTUATION

Before entering more deeply into this form of masora, we shall pay some attention to the system of vocalization and accentuation by which the correct reading in worship was to be fixed. Three main systems of vocalization and accentuation may be distinguished for Hebrew: 1. the Palestinian system; 2. the Babylonian system; 3. the Tiberian system.

Each of these can only be briefly discussed in this article. For further details we may refer to e.g. Dotan's comprehensive survey.[95]

1. The Palestinian system has not been fully elaborated, i.e. every manuscript shows a number of individual characteristics with respect to the signs.[96] The system is apparently still in development, as also becomes clear from manuscripts in which hardly any signs are found at all, besides others which show the system more *in extenso*. The vowel signs, which were put to the left of the letters, do not run parallel to the 'Tiberian' system, because they are embedded in a different reading tradition. The Palestinian system is essentially phonemic and does not discriminate anything beyond the five principal vowels. There are, however, two signs to mark the /a/. Apart from the vowel signs, there are diacritical signs to mark the different pronunciation of one and the same letter, (e.g. the letter *shin* or *dagesh forte*). These mostly consist of a single dot. Apparently, the punctuation and modulation of the biblical text posed a more difficult problem to the reader than its pronunciation. The accentuation signs differ from the vowel signs in seeming less controlled by fixed rules. In this respect, there are obvious and unsystematic divergencies between the manuscripts. As regards the division of the biblical verses, there are on the whole no differences between the Palestinian manuscripts and the Tiberian text.

2. The Babylonian system derives its name from its place of origin, but it was also found well out of Babylon. In Yemen, for instance, manuscripts following this system have been used up to this day. The earliest manuscripts using this system are a Geniza fragment from Cairo of the beginning of the tenth century and a complete manuscript of the Prophets of 916.[97] The texts with Babylonian vocalization show a prolonged development and they are accordingly sometimes classified according to certain periods and the kinds of pronunciations characteristic of them. There are in fact great differences within the system in the various manuscripts. The punctuation is incomplete, too, and varies according to the manuscripts. In the 'simple system', there are two sets of signs for the vowels: a. a regular Babylonian set, consisting of strokes which originated in letters, and supplemented with dots; b. a set which consists only of dots and is relatively rare.

---

[95]   Dotan, 'Masorah', 1433-71 (with a full bibliography, 1479-82).
[96]   Cf. for this system also: Revell, 'Biblical texts'; Chiesa, 'L'Antico Testamento'.
[97]   Cf. for the Geniza fragments now also: Yeivin, *Geniza Bible Fragments*, vols. 1-5.

The signs are usually put above the letters to the left (supralinear system). Because both systems have counterparts in the vocalization systems of Syriac (Western Syriac has vowel signs derived from [Greek] letters; the Eastern Syriac system consists only of dots), and some of the signs even have the same shapes and the same functions in both types of scripts, the question has arisen whether there may not have been mutual influence. This problem has not met with an adequate solution as yet. The compound vocalization system consists chiefly of graphemes made up of two signs. Just as do the other (Palestinian and Tiberian) systems, the Babylonian system has diacritical dots as well. The accent signs belong to a series of fixed symbols above the letters, which were, however, not combined with so-called conjunctive accents. If these do nonetheless occur in some manuscripts, they were derived from the Tiberian system, for instance by a secondary hand. The Babylonian verse division is sometimes at variance with that of the Tiberian system.

3. The Tiberian system of vocalization and accentuation – usually discussed at some length in the current grammar books of Biblical Hebrew, too – has come down to us as a consolidated, uniform and complete system.[98] There are seven vowels, for the most part written below the letters (sublinear system), for which eight signs are in use. Just as the systems mentioned before, this system too was used by various communities and by people of various traditions and pronunciations. Besides these eight, there is the sign of the *shwa* to denote the furtiveness of a consonant. As a diacritical sign, the dot above the *shin* to the left is in use. Besides, a dot in the six letters *bēt*, *gimel*, *dalet*, *kaf*, *pe* and *taw* marks the *dagesh lene*, a dot in all other consonants except the gutturals *alef*, *he*, *hēt*, *ayin* and *resh* marking the *dagesh forte*. With the former six letters, the situation in the context decides whether this dot is *lene* or *forte*. The *rafe*, a horizontal stroke over the letter, is the opposite of the *dagesh*, but it is only used sporadically or even omitted altogether in the manuscripts. Finally, a dot is sometimes found in the letter *he* which is called *mappiq*. A small vertical stroke, mostly to the left of a vowel sign, nowadays usually known as *meteg*, was traditionally called the *ga'ya*, which as *minor* and *maior* served as a reading aid, so as to improve the phonetical structure of a word.[99] Unlike the two systems mentioned before, the Tiberian system of accentuation is a complete system, consisting of disjunctive and conjunctive accents. Apart from dividing the verse into parts and fixing the melody to which the text is to be read, in the Tiberian system these signs also indicate where the stress in a word should be placed. This system of accentuation is therefore the only means of determining the intonation structure of biblical Hebrew. In this very subtle system, one proceeds from the principle that every division is a division in two (dichotomy). This dichotomy is continued in all of the resulting units until there remain only two words in the smallest unit, or until all the accent signs have been used up.

---

[98] For the Tiberian system, cf. also Yeivin, *Introduction*.
[99] See the discussion in Dotan, 'Masorah', 1450-53.

Geniza Fragment of *Masora* on Exod 17:2-15 (Ms. Heb. e 77 fol. 19 *verso,* Oxford, Bodleian Library).

Cf. Neubauer-Cowley, *Catalogue* 2, 323

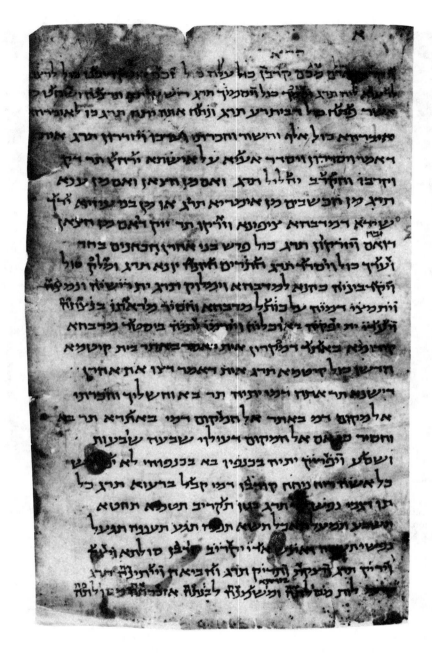

Geniza Fragment of *Masora* on the Targum of Onkelos, Lev 1:1-2:2 (Ms. Heb. d 62 fol. 45 *recto*, Oxford, Bodleian Library)

Cf. Neubauer-Cowley, *Catalogue* 2, 319. There are some superlinear vowel points; the consonants 'alef, 'ayin, waw and yod are used to represent ā, a, u and i. See Kahle, *Die hebr. Bibelhandschriften* 14 (16).

For the three poetical books (Psalms, Proverbs and Job), in certain cases other accents are used than in the remaining books.

It should be noted that in many manuscripts, graphemes of the Tiberian system are used in a way which deviates from the directions of the Tiberian vocalizers. This is described by Dotan as the 'Tiberian Non-Conventional' system.[100] An example of this is given by the *Codex Reuchlinianus* of the Prophets (written in 1105/6). This, however, and the mixing with still other systems cannot be further discussed. At least as important for the transmission of the biblical text, though, as its vocalization, punctuation and accentuation, is the work that can be regarded as the written masora given by the Masoretes.

In order to safeguard the accuracy of the transmission of the biblical text, the Masoretes devised certain mechanisms which developed into corpora of detailed notes concerning this text. The masora comprises everything outside the biblical text which concerns its correct reading and accompanies it. The almost universally accepted technical division is that into *masora parva* and *masora magna*, the latter being subdivided into *masora marginalis* and *masora finalis*.[101]

MASORA PARVA

The *masora parva* (Mp) was written between the columns of the biblical text. It consists in extremely brief notes, moreover often in the form of abbreviations. A small circle *(circellus)* or sometimes an asterisk was put over the word the note refers to. These masoretic notes usually refer to letters or words which could give rise to misunderstandings by the reader or copyists, e.g. a spelling with or without *mater lectionis*, certain vowels, accents, grammatical forms or unusual combinations of words which might be read or interpreted wrongly, etc. They mostly contain descriptive or comparative information, to the effect that the unusual form noted by the Mp at certain letters or words was also indicated for other places in the Bible, or books or parts of it. To mention an entirely arbitrary example: between the words אלהי and ישראל in Gen 33:20, a *circellus* is found above the open space between the two words (also in BHS). In the margin, the number '28' is given in Hebrew characters. This means that this same combination occurs twenty-eight times in the Bible. In G.E. Weil's edition of the *Massorah Gedolah*,[102] for instance, all these places are listed (under No. 2364). In the BHK or BHS editions, but also elsewhere, one can find lists of the signs and abbreviations of the Mp and their meanings.[103] The terminology used is generally Aramaic,[104] which may be indicative of its time of origin. It should, however, be noted that the Mp has not been handed down in identical form or with equal accuracy in all the manuscripts. Texts circulated

---

100 Dotan, 'Masorah, 1465.
101 For further details, see also Dotan, 'Masorah' 1419-29.
102 Weil, *Massorah Gedolah*.
103 In the BHS e.g. on pp. L-LV; see also Dotan, 'Masorah', 1422.
104 See also Morag, 'Some Aspects'.

with varying forms of Mp, and at a later time, when the Bible was printed, these made the confusion even greater, because the Mp was drawn from various sources. BHS and HUBP are trying to put an end to this confusion, in their editions after the best manuscripts.

Special attention must be made of the notation of the so-called cases of *ketiv* and *qere*, according to Robert Gordis, who devoted a special study to them, 'one of the most characteristic and interesting phenomena of the Masorah'.[105] In approximately fifteen hundred places – but the number sometimes varies with the manuscripts – the *masora* indicates that a word which is written (כתיב) in a certain way in the transmitted biblical text, should be pronounced (קרי) in another way, which is usually stated *in margine*. This different pronunciation usually also implies a different spelling of the word concerned, because different vowels generally correspond to a different consonantal text. Initially, every *qere* was placed in the margin of the text and the *ketiv* left unvocalized in the text. Later, the copyists collected these marginal readings in separate lists, which they added to the biblical books. Sometimes the entire body of variant readings was arranged by the Masoretes under various headings.[106] In the BHS, the vowels of the *qere* are put under the *ketiv*-forms in the text, while the consonants of the *qere* are to be found *in margine* and the *qere* is further indicated by means of the letter *qof* with a dot placed over it. In the course of time, many theories have been put forward about the origin and nature of the *ketiv-qere* cases, such as the opinion that they contain variants from very ancient manuscripts. Another opinion is that they are emendations replacing incorrect, difficult or unusual words or expressions.[107] In his study, Gordis presents a classification of the words with *ketiv-qere*, the number of which he estimates at 1350, and further demonstrates that, generally speaking, both forms are of equal weight. The *ketiv* need not always be inferior to the *qere*. According to Gordis's statistics, *qere* is superior to *ketiv* in only eighteen per cent of the cases, *ketiv* to *qere*, on the other hand, in twelve per cent of the cases. In sixty-two per cent of the cases, they balance each other out.[108] Therefore, the *qere*-forms are not variants of *ketiv*-forms considered problematic. Gordis discerns two stages in the development of the *qere*. The first stage marks the *qere* as a warning to the (public) reader, for instance to avoid blasphemy. In this connexion, one may think of the *qere perpetuum*, i.e. the *qere* which is not indicated separately but is always to be observed, e.g. the *tetragrammaton* YHWH, which occurs in the Bible 6823 times and is mostly pronounced as אדני, השם or something to that effect. In later times, the system of annotations in the margin was also used to record the variant readings of certain manuscripts.

---

[105] Gordis, *The Biblical Text*. The quotation is to be found on p. 2.
[106] Ginsburg, *Introduction*, 184f.
[107] For a historical survey, see: Gordis, *The Biblical Text*, 9-14.
[108] Gordis, *The Biblical Text*, XVI.

Apart from words in the text which were to be read differently according to the *qere*, there were also cases in which a word was to be read although it was not given in the text (קרי ולא כתיב), e.g. באים in Jer 31:38, the vowels of which are to be found in the text (e.g. of BHS), while its consonants have been placed *in margine*. This is one out of ten cases (Judg 20:13; 2 Sam 8:3; 16:23; 18:20; 2 Kgs 19:31, 37; Jer 31:38; 50:29; Ruth 3:5, 17). The opposite also occurs (כתיב ולא קרי), e.g. in Jer 51:3, where the combination of consonants ידרך occurs twice, but once without vowel signs, and where in the margin one finds the masoretic note: 'written, but not read'. This is one out of eight cases (the other cases are: 2 Sam 13:33; 15:21; 2 Kgs 5:18; Jer 38:16; 39:12; Ezek 48:16; Ruth 3:12). Besides these cases of *qere* and *ketiv*, there are a number of other categories, for instance that of a word which is written as one word but is read as two (15 times) (Gen 30:11; Exod 4:2; Deut 33:2; Isa 3:15; Jer 6:29; 18:3; Ezek 8:6; Ps 10:10; 55:16; 123:4; Job 38:1; 40:6; Neh 2:13; 1 Chr 9:4; 27:12) or the reverse (e.g. Lam 1:6; 4:3 etc.). Another case of *qere* is the linking of the final letter of a word with the next, as in Ezek 42:9: ומתחתה לשכות (*ketiv*), where the *qere* will have us read, more correctly, ומתחת הלשכות. The reverse of this can for instance be found in Ezra 4:12: (ושורי[א]). In the various manuscripts, the greatest number of mutual discrepancies with respect to *qere* and *ketiv* are found where *matres lectionis* are concerned. This is probably because in such cases the correct pronunciation of the biblical text is hardly or not at all at stake.

MASORA MAGNA AND FINALIS

Many of the annotations of the *masora parva* return in the *masora magna* (Mm) in greater detail, with the exception of the *qere*-notes and the unique forms. The latter masora was mostly written at the top or bottom of the page, in some manunscripts in the margins as well. If there was not enough space on a page, the copyists saved especially the long lists for the end of the book. The Mm contains, among other things, all the words or parts of verses which show an unusual form. Of these the Mp only records how often that form occurs, but not where. Combined with the masoretic data in BHS, Weil's book, mentioned before, gives an easily accessible picture of this. In the Mm, frequent use is made of *simanim* (mnemonic aids), fixed by the Masoretes in order to remember certain biblical passages.[109]

Finally, the *masora finalis* contains lists for which there was no space in the Mm. In the Babylonian system, Mm and Mp are also found, although to a lesser degree than in the Tiberian system. In the terminology used, there are differences with the Tiberian system to be discerned. In the vocalized Palestinian texts, hardly any masoretic notes are found.

---

[109] For examples, see e.g. Dotan, 'Masorah', 1424f.

From the above, it has become clear that the Masoretes, however ingenious the system was they developed in order to settle the accurate vocalization and accentuation of the text for the transmission of the consonantal text, leaned on the work done by their predecessors, whom we called *soferim*, in many respects (for instance in the cases of words in the text which could or should not be read). There is a clear tendency to be observed in the *traditio* of the MT which aimed at securing the *traditum* once and for all. At the beginning of the 16th century, Jacob ben Hayyim ibn Adonija of Tunis, a proof-reader at the printing establishment of Daniel Bomberg in Venice, prepared a new edition of the masora on the basis of a large number of biblical manuscripts, which was added to the well-known second edition of the Rabbinic Bible (Venice 1524/5).[110] With this statement, we are in fact entering the third period we shall discuss, which, however, though it may just as the second to some extent be distinguished from the other periods chronologically, can definitely not be separated from it. For this work, Jacob ben Hayyim had made use of a medieval compilation which is known by the title of *Okhla we-Okhla*, called thus after the initial words 'to eat' (1 Sam 1:9) and 'and now eat' (Gen 27:19), which contains a list of words occurring in the Bible twice, once with and once without conjunctive *waw*.[111] This is only one of the many works containing masoretic and grammatical data. Another famous work is that by Aaron ben Moses Ben-Asher of Tiberias, *Dikdukei ha-Te'amim*, which contains all sorts of grammatical rules, especially with regard to accentuation.[112] Ben Asher, as he is called for brevity's sake, is sometimes regarded as the definite authority on the reading of the biblical text. It might be said that with Ben Asher, the creative period of the masora had reached its close, and that he founded the study of Hebrew grammar, which was to rise to a high level of perfection.[113] The masora thus also became an essential auxiliary science for the study of grammar and exegesis. And in its return, it became itself an object of scholarly research and scientific criticism, as practised by a scholar like Elijah Levita (1469-1549), sometimes called the father of masoretic investigations, in his מסרת המסרת,[114] and continued to this day by

---

[110] Frensdorff, *Massorah magna*, compiled and put in alphabetical order that which was dispersed in Jacob ben Ḥayyim's edition.

[111] This list, too, has been edited by Frensdorff after a manuscript which is in Paris: *Das Buch Ochlah W'ochlah*. Diaz Esteban, *Sefer 'oklah we"oklah*, prepared a new edition, partially based on a manuscript from Halle; cf. Kahle, Cairo Geniza, 134; and *Masoretic Studies* 1 (1974), 131.

[112] Edited by S. Baer and H.L. Strack at Leipzig in 1879. A new and better edition has now become available in Dotan, *The Diqduqé Haṭṭeʿamim*. See further Revell, 'The oldest Accent List', 138-159.

[113] See Bacher, 'Die hebräische Sprachwissenschaft', 130f.

[114] See e.g. Weil, *Initiation*, 1-25. Kahle, *Masoreten des Ostens*, x, speaks less favourably of Levita: 'In Wirklichkeit ist dieser eitle Mann in seinen masoretischen Kenntnissen und Leistungen weit überschätzt worden, und diesem Umstande ist es zuzuschreiben, dass einige von ihm aufgebrachte Irrtümer bis heute unausrottbar scheinen'.

Gérard E. Weil and others in numerous studies. In the next chapter, we shall further discuss the compilators and investigators of the masora.

Maimonides gave the 'masoretic school' of Ben Asher an authoritative foundation in his own days and for the distant future in writing in his *Codex*, book 2, *Hilkhot Sefer Tora* 8:4, that with regard to masoretic matters, he based himself on a manuscript known in Egypt which contained the Bible in its entirety, 'which was formerly in Jersualem (serving to correct copies according to it), and everybody accepted it as authoritative, for Ben Asher corrected it many times. And I used it as the basis for the copy of the Pentateuch which I wrote according to the Law'.[115] Such scholars as Ben-Zvi and Goshen--Gottstein, who quote this passage by Maimonides, are of the opinion that this 'Mustercodex' that the great medieval scholar is here referring to, can only be the famous Aleppo Codex. At one time, this codex was well kept in the synagogue of Aleppo, but after the troubles in the middle of this century, it disappeared from this city and reappeared in Jerusalem damaged.[116] There it is being edited – as said above – in the Bible project of the Hebrew University (HUBP).

It is perhaps worth noting that, although in all probability Aaron from the famous Ben Asher family made the masoretic pointing and accentuation in the Aleppo Codex, the codex itself may have been written by another member of the family or of the Jewish community, just as was often the case with other manuscripts, too.[117] Thus Moses ben Asher made as 'punctator' (נקדן) the punctuation and accentuation system of the *Codex Cairensis*, a manuscript of the Prophets deposited in the Karaite synagogue of Cairo, in the year 895, and Aaron ben Moses ben Aaron that of the so-called *Codex Leningradensis*, on which BHK[3] and BHS are based.

In conclusion of this chapter we may draw attention to manuscripts in which the punctuation and accentuation system of the Ben Naphtali tradition is thought to be represented, and which deviate from those of the Ben Asher tradition in certain details. Kahle has paid attention to Ben Naphtali's text of the Bible and listed a number of manuscripts which, according to him, are important for this tradition.[118] We mention the so-called *Erfurter Codex* (now in the Deutsche Staatsbibliothek, Berlin) and the *Codex Reuchlinianus* (now in the Badische Landesbibliothek, Karlsruhe), a codex of the Prophets of the year 1105.[119]

---

[115] Quoted in Goshen-Gottstein, 'The Authenticity', 18 n. 1, cf. also Ben-Zvi, 'The Codex', 7; Kahle, *Cairo Geniza*, 107; Penkower, 'Maimonides', 39-128.

[116] See for the vicissitudes of this codex and the now missing parts the article by Ben-Zvi mentioned in n. 115, pp. 1-16.

[117] See Yeivin, 'Masora', 143; also Ben-Zvi, 'The Codex', 3-6.

[118] Kahle, *Masoreten des Westens*, vol. 2, 45*-68*.

[119] But cf. Brock, 'Bibelhandschriften I', 112. The punctuation of the *Codex Reuchlinianus* differs both from the tradition of Ben Asher and from that of Ben Naphtali. Sperber calls it 'pre-masoretic', Morag ('The Vocalization of Codex Reuchlinianus') calls it 'fuller Palestinian'.

The Period of Stabilization of the Masoretic Text

The final work on the biblical text which was done by the Masoretes of the families of Ben Asher and Ben Naphtali, not only meant that the outline of the biblical text, as we now know it in the editions of the Hebrew Bible, had been established for the future, but also that its vocalization and accentuation had been fixed. For since BHK[3] and BHS aim at reproducing every detail of the text and masora of the *Codex Leningradensis* and the same is attempted in the HUBP with regard to the *Aleppo Codex*, one may safely conclude that a certain stabilization of the Hebrew Bible has been achieved. By 'stabilization' we mean – as is perhaps needless to say – the fixation of the biblical text as regards length and number of pericopes, words, consonants, vowels, and accentuation, in brief: the fixation of the masora. However, we have not quite arrived at the end of the story of the transmission of the biblical text yet. Not only do there appear to be differences – though only minor – between the important manuscripts, but also the transmission of the biblical text after the period of the Masoretes of the Ben Asher and Ben Naphtali families had an interesting history of its own, which has been an object of scientific research to this day. Leaving aside the recent discoveries of Hebrew texts of the Bible in e.g. the Judaean desert or the Cairo Geniza, we may mainly refer to the invention of the art of printing, which has marked the transmission of the Bible for approximately five centuries, and thus should not go unnoticed in this survey. Obviously, we shall have to confine ourselves to some of the main issues of this history.

THE OLDEST PRINTED TEXTS OF THE BIBLE

In his *Introduction to the Massoretico-Critical Edition of the Hebrew Bible*, Ginsburg provides a comprehensive survey of the history of the printed text of the Bible, roughly up to and including the well-known second edition of the Rabbinic Bible, the so-called *editio princeps* with masora of Jacob ben Hayyim, edited by Bomberg in Venice (1524-1525).[120] Here we borrow some data from this survey.

As the first printed part of the Hebrew Bible, the Book of Psalms, probably printed in Bologna, appeared in 1477. As was usual in publishing texts in the fifteenth and sixteenth centuries, it was not indicated which manuscript(s) the publisher had used for his edition. Instead of the targum, Kimhi's commentary accompanied the biblical text. The book still clearly shows the problems the very first printers had to face. Thus after the first few psalms, the points which were to denote the vowels were replaced by a number of *matres lectionis*, inserted into the text in an arbitrary way. Besides, a large number of omissions can be discovered in the text, sometimes of entire verses, sometimes of only a

---

[120] Ginsburg, *Introduction*, 779-976.

single word. Other matters of this kind might be mentioned, but we shall confine ourselves here (and also in the case of subsequent printed copies) to referring to Ginsburg.[121] The *editio princeps* of the Pentateuch appeared in Bologna in 1482, accompanied by the Targum Onkelos in the so-called Rashi script in the narrow outer columns, and by Rashi's commentary in the upper and lower margins. The *editio princeps* of the Prophets was published in two volumes at Soncino, a small town in the duchy of Milan, in 1485-1486. Israel Nathan ben Samuel, of German origin, had settled in this town and, with his son Joshua Solomon, founded a printing establishment which concentrated on publishing Hebrew literature. For their business, they engaged Abraham ben Hayyim dei Tintori, who had already distinguished himself in the development of Hebrew typography at Ferrara and Bologna. The Soncino firm, which was to publish exceptional works, consisted of the said Joshua Solomon and his two nephews. The *editio princeps* of the third section of the Bible, the Hagiographa, appeared in Naples in the years 1486-1487 in three volumes. One of the peculiarities of this and also of the Soncino edition is the fact that out of reverence for the (names of) God, the tetragrammaton was reproduced as ידוה and *Elohim* as אלדים, the letter *dalet* replacing the letter *he*.

After the appearance in 1487 of a second edition of the Pentateuch at Faro, the *editio princeps* of the whole Bible was published in 1488. It appeared at Soncino again, and was provided with vowels and accents, but it contained no commentaries. The famous typographer Abraham ben Hayyim dei Tintori attached his name to this edition together with the owner of the printing firm. Just as some French and German manuscripts, this edition does not follow the set rules concerning open and closed sections. The masora was virtually neglected altogether by the editors, who were also rather careless about matters of *ketiv* and *qere*. Apart from that, there occur quite a few other omissions and *errores* in this edition.[122] After two editions of the Pentateuch (Ixar, 1490; Lisbon, 1491), the second edition of the entire Bible appeared in Naples in the years 1491-1493. Although it contains no colophon providing specific information to that effect, it may be assumed from the nature and execution of the typography that this is a Soncino product again.

In addition to and after the above-mentioned publications, editions of the complete Bible or parts of the Bible appeared at regular intervals. We mention the books of Isaiah and Jeremiah (Lisbon, 1492); the book of Proverbs (Leiria, 1492); the Pentateuch with the five *Megillot* and the *Haftarot* (Brescia, 1492); the third edition of the entire Bible (Brescia, 1494); the 'Former Prophets' with the commentary of Abravanel (Pesaro, 1510-1511); the same with the commentary of Kimhi (Pesaro, 1511); the 'Latter Prophets' with Kimhi's commentary (Pesaro, 1515); the books of Psalms, Proverbs, Job and Daniel (Salonica, 1515); the fourth edition of the entire Bible (Pesaro, 1511-1517).

---

[121] See Ginsburg, *Introduction*, 780-94.
[122] Ginsburg, *Introduction*, 820-31.

Now the time begins when the polyglots make their appearance, marking a new era in the history of the printed text of the Bible. The first polyglot, the *Complutensian*, which appeared at Alcalá (the *Complutum* of the Romans) between 1514 and 1517, was a Christian's undertaking: namely that of Francisco Cardinal Ximenes de Cisneros, Archbishop of Toledo.[123] This work consists of six folio volumes, the first four of which contain the OT. The first volume contains the Pentateuch in Hebrew, Aramaic (Targum Onkelos), Greek and Latin. The Hebrew text does have vowels, but as yet no accents, except for an indication of the penultimate stress. The second volume contains the books of Joshua, Judges, Samuel, Kings and Chronicles and the 'Prayer of Manasseh'. In this volume, the targum is omitted, just as, for that matter, in the subsequent volumes. The third volume contains canonical and deutero-canonical books in the following order: Ezra, Nehemiah, Tobit, Judith, Esther with apocryphal additions, Job, Psalms, Proverbs, Ecclesiastes, Song of Songs, Wisdom and Ecclesiasticus. The fourth volume contains the remaining canonical and deutero-canonical books. The printing of this last volume of the OT was completed on 10 July, 1517. The fact that this polyglot was a Christian product had some consequences for the Hebrew text. The Vulgate occupies the central position between the Hebrew and Greek texts. The form of the Hebrew text was adapted to this situation. Thus such books as Samuel and Kings, Ezra – Nehemiah and Chronicles were each divided into two books, the first two being called 1-4 Kings. The masoretic division of the text into sections was replaced by the Christian one into chapters, which in the beginning of the 13th century had been introduced into the Latin Bibles by Stephen Langton.[124] Also, the order of the books was revised according to that in the Vulgate. In addition, the accents of the Hebrew text were almost completely omitted and the vowel signs were sometimes altered irresponsibly. On the other hand, the consonantal text was reproduced with great accuracy and therefore became important for text-critical investigations. In this edition the manuscript(s) on which the text was based were again not specified. Ginsburg was of the opinion that a manuscript which he dated Toledo c.e. 1280 and which was written in a beautiful Sephardic hand – now deposited in Madrid, University Library, Codex No. 1 – must at least have been one of them.[125] Kahle has pointed out that the humanistically trained Spanish scholars are likely to have used the earliest manuscripts they could get hold of.[126] In addition, the editors of the Complutensian Polyglot used the Naples edition of the Bible as a standard.

In the years 1516-1517, the first edition of the Rabbinic Bible was published in Venice. This city was taking the place of Soncino, Naples and Pesaro, with Daniel Bomberg rivalling his predecessors in the art of printing Hebrew.

[123] See also Kahle, *Cairo Geniza*, 124-129.
[124] For the division of the Bible into chapters, see Ginsburg, *Introduction*, 25-31.
[125] Ginsburg, *Introduction*, 775f.; 918-25. Cf. also Kahle, *Cairo Geniza*, 125f.
[126] Kahle, *Cairo Geniza*, 126ff.; *idem*, 'Zwei durch Humanisten besorgte, dem Papst gewidmete Ausgaben der hebräischen Bibel', in: *Opera Minora*, 148-56.

Bomberg had emigrated from Antwerp to Venice, and his first contribution to a scholarly edition of the biblical text consisted in producing the above-mentioned edition in four volumes, prepared by Felix Pratensis. The title page may serve to show what is meant by the term 'Rabbinic Bible'. The Pentateuch, for instance, was printed with the Targum Onkelos and Rashi's commentary. The Prophets were provided with the Targum Yonatan and Kimhi's commentary. The Psalms had, in addition to the targum and Kimhi's commentary, the so-called commentary *Kav Venaki*, etc. Besides, the 'Jerusalem' Targum of the Pentateuch and the second Targum of Esther were printed as well, just as were treatises about the accents and the differences between the Ben Asher and the Ben Naphtali tradition concerning the Pentateuch. Felix Pratensis dedicated the work to Pope Leo X, who in his turn protected the former, and the printer Bomberg, against piracy. This work is the first in which the *qere*-variants are given in the margin. Also, the editor of this work has noted numerous variants regarding vowel signs, accents and consonants *in margine*, in addition to the cases of *ketiv* and *qere*. Other masoretic indications, too, are clearly shown in this edition, as opposed to all earlier printed works, for instance the words which were read by the *Soferim*, though not written in the text. It is beyond discussion that Pratensis must have consulted Hebrew manuscripts.

Simultaneously with this splendid large edition of the Rabbinic Bible, a small and accurate text of the Bibel was edited by Felix Pratensis in a quarto edition by Bomberg (1516-1517), destined, so to speak, for the 'layman' of modest means, and based on the biblical text of the large edition. For commercial reasons, the name of Pratensis – he was a Jew who had embraced Christianity – was omitted, just as was the dedication to the Pope, so as to create a market for this Bible among the Jews. The success of this edition necessitated a second edition in 1521, this time in the name of the brothers Adelkind, and even more geared to the needs of the Jewish market.

THE RABBINIC BIBLE OF BEN HAYYIM

The most famous edition of the biblical text, however, was to be the second edition of the Rabbinic Bible, i.e. the *editio princeps* of Jacob ben Hayyim with the masora (Bomberg, Venice, 1524-1525). This text of the Bible with the masora 'finally settled the Massoretic text as it is now exhibited in the present recension of the Hebrew Scriptures'.[127] Contrary to Pratensis, Jacob ben Hayyim was an orthodox rabbinic Jew. He convinced Bomberg of the importance of presenting the masora with the biblical text in an edition of the Bible, and the latter spared neither trouble nor expense to obtain the masora from far and wide. Ben Hayyim arranged the masoretic material in and accompanying the biblical text in such a way that the reader could easily understand and use it. The results of all this unparallelled labour were laid down in the four folio

---

[127]   Thus Ginsburg, *Introduction*, 956.

volumes of the Masoretico-Rabbinic Bible. Volume 1 contains the Pentateuch with the Targum Onkelos and the commentaries of Rashi and Ibn Ezra; besides, the Mm and Mp. The Targum Onkelos is provided with vowel signs and accents, too. Volume 2 contains the 'Former Prophets' with the Targum Yonatan and the commentaries of David Kimhi, Ralbag (= R. Levi ben Gershom) and Rashi. Volume 3 contains the 'Latter Prophets' with the targum and the commentaries of sometimes Kimhi (Jeremiah and Ezekiel), sometimes Ibn Ezra (the other books). The Hagiographa are contained in the fourth volume, of which the books of Daniel, Ezra-Nehemiah and Chronicles are without the targum, while for all books of this volume, commentaries by various Jewish exegetes have been included. As an appendix to this volume, Jacob ben Hayyim reproduced in 65 folios of four columns that part of the Mm which was too long for the upper and lower margins of the text. This edition of the Rabbinic Bible is the first – as far as cases of *ketiv* and *qere* are concerned – in which the consonants of the official readings are given in the margin, together with the letter *qof* provided with a dot: the so-called *qere*. The variants known as *sevirin* are also indicated clearly. Moreover, Ben Hayyim has stated the results of the collation of a number of manuscripts *in margine*. On the basis of this collation, he has made independent decisions. An example of this are the two verses of Josh 21 (vv. 36 and 37) which are included in numerous manuscripts and in all early printed editions, but omitted in a number of manuscripts, on account of *homoeoarcton*, but no less because of certain ideas held in masoretic circles. Jacob ben Hayyim likewise omits these verses in his edition.[128] In BHK[2,3] and BHS these verses are printed in a smaller type than the rest, in other editions it is usually indicated clearly that they are omitted in the masora.[129] In spite of the amount of knowledge Ben Hayyim managed to acquire, his work occasionally shows lacunae. Although Jacob ben Hayyim makes no mention of the edition of his predecessor Felix Pratensis, he appears to have made frequent use of it. In some respects his work even offers less than that of his predecessor (it omits, for instance, the so-called 'Jerusalem' Targum to the Pentateuch and the second Targum to Esther).

Despite the shortcomings of Ben Hayyim's work, the Rabbinic Bible remained a highlight in the history of the transmission of the Hebrew Bible for many centuries to come. First of all, a printed Bible was now available which paid sound attention to the masoretic punctuation and accentuation; secondly, it was considered by many later scholars to be a *textus receptus*, which could be relied on or which could be used as a basis for subsequent editions of the

---

[128] See Ginsburg, *Introduction*, 178ff.; 965.
[129] E.g. in Ev. van der Hooght's *Biblia Hebraica, ex recensione* Aug. Hahn, with a preface by Ern. Fr. Car. Rosenmüller, Lipsiae 1834; *Biblia Hebraica*[3] of Ev. van der Hooght, edited by K.G.W. Theile, Lipsiae 1902. Cf. also Kennicott, *Vetus Testamentum, ad locum*: 'Codices, pro hoc Opere, vel per totum vel in locis selectis collati, et in quibus est caput hoc *Josuae*, sunt 208. Ex his sunt 59, in quibus desunt (Masorâ sic jubente) duo commata inter 35 en 36: caeteri tamen codices 149 haec habent commata; in Textu 137, in Margine 12'.

Hebrew Bible. All things considered, the biblical text as edited by Ben Hayyim maintained its high authority until well into this century, even though in due course several attempts have been made to produce amended editions on the basis of the study of new manuscripts and of the masora. In conclusion, we would like to sketch the history of both tendencies: the study of the masora and the publishing of texts of the Hebrew Bible.

THE STUDY OF THE MASORA

In the preceding chapter, we have already seen that the masora is important not only for the accurate preservation of the text and the pronunciation and modulation in liturgical use, but also for the study of Hebrew grammar. We have already mentioned Elia Levita (Elijah Baḥur ben Asher ha-Levi), who in his מסרת המסרת (Venice, 1538, Bomberg), gave a historical survey of the masora in its many aspects. Unusual was his opinion that the accentuation and punctuation of the biblical text had not been given on Mount Sinai, but by the Masoretes, who lived after the talmudic period. He also published a survey of the various kinds of masora, its methods and its terminology, with a good deal of examples. This excellent work by Levita became the basis of a study by Johann Buxtorf Sr. (1564-1629), the well-known Christian Hebraist of Basle: *Tiberias, sive Commentarius Masorethicus ad illustr. Operis Bibl.* This work was published in Basle in 1620, and in it Buxtorf showed himself a master of the knowledge of the masora. He held, however, a more conservative opinion about the origin of the systems of vocalization and accentuation than Levita. The reader may only be reminded here of the disturbing controversy carried on between Buxtorf Jr. (1599-1664), who was just as conservative as his father, and L. Cappellus (1575-1658), who held a position similar to that of Levita.[130]

Quite a few activities, however, had already preceded the compiling of the masora before Levita.[131] Thus Meir ben Todros ha-Levi Abulafia (1180-1244) had dealt at length with the *defective* and *plene* spellings of Hebrew words in his book מסרת סיג לתורה. He arranged the words according to their *radices* in the form of a dictionary and added masoretic particulars. Another investigator of the masora was Jekuthiel ben Juda ha-Kohen 'ha-Nakdan' (= 'the punctator') who probably lived in the first half of the thirteenth century and wrote עין הקורא, a book which, contrary to that by Meir ben Todros, discussed accents and vocalization and may be regarded as a collection of grammatical and masoretic notes. This study relied on six Sephardic manuscripts and a number

---

[130] See e.g. Kraus, *Geschichte*, 48; Barthélemy, *Critique textuelle*, *10-*22; Cappellus' work *Arcanum punctationis revelatum sive de punctorum vocalium et accentuum apud Hebraeos vera et germana antiquitate* was published in two books at Leyden in 1624 by Th. Erpenius, without mention of the author's name. About the discussions concerning the integrity of the MT, cf. also: Keil, *Lehrbuch*, 632-35.

[131] In broad outlines, we follow here the descriptions given in Yeivin, 'Masora', 154ff., and Dotan, 'Masorah', 1476ff.

of older works, and became in its turn the starting-point for later grammarians and editors of the biblical text. A third name which should be mentioned in this connexion is that of Menahem ben Solomon ha-Meiri (1240-1306), the author of קרית ספר (two volumes). The first volume contains rules for writing a *tora*-scroll, the second offers grammatical rules with a view to the public reading of the Scriptures. These are followed by lists of words spelt *plene* or *defective*, open and closed sections and several further masoretic notes.

After the above-mentioned epoch-making work presented by Jacob ben Hayyim in his *Mikraot Gedolot* of 1524-1525 and the work of Elia Levita, the investigators of the masora can be seen to go back to these works again and again. Thus Menahem ben Juda di Lonzano (late 16th century), who in his אור תורה, arranged in the order of the biblical works, comments only on the Pentateuch, using Ben Hayyim's text as his basis. However, he introduces emendations into this text regarding orthography and especially vocalization and accentuation, on the basis of numerous manuscripts and the work of earlier scholars who have been mentioned above. But the most important book concerning the masora was written by Jedidia Solomon Raphael ben Abraham of Norzi (early 17th century) who in 1626 completed a book which he himself called גודר פרץ ('the repairer of the breach'), but which when printed for the first time in 1740-1742 (at Mantua) was given the title of מנחת שי (שי being the rendition of the – reversed – initials of Solomon Jedidia). This book contains an introduction to and a masoretic commentary on the whole of the Bible in the order of the biblical books. It does not only deal with vocalization, punctuation, etc., but also with the crownlets (תגין) on certain letters in the text. Every word and every letter about which one could possibly be mistaken, is discussed by him. In this way, his work becomes a kind of correction and emendation of the biblical text as given by Ben Hayyim. Later editors of the Bible have repeatedly revised the biblical text according to his directions.[132]

At approximately the same time, scholars occupied themselves with the masora in Yemen. Of those we shall only mention Yahya Ṣalih (latter half of the 18th century), who, in his book חלק הדקדוק, commented on the whole of the Bible on matters of accentuation, vocalization and other masoretic subjects. He had knowledge of many Yemenite manuscripts, and also of the targumim and of Saadya Gaon's Arabic translation. Among the Jews of Yemen, his book held the same high position as Jedidia Solomon of Norzi's מנחת שי among Western Jews.

Wolf Benjamin Ze'ev ben Simson Heidenheim (1757-1832) not only produced a number of new editions of the biblical text, but also systematically discussed all sorts of masoretic problems. He edited as many as five new editions of the Pentateuch. He also published the highly esteemed משפטי הטעמים (Rödelheim 1808). This is a book dealing with the accents, in which

---

[132] Cf. Kennicott, *Dissertatio generalis* (above, n. 45), 27 (§ 62); De Rossi, *Variae lectiones*, vol. 1, xl-xliii, §§ 37f.; Strack; *Prolegomena critica*, 4.

he constantly referred back to earlier masoretic authorities. In an edition of the Pentateuch (מאור עינים), he re-edited the above-mentioned עין הקורא, written by Jekuthiel ha-Kohen ha-Nakdan, in the margins.

SCHOLARLY EDITIONS OF THE BIBLE

In addition to these Jewish scholars, who intensified the study of the masora and attempted to create and publish a Hebrew text which was, in their view, as correct as possible, Christian circles increasingly engaged in the publishing of the biblical text after the edition of the *textus receptus* in the *Mikraot Gedolot*. We have already drawn attention to the polyglots in general, and have mentioned in this connexion the Complutensian Polyglot in particular, which had even been published before Ben Hayyim's *magnum opus*. Of the various polyglots which appeared after that, several are of some relevance to the subject under discussion, such as the *Antwerp Polyglot*, which was published at the expense of King Philip II (of Spain) by the well-known printer Christopher Plantin from 1569 to 1572 in eight volumes folio, and is accordingly sometimes called *Biblia Regia* after the former, sometimes *Biblia Plantinia* after the latter.[133] Its production was conducted by Benedictus Arias, also called Montanus, who was responsible for, among other things, the division of chapters into verses with Arabic numerals, which has become customary in our Bibles since this edition.[134] The first four volumes contain the OT, together with the eighth volume, but the latter also offers an interlinear Latin translation by Santes Pagninus. The critical value of the Hebrew text, however, is not very great, because it was not edited independently but derived from that of the Complutensian Polyglot and that of Ben Hayyim.[135] This verdict applies even more to the *Parisian Polyglot*, which appeared at Vitré's at the expense of Guy Michel le Jay in ten large-format volumes. In this case, the first four volumes are mere duplicates of the Antwerp Bible. As stated above, J. Morinus published the SamPent and its targum in this polyglot.

The most important polyglot is undoubtedly the *London Polyglot* in six folio volumes, published in London at Roycroft's between 1654 and 1657. This work was undertaken by Brian Walton (Bishop of Chester). As with former polyglots, renowned scholars and orientalists were called in, such as Edmund Castle (Castellus), who was also responsible for the *Lexicon Heptaglotton* (1669), two books in one volume folio, which was often added to the edition of this polyglot. This polyglot surpasses others of its kind in the great accuracy with which the texts were edited. In addition, the first volume of this work contains a historical critical introduction to the various texts and translations, written by Walton. Apart from the MT, the SamPent and its targum, the polyglot contains

---

[133] Nestle, 'Polyglottenbibeln', esp. 531f.
[134] See Ginsburg, *Introduction*, 107f.
[135] See e.g. Pfeiffer, *Introduction*, 99; cf. Hall, 'Biblical Scholarship, 54.

the LXX, fragments of the ancient Latin version, the Aramaic targumim and parts of the Ethiopic and Persian versions, all provided – where needful – with Latin translations. All these texts are moreover printed synoptically, and arranged very conveniently next to or below each other.

From the above survey it becomes clear that there hardly was general agreement among the scholars of the time about what would today be called a 'scholarly' edition of the Hebrew text of the Bible, and that the quality of an edition – and therefore the transmission of the Bible itself – depended on a number of circumstances. There was firstly the matter of the value and availability of the manuscripts on which one was going to base (partially) the text that was to be printed. Secondly, the question arose to what extent an editor ought to consider masoretic punctuation, accentuation and other indications relevant to his purpose. This is also related to the question for what purpose or for whom one intended the biblical text which was being edited: it made a difference whether the target group was of Jewish or Christian persuasions. It has become clear, though, that especially Jewish scholars came to prefer an edition based on the masoretic tradition as it had mainly been handed down by the Tiberian Masoretes. Ben Hayyim's second Rabbinic Bible of 1524-1525 was therefore often seen as the most easily accessible *textus receptus*. But there were other 'recensions' besides it, such as the above-mentioned edition by Gershom Soncino (Brescia 1494), a Hebrew text of the Bible on the basis of which M. Luther created his famous translation of the Bible. After having been revised in details according to other manuscripts, this text, which is highly inaccurate from a masoretic point of view, became the basis of not only the edition of the first Rabbinic Bible and the so-called Bombergian hand-sized editions; but also of the editions of the Bible by Robert Estienne (Stephanus; 1539; 1544-1546) and Sebastian Münster (Basle, 1535). Another 'recension' is the biblical text given in the Complutensian Polyglot, because it was produced from the manuscripts, independently of other editions of the Bible. This text has only vowel signs, no accents.[136]

These three original 'recensions' were at first only followed by editions which offered 'mixed' texts, such as the text of the Antwerp Polyglot and the editions dependent on it: the biblical texts in the lesser known *Hamburg* (1587) and *Nurnberg* (1599) Polyglots of Elias Hutter (1553-c.1609) and the *Leipzig Polyglot* (1750-51) of Chr. Reineccius.[137] The Bible editions of the above-mentioned Buxtorf Sr., both the hand-sized edition (Basle 1611) and his Rabbinic Bible in four volumes folio (Basle 1618-1619; vol. IV, 2 contains the masora) offer 'mixed' texts, because besides Ben Hayyim's text, he also used the text of the Complutensian Polyglot.

Editing practice with regard to the biblical text further developed along the indicated lines. We mention here the *Biblia S. Hebraea*, highly praised in the

---

[136]   See Jahn, *Einleitung*, vol. 1[2], 408; Buhl, 'Bibeltext', 726f.
[137]   Nestle, 'Polyglottenbibeln', 533f.

17th century, published in Amsterdam in 1661 (2nd impression 1667) by Jos. Athias and provided with a preface by the well-known professor Joh. Leusden of Utrecht. The Hebrew text was, as specified by the title, corrected according to and collated with a number of ancient manuscripts. But this edition, too, was substantially a 'mixed' text. In its turn, this text, prepared by Leusden and Athias, became the basis of other editions of the Bible, such as those of David Clodius (1677), revised by Joh. Heinrich May (1692); Everh. van der Hooght (Amsterdam 1705); H. Opitius (Kiel 1709); and Charles François Houbigant (Paris 1753, 4 vols.);[138] of Kennicott's above-mentioned work;[139] of the edition by Joh. Simonis (Halle 1752) and of editions of the Bible depending on the latter. Especially the influence of Van der Hooght's work continued to make itself felt in the – often numerous – reprints, because of its attractive shape and clear type, e.g. in the third edition of Joh. Simonis' *Biblia Hebraica Manualia ad praestantiores Editiones accurata* (Halle 1822), which was revised by E.F.K. Rosenmüller (fourth edition 1828); in the revision carried out by Aug. Hahn (1792-1863) of the edition by Athias – Leusden – Simonis – Van der Hooght (Leipzig 1832);[140] and in the *Biblia Hebraica ad optimas editiones imprimis Everardi van der Hooght accurate recensa et expressa* of Car. Godofr.-Guilielmus Theile (Leipzig 1849; 9th edition 1902), used by many generations of prospective OT scholars. The labour performed by M. Letteris (1800-1871) for the *British and Foreign Bible Society of London* (Vienna 1852; London 1866) should also be mentioned here. Even though he risked his reputation with the Jews by it, it was perhaps 'his most lasting achievement . . . as it resulted in innumerable editions of the "Letteris Bible" '.[141] In the United States of America, Van der Hooght's unvocalized text of the Bible became the first Hebrew Bible to be published (Philadelphia 1814, 2 vols.).[142]

Although also basing his edition of the biblical text (Berlin 1699, 4 vols.; 2nd edition 1772) on the text of Athias- Leusden, Dan. Ern. Jablonski (1660-1741) collated a great deal of other editions and several manuscripts. In its turn, his edition served Joh. H. Michaelis (1668-1738) as a basis for his own critical edition ('die Hallische Bibel'), for which he consulted nineteen printed editions and five manuscripts from Erfurt (Halle, 1720). Yet peculiar omissions can be pointed out in this edition, as would later be demonstrated by Joh. D. Michaelis.[143]

---

[138] See also Barthélemy, *Critique Textuelle*, *24.
[139] Kennicott, *Vetus Testamentum Hebraicum*, vol. 1, Praefatio (p.I): 'Imprimitur hic Textus *Hebraeus* secundum editionem *Everardi van der Hooght* Amstelodamensem, 8vo, 1705...'.
[140] One should distinguish between this and the *Biblia Hebraica ad optimas editiones inprimis Everardi van der Hooght ex recensione Aug. Hahnii expressa*, with a preface by Ern. Fr. Car. Rosenmüller, Lipsiae 1834. Several arbitrary textual emendations are to be found herein; see e.g. Keil, *Lehrbuch*, 631.
[141] See Weinberg, 'Letteris, Meir', 55; cf. also Snaith, 'The Ben Asher Text', 8.
[142] See Orlinsky, 'Prolegomenon', xi f.
[143] Michaelis, 'Von critischen Urkunden'.

It may be put that, as a result of the progressive developments in the field of printing but also in that of scientific research, some stability had been achieved by the middle of the previous century as regards the editing of the consonants and vowels of the biblical text and, to a lower degree, with respect to the masoretic accentuations and annotations, even though certain Bible publishers showed considerable ignorance at precisely this point. The masora and the variant readings, as far as they could be traced in manuscripts and other editions, were mainly recorded – as stated above – in the works of Ben Hayyim, Joh. Buxtorf, Everh. van der Hooght, J.H. Michaelis; in Norzi's שי מנחת, and in the works of Houbigant, Kennicott, De Rossi and others.[144]

THE PROGRESS OF SCIENTIFIC RESEARCH IN THE NINETEENTH CENTURY

In the middle of the previous century, however, scientific study of the biblical text and its masoretic traditions flourished, owing to various circumstances. Epoch-making studies were published in this field, the influence of which has kept making itself felt until well into this century and which should therefore be mentioned in connexion of our subject. In 1857, Abr. Geiger (1810-1874) published his book *Urschrift und Übersetzungen der Bibel in ihrer Abhängigkeit von der innern Entwicklung des Judentums*,[145] in which he attempted to demonstrate that in the period from the return out of the Babylonian Exile to the completion of the Talmudim, the history of religion and that of the biblical text have mutually influenced each other in Judaism. The pioneering aspect of Geiger's book consists in the author's being fully aware of his standing at the beginnings of a comprehensive view of the history of Judaism, which would also have consequences for the transmission of the biblical text. Geiger contrasted an independently transmitted biblical text from Babylonia with the Tiberian biblical text, which would eventually become the fixed text of the Bible. Geiger's work was to meet with approval, but also with a good deal of opposition. Meanwhile, the historical investigation of the transmission of the biblical text had also started in Jewish circles. In this article, we have already indicated Lagarde's contribution. In the end, historical and critical research was not going to leave unaffected those who had taken a conservative stand in the matter of the transmission of the biblical text.

Between 1869 and 1895, Seligman Isaac Baer (1825-1897), a pupil of the above-mentioned Wolf Heidenheim, edited a masoretic text of the Bible in several instalments in Leipzig at Bernh. Tauchnitz's, with the assistance of

---

[144] Keil. *Lehrbuch*, 631f., mentions further: J. Chr. Döderlein – J.H. Meisner (Leipzig 1839), who offer an extract from Kennicott's and De Rossi's works; cf. also Jahn, *Einleitung*, 460, who moreover points out that firstly the available manuscripts have been collated inaccurately and at random, and that secondly 'doch keine grosse Anzahl wichter Varianten zu erwarten steht', even after a meticulous and exhaustive collation of all the manuscripts.

[145] A second edition appeared in Frankfurt a/M in 1928, provided with an *Einführung* by Paul Kahle. This *Einführung* has in its turn been reprinted in Kahle's *Opera Minora*, 151-56.

Franz Delitzsch (1813-1890), who contributed, among other things, a preface drawn up in Latin. The volumes which appeared after Delitzsch's death (Libri Josuae et Judicum, 1891; Liber Samuelis, 1892) are obviously without this contribution. Owing to Baer's death, the books of Exodus – Deuteronomy could not be published any more. The first volume to appear was the book of Genesis (1869). As indicated by the titles of all these volumes, an attempt had been made to give a very accurate reproduction of the masoretic text *(e fontibus masorae varie illustravit, notis criticis confirmavit S. Baer)*. This work exhibits the spirit and influence of the nineteenth century also in the fact that several textual and conjectural emendations have been introduced into the text. Baer continued the work of his teacher Heidenheim which had resulted in the latter's work משפטי הטעמים, by publishing a book entitled תורת אמת(1852), in which he tried to give the precise rules for the accentuation of the three poetical books of Psalms, Proverbs and Job. Unlike Heidenheim's book, which exclusively relied on the ancient sources, Baer's book is a system of masoretic rules drawn up independently, which were supposed to generate eventually the 'correct' biblical text. With regard to the Bible an attempt was made to reconstruct the Hebrew text on the basis of the masora in such a way as to make it possible to bring the Ben Hayyim text still closer to the Ben Asher text, which was considered ideal. Kahle not unwittily calls the two producers of this text 'the last Masoretes',[146] and he offers two examples of the way in which they smoothed out difficulties or drew up rules which could not be found in the Ben Asher manuscripts, such as those concerning the placing of *meteg*.[147]

Another masoretic edition of the biblical text on the basis of the Ben Hayyim text was produced by the man who also wrote the *Introduction to the Massoretico-Critical Edition of the Hebrew Bible* which has already been quoted frequently above: Christian David Ginsburg (1831-1914). In 1894, a Hebrew Bible in two volumes appeared in London, sponsored by the *Trinitarian Bible Society*, which was reproduced in 1906 by the *Society for the Circulation of Uncorrupted Versions of the Word of God*. The *British and Foreign Bible Society* also published an edition of the Hebrew Bible in four volumes on the basis of the Ben Hayyim text, of which the Pentateuch appeared in 1908, the two volumes of the Prophets in 1911 and the Writings, only after Ginsburg's death, in 1926. For this edition of the Bible, Ginsburg (helped later by able assistants, such as A. Wright and H.E. Holmes) collated seventy-three manuscripts, of which sixty-one were in London in the British Museum. In addition he compared the Ancient Versions and the early editions of the Hebrew

---

[146] Kahle, *Cairo Geniza*, 113; about Baer, cf.: *idem, Der hebräische Bibeltext*; also Dotan, 'Masorah', 1478f.

[147] Baer's article 'Die Metheg-Setzung' strongly influenced the treatment of this subject in e.g. König, *Historisch-kritisches Lehrgebäude*, vol. 1, 86-90, and Bergsträsser, *Hebräische Grammatik*, vol. 1, § 11 ᵉ⁻ᵍ; cf. Kahle, *Cairo Geniza*, 114.

Bible.[148] These editions of the Bible have evoked a good deal of criticism notwithstanding Ginsburg's expert knowledge, firstly because uncritical use was made of the masora, and moreover because the manuscripts were used eclectically, without further classification or distinction of the readings. Roberts accordingly concludes: 'On the whole the work remains but another and poorer copy of the Ben Chayyim text'.[149] Yet Ginsburg was an expert in the field of the problems posed by the masora, as is witnessed by his *The Massorah. Compiled from Manuscripts, Alphabetically and Lexically Arranged* (London, 1880[1]-1905), a work in four volumes. In this he collected masoretic notes from numerous manuscripts and early printed editions of the Bible, which he arranged in alphabetical order and translated into English. But again, this work did not offer a comprehensive survey of the whole field of masoretic manuscripts, nor was full profit drawn from the latter. It may also be mentioned here that, apart from Ginsburg's 'Major Edition', the *British and Foreign Bible Society* edited two further editions containing the same text: a. an unpunctuated edition, also in four volumes, started in 1914 and completed in 1920, and afterwards reprinted many times; b. the 'Minor Edition', prepared by A.S. Geden,[150] started in 1916 and likewise completed in 1920. Both editions contain a selection from Ginsburg's apparatus, dealing only with cases of *ketiv* and *qere*, *defective* and *plene* spellings and *sevirin*, and omitting the references and names of the manuscripts employed. A less felicitous edition of Ginsburg's text was given in *The New Hebrew Bible*, Jerusalem 1953, revised, according to the title-page, by M. Cassuto on the basis of the Ben Asher masora, but in reality only a photographical reproduction of the edition of Ginsburg's work provided with notes by the late Cassuto, which were themselves made on the basis of the Letteris edition.[151]

KITTEL'S *BIBLIA HEBRAICA*

The Baer-Delitzsch edition of the Bible served as primary Hebrew text in education and in many scientific works, especially in Western Europe and in Christian circles. However, at the beginning of this century, a biblical text was published which has since been known as the *Biblia Hebraica* among many generations of students and scholars. At the basis of this edition stands Rudolf Kittel (1853-1929). In 1902 he published a text entitled: *Über die Notwendigkeit und Möglichkeit einer neuen Ausgabe der hebräischen Bibel*,[152] in which, quot-

---

[148] For further details, see Geden – Kilgour, *Introduction*. Among others, the German professors J.J. Kahan of Leipzig, H.L. Strack of Berlin and Eberh. Nestle of Maulborn assisted in going over the proofs.
[149] Roberts, *Old Testament Text and Versions*, 90; cf. also Kahle, *Cairo Geniza*, 136f.
[150] Alfred S. Geden also published a useful study: *Outlines*.
[151] See Kahle, 'The New Hebrew Bible'; Simon, 'The Jerusalem Bible', 109f.; Snaith in *Eleven Years of Bible Bibliography*.
[152] The subtitle is: *Studien und Erwägungen*, Leipzig 1902.

ing A. Klostermann, he points out the deplorable fact that academic students cannot but receive the impression of possessing in the Hebrew Bible *the* transmitted text, although the same students will use revised texts with variant readings when taught Greek or Latin. In order to fill this lack, Kittel decided on an edition of the Bible which would be 'critical', albeit not in the sense of P. Haupt's *The Sacred Books of the Old Testament* (the 'Rainbow-Bible'; begun in 1893 but never completed), in which textual and literary criticism were combined on the basis of a largely unpunctuated text. The real goal of an edition of the biblical text could not be 'kurzweg die Urschrift selber'. Its purpose was 'die Rückbildung des massoretischen Textes in der Richtung auf die Urschrift bis zu einem bestimmten, zwischen der Urschrift und der Massora liegenden, Punkte'.[153] In the *Prolegomena* to the first (Leipzig 1905-1906) and the second (Stuttgart 1912) edition of the *Biblia Hebraica*, edited by Rud. Kittel in association with his colleagues G. Beer, F. Buhl, G. Dalman, S.R. Driver, M. Löhr, W. Nowack, L.W. Rothstein and V. Ryssel, he wrote *inter alia* that this edition was characterized by the addition to the masoretic text of the principal *variae lectiones* of the Hebrew manuscripts and the *versiones antiquae* in the annotations, and furthermore of directions *ad emendandum textum*. There are two ways of approaching the biblical writers' own words *(verba scriptorum biblicorum ipsorum)*: a. to offer an emended text, which, however, if it is to be reliable, cannot go back behind a certain period *(paulo fere ante versionem veterrimam)*; or b. to offer a biblical text relying on the MT as the basis of the edition, which is, where necessary, provided with variant readings and directions for textual emendations in the apparatus. In this edition preference was given to 'b'. The biblical text on which the first two editions of the BHK were based was Jacob ben Hayyim's *Bombergiana* (1524-1525), though there are certain deviations from this edition, e.g. in the placing of *meteg*, on the strength of Baer's above-mentioned article.[154] A novelty in BHK which has unfortunately remained in BHS, was the fact that not only *variae lectiones* of Hebrew manuscripts (chiefly according to Kennicott's and De Rossi's specifications, though also according to those given by Baer and Firkowitsch[155]) and variant readings of the Ancient Versions were adduced in the so-called 'critical apparatus', but also suggestions for textual emendations on purely literary grounds. The latter obviously do not belong in a critical apparatus and have therefore been quite rightly criticized. They are, quite rightly again, omitted in the HUBP-edition.

---

[153] Kittel, 'Über die Notwendigkeit', 36.
[154] See *Prolegomena*, VI: 'Quod attinet ad *Meteg* scribendum, codex B saepe indiligenter et ex libidine se gerit'. In the books of Genesis – Joshua, for that matter, the *meteg* was written to the right of the vowel signs, owing to technical reasons.
[155] Abraham Firkowitsch, a Karaite leader, lived from 1786 to 1874. He was always eagerly and ambitiously looking for ancient manuscripts which could prove the antiquity and authenticity of the Karaites. Such scholars as H. Strack, A. Harkavy and others have demonstrated that Firkowitsch's material was not always equally genuine; c.f. Berkowitz, 'Firkovich, Abraham' 1305f.; Kahle, *Cairo Geniza* 5ff.; 31ff.

After many years of preparation, the third edition of the BHK was completed in 1937. Rud. Kittel himself would not live to see this complete publication, but he had initiated the important changes which this edition showed, and in the *Prolegomena* to the third edition in the Genesis volume (1929), he wrote: 'So wird denn in dieser Ausgabe an Stelle des Textes des ben Chaijim oder irgendeines anderen auf Handschriften des 13. und 14. Jahrhunderts n. Chr. ruhenden Masoretentextes erstmals der um Jahrhunderte ältere Text des ben Ascher in der Gestalt, in der ihn die Handschrift L gibt, dargeboten'.[156] The siglum L represents the *Codex Leningradensis* B 19[A] from the public library of Leningrad. The masoretic text was prepared and edited by Paul Kahle. The latter stated in his turn that he had hoped to be able to replace L in the course of his labour 'durch den Mustercodex des Ben Ascher selber, der sich in der Synagoge der Sephardim in Aleppo befindet'.[157] In his further discussion he points to the work of Mishael ben Uzziel, which appeared shortly after the death of the Masoretes of the families of Ben Asher and Ben Naphtali, and lists the differences between the texts of the two families. This list is older by many centuries than all other lists of masoretic discrepancies.[158] Anyhow, he considers Codex L a unique and pure masoretic text, written by Aaron ben Moses Ben-Asher, the great 10th-century Masorete.

It was not until the next edition, the *Biblia Hebraica Stuttgartensia* (1967-1977), which was prepared by K. Elliger and W. Rudolph with the assistance of several scholars (who had also worked on BHK[3]) and in co-operation with H.P. Rüger and J. Ziegler, that the MT was published together with the masora on the basis of Codex L. Kittel's promise had finally been fulfilled, and one of Kahle's ambitions realized. Although the critical apparatus accompanying the text certainly means an improvement on that of BHK, an important objection indicated above has not been removed: the apparatus goes beyond the text in adducing literary emendations and conjectural readings.[159] As regards the masora, the reader is offered *a* masoretic text on the basis of an ancient manuscript which is almost universally seen as a Ben Asher text. The same is true of the HUBP (also mentioned at the beginning of this article) which has up to now (partially) published the Isaiah text of the Aleppo Codex, and which moreover offers an excellent platform for scholarly discussion of masoretic matters in its *Annual of the Hebrew University Bible Project*, called *Textus*.

OTHER RECENT EDITIONS OF THE BIBLE

We have almost come back to the sketch of the situation given at the beginning

---

[156] *Biblia Hebraica*, Stuttgart 1937, III. Up to the publication of BHS, this edition has been reprinted many times.

[157] *Prolegomena*, VI.

[158] For the differences between the families of Ben Asher and Ben Naphtali, see also: Lipschütz, *Der Bibeltext*; *idem*, 'Mishael ben Uzziel's Treatise'; *idem*, 'Kitāb al-Khilaf'.

[159] Now also see Wonneberger, *Leitfaden*.

of this article. Before coming to a conclusion, however, we would like to mention two further editions of the biblical text of the latter part of this century which are often and widely used in scholarly studies. Firstly the Bible published by the *British and Foreign Bible Society* in London in 1958, edited by Norman H. Snaith. In 1933, the said society decided to replace the 'Letteris Bible'. Snaith was charged with the work involved in this. The Second World War caused the work to be considerably delayed. Snaith did not want to present a mere revision of the Letteris text, and wanted moreover to remain independent of the Ginsburg Bible. That is why he based his text on MS.Or 2626-8 of the British Museum, a beautifully illuminated Sephardic manuscript, formerly produced in Lisbon (1482). In addition to this he used a Yemenite manuscript, written between 1460 and 1480 (Ms.Or. 2375 British Museum), which contained only the Writings. A third consulted manuscript was the so-called Shem Tov Bible (1312) from David Sassoon's collection (no. 82). With the help of readings from Norzi's שי מנחת (mentioned earlier), which corresponded with the first hand in the Sephardic manuscripts, Snaith thought he would be able to approach as closely as possible a masoretic text of the Ben Asher tradition.[160]

A second edition is that published by *Koren Publishers* in Jerusalem in 1962 (5722), edited by D. Goldschmidt, A.M. Haberman and M. Medan. On the basis of a close study of ancient manuscripts, editions and masoretic lists, they established the published masoretic biblical text, 'the first Bible worked up and printed with vowels and accents in the Land of Israel'.[161] In a small and handy edition, this biblical text has been widely distributed and much used both within and outside Israel.

THE IDEAL OF THE ABSOLUTE MASORETIC TEXT

In conclusion: in his *Prolegomenon* to the reissue of Ginsburg's *Introduction*, Orlinsky repeatedly points out that *the* masoretic text cannot be referred to, for the simple reason that it has nowhere been recorded *which* or *whose* masora ought to be followed. He tries to prove his thesis with several examples, referring *inter alia* to comparisons of quotations from the Talmud with the manuscripts, or to matters of *ketiv* and *qere*. 'There never was, and there never can be, a single fixed masoretic text of the Bible!'[162] The only thing an editor might, according to him, claim with some right is his having edited the text of a single manuscript, provided that he is prepared to tell exactly where and why he has sometimes deviated from his original manuscript. In any case, an editor must keep in mind that no (average) masoretic text is superior to the above-mentioned editions by Van der Hooght, Hahn, Letteris and all the others. That

---

[160] See the *Preface* to the *Sefer Tora Nevi'îm ûKetûvîm*, London 1958; also N.H. Snaith, 'New Edition'; Roberts, 'The Hebrew Bible'.
[161] See Orlinsky, 'Prolegomenon', xv f.
[162] Orlinsky, 'Prolegomenon', xviii; cf. also xxiii f.

is why, still according to Orlinsky, partly on the basis of Lipschütz's analyses of Mishael ben Uzziel's work about the differences between the masoretic families of Ben Asher and Ben Naphtali, it should be condemned 'when scholars denigrate and dismiss the work of others . . .; I have in mind the derogatory remarks casually made of such scholars as Baer and Ginsburg'.[163]

Now one need not disparage the enormous amount of work done by former generations in order to admit that continuing research has made it clear that emendations can be and have been introduced into the editions of the text. One may with some justice doubt whether Maimonides' 'Mustercodex' was indeed the Aleppo Codex, and if it was, whether Maimonides' authority alone made it *the* pre-eminent masoretic text, yet one will not merely greet with pleasure such editions as are presented in BHS and in HUBP as examples of *an* authoritative MT, but also see them as monuments of the stabilization and standardization of the Hebrew text on the long road of its transmission. This stabilization has not yet been closed, at least as far as a general agreement on the scope and value of the masora is concerned, but since the beginning of the Middle Ages and even before that, the Hebrew consonantal text has been fixed, as one of the Hebrew texts which circulated at the beginning of the Common Era, and of which very clear specimens have been found at Qumran. The question what text lies before it, will probably never be answered. On the other hand, the *textus receptus* as we now know it in the editions of such manuscripts as the *Erfurt Codex*, the *Aleppo Codex* or the *Codex Leningradensis*, is more important for biblical exegesis than one is sometimes inclined to think, not only as regards their consonantal texts, but also with respect to their further divisions. There is a current exegetical school, called 'logotechnical', in which *inter alia* a numerical kind of structural analysis is applied to the biblical text.[164] Among other things, this analysis wants to open our eyes to the fact that the way in which according to the transmitted traditions the biblical text is subdivided and demarcated through *petuḥa* and *setuma* is not only very ancient, but also important for the determination of the structure of the text. This ingenious, perhaps artificial, structuralization of a distant past cannot but confirm that the stabilization of the biblical text which we now call the MT – although one should certainly distinguish between texts that still differ as to the masora – must have taken place at a time in which this text was already considered to be of canonical value, with respect to both form and content. It is therefore at this time that the text-critical work of Barthélemy and his colleagues sets in, already called, after BHS and HUBP, 'the third (text-critical) way'.[165]

---

[163] Orlinsky, 'Prolegomenon' xliv, n. 29.
[164] See e.g. Schedl, *Baupläne des Wortes*; Labuschagne, 'The Pattern of the Divine Speech Formulas'; *idem*, 'De literairkritische methode' (with a recent bibliography).
[165] See above, n. 43.

Bibliography

SURVEY OF SOME PRINTED (COMPLETE) HEBREW BIBLES*

* For further information concerning printed Hebrew Bibles or parts of the Hebrew Bible, see e.g.:
T.H. Darlow – H.F. Moule, *Historical Catalogue of the Printed Editions of Holy Scripture in the Library of the British and Foreign Bible Society*, 2, London 1903 (repr. 1963), 701-737. Also the relevant sections of *British Museum General Catalogue of Printed Books* and *The National Union Catalogue*.

1. First printed complete Bible *(editio princeps)*: 23 Feb. 1488, Soncino; ²1491 (Joshua Solomon Soncino), Naples; ³1494 (Gershom Soncino; used by Luther for his translation), Brescia.
2. Complutensian Polyglot (Cardinal F. Ximenez de Cisneros): 1514-1517 (OT: 4 vols.), Alcalá de Henarez.
3. First Rabbinic Bible: 1516-1517 (4 vols.; Felix Pratensis), Venice (Bomberg; also reprinted *in quarto*).
4. Brothers Adelkind: 1521 (2nd edition of *quarto*-edition of 1517), Venice (Bomberg; ³1528).
5. Second Rabbinic Bible; 1524-1525/26 (first edition with full *masora*; 4 vols.; Jacob ben Hayyim), Venice (Bomberg, ³ and ⁴1548; ⁵1617).
6. Seb. Münster: 1534-5 (2 vols.), Basle (Bebeliana).
7. F. Vatablus (*ex officina* Brothers Stephanus): 1539-1544 (13 books in 2 vols.).
8. Antwerp Polyglot (= Biblia Regia; Benedictus Arias Montanus): 1569-1572 (OT: 4 vols.; based on Hebrew text of Complutensian Polyglot), Antwerp (Chr. Plantin).
9. F. Vatablus – B.C. Bertramus – S. Pagninus: 1587 (2 vols.: Hebrew, Greek and Latin), Heidelberg.
10. E. Hutter: 1587, Hamburg (Lucius; ²1603).
11. J. Buxtorf Sr.: hand-sized edition 1611, Basle; sixth Rabbinic Bible (4 vols): 1618-1619, Basle (reprinted in seventh *Bibl. Hebr. Rabb. opera* Mosis Francfurtensis, 1714-1727, Amsterdam).
12. Parisian Polyglot (OT: 4 vols.; Guy Michel le Jay): 1629-1645, Paris.
13. Menasseh ben Israel: 1631 (³1639), Amsterdam (Laurentius).
14. London Polyglot (OT: 3 vols.; Brian Walton): 1654-1657, London.
15. Joh. Leusden – Jos. Athias: 1659-1661 (based on text of Buxtorf's edition; 2 vols.), Amsterdam.
16. J.G. Nissel: 1662, Leiden (A. Uchtmannus).
17. Joh. H. May: 1692; Frankfurt (revised by D. Clodius: 1677; ³1716 by G.C. Bürcklin; *'Biblia Clodiana'*).
18. D.E. Jablonski: 1699 (4 vols.; ²1772; based on Leusden-Athias edition), Berlin.

19. Everh. van der Hooght: 1705 (4 vols.), Amsterdam/Utrecht (almost entirely according to Leusden-Athias edition of 1667; several reprints, e.g. by Judah d'Allemand: 1817, London).
20. H. Opitius: 1709, Kiel.
21. Joh. H. Michaelis: 1720 (printed in three forms: *octavo; quarto; folio*; first critical edition), Halle (Magdenburg).
22. C. Reineccius: 1725 (2 vols.), Leipzig (^{3}1756).
23. Joh. Simonis: 1752 [reprint: 1753, Amsterdam (Jac. a Wetstein)], Halle (Magdenburg) (^{2}1767; ^{3}1822 by E.F.C. Rosenmüller; ^{4}1828).
24. Ch.F. Houbigant: 1753 (4 vols.), Paris.
25. B. Kennicott: 1766-1780 (2 vols.), Oxford.
26. J.C. Döderlein – J.H. Meisner: 1793, Leipzig (edited by C. Reineccius; with extracts from Kennicott and De Rossi).
27. Joh. Jahn: 1806 (4 vols.), Vienna.
28. B. Boothroyd: 1810-1816 (2 vols.), Pontefract.
29. S.I. Mulder: 1826-1838 (with a Dutch translation; uncompleted), Amsterdam.
30. Aug. Hahn: 1831, Leipzig (revision of Leusden – Simonis – Van der Hooght; reprinted many times).
31. C.G.W. Theile: 1849 (^{9}1902), Leipzig.
32. M.L. Letteris: 1852, Vienna; 1866, Berlin (and many subsequent editions).
33. S.I. Baer [-Franz Delitzsch]: 1869-1895, Leipzig (in instalments: Exodus – Deuteronomy are lacking).
34. P. Haupt: 1893-1904 ('Polychrome Bible'), Leipzig/Baltimore/London (incomplete).
35. C.D. Ginsburg: 1894, London/Vienna (2 vols.); 1908-1926 (4 vols.), London. Of this 'major edition' there appeared:
    a. unpunctuated edition: 1914-1920 (4 vols.; many reprints), London.
    b. A.S. Geden: 1916-1920 ('minor edition'), London.
    c. [U. Cassuto]: 1953, Jerusalem ('The New Hebrew Bible').
36. R. Kittel: 1905-1906, Leipzig (2 vols.; ^{2}1909 and reprints; the text is based on Jacob ben Hayyim's *textus receptus*).
37. [R. Kittel –] P. Kahle: 1929-1937, Stuttgart (and reprints; the text is based on the *Codex Leningradensis*).
38. A. Cohen et al.: 1946-1952 (14 vols.: 'Soncino Books of the Bible'), London/Bournemouth.
39. N.H. Snaith: 1958, London (based on Ms. Or 2626-8).
40. D. Goldschmidt – A.M. Haberman – M. Medan: 1962, Jerusalem.
41. 'The Hebrew University Bible Project': since 1965, Jerusalem (only Isaiah chs. 1-44 have so far been published [2 instalments, 1975; 1981]).
42. 'Biblia Hebraica Stuttgartensia' (K. Elliger – W. Rudolph): 1967-1977, Stuttgart.

STUDIES

In this article, several works have been discussed, quoted or used, which may be useful to the reader in further study. For the biblical text, I may yet then refer to the article by TALMON, 'Old Testament Text' *CHB* 1, 159-99, which presents an excellent survey (bibliography on p. 591 of the same work) within the framework of 'The Old Testament' (67-231), and to an article in Hebrew by the same author in the *EB* vol. 8, 621-41 (with bibliography), which deals at length with the (recent) history of textual studies. Many important articles have appeared or will appear in the journal *Textus*, the *Annual of the Hebrew University Bible Project* from 1960 onwards. Still very useful – among other things by its numerous references – is the work by ROBERTS, *Old Testament Text and Versions*. More recent surveys are to be found in encyclopaedias and (biblical) dictionaries. DOTAN's survey of the 'Masorah' in the *EJ* 16, 1401-82 (with bibliography) may be particularly recommended. In addition to WÜRTHWEIN'S *Der Text des Alten Testaments* one may now also refer to WONNEBERGER, *Leitfaden* (with a full bibliography), which offers an informative introduction to the practical use of the masora and the critical apparatus. Less exhaustive, but worth reading is DEIST, *Towards the Text of the Old Testament*. Re the masora the works of WEIL are especially commendable.

135

Bible Codex with *Haftarot,* Pentateuch (Gen 50:17 – Exod 1:15) and *Haftara* (1 Kgs 2:1-12) with *masora parva* and *masora magna* (Cincinatti, Hebrew Union College, Klau Library, HUC Ms. 1, fol. 21b).

136

Chapter Four

The Reading of the Bible in the Ancient Synagogue

Charles Perrot

General

The reading of the Tora on the morning of the sabbath was a universally accepted custom in the first century of our era both in Israel and the Diaspora. As Flavius Josephus wrote: '(Moses) ordered . . . that every week men should desert their other occupations and assemble to listen to the Law and to obtain a thorough and accurate knowledge of it . . .'.[1] Philo of Alexandria too mentions this reading of the sacred books, followed by explanation of passages still obscure.[2] Finally, the Acts of the Apostles says: 'From early generations Moses has had in every city those who preach him, for he is read every sabbath in the synagogues' (Acts 15:21). Hence the custom seems to have ancient roots, so much so that it could even be attributed to Moses himself. The inscription of Theodotus (discovered on the Ophel in 1914 along with the remains of an ancient synagogue for the use of Greek-speaking Jews of Jerusalem and pilgrims, and dating from before 70 of our era) also notes this reading: 'Theodotus, son of Vettenus, priest and archisynagogue, son of an archisynagogue, grandson of an archisynagogue, constructed the synagogue for the reading of the Law and the teaching of the commandments. . .'[3]

How was this reading done? It is hard to say. Reading practices seem still indistinct and lacking in uniformity at this early date. Many points remain obscure, though not to the point of excluding serious suggestions. The following exposition will work backwards, starting from what is sure and going to what is simply probable. We shall first then glance at the practice of the sixth to eight centuries of our era before gradually moving through earlier times. It will then be possible to date the beginnings of a 'continuous reading' of the Tora as a whole to some time probably in the second century. As for the time immediately before that, only a few suggestions can be made about the various reading practices. It seems that the reading of the Law was then done by taking 'selected readings' which followed the order of the biblical text. Reading of the Prophets was in fact always preceded by selected passages, at least in synagogues which

---

[1] Josephus, *Ag. Ap.* 2:175.
[2] Philo, *De Somniis*, 2:127.
[3] Cf. *CII* 2, 1404.

were under the influence of scribes belonging to the Pharisaic movement. Hence we shall first describe the main lectionary cycles, especially the Triennial Palestine Cycle (TC) without dwelling on the Annual Babylonian Cycle (AC) which is still used. We shall see more and more clearly that these cycles were not creations *ex nihilo*. But the amount of continuity that may be discovered in their formation should not obscure the gaps which mark their development.

The Main Reading Cycles

THE ANNUAL BABYLONIAN CYCLE

At the end of the talmudic period an annual cycle of Tora readings was already well established in Babylonia. It was to become dominant everywhere as time went on. Readings were distributed over the year in 54 weekly pericopes (*parashiyyot*; sg. *parasha*), many of which are quoted in the Babylonian Talmud.[4] Readings began on the sabbath after the feast of Tabernacles and were finished at Simḥat Tora, that is the feast of the joy of the Tora on the 23th of Tishri. The Law was accompanied each sabbath morning by a text from the Prophets (*haftara*; pl. *haftarot*). But these selected passages from the Prophets seem already less stable. At least between the various rites the different customs are relatively important, especially with regard to the length of the haftarot in question. N. Fried, in an appendix to his article 'Haftara' in the *Talmudic Encyclopedia*, gives a table of the readings of the AC with the various customs.[5] In a word, the AC seems to have been settled by the sixth century at least (if not as early as the fourth),[6] which leaves open, however, the question of its origin (Palestinian?) and early development.

The readings from the Prophets adopted by the Karaites show even more variations, proving certain contacts with the readings of the TC which will be discussed below. The Karaites, however, used an annual cycle, at least at a later stage of their history.[7] Anan, founder of the sect in eight century Palestine, accepted a six-monthly cycle with Genesis read in Tishri and Nisan.[8] Later Karaite practices seem to have diversified, till they settled down to an annual cycle, beginning on the sabbath of the festal week of Tabernacles or the following sabbath.

---

[4] *B.T. Megilla* 29b.
[5] Cf. Fried, 'Haftara' 1-31 and Appendix, 702-24.
[6] In *B.T. Megilla* 23b Rava (299-350) explicitly cites Jer 7:21f., which is the haftara of Lev 6:1f. in the Annual Cycle.
[7] Cf. Finkelstein, 'Prophetic Reading'. The lists referred to can be found in Perrot, *Lecture*, 50-52.
[8] See Mann, 'Anan's Liturgy'; other indications in Perrot, *Lecture*, 171-73.

THE TRIENNIAL PALESTINIAN CYCLE

In the Triennial Cycle of Palestine origin Tora readings are distributed over three years, in some 154 *sedarim* (sg. *seder*). But we must add at once that it would be more correct to say Triennial Palestinian *Cycles*, since the fine unity observable in the AC now seems less clear, in a tangle of customs still unstable.

Choice of sedarim and still more of haftarot can vary strikingly from one synagogue to another. The beginning of the readings can even take in three and a half years, and not just three. This shows how free the Palestinian synagogues were under the circumstances, though it was a relative liberty already channeled by traditions of readings. The readings of the TC are a little like the ancient Jewish prayers: freedom of formulation must be joined by the recurrence of motifs already established by custom. Synagogues were not at the mercy of their own fantasies.

We first name some sources which enable us to grasp better this complex situation and offer the possibility of reconstructing the TC (or TC's) in question. The Talmud quotes Num 28:2 a passage whose reading could not fall during the month of Adar in the AC,[9] while it would be possible 'for the people of Palestine who complete the reading of the Pentateuch in three years'.[10] In fact, with a TC beginning after the feast of Tabernacles, such a seder (Num 27:15 to 28:25) does indeed occur in Adar. The sedarim of the TC are indeed signalled in the margin of the manuscripts of the Tora by means of the letter *samekh* (ס).[11] Further, precious lists discovered in the Geniza of Old Cairo give the readings from the Tora and the Prophets as part of a TC.[12] Ancient poems *(piyyutim)*, as the *Kerovot* of Yannai, are adapted to this triennial cycle. And one must not of course forget the ancient books of homilies such as the *Tanḥumot* and the *Rabbot*, which partly follow the TC – before being reorganized to fit into the AC.[13] The importance of these last witnesses has been brought out in the fundamental book of Jacob Mann, *The Bible as Read and Preached in the Old Synagogue*.[14] Thus *Leviticus Rabba* generally bases itself on the TC though adding some homilies on otherwise unknown beginnings of readings.[15] However, none of these sources succeeds in obscuring the flexibility of reading

---

[9] This verse belongs to the Phinehas parasha, Num 25:10-30:1, in the Annual Cycle.

[10] *B.T. Megilla* 29b.

[11] This sign is noted in the margin of the Kittel-Kahle editions. See the lists of Mishael ben Uzziel and others in Perrot, *Lecture*, 41-44.

[12] See the lists of haftarot found in the Cairo Geniza and information on the piyyutim in Perrot, *Lecture*, 45-48; also Yahalom, *Collection*.

[13] See Theodor 'Midrashim' (1885-87); Bacher, *Proömien* (1913); Heinemann, 'Proem' (1971); Bregman, 'Perorations' (1981).

[14] Jakob Mann had meant to publish three volumes. The first appeared in Cincinatti, 1940, then in New York, 1971, with an important contribution from Ben-Zion Wacholder. Mann died in 1940, but the second volume was published in 1966, thanks to the efforts of Isaiah Sonne and of the Mann-Sonne Publication Commission after Sonne's death in 1960.

[15] On Lev 2:1f., for instance; see Strack, *Introduction*, 212, where Lev 2:3f. is mentioned; but see Sonne, in Mann-Sonne, *The Bible* 2, 156 n. 6.

139

traditions in Palestine. The scribes of the manuscripts of the Tora also often collect, in the margin or at the end, the number of the sedarim, which is generally 154, sometimes 141 or again 167 and even 175.

These very hesitations echo different customs in the choice of the opening of the seder. Some, for example, started the reading at Gen 12:1f., others at Gen 12:10f. (See the appended table on sedarim 10 and 10a where the letters signal different traditions). But this relative diversity of reading traditions should not prevent one's recognizing a certain overall unity. Once more, readers remained to some extent bound to their own tradition and, as we shall say further on, a beginning of a seder ordinarily coincided, as it seems, with the paragraphs which well before the destruction of the Temple already featured in the Bible scrolls. In any case a TC in the strict sense certainly existed in already firmly settled form. There is witness to this in some fragments of the Palestinian Targum discovered in the Cairo Geniza. There the readings of Exod 21:1f. and 22:24f. are clearly marked as the fifteenth and sixteenth sedarim of Exodus.[16]

The extra number of sedarim might give one to think of lectionary cycles going a little beyond the three years. And indeed a treatise from the time of the Gaonim, the *Hillukei Minhagim* (Treasure of Divergencies of Custom) notes that 'the people of Palestine celebrated the feast of Simhat Tora only once in three and a half years, and the day for reading a given section in a district is not the same as in another'.[17] This shows the lack of uniformity in Palestine, at least as seen by the astonished gaze of an author of a later age, accustomed to a fixed system. Nonetheless, the existence of reading traditions should not be called in question. They are attested by the sources enumerated above.

How then is the question to be clarified? More exactly: how to calculate the number of sabbaths available in the framework of a regular set of readings, non-festive, beginning after Tabernacles?[18] How to trace the contours of a cycle which overshoots three years? Does it begin in Nisan, in Tishri, or the contrary? Could these three and a half years have been later reduced to three only? Or, on the contrary, did certain Palestinian synagogues lengthen the period of readings to get in all the sedarim, never thinking of a fixed date for the beginning of the Tora? Questions, as one sees, abound. Personally, we think that the three year period was mostly the custom.

Here is the list of the Palestinian sedarim, with their haftarot. But, as has been said, the beginning of the sedarim and the choice of the haftarot can vary notably according to the age or to regional custom, while the relative stability of the whole must be acknowledged. In the list, the presence of a letter after the numbering of the seder implies no value judgment on the relative antiquity or diffusion of the sedarim so marked. Need one say that a synagogue beginning,

---

[16] See Kahle, *Masoreten* 2 (1930), Fragment A (1-5); photo 1.

[17] See Levin, *Trésor*, 36ff.; Heinemann, 'Triennial Lectionary Cycle', 42.

[18] A triennial cycle is three times fifty-two weeks, along with the intercalary month Ve-Adar, but minus three times the Four Special Sabbaths and sabbaths occurring during feasts.

for instance, a seder at Gen 6:5f. (S 4a) did not evidently follow the next sabbath by reading Gen 6:9f. (S 5)? So too, several haftarot are tacked on to the same seder, varying according to different customs. Apart from the scroll of the Twelve Prophets regarded as a whole, passages taken from several prophetic books were not read one after another. The length of the haftarot should also be remarked. No doubt, like the sedarim, a haftara could have at least twenty-one verses to start with, as the Talmud affirms,[19] but afterwards they were reduced to more or less ten verses and the reader was allowed to 'skip' so as to end with a resounding finale. In fact, these customary variations, including those of the sedarim, can often be explained by the wish to find a good opening, to avoid a weak ending, to avoid coinciding with a feast-day reading and to achieve a strong ending. Since the haftarot were often taken from Isaiah, had they not to announce 'the consolation' of Israel?

Readings of Genesis

Seder Genesis

1	1:1	Isa 65:17-25 (or 66:1)	24	26:12	Isa 62:8-63:7
2	2:4	Isa 51:6-16	25	27:1	Isa 46:3-47:4; 1 Sam
3	3:22	Ezek 28:13-19.25			4:15f.; 1 Sam 2:22f. (?)
4	5:1	Isa 29:18-24 and 30:18	26	27:28	Mich 5:6-13 (or 6:8); Hos 14:6f.
4a	6:5	Ezek 38:10f. (?)	27	28:10	Hos 12:13f.
5	6:9	Isa 54:9-17 (or 9-55:5)	28	29:31	Isa 60:15-61:3; 1 Sam 1:2f.
6	8:1	Hab 3:2-19; Jer 31:19f. (?)	29	30:22	1 Sam 1:11-22
7	8:15	Isa 42:7-15.21; Mich 7:9f. (?)	30	31:3	Jer 30:10-18 Mich 6:3f.
8	9:18	Isa 49:9-14 (or 23)	31	32:4	Obad 1-21; Isa 21:11f.
9	11:1	Zeph 3:9-17.20	32	33:18	Nah 1:12f.
10	12:1	Josh 24:3-10.14; Isa 51:1f. (?)	33	35:9	Isa 43:1-21 Isa 61:2-9 (or 1-9) (?)
10a	12:10	1 Kgs 8:37f.	34	37:1	Isa 32:18-33:15
11	14:1	Isa 41:2-13 (or 14)			Ezek 28:25f.
12	15:1	Isa 1:1-8; 2:2-3; Isa 40:10-21.31; 2 Sam 7:17f. (?)	35	38:1	Isa 37:31-38:6
			36	39:1	Isa 52:3-53:5
			36a	39:7	1 Sam 2:22-30.35 (?)
13	16:1	Isa 54:1-10	36b	40:1	Judg 18:1f.
14	17:1	Jer 33:25-34:5.12-13; Isa 54:10f.	37	41:1	Isa 29:8-14.18-19; Hag 1:1f. (?)
15	18:1	Isa 33:17-24; 35:10; Mal 3:19f. (?)	38	41:38	Isa 11:2-16
			38a	42:1	Isa 55:1f.
16	19:1	Isa 17:14-18:7; Judg 19:16-24; 20:27	39	42:18	Isa 50:10-51:11
			40	43:14	Jer 42:12-20
17	20:1	Isa 61:9-62:7.10-15; Judg 9:21f. (?)	41	44:18	Josh 14:6-15; 1 Kgs 18:36; Amos 9:13f.
18	21:1	1 Sam 2:21-28	42	46:28	Zech 10:6-11:7
19	22:1	Isa 33:7-16.22; Judg. 3:1f. (?)	43	48:1	2 Kgs 13:14-23
20	24:1	Isa 51:2-11; 1 Kgs 1:1f. (?)	44	49:1	Isa 43:22-44:2.5.
			45	49:27	Zech 14:1-11
21	24:42	Isa 12:3-14:2			1 Sam 9:1-10

[19] B.T. Megilla 23a.

22	25:1	2 Sam 5:13-6:1
23	25:19	Isa 65:23-66:8

Readings of Exodus

Seder Exodus

46	1:1	Isa 27:6-13	59	19:6	Isa 61:6-62:4
47	3:1	Isa 40:11-19.31	60	21:1	Isa 56:1-9; 57:19;
48	4:18	Isa 55:12-56:7 (or 8)			Isa 1:26f. (?)
49	6:2	Isa 42:8-21; 52:6f.	61	22:24	Isa 48:10-20 (or 49:3)
50	7:8	Joel 3:8-4:16 (or 18)	61a	23:20	Mal 3:1f.
51	8:16	Isa 34:11-35:4 (or 10)	62	25:1	Isa 60:17-61:6 (or 9);
52	10:1	1 Sam 6:6-14			Hag 2:8f. (?)
53	11:1	Mic 7:15-20; Nah 1:7	63	26:1	Isa 66:1-11
		Hag 2:6-15.23; Isa 6:13f.	64	26:31	Ezek 16:10-19
54	12:29	Isa 21:11-22:4.15;	65	27:20	Hos 14:7- Joel 1:14;
		2 Kgs 19:35f.; Zech 14:7			Jer 11:16-12:2; 15:15-16
55	13:1	Isa 46:3-13; 39:23f.	66	29:1	Isa 61:6-62:5
55a	13:17	Isa 45:13f.	67	30:1	Mal 1:11-2:7
56	14:15	Isa 65:24-66:10	68	31:1	Isa 43:7-15 (or 21)
56c	16:4	Isa 49:11-23; Josh 24:7f.	69	32:15	2 Sam 22:10-33 (or 51)
57	16:28	Isa 58:13-59:20	69c	34:1	1 Kgs 8:9f.
58	18:1	Isa 33:13-22	70	34:27	Jer 31:32-39
			70a	35:1	Isa 58:13f. (?)
			71	37:1	1 Kgs 8:9-22
			72	38:21	Jer 30:18-31:8
			73	39:33	Isa 33:20-34:8

Readings of Leviticus

Seder Leviticus

74	1:1	Mic 6:9-7:8; Isa 48:12-49:3; Isa 43:21f. (?)	88	15:25	Ezek 16:9f.; Isa 60:15f.; Isa 4:4f.
75	4:1	Ezek 18:4-17	89	17:1	Isa 66:1-11
76	5:1	Zech 5:3-6:14 (or 15)	90	18:1	Jer 10:2-10; Isa 40:18f.
76a	6:1	Mic 6:6f. (?)	91	19:1	Isa 4:3f.
77	6:12	Mal 3:4-12	92	19:23	Isa 65:22f.
78	8:1	1 Sam 2:28-31 and 3:5.20	93	21:1	Ezek 44:25f.
			94	22:17	Isa 56:7f.
79	9:1	Ezek 43:27-44:8.30	95	23:9	Joel 4:13-21
80	10:8	Ezek 44:21-27 and 46:3	95a	23:15	Josh 5:11f.
81	11:1	Isa 40:16f.	96	24:1	Hos 14:7f.; Jer 11:16f.
82	12:1	Isa 9:5f.; Isa 66:7f.	97	25:14	Isa 24:2-11; Isa 52:3f.
83	13:18	Isa 57:17f.	98	25:35	Isa 35:3-10
84	13:29	Isa 7:20f.	99	26:3	Isa 1:19f.
85	14:1	Isa 57:17f.; 2 Kgs 7:3f. (?); Jer 30:17f.	100	27:1	Judg 11:30f.
86	14:33	Isa 5:8-16			
87	15:1	Hos 6:1-9; Jer 17:14f.			

Readings of Numbers

Seder Numbers

101	1:1	Hos 2:16-25; Isa 35:1f.	115	17:16	Isa 11:1-11
102	2:1	Isa 49:5f.; Isa 8:18f.	116	18:25	Isa 62:8f.; Jer 2:3f.
			117	20:14	Obad 1f.

103	3:1	Isa 45:19f.; Isa 2:3f.; Mic 4:2f.	118	22:2	Mic 7:16f.; Isa 60:5f.
104	4:17	Isa 48:9f.; Zeph 3:7f.; Isa 56:5f.	119	23:10	Isa 49:23f.; Mic 7:17f.
105	5:11	Hos 4:14f.	120	25:1	Joel 4:18f.
105a	6:1	Judg 13:2f.	121	25:10	Mal 2:5f.
106	6:22	1 Kgs 8:54f.	122	26:52	Isa 57:13f.
107	7:48	Jer 31:20-32	123	27:15	Isa 40:13-26.31
108	8:1	Zech 4:2f.	124	28:26	Mal 3:4f.
109	10:1	Isa 27:13f.	125	30:2	Isa 45:23f.
110	11:16	Joel 2:16f.	126	31:1	Ezek 25:14f.
110a	11:23	Isa 50:2f.; Isa 59:1f.	127	31:25	Isa 49:24f.
111	13:1	Josh 2:1f.	128	32:1	Josh 22:8f.
112	14:11	Isa 52:5f.	129	33:1	Isa 11:16f.
113	15:1	Isa 56:7f.	130	34:1	Ezek 45:1f.
114	16:1	Hos 10:2f.	131	35:9	Josh 20:1f.

Readings of Deuteronomy

Seder Deuteronomy

132	1:1	Zech 8:16f.; Jer 30:4f.	145	16:18	Isa 1:26f.
133	2:2	Obad 21 and Jonah 1:1f.	146	17:14	Isa 32:1f.; Isa 33:22f.
134	2:31	Josh 10:12f.; Hab 3:11f.; Amos 2:9f.	146a	18:14	Mic 5:11f.
			147	20:10	Isa 66:12f.
135	3:23	Isa 33:2f.	147a	21:10	Isa 2:4f.
135b	4:25	Jer 31:20f.	148	22:6	Isa 31:5f.
136	4:41	Josh 20:8f.	149	23:10	Isa 1:16f.
137	6:4	Zech 14:9f.	150	23:22	Isa 19:21f.
138	7:12	Isa 54:10f.	151	24:19	Hos 10:12f.
139	9:1	Josh 1:10f.	152	26:1	Ezek 44:30f.
140	10:1	1 Kgs 8:9f.	153	28:1	Isa 55:2f.; Jer 33:10f.
141	11:10	?	154	29:9	Josh 24:1f.
142	12:20	Isa 54:2f.	155	30:11	Isa 48:18f.
142b	13:2	Zech 13:5f.	156	31:14	1 Kgs 2:1f.
143	14:1	Isa 46:1f.; Isa 63:8f.	157	32:1	Isa 1:2f.
144	15:7	Isa 29:19f.; Amos 8:4f.; Isa 35:3f.	158	33:1	Josh 1:1f.

The Establishment of Reading Cycles

The preceding section relies on a difficult documentation but a solid one. The following pages will bring in assured elements, data from the Mishna for instance, but the element of hypothesis grows larger. The situation is easily explained by the suppleness of the traditional readings, most marked in the TC. Thus the Mishna furnishes precious information on the manner in which the lessons may be read, but never says what the sabbath ordinances are in the choice of readings. It is as if reading custom or customs were master of the situation, even in their freedom, with no call for intervention, unless a change occurred in the customs of the place.

READINGS ACCORDING TO THE MISHNA

We shall first collect the data in tractate *Megilla* 3 and 4 of the Mishna.

143

Mentioning also the blessings pronounced before and after the lessons,[20] this tractate defines the number of readers of the Tora. They are seven on the sabbath morning: 'This is the general rule: when the Additional Prayer is appointed and it is not a Festival-day, the Law is read by four. On a Festival-day it is read by five, on the Day of Atonement by six, and on the Sabbath by seven. They may not take from them but they may add to them, and they close with a reading from the Prophets. He that begins the reading from the Law and he that completes it say a Benediction the one at the beginning and the other at the end.'[21] According to Rabbi Akiva however there had to be at least six readers on the sabbath.[22] A prophetic haftara was to follow the reading of the Tora on the morning of the sabbath, on feasts and on the Day of Atonement, but not so after the afternoon readings of the sabbath, Monday and Thursday. The number of verses to be read by each reader is prescribed: at least three, giving twenty-one verses in all, as the Talmud was to say.[23] It should not be forgotten here that the verses in question cannot entirely be identified with our present-day ones, which only came in with the Middle Ages.[24] No passage in the Tora may be skipped unlike the Prophets. 'A passage may be skipped in the reading of the Prophets, but not in the Tora.'[25] During the reading from the Tora each verse, read out in Hebrew, could be translated into Aramaic, but by some other than the reader. In the case of the Prophets, the translator comes in after a group of three verses. Only a few passages of the Tora are not to be translated: the story of Reuben (Gen 35:22f.); the end of the story of the golden calf (Exod 32:21f.); the Priestly Blessing (Num 6:24-27). The same holds for some prophetic texts about David (2 Sam 11:2-17) and Ammon (13:1f.). It was deemed sufficient to read them, but not to give the translation. The case of Ezekiel was graver: 'They may not use the chapter of the Chariot (Ezek 1)[26] as a reading from the Prophets; but R. Yehuda permits it. R. Eliezer says: They do not use the chapter *Cause Jerusalem to know* (Ezek 16:1f.) as a reading from the Prophets.'[27] The Mishna wants the readings done from leather scrolls written in the Hebrew 'square script',[28] not with the ancient Hebrew characters still known in the time of Bar Kokhba (died 135).

[20] See *M. Megilla* 4:1-2; *P.T. Berakhot* 7 (11a); *B.T. Berakhot* 11b; also Heinemann, *Prayer.*

[21] See *M. Megilla* 4:2; *T. Megilla* 4:11.

[22] *B.T. Megilla* 23a.

[23] *B.T. Megilla* 23a.

[24] The *Tractate Soferim*, of Palestinian origin, counts 15.842 'verses' in the Tora. *B.T. Kiddushin* 30a gives 5888 . . .

[25] *M. Megilla* 4:4 and *T. Megilla* 4:4.

[26] Possibly also Ezek 8 and 10 according to Gruenwald, *Apocalyptic and Merkavah Mysticism*, 74.

[27] *M. Megilla* 4:10 and *T. Megilla* 4:31.

[28] *M. Megilla* 2:2.

CONTINUOUS READING

According to the Mishna, the modalities of the readings are thus clear enough at the end of the second century, with no question of a fixed cycle of readings, or, more exactly, of an already fixed list of sabbath readings. The prohibition of skipping passages in the Tora has however been noted. It implies the existence of a continuous reading of the text. Was this always the case? This is open to doubt. The very fact of stipulating that the whole Tora should be read, including certain delicate passages, gives one rather to think that readers abstained in these cases. If the Mishna insists on the point, there is a reason. More precisely still, the explicit mention of an 'order' of readings (literally, a *seder*) in the Mishna must be noted.[29] Hence it cannot only be a matter of simple 'selected passages' read according to the wishes of readers, as was the case at least since the end of the second century. Now, the Mishna suggests the existence of this 'ritual' when there is in fact coincidence with other readings. The order of sabbath readings must be interrupted to make way for readings more suitable for feast days, half feasts, watches, new moon, fasts and the Day of Atonement.

During the month of Adar, the regular order of the readings must give way to the Four Special Sabbaths which prepare in a way the feast of Passover, with special readings (for which see lists, below). The readings of the *Shabbat Shekalim* recall the offering to be made to the Temple. The *Shabbat Zakhor* brings up the memory of the Amalekites and prepares directly for the half-feast of Purim. The *Shabbat Para* speaks of the red cow, of which the ashes serve in the preparaton of lustral water. The *Shabbat ha-Ḥodesh* finally, declares early the rules to be followed as the Passover approaches.

As can be seen, the very establishment of a *lectio continua* of the Tora soon brings up the question of the clashing of festive readings with others which follow the principle of the 'selected pieces', the better to be adapted to each circumstance as it occurs. Now the question raised by such coincidence can only have been heard after the Destruction of the Second Temple, at the time of the reorganization and unification of Judaism which featured in the second century of our era, at the time when the synagogues revived by adapting some usages of the former Temple. In fact, the Four Sabbaths termed special are not mentioned in the ancient Jewish writings, called apocryphal, of the period before the Destruction of the Temple. It was only after this that the highest authorities of the synagogue had control of the calendar with power to determine the month to be added, powers formerly belonging to the Temple officers. The sabbaths in question could then be determined, doubtless in the light of ancient traditions. These special sabbath readings would more or less stand in for gestures now impossible such as the strangling of the Red Cow. The case of the feast-day readings seems even clearer. While the Temple was functioning, there was certainly no question in Jerusalem of going to the synagogue to hear feast-day readings. The liturgical texts were at the time used in the Temple,

---

[29] *M. Megilla* 3:4.

where they attracted many. Of course there was no wish to double the worship by having readings outside the sacred precincts. In any case, the synagogue is primarily the 'house of the sabbath' (Greek *sabbateion*), as is said in a decree of August cited by Flavius Josephus.[30]

Mishna *Megilla* 3:5-6 mentions only a few readings: at Passover, Lev 22:26ff.; Pentecost, Deut 16:9f.; Rosh ha-Shana, Lev 23:23f.; Day of Atonement, Lev 16:1ff.; Sukkot, Numb 29:2f.; Ḥanukka, Numb 7:1ff.; Purim, Exod 17:8f. Such a list indicates the importance of these cultic texts, first used in the Temple, with no attempt to make them simple synagogue readings – before 70 C.E. at least. It was both the end of the Temple and the establishment of a regular order for sabbath readings that in my opinion occasioned the insertion of the festal readings in the Mishna, as a novel problem which had to be resolved. To say this is not to question the great antiquity of the festal readings. It merely places them elsewhere than in the morning service of the sabbath.[31] What we reject is the theory of I. Elbogen in particular.[32] He maintains that the festal readings which appeared as early as the third century before our era, at the pilgrimage feasts, at the Day of Atonement and New Year, where then introduced into synagogue services even before the Destruction of the Temple. He further says that the readings of the Four Sabbaths held to be special prevailed in the same situation before it was customary in the synagogue to read them at each sabbath throughout the year. This apparently logical development cannot be proved to have taken place. One rather thinks of customs of various origins which after the calamities of 70 had to be accomodated as best they could in any given synagogue. The text of the Mishna is in a way testimony to this novelty in fidelity to hitherto sporadic customs.

The festal readings mentioned in the Mishna are no more than an initial effort. Later customs enlarged them greatly. The festal readings, the semi-festal and others, as still usual today, follow the Babylonian tradition. They are quite well known in the Babylonian Talmud[33] and in later rituals. Here we give only the list of Palestinian readings, which are less common. It will be seen that this list begins with Tishri, and not with Nisan as in the Babylonian tradition.[34]

Rosh ha-Shana (New Year): Lev 23:23f.; Joel 2:1f.; Gen 21:1f.; 1 Sam 1:1f.

[30] Josephus, *Ant.* 16:164.
[31] About the end of the first century, according to *B.T. Beitsa* 15b, R. Eliezer ben Hyrcanus spent the whole feast-day reading the laws on the feasts (Lev 23).
[32] Elbogen, *Gottesdienst*, 155-74.
[33] *B.T. Megilla* 31a/b; cf. *T. Megilla* 4:5; *Tractate Soferim* 17:6.
[34] On the beginnings of these festal-readings in Palestine, see Mandelbaum, *Pesikta de-Rav Kahana*, 2, XIV-XVII.

Shabbat Shuva (Repentance Sabbath): Deut 30:1f.: Hos 14:2f.

Yom ha-Kippurim (Day of Atonement): Lev 16:1f.; Isa 57:15f.

Sukkot (Tabernacles): First day, Lev 22:26f. and Zech 14:1f.; Lev 23:40f. and Jer 17:7f.; Second to seventh day, Num 29:17-34; Eight day, Num 29:35f.; 1 Kgs 8:54-61.66; Sabbath of the feast, Deut 14:22f.; Mal 3:10-24.

Hanukka (Dedication): Num 7:12-8:4, during the eight days; sabbath of the feast, Num 7:1-8:4; 1 Kgs 7:51f.

Shabbat Shekalim: Exod 30:11-16; 2 Kgs 12:1f.; Ezek 45:12f. (?)

Shabbat Zakhor: Deut 25:17-19; 1 Sam 15:2-9.31.

Purim (half-feast): Exod 17:8-16.

Shabbat Para: Num 19:1-22; Ezek 36:25 and 37:14.

Shabbat ha-Hodesh: Exod 12:1f.; Ezek 45:18f.; Isa 41:27-42-9.

Pessah (Passover): First day, Lev 22:26f.; Josh 5:2-12; Second day, Lev 23:9.; Third day, Exod 12:43f.; Fourth day, Num 9:1f.; Fifth day, Deut 16:1f.; Sixth day, Exod 22:24f.; Seventh day, Exod 14:30f.; Judg 5:1-20 or Isa 10:32f. (?) or Isa 19:1-25; Sabbath of the feast, Deut 14:22f.; Mal 3:10-24 or Exod 13:17f. (?), Ezek 37:1f. (?).

Shavuot (Pentecost): Deut 16:9f.; Exod 19:1f.; Hab 3:3-11 (and Zeph 3:20).

Fast of Tisha be-Av (the Ninth of Av): Lev 26:14f.; fasts: Exod 32:11-14; 34:1f.; Lev 26 and Deut 28.

Rosh ha-Hodesh (New Moon): Num 27:11-15; on a sabbath, Num 28:9-10.11-15 and Ezek 46:1f.

Esther was read from Adar 11 to 15, as laid down in the Mishna, *Megilla* 1:1f. Reading the other scrolls became customary only later.[35] Canticles at Passover; Ruth at Pentecost; Ben Sira at Sukkot; Lamentations was read on the Ninth of Av to recall the fall of Jerusalem, and this practice may have been older.[36] These pious readings clearly did not form part of the morning service on the sabbath. Other series of sabbath readings also became customary but at a late date. The three 'Rebuking' sabbaths preceding the Ninth of Av used Jer 1:1f.; 2:4f. and Isa 1:21f. For the seven 'Consolation' sabbaths which followed, the choice fell on Isa 40:1f.; 49:14f.; 54:11f.; 51:12; 54:1f.; 60:1f. and 60:10f.[37] The book of festal homilies *Pesikta de-Rav Kahana* is based on these readings, but cannot be exactly dated (fifth century on?).

---

[35] See *Tractate Soferim* 14:3; Elbogen, *Gottesdienst*, 184-86.
[36] According to *P.T. Shabbat* 16 (15c) the Writings could only be read on the sabbath evening. Lamentations is said to have been read the sabbath before the 9th of Av by R. Hiyya and R. Yishmael ben Yose (after 150).
[37] See Barth, 'Rebuke'.

ESTABLISHMENT OF CYCLES OF READINGS

Another custom occasioned an important change in the arrangement of readings. According to the Mishna,[38] it became customary to read the Tora on the afternoon of the sabbath as well as on the market days Monday and Thursday. Thus people too far from the synagogue on sabbath mornings could have the benefit of Tora readings, though they lacked the accompanying haftara. Later this institution was attributed to Ezra[39] or the Elders who preceded the Great Synagogue.[40] In fact there is scarcely any trace of this custom before the Destruction of the Second Temple; at least, earlier documentation never mentions it. But the inauguration and spread of this custom soon caused no slight upset. How could these new reading days be fitted into the *lectio continua* of the Tora? In the middle of the second century C.E., an important discussion opposed Rabbi Meir to his contemporary Rabbi Yehuda bar Ilai. According to the former, all the pericopes of the Tora should be read in succession on the days of reading: 'On the evening of the sabbath, reading is begun were it left off in the morning; on Monday, it begins where it left off on the evening of the Sabbath; on Thursday, where it left off on Monday. Finally, on the morning of the next sabbath, it begins where it left off on Thursday.'[41] R. Yehuda on the contrary held that the sabbath morning reading should not be deducted from the passages read before that; which custom was to be ratified in the Mishna.[42]

It is hard to escape the conclusion that this divergence in custom was the basic cause of the later AC and TC. Once the principle of the *lectio continua* with fixed beginnings of pericopes had been in the main admitted and preeminence accorded to the sabbath morning readings, the Annual Cycle can be seen as the natural sequence of the custom followed by R. Meir and the Tosefta. The Cycle known as Triennial fits in well as the prolongation of the custom accepted by R. Yehuda. If the initial words of the readings are kept identical, a period at least three times as long is needed to use up all the readings in this system. Hence both the AC and the TC may have been started in Palestine itself. The AC was undoubtedly to flourish to the full in Babylonia but the Karaite Jews could also preserve an ancient Palestinian cycle of an annual type, to say nothing of the Samaritans. But clearly part of the preceding demonstration rests on the hypothesis that the openings of the Tora readings were already more or less fixed at this early stage. We insist emphatically on the words 'more or less' because we do not want to deny the diversity of reading customs as argued before. Careful search is thus necessary to discover the beginning of a section as Shimon ben Yohai says at the end of the Second Century according to *Sifrei Deut.* 48, p. 108-09 (on Deut 11:22). Nevertheless, this does not call into

---

[38] *M. Megilla* 4:1.

[39] *P.T. Megilla* 4 (75a); *B.T. Bava Kamma* 82a.

[40] *Mekhilta de-R. Yishmael, Wayassa* 1, p. 154 (on Exod 15:22).

[41] *T. Megilla* 3:10; *B.T. Megilla* 31b and the *Tractate Soferim* 10:4.

[42] *M. Megilla* 3:6; see Heinemann, 'Triennial Lectionary Cycle', 45; but also Goldenberg, *Sabbath-Law*, 168-69.

question the very existence of the beginnings of these readings. Is there real proof of this? Before answering this question, we shall consider in general Tora reading before the fall of the Second Temple.

Bible Reading Before 70 C.E.

Judaism is known to have varied greatly according to social and religious milieu before the fall of the Second Temple. Under these circumstances, is it practical to ask about synagogue readings at the time? One might of course appeal to the tradition which makes Moses the creator of such readings, but this means mainly the great reverence accorded to the custom in the first century.[43] And what of the diversified origins of the biblical texts? If at certainly different dates, the biblical traditions were commited to writing, that was surely to have them read, and publicly at that. Writing calls for reading and in ancient times reading was done out loud before a group. Should one therefore point more particularly to the assemblies of the ancient Babylonian Diaspora, before stressing Ezra's predominant role in the matter? Finally, there are the origins of the *proseuchae* (houses of prayer) in the Egyptian Diaspora to be considered, existing from the third century B.C.E. And it seems that synagogues in Palestine became more and more numerous from the middle of the second century B.C.E. on. In any case, the custom of reading the Law of Moses was well established in the first century C.E., both in Israel and the Diaspora. Still, that tells us hardly anything about the modalities of Tora readings, on sabbath mornings in particular.

READINGS AT FEASTS AND ON THE SABBATH

Several biblical texts explicitly mention the fact or the obligation of readings. According to Deut 31:9-11 the Tora was to be read at Tabernacles, at the end of the sabbatical year. In Neh 8:1-18, where one can see in a way the prefiguration of the synagogue, Ezra reads 'the law of Moses' to prepare directly for the feast of Tabernacles with readings from the first to the seventh day (Neh 8:18). This shows the importance of this feast in the matter of readings; see too 2 Kgs 23:1-3. Also at Tabernacles, as now the Mishna says,[44] the king was to read out a large section of Deuteronomy, going on to the end of the book. And in the year 40-41 C.E., King Agrippa did this reading. Then, according to the Greek Book of Baruch, the people of Jerusalem were asked for a public reading of Jeremiah, to be done 'In the House of the Lord, on the day of the feast (Tabernacles) and the days of the opportune time (Or: the days of assembly).[45] Finally, at the Day of Atonement, in the month of Tishri still, the High Priest read out the law in

---

[43] Josephus, *Ag. Ap.* 2:175; Acts 15:21; *Sifrei Deut.* 127 (p. 185-86) on Deut 16:1; *P.T. Megilla* 4 (75a) etc.

[44] *M. Sota* 7:8.

[45] Baruch 1:14; see Bogaert, 'Personnage', 73-81.

the courts of the Temple.[46] The Temple, we see, remained the site of the Word and hence of teaching. In keeping with tradition the scrolls of the Tora were kept there as models, and religious discourses were listened to in the forecourts.[47] Other readings are mentioned in Exod 24:7 and Josh 8:12-34 in the context of the Renewal of the Covenant. None of these instances, however, says that the reading took place on the sabbath. Still, sabbath readings there were, from the middle of the second century B.C.E. at least, so much so that they could be seen as an ancient institution in the first century C.E., already attributed to Moses. But it is still hard to say when exactly the custom of a weekly assembly on the sabbath morning was linked to a regular reading of the Tora. In reality, the two customs go together. The Bible can be read apart from a sabbath meeting, but is a sabbath meeting thinkable without such reading, which really makes it what it is? The sacred sabbath assembly (*Miqra'* Exod 12:16f.) calls for reading (*Miqra'*, Neh 8:8). This takes us back to the middle of the second century B.C.E and after, when synagogue after synagogue was being built in Palestine mainly under the influence of scribes of the Pharisee persuasion. But here perhaps one must invoke another custom. Each of the twenty-four districts of Israel sent, from the beginnings of Tishri on, a delegation *(mishmar)* of priests, Levites and Israelites to Jerusalem for the service of the Temple: that is, two weeks the whole year round. And during this double period of service beginning on a sabbath, the people of each county town concerned met on the local square and read each day one of the seven sections of Gen 1:1-2:4. These meetings, called *ma'amadot* or Watch Stations must probably have consolidated if they did not create the custom of regular assemblies.[48] It still remains difficult to date this custom, which was certainly in existence before the fall of the Temple.

There is another point. Reading and teaching go hand in hand, as is mentioned in the inscription of Theodotus quoted at the beginning of this article. Teaching calls for reading and vice versa. May it not be said that unlike the *proseuchae* perhaps of the Diaspora, which appeared primarily as 'houses of prayer', the Palestinian synagogues aimed originally at responding to a need for instruction? Not enough attention has been paid to the layout of these buildings of before 70 C.E. which are in all probability to be designated synagogues – at Gamla, Masada and the Herodion. They may be said to 'petrify' as it were the seating arrangements of the disciples in a circle around their master. These ancient synagogues were not oriented towards Jerusalem but towards the reader and lecturer in the middle of the building. And of course, these masters taught on the sabbath above all.[49]

---

[46] *M. Yoma* 7:1; see also on the 24th of Tishri the reading for a fast according to Neh 9:1.
[47] *M. Moed Katan* 3:4; for the discourse see John 7:14; Acts 3:11f.
[48] See Hruby, 'La synagogue' 473-514 quoting *M. Taanit* 4:1 etc.
[49] See the link between law and sabbath, Neh 9:14.

VARIOUS READING CUSTOMS

The author of the *Acts of the Apostles* describes as follows the sabbath order at Antioch of Pisidia: 'After the reading of the law and the prophets, the rulers of the synagogue sent to them, saying, Brethren, if you have any word of exhortation for the people, say it' (Acts 13:15). One recognizes here the customary order of a reading of the Tora followed by a reading of the Prophets and finally the homily or exhortation. But it must be said at once that this description should not be forced so far as to make it the model followed everywhere. Still less should the three elements be considered of the same importance. The Tora is primary. It alone is normative. The reading from the prophets follows, but secondarily, as the first divinely authorized interpretation of the text of Moses. As for the homily, where there was one, its form and place could vary considerably under various circumstances.

Later the sermon will be seen splitting off from the morning readings, to be given only on the sabbath afternoon or sometimes even on the Friday.[50] From the third century on in particular, one type of homily called *Proem* became very popular and was delivered at the start of the morning service. This is an instance of how custom could vary with circumstances. It is easy to guess how much more difficult it is to grasp the situation in the first century. In fact, the practice reported in Acts does not seem to have been universally accepted in Israel and the Diasporas, even though it prevailed, very probably, in synagogues influenced by scribes of the Pharisaic movement. Other practices seem to have been known, which we can only evoke here. The point is important, since each of the practices shows in fact a different way of addressing the Bible text which is in question. Even the manner of reading the Bible can have its own personal or community note. In each case the scriptural reference plays a different role. Here are a few instances, greatly simplified:

1. Very little is known about how the ancient Samaritans read scripture. Did they, in the beginning, use selected verses of the Tora in the sort of abridgements known as *Qetafim*? Only later on, but at least from the twelfth century, the Samaritans read the whole Tora in a year, beginning on the Sabbath after Tabernacles.[51] The cycle differs greatly from the Annual Babylonian Cycle.

2. Sadducee practice remains unknown. One can only conjecture that a (possible) reading of the Tora was given a very literal interpretation, with no appeal to the Prophets to support it.[52] Happily, the following practices are less obscure:

3. In the Egyptian Diaspora and at Alexandria in particular according to Philo,[53] the reading of the Law, done at once in Greek, seems to have been

---

[50] *P.T. Sota* 1 (16d); *Lev. Rabba* 9:9, p. 191.
[51] See Cowley, 'Samaritan Liturgy' and especially Baillet, 'Récitation de la Loi'; Perrot, *Lecture*, 169-71.
[52] See Le Moyne, *Les Sadducéens*, 357-79; Beckwith, above, pp. 73-76.
[53] See Perrot, 'Lecture de la bible'.

followed by a commentary of the allegorical type. The text of the Prophets seems to play no role, at least according to what Philo says, whose treatises, though not homilies strictly speaking, do reflect the practice or one of the practices of Alexandria. In the main his treatises follow the major sections of the readings of the law. *De Mundi Opificio* is on Gen 1:1f.; *Legum Allegoriae* is on Gen 2:1f.; *De Cherubim* is on Gen 3:24ff.; *De Gigantibus* is on Gen 6:1f. – and so on. Further Philo quotes by means of a title various sections of reading; 'On the bush' for instance[54] also mentioned in Mark 12:26, meaning Exod 3:1f. This does not mean that the Jews of Egypt neglected the Prophets or the Hagiographa (the Writings), but that the reading of these texts with a different status was done in a different context. It must be noted, however, that the Egyptian Therapeuts of whom Philo speaks in *De Vita Contemplativa*, devoted attention to 'the Laws, the Oracles gathered from the lips of the Prophets, Hymns, and all that enables knowledge and piety to increase and attain their fulness'.[55] The Fourth Book of Maccabees, written in Egypt (?) between 40 and 118 more or less, expressly mentions the reading of the Law accompanied by reflections taken from the Prophets, the Psalms and the Hagiographa (4 Macc 18:10-18). Hence, even though the reading of the Law had privileged status, the other books already had the quality of doing something to bring out its value.

4. At Qumran, among the 'Covenanters', Jews very probably of Essene leanings, the reading and explanation of the Tora played a considerable role. We may quote Philo on the Essenes: 'They use these laws (those of the Pentateuch) to learn from at all times, but especially each seventh day, since the seventh day is regarded as sacred. On that day they abstain from other work and betake themselves to the sacred places which are called synagogues. They are seated according to age in fixed places, the young below the old, holding themselves ready to listen with the proper good manners. Then one of them takes the books and reads. Another, from among those with most experience, comes forward and explains anything that is not easy to understand . . .'[56] So too at Qumran, the reading of the Tora is the main preoccupation, so much so that these sectarians had to watch 'one third of the nights of the year to read the book, to study the Law and to pray together'.[57]

No special value is here attributed to the readings on the sabbath morning. But the Prophets were read and commented on attentively, as the *Pesharim* discovered at Qumran prove. We must insist however on the following point:

---

[54] Philo, *De Somniis* 1:194.
[55] Philo, *De Vita Contemplativa* 25; see paragraphs 30-33 on the meeting on the seventh day and paragraphs 75-77 on the commentary on the scriptures; cf. Ellis, below, pp. 657-58; Nikiprowetzky, *Commentaire*; Harl, *La Bible d'Alexandrie*. For quotations from Hagiographa and Prophets in Philo, see Beckwith, above, pp. 47-48, 54-55.
[56] Philo, *Quod Omnis Probus Liber Sit* 81-82.
[57] See *1QS* 6:6-8. The 'book' is the Tora, as in Ezra 6:18; Neh 8:1f.; Mark 12:26. According to Fishbane, below, p. 344 there is no indication of a synagogue lection at Qumran.

though the Qumranites often mingled in their interpretations of florilegia elements drawn from the Tora, the Prophets and other writings, they also liked commenting prophetic books in a continuous sequence, as the *Pesher on Habakkuk* shows. Then the prophetic text is read and explained for its own sake, in its continuity, to gain a more vivid and immediate interpretation of the text in terms of the life of the group. We think that a like phenomenon is wanting in the ancient synagogue influenced by scribes of the Pharisaic party. No doubt the texts of the prophets were also read but that was primarily in terms of the Tora. The synagogue, meaning the Pharisee synagogue, only used selected passages taken from the Prophets. Then the prophetic text is read as an interpretation of the Tora, remaining itself outside the ambit of interpretation. Scribes of the Pharisaic party did not, apparently, give continuous commentary on the Prophets independently of the Tora. One last point still: until the end of the first century c.e. at least, the Book of Ezekiel was rather 'hidden', not exploited as at Qumran.[58] And also – is it merely by chance that the *pesharim* so far discovered are only of Isaiah, the Twelve Prophets and the Psalms?[59]

5. The link established between the Tora and the prophetic text in the sabbath morning readings is one of the innovations, both humble and extraordinary, made by the ancient scribes, whose practice enriches still synagogue and church. This reading 'in a mirror' enables an interpretation to be given which is respectful towards the first Word and full of prophetic warmth. It is no doubt difficult to give the date and birthplace of this practice. Possibly the oldest mention is in 2 Macc 15:9 where Judas Maccabeus 'encouraged' the people 'from the Law and the Prophets'. This custom, introduced on the sabbath morning in the synagogue, meant that the text of Moses was seen in its brightest colours, being understood partly through the 'prism' of the prophetic texts and then, by means of the homily, through the aid of all the other 'Writings', the better to express the Word of God. Finally, the whole Bible was called upon, and the synagogue transformed into a sort of immense 'living concordance' of the sacred text.

The eligible passages from the Prophets so suit the text of Moses and to explain it clearly had still to be found. This basic link is perfectly illustrated by a Palestinian designation of the reading from the Prophets: the Aramaic *ashlemata*, 'achievement' or 'accomplishment'.[60] The Prophet was the fulfilment of Moses. The ordinary term, haftara, first meant rather 'the conclusion' of the reading or 'the word of farewell'.[61] Thus some verses from the Prophets could be the ending of the sabbath service: 'The reading of the law is closed with the prophet' *(le-haftir ba-nabi)*. It is another warning not to insist too rigidly on the

---

[58] So the *Damascus Document* 3:21, 7:21 and *4QFlorilegium*. The author or rather glossator of 2 Cor 6:14-7:1 quotes Ezek 37:27 in an obviously Essene passage. The Book of Revelation alludes very often to the text of Ezekiel.

[59] See Horgan, *Pesharim*.

[60] See Mann, *The Bible* 1, 555-60; Perrot, *Lecture*, 186; Safrai, 'Synagogue', 928.

[61] *P.T. Berakhot* 4 (7d).

Tora-Prophets-Homily ritual. In the first century C.E. and also afterwards, customs were supple. The link between Tora and Prophets remains nonetheless certain, not to mention the use of the Psalms, as in Luke 24:27 and 45. Here too, Isaiah and the Twelve Prophets, along with the Psalms, seem to have been commonest. So with the apostle Paul, the former Pharisee, as in the haftarot of the Triennial Cycle. Which does not mean that other writings, including those now classed among the Apocrypha, did not play their part in the homily or in the pious readings done apart from the sabbath morning. The scribes close to the Pharisaic movement were already able users of the Wisdom literature. The same holds true of Paul. Suffice it to quote the *Syriac Apocalypse of Baruch*, from shortly after the fall of the Temple, where the author asks: 'When therefore you receive this letter, read it attentively in your gatherings, and think on it especially on the days of your fasts' (*2 Baruch* 86:1-2).

SABBATH DAY READINGS

Can some details be given about the nature of the readings in the synagogue on the sabbath morning before 70 C.E.? Who did the reading and how were the Tora and the Prophets read?

THE READING. We must recall to begin with that contrary to the rich and important *proseuchae* or synagogues in Antioch or Alexandria, the buildings housing synagogues in Israel must have seemed meagre and poor, with no great architectural quality. But they were numerous, especially in Jerusalem, and even in remote places like Nazareth. Under these circumstances one can guess how hard it was to find large numbers of readers and commentators, at a time when schooling had barely begun to develop. It seems that one reader was enough for the sabbath morning. This at any rate is what Philo gives us to understand, as do some later Jewish sources.[62] If a priest was present, he could be asked first to take on the task,[63] providing of course that he could read. In any case, there was not the breach between temple and synagogue such as is sometimes imagined.

The 'minister' of the synagogue, mentioned for instance in Luke 4:20, first went to fetch one of the five scrolls of the Tora, kept in a portable chest or a special niche.[64] All synagogues must surely have possessed the whole Tora in its five volumes (Aristeas, second century B.C.E., says 'cases')[65] and some other Bible scrolls, like Isaiah and the Twelve Prophets, and no doubt the Psalms.

---

[62] Philo, according to Eusebius, *Praeparatio Evangelica* 8:7, 13; see also *T. Megilla* 4:13 (at least exceptionally) and *P.T. Megilla* 4 (25a).
[63] So for Philo, see note 62 and *M. Gittin* 5:8 – 'A priest reads first, and after him a Levite, and then an Israelite in the interests of peace'.
[64] Or again 'in a corner' *B.T. Kiddushin* 66a, or in jars at Qumran.
[65] *Aristeas* 179 and 310 describe the Tora with the aid of the term *teuchè* probably signifying the Cases of Papyrus.

These were the books most in use. The Palestinian synagogues, small and numerous, could probably not afford all the scrolls, which were in any case expensive. So the minister could quickly find the scroll desired, if only because of its form. The scrolls of the Tora, the Twelve Prophets and the Psalms found at Qumran stand out easily from the other scrolls by their height or the carefulness of their script.[66]

The minister gave the scroll to the reader, who, once the blessing was said after Ezra's example (Neh 8:6), 'opened' the scroll, that is, unrolled it. He had not the sticks which are now used to hold it.[67] Then, standing on a wooden platform like Ezra, he read the text in Hebrew. But in the Diaspora, Egypt especially, reading must have been simply in Greek, using the text of the Septuagint.[68] Obviously this meant giving great weight to the Greek scroll. Philo, not knowing Hebrew, very probably, puts the two versions on the same level: 'They (the Jews of Alexandria) regard them with admiration and respect, like two sisters, or rather, as one and the same work, both in form and substance . . .'.[69] Still one may suppose that in the 'synagogues of the Hebrews' which are mentioned several times in connection with the Diaspora at Rome and Corinth, reading was also in Hebrew.

In Israel, outside the Synagogues of Greek-speaking Jews probably,[70] the reading was in any case in Hebrew. But is it certain that at this early period the Hebrew was followed by an Aramaic targum? Later, the *meturgeman* would be asked to speak lower than the reader, while translating from memory, without the aid of a written text, each verse read from the Tora.[71] In fact, there is no proof that this custom existed before 70 c.e. No doubt Ezra read the law 'clearly *(mephorash)* and gave the sense' (Neh 8:8). But must one see here an allusion to the targum as the Talmud says?[72] The language of the Palestinian Targum, and especially that of Codex Neofiti, reflects perhaps the language of the first century, and the traditions assembled here may well echo more ancient interpretations. But this does not oblige us to postulate a systematic practice of translation in the first century on the sabbath morning. It might be more correct to regard the targum as an early form of homily or commentary,[73] and not as a translation strictly speaking which would be a sort of 'double of' the Hebrew.

---

[66] See Perrot, *Lecture*, 117-27.

[67] At least the finds at Qumran do not testify to this.

[68] *M. Megilla* 1:8 and 2:1 mention the existence of scrolls written in other languages than Hebrew, even though *M. Yadayim* 4:5 condemns this practice. *T. Megilla* 4:13 asks for the beginning and end of the reading to be in Hebrew.

[69] Philo, *De Vita Mosis* 2:40.

[70] The inscription of Theodotus is in Greek. Greek was surely spoken in the Hellenistic synagogues of Jerusalem mentioned in Acts 6:8.

[71] See *T. Megilla* 4:21 and *P.T. Megilla* 4 (74d); see Alexander, 'Rabbinic Lists'; Alexander, below, pp. 238-39.

[72] *B.T. Megilla* 3a.

[73] See York, 'The Targum' who also emphasizes the link between targum and commentary. Cf. Alexander, below, p. 239.

THE READINGS AND THE SELECTED PASSAGES. The lector first reads a 'selected passage' of the Tora, not one picked according to his fancy but some notable text. He was not obliged to read the Tora as a continuity. The principle of the *lectio continua* only prevailed since the second century C.E. The Talmud[74] still remembers the existence of short readings in the time of Ezra, consisting of three to ten verses. Still more exactly, some midrashim mention that R. Eliezer ben Hyrcanus preached on Gen 14:1f., before 70 C.E. The midrash *Tanḥuma* designates this reading by the Hebrew word *'inyan*, that is, selected paragraph or passage.[75] But is it still possible to identify the texts chosen at this early period?

The titles given to the readings sometimes enable us to distinguish them better, like the mention of 'about the bush' in Mark 12:26, or 'about Elijah' in Rom 11:2, referring to the prophetic reading of 1 Kgs 19:10. Then there are a dozen similar titles in Philo:[76] 'the song' Exod 15; 'the church' Exod 19; 'the great vow' Num 6, etc. But there is another clue in the fact that the readings are marked out in manuscripts, including those of Qumran. These divisions are very ancient, even if different reading traditions have often been mixed up in the old manuscripts. Later their structure can be used to distinguish *petuḥot* and *setumot*, that is, open sections and closed sections.[77] But methods of writing allow the various qualities of the paragraphs to be distinguished, as early as Qumran. It is difficult not to see the constant coincidence of these divisions with the selected passages of before 70, and then with the sedarim of the TC and the *parashiyyot* of the AC. It is the natural thing. A reader could not start just where he liked. Starting-points were obvious and practically unavoidable. Later developments in these readings show frequently the effort to find a good place to start and then to end on a good finale. Hence one must conclude – without questioning the novelty of customary cycles of readings adopted after the second century C.E. – that there was a real continuity between ancient practice and later cycles. The choice of openings, very numerous to begin with, like the *petuḥot* which mark out the Tora, was to be more and more restricted in the triennial cycles and finally the annual cycle.

It was partly the same with the Prophets, which were read also each sabbath, as is said in Acts 13:27. Here too the paragraphing, *petuḥot* and *setumot*, mark out the text, even more systematically than with the Tora.[78] The frequency of the divisions seems to suit perfectly a continuous reading of the Prophets, the better to stress the structure and guide the reading of the whole. It is not

---

[74] *B.T. Bava Kamma* 82a.

[75] See Midrash *Tanhuma-Buber*, *Lekh Lekha* 10 (35a) and *Gen. Rabba* 41:1, p. 397-98.

[76] See the list in Perrot, *Lecture*, 149.

[77] Perrot, 'Petuhot et Setumot' and Oesch, *Petucha und Setuma*.

[78] So in *1QIsaᵃ*. Oesch, *Petucha und Setuma* insists strongly on this point. I see the case of the divisions of readings in the Tora as a little different. They are less systematic (Thus, no 'open section' between Deut 22:6 and 25:17) and they often agree with the openings of a seder and of festal readings.

surprising, therefore, that the openings of the haftarot, known from the TC and AC, should coincide relatively less often with these divisions of reading, which were indeed very numerous and more moveable. This is easily explained. The haftarot were always, then as now, selected passages apt to bring out the value of the Tora text. The prophetic text complements that of the Tora to clarify its meaning. Hence a section from the Pentateuch cannot be accompanied by any random prophetic text. A verbal and thematic link between them was needed, so that the passage from the prophet 'resembled' the passage from the Tora, as was to be affirmed by the Talmud.[79] It was precisely this similarity which was to give some of its later dynamism to the homily. But this 'magnetizing of texts' existed already before the fall of the temple.

Examples can only be given indirectly. That is, a magnetization of the same type can be seen in some texts previous to 70 C.E.. After the reading of Exod 21:1f. the haftara of the TC is Isa 56:1f., with a good finale in 57:19. Verbal and thematic links are obvious between the beginnings of the two items – especially the word *mishpat*, order. Later, according to the midrashim, the preacher of the homily brings out clearly the theme of the stranger (Exod 21:8 and Isa 58:3f.) to show how God never shows undue favour. In 95 C.E., at Rome, four celebrated rabbis were already preaching on these texts.[80] It is no surprise therefore when the author of Eph 2:11-22 also exploits this text from Isaiah (Isa 56:14; 57:19). Gentile Christians must no longer feel strangers, since Christ has taken away the 'barrier', that is, 'the law of commandments and ordinances' (Eph 2:15). Another example comes from the TC, which said that two sabbaths, at least, signalled the exceptional birth of great men: Gen 16:1f., the birth of Ishmael, followed by Isa 54:1f., 'Cry for joy, thou barren one!' and Gen 21:1f., (Isaac), and then 1 Sam 2:21f. (Samuel). Now in Gal 4:21-33 Paul relies on Gen 16 and quotes Gen 21:10 and Isa 54:1 – to speak of the birth of the Gentile Christian Church.

These few hints should not make us deduce the existence of a fixed cycle of readings before 70 C.E. But some prophetic texts seem already to gravitate around some texts of the Tora. A reader could not start reading anywhere he liked in the Tora. Thus he could not conclude his Tora reading by just any accompanying prophetic text. And if ancient reading divisions ended to some extent in the sedarim and parashiyyot, must not certain haftarot also be inheritors of an ancient reading tradition? Beyond the gaps in history, there are continuities to be recognized. Can one go further? There was undoubtedly great freedom of choice in selected readings, but note must be also taken of the very firm tradition which stressed the importance of the month of Tishri, and especially of Tabernacles. The king finished reading Deuteronomy at the end of

---

[79] *B.T. Megilla* 29b, *dedamē lēh*, 'resemble him'.
[80] See Mann, *The Bible* 1, 472. *Exodus Rabba* 30:9 says that R. Gamliel II, R. Yehoshua ben Hananya, R. Elazar ben Azaria and R. Akiva preached at Rom at the end of Domitian's reign; see also Perrot, 'Lecture synagogale'.

the sabbatical year, at Tabernacles. A new reading of the Tora must probably have started in terms of a seven-year cycle. Moreover, if it is necessary to recognize a beginning of the reading, that does not imply that a certain order was already respected for the reading of the chosen passages of the Tora as well. However, it is this point precisely that is reflected in the Palestinian Apocrypha, like the *Biblical Antiquities* of Pseudo-Philo at the end of the first century. This book follows selected readings according to the order of the Tora.[81]

At Nazareth, according to Luke 4:16-30, Jesus read Isa 61:1f., which in fact spoke of the liberation brought by the sabbatical year. Then he sat down, giving the scroll back to the minister, and claimed to be himself the 'accomplishment' of this prophecy of accomplishment. Luke does not mention here the preceding reading from the Tora; possibly because early Christian exegesis devoted itself very quickly to reading and commenting on the Prophets (as at Qumran), without relying much on the Tora. In any case, this gesture of Jesus bases Christian reading of the Bible on the imperative heritage of Jewish reading of the Word of God. After reading Isa 61:1f., with an element from the reading for the fast mixed in (Isa 58:6),[82] Jesus gives a sort of homily linked partly by verbal echo and content to the text of scripture. Later, Paul was also to start from the scriptures to speak of the Messiah on three successive sabbaths (Acts 17:2). But it is still difficult to make out the form or forms of homiletics at this early stage.

Very little is known of ancient homiletic practice till the time of the Talmud. The homiletical midrashim reflect to some extent, no doubt, actual sermons. But this would be in abridged form, with often diverse material and greatly reorganized. These midrashim were used primarily to make other sermons. The date of their final redaction is obviously late. Hence we avoid taking up such a subject here, difficult in any case and a constant matter of dispute. We note only the sermons called *Yelammedenu*, which however are hardly earlier than the fifth century C.E..[83] We note also just the *Proem* homily mentioned earlier.[84] The preacher begins with the help of a verse called *petiḥta* – opening verse – often taken from the Hagiographa (the Writings). Sometimes this verse has little bearing on the theme brought out by the day's readings. But the preacher, in a series of expositions, cleverly weaves all these biblical texts into one tissue, before ending with the verse which is to be the opening of the sabbath reading. Sometimes the sermon began by asking a question concerning the halakha. Again, the opening of the reading of the day could be used as starting-point, to be followed by an exposition where texts from the whole of Scripture were formed into a long chain. Custom therefore varied according to circumstances, making research into the matter all the more difficult. The commentator on the

---

[81] Perrot, *Pseudo-Philon*, 33-39.
[82] Isa 58 was to be the reading on the Day of Atonement fast (really, Isa 57:15f.). But this day also marks the beginning of the Jubilee year of Isa 61, which last text is also quoted in *11QMelchizedek* and *1QH* 18.
[83] Böhl, *Aufbau*, puts this type of sermon between the 5th century and the writing of the *Pesiktot*.
[84] See Heinemann, 'Proem'.

New Testament might well be tempted to explain by this type of preaching certain series of scriptural quotations, taken over by the apostle Paul and others, and also some discourses in Acts (Acts 2 and 13 for instance).[85] Here perhaps a show of prudence should be the rule, at least as long as research into the ancient homily has failed to reach more solid conclusions on literary and historical grounds.

Selective Bibliography

General works on the reading in the Synagogue are: BILLERBECK, 'Ein Synagogengottesdienst'; ELBOGEN, *Der jüdische Gottesdienst*; HRUBY, 'Le Sabbat et sa célébration'; HRUBY, 'La Synagogue'; SAFRAI, 'The Synagogue'; SCHÜRER, *History* (Rev. ed.) 2, 423-63; ZUNZ, *Gottesdienstlichen Vorträge*. Important discussions of the different cycles of reading are to be found in BARTH, 'The "Three of Rebuke" '; BREGMAN, 'Triennial Haftarot'; BÜCHLER, 'Reading of the Law'; FRIED, 'Haftara'; FRIED, 'List of Sedarim'; FRIED, 'Triennial Cycle'; HEINEMANN, 'Triennial Cycle' and 'Triennial Lectionary Cycle'; KLEIN, 'Four Notes'; MANN, *The Bible as Read and Preached* 1-2; PERROT, *La Lecture*; ROSENTHAL, 'Torah Reading'; THEODOR, 'Die Midraschim zum Pentateuch'; YOEL, 'Bible manuscript'.

A description of the ancient divisions, *petuhot* and *setumot*, is presented in the works of LANGLAMET, 'Le Seigneur dit à Moïse'; OESCH, *Petucha und Setuma*; PERROT, 'Petuhot et Setumot'.

On reading of the Tora in the Samaritan tradition, see the studies of BAILLET, 'La récitation', COWLEY, 'Samaritan Liturgy', MACDONALD, 'Comprehensive and Thematic Reading'. Reading of the Law and Prophets in Karaite circles is discussed by FINKELSTEIN, 'Prophetic Reading' and MANN, 'Anan's Liturgy'. Important studies on reading methods in the Hellenistic world have been published by BOGAERT, 'Le personnage de Baruch'; HARL, *La Bible d'Alexandrie*; NIKIPROWETZKY, *Le commentaire*; PERROT, 'La lecture de la Bible'. Studies on the function and form of the homily are: BACHER, *Proemien*; BÖHL, *Aufbau*; COHEN, 'Leviticus Rabba'; HEINEMANN, 'Proem'; MANDELBAUM, *Pesikta de Rav Kahana*; SARASON, 'Petihtot'; STEIN, 'Die Homiletische Peroration'; THYEN, *Der Styl*.

On the relations of the lectionary cycles with the New Testament the following studies particularly deserve mention: CROCKETT, 'Luke 4:16-30'; GOULDER, *Midrash and Lection*; GUILDING, *Fourth Gospel*; MORRIS, *New Testament*; PERROT, 'La lecture synagogale' and 'Luc 4, 16-30 et la lecture biblique'.

---

[85] Cf. Bowker, 'Speeches in Acts'; Dumais, *Language*.

Chapter Five

The Septuagint

Emanuel Tov

General

NAME

The name of the Septuagint derives from the legend that 72 (70) elders translated the Pentateuch into Greek. In the second century C.E. this tradition was extended to alle the translated books of the Bible, and finally the name 'Septuaginta' referred to all the books contained in the canon of the Greek Bible, including books that are not translations of an original Semitic text.

Ancient sources mention 72, 70 or 5 translators of the Pentateuch. The main tradition – which is found in rabbinic, Jewish-Hellenistic and Christian sources[1] – mentions 72 or 70 elders, and only a few sources (e.g. *Avot de-Rabbi Natan* B 37, 94f.) mention 5 translators. The numbers 70 and 72 are probably legendary and the precise relationship between them is unclear. Possibly the original tradition referred to 72 translators (6 elders from each tribe as mentioned in the *Epistle of Aristeas*) and this number was then rounded off to 70. But it is also possible that seventy, which often serves as a typological number, was the original one: to the tradition that seventy elders translated the Pentateuch into Greek one can compare the 'seventy of the elders of Israel' who went up to the mountain of Sinai together with Moses (Exod 24:1,9), the seventy elders who were appointed to assist Moses (Num 11:16ff.) and the seventy members of the Sanhedrin.[2]

The name 'Septuagint' denotes both the first Greek translation of the Bible and the collection of Jewish-Greek Scripture, containing *inter alia* this translation. The latter usage is imprecise because this collection contains also late revisions of the original translation and books that were originally written in Greek. In order to distinguish between the two usages of the word, the collection of Jewish-Greek Scripture is generally called the 'Septuagint', while the first translation of the Bible is often named 'the Old Greek (translation)'.

---

[1] The rabbinic sources have been collected and described by Müller, 'Rabbinische Nachrichten', 73-93. The Greek and Latin sources have been collected by Wendland, *Aristeae ad Philocratem Epistula*.

[2] Cf. Metzger, 'Seventy or Seventy-two'.

161

SCOPE, ORDER AND NAMES OF THE DIFFERENT BOOKS

The canon of the Septuagint contains three types of books: a) A Greek translation of the 24 canonical books of the Hebrew Bible. b) A Greek translation of books not included in the Hebrew canon. c) Books written in Greek as the Wisdom of Solomon and the Additions to Daniel and Esther.

The latter two groups together form the so-called Apocrypha.

The Septuagint canon is arranged differently from the Hebrew canon. While the Hebrew books are arranged in three groups reflecting different stages of the process of canonization, the books of the Greek Bible are arranged according to their literary character: a) Pentateuch and Historical books. b) Poetical and Sapiential books. c) Prophetical books.

Within each group the sequence of books does not correspond to that of the Hebrew canon.

The names of many of the books of the LXX differ from their counterparts in the Hebrew Bible, but they, too, reflect early Jewish traditions. For example, the Greek name of the fourth book of the Pentateuch, 'Ἀριθμοί, 'Numbers', has its counterpart in the Mishna and Talmud as חומש הפקודים (Hebrew Bible: במדבר).

TIME OF COMPOSITION

Only a few data are known concerning the time of composition of the translations contained in the canon of the 'LXX'. According to the *Epistle of Aristeas* the Pentateuch was translated in the third century B.C.E.; this seems plausible in the light of the early date of some papyri of the Pentateuch (middle or end second century B.C.E.). The books of the Prophets and Hagiographa were translated after the Pentateuch, since in them extensive use is made of its vacabulary and it is often quoted. As for the *terminus ad quem*, since the grandson of Ben Sira knew the translation of the books of the Prophets and part of the Hagiographa (132 or 116 B.C.E., according to different computations), these translations were probably finished before the first century B.C.E. Most of the books may have been translated at an early stage (beginning second century B.C.E. or earlier). One may note that the following books are quoted in early sources: Chronicles is quoted by Eupolemus (middle second century B.C.E.) and Job by Pseudo-Aristeas (beginning first century B.C.E.). Additionally, Isaiah contains allusions to historical occurrences which indicate that it was translated in the middle of the second century B.C.E.[3]

The Septuagint canon also contains some revisions of 'Old Greek' translations, dating from the first century B.C.E. until the second century C.E.. Thus some 400 years passed from the time of the first translation contained in this canon until the time of the last one.

---

[3] Cf. Seeligmann, *Septuagint Version*, 76-94.

POSITION WITHIN JUDAISM AND CHRISTIANITY

Originally the LXX was a Jewish translation (see below), and hence was quoted by Jewish historians (Demetrius, Eupolemus, Artapanus, Josephus), poets (Ezekiel) and philosophers (Philo). Especially the Pentateuch was also used in the synagogue service. However, at the end of the first century C.E. many Jews ceased to use the LXX because the early Christians had adopted it as their own translation, and by then it was considered a Christian translation. This explains the negative attitude of many Rabbis towards the LXX, which is reflected *inter alia* in *Massekhet Soferim* 1:7

> It happened that five elders translated the Pentateuch into Greek for King Ptolemy. That day was as hard for Israel as the day the calf was made, because the Pentateuch could not be translated properly.

This negative approach is visible also in the view of the Rabbis who explained the differences between the MT and LXX as alterations of the latter.[4]

The LXX influenced the NT at various levels. Firstly, many of the terms used and partly created by the LXX translators became part and parcel of the language of the NT. Furthermore, the NT quotes the LXX frequently, and some of its theological foundations are based upon the wording of passages in the LXX. Conversely, the NT influenced the transmission of the LXX but little. Allegedly several Christian changes were inserted at one time in LXX manuscripts, but few have survived to date. A much quoted example to this point is the adition to ὁ κύριος ἐβασίλευσεν, 'the Lord reigned' (Ps 96 [95]:10) of ἀπὸ τοῦ ξύλου, 'from the wood', i.e. from the cross, which has been preserved in only a few sources.

As has been said, within Judaism the LXX was never esteemed as much as in Christianity, because the Jews possessed an inspired *Hebrew* Bible, while to most of the Christians the LXX was the only sacred source of the OT and to some of them it was their main source. At an early stage the belief developed that this translation was divinely inspired and hence the way was open for several Church Fathers to claim that the LXX reflected the words of God more precisely than the Hebrew Bible.[5]

The LXX remained the Bible of the Church also through its Latin translation, the Vetus Latina, which was later replaced by Jerome's Vulgate. Today, the LXX is still considered a sacred book by the Greek Orthodox Church.

IMPORTANCE FOR SCHOLARSHIP

From the LXX we learn much important information concerning the translators and their techniques, their linguistic knowledge and methods of exegesis, the

---

[4] See Tov, 'Rabbinic Tradition'.

[5] Thus Justin Martyr, *Dialogue with Trypho* 73:1 claimed originality for the aforementioned addition to Ps 96(95):10 and similar ones. For the whole question, see Benoit, 'Inspiration'.

Greek language of Egypt in the third and second centuries B.C.E., as well as the intellectual and cultural background of the translators. For OT scholarship the main significance of the LXX lies in its supposed Hebrew *Vorlage*. The LXX is the earliest written translation of the OT, and, until recently its MSS were the most ancient witnesses of the biblical text. Also after the recent finds of Hebrew MSS at Qumran, the LXX remains – after the MT – the most important, complete, source for the text of the Bible.[6]

Origin and Original Form of the Translation

INTERNAL EVIDENCE

Internal evidence concerning the origin of the LXX is not plentiful and some of it is open to different explanations. However, a few conclusions can be drawn:
1. The Pentateuch was translated by *Jewish* translators. Some of the other books of the LXX also reflect exegesis which may be characterized as 'Jewish', but the Jewish origin of every individual book cannot be proven.
2. The LXX originated in *Egypt* as can be demonstrated by its vocabulary (see note 47).
3. The vocabulary of the individual books of the LXX shows that *different* translators participated in its translation.

EXTERNAL EVIDENCE

There are many external data concerning the origin of the LXX, but most of it depends on two early versions of one story. All known sources are legendary and their historicity is the subject of much debate.

The most extensive descriptions are found in the *Epistle of Aristeas*,[7] one of the Pseudepigrapha, probably written in the second century B.C.E., and in Epiphanius' treatise *On Measures and Weights*, written in the fourth century C.E. The *Epistle of Aristeas* describes how a King Ptolemy (apparently Ptolemy II Philadelphus who reigned from 285 until 247 B.C.E.) summoned 72 Jewish elders from Palestine and how they translated their Holy Book for the library of Alexandria in 72 days. The story is dominated by its many legendary details; these elements are even more manifest in Epiphanius' description. According to the latter, 36 pairs of elders translated all the books of the Bible; upon completion they compared their translations and it so happened that the various translations coincided in all details. It should be pointed out that the evidence of

---

[6]   On this aspect of the LXX – which is not discussed here –, see Tov, 'Septuagint, The Contribution of'; Tov, *Text-Critical Use*.
[7]   Cf. Nickelsburg, 'Bible Rewritten', 75-80.

the *Epistle of Aristeas* refers only to the Pentateuch, while that of Epiphanius, and of several sources before him, refers to the whole Bible.

The tendentious character of the *Epistle of Aristeas* is evident in many details. It extolls the LXX, it speaks apologetically about the laws of the Jews and it praises highly King Ptolemy. Consequently, it seems improbable that all details of its description are trustworthy; it seems, however, plausible that at least the kernel of its story is historical: someone, possibly the king himself, commissioned a group of Jewish elders to translate their Holy Book into Greek. This assumption is supported by outside evidence concerning the interest shown by Ptolemaic kings – as well as by learned men in their time – in various foreign cultures. Some scholars, however, also attach historical value to other elements contained in the *Epistle*, while others reject the entire story.

MODERN THEORIES

THE 'URTEXT' THEORY. De Lagarde was the first scholar to discuss the principles involved in reconstructing the original form of the LXX.[8] According to him, all manuscripts of the LXX derive from one prototype, a theory similar to that which he holds for the MT. However, while his assumption for the MT is based on actual evidence, that is, on unique common features found in all MSS (e.g., *puncta extraordinaria* and other diacritical signs of the Masoretes), his views on the LXX are based merely on analogy with the MT. It should be noted that de Lagarde did not distinguish between the reconstructed prototype of all MSS of the LXX and the assumed original translation, so that in his discussion the term *Urtext* refers to both.

De Lagarde did not content himself with the mere formulation of abstract principles but he also applied them to the texts themselves. According to his system, one needs first to reconstruct the original form of each of the three main textual branches of the LXX (the Hexapla and the revisions of Lucian and Hesychius),[9] from which the *Urtext* of the LXX can then be reconstructed. De Lagarde's aim, namely to reconstruct the *Urtext* of the LXX from its main textual branches, does not seem to be obtainable, but, more importantly, neither the Lagarde[10] nor any of his followers succeeded in reconstructing the *Urtext* of any one of the three revisions. The best application of de Lagarde's principles is found in the edition of Joshua by Margolis,[11] but he, too, was not successful in reconstructing in a convincing way the original text of the textual families of this book.[12]

---

[8] De Lagarde's seminal remarks are included in the introduction to his *Anmerkungen*, 1-4 and are repeated with additions in his *Mittheilungen*, 19-26.

[9] See below, n. 64.

[10] See de Lagarde's reconstruction of the Lucianic revision in his *Librorum Veteris Testamenti canonicorum pars prior graece*.

[11] Margolis, *Book of Joshua*.

[12] See also Tov, 'Fifth Fascicle'.

Despite the mentioned reservations, de Lagarde's assumption that all extant LXX manuscripts are based on one prototype has been accepted by the majority of scholars; however, not all agree that the underlying text should be called the *Urtext* of the LXX.

MULTIPLE TRANSLATIONS. The first scholar who questioned the existence of an *Urtext* of the LXX was Kahle. His theories have been formulated in various and discordant ways between 1915 and 1962 and they have become known especially from the three editions of his book *The Cairo Geniza*.[13] Kahle's views center around two closely connected points:

1. The present textual uniformity of the LXX developed from an earlier multiplicity of translations. Therefore the task of LXX textual criticism is to *describe* its manifold textual traditions, and not to reconstruct an assumed *Urtext*, for such a text has never existed in reality.

2. None of the many translations was considered authoritative in pre-Christian times; consequently all were used and quoted. The early Church, however, chose one textual tradition as authoritative (the nature of which was not defined by Kahle). Therefore, over against a multiplicity of early Jewish translations, one notes a textual uniformity from the first century C.E. and onwards. This unity was disturbed in the next centuries by the appearance of the revisions of the LXX whose influence was felt in all MSS.

Kahle himself provided some arguments against his first thesis. Among other things he maintains that one should posit for each book of the LXX an initial attempt at translation which was revised time and again. This first translation could be called an 'Urtext', writes Kahle,[14] but such a term would not be an appropriate designation for the fluid textual condition of the LXX in its initial stage. Nevertheless Kahle admitted the existence of an original form of the LXX, even if it cannot be reconstructed.

Just as the model for de Lagarde was the MT, Kahle often compared the development of the LXX to the growth of the Aramaic targumim. He hypothesized that various formulations of the LXX, initially oral and later written, existed in Egypt, similarly to those of the targumim. However, the comparison with the targumim is not supported by any explicit evidence.

Kahle based his view to a great extent on two indications of the multiplicity of early translations, both of which are problematic and open to different explanations:

1. Unlike other scholars, Kahle argued that the *Epistle of Aristeas* does not mention a *new* translation of the Pentateuch, but an official *revision* of earlier translations. According to Kahle, the evidence contained in the *Epistle* agrees with his hypothesis of multiple translations. His view is based primarily on *Ep. Arist.* 30 which says that the writings of the Jews previous to

---

[13] Kahle, *Cairo Genizah* (1947, 1959; German edition, 1962). See further his 'Untersuchungen'.
[14] See especially 'Die Septuaginta', 177.

the time of the official translation 'σεσήμανται carelessly'. Kahle explained the verb as 'were translated', and accordingly the *Epistle* mentions earlier Jewish *translations*. But, according to other scholars the *Epistle* speaks about 'editing', 'copying', 'writing' or 'transmitting', and this description refers to *Hebrew* writings.[15] Moreover, if the *Epistle* had referred to a revision of earlier translations, most probably this would have been explicitly stated.

2. From the beginning of the 20th century, several Greek textual traditions have become known that differ significantly from the tradition contained in MSS A, B and S of the LXX. According to Kahle, this textual variation proves the very existence of multiple *translations*. Time and again Kahle expressed his disagreement with the majority of scholars who claim that these traditions reflect mainly early revisions of the LXX (e.g., Pap. Ryl. Gk. 458 and the Minor Prophets Scroll found in *Naḥal Ḥever*).

Kahle's opinion has remained unsupported by other scholars, with the sole exception of his pupil A. Sperber.[16]

MULTIPLE TEXTUAL TRADITIONS. In the views of de Lagarde and Kahle one finds both correct elements and serious shortcomings; newly found data allow for the formulation of an intermediary position which is reflected in an embryonal status in an article by Bickerman.[17]

It is reasonable to assume with de Lagarde that behind the majority of the books of the LXX (if not all of them) there was one translation. However, the original wording of this translation has not been preserved in a pure form for a long period because with the beginning of its transmission in different scrolls it diffused to several secondary textual traditions: in the pre-Christian period and to a lesser extent in the first centuries of our era scribes and editors inserted in every scroll corrections of various types.[18] Bickerman stressed that in these early times there were not in existence two identical scrolls of any one of the books of the LXX.

On the basis of this description, the following four stages can be recognized in the development of the text of the LXX:

1. The original translation.
2. A multitude of textual traditions, resulting from the insertion of corrections (mainly towards the Hebrew) in all known individual scrolls in the pre-Christian period, and to a lesser extent in the first century C.E.
3. Textual stabilization in the first and second centuries C.E., due to the

---

[15] For a summary of the opinions, see Gooding, 'Aristeas'.
[16] *Septuaginta-Probleme*; 'New Testament and Septuagint'; *Historical Grammar*, 321ff.
[17] Bickerman, 'Some Notes'.
[18] Recently published papyri show the complexity of the situation. Even when all the unicial manuscripts agree, their common text may have been created by revisional activity, while the original text is contained in an early papyrus, such as *4QLXXLev*ᵃ, analyzed by Skehan, 'Qumran Manuscripts', and Pap.Ryl.Gk 458 of Deut, analyzed by Wevers, 'The Earliest Witness'.

perpetuation of some textual traditions and the discontinuation of others.

4. The creation of new textual groups and the corruption of existing ones through the influence of the revisions of Origen and Lucian in the third and fourth centuries C.E.

A LITURGICAL APPROACH. Thackeray,[19] like Kahle, posited that the LXX translation originated from the internal needs of the Jewish community of Alexandria, which required a translation of the Pentateuch for the synagogue reading. Thackeray further surmised that parts of the Prophets and Hagiographa were translated for the same purpose. The transmitted form of the LXX is based on these partial translations.

The original vocabulary is still visible in Ezek 36:24-38 and in the so-called Barberini version of Hab 3 whose wording differs from that of the surrounding chapters. Thackeray's theory seems plausible, especially for the Pentateuch, but it cannot be proven.

THE TRANSCRIPTION THEORY. According to Wutz,[20] the early translators used manuscripts of the Hebrew Bible written in Greek characters and not, as expected, in Hebrew. His assumption is based, among other things, on the fact that the second column of the Hexapla contains a transcription of the whole Hebrew Bible and it thus stands to reason that such texts were in existence before Origen's time. Wutz attempted to prove his theory with hundreds of examples, but most of them have been rejected by scholars; consequently the theory cannot be upheld.

The Character of the Translation

Before we start to discuss 'the character of the translation' and 'the intellectual and cultural background of the translators' (below), we have to remark that these subjects have not been described in the scholarly literature with regard to the *whole* of the LXX, but important aspects have been discussed[21] with regard to individual books.[22]

---

[19] Thackeray, *Jewish Worship*, 'Primitive Lectionary Notes'.

[20] Wutz, *Transkriptionen*. Reactions on Wutz' theory are listed in Brock-Fritsch-Jellicoe, *Classified Bibliography*, 43-44.

[21] Some studies are referred to in the notes; for more complete references, the reader is referred to Brock-Fritsch-Jellicoe, *Classified Bibliography*.

[22] Of the more important studies on individual books of the LXX see the following ones, listed in chronological sequence (for bibliographical details see Brock-Fritsch-Jellicoe, *Classified Bibliography*): Frankel on the Pentateuch, de Lagarde on Proverbs, Scholz on Esther, Streane on Jeremiah, Flashar on Psalms, Holmes on Joshua, Kaminka on the Minor Prophets, Ziegler and Seeligmann on Isaiah, Gerleman on Job, Chronicles and Proverbs, Soisalon-Soininen and Schreiner on Judges, Wevers on Samuel-Kings, Orlinsky on Job, Ziegler on Jeremiah and Allen on Chronicles.

THE APPROACH TO THE ACT OF TRANSLATING

The LXX was one of the great translation enterprises of antiquity.[23] It was the first major translation from an oriental language into Greek and it was also the first written translation of the Bible. It follows that the first translators had to cope with many problems which had not yet been tackled, among them the shift from a Semitic to an Indo-European language and the transposal of concepts from one culture into another.

In Ptolemaic Egypt two different kinds of translation techniques were known: precise translations, needed for commercial and judicial transactions (undertaken by people from different origins) as well as free translations of literary works. The LXX translators generally used translation techniques which were somewhere between these two extremes.

THE HETEROGENEOUS CHARACTER OF THE LXX

The canon of the 'LXX' contains not only original translations of the biblical books, but also some revisions of earlier translations. The book of Daniel included in the canon was translated by Theodotion, and Ecclesiastes probably by Aquila. Revisions are found even in sections of books: e.g., parts of Samuel-Kings contain the *kaige*-Theodotion revision (see below). This mixture probably originated in the time when scribes started to compose large scale codices copied from scrolls of apparently variegated character.

The heterogeneous character of the LXX derived not only from the aforementioned external conditions, but also from differences in translation techniques between the various books. To give a few examples: the phrase 'ה צבאות has been rendered in the Latter Prophets (except Isaiah) by κύριος παντοκράτωρ, in Isaiah by κύριος Σαβαωθ and in other books by κύριος τῶν δυνάμεων. In the Pentateuch and Joshua the word פלשתים is transliterated as φυλιστιειμ, while in subsequent books it is rendered by ἀλλόφυλοι.[24] Therefore, when discussing the translation character of the LXX, one should take into consideration the special character of each individual book. In fact, the maximal entity which can be considered as separate translation unit is a single book and at times only part of a book.

SOURCES OF INFORMATION FOR UNDERSTANDING THE HEBREW

There is no concrete evidence that the translators possessed either dictionaries or word lists. Thus, when attempting to determine the meaning of a word, they resorted to various sources of information:

---

[23] For this section, cf. Bickerman, 'Septuagint'; Rabin, 'Translation Process'; Brock, 'Phenomenon'; Orlinsky, 'Septuagint as Holy Writ', 103ff.; Brock, 'Aspects'.

[24] For additional examples of this kind, see Hatch, *Essays*, 20-23; Thackeray, *Grammar*, 6-9.

a. *Exegetical traditions.* The exegesis reflected in the LXX is often paralleled elsewhere. The translators must therefore have known several exegetical traditions. For example, in Exod 12:13,27 פסח has been rendered by σκεπάζω (to pity), similar to the tradition found in rabbinic sources, Tg. Onkelos, and some Jewish grammarians.

In Gen 33:19, Josh 24:32 and Job 42:11, קשיטה (a unit of unknown value) has been rendered as 'lamb' in the LXX, Tg. Onkelos, and the Vulgate. In *Genesis Rabba* it has been explained similarly.[25]

b. *Context.* Translators frequently inferred the meaning of an unknown word from the context. Often this procedure was little more than guesswork, and the number of guesses of this kind is larger than generally thought. This applies especially to rare and unique words. Thus the translator of Isaiah rendered the rare word נשף (twilight) three times according to its context, each time differently: Isa 5:11 τὸ ὀψέ (late); 21:4 ψυχή (soul); 59:10 μεσονύκτιον (midnight). In the book of Jeremiah four different verbs which were understandably difficult for the translator have been rendered by the general verb παρασκευάζω (to prepare): Jer 6:4; 12:5; 46 (26):9; 51 (28):11.

c. *Etymology.* Often the translators were guided by etymological considerations. Thus the word מועד in the phrase אהל מועד (tent of meeting) has always been rendered as μαρτύριον (witness) as if it were derived from עוד, rather than יעד; and ערבה (desert plane) has sometimes been rendered as if connected with מערב (west).[26]

d. *Postbiblical Hebrew.* Most of the translators seem to have been well-acquainted with postbiblical Hebrew, more so than with biblical, and at times their translation equivalents are better understood against this background. For example, the word ארמון (palace, citadel), occurring frequently in the Bible, is rare in later Hebrew. This may account for a variety of guess-translations in the LXX (house, city, land, cave, fundaments, tower, etc.).

At times the translators rendered a certain word according to its meaning in postbiblical Hebrew even though in the Bible the word occurred in a different sense. של, although occurring a few times in the Bible, is basically a postbiblical word, and the rendering of Gen 49:10 must be viewed against that background: עד כי יבא שילה 'until (he?)comes (to?) Shilo'–ἕως ἂν ἔλθῃ τὰ ἀποκείμενα αὐτῷ 'until there come the things stored up for him' = עד כי יבא שֶׁ(לֹ)לה.

e. *Aramaic.* When the Greek translations were made, Aramaic was the lingua franca of many of the inhabitants of Egypt and Palestine. Within the LXX this becomes evident from transliterations reflecting Aramaic rather than Hebrew forms of words: γιώρας (גיורא), representing גר; πάσχα (פסחא), representing פסח; μαννα (מנא), representing מן.

At times, the translators' knowledge of Aramaic misled them when the meaning of a Hebrew root differed from its Aramaic counterpart. For example,

---

[25] See *Genesis Rabba* 79:7 (pp. 946-49).
[26] See Tov, *Text-Critical Use*, 241-48.

in Ps 60 (59):10 and 108 (107):10, סיר רחצי (my wash basin) has been rendered as λέβης τῆς ἐλπίδος μου (basin of my hope) according to the meaning of the root רחץ in Aramaic.[27]

f. *Translation of the Pentateuch.* Translators of the later books were sometimes guided by that of the Pentateuch. Thus the word זועה/זעוה (terror) has been rendered in Jer 34 (41):17 by διασπορά (diaspora) according to the LXX of Deut 28:25. On four occasions in Jeremiah אההּ (alas) has been translated by ὦ ὤν (he who is) following the LXX of Exod 3:14 אהיה אשר אהיה – ἐγώ εἰμι ὁ ὤν.[28]

In spite of these sources of information, often the renderings themselves must be described as guessing, and this occurred into a much larger extent than is generally assumed. Such guesses are visible in various groups of renderings, described elsewhere:[29] contextual guesses, contextual 'changes', reliance on parallelism, employment of general words and etymological renderings. In addition to these types of renderings, some words were left untranslated because the translator did not know their meaning, such as הברקנים (briers?) in Judg 8:7, 16 (βαρκοννιμ and sim.). Most of these words are objectively difficult, because they are *hapax legomena* in the Bible or in the book under consideration.

THE CHOICE OF TRANSLATION EQUIVALENTS

It was a difficult task for the first translators to form and partly to invent a vocabulary which would express the content of the Pentateuch (however, evidence suggests that several equivalents had already been determined by previous generations). This search for equivalents was basically a process of linguistic identification, but exegetical factors played an important role.

The results of the translators' search for equivalents are not equal in the different books, nor in the various semantic fields. Many of the lexical choices were employed as equivalents of their Hebrew counterparts in the whole of the LXX, while others were invented *ad hoc*. When according to the translators a given Hebrew word could not be expressed adequately by an existing Greek word, sometimes new words (neologisms) were coined such as σαββατίζω (keep Sabbath = שבת), προσήλυτος = גר (see p. 175), and ἀκροβυστία (= ערלה).[30] For a relatively small group of technical words no appropriate equivalents at all could be found, so that they were transliterated as such into Greek: e.g. μαναα (מנחה), ἐφουδ (אפוד) and γομορ (עמר) – some of these transliterations were probably used as such in the daily speech of the Greek

[27] Ibid., 249-50.
[28] See Tov, 'The Impact of the LXX Translation'.
[29] Cf. Tov, 'Septuagint Translators'.
[30] Hatch, *Essays*, 12-13 and especially Lee, *A Lexical Study*.

speaking Jews of Alexandria, e.g. γειώρας, based upon the Aramaic counterpart of the biblical גר, viz. גיורא.

Within the various books of the LXX there are opposing tendencies with regard to the representation of individual Hebrew words and syntagmata, deriving from differences in translation character between the various books, ranging from (very) literal to (very) free. When analyzing translation techniques from the point of view of the translator's attitudes towards the Hebrew text, it is probably best to take the criteria for literalness as the point of departure since these can be defined more easily than criteria for free renderings. In recent scholarship, attempts at defining such criteria have been formulated by Barr and Tov.[31] According to the latter, one of the main criteria for defining the literalness of translation units is the recognition of the consistency in the translation. Many translators rendered all occurrences of a given Hebrew word, element (e.g., preposition), root or construction as far as possible by the same Greek equivalent, often disregarding the effect of this type of translation upon its quality. This tradition (rather than system) of consistently representing words and roots by the same equivalents probably developed in a school-type milieu and may reflect the belief that the words of the Holy Bible should be rendered consistently in order to remain as faithful as possible to the source language. Although consistent representation, usually called 'stereotyping'[32] needs to be studied in greater detail, it is probably true to say that from the outset a tendency towards stereotyping was the rule rather than the exception. Thus, once the initial lexical choice of a certain equivalent had been made, either in an earlier translation unit, or by a preceding generation, or by the translator himself, it was used wherever possible. Failure to stereotype was conditioned by the context, the limitations of the Greek language, and above all, by the inclinations of individual translators.

It has yet to be examined which types of words and elements were rendered stereotypically, in which books and under which circumstances. A good example of a stereotyped rendering is the equivalent ברית – διαθήκη which occurs in 99 per cent of the occurrences of the Hebrew and Greek words. Other examples are 'ה – κύριος, אלהים – θεός, אח – ἀδελφός, תורה – νόμος. Often different stereotyped renderings were used in different translation units, as might be expected in such a heterogeneous composition as the LXX. In this way a translators' jargon developed in which Hebrew words and roots were generally represented with their standard translations. This system facilitated the trans-

---

[31] Barr, 'Typology of Literalism', 11; Tov, *Text-Critical Use*, 50-66. For the last developments in this area, see Tov-Wright, 'Computer Assisted Study'.
[32] To the best of my knowledge, the use of the term 'stereotyped' within LXX research derives from Flashar, 'Exegetische Studien', 105. Rabin, 'Translation Process', 8ff. names the phenomenon under investigation 'verbal linkage'. For a brief discussion of some types of words which have been rendered stereotypically, see Heller, 'Grenzen sprachlicher Entsprechung', 240ff. See further Tov, 'Three Dimensions', 529-44.

lation process and was also of help to the reader. For one thing, variation in the representation of technical words often confused the reader of the LXX.[33]

TRANSLATION TECHNIQUE AND EXEGESIS

The collection of LXX books contains both literal and free translations. Typical examples of free (and sometimes paraphrastic) translations are Job, Proverbs, Isaiah, Daniel and Esther; literal translations are the books of Judges (B text), Psalms, Ecclesiastes, Lamentations, Ezra-Nehemiah and Chronicles, as well as those parts of Samuel-Kings which are ascribed to the *kaige*-Theodotion revision. All other books, and they form the majority, are found somewhere between these two extremes. There are, however, certain exponents of the translation technique which are common to all books, although the frequency of their occurrence is determined by the character of the translation. This applies in particular to certain renderings which could be considered 'deviations' from the MT from a purely formal point of view, but a closer look at their nature reveals that they are, in fact, a direct result of the nature of the undertaking as understood by the translator.

EXEGESIS. It has become a commonplace to say that all translations reflect exegesis, but a correct understanding of these exegetical elements necessitates a specific description of their nature. This may be divided into linguistic and contextual exegesis. Every translation reflects linguistic exegesis, which is an integral part of the act of translation. Linguistic exegesis involves the grammatical identification of all words (especially forms of verbs and nouns) in the source language as well as their semantic interpretation. On the other hand, not every translation contains additional forms of exegesis. A translation like Aquila's, for example, reflects mainly linguistic exegesis, since Aquila was interested only in the linguistic identification of the Hebrew words, and did not introduce any exegetical elements in his translation. This tendency is visible in his choice of equivalents which was stereotyped throughout the translation, irrespective of the context.

Admittedly, the translation of Aquila is an unicum, but within the canon of the LXX there are also several translation units which are remarkably consistent in their choice of equivalents. That is to say, their lexical choices were less influenced by the context than were those of other translation units.

Leaving aside the linguistic exegesis found in all translation units, we now turn to other forms of exegesis. In a way, all forms of exegesis might be called 'contextual exegesis', because the translators' concept of 'context' was wider than ours. They referred to the relationship between the words not only in their immediate, but also in remote contexts. Furthermore, the translation might contain any idea the source text called to mind.

---

[33] This was shown with regard to technical terms in the Pentateuch by Gooding, 'Account'.

The analysis of such exegetical elements deals with all elements that deviate from the literal sense of a given word, phrase or sentence. They add elements to the MT and omit them as well as introduce certain changes in the text. Most exegetical elements, however, are reflected in the lexical choices themselves, which were influenced by the immediate context and the conceptual world of the translators.

Thus regular or contextual exegesis reveals itself often in the choice of unusual equivalents, in the connections made between words, and in the adaptation of Hebrew to Greek diction, for example when idiomatic Hebrew phrases are translated into Greek. For instance, Exod 6:12 ערל שפתים 'of uncircumcised lips', is translated by ἄλογος, 'speechless' and Hos 8:8 כלי אין חפץ בו, 'a vessel in which there is no desire', is rendered by σκεῦος ἄχρηστον, 'a useless vessel'. Other 'deviating' translations result from a translator's legitimate exegesis of certain words or phrases. In this way, Gen 1:2 תהו ובהו, is rendered by ἀόρατος καὶ ἀκατασκεύαστος, 'invisible and shapeless', and Isa 9:13 כפה ואגמון 'palm branch and reed', is rendered by μέγαν καὶ μικρόν, 'great and small'.

Likewise, the translators added various elements to the translation which served to improve its readability from a linguistic and contextual point of view, clarifying Hebrew or Greek words and explaining their content. Translators also omitted various elements which they considered superfluous.

CONTEXTUAL ADJUSTMENTS. In addition to the exegetical elements described above, translators felt free to make certain contextual adjustments in small details which belong to the precise wording of the translation and not to its content as described above. This applies to contextual adjustments between the plural and singular forms of verbs and nouns, between different pronouns and nouns, and also to the addition and omission of such elements in order to produce a translation which would be smoother than the source text itself. (For a more detailed description of the nature of these elements, the reader is referred to the monographs in n. 22.)

The Intellectual and Cultural Background of the Translators

A translation generally contains information about the intellectual background of its translator(s) – this information can be recognized through reflections of ideas and knowledge which may be attributed to him personally – as well as about his cultural environment, through terms and ideas which the translator had appropriated. It is very hard to identify such elements and to distinguish between the two strands, even more so in the case of the LXX, since its Hebrew *Vorlage* is not sufficiently known.

Despite these methodological difficulties one can perceive some aspects of the intellectual and cultural background of the translators, reflected in some translation options as well as in forms of tendentious exegesis. One will recognize in the LXX certain *theologoumena* which differ from book to book; they cannot be combined into a detailed theological system and therefore one can not crystallize a 'theology' of the LXX translation as a whole.[34]

THE CHOICE OF CERTAIN TRANSLATION EQUIVALENTS

The majority of translation equivalents derive from linguistic identifications of a given Hebrew root or word with a Greek equivalent; as such they are of importance for our understanding of the linguistic knowledge of the translators, but are of limited importance for our understanding of their conceptual world.

An analysis of some *standard* equivalents shows the complexity of the situation: An inevitable result of the process of linguistic identification is, among other things, the lack of overlapping between words in the source language and in the target language. It is but natural that a given Hebrew word possesses meanings which are not reflected in its Greek translation, and the same is true for the relationship between a given Greek word and its biblical counterpart. For example, the identification of the root צדק with δικαιο – (thus, צדיק – δίκαιος) was accepted by most of the LXX translators probably because the two words cover each other fairly well. This lexical choice has given rise to an interesting semantic development within the Greek language. In classical Greek the stem δικαιο – is used mainly with regard to the relationship between human beings, but in the LXX (as a result of its Hebrew source) it refers predominantly to the relationship between man and God. Therefore, the special use of δικαιο – in the LXX does not reflect any theological tendency of the translators, but it is an inevitable result of the identification of צדק and δικαιο –.

A slightly more complicated case is the standard LXX translation of גר with προσήλυτος. In the OT גר denotes the 'stranger', but in postbiblical Hebrew it was used as 'someone who joined the religion of the Israelites', especially in the phrase גר צדק (cf. also the Aramaic גיורא 'proselyte'). The Greek translators represented גר in accordance with the linguistic reality of their own times almost exclusively by προσήλυτος, a word which apparently was coined to denote the special meaning of גר in postbiblical times. It is inconceivable that the translators used this rendition because of missionary tendencies,[35] because the use of προσήλυτος in a verse like Exod 22:21 ἦτε γὰρ προσήλυτοι ἐν γῇ Αἰγύπτῳ, 'for you were "proselytes" (MT: strangers) in the land of Egypt' is highly inappropriate. Rather, the equivalence גר – προσήλυτος reflects the linguistic background of the translators.

In a relatively small number of instances, however, the thought-world of the translators reveals itself in the choice of certain translation options; this is true both of renderings occurring throughout the LXX and of renderings which occur

[34] For a detailed discussion see Tov, 'Die Septuaginta'.
[35] Thus Schreiner, 'Hermeneutische Leitlinien', 391.

only occasionally.[36] For example, different kinds of transgression (און, שקר, עולה, חמס, זמה, etc.) are rendered uniformly by the translators of the Psalms by ἀνομία. Thus, according to this translator all these transgressions constitute sins against the νόμος, the Law. A similar trend is visible in Isa 57:4 where זרע שקר 'offspring of deceit' is rendered by σπέρμα ἄνομον, as well as in various places in the book of Proverbs such as 29:8 אנשי לצון, 'scoffers' – ἄνδρες ἄνομοι.

The translators of the Pentateuch made a distinction between a Jewish altar (מזבח – θυσιαστήριον) and a pagan altar (βωμός); the Aramaic targumim similarly distinguished between the Jewish מדבחא and the pagan אגורא.

The translator of Isaiah frequently used the word δόξα, 'glory', not only as the standard translation of כבוד, but also as an equivalent of several other words, especially with reference to God (און, גאות, הדר, הוד, חסד, יפי, עז, תפארת, etc.). He even inserted it in the translation against the MT, e.g. Isa 6:1 'and his train filled the temple', LXX: 'and the house was full of his glory (δόξα)'. Hence, for the translator of Isaiah, δόξα is one of the central characteristics of God.

VARIOUS TYPES OF EXEGESIS

The personality and background of the translators may reveal themselves in various types of exegesis not necessitated by the context but inserted extraneously by the translators. The translators were certainly aware that they added elements to the translation which were not found in their Hebrew *Vorlage*; but apparently religious motivations, adherence to certain exegetical traditions as well as didactic considerations allowed them to translate in a manner often similar to that of the targumists. The following sections discuss three types of such exegesis which, when contrasted with the regular exegesis described above, should be considered tendentious.

THEOLOGICAL EXEGESIS. Theological exegesis may relate to the description of God and His acts, the Messiah, Zion, the exile as well as various religious feelings. It may be expressed through theologically motivated choices of translation equivalents, as well as through additions and omissions of ideas considered offensive. Theological tendencies are apparent throughout the LXX, but they occur more frequently in 'free' translation sections, such as the book of Isaiah.[37] For example, the idea that God brings σωτήριον, 'salvation', referring

---

[36] Detailed discussions of theological connotations of LXX words are found in Kittel-Friedrich, *Theologisches Wörterbuch*, as well as in a series of articles by Bertram (see Brock-Fritsch-Jellicoe, *Classified Bibliography*, 17-19). It should be remarked, however, that both tend to discover theological tendencies also in natural Greek equivalents of Hebrew words. Against this trend see especially Barr, *Semantics*.

[37] See Seeligmann, *Septuagint Version*, 94-121 ('The translation as a document of Jewish-Alexandrian theology').

particularly to salvation from the exile, has often been inserted into the LXX against MT. E.g., Isa 38:11 'I shall not see the Lord, the Lord', has been rendered as 'I shall no more see at all the salvation of God . . .'. Isa 40:5 '(And the glory of the Lord shall be revealed) and all flesh shall see it together' has been rendered as 'and all flesh shall see the salvation of God'.

In many verses the translators added religious colour to secular descriptions. E.g., Isa 5:13 '(Therefore my people go into exile) for want of knowledge . . .' is rendered as '. . . because they do not know the Lord'. This phenomenon is particularly frequent in Proverbs. E.g., Prov 13:15 'Good sense wins favour' is represented by 'sound discretion gives favour, and to know the Law (νόμος) is the part of a sound understanding'. It stands to reason[38] that in this double translation, the free one mentioning νόμος is original, while the literal one was added subsequently.

Although the translators generally felt free to render literally verses or words in which God is portrayed anthropomorphically, in some instances[39] these were avoided. To give a few examples: Num 12:8 'and he beholds the form of the Lord' has been changed in the translation to 'and he beholds the δόξα of the Lord'. Exod 4:24 'the Lord met him' has become 'the angel of the Lord met him'. Exod 24:10 'and they saw the God of Israel' has been changed to 'and they saw the *place* where the God of Israel stood'.

MIDRASH-TYPE EXEGESIS. Many of the translated books contain midrash-type exegesis. Those elements are considered midrashic which deviate from the plain sense of the MT and either reflect exegesis actually attested in rabbinic sources or resemble such exegesis but are not found in any midrashic source. Further study is needed in order to solidify our criteria for the identification of midrash-type exegesis in the LXX[40] and for the distinction between midrashic elements which entered the translation on the Greek level and such elements as were found as variants in Hebrew MSS.

Several midrashic elements in the LXX clarify the Pentateuchal laws. Thus to Exod 22:19 יחרם the LXX added θανάτῳ as in *B.T. Sanhedrin* 60b. To Exod 22:7 'the owner of the house shall come near to God', the translator added 'and shall swear' (cf. *B.T. Bava Kamma* 63b). מלאתך ודמעתך in Exod 22:28 has been explained as 'the first-fruits of your threshing floor and wine-press'.

Other midrashic elements are of haggadic nature. 'The tree' in Isa 65:22 has been explained in the LXX as 'the tree of life'. In Isa 1:13 קרא מקרא 'the calling of the assembly' has been explained as ἡμέραν μεγάλην, i.e. יומא רבא, one of the appelations of the Day of Atonement in the Talmud. חרבות צרים, 'flint knives' in Josh 5:2 has been translated by μαχαίρας πετρίνας ἐκ πέτρας

---

[38] See de Lagarde, *Anmerkungen*, p. 3 (rule III).

[39] Cf. Fritsch, *Anti-anthropomorphisms*.

[40] Cf. Frankel, *Über den Einfluss der palästinischen Exegese*; Prijs, *Jüdische Tradition*; Gooding, *Relics of Ancient Exegesis* and Gooding's earlier articles mentioned there; Tov, 'Midrash-Type Exegesis'.

ἀκροτόμου 'stone knives of flinty rock'; the second element of this doublet reflects a midrashic translation of the Hebrew phrase (cf. Deut 8:15 צוּר(מ) החלמיש, πέτρας ἀκροτόμου).

As a rule, the midrashic deviations of the LXX are not as extensive as those of the Palestinian targumim, but there are some exceptions. Thus the translation of Proverbs is often more a Jewish-Hellenistic midrash to its Hebrew source than a Greek translation.[41] Its translator often changed the imagery of MT, e.g. Prov 13:10 'By insolence the heedless make strife, but with those who take advise is wisdom', LXX: 'A bad man does evil with insolence, but they that are judges of themselves are wise'. Many of the secular descriptions in Proverbs are given a religious colour (e.g. Prov 13:15), and the רשעים and the אוֹלים in this book are often seen as sinners against the Law (ἄνομοι) or against religion (ἀσεβεῖς).

Midrashic changes on a larger scale have been discussed by Gooding who hypothesized that the deviating arrangement of the LXX text in 1 Kings derives from a wish to rearrange the sections of the text in order that it may serve as a proof for Solomon's wisdom.[42] According to Gooding, this translation also reflects a tendency to absolve David, Solomon and Ahab of their sins.

ACTUALIZATIONS. In order that the subject matter of the translation should be understood by the readers, the LXX translators used words and terms taken from daily life in Egypt and also made actualizing changes. E.g., in Isa 9:11 'Aram on the east and the Philistines on the west' has been changed to 'Syria on the east and the Greeks on the west'. In this translation the names of the enemies of Israel in the time of the OT have been changed to conform with the situation existing during the Hellenistic period (for this technique, cf. that of the *pesher* in Qumran). The new enemies are the Hellenistic cities on the shore of the Mediterranean and the Seleucid kingdom in the East. In Isa 46:1 'Bel . . . Nebo', the last name has been changed to Δαγων. Seeligmann ascribes this change to a Hellenistic source which knew Dagon as a Babylonian godhead side by side with Bel.[43] From a similar source the translator possibly also derived the translation of 'Ararat' in Isa 37:38 as 'Armenia'.

The Language of the LXX

HEBRAISMS

The LXX was written in the Hellenistic dialect of the Greek language, named κοινὴ διάλεκτος, i.e. the 'dialect' which was 'in general use' by those who

---

[41] See de Lagarde, *Anmerkungen*; Gerleman, *Studies in the LXX*.
[42] Gooding, 'Problems of Text and Midrash'.
[43] See Seeligmann, *Septuagint Version*, 77.

spoke Greek from the 4th century B.C.E. onwards.[44] Research into the language of the LXX is important for the study of the κοινή, since it forms the largest literary source which has been written in this dialect. However, the study of the language of the LXX as a document of the κοινή is complicated by its linguistic isolation from other witnesses of the κοινή because of its many lexical and syntactic 'Hebraisms'. A Hebraism may be defined as a Greek word, phrase or syntagma which transfers certain characteristic Hebrew elements into Greek in an un-Greek fashion (this phenomenon is a direct result of the technique of stereotyped translation described above).[45]

The phenomenon of 'syntactical Hebraisms' may be demonstrated by the following examples. In classical Greek the verb ὄμνυμι governs the dative, accusative or the preposition πρός. However, because its Hebrew counterpart (נשבע) governs –ב (usually rendered by ἐν), in the LXX the verb generally governs the preposition ἐν. Similarly, the frequent use of καί in places where classical Greek uses the particle δέ resulted from the stereotyped translation of the connective *waw* by καί.

Another type of Hebraism found in the LXX is the so-called 'lexical Hebraism', i.e. the un-Greek use of a Greek word caused by the stereotyped representation of its Hebrew counterpart. It must be realized that these stereotyped renderings do not function as ordinary Greek words possessing Greek meanings, but rather are used by the translators as mere *symbols* representing Hebrew words. This situation is exemplified by a well-known equivalence, namely that of שלום and εἰρήνη. In the LXX, שלום is rendered by εἰρήνη in 178 instances and further by 18 different equivalences all of which occur only once or twice. Conversely, εἰρήνη represents nearly exclusively שלום; εἰρήνη is thus clearly the main equivalent of שלום, often used automatically. The choice of εἰρήνη was natural since the most frequent meanings of שלום, 'peace (from war)' and 'tranquility' are well represented by the most frequent meaning of the Greek word, viz., 'peace from war'. However, not infrequently שלום is also used as 'welfare' and 'health', and these meanings should have been rendered into Greek by words other than εἰρήνη. Nevertheless, the wish for stereotyped representation often led a translator to render such occurrences of שלום also with εἰρήνη. A manifest example is 2 Sam 11:7 . . . (וישאל) ולשלום המלחמה – καὶ ἐπηρώτησεν . . . εἰς εἰρήνην τοῦ πολέμου, 'and he asked . . . how the war prospered'.

---

[44] Grammars and grammatical studies on the language of the LXX are mentioned in Brock-Fritsch-Jellicoe, *Classified Bibliography*, 23-28 and in Tov, *Classified Bibliography of Lexical and Grammatical Studies*. The most extensive grammar of the LXX is Thackeray, *Grammar* (Phonology and morphology only).

[45] Many studies have been written on Hebraisms in the LXX. See especially Helbing on the syntax of the verbs, Johannessohn on prepositions and cases of nouns, Soisalon-Soininen on infinitives, and Sollamo on semiprepositions. Lexical Hebraisms have been studied especially by Gehman in a series of articles, Rapallo, *Calchi ebraici*, Walters, *The Text of the Septuagint*, 155ff. For further studies and bibliographical details, see the bibliographies mentioned in the previous note.

A similar situation obtains with regard to other words in the LXX. υἱός follows בן, even in such combinations as 1 Sam 26:16 בני מות, 'those who deserve to die', literally: 'sons of death' – υἱοὶ θανατώσεως. יד, 'hand' is usually translated by χείρ ('hand' as part of the body), even when the Hebrew word denotes 'monument'. Also phrases characteristic of Hebrew such as . . . גלה את אזן, ('uncover the ear of . . .', i.e. 'reveal to . . .') have been rendered by the standard equivalents of each word (ἀποκαλύπτω τὸ οὖς τινος).

THE CHARACTER OF THE LANGUAGE

Until the end of the 19th century two main opinions existed concerning the nature of the language of the LXX. On the one hand, many scholars asserted that the language of the LXX differed from the other witnesses of the κοινή because the Egyptian Jews spoke a special Greek dialect ('Jüdengriechisch') which contained many elements deriving from the Hebrew language. On the other hand, there were those claiming that the LXX was written in classical Greek. There were even those who claimed that the special character of the language of the LXX derived from its being the language of the 'Holy Spirit'.[46] The investigations of Deissmann[47] brought the controversy to a temporary end. When around the turn of the century Greek papyrus fragments from the Hellenistic period were discovered in Egypt, Deissmann immediately recognized that many words which were previously considered 'Hebraisms' were in fact indigenous to Hellenistic Egypt.[48] It was thus the Hellenistic Egyptian 'couleur locale' which made the language of the LXX appear different from other documents written in κοινή-Greek.

The line of investigation started by Deissmann has been accepted by many scholars,[49] albeit with a major reservation: Even if an isolated parallel to the Hebraism may be spotted in a secular Greek source, the word or element in question should nevertheless be considered a Hebraism if the large frequency of its occurrence is conditioned by Hebrew rather than Greek usage. This is true, e.g., for the many occurrences of καί instead of δέ, of ἰδού (translating הנה), and for εἰς τὸ ὄνομα (translating . . . לשם).

However, beyond the views ascribed above, it must be stressed that the special character of the language of the LXX derived mainly from the translators' close adherence to the source language. The LXX indeed reflects several ele-

---

[46] For a review of the opinions, see especially Vergote, 'Grec Biblique'; Ros, *Studie van het Bijbelgrieksch*. These studies as well as others reflect an almost unavoidable mixture in terminology referring to both the LXX and the NT as 'biblical Greek'.

[47] Deissmann, *Bibelstudien; Neue Bibelstudien*.

[48] E.g., technical terms from the cult, such as παστοφόριον and κώδωνες and from the administration such as διάδοχος and ὑπομνηματογράφος.

[49] See especially Lee, *Lexical Study*. Similar investigations in the field of syntax have been carried out by Thumb (Brock-Fritsch-Jellicoe, *Classified Bibliography*, 23). Especially noteworthy is the dictionary by Moulton-Milligan, *Vocabulary of the Greek Testament*.

ments of the Egyptian branch of the κοινή, but this situation determined the special character of the language of the LXX to a lesser extent than the translation techniques employed.

Revisions of the LXX

GENERAL

A given textual tradition can be considered a revision of the LXX if the following two conditions are met:
a. The LXX and the revision share a common textual basis, established by the existence of distinctive agreements.
b. The supposed revision was revised into a certain direction, generally towards a more precise reflection of its Hebrew source. However, the purpose of some revisions was the clarification and stylistic improvement of the wording of the original translation, without any connection to the Hebrew *Vorlage*.

Scholars have not always paid attention to these two conditions, and consequently the revisional nature of some textual traditions has not been established without doubt.

It would be useful to distinguish between the following three types of revisions (however, this distinction cannot always be made):
a. Textual branches of the LXX into which occasional changes have been inserted.
b. Revisions which have a large basis in common with the LXX.
c. Revisions whose common basis with the LXX cannot always be demonstrated easily (as in the case of the 'Three') and in fact are nearly independent translations.

In the last two decades, older terms (as well as the views behind them) have become extinct, while new terms have been introduced into the scholarly discussion. Thus, with the unraveling of a series of subsequent revisions of the original Greek translation, it has become customary, especially among American scholars, to refer to the oldest recoverable translation as the Old Greek, to be distinguished on the one hand from the term 'LXX' proper (Pentateuch) and on the other from later editorial activity. As for newly discovered revisions, see below. In modern research the term Ur-Theodotion hac become extinct, as has Ur-Lucian, but the latter has been replaced by proto-Lucian, referring to a different entity.

Trying to determine the factors behind the revisions of the LXX, we may point to the following:
a. The translation of the LXX often differed from the Hebrew text as it was established in later times; therefore the LXX 'needed' to be changed in order to confirm with this Hebrew text.

b. Jews felt the necessity to remove 'Christian' elements from the LXX.

c. Evidence suggests that the need was felt to integrate 'Jewish' exegesis in the LXX.

DESCRIPTION OF THE REVISIONS

Revisions have been recognized in various places: papyrus and vellum fragments as well as manuscripts of the LXX, citations from the 'LXX', the substratum of certain textual traditions. In some books revisions are contained in the canon of the 'LXX' itself. The revisions are subdivided into the following three groups: a. Proto-Hexaplaric revisions; b. The Hexapla; c. Post-Hexaplaric revisions.

The Hexapla is the center of this classification because of its paramount importance for the textual history of the LXX.

PROTO-HEXAPLARIC REVISIONS. The revisions of *kaige*-Theodotion, Aquila and Symmachus are referred to in both ancient sources and modern research as the 'Three' (οἱ γ'). The 'Three' were included in the Hexapla (see below), and are often quoted *en bloc* in Hexaplaric MSS. Upon analyzing their readings, one realizes that the 'Three' agree more frequently than one would expect of independent translations. Since, however, the revisions of both Aquila and Symmachus were based upon *kaige*-Theodotion (as has been shown by modern scholarship), the large number of agreements is not at all problematic.

(1) *Kaige-Theodotion*

The discovery of a Greek scroll of the Minor Prophets at *Naḥal Ḥever* (1953) caused its editor Barthélemy,[50] to undertake a thorough investigation of the relationship between the vocabulary of the scroll and other sources. He discovered that the scroll contains an early revision of the LXX, and that a similar revision is found in several additional sources: marginal notes deriving from the sixth column of the Hexapla (attributed to Theodotion), parts of the 'LXX' of Samuel-Kings (2 Sam 11:1 [10:1?]-1 Kgs 2:11; 1 Kgs 21-2 Kgs), the *Quinta* column of the Hexapla, part of the textual tradition of the 'LXX' of Judges, etc. Barthélemy named the anonymous revision 'καίγε' because one of its distinctive features is that the word גם is always translated with καίγε ('at least'), apparently following the rabbinic hermeneutic rule that each גם in the Bible refers not only to the word(s) occurring after it but also to one additional element (one of the 32 hermeneutical rules of R. Eliezer ben Yose ha-Gelili, which is called 'inclusion and exclusion'). In scholarship this anonymous revision is often called the *kaige*-Theodotion revision because it was ascribed in antiquity to Theodotion who allegedly lived at the end of the second century C.E.

The *terminus ad quem* of the revision has been determined by Barthélemy as approximately 50 C.E. (i.e., the palaeographical date of the *Naḥal Ḥever* scroll).

---

[50] Barthélemy, *Les devanciers*.

It is quite possible, though, that the revision was made somewhat earlier, viz. towards the end of the first century B.C.E. This early dating solves a problem which has long preoccupied scholars: Quite unexpectedly, the revision of Theodotion is quoted in several sources which antedate the time of the 'historical' Theodotion.[51] This situation had led scholars to posit a 'proto-Theodotionic' translation from which the quotations derived and on which Theodotion's revision was based. After the 'discovery' of the *kaige*-Theodotionic revision the assumption of a proto-Theodotionic translation (Ur-Theodotion) became superfluous.

Barthélemy's assumption has generally been accepted by scholars. However, there remain many questions, some of which have been the subject of subsequent discussion.[52]

More than other translators, *kaige*-Theodotion aimed at a stereotyped representation of the Hebrew words such as the translation of איש with ἀνήρ ('man'), even when the word appears in the meaning of 'everyone'. He also paid much attention to the etymological structure of the Hebrew words. On the other hand, he invented non-stereotyped translation options in order to avoid two different Hebrew words being rendered by one Greek word. E.g., he translated אני with ἐγώ and אנכי with ἐγώ εἰμι ('I am'), thus creating un-Greek translations such as 2 Sam 12:7 ואנכי הצלתיך – καὶ ἐγώ εἰμι ἐρρυσάμην σε ('And *I am* delivered you').

A special characteristic of Theodotion and the 'LXX' translation of 2 Kgs (which is assigned to the *kaige*-Theodotion revision) is the appearance of many transliterations, especially of words which were presumably unknown to the reviser. In these cases the reviser apparently preferred to transliterate the unknown word[53] rather than to guess at its meaning.

(2) *Aquila*

According to Silverstone, Aquila is identical with the Onkelos who is mentioned in the Talmud (*B.T. Megilla* 3b and elsewhere) as the translator of the Targum of the Pentateuch.[54] However, although the names Aquila and Onkelos are closely related, there is no proof that one person both revised the LXX and translated the Pentateuch into Aramaic. Both translations are exact, but the precision of the Greek translation is much greater than the Aramaic translation.

Aquila prepared his revision approximately 125 C.E. In some books he issued two 'editions', but the relationship between them is not known.

Aquila inherited his approach to Scripture from his teacher Rabbi Akiva. According to the latter's system, every letter in the Bible is meaningful, and

---

[51] The evidence is listed by Schmitt, 'Stammt der sogenannte „ϑ"-Text bei Daniel wirklich von Theodotion?'.

[52] See, i.a. Shenkel, *Chronology and Recensional Development*; O'Connell, *The Theodotionic Revision*; Bodine, *The Greek Text of Judges*; Greenspoon, *Textual Studies*.

[53] Cf. Tov, 'Transliterations of Hebrew words'.

[54] Silverstone, *Aquila and Onkelos*.

therefore Aquila made an attempt to represent precisely and separately all words and particles and even morphemes.[55] For example, he translated the *nota accusativi* (את) separately with σύν and he represented the three elements composing the word למרחוק (2 Kgs 19:25) with three separate words εἰς ἀπὸ μακρόθεν. Aquila, in a manner very similar to *kaige*-Theodotion expressed the etymological structure of the Hebrew words in his translation in an extreme way. E.g., considering (ב)ראשית ('beginning') in Gen 1:1 as a lengthened form of ראש ('head'), he translated it with a derivative of κεφαλή ('head'), viz. κεφάλαιον, even though that Greek word has a different meaning ('main point').

Apparently Aquila made a special effort to replace renditions which had become 'Christian' terms. Thus the translation of משיח (χριστός) was replaced with ἠλειμμένος. Partly because of this, his translation was well-liked among Jews, while avoided by Christians.

(3) Symmachus

Conflicting data have been transmitted concerning Symmachus' biographical details. According to Epiphanius he was a Samaritan who had become a proselyte; according to Eusebius and Jerome, however, he was an Ebionite. Schoeps attempted to prove that Symmachus was an Ebionite by showing that some of his renditions reflect Ebionite views. On the other hand, according to Barthélemy,[56] the biblical translator Symmachus is identical with Rabbi Meir's disciple סומכוס, mentioned in *B. T. Eruvin* 13b. In any event, Symmachus was conversant with many midrashim that are also reflected in rabbinic literature.[57] On the basis of some descriptions from antiquity, Symmachus' revision is usually dated at the end of the second century C.E.

Two tendencies in direct opposition to each other are visible in Symmachus' revision. On the one hand he was very precise (like Aquila, he based his revision on *kaige*-Theodotion), but on the other hand he very often translated *ad sensum* rather than representing the Hebrew words with their stereotyped renderings. These contextual translations of Symmachus were much favoured by Jerome, and therefore he often followed him. Symmachus' translation technique has been described in detail by Busto Saíz.[58]

In addition to the aforementioned revisions, which are rather well evidenced in certain books, several partial revisions are known, none of them well documented. E.g., papyrus Chester-Beatty-Scheide 967 of Ezekiel, *4QLXXNum*,[59] MSS AFM . . . of Exod-Deut,[60] etc.

---

[55] For an analysis of Aquila's translation technique, cf. especially Reider, *Prolegomena*; Hyvärinen, *Übersetzung*.
[56] Barthélemy, 'Qui est Symmaque?'.
[57] See Schoeps, 'Ebionitisches'; 'Mythologisches'; 'Symmachus Studien III'.
[58] Busto Saíz, *La traducción de Símaco*.
[59] See Skehan, '4QLXX^Num'; Wevers, 'An Early Revision'.
[60] See Gooding, *Recensions*.

THE HEXAPLA. The Hexapla is the six column edition of the Hebrew Bible and its Greek versions, prepared by Origen in the middle of the third century C.E., mainly as a basis for discussions between Jews and Christians who needed to know the exact differences between each other's Bibles.

Ancient sources contain some evidence that Origen also issued a Tetrapla, i.e. a separate edition of the third to the sixth column, whose appearance apparently preceded the Hexapla.[61]

Scholars have often wondered about the sequence of the six columns, which, for one thing does not reflect their chronological order. Possibly Origen wanted to supply his readers with an aid for reading and understanding the Hebrew Bible: the first column contains the Hebrew source, a Greek transcription of the Hebrew found in the second column facilitated the reading of the unvocalized first column, the third column (Aquila) provided the meaning of the *words*, the fourth column (Symmachus) explained the *content* and the fifth column provided detailed information about the differences between the LXX and MT.[62] The remaining columns provided additional information; of them only the sixth column is preserved in all books.[63] This column is ascribed to Theodotion, but it contains translations of various sources.

In the beginning of the fourth century the fifth column ('LXX') was published separately by Eusebius and Pamphilius, and it soon dominated the textual transmission of the LXX in Palestine.[64]

The importance of the Hexapla for scholarship lies in its preservation of the 'Three' and in the precise notations of Origen in the fifth column comparing the LXX to the Hebrew Bible. Leaving aside most of the qualitative differences, he focused on quantitative differences (omissions, additions) between the two sources. Thus he denoted with obelus signs ($\div$) elements extant in Greek, but not in Hebrew; and elements extant in Hebrew, but not in the LXX, which were added from one of the other columns (mainly from the sixth) were denoted with an asterisk sign ($*$).[65] These diacritical signs are preserved by a few manusripts which contain the Hexaplaric recension (fifth column). However, recently discovered fragments of the *complete* Hexapla, especially the Psalm fragments published by Cardinal Mercati,[66] show no Hexaplaric signs in the fifth column.

---

[61] For the whole section, cf. especially Barthélemy, 'Origène'.

[62] Cf. especially Emerton, 'Purpose' and previously Orlinsky, 'Some Corruptions'.

[63] Some readings of other columns *(Quinta, Sixta, Septima)* have been transmitted in a few books of the OT.

[64] See the introduction to Jerome's translation of Chronicles: 'Alexandria et Aegyptus in Septuaginta suis Hesychium laudat auctorem, Constantinopolis usque Antiocham Luciani martyris exemplaria probat, mediae inter has provinciae palestinos codices legunt, quos ab Origine elaboratos Eusebius et Pamphilius vulgaverunt, totusque orbis hac inter se trifaria varietate conpugnat'. Though the assumption of a 'trifaria varietas' of LXX MSS was probably correct for the time of Jerome, at present no distinctly Hesychian text type can be isolated (see however, Jellicoe, 'Hesychian Recension').

[65] Cf. especially Soisalon-Soininen, *Der Character*.

[66] Mercati, *Psalterii Hexapli Reliquiae*.

Hence scholars have hypothesized that the original Hexapla did not contain these signs, and that these were inserted subsequently in a separate edition of the fifth column of the Hexapla.

POST-HEXAPLARIC REVISIONS. The most important post-Hexaplaric revision is that of Lucian († 312 C.E.). Lucian's text was rediscovered in the last century when Ceriani, Field and de Lagarde successfully identified the manuscripts containing the Lucianic tradition which is most clearly visible in the historical books (MSS boc$_2$e$_2$ from Ruth 4:11 and onwards). In most books the Lucianic revision clearly elaborates on the Hexapla (e.g., in the Latter Prophets), but in some books it also reflects elements which antedate the time of the historical Lucian and of the Hexapla (Origen). In some books no Lucianic group can be detected at all.[67]

Scholars have always shown a keen interest in the Lucianic tradition because of the opposing tendencies reflected in this text, because of the 'proto-Lucianic' readings, and because of its agreements with Hebrew scrolls recently found at Qumran, especially of Samuel.

At the present state of research, scholars are divided in their opinion on the nature and origin of the Lucianic tradition, especially in the historical books where the problems are most urgent. The four main positions[68] with regard to 1-2 Sam and 1-2 Kgs (1-4 Reigns in the LXX) are summarized here, although it should be stressed that any conclusion reached with regard to these books cannot automatically be applied to other ones.

In this study of 1-2 Kgs,[69] Rahlfs showed how, on the one hand, Lucian brought the Old Greek into conformity with the Hebrew, while, on the other hand, he removed the Old Greek from the MT by freely revising its language and style. Rahlfs further realized, as had a few scholars before him, that Lucian's fourth century revision reflects many ancient, proto-Lucianic, elements which are also found in various sources antedating the historical Lucian by several centuries. Rahlfs' study forms the basis for most descriptions of Lucian in the handbooks on the text of the OT.

A completely novel view of the Lucianic problem was offered in 1963 by Barthélemy[70] who contended that the 'Lucianic' MSS (boc$_2$e$_2$) in 2 Sam 11:2-1 Kgs 2:11 (section 'βγ') comprise the Old Greek translation and that the other MSS, hitherto considered the 'LXX', contain the *kaige*-Theodotion revision). Barthélemy thus turned the relationship between boc$_2$e$_2$ and the other MSS upside down, basing this reversal on a detailed description of the relationship between individual translation options in both traditions. Although Barthélemy did not deal with the problem of the 'Lucianic' MSS in other books, he found

---

[67] For Genesis, see Wevers, *Text History*, 158-75.

[68] See also Muraoka, 'The Greek Text of Samuel-Kings'. For a detailed review of the research, see Van der Kooij, 'De Tekst van Samuel'.

[69] Rahlfs, *Lucians Rezension*.

[70] Barthélemy, *Les devanciers*.

reasons for a complete rejection of the historical evidence relating to the Lucianic revision.

In 1964[71] Cross attacked the issue of the Lucianic problem from a completely different angle. He realized that *4QSam*[a] contains many proto-Lucianic readings, especially in 2 Sam 11:2-1 Kgs 2:11. Retaining the idea that MSS boc_2e_2 contain a revision, Cross now suggested that these MSS are composed of two different layers: a substratum containing a proto-Lucianic revision of the Old Greek towards a Hebrew text like *4QSam*[a], and a second layer consisting of the historical Lucian's corrections.

In 1972[72] Tov claimed that the hitherto published data do not justify the assumption of a proto-Lucianic *revision*. According to his synthesis, the text of boc_2e_2 is composed of two different layers: the second layer contains revisional elements which were presumably superimposed on the first layer in the time of the historical Lucian. Elements of the first layer are evidenced in many pre-Lucianic sources with such a wide geographical range that this substratum probably contained the Old Greek translation, as has been suggested by Barthélemy for the whole of boc_2e_2.

Bibliography

The most detailed *introduction* to the LXX is: SWETE, *An Introduction to the Old Testament*, updated by JELLICOE, *The Septuagint and Modern Study*. The major issues preoccupying LXX research have been reviewed by SEELIGMANN, 'Problemen en perspectieven'; ORLINSKY, 'Current Progress and Problems' in WILLOUGHBY (ed.), *The Study of the Bible*, 144-61; KATZ, 'Septuagint Studies in the Mid-Century' in DAVIES-DAUBE (eds.), *The Basckground to the New Testament and its Eschatology*, 176-208; WEVERS, 'Septuaginta Forschungen'; Ibid., 'Septuaginta Forschungen seit 1954'; HOWARD, 'The Septuagint: A Review of Recent Stdies'; JELLICOE (ed.), *Studies in the Septuagint*; FERNANDEZ MARCOS, 'Los estudios de "Septuaginta". Visión retrospectiva y problemática más reciente'; Idem, *Introducción a las versiones griegas de la Biblia*.

CRITICAL EDITIONS: BROOKE-MCLEANE-THACKERAY, *The Old Testament in Greek*, (diplomatic edition of codex B; not complete); *Vetus Testamentum graecum auctoritate societatis litterarum gottingensis editum* (eclectic edition); RAHLFS, *Septuaginta, Id est Vetus Testamentum graece iuxta LXX interpretes* (eclectic edition, 'Handausgabe' of the Göttingen edition); FIELD, *Origenis Hexaplorum quae supersunt*.

---

[71] Cross, Jr., 'History of the Biblical Text'. See further his 'Evolution of a Theory of Local Texts'. The views of Cross have been further developed in a series of monographs written by his students. On the relation between *4QSam*[a] and the so-called Lucianic MSS, see especially Ulrich, *The Qumran Text*; Tov, 'The Textual Affiliations'; Tov (ed.), *The Hebrew and Greek Texts of Samuel*.

[72] Tov, 'Lucian and proto-Lucian'.

GRAMMAR: THACKERAY, *A Grammar of the Old Testament in Greek.*

LEXICON: SCHLEUSNER, *Novus thesaurus philologico-criticus.*

CONCORDANCE: HATCH-REDPATH, *A Concordance to the Septuagint.*

Selected *bibliography* can be found in the notes of this article. A nearly exhaustive bibliography (1860-1970) is found in BROCK-FRITSCH-JELLICOE, *Classified Bibliography.*

Chapter Six

The Samaritan Targum of the Pentateuch

Abraham Tal

General

The Samaritan Targum of the Pentateuch arose, much like other targumim, as a response to the linguistic changes which took place in Palestine during the last centuries B.C. and the first centuries C.E. The slow but uninterrupted penetration of Aramaic in the western part of the 'fertile crescent' began with the enthroning of the so-called 'Reichsaramäisch' as the official administrative language of the Persian Empire and continued by being adopted, first by educated and privileged upper classes, followed by the middle class of merchants and urban artisans and finally permeated wide circles of the whole population. It is generally agreed that while at the beginning of the Christian Era Hebrew was still in use in Palestine, with Aramaic in symbiotic relationship,[1] by the third century Aramaic had become the principal if not the only language spoken and written in the entire area. It was only natural that such circumstances should give rise to a variety of Aramaic versions of the Holy Script amidst the various communities in Palestine.

Indeed, the community of Qumran used such versions at an early date, only fragments of which resisted the vicissitudes of time and nature conditions. Their early origin is attested by their relatively old Aramaic which is very close to 'Reichsaramäisch'. Nevertheless, even these versions contained developed linguistic forms, forerunners of those which came into common usage in the period known as 'Middle Aramaic'. Similarly, (non-sectarian) Judaism used a targum of nearly the same linguistic age: Onkelos for the Pentateuch and Yonatan for the (former) Prophets.[2] No Samaritan Aramaic targum of this period has been preserved, if one ever existed.

In the course of time, with the expansion of Aramaic and its propagation throughout the entire population of Palestine, new Aramaic versions arose, each reflecting the contemporary stage in the linguistic evolution of Aramaic. It is very likely that towards the middle of the third century the so-called Targum

---

[1] Fitzmyer believes that Palestine was at that time tri-, or even quadrilingual. See his erudite article in 'Languages of Palestine'. Compare also Rabin, 'Hebrew and Aramaic', 1033ff.

[2] Tal, *Former Prophets*, 13-23, 30 (Hebrew section); 213-16.

Yerushalmi[3] arose in the Jewish community. It would appear that the Samaritan community elaborated its own targum at the same time, for its linguistic character is virtually identical to the Jewish version, as far as the oldest type of the Samaritan Targum is concerned (v. infra). Both Jewish and Samaritan targumim represent a younger Aramaic layer, which differs from that of Qumran and Onkelos.[4]

The present state of targumic studies does not provide us with sufficient criteria on which a clear relationship between the various targumim of the Pentateuch can be established. It is difficult to say with certainty that Codex Neofiti 1,[5] the Geniza Fragments [6] and the multitude of recensions of the Fragmentary Targum[7] are variants of the same literary composition, namely the Jewish 'Targum Yerushalmi', although in view of their linguistic similarity and common literary approach, this assumption does indeed seem plausible.[8] The Samaritan Targum presents us with a similar problem. At the present state of documentation no positive answer can be given to the question whether the extant manuscripts of the Samaritan Targum are variants of one basic recension, although many clear indications of filiation relationship between certain manuscripts exist.[9] Nevertheless, there are sufficient reasons to assume that the great diversity of the manuscripts of the Samaritan Targum is a result of a long and continuous process of adaptation to the changing external conditions, both linguistic and literary. In other words, the various types of manuscripts represent stages of linguistic evolution of Samaritan Aramaic on the one hand and literary-theologic development on the other. This metamorphosis of the Samaritan Targum is in the background of the ensuing discussion.

History of the Samaritan Targum.
The Linguistic State of its Extant Manuscripts

Only a few manuscripts of the Samaritan Targum survived the vicissitudes of time. Several factors contributed to their scarcity, the major one being the long chain of persecution inflicted upon the tiny Samaritan communities that existed in the Middle East by their hostile neighbours. The few centres in Damascus,

---

[3] This is the name of the Jewish Palestinian Targum according to Jewish medieval sources. In recent literature it is often called 'Palestinian Targum'.

[4] For the problem of the dating of these targumim, see Tal, 'Stratigraphy', idem. 'Demonstrative Pronoun', idem. 'Infinitive'. See Alexander, below, pp. 242-47.

[5] Recently edited by Díez Macho, Neophyti 1.

[6] Edited by Kahle, Masoreten des Westens. A new edition has been published by Klein, Genizah Manuscripts.

[7] Edited by Ginsburger, Das Fragmententhargum, and recently by Klein, The Fragment-Targums.

[8] The so-called Pseudo-Yonatan is not included in this category, being a compilation of sources, some of them non-targumic. See the footnotes of its editor: Ginsburger, Pseudo-Jonathan, passim. Cf. Tal, Former Prophets, p. 22 (Hebrew section). For a different view, see Le Déaut, Introduction, 94ff. and Alexander below, p. 219; ibid. p. 251 for recent editions of this targum.

[9] Tal, Samaritan Targum, Introduction, 32-37.

Askalon, Gaza, Cairo, etc., gradually disappeared during the course of the last centuries and of all their written treasures only a few manuscripts copied in Damascus have survived and even these owe their survival to the fact that they were sold some time prior to the extinction of the community. Another factor was the diminishing importance which the Samaritans attached to their targum in the last centuries. As Arabic increasingly replaced Aramaic as the vernacular, the targum declined in importance and in the course of the fourteenth century it was removed even from the liturgy.[10] In fact Samaritan scribes did continue to copy targumic manuscripts until the sixteenth century as a traditional activity, but with no intention of meeting any spiritual needs. Since bi- and trilingual manuscripts written in parallel columns (Hebrew, Aramaic and Arabic) and once been in use, scribes continued copying them as though the Aramaic columns were still equal in importance with the two others. Occasionally, the targum was even copied separately.[11] Consequently, the entire amount of extant manuscripts of the Samaritan Targum consists of eight manuscripts, the oldest one being copied in the twelfth century, as far as explicit evidence regarding their age has been preserved.[12] No manuscript copied during the lifetime of Samaritan Aramaic exists. Only one manuscript is complete – the others are, to a larger or smaller extent, in a fragmentary state.

In spite of their state and scarcity, from what has remained valuable information can be elicited regarding the evolution of the targum. At least part of the manuscripts descends from a time when Aramaic was still known by the learned members of the community and used in the liturgical service by the entire community. The scribes of that period, undoubtedly belonging to the learned circles, were reliable agents of transmission so that their work constitutes clear evidence of the character of the Samaritan Targum. The prototypes of their copies originated at various periods of evolution so that the products of their labour reflect those same stages of development of Aramaic in Palestine. However, the remainder of the manuscripts was copied in the period when Aramaic was no longer properly understood. The scribes of that period were strongly influenced by Arabic, their spoken language, on the one hand, and by Hebrew, the language of the Holy Script, on the other. Both penetrated deeply into the copies they made. Moreover, their ignorance of Aramaic gave rise to a plethora of scribal errors which totally distorted the targum they produced.[13]

THE OLDER MANUSCRIPTS

The first of the above-mentioned categories consists of two small groups of

---

[10] *Ibid.*, p. 14, n. 3.
[11] Apparently, the scribal activity was renewed at the end of the nineteenth century, when a number of manuscripts, copies of those of Shechem Synagogue, were produced.
[12] Not all the manuscripts have such evidence.
[13] From the seventeenth century on, such a manuscript became the representative of the Samaritan Targum, being reproduced in the Polyglots of Paris and London successively.

manuscripts. The first one, comprising MSS J, M and N,[14] represents the oldest form of the Samaritan Aramaic as handed down to our generation, their language being very close to Jewish targumic Aramaic.[15] The second, namely MSS C and V,[16] is representative of a developed type of Aramaic, closely related to the later language of the Jewish midrash and (Palestinian) Talmud. A few examples are given below in order to illustrate the differences in the language of these two groups.

THE VOCABULARY. New words, unknown in the epoch to which the first group belongs, appear in the second. They are also frequent in the Samaritan midrash known as *Memar Marka*[17] and in the Samaritan liturgy.[18] As far as non-Samaritan sources are concerned, they are characteristic of the Jewish Aramaic of the Palestinian Talmud and the midrash. Some of them occur in Syropalestinian Aramaic whose literary expression starts in this period as well.

Instead of the older זעור, 'few', 'little', characteristic of the first group, a new form ציבחד appears in the second, e.g. Gen 43:2 ומורו לן ציבעד מזון, 'buy us a little food' (V);[19] Exod 17:4 ציבעד וירגמוני עורי, 'they are almost ready to stone me' (C). ציבחד is common in *Memar Marka*: והוא סליק ציבעד ומשתאם לאחריו, 'and he (Moses) was ascending a little and looking behind himself'[20] and in the liturgy, ואנדיך.בציבעד כל הצריך לעלם, 'and you created in little time all that the world needs'.[21] It is not attested in Palestinian Jewish Aramaic before the talmudic period. It occurs frequently in the Palestinian Talmud, e.g.: מן גו דאינון ציבחד הוא מכוין, 'since they (the first three verses of the Shema) are small in number he prays with devotion' (*P.T.*

---

[14] J – British Library Or. 7562; M – British Library Or. 1442; Trinity College (Cambridge) R 15.56, Leningrad Sam 182; N – Bodley (Oxford) add 8v 29; Leningrad Sam 183. See Tal, *Samaritan Targum*, Introduction, 16.

[15] In the articles mentioned above (note 4) an attempt to differentiate between several layers of Jewish Palestinian Aramaic has been made. In accordance with phonological and morphological criteria a chronological distinction has been made between the Aramaic of the Palestinian Targum and the later Aramaic of Talmud and Midrash.

[16] A. Tal, *Samaritan Targum*, Intr., 16. C = Shechem Synagogue No 6; V = Vatican Cod. Barberini Or 1.

[17] Composed in its major part in the fourth century C.E. It was recently edited by Macdonald, *Memar Marqah*, 1-2 (1963). A new edition, annotated, translated and commentated is being prepared by Z. Ben-Hayyim.

[18] Similar to *Memar Marka*, the most ancient liturgic hymns belong to the fourth century. Both are later than the oldest form of the targum which, according to Ben-Hayyim is the oldest literary composition of the Samaritans: Review of J. Macdonald, *Memar Marqah*, p. 185. Editions of parts of the liturgy have been published *inter alii* by Gesenius, *Carmina Samaritana* (1824); Cowley, *The Samaritan Liturgy* 1-2 (1909); Ben-Hayyim, *Literary and Oral Tradition* 3b (1967).

[19] The guttural consonants have been lost in Samaritan Aramaic as well as in Hebrew. Consequently, the 'guttural' letters are used in writing in an arbitrary manner. See Tal, Samaritan Targum, Intr., 133-46.

[20] Macdonald, *Memar Marqah*, 129.

[21] Ben Hayyim, *Literary and Oral Tradition*, 3b, p. 356.

Shabbat 1, 3a). Similarly, in Syropalestinian עוד ציבחד, 'almost' (Exod 17:4), etc.

תלים[22] is the equivalent of the Hebrew אח, 'brother' in several verses of the second group while in the first the old Aramaic אח persists. E.g. Gen 14:6 לוט תלימה, 'Lot his brother' (c); Exod 4:18 ליד תלימי דבמצרים, 'to my kinsmen in Egypt' (V). תלים is common in *Memar Marka*, e.g.: יוסף עם תלימיו, 'Joseph and his brethren'.[23] It is attested in the Palestinian Targum of Gen 49:5 (according to Codex Neofiti 1 and to the Fragmentary Targum): שמעון ולוי אחין תלימין, 'Simeon and Levi are brethren'. Obviously, a marginal gloss has been absorbed into the text.
gloss has been absorbed into the text.

Another category of lexical differences appears in words occurring in both groups. However, in the latter they differ in meaning as a result of semantic changes that took place during their use in living speech; a narrow semantic area became broad, an abstract noun became concrete and so on. Obviously, such changes are the products of the evolution of Aramaic over the generations that passed between the two periods. The same, or parallel, changes in meaning occurred in the adjacent Aramaic dialects in Palestine.

The verb קרא has a twofold meaning in old(er) Aramaic:
1) 'to summon', as in *Genesis Apocryphon* 20:26 וקרא לי אליו, 'and he summoned me to him';[24]
2) 'to name', see the *Wisdom of Ahikar* 117: אריה [לא אי]תי בימא, על כן יקראון לקפא לבא 'there is no lion in the sea therefore they call the קפא lion' (?).[25]

In the sources of old(er) Aramaic זעק has the sense 'to cry', cf. Dan 6:21 בקל עציב זעק, 'he cried with a sad voice'. Samaritan Aramaic as represented by the first group of manuscripts differentiates between these two meanings. קרא is used in thes sense 'to name', e.g. Exod 2:10 וקרת ית שמה משה, 'she named him Moses' (J), whereas 'to summon' is attributed to זעק, Exod 1:18 וזעק פרעה למילדאתה ואמר לין, 'Pharaoh called the midwives and said to them' (J). צווח translates the Hebrew צעק, Gen 27:34 ויצבע צבעה, 'he cried out' (J). This distinction is occasionally ignored in the second group where the verb זעק occurs in both senses, cf. Exod 17:15 ובנה משה מדבח וזעק שמה ה' נצועה, 'Moses built an altar and called the name of it God is victorious' (V). The new sense of זעק occurs in *Memar Marka* as well: זעק יתן בנים בכורים, 'he named us firstlings',[26] etc. A parallel evolution took place in Jewish Aramaic. קרא had formerly both senses, as in the Palestinian Targum (according to Codex Neofiti 1): וקרא לרחל וללאה לאפי ברא, 'and he called Rachel and Lea into the field' (Gen 31:4); קרא שמיה

---

[22] This is an Akkadian loan: *talīmu*. Von Soden, *Akkadisches Handwörterbuch*, 1310a.

[23] Macdonald, *Memar Marqah*, 144.

[24] Avigad-Yadin, *A Genesis Apocryphon*, 44.

[25] Cowley, *Aramaic Papyri*, 216.

[26] Macdonald, *Memar Marqah*, 136.

גלעד, 'he named it Galeed' (Gen 31:48). צווח means in these texts 'to cry': וצווחית בקל רם, 'and I cried out loudly' (Gen 39:14). However, in talmudic and midrashic Aramaic צווח replaced קרא in its second sense: בערביא צווחין לתרנגלא סכויא, 'in Arabia a cock is named SAKOYA'.[27]

A distinction is made in the first group between אבן, 'stone', and כיף, 'rock'. Cf. Gen 28:11 ונסב מן אבני אתרה, 'and he took one of the stones of the place' (J), vs. Num 20:8 ותמללון עם כיפה, 'speak to the rock' (J), etc. This distinction has been partially abandoned by the second group which sporadically adopted כיף for 'stone' as well, Exod 7:19 ובקצמיה ובכיפיה, 'in vessels of wood and in vessels of stone' (CV); Deut 4:28 עובד אדי אנש קיצם וכיף, 'the work of men's hands, wood and stone' (C). In Jewish Aramaic the same expansion in the use of כיף occurs. In older sources, such as Onkelos, the distinction is maintained. Thus Onkelos has in the above mentioned verses: ותמללון עם כיפא ; ונסיב מן אבני אתרא respectively. Similarly, the Targum of Job from Qumran has אבן for 'stone' (38:6; 41:16) and כפא for rock (39:1). In later sources, however, כיף occurs in the sense of 'stone', cf. *P.T. Avoda Zara* 4, 43d בחיין דאת מרים אילין כיפיא, 'please remove these stones'. The same is true with respect to Syropalestinian Aramaic where כיף means 'stone', Exod 15:5 נחתו לעומקא הין כל מא דכיפא, 'they went down into the depths like a stone'.

GRAMMATICAL FEATURES. The 1st person plural of the pronoun prevalent in the first group is אנחנן, a developed form of the old Aramaic אנחנא attested by Onkelos and the documents of Qumran.[28] It was produced by the nazalization of the final vowel.[29] In several verses MS v which belongs to the second group has אנן, e.g. Gen 42:21 חיבין אנן, 'we are guilty'. This pronoun is already found in the Palestinian Targum, cf. Num 20:4 (according to Codex Neofiti 1): אנן ובעירין, 'we and our cattle', and in Syropalestinian Aramaic, Gen 19:13 לבדיל דאנן מיבדין אתרא הדן, 'for we are about to destroy this place'.

The demonstrative pronouns (possibly pointing at distant objects) that prevailed in the pre-talmudic period in Palestinian Aramaic, ההוא, 'that' (masc.), ההיא, 'that' (fem.), האנון, 'those' (masc. pl.), האנין, 'those' (fem. pl.), are the only ones to be found in the first group of manuscripts. The second group presents several cases of a new series of demonstrative pronouns constructed by means of the *nota accusativi* ית, Lev 22:30 ביתה יומה, 'on that day' (C); Gen 48:20 ביתה יומה (V). *Memar Marka* is very rich in this pronoun: דחלו ביתה יומה, 'they feared that day'.[30] The use of ית with pronominal suffixes to denote demonstratives is common in talmudic and midrashic literature, as in *P.T. Bikkurim*, 3, 65d אמר יתיה דמן רבנן, 'that (man) of the Rabbis said';

---

[27] Cf. *Lev. Rabba* 25:5, p. 575.

[28] Cf. the older Syriac אנחנן as compared to the younger חנן.

[29] A process that developed further in the talmudic period, when all the final long vowels became nasalized. See the first article mentioned above, note 4.

[30] Macdonald, *Memar Marqah*, 11.

Genesis Rabba 56:5, p. 600 כפתייה יתהון יתשתרון איש, 'let those tied to be released'. It also occurs in Syropalestinian Aramaic, Isa 25:9 ביתה יומה, 'on that day'.

The verb יהב, 'to give', is defective in 'classical' Aramaic. Up to the talmudic period only its perfect יְהַב, participle יָהֵב and imperative הַב existed. In the remaining verbal forms it was supplemented by the verb נתן : יִתֵּן – imperfect; לְמִתֵּן – infinitive. This is the case with the manuscripts of the first group as well. However, in the manuscripts of the second group traces of a new development are detectable, namely, יהב expanded its territory to encompass the imperfect and infinitive area. Cf. Gen 47:24 ותהבון חמושה לפרעה, 'you shall give a fifth to Pharaoh' (C); Exod 32:13 דאמרת אהב (!) וכל ארעה הדן לזרעכון, 'and all this land that I have promised will I give to your descendants' (V). These new forms are very common in talmudic and midrashic Aramaic, e.g. *P.T. Berakhot* 4, 7b תיהב לי גולתי, 'you will give me my cloak'; *P.T. Kilayim* 9, 32b/c מאן בעי מיהב ליה, 'who wants to give him', etc. Similarly, in Syropalestinian Aramaic, Joel 2:10 ומרא ... יחשכון ושמשא וזהרא יהב קלה, 'the sun and the moon are (literally: will be) darkened . . . and the Lord utters (lit.: will give) his voice'.

These late words and grammatical forms did not replace the previous ones. They are few in number and there are rarely more than two occurrences of each in any given manuscript of the second group, where the older forms actually dominate. Consequently, it may be inferred that the prototypes of the manuscripts in question originated in the same period as those belonging to the first group. However, in the course of their transmission, the scribes who copied them were not always meticulous enough to avoid the influence of the more developed Aramaic spoken in their times, which therefore occasionally penetrated into their copies. This is particularly true of the talmudic period. On the other hand, it is possible that these linguistic innovations were introduced intentionally in order to adapt the targum to the contemporary linguistic conditions (in the same way as later copyists adapted the younger manuscripts discussed below). In this case, however, there is no satisfactory explanation as to why they realized their intentions on so few occasions. Nevertheless, it is the presence of these novelties which establishes the younger age of this group.

THE LATER MANUSCRIPTS

The group of manuscripts consisting of MSS A, B and E[31] belongs to a much more recent period. They were copied during the fifteenth and sixteenth centuries when, due to the domination of Arabic, Aramaic lost its position among the Samaritans and became extinct. A new language, used exclusively for literary purposes, arose in the fourteenth century. This somewhat artificial

---

[31] A – Shechem Synagogue No. 3; B – Shechem Synagogue No. 4; E – Vat. Cod. Sam No. 2; Cf. Tal, *Samaritan Targum*, Intr. 16.

language, a blend of Aramaic and Hebrew strongly influenced by Arabic, became the 'official' language of the Samaritan community, and many liturgical poems were composed in it, as well as considerable parts of *Memar Marka*.[32] Furthermore, as it was fashionable at the times when the manuscripts of this group were copied, it had a considerable influence on their scribes, who made visible efforts to adapt the targum they copied to the new linguistic standards. The language they produced was basically Aramaic with a great number of Hebrew borrowed grammatical patterns. Several examples of those patterns, occurring in the late manuscripts of the targum are given below.

1. The second and the third person plural of the imperfect of the verb lack the common Aramaic final *nun*: Exod 12:4 תמנו, 'you shall count' (AB); Exod 16:5 ויכבנו, 'they shall prepare' (A); Exod 23:11 וייכלו, 'they shall eat' (E), etc.

2. A *waw* was appended to the second and the third person plural of the imperfect of the verb הוה, 'to be'; Exod 19:5 תהוונו, 'you shall be' (AB); Gen 48:6 וידהונו 'they shall be' (E), etc.

3. Several verbs *primae nun* act as bi-radicals. This peculiarity is found in A alone, cf. Gen 25:26 ובתר כן פק תלימה, 'afterwards his brother came forth (= נפק)'; Gen 43:24 ותן כסה לחמורידהון, 'and (he) gave provender to their asses' (= ונתן), etc.

4. The first person singular suffix of the perfect תי־ frequently replaces the Aramaic ת־, cf. Gen 21:30 חפסתי, 'I dug' (A); Gen 21:23 עבדתי, 'I have done' (B); Gen 30:27 נסתי, 'I have learned by divination' (E).[33] Such forms occur in the late liturgy as well.[34]

Among the innovations of non-Hebrew origin two are worth mentioning:

1. A new plural of the noun פם, 'mouth', arose: פממין. E.g. Num 32:34 מפממיכון, 'from your mouth' (A);[35] Deut 31:19 פממידהון, 'their mouth' (E).

2. The *resh* of the singular בר, 'son', was generalized to replace the *nun* of the plural. Consequently, the forms ברין, ברי־, etc., appeared frequently instead of the old forms בנין, בני־, cf. Gen 5:26 ברין וברן, 'sons and daughters' (A); Exod 16:1 ברי ישראל, 'the sons of Israel' (BE).

Those late grammatical phenomena, products of the deterioration of the structure of Aramaic which took place from the fourteenth century on, should not distract one's attention from the effects of the natural linguistic evolution that

---

[32] It is described by Ben-Ḥayyim in 'Liturgical Poems', 333-36 and recently in *Literary and Oral Tradition*, 3b. See especially pp. 11, 27, 71, 108. See also Cowley, *Samaritan Liturgy*, XXXIV.

[33] Although תי־ as the suffix of the 1st person of the perfect is regular in the Aramaic of Onkelos, it is however restricted to the verbs *tertiae yod*.

[34] Ben-Ḥayyim, *Literary and Oral Tradition* 3b, 296. Cf. the editor's note.

[35] This is a good example of the scribe's work of adaptation, for the whole part of A, from Num 30 on, is a faithful copy of J. Yet, J has מפמכון in this verse. Regarding the nature and age of A see Tal, *Samaritan Targum*, Introduction, 22ff.

originated in the talmudic period, and of which there are copious examples in the manuscripts of the third group.

Consequently, אנן as the first person plural pronoun, the demonstrative ־ית, the imperfect and the infinitive of the verb יהב are far more abundant in the third group than in the second. These grammatical markers point to the fact that the manuscripts of this group were copied from prototypes whose final redaction took place in the period of living speech.

The vocabulary in the manuscripts of the third group provides clear evidence of their more recent vintage. Firstly, the innovations of the talmudic period discussed above occur much more frequently in this group. Accordingly, ציבחד, תלים are very common in A, E and (less no) in B. Secondly, other words which arose in the same period occur, attesting to their linguistic background. A small selection is given below.

The verb חזה, 'to see', prevalent in the Old Aramaic and *Reichsaramäisch*, continued its existence during the first centuries C.E., as attested by Qumran Aramaic and Onkelos. Later, it was superseded by חמה, first in the Palestinian Targum, then in the talmudic and midrashic literature.[36] It is also dominant in Syropalestinian Aramaic. Its first appearance in Samaritan Aramaic is in this group of manuscripts,[37] cf. Exod 2:6 ועמת ית ילידה, 'she saw the child' (A); Exod 33:10 ויחמון כל עמה, 'all the people saw' (B); Deut 32:36 כד יעמי אן אזלת יד, 'when he sees that their power is gone' (E), etc. חמה is also used frequently in *Memar Marka*, e.g.: לא עמיתון מיום דנפקת מן אקרון, 'I have not seen them since I left them',[38] and in the liturgy, ועמין למאורה סלק, 'they saw the ligt rising'.[39]

פסקול renders ברית, 'covenant', instead of the common Aramaic קיאם in many verses. E.g. Exod 2:24 ודכר אלהה ית פסקוליה עם אברהם, 'God remembered his covenant with Abraham' (A); Deut 31:16 ויבטלו ית פסקולי, 'they will break my covenant' (E). פסקול is also frequent in *Memar Marka*: דלה תלתה פסקולין, '(Israel) has three covenants'.[40] The verb פסקל is found *P.T. Pea* 1, 15c (according to MS Leyden):[41] עמיה במאה דינר ופסקלוניה, 'they agreed with him (to pay) hundred denarii'. Similarly in Syropalestinian Aramaic: פסקל עם פעליא, 'after agreeing with the labourer' (Matt 20:2).[42]

The change in meaning of אבן, כיף, etc, which took place during the talmudic period, is much more evident in the third group than in the second. Moreover, the list of words of changed meaning is much larger in this group.

---

[36] Tal, *Former Prophets*, 199, n. 24.

[37] In this respect, as in the case of אנחנן, the first group of manuscripts attests to a somewhat older stage of Aramaic than the Palestinian Targum.

[38] Macdonald, *Memar Marqah*, 10.

[39] Ben-Ḥayyim, *Literary and Oral Tradition*, 3b, 56.

[40] Macdonald, *Memar Marqah*, 6.

[41] Lieberman, *Greek in Jewish Palestine*, 176.

[42] Smith-Lewis and Dunlop-Gibson, *The Palestinian Syriac Lectionary*, 276.

For example, all of them have נוף as a translation of זרע in the sense of human offspring, such as Gen 15:3 הן לי לא יהבת נוף, 'behold thou hast given me no offspring' (A); Exod 32:13 סגוי אסגי ית נופכון, 'I will multiply your descendants' (B); Deut 31:21 לא תתנשי מפם נופה, 'for it shall not be forgotten out of the mouth of their descendants' (E).

Moreover, many words are employed with a deteriorated meaning in this group due to the ignorance of Aramaic which is characteristic of this period. A small selection of examples is given below.

Biblical Hebrew makes no distinction between the two senses of the verb שלח: 'to send' and 'to extend'. Only in later parts of the Bible does one find: לבד מאשר יושיט לו המלך את שרביט הזהב, 'except the one to whom the king holds out the golden scepter' (Esther 4:11). The verb הושיט is frequent in post biblical literature where it signifies 'to extend' (occasionally with the complement ידו), c.f. T. Demai 2:24 לא יושיט אדם כוס יין לנזיר, 'one should not extend a glass of wine to a Nazirite'. This verb is very frequent in Jewish Aramaic with the same peculiar meaning, as in Onkelos to Gen 22:10 ואושט אברהם ית ידיה ונסיב ית סכינא, 'then Abraham put forth his hand and took the knife' which translates: וישלח אברהם את ידו ... . Any other שלח of the Hebrew text is translated as שלח. This distinction between שלח and אושט is present in the first and the second group, but not in the third, ואושט occurring with the sense of 'to send' as well. See Gen 27:42 ואושטת וזעקת ליעקב, 'she sent and called Jacob' (A); Gen 45:5 הלא לשארות אושטני ה', 'for God sent me (to Egypt) to preserve life' (A).

לחם has two meanings in biblical Hebrew, the first refers to food in general and the second to baked dough. Both senses are rendered by ancient targumim as לחם, e.g. Onkelos to Gen 47:12 וזן יוסף ית אבוהי לחמא, 'Joseph provided his father ... with food', vs. Gen 18:5 ואיסב פתא דלחמא וסעודו לבכון, 'I will fetch a morsel of bread, that you may refresh yourselves'. Similarly, the Targum of Job from Qumran uses לחם in its general meaning: ואכלו עמה לחם בביתה, 'they ate with him bread in his house' (42:11). This is true for the manuscripts of the first two classes which use לחם in the same manner, although in several verses מזון appears with the meaning of 'food', when the Hebrew text has אכל לחם, e.g. J in Gen 42:10 עבדיך אתו לממור מזון, 'your servants come to buy food'.[43] It seems that over the years מזון replaced לחם in this sense, while the latter was restricted to mean 'bread' only. Cf. the Fragmentary Targum of Gen 3:19 בזיעת (!) אפך תאכל מזון, 'in the sweat of your face you shall eat food' (the Hebrew text has לחם). However, in the manuscripts of the third group this differentiation has been nullified by the expansion of מזון to the sense of 'baked dough', as in Exod 29:23 וככר לחם אחת, 'and one loaf of bread', is translated as ודחפין מזון חד (A); Lev 7:13 חלת לחם חמץ, 'loaf of leavened bread', as חלת מזון חמי (A); Exod 29:23 ככר לחם, 'a loaf of bread', as ככר מזון (B), etc.

---

[43] מזון occurs twice in Onkelos in this sense. Deut 10:18 מזון וכסו, 'food and clothing'; Deut 24:6 מזון לכל נפש, 'food for every soul'.

Another characteristic of the late group of manuscripts is the large measure of Arabic elements in their text. Although almost every manuscript suffers from accidental encroachements of the scribe's spoken language,[44] members of the first two groups contain few instances of Arabic. Manuscripts of the third group, however, contain considerable numbers of Arabic words and arabisms. MS A is outstanding in this respect, with more than 120 Arabic words,[45] e.g.: אללה, 'God' – اللّٰه (Gen 5:1, Exod 7:1); גרם, 'offense' – جرم (Gen 31:36; Exod 22:8); עגין, 'cake' – خبين (Num 15:20), etc. MSS B and E abound in Arabic words as well: כרים, 'generous' – كريم (Exod 35:22) – B); פוסטטה, 'his tent' – فسطاط (Exod 35:11 – B); חרבה, 'war' – حرب (Exod 13:17 – E); עקור, 'wine' – عقار (Deut 32:14 – E) Arabisms produced by minor changes in the letters of words are quite numerous in these manuscripts, e.g.: חמס, 'five' – خمس, instead of חמש חמש (Gen 7:20 – A), etc.

RÉSUMÉ

Thus far we have discussed the history of the text of the Samaritan Targum as reflected by its linguistic patterns. The manuscripts that survived to the present day can be divided linguistically into three groups representing three periods. The first contains manuscripts that reflect the period of the beginning of the Aramaic expression of Samaritan literary activity. This language bears a close resemblance to that of the Palestinian Jewish targum(im) and is in certain respects even older than it. The second parallels the talmudic and midrashic era, by which time Aramaic had evolved still further and left traces on the manuscripts originating at that time. The third group reflects the period of Arabic domination, when Aramaic was largely forgotten and a new 'Samaritan' arose, formed out of Aramaic and Hebrew with strong Arabic traces. To a large extent scribes of that period adapted the targum they copied to this contemporary 'literary' language.[46]

The dynamic character of the Samaritan Targum can therefore be detected. Indeed, the scribes of the Samaritan community never considered the targum immune from external influences, and therefore never refrained from 'modernizing' the text they copied. We refer especially to the later scribes whose intervention is largely visible. However, the work of adaptation by the scribes, who were part of the learned members of the community and sometimes

---

[44] J, the oldest manuscript, has an entire passage accidentally copied from the parallel Arabic column into the Aramaic one: Lev 17:13-14.

[45] Some scholars attribute many items of its vocabulary to Arabic. See Kohn, *Samaritanische Studien, passim*; Kohn, *Zur Sprache, passim*.

[46] For a detailed exposé of the language of the Samaritan Targum see Tal, *Samaritan Targum*, Introduction, 52ff.

descended from priestly families, is by no means restricted to the linguistic level, for in fact they also very often expressed the theological views of their times by introducing (small) changes into the text of teh targum.

The Hermeneutical Character of the Samaritan Targum

Compared to the Jewish targumim, which are very often paraphrastic, the Samaritan Targum appears to be a word-for-word translation. Rabbi Yehuda's dictum המתרגם פסוק כצורתו הרי זה בדאי, 'he who translates a verse literally is a liar' (for he misrepresents its real sense),[47] was taken into consideration with relative seriousness by Onkelos and therefore, its departures from the text of the Pentateuch are relatively rare, occurring mainly in cases where traditional interpretation requires small paraphrastic additions or alterations. The Palestinian Targum on the other hand did not see itself bound by any degree of restriction and very often included in its translation many midrashic augmentation, whether crucial to the proper understanding of the passage or not.[48] Finally, Pseudo-Yonatan, which is even more 'developed', resembled a collection of aggadic and even halakhic traditions, much of which existed in the commonly known rabbinic sources.[49]

LITERALNESS

The Samaritan Targum differs from any of the Jewish targumim in that its translation procedures are in (incidental?) accordance with the second half of Rabbi Yehuda's dictum: והמוסיף הרי זה מגדף, 'and he who adds is a blasphemer'. Indeed, its correspondence to the Hebrew original is so great, that scholars have often formulated grave accusations concerning its so called 'slavish' devotion to the Hebrew text. 'Bekannt ist, dass alle samaritanischen Übersetzer sich sklavisch an den Text des samaritanisch-hebräischen Pentateuchs gehalten haben', claimed P. Kahle in his doctoral dissertation,[50] following S. Kohn's statement: 'Das sam. Targum ist eine wörtliche, am Buchstaben klebende Uebersetzung, welche den sam.-hebräischen Bibeltext mit sklavischer Treue, aber gedankenlos und unverständig und mit mangelhafter Kenntniss des Hebräischen wiedergibt'.[51] Both are in line with J.W. Nutt's words: 'It is minutely literal . . . falling occasionally into the most grotesque blunders . . .'.[52]

---

[47]   T. Megilla 4(3):41.
[48]   See for example the large midrash included in Codex Neofiti 1 and the Fragmentary Targum to Gen 15:1.
[49]   From which they sometimes seem to be quoted. See above, n. 8.
[50]   Kahle, Textkritische und lexicalische Bemerkungen, p. 7f.
[51]   Kohn 'Samaritanische Pentateuchübersetzung', 686.
[52]   Nutt, Fragments of a Samaritan Targum, 110ff.

However, the 'slavish' literalness often produced only what appear to be 'grotesque blunders' for on closer examination one can discern subtle midrashic interpretations beyond the apparently mechanical translations. Thus, in Gen 41:2 ותרעינה באחו, 'they feed in the reed grass', is translated by J as ורעיניין בתלימו. תלים equals אח, 'brother' *(v. supra)* in Aramaic; apparently, the targum has misunderstood the vocable אחו, 'reed grass' and, ascribing it to אח, created a 'grotesque blunder', תלימו, which imitates the Hebrew model attaching a final *waw* to תלים.[53] On closer examination, the echo of a midrash can be detected, as the one formulated in *Genesis Rabba* 99:4 (p. 1090-91) באחו . . . בשעה שהשנים יפות הבריות נעשים אחים אילו לאילו (91 אהבה ואחווה בעולם - , 'when years are prosperous, people fraternize . . . באחו – love and fraternity reside in the world'. Consequently, the final *waw* is not an imitation of the Hebrew original but the well-known termination of the Aramaic *nomina abstracta* transforming תלים, 'brother', into תלימו, according to the midrashic interpretation of אחו. This kind of 'concealed' midrash is quite frequent in the various manuscripts of the Samaritan Targum. Another example of misunderstanding of the Samaritan 'literal' approach to the Hebrew text is the targum of Exod 20:22 (MT 20:26) ולא תסק בשקרין על ולא תעלה נמעלות על מזבחי דלא תגלה ערות עליו which translates מדבחי אשר לא תגלה ערות עליו, 'and you shall not go up by steps to my altar that your nakedness be not exposed on it'. The targum renders במעלות, 'by steps', as בשקרין, 'in fraud', which led S. Kohn to assume that 'eine der gewönlichen Uebersetzungssünden' occurs.[54] The ancient legislator was indeed concerned with decency at an epoch when men wore long gowns, and underwear had not yet been popularized.[55] Onkelos (20:23) followed him faithfully: ולא תסק בדרגין (דרג = step). The Samaritan Targum, however, even in its oldest version, could no longer see the necessity of such an admonition (it seems that men's fashion had changed by its time) and gave it a wider interpretation. By including the *mem* of במעלות into the root (originally עלי), the word מעל, 'fraud', was created whose plural is מעלות. Thus a moral imperative was obtained: 'you shall not go up to my altar with fraud (in your heart)'. This interpretation does not contradict the traditional reading of the Hebrew text of the Samaritan Pentateuch, since *bāmālot* fits both senses. Moreover, the following ערותך does not preclude such interpretation, since ערוה has also an abstract sense. Cf. Deut 24:1 . . . כי יקח איש אשה . . . והיה אם לא תמצא חן בעיניו כי מצא בה ערות דבר . . ., 'when a man has taken a wife . . . if then she finds no favour in his eyes because he has found some undecency in her'.[56] However, a late scribe of the Samaritan Targum substituted the ambiguous ערותך by a more precise גנותך, 'your disgrace' (A), in

[53] Geiger, 'Neue Mittheilungen', 732.
[54] Kohn, 'Samaritanische Pentateuchübersetzung', 665 n. 2.
[55] Moses was commanded to make a special wardrobe for the priests. See Exod 28:42.
[56] 'La Sainte Bible' translates *ad sensu*: 'et il a découvert une tare à lui imputer'.

accordance with the above mentioned verse where עֶרְוָה has the abstract sense of 'disgrace' and the targum invariably uses גנו.[57] Therefore בשקרין is not a result of a confusion of two different Hebrew roots. In fact the scribe played the role of the adaptor, as he did elsewhere.

Nevertheless, the Samaritan Targum does have a literal character, in the sense that it is based on the rule of word-for-word translation, i.e. the targum has only one Aramaic word for each Hebrew word of the Pentateuch. Only rarely does a scribe deviate from this rule by adding a word to the 'literal' translation in order to express an exegetic idea. Cf. Exod 15:27 ויבאו אלימה ושם שתים עשרה עינת מים ושבעים תמרים, 'they came to Elim where there were twelve springs of water and seventy palm trees'. The verse poses a problem: how was it possible that a place, so abundant in water could support seventy palm trees only? MSS V adds one word: ‎עים גוני תומרים ושב‎, i.e. 'and seventy sorts of palm trees', which appears far more plausible.[58]

However, the hermeneutical aspect of the Samaritan Targum varies greatly from manuscript to manuscript. The younger a manuscript is, the more paraphrastic it is. J which, as we have seen above, represents the oldest stage of the Samaritan Targum as far as its language is concerned, is the poorest manuscript with respect to paraphrastic translations, whereas A, which represents the youngest targumic manifestation abounds in such material. Yet a coherent division of the manuscripts based on their interpretative activity compared to their age cannot be made for, as in the case of linguistic innovation (discussed above), the intervention of the scribes at various stages of transmission of the targum was quite inconsistent. However young a manuscript is, if its scribe was faithful to his model, the measure of adaptation of the text to the changing theological views of the Samaritan society was very small (as is the case of MS E which is in its greater part a copy of a manuscript of the type of the old MS C). On the contrary, an older manuscript can exhibit a large amount of hermeneutic interpretations, if its scribe was open to the current religious inclinations of his time and took the liberty to intervene in the text he produced (as is the case of MS V). In spite of this inconsistency, the distinction between the groups of manuscripts, as established above, is valid for the present domain as well.

TRANSLATION OF ANTHROPOMORPHIC EXPRESSIONS

The difference in approach is best illustrated in cases in which anthropomorphic and anthropopathic descriptions of God and His deeds appear in the Hebrew text. והייתם כאלהים, 'and you will be like God' in Gen 3:5 is rendered in MS

---

[57] The Karaite Ben Zuṭa Abu Al-Surri explained the passage of Exod 20:22 in the same way and was the subject of a scathing attack by Ibn-Ezra.

[58] This verse produced the same perplexity amongst Jewish circles, for the *Mekhilta de-R. Shimon bar Yohai, Beshallah* 15, p. 105 says: שהרי ... מגיד שהיה אותו מקום מקולקל היו שם שנים עשר מבועים ולא סיפקו אלא שבעים דקלים, 'it says that the place was damned . . . for there were twelve springs in it which supplied water for seventy palm trees only'.

A as ותהונו כמלאכיה, i.e. as angels. Similarly, in Gen 5:1 בדמות אלהים, 'in the likeness of God' is rendered as בתשבית מלאכיה. כי לקח אתו אלהים, 'for God took him' (Gen 5:24) as הלא נסבתה מלאכיה; בני האלהים, 'the sons of God' (Gen 6:2, 4) as ברי שלטניה, 'the sons of the rulers'; בצלם אלהים, 'in the image of God' (Gen 9:6) as בצורת מלאכיה. MS J makes no attempt to deface this rough personification of God and uses אלהים in all these instances. There is little doubt that A's scribe was influenced in these cases by the Arabic Versions of the Pentateuch, the oldest of which probably dates to the eleventh century,[59] which renders אלהים in these verses as אלסלאטין, מלאך אללה, respectively. In Exod 8:15 אצבע אלהים הוא, 'this is the finger of God', is rendered in MS A as יכלתה דאללה, i.e. 'the potence of God', with which MS V is in line: יכלות אלהים, both of them in accordance with some of the Arabic Versions: קדרת אללה.[60] In the same way, 'ימינך ה, 'thy right hand, O Lord' (Exod 15:6) is rendered by MS A as יכלתך.[61] The older manuscripts have ימינך, אצבע, respectively. MS A however, is not consistent in avoiding the personification of God. ושכתי כפי עליך . . . והסירותי את כפי, 'I will cover you with my hand . . . and I will take away my hand . . .' (Exod 33:22, 23), is rendered כפי by all the manuscripts, except B which has ואטלל בטללי in the first case and ואסטי עני in the second (i.e. 'I will throw my shadow . . . I will take away my cloud').[62] Similarly, MS A translates 'ה וירד, and the LORD descended', as ונחת (Exod 34:5); 'ויעבר ה, 'and the LORD passed', as וגע (ibid., v. 6) as do all the other manuscripts. V alone tries to avoid the personification: 'וגע מלאך ה, 'ונעת מלאך ה, respectively, according to its Arabic column: ואנחדר מלאך אללה, ועכר מלאך אללה.

However, circumlocutions do exist in the old manuscripts. They translate anthropomorphic expressions in the Hebrew text in cases where their metaphoric character is obvious. Gen 17:1 where God says to Abraham: התהלך לפני והיה תמים, 'walk before me and be perfect', is rendered by MS J as התהלך לרחותי, 'walk in accordance with my desire'. It is not avoidance of anthropomorphism that determined this translation; it is rather the somewhat uncalled metaphor, to the translator's (or scribe's) taste. After all, men, even the righteous, do not walk *before* God; they act according to His moral requirements. Similarly, in Gen 48:15 האלהים אשר התהלכו אבותי לפניו, 'God before whom my fathers walked', is rendered by MS J as לרעותה. In Exod 33:14, 15 פני ילכו והנחתי לך ויאמר אליו אם אין פניך הלכים אל תעלנו מזה, 'My presence (lit. My face) will go (with you) and I will give you rest. And he said unto him, if Thy presence (lit.: face) will not go (with us) do not carry us up hence', is rendered רעותך, רעותי, respectively, not only by J

---

[59] The latest was compiled by Abu Sa'īd in the thirteenth century. For a detailed survey of the Arabic versions of the Samaritans see Sheḥade, *The Arabic Translation*.

[60] Cf. قدرة , 'power', 'ability'.

[61] The Arabic versions have קדרתך.

[62] In accordance with the Arabic versions. Cf. the Arabic column of MS V: ואטלל בעמאמי . . . . ואזיל עמאמי

but by all the manuscripts (except C which has in the first case a hebraism: פני).
In Num 6:25, the blessing of the priests: יאר ה' פניו אליך, 'the LORD make
His face to shine upon you', is rendered by all the manuscripts (except A) as
יניר ה' רחותה לידך. Similarly, in Deut 4:37 ויוצאך בפניו בכחו הגדול
ממצרים, 'and brought you out in His sight with His mighty power out of
Egypt', פניו was understood, as in the cases cited above, as the (good) will of
the almighty God and translated by all the manuscripts as ברעותה.[63]

On the other hand, when the face of God expresses His anger, the Samaritan
Targum, even in its oldest manuscripts, renders פנים as רוגז, again in order to
materialize the metaphor in keeping with the contemporary literary style, and
certainly not in order to avoid anthropomorphisms. Lev 20:3 ואני אתן את
פני באיש ההוא והכרתי אותו מקרב עמו, 'and I will set My face against
that man and will cut him off from among his people', is rendered ואנה אתן ית
רגזי ... by MSS B, C, E, J, M and V. A alone has ית אפי, probably an
aberration, for in verses 5 and 6 it joins the other manuscripts reading רגזי for
פני.

The position is different in cases where the face of God has no metaphoric
sense. In Exod 33:23 ופני לא יראו, 'but My face shall not be seen', MSS A, C
and J translate ואפי לא יתחזון. E, M and N have a variant: וקדמי.[64]

Another clear case in which old, as well as more recent manuscripts manifest
the repulsion of the Samaritans for the personification of God is Num 12:8
where Moses' particular position is emphasized: ותמונת ה' יביט, 'he beholds
the form of the LORD' MSS A, C, E, J and M render ותמונת as ונעירות (=
ונהירות) as if the passage means 'the wisdom of God'. Thus תמונה, 'image',
was interpreted as תבונה, 'wisdom', by means of a slight change in the
phonetic structure of the word (m and b being both voiced bi-labials the change
is minimal). Indeed, תבונה in Deut 32:28 is translated נהירו as well as in

---

[63] In this passage רעותה, 'God's (good) will' may have a wider sense. The Samaritans divide the
history of mankind into three eras. The first begins with the Creation and ends with the schism that,
after the instalment of the Tabernacle on Mount Garizim, divided the people of Israel and established the erring cult in Shilo. This era is named רעותה, the Golden Age of the Children of Israel
which culminated in the Exodus from Egypt and the conquest of Canaan. The second era is פנותה,
the era in which God 'concealed His face' from the Children of Israel because of this sin. Cf. Deut
31:17 והסתרתי פני מהם ... וחרה אפי בו, 'then my anger will be kindled against them . . . and I
will hide my face from them', which is rendered by the targum as ואכסי רעותי מנן. The רעותה
will return with the תהב (Messiah) in the far future. See Geiger, 'Neuere Mittheilungen', 179, n. 23;
Kohn, Zur Sprache, 47-51; Ben-Ḥayyim, Literary and Oral Tradition, 3b, 47. A small annotation in
the margin of MS M in Gen 41: 45 reveals the Samaritan belief that רעותה is hidden away: Pharaoh
delighted by Joseph's wisdom, named him צפנתי פענה (according to the Samaritan Hebrew text),
i.e., 'he deciphered my secret'. The marginal annotation reads: גנ[י]זה דרחותה (גלה), 'he
(Joseph) revealed the hiding of the רעותה'.
[64] It is B alone that makes a circumlocution: קנומי, 'myself'. Cf. Abu-Saʻīd: דאתי, 'my essence'.

Exod 31:3. Interesting enough, *Hamelits*,[65] quoting our *hapax*, puts תבונת in the Hebrew column, although its parallel Aramaic column has דמות, similar to MS B in our verse.

Even euphemistic translations of passages in which the epithet אלהים is attributed by the Hebrew text to human beings are not customary in the old manuscripts. In Gen 42:28 מה זאת עשה אלהים לנו, 'what is this that God has done to us' is an expression of perplexity towards the confusing events that happened to Joseph's brothers in Egypt. MSS A and V could not admit that God was directly involved in the course of events and, attributing them to Joseph's initiative, translated שלטנה, in line with the Samaritan Arabic Version: אלסלטאן, 'the ruler'. An interlinear annotation in MS M reads: שליטה; on its margin another one reads: מלכה. The old manuscripts, including B (the copy of M) and E (the copy of a manuscript of C's type) remained unchanged: אלהים (unless they considered the events as emanating from God's will. Cf. Rashi's comentary *ad loc.*). The ironic answer of Jacob given to his childless wife Rachel in the form of a rhetorical question: התחת אלהים אנכי, 'am I in God's stead' (Gen 30:2), is translated literally by MSS J and E: החליפת, and similarly by M and its copy B: התחת. A has דחול אלהה אנה, 'I am God-fearing' (i.e. pious).[66] Of the old manuscripts only C has דחל מן אלהים אנה. This interpretation, which avoids the insolence of Jacob's answer, was made possible by the closeness, in Samaritan pronunciation, of התחת אלהים – *ā'tat ēluwwəm* ('in God's stead', to which *he interrogativum* is prefixed) and חתת אלהים – *ātat ēluwwəm* ('the terror of God'), e.g. Gen 35:5 which is rendered by all the manuscripts as דחלת אלהים. This interpretation is shared by MSS V and M (with its copy, B) in the parallel passage, Gen 50:19 (Cf. Onkelos: 'דה אנא דחלא).

DEFENCE OF THE IMAGE OF THE FATHERS

Apology was one of the main concerns of the young manuscripts of the Samaritan Targum. Whenever a passage contained an expression that could prejudice the image of one of the Fathers of the Nation, hermeneutical devices were employed in order to soften its effect by blurring the candour of the Hebrew original. This is best exemplified by the narrative of Jacob's escape from Laban. Both Jacob and Rachel committed a moral (as well as penal) offence, incompatible with their position in the Nation's conscience. In two successive verses both are involved in theft: ותגנב רחל את התרפים אשר לאביה; ויגנב יעקב את לב לבן ... 'and Rachel stole her father's houdehold idols;

---

[65] The vocabulary compiled by the Samaritans in the eleventh century. It is disposed in three parallel columns; the first contains an alphabetical list of words of the Hebrew text of the Pentateuch, the third their Aramaic parallels, as collected from the manuscripts of the targum that the compiler had before him and the second an Arabic translation of the Aramaic column. See Ben Ḥayyim, *Literary and Oral Tradition*, 1, 61ff.

[66] In accordance with the Arabic Version of Abu Sa'īd: חאיף.

and Jacob outwitted Laban (litt.: stole his heart) . . .' (Gen 31:19-20). The Samaritan Targum according to MS A could not support such a description of Joseph's parents.[67] Moreover, these verses contradict the epithet given to Jacob: איש תם, 'a plain man' (Gen 25:27). As for Rachel, the mother of the righteous Joseph, it was inconceivable that she could possibly commit a twofold crime, namely theft and, even worse, idolatry (for, otherwise it was unlikely that she be interested in her father's idols). Consequently, MS A rendered the verb גנב, 'to steal', as נסב, 'to take': ונסבת רחל . . . ונסב יעקב,[68] even though Jacob is still to be blamed, for he is still guilty of trickery. However, A's scribe was not alert enough to avoid גנבתון in v. 32. The other manuscripts did not hesitate to use the verb גנב in all these cases. Moreover, the question of the תרפים remains. Obviously they are idols, for later, when Laban meets Jacob, he accuses his son-in-law: למה גנבת את אלהי, 'why did you steal my Gods? (Gen 31:30; cf. v. 32). Again, A intervened by substituting תרפים and אלהים by 'harmless' words: למה גנבת ית אצטרלבי! (v. 19);[69] ונסבת רחל ית סלקקידה (v. 30), in accordance with the Arabic Versions: אצטרלאבי, 'my astrolabes'.[70] The integrity of Jacob is assured by A when, according to the Hebrew text, doubt exists, as for example in the narrative concerning Isaac's blessing, when Rebecca's instigation to commit fraud was met with too feeble resistance on Jacob's part: הן עשו אחי איש שעיר ואנכי איש חלק, 'Esau my brother is a hairy man and I am a smooth man' (Gen 27:11). A's scribe did not consider Jacob's expression of fear of being recognized as a sufficient objection to his mother's dark intentions and reinforced it by rendering חלק, 'smooth', as חסיד, 'pious', in accordance with the epithet איש תם mentioned above.[71] Furthermore, when Isaac discovers the fraud and says to Esau (v. 35): בא אחיך במרמה, 'your brother came with guile', A's hand intervenes: באמנו, 'with skill', i.e. being more skillful than you, he forestalled you.[72] A consistently used the same vocable to render the passage of Gen 34:13 where Jacob's sons

---

[67] The Samaritans consider themselves the descendants of the tribes of the sons of Joseph, namely Manasseh and Ephraim, and of Levi.

[68] Although Abu Sa'īd's Arabic version could not inspire its translation: וסרקת, 'she stole'. . . ואחתלס, 'he cheated'.

[69] An unknown vocable, perhaps a purposely distorted word for the sake of euphemism.

[70] The astrolabe was very popular amongst Arab navigators. Thus MS A attributed to Rachel the intention to provide her husband with instruments of orientation for the planned journey. The Jewish medieval exegesis was also concerned with these problems and made attempts to alleviate the discomfort produced by these passages. Ibn Ezra says in his commentary: יש אומרים שהוא כלי נחשת העשוי לדעת חלקי השעות, 'some say that it (the תרפים) is a tool made of copper, to find the division of the hours'. Cf. Nahmanides ad loc. According to Genesis Rabba, 74:3, p. 863, Rachel stole the idols in order to prevent her father from idolatry.

[71] This procedure is shared by the Jewish midrash, as expressed by Genesis Rabba 65:9, p. 726: ואנכי איש חלק, כמה דאת אמר כי חלק ה' עמו, which connects חָלָק with חֵלֶק of Deut 32:9.

[72] Cf. Onkelos ad loc.: בחוכמה, 'with wisdom'. This reading is reproduced in a marginal note of MS M. For the relation of M's annotations to Onkelos see Goldberg, Das samaritanische Pentateuchtargum, 28-34.

deceitfully treated with Shechem and Ḥamor about Dina's marriage: ויענו
בני יעקב ... במרמה, 'and the sons of Jacob answered ... deceitfully'
ואגיבו ברי יעקב ... באמנו. The other manuscripts have במרמה in both
cases. Sarah's lie ותכחש שרה, 'Sara denied' (Gen 18:15) which is rendered by
MSS C, J and M as וכדבת, 'lied', a translation unacceptable to A, was softened
by him to ואנכרת, 'denied'.[73]

Yet paraphrastic translations for the sake of apology are not the exclusive
occupation of A. Occasionally the old manuscripts display also such translations, as in the case of Joseph whose reputation as a righteous man (cf. Gen
39:7-13) was somewhat diminished by the narrative of Gen 44:5,15 which
describes him as practising divination: והוא נחש ינחש בו, 'by this that he
divines'. This is a flagrant offence according to Lev 19:26 לא תנחשו, therefore
all of our manuscripts translate: נסוי ינסי. The meaning of the verb נסה is
'to examine' with no connotation of magic. Onkelos translates: בדקא יבדק in
the same way, its translation being reproduced in a marginal note of MS M.
Similarly, in Gen 30:27 Laban's words נחשתי ויברכני ה', 'I divinated and
God blessed me' are translated by J as: אתנסית וברכני ה', for no translator
would attribute Laban's success to divination. Cf. Codex Neofiti 1: נסיית,
Onkelos: נסיתי. Yet no other verse containing the verb נחש has been similarly altered in any manuscript. Thus, in Deut 18:10 מנחש, 'diviner', is rendered מנחש, etc.[74]

DEFAMATION OF UNPOPULAR PERSONS

These attempts at saving the faces of the prominent personages of the Holy
Script are only one aspect of the perseverent and tireless attempt to harmonise
the scriptures. Improper behaviour of such a person has to be attenuated in
order to avoid any contradiction with his image, as presented in other parts of
the Pentateuch.[75] Conversely, persons are defamed in accordance with their
disgraceful image as depicted in other parts of the scripture, as for example
Laban whose warm welcome of Jacob (Gen 29:13) produced grave suspicion, in
view of his deceitful behaviour (v. 18-29): וירץ לקראתו ויחבק לו
וינשק לו ויביאהו אל ביתו, 'he ran to meet him and embraced him and
kissed him and brought him to his house'. A lost manuscript of the targum
whose traces are preserved by the Aramaic column of *Hamelits* (v. *supra*)

---

[73] Cf. Abu Saʿīd's version: וגהדת, 'she denied'.
[74] Except MS A which by an excess of zeal interpolates לא תנסו in Lev 19:26. The other
manuscripts have invariably לא תנחשון. However MS J is to be suspected, its version being of
secunda manus.
[75] This is a part of a long traditional activity that had already begun with the redaction of the
Samaritan Pentateuch. One can easily detect the multitude of additions that occur wherever the
masoretic text seems to be defective.

translates ויחבק, 'to embrace', as וגשש. The verb גשש means 'to explore'.[76] Its use suggests a well-known Jewish midrash: כיון דלא חמא אפיסטקיתיה ויחבק לו, אמר דלמא דינרין אינון ויהיבין בחרציה, 'since (Laban) did not see his (Jacob's) purse (ὀψοθήκη), he embraced him thinking: perhaps denarii does he bear in his bossom' (*Genesis Rabba* 70:13, pp. 812-13).

Nimrod is another unpopular figure. Gen 10:8-9 narrates: 'and Cush became to be father of Nimrod; he was the first on earth to be a mighty masn; he was a mighty hunter before the LORD, therefore it is said: Like Nimrod a mighty hunter before the LORD'. The Samaritan Chronicles depict this person in very unpleasant terms. According to *The Book of Asaṭir*,[77] he was a wicked king of Erekh who foresaw the birh of an offshot of Arpakhshad who would destroy all the idols. He tried to prevent Arpakhshad's sons from giving birth by separating the males from the females but Terakh escaped and thus Abraham was born. Nimrod cast Abraham into a burning furnace, etc. Such a villain was not sufficiently defamed by the Joly Script, according to later views. Furthermore, in biblical times hunting was not as discrageful a profession as it probably was in later days, as an annotation found in the interlinear space of MS M attests, which renders ציד, 'hunt', as אנוס, 'robbery' (Gen 25:27).[78] This attitude towards hunting is manifested again by the meaningless vocables used by MS A for ציד in Gen 27: שרבלותי (v. 19); פצפצותי (25); צפצפות (30); ציוף (33). All these lexical monstrosities are intended to blurr Isaac's greediness for the detested hunt. In view of this attitude, a hunter (whose name, נמרוד, suggests מרד, 'rebellion') cannot be connected with the following wording: לפני ה for, as we have seen above, only a righteous person 'walks before God'. It was therefore only natural that MS C would substitute ציד by עצאי, 'rebel'.[79] Thus the shame of Nimrod was established for eternity.

For the sake of harmonization, the role of Ḥobab, Moses' relative, has been diminished. This honourable Midianite accompanied the children of Israel during their wandering across the desert exploring for them the wilderness as an experienced scout. On the eve of their installment in the Promised Land, Moses gratefully mentions Ḥobab's assistance and asks him to share Israel's fate: אל נא תעזב אתנו כי על כן ידעת חנותנו במדבר והיית לנו לעינים 'do not leave us, I pray you, for you know how we are to encamp in the wilderness

---

[76] Ben-Ḥayyim, *Literary and Oral Tradition* 2, 460. Cf. Num 13:2 ויתרו, 'that they may search', rendered by MS A as ויגששון.

[77] Ben-Ḥayyim, 'Book of Asaṭir', 117ff. A similar aggada exists in Jewish sources. See *Genesis Rabba* 38:12, p. 363.

[78] A trace of a lost manuscript, preserved in *Hamelits*, has the same word. See Ben-Ḥayyim, *Literary and Oral Tradition*, 2, 572.

[79] The same meaning was attributed to ציד by Pseudo-Yonatan גיבר מרוד, playing on Nimrod's name. The verb עצה also means 'to rob', 'to oppress', e.g. Lev 5:21 בגזל, '(taken away) by force', is rendered by the Samaritan Targum as בעציאן.

and you will serve as eyes for us' (Num 10:31). This important function of Ḥobab, as formulated by Moses, contradicts the role of 'the ark of the covenant of the LORD' which 'went before them . . . to search out a resting place' (v. 33) and also the role of God's guidance (cf. Exod 13:21; Num 14:14). Consequently, the Samaritan Targum in all its manuscripts translates לעינים, 'as eyes', as if it was לעניים, 'as poor men': לצרכים, 'in need', in line with the generosity expressed by the following verse: הטוב ההוא אשר ייטב ה' עמנו והיטבנו לך, 'whatever good the LORD will do to us, the same will we do to you'.[80]

PRESERVING THE HONOUR OF ISRAEL

The harmonization sought by the Samaritan Targum is by no means limited to the character and behaviour of the personages of the Pentateuch. In fact it is practised throughout the Holy Script. Thus, the allegoric description of Israel in Bileam's prophecy arouses horror: לא ישכב עד יאכל טרף ודם חללים ישתה, 'it does not lie down till it devores the prey and drinks the blood of the slain' (Num 23:24). It is unconceivable that a righteous people about which the same prophecy says: לא הביט און ביעקב, '(God) has not beheld iniquity in Jacob' (v. 21), would violate the commandment formulated in Deut 12:16 רק הדם לא תאכלו, 'only you shall not eat the blood'. Therefore the MSS A, B, E, J and N rendered ישתה as יגר, the imperfect of the verb נגד, 'to draw', 'to make to flow',[81] thus giving an entirely different meaning to the passage: 'and shed the blood of the slain'.

It is important to emphasize the fact that the Samaritan Targum is based on the Hebrew text of the Pentateuch, but was amended to incorporate and reflect the Samaritan tradition which differs in many cases from the Jewish masoretic text. Some of these differences are of a hermeneutic nature as are their translation into Aramaic. For example in Gen 49:5 Jacob characterises his sons Simeon and Levi as revengers who retaliate against Shechem, the raper of their sister, Dina: כלי חמס מכרתיהם.[82] This is rendered by J and other manuscripts as: אסכמו שקר בקיומיון, 'they put an end to the wrong deeds (of Shechem) by their covenants' (proposed to the people of Shechem, Gen 34).[83] This interpretation was made possible by the verb כלו, the third person plural of the perfect of כלה 'to put an end to' and by the interpretation of מכרתיהם as the

---

[80] The Jewish targumim treat Ḥobab with a similar tendency. Onkelos says: וגבורן דאתעבידא לנא חזיתא בעיניך, 'you saw the miracles made to us with your eyes'; Pseudo-Yonatan: ודהוית חביב עלן כבבת עינא, 'you were dear to us as the pupil of our eye'; Codex Neofiti ותהוי לן לסהדותה, 'you shall be our witness'.

[81] Cf. Syriac נגד (Brockelmann, *Lexicon*, 413a).

[82] As against the masoretic text: כלי חמס מכרתיהם, 'weapons of violence are their swords' (Cf. King James' Version: 'instruments of cruelty are in their habitations').

[83] A slightly different sense is given by the reading of MSS C and N: קיאמון, 'of their covenant'. M and B read מקעימידון, probably intending the sense 'their cutting off'. Cf. Septuagint *ad loc*. See Ben-Ḥayyim, *Literary and Oral Tradition* 3a, 33. Abu Saʿīd's version is מקאטיעהמא, 'their decision'.

plural of מכרת, a derivative of כרת, 'to make a covenant'. Consequently, in verse 7 Jacob does not curse them, as it does according to the masoretic text: ארור אפם, 'cursed be their anger'. On the contrary, he praises them: אדיר אפם, 'their anger is mighty'. This is translated by ms J: משבח רגזון. A's version is slightly different: חסין רגזון.

SAMARITAN READING OF THE HEBREW TEXT

However, these differences between the two traditions which gave birth to the translations illustrated above are not always immediately visible. Numerous textual peculiarities which are in many cases interpretative are revealed in the Samaritan traditional pronunciation, but hidden by the consonantal writing of their Pentateuch. Only the knowledge of the Samaritan tradition of the reading of the Tora can reveal these peculiarities and explain the apparently 'unskilled' translations. It is therefore with the *reading* of the Tora that the targum has to be confronted.[84] For example in Gen 37:3 וישראל אהב את יוסף מכל בניו כי בן זקנים הוא לו, 'Israel loved Joseph more than any other of his children because he was the son of his old age', is rendered by ms J as: . . . בר חכמה is הלא בר חכמה הוא לה (B, C and E have similar translations).[85] is based on the interpretation of זקנים as 'elders', i.e. 'sages' (plural of זקן), according to the pronunciation of the word in the Samaritan tradition: za-qīnəm.[86]

Another paraphrastic translation resting on the Samaritan particular reading of the Hebrew text is in Gen 49:14 יששכר חמור גרם רבץ בין המשפתים. The masoretic vocalization גרם and משפתים points to the possible meaning of 'Issachar is a strong ass crouching down among the sheepfolds'. Yet, the Samaritan interpretation of these two words is different. The first is pronounced gīram, i.e. 'strangers', the second ammašfātəm, i.e. 'nations', 'languages';[87] consequently, the verse is translated by mss B, J and M as: יששכר חמור תותבים רבע בין כרניה. C, E and V have a synonym for the latter: לשניה.[88] Thus, Issachar is characterized as a tribe which, like an ass, 'bears' the strangers and lives between the nations. This calls to mind a Jewish midrash that describes Issachar as חמור לגרים, a tribe of renowned scholars whose

---

[84] An immense contribution to the understanding of the Samaritan Targum has recently been made by Ben-Ḥayyim who published the traditional reading of the Samaritan Pentateuch in phonetic transliteration in *Literary and Oral Tradition* 4 :1979).

[85] Cf. Onkelos: ארי בר חכים הוא ליה, 'for he is his wise son'.

[86] Contrary to the masoretic vocalization זְקֻנִים, 'the old age'. Cf. Gen 21:2 ותלד שרה לאברהם בן לזקניו, 'Sarah bore Abraham a son in his old age'. In this case both traditions agree; the Samaritan reading alzāqāno is translated לסיבותה, in similarity with Onkelos: לסיבתוהי.

[87] Cognate of שפה, 'lip', 'language'. The Samaritan pronunciation does not distinguish between *shin* and *sin*, both being pronounced as *š*. See below.

[88] כרניה can also be considered as a result of the attribution of משפתים to משפחתים, for no guttural consonant exists in Samaritan pronunciation in such conditions.

wisdom produced the admiration of many gentiles who came to his land and became proselytes – גרים (*Genesis Rabba* 98:12, p. 1263).

Occasionally phonetic changes led to different approaches to the contents of a passage and produced a particular translation, an example of which is the interchange of the palatal consonants *k* and *g* which gave birth to forms as שרוג, עגבר, דוגיפת, etc.[89] In Gen 42:9-16, Joseph's charge against his brothers, מרגלים אתם, 'you are spies', could be pronounced either *am-raggēlam*, 'spies' or *amrakkēlam*, 'gossipers', 'calumniators'. This somewhat less grave charge was probably more acceptable to the scribe of MS A whose version is טפילין, 'slanderers' (v. 9),[90] משמצין, 'defamers' (v. 11).[91] Only in v. 16 does A have שחודין, 'spies'.[92] In the interlinear space and in the margin of MS M a later hand noted: מדגלין, 'liars' (v. 9, 11).[93] The old manuscripts have מיללין (J), אלילין (C, M), גשושין (V), all of them having the meaning 'spies', in keeping with the version *amraggēlam*.

Shin (š) and *sin (ś)* merged in Samaritan Hebrew resulting in *š*. Consequently in Num 5:12 איש איש כי תשטה אשתו, 'if a man's wife goes astray (is faithless)', was pronounced *tišti* and attributed accordingly to the post biblical root שטה, 'to act foolishly' and translated as תשתטה by MSS A, B, N and V (cf. vv. 19, 20, 29). However, this phonetic shift probably took place at a relatively late date, since MS J, the oldest version, has תסטי which attests to a stage of Samaritan Hebrew when ש still had its peculiar phonetic status, equating Aramaic ס (s). The same is true for MSS C and E in all these instances, and partly in M and N.

The loss of the guttural consonants in Samaritan Hebrew produced the fusion of different roots in many instances, as in the case of Gen 18:12 ותצחק שרה בקרבה לאמר אחרי בלותי היתה לי עדנה, 'Sarah laughed to herself saying, after I have grown old shall I have pleasure (rejuvenation)'. The Samaritan pronunciation of ותצחק is *wteṣā‘aq* which can be taken as ותצעק, 'she cried', 'she sobbed', etc., as indeed was A's interpretation, judging by its rendering: וקטרגת שרה 'Sarah reproached'. It is a bitter reproach that she uttered 'within herself', according to this interpretation.[94] Similarly, a peculiar interpretation from the loss of *ayin* in Gen 49:7 where Jacob speaks about Simeon and Levi: ועברתם, 'and their wrath', according to the masoretic text. The Samaritan tradition which does not discern between *ayin* and *ḥēt* attributes the pronuncia-

---

[89] The masoretic text has שרוך, עכבר, דוכיפת, respectively. Cf. Ben-Ḥayyim, *Literary and Oral Tradition* 5, p. 23.

[90] Cf. Syriac טפל, 'to defile' (Brockelmann, *Lexicon*, 285b). See also Ps 119:69 טפלו עלי שקר, '(the godless) besmear me with lies'.

[91] Cf. Hebrew שמצה, 'blemish', 'disgrace' (Jastrow, *Dictionary*, 1600b).

[92] Cf. Deut 1:22 ויחפרו, 'and they may explore (the land)'; C וישחדון.

[93] Cf. Syriac דגל, 'to lie' (Brockelmann, *Lexicon* 141b).

[94] Kohn, *Samaritanische Studien*, 80-81.

211

tion *wābāratimma* to וחברתם, 'their company'. This is translated accordingly ודביקתון.⁹⁵

Not only phonetic changed produced interpretative translations. As we have seen above, the Samaritan Pentateuch often differs from the masoretic text in morphology giving rise to peculiar interpretations. A most interesting passage in this respect is Gen 30:3, where Rachel, having seen that she is childless, asked Jacob to 'go unto' Bilhah, her maid, so that: ותלד על ברכי, 'she may bear upon my knees'. So far the masoretic tradition. The Samaritan Pentateuch, though identical in orthography, has the pronunciation *birruki* which means 'my blessing'.⁹⁶ Indeed, this nominal form implies a different interpretation which is expressed clearly by MS A: ותלד על ברכתי, 'she will bear according to my blessing'. MSS B, E and M have similar readings: על ברוכי. The same grammatical form with the same interpretation is found in Gen 48:12, where the masoretic text has ויוצא יוסף אתם מעם ברכיו, 'Joseph removed them (his sons) from his (father's) knees'. The Samaritan again has ברוכיו, pointing to Jacob's blessing (cf. v. 19ff.). Accordingly, MSS B and M have ברוכה. However, MSS C and J do not follow the Samaritan text which in these cases is probably the result of a hermeneutic evolution and thus render ברכיו, ברכי respectively, in accordance with the masoretic text.⁹⁷ Given the age of the version that is contained in these manuscripts, it is evident that in the remote past the Samaritans shared the reading represented by the masoretic text, ברך and, naturally, its interpretation: 'knee'.⁹⁸

An intriguing instance of divergent traditions within the Samaritan Targum concerns one of the most important principles of Samaritanism, as expressed by the text of the Samaritan Pentateuch, namely in Exod 20:24 מזבח אדמה תעשה לי . . . במקום אשר אזכרתי (!) שמי שמה אבוא אליך וכרכתיך, 'an altar of earth you shall make for me . . . in every place where I recorded my name there I will come to you and I will bless you'. The perfect אזכרתי, *ēzākarti*, means, according to the Samaritan dogma, that God has already chosen His holy place as specified in the Samaritan version of Deut 27:4-6 תקימו את האבנים האלה . . . בהר גריזים . . . ובנית שם מזבח והעליתה עליו עלות . . ., 'you shall set up these stones . . . on Mount Garizim . . . and there shall you build an altar . . . and you shall offer burnt offerings'. The masoretic text has in Exodus בכל מקום אשר אזכיר את שמי, etc., 'in all places where I will record my name', for the holy place has not yet been chosen. In any event, it is by no means mount Garizim; in Deut it has הר עיבל, 'Mount Ebal'. This crucial difference between Samaritanism and Judaism is expressed in Deut 12: 5, 11, 14, etc., where the Samaritan text has invariably המקום אשר בחר, 'the place which the LORD chose', whereas the

---

⁹⁵ דבק means 'to stick', 'to be attached', hence דביקה means 'company'.
⁹⁶ As against הברכים, *abbārākəm*, 'the knees', Deut 28:35.
⁹⁷ In the second case E joins them as well as V: ארכביו, 'knees'.
⁹⁸ The Arabic version of Abu Sa'īd is ברכתי, 'my blessing'.

masoretic text has יבחר, 'will choose'. Yet MS J renders the passage in Exod
20:24 as: ובאתרה דאדכר ית שמי, 'in the place where I will record my name',
etc., in distinct contrast to the other manuscripts which follow the Samaritan
tradition of using the perfect: דאדכרת. MS A appears to be corrupted: דתדכר,
unless a 'neutral' interpretation intended: 'where you shall remind my name'.[99]
Does J's reading allude to an early stage of development of the Samaritan
Pentateuch when Samaritan dogma did not yet involve the text of the Tora in its
entirety? At the present state of study it is impossible to draw conclusions with
any degree of certainty.[100]

SAMARITAN HALAKHA

The existence of a Samaritan halakha is also attested by several manuscripts of
the Samaritan Targum. A good example is Lev 11:40 והאכל מנבלתה יכבס
בגדיו וטמא עד הערב. According to the masoretic text this passage means:
'he who eats of its carcass (the dead animal) shall wash his clothes and be
unclean until the evening'. The Samaritan tradition distinguishes between this
occurence of the verb אכל which is pronounced *wakkəl*, giving it a peculiar
form,[101] and the regular אכל, pronounced *akəl*.[102] This peculiar form is bound to
have a peculiar meaning, for several manuscripts of the Samaritan Targum,
namely MSSA, C, E and J render it as ודגרף, 'he that flays', while V has
ודמאכל, 'he that feeds', and B: ותגר, 'he that trades'.[103] No doubt, an
interdiction to deal with carcasses underlies the peculiar pronunciation revealed by these various translations.[104]

Another halakhic translation is A's rendering ואגאה of the Hebrew ויקב in
Lev 24:11 ויקב בן האשה הישראלית את השם, 'and the Israelite woman's son
blasphemed the Name (of God)'. MSS C and E have ואגה, ואגהה respectively.
All these are various orthographies of the verb הגה, 'to utter'. B, M and N use

---

[99] On the Jewish-Samaritan dispute regarding the Holy Place see Kohn, *Samaritanische Studien*,
84ff.; Kohn, *Zur Sprache* 190ff.; Kippenberg, *Garizim und Synagoge* 227.

[100] To assume an interpolation of Jewish origin would be to oversimplify the problem. One has to
keep in mind that the passage in question is situated in one of the central parts of the Pentateuch. A
scribe is bound to be alert when he copies a text which has a particular ideological significance, as in
our case, in which the ancestral polemic with Judaism is expressed. It is worth mentioning the quite
unusual orthography of the Hebrew *Hiph'il* with the prefix *'Alef*. The whole problem can apparently
be solved by assuming a *Hitpe'el* with assimilated t in MS J:דאדכר.The inconvenience of a direct
object after a *Hitpe'el* is a minor problem since that form functions as an active as well. Cf.
Ben-Ḥayyim, *Literary and Oral Tradition*, 3b, 112; 5, 80 and 206 (n. 40).

[101] Participle of *Pi'el* without the regular prefix *mem*. Cf. Ben-Ḥayyim, *Literary and Oral Tradition*,
5, 142 and n. 131.

[102] Participle of *Qal*. Cf. Gen. 39: 6, etc.

[103] Cf. also the translation of similar cases in Lev 14:47; 17:15; 22:8 where synonyms of גרף occur in
various manuscripts: שלע, קלף, טלק (= שלח).

[104] Cf. Kohn, 'Samaritanische Pentateuchübersetzung' 67ff.; Ben-Ḥayyim, *Literary and Oral Tradition* 3a, 69. Abu Sa'īd's version has ואלמנטף, 'he that cleans'.

the variant וכרז,[105] whereas J has ולעט, 'he cursed', (the perfect of the verb לוט). J's translation seems to be based on the interpretation of ויקב, *wyiqqav*, as the imperfect of קבב, 'to curse'.[106] However, this particular translation of J in v. 11 does not represent a divergent view concerning the pronunciation of God's name, being rather a result of the following ויקלל, 'and he cursed', for in v. 16 J renders 'ונקב שם ה, 'he that utters God's name', as וכרז.[107] The use of the verb הגה in connection with the interdiction in question reminds of *M. Sanhedrin* 10:1 where Abba Shaul includes ההוגה את השם באותיותיו, 'he that utters the name (of God) by its letters' among those who 'have no share in the world to come'.[108] At any rate, the Tetragrammaton is substituted in the traditional Tora reading of the Samaritans by the word *šēma*, 'the name', an Aramaic vocable, parallel to the Hebrew השם used by Jews.

It is probably in connection with the Samaritan's inclination to avoid any mention of God's name that several manuscripts render אל שדי as חיולה ספוקה (alternatively חילה ספקה, etc.). חיולה is the *nomen agentis* derived from חיל, 'strength' and means 'the powerful'. It appears in MS A even when no connection with שדי exists. Thus, אל ראי (Gen 16:13), 'the LORD that sees me', is rendered as חיולה חזוה; אל קנא, 'a jealous God' (Exod 20:5), as חיולה קנאה, etc. Only in 5 instances out of a possible 40 does A render אל by אל or אלה. Conversely, J has only 7 out of 53 possible instances of חיולה. Being of older vintage, it is undoubtedly less commited to the later efforts to avoid mentioning God's name, even indirectly.[109] However, חיול with its variants, חיאל, חיל, as epithets of God is of a quite ancient origin: it is attested under the synonym form גבורה (i.e. 'strenght') in Jewish sources.[110] As for ספוקה, the *nomen agentis* which translates the Hebrew שדי, it originates in the hermeneutic division of the word into ש־די, 'he that supplies'.[111] Although it is used exclusively by MS A[112] and totally unknown in J, the expression probably has old origins, as a Jewish midrash attests: אני אל שדי ־ אני הוא שאמרתי לעולם די, 'I am El Shadday: It is I who said to the world "day" (enough)'

---

[105] Cf. Num 1:17 את האנשים . . . אשר נקבו בשמות, 'these men . . . who were expressed by their names', is rendered by MSS C, E, M and J as דאכרזו; B and N have דכריזו.

[106] In line with Jewish targumim which have וחרף (Cod. Neofiti [M], the Fragmentary Targum and Pseudo-Yonatan, but not with Onkelos: ופריש, 'expressed').

[107] MSS A, C and E differ somewhat: ומקסם 'he that enchants', apparently introducing an explicit reference to the interdiction to use God's name for purposes of sorcery and magic. RSV: 'he who blasphemes'.

[108] On the whole matter see Kohn, *Samaritanische Studien* 75ff. See also Ben-Ḥayyim, 'Pronunciation' 147-54.

[109] Two of the seven occurrences of חיולה are cases of God's self introduction (Gen 31:13; 46:3); the other of invocation (Gen 33:20; 35:1, 3; Exod 15:11; Num 12:13).

[110] Urbach, *The Sages*, 83ff. Cf. Kippenberg, *Garizim und Synagoge*, 80-96. However, the later יכבלה, יכלה (MS V in Gen 43:14; 49:25 and perhaps A in Gen 31:29) is probably due to Arabic influence. Cf. Saadya's version as well as Abu Sa'īd's: אלקאדר. Is it the same ancient tradition that produced Jerome's translation *Omnipotens*?

[111] Kohn, *Zur Sprache* 179; Kohn 'Samaritanisch Pentateuchübersetzung', 674.

[112] Gen 17:1; 28:3; 35:11; 43:14; 48:3; 49:25.

(*Genesis Rabba* 46:3, p. 460). In the following, the midrash cites Aquila: איקנוס (ἱκανος).[113] MSS C and V occasionally use the variant ספקה for שדי.[114] On the other hand there is no difference between the various manuscripts with regard to the rendering of Bileam's words who, speaking about his own abilities says: מחזה שדי יחזה, 'who sees the vision of the Almighty' (Num 24:4, 16, according to the masoretic text). The possibility that the villain who sought to curse the Children of Israel (Num 22ff.) and provoked them to sin (Num 30:8) could have divine revelations similar to Moses' was inconceivable to the Samaritans. שדי has therefore been interpreted as שדה, 'field', and translated accordingly: דמחזי ברה יחזי, 'which has visions (in) the fields'. However, B's scribe alone has: ספוק.[115]

TRANSLATION OF PROPER NAMES

It was not common practice to translate proper names in the Samaritan Targum. Yet, hermeneutically altered names do occur occasionally, for example in Gen 30:21 MS A has חכמה for דינה, Jacob's daughter, translating the appelative דין, 'judgement'. In Exod 1:15, one of the midwives who saved the children of the Israelites, thereby disobeying Pharaoh's orders, is named by MS A עטרה, 'the beautiful one'. This name is recorded in an interlinear annotation of MS M[116] which has also a surname for the second midwife כשירה: שפרה, 'the fair one' which MS A however failed to adopt in its text. [ארץ] אדום in Num 20:18 is rendered by MS A as ארומה and in v. 23 as רומה, both in accordance with the Jewish tradition of associating the name of Edom with the detested empire of Rome.[117] MS M has many interlinear and marginal annotations containing epithets given to various personages. Thus, for example, Reuben is surnamed חטיאי, 'sinner' in view of his misconduct with Bilhah (narrated in Gen 35:22); Jehuda is called נגדה, 'ruler' (according to Gen 49:10); Issachar is מגיר, 'converter' (cf. *ibid.*, v. 14); Dan is מדין and פשור, 'judge' (*ibid.*, v. 16); Asher is משבח, 'praised' (*ibid.*, v. 20), etc. All these epithets are annotated in the list of the heads of the tribes given in Num 1:5-14.

CONCLUSION

The sketch given in the above lines does not intend to draw definitive conclu-

---

[113] Cf. the Septuagint translation of Job 21:15. The Arabic versions of Saadya and Abu Saʿīd represent the same tradition rendering שדי as אלכאפי, 'the supplier'.

[114] Marginal and interlinear annotation of MS M render שדי as מינקה, 'breast feeder', a midrashic interpretation of the word as derived from שדים 'breast' (the Samaritan pronunciation makes no distinction in structure between שדי – *šiddi* and שדים – *šiddəm*).

[115] Cf. Saadya's translation: מנאטר אלכאפי.

[116] As well as in the Samaritan Glossary *Hamelits* (Ben-Ḥayyim, *Literary and Oral Tradition*, 2, 568).

[117] Kohn, 'Samaritanische Pentateuchübersetzung', 675. Cf. Jastrow, *Dictionary*, 16a.

sions regarding the hermeneutical approach of the hands that composed, re-dacted and copied the Samaritan Targum, from its inception to its present variated forms. Such a conclusion has to emanate from an extensive study taking into consideration the other products of the Samaritan spiritual activity: *Memar Marka*, the liturgy of the Samaritans, their Chronicles and, obviously, their Arabic Versions of the Pentateuch. This study is, for the time being, a desideratum.

Bibliography

EDITIONS

The first edition of the Samaritan Targum ever made is that of MORINUS, *Biblia Polyglotta* (1645), which reproduces a Vatican manuscript, namely Vat. Sam. 2. It was reproduced with unnecessary emendations in WALTON, *Biblia Sacra Polyglotta* (1657). The same manuscript was published in Hebrew characters: BRÜLL, *Das samaritanische Targum zum Pentateuch* (1873-76). The first critical edition based on several manuscripts is: PETERMANN-VOLLERS, *Pentateuchus Samaritanus* (1872-91). A recent critical edition is: TAL, *The Samaritan Targum of the Pentateuch* (1980-1983) with an introduction.

STUDIES

The most important studies concerning the Samaritan Targum are the essays of KOHN: *Samaritanische Studien* (1868), *Zur Sprache* (1876) and his severe crit-icism of Petermann-Voller's edition: 'Die samaritanische Pentateuch-Überset-zung' (1893). A very important study concerning the problematic of the manu-scripts of the Samaritan Targum is: GOLDBERG, *Das samaritanische Pentateuchtargum* (1935). Very instructive for the lexicography of the targum are the rich notes of BEN-HAYYIM in his edition of the medieval Samaritan Glossary, namely *Hamelits: Literary and Oral Tradition* 2. A modern grammar of Samaritan Aramaic largely based on the material of the targum is: MACUCH, *Grammatik des samaritanischen Aramäisch* (1982). So far, no dictionary of the Samaritan Aramaic has been published. The Samaritan material of CASTELLUS, *Lexicon Heptaglotton* (1686), is obsolete. A dictionary is being prepared by A. Tal.

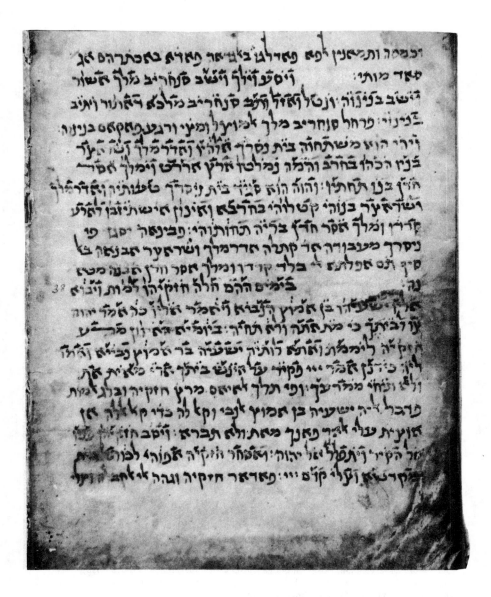

Bible Codex, Prophets with Targum Onkelos and Arabic Translation in Hebrew Characters of Saadya Gaon, Isa 37:37-38:2, 12th-13th c. (JTS 240, EMC 73, f. 8b).

Cf. A. Díz Macho, *Textus* 1 (1960) 132-43; *idem, Manuscritos hebreos* 175-77. 253-68.

Geniza Fragment from the Taylor-Schechter Collection, Exod 39-39-40:17 with Babylonian *masora* and *masora* on targum Onkelos (Cambridge University Library, MS T -S B4.12 *verso*).
Cf. Kahle, *Masoreten des Ostens* 6, 106. According to A. Díez Macho (*Estudios bíblicos* 16, 1957, 249) the fragment dates from the 9th-10th century.

Chapter Seven

Jewish Aramaic Translations of Hebrew Scriptures

Philip S. Alexander

The Extant Rabbinic Texts

THE PENTATEUCH: ONKELOS

Targum Onkelos (= Onk) was the official targum of Babylonia: the Babylonian Talmud refers to it as 'our targum' (*B.T. Kiddushin* 49a), and introduces quotations from it with the phrase 'as we translate' (e.g. *B.T. Sanhedrin* 106b). On halakhic matters Onk is in close agreement with the Mishna, at least as the Mishna was understood in the Babylonian academies, and the Bavli cites it as an authority even on halakha (see e.g. *B.T. Nazir* 49a, quoting Onk to Num 6:4). Onk offers a simple, non-expansive version. It does contain some aggada, but this, where it occurs, is presented in highly allusive, abridged form.[1]

The traditional attribution to Onkelos is based on a single passage in the Bavli; the parallel in the Yerushalmi, however, speaks of *Aqilas*:

Bavli Megilla 3a	*Yerushalmi Megilla* 71c
R. Yirmeyahu – or some say R. Hiyya b. Abba – also said: The targum of the Pentateuch was composed by Onkelos the proselyte under the guidance of R. Elazar and R. Yehoshua.	R. Yirmeyahu said in the name of R. Hiyya bar Ba (= Abba): Aqilas the proselyte translated the Pentateuch before R. Eliezer and R. Yehoshua, and they praised him and said: *Yopyāpîtā mibbᵉnê 'ādām* (Ps 45:3).

Two points are clear. First, the form *Onkelos* is simply a corruption of *Aqilas*: the corruption is found elsewhere in rabbinic literature (cf.e.g. *T. Demai* 6:13 with *P.T. Demai* 25d). Second, the Yerushalmi is referring to the *Greek* version of the Pentateuch known as Aquila, which it cites on a number of occasions (e.g. *P.T. Sukka* 53d). This is clear from the context which is concerned with the dictum of R. Shimon ben Gamliel that it is permissible to write the Sacred Books only in Greek, and from the recherché pun on *yopyāpîtā mibbᵉnê 'ādām*, which is taken to mean, not 'you are fairer than the sons of men', but 'you have used the language of Japhet better than the sons of men', the 'language of

---

[1] For examples of aggada in Onk see Vermes, 'Haggadah in the Onkelos Targum', and Bowker, 'Haggadah in the Targum Onkelos'.

Japhet' being Greek: see Gen 10:2, where Javan (= Greece) is put among the sons of Japhet, and compare *B.T. Megilla* 9b (parallel: *Genesis Rabba* 36:8, p. 342), where 'the words of Japhet' mean Greek. If this interpretation of *P.T. Megilla* 71c is correct, then the Bavli parallel becomes problematic, for it is obvious in context that it refers to an *Aramaic* version. The simplest solution is to suppose that the Babylonians misunderstood the logion of R. Yirmeyahu, and took it as conveying information about their own anonymous Aramaic translation of the Tora.[2]

Compared to the Palestinian targumim, Onk has come down to us as a highly unified, stable tradition. It even has its own masora, which includes a list of readings where the tradition of Nehardea differs from that of Sura. All the evidence points to some sort of official recension of the text in Babylonia in the talmudic period. Already among the Geonim Onk was received as being of the highest sanctity. There are, nonetheless, significant divergences between its MSS. The aim of the text-critic must be to recover the Babylonian form of the targum. This may be possible through Yemenite MSS which preserve strongly the Babylonian tradition. Of these MSS 131 (EMC 952), 133a (ENA 1705), 152 (ENA 80), and 153 (EMC 48) of the Jewish Theological Seminary of America, New York, and Ms. Ebr. 448 of the Vatican Library are particularly important.

THE PENTATEUCH: PALESTINIAN TARGUMIM

NEOFITI 1. In 1956 A. Díez Macho discovered a copy of the Palestinian Targum of the Pentateuch (Codex Neofiti 1 [= Neof]) in the Vatican Library, where it had lain largely unnoticed because it had been miscatalogued as Targum Onkelos.[3] The text, written by three main hands, is virtually complete. A colophon states that it was copied at Rome in (5)264 A.M. = 1504 C.E. for Giles of Viterbo. It is possible to trace this recension back much earlier for it has been shown to agree significantly with the Palestinian Targum quotations in earlier Jewish writings (e.g. the *Arukh* of Nathan ben Yeḥiel of Rome, d. 1106), where these cannot be paralleled in other extant texts of the Palestinian Targum.[4] On the whole the translation is restrained and sober, the aggada being less extensive than that in either the Fragmentary Targum or Pseudo-Yonatan. Neof is richly supplied with glosses, both marginal and interlinear, in about ten different hands. These are, in the main, alternative Palestinian Targum readings. Different sources were drawn upon. Note, e.g. Gen 10:4 where there are two variants, the second of which is introduced by *L'''* = *lashon 'aher*, 'another

---

[2] The rabbinic traditions are discussed by Friedmann, *Onkelos und Akylas*, and Silverstone, *Aquila and Onkelos*, but see especially Barthélemy, *Les devanciers*, 148-56.

[3] Díez Macho, 'The Recently Discovered Palestinian Targum'.

[4] See Speier, 'Relationship'.

reading'. The glosses sometimes agree with Pseudo-Yonatan, sometimes with the Fragmentary Targum, sometimes with the Cairo Geniza fragments, and sometimes with Onk. A number of them are textually unique.

PSEUDO-YONATAN. The title of this work found in the *editio princeps*, viz. 'Targum of Yonatan ben Uzziel', is a misnomer which came about through a false resolution of the abbreviation T"Y as *Targum Yehonatan* instead of *Targum Yerushalmi*. The mistaken ascription of this targum to the supposed author of the Babylonian Targum to the Prophets may go back to Menaḥem b. Benjamin Recanati in the 14th century. The work is, in fact, a recension of the Palestinian Targum of the Pentateuch, which, save for a few verses, is complete.

Pseudo-Yonatan (= Ps-Y) is the most paraphrastic of all the Pentateuchal targumim: it is estimated to be about twice the length of the original Hebrew text. It is a highly mixed tradition, an amalgam of interpretations from widely different periods. It has been argued that it contains at once some of the earliest and some of the latest dateable targumic material. Some of its aggadic traditions are not attested elsewhere in rabbinic literature. In its final state the collection has been worked over with some care, and in many ways Ps-Y is the most literary of the Palestinian targumim. That its final redaction cannot have been earlier than the 7th cent. C.E. may be deduced from its rendering of Gen 21:21:

Hebrew text	*Pseudo-Yonatan*
And he (Ishmael) dwelt in the wilderness of Paran: his mother took for him a wife out of the land of Egypt.	And he dwelt in the wilderness of Paran, and he took as wife 'Adisha [v.l. Ḥadisha; Ginsburger proposes 'Ayesha] and he divorced her; and his mother took for him Fatima as wife from the land of Egypt.

The same aggada is found in more expanded form in *Pirkei de-Rabbi Eliezer* 30. The names of the two wives of Ishmael (the supposed progenitor of the Arabs) correspond to those of a wife and daughter of Muhammad: Fatima was the daughter of Muhammad by his first wife Khadijah; 'Adisha/Ḥadisha may be Khadijah, or, if we read 'Ayesha with *Pirkei de-Rabbi Eliezer* 30 (as Ginsburger suggested), the reference could be to another wife, 'Ayisha. Counterbalancing such late elements, however, are early ones, and there is sufficient evidence of internal contradiction, reworking and glossing in this targum for us to see that in its present state it is the culmination of a very long process of evolution. There are two witnesses to the text: (1) the *editio princeps* in *Ḥamishah ḥumshe Torah* published by Asher Forins, Venice 1590-91 (on which see M. Steinschneider, *Catalogus librorum hebraeorum in Bibliotheca Bodleiana*, Berlin 1852-60, no. 295); and (2) Ms. Add. 27.031, British Library, London, which bears the signature of the censor Dominico Gierosolomitano and the date 1598. The disagreements between these two texts establish their independence; their large measure of agreement indicates that they are derived from a common archetype.

CAIRO GENIZA FRAGMENTS. 7 MSS recovered from the Cairo Geniza containing extensive passages from the Palestinian Targum appear to be remnants of once complete targumim to whole books of the Pentateuch, or even to the whole Pentateuch. One MS (Kahle D) still preserves parts of Genesis, Exodus and Deuteronomy. Some MSS give the full text of the original, Hebrew and targum alternating, verse by verse. Others present only abbreviated Hebrew lemmata. The significance of this difference (which extends to other targum MSS) is not obvious. The Cairo Geniza fragments (= CG) are the earliest extant witnesses to the text of the Palestinian Targum, the oldest of them (Kahle A) dating from the 8th/9th cent., at the latest. The texts show all the characteristic features of the Palestinian Targum, aggadic passages alternating with sections of more or less literal translation. The MSS do not agree precisely with any of the other recensions of the Pal. Targ., nor even with each other, in the few instances where they overlap. This is eloquent testimony to the extreme fluidity of the text of the Pal. Targ.

FRAGMENTARY TARGUM. The *editio princeps* of the Fragmentary Targum (= FT) was published under the title 'Targum Yerushalmi' in the first edition of Bomberg's *Biblia Rabbinica*, Venice 1516-17 [= Bomb 1]. Five MSS closely related to the Bomberg text are now known:
(1) V = Ebr. 440, fols 198-227, Vatican Library (13th cent.);
(2) N = Solger 2,2°, fols 119-47, Stadtbibliothek, Nürnberg (1291 C.E.);
(3) L = B.H. fol. 1, Universitätsbibliothek, Leipzig (13th/14th cent.);
(4) M = Ms 3 of the Günzburg Collection, Moscow (16th cent.);
(5) S = Ms 264 of the Sassoon Collection (17th cent.).
Klein has demonstrated the inter-relationship of these various textwitnesses.[5] Bomb 1 and M are both transcriptions of N. S is copied from Bomb 1, or possibly from the second edition of the *Biblia Rabbinica*, Venice 1524-5 [= Bomb 2]. V and L are both independent of N, and of each other. V contains 908 verses of the Pentateuch (taken from all five books), N 833 verses, and L 293 verses. Though V, N and L differ in length, it appears from their overlaps that they constitute a single recension of FT and, presumably, ultimately go back to a common archetype. FT as represented by these MSS has three distinguishing features: *first*, it is a Palestinian Targum, in western Aramaic; *second* it covers only selected verses of the Pentateuch (hence its name); *third*, although it contains numerous aggadic expansions, it also contains a significant number of verses where the translation is literal.

---

[5] Klein, 'Extant Sources'.

There are four other MSS, which cannot be related stemmatically to the Bomberg group, though they show all the characteristics of the FT. These should be regarded as four further recensions of FT. The MSS are:

(1) P = Hébr. 110, fols 1-16, Bibliothèque Nationale, Paris (15th/16th cent.): 589 verses of the Pentateuch;

(2) J = Ms 605 (ENA 2587), fols 6-7, Jewish Theological Seminary of America, New York (14th/15th cent.): Exod 14:1, 13, 14, 29-31; 15:1-2; 17:15-16; 19:1-8;

(3) B = Or. 10794 (Gaster collection), fol. 8, British Library, London (? 12th/13th cent.): Deut 1:1 - 5:9;

(4) C = T-S AS 72.75,76,77, University Library, Cambridge (9th/10th - mid 11th cent.): Deut 23:15 - 28:5; 32:35 - 33:9.

There are, then, in all some five different recensions of the targum-type known as the Fragmentary Targum.

Why did the FT text-form evolve? Why should anyone make such a collection of Palestinian Targum fragments? It is hard to say. Some have seen FT as a set of variant readings intended to supplement a complete text of the Palestinian Targum. In support of this idea it should be noted that if the marginal glosses of Neofiti 1 were collected and published separately they would constitute a kind of FT. On the other hand, it is arguable that, like the targumic Toseftot (on which see below), the collection was made to supplement Onk. Both the Toseftot and the FT may have arisen at a time when Onk was becoming the dominant targum in the west. Since Onk is, on the whole, a non-aggadic targum, the need was felt to preserve the aggadic material of the Palestinian Targum. The Toseftot may be rather random Palestinian traditions known to scribes who copied Onk. FT, however, looks like something more systematic: it has probably not arisen through collecting traditions from different sources, but by deliberate abridgement of complete recensions of the Palestinian Targum. Complete Palestinian targumim were collated against Onk, and the non-aggadic passages removed. This view gains support from the fact that the verses which are not represented by any of the recensions of FT are usually rendered more or less literally in at least one of the complete recensions of the Palestinian Targum.

TARGUMIC TOSEFTOT. Here and there in the MSS of Onk aggadic passages are to be found under the rubric 'Tosefta' or 'Tosefta Yerushalmi'. These passages are clearly interpolations, derived from the Palestinian Targum, which were meant to embellish the literal version of Onk. The Toseftot may be inserted into the text of Onk at the appropriate place, or written in the margin, or gathered together at the end of the main text. Separate collections of Toseftot are also attested. The Toseftot differ from FT in two respects:

(1) they are always expansive, whereas FT contains a significant number of verses which are translated literally; and

(2) while FT's western Aramaic dialect has been preserved more or less intact,

the dialect of the Toseftot has been deliberately corrected (with varying degrees of consistency and success) to conform to the dialect of Onk. This linguistic recasting is a feature not only of the Toseftot inserted into the Onk MSS, but also of the separate collections of Toseftot as well, thus showing that the latter too were intended to supplement Onk. Where the Toseftot overlap with other Pal. Targ. texts they often prove to represent independent recensions of the Pal. Targ.

FESTIVAL COLLECTIONS. Some MSS contain collections of targumim covering the Tora lections for the festivals and special Sabbaths. The nature of this type of text is well illustrated by Bodleian Ms Heb. e 43, fols 57-67 (= Kahle F), the colophon of which states: 'This is the notebook *(diftar)* of Jacob, son of Ṣemaḥ . . . It contains the targum of the additional readings *(musafim)* for all the Festivals, and the targum for Hanukka' (fol 57r). The relationship between these Festival Collections and the complete Palestinian targumim such as Neof is analogous to the relationship between the homiletic midrashim (e.g. *Pesikta de-Rav Kahana*) and the straightforward exegetical midrashim (e.g. *Mekhilta de-R. Yishmael*). The Festival Collections differ from each other both as to content and as to textual reading. There is nothing to suggest that they go back to a common archetype, or archetypes, or that there was any attempt to produce a standard collection.

TARGUMIC POEMS. The character of these Aramaic compositions is well illustrated by the poem *'Ezel Moshe*, which gives, in the form of an alphabetic acrostic, a dramatic version of Moses' encounter with the Red Sea during the Exodus from Egypt. Though not strictly a targum, there is evidence connecting the poem to the targum of the Tora reading for the 7th day of Passover (Exod 14-15). It is inserted into the targum after Exod 14:29 in MS Paris 110, and interwoven with the verses of the targum in MS 335 of the University Library, Hamburg. The poem represents, in rather extreme form, the sort of aggadic embellishment of the biblical narrative which is common in the Palestinian targumim. The different ways in which it is presented in the Paris and Hamburg MSS in relation to the targum, may reflect different ways of reciting the poem in synagogue. The antiquity of the *'Ezel Moshe* is confirmed by the fact that a 4th/5th cent. papyrus fragment of it is extant.[6] A number of other Aramaic poems relating to the 7th day of Passover are known, as well as to Shavuot, to *Shabbat ha-Ḥodesh*, and to the story of the death of Moses (Deut 34).[7] These poems throw light on the aggada of the targum, and on its liturgical presentation in synagogue.

[6] Yahalom, "Ezel Moshe', edits the papyrus and compares it with the medieval versions of the poem.
[7] The most extensive listing of these poems is still Zunz, *Literaturgeschichte*, 18-22, 74-80, 150-51.

THE PROPHETS: YONATAN

Targum Yonatan [= Yon] is the counterpart of Onk on the Pentateuch; it is the official Babylonian targum to the second division of the canon. The attribution to Yonatan ben Uzziel is based on *B.T. Megilla* 3a: 'R. Yirmayahu – or some say R. Ḥiyya bar Abba – said: . . . The targum of the Prophets was composed by Yonatan ben Uzziel from the mouth of [= under the guidance of] Haggai, Zechariah and Malachi'. Yonatan is a shadowy figure. According to *B.T. Sukka* 28a (cf. *B.T. Bava Batra* 134a; *P.T. Nedarim* 39a; *Avot de-Rabbi Natan* A14, 29a) he was the most distinguished of Hillel's pupils; but here he is made a contemporary of Haggai, Zechariah and Malachi, the last of the prophets.[8] Barthélemy has argued that in fact the reference in *B.T. Megilla* 3a is not to an Aramaic version, but to the Greek version of Theodotion (= Yonatan). He points out that on a number of occasions elsewhere in the Talmud the Targum of the Prophets is, by implication, attributed to Rav Yosef bar Ḥiyya (c. 270-333 c.e.), the head of the Academy of Pumbeditha – a scholar reputed to have made a special study of targum. Thus Targ. Isa 5:17 is cited in *B.T. Pesaḥim* 68a, and Targ. Obad 6 in *B.T. Bava Kamma* 3b, under the rubric, 'as Rav Yosef translates'. (See also Ḥai Gaon's commentary on *Toharot* quoted in the *Arukh*, ed. Kohut, II pp. 293a, 308a.)[9] The tradition is cited in the name of R. Yirmeyahu and R. Ḥiyya b. Abba (both third century Palestinian authorities), so it could well have referred originally to Theodotion. There can be no doubt, however, that in Babylonia it was taken as referring to an Aramaic version. The mistake would be analogous to the transfer to the Targum of the Pentateuch of a tradition originally about the Greek version of Aquila.

Yon was held in high esteem in Babylonia and is cited as authoritative in the Bavli. On several occasions quotations from it are introduced by the formula: 'Were it not for the targum of this verse we should not know what it means' (*B.T. Megilla* 3a; parallels: *B.T. Moed Katan* 28b; *B.T. Sanhedrin* 94b; *B.T. Berakhot* 28b). It has close affinities with Onk both in language and in the character of its translation, though it is rather more aggadic than Onk, and in poetic passages can be quite expansive (see e.g. Judg 5 and 1 Sam 2:1-10). It has all the marks of thorough editing, its renderings being, on the whole, consistent. Yon was probably redacted in Babylonia about the same time as Onk. Though, like Onk, its text is very stable there are significant textual variants in the MSS. The major text-critical problem is the relationship of the Yemenite MSS with supralinear vocalisation (e.g. Mss Or. 2210 and Or. 2211 of the British Library, London) to western MSS with Tiberian vocalisation (e.g. Codex Reuchlinianus). There appear to be two slightly different recensions of the targum – a western and a Yemenite. It is generally assumed that the Yemenite MSS take us closer to the Babylonian form of the targum.

---

[8]   An analysis of the rabbinic traditions regarding Yonatan may be found in Neusner, *Development*, 90 and *Rabbinic Traditions* 1, 198-200, 206-7, 393.

[9]   Barthélemy, *Les devanciers*, 90.

Codex Reuchlinianus contains about 80 passages (in both the Former and the Latter Prophets) under the rubric 'Targum Yerushalmi' or 'Targum 'Aḥer'. These are probably remnants of a recension, or recensions of a complete Palestinian Targum of the Prophets. Other fragments are found in other sources, sometimes called 'Tosefta of the Land of Israel', or simply 'Tosefta'. Like the Palestinian Toseftot to Onk these Toseftot were presumably intended to supplement Yon's literal version. Though Palestinian in origin they are often recast in the Aramaic dialect of Yon. They presumably arose at a time when Yon was displacing the Palestinian Targum of the Prophets as the authoritative liturgical version, and represent an attempt to salvage some of the more interesting Palestinian traditions.

THE WRITINGS

According to *B.T. Megilla* 3a Yonatan ben Uzziel wanted to translate the Writings, but was forbidden: 'He (Yonatan ben Uzziel) further sought to reveal (by) a targum (the inner meaning) of the Writings, but a *bat qôl* went forth and said, Enough! What was the reason? – Because the date of the Messiah is foretold in them.' This might suggest that in talmudic times no targum of the Writings was known, or in use, in Babylonia. Yet targumim for all the Writings are extant (with the predictable exception of Ezra, Nehemiah and Daniel), some of which are ascribed in rabbinic literature to the Babylonian scholar Rav Yosef. Thus *Soferim* 13:6 introduces a quotation from the *Targum Sheni* to Esther 3:1 with the words, 'Rav Yosef translated'. This may be yet another case of attributing an anonymous targum to the great Babylonian targum expert. Mediaeval writers, more reasonably, refer to the targumim of the Writings as 'Targum Yerushalmi'. The aggadic nature of many of these targumim, their basic dialect, and their translational equivalents tend to bear out this classification.

The targumim of the Writings have not been studied as intensively as the Pentateuchal targumim, and many fundamental textual problems still remain unresolved. There is evidence everywhere of great textual fluidity – a lack of textual stability reminiscent of the Pal. Targ. to the Pentateuch. Quite diverse recensions exist for most of the targumim of the Writings. Targ. Lamentations is a case in point: at least two recensions of this are extant – one in the Yemenite mss (e.g. Or 1476 of the British Library, London), the other in western mss (e.g. Codex Urbinas 1 of the Vatican Library). Comparison of these two recensions leads to the unexpected conclusion that, if we ignore the superior vocalisation of the Yemenite mss, the western recension is arguably older and better than the Yemenite.[10] This distinction between western and Yemenite recensions seems to extend to Targum Canticles and Targum Qohelet as well. Mss both of

---

[10] This is argued at length by Alexander, 'Textual Tradition'.

western and Yemenite provenance exist for the other two Megillot (Ruth and Esther), but there the recensional picture is very unclear. The case of Esther is particularly difficult. Bomberg in his Rabbinic Bible distinguished two targumim to Esther – one of which he called 'Targum' and the other 'Targum Sheni'. There are Yemenite MSS (and, apparently, some western MSS) which do not observe this distinction, but present texts displaying a mixture of both recensions of the Targ. Esther. There is also the so-called 'Third Targum' to Esther, found only in the Antwerp Polyglott (1569-72).

The targumim to Psalms, Job and Proverbs form an interconnected group. In Job, and to a lesser degree in Psalms, two (sometimes three or even four) targumim are given for a single verse, the first being more or less literal, the second, introduced by the formula 'Targum 'Aḥer', being aggadic. These targumim were presumably created by deliberate and systematic fusion of originally different recensions. They mark the confluence of originally different streams of tradition. Targum Proverbs has significant affinities to the Peshitta of Proverbs. It is not clear whether the targum depends on the Peshitta, or the Peshitta on the targum, or whether both draw on a common source.

No targum of Chronicles was known to the editors of the early Rabbinic Bibles and the Polyglotts. The *editio princeps* did not appear till 1680-83.[11] Three MSS are extant:

(1) E = the Erfurt Codex (now Ms. or. fol. 1210 and 1211, Deutsche Staatsbibliothek, Berlin);
(2) C = Ms. Or. Ee. 5.9, University Library, Cambridge;
(3) V = Codex Urbinas 1 (Urb. Ebr. 1, Vatican Library).

A fourth MS was destroyed in 1945: all that survives is a charred block in the Sächsische Landesbibliothek in Dresden (Mscr. Dresd. A 46). The MSS appear to represent two different recensions of the targum – one found in C and V, the other in E. Targum Chronicles shows strong affinities to the Pal. Targ. of the Pentateuch, particularly Ps-Y (cf. e.g. Targ. 1 Chr 1:4-24 with Ps-Y Gen 10:1-32).

In character the targumim of the Writings differ from each other. Proverbs and Chronicles are non-expansive. Psalms and Job contain numerous aggadic plusses. However, it is in the Megillot that the greatest degree of paraphrase is to be found, particularly in Lamentations, Song of Songs and Esther. *Targum Sheni* to Esther is the most expansive of all the targumim.

The Character of the Targum

TRANSLATION TECHNIQUES

A literature as vast and diverse as the targumim defies easy generalization. One

---

[11] It was published by M.F. Beck at Augsburg. Beck used the Erfurt ms.

common approach to characterizing the targum is to identify and list its various translation-techniques. The implication is that these techniques in sum should suffice to define the phenomenon of 'targumism'. The following are some of the more important translation-techniques which have figured in the discussion:

(1) *Treatment of anthropomorphism*

The targumim on many occasions soften anthropomorphic expressions used of God. E.g.
1. Gen 11:5, 'The Lord came down to see the city and the tower';
   Neof, 'The Glory of the Shekhinah of the Lord was revealed to see the city and the tower'.
2. Gen 3:5, 'For God knows';
   Neof, 'It is revealed and known before the Lord'.
3. Exod 3:20, 'I will put forth my hand and smite the Egyptians';
   Neof, 'I will send the plague of my punishments and put to death the Egyptians'.
4. Exod 15:8, 'With the blast of Your nostrils the waters were piled up';
   Ps-Y, 'By a Word [*memar*] from before you, the waters were transformed into heaps and heaps'.
5. Gen 26:3, 'Sojourn in this land and I will be with you';
   Ps-Y, 'Sojourn in this land and my Word [*memri*] will assist you'.

Since the time of Saadya it has been argued that such translations are motivated by doctrine and arise from a desire to defend the transcendence and spirituality of God. The problem is that the targumim are not consistent: they also translate literally many anthropomorphic terms. No one has yet discovered a pattern in this inconsistency, or offered a convincing explanation for it. It is unlikely that dogma played a significant role. In rabbinic literature contemporary with the targumim God can be spoken of in strikingly anthropomorphic language. The translations quoted above are sonorous, and, presumably, intended, in a general way, to be reverential. They are characteristic of the style of the targum – to the extent that at certain points in targumic literature the style almost becomes parody.[12]

(2) *Actualisation*

The targumim have a tendency to 'update' Scripture. E.g. they regularly identify biblical peoples and places with peoples and places from their own times. All the Palestinian Targumim systematically interpret the names on the

---

[12]   Klein gives the most balanced treatment of anthropomorphism in the targumim. See especially his *Anthropomorphisms and Anthropopathisms*. Further, Hayward, *The Memra*, and Muñoz León, *Dios Palabra* and *Gloria de la Shekina*.

Table of the Nations in Gen 10. Thus Gen 10:2 becomes in Ps-Y: 'The sons of Japhet were Gomer, Magog, Madai, Javan, Tubal, Meshech, and Tiras, and the names of their provinces are: Phrygia, Germania, Media, Macedonia, Bithynia, Asia, and Thrace'. The targumic treatment of Gen 10 gives a map of the world as known to the meturgemanim. In similar fashion they identify many of the places mentioned in the definition of the borders of the Promised Land in Num 34:3-12, and so provide a targumic map of Erets Israel. Later institutions, such as the synagogue and the Beit ha-Midrash, are introduced into the narratives of the patriarchal period (see e.g. Ps-Y to Gen 9:27, and Neof to Gen 30:13). In general the phenomenon of actualisation may be compared to the practice in 17th century Dutch art of painting biblical scenes in 17th century Dutch costumes and settings.

(3) *Doublets*

In a doublet the original is translated twice. E.g. Gen 18:3: MT, 'If now I have found *favour* in your eyes'; Neof, 'If now I have found *grace and favour* in your sight'. Exod 15:1: MT, 'I will *sing* to the Lord'; Neof, 'Let us *praise and extol* before the Lord'. In these two cases one word in the original is involved. Sometimes it is a phrase. E.g. Gen 4:4: MT, 'The Lord favoured Abel'; Ps-Y, 'It was pleasing before the Lord, and the Lord favoured Abel'. There may be different reasons for doublets. It may be simply a matter of style. Or a pair of words may have come to form a cliché: for 'grace and favour' see Esth 2:17, and for 'praise and extol' see Dan 2:23. In some cases doublets can arise through the conflation of different textual traditions. In the doublets considered here the second element is synonymous with the first. There are, however, examples of double translation where the second element offers a different, perhaps even contradictory, rendering of the Hebrew from the first. Note Ps-Y's double rendering of the Hebrew *nᵉśô* in Gen 4:13 as 'tolerate', and 'forgive' (see further below). Such antithetic doublets are, perhaps, aimed at maximizing the sense of Scripture.

(4) *Associative translation*

Associative translation[13] occurs where in translating text A the meturgeman is influenced by similar phraseology in text B. E.g. Exod 16:31 states with regard to manna that 'the taste of it was like wafers (made) with honey' [Hebrew: *ṭaʿmô kᵉṣappîḥit biḏᵉḇāš*]. Neof translates: 'its taste was like pancakes [*šišin*] with honey'. The parallel text in Num 11:8 describes the taste of the manna as being 'like the taste of a cake baked with oil' [Hebrew: *kᵉṭaʿam lᵉšad haššemen*]. There

---

[13]   See Klein, 'Associative and Complementary Translation'. Klein's various essays analysing the translation techniques of the targumim are particularly commendable. Further, Sperber, *The Bible in Aramaic*, 4B, 37-264.

too Neof has, 'like the taste of pancakes with honey'. The psychological mechanism of associative translation is not always clear. In some cases the influence of the parallel text seems to be subconscious: there is no deliberate harmonisation; the parallel simply echoes at the back of the translator's mind. In other cases the association may be more calculated, perhaps triggered by a linguistic problem. In the example just given the meturgeman may have been puzzled by the expression *lᵉšad haššemen* in Num 11:8, and simply for convenience re-used the translation of the parallel passage in Exod 16:31.

(5) *Complementary translation*

This is a variant of associative translation. However, instead of an element from text A displacing the parallel element in text B, the parallel elements are combined and a composite translation worked out which is used in *both* texts. E.g. Cain is described in Gen 4:2 as 'a tiller of the soil' [*'ōḇēd 'ᵃḏāmā*]; Noah is called 'a man of the soil' [*'îš 'ᵃḏāmā*] in Gen 9:20. Ps-Y translates in both cases, 'a man tilling the soil'.

(6) *Converse translation*

In converse translation[14] the targum appears to give a sense opposite to the plain meaning of Scripture. This frequently involves the insertion or deletion of a negative. E.g. Gen 4:14, 'Behold, you have driven me this day from the face of the ground; and I shall be hidden from your face'; Neof, 'Behold, you have banished me this day from the face of the earth, and it is not possible for me to be hidden from before you'. In some of these cases the targum has reversed the sense of Scripture by treating positive statements as questions without an interrogative particle, to which the implied answer is 'no'. Note Ps-Y's translation of Gen 4:14, 'Behold, you have banished me this day from the face of the earth; yet is it possible that I should be hidden from before you?' Converse translation in this instance is motivated by doctrinal concerns: the plain sense of Scripture appears to call into question the omniscience of God.

DIFFERENT TYPES OF TARGUM

Analysis of the translation-techniques of the targum is an important subject, but its limitations should be clearly recognized. It very rapidly ends up in subjectivity: we find ourselves trying to guess what was going on in the minds of the meturgemanim. (Note, particularly the problem of associative translation.) Moreover a definition of targumism in terms of translation-techniques can hardly be adequate because it fails to discriminate between texts, and it ignores fundamental questions of literary form. There are, in fact, quite different types

---

[14] Klein, 'Converse Translation'.

of translation found within the confines of the targumic corpus. A distinction is commonly drawn between 'paraphrastic' and 'literal' targumim, by measuring the relative lengths of the targumim against the original. That is not a very meaningful approach, for it obscures the fact that paraphrastic translations may differ fundamentally from each other, and that a paraphrastic and a literal targum may, formally speaking, have more in common than two paraphrastic targumim. There are more important classifications to be made. Two basic types of targum – type A and type B – should be distinguished. To illustrate their character we will present an extensive sample of each.

Type A Targum

TARGUM PSEUDO-YONATAN, GENESIS 4:3-16

4:3, MT: *It came to pass in process of time, that Cain brought of the fruit of the ground an offering to the Lord.*
TARGUM: *It came to pass in process of time*, on the fourteenth of Nisan, *that Cain brought of the produce of the ground*, of the seed of flax, *an offering* of first-fruits *before the Lord.*

4:4, MT: *And Abel, he also brought of the firstlings of the flock and of the fat thereof, and the Lord favoured Abel and his offering.*
TARGUM: *And Abel, he also brought of the firstlings of his flock and of the fat thereof,* and it was pleasing before the Lord, *and the Lord favoured Abel and his offering.*

4:5, MT: *But Cain and his offering he did not favour. And Cain was very angry and his countenance fell.*
TARGUM: *But Cain and his offering he did not favour. And Cain was very angry and* the expression of *his countenance fell.*

4:6, MT: *The Lord said to Cain: Why are you angry, and why has your countenance fallen?*
TARGUM: *The Lord said to Cain: Why are you angry, and why has* the expression of *your countenance fallen?*

4:7, MT: *If you do well, is there not lifting up [šᵉ'ēt]? But if you do not do well, sin crouches at the door; to you is its desire, but you shall rule over it.*
TARGUM: *If you will amend your deeds, shall not your guilt be forgiven you?* But if you will not amend your deeds in this world, your sin is kept till the great day of judgement. Sin *crouches at the doors* of your heart, but into your hand I have given authority over the evil inclination; *to you shall be its desire, but you shall rule over it,* whether to act justly or to sin.

4:8, MT: *And Cain said to Abel his brother . . . And it came to pass, when they were in the field, that Cain rose up against Abel his brother, and killed him.*

229

TARGUM: *Cain said to Abel his brother:* Come, let us both go out into the field. *And it came to pass, when they had gone out,* both of them, *into the field, that* Cain answered and said to Abel: I see that the world has been created through mercy, but it is not ordered according to the fruit of good deeds; and that there is partiality in judgement. Otherwise why was your offering accepted with favour, whereas my offering was not accepted from me with favour? Abel answered and said to Cain: The world has been created through mercy, and it is ordered according to the fruit of good deeds, and there is no partiality in judgement. It is because the fruit of my deeds was better than yours and preferable to yours that my offering was accepted with favour. Cain answered and said to Abel: There is no judgement, no judge, no other world; there is no fair reward given to the righteous nor punishment exacted from the wicked. Abel answered and said to Cain: There is judgement, there is a judge, and another world; there is a fair reward given to the righteous and punishment exacted from the wicked. On account of these matters they were quarreling in the open field, and *Cain rose up against Abel his brother,* drove a stone into his forehead, *and killed him.*

4:9, MT: *The Lord said to Cain: Where is Abel your brother? He said: I do not know; am I my brother's keeper?*

TARGUM: *The Lord said to Cain: Where is Abel your brother? He said: I do not know; am I my brother's keeper?*

4:10: MT: *He said: What have you done? The voice of the bloods of your brother cries to me from the ground.*

TARGUM: *He said: What have you done? The voice of the bloods of* the killing of *your brother* that were swallowed up in the clay *cry before me from the ground.*

4:11, MT: *And now cursed are you from the ground, which has opened its mouth to receive the bloods of your brother from your hand.*

TARGUM: *And now,* because you have killed him, *cursed are you from the ground, which has opened its mouth to receive the bloods of your brother from your hand.*

4:12, MT: *When you cultivate the ground, it shall not henceforth yield its strength to you; a fugitive and a wanderer shall you be in the earth.*

TARGUM: *When you cultivate the earth, it shall not henceforth yield the strength* of *its* fruits *to you; a fugitive and a wanderer shall you be in the earth.*

4:13, MT: *Cain said to the Lord: My sin is too great to bear.*

TARGUM: *Cain said before the Lord: My rebellion is* far *too great to be borne,* yet before you is the power to forgive it.

4:14, MT: *Behold, you have driven me this day from the face of the ground; and I shall be hidden from your face. I shall be a fugitive and a wanderer in the earth; and it shall come to pass, that anyone finding me will kill me.*

TARGUM: *Behold, you have banished me this day from the face of the earth; yet is it possible that I should be hidden from before you? And if I shall be a fugitive and a wanderer in the earth, any* just *man who will find me will kill me.*

4:15, MT: *The Lord said to him: Therefore, whoever kills Cain, sevenfold shall vengeance be exacted from him. And the Lord set for Cain a sign, lest anyone finding him should strike him.*

TARGUM: *The Lord said to him: Therefore, whoever,* for seven generations, *kills Cain, punishment shall be exacted from him. And the Lord inscribed upon* the face of *Cain a letter* from the great and glorious Name, *so that anyone who found him,* when he saw it, *should not kill him.*

4:16, MT: *And Cain went out from the presence of the Lord, and dwelt in the land of wandering, before [*qidmat*] Eden.*

TARGUM: *And Cain went out from before the Lord, and dwelt in the land of the wandering* of his exile, which had been made for him *from of old [*milleqadmin*], like the Garden of Eden.*

Even a cursory reading of this passage from Pseudo-Yonatan will show that it does not offer a translation of the Hebrew, in any normal sense of that term: it is a paraphrase. Two important points about the nature of this paraphrase should be noted. *First*, when expansions occur they are presented in such a way that they can be bracketed out, leaving behind a viable one-to-one rendering of the original. This is the distinguishing characteristic of type A targum: it consists of a base translation + detachable glosses. In the targum translation above the base translation is indicated by the use of italics. *Second*, the expansions are unevenly distributed. Sections of the text are rendered more or less literally; others are expanded many times over. The most striking expansion is at verse 8. The effect of this within the targumic retelling of the story is to focus attention on this point of the narrative. The meturgeman saw the events of verse 8 as marking a crisis in the unfolding drama, as holding the key to its meaning. The additions in Ps-Y to Genesis 22:10 and 14 perform a similar literary function in the targumic version of the Akeda.

The additions at Gen 4:8 have been generated by a lacuna in the biblical narrative: the Bible fails to tell us what happened in the field which led to Cain murdering Abel. The targum supplies the omission: Cain and Abel had an argument – a profound theological argument about the relationship between the divine attributes of mercy *(raḥamim)* and justice *(din)*. The narrative lacuna in the Bible provides the meturgeman with the chance to read into Scripture some of his own theological concepts. Abel takes the classic rabbinic view that in his governance of the world God holds justice and mercy in balance. If Abel has been favoured, it is because God is rewarding his good deeds. Cain on the other hand denies that justice operates: there is only mercy, which, in the absence of the counterweight of justice, becomes perverted into partiality and

231

favouritism. God has accepted Abel's sacrifice on an arbitrary whim. By introducing this debate the meturgeman universalizes the story: Abel becomes the prototype of the martyr who dies for the profession of his faith; Cain the prototype of the heretic who persecutes the faithful. Some have detected an anti-Sadducean polemic here.[15] This is speculative. There is only one element in Cain's position which is arguably distinctively Sadducean, viz. the denial of the world to come. But it should be noted that there is no stress on this: it comes in incidentally, in the context of the denial of divine justice.

At a number of other points the targum fills in narrative lacunae.

(1) The Bible fails to give a satisfactory reason why Abel's offering was accepted, and Cain's rejected, thus leaving dangerously open the possibility that God acted arbitrarily. Two small additions in the targum of verse 1 are addressed to this problem. The targum asserts that the events took place on the 14th of Nisan, i.e. at the time of Passover, and that the offering brought by Cain was 'the seed of flax'. The implication is that Cain and Abel were celebrating a primitive Passover: Abel's offering was appropriate ('the firstlings of the flock'), but Cain's was not ('produce of the ground').

(2) At the beginning of verse 8 the masoretic text states that 'Cain said to Abel his brother', but does not tell us what he said. The targum renders: 'Cain said to Abel his brother: Come, let us both go out into the field'. It is possible that the meturgeman actually had a Hebrew text which read the additional words (cf. LXX and Peshitta); the MT may simply be defective. In this case we would have a textual rather than a narrative lacuna. However, it is equally possible that the meturgeman had the MT before him and deduced the missing words from the context.

(3) At the end of verse 8 the targum supplements the Bibly by suggesting *how* Cain killed Abel: 'he drove a stone into his forehead'. This tradition, which may have been influenced by a memory of Exod 21:18 ('if men contend, and one smites the other with a stone . . .'), is as old as *Jub* 4:31.

(4) The targum identifies the 'sign' which the Lord set for Cain (verse 15) as a letter from the 'great and glorious Name' (= the Tetragrammaton), which God inscribed on his face (i.e. presumably on his forehead). The letter of the divine name acted like an amulet to shield him from harm.

In each of these instances the meturgeman has supplied the sort of circumstantial detail which an audience would demand from a retelling of the Bible story, though at the same time he never misses an opportunity to impose his own theology on the text. At other points he expands the text to cope with more immediate exegetical problems. Verse 7 is a case in point. The meturgeman produces a coherent, and in its way convincing, resolution of this *crux interpretum*. He takes the ambiguous s^e'$\bar{e}t$ as = s^e'$\bar{e}t$ '$\bar{a}w\bar{o}n$, 'removal of guilt', i.e. forgiveness (cf. Psalm 85:3). So the sense of the first part of the verse becomes: If you amend your ways – in effect, if you repent – you will be forgiven. The

---

[15] Isenberg, 'An Anti-Sadducee Polemic'.

converse is then added: If you do *not* repent, your sins will be judged on the day of judgement. 'Sin crouching at the door' is read as an image of temptation – as an allusion to the evil inclination *yeṣer ha-ra'*). The 'doors' are the doors of the heart. Sin desires to enter and dominate, but it lies entirely within man's power whether he does good or evil. Once again the meturgeman has skilfully worked his own ideas into the text. In this case it is the doctrine of the two inclinations, in particular the notion that man can subdue the evil inclination and choose to do good.

Repentance is a major motif in the targum's reading of the story. Cain is a notable example of repentance, as well as of heresy. At verse 13 Cain acknowledges the heinousness of his crime: 'My rebellion is far too great to be borne'. The sense appears to be that it is intolerable to *God*, as the translation 'rebellion' *(meroda)* for the Hebrew *'āwōn* indicates. Yet God's power of forgiveness transcends even Cain's sin. Verse 13 is read as a prayer for pardon. In effect it involves a double rendering of the Hebrew *n'śô'* – as 'bear/tolerate' and as 'forgive'. Cain's repentance explains the suspension of divine punishment 'for seven generations' (perhaps to allow him to prove the sincerity of his change of heart), and the protection of the divine name – a privilege which would not have been granted to an impenitent scoundrel (cf. *Canticles Rabba* 4:12, 2: 'The weapons which were given to them at Horeb had the ineffable Name inscribed on them, and when they sinned it was taken away from them'). The Hebrew *šiḇ'āṯayim* ('sevenfold') in verse 15 has been interpreted as 'for seven generations', and, contrary to the masoretic accentuation, has been joined with the preceeding phrase ('whoever kills'), rather than with the following verb ('punishment shall be exacted'). That this is the intention of the targum becomes clear from Ps-Y to Gen 4:24: 'If for Cain who sinned and returned in repentance, (judgement) was suspended for seven generations, for Lamech, the son of his son, who did not sin, it is right that (judgement) should remain in suspense for seventy-seven generations.'

It is not possible to go into detail here as to Ps-Y's relationship to the other targumim of this passage. Two brief notes must suffice.

(1) At vers 16 the sense of the targum is not immediately clear. The meaning is probably *not* that the land of Cain's exile was one of the special things, like the Garden of Eden, created at the beginning of the world.[16] Rather the idea is that before Cain's sin the earth was like the Garden of Eden. His sin had a disastrous effect on nature. God's curse on the earth (Gen 3:17-18) was suspended, and only became operative after the murder of Abel. The meturgeman saw a parallel between Cain's exile and Adam's expulsion from Paradise, between the curse of Gen 3:17-18 and the curse of Gen 4:12. The sense of the targum then is: Cain dwelt in the land of his exile, which had been to him formerly like the Garden of Eden. Some of the other targumim are more explicit: 'Cain went out

---

[16]   As argued by Bowker, 'Haggadah in the Targum Onkelos', 54-55. The parallel with Ps-Y Gen 2:8 is not compelling.

from before the Lord and dwelt as an exile and a wanderer in the land east of the Garden of Eden. Until he killed Abel the earth had borne him fruit like the fruit of the Garden of Eden, but after he sinned and killed Abel, it changed and bore him thorns and thistles' (Neof). Ps-Y's interpretation is allusive. The obscurity of its translation has come about because it is abbreviating a fuller tradition.

(2) At verse 10 Ps-Y surprisingly does not exploit the plural 'bloods' (dāmîm). There was an old and widespread tradition (found in M. Sanhedrin 4:5, and in the other targumim to this verse) that the plural alludes to Abel's righteous progeny whom Cain aborted by murdering his brother. The omission is surely significant, even though the precise reason for it is unclear. Perhaps the meturgeman did not want to blacken Cain too much, and so make his repentance and forgiveness less plausible.[17]

Type B Targum

Type B targum, like type A, is paraphrastic, but it displays a fundamental difference in form. In type A a viable one-to-one translation of the Hebrew can be extracted from the paraphrase by bracketing out the additions. In type B a base translation cannot be recovered: the translation is dissolved in the paraphrase. Type B targum may be illustrated from the description of the body of the beloved in Canticles 5:10-16.

TARGUM CANTICLES 5:10-16

5:10, MT: dôdî ṣaḥ wᵉ'ādôm dāgûl mērᵉḇāḇā.
My beloved is white and ruddy, pre-eminent above ten thousand.
TARGUM: Then began the Assembly of Israel to speak of the praise of the Lord of the Universe, and thus she said: That *God do I desire* to serve who in the day is wrapped in a robe *white* as snow, and is occupied with the Twenty Four Books – the words of the Law, and the words of the Prophets and the Writings; and by night he is occupied with the six Orders of the Mishna. The splendour of the glory of his face shines like fire, on account of (his) great wisdom and powers of argument, for he promulgates new decisions every day, and he will disclose them to his people on the Great Day. And his *banner* [ṭiqsa] is over *ten thousand* myriads of angels who minister before him.

5:11, MT: rō'šô keṯem pāz qᵉwuṣṣôṭāyw taltallîm šᵉḥōrôṯ kā'ôrēḇ.
His head is as the most fine gold, his locks are curled, and black as a raven.
TARGUM: *His head* is the Law, which is more precious than *pure gold*; and [*his locks* are] the interpretation of the Words (of the Law), in which are *heaped up*

---

[17] The best discussion of this passage is Vermes, 'Targumic Versions'. For an earlier treatment see Grelot, 'Les Targums du Pentateuque'.

234

reasons and precepts. To those who keep them, they are white as snow, but to those who do not keep them, they are *black* like the face of *the raven.*

5:12, MT: *'ênāyw kᵉyônîm 'al-'ᵃpîqê māyim rōḥᵃṣôṯ beḥālāḇ yōšᵉḇôṯ 'al-millē'ṯ.*

His eyes are like doves beside the water-brooks; washed with milk, and fitly set.

TARGUM: *His eyes* look constantly upon Jerusalem, to do good to her and to bless her, from the beginning of the year to its end (*like doves* that stand and look at *fountains of water*) – through the merit of those *sitting* in the Sanhedrin, who busy themselves with the Law, and make justice shine/flow [*manharin*], so that it is smoothe like *milk*, and (through the merit) of those sitting in the Houses of Study, who are circumspect in judgement, till they reach a decision to acquit or to condemn.

5:13, MT: *lᵉḥāyāw ka'ᵃrûgaṯ habbōśem migdᵉlôṯ merqāḥîm śip̄ᵉṯōṯāyw šôšannîm nōṭᵉp̄ôṯ môr 'ōḇēr.*

His cheeks are as a bed of spices, as banks of sweet herbs; his lips are as lilies, dropping with flowing myrrh.

TARGUM: The *two tablets [luḥe]* of stone which he gave to his people are written in ten lines, similar to the lines in a *spice-garden,* and *produce [merabbin]* subtleties just as the garden produces *spices.* And the *lips* of his sages, who busy themselves with the Law, *drip* reasons on every side, and the utterance of their mouths is as *choice myrrh.*

5:14, MT: *yāḏāyw gᵉlîlê zāhāḇ mᵉmullā'îm battaršîš mē'āyw 'ešeṯ šēn mᵉ'ullepeṯ sappîrîm.*

His hands are as rods of gold set with beryl; his body is as polished ivory overlaid with sapphires.

TARGUM: The *twelve tribes* of his servant Jacob were *enrolled [gelilan]* upon the breast-plate, the *golden* ornament of holiness - engraved upon twelve gems, along with the three Patriarchs of the world, Abraham, Isaac and Jacob. Reuben was engraved on carnelian; Simeon was engraved on topaz; Levi was engraved on smaragd; Judah was engraved on carbuncle; Dan was engraved on sapphire; Issachar was engraved on emerald; Gad was engraved on jacinth; Asher was engraved on agate; Naphthali was engraved on amethyst; Zebulun was engraved on *beryl;* Joseph was engraved on onyx; Benjamin was engraved on jasper. (These were) like the twelve signs of the zodiac, shining like a *lantern ['ašašit],* resplendent in their workmanship as elephant's tusk, and shining like *sapphires.*

5:15, MT: *šôqāyw 'ammûdê šēš mᵉyussāḏîm 'al-'aḏnê-p̄āz mar'ēhû kallᵉḇānôn bāḥûr kā'ᵃrāzîm.*

His legs are as pillars of marble, set upon sockets of fine gold; his aspect is like Lebanon, excellent as the cedars.

235

TARGUM: *The righteous are the pillars of the world, resting on supports of fine gold,* that is to say, on the words of the Law with which they busy themselves, and by means of which they admonish the people of the House of Israel to do his will. Comely is he, and filled with compassion towards them as an Ancient One, and he makes the guilt of the House of Israel *white* as snow. He is ready to wage triumphant war against the nations who transgress his word, like *a young man*, mighty and strong *as cedars*.

5:16, MT: *ḥikko mamᵉṭaqqîm wᵉkullô mahᵃmaddîm zeh dôdî vᵉzeh rēʿî bᵉnôṯ yᵉrušālāyim.*

> *His mouth is most sweet; yea he is altogether lovely. This is my beloved, and this is my friend, O daughters of Jerusalem.*

TARGUM: *The words of his palate are sweet* as honey, and *all* his precepts are more *desirable* to his sages than gold or silver. *This is* the praise of God, *my beloved*, and *this is* the strength of the might of the Lord, *my friend, O you prophets*, who prophesy in *Jersualem*.

The targum's reading of the original is highly coherent. Following the general lines of rabbinic exegesis of Canticles, the speaker is taken as the Assembly of Israel, the Beloved as God. The emphasis in the targum is notably unmystical: the relationship between God and Israel is defined in classic fashion in terms of Tora and commandments. Like much of targum Canticles, this whole passage is presented as a paean of praise to the study of the Oral and Written Law. God himself sets an example: he spends the day studying Scripture, and the night studying Mishna!

At first sight the targum appears untrammelled. Closer analysis suggests that behind it lies a disciplined and exact exegesis of the biblical text. Each element in the original is taken as a symbol or cypher to be decoded and arranged in a coherent story, within the broad hermeneutical perspective that the text is an allegorical statement about God's relationship to Israel through Tora. Canticles 5:13 illustrates the method. 'Cheeks' *(lᵉḥāyayim)* in the Hebrew is interpreted, on the basis of similarity of sound, as alluding to the 'two tablets *(luḥot)* of the Law'. But how can the tablets of the Law be like 'a bed of spices'? The comparison must be between the orderly rows of plants in the herb-garden, and the lines of writing on the tablets. The meturgeman's interpretation of the next word seems to turn on a repointing: for the masoretic *migdᵉlôṯ* he reads *mᵉgaddᵉlôṯ*, 'producing'. *Merqāḥîm* is then given a twofold sense: literally as 'spices', and allegorically as 'the subtleties of the Law'. Hence: 'The Law produces subtleties, just as a herb-garden produces spices'. God's 'lips' are taken naturally as referring to his spokesmen, the Sages, and the 'myrrh' which flows from the lips as the pronouncements of the Sages on matters of Law.

The exegesis underlying the targum is not always obvious. Sometimes it appears to ignore elements in the original. At other times, where the correspondence between the targum and the Hebrew is fairly certain, the basis of the correspondence is not clear. E.g. in Targum Canticles 5:13 what has happened to the biblical 'lilies *(šôšannîm)'*? One suspects it is represented by 'the Law' in the phrase 'who busy themselves with the Law'. But on what grounds has this equation been made? *Canticles Rabba* 5:13, 1 comments: '*His lips are as lilies:* This is the scholar who is fluent in his Mishna'. This clearly implies a correspondence between *šošanna* and *mišna*. Perhaps a similar idea lies behind Targum Canticles, but we cannot be sure. It is similarly unclear why in verse 11, 'head' is equated with 'Law', and 'locks' with 'the interpretation' of the Law, or why in verse 14, 'the twelve tribes of his servant Jacob' should stand against 'his hands'. The reason for these uncertainties is simple. The meturgeman has not made clear his exegetical reasoning, and he has not done so because he remained conscious that, despite the large element of paraphrase which he was introducing, he was producing a text in the form of a translation, not in the form of a midrash. Sometimes he sails close to midrashic form, as at the beginning of verse 11, but his discipline and restraint are quite remarkable. There are a sufficient number of clear correspondences between the targum and the original (shown in italics in the targum translation above) to reveal the basic pattern: each element of the original is taken in its proper order and expounded, and *all* elements of the original are represented. In those cases where elements appear to be 'lost', we may give the meturgeman the benefit of the doubt. It is simply due to our ignorance of the underlying exegetical processes. So then, type B targum, as to general method, turns out to be similar to type A: both types aim to exegete every element in the biblical text in proper, serial order. The difference comes down in the end to one of form. From type A a straightforward, one-to-one rendering can be extracted; from type B it cannot: the original is dissolved in the paraphrase.

The ingenuity and learning of the meturgeman in Targum Canticles should not be underestimated. To sustain this sort of paraphrase over the whole book is a *tour de force*. Targum Canticles is not 'folk' literature: it is a highly learned book, displaying a degree of coherence which suggests that the basic scheme must have been worked out by a single author. Who he was, or where and when he lived it is impossible to say. His originality is shown when we compare his targum with the great compendium of rabbinic interpretation on Canticles, *Canticles Rabba*. There are overlaps between the two works: that is hardly surprising. More significant are the numerous cases where Targum Canticles offers an interpretation *not* found in *Canticles Rabba*. E.g. *Canticles Rabba* is totally unaware of the targum's view that Canticles 5:14 alludes to the high priest's breast-plate, engraved with the names of the twelve tribes. Though Targum Canticles and *Canticles Rabba* drew at certain points on a common tradition of exegesis, it is unlikely that either work is directly dependent on the other.

Sitz im Leben

In what circumstances did these Aramaic versions of the Bible originate, and how were they used? These questions bring us to the Sitz im Leben of the targum.

The targum was a flourishing institution in the period of the Talmud, and a large number of statements scattered through classic rabbinic literature reveal something of its character, use and purpose. These statements must be treated with caution: they are often prescriptive, i.e. they indicate what the rabbinic authorities thought *ought* to happen rather than what was in actual fact the case, and they come from different periods and diverse regions. But they are our only real evidence on the Sitz im Leben of the targum, and they must be the starting-point of any discussion on this subject. Rabbinic literature points to the use of the targum in three distinct settings: (a) synagogue; (b) private devotion; (c) school.[18]

The primary setting for the targum was the synagogue. The majority of the rabbinic references relate to its use in this context. It formed part of the institution of the public reading of the Tora. As the biblical lessons were read out (both Tora and Haftara) they were simultaneously rendered into Aramaic. The rabbinic rules for the delivery of the targum express some very clear ideas as to the targum's nature and function. Targum belonged to the category of Oral Law *(Tora she-be'al pe)* and the way in which it was to be delivered neatly illustrates the rabbinic view of the relationship between Oral and Written Tora *(Tora she-bikhtav)*. Every effort had to be made to avoid confusing the targum with the written text of Scripture. The Scripture reader and the translator *(meturgeman, turgeman, ha-metargem)* must be two different people. The Scripture reader had to be clearly seen to be *reading* from the scroll; the translator had to recite the targum from memory: he was not allowed to use a written text in synagogue, nor was he permitted to glance at the Tora scroll – 'lest the people should say that the translation is written in the Tora'.[19] Nor was the reader allowed to prompt him if he faltered. Translation was simultaneous, but targum was not allowed to overlay Scripture: Scripture and targum were delivered alternately; in the case of the Pentateuch, each verse of Scripture was followed by the corresponding verse of targum, in the case of the Prophets up to three verses could be read before the targum was given.

The underlying purpose of these rules is obviously to keep Scripture and targum apart. At the same time a contrary tendency can be observed – to bring Scripture and targum closely together. The reader and translator stood side by

---

[18] See Alexander, 'Rabbinic Rules', and York, 'The Targum in the Synagogue and in the School'. The major rabbinic references on the use of the targum in synagogue are: *M. Megilla* 4:4, 6; *T. Megilla* 4(3):20, 21; *P.T. Megilla* 74d, 75a; *B.T. Megilla* 21b, 23a/b, 32a; *B.T. Berakhot* 45a; *B.T. Soṭa* 39b; *Pesikta Rabbati* 5 (p. 14a/b) = *Tanḥuma Buber* II, 87-88 (*Wayera* 6). The rules are summarized by Maimonides in *Hilkhot Tefilla*, 12:10-14. The *locus classicus* for the targum in school is *Sifrei Deut.* 161, p. 212.

[19] *B.T. Megilla* 32a.

side. Only small portions of the original were read against the translation, and while translation and original were not allowed to overlap, ideally there should be no pause between Scripture and targum; Scripture and targum were intended to form one continuous, seamless text; they interlocked to make a single unit. The rabbinic view of the function of the targum does not envisage it as an independent version: targum should always stand in the presence of Scripture; original and translation should always be juxtaposed and live in dialectical tension. Again a twofold purpose is discernible. On the one hand the Rabbis were concerned to prevent targum taking off into a life of its own, and so, possibly, replacing Scripture: Scripture had absolute priority; targum was only a bridge to the understanding of Scripture. Once one had crossed over to a secure understanding of Scripture, the bridge could, in theory, be ignored. On the other hand targum offered a useful means of imposing a certain reading on Scripture, without resorting to the drastic expedient of altering the text of the original – a reading that would be in keeping with rabbinic theology and that would exclude other readings (e.g. Christian) of which the Rabbis disapproved. The fact that Scripture was in Hebrew and the targum in Aramaic was a help. The two texts were easily distinguished on linguistic grounds, so in bringing targum close to Scripture there was little danger of one being confused with the other.

There is clear evidence that the Rabbis viewed the targum as more than translation in any narrow sense: its purpose was to exegete and to interpret Scripture. Significantly they traced the inauguration of the targum back not to Sinai, but to the re-presentation of the Law to Israel by Ezra after the exile in the square before the Water Gate (Nehemiah 8):

> What is the Scriptural justification *(minnayin)* for the targum? R. Zeira said in the name of Rav Hananel: *And they read from the book, from the Law of God* – this refers to Scripture; *clearly [meʿpōrāš]* – this refers to targum; *and they gave the sense* – this refers to the accents; *so that the people understood the reading* – this refers to the traditional text; some say it means the decisions, others the beginnings of the verses.
> (*P.T. Megilla* 74d)

The targum, then, makes the Scripture 'clear' *(meʿpōrāš)*: it contains an element of *perush*. The *meturgeman* performs a Levitical role. The sense of the word 'targum' itself should be noted: its semantic field corresponds closely to that of the Latin *interpretatio*, i.e. it covers both *translation* from one language into another, and *explanation* of a text in the same language. When Joseph was feigning ignorance of Hebrew he spoke to his brothers through a *meturgeman* (Neof and Ps-Y Gen 42:23). Equally Aaron, when acting as Moses' spokesman to Pharaoh and the Israelites, is referred to as Moses' *meturgeman* (Neof Exod 7:1, cf. *Exodus Rabba* 8:3). All the evidence suggests that both these elements of *interpretatio* – translation and commentary – were meant to be present in the targum.

The use of the targum in other settings – in private devotion and in school – is closely related to its basic liturgical use in synagogue. The *locus classicus* for the use of targum in private devotion is *B.T. Berakhot* 8a (end): 'Rav Huna bar Yehuda said in the name of Rabbi Ammi: A man should always complete his *parashiyyot* with the congregation – twice in the Hebrew and once in the Targum'. The idea is that one should prepare oneself in the privacy of one's own home to hear the public reading of Tora in synagogue by going through the relevant section both in the Hebrew original and in the Aramaic translation. The aim presumably was to be able to follow the public reading with understanding. Besides being able better to understand the Hebrew one would have been in a position to vet the targum – a point to which we shall return presently. Note once again, as with the liturgical presentation of targum in synagogue, Scripture and targum are juxtaposed, a relationship of interdependence is established. However, the priority of Scripture is maintained by having it read twice, as against the one reading of the targum.

The staple of primary education in the school *(beit ha-sefer)* was the Hebrew Bible. The Bible was approached through the targum. Besides giving the pupils an approved interpretation of the original, the targum would have played a fundamental role in the acquisition of Hebrew by forming a bridge between the vernacular and the sacred tongue. Yet again the fundamental fact shines through: the targum was meant to function only side by side with Scripture. The school setting was probably of vital importance for the transmission of the targum. The targum was largely passed on by oral means. Though there seems to have been no strong objection to the use of written texts of the targum in private devotion or in school, it is unlikely that many copies of the targum would have been in circulation. In general books were rare and expensive. Apart from the schoolmaster few would have owned a copy of the targum. Following normal paedogogical practice the targum would have been learned off by heart in school. It was there that boys first acquired a knowledge of the text which they might later be called upon to recite in synagogue.

Rabbinic literature has little to tell us as to who was responsible for the targumim, or when they originated. The tradition noted earlier about the inauguration of the targum in the time of Ezra should be seen more as a statement about the nature and function of the targum than as straighforward historical fact. The traditions attributing the Pentateuchal Targum to Onkelos, the Prophetic Targum to Yonatan ben Uzziel, and the targumim of several of the Writings to Rav Yosef, are, as we saw, totally unreliable. One point, however, is clear: the rabbinic authorities were aware of the influence these versions could exert, and attempted to control not only the manner of their delivery but their content as well. It was forbidden to translate certain sensitive portions of Scripture, and certain translations were explicitly censured. The congregation was encouraged publicly to rebuke or to silence a translator who gave an unauthorized translation.[20] This should be seen in the light of the fact that all the males would have learned the targum in school, and would have refreshed their memories of it before coming to synagogue, if Rabbi Ammi's rule ('twice in Scripture, once in targum') was at all widely observed. The way in which the targum was transmitted would have made strict standardization difficult. It would be a mistake, however, to suppose that the *meturgeman* would have been free to translate more or less as he chose. The targum was a 'text', and its content would have been fairly comprehensively determined by tradition.

How do the extant targumim relate to the targum in the talmudic period as reflected in classic rabbinic literature? Can we assume that the texts as they now stand go back to the talmudic period and that they represent direct transcripts of targumim actually used in synagogue? There is clear evidence that at least some of the extant texts did play a liturgical role. Thus, a number of the Cairo Geniza MSS have been marked with the *sidrot* for the triennial lectionary cycle, and it is natural to assume that the Festival Collections of targumim, consisting exclusively of readings for festivals and special Sabbaths, were put together for liturgical use. The Aramaic poems, such as *'Ezel Moshe* clearly formed part of the liturgy, and, as we have seen, they are often intimately bound up with the targum. Onk and Yon were certainly recited in synagogue, and the liturgical use of a number of other targumim has continued in Yemenite synagogues down to the present day. There can be no doubt that most of our texts are ancient (the oldest Cairo Geniza fragments date to the 8th/9th century), and that they give us access, sometimes very directly, to the targum as delivered in the old synagogue in the talmudic era. But it would be wrong to generalize: not all the targumim had a liturgical role, and it is unwarranted to make liturgical use integral to the definition of targum. Some simple facts should be borne in mind. Yon covers the whole of both the Former and the Latter Prophets, despite the fact that only part of the second division of the canon would ever have been read in synagogue. A similar situation pertains in the Writings: there are, for example, targumim for Job and Proverbs, even though it is hard to imagine that these books had a liturgical use. The targum had a role in the Beit ha-Midrash, which, though overshadowed by its synagogue role, was not dependent on it. The targumim continued to be copied, and, possibly augmented and altered, in the middle ages, long after the targum had ceased to function as a liturgical version in most synagogues. They were valued as convenient repositories of traditional exegesis, as readings of Scripture. They had a life as purely written texts. Targum became solely a literary genre. Indeed, it is not inconceivable that some of the later targumim were composed in the early middle ages purely for private use.

---

[20] See Alexander, 'Rabbinic Lists'. The main rabbinic references are: *M. Megilla* 4:9, 10; *T. Megilla* 4(3):31; *B.T. Megilla* 25a/b.

History of the Targumim

INTERRELATIONSHIPS

In attempting to reconstruct the history of the targumim the first point to be clarified is the interrelationship of the texts. Most of the work done on this subject relates to the Pentateuchal targumim, which have been subjected to detailed internal analysis and synoptic comparison. As our survey indicated the Pentateuchal targumim fall into two groups: group 1 consists of Onk; group 2 of Neof, Ps-Y, FT, CG and the other representatives of the Palestinian Targum. The distinction between the groups has to do partly with the nature of the translation: Onk is on the whole literal, whereas the Palestinian Targumim tend to be paraphrastic. It is also, in part, a distinction as to dialect: Onk is in a type of Standard Literary Aramaic[21]; the Palestinian Targumim display a number of varieties of Galilean Aramaic. A third factor is provenance: Onk was the official targum of Babylonia, and there is good evidence that it reached its present form there; the Palestinian Targumim, as their name suggests, circulated in Palestine. However the distinction as to provenance should not be pushed too far, for analysis suggests that Onk is, in fact, Palestinian in origin. The dialect of Onk is not Babylonian (that is to say, it differs from that in the Babylonian Talmud). Though as a type of Standard Literary Aramaic it could, in principle, have been written either in the east or the west, it has been shown to display certain linguistic traits which point to a western origin.[22] Its Aramaic is close to that of the *Genesis Apocryphon* from Qumran. Moreover, Onk, though generally non-expansive, does contain a certain amount of aggada. This aggada, which as to content appears to be of Palestinian origin, is often presented in a highly allusive form which suggests that a fuller tradition is being abridged.[23] The fuller tradition is frequently attested in the Pal. Targ. The most economical explanation of the facts is that Onk has evolved from a fuller Palestinian Targum, which was shortened, perhaps with a view to bringing it into closer conformity to the Hebrew text. It should be noted that, although mistaken as to the precise authorship of the targum, Babylonian tradition does recognize Onk as a product of the west. The interrelationships of the Pentateuchal targumim are displayed on Fig. 1.

The situation in the second division of the canon is probably analogous. Yon, the official targum of Babylonia is in a dialect similar, if not identical to, that on Onk[24], and like Onk it probably originated in the west. The Toseftot, despite

---

[21] On the character of this type of Aramaic see Greenfield, 'Standard Literary Aramaic'.

[22] See Kutscher, 'The Language', especially p. 10.

[23] This is argued persuasively by Vermes, 'Haggadah in the Onkelos Targum'. See further Kuiper, *The Pseudo-Jonathan Targum*. The aggada is not exclusive to the targumim, so it could be argued that Onk has drawn independently on the same aggadic traditions as the Palestinian Targumim. However, the hypothesis that it is shortening a fuller Pal. Targ. is more economical.

[24] For a discussion see, Tal, *The Language of the Targum of the Former Prophets*.

attempts to recast them in the dialect of Yon, were originally in Galilean Aramaic, and are remnants of a Pal. Targ. similar to the Pal. Targ. of the Pentateuch.

As for the third division of the canon, a distinction between 'Babylonian' and 'Palestinian' does not seem to apply: all the texts are Palestinian in origin. There are, indeed, different recensions extant of the various books, analogous perhaps to the different recensions of the Pal. Targ. to the Pentateuch, but the requisite work has not yet been done to clarify their interrelationships. As was indicated earlier, a grouping of the targumim of the Writings, on the basis of translation-equivalents and style, is widely recognized: three groups are distinguished: (1) the Five Megillot; (2) Job, Psalms and Proverbs; (3) Targum Chronicles. Affinities between some of the targumim of the Writings, and the targumim of the Pentateuch and the Prophets, have been clearly demonstrated: e.g. Targ. Chron. in dialect, translation-equivalents and aggada is particularly close to Ps-Y. However, it is hard to establish in such cases which text has priority, and one should be careful not to jump to conclusions.

DATING CRITERIA

Literary analysis and synoptic comparison establish the genealogical relationships between the targumim, and give some indication as to their relative dates. They do not, however, furnish us with absolute dates. The wide divergence of opinion among the experts shows that dating the individual targumim is by no means an exact science. It simply has to be conceded that, in the case of the Aramaic targumim, objective dating criteria (apart from the *terminus ante quem* provided by the dates of the MSS) simply do not exist. The major problem lies with the extremely fluid nature of the texts. Apart from Onk and Yon there is little to suggest that any of the texts was redacted or standardized at a definite point in time. Most of the texts underwent change and development over long periods, with the result that they are all composite – amalgams of elements of very different date. Few of the targumim have an absolute date.

Despite the difficulties there are a number of methods which have been widely applied to the problem of the dating of the targumim. Three in particular are worthy of note – analysis of the aggada, analysis of the halakha, and analysis of the geographic equivalents in the targumim. It should be stressed that none of these methods can yield an absolute date. However, if used with circumspection they do provide clues as to the history of the targumim.

ANALYSIS OF AGGADA. It can often be established from datable early Jewish texts (such as the Dead Sea Scrolls, Philo, Josephus, and certain of the Pseudepigrapha) how early a given àggadic tradition was current. If it can be shown that a targum contains a large number of early traditions, then there is at least a *prima facie* case for seeing a stratum of that targum as early. This method can be refined in a number of ways. A more rigorous approach is to trace how the

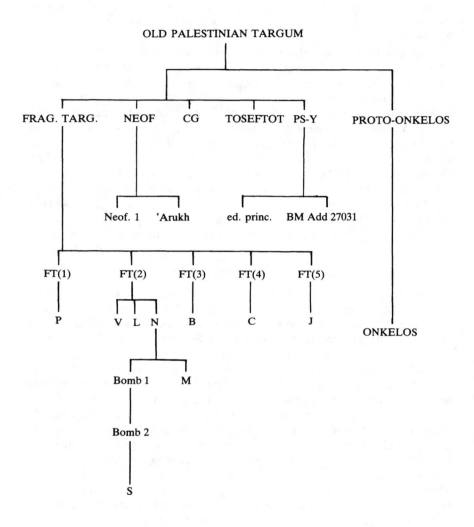

Fig. 1. The genealogical relationships between the recensions and manuscripts of the pentateuchal targumim.

interpretation of a particular biblical verse develops through early Jewish and Christian literature, and then find out where the targumic exposition fits into this development. E.g. a survey of the earliest aggadic sources (the Pseudepigrapha, the NT, the Dead Sea Scrolls) establishes that at the turn of the eras the expression *b^{e}nê 'ᵉlōhîm* in Gen 6:3 was taken to mean 'angels'. Later, however, probably for doctrinal reasons, a reaction to this view set in both in rabbinic and Christian circles: it was taught that the reference was not to heavenly beings, but to mortal men. The standard rabbinic view became that the *b^{e}nê 'ᵉlōhîm* were 'sons of the judges', or 'sons of the nobles'. Christian reaction against equating the *b^{e}nê 'ᵉlōhîm* with angels seems to begin in the late second century C.E. In rabbinic circles, however, this exegesis came under attack a little earlier, if *Genesis Rabba* 36:5, p. 247 is to be believed: 'R. Shimon ben Yoḥai called them (i.e. the *b^{e}nê 'ᵉlōhîm*) the sons of the judges. R. Shimon ben Yoḥai cursed all who called them sons of God.' The targumim have the following translations: Onk, 'sons of the nobles'; Neof, 'sons of the judges'; Neof margin, 'angels'; Ps-Y, 'sons of the nobles'. Onk and Neof agree with the newer exegesis, Neof margin with the older. Ps-Y, at first sight, also agrees with the newer exegesis, but in fact its text is mixed, for a little later (in 6:4) it renders *hann^{e}pilîm* by 'Shamḥazai and 'Aza'el, who fell from heaven'. Shamḥazai and 'Aza'el were two notable angels in early Jewish angelology, the leaders, according to 1 Enoch 6-11, of the angels who rebelled against God. There are other elements in Ps-Y at this point which recall the traditions found in 1 Enoch 6-11. So Ps-Y's 'sons of the nobles' appears to be a later revision of the targum, possibly in the light of Onk. This sort of analysis discloses the mixed nature of the targumim: the majority of the texts reflect an exegesis that became current probably after 150 C.E.; however, there are also traces of an earlier stage of the targum which has escaped the reviser's hand.[25]

ANALYSIS OF THE HALAKHA. The targumim translate the halakhic portions of the Pentateuch, and in doing so interpret the halakha. Their halakhic interpretations can be compared with the halakha in the Mishna (compiled around 200 C.E.). In cases where the targumim disagree with the Mishna, the possibility is worth considering that they represent an exegesis that arose prior to the redaction of the Mishna and its acceptance as authoritative. This argument must, obviously, be used with caution: it would be a mistake to imagine that the Mishna imposed a monolithic uniformity on all subsequent halakha. The Mishna itself quotes divergent rulings. However, the method does have its use, and a significant number of such disagreements between the Mishna and a text intended to explain Scripture in the synagogue, may reasonably be taken as an indication of the presence in the targum of early, possibly pre-mishnaic material. E.g., the Mishna established as the standard rabbinic interpretation of Exod 22:5-6 (Hebrew text 22:4-5) that Exod 22:5 refers to the case of a man who lets

[25] Further, Alexander, 'Early Exgesis of "Sons of God" '.

his cattle crop his neighbours field or vineyard, whereas Exod 22:6 refers to the case of a man who lights a fire and it burns the standing corn in his neighbour's field. This interpretation involves a play on the root *b'r*, which in verse 5 is taken to mean 'graze cattle', but in verse 6 as 'to burn'. In the Palestinian Targum as represented by Neof and by CG, Kahle A (though the text of the latter is rather confused) the root is given the sense of 'burn' in both verses. The divergence of these texts from the halakha may be illustrated by contrasting Neof's rendering of Exod 22:5 with Onk's of the same verse, which predictably agrees with the Mishna:

Onk Exod 22:5	*Neof Exod 22:5*
If a man causes to be eaten a field or a vineyard, and sends his cattle and they eat in the field of another, he shall give in restitution the best of his field and the best of his vineyard.	If a man sets fire to a field or a vineyard and lets the fire spread, and causes fire in the field of another, he shall give in restitution the best of his field and the best of (his) vineyard.

Once again the Palestinian Targum contains a mixed tradition: Ps-Y concurs with the mishnaic view, whereas Neof and CG disagree. It is a reasonable postulate that the divergent targumic interpretation is the earlier and arose prior to the Mishna being established as the authoritative statement of rabbinic halakha.[26]

ANALYSIS OF GEOGRAPHICAL EQUIVALENTS. The tendency of the targumim to 'actualize' Scripture by identifying peoples and places provides opportunities for dating traditions, since the targumic equivalents are presumably from the world and the time of the meturgeman. Few geographical terms in the targumim of the Pentateuch relate exclusively to the Byzantine or Arabic geographical onomastica:[27] the vast majority belong to an earlier period. E.g. the equivalents which Neof gives for the Table of the Nations in Gen 10 fit best with the world of the 3rd to 4th centuries C.D. As with analysis of aggada this approach can be improved if it is combined with a history of traditions. The possibilities may be illustrated from Num 34 which contains a cluster of geographical terms defining the borders of the Land of Israel. There is evidence of reworking in the Palestinian Targumim at this point, but from each targum a primary literary stratum with a set of border points can be extracted. The

---

[26] This type of argument must be applied with full sensitivity to the diversity of early rabbinic halakha. The crude rule of thumb that what is anti-mishnaic is pre-mishnaic is virtually meaningless. On targum and halakha see: Albeck, 'Aprocryphal Halakha'; Schelbert, 'Exodus XXII 4'; Heinemann, 'Targum Exodus 22:4'; idem, 'Early Halakha'; Jackson, 'The Fence-Breaker'; Itzchaky, *The Halacha*; Maori, 'Relationship'.

[27] The name ZYNG'Y in Ps-Y Gen 10:7 looks like an example of a name which first appears, at least in this form, in the onomasticon during the Islamic era. It is clearly related to the Arabic *zandj* or zindj which denoted the negro tribes of east Africa: see e.g. Abulfeda, *Geographica* IV, p. 151.

borders of the Land of Israel as defined by each of the Palestinian Targumim prove to be the same. These targumic borders can be compared with the rabbinic definitions of Erets Israel. The Rabbis showed interested in this subject because it affected the operation of the 'commandments pertaining to the Land (*miṣwot teluyyot ba'areṣ*)'. A line of development can be traced through the rabbinic pronouncements, running from a boundary-formula contemporary with Gamliel II (c. 100 C.E.) (*M. Halla* 4:8; *M. Sheviit* 6:1), through a boundary formula of Yehuda bar Ilai (c. 150 C.E.) (*M. Gittin* 1:2; *B.T. Gittin* 8a), to the Tannaic Boundary List (c. 200 C.E.) (*Sifrei Deut.* 51, p. 117; *T. Shabbat* 4:11; *P.T. Sheviit* 36c). The general tendency is to retract the borders of the Land as time goes on, those in the time of Gamliel being much wider than those described in the Tannaic Boundary List. The targumic borders agree with those defined in the time of Gamliel, and diverge from the other definitions. An early date for the Palestinian targumic borders is confirmed by the fact that almost identical borders for Erets Israel are found in the *Genesis Apocryphon* (*1QGenAp* 21:14-19). The revised nature of Onk also emerges from this analysis: Onk offers only one identification in this whole passage (viz. Kadesh Barnea = Reqem Ge'ah, i.e. Petra). This happens to be the sole point where the Pal. Targ. border definition and the Tannaic Boundary List coincide.[28]

Concluding Synthesis

We are a long way yet from writing a definitive history of the vast and complex corpus of the targumim. The following concluding notes offer a tentative synthesis of the results so far achieved.

(1) The practice of translating the books of the Bible into Aramaic began in the late Second Temple period. This is proved beyond all doubt by the existence of the Qumran Targumim of Job and Leviticus, as well as by the *Genesis Apocryphon*, which, though doubtfully a targum in the rabbinic sense, does attest the practice of paraphrasing the Bible into Aramaic. Corroboration for such an early date for the institution of the targum can be drawn from the rabbinic targumim. There is now a wealth of evidence that all the rabbinic targumim contain early aggadot, and converge significantly as to their Bible interpretation with datable early texts (e.g. Josephus, Philo, and the NT). Moreover, given their dialect, it is highly unlikely that Onk and Yon (at least as to their basic text) could have originated after 135 C.E..

(2) It is impossible to say how much of the Bible was available in Aramaic in the late Second Temple period. It is natural to assume that the Pentateuch would have been translated first. However, it should be remembered that we have excellent evidence for very early translations of the Writings into Aramaic. There is not only the direct evidence of the Job Targum from Qumran,

---

[28] Further, Alexander, *Toponymy*.

but indirect evidence from rabbinic literature of early Aramaic versions of Job and Esther.[29]

(3) From the beginning the institution of the targum had a twofold setting – in both the synagogue and the study. It is a mistake to overstress its liturgical function. Aramaic versions were used not only to translate the biblical lections in synagogue; they were used as a way of offering an interpretation of Scripture for the Bible student, and bridging the gap between his vernacular and the original Hebrew. As a type of Bible commentary the targum has a number of advantages: it allows the original to be left intact; the interpretation is carried by a separate text, which, for simple linguistic reasons, is immediately distinguishable from original Hebrew. The antiquity of the Beit ha-Midrash setting of the targum is once again indicated by the Qumran Job Targum: it is hard to conceive of any liturgical use for Job.

(4) The Old Palestinian targumim were probably in Standard Literary Aramaic. This is the dialect of the Qumran targumim. It is also the dialect of Onk and Yon. Their language was literary, and probably did not correspond precisely to spoken Aramaic, either in Judaea, or (a fortiori) in Galilee. It is a mistake to suppose that in dialect, or linguistic register, a targum must correspond precisely to the vernacular. There is clear evidence of targumim being used liturgically where the language does *not* correspond to the vernacular: Onk and Yon in Babylonia are a case in point. An important observation flows from this: the targumim are learned versions. By overstressing the targum's function to translate the Bible into the vernacular, the impression can be given that they are popular in origin, that they constitute a kind of folk-literature. This is *not* borne out by close analysis. Though some targumim may have been aimed at 'the common man', they are deeply learned versions, the work of scholars. By the same token it is wrong to suppose that the targum in synagogue was ever a spontaneous rendering. The translation was always likely to be traditional and to a large measure predetermined.

(5) It is hard to say whether the Old Palestinian targumim were expansive or non-expansive. The evidence suggests that both types of targum were known. The Qumran Job Targum is 'literal', whereas the *Genesis Apocryphon* is expansive. There are indications that Onk at least was derived from a more expansive targum, and it has been shown that some of the aggadic additions in the extant Palestinian Targumim are of a very early date. In the light of this evidence one should avoid the facile rule of thumb that the shorter and simpler a version, the earlier it is.

(6) At some point the Old Palestinian targumim in Standard Literary Aramaic were recast in the younger dialect of Galilean Aramaic. This probably happened after the Bar Kokhba war when the centre of Jewish cultural life moved from Judaea to Galilee. However, the change was not solely connected with a change in the spoken dialect of Aramaic. As was stressed earlier, the

---

[29] Job: *B.T. Shabbat* 115a; Esther: *M. Megilla* 2:1.

language of the targumim (either in register or dialect) probably never coincided precisely with the vernacular. Moreover there is reason to believe that the main features of the so-called Galilean dialect had already emerged in Galilee *before* the Bar Kokhba war. The linguistic change probably reflects the new-found acceptability of Galilean Aramaic, which, as the Gemara of the Palestinian Talmud shows, was now widely used in the schools for the discussion of halakhic questions. The implication of this argument is clear: none of our extant Palestinian Targumim, as to their basic *linguistic* form, can be earlier than the late second century c.e.

(7) The Palestinian Targumim were never standardized. This is evident from the number of recensions now extant. Though the various targumim clearly belong to the same tradition, and often overlap in content, no official text of the targum emerged in Palestine. There was some attempt by the rabbinic authorities to control the content of the targum: certain texts were not allowed to be translated in public, and certain translations of individual verses were censured; but rabbinic control was neither extensive nor all that successful. The rabbinic injunctions are sometimes ignored. Targumim were in circulation which took up halakhic positions diverging from those advocated in the Mishna. It is impossible to say whether, broadly speaking, the various extant recensions of the Palestinian Targumim represent successive revisions of the targum, or were contemporaneous forms which differed due to regional variation. The latter is more likely to be the case. The regional diversity in the text of the targum would be analogous to the regional diversity in the text of the standard synagogue prayers (the *Amida* and the *Shema*).

(8) A recension of the Old Palestinian Targum (both to the Pentateuch and the Prophets) was taken to Babylonia, probably before the Bar Kokhba War, i.e. before the Old Pal. Targ. began to be recast into Galilean Aramaic. There it was subjected to a thorough revision and standardization which resulted in the emergence of Onk and Yon. The Babylonian revision of the Old Pal. Targ. involved two things: first, a shortening to bring the targum into close conformity to the Hebrew text, and second, a thorough revision of the halakhic aspects of the targum to bring it into agreement with the halakha of the Babylonian schools. The Babylonian revision did not, however, involve a radical recasting of the targum into the Aramaic dialect of Babylonia: the targum remained basically in its original dialect – a western form of Standard Literary Aramaic. The preservation of the original dialect of the targum probably reflects conservatism on the part of Babylonian Jewry, as well as the prestige of the original version brought to Babylonia. It arrived with a certain sanctity, at a time when the spiritual authority of Erets Israel was paramount in Babylonia.

(9) In the post-talmudic period the Babylonian recension of the Old Palestinian Targum (i.e. Onk and Yon) returned to the west. This return reflects the growing authority of the Babylonian Gaonate in the early middle ages, and its spiritual hegemony over world Jewry. Onk and Yon did not, it seems, totally displace the Palestinian Targumim, but their arrival did have profound affects

on the targum in the west. First, it led to the emergence of truncated forms of the Pal. Targ. which were designed to supplement Onk and Yon. The so-called Fragmentary Targum, and the targumic Toseftas illustrate this phenomenon. These forms of the Pal. Targ. presumably arose in a milieu where Onk and Yon had become the dominant targum. Second, the arrival of Onk and Yon led to extensive linguistic contamination of the Palestinian Targumim from the dialect of Onk and Yon. This is seen at its most extreme in certain targumic Toseftot where the original Palestinian Targum has been systematically recast into the Onk/Yon dialect. It is also illustrated by Ps-Y which is dialectally mixed – i.e. it contains features of both Galilean and Onk-type Aramaic. The targumim of the Writings are in a mixed dialect, broadly similar to that of Ps-Y.

(10) The liturgical use of the targum began to die out in the middle ages. An important factor in this development was the rise of Islam and the emergence of Arabic as the vernacular of the Jews in the middle east. It is possible that Saadya's *Tafsir* took over the liturgical function of the targum in some synagogues. The liturgical use of the targum continues in Yemenite synagogues to this day: it is hard to say whether this represents a genuine historical continuity with talmudic and post-talmudic practice, or a revival of the institution of the targum. After its liturgical demise the targum continued to be widely used as an aid to the study of the Bible: it never lost its place in the Beit ha-Midrash.

Bibliography

For bibliography on the targumim see: B. GROSSFELD, *A Bibliography of Targum Literature*, 1-2, Cincinnati/New York 1972-77. DÍEZ MACHO, in the introductions to his edition of Codex Neofiti 1, gives exhaustive surveys of current work on the targumim.

EDITIONS

A. THE PENTATEUCH

Onkelos
BERLINER, A. *Targum Onkelos*. 1-2. Berlin 1884.
SPERBER, A. *The Bible in Aramaic*. Vol. 1, *The Pentateuch According to Targum Onkelos*. Leiden 1959.
Targum Onkelos to the Pentateuch: A Collection of Fragments in the Library of the Jewish Theological Seminary of America, New York. 1-4. Introduction by D. Boyarin. Jerusalem 1976 [Facsimiles of MSS 152, 153, 131, 133a].
The Pentateuch, with the Masorah Parva and the Masorah Magna and with the Targum Onkelos: MS Vat. Heb 448. 1-4. Introduction by A. Díez Macho. Jerusalem 1977.

For the Masora to Onkelos see: A. BERLINER, *Die Masorah zum Targum Onkelos*, Leipzig 1877; S. LANDAUER, *Die Masorah zum Targum Onkelos*, Amsterdam 1896.
Further: G.E. WEIL, *ALUOS* 5 (1963) 114-31; idem, *Textus* 4 (1964) 30-54; idem, in *In Memoriam P. Kahle*, ed. M. Black and G. Fohrer, Berlin 1968, 241-53.

Neofiti 1
DÍEZ MACHO, A. *Neophyti I: Targum Palestinense MS de la Biblioteca Vaticana*. 1-6. Madrid-Barcelona 1968-79.
A photocopy of the complete MS has been published in two vols by Makor, Jerusalem 1970.

Pseudo-Yonatan
Ḥamishah Ḥumshe Torah, Venice 1590-91. The *editio princeps* (reprinted in the London Polyglot, Vol. 4).
GINSBURGER, M. *Pseudo-Jonathan (Thargum Jonathan ben Usiel zum Pentateuch). Nach der Londoner Handschrift*. Berlin 1903 repr. Hildesheim – New York 1971.
REIDER, D. *Pseudo-Jonathan: Targum Jonathan ben Uziel on the Pentateuch copied from the London MS (British Museum Add. 27031)*. Jerusalem 1974.
CLARKE, E.G. *Targum Pseudo-Jonathan of the Pentateuch: Text and Concordance*. Hoboken, New Jersey 1984.

Cairo Genizah Fragments
KAHLE, P. *Masoreten des Westens* 2, Stuttgart 1930 repr. Hildesheim 1967.
KLEIN, M.L. *Genizah Manuscripts of Palestinian Targum to the Pentateuch*. 1-2 Cincinnati 1986.

Fragmentary Targum
KLEIN, M.L. *The Fragment-Targums of the Pentateuch* (Analecta Biblica 76). Rome, 1980.
— *Genizah Manuscripts*, passim.

Toseftot
KLEIN, M.L. *Genizah Manuscripts*, passim.
Further: A. EPSTEIN, *REJ* 30 (1895) 44-51; M. GINSBURGER, *Das Fragmententhargum*, Berlin 1899, 71-74; A. DÍEZ MACHO, *Sefarad* (1956) 314-24; P. GRELOT, *REJ* N.S. 16 (1957) 5-26; idem, *REJ* N.S. 18 (1959-60) 129-30; idem, *RB* 79 (1972) 511-43; SPERBER, *Bible in Aramaic* 1, 354-57; R. KASHER, *Sinai* 78 (1975) 9-17; M. KLEIN, *JJS* 26 (1975) 61-67.

Festival Collections
KLEIN, M.L. *Genizah Manuscripts*, passim.

Targumic Poems

KLEIN, M.L. *Genizah Manuscripts*, passim.

YAHALOM, J. ' "Ezel Moshe" – According to the Berlin Papyrus'. *Tarbiz* 47 (1978) 173-84.

Further: L. ZUNZ, *Literaturgeschichte der synagogalen Poesie*, Berlin 1865, 18-22, 74-80, 150-51; M. GINSBURGER, *ZDMG* 54 (1900) 113-24; idem, *REJ* 73 (1921) 14-26, 186-94; S. HURWITZ, *Machsor Vitry*, 2nd ed. Nürnberg, 1923, 305-44; Y. KOMLOSH, *Sinai* 45 (1959) 223-28.

B. THE PROPHETS

Yonatan

DE LAGARDE, P. *Prophetae Chaldaice*. Leipzig, 1872.

SPERBER, A. *The Bible in Aramaic*. Vol. 2, *The Former Prophets according to Targum Jonathan*. Vol. 3, *The Latter Prophets according to Targum Jonathan*. Leiden, 1959-62.

Targum to the Former Prophets: Codex New York 229 from the Library of the Jewish Theological Seminary of America. Introduction by A. Díez Macho. Jerusalem, 1974 [Facsimile].

Corpus Codicum Hebraicorum Medii Aevi, Pars II: The Pre-Masoretic Bible. Vol. 1, *Codex Reuchlinianus*. Introduction by A. Sperber. Copenhagen, 1956 [Facsimile of Codex Reuchlinianus 3 of the Badische Landesbibliothek, Karlsruhe].

RIBERA FLORIT, J. *Biblia Babilónica: Profetas Posteriores (Targum)*. Barcelona, 1977.

STENNING, J.F. *The Targum of Isaiah*. Oxford, 1949.

LEVINE, E. *The Aramaic Version of Jonah*. Jerusalem, 1975.

Toseftot

DE LAGARDE, P. *Prophetae Chaldaicae*, pp. VI-XLII.

STENNING, J.F. *Targum to Isaiah*, 88-105.

SPERBER, A. *Bible in Aramaic*. Vol. 2, p. IX, Vol. 3, p. XII.

See further: A. DÍEZ MACHO, *Sefarad* 27 (1957) 237-80; idem *Estúdios Biblicos* 15 (1959) 287-95; idem, *Biblica* 39 (1958) 198-205; P. GRELOT, *RB* 73 (1966) 197-211.

C. THE WRITINGS

DE LAGARDE, P. *Hagiographa Chaldaice*. Leipzig, 1873.

SPERBER, A. *The Bible in Aramaic*. Vol. 4A. Leiden, 1968 [Chronicles, Ruth, Canticles, Lamentations, Ecclesiastes].

The Targum to the Five Megillot, Ruth, Ecclesiastes, Canticles, Lamentations, Esther: Codex Vat. Urb. I. Introduction, notes, translations and indices by E. Levine. Jerusalem, 1977 [Facsimile of Codex Urbinas 1].

LEVINE, E. *The Aramaic Version of Ruth* (Analecta Biblica 58). Rome, 1973.

VAN DER HEIDE, A. *The Yemenite Tradition of Targum Lamentations* (Studia Post-Biblica 32). Leiden, 1981.

LEVINE, E. *The Aramaic Version of Lamentations*. New York, 1976.

MELAMED, R.H. *The Targum to Canticles according to Six Yemenite MSS*. Philadelphia, 1921.

DÍEZ MERINO, L. 'Targum al Cantar de los Cantares'. *Annuario de Philologia*, Universidad de Barcelona, Facultad de Filología, Barcelona, 1981.

LEVY, A. *Das Targum zu Koheleth, nach südarabischen Handschriften*. Breslau, 1905.

KNOBEL, P.S. *Targum Kohelet: A Linguistic and Exegetical Inquiry*. Ph.D. Dissertation. Yale, 1976.

LEVINE, E. *The Aramaic Version of Qohelet*. New York, 1979.

DAVID, M. *Das Targum Scheni nach Handschriften herausgegeben*. Berlin, 1898.

Biblia Regia, Antwerp 1567-72, Vol. 3, for the 'Third Targum' to Esther.

DÍEZ MERINO, L. *Targum de Job: Edición Príncipe del Ms. Villa-Amil n.5 de Alfonso de Zamora*. Madrid, 1984.

-- *Targum de Salmos: Edición Príncipe del Ms. Villa-Amil n.5 de Alfonso de Zamora*. Madrid, 1982.

BECK, M.F. *Paraphrasis Chaldaica I Libri Chronicorum, Paraphrasis Chaldaica II Libri Chronicorum*, Augsburg, 1680-83 [The *editio princeps*.]

LE DÉAUT, R. and ROBERT J. *Targum des Chroniques* (Analecta Biblica 51). Rome, 1971.

TRANSLATIONS

Translations of most of the targumim are available in European languages. Particularly noteworthy is R. LE DÉAUT, *Targum du Pentateuque* 1-5. Paris 1978-81 [French translations of Neofiti 1 and Pseudo-Yonatan]. English, French and Spanish versions of Neofiti 1 are given in Díez Macho's edition. Klein gives excellent renderings of the texts in his *Fragment-Targums* and his *Genizah Manuscripts*. Levine's translations in his various editions are rather unreliable. A complete English version of all the targumim is being prepared under the editorship of M. McNamara (*The Aramaic Bible*, Edinburgh 1987-).

Peshitta, *Codex Ambrosianus* B. 21. INF. f. 158 *recto* (Milano, Biblioteca Ambrosiana). Isa 66:6 – Jer 2:6.

See p. 257.

Chapter Eight

The Old Testament Peshitta

Peter B. Dirksen

Introduction

To say that very little is known about the origin and early history of the Old Testament Peshitta will be one of the few statements about this translation which will go unchallenged. The earliest references to the Peshitta are from the fourth century and from these we learn little more than that this version was in use as the Bible translation of the Syriac speaking Christians. Aphrahat (wrote between 336 and 345) and Ephraim Syrus (d. 373) made use of it. Theodore of Mopsuestia (d. 428) refers to the Syriac translation in his commentary on Hab 2:11. He appears to hold this translation in much less esteem than the Septuaginta. In his exposition of Zeph 1:5 he again deprecatingly refers to the Syriac translation, adding that 'till today it is not known who he [viz. the translator] was'. A little further he refers to the translator as 'an obscure person who translated the Hebrew text into the language of the Syrians'.[1]

If at so early a stage the origins of the Peshitta had been forgotten it is no surprise that references to it in later writers have no historical value and are purely legendary. Ishoʿdad of Merw, (ninth century) says that some books of the OT were translated into Syriac in the time of King Solomon at the instigation of King Hiram of Tyre, whereas the other books of the OT and the NT were translated during the reign of King Abgar. He also mentions the opinion of others who held that the translation was made by a priest Asya who was sent to Samaria by the king of Assyria.[2] These opinions with minor variations (e.g. Asa instead of Asya) are also found in other writers, as in the introduction to Bar Hebraeus's (d. 1286) commentary *Auṣar Raze*[3] and his *Chronography*.[4]

The name 'Peshitta' is found for the first time in the *Hexameron* of Moses bar Kefa (d. 903), who mentions that in the Syriac language there are two translations, namely the Peshitta, based on the Hebrew text and made in the time of

---

[1] Migne, *PG* 66, col. 237/8, 451/2, 453/4. A more recent edition is Sprenger, *Theodori Mopsuesteni Commentarius* (1977). Weitzman, 'Origin', 277f., note 2 argues that it is not always clear that Theodore's translation of the 'Syrians' is in fact that of the Peshitta, especially in the case of Zeph 1:5.
[2] Cf. Vosté-van den Eynde, *Commentaire d'Išoʿdad de Merv*, 3.
[3] For text and translation see Wiseman, *Horae Syriacae*, 92-94.
[4] Cf. Wallis Budge, *The Chronography* 2 (text) p. 8; 1 (transl.) p. 24.

King Abgar, and Paul of Tella's translation from the Greek. The latter translation was made in 617-618 and is known as the Syro-Hexaplaric version, since it is based on the Greek text of Origen as found in the fifth column of his *Hexapla*[5]

The word 'Peshitta' is the feminine form of the passive participle of the verb *pešat*, 'to stretch out', 'to extend'. This passive participle often functions as an adjective meaning 'simple'. As the name 'Peshitta' it presupposes *mappaqta*, translation. There is no unanimity as to the exact meaning of this name. A number of scholars, e.g. Eb. Nestle,[6] have followed L. Bertholdt, who proposed the meaning '(the translation) in common use', the 'vulgata', as against its rival, the Syro-Hexaplaric version.[7] Another opinion is that it reflects the contrast between this 'simple' translation and more paraphrastic translations. This possibility was favoured by W. Gesenius,[8] and by Nestle in an earlier publication[9] with reference to Bar Hebraeus. The latter wrote: 'This translation of the Seventy is held in esteem with our learned men and it is in the hands of the Romans/Byzantines *(ar-rum)* and the other denominations of the Christians except for the Syrians, especially those of the East, for their translation, called Peshitta (Arabic: *basita*) because it abstains from eloquent language in its translation, agrees with the text of the Jews'.[10] A third opinion is that of F. Field, who proposed an analogy to *haplous*, which refers to a MS with only the text of the LXX as against the *Hexapla*.[11] In this suggestion Field was followed by J. Wellhausen[12] and Th. Nöldeke.[13]

TEXT EDITIONS AND TEXTUAL CRITICISM

Since there is no outside information about the early history of the Peshitta all inferences about it have to be made on the basis of its text as it has become known to us. A major handicap in all research into the early text and history of the Peshitta has been that no reliable edition of it existed. The first printed edition of the Peshitta was that of the *Paris Polyglot* of 1645.[14] This text was based on a poor seventeenth century MS, Paris, Bibl. Nat., Syr. 6 (17a5 in the Leiden edition). The *Paris Polyglot* was reproduced in the *London Polyglot* of 1657 with the addition of a number of variant readings from a few London MSS. From the *London Polyglot* the text passed into S. Lee's edition of 1823. Two widely used text editions were primarily meant for use in Syriac speaking

[5] A translation of the passage by J.P.P. Martin is cited in Duval, *Littérature Syriaque*, 25f.
[6] Nestle, 'Syrische Bibelübersetzungen', 169f.; Ibid. 'Zum Namen', 159.
[7] Bertholdt, *Historischkritische Einleitung*, 593.
[8] Gesenius, *Commentar*, 81.
[9] Nestle, review of I. Prager, col. 281.
[10] Wiseman, *Horae Syriacae*, 92-94.
[11] Field, *Origenis Hexaplorum*, IX.
[12] Wellhausen (-Bleek), *Einleitung*, 602.
[13] Nöldeke, review of Wellhausen (-Bleek), 589.
[14] For the printed editions see besides the literature mentioned in the bibliography: Bloch, 'The Printed Texts'; Roberts, *Text and Versions*, 214-17; Emerton, 'The printed editions'.

churches, the Urmia edition of 1852, made by American Presbyterian missionaries in Urmia in Persia, near the Turkish border, and the Mosul edition of 1887, made by the Dominicans in Mosul. The problem with these two editions is that it is not known on what authorities they were based. According to Barnes[15] the Urmia text of Chronicles 'is a reproduction of L [Lee's edition] in Nestorian characters with Nestorian vowels and with improved spellings', which is explained by the fact that Chronicles 'was not well known among the Nestorians, perhaps was not regarded as Canonical,. . .'[16] In general it seems that for the Urmia edition MSS have been used along with Lee's edition.[17] The Urmia edition in its turn was used for the Mosul edition, for which also MSS were used. In the meantime Ceriani's important facsimile edition of the seventh century Ambrosianus had appeared.[18] This was a great improvement on the existing editions, though not easily available. Old and important though the Ambrosianus may be, it does not give us the best text of its own time. It contains a good number of mistakes and readings peculiar to itself which have no claim to textual priority, and it needs comparison with other ancient MSS when used for text-critical purposes.

The long-felt need for a critical edition of the Peshitta is now being met by the Peshitta Institute of Leiden University. Under the auspices of the International Organization for the Study of the Old Testament (IOSOT) this Institute is editing an edition of the Ambrosianus, emended in a number of places, with a critical apparatus which includes the variant readings of the MSS up to and including the twelfth century.[19] For the study of the history of the Peshitta text this edition is a major step forwards. For the early period, however, we are left without any MS evidence. There are only two MSS from the fifth century, one containing Genesis and Exodus,[20] and the other, a palimpsest, containing parts of Isaiah and Ezekiel.[21] For all parts of the OT there are a few MSS from the sixth century to the ninth century. This means that at best we may be able to reconstruct the development of the text from the sixth century onward. For the preceding period we have little more than hypotheses.

But even for the period for which we have MS evidence the textual critic's task is far from finished, although during the last few decades some new insights have come to the fore.

---

[15]   Barnes, *An Apparatus Criticus*, XV. J. Bloch erroneously applied this conclusion also to Song of Songs (cf. Emerton, 'The printed editions', 424).
[16]   Barnes, *The Peshitta Psalter*, XXXII, XXXIII.
[17]   See Haefeli, *Die Peschitta*, 66-68; Barnes, *The Peshitta Psalter*, XXXII, XXXIII; Diettrich, *Ein Apparatus criticus*, XV-XVII; Albrektson, *Studies in . . . Lamentations*, 4-6.
[18]   Its date is unknown. The seventh century is an educated guess as expressed in its siglum 7a1 in the Leiden Peshitta edition.
[19]   *The Old Testament in Syriac according to the Peshiṭta Version*, Leiden 1972-19.... To date eleven volumes have appeared. Six more volumes are expected to appear in the next few years.
[20]   London, Nat. Libr. Add. 14,425 (5b1 in the Leiden edition). The MS also contains the greater part of Num and Deut, but these books are from a different, and possibly later hand.
[21]   London, Nat. Libr., Add. 14,512 (5ph1 in the Leiden edition).

The Peshitta MSS present the textual critic with an enormous number of variant readings, due partly to clerical errors, and partly to the freedom many copyists allowed themselves in improving Syriac style and idiom, or at least adapting it to their personal preferences. These differences occur not only in later MSS, but also in older MSS. In the past much attention was paid to the younger MSS in text-critical studies. This was partly due to the fact, mentioned above, that it was the text of a late MS which was most easily available through the printed editions. Another reason was their supposed significance for the study of the history of the text. It was widely thought that, as A. Rahlfs had argued,[22] the Syriac text tradition had divided into two separate streams, a Western and an Eastern text. This division was thought to have been the result of the withdrawal of the East Syrians, or Nestorians, to the East by the end of the fifth century. Within the West Syrian tradition three subdivisions had grown up: a Jacobite, a Melkite, and a Maronite tradition. It was thought that these different confessional communities had few contacts with each other, and that in each community a text tradition developed more or less in isolation from the others. On the basis of these assumptions the textual critic's task seemed to be to establish the text of the two main text traditions, the Eastern text and the Western text, the latter by first establishing the text of its three branches and then comparing these texts among themselves. By next comparing these two text traditions, one could hope to establish, at least to a great extent, the pre-schismatic text as it existed by the end of the fifth century.

In recent years this position has been challenged on two counts. On the one hand the division of the text in more or less isolated streams along confessional lines has been denied by several scholars, while on the other hand it has been argued that in general the younger MSS contribute little to establishing the oldest text of the Peshitta as far as MS evidence is concerned. These insights were the result of a study of much more MS material than previously had been available.[23] A practical result of this development has been that in the critical apparatus of the 'Leiden Peshitta', referred to above, only MSS up to and including the twelfth century are included.[24]

IMPORTANCE FOR SCHOLARLY RESEARCH

The most important stimulus for Peshitta studies has been its possible value for OT textual criticism. In the study and use of ancient versions pride of place goes, of course, to the LXX, which may reflect a Hebrew text older than, or at least different from the masoretic text known to us. In general this is not the case with the Peshitta. A great many studies on the relation between the text of the Peshitta and MT, agree that the Hebrew text which is reflected in the Peshitta is

---

[22] Rahlfs, 'Beiträge zur Textkritik'.
[23] For a fuller discussion of these two points see the present writer's article: 'East and west'.
[24] The only exception is the first volume, IV,6, which appeared in 1972.

practically identical with MT, or at least very close to it.[25] This suggests that the Peshitta originated after the early masoretic text had more or less been established, which means after the middle of the first century C.E.

Yet there are a number of places where the Peshitta together with LXX, the targum(s), or both, perhaps even alone, may well reflect a text different from MT. Whether those readings are to be preferred to the text of MT is a question which cannot be answered in general, but only on the basis of the merits of the readings involved in each particular case. M.H. Goshen-Gottstein[26] cautions that in the case of readings in the Isaiah scroll of Qumran which differ from MT, but are parallelled in one or more of the ancient versions 'we have to accustom ourselves to looking at different versions not as after each other but as beside each other'. He gives a list of readings found in the Isaiah scroll which differ from MT but are supported by the Peshitta, the targum, or both, and sometimes also LXX.

There are two aspects of the Peshitta which, because of their importance in textcritical studies, may be mentioned at this point.

1. Scholars who have argued that for a specific book the Peshitta goes back to a Hebrew text close to MT generally agree that the translation of the Peshitta is not slavish. There is a good measure of freedom in the treatment of the Hebrew to meet the demands of Syriac idiom. The most recent confirmation of this tendency is given by A. Gelston,[27] who gives examples of a number of stylistic modifications among which are pluses, minuses, inversion of the order of words, avoidance of the construct state, modifications in tense, number, person, and suffixes, and avoidance of rhetorical questions. Differences may also be due to exegetical, theological modifications, of which Gelston gives a number of examples. By way of illustration his second example may be mentioned. In Hos 14:9 the Hebrew reads: 'O Ephraim, what more have I to do with idols?' By adding *wenemar* the Peshitta makes Ephraim the speaker instead of God: 'And Ephraim says: what more . . .'[28]

Another type of difference between the Peshitta and MT is due to the influence of Jewish exegetical traditions, a point which will be dealt with more fully below. The passage just mentioned, Hos 14:9, may be an illustration of this influence, since the same addition is found in Tg. Yonatan. Another influence exercised on the Peshitta is that of LXX, although it is not always clear whether this influence goes back to the translator himself, or to later adaptation. In either case, of course, the Peshitta in its agreements with LXX has no independent value as a witness to a possible Hebrew *Vorlage*.

---

[25] For a survey of the relevant literature see e.g. Van Puyvelde, 'Versions Syriaques' and Mulder, 'The Use of the Peshitta'. To this literature may now be added Gelston, *Twelve Prophets*, according to whom the Hebrew Vorlage of the Peshitta was 'very nearly identical with MT' (p. 118).

[26] Goshen-Gottstein, 'Die Jesaia-Rolle'.

[27] Gelston, *Twelve Prophets*.

[28] The examples referred to are found on pp. 131-56.

2. These matter of translation technique and external influence have to be studied for each book or group of books separately. The Peshitta, as is generally acknowledged, is not the work of one hand, but of many hands, and each translator had his own way of going about his task. To mention only a few examples: the translation of Judges follows the Hebrew closely, whereas that of Chronicles is very free. There is little influence, if any, of the LXX in the Pentateuch, but in Psalms this influence is very clear. The Pentateuch clearly shows use of Jewish exegetical traditions.[29] This means that the character of the Syriac translation has to be established before any conclusions as to the Hebrew *Vorlage* can be drawn.

The approach just referred to is valid on the assumption that the Peshitta is a translation from the Hebrew. This basic assumption, however, has been challenged by a number of scholars who hold that at least Peshitta Pentateuch but possibly other books as well are not independent Syriac translations, but developed out of the Jewish targumic tradition. In this approach free or paraphrastic renderings and agreements with Jewish exegetical traditions are not considered as matters of translation technique, but as survivals of the Peshitta's targumic past. This position will be dealt with more fully below. It will be clear that in this approach the relation between the Syriac and the Hebrew texts is less direct, which should lead to even greater caution in using the Syriac for text-critical purposes.

This position leads to the second, though less prominent, stimulus of Peshitta studies: interest in the Peshitta as an expression of the religious tradition of the community or communities from which it originated. In his dissertation of 1859 Perles, whose name will be mentioned several times further on, considered the Peshitta, especially the Pentateuch, as a collection of Jewish exegetical traditions, and therefore argued for a Jewish origin. Since then the perennial questions have been: Did the Peshitta or its various parts originate in Jewish or in Christian circles? Where was it made? What is the relation between the Peshitta and Jewish exegesis in general and to the targums in particular? These questions, of course, are interrelated. Those who suppose Christian origin usually locate the translation in Edessa, the present Urfa in the South of Turkey. On the assumption of Jewish origin, however, we may think either of Edessa or of Adiabene, the Jewish kingdom east of the Tigris.

This article will not go into matters which concern the text of the various MSS or the development of the text as found in the available MSS. Rather, it will concentrate on the Peshitta as a work which originated in the borderland between the Jewish and the Christian communities and traditions. It will attempt to indicate the positions of the various scholars in the ongoing research into the early text and history of the Peshitta which have been held or are being

---

[29] For literature see note 25. In his study 'Origin' Weitzman argued that in the Psalms the influence of LXX goes back to the translator himself.

held, and to the underlying issues which explicitly or implicitly have played a role in this discussion.

Jewish or Christian Authorship?

One of the most intriguing questions in Peshitta studies up to the present day has been that concerning its origin: Was the Peshitta, wholly or partly, a Jewish or a Christian translation? The only way to answer this question is to try to find typically Jewish or Christian elements in the Peshitta which are not explained by the corresponding Hebrew text. Some scholars have argued for a Jewish origin, others have advanced arguments for a Christian origin, whereas a third group took a mediating position in assuming the translators to have been Jewish-Christians.

ARGUMENTS FOR A CHRISTIAN ORIGIN

Among the texts which have been adduced in favour of a Christian origin either of the Peshitta as a whole or only of the book in question, the best known is Isa 7:14, where the Hebrew word *ᶜalma*, 'young woman', is translated by *bᵉtulta*, 'virgin', instead of *ᶜelaymᵉta*, as elsewhere. This argument is adduced by W. Gesenius.[30] The protagonists of a Jewish origin are not impressed and explain this rendering as a later Christian adaptation. A. Vööbus says in connection with this verse: 'Aber solche Behauptungen sind wertlos für die Forschung, denn die Frage ist ja ob diese Elemente wirklich der Original-gestalt angehört haben, oder eher dem Prozess der fortschreitenden Veränderungen, . . .'[31] A later Christian adaptation is, of course, not to be excluded *a priori*, but no evidence that any such adaptation actually has taken place, has been adduced. As another example Gesenius adduces Isa 53:8, where the Hebrew word *lamo*, '(the stroke was) on them', is rendered by the singular: 'on him', viz. the suffering servant.

The number of places which might indicate Christian authorship is small, and it is not surprising that scholars have also brought forward more general considerations. Gesenius advanced the argument that Syriac developed as a Christian language without there being any indication that Jews ever made use of it.[32] Close to this is Th. Nöldeke's argument that the language of the Peshitta of the OT is the same as that of the NT, i.e. Christian.[33] Another argument with respect to some books is the translator's alleged poor knowledge of the Hebrew language, advanced, e.g., by J.M. Salkind for Song of Songs.[34]

---

[30] Gesenius, *Commentar*. The discussion of authorship on pp. 85-7.
[31] Vööbus, *Peschitta und Targumim*, 108, n. 13.
[32] Gesenius, *Commentar*, 86.
[33] Nöldeke, *Alttestamentliche Litteratur*, 262.
[34] Salkind, *Die Peschitta zu Schir-haschirim*, 14.

261

Apart from some passages which are thought to have a Christian colouring, the only important argument for Christian authorship derived from the Peshitta text was advanced by L. Hirzel in 1825.[35] His argument is based on the Syriac translation of the list of unclean birds and names of locusts in Lev 11 and Deut 14. Instead of giving an exact Syriac equivalent for every Hebrew word the Syriac translation has sometimes transliterated instead of translated, and, moreover, has omitted some of the birds mentioned in the Hebrew text. It is argued that such a measure of negligence could hardly be expected from a Jewish translator, who would rather have been careful in translating such an important text. This argument has been accepted by other scholars, e.g. B.J. Roberts.[36] On the other hand, its validity has been questioned, first by J. Perles in 1859,[37] and more recently and in more detail by J.A. Emerton.[38] According to Emerton, the differences between the Hebrew and the Syriac texts can be explained by assuming in some instances that the Syriac translator considered two Hebrew words to be covered by one Syriac word, while in other instances the translator may just have omitted a Hebrew word which he did not understand. There is no reason why a practising Jew should not have been ignorant of the meaning of some rare Hebrew words. Therefore the translation of this portion does not point to a Christian author.

A JEWISH BACKGROUND

On the other hand, arguments have been advanced for a Jewish background of the Peshitta. An early defender of this view was J. Perles.[38a] His doctoral thesis of 1859, *Meletemata Peschitthoniana*, may well be considered one of the most important studies in the history of Peshitta research, indebtedness to which is acknowledged in many later studies. The stimulus of this study has moved in various directions: those who have argued for influence from Jewish exegetical traditions, as well as the advocates of a special relation between the Peshitta and the targumic tradition in general or a specific targum in particular, may all appeal to this basic study by Perles.

Perles gives an impressive list of cases where the Peshitta rendering can be understood only from the background of Jewish halakhic and aggadic traditions. This Jewish influence can be traced throughout the Peshitta, but in a relatively large measure in the Pentateuch.

A few examples may be given.[39] In Ezra 9:4f 'until/at the evening sacrifice' is rendered by 'till/at 9 o'clock'. This time indication agrees with that of the time of

---

[35] Hirzel, *De Pentateuchi*, 126-32.
[36] Roberts, *Text and Versions*, 221.
[37] Perles, *Meletemata*, 40.
[38] Emerton, 'Unclean Birds'.
[38a] In a number of bibliographical references the author is wrongly referred to as F. Perles. The latter was his son.
[39] The first two examples in Perles, *Meletemata*, are found on p. 16, the latter two on p. 28.

the afternoon prayer after the sacrificial worship had ceased to exist, cf. *B.T. Berakhot* 26b. In 2 Chr 33:7 the Hebrew reads: 'He also placed a graven and a molten statue . . .'. This is rendered by: 'and he put a statue of four faces (*l^etsalma d'arba^c 'appin)'*. This translation is elucidated by *B.T. Sanhedrin* 103b which says in a comment on this place and vs. 22: 'There is written an idol and there is written idols. Rabbi Yohanan said: 'first he made one face for it and later on he made four faces for it in order that the Shekhina might see it and become angry'. In Gen 30:28 *noqba*, 'define', is translated by the unusual *p^eruš*, the verb meaning 'to set apart, separate', which agrees with Tg. Onkelos (*p^eriš*) and *Gen. Rabba* 73:8 (p. 851). In Gen 8:4 the name Ararat is rendered by Qardu, as in Tg. Onkelos and *Gen. Rabba* 33:4 (p. 309). According to Perles so many Jewish traditions have been preserved in the Peshitta that its origin must have been in Jewish circles.

This line of argument has always remained the most prominent in assuming a Jewish background for the Peshitta. Yet, those who advocate a Christian background are not convinced, and argue that the Jewish influence can be adequately explained by assuming a Jewish-Christian translator, or Jewish influence on a Christian translator, as was done by E. Nestle.[40]

Other arguments for a Jewish origin concern details. One example is N. Walker's observation that in the majority of places 'Aram/Arameans' has been rendered by 'Edom/Edomites', the difference in Syriac being only the place of a diacritical point.[41] This, according to the writer, is understandable from a Jewish point of view: the Jewish scribes wanted to avoid the name of Aram, ancient Israel's adversary, since the Syrians were their neighbours and co-patriots in the second/third century C.E. This interesting observation was taken up and modified by A. van der Kooij,[42] who notes that in Tg. Yonatan and in Aphrahat's writings Edom is a cover-name for Rome. It may be assumed that also the Syrian translator rendered 'Edom' as a reference to the Roman power in the province of Syria. Van der Kooij argues that this was done by a Jewish-Christian translator in Edessa about 162 C.E.

OTHER OPINIONS

As has already been indicated, a third position is held by those scholars who, acknowledging the validity of the arguments of both sides, hold that the translators were Jewish-Christians. This view was defended, e.g., by Th. Nöldeke.[43] It may be noted that this view is more than a compromise between the other two opinions and a combination of their arguments. There is an *a priori* probability that in Edessa the early Christian community counted among

---

[40] Nestle, review of I. Prager, col. 281.
[41] Walker, 'The Peshitta Puzzle'.
[42] Van der Kooij, *Die Alten Textzeugen*, 293-95.
[43] Nöldeke, *Alttestamentliche Litteratur*, 262f.

its adherents a number of converted Jews, who with their knowledge of the Hebrew OT were well equipped to undertake the translation into Syriac, and who would be expected to have contributed to it elements from their own religious heritage.[44]

A fourth possibility has been suggested by M.P. Weitzman,[45] viz. that part of the Peshitta originated in a (possibly sectarian) Jewish community and another part in that same community after it had converted to Christianity. Thus, while he accepts the opinion that the Peshitta Pentateuch is a Jewish translation, he finds signs of a Christian background in the Psalter. This suggests the possibility that 'the Pentateuch was translated while that community was yet Jewish, and the Psalter when its evangelisation was well under way if not complete'.

Peshitta and Jewish Traditions: The Pentateuch

INTRODUCTION

PERLES's study, which has already been referred to, has been important not only because of its thesis that the Peshitta is of Jewish origin, but also, and perhaps even more so, because of the evidence it adduced that the Peshitta had been greatly influenced by Jewish exegetical traditions and that many a Peshitta reading could be well understood only against this background. This influence can be found in the whole Peshitta, but especially in the Pentateuch. Accordingly, in the first part Perles gives examples from the Pentateuch and from other books, and in the second part exclusively from the Pentateuch.

Perles adduces a great number of Peshitta readings which are thought to reflect Jewish aggadic or halakhic traditions. A few examples have been mentioned already. Besides these there are other, though less prominent, indications of a Jewish background. As one of them Perles lists a number of euphemistic translations as are well-known from Jewish literature. Two examples are the following: in Judg 2:18 'for the Lord was moved to pity *(yinnaḥem)* by their groans' is translated: 'the Lord heard their groans', and in Gen 21:6 'God has made laughter for me' by: 'the Lord has made great joy for me'.[46] In the second part Perles often refers to the agreement between Tg. Onkelos and the Peshitta. He does not, however, infer a dependence of the Peshitta on Tg. Onkelos, (the latter being younger than the Peshitta) but considers that 'the Aramaic and the Syriac translations do not contain anything but a deposit of individual interpretations which were (orally) current in that time among all people and which have been preserved for us to a great extent in halakhic and aggadic writings of that age'.[47]

---

[44] Cf. Drijvers, 'Edessa'.
[45] Weitzman, 'Origin'.
[46] Perles, *Meletemata*, 18 and 33.
[47] Ibid. p. 27.

Perles's approach initiated a line of research that has been kept up till the present day and which is marked by a long list of scholarly studies which all profess to follow his lead. These studies agree in recognizing influence from Jewish traditions and translation techniques in the Pentateuch and possibly in other books as well. The question is how this influence is to be accounted for. In answering this question the investigations take divergent directions. In the main we can distinguish between the following lines of approach in connection with the Pentateuch:

1. Peshitta Pentateuch originated from the targum tradition:
   (a) It originated from a Palestinian targum;
   (b) It originated from an Eastern targum.
2. Peshitta Pentateuch is an independent translation of the Hebrew, but the translator consulted a written copy of Onkelos.
3. The translator was influenced by Jewish exegetical traditions.

PESHITTA PENTATEUCH ORIGINATED FROM A PALESTINIAN TARGUM

In 1875 PRAGER published a study on the question as to the Jewish or Christian origin of the Peshitta.[48] With Perles he finds strong Jewish influence in the Peshitta, but he disagrees with Perles in the way of explaining this. According to Prager there are linguistic elements in the Peshitta which are alien to Syriac and which point to West-Aramaic. His conclusion is that the Peshitta originated as a Palestinian Jewish targum. But, as E. Nestle observed in his (critical) review of Prager's study, his conclusions are lacking in preciseness and clarity.

Prager's arguments and conclusions failed to exercise much influence on scholarly opinion, and it was only after more than half a century that Prager's ideas as to the origin of the Peshitta were put forward again in a new way on the basis of new material: the Cairo Geniza targum fragments. The study of these fragments led the two scholars BAUMSTARK and KAHLE to what has become known as the Kahle-Baumstark hypothesis, according to which the Peshitta originated from a Palestinian, West-Aramaic targum. To put the names of these two scholars together is justified as far as a West-Aramaic background is concerned. The two scholars differ, however, as to what type of Palestinian Targum text this was, and what the connection was between the Peshitta and Tg. Onkelos, at least after Baumstark had reconsidered his earlier position.

In his well-known *Geschichte der syrischen Literatur* (1922) Baumstark gives as his opinion that the Peshitta goes back to the Hebrew text in a form close to that which was known to and used by Jerome. There has been influence on the Peshitta from the targum tradition, especially Onkelos, which points to a Jewish origin, but Baumstark, explicitly rejects Prager's thesis that the Peshitta was originally a Palestinian targum.[49]

The Cairo Geniza fragments made Baumstark change his position. He had the opportunity to study these fragments before their publication by Kahle in

[48] Prager, *De Veteris Testamenti Versione*.
[49] Ibid. p. 18, n. 19.

1930.[50] The result of this study was presented in his article 'Wege zum Judentum des neutestamentlichen Zeitalters' of 1927, in which Baumstark suggested some ways of access to a better knowledge of the Jewish traditions in the NT era. He mentions that he has found many agreements between the Peshitta and these Geniza fragments and advances the view that Peshitta Pentateuch was 'die schriftliche Fixierung einer im engsten Zusammenhang mit Palestina stehenden Targumtradition'. The Peshitta and the Palestinian Targum go together as against MT as 'Zwillingspaare von Zeugen der textgeschichtlichen Entwicklung'. To explain this, Baumstark takes up a suggestion made by J. Marquart in 1903.[51] The latter deals with the Jewish communities in former Assyria and pays special attention to the conversion of King Izates of Adiabene, East of the Tigris, and his wife, Queen Helena, to the Jewish faith, c. 40 C.E. This could well have provided the historical background of the Peshitta since the 'bekannte, bisher indessen unerklärte Thatsache, dass die Übersetzungen mehrerer alttestamentlicher Bücher in der Peshitta, namentlich des Pentateuchs, sowie der Chronik, nicht viel weiter sind als aramäische Targume' could easily be explained by the Peshitta having originated in a Jewish or Judaized population which even had been governed by a Jewish dynasty. This hypothesis is modified by Baumstark to the effect that in the days of Izates and Helena a West Aramaic targum tradition is thought to have been taken from Palestine to Adiabene.

Baumstark gives his view in very general terms, in conformity with the article as a whole, without giving textual evidence for the supposed close relationship between the Peshitta and the Palestinian Targum tradition, and without being specific as to the development from this tradition into the Peshitta as we have it.

In 1930 Kahle published the Geniza fragments in his *Masoreten des Westens* 2.[52] In the introduction to these texts he expressed the same view as Baumstark. The Geniza fragments witness to the ancient Palestinian Targum, a copy of which was taken to the East and there re-written *(umgeschrieben)* in East-Aramaic. The need for an East-Aramaic Bible translation had arisen with the conversion of the royal house of Adiabene.[53] It is to this 'Umschrift' that the Peshitta goes back. Kahle never followed up his remarks by giving specific material to substantiate his point of view or by further developing it. Baumstark did so in his important article 'Pešiṭta und palästinensisches Targum', 1931. This article marks a further development of his point of view. The relationship between the Peshitta and the Geniza fragments appears to be less close than had been suggested first by himself in his 1927 article and after that by Kahle,

[50] Kahle, *Masoreten des Westens* 2.

[51] Marquart, *Streifzüge*, 299. In a different way king Izates has been connected with Peshitta origins by Wichelhaus, *De Novi Testamenti Versione Syriaca Antiqua*, 92ff., who equated this king with the legendary king Abgar.

[52] Recently a new edition has been published by M.L. Klein *(Genizah Manuscripts)*.

[53] More attention was paid by Kahle to this supposed historical background in his *Schweich Lectures* of 1941, published in 1947 as: *The Cairo Geniza*, 179-97 (= 1959², pp. 265-83).

although only the latter is explicitly mentioned as defending that point of view. Baumstark now states that the relationship between the Peshitta and these Geniza texts is no different from that between the Peshitta and the other Palestinian Targum texts, Pseudo-Yonatan and the Fragmentary Targum. On the one hand there are agreements between the Peshitta and the Geniza fragments, but on the other hand there are large portions where there seems to be no contact between the two texts at all.

Yet, Baumstark remains convinced that the Peshitta ultimately goes back to a West-Aramaic targum tradition. To argue his case, he adduces a linguistic argument, to the effect that a few Peshitta readings can only be explained on the basis of a West-Aramaic word from a region where the difference in pronunciation between the laryngals had been blurred, to wit Palestine. From the two examples which are adduced one may be mentioned here: In Deut 1:19 Hebrew *derekh*, 'way', is rendered in the Peshitta by *'ar῾a*, 'land', which must be a scribal error for targumic *'urḥa*, 'way' (῾*ayin* for *ḥēt*). The conclusion to which Baumstark is led is that the Peshitta goes back to a targum text that did not stand beside that of the Geniza fragments, but was much older than it. The Peshitta, then, is an indirect witness to an older stage of development of the Palestinian Targum tradition. To further substantiate his case, Baumstark advances first Lev 22:28. In the Geniza fragments we have a later development of the text found in Tg. Pseudo-Yonatan which proves that the Geniza fragments do not represent the old Palestinian Targum. Next Baumstark adduces four passages where the Peshitta supposedly reflects an older targum tradition than found in the Geniza fragments, Gen 38:5; Lev 18:21; Gen 14:13; Gen 7:4. Finally, an observation to be taken into account is that Tg. Onkelos and the Peshitta seem to go back to one and the same source. For this Baumstark adduces Exod 4:25 and 2:18, where the reading of the Peshitta and Tg. Onkelos (in 2:18 also Tg. Pseudo-Yonatan) is thought to reflect one and the same source-text, different from MT. That source-text can easily be explained as a misreading of a Syriac text written in Estrangela, then current in Mesopotamia. All these considerations together led Baumstark to the following hypothesis: A recension of the original Palestinian Targum ('Urtargum') was taken to the East, where it was re-written in the Estrangela script. From this text two revisions developed, first the Peshitta and later on Tg. Onkelos; in both the paraphrastic character of the Palestinian Targum was suppressed. In Palestine the original targum had a development of its own, of which the Geniza fragments are a later witness.

In passing it may be noted that this connection between the Peshitta and Tg. Onkelos shows up a difference between Kahle and Baumstark. Whereas, according to the latter, Onkelos developed from a Palestinian Targum tradition – as did the Peshitta –, Kahle does not see any connection between Tg. Onkelos and the Western Palestinian Targum, and, consequently, none between Onkelos and the Peshitta.

In an article from 1935[54] Baumstark reiterates his hypothesis without giving (or intending to give) further specific proof for it. For this he refers to the, then forthcoming, dissertation of his student Curt PETERS. This dissertation actually appeared the same year.[55] From the very beginning, Peters makes it clear that his thesis aims at giving support to Baumstark's hypothesis. He intends to do so by studying the agreements between the Peshitta and all or any of the known targum texts as far as these differ clearly from MT. In the first part Peters lists some 230 agreements between the Peshitta and all extant targum texts against MT, and in the second part over 300 agreements between the Peshitta and part of the targum texts against MT. Many of these examples already occurred, as is to be expected, among those presented by Perles. Peters's conclusion is that this material indicates that the Peshitta and the targums are related and that this relation 'of course can only mean dependence, one way or the other'.[56] Since it is unlikely that a translation of the Bible has later been adapted to a targum, the reverse must have been the case: the original targumic form of the Peshitta must have been adapted to MT. However, the Peshitta does not side with any specific targum, but may agree with any targum individually, or with more targums in various combinations, which indicates that the text of the Peshitta does not reflect the targum tradition in any known form, but in a form that underlies all extant forms. This older targum ('Grundschicht') is 'der ruhende Pol in der Erscheinungen Flucht', to which all known targums have to be measured.[57] In short, Peters has given us the textual material necessary to test the validity of Baumstark's thesis, under the approving eye of the master himself. The extent to which the latter identified with Peters's material and conclusions is well expressed in his remark: 'Den Beweis hierfür [i.e. for his own hypothesis] habe ich . . . in der noch ungedruckten Dissertation eines vielversprechenden Schülers Curt Peters erbringen lassen'.[58]

In evaluating the wealth of material presented by Peters it will first be necessary to sift out the many cases which concern only grammatical or syntactical details such as verb forms, suffixes, and conjunctive *waw*. In general this kind of agreement does not carry any weight. In a number of cases the agreement between the Peshitta and targum(s) could be explained on the basis of a Hebrew *Vorlage* different from MT, as Peters himself is well aware. Peters does not compare his material with the readings of LXX and SamPent. P. Wernberg-Møller, in a critical appraisal of Peters's material,[59] lists some examples of readings which are presented as exclusive agreements between the Peshitta and the Palestinian Targum, but which are actually found also in LXX and/or SamPent. Cases like these cannot be used to argue a dependence of the

[54] Baumstark, 'Neue orientalistische Probleme'.
[55] Peters, 'Peschittha und Targumim'.
[56] Ibid. p. 40.
[57] Ibid. p. 41.
[58] Baumstark, Neue orientalistische Probleme', 91.
[59] Wernberg-Møller, 'Some Observations', 138-40.

Peshitta on targumic material. Wernberg-Møller's conclusion as to Peters's material, as far as it concerns a possible dependence of the Peshitta on the Palestinian Targum tradition, is that it is 'unimpressive and unpersuasive'.

This, however, does not leave Peters's material without value. After all possible reductions have been made, there remain a number of agreements between the Peshitta and the targums against MT which suggest that some form of a relationship between them does indeed exist. One example may be given: In Deut 32:17 the Hebrew *ba'u*, '(gods, who had) appeared', is translated in both the Peshitta and Tg. Onkelos/Fragmentary Tg. by the *'etp^{e}el* of *^{e}bad*, 'were worshipped'.[60]

It is, of course, very well possible that in a number of cases the Peshitta and the targums happen to give independently the same interpretative rendering of the Hebrew, but the number of cases suggests more than accident. Peters's material, however, offers no convincing proof of dependence of the Peshitta on a hypothetical targum and there seems to be no reason to go any further than to assume with Perles that both the Peshitta and the targums made use of generally known Jewish exegetical traditions.

In the same year that Peters published his dissertation to substantiate Baumstark's thesis, another dissertation appeared, written by a student of Kahle, WOHL, to defend Kahle's hypothesis of the origins of the Peshitta.[61] As is clear from the title, Wohl's claim is twofold: to study the relation of the Palestinian Targum to other targums and to the Peshitta. As could be expected, in the focus of attention stand the Geniza fragments with which other targum texts are compared. The conclusion from this comparison is that the Fragmentary Targum is a collection of Palestinian Targum traditions, that Tg. Pseudo-Yonatan too preserves Palestinian traditions, and that some Palestinian material has even found its way into Tg. Onkelos.

In various lists Wohl gives agreements between the Peshitta and Palestinian Targum traditions, some of which overlap with Peters's material. His conclusion is that the Peshitta ultimately goes back to a West-Aramaic targum. He agrees with Baumstark that this targum preceded the text found in the Geniza fragments, but maintains that it is much nearer to these fragments than was assumed by Baumstark. It may be noted here that on one point Wohl takes a different position from Kahle. Wohl accepts that there is a relation between Tg. Onkelos and the Palestinian Targum. Tg. Onkelos originated in Babylonia but on the basis of Palestinian targumic material. Most of this Palestinian material was lost when later on Tg. Onkelos was adapted to MT, but some of it was preserved. This explains how Onkelos may on points agree with the Peshitta, either exclusively or together with the Palestinian Targum. Wohl lists some thirty cases of exclusive agreement between these two versions, and twelve

---

[60] Peters, 'Peschitta und Targumim', 9.
[61] Wohl, *Das Palästinische Pentateuch-Targum*.

cases in which these two are joined by the Palestinian Targum. These are followed by ten examples of agreement between Onkelos and the Palestinian Targum. Wohl does not infer direct influence from Onkelos upon the Peshitta. If he had, argues P. Wernberg-Møller, this 'would have disrupted his general argument, and would have ruined utterly his case for a Palestinian origin of P.'[62] This judgement may go too far: Wohl's hypothesis is not *a priori* impossible, because Tg. Onkelos and the Peshitta could both, but independently, have used Palestinian traditions. One must nevertheless concede to Wernberg-Møller that Wohl neglected the relationship, amply attested by his own material, between Onkelos and the Peshitta.

The importance of Wohl's study is parallel to that of Peters in that it gives us the material which should substantiate Kahle's hypothesis of a close connection between the Peshitta and the targum tradition embodied in the Geniza fragments. This remains the important contribution of this study although its conclusions have found little acceptance in spite of Baumstark's approval. In 1942 the latter wrote that it 'could no longer be doubted' that the Peshitta had originated from a Palestinian Targum, rewritten into East-Aramaic. 'Neben eigenen Äusserungen darf ich auf zwei Dissertationen von C. Peters und Sch. Wohl verweisen deren eindeutige Ergebnisse in dieser Richtung slechthin überzeugend wirken'.[63] A number of cases listed by Wohl concern only grammatical or syntactical details, which should be left out of consideration. But also many other examples are open to other explanations. In his critique of Wohl's study[64] Wernberg-Møller chooses six examples in which the supposed special agreement between the Peshitta and the targum does not exist or can be explained by assuming independent translation of the Hebrew in both versions or a common Hebrew Vorlage different from MT. The latter possibility is to be reckoned with especially in those cases where LXX shares the reading of the Peshitta and the targum, a consideration not included by Wohl in his study.

SYRIAC TRANSLATION LITERATURE AND PATRISTIC TEXTS. In the foregoing studies the supposed targumic background of the Peshitta was shown by a comparison between the Peshitta text and that of the targums. Another line of approach was found in Syriac translation literature and patristic literature. In Syriac translation literature the possibility is to be reckoned with that the translator did not translate Greek Bible quotations into Syriac but quoted directly from the Syriac Bible familiar to him. This Syriac Bible text could be older than the Peshitta text known to us. As to Syriac patristic literature, part of which is older than our oldest Peshitta MSS, the question may be asked whether in Bible quotations a Peshitta text is quoted or reflected which is older than that found in our MSS.

---

[62] Wernberg-Møller, 'Prolegomena', 263.
[63] Baumstark, 'Ps.-Jonathan', 101f.
[64] Wernberg-Møller, 'Prolegomena', 256-59.

BAUMSTARK was the first to draw from these two sources to strengthen his case. In 1933 he investigated some examples of Syriac translation literature.[65] The Syriac translation of *Didaskalia* does not allow clear conclusions as to the character of the Bible quotations. The Syriac translation of Titus of Bostra's (d. 357) treatise against the Manicheans does give some OT texts in a form older than the present Peshitta text. The results from the Syriac translation of Eusebius's *Church History* are inconclusive but the translation of his *Theophany* does provide us with some old Peshitta variants.

The question of patristic literature was dealt with by Baumstark in two articles, from 1935 and 1942/3.[66] In the first article he gives a few instances taken from Ephraim and Aphrahat, both fourth century, which, he claims, show a text older than our Peshitta text and nearer the Palestinian Targum tradition. In the second article Baumstark deals exclusively with Aphrahat. It is argued that in Aphrahat's quotation of Deut 34:6 we find remnants of an older, more targumic text. Other biblical quotations, too, reflect a Syriac text which differs from our Peshitta text and shows an earlier phase in its development. As a 'wilder' text it is closer to the targumic origins of the Peshitta, and this is corroborating evidence for what was already clear from a direct comparison between the Peshitta and the targum. In Baumstark's first example, Deut 34:6, the Peshitta reads with MT 'and they buried him in the valley of Moab, opposite Beth Peor'. Aphrahat adds to this the words 'where Israel sinned'. This is considered by Baumstark as reflecting the tradition found in Tg. Pseudo-Yonatan, where Beth Peor, a geographical name, has become the deity Peor. Aphrahat, therefore, is thought to have taken this text from the East-Aramaic text out of which the Peshitta developed.

In this connection it is of crucial importance to know whether Bible citations have been taken *verbatim* from a biblical text or are more or less free allusions to a biblical passage. Baumstark admits that in Aphrahat's quotations memory may have played a role, but nevertheless he is confident that many differences between his text and that of the Peshitta can be explained by assuming that Aphrahat actually used a Syriac text different from our Peshitta text. This question was thoroughly dealt with by OWENS in his book on Aphrahat's Genesis and Exodus citations, 1983. He examines 221 citations and allusions to Genesis/Exodus passages in Aphrahat's *Demonstrations*. His conclusion is that from these 221 passages only twenty-five are 'recognizable as being literal'. 'I found', he writes' 'no quotation which I can be sure was made by consulting a MS.' Owens, therefore, disagrees with Baumstark's evaluation and use of Aphrahat's quotations and, on the contrary, states that Aphrahat's citations do not give any indication of an earlier, more expanded text, but presuppose basically the Peshitta text as we know it.

In this connection mention may be made of another aspect of the way in which Bible quotations may be given, viz. that of metrical constraint. This point

---

[65] Baumstark, 'Das Problem der Bibelzitate'.
[66] Baumstark, 'Neue orientalistische Probleme', and Baumstark, 'Ps.-Jonathan'.

was made by WEITZMAN in his discussion of Peters's use of Ephraim in his study of the Peshitta Psalter, which will be dealt with later.

Baumstark's approach was followed up and applied in a more expanded form by VÖÖBUS. In 1958 his book *Peschitta und Targumim des Pentateuchs* appeared, which was a comprehensive attempt to reach an older Peshitta text by way of other material. In the first chapter he analyses a number of Pentateuch citations found in Syriac literature from the fourth down to the thirteenth century. These citations differ from the Peshitta, LXX, and MT, but agree with a targumic tradition, and therefore are considered traces of an earlier targumic text. In ch. 2 and 3 he investigates two portions, Exod 15:1-21 and Deut 32:1-43. For each of these two portions he compares the Peshitta text first with the various targumic texts and after that with the Arabic translations of the Peshitta and with Syriac patristic texts. The result of this comparison consists of lists of Syriac and Arabic words and groups of words which agree with the rendering in one or more targums and which, according to Vööbus, show the targumic 'pigment' or 'profile' which was characteristic of the early text of the Peshitta. He whole-heartedly endorses Baumstark's hypothesis of a targumic origin of the Peshitta, but disagrees with the latter on one point: whereas Baumstark thought that the originally west-Aramaic targum was more or less stripped of its targumic paraphrastic extras when it was rewritten into East-Aramaic, Vööbus is of the opinion that the measure of targumic 'pigment' he has found shows that the targumic 'Grundschicht' of the Peshitta lost its paraphrastic character only gradually and developed into the present Peshitta text over a long period of time. The material which he examined proved to be a 'Fundgrube für das targumische Gut im Syrischen', and this result, as Vööbus confidently says, introduces 'eine neue Epoche für das Studium der Vorgeschichte der Peschitta'.[67]

Vööbus's approach and conclusions met with both approval and scepticism. J.B. Segal agrees with him and states that he 'has established firmly the Targumic *Grundschicht* of the Syriac Pentateuch,[68] whereas E. Würthwein says: 'Diese These [viz. the targumic origins of the Peshitta] wird von dem Verfasser . . . zur Evidenz erhoben'.[69] More cautious is M.H. Goshen-Gottstein, according to whom most of the non-Peshitta readings adduced by Vööbus do not support the latter's thesis. Some examples of agreement between the Peshitta and the targums, however, are striking and offer further proof of the 'targumic affinities' of the Peshitta.[70]

---

[67] Vööbus, *Peschitta und Targumim*, 105.
[68] Segal, review of Vööbus, *Peschitta und Targumim*.
[69] Würthwein, review of Vööbus, *Peschitta und Targumim*.
[70] Goshen-Gottstein, review of Vööbus, *Peschitta und Targumim*. Isenberg's statement that 'M. Goshen-Gottstein has accepted his (viz. Vööbus's) conclusion without reserve' ('Jewish Palestinian Origins', 70) does not convey a correct impression of Goshen-Gottstein's independent point of view.

Serious reservations about the validity of Vööbus's arguments have been expressed by M.D. Koster,[71] who examines in detail Vööbus's method and examples, and as a result of this rejects Vööbus's conclusions, leaving only a very small number of places which may, but not necessarily do, point to a relationship between the Peshitta and the targum tradition. The present writer is inclined to agree with Koster, which is not to deny that Vööbus's study is an important one in the discussion about the origin of the Peshitta and its relation to the targums. This kind of investigation had to be made, if only for this once, and certainly Vööbus's adduces every bit of evidence he can find for his case, and leaves one confident that little more remains to be found. Therefore this material is valuable even for those who would deny Vööbus's thesis.

Another major attempt to establish a targumic origin of the Peshitta was the doctoral thesis of ISENBERG of 1968.[72] Isenberg's position is close to that of Baumstark. Just as Baumstark inferred the early existence of an 'Urtargum', Isenberg argues for a 'Proto-Targum', which served as the basis for all extant targums to which also the Peshitta is reckoned. On the basis of this 'Proto-Targum' a Palestinian and a Babylonian targum tradition developed, the latter being represented by Tg. Onkelos and the Peshitta. The *Vorlage* of this 'Proto-Targum' was a Hebrew text different from MT.

The main evidence adduced for this twofold conclusion consists of three places in which the targums, LXX, and SamPent agree in a reading different from MT and thus point to a different Hebrew *Vorlage*, and ten places where all targums agree in a reading which is secondary to MT and thus show their common background. Isenberg himself admits that 'What is striking is the paucity of significant variants . . .'[73]

Elsewhere in his study[74] the question is touched upon as to whether one or more targums might be completely dependent on MT and therefore later than the other targums. This possibility is rejected because each of the targums preserves at least one (!) significant pre-masoretic variant. In spite of this slender evidence, however, Isenberg is confident that the common origin of all targums and the Peshitta is clear enough.

The relation between the Peshitta and the targum tradition is discussed in the third chapter. First Isenberg quotes with approval some examples from previous studies which show a relation between the Peshitta and the targums. The first is Perles from whom five examples are quoted, the difference being that, whereas Perles assumes a common oral tradition, Isenberg believes in a literary relation between the Peshitta and the targum tradition. As is to be expected, Baumstark is fully endorsed. His 1931 article 'Pešiṭta und palästinensisches

---

[71] Koster, *The Peshiṭta of Exodus*, 198-212.
[72] Isenberg, *Jewish Aramaic Translations*. Isenberg's point of view as to the origin of the Peshitta is also expressed in his article 'Jewish-Palestinian Origins'.
[73] Isenberg, *Jewish Aramaic Translations*, 117-25; quotation from p. 127.
[74] Ibid. p. 135.

Targum' is extensively discussed and his conclusions are accepted, although Isenberg is critical of Baumstark's linguistic arguments.

Qualified support is given to Wohl and Peters. Wohl's method is criticized to the effect that only those agreements between the Peshitta and the targums should have been used in which they differ from LXX and SamPent. Some of Wohl's examples, however, are useful to prove a relation between the targums and the Peshitta and five of them are quoted. Although Peters's method is considered more adequate by Isenberg, many of his examples are held to be invalid because they concern only details which can easily be explained by scribal activity. There remain, however, a number of agreements which do establish a relationship, and many of them are quoted. This section is closed with an approving reference to Vööbus, with whom he agrees in that the Peshitta is related to the targumic tradition in general but not especially to any of the known targums.

CRITICAL ASSESSMENT OF KAHLE-BAUMSTARK. The Baumstark-Kahle approach has had and still has its defenders, but in no less degree it has found its opponents too. Two of them may be mentioned here: A. Sperber and P. Wernberg-Møller.[75] The position of these two scholars will be dealt with in the following sections. Before arguing their own case, however, they both discuss the Baumstark-Kahle hypothesis.

SPERBER asks the very basic question: how could what Baumstark suggested in his theory actually have taken place? We must assume that first the West-Aramaic targum which had been taken to the East was stripped of its paraphrases, to adapt it to the Hebrew text. This task having been completed, the remaining targum text ('Rumpftargum') was translated from West-Aramaic into Syriac. That this was no easy task is well illustrated by Sperber, who draws up a synopsis of four texts of Gen 48:11-21, MT, the Palestinian Targum, the Peshitta and Tg. Onkelos. At first glance it becomes clear that the Palestinian Targum and the Peshitta are two very different texts. After this survey Sperber goes on: 'And now I ask, why would these men, who knew Hebrew well enough to complete this laborious task in eliminating the paraphrases on the basis of the Hebrew text . . ., and who had enough philological sensitivity not to be de-railed in translating the West-Aramaic text into East Aramaic – why would they have gone to so much trouble to change the Palestinian form of the Targum in view of the fact that it would have been much easier and simpler to translate directly from the Hebrew into East-Aramaic?' (my translation).

To override this very basic objection to Baumstark's theory one would need strong and unambiguous textual evidence. As was already indicated above Baumstark hardly gave textual evidence to support his thesis, Kahle not at all. Did their pupils Peters and Wohl? Reference was already made to WERNBERG-MØLLER's critique of the work of these two scholars. In his two articles Wern-

[75] Sperber, 'Peschitta und Onkelos'; Wernberg-Møller, 'Some Observations' and 'Prolegomena'.

berg-Møller is not in the first place concerned with the validity of individual cases but with the question of methodology: How can we prove a literary dependence of the Peshitta on any targum tradition? The answer is: only through 'phraseological similarity'.[76] Similarity in details and in isolated words is not sufficient. This criterion also excludes as evidence similarity in halakha if in this respect the Peshitta differs from the official halakha as found in Tg. Onkelos while agreeing with the Palestinian tradition. Halakhic traditions contrary to the official halakha which existed in the West may as well have existed in the East, where they could have influenced the translator(s) of the Peshitta.[77] Finally, agreements based on differences or affinities between Aramaic dialects have no cogency. We do not know enough of these dialects to use them for establishing dependence of an East-Aramaic text on a West-Aramaic text.[78]

In his own comparison between the Peshitta text of Genesis and the Geniza fragments, Wernberg-Møller has found eleven places which, at least at first sight, show an agreement between these two texts in which they differ from MT and Tg. Onkelos. In eight of these cases the agreement can easily be explained without assuming literary dependence. In three cases no such explanation can be given, but in two of them the agreement is not impressive. Only in one case, Gen 48:16, Wernberg-Møller admits to having no satisfactory solution.[79] The paucity of agreements between the Peshitta and the Palestinian Targum all but excludes the possibility of the Peshitta having any literary relation to the latter.

It may be noted that this negative conclusion does not affect Baumstark's theory, but only Kahle's. It actually concurs with Baumstark's (later) opinion, as opposed to Kahle's that the Peshitta does not show any remarkable agreement with the Palestinian Targum. Wernberg-Møller and Baumstark only go in opposite directions after having reached this conclusion, Baumstark taking refuge in a hypothetical older targum, and Wernberg-Møller denying any direct relation between the Peshitta and the Palestinian Targum.

Wernberg-Møller finds corroboration for his conclusion in another observation, viz. that many cases testify to the Peshitta's independence of the targumic traditions. He is right in paying attention to this side of the argument. In previous studies exclusive attention was given to agreements between the two versions. Agreements may point to literary contacts, but if it is claimed that one of the two versions ultimately goes back to the other, then evidence of this version being independent should also be taken into account. Wernberg-Møller presents forty-four examples of the Peshitta's independence of the targums.

---

[76]   e.g. Wernberg-Møller, 'Some Observations', 132.
[77]   Wernberg-Møller, Prolegomena', 255.
[78]   Ibid. p. 255f., 260f. For a discussion of the linguistic arguments see also Rosenthal, *Die Aramaistische Forschung*, 199-206.
[79]   Wernberg-Møller, 'Some Observations' 144.

The difference may be between two interpretations of the Hebrew, or between a literal translation in the Peshitta and a non-literal translation in the targum. In a number of cases the Peshitta does not use a word found in the targums although this word existed also in Syriac, and could have been used. Finally the Peshitta may show its independence by giving a free translation, or even a faulty one, whereas the Palestinian Targum and Tg. Onkelos are faithful to the Hebrew. By way of illustration one example may be given. In Gen 37:30 *'enennu* is correctly translated 'he is not there' in the Palestinian Targum and in Tg. Onkelos, in the Peshitta, however, incorrectly by 'where is he?'[80]

PESHITTA PENTATEUCH ORIGINATED FROM AN EASTERN TARGUM

Opposition to the Baumstark-Kahle approach does not necessarily mean denying a targumic origin of the Peshitta. There remains the possibility of the Peshitta having originated from an East-Aramaic targum. This is the position of SPERBER. In the article mentioned before he asks the question as to the relation between the Peshitta and Tg. Onkelos. The best and surest way to establish a relation between these versions is to show that there are readings in either version which can only be explained by referring to the other version. Sperber adduces four cases where an Onkelos witness is thought to have a composite text, one of the two renderings being found in one or more other Onkelos witnesses, and one in the Peshitta. This means that the composite Onkelos text can be explained only by a reference to the Peshitta, and from this Sperber concludes that there must be a close relationship between the Peshitta and Onkelos. However, there are many differences between Onkelos and the Peshitta. Both give basically a literal rendering of the Hebrew text, but Onkelos deviates from this quite often, because of his inclination to avoid anthropomorphisms and because of the requirements of rabbinic exegesis. These deviations are only incidentally found in the Peshitta. This leads Sperber to the conclusion that the Peshitta reflects an East-Aramaic literal targum (as opposed to the more paraphrastic West-Aramaic targums) as it existed before it developed into Tg. Onkelos by way of elimination of anthropomorphisms and adoption of Jewish exegesis. This older form of an East-Aramaic targum was put ('Übertragen') into Syriac and so has come to us in the form of the Peshitta.

It is a pity that Sperber has nowhere followed up this short treatment of the relationship between the Peshitta and Tg. Onkelos and given more examples to support his case. Now we are left with only four places from Genesis to shoulder the burden of proof. Moreover, with respect to each of these examples doubts may remain as to whether the Peshitta reading, in all cases a straightforward and correct translation of the Hebrew, is indeed so evidently necessary to explain the targum reading. One example may be quoted. In Gen 3:5 Hebrew *yod[ec]e*, 'knowing', is translated in most Onkelos witnesses by *ḥakhmin*, 'wise,

---

[80] Ibid. p. 156f.

knowing'. The Peshitta has the exact equivalent of the Hebrew: *yadᶜay*. One Onkelos witness has *ḥakhmin lᵉmidaᶜ*, 'wise to know'. According to Sperber this reading is composed of the first two renderings, one of them being that of the Peshitta.

A comparison between the views of Sperber and Baumstark brings to light the extent to which the question of Peshitta origins is tied up with the broader question as to the relation between the various targums. As already mentioned, Baumstark holds that both Tg. Onkelos and the Peshitta developed from a West-Aramaic targum which was taken to the East. Sperber assumes a completely separate development of two targum traditions, a paraphrastic one in the West, a literal one in the East. In both views there is a strong hypothetical element: in Baumstark's view the Palestinian Targum, which he supposed to have been taken to the East, is purely hypothetical, both in its text and in its very existence; in Sperber's view the early form of a literal Eastern targum from which Onkelos developed is a postulate. In the first case Tg. Onkelos was the result of a narrowing down of the paraphrastic Palestinian Targum to a more literal rendering, in the second case Tg. Onkelos resulted from a process of adapting a very literal targum to the requirements of piety and exegesis.

THE TRANSLATOR(S) OF PESHITTA PENTATEUCH USED TARGUM ONKELOS

It should come as no surprise that the relation between Tg. Onkelos and the Peshitta has been a special object of study, apart from the question as to the relation between the Peshitta and the targums in general. Although its roots may have been in the Palestinian Targum tradition, it is generally held that Tg. Onkelos developed and received its final form in Babylonia.[81] Just like the Peshitta, it was written in a form of East-Aramaic. Therefore there would be an *a priori* probability that if there were any dependence on the targumic tradition this would show especially in agreements with Tg. Onkelos.

As was already mentioned earlier, Perles drew attention to agreements between the Peshitta and Tg. Onkelos without positing dependence of the Peshitta on the latter. Ever since, scholars could not fail to see points of contact and try to account for it. Baumstark and Isenberg did this by considering both versions as separate developments from a Palestinian targum after it had been taken to the East, Sperber by assuming a common East-Aramaic sourcetargum.

It was SCHÖNFELDER who in his *Habilitationsschrift*[82] of 1869 posited a direct dependence of the Peshitta on Tg. Onkelos in a number of cases. As is clear from the subtitle of his study, Schönfelder's primary concern was to establish the age of Tg. Onkelos. The Peshitta is important in this respect because it appears that the Peshitta has used Onkelos and that therefore the latter is older

---

[81] For a recent protest against this assumption see Greenfield, 'Standard Literary Aramaic', 287.
[82] Schönfelder, *Onkelos und Peschittho*.

than the Peshitta. In the first chapter Schönfelder gives a great number of agreements between the Peshitta and Onkelos, many of which had already been mentioned by Perles. These agreements prove that the Peshitta has used a written copy of Onkelos. This is confirmed by the agreements in translation technique, dealt with in chapter 2. An example of this is the use of q^edam, 'before', in expressions as 'to serve before God', as a rendering for the Hebrew 'to serve God'. In general anthropomorphisms are avoided. This translation technique is followed systematically in Onkelos, but only in a limited number of cases without pattern in the Peshitta, which indicates that the Peshitta used Onkelos, not *vice versa*. In the third chapter attention is paid to aggadic and halakhic elements common to Onkelos and the Peshitta. Schönfelder gives seven examples of which at least four had already been mentioned by Perles. In chapter 4 he discusses some passages from the Talmud and Onkelos itself which should corroborate the thesis of Onkelos having originated in the early beginning of our era.

Schönfelder expresses his indebtedness to Perles, but differs from the latter on an important point: whereas Perles saw Onkelos and the Peshitta as two 'deposits of Jewish interpretations and traditions', Schönfelder is convinced that the agreements are the result of the Peshitta having used Onkelos. Schönfelder is aware that the traditions in which both versions agree may also be found in rabbinic sources, but this may be explained by assuming that the latter are dependent on Onkelos instead of being the source of both the Peshitta and Onkelos. This point is not explicitly dealt with, but only stated. In his discussion of Gen 30:27 the writer says, in so many words rejecting Perles's opinion: 'Ich wüsste nicht, mit welchem Rechte man Schriften, wie Gen. Rabba oder ähnliche, oder deren Traditionen-Inhalt für älter als das erste Targum ausgibt, und was uns verbieten könnte, das Targum als Quelle für die Talmudisten oder die rabbinische Literatur uns zu denken.'[83] Although the assumption of the rabbinic sources or their traditions being younger than Onkelos is crucial for Schönfelder's argument, no supporting evidence is given and therefore it remains a weak point in his discussion of the relation between the Peshitta and Tg. Onkelos.

In his introduction Schönfelder rightly states that agreements between the Peshitta and Onkelos are not necessarily proof of dependence and may be explained e.g. by their using a common tradition. In dealing with these agreements, however, Schönfelder does not actually honour this *caveat*, probably because he builds his case on the assumption of Onkelos being older than the rabbinic sources. One of many examples is Gen 2:8. According to MT God planted a garden in Eden, in the East *(miqqedem)*. The Peshitta translates 'God planted Paradise in Eden in former times *(men q^edim)*'. Schönfelder only mentions – besides the readings of LXX and Vulgate – the rendering of Onkelos: *mill^eqadmin*, 'in former times', which is supposed to be the source of the reading

---

[83] Ibid. p. 40f.

of the Peshitta. Ch. Heller, in a critique of Schönfelder's study,[84] discusses this verse and mentions a number of passages in talmudic sources which should make clear that there was a popular tradition that Paradise was created before the world came into existence. This tradition, according to Heller, must have been used here by both the Peshitta and Onkelos. The same background for this rendering is adduced by Y. Maori in his study which will be dealt with below.

If Schönfelder has not proven dependence of the Peshitta on Onkelos, he has at least given us an important addition to the material supplied by Perles, and given further proof that in many respects the two versions reflect the same tradition of translation and interpretation.

In 1931 SILVERSTONE published his study 'Aquila and Onkelos', which, as far as the Peshitta is concerned, runs very much parallel to Schönfelder's work. Silverstone sets out to prove that Aquila was the author not only of the Greek translation known by his name, but also of Tg. Onkelos. One of his arguments is found in the relation between the Peshitta and Onkelos. It appears that between these two versions there is a relation of dependence: one of the two has been using the other. A number of agreements can be explained by the Peshitta having used Onkelos, not the other way round. Since the Peshitta was written c. 150 C.E., Onkelos must have been written not later than c. 140 C.E., that is in Aquila's lifetime.

In arguing his case, Silverstone cites yet more examples of agreement between the Peshitta and Onkelos besides a number of passages which had been adduced in earlier studies. His first example consists of seventeen places (besides a reference to more) where the Hebrew text has the verb *laqaḥ*, 'to take', and the Peshitta and Onkelos agree in translating this verb by either *nᵉsab*, in connection with inanimate objects and when it refers to 'taking' a wife, or *dᵉbar*, when used with human beings. The agreement is indeed remarkable.[85] Yet the question may be asked whether especially an example like this points to the Peshitta actually having used Tg. Onkelos or, rather, to a translation tradition known to both.

WERNBERG-MØLLER has already been referred to a couple of times as an opponent to the Baumstark-Kahle hypothesis. His own view puts him into line with Silverstone and Schönfelder. Wernberg-Møller is of the opinion that the Peshitta, as far as can be concluded from the text of Genesis, is an independent translation of the Hebrew. In a number of places, however, the translator has made use of a written copy of Tg. Onkelos in a text form differing to a limited extent from the one known to us.

---

[84] Heller, *Untersuchung über die Peschitta*; Schönfelder's material is discussed on pp. 4-7.
[85] Cf. Wernberg-Møller's comment in 'Some Observations', 175f.

Wernberg-Møller argues his case in general terms.[86] It appears (a) that there are *many* examples of agreement between the Palestinian Targum, Tg. Onkelos, and the Peshitta, (b) that in *other cases* the Peshitta agrees with Tg. Onkelos against the Palestinian Targum, and (c) that in *very few* instances the Peshitta agrees with the Palestinian Targum against Tg. Onkelos. The first agreements (a) make it probable that Tg. Onkelos goes back to the Palestinian Targum, and the Peshitta in its turn to Tg. Onkelos. This is confirmed by the agreements of (b), and not contradicted by those of (c). These latter agreements with the Palestinian Targum against Tg. Onkelos may be accounted for by assuming that in the Peshitta use was made of a text of Onkelos which in detail differed from the present text. In another article[87] the author gives a number of examples to substantiate his opinion. These examples, according to the author, show that if there is a literary relation between the Peshitta and either Tg. Onkelos or the Palestinian Targum, the first possibility obtains.

The examples which Wernberg-Møller adduces are indicative of the complexity involved in comparing the Peshitta text with that of the targums. In his discussion of the studies of the Baumstark-Kahle school, the writer rightly stresses that agreements between the Peshitta and the targums should not too easily be taken as indications of dependence. There may be other explanations for them. Over against agreements in details or isolated words, Wernberg-Møller requires 'phraseological similarity' to prove dependence. It does not, however, become clear from his own examples what is characteristic of this 'phraseological similarity'. And the question still remains as to which agreements can actually be considered as proofs of a literary relation. As an illustration of the problem one example may be given. According to Wernberg-Møller one of the 'very striking instances of agreement' is the way the Hebrew verb *šaraṣ*, 'to swarm, teem', is translated in the Peshitta and in Tg. Onkelos. In Gen. 1:20, 21; 7:21 both have the verb *rᵉḥaš*, 'to swarm', in Gen 8:17; 9:7 both use the root *jld*, Onkelos in the *'itpᵉᶜel*, 'to be brought forth', the Peshitta in the *'aphᶜel*, 'to bring forth'. At first sight one may be inclined to agree with the author, that 'the remarkable agreement between Onk and the Peshitta here can hardly be accidental'. However, at closer look doubts may arise. In the first three places we find the same translation of the Hebrew word which is used elsewhere (Exod 7:28; Lev 11:29, 41, 43, 46; Ps 105:30). This translation is the natural one which we would expect, and there is no reason to assume that the Peshitta has consulted the targum here. Moreover, in the first of these places, Exod 7:28, Onkelos has a different translation (*wirabbe*, 'make many, multiply'), which excludes dependence. In the other two places, Gen 8:17; 9:7, where the root *jld* is used, the verb stands along other verbs meaning 'to be fertile/to multiply', and the translation in both Onkelos and the Peshitta is very appropriate, the other Syriac verb *(rᵉḥaš)* hardly making sense here. Both the Peshitta and

---

[86] Wernberg-Møller, 'Prolegomena'.
[87] Wernberg-Møller, 'Some Observations'.

Onkelos may well have come to this correct translation independently, which may be indicated also by the difference in verb form. It may be added that in the book of Ezekiel the *'aphᶜel* of *jld* is used as a translation of *šaraṣ*: in Ezek 47:9 *'ašer jišroṣ* is rendered *dᵉmawlᵉda*, whereas Tg. Yonatan uses the other verb, *rᵉḥaš*. This example may confirm what Wernberg-Møller himself strongly defended in his two articles, that great caution has to be taken in positing a direct literary relationship between the Peshitta and Tg. Onkelos or any other targum. The agreement may only reflect the common demands of the two East-Aramaic dialects. Another possibility that must be taken into account is that both Tg. Onkelos and the Peshitta make use of Jewish exegetical traditions.

In the previous section reference was made to the connection between theories about the Peshitta and those about the history of the targum tradition. This connection may also be noted in the views dealt with in this section.

Schönfelder, on the basis of agreements between the Peshitta and Tg. Onkelos, is convinced that the first made use of a written copy of Tg. Onkelos, and consequently places Tg. Onkelos in the beginning of our era. This whole theory, however, becomes untenable if on other grounds it is established that Tg. Onkelos is the result of a long development and, in the form we know it, of a much later date than the Peshitta. Th. Nöldeke, in his review of Schönfelder's study therefore, rejects Schönfelder's main thesis and accepts his material, as far as his examples are valid, only as a supplement to the material already supplied by Perles to prove influence of Jewish exegetical exegesis on both Onkelos and the Peshitta.

Silverstone, too, has the Peshitta use a copy of Tg. Onkelos, which is thought to have been completed mid-second century.

If Onkelos is dated much later, than the reverse position, that of Onkelos being dependent on the Peshitta, becomes a possibility. This was actually defended by, among others, M. Seligsohn.[88] Wernberg-Møller's position is more flexible: Tg. Onkelos is the result of a long development on the basis of Palestinian material. The Peshitta used Onkelos in a form which preceded its final shape, and this would explain how Palestinian material could penetrate the Peshitta by way of Onkelos even in cases where Onkelos itself no longer has this material.

THE TRANSLATOR WAS INFLUENCED BY JEWISH EXEGETICAL TRADITIONS

The first study that should be mentioned here is that of PERLES of 1859, which has already been referred to before.[89] His was a real pioneer's work, which has greatly stimulated further research into the origins of the Peshitta, although

---

[88] Seligsohn, 'Peshitta', referred to by Silverstone, *Aquila and Onkelos*, 127.
[89] Perles, *Meletemata*.

many scholars after him were led to other conclusions by positing targumic origins or use of Tg. Onkelos. Support for his position was given by HELLER in his thesis of 1911.[90] According to Heller the rules of interpretation and the translation technique of the Peshitta reflect the spirit of the Talmud. The author rejects Schönfelder's thesis of a literary relation between the Peshitta and Onkelos, discussing some of the latter's examples in detail. The Peshitta as a whole is to be understood from a Jewish background, and is, therefore, either a Jewish translation, or a Christian translation to which Jews contributed.

It is an interesting and a remarkable fact that after the intensive research and the lively debate that have been going on since Perles wrote his now classical study, a major study was written by MAORI which basically takes the same position as did Perles.[91] According to Maori Peshitta Pentateuch is basically a literal translation of the Hebrew, but the translator(s) made use of Jewish exegetical traditions in a number of places. Maori agrees with Perles that there is no reason to posit dependence of the Peshitta on any targum where they agree. The agreement may be explained on the assumption that both share the same exegetical tradition. The differences between the two scholars concerns a secondary point: whereas Perles speaks of the use of Jewish exegetical traditions that were current in oral form, Maori argues that 'P's choice of words demonstrates that P. was influenced by written stylized literary materials, or at least was familiar with oral, exegetical-midrashic traditions that were already stylistically formalized'. The scholarly work previous to his own study has led Maori to methodological carefulness. In chs. 3-5 he deals with the methodological questions concerning his study. It will be limited to 'clear-cut cases', excluding all cases where an agreement between the Peshitta and rabbinic sources may be explained otherwise than by the Peshitta being dependent on the latter. The translation of the Peshitta may be the result of the demands of the Syriac language, of independent assimilation to other biblical passages, or of independent interpretation of the Hebrew. A further restriction is positing dependence only in those cases where the particular explanation of a given passage actually occurs in rabbinic sources. This 'minimalistic methodology' is a strong point in Maori's study. In the main chapter of the book, ch. 6, he adduces 106 cases where direct dependence on rabbinic sources is posited. One example may be given. In Gen 30:27 the Hebrew word *niḥašti*, 'I learned through divination', is translated *nassit*, 'I have experienced'. This is done only here; everywhere else the Hebrew word is translated by the same root in Syriac. The same is true for Tgs. Onkelos and Neofiti. Apparently we have here the same Jewish exegetical tradition which is found in *Gen. Rabba* 73:8 (p. 851), where exactly the same interpretation of *niḥašti* is given. This rendering may be explained as a conscious attempt to prevent the meaning of divination here

---

[90] Heller, *Untersuchung*.
[91] Maori, *The Peshitta Version*. The English quotations have been taken from the English summary, pp. XIV, V, XVIII.

being given to the Hebrew word, since it is deemed unsuitable in view of the following words.

The last work to be mentioned is that of COOK.[92] In the introduction of his study Cook is critical of the Baumstark-Kahle school because of their 'ad hoc approach' to the question of a possible relation of the Peshitta to the targums. Cook pleads for a 'contextual analysis', that is: studying the text in the light of the translator's aim and the resulting translation technique. The Pentateuch is basically a literal translation of the Hebrew, but the translator(s) wanted to give an understandable translation which in a number of cases lead to interpretative renderings. This is done in a 'minimalistic way', i.e. not more than is necessary for the sake of clarity, in contrast to the more paraphrastic targums. In studying the Peshitta text one has to reckon with various internal and external criteria which may account for the Peshitta rendering deviating from the Hebrew. The internal criteria are a possible different Hebrew *Vorlage*, (which Cook is hesitant to resort to), Syriac style and grammar, and harmonization with nearby or parallel passages. External criteria are influence from Jewish exegesis, from LXX, and from the targums. This emphasis on the need of studying the translation technique and the resulting caution in drawing conclusions from external agreements is an important aspect of Cook's study, irrespective of whether or not one agrees with his conclusions in detail.

The introduction is followed by two chapters in which the author applies his 'contextual analysis' to a great number of renderings from Genesis and Exodus, further enriching the comparative material earlier collected by other scholars. In accordance with the writer's basic rules the Syriac rendering is explained on the basis of the translation technique, which includes use of LXX or one or more targums in difficult places. It is probable that the translator used a written copy of the targums and other written exegetical literature, and not just oral traditions since 'his nuances are too book-directed (boek-gerig)',[93] a conclusion in which Cook stands close to Maori. At the end of his work Cook poses the question as to Jewish or Christian authorship. His conclusion is that the Jewishness of the translation is an indisputable fact ('Die Joodsheid van hierdie vertaling staan soos 'n paal bo water'). This is clear from the use of Jewish exegesis, of the targums, and also of LXX. It is true that later on LXX was rejected because of its use by Christians, but it is not certain that this negative attitude which existed in the West was also found in the East.

FINAL REMARKS CONCERNING PESHITTA PENTATEUCH

It will be clear that the first hypothesis (The Peshitta originated from the targum tradition) on the one hand and the second (The Peshitta used Tg. Onkelos) and

---

[92] Cook, *Ondersoek*.
[93] Ibid. p. 131.

the third one (influence of Jewish exegesis) on the other hand are mutually exclusive. The Peshitta (Pentateuch) is either a translation or reworking of an Aramaic targum, or a translation from the Hebrew. The second and third hypothesis, however, could well go together. A translator who would be acquainted with Jewish exegesis could well have consulted Onkelos, and *vice versa*. Both possibilities have to be proved or disproved independently of the other. On the basis of available evidence it may be difficult to draw a sharp line. An illustration of this is given by LEVINE. In his detailed study of Gen 4:1-16[94] the writer aims at bringing to light the Jewish-exegetical background of the translation of the Peshitta. In his conclusions he says (italics mine): 'A knowledge of both the Hebrew original and *the Jewish exegetical tradition* is so apparent, that there can be no doubt of *Jewish influence* on the Peshitta. The translator(s) consulted *Jewish-Aramaic* tradition which was available to them in *the targums*. The Syriac Pentateuch, . . . is an important asset in the study of the *targum texts* that are currently available. Conversely, *targumic and midrashic texts* may frequently illuminate the broad outlines of the Peshitta's intent and meaning'.

As one surveys the material, there can hardly be any doubt that in a considerable number of places Peshitta Pentateuch exhibits influence from Jewish exegesis as known from and exemplified by targum and midrash. This conclusion, to which Perles was led in the first study of a long line of scholarly works, was confirmed by the recent study of Maori. As to a possible dependence on Onkelos the evidence is less clear. As was already indicated above, caution is needed before an agreement between the Peshitta and Onkelos can be taken as an indication of dependence. Many agreements may be explained by the demands of the two related languages, of common translation techniques or otherwise. A main problem in proving dependence is that agreements between the Peshitta and Onkelos which do not seem to be accidental do not necessarily point to dependence and may as well be due to common exegetical traditions. In this respect the lists provided by different scholars may be mutually corrective and complementary. Put together they now form an almost bewildering variety in the choice of examples and interpretation of these. For optimal use of them one would wish to have a concordance to them available. Two examples, already referred to earlier, may be given. In Gen 8:4 the rendering of 'Ararat' by 'Qardu' is listed by Peters as one of the examples of the Peshitta being linked to the targum tradition in general (Tg. Onkelos, Palestinian Targum, Tg. Yonatan),[95] as was done by Isenberg, who added Tg. Neofiti.[96] Schönfelder gives it as one of the examples which show dependence of the Peshitta on Onkelos.[97] Wernberg-Møller, too, notes the agreement between the Peshitta and the targums. In his opinion the Peshitta has been influenced by Onkelos,

---

[94] Levine, 'Syriac version'.
[95] Peters, 'Peschitta und Targumim', 11, 14.
[96] Isenberg, *Studies*, 197.
[97] Schönfelder, *Onkelos und Peschittho*, 5.

whereas Onkelos goes back to the Palestinian Targum tradition as found in the Geniza fragments.[98] Perles, as cited before, had already mentioned that the same rendering is also found in *Gen. Rabba* (33:4, p. 309) and expressed as his opinion that common knowledge of Jewish exegesis is the source of this rendering.[99] The same view is held by Maori, who adds the interesting observation that the identification of Ararat with Qardu in this verse is also found in Josephus's *Antiquities*.[100] Cook lists this place as an example of the translator having consulted a written targum.[101]

The other example is Deut 32:17. Hebrew *ba'u*, 'they came', is rendered by 'they were worshipped' in the Peshitta and the targums. Schönfelder mentions the agreement as an example of the Peshitta being dependent on Onkelos.[102] Peters, as cited above, gives the agreement with Tgs. Onkelos and Yonatan as pointing to the Peshitta's relation to the targum tradition in general.[103] Maori adduces a tradition in *Mekhilta de-R. Yishmael* (*Bahodesh* 6, p. 224), which could well explain this translation in both the Peshitta and the targums from the background of Jewish exegesis.[104] Many more examples could be given, but these two may suffice to make clear that the evidence is not always unequivocal as to the source of the Peshitta's rendering. Since the influence of Jewish exegesis is clear in many cases where Onkelos does not agree with the Peshitta, this same influence may well have been at work also in cases where the two do agree, irrespective of whether in a given place such an exegetical tradition is known from other sources, since not all Jewish exegetical traditions have been preserved. This does not exclude the possibility that the translator of the Peshitta may incidentally have made use of Onkelos. Wernberg-Møller's warning that agreement is not enough, and that 'phraseological similarity' is needed to establish literary dependence, should be kept well in mind.

Peshitta and Jewish Traditions: Books Outside the Pentateuch

There has not been such extensive discussion of the possible Jewish origin of those books of the Old Testament that fall outside the Pentateuch. This is not surprising, since the Pentateuch is the most important part of the OT and the first to be translated by Jews in another language. Yet, the same questions have been asked and the same answers given in relation to books outside the Pentateuch. The only difference between the Pentateuch and the other books of the OT is a matter of *a priori* probability. The more probable it would seem that Peshitta Pentateuch had a targumic origin or was influenced by Jewish

[98] Wernberg-Møller, 'Some Observations', 163f.
[99] Perles, *Meletemata*, 28.
[100] Maori, *The Peshitta Version*, 74.
[101] Cook, *Ondersoek*, 47, 93.
[102] Schönfelder, *Onkelos und Peschittho*, 27.
[103] Peters, 'Peschittha und Targumim', 9.
[104] Maori, *The Peshitta Version*, 179, n. 4.

traditions, the more one could reckon with the possibility of this being the case also for other books of the OT, and, conversely, the more one is disinclined to accept a targumic background or a Jewish origin for Peshitta Pentateuch, the less one would expect this to be the case in other books.

A TARGUMIC BACKGROUND OF I SAM AND THE PSALMS

One of the scholars mentioned in relation to the Pentateuch has extended his researches into a possible targumic background into books outside the Pentateuch, viz. PETERS. In two articles he argues for a targumic background of the Psalms and 1 Sam respectively. The first article appeared in 1939, the second in 1941.[105]

In his article on the Psalms Peters adduces ten examples of agreement between the Peshitta and Tg. Psalms over against MT. The writer acknowledges that this is scant evidence but nevertheless he is confident that further research will result in many times the number of examples and that it would lead to the 'inevitable conclusion' that the Peshitta originated on the basis of a targumic tradition. Further evidence is found in psalm quotations in Syriac literature, either original or translated from the Greek, and in Arabic literature translated from Syriac. In the article on 1 Sam the *pièce de résistance* is a list of thirty cases of agreement between the Peshitta and Tg. Samuel against MT. These agreements, together with other corroborating evidence, lead Peters to the conclusion that Peshitta Samuel is rooted in a targumic tradition, although the ultimate form of that targum is not necessarily that of Tg. Samuel as we know it.

This is not the place to deal with Peters's material in detail. A few examples may, however, be mentioned to exemplify the problems and traps which are inherent to a comparison between the two texts. In his article on Psalms his first example is Ps 5:7. The Hebrew *'iš damim*, 'a man of blood(shed)', is rendered in the Peshitta by *gabra 'ašed dᵉma*, 'a man who sheds blood', in which it agrees with the targum. If, however, we do not isolate this place, it becomes evident that the addition of 'who sheds' does not indicate a literary relationship, but reflects a common translation technique: to prefer good idiomatic Syriac/ Aramaic to a strictly literal translation. The same translation 'who sheds blood' is found elsewhere in the Peshitta (2 Sam 16:7, 8; Ps 55:24; 59:3; Prov 29:10). In the last place the targum agrees with the Peshitta, in the other places it has a different, though adequate translation.

For the use which Peters makes of Syriac and Arabic literature reference may be made here to Weitzman's discussion of it.[106] Weitzman argues that free, so-called targumic citations of OT texts in Syriac poets like Ephraim, may in fact be due to metrical constraints. Again, the Arabic authors who yield 'targumic'

---

[105] Peters, 'Pešitta-Psalter' and 'Zur Herkunft'.
[106] Weitzman, 'Origin'.

286

citations from the OT cite the NT equally free, so that the freedom must be due to the Arabic writers rather than any 'targumische Grundschicht'.

One of the examples in the article on 1 Sam is 5:3. MT has *nofel*, part of *nafal*, 'to fall'. Both the Peshitta and the targum render it by *rᵉme*, pass. part. of *rᵉma*, 'to put'. The translation problem is, that Hebrew *nofel*, besides 'falling', also means 'fallen, lying'. This double meaning is not found in Syriac/Aramaic, which regularly uses *rᵉme* in the latter meaning, e.g. Deut 21:1, Judg 3:25. Thus, both the Peshitta and the targum give the expected equivalent of *nofel* quite independently of each other.

A case of common translation tradition, finally, is Peters's third example. In 1 Sam 2:2 MT has 'there is no Rock'. Both the Peshitta and the targum have 'there is no Strong One'. This agreement may at first sight seem remarkable, but instead of being an isolated case it is rather an example of a standard translation. Elsewhere, where 'rock' is used for God, we find the same rendering, both in the Peshitta and in the targum, e.g. 2 Sam 23:3; Isa 17:10.

In his article on 1 Sam Peters wishes to offer a corrective to P.A.H. de Boer's earlier study of the text of 1 Sam.[107] In his study De Boer discusses successively the way the targum, the Peshitta, and LXX have rendered the Hebrew text. In his chapter on the Peshitta he notes the pluses, the minuses and other alterations. In a number of places he notes an agreement between the Peshitta and the targum, but these do not point to a literary relationship between the two.

Peters has reservations as to De Boer's 'casuistic approach'. Over against this approach he sets out to give in a 'systematic comparison' an overall picture which is supposed to 'point unmistakably to a targumic origin of the Peshitta'.

In his polemic remark Peters touches upon the basic question of methodology in this type of research, although he does not enlarge upon it. The two studies of De Boer and Peters exemplify two different approaches. In the former we find a treatment of the Peshitta text in its own right in which no dependence on an outside source is posited if there is no compelling reason to do so. In Peters's study, however, a hypothesis, or at least a working-hypothesis, is tested out on the material and found valid. It may be remarked that *a priori* there is nothing to find fault with in Peter's method. The only sure way to establish a literary relationship of any kind is to register agreements between the two versions where they together deviate from MT, and to investigate whether a clear pattern is discernible. The crucial point, however, is that these agreements can only be used for arguing a literary relationship if they cannot be explained otherwise, and if the agreements show a remarkable frequency. De Boer does not see any such pattern, and Peters's examples, rather than challenging this conclusion, would seem, both in type and in number, to fall short of supporting his far-reaching conclusion.

---

[107] De Boer, *Research*. This study was followed by '1 Sam. XVII' and 'The text of 1 Samuel XVIII-XXXI'.

A TARGUMIC BACKGROUND OF ISAIAH?

A major study in the same line of research is the doctoral thesis of RUNNING on the book of Isaiah.[108] In the Introduction of her thesis the writer states the aims of her investigation. The three main purposes are: '1. To find traces of the Aramaic Targum underlying the Syriac text and thus 2. to go behind the Peshitta revision to the Old Syriac text forms, following the type of work done by Arthur Vööbus in the area of the Pentateuch . . 3. To show the support given by the Syrian authors to variants from the Peshitta text, especially in the writings of the earliest, Aphrahat of Persia, and St. Ephraim of Edessa . . ., which may well lead toward reconstruction of the Vetus Syra text, as is also indicated by Vööbus'.

The sixth chapter is in view of the writer's aim the most important since 'In this chapter the more important variants are discussed in some detail as to the possibility of their being traces of the Targum substrata and Old Syriac text forms'.[109] In this chapter 101 variants have been selected for further discussion. These variants may be the result of scribal errors, but also traces of the earlier 'varied, individualistic, wilder' text of the Old Syriac with its targumic characteristics, as against the 'rather rigid, standardized revision represented by the Peshitta'.[110] Since in individual cases it may be difficult to ascertain which possibility applies, a regular comment upon a variant is: 'It could be a scribal error or Old Syriac.' In the eighth chapter a summary and conclusions are given. It appears that from the 101 variants '20 could be either Old Syriac text form or scribal error;' 11 may be Old Syriac hiding in the Peshitta; 23 are most likely scribal errors; 47 are probably genuine traces of the older text form, and about half of these, 24 are really traces of the Targum'.

It is impossible to do justice here to the rich amount of material and statistics collected in this study. But from the above Running's position will be clear. She shares Vööbus's point of view and approach, and is led to concurrent conclusions. From this it also follows what the difference is between her approach and that of Peters, mentioned earlier. Peters compares the texts of the targum and the Peshitta in order to find proof of a literary relationship. Running, on the other hand, convinced that the specific relation between the two versions as argued by Vööbus exists, aims at adducing evidence for an older and 'wilder' text. Agreement with the targum is not necessary, but if the targum does agree with a Peshitta reading, then hardly any doubt remains: 'Where support for a variant can be found in the Targum, and in that alone, it is quite surely a genuine trace of the original stratum underlying the Syriac Old Testament text.'[111]

Those who share the hypothesis of an older targumic text of the Peshitta and find it borne out by Vööbus's approach may well find additional evidence for it

---

[108] Running, *An Investigation*.
[109] Ibid. p. 249; the material is also given in Running 'An Investigation' (part II) 43-54.
[110] Running, *An Investigation*, 250 and 'An Investigation' (Part II) 42.
[111] Running, *An Investigation*, 298 and 'An Investigation' (Part III) 148.

in Running's material. Those, however, who are sceptical of this hypothesis will find no convincing evidence for it in this study, and will rather be inclined to find other explanations for the variants which are adduced. At this point it may be remarked that the systematic collations of MSS in connection with the Peshitta Project have made it clear that the transmission of the text of the Syriac Bible is not generally characterized by great care on the side of the copyists and, moreover, that the copyists have allowed themselves a good measure of freedom with regard to idiomatic details which do not affect the meaning of the text. These two factors have led to a good many variant readings in even the earliest Syriac MSS. This fact should caution us in a search for older, more targumic readings among variants in single MSS.

This more cautious approach is found in VAN DER KOOIJ's evaluation of Running's material.[112] In his study Van der Kooij discusses LXX, *1QIsa*ᵃ, *1QIsa*ᵇ, Theodotion, Aquila, Tg. Yonatan, Symmachus, Peshitta, and Vulgate. In his chapter on the Peshitta he pays ample attention to Running's study and discusses all the variants taken from ancient Peshitta MSS. Van der Kooij is of the opinion that in every single case the variant reading can be explained as having originated in the process of text transmission, as idiomatic change, assimilation to other verses, scribal error, etc.

The last study that should be mentioned here is that of DELEKAT.[113] Delekat notes that in the book of Isaiah there are a good number of agreements between the Peshitta and LXX. Moreover, there are contacts ('Berührungen') between the Peshitta and Tg. Yonatan, and between Tg. Yonatan and LXX. There is no reason to assume that any of the three versions made us of either of the other two. This leads to the hypothesis that both the Peshitta and Tg. Yonatan go back to an older targum on which also LXX was in a large measure dependent.

THE SYRIAC TRANSLATOR USED A WRITTEN COPY OF TARGUM YONATAN

The second possibility – that the Syriac translator worked from a Hebrew text but also consulted a written targum – is argued by MAGER in his dissertation on Peshitta Joshua of 1916.[114] Explicit attention is paid to the relation between the Peshitta and Tg. Yonatan. From a list of thirty-five cases of agreement between the two versions Mager draws the conclusion that the Peshitta must have used a written copy of Tg. Yonatan. The nature of these agreements, however, is far from compelling. Scholarly discussion of later years has made us cautious in positing a literary relationship between the two versions. Agreement in omitting or adding prefixed *waw*, as is adduced in two places, means nothing. In

---

[112] Van der Kooij, *Die alten Textzeugen*.
[113] Delekat, *Die Peschitta zu Jesaja*.
[114] Mager, *Die Peschiṭṭho zum Buche Josua*, see esp. pp. 60-63.

other cases both the targum and the Peshitta give natural renderings of the Hebrew, and the agreement is easily explained by the closeness of the two dialects to each other. Yet, there are two examples in Mager's list which are worthy of notice. In Josh 10:41 the name 'Kadesh Barnea' has been rendered in both the targum and the Peshitta by *rᵉqem dᵉgaya*, and in Josh 9:10 'Bashan' by *matnin*. Since, however, in the first case this rendering occurs everywhere else, and in the second case also in a few other places, there seems to be no reason to posit dependence of the Peshitta on Tg. Yonatan. Rather, both versions are making use, here and elsewhere, of a current Jewish translation tradition.

Mager's list reminds us of the need of what Wernberg-Møller called 'phraseological similarity' to establish a literary relation. This is an important criterion. Besides, another question should be asked. If the translator of the Peshitta consulted the targum, then we would expect him to have done so in places which caused specific difficulties, either because of linguistic problems or for theological reasons. Therefore, as the convincing touch to external agreements, there should be the plausibility of the translator having used the targum in a particular place.

INFLUENCE OF JEWISH EXEGETICAL TRADITION

Apart from the studies already mentioned, no major studies have been written on the relation between the Peshitta and the targum tradition or Jewish exegesis for the books of the OT outside the Pentateuch. A few articles deal with this subject, and otherwise, it is treated within the framework of a wider study. The studies made on the various books of the OT agree in the conclusion that the Peshitta was a translation of a Hebrew text which was close to MT, the only exception being the book of Chronicles. Allowance is made for the possibility that the translator of a particular book has used a targum or has been guided by Jewish exegetical tradition or both.

As early as 1827 CREDNER wrote his doctoral thesis on the Peshitta of the Minor Prophets with special attention to Hosea. He lists a number of readings in which the Peshitta and Tg. Yonatan agree against MT[115] and concludes that at least for Hosea the translator has made use of the targum. Some of Credner's examples are indeed notable, e.g. his first one, Hos 2:9, where Hebrew *lᵉkassot*, 'to cover', has been rendered in the targum and the Peshitta literally the same: *dᵉjehbet lah datkasse*, 'which I have given her to cover'. It may be added, though, that any translator inclined to a more paraphrastic rendering to make the meaning of the Hebrew more explicit, could hardly have thought of another translation into an Aramaic language. Another notable example is his third: in 4:14 *haqqᵉdešot*, 'the (sacred) prostitutes', is translated in both versions by 'those who go outdoors'. In the targum this rendering *(nāpqat bara)* is used also in some other passages (1 Kgs 14:24; 15:12; 22:47), in the Peshitta *(nāpqat šuqē)*

---

[115] Credner, *De Prophetarum Minorum Versionis Syriacae*, 96-100.

only here. The Peshitta rendering, however, may well have been a Syriac idiom, just as the targum rendering was apparently a well-known Aramaic idiom.

The closing two decades of the last century saw a steady flow of short dissertations which deal with the text of the Peshitta in its relation to MT, LXX, and in most cases also the targums. Generally they follow the same pattern: the main body of these studies consists of a list of Peshitta readings which are thought to deviate from MT, with a characterization of the difference, its possible cause, and a comparison with LXX and the targum. In an introduction or at the end of the study the writer gives his opinion as to the way the translation was made and its possible dependence on LXX and/or targum. In 1887 SEBÖK (SCHÖNBERGER)'s dissertation on the Dodekapropheton appeared.[116] He mentions a number of agreements between targum and Peshitta, and expresses as his opinion that these reflect Jewish exegesis as was generally known and orally transmitted. The year 1891 saw the publication of OPPENHEIM's thesis on Ps 107-150.[117] In the introduction the writer only says: 'Der Einfluss des Targums tritt auch an vielen Stellen deutlich zu Tage'. In his thesis on Job, 1892, MANDL deals with the relation of the Peshitta with LXX and targum in the last few pages.[118] His conclusion is that the translator, while translating from the Hebrew, made use of the targum once in a while. A number of agreements should point in that direction. Serious doubts about the validity of these agreements as proof for a literary relationship were expressed by Th. Nöldeke in his review of this study.

In the following year, 1893, WEISS's dissertation on Deutero-Isaiah was published.[119] Weiss does not find any use of Jewish exegesis. On the contrary, there are clear examples of a Christian interpretation in Isa 52:15; 53:2, 4, 5, 7, 8, 9, 10. In his dissertation on Lamentations of 1895 ABELESZ concluded that the translator had made no use of the targum.[120] In 1897 no less than three dissertations of this kind appeared. WARSZAWSKI wrote a thesis on Isa 1-39[121] in which he concludes that there are a good number of contacts between the Peshitta and Tg. Yonatan. These do, however, not point to use of the targum by the translator, but to knowledge and use of Jewish exegetical traditions. In his dissertation on 1 Sam SCHWARTZ comes to the very general conclusion that 'P. mit Trg. oder Tradition sich berührt',[122] whereas, also in general terms, BERLINGER states in his thesis on 1 Kings that the translator may have used Tg. Yonatan in isolated difficult places.[123]

---

[116] Sebök (Schönberger), *Die syrische Übersetzung der zwölf kleinen Propheten*.
[117] Oppenheim, *Die syrische Übersetzung des Fünften Buches der Psalmen*.
[118] Mandl, *Die Peschittha zu Hiob*.
[119] Weiss, *Die Peschitta zu Deuterojesaia*.
[120] Abelesz, *Die syrische Übersetzung der Klagelieder*.
[121] Warszawski, *Die Peschitta zu Jesaja*.
[122] Schwartz, Die syrische Übersetzung des ersten Buches Samuelis.
[123] Berlinger, *Die Peschitta zum I.(3.) Buch der Könige*.

A book which has received a good measure of attention is Isaiah. Four studies have already been mentioned: those of H. Weiss (1893), L. Warszawski (1897), L. Delekat (1957), and L.G. Running (1964-1966). Three more studies deal with the whole or part of this book, those of H. Hegermann, A. van der Kooij and E.R. Rowlands.

The sixth chapter of HEGERMANN's study on the text of Isa 53 and § 5 of his conclusions deal with the Peshitta.[124] In a detailed verse by verse investigation of Isa 52:13-53:12 Hegermann is led to the conclusion that the Peshitta is not a Christian translation, and rather reflects a Jewish messianic interpretation. In the Introduction he explicitly refutes Weiss's interpretation of some Peshitta renderings as typically Christian. To mention one example: in 53:4 Hebrew *nagu^c*, 'stricken', is rendered in the Peshitta by *k^{e}tiša*, 'beaten'. Weiss translates 'cruciatus', 'crucified', and sees in it a clear Christian interpretation. Hegermann rightly objects that the translation 'crucified' is wrong, and that in the NT Peshitta for 'to crucify' always another verb is used.

VAN DER KOOIJ, on the other hand, is of the opinion that some passages in the book of Isaiah point to a Christian translator.[125] He mentions 25:6-8; 49:1,4a; 52:15; 53:2. In the last verse Hebrew *w^{e}nehm^{e}du*, 'that we should desire him', is translated *w^{e}daggelnay*, 'and we acted treacherously toward him'. Weiss had considered this to be a Christian rendering. To this Hegermann objected that no Christian translation has this rendering, an argument which has little force. Van der Kooij agrees with Weiss. He translates the Peshitta rendering with: 'und wir beschuldigten ihn der Lügenhaftigkeit', and comments that this probably refers to (the) Jews failing to acknowledge Jesus as the promised Messiah. Since, however, the translator was well versed in Hebrew, and moreover there are some points of contact with Tg. Yonatan, this translator was probably a Jewish-Christian. Van der Kooij mentions a few examples of agreement between the Peshitta and the targum which could point to the translator of the Peshitta being familiar with the targum. One of the examples is the translation of Hebrew *r^{e}fa'im*, 'ghosts of the dead', in 14:9 by 'heroes' in both versions. Van der Kooij's examples are well worthy of note. The meaning of the Hebrew words involved may indeed not have been immediately clear, and any translator may be prone to be influenced by an outside source. It is, however, hard to decide whether this source was the targum or current Jewish exegesis.

The third study, that of ROWLANDS, finally, deals exclusively with the relation between the Peshitta and the targum.[126] The writer gives seven examples of readings in the Peshitta which show similarity to the rendering in the targum, besides a few places where there is a correspondence between the targum and only one or more Peshitta MSS, and a few readings where agreement of the Peshitta with LXX may indicate common use in the Peshitta and LXX (and

---

[124] Hegermann, *Jesaja 53*.
[125] Van der Kooij, *Die alten Textzeugen*.
[126] Rowlands, 'The Targum and the Peshitta Version . . . of Isaiah'.

targum) of current exegesis. The agreements between the Peshitta and the targum may indicate that 'both had some connection with a common method of interpreting the Biblical texts'. An example is 6:10, where Hebrew *w^erafa*, 'and he will be healed', is rendered in both versions by the *itpe 'el* of *šbq*, 'he will be forgiven'. The writer is well aware that his examples are not unambiguous, and that other explanations of the agreements are possible, so, e.g., in 3:7, where Hebrew *ḥobeš*, 'physician', is rendered *riš*, 'head', in the Peshitta, and *k^esar lemehye riš*, 'as a prince to be head', in the targum. This rendering could well have presented itself as the most adequate independently to both translators. As the author himself notes, the same rendering is found in LXX *(archegos)*. The writer states that he gives 'a selection of instances'. Yet, a few lines further he admits that 'the connection is very sporadic, affecting the renderings of words, phrases and ideas here and there'.

Other studies on individual books to be mentioned are those of L. Kruse-Blinkenberg, A. Gelston and H. Pinkuss. KRUSE-BLINKENBERG compared the Peshitta text of Malachi with that of MT, Tg. Yonatan, and LXX.[127] In some places the Peshitta differs from MT, while wholly or partly agreeing with the targum. Differences between Peshitta and targum indicate that the Peshitta is an independent translation of the Hebrew. Because of the agreements between Peshitta and targum, however, 'there must be some kind of connection', without it being possible to say anything more specific as to this common source.

The Peshitta of Dodekapropheton as a whole was studied in the latest major monograph on the Peshitta, GELSTON's doctoral dissertation, already referred to in the Introduction.[128] The eighth chapter deals with 'The Peshiṭta and the Targum'. Gelston's conclusion of his study of the relation between the two versions is that there is no evidence of dependency, but there are some suggestive agreements which point to the same exegetical background.

A detailed study on Proverbs by PINKUSS was published in 1894.[129] This study stands apart from those just mentioned in that not a dependency of the Peshitta on Tg. Proverbs is argued, but *vice versa* of Tg. Proverbs on the Peshitta. In this opinion he had been preceded by others to whom he refers in the introduction: J.A. Dathe, Th. Nöldeke, J.G. Eichhorn and F. Hitzig. The opposite opinion, that of the Peshitta being dependent on the targum, had also been proposed, viz. by S. Maybaum in 1871.[130] Although in this study many valuable observations are made, the conclusions which Maybaum draws from them have found no following.[131] The most important reasons advanced by Pinkuss for positing

---

[127] Kruse-Blinkenberg, 'The Pešitta . . . of Malachi'.
[128] Gelston, *Twelve Prophets*.
[129] Pinkuss, 'Die syrische Übersetzung der Proverbien'.
[130] Maybaum, 'Über die Sprache des Targums zu den Sprüchen'.
[131] A discussion of Maybaum's article was given by Nöldeke in his article 'Das Targum zu den Sprüchen'.

dependence of Tg. Proverbs on the Peshitta are the lack of aggadic interpretations and paraphrastic renderings, the Syriac colouring of the language, and the more than 100 places where the targum agrees with Peshitta and LXX. Since Tg. Proverbs will not have used LXX, it must have made use of the Peshitta in these places. The Peshitta itself does not exhibit typically Jewish or Christian traits which would point to its origin.

In the remaining studies the relation between the Peshitta and the targum is only marginally dealt with. Some examples are the following.

In his well-known study of the books of Samuel[132] DRIVER mentions a number of places where God is referred to by circumlocution as is well-known from the targums, e.g. 'they served God' is rendered 'they served before God', and 'they prayed to God' as 'they prayed before God'. Cases like these indicate that there has been some Jewish influence on the Peshitta.

In the Prolegomena' of his Ezekiel commentary of 1886[133] CORNILL mentions some renderings in the Peshitta which are typically targumic in that references to God are modified so as to be felt as more reverential, by means of the preposition q^edam, as in 20:27, where $gidd^ef u'$ oti, '(your fathers) blasphemed me', has been rendered by $gadd^ef(w)$ q^edamay, '(your fathers) blasphemed before me', or otherwise as 14:8; 15:7, where $w^enatatti panay$, 'and I will set my face (against that man)', is rendered by $wettel rugzi$, 'I will put my anger . . .'. His conclusion is that examples like these show the same 'jüdische Geistesrichtung' as is found in the targum.

A special case is Chronicles. As early as 1870, TÖTTERMAN noticed in his dissertation on 1 Chr that the Peshitta agrees with Tg. Chronicles in its translation technique: the translator has rendered freely, deviating from the Hebrew in a number of places, omitting and adding words, and rendering in an interpretative way. This points to a Jewish translation.[134] His conclusions were confirmed by FRÄNKEL, who gives a detailed comparison of the Peshitta with MT.[135] The result is a long list of cases where the Peshitta differs from MT, in paraphrastic renderings, in additions, in omissions, in assimilations to parallel passages, sometimes following MT, but in most cases Tg. Yonatan, and in avoiding anthropomorphisms. A few examples may be given: In 1 Chr 12:1 the Hebrew text beginning with w^ehemma, 'they . . .' is rendered in the Peshitta by' 'and they stood before David valiantly, and if he had so desired they would have killed Saul, the son of Kish, because they were champions and warriors'. In 12:16 (Peshitta vs. 15) 'the first month' has been translated by 'the month of Nisan'. In 28:2 'for the footstool of our God' has been rendered: 'and for the place of the $š^ekhina$ of our God'. The conclusion is that Peshitta Chronicles is

---

[132] Driver, *Notes on the Hebrew Text*; The Peshitta is discussed on pp. xlii, lxxii-lxxvii (1st ed., 1890; pp. li-lii, lxxi-lxxvi (2nd ed., 1913).
[133] Cornill, *Ezechiel*. The Peshitta is discussed on pp. 137-56.
[134] Tötterman, *Pelguta qadmayta d^ebaryamin*, 6f.
[135] Fränkel, 'Die syrische Übersetzung . . . der Chronik'.

'ein reines und unverfälschtes jüdisches Targum'. It was probably made by a Jew in Edessa, about 200 C.E.

Epilogue

Surveying the studies mentioned above one will find it difficult to formulate well-defined conclusions. There is little doubt that Peshitta Pentateuch contains many examples of Jewish exegesis. Peshitta Proverbs has contributed to the genesis of a Jewish targum of that book and conversely, Peshitta Chronicles seems to be based on a Jewish targum, or at least has all the characteristics of it. In other books there is some influence from Jewish translation and interpretation tradition. Besides, there is the possibility that in some books the translator has made use of a written targum, a possibility which has been argued in particular for the Pentateuch. The studies which arose out of the Baumstark-Kahle school have richly provided us with material relevant to the relation of the Peshitta to Jewish exegesis, but the hypothesis of a targumic origin of Peshitta Pentateuch and other books still lacks convincing evidence.

The Peshitta has come to us as the translation of the OT in use with the Syrian Christians. Yet, its roots have drawn from the nutritive matter of the Jewish religious heritage. But did it partly or wholly originate in Jewish circles? The answer to this intriguing question must remain open. No decisive arguments for either Christian or Jewish authorship have been advanced. The case for a Jewish origin is strongest with respect to the Pentateuch. As is to be expected, this is generally favoured by scholars who argue for a targumic origin of the Peshitta. Baumstark and Kahle connect this targumic origin with the need for a Syriac translation in Adiabene after the conversion of the royal house. Wohl, Peters, and Sperber do not deal with the question of Jewish or Christian origin explicitly, but they seem to presuppose Jewish origin. Isenberg only states in his summary that the Peshitta must be considered of 'Palestinian and probably Jewish origin'. Vööbus, too, favours Jewish origin, but admits that, lacking definite proof, it remains a hypothesis.[136] Among the scholars who consider Peshitta Pentateuch an independent translation from the Hebrew, Wernberg-Møller assumes Christian origin: the Christian translator used the Jewish Tg. Onkelos.[137] Other scholars favour Jewish authorship. Silverstone assumes it without discussing the question.[138] For Maori the Jewish exegetical material and rabbinic influence found in the Peshitta point to a Jewish origin.[139] Cook, too, holds that the Peshitta was originally a Jewish translation.[140]

The Jewish influence on Peshitta Pentateuch excludes the possibility of it being the work of a Christian unfamiliar with Jewish traditions. It remains,

---

[136] Vööbus, Peschitta und Targumim', 108f.
[137] Wernberg-Møller, 'Some Observations', 180.
[138] Silverstone, *Aquila and Onkelos*, 124.
[139] Maori, *The Peshitta Version*, xx.
[140] Cook, *Ondersoek*, 134.

however, difficult to choose between Jewish authorship and authorship of a Jewish-Christian, who, in translating the Pentateuch, would certainly have made use of his Jewish heritage.

In the other books of the OT too, there are indications of Jewish influence but to a less extent than in the Pentateuch, and the case for a Jewish origin of the various books is weaker. As has been mentioned above, a few scholars argue for a targumic origin of one or two books: Peters for Samuel and Psalms, Delekat and Running for Isaiah. In his two articles Peters does not explicitly posit Jewish authorship, but seems to imply it. Running favours Jewish authorship for Isaiah, though without discussing the issue.[141] Delekat holds that Peshitta Isaiah (and as seems the whole OT) was of Jewish origin and later on taken over by the Christians.[142]

If this hypothesis of a targumic background is not accepted the question concerning origin can only be answered, if at all, on the basis of specific Jewish or Christian elements in the various books. How difficult it is to find unambiguous evidence is clear from the book of Isaiah, for which some writers defend Jewish, and other writers Christian authorship. The lack of clear evidence is also attested by the latest contribution to the subject, that of Gelston. In the closing chapter of his study, mentioned earlier, Gelston discusses 'The Origins of the Peshiṭta' and states: 'We have borne in mind the question whether the Peshitta of the Dodekapropheton is of Jewish or Christian origin, and while we have found no conclusive evidence we have found nothing positively to suggest a Christian origin and nothing to make a Jewish origin improbable'. Some evidence, however, though not conclusive, is thought to point in favour of a Jewish origin. This evidence is (a) that the Peshitta rendering of Hos 6:2 is 'less susceptible of a Christian interpretation than either the MT or the LXX, (b) that the translator(s) 'showed no consistent preference for readings of the LXX rather than those of the MT', and (c) that both Tg. Yonatan and the Peshitta show dependence on a common exegetical tradition.[143]

The present writer is inclined to favour the hypothesis of Jewish-Christian authorship, at least for those parts which show influence of Jewish exegetical traditions. Lacking decisive evidence, however, we can do no more, at least for the time being, than outline the possibilities.

Bibliography

In the preceding article mention has been made of most of the relevant literature as far as it concerns specific problems in general or related to individual

---

[141] Running, *An Investigation*, 4; 'An Investigation' (part I) 141.
[142] Delekat, 'Die Peschitta zu Jesaja', 193.
[143] Gelston, *Twelve Prophets*, 193.

books of the OT. The following is a survey of the most important titles related to the Peshitta as a whole.

For the study of the Peshitta text and its history the older text editions are unsatisfactory. For most of the OT books we have now *The Old Testament in Syriac according to the Peshitta version*, Leiden, 1972 . . . The remaining books are expected to appear in the next few years.

A survey of all known Peshitta MSS was published by the Peshitta Institute as: *List of Old Testament Peshitta Manuscripts (Preliminary Issue)*, Leiden 1961. Supplements to this *List* were published as *Peshitta Institute Communications* in *VT* 12 (1962) 127f., 237f., 351; 18 (1968) 128-43; 27 (1977) 508-11; 31 (1981) 358; 35 (1985) 466f.

A still useful, though inevitably somewhat dated, introduction to the Peshitta is HAEFELI's *Die Peschitta des Alten Testaments* (1927). Detailed encyclopaedia articles are those of NESTLE, 'Syrische Bibelübersetzungen' (1897), VAN PUYVELDE, 'Versions Syriaques' (1960) and BROCK 'Bibelübersetzungen, 4. Die Übersetzung ins Syrische' (1980).

Surveys of recent literature are: VAN DER PLOEG, 'Recente Pešiṭta-Studies (sinds 1927)' (1952); HOSPERS, 'The Present-Day State of Research on the Pešiṭta (since 1948)' (1964); VAN DER PLOEG, 'The Peshitta of the Old Testament' (1970); HOSPERS, 'Some Remarks with regard to the Text and Language of the Old Testament Peshitta' (1982).

Chapter Nine

The Latin Translations

Benjamin Kedar

Old Latin Versions

HISTORICAL AND TECHNICAL DATA

The spread of Latin as the official, commercial, and military language of the ancient world was concurrent with the growth of the Roman state and the advance of its armies. Hellenistic Greek maintained, however, for a relatively long time its position as the language of literature, philosophy and religion. The educated Romans as well as significant sections of the population in the provinces were bilingual, the Greek and Latin languages strongly influencing each other in their further development until finally Latin became predominant.[1]

This provides the linguistic setting for the operations of the early Christian Church. In the beginning Greek was the cultural language of Christendom, it was then forced to make room for Latin which finally gained absolute dominance. The one consequence of this process that concerns us here is the growing demand for Latin Bible translations, which probably was first felt in the provinces such as North Africa or Southern Gaul but subsequently even in the city of Rome.[2]

The first tangible evidence for the existence of a Latin version dates back to the middle of the second century C.E. when Christian writers began to write their treatises in Latin, citing biblical verses and passages in this language. Tertullian (c. 130-230 C.E.) though he himself wrote in both Greek and Latin, testifies to the exclusive use of the Latin language in the African church of his time. In his Latin works we find long scriptural quotations which, however, exhibit such lack of textual consistence that they hardly point to one authoritative version. Some scholars think they have been able to detect two different versions at the basis of Tertullian's quotations while others assume that the

---

[1] Palmer, *Latin Language*, 148-80. On the mutual influence cf. Debrunner-Scherer, *Geschichte der griechischen Sprache* 2, 77-78, 82-88. Josephus, *Ant.* 14:196-98, 319-22 testifies that inscriptions and official proclamations in the two languages mentioned, were quite common in Palestine.

[2] Kaulen, *Geschichte der Vulgata*, 138-39; Stummer, *Einführung*, 15-17; Sparks, 'Latin Bible', 101. In the middle of the 3rd century C.E. Novatian at Rome wrote Latin, the Roman bishop Cornelius, Greek; cf. Roberts, *Text and Versions*, 237.

Latin Father offered ad-hoc renderings from the Greek Bible.[3] Be this as it may, there still exists a sufficient measure of uniformity in Tertullian's biblical extracts and of concurrence with other known Latin textforms as to lead us to believe that Tertullian was acquainted with Latin Bible translations, possibly quoting them from memory. The first Latin Father to cite a very precise text of long passages from the Bible was Cyprian (d. 258), followed by a long line of Latin Fathers, among them Augustine (354-430) and Jerome (d. 420), whose works contain ample extracts from Latin Bible versions. From a somewhat later time there exists the direct evidence of MSS, unfortunately fragmentary, that contain old versions which are not Hieronymian, and finally not a few manuscripts of the Vulgate present an old Latin text in some biblical books or passages, or as marginal glosses. In addition to this, also in the liturgy many an old wording has been preserved.[4]

This multiplex material that gives fragmentary and sometimes contradictory evidence of old Latin Bible translations is subsumed under the name 'Old Latin' (= OL) or 'Vetus Latina'.[5] This term is not meant to suggest the notion of originally one complete Latin Bible. It is merely a convenient reference term for any Latin text-form independent of the Vulgate. There is not extant, then, a single MS that covers the whole range of biblical books, and indeed, only when a purely scholarly interest arose long after the Vulgate had gained the lead, attempts were made to compile the innumerable pieces of evidence from all such disparate sources as are at our disposal and to arrange them consecutively according to the order of the biblical books. Worthy of mention is the work of P. Sabatier in the middle of the 18th century and its new edition, extensively enriched and improved though incomplete as yet, by the *Vetus Latina Institut* at the Erzabtei Beuron (Germany).[6]

In view of the complex textual evidence the following question, much debated also with regard to other classical versions and even the Hebrew Bible for that matter, presents itself in relation to the Latin Bible: Should we assume that originally there existed only one translation which subsequently branched out

[3] Campenhausen, *Western Church*, 4-35 (Tertullian), 36-60 (Cyprian). Braun, *Deus Christianorum*, 21; Gribomont, 'Vetus Latina', 1178.

[4] Kennedy, 'Latin Versions', 49-53, offers an extensive list of the extant authorities for non-Hieronymian Latin Bible texts. This list should be supplemented according to Fischer, *Vetus Latina 1-Verzeichnis*, and Ayuso Marazuela, *Vetus Latina Hispana – Prolegómenos*. A concise enumeration of the important MSS and editions is given by Noth, *Welt*, 272-74. Concerning the NT, cf. Birdsall, 'Latin Versions', 370-74.

[5] The Latin Fathers mention *vetus editio, antiqua translatio, vulgata editio* and the like. Whether *(vetus) itala* refers to a Latin version used in Italy (Stummer, *Einführung*, 55) or to Jerome's translation (Burkitt, *Old Latin*, 55-65) is a moot question.

[6] Cf. Sabatier, *Vetus Italica* and Fischer, *Vetus Latina*. A certain Flaminius Nobilius at Rome antedated Sabatier by almost two centuries attempting to collect and edit the fragments of ancient Latin texts. The *Vetus Latina Institut* of Beuron possesses a complete card-index, verse by verse, of all witnesses to an OL text. Kind permission has been granted to the present writer to consult it. Important text-editions are those by Fischer, Robert, Ranke, Dold, Belsheim, Weber, Schildenberger, from which our quotations are taken.

into the extant variety of text-forms, or rather that right from the beginning a number of distinct versions existed which to some extent were later brought into line. It is a question that has not been decided definitely and probably will never be. Rather strong arguments can be mustered for either thesis.[7] On the one hand, there are undeniably innumerable passages on which our witnesses, MSS and patristic quotations, differ; even the most casual comparison reveals lexical and grammatical variations, to say nothing of the differences of spelling. Indeed, Augustine, who speaks of the 'unlimited variety of Latin translators' seems to testify expressly to the existence of many separate Latin versions when he contrasts the small group of translators who rendered the Hebrew Bible into Greek with the countless number of persons who dare translate the Scripture into Latin from any Greek codex they come across.[8]

Jerome, occasionally, gives the impression of sharing this view, e.g. when he criticizes his predecessors, the 'unskilled translators'. Yet on closer inspection it seems that he, though complaining of the textual variety and corruption caused by the ignorance and carelessness of revisers and copyists, presumed that once a single genuine version had existed.[9] This, then, brings us to the arguments in favour of such presumption: the amount of variation may after all be explained as the result of the many local recensions and the incessant copying to which the text was subjected. Moreover, the variants appear of relatively minor importance when viewed against the stock all witnesses seem to share, namely an identical wording of a good many verses and passages, some lexical and grammatical peculiarities, and – as we shall see shortly – a very characteristic translation technique.

Although the origin of the Latin Bible cannot be traced, we may attempt to sketch out the lines along which it developed and spread. The desire for a Latin Bible among many sections of the population of the Roman Empire must have been growing as the knowledge of Greek dwindled, probably first in the remote provinces. A Latin text was needed as well for the instruction of the faithful as for the sermon, liturgy and pious edification. At this stage we must reckon with a great number of fragmentary translations, frequently oral or crudely written

---

[7] Among those who assume the existence of several distinct versions are Kaulen, *Geschichte der Vulgata*, 107-44; Ziegler, *Bibelübersetzungen*, 4-8; and Mechineau, 'Latines (Versions)', 113-19 ('de la pluralité des versions'). the one-version theory is summarized by Watson, 'Style and Language', 194: 'There never was more than one original Old Latin version', and Birdsall, 'Latin Versions': 'The studies of the team of scholars working at Beuron have shown . . . that the Old Latin is basically one version'.

[8] '. . . cuique primis fidei temporibus in manus venit codex Graecus . . . ausus est interpretari' (*De Doctrina Christiana* 2:11). Cf. Ziegler, *Bibelübersetzungen*, 6-10.

[9] Jerome complains that the Jews mock at the many variations in the Latin versions ('solent enim ridere de nobis . . . si verborum dissonantiam in nostris codicibus potuerint demonstrare', 5, 432 [cf. n. 18]); and indeed variety there was among those many copies of the Scriptures dispersed all over the earth ('exemplaria scripturarum toto orbe dispersa . . . inter se variant'; *Prol. in Evang.*); he speaks of the many incompetent translators ('imperiti translatores'; *Praef. in Prov.*) but on the other hand puts the blame on the copyists ('scriptorum vitio depravata interpretatio antiqua'; *Prol. in Iob*).

down, of unequal merit. They were borrowed and eagerly copied. Later, at some centre or centres, the need was felt to collect these isolated efforts and unify them. Whether this center was North Africa, as the majority of scholars assume, or Antioch in Syria, as others try to prove, or somewhere else (even Rome, though less likely, cannot be ruled out) we cannot know. But Cyprian's treatment of biblical texts presupposes a Latin standard version which is reflected in most, if not in all subsequent old Latin texts. This text, however, was continuously subjected to local recensions, dialectical copying and permanent textual meddling including substitution of older, local translations and insertion of glosses; thus the notion arose of widely divergent, if not absolutely separate versions. With the gradual acceptance of Jerome's Latin Vulgate, the Old Latin was more and more neglected, most of its MSS were damaged or lost and its text carelessly mixed with Vulgate readings.[10]

The OL deserves our attention for many reasons. First, it is the product of an admirable intellectual labour. As every translation it rests upon the decoding of a message expressed in one specific set of linguistic symbols and its restatement by means of a structurally different code. Being based mainly, if not exclusively, on the Greek Septuagint, the OL may help us in reconstructing a Greek reading prior to that contained in the MSS of the Septuagint which, generally speaking, are of a later date than when the Latin translation was made.[11] The OL, through its extremely faithful renderings, may help to elucidate words peculiar to Hellenistic Greek, or at least indicate how these were interpreted at the time. Its language is the foremost witness to Late-Latin. Lastly, its most important contribution, the OL reflects the beliefs and traditions of its period or even earlier times.

THE OLD LATIN AS A VERSION

Latinity and Translation Technique
If one wishes to reach an adequate understanding and a fair appraisal of the Latinity of the OL, one has to take into consideration the various factors that have generated its traits and peculiarities.

First of all, we deal with Late-Latin quite removed from Ciceronian standards. Whether the latter had ever guided people in their everyday speech need

---

[10] Cf. e.g. Fischer, *Vetus Latina 2. Genesis*, 6* (on MS 100 Lyon): '. . . zahlreiche Randeinträge . . . zwei ganze Lesungen sind eingetragen . . . ihr Text ist Vulgata . . . Korrekturen . . . Angleichungen an die Vulgata', and 10* (on one passage in MS 102): '. . . ein merkwürdiges Gemisch aus Vulgata und Vetus Latina'. On a gradual introduction of changes cf. Ranke, *Fragmenta*, 51.

[11] The question of the Greek text-form on which the OL was dependent has no simple answer; each portion must be scrutinized separately, cf. Kennedy, 'Latin Versions', 58-62; Burkitt, *Old Latin*, 5-9; Ziegler, 'Zur griechischen Vorlage', 175-291; Schildenberger, *Altlateinische Texte*, 9-10, 84-86. Vercellone, *Variae Lectiones* 2, 436, remarked on points of contact between the OL of the OT and the so-called Lucianic readings; his observation has subsequently been confirmed by many scholars (Wellhausen, Driver, Burkitt *et al.*).

not concern us here; at any rate, in the first centuries C.E. neither pagan nor Christian authors adhered to the old style and rules in their writings, let alone in their speech. Naturally, the language had developed: pronunciation was constantly changing, especially in the conquered territories; new words had been coined and loan-words been taken from Greek and other languages and thus the vocabulary been enriched; the meaning of many words had somewhat shifted; analogies had brought about simplifications in the grammatico-syntactical structure. The language of the OL basically agrees with the common idiom of the times.[12] In some cases this may be due to the educational background of the translator, in other cases to his intention to reach an audience lacking stylistic refinement. But mostly the reason seems to be more profound: Christians, distrustful of pagan education and classical rhetorics, prided themselves upon the 'humble speech' *(sermo humilis)* of the Church. Of course, the Christian authors had received generally the same solid classical training as their pagan contemporaries; this becomes clear from their eloquent writings. And yet, demanding whole-hearted allegiance to the new culture of Christianity, they tended to condemn the old education as the work of the devil.[13] Consequently, popular usage gained entrance much more easily.

Moreover, the new faith was in need of an adequate linguistic medium. Specific terms from ecclesiastic Greek or, through the latter, from the Hebrew, were incorporated into Latin; and the process of creating new words or bestowing new meanings on some items of the vocabulary mentioned above, was now diverted into the realms of Christian culture. The OL is at the same time the product of Christian Latinity as well its major producer.[14] The cardinal point, however, is the fact, that the OL displays a translation idiom based upon a very definite philosophy of translating. In the ancient world we find the free flow of literary motives from one culture to another but, on the other hand, the translation of documents exhibits more often than not the crudest literalism. In the case of the Bible, the translators dared not think of it as a literary work the stylistic devices of which had to be properly transferred; the Book they set out to render into Latin, contained the divine revelation; it was God's Word. The authority of the Bible in which every word counted and even the order of the words was of importance demanded that the humble translator agreed to be 'in servitude to the words' and presented a 'word-for-word' translation. The Greek

---

[12] Kaulen, *Handbuch zur Vulgata*, 3-8; Palmer, *Latin Language*, 148-285. Storehouses of information are the works: Rönsch, *Itala und Vulgata*; Mohrmann, *Études*; Blaise, *Manuel*.

[13] Clarke, *Rhetoric*, 148-55. Augustine, *De Doctrina Christiana* 2:13, 19-20; 3:2-3; 'melius est reprehendant nos grammatici quam non intelligant populi' (*In Ps* 138:70). Jerome: 'Rhetores . . . quorum artis est verisimilia magis quam vera dicere', *Ep.* 48:13; 'Domine, si umquam habuere codices saeculares, si legero, te negavi', *Ep.* 22:30.

[14] On the evolution and changes in Christian Latin cf. Billen, *Old Latin Text*, 6: '. . . the history of a few renderings (contains) hints of modification in religious ideas during the third century . . . evidently not unrelated to the development of thought in the Christian Church'; Janssen, *Kultur und Sprache*, 241: 'Das christliche Latein des Cyprian ist gegenüber Tertullian kräftig weiterentwickelt, viele Wendungen sind zu fester Terminologie der christlichen Sondersprache geworden'.

Septuagint had already opted for such adherence to the structure of the sacred original; now the OL followed suit.[15] It will be our task now to demonstrate the characteristic features by means of a few examples chosen.

The *carelessness in the pronunciation* of vowels and consonants can be learned from peculiarities of spelling: *famis* 'famine' (Gen 41:57) instead of *fames*; *veatores* 'wayfarer' (ib. 37:25) for *viatores* (from *via* 'way'); *aput* 'with, near' (ib. 42:33) for the more usual *apud*; *bellicans* 'to pluck, nip' (Amos 7:14) for *vellicans* (from *vello* 'to pluck') and the like. Besides the spelling *Israel* we find *Istrahel* and *Israhel* (Gen 46:8, 49:16). In the vocabulary we find the vulgar use of *plebs* 'people' (Amos 7:15), with no accessory notion of contempt (the people of Israel is referred to; cf. Luke (2:32); and the Low-Latin *manducare* 'to eat' (Hos 9:3) for *comedere*. As neologisms of the later idiom we may adduce *refrigerium* 'recovery, rest' (Hos 12:8), *contribulatio* 'contrition' (Isa 65:14; cf. Tertullian, *Adversus Iudaeos* 13). A long list of Greek loan-words could easily be drawn up, beginning with *agonia, agonizare* 'agony; to struggle' (Luke 22:43; Sir 4:33 [28]) and ending with *zelus* 'zeal' (Wis 5:18 [17]). A good many new words imported or imitated a Greek model: *paranymphus* 'bridesman, friend' (Gen 26:26) for Greek *nymphagōgos*; *pervindemiaverunt* 'to gather the vintage' (Amos 6:1), Gk. *apetrygēsan*. Aramaic loan-words seem to be: *abra* 'maid' (Judith 10:10) from *ḥbr' ,ḥbrt'* 'associate, friend', *mammona* 'riches' (Matt 6:24) and so on.[16]

As regards the *divergence from classical usage* in grammar and syntax one should mention the irregular comparison by the use of adverbs (*magis, plus*, etc.): *magis bonus* 'extremely good' (Wis 8:20), *plus lucidiores* 'brighter' (Sir 23:28 [19]); the frequent use of the indicative instead of the subjunctive mood and the substitution of object clauses introduced by *quod, quia* and the like instead of the classic construction of accusative with infinitive: *et vidit deus lucem quia bona est* (Gen 1:4; Vg . . . *quod esset bona*) 'and God saw the light, that it was good'.

An extract from the OL, chosen at random, shall illustrate its general character.

Gen 37:18-20, 23-25.

And when they saw him afar off, even before he came near unto them, they conspired against him to slay him. And they said one to another, Behold, this dreamer cometh. Come therefore, and let us slay him . . . And it came to pass, when Joseph was come unto his brethren, that they

---

[15] Bickerman, 'Septuagint', 11-28; Kedar, *Vulgate*, 30-46; Ceresa-Gastaldo, *Latino*, 32-38 (with ample bibliography).

[16] *Paranymphus* is also Greek, of course, but had become an accepted loan-word and as such substitutes for the foreign *nymphagogos*; yet pure Latin variants exist: *pronobus, gener* etc. (cf. Fischer, *Vetus Latina 2. Genesis*, 280). Kaulen, *Handbuch zur Vulgata*, 30, 83, 95. Rönsch, *Itala und Vulgata*, passim.

stripped Joseph out of his coat, his coat of many colours that was on him;
And they took him, and cast him into a pit: and the pit was empty, there
was no water in it. And they sat down to eat bread and they lifted up their
eyes and looked and, behold, a company of Ishmaelites came.

MT		LXX	OL	Vg.
(18)	וייראו אתו	προείδον δε αυτον	providerunt autem eum	qui cum vidissent eum
	מרחק	μακρόθεν	de longe	procul
	ובטרם	πρὸ τοῦ	priusquam	antequam
	יקרב	ἐγγίσαι αὐτὸν	adpropiaret	accederet
	אליהם	πρὸς αὐτούς	illis	ad eos
	ויתנכלו אתו	και ἐπονηρεύοντο	et insaeviebant	cogitaverunt
	להמיתו	τοῦ ἀποκτεῖναι ἀυτόν	occidere eum	illum occidere
(19)	ויאמרו	εἶπαν δε	dixerunt autem	et mutuo loquebantur
	איש	ἔκαστος	singuli	
	אל	πρὸς	ad	
	אחיו	τὸν ἀδελφὸν αὐτοῦ	fratrem suum	
	הנה	ἰδου	ecce	ecce
	בעל החלמות	ὁ ἐνυπνιαστὴς	somniator	somniator
	הלזה	ἐκεῖνος	ille	
	בא	ἔρχεται	venit	venit
(20)	ועתה	νῦν οὖν	nunc ergo	
	לכו	δεῦτε	venite	venite
	ונהרגהו	ἀποκτείνωμεν αὐτὸν	occidamus illum	occidamus eum
			......	......
(23)	ויהי	ἐγένετο δε	factum est autem	confestim igitur
	כאשר בא	ἡνίκα ἦλθεν	postquam venit	ut pervenit
	יוסף	Ιωσηφ	Ioseph	
	אל אחיו	πρὸς τούς ἀδελφους αὐτοῦ	ad fratres suos	ad fratres suos
	ויפשיטו	ἐξέδυσαν	exuerunt	nudaverunt
	את יוסף	τὸν Ιωσηφ	Ioseph	eum
	את כתונ	τὸν χιτῶνα	tunicam	tunicam talari
	את כתנת הפסים	τὸν ποικίλον	variam	et polymita
	אשר עליו	τὸν περί αὐτον	quam indutus erat	
(24)	ויקחהו	και λαβόντες αὐτον	et adpraehensum eum	
	וישלכו אתו	ἔρριψαν	proiecerunt	miseruntque
	הברה	εἰς τόν λάκκον	in lacum	in cisternam
	והבור	ὁ δὲ λάκκος	lacus autem	
	רק	κενός	vacuus erat	
	אין בו מים	ὕδωρ οὐκ εἶχεν	sine aqua	quae non habebat aquam
(25)	וישבו	ἐκαθισαν δὲ	et sederunt	et sedentes
	לאכל	φαγειν	ut manducarent	ut comederent
	לחם	ἄρτον	panes	panem
	וישאו	και ἀναβλεψαντες	et adlevatis	
	עיניהם	τοῖς ὀφθαλμοις	oculis	
	ויראו	εἶδον	viderunt	viderunt
	והנה	και ἰδού	et ecce	
	ארחת	ὁ δοιπόροι	veatores	viatores
	ישמעאלים	Ισμαηλιται	Ismaelitae	Ismahelitas

The scrupulous adherence of the OL to the Greek text is most conspicuous. Particles find their equivalents (Greek *de, nyn oun, pro[idein]* Latin *autem, nunc ergo, pro[videre]*, respectively); repetitions are imitated (v. 23 the name Ioseph, v. 24 the mention of the cistern) and the like. Consequently, since the Septuagint is a version that also closely follows the original, the idiom of the OL strikes us – in contradiction to the Vg – as outlandish, Hebraic. There is the paratactic arrangement of the clauses; there is the un-Latin word-order; and there are the direct reflections of Hebrew idiomatic expressions. As to the Low-Latin character we have the lexical evidence of *manducare* 'to eat', *insaevire* 'to fall into a passionate rage', *adpropiare* 'to draw near'. Being only human, the Latin translators do occasionally diverge from their basic policy and go their own way; one must not overlook these small indications of some independence: The choice of the emotionally loaded verb *insaevire* for the hackneyed Greek *ponēreuesthai*; the rendering *quam indutus erat* '(the coat) he was dressed in' against the Greek and Hebrew '(the coat) which upon him' and the like bear witness to the interpreters' common sense.

Such features can be discerned throughout the OL. The dependence upon the Septuagint strikes the reader especially when the Latin version faithfully copies blunders of the Greek. The Hebrew words *'ûlām lûz* 'but Luz . . .' (Gen 28:19) are mistakenly taken by both versions as one word, a place-name: *Ulamaus*; similarly, *maḥmād* 'preciosity' (Hos 9:6), is confused by both with the locality *machmas*. Both versions offer a mistaken rendering, based upon a vocalization divergent from the MT when they translate the consonants *mṭh* as 'a staff' (OL *virga*), reading *maṭṭeh* 'a rod, staff', instead of *miṭṭâ* 'bed' in the verse Gen 47:31 (though a little later – ib. 48:2 – they read the identical consonants correctly [OL *lectum or lectulum*]); this erroneous rendering, as is well known, has been perpetuated in Heb 11:21.[17]

The OL commits its own blunders which sometimes have a bearing on the exegesis of a specific verse. Hos 14:3 the Hebrew has (literally) 'and let us render bullocks our lips', generally taken to mean 'we will render for bullocks the prayers of our lips' (Jerome: *vituli autem labiorum laudes in Deo sunt* 'the bullocks of the lips are the praises to God'; 6, 158);[18] this had been rendered by the LXX 'we will render the fruits of our lips', reading Hebrew *pěrî* 'fruit' for *pārîm* 'bullocks'. The OL rendering of this clause is as follows: *et retribuemus fructum laborum nostrorum*, 'we will render the fruits of our labours'. Obviously a scribal error, *laborum* 'of the labours', for *labiorum* 'of the lips', has given rise to such radically new interpretation. In Hos 9:11 the prophet threatens Ephraim that its glory shall be taken away 'from the birth, and from the

---

[17] Cf. Jerome's critical remarks on these blunders 3, 349 and 3, 371-72 (cf. note 18), respectively. His philological honesty and his courage ('audacter dico') to depart from the NT reading, are noteworthy.

[18] If not stated otherwise Jerome's words are quoted from Vallarsi, *Sancti Hieronymi..Opera*: vol. 1 contains his letters; vol. 3 his commentaries on Genesis and Ecclesiastes; 4-6, his commentaries on the Prophets.

womb, and from the conception'. The LXX had rendered the Hebrew words properly: *ek tokon kai ōdinōn kai syllēmpseōn*. However, *tokos* has an additional meaning besides 'childbirth', namely 'the produce of money; interest' while *ōdines* 'throes of child-birth', may denote metaphorically 'any pains, travail'. The Latin translators gave preference to these secondary meanings and rendered thus: *ex usuris et ex iniquitatibus* which then bestowed the meaning on the verse 'their glory will desert them because of usury and iniquity'. The third word, *syllempsis*, being unambiguous, was correctly rendered 'conception': *ex conceptionibus*. One MS, however, under the impression of the preceding words exhibits the scribal error: *ex conspectionibus* 'because of their looks'.

The ingenuity of the translators, on the other hand, should also be noted. Frequently no simple Latin equivalent of a given Greek term was available; e.g. for the word *sympasa* 'all together; the totality' which the LXX equates with Hebrew *hā'āreṣ* 'the earth' (Isa 11:9) and *tēbēl* 'the whole inhabited world' (Nah 1:5), the OL sensibly puts *universa terra*. The prophet's complaint that the Israelites had 'set up kings' and 'made princes' (Hos 8:4) not in accordance with God's wish, is expressed in Hebrew as well as in Greek by purely verbal constructions: *himlîkû . . . hēśîrû*, and *ebasileusan . . . erxan*, respectively (the latter in the active sense 'they reigned . . . they ruled'). The OL offers a sound, periphrastic rendering, restoring on its way the causative sense: *regem constituerunt . . . principatum egerunt*. Such periphrastic rendering, *interpretatio per circuitum*, as Augustine called it (*De Doctrina Christiana* 2) is quite frequent: *asebein* 'to act impiously', becomes Latin *inpie agere* (Hos 8:1); *pneumatophoros* '(the man) possessing-the-wind/spirit' (ib. 9:7), becomes *(homo)qui spiritu fertur* 'carried by the spirit', or *spiritalis* 'spiritual, inspired'; *teteichismenai* is rendered *(civitates) muris circumdatas* '(cities) surrounded with walls' (ib. 8:14); *archioinochoos* 'the chief of the butlers', and *archisitopoios* 'the chief of the bakers' (Gen 40:2), are rendered *princeps vinifusorum* and *princeps pistorum* or even *qui erat super vinum* and *qui erat super pistores*; and so on.

Very rarely does the OL dare to introduce lexical variation; e.g. Hos 9:1-2 where the MT and the LXX use twice the same vocable, signifying 'cornfloor', whereas the OL varies: *messis* 'the harvest', and *area* 'a threshing-floor'; but double renderings can be found here and there: for Greek *oikos* 'a house' the OL has *domus habitationis* 'the house for habitation' (Mic 5:2).

Insertions, though quite rare, may have a bearing on exegetical traditions embedded in this version and shall be discussed below. Concluding this paragraph we feel it is only fair to give the OL as a version higher marks than is has commonly received after the Vg. emerged to its dominant position.[19] Granted the premises as stated above, this Latin version, in no lesser degree than the

---

[19] Thus, eg. McKenzie: 'No great merit can be attributed to the Old Latin. It was made from the LXX and the translators had little Latin and less Greek. It was slavishly literal and often unintelligible. The translators were not educated men and produced without intending it one of the greatest monuments of vulgar unlettered Latin of the period' (*Dictionary of the Bible*, New York 1975[10], 917).

LXX, achieved its goal, namely that of providing the Latin-speaking reader with a meticulously produced replica of what was considered to be the authentic Bible text.

Traces of Jewish Traditions

Since all indications point to the fact that the OL is not the product of a single effort, the question arises whether strands of pristine translations, or at least early interpretative traditions can be detected in it. Setting out some evidence why this question may be answered in the affirmative, we must enter a caveat. Given the extreme literalism of the version under review, one must not expect any glaring instances of hermeneutics as are found e.g. in some of the Aramaic targums. One has to read between the lines, so to speak, in order to perceive echoes of exegetical traditions; in other words, the minute details of lexical equivalents and idiomatic renderings in each single verse have to be scrutinized. This is a task yet to be done systematically; the examples adduced in the following discussion are merely meant to serve as illustration.

A priori one may feel entitled to presume that Jewish Bible translations into Latin existed in relatively early times. It had been the custom of the Jews before the period under review to translate biblical books into their vernacular; such translations, sometimes made orally but frequently also written down, were needed for public reading in the synagogue and for the instruction of the young. Since we know of Jewish communities in many corners of the Roman Empire and in Rome itself, it is plausible to ascribe some translational efforts to them. Moreover, there does exist tangible evidence: In Jewish catacombs of ancient Italy a third of the inscriptions quote biblical verses in Latin: The grave is called *domus aeterna* 'the eternal home' (cf. Eccl. 12:5), and in memory of the deceased it is said *ligatus in ligatorium vitae* 'bound in the bundle of life' (1 Sam 25:9), and *memoria iustorum ad benedictionem* 'the memory of the just is blessed' (Prov 10:7).

Indeed, a number of scholars are inclined to believe that the OL has at its base pre-Christian translations made from the Hebrew. The proofs they adduce are, however, far from conclusive. Isolated linguistic or exegetic points of contact with Jewish idioms or targumic renderings do not necessarily prove a direct connection between the OL, or its early sections, and Jewish traditions.[20] Some similarities may be accidental, others the outcome of intercourse between Christians and Jews at much later times. The thesis, therefore, should be formulated with more caution. The OL, though in general being the author-

---

[20] The assumption of a Hebrew original as the ultimate source of the OL is defended by Blondheim, *Les parlers*, xxxiv-lxix; Cassuto, 'Hattargûm hayyehûdî', 205-16; and in a modified form: Baumstark, 'Orientalische Probleme', 89-114; Sparks, 'Latin Bible', 102-03; Schildenberger, 'Altlateinische Texte', 51. Rahmer, *Hebräische Traditionen*, 12-13 points to some midrashic remarks that speak of a Latin Bible version. Mohrmann, 'Linguistic Problems', 22-29 has doubted the assumption mentioned, pointing out that Christian Latinity flourished after the rupture between Christians and Jews.

itative version of the ancient Western Church and in general being based on the LXX, exhibits quite frequently an independence of the Greek version as we know it, relying instead on the Hebrew text and Jewish traditions. A few examples out of a larger collection shall demonstrate this fact. Of course, it could be argued in each case that the deviation from the LXX and agreement with the Hebrew text does not originate with the Latin version but rather with a Greek *Vorlage* unknown to us. This admittedly may be the case here and there. It would be unwarrented, however, to attribute the totality of these numerous and quite diverse instances to one hypothetical MS or to a number of MSS all of which, supposedly, were lost.

First one may mention those blunders of the translators that can be explained only from the Hebrew. The OL has Edom for Aram (2 Chr 20:2) – correctly rendered 'Syria' by the LXX and Vg – due to a confusion of the Hebrew consonants *Rēš* and *Dālet* that graphically especially resemble each other. The consonantal sequence *gmlym* (ib. 20:11), according to the MT to be read *gomlîm* 'they retribute', becomes in the OL *cameli*, based on the mistaken vocalization *gĕmallîm* 'camels'. Hebrew *dĕvarîm* (Hos 14:3), correctly translated into Greek *logoi* 'words', is rendered *multi* 'many', reflecting a reading *rabbîm*. Hebrew *middûr* 'from dwelling' (Ps 84[83]:11) is rendered *a generatione* 'from the generation', i.e. *middôr*; *šām* 'there' (ib. 87[86]:4) > *nomen* 'name', i.e. *šēm*.

Blunders and errors these may be, yet they prove the point under discussion. Then there are the cases of Hebrew erudition, genuine or otherwise. In the verse just mentioned (Hos 14:3) the OL renders the words 'Take away all iniquity': *potens es dimittere peccata* 'powerful thou art to forgive sins', a rendering that equates *kl* 'all', with *ykl* 'to be able, strong'. Hebrew *baḥûrîm* 'young men' (Amos 8:13) – LXX, correctly: *neaniskoi* – is translated: *iuvenes electi* 'chosen young men', reflecting the meaning of the verbal root *bḥr* 'to choose'. Similarly, the name Tabor (1 Sam 10:3), rendered *thabor electae*, is derived from the root *brr* 'to select'.

The OL quite correctly renders the MT: *et ideo sic* 'and therefore' (1 Sam 3:14), where the LXX misreads the Hebr (*lō'kēn* 'not like this' instead of *lākēn*); *foveam* for Hebrew *tĕ'ālā* (1 Kgs 18:32) where the LXX merely offers a transliteration *(thaala)*; but the OL transliterates *aoth* (*ḥawwōt*; Judg 10:4) where the LXX offers a translation. The Hebrew *ḥesed* 'mercy' (2 Chr 35:26) had received an extraordinary rendition in the LXX: *elpis* 'hope'; the OL returns to the standard equivalent *misericordia*.

An echo of Jewish halakhic law we seem to detect when the OL omits the conjunction, found in the LXX between the second item and the third: *ma'ăyān ûbôr miqweh mayim* 'a fountain and a pit, full of water' (Lev 11:36) > *lacu collectionis aquae*. According to the Greek text there are mentioned three different things: a fountain and a pit and a gathering of waters. The OL distinguishes between two, namely the fountain and the pit which is a 'collection of water'; the identical distinction is made in *M. Mikwaot* 1:7.[21]

The OL occasionally inserts a clause, a fact which is of special interest since here the translator, or some interpolator, offers a clue to his beliefs, his religious vocabulary, or his knowledge of the Bible. The prophet had warned his people: 'Rejoice not, o Israel, for joy, as (other) peoples' (Hos 9:1). The last word *ka'ammîm* 'like the nations', is rendered: *sicut populi terra* 'like the nations of the world', an expression that recalls the denotation of the heathens in later Judaism.[22] In the book of Jeremiah we find in the same context two interpolations: 'he that getteth riches' (Jer 17:11) is explained: *multos pariat sibi filios adquirens divitias suas* 'he begets many sons acquiring his wealth'; and 'they that depart from me shall be written in the earth' (ib. 17:13) is explained: *qui discesserunt a terra scribantur in libro mortis*, '. . . the earth they shall be written in the book of death'. On both verses the rabbinic commentators offer very similar explanations. It is obvious that the latter verse contains a negative allusion to the 'Book of Life, of the Living' (Ps 69[68]:29. Cf. Jerome 4, 961 *deleti de libro viventium* 'stricken from the book of the living').[23]

Considerations of space prevent us from presenting additional material which at any rate would have done little more than give support to the conclusions one may attempt to draw from the limited survey presented above. There can be no question at all that the influence of a Hebrew text-tradition is noticeable in the OL; the traces of such influence are relatively rare, in other words, they occur embedded in wide stretches of a text that closely follows the Septuagint. It also seems, that these Hebrew-influenced patches have the tendency to appear in bundles; many of these patches do not testify to the solid work of an erudite Hebraist, but rather give the impression of improvised remarks by a half-learned person. This leads us to believe that most of these points of contact with the Hebrew text, or with Jewish exegesis, are not remnants of an old Jewish Latin version – some, of course, may be such – but rather the result of later corrections and insertions at the hand of persons who

---

[21] For the sake of clarity contrast the following:

LXX	OL
kai lakkou	et lacus
kai synagogēs hydatōs	aquae congregatio

(Vg et cisternae *et* omnis aquarum congregatio). As to the Jewish interpretation cf. also *Sifra, Shemini* 8, 1-3 (p. 54d) and Ibn Ezra *ad loc.* who explains 'a pit, i.e. a gathering of water' but then remarks 'some say that "and" is missing' (i.e. 'a pit *and* a gathering of water').

[22] The frequently employed expression is *'ummōt hā'ōlām* 'the nations of the world', i.e. the gentiles, heathen.

[23] The targum, Rashi and Kimhi take v. 11 as reference to a certain bird (the partridge or the cuckoo) that supposedly collected as many eggs, or drew after it as many chickens as possible from other birds. V. 13 is interpreted by the targum as referring to the fall of the wicked into the Gehenna while Rashi comments that they shall be written in the graves situated in the depth of the earth. Another commentary *(Metsudat David)* expressly mentions 'the book' in which their fate shall be written down.

had sufficient knowledge of the respective languages to notice the many imperfections of the version, yet did not possess sufficient skill nor authority to perform a thorough job.[24]

Christian Exegesis

Obvious christological amplifications in the translation of the OT are easily recognized as later interpolations; not all the MSS contain them. A famous example is the verse Ps 96(95):10 'Say among the heathen that the Lord reigneth', for which many MSS of the ancient Latin Psalter have: *dicite in nationibus dominus regnavit a ligno*, i.e. '. . . the Lord reigns from the cross.' This addition, also known from the Greek and Latin Fathers, was regarded by many Christians as authentic and yet did not glide into each and every MS.[25] Then there is this interpolation found in Greek Patristic commentaries on the Psalms and in many MSS, followed by the OL: verses from Rom 3:13-18 were incorporated into Ps 14(13):3.

However, the influence of the Christian faith makes itself felt in a much subtler way. First, there is the linguistic impact which has two major aspects: the penetration of Greek loan words with a very specific meaning attached to them, and secondly, the lexical and semantic restructuring of the Latin vocabulary.

One should bear in mind that a loan-word, even when originally assigned for the same task it fulfills in its original language, can never occupy an identical position within the framework of its adoptive language. Even a term as 'prophet' must have conveyed slightly different connotations to the Greek-speaking reader who somehow was acquainted with the word's etymology and history, on the one hand, and on the other hand, to a Latin-speaking person to whom the opaque word meant some sacred title; suffice it to mention the orthographic inconsistency in Latin: *profeta* (Amos 7:14) vs. *prophetabis* (ib. 7:16). The linguistic impulse is much more noticeable when through the introduction of a loan-word a semantic rearrangement takes place in the target language. Thus e.g. the Greek word *angelos* 'messenger', which in the LXX stands for Hebrew *mal'āk* with the same meaning, was taken over into Latin as *angelus*. This loan-word, however, was almost exclusively used when the context mentions a 'messenger from Heaven', i.e. 'an angel', while elsewhere the Latin word *nuntius* 'messenger' is introduced. Thus we encounter this situation:

Gen 32:4	And Jacob sent messengers
LXX	apesteilen de Iakōb angelous
OL	misit autem Iacob nuntios
against	
Gen 32:2	and the angels of God met him

---

[24] Sparks, 'Latin Bible'. Plausibly, the need to correct the Latin text according to the Hebrew Bible also arose from religious disputations between Jews and Christians.

[25] Cf. Vallarsi's *(Sancti Eusebii Hieronymi..Opera)* note 10, 311.

LXX	kai synēntēsan autō hoi angeloi tou theou
OL	et occurrerunt ei angeli dei

In other words the OL, having adopted the Greek word, generates a lexical differentiation in order to bring into relief the semantic ambiguity of the Greek – and Hebrew – lexeme. This in itself constitutes a rather decisive intervention: the 'angel' in the subsequent history of religion removes itself more and more from the notion of the simple messenger, created *ad hoc* and of human appearance, who carried God's message to men, to become a celestial, semi-divine being. A still more significant consequence follows: If there exists such lexical specification, then in each specific case a decision must be reached which of the two terms be the appropriate. Thus e.g. the prophet Haggai has been granted the title *angelus* (Hag 1:13) by the OL, while the Vg. recognizes him only as *nuntius*.

A similar case is that of the verb *evangelizare*, a loan-word which stands side by side with the calque translation *bene nuntiare* 'to announce'. Whereas the LXX consistently employs the vb. *euangelizein*, the old Latin versions vacillate between the Greek and Latin verb. In view of the very specific way in which the NT mentions *evangelium* and *evangelista*, there is a glaring difference between: *bene nuntiate de die in diem* 'announce from day to day' (Ps 96[95]:2), and: *dominus dabit verbum evangelizantibus* (ib. 68[67]:12), which will be understood to mean 'God gives the word to those that announce the gospel'. A like dichotomy has developed in the OL in the wake of, but in contradistinction to the LXX concerning many other words, such as *diabolus* vs. *adversarius* 'devil, adversary'; *psallmare* vs. *cantare, canere* 'to praise, sing'; *synagoga* vs. *congregatio* 'congregation'; *eleemosyna* vs. *iustitia* 'justice, alms', and so on. The incorporation of the loan-words of a narrowly defined applicability side by side with their Latin equivalents that continued to fulfill the broader functions was one of the ways by which the OL aided in creating a unique idiom of Christendom.

Another way was the moulding of a Latin, lexically and semantically enriched, out of the old language. Suffice it to remind us of the new, additional meanings some well known words assumed having passed into the Latin Bible: *fides* 'trust, reliance', also denotes 'the religious faith' (Hab 2:4; 1 Tim 1:2); *gentes* 'nations' denotes 'the heathen' (Ps 79[78]:10), *peccatum* 'a fault, blunder', becomes the term for 'sin, guilt' (Gen 18:20), *testamentum* 'a will, testament', stands for covenant' (ib. 17:2), *saeculum* 'a generation, an age', denotes 'forever, in all eternity' (Ps 37[36]:27).[26]

---

[26] Blaise, *Manuel*, 11-15. Souter, *Glossary*, *passim* e.g. on *peccatum* p. 290. Jerome deemed it necessary to explain the broadened meaning of *testamentum* in Christian Latin: 'In plerisque Scripturarum locis testamentum non voluntatem defunctorum sonare, sed pactum viventium' (5, 957 *ad Mal* 2:4; 'In many biblical passages testamentum does not denote the last will of the deceased but rather a covenant of the living').

Now and then his Christian faith seems to have dictated the wording to the translator. Thus he renders – against the MT and LXX – the key word in the clause 'the fruit of his deeds' (Jer 17:10): *cogitatio* 'a thought, design'; thus the prophet's saying comes to mean that God who searches the heart, giveth every man according to his inner thoughts (cf. Jerome ad loc. *quod nullus cog-itationum secreta cognoscat nisi solo deus*, 'because no one save God knows the secret thoughts'; 4, 960). The rendering *thronus virtutis* 'a mighty throne' (ib. 17:12) for Hebrew *kissē' kābôd* and Greek *thronos doxēs* 'a glorious throne' (Vg. *solium gloriae*) may be based on 2 Thess 1:7, 9 where 'glory' and 'might' are combined *(et a gloria virtutis eius)*. The wording *avulsi sumus in eis* 'we are removed (i.e. we die) in them (the bones)' (Ezek 37:11) may refer to the belief in a resurrection of the flesh. The prophet Amos in very harsh words condemns the 'pride' of Jacob: '. . . saith the Lord . . . I abhor the excellency of Jacob' (Am 6:8). The word for 'excellency, pride', Hebrew *gā'ôn*, Greek *hybris*, is not rendered *superbia* as one would expect but instead the OL has: *iniuria* 'injustice, injurious act'. According to this translation, it is not Jacob's splendour that has caused God's wrath but rather his actions done contrary to justice. The OL of Hos 14:3(2) has the following addition: *et aepulabitur in bonis cor vestrum* 'and your heart shall feast upon the good things'; this is reminiscent of 1 Cor 5:8.[27]

The commonplace statement that every translation is an interpretation could be given a sharper edge: Even a translation that aims at literalism offers the translator an opportunity to introduce something of his personal thoughts and beliefs. In the case of the OL, though, it is not the voice of a single person we think to discern but rather the sounds of an historic workshop that has been continuously engaged in transferring the Scriptures into Latin.

Jerome and the Vulgate

JEROME, THE TRANSLATOR

Education; Qualifications
As the Old Latin version accompanied the growth of the victorious Western church the number of its copies, revisions and recensions grew to such an extent that the need was felt for the establishment of one authoritative Latin Bible-text out of the many text-forms in circulation. Such reliable text was to be used not only for instructional and liturgical purposes but also in controversies with heretics and Jews. This task of preparing a revised Latin version, of the NT as a

---

[27] Hos 8:3 has the following interpolation: '(istrahel avertit bona) haec dicebant propter quod non interrogabant dom' (inimicum persecuti sunt)'. The problem to be solved was this: In contradis-tinction to the MT, the LXX seems to say that Israel shall pursue and give chase to its enemy; this hardly makes sense in this context. The OL through its interpolation ('since they have not consulted God') makes it clear that here *persecuti sunt* does not mean 'pursued victoriously with intent to kill' but rather 'followed, went after as admirers'.

first step, was entrusted to Eusebius Hieronymus, or Jerome as later ages would call him, in c. 382 who at that time had already won a fame in Rome as scholar and writer.[28]

In the present context only those biographical details are significant that help to explain his tireless occupation with philological material and testify to his abilities and qualifications to perform the gigantic task of translating the Bible.

As son of wealthy parents Jerome received a good education which included the study of Latin grammar and literature, rhetoric and Greek. Though later, having begun serious theological studies, he felt strong qualms about his being attracted so much by classical culture, his works, all of them dedicated to ecclesiastical and biblical subjects, not only bear witness to his classical training but also betray a continued affection toward it. In one of his letters (*Epistulae* 53:6) he mentions grammar, rhetoric, philosophy, geometry, dialectics, music, astronomy, astrology and medicine as useful skills; he cites Horace and praises Vergil (5, 11-13); and in connection with Ezekiel's vision (Ezek 1) he mentions Hippocrates' doctrine of the four elements fire, air, water, earth (ib.). For identification of the precious stones mentioned by Ezekiel (28:11-19) he sends his diligent readers to Pliny's *Natural History* (*diligens a nobis mittendus est lector*; 5, 334). He informs us of the extensive concurrence of Christian dogma and Stoic doctrine (4, 159). In his translation from the Hebrew we find terms taken from pagan mythology: *gigantes* (Gen 6:4), *pythones, aruspices* (2 Kgs 21:6), (the goddess) *fortuna* (Isa 65:11), *sirenes* (ib. 13:22), *lamia, onocentaur* (ib. 34:14), *fauni ficarii* (Jer 50:39) and so on. We may suspect that the extraordinary rendering *populus* for *šā'ôn* 'a noise, tumult' in the verse *vox populi de civitate . . . vox domini* 'a voice of noise from the city, . . . a voice of the Lord' (Isa 66:6) is due to a reminiscence of the Latin proverb: *vox populi vox dei*.[29] Jerome's translation not infrequently assumes the sonority and rythm of poetry. Contrast the following passage in his work, the Vulgate, with the OL.

Gen 37:34
Jacob rent his clothes and put sackcloth on his loins, and mourned for his son many days.

Vg	OL
scissisque vestibus	et conscidit Iacob vestimenta sua

[28] Quotations of Jerome's words in the present study are from Vallarsi; see note 18. Bardenhewer, *Geschichte* 3, 605-55; Lietzmann, 'Hieronymus', 305-25; Campenhausen, *Western Church*, 129-82. We learn of Jerome's commision from his Preface to the Gospels which is phrased as a letter to Pope Damasus (c. 304-384).

[29] The ultimate source of this proverb may be Hesiod, *Works and Days*, 763-64; the Latin rephrasing, however, is quite old (cf. Walter, *Lateinische Sprichwörter*, 911). Jerome comments (4, 804) that the one voice is that of Jerusalem's wailing population when the city is attacked by the Romans while the other voice is that of the punishing God. It should be noted that the lemma corrects the inaccurate rendering, substituting *(vox) fremitus* for *(vox) populi*.

indutus est cilicio	et posuit saccum super lumbum suum
lugens filium	et flebat filium suum
multo tempore	diebus multis

Having moved to the desert of Chalcis, east of Antioch, (374), leading a life of ascetism and study, he took up Hebrew studies; a convert to Christianity taught him 'the hissing and puffing words' of that language until he was able to harvest 'sweet fruits from the bitter seed' (*Epistulae* 125:12).[30] After many years there and in Antioch where he undoubtedly perfected his Greek but also continued to learn from Jewish masters (*Epistulae* 18:10), he returned to Rome (382). There he established contact with a Jew who supplied him with Hebrew texts, taken secretly from the synagogue. In the year 385 Jerome left Rome for Palestine and after a journey through that country in order to acquaint himself with its geography and history,[31] he finally settled at Bethlehem (385). Again he succeeded in finding a number of Jewish teachers with whom he discussed the minutiae of the Hebrew Bible. Frequently in his commentaries he tells us that he had asked a Jew to explain the meaning of a word or a phrase to him (6, 934; 4, 291; 5, 94) because 'whenever someone opines something better and more correct, we should gladly accept it' (6, 814) and 'when in doubt, ask the Jews' (*sicubi dubitas, Hebraeos interroga*; *Epistulae* 112:20; cf. *Adversus Ruffinum* 2:25, 28, 30 where he quotes from his earlier writings). Jerome mentions one of his teachers by name (Baranina i.e. Bar-Hanina; 2, 469) and calls others by their titles, such as *deuterōtēs* (i.e. *Tanna*), *scriba* (i.e. *sôfēr*), *sapiens* (i.e. *hākām*). It is inconceivable that such persistent efforts should not produce results. Against those who maintain that Jerome's knowledge of Hebrew has been overestimated, it must be stressed that he was, indeed, proficient in this language. In conjunction with his monumental translation, the Latin Vulgate, innumerable remarks on Hebraic philology witness to this proficiency.[32]

For Jerome Hebrew was 'the progenitress of all the other languages' (*matrix omnium linguarum*; 6, 730), the language of creation (*ad Isa* 13:10; 4, 240, *ad Amos* 5:8-9; 6, 288-89). The Greek and Latin names of the stars bear witness to the ridiculous fables of the heathen; the Hebrew language possesses its own vocabulary. That is how God called the light 'day'; the firmament 'heaven'; the dry land 'earth'; the gathering of the water 'sea'; and thus he bestowed on each star its name. Jerome names the twenty-two letters of the Hebrew alphabet (*Epistulae* 30:5) and is acquainted with the old Hebrew script; he notes that in

---

[30] Barr, 'St Jerome's Appreciation', 283-302.

[31] Jerome, probably, was the first to stress the need to get acquainted with the geography of Palestine in order to better understand the Scriptures (*Prol. in Paralip.*) Miller, 'Aufenthalt' 40-54.

[32] Burkitt, 'The Debt', 91: '. . . the Latin Vulgate is not, strictly speaking, a new translation . . . (Jerome's) knowledge of Hebrew was not profound'. The first part of this statement is obviously wrong, if only because it ignores the heterogeneity of the work; the second part is disproved by the translator's achievement. As to his perseverance with regard to his Hebrew studies cf. Rahmer, *Hebräische Traditionen*, 5-15; Barr, 'St Jerome and the Sounds' and 'St Jerome's Appreciation'; Bardy, 'Saint Jérôme', 145-64; Kedar, Vulgate, 50-51, 296 n. 61.

this script the letter *Tāw* (Ezek 9:4) has the shape of a cross (5, 95-6). He admires the Hebrew language and deems, as compared with it, the Latin and Greek languages poor in their vocabulary (*propter . . . ad comparationem linguae Hebraeae, tam Graeci quam Latini sermonis pauperiem*; 4, 488). When a mistaken LXX rendering is based on a scribal error in the original, he comments on the resemblances of Hebrew letters, e.g. the letter *Rēš* and the letter *Dālet*; thus *amicitia* 'friendship' *(r')* might easily be confused with *scientia* 'knowledge' *(d')* (*ad Jer* 15:12; 4, 947). Doubts as to Jerome's knowledge of Hebrew have been voiced inter alia because he apparently did not distinguish between *š* and *ś*: he explains the ambiguity of the consonantal sequence *sb'* that it can be taken to mean either 'seven' or 'satiated' (4, 873) ignoring that the first is pronounced with a *š (šeba')* the other with a *ś (śābēa')*. But since Jerome dealt with the problems the ancient translator faced who had a text, unvocalized and without diacritical marks, before him, the confusion as indicated by him could indeed take place. Moreover, Latin has no equivalent, neither phonetic nor graphic, for *š*. At another occasion he does point out 'the different accentuation' (*pro diversitate accentum*; 4, 786) of the two sibilants; is he to blame that he did not find a way of proper transliteration?[33]

Jerome's seriousness and philological precision in reading the Hebrew text finds its expression when he is ready to forgo a christological interpretation of a verse because one silent letter is in the way: '(The Lord) declares to man what is his thought' (Am 4:13) had been rendered by the LXX (in Jerome's Latin translation): *annuntians in homines Christum suum* '. . . announcing his Christ to men'. Had the Hebrew letters been *mšyḥ* he expounds, it could have stood for *mašîaḥ* 'Messiah'; since, however, the sequence had a superfluous *Hē'* as second letter, i.e. *mh šyḥ* (*HE secundum literam plus habens*; 6, 278) Jerome feels obliged to correct this rendering (Vg *adnuntians homini eloquium suum*). Though having before him an unvocalized text, he frequently comments on the proper vocalization: *MEM, JOD, MEM-si legatur MAIM 'aquas' significat, si MEJAM 'de mari'*, 'if the sequence *m-y-m* is read *mayim*, it means 'water', if *miyyām* 'from the sea' (6, 131).[34]

The fact that Jerome can compare three languages and the problems he faces as a translator, make him a keen observer of linguistic phenomena.[35] He raises fine points of grammar and semantics. He notices the lack of the definite article in Latin (7, 503) and comments on number and gender of nouns. Hebrew *RUA* 'spirit' is feminine; however, nobody should find this, in view of the Holy Spirit, scandalous: in Latin the word is masculine, in Greek neuter, so that we learn that deity has no sex (*in divinitate enim nullus est sexus*; 4, 485-486). Jerome is

---

[33] Cf. Siegfried, 'Aussprache', 34-83; Sutcliffe, 'St Jerome's Pronunciation', 112-25; Sperber, 'Hebrew', 103-274.

[34] Obviously, the many transliterations in Jerome's works are not trustworthy from a text-critical point of view. Copyists, ignorant of Hebrew, inevitably introduced many scribal errors.

[35] Jerome prides himself: 'ego philosophus, rhetor, grammaticus, dialecticus, hebraeus, graecus, latinus, trilinguis' (2, 537); the order of the languages enumerated is noteworthy.

capable of making nice semantic distinctions between Hebrew synonyms (though he does not always pay attention to them in his translation): *nĕbēlâ* is the corpse of a beast which has died without shedding blood, *ṭĕrēpâ* is a corpse torn by beasts (5, 45). The verb *znh* 'to fornicate' denotes the conduct of a woman who lies with many men, *n'p* 'to commit adultery', a woman that deserts her husband for someone else (6, 14). *'āwôn* 'iniquity', antedates the law, *ḥēṭ'* 'sin', occurs after the law (6, 89). Jerome remarks on the polysemy of words: *rûaḥ*, according to the context, may mean either *spiritus* 'spirit', or *anima* 'soul', or *ventus* 'wind' (5, 7). *reḥem* denotes *vulva* 'womb' and *misericordia* 'mercy' (6, 235).

There are hundreds of examples of the above kind. Jerome inadvertently demonstrates that he is able to find easily a Hebrew equivalent for a given Greek word whenever, in correcting the wording found in the LXX, he states what the Hebrew vocable, not found in the MT, should have been, were the LXX correct (e.g. 4, 470).[36] And thus we may believe him, that when he translated the Aramaic text of Tobit, he asked a Jew to give an improvised Hebrew rendering of it which Jerome, in his turn, dictated on the spot in Latin to his scribe *(Prologus Tobiae)*. If we accept this evidence, it proves a high degree of proficiency.

It is probable that Jerome had acquired a fair knowledge of Aramaic or Syriac and a smattering of Arabic, yet the evidence (*Epistulae* 17:2; *Prologus in Danihele; Prologus in Iob*) is not conclusive. But that his inquisitive mind always turned to languages which might help to elucidate a biblical text, cannot be doubted: Jerome tells us of his inquiries into the Egyptian and Punic languages (4, 291; 6, 425).

What then shall we make of the alleged mistaken renderings and errors in Jerome's translation? To begin with, most of the so-called mistakes, if not all, commonly adduced are definitely not blunders but conscientiously chosen renderings in agreement with philological notions current in his times. Indeed, it is easy to find support for his renderings in Jewish versions and commentaries. As we shall return to this question later, suffice it to adduce an example or two.

As is well known, Jerome derived the verb *qrn* (Exod 34:29) not from *qeren* 'a ray', but from *qeren* 'horn', and thus aided in creating the image of a 'horned' Moses: his face was horned *(cornuta)*. This, however, is not a haphazard rendering: Jerome could have copied the LXX ('glorified'), had he wanted it. Yet his way of translating is a replica of Aquila's etymologizing rendition and was meant as a glorification of Moses: horns are the insignia of might and majesty (6, 321; 4, 68). Jerome overlooking the homonym presents the usual translation *costa* 'a rib' for *ṣela'* (Job 18:12) instead of 'a fall, ruin' (calamity is

---

[36] E.g. Isa 38:9. For Hebrew *miktāv* 'A writing, letter' the LXX had *proseuchē* 'a prayer'. Jerome comments (4, 470): 'Miror quomodo soli Septuaginta pro "scriptura" "orationem" posuerint, quum "oratio" THEPHELLAT dicatur et non MACHTTAB quae in praesenti loco scribitur'; in other words, Jerome easily, i.e. without contextual aid, was able to find the lexical equivalents Greek *proseuchē* > Latin *oratio*, and *oratio* > Hebrew *tĕfillâ*.

ready for his ruin). Yet Jerome elsewhere knew how to translate the homonym correctly: *plaga* (Ps 38:18), and on the other hand, the Jewish medieval commentators support Jerome's interpretation of our verse; Ibn Ezra says the word here means 'the side', while Rashi thinks 'the rib' refers to 'a man's wife'. The vocable *'ûbāl* occurs three times in the same context: Dan 8:2, 3 and 6. The Vg has for this *porta* 'gate', *palus* 'pool', and again *porta*. Is Jerome so insecure? He is not; a glimpse into rabbinic commentaries reveals the existence of two traditions: 'the entrance gate' (Saadya) and 'a stream of water' (Ibn Ezra).

Of course, Jerome did err a few times. In his commentary (6, 120) he confuses Shalman (Hos 10:14) with Zalmunna, the Midianite king (Judg 8:5). He also seems to have confused now and then the gutturals *'Alef* and *'Ayin*; thus *n'mnym* 'pleasant' > *fideles* 'faithful', as if spelled with an *'Alef* (Isa 17:10); *bā'ēr* 'to destroy' (ib. 6:13) >*in ostensionem* 'for exposing, manifestation', as if written *b'r*. In his commentary Jerome not only corrects these mistakes (4, 196, 283, 99) but appears to be astonished at the erroneous translations. Yet they are not so surprising. Jerome generally worked in great haste and obviously did not look up every Bible verse he wanted to quote; or somebody unable to pronounce the gutturals read the passage to him whereupon Jerome dictated his Latin rendering.[37] We submit therefore, that this kind of error, paradoxically, constitutes additional proof of Jerome's expertise.

Scholarly Works

Jerome was a prolific author. It would be futile to enumerate his works, the more so since we would necessarily limit ourselves to a list of the extant writings; it seems, however, that he had written more but part of it has perished without trace except a few remarks in Jerome's extant writings. Thus we shall mention only some of the more important treatises directly relating to the interpretation of the Bible text.[38]

At the outset Jerome translated biblical treatises by renowned Greek Fathers (c. 381) – an activity which he continued to practice now and then in later years – but soon contributed works of his own. The 'Book on Hebrew Names' *(De Nominibus Hebraicis)* was meant to be a revision of Origen's book on this subject but contains Jerome's incisive criticism based upon his Hebrew learning. His 'Book of Hebrew Questions on Genesis' *(Liber Quaestionum Hebraicarum in Genesim)* deals only with the more difficult and important passages, yet it offered its author the opportunity to point out the grave defects of the old version and thus the obligation to return to the original text (c. 389). At about the same time he composed his commentary on Ecclesiastes *(Commentarius in Ecclesiasten)*, a discussion and explanation of the Hebrew text which is rendered in an ad-hoc Latin translation. Jerome repeats here thoughts contained in

---

[37] Kedar, Vulgate, 52-53. Jerome kept complaining about his bad eyesight *(Ep.* 21:42) which made him dependent upon people who read the texts aloud for him.
[38] Bardenhewer, *Geschichte*, 612-27.

Origen's writings but added some remarks as made by his Jewish teachers. A little later (c. 392) Jerome wrote his *Commentarioli* on the Psalter – in the main, again, a translation and complementary edition of Origen – but also began composing his extensive commentaries on the Prophets, a labour in which he would be engaged almost thirty years: By the years 392 he had completed his treatises on Nahum, Micah, Zephania, Haggai and Habakkuk *(Comm. in Amos; Prol.)*; about three years later he interpreted Jonah and Obadiah but only as late as 406 he had completed the Dodecapropheton. He then turned to Daniel (c. 407), Isaiah (408-420), Ezekiel (410-415), and Jeremiah (415-420) the commentary of which remained incomplete because of Jerome's death. This chronology, as compared with the dates of Jerome's translational activities, is of importance because from textual divergences and interpretational discrepancies between the two sets one may attempt to draw some conclusions as to changes in the material at Jerome's disposal and in his philological conception. Of the NT Jerome commented on four of the Pauline epistles (c. 387) and in the year 398 he dictated a commentary on the Gospel according to St. Matthew.

The scholarly work of Jerome is, like the man himself, full of contradictions but at the same time – one might be tempted to say: because of them – of greatest historical interest. Jerome preached Christian virtues and led the life of an ascetic yet he displayed a malicious disposition towards his many adversaries among whom he counted intimate friends of days past. He despised the rhetoric of the heretics (6, 138) but made use of every possible rhetoric device in his controversies. He prided himself to be a humble person and to have a fame as such *(Epistulae* 45:3). He eagerly sought the scholarly guidance of the Jews but also mocked at their exegetical fantasies (6, 498).

In his works we encounter similar disparities. Jerome quotes, sometimes critically more often without making clear his own preference, previous commentators; contradictory renderings of his Greek predecessors; exegetical interpretations of Jews and Christians. His own opinions about the proper citation of particular passages were variable; in principle he admits the 'historic' explanations of the Jews as well as the 'allegoric' ones of the Christians *(historiae hebraeorum tropologiam nostrorum miscere; Comm. in Zech., Prol.).* Jerome, as we shall have to discuss in a moment, grew more and more critical of the LXX, and yet, having refuted it on philological grounds, he usually still explains its wording in full.[39]

Notwithstanding the lack of clear and solid principles in Jerome's exegetical work, it testifies to the vast learning of the man. His writings and especially his commentaries on biblical books, are a storehouse of information on textual, philological, and exegetical questions.

---

[39] Jerome explicitly defends the use of both texts, the Hebrew and the Greek, so that they would elucidate each other ('unde et utramque editionem posui: ut quod in altera videtur obscurum, alterius lectione reseretur'; 4, 561). Bardenhewer, *Geschichte,* 627-30, 652-53; Campenhausen, *Western Church,* 162-66; Sparks, 'Jerome', 535-39.

Historical and Technical Data

In view of the confusion caused by the innumerable Latin text-forms, Jerome was commissioned by Damasus, bishop of Rome, to revise the Latin Bible, in other words to prepare an authoritative text in the light of the Greek. Whether this revision was to be limited to the NT or was meant to include the whole Bible, is a moot question. The latter seems more plausible since we know of a revision of some books of the OT, first and foremost the Psalter, which Jerome emended from the Greek of the LXX. In the main, however, the product of this revision is the text of the NT as we find it in the Vulgate. The revised four Gospels appeared in 383, the remainder received a rather cursory revision at best. As regards the OT the revision, or the planning of such, soon yielded to a much more ambitious design, namely that of a fresh translation directly from the Hebrew original. Admittedly, Jerome did not execute this ambitious plan in a prefixed, logical sequence; there also was no official commission for it. But his growing awareness of the enormous discrepancy between the Hebrew and the Greek Bible texts and his wish, at the request of friends, to produce a reliable translation, determined Jerome's basic attitude towards the canonical books of the OT as disparate as the various portions of his Vulgate may be in other respects: In order to obtain the sense of the biblical message, recourse must be had to the original 'truth' of the Hebrew text *(hebraica veritas)*.

This bold conception entailed the discarding of the authenticity of the LXX as maintained by Church autorities such as Augustine who had whole-heartedly favoured the NT revisions but strongly opposed Jerome's abandonment of the Septuagint and his unconditional acceptance of the Hebrew text.[40] Now and then, especially in the prefaces to the translated books, Jerome attempts to convince his audience that it is not his intention to disparage the LXX but rather to render the Hebrew as faithfully as possible. But obviously, prudence and expedience, besides a natural attachment to the traditional belief, dictated such pronouncements. Gradually Jerome became more outspoken in his views until, at the end, he rejects the view of the LXX as being an inspired version. The report about the miraculous production of the Greek version is an unfounded legend, Jerome maintains; the apostles' quotations of the OT did not agree with the Greek text.

Jerome dedicated fifteen years to the new translation (c. 390-405). One can establish, in the main, the sequence of the books translated; some details are still debatable. In 393 he had accomplished the translation of the books of the Prophets, Samuel and Kings, the Psalms, and Job *(Epistulae* 49:4). It is commonly supposed that the 'four books of Kings' constitute the first step; the *Prologus Galeatus*, the 'Preface with a Helmet' attached to this portion appears to be an introduction to the whole work. However, these prefaces seem to have a history of their own. Thus, e.g., in his preface to the book of Joshua, Jerome

---

[40] Schwarz, *Biblical Translation*, 30-33 (Jerome), 37-42 (Augustine).

mentions as a task lying ahead the translation of Judges, Ruth, and Esther; he also mentions the death of his aristocratic sponsor Paula. His preface to the book of Esther, however, is dedicated to this lady. It follows that the preface to Esther was written prior to, and independently of the translations. The evidence of the *Prologus Galeatus* should thus not be overestimated; it is conceivable, that this prologue was sent out later. From the point of view of the mode of translation it seems that the Prophets and the Psalter were the first books to be translated; they are also the theologically most important books.[41] Be this as it may, in 394-396 Ezra, Nehemiah and Chronicles are translated; 398 Proverbs, Ecclesiastes and Song of Songs follow; 398-405 the work is completed with the translation of the Pentateuch, Joshua, Judges, Ruth and Esther. Of the Apocrypha – Jerome was rather suspicious of the apocryphal books – he translated Tobit and Judith from the Aramaic but left other books (Wisdom, Ecclesiasticus and Maccabees) unrevised.[42]

The reception of this new Latin translation was anything but enthusiastic; clergy and laity tended to cling to the old version they were used to hear and quote, and to look with suspicion upon any attempt to produce a new Latin Bible-text which, moreover, involved a depreciation of the LXX and the acceptance of the Hebrew Bible of the Jews. After the great scholar's death, however, his translation from the Hebrew was gradually adopted, first side by side with the OL, until it won a complete victory: in the year 1546 the Council of Trent officially elevated it to the position of the authoritative text *(textus auctoritate plenus)*. From that time on Jerome's version has been indeed the *Biblia Vulgata)*, i.e. the commonly used edition of the Holy Scriptures regarded as the ultimate authority by the Latin-speaking Catholic Church.[43]

Translation Technique
Among the classical Bible versions the Vg occupies a unique position insofar as it is the fruit of one man's labour; his biography as well as the circumstances under which he produced his translation are known to us; and he describes in detail the problems he faced as a translator and the solutions he found best.

---

[41]   The commonly accepted chronology is given by Bardenhewer, *Geschichte*, 617. White, 'Vulgate', 875-76; Cavallera, *St. Jérôme* has suggested a divergent sequence, namely that the Prophets were translated before Kings: In his prologue to Isaiah Jerome justifies his presenting the text *per cola et commata*, a remark which would be appropriate at the beginning of his work. Moreover, in his preface to Daniel he expounds the tripartite arrangement of the Hebrew Bible; why does he not refer to the *Prologus Galeatus* where the identical information is given, if indeed it did already exist? Kedar, *Vulgate*, 280-85, has attempted to support Cavallera's assumption from a different angle, that of changes in Jerome's translation technique.

[42]   Sparks, 'Jerome', 532-35.

[43]   On the name 'Vulgata' cf. Sutcliffe, 'Vulgate', 345-52. This new Vulgate was, of course, exposed to the usual process of textual corruption. Several attempts were made to reconstruct one reliable text-form out of the bewildering amount of MSS at variance with one another (cf. Berger, *Histoire*; White, 'Vulgate', 877-82.) As to the critical editions at our disposal nowadays cf. *Biblia Sacra* and *Novum Testamentum* in the bibliography.

Jerome's testimony is, admittedly, to be taken with more than a grain of salt; he is prone to exaggerate and to be misled by his memory when attempting to explain processes that had taken place many years ago. With this reserve we may try to put the puzzle together. It has already been said that Jerome made the translation at the request of others; the prefaces to the individual books mention the respective sponsors. Sometimes these people, or their messengers, were waiting for the product while Jerome was working on it. Thus he wrote, or rather dictated in great haste, his amanuensis becoming restless whenever Jerome paused to consider the passage: 'I dictate what comes into my mouth' (*Comm. in Gal.* 3, *Prol.*; *Comm. in Isa.* 5, *Prol.*; *Ep.* 75:4).[44] There seemed to be no time to revise the dictation, let alone turn over the leaves of old codices or scrolls. In extreme cases then, Jerome's rendering was based on the knowledge stored up in his mind, in others, of course, he had recourse to a variety of written sources.

The Hebrew text he had before him was much closer to, but by no means identical with the MT. It is interesting to note that Jerome who permanently censured the Greek and Latin Bible texts had utmost confidence in the reliability and constancy of the Hebrew; he seems to have assumed that the current Hebrew text-form was identical with that underlying the LXX. This can best be explained as consequence of the impression the relatively stabile text of the Hebrew OT made on any person who compared this situation with that prevailing in the area of the Greek and Latin versions. He mentions minor variants, though. On the verse 'no breath at all in the midst of it' (Hab 2:19) he remarks that in some Hebrew MSS the word *kol* 'all' does not appear; this parallels Aquila's rendering *et spiritus eius non est in visceriibus eius* (6, 630); yet in the Vg he renders: *et omnis spiritus* . . . He also comments on the variant reading of the proper name Efron vs. Efran found in MSS of his day (*Quaest. Hebr. in Gen.* 23:16-17). There seems to be some agreement between Jerome's Hebrew text and the Qumran scroll of Isaiah; e.g. 'for signs and wonders' (Isa 8:18) the Vg, like the scroll, have the singular 'for a sign and wonder' (*in signum et in portentum*). It should be noted that in his commentary, composed c. 17 years later, Jerome introduces the plural forms echoing the MT (*signa..portenta*).[45] The Vg reveals a variant parallel to one found in the Talmud: Job 14:16 *tu quidem gressus*, reading *'attâ* 'thou' like *P.T. Berakhot* 5:1 (9a) instead of *'attâ* 'now' as in the MT. Most of what is known as emendations of the Scribes and Masoretes are introduced into the Vg but not all. As far as the vocalization is concerned, the Vg not infrequently strays from the MT. Since there did not yet exist Hebrew vowel signs, Jerome though certainly acquainted with the reading traditions, to a certain extent felt free to improvise. For *ṣaddîq* 'the righteous

---

[44] *Ep.* 75:4 contains a vivid description as to the technical aspect of bookproduction in those days: From Spain six short-hand writers *(notarii)* had arrived in order to copy Jerome's works for their wealthy patron.

[45] Kedar, 'Divergent Hebrew Readings', 176-78.

man' (Prov 18:5) he reads ṣedeq 'righteousness'; for lāʿad 'forever' (Isa 30:8) he read lĕʿēd 'in testimony' and the like.[46]

Entering the stage of translating Jerome had recourse to the information offered by several sources. First probably occurred to him the version of the OL. In some instances, plausibly for reasons of Church tradition, he left it intact. Thus the verses Isa 11:1-3a are identical in the OL and the Vg.[47] The same occurs with regard to the clause Gen 49:10 that was applied to the Messiah (*et ipse erit expectatio gentium* 'he is the hope of the nations'). Then there was the Septuagint and the three later Greek translations by Aquila, Symmachus and Theodotion. Much has been made of Jerome's dependence on these, especially on Symmachus. However, such impression of dependence prevails only as long as we look for points of contact between the Vg and any particular source. The moment we survey the overall picture, his relative independence becomes apparent: He never agrees with one of his informants for more than a short clause. In other words, Jerome made use of the works of his predecessors in a way a modern scholar has recourse to a concordance, a dictionary, a grammar and scholarly commentaries. This, of course, also applies to the information he gathered from his Jewish instructors. The final decision rests with Jerome and he reaches it having weighed the evidence.[48]

The Process of Linguistic Transfers

These were the mechanics of translation; now comes its philosophy. The transfer of a message from one linguistic code into another can be carried out, roughly speaking, either in the direction of the target language or towards the source language. In other words, either the sense of a message is figured out and then encoded according to the rules of the target language, or else the constituent morphemic and lexical elements contained in the message are decoded and then represented by their approximate counterparts in the target language. When carried to excess, both modes become absurd: the first disrupts the connection with the original, the other produces unintelligible statements. Translational practice follows one of the many passable routes between the two extremes, yet taking one of them as guideline.

Concerning this question Jerome displays extreme contradictions.[49] Not only do we find in his writings conflicting theories about the commendable method

---

[46] In many such cases Jerome, it is true, agrees with other versions; the very inconsistency in this respect provides an indirect proof that the final decision was always his own.

[47] Ceresa-Gastaldo, *Latino*, 73-75.

[48] Stummer, *Einführung* 90-124; Ziegler, *Jüngere griechische Übersetzungen*; Cannon, 'Jerome' 191-99. Remarks on and references to the later Greek versions abound in Jerome's writings (4, 122; 5, 932; 6, 258; 9, 1100 and many, many more).

[49] The classic formulation of the translator's dilemma was put forward by Franz Rosenzweig: '. . . wie sich das Herrschgebiet der beiden Prinzipien, das der Bewegung des Texts zum Leser und das der Bewegung des Lesers zum Text, gegeneinander abgrenzt' (*Kleinere Schriften*, 144). Stummer, 'Beobachtungen', 3-30; Johannessohn, Entstehung', 90-102.

of translating; not only do we encounter opposite practices in his version; but he speaks of the need to translate according to the sense at a moment when he offers very literal renderings (*Epistulae* 57:5-10) and prides himself of literalism in connection with a biblical book. Esther, that can serve as a model of paraphrastic translation *(Prologus Hester)*.

In one of his letters (*Epistulae* 106:3) he defines as the translator's task to render idiomatic expressions of one language into suitable expressions peculiar to the other. The translator had to represent the sense of the original rather than its wording (cf. above *Epistulae* 57:10): *non verba in Scripturis consideranda sed sensus*. In some of the prefaces the voices similar sentiments (e.g. *Prolegomenon in Paralipomenon*). On the other hand he maintains, in the Holy Scriptures every word is sacred and even the wordorder, a mystery (*Epistulae* 53:8; 57:5). Thus it seemed imperative for the translator to preserve the peculiarities of the original. It remains to be seen to what extent these conflicting principles exerted their influence on Jerome's practice.

Linguistic equations that juxtapose Hebrew and Latin words do exist in the mind of all who have knowledge of both languages; they certainly were present to Jerome's mind. Examples of lexical equations are: *bayit* 'house' > *domus*; *'iššâ* 'woman' > *mulier*; *milḥāmâ* 'war' > *bellum*; *yôm* 'day' > *dies*; *māwet* 'death' > *mors*; *kôs* 'cup' > *calix*; *'kl* 'to eat' > *comedere*; *bnh* 'to build' > *aedificare*; *gādôl* 'great, large' > *magnus*; *ḥākām* 'wise' > *sapiens*; *ṭôb* 'good' > *bonus*, and many others like these. But also grammatical morphemes, such as the ending -*îm* indicating the plural, or the hiph'il conjugation denoting the causative, and syntactical constructions, e.g. the construct state or relative clauses, had found Latin counterparts. Complications occured, of course, as when the polysemy of a Hebrew lexeme, e.g. *kesef*, 'silver' and 'money' had to be clarified by translating either *argentum* (Gen 24:35) or *pecunia* (Jer 32:44); or when two Hebrew words had to be represented by one and the same Latin word, e.g. *minḥâ* 'gift', and *šōḥad* 'a bribe', both by *munera*; or when a very specific Hebrew term had to be rendered periphastically,e.g. *gāzît* 'a hewn stone' > *lapis quadrus*; *bṣr* 'to gather grapes' > *colligere quasi vindemiam*. But these questions are peripheral; the crucial dilemma of the translator lies elsewhere: At what point is he ready to forgo the standard equation replacing it by semantically, but not formally, suitable substitutes.[50]

An extremely free translation ignores all the established equations even where they would serve their purpose; an extremely literal translation sticks to those equations even in a context where they do violence to the character of the target language. As we have said, most translations move somewhere between the two extremes wherefore their position can be determined by the ease with

---

[50] In other words, at what point does the translator lay aside the usual equation *bayit* 'house, building' > *domus*, replacing it by *domestici* since the context requires the sense 'people of the house', i.e. family or domestic servants (Prov 31:15 vs. 2 Kgs 8:2). The list of periphrastic renderings is quite long'; cf. Kedar, *Vulgate*, 99-100.

which they abandon the standard equations. We shall find that the Vg in this respect displays extreme variability.

As to the rendering of a grammatical morpheme there exists on the one hand its analytical transfer, on the other hand, its semantic recasting: *hišmîa'* 'to let hear, announce' > *auditum facio* (Amos 3:9) vs. *adnuntio* (Jer 48:4) or *nuntium mitto* (1 Kgs 15:22); *hiškîn* and *hiškîb* 'to lead somebody to (a place of) rest' are rendered *habitare facio* (Ezek 32:4) and *dormire facio* (Hos 2:20[18]), respectively, or *conloco* (Gen 3:24; 1 Kgs 3:20).[51] The morpheme of a plurale tantum is either transferred into Latin, against the usage of this language, or disregarded: *šāmayim* 'heaven, sky' becomes either *caeli* (Isa 1:2) or *caelum* (Gen 1:1). The Hebrew word for 'blood' can be used in the sing., *dām*, or in the pl., *dāmîm*. The latter form is translated *sanguines* (Ezek 9:9; Mic 3:10) or *sanguis* (Deut 19:10).

Still more informative in this connection are the divergent renderings of lexemes. Only a few examples can be adduced. *leḥem* 'bread' means metonymically: 'sustenance, subsistence'; Vg has *panis* (Amos 7:12) vs. *esca* (Ruth 1:6), *victus* (Deut 10:18), *necessaria* (Prov 27:27). *dābār* 'a word, an event' is generally rendered *verbum, sermo* or *res* but sometimes a semantic specification is offered instead: *concilium* 'advice' (Gen 41:37; OL *verba*); *promissum* 'a promise' (Judg 11:10; OL *verbum*); *propositum* 'a plan' (1 Kgs 18:24; OL *verbum*). *bayit* 'a house, home', is generally rendered *domus*, occasionally translated into *domestici* 'domestics' (Prov 31:15), *intrinsecus* 'inside' (Gen 6:14); or *templum* (2 Kgs 10:25), *fanum* (Judg 9:27), *delubrum* (Jer 43:12) when the word refers to a sanctuary (but Hag 1:4 *domus*. Cf. Mic 3:12 vs. 4:1). The standard rendering for *bāśār* 'flesh, meat', *caro*, has been maintained even where the Hebrew word refers to 'all living creatures': *finis universae carnis* 'the end of all flesh' (Gen 6:13; noteworthy that the OL, following the LXX, reads *tempus omnium hominum* 'the time for all men'), but *bāśār* > *verenda* 'the private parts' (Lev 16:4). *lēb* 'heart' generally becomes *cor* (Hos 2:16) but also *mens, anima, conscientia* (Eccl 1:16, 7:26, 23), *cogitatio* (Deut 18:21), and can altogether be lexically disregarded (Gen 50:21; 2 Sam 19:8). Idiomatic expressions are either rendered literally or are transformed: 'in the ears of the people', i.e. with the people listening > *in auribus populi* (Jer 36:13), or *audiente populo* (ib. 36:14); *'iš 'el 'āḥîw* 'a man to his brother', i.e. to one another > *vir . . . frater* (Isa 9:18), or *ad invicem* (Exod 16:15) and *mutuo* (Gen 37:19); similarly, *'iš 'el rē'ēhû* > *vir . . . collega* (Jonah 1:7), or *mutuo* (Exod 18:7). It must be remembered, though, that strange as the literal renderings must have sound to Roman ears unaccustomed to biblical idiomatic usage, after a while, through constant use, the extended meanings were absorbed by the target language, a process which had taken place long before the publication of Jerome's translation. Thus the noteworthy fact is the latter's gradual breaking away from such strange

---

[51] Kaulen, *Handbuch zur Vulgata*, 236. Kedar, 'Wiedergabe'.

sounding literalism rather than his original attachment to it.[52] As a curiosity we may add that the Hebrew idiom 'lay thine hand upon thy mouth' i.e. be silent, was once translated literally (Prov 30:32) but twice the key-word underwent a change from 'hand' to 'finger': *pone digitum super os tuum* (Judg 18:19; OL *impone manum tuam super os tuum*), *superponite digitum ori vestro* (Job 21:5; OL . . . *manum* . . .), obviously in accordance with the more refined Roman manners.

As to literalism in syntactical constructions, suffice it to observe instances of juxtaposition of clauses, and of paronomastic linkage and their linguistic transformation.[53] In Jonah 1:14-16 we find, in close imitation of the Hebrew: *et clamaverunt . . . et dixerunt . . . et tulerunt . . . et miserunt*, whereas in Ruth 4:1d-3a the formally similar verbal forms are rendered thus: *qui divertit . . . et sedit . . . tollens . . . dixit . . . sedentibus . . . locutus est.* ḥlm ḥālôm 'to dream' > *somnia somniare* (Joel 3:1) but *videre somnium* (Gen 40:5); similarly, *laetatus est laetitia magna* 'to rejoice greatly' (Jonah 4:6) but *laetatus est gaudio magno* (1 Chr 29:9), and dozens like that.

In fine, Jerome's translation displays an unevenness with regard to the guiding principle to an extent unknown from any other classical Bible version. Moreover, this unevenness, though somewhat observable in each individual book, becomes most conspicuous on comparing the books with one another. Psalter and Prophets exhibit adherence to the linguistic structure of the source language while Joshua and Judges, Ruth and Esther abound in free renderings. It can hardly be a coincidence that the former were the early products of Jerome's labour, the latter constitute the concluding part: step by step, as Jerome grew more and more assured and practised, he turned his attention to the sense of the complete statement, leaving aside its linguistic constituents.

In order to bring this fact into full relief we first adduce a passage from Jerome's early translation which is yet quite close to the OL.

Jonah 1:5-6

> Then the mariners were afraid, and cried every man unto his god, and cast forth the wares that were in the ship into the sea, to lighten it of them. But Jonah was gone down into the sides of the ship; and he lay, and was fast asleep. So the shipmaster came to him and said unto him etc.

---

[52] A well-known stylistic tendency to be observed in the Vulgate is that of lexical variety; Plater-White: 'Jerome has the tantalizing habit of translating the same Hebrew word by different Latin equivalents' (*Grammar*, 7). Rehm, 'Bedeutung', 192: 'Hieronymus vermeidet es, in inmittelbarer Aufeinanderfolge mehrmals das gleiche Wort zu gebrauchen'. Reuschenbach, 'Hieronymus als Übersetzer', 31-57. Stummer, *Einführung*, 114.

[53] Kedar, *Vulgate*, 252-58.

MT	OL	Vg
וייראו המלחים	et timuerunt nautae timore magno	et timuerunt nautae
ויזעקו	et proclamaverunt	et clamaverunt
איש אל אלהיו	unusquisque ad dominum suum	viri ad deum suum
ויטלו את הכלים	et iactum fecerunt vasorum	et miserunt vasa
אשר באניה	quae erant in navi	quae erant in navi
אל הים להקל מעליהם	in mare ut aleviarentur ab eis	in mare ut adleviaretur ab eis
ויונה ירד	Ionas autem discenderat	et Ionas descendit
אל ירכתי הספינה	in ventrem navis	ad interiora navis
וישכב וירדם:	et dormiebat et stertebat:	et dormiebat sopore gravi:
ויקרב אליו רב החבל	et accensis ad eum gubernator	et accessit ad eum gubernator
ויאמר לו	et dixit ei	et dixit ei

The overall similarity is obvious: The Vg, indeed, gives the impression of a mere recension. Thus it omits the amplification *timore magno* and corrects *stertere* 'to snore' into *sopore gravi* 'a heavy sleep' (cf. Jerome's remark: *Thardema . . . id est gravem et profundum soporem, 'tardēmâ* i.e. a heavy and deep sleep'; *Quaest. Hebr. in Gen 2:21*). From the point of view of Latinity the improvements are: *miserunt,* a synthetic rendering, instead of the analytic *iactum fecerunt* which imitates the causative Hebrew *hiph'il*; and *interiora navis* 'the interior of the boat' instead of *ventrem navis* 'the belly of the boat'. On the other hand, the Hebraism *vir* 'man' for 'everyone', imitative of Hebrew *'îs* 'man; everyone, each' should be noted. This juxtaposition should be compared to that of Gen 37:18-25 cited above where the Vg boldly diverges from the beaten track.

We now proceed to contrast two widely divergent ways of rendering linguistic features as can be observed in the following parallel passages.

		Isa 36:2-38:3	2 Kgs 18:17-20:3
prepositions			
	בתעלת־(הברכה)	36:2 in aquaeductu	18:17 iuxta aquaeductum
	(מרדת) בי	36:5 a me	18:20 Ø
	ביד־(עבדיך)	37:24 in manu	19:23 per manum
	בדר . . . בה	34 in via . . . per eam	33 per viam . . . Ø
lexemes			
	בחיל כבד	36:2 in manu gravi	18:17 cum manu valida
	אשר על הבית	3 qui erat super domum	18 praepositus domum
	תשיב את פני־(פתח)	9 sustinebis faciem	24 potestis resistere
	דבר נא	11 loquere	26 precamur ut loquaris
	באזני העם	in auribus populi	audiente populo
	לא תנתן (העיר)	15 non dabitur	30 non tradetur
	עשו אתי ברכה	16 facite mecum benedictionem	31 facite mecum quod vobis est utile
	דבר	21 verbum	36 quicquam
	ונשאת (תפלה)	37:4 leva	19:4 fac
	נתן (בו רוח)	7 dabo	7 inmittam
	ונתן באש	19 dederunt . . . igni	18 miserunt . . . in ignem
	אחריך	20 post te	21 post tergum
	קצרי יד	27 breviata manu	26 humiles manu
	והטוב בעיניך	38:3 quod bonum est in	20:3 quod placitum est

		oculis tuis	coram te
an euphemistic emendation *(qĕrê)*	שיניהם/מימי רגליהם	36:12 urinam pedum	18:27 urinam
syntactical constructions	וישלח	36:2 et misit	18:17 misit autem
	ויצא	3 et egressus est	18 egressus est autem
	ויאמר	4 et dixit	19 dixitque
	ויהי כשמע	37:1 et factum est cum audisset	19:1 quae cum audisset
	וישכימן בבקר	36 et surrexerunt mane	35 cumque diluculo
	והנה כלם(פגרים מתים)	et ecce omnes	surrexisset vidit omnia
	ויהי הוא משתחוה	38 et factum est cum adoraret	37 cumque adoraret
a paronomastic construction	הבטחון אשר בטחת	36:4 fiducia qua confidis	18:19 fiducia qua niteris
idiomatic redundancy	איש ... איש ... איש	36:16 unusquisque . . . unusquisque . . . unusquisque	18:31 unusquisque . . . Ø Ø
	איש	18 unusquisque	32 Ø
	כי מצות המלך לאמר	36:21 mandaverat enim rex dicens	36 siquidem preaceptum regis accepterant
	כה תאמרון ... לאמר	37:10 dicetis . . . loquentis	19:10 dicite . . . Ø
explanatory additions	ובא בכפו	36:6 intrabit in manu eius	18:21 comminutus ingreditur manum eius
	המבלעדי ה'	10 sine Domino	25 sine Domini voluntate
	כי שמעים אנחנו	11 intellegemus enim	26 siquidem intellegimus hanc linguam
	ואתה תנצל	37:11 et tu poteris liberari	19:11 num ergo solus poteris liberari
	אלהי הגוים	12 dii gentium	12 dii gentium singulos
	והחרישו	21 et siluerunt	36 tacuit itaque
	לפני קמה	27 antequam maturesceret	26 antequam veniret ad maturitatem
redundant information	וירק דשא	27 gramen pascuae	26 virens herba
	תציר גגות	et herba tectorum	tectorum
	פלטת בית יהודה	31 id quod salvatum de domo Iuda	30 et quodcumque reliquum fuerit
	הנשארה	et quod relictum est	de domo Iuda

Evidently, Isa keeps much closer to the Hebrew structur than Kgs. As said before, each method of translating has its merits; and it is precisely in many a literal rendering that Jerome imparts invaluable linguistic insights. This must be said in response to those who limit their praise of the Vg to those portions that are smooth and elegant from the point of view of Latin letters, overlooking the fact that undoubtedly much of the original's pungency has been blunted in such passages; the flavour of the Hebrew Bible seems best preserved in Vg passages that do not give the text in an arbitrary clarity and stylistic elegance. At any rate, with regards to the varying modes of translating within the Vg, suspending judgement, we should content ourselves to register the facts. It may be that in its very variability, linguistic and translational, there lies the attraction of the Vg.

The Imprint of Christian Tenets

The need to amplify a verse where the Hebrew seemed too concise or cryptic; the possibility to compress one that contained redundant constituents; but first and foremost, the ambiguity inherent in each and every linguistic expression, left ample room for interpretations of the text by even such a conscientious a translator as Jerome. Many of these interpretations were, of course, not Jerome's own innovation but rather the reflection of exegetical traditions that had grown through the centuries.

Of the Christian application of the OT Jerome was deeply convinced; specific evidence if one needed it, is amply found on every page of his commentaries: e.g. on Isa 19:3-15 (4, 203-206) Jesus Christ is mentioned not less than eight times. The Bible text, as interpreted by Jerome, also proves, of course, that the Christian Church holds the true faith whereas the Jews, their prayers and customs, are of the devil (6, 14, 22 etc.).[54] Thus he remarks on the verse 'That unto me every knee shall bow' (Isa 45:23) that such indeed was the custom of Christians while the Jews, revealing their haughty mind, did not practice it (4, 543). Another example: Jerome, in his rendering of the Psalter had substituted the terms *congregatio, coetus* 'congregation, assembly' for the loan-word *synagoga* of the OL; only once did he leave this word intact, namely Ps 106 (105):18-19 where the word refers to the party of Dathan and Abiram who rebelled against the leadership of Moses, i.e. against God's will; for such a rebellious crowd the word *synagoga* appeared to him appropriate.

It is the more remarkable then, in view of his fervent belief and unshakeable convictions, that Jerome admitted, nay kept insisting that the OT also contained information about actual historic events besides predictions of the coming of

---

[54] Jerome was ever ready to condemn violently and indiscriminately whatever, at that precise moment of his theological career, appeared to him like heresy. It is not surprising therefore, to find in his writings many venomous statements against Judaism and the Jews: their stubbornness is the outcome not of any innate inclination but of their own volition (7, 88); God, far from being their protector, has become their enemy and rejects them (4, 745; 6, 104); their synagogue is equal to fornication and adultery, their ceremonies are harmful to Christians (6, 14; 1, 741), in their traditions lurks the Antichrist (4, 705); they persecute the Church (7, 389). The Jews attempt to remove any christological reference from the Prophets' words (4, 580) but their knowledge and learning is in vain (7, 734), and so on.

Christ; and that any christological interpretation was admissible only to the extent that it was philologically justifiable. On Isa 17:7-8 he censures those who deem the words to be fulfilled in the time of Christ: the interpreters' pious disposition had eclipsed the historic dimension (4, 195). In the same vein he disapproves of the current popular etymology according to which Aramaic *Pascha* 'Passover; Easter' derives from Greek *paschein* 'to suffer', and thus denotes the Passion; the word comes from Hebrew *psḥ* 'to pass by', Jerome explains (4, 423-424), and thus means *transitus* 'a going over; a passage'. The Latin spelling of the place-name *Boṣrâ*, namely *Bosra*, had misled many to combine it with Hebrew *bâśâr* 'flesh' and find in it a reference to Christs' body. This widespread pious error (*multi pio errore lapsi*; 4, 746) is due, as Jerome points out, to a confusion of *Ṣādê* with *Śîn*. Even discussing the crucial verse 'Behold, a virgin shall conceive' (Isa 7:14) Jerome admits that the Hebrew word *'almâ*, employed in this verse, was not the usual one for 'virgin'; this would have been *bĕtûlâ*. Yet, according to Jerome (4, 108), the proper etymology of *'almâ* vindicates the Christian interpretation: The root *'lm* means 'to hide, conceal' and thus the word under review denotes 'a maiden hidden from the view of men', i.e. a virgin.

Wherever language leaves room for a Christological acceptation, Jerome of course propounds it. Thus he tends to render the homonym *kar* – which denotes either 'a lamb' or 'pastures' – *agnus* 'a lamb', even where the other meaning seems appropriate (Isa 30:23). The Christological application of the word under review is brought into relief Isa 16:1; Jerome rejects the historically legitimate rendering 'send a lamb to the ruler' (*emitte agnum dominatori*; 4, 269) but rather equates the lamb with the ruler: *emitte agnum dominatorem terrae*, 'send the lamb, the ruler of the earth', a translation which is meant to confirm the tenet that judgement of this world has been given to the Son by the Father (*non enim pater iudicat quemquam, sed omne iudicium dedit filio*; 4, 271). An explicit reference to the death of Jesus is introduced into the translation of the verse 'and his rest shall be glorious' (Isa 11:10) where the Vg has 'his sepulchre' (*sepulcrum eius*) for 'rest, resting-place'. Jerome admits that by substituting 'grave' for 'sleep, rest' (*pro dormitione et requie*) he intended to make the sense clearer to the reader (4, 161). Jerome who takes Prov 8:22 as referring to Jesus explains that the Hebrew verb *qnh* which may denote either 'to create' or 'to possess' should be understood in the latter sense in this context (4, 351; Vg *dominus possedit me*); thus the Arians' conception is philologically refuted. In the same vein Jerome introduced the following correction: Ps 8:6 states that the human being, or rather 'the son of man', is only a little lower than *'elōhîm* 'God'. The latter word had been rendered by the ancient Latin Psalters – in the wake of the LXX – 'angels' (*paulo minus ab angelis*); Jerome in whose opinion the Ps alluded to Jesus (7, 461) who is God made man, felt free to restore the original wording: *paulo minus a deo*.

The root *yš'* offered Jerome the opportunity to introduce the name of Jesus into the text of the OT: Hab 3:18 'I will joy in the God of my salvation (*yš'y*); Vg

. . . *in deo iesu meo* 'in God, my Jesus'. Previously (5, 13) there had been mentioned the *māšîaḥ* 'the anointed (ruler)' as the object of God's deliverance. Jerome renders the word as usual, *christus*, but through a linguistically forced interpretation of the nota accusativa *'et* as 'with' turns the Anointed into the active saviour: *egressus es . . . in salutem cum christo tuo* 'Thou art come forth . . . for the deliverance with Thine Christ'. Jerome is happy to note that even Aquila who generally preferred the Greek rendering *eleimmenos* 'an anointed one', this time had opted for *christos* (6, 655-656).

It is in consequence of the Christian faith in the OT that Jerome hated and bitterly attacked people like Marcion and the adherents of Manichaeism who refused to accept this old portion of the Scriptures and 'with rabid mouth tear the Old Law to pieces' (3, 480).

The Influence of Jewish Exegesis

If Christian faith proved the fundamental exegetical guide, the influence of Jewish exegetical traditions is noticeable in innumerable smaller details of Jerome's translation and commentaries. Considerations of space permit us to adduce no more than a handful of examples out of the practically unlimited stock.

Already in his treatise on Hebrew names, Jerome had displayed his philological interest which, crude as it was, faithfully reflected conceptions and methods of his Jewish contemporaries; he remained faithful to this way of linguistic interpretation. The name of the land Hadrach (Zech 9:1) is explained: 'sharp and gentle' (*acutum, molle*; 6, 856) on the base of Hebrew *ḥad* and *rak*, respectively; the words of the Lord are sharp to the wicked and gentle to the just, he remarks. Jewish tradition offers an almost identical exposition: sharp to the heathen, gentle to Israel (*Sifre Deut* 1, p. 7; Rashi *ad loc*).

Proper names are of course usually transliterated in the Vg but sometimes an explanatory remark is added (e.g. Ruth 1:20) or an etymologizing rendition is given: Thus the city name *'ûr kaśdîm* 'Ur of the Chaldees' is transliterated *Ur Chaldeorum* in Genesis (e.g. 11:28) but somehow etymologically interpreted *de igne Chaldeorum* 'out of the fire of the Chaldees' in Nehemiah (9:7); the latter reflects an old midrash (cf. Rashi on Gen *loc. cit.*).[55] Similarly, the place-name Achzib is explained as derived from the root *kzb* 'to lie': *(domus) mendacii* '(house) of falsehood' (Mic 1:14) to which Ibn Ezra's comment that the word is not to be taken as a place-name should be compared. When Jerome translates the name Elhanan, the son of Jaare: *adeodatus filius saltus* (2 Sam 21:19), this constitutes an implicit commentary that this is not really a person's name but rather a sobriquet of David (cf. Tg. Yonatan and Rashi). Jerome transliterates

---

[55] In his commentary on Genesis Jerome elaborates the Jewish tradition ('tradunt autem Hebraei . . .') according to which Abraham, having refused to worship the fire, was thrown into the flames but saved by God ('dei auxilio liberatus de idololatriae igne profugerit'; 3, 323); cf. *Pirkei de-R. Eliezer* 26.

the cryptic name *šēšak* (Jer 25:26; 51:41) but he is acquainted with the rabbinical tradition that takes it as a cypher for Babel on a system that substitutes the last letter of the alphabet for the first, the penultimate (s) for the second (b) and so on (4, 1019). On philological grounds, mistaken though, he renders *nešef* (Isa 21:4) Babylon since he thought to find the same root in the word *nišpeh* (ib. 13:1-2) which refers to Babel. Jerome is prone to offer etymological renderings when a word is rare and difficult. *sōkēn* 'a steward' is rendered *qui habitat in tabernaculo* (Isa 22:15), as if derived from *sukkâ* 'a tabernacle'; the same derivation is found in Aquila and Symmachus (*skēnounta* and *skēnopoiounta* respectively, from *skēnē* 'a tabernacle'). *rōzēn* 'a prince' is translated *princeps* (Judg 5:3) but also *secretorum scrutator* 'an investigator of secrets' (Isa 40:23), as if this word and *rāz* 'secret' were linked. This assumed etymology also explains the Latin wording for *rāzî lî rāzî lî* (Isa 24:16) 'my leanness, my leanness (? or 'I waste away, I waste away'?): *secretum meum secretum meum* 'my secret . . .' This indeed is also the view of Jewish translators (Tg. Yonatan, Symmachus) and commentators (cf. Rashi. But Kimhi differs). Now and then Jerome attempts to reflect the presumptive etymology of a verb in a periphrastic rendering. Thus *šḥr* 'to seek' *desiderare* (Prov 7:15), *vigilare* (Job 24:5) but also *consurgere diluculo* 'to rise in the morning' (Prov 11:27), *de mane vigilare* 'to watch from early morning' (Isa 26:9) because of *šaḥar* 'the dawn'; similarly, *plh* 'to distinguish' > *miraculo dividere* 'to distinguish by a miracle' (Exod 11:7; but cf. ib. 33:16) because of *pele'* 'a miracle'; and *mrh* 'to rebel' > *ad amaritudinem concitare* 'to rouse up into bitterness' (hos 14:1; but cf. Num 14:9) because of *mar* 'bitter'.[56]

Many words are translated according to rabbinic explanation; in some instances Jerome explicitly states this to be the case, while in others it becomes obvious from parallel expositions in Jewish writings. The word *geber* 'man', usually rendered *vir* or *homo*, is once translated *gallus gallinaceus* 'a poultry-cock' (Isa 22:17) – *geber* 'cock' is attested only in post-biblical Hebrew – because, as Jerome tells us, 'the Hebrew who instructed me in the studies of the oT had offered this explanation' (4, 318); the medieval commentators, one should add, know of this lexical equation and some accept it (cf. Rashi and Kimhi *ad loc.*) *'rṣ* 'to fear; to frighten' is rendered *praedicare* 'to praise' (Isa 29:23) to which *Pirkei de-R. Eliezer* 4 should be compared. The rendering *ništā 'â* > *loquamur* 'let us talk' (ib. 41:23) against the usual *š'h* > *respicere* 'to look about', is based upon the Aramaic sense of the root; this parallels the explanation given by Rashi and Kimhi. Jerome having asked his Jewish informant, was instructed that the meaning of *qeset* (Ezek 9:2-11), was that of Greek

---

[56] Jerome who mockingly criticizes Aquila's attempts to render not just the foreign vocable but also its etymology (*Ep.* 57:11), is himself prone to etymologizing rendition: *qāmâ* 'corn' > *seges* Deut 16:9 but *stantes segetes* 'standing corn' (Exod 22:6) because of *qwm* 'to stand'; *mělûnâ*, 'hut, cottage' > *tugurium* (Isa 1:8) but also *tabernaculum unius noctis* 'a hut for one night' (Isa 24:20) because of the linkage to *lyn* 'to pass the night'; *(ša'ar) šalleket* > *(porta) quae duxit* '(the gate) leading to . . .' deriving it from *lkt* 'to walk, go' and the like.

kalmarion (*graeco sermone apellari kalmarion*; 5, 94), i.e. 'an inkstand' which he then rendered *atramentarium*. In passing it should be mentioned that the loan-word *kalmarin* 'inkstand' occurs in the Mishna.[57] Some important conclusions regarding his reliance upon Jewish informants may be drawn from Jerome's report just mentioned. First, he was in a position to receive what appears an on-the-spot information from a learned Jew when he needed it, and secondly, their common language sometimes, if not always, was Greek. These conclusions are confirmed by additional observations. On the *hapax legomenon kāpîs* (Hab 2:11) Jerome remarks that it denotes 'a beam in the middle of a building to uphold its walls; in common Greek language *himantosis*' (6, 617). The Latin paraphrase of the Greek word (on which cf. Sir 22:16) makes the impression of an ad-hoc Latin translation of an oral Greek explanation; the Vg puts it somewhat more elegantly: *(lignum) quod inter iuncturas aedificiorum est*. A conclusive indication as to Jerome's work-procedure we may find in the following instance of a mistaken translation: The word *ḥôl* 'sand', in the verse 'I shall multiply my days as *ḥôl*' (Job 29:18) is rendered *palma* 'a palm(-tree)': *et sicut palma multiplicabo dies*. This deviation cannot be explained as dependent upon the LXX (though the verse contains *stelechos phoinikos* 'the stem of a palm-tree', it diverges widely from the Hebrew text and the Vg); Jewish tradition, however, offers a clue since it also ascribes an extraordinary meaning to the word *ḥôl* in this verse, namely as denoting the miraculous bird that is consumed by a fire in its nest but then comes to life again (cf. *B.T. Sanhedrin* 108b; Jewish commentators; *Gen Rabba* 19:5, p. 174: '. . . .except one bird called *ḥôl* etc.'). This, of course, corresponds with the fabulous bird Phoenix, the *phoinix* of the Greek. This Greek word, however, did have an additional meaning: 'a palm-tree'.[58] It seems, then, that Jerome's Jewish consultant pointed out that the usual equation *ḥôl* 'sand' was not appropriate in this case and then explained the required sense in Greek: *phoinix*, meaning the bird, of course. Jerome, however, – perhaps with the LXX in the back of his mind – misinterpreted the information, thinking of the alternative meaning 'a palm-tree' and translated accordingly. This again testifies to the oral consultations and also to the haste in which they were conducted. Indeed, not infrequently we find evidence that Jerome did not bother – or find the time – to look up passages he wanted to quote. On Hos 4:14 where he had translated *qĕdēšôt* 'harlots', *effeminati* ('effeminates that submit to unnatural lust'), Jerome reminds his readers (6, 41) that Isa 3:4 also contains the word *effeminati* – which is correct – as a translation of Hebrew *qĕdēšîm* – which is not correct! The Hebrew word there is a completely different one *(ta'ălûlîm)*. Evidently he had reconstructed the text from memory.

---

[57] '. . . the *qalmarin* ('inkstand') of Yosef, the priest' (*M. Mikwaot* 10:1).
[58] LXX *stelechos phoinikos*; this composite expression is rendered by Jerome *arbor palmae* (*Iob ex Graeco*; 10, 82). This and the widely divergent wording of the whole verse in the LXX make it highly improbable that Jerome followed the Greek.

Analytical renderings of supposed compounds reflect Jewish tradition: *ṣlmwt* > *umbra mortis* 'shadow of death' (Job 3:5 and freq.) parallels the Greek versions and the masoretic vocalization; *qiqālôn* 'utter disgrace' (Hab 2:16; probably an emphatic form of *qālôn* 'disgrace' > *vomitus ignominiae* 'the vomitting of disgrace' as if spelled *qî' qālōn* parallels *Esther Rabba* 3 and Kimhi *ad loc.*[59] Many amplifications in the Vg betray their Jewish origin. The word *hamma'ămîqîm* 'those that go deep' (Isa 29:15) is rendered *qui profundi estis corde* 'who are deep in their heart'; this corresponds exactly with Ibn Ezra's comment: '. . . in the depth of their heart'. The clause 'where is he that weighed' (ib. 33:18) is expressed in Latin: *ubi legis verba ponderans* 'where is he that weighs the words of the law'; exactly like *B.T. Hagiga* 15b: 'they weighed the light and the grave matters of the Law'. The words 'too short is the bed to stretch oneself on it' (ib. 28:20) are rendered thus: *coangustum est enim stratum ut alter decidat* 'the bed is so narrow that one of the two will fall'; thus also *B.T. Yoma* 9b: 'too short . . . as that two friends could stretch themselves on it at the same time'. In his commentary Jerome explains this saying slightly differently (4, 382): 'This is a metaphor . . . the husband says to his adulterous wife: The one bed cannot hold myself and the adulterer with you'. A like elaboration on this verse we find *Lev Rabba* 17:7 'The bed cannot hold a woman and her husband and her lover'.

It probably was his acquaintance with the actual conditions prevailing in Palestine that caused explanatory renderings such as *kěna'ănî* > *mercator* 'merchant' (Zech 14:21) instead of the usual *chananaeus* 'Canaanite'; *'ărābî* > *latro* 'robber' (Jer 3:2) instead of the usual *arabs* 'an Arab'; and the explanation of Hebrew *bōrît* 'soap' (Jer 2:22) as a vegetable used by the walkers in the Palestinian province (4, 851).

Jerome was well aware of rhetoric devices employed in the Bible and he points out metaphorical and metonymical figures of speech as well as irony and hyperbole (6, 596, 956; 7, 620 and passim). It is not surprising then to find the clear recognition of the fact that the Bible employs words and measurements according to human custom: *humanae consuetudinis verbis utitur atque mensuris* 4, 487). He is referring to the description of God's workmanship Isa 40:12. On this same verse Kimhi remarks that it has to be taken metaphorically. The Christian father and the Jewish erudite agree with the talmudic dictum: 'The Scriptures speak the language of man' (*B.T. Berakhot* 31b).

The Contribution of the Latin Versions

In conclusion, the influential role played by the Latin translations in the cultural history of mankind deserves to be mentioned. Through the Old Latin version – or versions –, region after region of the greatest empire the West had ever seen,

---

[59] Kimhi: '*qiqālōn* is composed of *qî* 'vomitting' and *qālōn* 'disgrace'; this refers to the drunkard etc.'; *Esther Rabba* 3: 'vomitting on his upper body, disgracing his lower parts'.

became acquainted with the Bible. The Old Latin was perhaps the base of the Old Slavonic translation, and portions and whole books of it found their way into what later on became the standard Latin Bible, the Vulgate. This latter version, with regard to the books of the OT one man's translation made from the Hebrew, must be considered a great and definitely a most influential literary accomplishment. Jerome's Vulgate accompanied the Western Church as it emerged to its dominant position; it was the focus of theological debates and scholarly studies. The early Bible translations into European vernaculars are based upon it. This is not merely a matter of quantitative diffusion: Europe had risen to predominance in human history, a rank it would hold for centuries to come. Consequently, it was the world which the Scriptures in their Latin dress set out to conquer. Israelite and Jewish emotion and thought from earliest beginnings on down to the times of Jesus, were passed on unto the new centres of civilization and their letters. Dozen of fundamental concepts and a thousand phrases were transferred from Hebrew into Latin, and then from Latin into modern tongues.[60] The Hebraic spirit, its essence and its form, poured into Latin molds put its imprint on all subsequent human affairs.

Bibliography

TEXTS

SABATIER, *Bibliorum Sacrorum Latinae Versiones Antiquae* (1739-1743, the so-called new edition, Paris 1751, is a mere reprint). This work, published in three volumes, remains the only full collection of the fragments of the Old Latin translations of the OT – vls. 1 and 2 – and the NT. In view of the ample material that has come to light since those days it is very antiquated. As to an updated edition cf. Vetus Latina.

Novum Testamentum Domini . . . latine, ed. WORDSWORTH-WHITE et alii (1889-1954). This text-critical edition of the NT Vulgate adduces the ancient variants in its apparatus criticus.

Itala, ed. JÜLICHER-MATZKOW-ALAND (1938-1963; 2nd ed. 1970-76). This edition of the Gospels summarizes the relevant textual studies.

Vetus Latina, ed. FISCHER et alii (1949-   ). The Benedictine abbey at Beuron has undertaken to publish an updated 'Sabatier' utilising the new material available and conforming to stricter standards of textual criticism. Thus far besides volume 1 describing the MSS there have been published from the OT Genesis, and from the NT the Catholic Epistles.

Vetus Latina Hispana, ed. AYUSO MARAZUELA (Madrid 1953-   ). The editor who maintains that there existed an independent ancient Latin translation in

---

[60] The medieval Jewish Bible exegetes and commentators were well acquainted with Jerome's Vulgate; cf. Rahmer, *Hebräische Traditionen*, 13.

Spain has undertaken to publish the relevant MSS. Besides the introductory vol. 1 there have been published the vols. on the Octateuch and the one on the Psalter.

Biblia Sacra . . . ad codicum fidem . . . ord. S. Benedicti edita (1926-   ). This edition of the Vulgate offers an almost complete picture of the variant textual traditions in its comprehensive apparatus criticus. Sixteen vls. have been published; the portion of the OT and the Apocrypha is practically complete. On the principles that guided the Benedictine scholars responsible for this monumental work cf. GASQUET, 'Vulgate', 515-20 and QUENTIN, *Mémoire.*

Biblia Sacra iuxta Vulgatam versionem, ed. WEBER et alii (1969). A masterly executed and convenient hand edition of the Vulgate.

VERCELLONE, *Variae Lectiones Vulgatae Latinae Bibliorum Editionis* (1860-64). A collation of variants of a portion of the Vulgate, namely the Historical Books as far as Kings.

The commonly printed text of the Vulgate is that of the Catholic Church's official edition prepared under pope Clement VIII (1593). This Clementine edition differs in many details from Jerome's genuine translation. A reliable reprint of the Clementine Vulgate Bible was published by VERCELLONE, *Biblia Sacra Vulgatae Editionis* (1861).

There are thousands of extant Vulgate MSS; cf. the extensive list of the most important ones and their description WHITE, 'Vulgate', 886-89. A collation of the ancient Codex Amiatinus throughout the OT was published by HEYSE and TISCHENDORF in 1873 *(Biblia Sacra Latina).*

Old Latin texts of the OT supplementing Sabatier's edition were published and commented by RANKE (fragments of the Pentateuch and the Prophets), ROBERT (parts of the Heptateuch), DOLD (Prophets, also portions of the Gospels), BELSHEIM (parts of Gen, Exod, Lev), SCHILDENBERGER (Prov), WEBER (Ps; Chr). Cf. also KENNEDY, 'Latin Versions', 49-53. Since 1940 *Biblica* has reported in a special section of its bibliographical review on newly published Old Latin texts.

HISTORY

KAULEN, *Geschichte* and STUMMER, *Einführung* describe origin and history of the Vulgate but are also informative with regard to the Old Latin version. BERGER, *Histoire* is the classic work on the history of the Vulgate after Jerome's death; it also adduces many examples of mixed text-forms in MSS, i.e. Vulgate MSS which exhibit Old Latin texts in marginal notes or conflate readings, and sometimes in entire books of the Bible. On the history of the Old Latin version also cf. SCHÄFER, *Die altlateinische Bibel* and STENZEL, 'Zur Frühgeschichte'.

With regard to the biographical background of Jerome's work his biographies by BARDENHEWER, *Geschichte*, GRÜTZMACHER, *Hieronymus* and CAVALLERA, *St. Jérôme* should be consulted. His scholarly competence is discussed by SPARKS,

'Jerome' and BARR, 'St. Jerome'. Jerome's philological principle of translation (vs. Augustine's inspirational principle) is accurately brought out in full relief by SCHWARZ, *Principles*, 25-37.

For the works of Jerome the edition of Vallarsi (11 vols. 1734-42) is still valuable. The new edition within the *Corpus Christianorum (Series Latina)*, CCL vols. 73 (1959) – 79 (1982) is critically an improvement upon Vallarsi but incomplete as yet; vol. 73, pp. IX-LII contains a very extensive, classified bibliography.

PHILOLOGY

On Christian Latinity cf. SOUTER, *Glossary*, BLAISE, *Manuel* and the thorough study by MOHRMANN, Études. With regard to the lingual peculiarities found in the Latin versions the following studies should be consulted: RÖNSCH, *Itala und Vulgata*, KAULEN, *Handbuch zur Vulgata* and PLATER-WHITE, *Grammar*. BILLEN, *Old Latin Texts* offers a detailed study of the vocabulary found in the texts of the Heptateuch. Most of the above mentioned editors of OL texts comment on linguistic facts: ROBERT offers an examination of the grammar, the spelling, and the neologisms of the text (pp. XLI-LXXXV, CXXIII-CXXVIII), RANKE supplies many notes on grammar (pp. 412-27).

The view that the earliest Latin translation was based on an original Hebrew text was put forward by BLONDHEIM, *Les parlers* and accepted in a modified form by others; cf. ROBERTS, *Text and Versions*, 238-39, STUMMER, 'Lateinische Bibel'. Jewish traditions in Jerome's translation and commentaries have been discussed by RAHMER, *Hebräische Traditionen* and STUMMER, 'Spuren', 'Beiträge'.

The process and methods of translation with regard to the Vulgate were examined and described by REUSCHENBACH, *Hieronymus als Übersetzer*, REHM, 'Bedeutung', KEDAR, *The Vulgate*. A moot question is the text-critical aid to be derived from the Latin versions. In view of the variety of text-forms it is impossible to establish a linkage between the one hypothetical Old Latin and one specific Greek text-tradition; what is needed is an examination of the text-forms for each individual book. Thus, despite the fact that the earliest Latin translation of the OT must have been made from a pre-hexaplaric Septuagint, it has been noted that the OL text of Sam and Kgs often coincide with Lucianic readings; cf. FISCHER, 'Lukian-Lesarten'. The value of Jerome's Vulgate for the textual criticism of the Hebrew Bible has frequently been denied, e.g. STUMMER, Einführung, 123; NOTH, *Welt*, 257 and 284; DE SAINT-MARIE, *Richesses*, 151 and many others. This view, however, oversimplifies the issue: in innumerable minute details the Vulgate points to Hebrew variants; cf. NOWACK, *Bedeutung*; SMITH, 'Value'; MARKS, *Textkritische wert*; KEDAR, 'Divergent Hebrew'.

Further reference should be made to the standard works and encyclopaedic articles on Bible versions of which the following deserve special mention; they also embody copious bibliographies. ROBERTS, *Text and Versions*, 237-46 (Old Latin), 247-65 (Vulgate), 310-14 (bibliography). *A Dictionary of the Bible* (ed. Hastings): KENNEDY, 'Latin Versions', 3, 47-62, WHITE, 'Vulgate', 5, 873-90. *Dictionnaire de la Bible*: MÉCHINEAU, 'Latines (Versions)', 4, 96-123; MANGENOT, 'Vulgate', 5, 2456-99. *DBS*: BOTTE, 'Vulgate', 5, 334-47. *Theologische Realenzyklopädie*: REICHMANN, 'Vetus Latina (NT)', 6, 172-76; BROCK, 'Vetus Latina (AT)' ib. 177-78; REICHMANN, 'Vulgata', ib. 178-81.

Chapter Ten

Use, Authority and Interpretation of Mikra at Qumran

Michael Fishbane

Introduction

Almost with the first publication of the documents found in and around the
Dead Sea, attempts were made to appreciate and evaluate their exegetical
content.[1] As Dupont-Sommer, one of the early writers on the Qumran scrolls
was quick to observe, in this remarkable corpus Mikra was subject to an
'immense labeur exégétique'.[2] Here, then, one could begin to glimpse something
of the context out of which ancient Judaism, and its vast exegetical enterprise,
was formed. To be sure, a sense of this had long been noted and its value
assured. Quite well known, for example, were the inner-controversies among
the earliest Pharisaic sages on assorted exegetical points;[3] the diverse (if not
highly stylized) exegetical contestations between the Pharisees and other
groups (like the Sadducees, Samaritans and Boethusians);[4] and the other
exegetical productions – like the book of *Jubilees* – whose homiletical style and
legal content could not easily be aligned with the known Pharisaic literature.[5]
Indeed, even the historical work of Josephus, in which is found the famous
account of several ancient Jewish 'philosophies' (the Pharisees, Sadducees and
Essenes) distinguished by exegetical differences, is itself replete with exegetical
features and traditions.[6] What the evidence of the Dead Sea scrolls offers then –
and, indeed, offers in abundance – is primary and hitherto unknown documentation from this milieu of ancient Jewish exegesis. Not only is this material
distinct from the Pharisaic mainstreams known to us, but it also provides direct

[1] Cf. Brownlee, 'Biblical Interpretation'; Wieder, 'Habakkuk Scroll'; Vermes, 'Commentaires
bibliques'; Brownlee, 'Habakkuk Midrash'; and Osswald, 'Zur Hermeneutik'.
[2] Dupont-Sommer, *Les Ecrits esséniens*, 319.
[3] Cf. e.g. *M. Eduyot* 1:1-3; *M. Yadayim* 4:6-8; *B.T. Shabbat* 17a, 88b. In *Avot de-R. Natan* A12
(end p. 56), an individual who did not know the exegesis of purity as practiced in R. Yohanan's circle
was chided: 'If this is how you have practiced, you have never eaten heave-offerings in your life'.
[4] Cf. e.g. *M. Menahot* 10:3; *T. Menahot* 10:23; *B.T. Menahot* 65a-66b; *B.T. Rosh ha-Shana* 13a;
and Jos. *Ant.* 13:293-98.
[5] See Albeck, *Das Buch der Jubiläen*. Cf. Nickelsburg, 'Bible Rewritten' 99-100.
[6] See I. Heinemann, 'Josephus' Method'; and Rappaport, *Agada und Exegese*. Cf. Feldman,
below, pp. 000-00.

attestation to the vital role played by the interpretation of Mikra in the formation of ancient Jewish communities.

For the communities in and around Qumran, the Mikra of ancient Israel was
a cherished inheritance. Virtually every book of this corpus is attested in long
scrolls or assorted scraps (save the scroll of Esther), and were subject to a vast
labor of learning and elaboration. This was no mere antiquarian exercise on
their part. For the covenanteers who called their community a 'house of Tora'
(*CD* 7:10), this effort was rather part of a living commitment to the truth and
significance of Mikra, a corpus of divine teachings whose correct interpretation
provided *the* way of salvation (*CD* 14:1f.) and *the* knowledge of the divine plan
for history (*1QpHab* 2:6-10). Mikra thus contained the concrete basis for
proper action and requited hope, not solely because it contained the revealed
teachings of God through Moses and the prophets, but particularly because the
community believed itself alone to possess the proper understanding of the
ancient laws and prophecies contained therein. The covenanteers of Qumran
thus lived the Law of Moses and longed for the Day of the Lord: in resolute
confidence that their interpretation of Mikra were true and certain.[7]

The documents of Qumran thus attest to a dual commitment: a commitment
to the truth of the Tora and the prophecies (that of Moses and his prophetic
successors), and a commitment to the truth of their interpretation of the Tora
and the prophecies (that of the founding 'Interpreter of the Tora' and his
succesor[s] the 'Teacher of Righteousness'). There was, then, both Mikra and
its Interpretation, as guided by the head teacher and those authorized to
interpret under his guidence (or the exegetical principles laid down by him). In
this matter, too, the Qumranians were part and parcel of the exegetical milieu
of nascent Judaism. Like them, the different Pharisaic fellowships were also
organized around teachers and their interpretations of Mikra. Indeed, even
within the fairly broad consensus of ancient Pharisaic teachings, and the (eventually formulated) ultimate divine authority for its modes of interpretation (*M.
Avot* 1:1), sharp disagreements and even disarming confusion over its diverse
results abound.[8] Depending on the issues, differences of interpretation could
also be – and were – the basis for communal subdivisions and splits.[9] Such
features are also highly characteristic of our Qumran sources, as we shall yet
see, and many other contemporary analogues could be adduced. Here it may
suffice to recall that in the traditions that developed around Jesus and his
followers a main ingredient was the centrality of the Teacher, along with the
convincing or distinctive character of his interpretations of Mikra.[10] Clearly, at

---

[7] This was the normative ideology, from which those of 'little faith' defected; cf. *1QpHab* 2:1-10.

[8] See above, n. 3.

[9] This is particularly true in matters of food piety, around which a special Pharisaic fellowship
developed. For the pertinent rabbinic sources and a comparison with Qumran materials, see Rabin,
Qumran Scrolls.

[10] Cf. Matt 15:1-3; Mark 7:1-3; 1 Tim 6:3-4; Col 2:8.

this time, neither the shape of Pharisaic Judaism nor the temper of its exegetical program had been definitively set. Still and all, two points are abundantly clear:

(1) the style of Judaism which one chose was directly related to the style and methods of its exegetical tradition; and

(2) the authority of this tradition was the basis for the contentions anent the value and truth of the Judaisms at hand.

We are thus presented with a vast exegetical *oeuvre* in ancient Judaism – one of intense and immense significance – of which the productions of the Qumran covenanteers is a valuable addition. It will therefore not be surprising to observe that these interpreters of Mikra utilized many modes of exegesis characteristic of the early Pharisaic sages. For despite the more formalized character of the latter, the fact is that their earliest exegetical efforts overlap with those of the covenanteers. In addition, precisely because of the more formal character of the Pharisaic traditions, these latter provide a foil against which the more rudimentary expressions of Mikra interpretation in the scrolls can be perceived. The issue, then, is not to project Pharisaic methods of interpretation into the Qumran sources, but to utilize them (where appropriate) for reconstructing or isolating related (and contemporary) exegetical features. By the same token, both the Pharisaic and Qumran exegetical traditions can also be viewed as heirs to the earlier exegetical efforts of ancient Israel, efforts which, in their final creative and editorial stages at least, overlap these productions of ancient Judaism. For indeed, if the exegetical works of the Pharisees and Qumranians presuppose a received and authoritative Mikra, this latter is also a repository of the exegetical labor of the scribes and sages of ancient Israel. And if the former represent the earliest interpretations of Mikra as a foundation document *for* Judaism, 'inner-Biblical' exegesis represents interpretations of Mikra as a document *in formation*.[11] It will therefore be of interest to place the interpretations found in the scrolls at the cross-roads of these two great cultural stadia: ancient Israel and rabbinic Judaism. Hereby, its common and unique exegetical patterns and assumptions, the use, interpretations and notions of authority of Mikra at Qumran, can be brought into comparative perspective.

A final introductory word is in order about the categories to be employed here. For while such terms as 'use', 'authority' and 'interpretation' (in the title) provide the means for an analytical description of the role of Mikra at Qumran, such a classification must not obscure the fundamental interrelationships between them. Every use of Mikra, it may be argued, is also a reuse of it in some way, and presupposes certain notions of authority. Similarly, the notions of authority of Mikra which exist variously condition the nature, style and manner of presentation of the interpretations brought to bear on it. Accordingly, the static nature of the categories taken separately consistently presupposes their

---

[11] On the whole phenomenon, see Fishbane, *Biblical Interpretation*.

dynamic correlation. This consideration is all the more vital given the variety of materials to be analyzed. They differ in genre and form; in technique and terminology; and in time and tradition. Accordingly, to speak of the Qumran scrolls in monolithic terms – whether in ideology, communal formation, or uses of Mikra – would be to blanche the evidence. Moreover, if the texts are themselves diverse, their historical attribution is, in many cases, well-nigh inscrutable. For whether the *Rule Scroll* and the *Damascus Document* represent two phases of one community, or the disciplines and ideologies of several, and whether or not the contents and styles of these latter are related to the so-called *Temple Scroll*, are not matters given to clear or final determination. But since some estimation of these social-historical questions – further compounded by the questionable relationship between the covenanteers and the Essenes, based on what is known about them from Josephus and Philo – has a vital bearing on the problems to be discussed here, it seems prudent to use the diverse materials at hand primarily as evidence for *types* of use, authority and interpretation of Mikra in and around Qumran, not as evidence for one sectarian community at any one time.

Mikra and its Uses

MIKRA AS A TEXTUAL ARTIFACT

A consideration of the uses of Mikra in the Qumran scrolls must begin with a recognition of its priviledged presence as a *textual artifact*. As is well-known, the caves of the Judaean desert have yielded a vast treasure trove of hand copies of 'biblical' books. These represent the oldest manuscripts of the Hebrew Bible in our possession, with all the books of the later masoretic canon represented except for the scroll of Esther. Most of these manuscripts are preserved only in smallish scraps, or at best in several columns of texts representing a short sequence of chapters, sometimes continuous, sometimes not (depending on whether the columns are from one section of leather or from several which melded as the rolled document decomposed). The preservation of an entire book, like the great Isaiah scroll *(1QIsaᵃ)*, is a rarity. But despite the inconsistent and incomplete evidence, there is no doubt that the preservation of Mikra was a matter of great scribal care and tradition. Great care was taken to write the texts in a clear hand; and, despite some paleographic variations over the course of time, the so-called square script in the Herodian style shows signs of stability and conventionality. The use of the older paleo-Hebrew script for writing the Tetragram in some of the sectarian compositions[12] probably represents a convention for rendering the Divine Name in a nonsacral manner, alongside such other conventions as marking four dots or writing the eu-

---

[12] Siegel, 'Paleo-Hebrew Characters'. Cf. Demsky, above, p. 10.

phemistic *hw'h'* (*1QS* 8:14). The consistent use of the paleo-Hebrew script in some manuscripts of biblical books, like *4QpaleoEx^m* (on Exodus), presumably derives from other Palestinian scribal traditions,[13] and is quite different from the majority of Pentateuchal manuscripts found at Qumran.[14]

Evidence for scribal care and conventionality in the treatment of *Mikra-as-artifact* is also reflected in such matters as the incising of transverse lines and the way the letters were 'hung' on them, as well as in such matters as line-length and spacing between letters and words. Such considerations were of very great concern to ancient Jewish scribes, as one can estimate from the material preserved in the (non-canonical) post-talmudic tractate known as *Massekhet Soferim*. Indeed, the fortunate fact that many texts (like the large Isaiah scroll) are not preserved in clean copy, and preserve many errors, erasures and over-writings intact, show how great was the concern to preserve the literary tradition in the proper, i.e. conventional and authoritative, manner. In addition, the artifacts also reveal that these texts were copied in a way to render them meaningful for the community which used them. As we shall see below, the concern for paragraphing, by joining or separating rhetorical units, reflects a clear concern by the tradents to isolate coherent thematic units; similarly, the resolution of syntactic ambiguities, by one means or another, also demonstrates that texts were not simply copied or read, but done so in an authoritative and conventional manner.

Presumably, then, it is an intense preoccupation with a text important to the community, and no mere off-hand regard for the authority of its formulations, which accounts for the expansions and harmonizations which can be found in a whole variety of Mikra manuscripts from Qumran. The complexity of these materials do not lend themselves to neat groupings of text families corresponding to such later text-types as 'Masoretic', 'Samaritan', and 'Septuagint'. There are, too be sure, observable correspondences between these types and the Qumran evidence; but the multiple alignments make any final categorization premature at this stage.[15] But the variety attests to a great fluidity in the state of the text at this time, and considerable allowances for filling-in gaps of content and resolving diverse formulations. In this regard, it has even been suggested that the phenomenon of biblical paraphrases found in such MSS as *4Q154* – where diverse passages are brought together along with connecting exegetical comments – may, in fact, be 'the actual forerunner of biblical *manuscripts*'; that is, 'the scribes were influenced by literary compositions in which the editorial procedure behind the act of harmonization was already accomplished and on which the actual harmonization was based.[16] This is not certain by any means, and it is just as likely that we have different attempts in different genres to add

---

[13] See Skehan, 'Samaritan Recension'.
[14] For a reevaluation of these matters, see Tov, 'Modern Textual Outlook'.
[15] Ibid.
[16] Tov, 'Harmonizations', 15f.

to the coherence of the Mikra tradition at hand. It might even be the case that the paraphrases reflect speculations on textual harmonizations in scribal circles where there was greater hesitancy to insert the additions and comments into the pentateuchal text. Indeed, despite the variety of texts (in fact, precisely because of them) one is left in doubt about the attitude of the Qumran covenanteers themselves. Do the variety of texts simply reflect a diversity of materials brought to their library for examination or collection (by members who came from Jerusalem priestly circles and elsewhere), *even though* the sectarians themselves only considered one fairly stable text-type to be authoritative? Or do the various Mikra manuscripts indicate a more fluid notion of the authority of the textual artifact itself, perhaps something along the lines of 'official' vs. 'vulgar' text-types?

Some of these questions could certainly be resolved if we had any indication whether Mikra was read-out in a synagogue liturgy. For were this the case, there would undoubtedly have been a preference for one text-type or another. Moreover, if Mikra was used in a lectionary setting at Qumran, this would also provide some context for the targum manuscripts found there, on the assumption (following later explicit rabbinic tradition)[17] that such texts as *11QtgLev* reflect a simultaneous translation during a prayer service. But despite the enormous importance of the Tora of Moses for study and observance at Qumran (as we shall see), there is as yet no indication of a synagogue lection, and thus no ritual setting for targumic renditions of it. This is all the more remarkable, on the one hand, given that a lectionary setting (with accompanying textual interpretation) is actually preserved in our early post-exilic sources (Neh 8), and that the very record of this event suggests that it is based on an even older liturgical procedure (possibly of exilic provenance).[18] Moreover, it is also notable that rabbinic sources have preserved a tradition on this text to the effect that the custom of targumic renditions was practiced in the time of Nehemiah.[19] While this specific tradition may stretch the linguistic evidence, the antiquity of vernacular renditions of Mikra need not be doubted. Indeed, the suggestion that the earliest Septuagint sources reflect a diglossic translation in a liturgical context strongly commends itself.[20] In any event, the targum to Leviticus (like that to Job, and others still unknown) indicate a living context of study of Mikra at Qumran, a matter which, of course, lies at the heart of the scribal enterprise as a whole.

Knowledge and study of the Tora of Moses was thus a basic prerequisite for the proper understanding and faithful performance of the commandments. Contemporary Stoics queried about the relative importance of theory and practice; and our early Pharisaic sources show a Jewish adaptation of this *topos*

---

[17] See *M. Megilla* 4:4.
[18] Fishbane, *Biblical Interpretation*, 113.
[19] *B.T. Megilla* 23a, commenting on Neh 8:8.
[20] Cf. Rabin, 'Translation Process', 17f.

in the recurrent debates over the relative importance of study (of Tora) and practice (of the commandments). A famous rabbinic resolution of this dilemma was to prefer study, and to say that 'Tora is (the) great(er), for it leads to practice.'[21] Such a dilemma would have been resolved quite differently by the Qumran covenanteers. Faced with the question, they would have said that *both* are 'great', but that study of Tora is the greater, for without it there can be no true and proper religious practice. Study of the Tora is thus its correct study and interpretation; and only on this basis can there be legitimate and divinely authorized observance of the commandments.

The fundamental interrelationship of these themes recur in the sources. It is mentioned at the very outset of the *Rule Scroll*, where members of the community are enjoined 'to do (i.e., perform) what is right and proper before [God], in accordance with what He commanded through Moses and all His servants, the prophets . . . to perform the statutes of God . . . [and] to clarify their knowledge in the truth of the statutes of God' (*1QS* 1:3, 8, 12). And an initiate is subject to a period of examination with respect to 'his understanding and practice' (6:14), and cannot become a full member until a noviate period is passed and he is again thoroughly examined with respect to 'his spirit and practice' (6:17-18). These initiates into proper wisdom and practice are also called, in a textual variant (to 6:24), 'men of the Tora'.[22] Like all members, they must ever after continue their study of the Tora and be scrupulous in performance of the rules, as revealed in the text and as exegetically derived therefrom. 'And in any settlement where there obtains [a communal quorum of] ten let there not be lacking a person who Interprets the Tora (דורש בתורה) continuously, day and night (יומם ולילה), in shifts among the fellows; and the Many shall engage diligently together one-third of every night of the year: studying the book (Mikra), and interpreting rule(s), and blessing together' (6:6-8).

Quite clearly, this legal injunction of continuous study for those who have separated themselves from sinful practices is itself an exegetical adaptation of the sapiental exhortation in Ps 1:1-2. There the truly happy person is portrayed as one who forsakes the way of the sinners and does not dwell among scoffers: 'but whose delight is the Tora of the Lord and in His Tora (בתורתו) he meditates (יהגה) day and night (יומם ולילה)'. The verb 'not be lacking' (ואל ימש) is not found in the psalm, but is found in Josh 1:8 (together with the other language of our scroll).[23] Another adaptation of this 'biblical' language occurs in a related context in the *Damascus Document*, which states that 'in any settlement where there obtains a [communal quorum of] ten let there not be

---

[21]   *Sifrei Deut.* 41, p. 85.

[22]   So Milik, reported in *RB* 63 (1956) 61.

[23]   Josh 1-8 is itself an exegetical reworking of an earlier passage; see Fishbane, *Biblical Interpretation*, 384.

lacking (אל ימש) a priest versed in the book of הגו' (CD 12:2-3). The background of this language in Psalms and Joshua suggests that this text is nothing other than the 'book of Meditation' *par excellence*, the Tora of Moses.[24] But the passage from *1QS* 8:6-8 is important in another respect. For just this regulation may indicate the liturgical context of lection and exegetical study queried about earlier. This possibility is, in fact, rendered quite plausible in the light of Nehemiah 8 itself. For just as there Ezra (a priest able 'to inquire [לדרש] into the Tora of the Lord' [Ezra 7:10]) convened the people to hear the Tora recited, which 'reading' (verb קרא) was preceeded by a 'blessing' (verbברך) and extended by interpretations (vv. 2-9; 13-16), so does the *Rule Scroll* state that the community was convened continuously 'to read (לקרוא)' the Tora, 'to interpret/inquire (לדרוש)' into the law, and 'to bless (לברך)' together. The specific language found in 7:6-8 may therefore be more than a mere stylistic conceit, and point to the liturgical tradition of considerable antiquity.

The need 'to return' in faith 'to the Tora of Moses', and to study it intensively, is 'because in it *everything* can be learnt' (CD 16:1-2; כי בה הכל מדוקדק). This striking expression is somewhat reminiscent of the nearly contemporaneous remark attributed to one Ben Bag-Bag, in a classical Tannaic source: 'Turn it (the Mikra), and turn it (again), because *everything* is in it' (M. *Avot* 5:22; דכלה בה). Indeed, for both the early Pharisees and the covenanteers of Qumran everything could be found in Mikra *through exegesis*. Concerned that they 'proceed in accordance with the Tora' (*1QS* 7:7), the sectarians studied the 'revealed text' (נגלה) for its 'exact formulation' (פרוש; cf. CD 6:14, 18, 20; 12:6) and explicit 'ordinance' (משפט; CD 7:7). Where this was not forthcoming, they proceeded to uncover its 'hidden' content (נסתר), according to the exegetical principles of the group (see below). In this way, everything necessary for proper legal-ritual practice could be derived from the books of Moses.

In a similar way, study of the nonlegal portions of Mikra, particularly the narratives, the psalms, and the prophecies – involved instruction in the manifest and hidden content. Thus, in group study or in homiletical exhortations, 'the Preceptor' might 'inform the Many in the way of God; instruct them in His wondrous might; and recite before them the נהיות' (CD 13:7-8). This last phrase alludes to the metaphysical teachings of the Spirits and their enmity in the heavens (among the angels) and on earth (among mankind) until the final divine Judgment (see *1QS* 3:15-4:14; and נהייה at 3:15). These teachings bear on the relationships between cosmic and historical events, and are concerned with future events. In the same way, recollections of the mighty acts of God include both a celebration of past deeds and instruction in the events to come. What such exegetical instruction might have been like can be gauged from the material at hand. In a text like the *War Scroll*, for example, a long prayer is recited to God (*1QM* 9:17-16:1) in which certain past acts of power –

---

[24] For interpretations of this difficult term, see Rabin, *Zadokite Documents*, ad loc. Cf. also Dimant 'Qumran Sectarian Literature', 493 n. 57; 527.

the defeat of Pharoah at the exodus and the defeat of Goliath by David – are used as *paradigms* for future acts of divine salvation (11:2-3, 9-10). Presumably instructions in such events, presenting them as the antitype of future divine deed, was part of ancient uses of Mikra. Similarly, a number of older prophecies recalled in this source as bearing on future events were also part of such instructions (see 10:2-5, citing Deut 20:2-4; 10:7-8, citing Num 10:9; 11:6-7, citing Num 24:17-19; and 11:11-12, citing Isa 31:8). Significantly, the *prophetic application* of these texts to future events is made *grosso modo*, and not by means of an atomization and reinterpretation of particular words, as is characteristic of the *pesher*-genre, which, of course, is also the result of intensive study of the hidden intent or true application of prophetic lemmata. Thus, just as the true application of the laws is the result of interpretative techniques and meanings revealed to the Interpreter of the Tora and his followers, so also the true application of the prophecies is the product of techniques and meanings revealed to the Teacher of Righteousness and his followers (see below).

USE OF CITATIONS AND CITATION-FORMULAE

The authority of Mikra is furthermore evident through the variety of citations and citation-formulae employed in the scrolls, and through the various ways lemmata and comments are correlated.[25] Indeed, the citations are used to give both *prestige* and *authority* to the legal, homiletical or prophetic comments which precede them. The materials from Mikra are introduced as that which is 'written' (כתוב) in a particular book; or they are presented as that which God, or Moses, or one of the prophets has 'said' (אמר), 'spoken' (דבר), 'told' (הגיד), 'taught' (למד), 'announced' (השמיע). The first three terms are by far the most prevalent, and begin to reflect the diversity of citation formulae characteristic of Jewish texts of the period.[26] In particular, one can note the emergence here of terms found in Pharisaic and classical rabbinic sources, such as the introduction of Mikra citations by כמו שכתוב ('as it is written'); כמה שנאמר ('as is said'); מגיד הכתוב ('Scripture [lit., "the writ"] tells'); and תלמוד לומר ('Scripture [lit., "the teaching"] says'). This latter is strikingly adumbrated in the scrolls in connection with the false teaching of the opponents (cf. *4QpNah* 2:8).[27] Sometimes the citation formulae are used in the scrolls without any further attribution (e.g., *CD* 9:2, 5; 15: 6-7). More commonly, the writer indicates his source, either by referring to a specific 'book' (e.g., of Moses, *4QFlor* 1:1; Isaiah, *4QFlor* 1:16; or Ezekiel, *4QFlor* 1:16), or to the

---

[25] A seminal early study on the citations and their use is Fitzmyer, 'Explicit Old Testament Quotations'. As I have not found his classification flexible or complex enough, it has not been used here. Earlier and contemporary studies on (explicit and implicit) citations in specific texts was done by Carmignac. See his 'Citations . . . dans la "Guerre" '; and id., 'Citations . . . dans les "Hymnes" '. A more formal analysis is that of Horton, 'Formulas of Introduction'.

[26] Cf. Metzger, 'Introducing Quotations'. Ellis, below, pp. 692ff.

[27] See the proposal of Wacholder, 'Qumran Attack', with earlier literature cited.

name of an ancient authority (e.g., Moses, *1QM* 10:6; *CD* 8:14; Isaiah, *CD* 4:13-14, 6:7-8; Ezekiel, *CD* 3:21, 19:11-12; or Zechariah, *CD* 19:7).

Among the *explicit* citations, two broad types of use can be discerned. In the first, the citation follows a point previously made in the text and is used to *justify* it. It therefore functions, formally, as a prooftext. But what is of particular interest is that these citations can almost never be read according to their plain-sense. Due to their recontextualization, they must each be construed relative to the point which precedes them. This is not necessarily to say that the lemmata have exegetically sponsored the point at issue, but solely to indicate that the original sense of the prooftext must be disregarded in order to understand how the writer has exegetically appropriated it. The question as to whether Mikra citation sponsors or supports the new issue must be ascertained in each separate instance: no generalization is possible. Without engaging in the specifics of exegetical practice and technique here (see below), several instances can nevertheless serve to illustrate this important matter.

LEGAL CITATIONS. At the beginning of a long list of Sabbath rules in the *Damascus Document*, the covenanteer is told: 'Let no man do work on Friday from the time when the orb of the sun is distant from the gate by its own fulness; for that is what He (God) said: Guard (שמור) the Sabbath Day to keep it holy' (*CD* 10:14-15). Clearly, this citation from the Decalogue (Deut 5:12) has been adduced to justify sectarian rules concerned with determining the onset of the Sabbath day. The matter is not considered in the Mikra. But now, by determining that one should 'guard' the onset of the Sabbath by beginning it when the sun is the distance of its own orb from setting, and relating that customary procedure to Deut 5:12, Mikra is used to support the ruling. Indeed, by reading שמור as 'guarding' the onset of the holy day, and not in terms of 'heeding' the Sabbath rest (the contextual consideration in the Decalogue and the succeeding rules of the *Document*), the new rule is impliedly shown to be 'found' in the Mikra. Presumably, the custom described here preceded the biblical proof; but the rule has been so presented ('for that is what He said') as to suggest that it has been exegetically derived from the older divine law.

At the conclusion of the Sabbath rules (11:17-19), the community is enjoined: 'Let no man offer on the altar on the Sabbath except (כי אם) the burnt-offerings of the Sabbath; for thus it is written: Apart from (מלבד) your Sabbath-offerings.' In this case, the legist is concerned to restrict offerings on the Sabbath and to justify the innovation on the basis of Mikra (Lev 23:38). However, it will be observed that in its original context the adverb מלבד ('apart from') means something like 'besides'; whereas in the new rule the term has been construed in a restrictive sense (as one can also see from the words כי אם which *preceed* the citation). As in the preceding case, Mikra is ostensibly utilized to authorize the rule; and the passage is presented *as if* it represents the plain-sense of the Mikra, not its reinterpreted sense. Accordingly, one must be cautious in assuming that where the new rules are linked to Mikra they were *in the first instance* exegetically derived from them. It is just as likely that the prooftexts, *even* where an exegetical dimension is predominant, are secondary justifications of customary, non-biblical procedures. This seems all the more likely where different sectarian legal injunctions are justified by nonlegal texts (cf. *CD* 11:40; *1QS* 5:17-18). The more puzzling matter is why only certain rules are (exegetically) justified, ones which are certainly not the most obvious or (to judge by rabbinic procedures), even the most conducive.

NONLEGAL CITATIONS. As just noted, rules or directives to the community are sometimes justified by nonlegal citations. These are clearly of a *post hoc* nature. Thus *1QS* 5:7-20, which prohibits consociation with nonmembers in all matters, supports its injunctions of separation with two prooftexts. The first (at 5:15), after justifying nonrelations with nonsectarians with the moral exhortation 'for he should be far (ירחק) from him in every matter (בכל דבר), goes on to justify that point with a Mikra citation: 'for so it is written: "you shall be far (תרחק) from every false thing (מכל דבר)" '. This citation, which derives from the moral approbation to judges in Exod 22:7, is now used to support separation from persons who can transmit impurity to a covenanteer, simply on the basis of similar terms! The citation is thus made to serve an entirely new purpose; and the transformed reuse of the passage is not further explicated. In this respect, it stands apart from the second justification (at 5:17-18). For there further rules of noninvolvement are justified by a citation from Isa 2:22: 'as is written: "cease (חדלו) from Man who only has breath in his nostrils, for by what does he merit esteem (נחשב)"?'; and this citation *is* exegetically justified by the comment: 'for all those who are not accounted (נחשבו) in his covenant, it is necessary to separate (from) them and all that is theirs.' In this striking case, a citation which speaks of the vain-glory of mortal humans is reinterpreted – on the basis of the verb נחשב (the standard term for being accounted a member, cf. 5:11) – to support separation from the impure. Remarkably, too, the universal 'Man' of the Isaiah passage is now transformed to indicate particular men, nonsectarians, in fact.

This support of one justification through a quite explicit reinterpretation of it, calls to mind *1QS* 8:13-15. In this passage, the covenanteers are told of their imperative to separate from evil and 'to go to the desert, to prepare there the way of the Lord'. The language of this injunction is contrived to anticipate the supportive citation from Isa 40:3 'as is written: "in the desert prepare the way (of the Lord), straighten a highway to our God" '. Now the first clause of this citation is clearly a straight-forward biblical justification of the covenanteer's decision to built a community in the Judaean wilderness. The second, however, is given a new meaning: for the word 'highway' is explicated to mean the 'study of the Tora (מדרש התורה)' in the special manner of the sect. The original rhetorical parallelism has thus been broken-up and distributed with two different senses, a regular feature, in fact, of rabbinic aggadic midrash.

PROPHETIC CITATIONS. Certainly the foregoing citation-plus-commentary from the *Rule Scroll* may be understood as the reuse of an ancient prophecy in the course of a rhetorical discussion. Many comparable instances can be found in the *Damascus Document*. There the rhetor repeatedly reviews the comments with explicit citations from Mikra, which are then reinterpreted (word-by-word) with respect to sectarian law and ideology. For example, in *CD* 3:18-4:4 the speaker describes how God 'made reconciliation' with sinful Israel and established a 'sure house', that those who hold fast to it have 'eternal life', *as was promised* to the prophet Ezekiel in Ezek 44:15. This passage is then explicated in terms of the sect, so that the special nature of sectarian triumphalism is justified *through the Mikra*. Or again, just following this passage, the sins 'let loose' within the post-exilic community are presented as that of which God 'spoke by the hand of the prophet Isaiah son of Amoz.' Isa 14:21 is then cited and explicated with respect to archetypal sectarian sins: 'whoredom', 'wealth', and 'pollution of the Sanctuary' (4:13-18). Through these boldly reinterpretated citations, the communal sense of history and destiny is justified and vindicated. Of the many other examples that occur, we may simply add at this point such passages as 7:9-10, where a Mikra citation adduced to justify a comment *on the basis of its reinterpretation*, is itself justified via another citation from Mikra. A parade instance where a series of Mikra citations, appropriately reconstrued, are used to justify sectarian hopes may be found in *4QFlor* 1-2.[28]

The second type of explicit citation in the scrolls presents Mikra first, with the comment or comments following thereafter. While there is little doubt in these cases that Mikra is being used, the citations occur in a variety of literary forms – and this effects the presentation of the lemmata. We may, accordingly, speak of the pseudepigraphic, the pesherite, the anthological, and the explicatory form in this regard. Specific exegetical examples will be considered below.

PSEUDEPIGRAPHIC FORM. In the *Temple Scroll*, related but different legal texts are variously integrated into thematic units, with their differences harmonized and exegetical innovations interpolated throughout. For example, in *11QTemp* 11-29 a block of materials dealing with cultic festivals and procedures is culled from Num 28-29 (with elements from Lev 23 and other sources). Similarly, in columns 40-66 civil laws are culled primarily from the book of Deuteronomy (chapters 12-23), though with related Mikra texts worked-in. In either of the two units, the attentive reader can easily observe how the base text (Num 28-29 or Deut 12-23, respectively) organizes the diverse materials, and how the entire ensemble is reauthorized as the word of God *in just this new form*. They are thus pseudepigraphically represented as the instructions of God to Moses, even those Deuteronomic units where Moses (in the Tora) reports the divine word. In *11QTemp* it is not Moses who reports God's instructions, but God Himself

---

[28] On this text, see now Brooke, *Exegesis at Qumran*.

350

who is the speaker. Through this reauthorization (of old laws and new interpretations) it is a rewritten book: a new Tora. In this way, the pseudepigraphical procedure in *11QTemp* differs notably from that found in the masoretic text itself, where exegetical innovations and textual blends are worked into the revealed instructions presented through (Exod-Num) or reported by (Deut) Moses. A comparative examination of the practice suggests a more restrained pseudepigraphical attitude in ancient Israel, since there the examples are occasional and often stylistically unwieldy. In *11QTemp*, on the other hand, the practice shows thematic and stylistic consistency. In fact, in those few cases where the pseudepigraphical transformation would result in a theologically awkward or stylistically confusing text (as, at *11QTemp* 55:2ff. and 63:7-8) the formulation found in the book of Deuteronomy was left intact.[29] In the *Temple Scroll*, therefore, the reader confronts the text as a *new* Tora, even while perceiving the biblical base around which the sources and innovations were integrated. One may confidently surmise that this was the very hope and intent of the author.

PESHERITE FORM. In the so-called *pesher*-literature, as well, large blocks of Mikra are presented prior to their reinterpretation. Moreover, as also in the preceding type, the base text, now those with a prophetic focus (e.g., the words of the prophets and selected psalms), determines the structure and developments of the new text. But here the issue is not the reinterpretation of a consecution of laws, but the elucidation of consecutive lemmata from the text at hand (usually after full citations, though also after repeated citations of half-verses) with references to the present and future life of the community. The lemmata are separated from the interpretations by commentary formulae of several related types (e.g., 'its *pesher* [eschatological sense] is').[30] In this way, Mikra is presented as the authoritative prophetic word of God; and the commentaries on it are authorized as the true meaning or application of that word for the times at hand. Hence, whereas in the *Temple Scroll* the Pentateuch (primarily) was used as the source of new legal truth; in the *pesharim*-texts the Prophets (primarily) were used as the source of new eschatological truth. In both cases, it must be stressed, the pertinent truth is for the sectarians, and is a *reworked* and *interpreted* truth.

ANTHOLOGICAL FORM. Limited and also more extended types of anthological reuse of Mikra can be found among the Qumran scrolls, where Mikra is presented alone or before comments upon it. Among the more limited types, examples of a legal, liturgical, narrative, and prophetic character are known. Thus as part of the phylacteries found at Qumran, the four major Pentateuchal

---

[29] Discussion of the pseudepigraphic features of *11QTemp* appear in the Introduction (vol. 1) and throughout the notes of the critical edition of Yadin, *Temple Scroll*. A valuable discussion of various pertinent matters can be found in Brin, 'Mikra in the Temple Scroll'.

[30] On the formulary and its relation to Mikra and contemporary Jewish Literature, see Fishbane, 'Qumran Pesher'; and id., *Biblical Interpretation*, 444-57, and notes.

sections used in Pharisaic *tefillin* (Exod 13:1-10; 13:11-16; Deut 6:4-9; 11:13-21) are also found along with several other passages, including the Decalogue.[31] Clearly this liturgical collection is unified thematically: all four refer to teachings which should be signs on the hand and frontlets between the eyes (Exod 13:9, 16; Deut 6:8; 11:18); and presumably the addition of the Decalogue (introduced with the words *ha-devarim ha'eleh*, 'these words', in Exod 20:1) to the ensemble is because Deut 6:4-9, which follows a recitation of the Decalogue (Deut 5:6-18), instructs the Israelite to bind *ha-devarim ha'eleh* to their arm and head. A hybrid anthology (of the versions in Exod 20 and Deut 5) has long been known in the form of the Nash papyrus;[32] and now, in *4Q149* a mixed text of the two versions of the Decalogue has been found in an ancient *mezuza*.[33]

The materials found in *4Q158* provide a different case. Here there are ensembles of running text which include a number of exegetical additions. Thus in fg. 1-2 of this *siglum*, sections from Gen 32 are juxtaposed to Exod 4:27-28, along with exegetical additions; although the meaning of this juxtaposition is not immediately apparent.[34] More striking is the sequence in fg. 6-12, where the following ensemble is found: Exod 20:19-21; Deut 5:28-29; Deut 18:18-22 (fg. 6); Exod 20:12, 16, 17; Deut 5:30-31; Exod 20:20-26; Exod 21:1, 3, 4, 5, 6, 8, 10. Along with this running text a small number of exegetical additions can also be noted. Presumably, we have here an attempt to harmonize and integrate various texts on the theme and sequence of the revelation, the role of Moses, and the authority of his successors. In the text preserved here, this ensemble has been judged closer to the so-called Samaritan text than to the Masoretic.[35] Indeed, it is striking that also in the received Samaritan text the Decalogue in Exod 20 is supplemented with materials from Deut 5 and 18, as well as from Deut 27:4-7. This latter is also transformed by an addition which legitimates the Samaritan sanctuary of Shechem. This matter is lacking in *4Q158*, so that a

---

[31] Milik, *Qumran Grotte 4*; Yadin, *Tefillin*.

[32] According to Greenberg, 'Nash Papyrus', 'the combination of the Decalogue and the *Shema* indicates that the text of the papyrus represents the Tora readings included in the daily morning liturgy of Second Temple times (cf. Tam. 5:1: "they recited the Decalogue, the *Shema*, etc.")'.

[33] See Milik, *Qumran Grotte 4*, 80.

[34] According to Tov, 'Harmonizations', 17, they are juxtaposed 'for no clear reason'. But it would appear that this *semikhut parashiyyot*, or linkage of pericopae, may be due to several lexical and thematic considerations. For if we look at the preserved texts *and* their immediate context, there appears to be an (exegetical-homiletical?) attempt to draw a connection between several encounters: the mysterious divine encounters ((attacks?) and the woundings of the 'leg' in Gen 32:25-33 and Exod 4:24-26, on the basis of the common verbs *naga'* and *pagash*; and the fraternal encounters (reunions) in Genesis 33 (Jacob and Esau) and Exod 4:27-31 (Moses and Aaron), on the basis of the common verbs *nashaq* and *pagash*, and the common adverb *liqra't*. Notably, Exod 4:24-26 is followed by vv. 27-31; and Gen. 32:25-35 is followed by ch. 33. The writer of this Qumran fragment was obviously struck by the multiple concordances (divine and fraternal encounters, with similar terminology, in both cases). Such correlations would suggest a whole area of exegetical imagination and interest.

[35] But *4Q158* and the Samaritan text in question (analyzed by Tigay, 'Documentary Hypotheses') are not parallel anthologies, and derive from different traditions.

cultic tendentiousness is not yet in evidence in the Qumranite anthology. Whether the latter anthology had any liturgical use is impossible to say. On the contrary, it is more probable that this integration was motivated by exegetical-harmonistic considerations. Faced with confusing elements regarding the sequence of the Sinai revelation, and the role of Moses, some sages may have tried to rewrite Mikra in order to produce a more integrated text, though its communal status remains unclear. The *Temple Scroll*, to which we turn next, is the consummate early Jewish expression of this concern for anthological integration. It achieved this through a 'rewritten Tora'.

The anthological reuse of explicit Mikra texts in *11QTemp* has several forms and variations.[36] In this context, we shall focus on what appears to be the two most dominant classes: (a) the limited type of reuse, where two or more texts bearing on a specific legal topic are integrated to produce a new Tora rule (with and without exegetical comments); and (b) the more extended type of reuse, where a series of the former type are unified by an older Tora sequence (e.g., the sequence of laws in Deuteronomy) to produce a new Tora.

(a) *The limited type.* The rule in *11QTemp* 66:8-9 provides an instructive case in point. There we read that 'If a man seduces a young virgin who had not been betrothed – *and she is permitted to him [in marriage] according to the law* – and he lies with her and is caught, let the man who lies with her give 50 pieces of silver to the father of the maiden. And she shall become his wife because he raped her. He may never divorce her.'[37] It is obvious that here the legist has harmonized two distinct formulations, one rule from Exod 22:15, dealing with seduction, the other from Deut 22:28-29, dealing with rape, evidently because both deal with a young virgin who had not been betrothed. Combining related but essentially different rules, and rewriting them as one, is certainly not an innovation of our legist. Similar features are found within Mikra itself, along with exegetical comments similar to that added here (the emphasized phrase).[38] What is distinctive here is the consistency of this anthological reuse of Mikra in order to produce new rules. Indeed, both the deliberateness and the dexterity of the procedure suggest that for the author of *11QTemp* this was much more than a stylistic conceit. Presumably, this procedure is much more related to his concern for an authoritative representation of earlier revelations and authoritative rules. This comes through even more where the new law is presented through a vast texture of older rules (as, e.g., in the prescriptions concerning

---

[36] Brin, 'Mikra in the Temple Scroll', has offered a helpful list and analysis of types; the categorization of the 'anthologized uses' of Mikra offered by Kaufman, 'Temple Scroll', is much more nuanced but not, therefore, always more helpful. Limitations of space have led to a simpler classification here.
[37] On the translation of *'orasa* as 'who had not been betrothed' I follow D.W. Halivni, 'Note'. And see now his extended analysis of this rule against the background of ancient Jewish law and terminology, in *Midrash, Mishnah, and Gemara*, 30-34 and notes.
[38] See Fishbane, *Biblical Interpretation*, 188-97, 216-20, 228-30.

the festival of unleavened bread, which integrates citations from Lev 23:6-8; Num 17:10-16; 28:17-25; Deut 16:8; and Ezra 16:8).

(b) *The extended type.* A brief example of the 'running anthology' may be found in *11QTemp* 51-52. The base text here begins with Deut 16:16ff. (rules about judges). After taking this up, the legist then provides some exegetical additions to it. Then, before continuing with the rules in Deut 16:21 (prohibiting the planting of sacred poles near the altar), the writer adds a new introduction which contains a summary of the laws which follow in 51:19-21. Upon returning to the base text of Deuteronomy, the writer cites Deut 16:21 and 22 (52:1-2) and then, quite unexpectedly, Lev 26:1 (52:2-3). This latter rule prohibits incising forms on altar stones, and is not mentioned in Deut 16:21-22. The legist was evidently drawn to it by association: since the same phraseology is used in both Deut 16:22 and Lev 16:1 to prohibit the erection of stelae by Israelites. In this manner, the writer was able both to integrate related rules in one place *and* to produce a Scripture without duplication. This done, the text (52:3-4) continues with the Deuteronomic issues found in Deut 17:1. Once again, it is only after a complex series of associations to other Pentateuchal passages (including those dealing with vows) that the legist in col. 55 returns to his base text, now at Deut 17:2. Clearly, the ancient Tora of Moses was of very great importance to him. One might even conclude that the very 'Mosaic' form of *11QTemp* reflected one of his principle ideological concerns: to preserve the older teaching while representing it in a new and *reinterpreted* form. That is, the legist was concerned to retain the ancient Tora, though in accordance with the truth of Mikra as he and his fellows understood it and practiced it. One might further suggest that just this (anthological) form was used by the author to *justify* his extensive exegeses and reuse of Mikra.

EXPLICATORY FORM. There are a number of occurences in the *Damascus Document* where a text from the Mikra is first cited in order to introduce a rule or idea, which latter is then subsequently explicated. In this way, it is again not Mikra *per se* which commends assent by the covenanteers, but Mikra as exegetically clarified. In the preceding section, we saw that Mikra was cited after the presentation of a new rule or idea in order to justify it or give it legitimacy. In the following cases, the citation also serves to justify the new rule or idea – though now the citation comes first and the explication follows. In these cases we have, in fact, something akin to proto-midrashic (legal and homiletical) discourses.

(a) In *CD* 9:2-5, after an apodictic rule dealing with judicial execution (9:1), which is neither justified or explicated, the legist turns to a new case: 'And as to that which is said [in Scripture, Lev 19:18]: "You shall not take vengeance (לא תקום) nor bear rancor against your compatriot (בני עמך)", and every person among the covenanteers who will bring an accusation against his neighbor (רעהו), without [first] reproving [him] before witnesses, or brings it up when enraged, or tells his elders to make him contemptible: he takes vengeance

(נוקם הוא) and (bears) rancor. For it is expressly written: "He takes vengeance (נוקם הוא) on his adversaries, and he bears rancor against his enemies" (Nahum 2:1)." '

It will be observed that the concern of the rule, to establish procedures for reproving fellow sinners without rancor, does not follow directly from Lev 19:18, the opening citation. That Tora passage is rather explicated with reference to the sectarian rules which (presumably) preceeded it, but which it now serves to justify. In order to make his point, the exegete transforms the Mikra text into a more popular idiom. In his view, one who does not follow the rules of reproof, but delays this procedure, acts with vengeance (explained as rage) and rancor (explained as intent to contemn). There then follows a further passage, from Nahum 2:1, which justifies the explication and butresses the first citation in a most interesting way. Most commentators read the Nahum citation as a direct and ironical use of Mikra; i.e. *you*, a covenanteer, must not bear vengeance, etc., *even though* God ('He', understood as a euphemism for the Tetragram) does. But two points suggest a different explanation. The first point is that the citation from Lev 19:18 is already read by the legist in a narrow sense (the 'compatriot' is not any Israelite, but a sectarian); the second is that just before the second lemma the legist adds that one who does not follow the new procedure of reproof, and brings the accusation up later 'takes vengeance (נוקם הוא).' Since just this latter expression is also the (purported) reading of Nahum 2:1, which goes on to refer, vengence, etc. with respect to Israel's 'adversaries' and 'enemies', one may justifiably understand this prooftext to serve an entirely new conclusion; viz., to neutralize the divine statement and reapply its content (viz., sanction) to the covenanteers. The underlying argument would thus be as follows: since Scripture itself (in Nahum 2:1) says that vengeance and rancor are emotions directed against one's enemies, it must follow that the exegetical reading of Lev 19:18 as condemning such practices towards own's sectarian compatriots is fully justified. Mikra is thus exegetically used here to both establish and vindicate a new judicial procedure. Presumably, the procedure long preceeded this 'midrashic proof'.[39]

(b) A second example comes from the homiletical sphere. In *CD* 8:14-18, after a condemnation against those contemporaries who have falsely 'built the wall' (8:12-13), that is, who interpret and practice the Tora differently from the sect, the preacher quotes from Scripture: 'And as for that which Moses said [to Israel]: "Not for your righteousness or uprightness of heart do you disposses these nations, but [rather] because He [God] loved your fathers and kept the oath" – this is the case (וכן המשפט) with regard to the repentant ones of Israel who departed form the way of the people: because of God's love for the ancestors . . . He loves their decendents . . .' As in the preceding case, Mikra is first adduced and then explicated. Ostensibly, the preacher has simply cited the

---

[39] See Rabin, *Zadokite Documents*, ad loc.; for a broad review and analysis, see Schiffman, *Sectarian Law*, ch. 6.

words of Moses. Closer examination, however, shows that Mikra has been reused in a more deliberate way. For in blending together (a selected composite from) Deut 9:5a and (a stylized rephrasing from) 7:8a the preacher has used the authority of the Tora in order to emphasize the nature of divine grace in the present era. The older words of Moses, dealing with the generation of Conquest, are now reapplied to the sectarian community and its anticipated displacement of the foreign oppressor then in the land. Indeed, those Jews who have repented and joined the community are told that their victory will not be the result of their own merit, but solely due to God's love and promise to the ancestors. The preacher thus utilizes the Mosaic lemmata and redirects their meaning to his own day. The community is likened to the ancient generation of wandering in the desert: like them they will victoriously inherit the land; and, again like them, they will be vindicated because of God's faithfulness to his ancient oath. Having reused Mikra in this exhortatory manner, the preacher closes with a repeated denunciation of the 'builders of the wall' (8:18), itself an allusion to Ezek 13:10.[40]

REUSE OF BIBLICAL LANGUAGE

The sectarian ideology that it alone is the true Israel, heir of the ancient past, is no where so pervasive as in the predominance of biblical language and form throughout the scrolls. Indeed, virtually every page of text is replete with extensive uses of Mikra as a *model* of one sort or another. To explore this topic in detail would actually require a review of almost every line of sectarian composition. This is clearly beyond the scope of the present enterprise. We shall therefore limit ourselves here to three broad areas.

(1) *Mikra as Model for Language.* The dense reuse of biblical language is especially evident in the paraenetic sections of the *Damascus Document*,[41] the prayers of the *Hodayot* collection, and the discursive narrative of the *War Scroll*.[42] The interweaving of passages from all the compositions of ancient Israel not only creates a thick archaic texture, dramatizing the biblical inheritance and character of the sect; but these passages also generate a network of intertextual associations that give special resonance to the sectarian compositions. In fact, the implicit citations embedded in these texts produce a tableaux of interlocking allusions: a *new biblical composition*. Choosing somewhat randomly, let us simply cite one of the sentences that precedes the Deuteronomic

[40] On this textual image in its original context, see Fishbane-Talmon, 'Structuring of Biblical Books' 131-36.
[41] Cf. Rabin, *Zadokite Documents*, IX (preface), 'I am convinced that the Admonition (pp. i-viii, xx) is all of it a mosaic of quotations, both from OT and other, now lost, writings, a clever presentation of *testimonia*, not a history of the sect'.
[42] On this text, see Carmignac, 'Citations . . . dans la "Guerre" '. On *1QS*, see Wernberg-Møller, 'Some reflections'.

citations in *CD* 8:14-18, just considered. In 8:7-9 the preacher begins: 'And they did each one what was right in his eyes and preferred each one the stubbornness of his heart, and did not withdraw from the people [of the land and their sin], but rebelled highhandedly by walking in the ways of the wicked.' There is nothing complicated about this rebuke: it is manifestly unified in both theme and concern. No complicated or ironic clash of images is found. Nevertheless, through its composite of textual allusions, a sharper charge is generated. For one thing, the imagery of doing what is 'right in one's eyes' is standard Deuteronomic language for religious anarchy (cf. Deut 12:8; Judg 21:25), just as stubborness of heart is a recurrent expression which conveys a censure of personal will and divine disregard (Deut 29:18; Jer 9:13). Then, too, the language of withdrawing (נזרו) is used technically of removal from Israelite holiness (Lev 22:2) or towards pagan activity (Hos 9:10), and the choice of the verb פשע to express rebellion and the image יד רמה to convey (highhanded) intention, respectively convey the rebellion at Sinai (Exod 32:25) and the deliberate rejection of divine commandments (Num 15:30f.). Finally, the image of going in the way of the wicked recalls the idioms of Ps 1:1, where such sinners are juxtaposed to those who follow the Tora.

It is certainly not necessary to argue that the preacher of *CD* 8:7-9 had just the aforenoted passages in mind (though in several cases the language is unique) to recognize that his choice of expression is deliberately allusive and richly biblical. Little would be gained by dismissing this 'biblical texture' as so much linguistic archaizing or stylistic conceit. For to separate verbal form from ideological content would be unnecessarily artificial. Since the community believed itself to be the new Israel, it also came to express itself in this authoritative manner. Thus not only through explicit citations and applications, but also through a chain of textual allusions and associations, the authority of Mikra for the covenanters' self-understanding is dramatically asserted.

(2) *Mikra as Model for Composition.* In taking up this subject, it will be well to distinguish between more narrow and more extensive uses of compositional forms found in the Mikra. An example of the former is the liturgical recitation found in *1QS* 2:2-10. This liturgy is part of a ceremony of induction for initiates. In the course of the procedure, the priests bless the lot of those pure in practice while the Levites curse those that share the lot of Belial. What is particularly striking about these recitations is that the first is worked around a reuse of the Priestly Blessing found in Num 6:24-26, whereas the second is its inversion. The biblical form is particularly evident in the first case, though the lemmata are recited without citation formulae and supplemented asyndetically. Thus we read: 'May He (the Lord) bless you *with all good*; may He protect you *from all evil*; may he enlighten *your heart with the wisdom of life*; may He be gracious to you *with everlasting knowledge*; and may He raise up for you the face *of his pious ones for everlasting* peace (2:3-4).' As in many cases in Mikra and early

rabbinic literature, the ancient Priestly Blessing serves as the structure and basis for a new liturgical composition.[43]

Another type of implicit use of Mikra deserves mention. And that is the 'anthological' composition found in many legal texts. As noted earlier, the *Temple Scroll* is particularly characterized by the coordination of related Mikra passages to expand or harmonize certain topics, and to authorize innovations through deliberate changes. For example, the rules of the paschal-sacrifice incorporate Exod 12:47-48; Num 9:3; and Deut 16:7 into a new legal mosaic. In addition, Exod 12:47, which explicitly states that '*all* the congregation of Israel shall do it (viz., the sacrifice)', is supplemented by the remark (utilizing Mikra language concerning the valid age of priestly service): 'from the age of twenty and upwards they shall do it.' By this qualifying addition the previous assertion is manifestly undercut. But by weaving it into the known rules for the paschal rite, the author has also justified his procedure in the light of his (here implicit) ideology that Israel is a 'kingdom of priests'. A more limited and also more subtle form of such legal creativity can be found in the *Damascus Document*. For example, in the continuation of the aforenoted example regarding reproof (*CD* 9:6-8), the light indicates that vengeance involves witholding reproof '*from one day to the next* (מיום ליום)', he is drawing an analogy to the law of vows in Num 30:15 where the very same phraseology occurs. In this way, the legist is able to innovate or justify a time-limit for proper reproof *on the basis* of the laws of Moses.[44] The Mosaic interpretation establishes an analogy: just as in the one case the vow of an unmarried or married woman is valid unless invalidated within a day by her father or husband (respectively), so is reproof valid only for the same period of time. The words מיום ליום are therefore no mere phrase. For the legist of *CD* it is an operative legal expression intentionally used to justify his exegetical innovation. This procedure of legal validation is quite common to the *Damascus Document*, where the technique of explicit legal justification is used as well.[45]

On a more extensive plane, the broad impact of a compositional form from the Mikra is attested in different genres of the sectarian scrolls. We have already mentioned the use of the legal sequence of the book of Deuteronomy on the composition and editing of the *Temple Scroll*. We may now add that Deuteronomy strongly influenced the style and structure of the *Damascus Document*, as well. Thus, like Deut 1-11, *CD* opens (1-8) with a collection of paraenetic reviews of the national past, and begins various subsections with the exhortation '(and) now hear' (1:1; 2:1; 3:14). This introductory statement is also found in Deut 4:1; 6:4; 9:1; 10:12. In addition, just as Deuteronomy follows its

---

[43] See Fishbane, *Biblical Interpretation*, 329-34.

[44] See the analysis of the rabbinic literature, and the overall treatment of Schiffman, *Sectarian Law*, ch. 4.

[45] Schiffman, *Sectarian Law, passim*, and earlier in *Halakha at Qumran, passim*, has forcefully argued that the halakha (as against sectarian organization rules) was not only justified through the inspired interpretation of biblical texts, but derived from it as well.

historical retrospectus with a corpus of cultic and civil rules (ch. 12-26), the historical review in *CD* is also continued by a corpus of cultic and civic rules (9-16). No blessings and curses follow these rules, however, as they do in Deut 27-28. Instead, such a procedure is found in *1QS* 2:208 in the liturgical recitation just discussed.

(3) *Mikra as Model for Practices or Procedures*. The dominant impact of Mikra on the covenanteers is also evident in their reuse of it to determine the nature and structure of their judiciary, for example, or the ages of service of the officers of the community in their encampments and during the final eschatological war. In this latter battle, the structural arrangement of the tribes is also modeled on the deployment of the tribes around the portable ark in the wilderness, as described in the opening chapters of the book of Numbers.

As a final example, we return to *1QS* 2. It will be recalled that this text includes the blessings and curses of a covenant initiation ceremony. But the reuse of Mikra goes beyond a reuse of the Priestly Blessing and a mere allusion to the blessings and curses of Deuteronomy. For the blessings and curses are recited by cultic officers deployed in two groups, just as in the covenant ceremony described in Deut 27:9-26 (and enacted in Josh 8:33-34). Like the latter, moreover, the new covenanteers respond to the recitation with the words 'Amen, Amen' (2:10). Accordingly, just as this ancient ceremony was prescribed in the wilderness and performed by the people of Israel and entered the land in the days of Joshua, so it now serves as the model for all those who would go out to the wilderness and enter the special covenant of the true Israel. This reappropriation of the ceremony by the sectarian community is both more bold and more consequential than the rhetorical reuse of it centuries earlier, by the prophet Jeremiah (11:1-5).

To conclude: virtually the entirety of Mikra is used and reused by the writers of the Qumran scrolls in order to author, reauthor, and – ultimately – to authorize their practices and beliefs. In any specific composition, many diverse texts might be adduced; just as many diverse texts might be adduced to support any one point. Indeed, the justification of a line of argument from several biblical sources at once demonstrates the wide-ranging literary imagination of the composers, and the authority of *the totality* of Scripture for them. Further, it is instructive to note that certain texts were variously employed in different genres. Thus the book of Isaiah was copied for itself, and reused both in pesherite comments found in *CD* and in special *pesher*-compositions. Comparably, the book of Leviticus was copied for itself (even in paleo-Hebrew script), translated into Aramaic in targum form *(11QtgLev)*, and reused to justify prophetic pronouncements (in *11QMelch*). And finally, the book of Genesis was copied for itself, rewritten in an expanded and legendary manner in Aramaic *(1QGenApoc)*, and used for prophetic pronouncements. Quite evidently, the use of a text in one genre did not preclude its use in another; and the predilection for certain texts overall (like Deuteronomy, Isaiah, or Daniel),[46] as well as specific ones (like the diverse reuses of the prophecy in Num 24:17),[47] suggests that within the sectarian communities there was something like a 'canon-within-a-canon', something of a hierarchical preference for certain texts over others. However this be, the significant matter is not solely the use or reuse of given texts, but rather their employment by authoritative teachers in authoritative ways. It is to such matters that we now turn.

The Authority of Mikra

Several distinct, though related, levels of authority recur throughout the Qumran scrolls. To begin, it must be stressed that the principle source of authority of Mikra is that it is the revelation of God, 'which He commanded through Moses and through all his servants the prophets' (*1QS* 1:3; cf. 8:15-16). There are thus two categories: the inspired words of Moses (the Tora) and the inspired words of the prophets (the predictions of the prophets). This bifurcation also covers the explicit citations of Mikra. As we have seen, the words or books of Moses and the Prophets (like Isaiah, Ezekiel, and Zechariah) are adduced both to justify new teachings anent the Tora of Moses, and to validate new understandings of the ancient prophecies. But this valorization of Moses and the Prophets should not obscure the central fact that God alone is the principle source of authority for the community. Indeed, it is precisely because of their revealed aspect (cf. *1QS* 8:15-16) that the teachings of Moses and the Prophets have any authority whatever. Thus, with respect to the inheritance of Mikra, the sectarians might speak of a twofold *chain of authority*: God and His authoritative spokesmen.

But as we have repeatedly observed, the authority of the Law and Prophecies for the sectarians cannot be separated from the way in which they were interpreted. It was, in fact, precisely in the special way that the old laws were reinterpreted or extended, the old predictions reapplied or decoded, and the institutions of ancient Israel restructured or regenerated, that the covenanteers of Qumran saw themselves as distinct from other contemporary Jewish groups. Moreover, just because these reinterpretations of the ancient revelations were claimed to be the *true meaning* of God's word, a proper appreciation of the authority of Mikra for the sectarians would have to supplement the aforementioned chain of authority. In addition to a chain starting with God and extending to Moses and the Prophets, one must therefore also speak of their successors: the authoritative teachers of the community. As in the earlier

---

[46] Cf. e.g., Bruce, 'Book of Daniel'; also Brownlee, *The Meaning of the Dead Sea Scrolls*.
[47] See *CD* 7:18-21; *4QTest* 9-11; and *1QM* 11:5-7; also *Test. Levi* 18:3; *Test. Judah* 24:1; *P.T. Taanit* 4:2, 67d; *Rev* 22:16.

bifurcation, here too a distinction may be made between legal and prophetical interpretations.[48]

AUTHORITY OF THE TEACHER

The scrolls are very clear about the pivotal position of authoritative teachers in the history of the community. The group is founded by one called the Unique Teacher (מורה היחיד; *CD* 20:1);[49] and a turning point in the history of the sect is when God raises up 'men of understanding' from Aaron and 'men of discernment' from Israel to dig the 'well', i.e., to study and interpret the Tora (*CD* 6:2-11). Further reinterpreting the phrases of Num 21:18, *CD* goes on to speak of the true community of penitents who went out to the wilderness, where they 'sought [God]' (דרשוהו) and were instructed by the Interpreter/Inquirer of the Tora (דורש התורה). This same ideology is reflected in *1QS* 8:13-16, where reference is made to those who would separate themselves from sin and go to the wilderness, in accordance with the prophetic word of Isaiah 40:3; 'Prepare in the wilderness the way of * * * * (the Lord), straighten a highway in the wasteland for our God.' The last clause ('straighten a highway') is further interpreted to refer to 'the interpretation of the Tora (מידרש התורה) [which] He commanded through Moses, to do all that which has been revealed at each period, and which the prophets have revealed through His Holy Spirit.' Significantly, the aforementioned *CD* passage concludes with the remark that 'without [the "Staff" of Instruction] they [the sectarians; and all others] will not grasp [the meaning of the revelations of God] until there arises one who teaches righteousness (מורה הצדק) in the end of days.'

The role of the Teacher is equally important in the interpretation of the prophecies, as is explicitly remarked in a comment in *1QpHab* 2:1-9. Here we read of '[. . . the words of] the Teacher of Righteousness from the mouth of God.' These are words which explicate 'all that which will co[me up]on the final generation'; words 'of [under]standing which God put in [his heart], to interpret (לפשור) all the words of His servants the prophets.' Elsewhere, in the same text, we read that 'God informed him [the Teacher] concerning all the mysteries (רזי) of His servants the prophets . . . which the prophets spoke; for the mysteries of God are wondrous (7:4-5, 8).' Indeed, the true meaning of the ancient prophecies were not even known to the authoritative spokesman of God who revealed them in past times. Only through the interpretations of the Teacher will the community know of the final day and their ultimate vindica-

---

[48] For an attempt to place the Qumran 'chain' comparatively within the context of early Tannaic traditions, see Herr, 'Chain of Transmission'.

[49] Or, emending *yahid* to *yahad* (i.e. 'Teacher of the Community'). However, *CD* 20:32 also reads 'men of the *yahid* (Unique [one] who listen to the Teacher of Righteousness'. The variation *yahid/yahad* may therefore be inconsequential, with 'community' (*yahad*) the sense in both instances. This parallelism would also align the Teacher of 20:1 with the Teacher of Rigtheousness otherwise a thorny problem.

tion. Without them, the true intent of the prophetic 'words' will also not be grasped. Or, in the exultant words of one member: 'You (God) have informed us about the final ti[mes] of the (eschatological) Wars *through Your Annointed Ones, the Visionaries of the Fixed Times*' (*1QM* 11:7-8).[50]

REWRITING OF TORA RULES

The cumulative impression of the Qumran scrolls, then, is that its primary text, Mikra, is the product of divine revelation; and that its own texts, which extend and develop the teachings of God, in various legal-sectarian collections and in various pesherite commentaries, are *also* the product of divine revelation. But here a certain qualification is necessary. For while one must agree that the authority for the various legal exegeses in the *Damascus Document* and the *Rule Scroll* lies in their being the product of *divine inspiration through teachers and communal members*, the authority of the legal exegeses in the *Temple Scroll* lies in their purportedly being *an original revelation of God* (i.e., not an inspired interpretation). One may therefore see in *11QTemp* a quite different notion of exegetical authority: one which does not allow the interpretations of Mikra to appear separate from the Tora – be that through explicitly or implicitly justified exegesis, as commonly in *CD* – but deems it necessary to rewrite the Tora text itself.

The ideology of *11QTemp* that all reinterpretations of the Tora must be *part* of the Tora, and not simply related to it through exegetical justifications or verbal allusions, is evident not only in the *form* of this text, *a Tora revealed by God to Moses*, but also through exegetical features *within* the text. Of principle interest here is the reworking of Deut 17:10 ('and you will do *according to the word* which they shall tell you from the Place . . .') in *11QTemp* 56:34. The Pentateuchal source simply advises Israelites who proceed to the high courts to follow the adjudication of the priests and other judicial officials there. In *11QTemp* a strikingly different reading is found: 'and you will do *according to the Tora* which they shall tell you, and *according to the word* which they shall teach you *from the book of the Tora*, and tell you *in truth* from the Place . . .' Clearly, the authority of the adjudicatory words of the Pentateuchal text have been transformed in the sectarian version to mean the words *found* in the Tora. Indeed, all instruction must proceed from these *divine* words, the Tora book at hand, *11QTemp*, not from the human words of the judicial officiants. *11QTemp* is thus the *true* Tora, for in it all things are to be found. Certainly there is reflected here a different attitude towards writing new laws – *no matter how justifiable be their relation to the ancient Tora* – than that known from *CD*. Moreover, it is also quite possible that we also have here a critique of the early

---

[50] The technical term 'fixed times' *(te'udot)* is also used in legal contexts; cf. *1QS* 1:9.

Pharasaic position.[51] For at this time Pharisaic sages did not permit the writing down of new biblically based or justified) laws, as they did later. They rather required that the new rules be derived from the Tora or related to it, *but be transmitted orally*. It is therefore of much comparative interest to observe that one of the most notable Pentateuchal sources from which the early rabbis midrashically justified their ideology was Deut 17:10f![52] Presumably, ancient polemics centered on its proper interpretation.

In the light of the foregoing, three types of exegetical authority may be noted. 1. the writing down of new rules together with their (explicit or implicit) Scriptural justification *alongside the Tora of Moses*, as is common in the *Damascus Document*; 2. the writing down of new rules together with their Scriptural justification *within a new Tora of Moses* – as is characteristic of the *Temple Scroll*; and 3. the preservation in oral form only of new rules (at first with their Scriptural justification, later without them) *alongside the Tora of Moses*. Whether types 1 and 2 are so distinct as to suggest their basis in different and quite unrelated communities, is a matter for further consideration, to be weighed alongside the other linguistic and thematic considerations which distinguish *CD*, *1QS* and *11QTemp*.[53] Nevertheless, it is also clear that their relationship is closer than that between either of them and the Pharisaic position; or between any of these three and the Sadduceean alternative. For if we can trust later rabbinic tradents, the Sadducees allowed themselves to write down new rules alongside the Tora of Moses, but were not willing to justify these fixed laws on the basis of divine Scripture.[54] Finally, these four types may be compared with a fifth: that found in the masoretic text itself, where reinterpretations and ammendments to the rules of the Tora were pseudepigraphically incorporated into the text on a regular basis. The authority for these ancient Israelite innovations was thus the divine word to Moses, or Moses' own authority as teacher of the Law.[55] Only in some late circles is there the slightest hint of inspired legal exegesis.[56] On the other hand, the notable example of a divinely inspired interpretation of prophecies in Dan 9-11 is the near contemporary of this same phenomenon in the Qumran scrolls.[57]

---

[51] See the remark of Yadin, *Temple Scroll* 1, 56 and 2, 17; cp. the comments of Wacholder, *Dawn of Qumran*, 19.

[52] Cf. Tg. Pseudo-Yonatan *ad* Deut 17:10-11; esp. v. 11, *'al memar oraita deyalfunkhon we- 'al hilkhat dina' deyemerun lekhon*, 'according to the word of the Tora which they shall teach you, and according to the halakhic rule which they shall say to you'.

[53] See the arguments of Levine, 'Temple Scroll'; and also Schiffman, 'Temple Scroll in . . . Perspective'.

[54] See now the discussion of Weiss Halivni, *Midrash, Mishnah, and Gemara, passim*.

[55] See Fishbane, *Biblical Interpretation*, 257-65, 530-33.

[56] Ib., 539-42.

[57] On inspired exegesis in Daniel 9-11, see id., 479-95.

ONGOING DIVINE REVELATIONS

The inspired interpretations at Qumran are also authoritative insofar as it is *only* these interpretations which carry the true divine intent of the Tora of Moses and the words of the prophets; i.e., it is *only* on the basis of the law as interpreted by the Teacher and Interpreter (and their inheritors), and *only* on the basis of the prophecies as interpreted by the Teacher, that God's will can be fulfilled and known. The sectarians believed that only they were the bearers of the esoteric sense of the ancient revelations. Thus, whereas the Tora of Moses explicitly stated that 'the hidden things (נסתרת) are the Lord's and the revealed things (נגלת) are ours and our children's forever, to perform all the words of this Tora' (Deut 29:28), the ideology at Qumran was significantly different. There the 'revealed things' were for all Jews, but the 'hidden things' were for them alone.[58] Indeed, on their view, God revealed to the sect the hidden interpretation of the Law by which all Israel, including even its great leaders, like David, unknowingly went astray (*CD* 3:13; cf. 4:13-6). By following the true meaning and practice of the Law, the sectarians believed that they would not sin and would be guaranteed salvation. 'And all who will no according to the oath of God's [true] covenant, there will be surety (נאמנות) for them *to save them* from all the snares of Doom' (*CD* 14:1-2); 'those who perform the Tora [according to its true interpretation] . . . [will be saved] because of their labor and trust (אמונתם) in [the teachings of] the Teacher of Righteousness' (*1QpHab* 8:1-3). The nonsectarians, on the other hand, will be doomed: 'for they have not been numbered in the [true] covenant . . . nor sought Him (God) by His Law, to know the hidden things (הנסתרות) by which they have gone astray for their guilt; and (indeed even) the revealed things (הנגלות) they have transgressed insolently' (*1QS* 5:11-12).

There is a second significant divergence between Deut 29:28 and sectarian ideology. For whereas the Pentateuchal passage refers to the performance of the 'revealed things' of the Tora 'forever', the sectarians believed that the 'hidden things' constituted a *new* revelation of interpretations of the Law. The original Law, with its conventional and traditional interpretations, was thus not abrogated but rather superceded through innovative and ongoing revelations of its meaning. It was thus not the 'revealed things' alone which had authority over sectarian practice, but the ancient revelations as understood through the inspired interpretation of its 'hidden' sense. Thus the 'chain of authority' mentioned earlier is also a 'chain of ongoing divine revelations'. Initially the Tora of Moses was revealed (and also the words of the prophets); subsequently, through the founding teachers and ongoing study of the covenanteers, the hidden meanings of the Law (and Prophets) were revealed. This sectarian position is repeated in various forms. The *Damascus Document*, for example, refers to a hidden 'book of the Tora' which had been sealed up in the Ark since

---

[58] Agreeing with analysis of Schiffman, *Halakha at Qumran*, 22-32; contra Wieder, *Judean Scrolls and Karaism*, 53-62.

the days of Joshua, a matter which lead to many serious sins of marital impurity (4:21-5:11);[59] and, after referring to the special revelation of new meanings of the Law through the Interpreter of the Tora *'for the whole epoch of wickedness*, and without which [the sectarians and others] will not grasp [its meaning] *until* he who teaches righteousness will arise in the End of Days' (6:4-11; see above), the sectarians are exhorted to 'take care to do according to the exact statement (פרוש) of the Law *for the epoch of wickedness'* (6:14). Similarly, in the *Rule Scroll* the sectarians are told to go to the wilderness and engage in the 'elucidation (מדרש) of the Tora [which] God commanded through Moses: to perform – [in accordance with] all that has been revealed *at each period* (עת בעת; 8:15-16, and cf. 9:19-20).

It would thus appear, according to these sources, that the community believed in a progressive revelation of the meaning of Mikra (the Law and the Prophets); indeed, this revelation was the sole basis for the comprehension of Mikra until the End of Days. At that time, with the fulfillment of the prophecies and the correct performance of the Tora (among the sectarians), a new epoch would be inaugurated, one which entailed either the abrogation of the Law entirely or its dispensation in some new form, depending on how one interprets *CD* 6:10-11 (cited just above). On the one hand, there were certainly contemporary views which expected the abrogation of the Law in the final days (1 Macc 14:41); and *4QpBless* 3-5 even has a most striking formulation in this regard. But it is just as likely that the community believed in the ongoing authority of the Tora of Moses, but anticipated that its true meaning (already known to them) would in the End be revealed to all. Such a view would help explain the role of the *Temple Scroll* among the sectarian scrolls. For it would suggest that while in the present epoch of wickedness the true 'hidden' sense of the Law would be circulated privately in special sectarian pamphlets (like *CD* and *1QS*), a new Tora of Moses, incorporating all the true meanings of it in a revised form, would be the property of all those Jews who would survive the Final War. On this view, the *Temple Scroll* would thus be the Tora for the New Age: 'the *second* Tora' which 'is written on the tablets' (*4Q177* 1:12, 14) and hidden from of old. It is therefore striking to note, in this regard, that the very group of sins mentioned in *CD* in connection with transgressions performed *because* this document was 'sealed up' – (1) marital impurity; (2) conveying uncleanness to the Sanctuary; and (3) gross accumulation of wealth (see 4:17-18; also 4:20-5:11 – are those emphasized in *11QTemp* (for [1], see 51:17-18 and 60:15-16; for [2], see 35:10-14 and 48:14-17; and for [3], see 57:20-21). In any event, three distinct periods bearing on the ongoing and changing authority of Mikra can be discerned: Period One, when God revealed the Tora of Moses and the Prophecies to ancient Israel (the 'revealed things'), for the establishment of the Covenant and the people's salvation; Period Two, when, after sin and exile, God revealed the true Meaning of the Tora and the Prophets to the Instructor in

---

[59] Wacholder, *Dawn of Qumran*, 117, has interpreted this as referring to *11QTemp*.

Tora and the Teacher of Righteousness, and their repentant followers (the 'hidden things'; the 'mysteries'), for the establishment of a New Covenant and the salvation of the New Israel faithful to it; and Period Three, when, after the sin and destruction of nonsectarians, God would reveal His New Instruction (possibly the *Temple Scroll*) through the one who would teach righteousness, for the salvation of all (*CD* 20:20).[60]

The Interpretation of Mikra

As we have seen, the sectarians believed themselves in possession of the True Interpretation of Mikra during the epoch of wickedness. In a sustained and repeated image, this revelation of true interpretations for the faithful is likened to a well of living water. Thus, at the outset of the *Damascus Document*, the people are told how 'God revealed' to those 'who were left over' after the exile, 'and who held fast to the commandments', 'hidden things regarding which all Israel had gone astray . . . His righteous testimonies which man shall perform and live thereby . . ; *and they digged a well for much water*' (*CD* 3:12-16). Later on it is stressed how God 'raised' up 'men of understanding' and 'wisdom . . . *and they digged the well . . . with the staff: the Well is the Law . . . and the Staff is the Seeker* (דורש) *of the Law*'; for 'without' this Well and Teaching no one can 'grasp' the true meaning of the Tora (*CD* 6:2-11). Thus the sectarian can exult: 'You have established within my heart a true foundation, *waters of well* for those who seek it (דורשיה; *1QH* 6:9);[61] while nonsectarians, even those who 'have forsaken the *well of living water*' will be bereft on the Day of Judgement (*CD* 8:21a).

A vigorous dedication to the interpretation of Mikra was thus cultivated by the sectarians. They were concerned to observe the laws according to their 'exact meaning (מדוקדק; *CD* 6:14, 16, 20)', for in the Tora of Moses 'every-thing is stated precisely (פרוש; *CD* 13:1-2)'; just as they were concerned to 'determine (פרוש) the seasons' precisely, for such is 'stated precisely (מדוקדק) in the book of the Divisions of the Periods' (*CD* 16:2-3). With this knowledge the community was distinguished from all others. 'For everything hidden from all Israel' might be 'found by one who seeks (הדורש) [Scripture] properly' (*1QS* 8:11-12); but all others will be confounded, 'for . . . they have not sought Him (דרשוהו) [God] according to His Law to know the hidden things' (*1QS* 5:11). The sectarians regarded themselves as 'scholars (מלומדי) of the Law' (*1QM* 10:10; cf. *1QH* 2:17); but considered all others, 'who seek (דרשו) facilely' (*CD* 1:18), as ones 'whose falsehood is in their study (בתלמוד); (*4QpNah* 2:8).[62] Similarly, the sectarians regarded their interpret-

---

[60] Lit., 'Observe the covenant until the Messiah of Righteousness comes . . . the Tora with the men of the community'.
[61] Interpreting *wmyh bryt* as *my brwt* (i.e., *may borot/be'erot*), with Wallenstein, 'A Hymn', 280 (and n. 9).
[62] On this phrase, see above n. 27.

ers of prophecies as 'visionaries (חוֹזֵי) of truth' (*1QH* 2:15); but considered the interpretations of all others, who do not interpret 'by the Holy Spirit', as 'visionaries (חוֹזֵי) of deceit' (*1QH* 4:10) and 'falsehood' (4:20). Such polemical point-counterpoint underscores the centrality of true interpretation in the proper understanding and performance of Mikra.

In earlier sections, we had the occasion to indicate the various literary forms utilized among the sectarians for the interpretation of Mikra (lemmatic, anthological, and pseudepigraphic forms, among others), as well as several of the techniques employed in their vast exegetical enterprise (scribal, legal, homiletical and prophetic). In order more fully to appreciate this achievement, a more specific focus on the *techniques of interpretation* will be offered. These techniques will be considered in a somewhat formal way, with examples drawn from earlier sections, where the texts were cited.

SCRIBAL EXEGESIS

In the course of scribal transmission, several types of exegesis were registered in the scrolls, most probably on the basis of prolonged study and reflection.[63] Concern for divine honor or sanctity, for example, resulted in *euphemistic* renderings of the Tetragram. Thus in *1QS* 8:14, the citation from Isa 40:3 renders the Tetragram with four dots ('the way of * * * *'); whereas just earlier, where this citation is alluded to with an interpretation (to go to the wilderness), the Divine Name is rendered by the pronoun *hw'h'* (8:13-14), a circumlocution also found in *CD* 9:9 and Tannaic sources *(M. Sukka 4:5)*. On the other hand, in *CD* 15:1 the sectarians prohibited the substitutions *alef we-lamed* (for El, Elohim) and *alef we-dalet* (for Adonai) in oaths, as comparably in other Tannaic regulations (*M. Shevuot* 4:13). In one notable instance, *CD* 8:16 restylizes Deut 7:8 in order to avoid the divine Name; and an attempt to avoid anthropomorphic renderings results in the substitution 'before the Lord' for 'the eyes of the Lord' in *11QTemp* 53:7-8; 55:12-14), a change common in Targum Onkelos and Yonatan, and quite possibly in the masoretic text as well.[64]

With respect to the substance of lemmata, scribes might indicate 'sense' by means of *paragraphing*, as in the 'unit' *1QIsa* 51:17-52:6).[65] Relatedly, scribal sense might be achieved via *phrasing*. Thus, in the aforenoted citation, from Isa 40:3 in *1QS* 8:14-15, the deletion of the introit 'a voice calls' allows the teacher to use the verse to exhort the sectarians 'to prepare a way in the wilderness', i.e. to establish a community there. A similar verse-division is found in the medie-

---

[63] For scribal exegesis within the Hebrew Bible, see Fishbane, *Biblical Interpretation*, Part 1.

[64] On anthropomorphisms in the targumim, see Komlosh, *Aramaic Translations*, 103-07; Alexander, above p. 226. As regards the masoretic text, the variations between 2 Sam 22:7b and Ps 18:8b are suggestive of earlier parallels to this phenomenon.

[65] Cf. Brownlee, 'Background' 189-93.

val Masora, which presumably also reflects the original syntax of the exhortation, though for the post-exilic community in Babylon this exhortation would have been understood as an appeal to prepare for the journey through the desert to the Homeland. The rendering 'a voice calls *from* the wilderness . . .' in Matt 3:3, which joins the introit to the first stich of the parallelism, is thus an exegetical reworking of the lemma to support the call of John from that place. In other instances, syntactic ambiguities regarding whether a word was to be read with the preceding or following clause, a problem of syntactic determination known as *hekhre'a ha-katuv* in Tannaic sources,[66] was resolved quite differently from the masoretic procedure. Whereas in the latter tradition two words of a syntactically ambiguous construction were joined by conjunctive accents (so that the words are to be read with the preceding clause), in some Qumran texts a disjunctive *waw* may be found before the second word (so that it was to be read together with a new phrase).[67] This method of resolving ambiguity is confirmed through a comparison of the Samaritan, masoretic and Septuagint versions on certain verses;[68] and it is mentioned in talmudic and medieval Jewish sources.[69] We thus see that, even at the basic level of reading, the interpretations of a community and its teachers play a strategic role.

LEGAL EXEGESIS

As we have seen, the legal regulations of the covenanteers are found in different genres; in topical collections, like the *Damascus Document*, and in biblical-style collections, like the *Temple Scroll*. In addition, these legal regulations are presented in diverse forms: with and without explicit justifications from Mikra, and within and alongside full or abbreviated Mikra citations. Quite certainly, a highly developed range of hermeneutical techniques were utilized, and it is to a review of some of these that we now turn.[70] Admittedly, these techniques are incorporated within the regulations without conceptual elaboration or terminology. It will nevertheless be of some historical interest to categorize them along the lines and terms found in the more developed Tannaic and Amoraic traditions. For by doing so, the place of Qumran interpretation within the context of ancient Jewish exegetical techniques can be more formally and comparatively observed.

1. *Linguistic precision.* Earlier, we had occasion to refer to the citation of Deut 5:12 ('Observe [שמור] the Sabbath day') in *CD* 10:14-15, in connection with a determination of the onset of the holy Sabbath day; and to the citation of

---

[66] The *locus classicus* is *Mekhilta de-R. Yishmael, Beshallah* 1, p. 179 (*ad* Exod 17:9). Further on this matter, based on evidence in *Minhat Shai*, see Blau, 'Massoretic Studies', 139.

[67] See Eliner, 'Ambiguous Scriptural Readings'.

[68] See Fishbane, *Biblical Interpretation*, 82.

[69] On the *'itture soferim*, see *B.T. Nedarim* 37b, and *Arukh Completum*, 6, 189. Cf. Mulder, above p.92.

[70] For the phenomenon in the Hebrew Bible, see Fishbane, *Biblical Interpretation*, Part 2.

Lev 23:28 ('Apart from [מלבד] your Sabbath-offerings) in *CD* 11:17-19, in connection with a concern to restrict sacrifices on the Sabbath to the special burnt-offering of the Sabbath. In the first case, the citation preceded the sectarian determination; in the second, it followed it. Nevertheless, in both cases a ruling of Mikra was used to justify the new regulation on the basis of a *diyyuq*, or close linguistic examination. In *CD* 10:14-15 the unspecific and admonitionary verb שמור was constructed to mean 'be watchful' (with respect to the setting sun; i.e., the temporal boundaries of the day), not merely 'be heedful' or 'attentive'. Similarly, in *CD* 11:17-19 the broadly inclusive adverb מלבד was reinterpreted more restrictively to mean 'except'. In this instance, the semantic nuance of the word is not at stake; it has rather undergone a complete change of meaning in this later period. Hence the *diyyuq* here is somewhat akin to the more formal rabbinic אינו . . . אלה technique, where a later meaning of a word replaces an earlier one (i.e., the word under discussion 'means, in fact, *x*').[71]

2. *Analogical extension or correlation.* Quite frequently in the masoretic and Samaritan versions extensions to laws are formally marked by technical terms.[72] Similar procedures are found in the Qumran scrolls. Thus, in connection with a denunciation of forbidden marriages, *CD* 5:8-10 cites a version of Lev 18:13 'And Moses said: you shall not approach your mother's sister; she is your mother's kin', a rule which prohibits marriages between nephews and aunts. In Mikra, the opposite is not stated; and the Pharasaic ruling accordingly permitted marriages between neices and uncles. However, our sectarians believed that proper understanding of the meaning of Scripture led the nation to practice *zenut*, 'harlotry', by which was meant incest. The proper ruling is therefore given straightaway along with the operative principle: 'now the rules of incest are written [in Mikra] with reference to males, *and apply equally to women* (lit. 'and like them [כהם; viz., the males] are the women'). Only given here, this far-reaching principle may be assumed to have been operative elsewhere in Qumran exegesis. It would be an instance of what the rabbis called *revuta'*, by which a feature of the written text – here, the masculine pronoun – was understood to 'include' something else.

Another type of legal exegetical extension may be found in the anthology of *11QTemp* 52:1-3. In it, a reference to the law in Deut 16:21 prohibiting the erection of stelae is followed by a citation from Lev 26:1. It was pointed out earlier that the link between these passages is the occurence of the same prohibition *in the same language*. But the legist had further reason to cite Lev 26:1 here, since this latter also prohibits incising forms on altars. Thus the Deuteronomic rule is extended on the basis of the priestly rule which is partly

---

[71] E.g. *Mekhilta de-R. Yishmael*, Bo 6, p. 20 (*ad* Exod 12:9); and ibid. *Yitro* 4, p. 218 (*ad*) Exod 20:1).

[72] For the Masoretic Text, see Fishbane, *Biblical Interpretation*, 170-87; for the Samaritan Text, see Daube, 'Zur frühtalmudischen Rechtspraxis', 148.

identical to it in language. Such terminological analogies, known as *gezera shawa* in rabbinic literature, served as the basis to correlate legal formulations and extend one of them on the basis of the other. If we were to articulate the preceding exegesis in rabbinic terms, the following hermeneutical proof might be stated: since Lev 26:1 and Deut 16:21 both prohibit the erection of stelae using similar language (*x*), though only the former text explicitly prohibits altar incisions (*y*) we must infer this prohibition also in the latter text. Thus again, on the basis of a linguistic feature, more is attributed to a given passage than directly, or explicitly, stated.

In the case of *CD* 9:6-8, cited earlier, the legist also drew and analogy between the law of reproof (his central concern) and the laws of vows by utilizing the language of the latter ('from one day to the next') in establishing the time-limit for valid reproof. This latter is not so much a *gezera shawa* between *CD* 9:6-8 and Num 30:15 as an allusion to the latter, in order, on that basis, to establish a 'Mosaic' regulation with respect to the sectarian law of reproof. Such a use of the Mikra to support new regulations is closer to the rabbinic hermeneutical technique called *zekher la-davar*. A related instance of this form of intertextuality is *CD* 10:17-20. Hereby, the covenanteer is admonished to obey the Sabbath and: 'not speak a foolish or empty word (. . . ידבר דבר); . . . [and] not lend anything . . . [or] dispute about property and gain . . . [and] not speak about matters (ידבר בדברי) of work and labor to be done (לעשות) on the morrow; . . . [and] not go out to the field to do (לעשות) the work he desires [to complete, etc.]. . .' As the language makes clear, these new regulations are loosely derived from (or correlated with) the language of Isa 58:13. In this text, true Sabbath behavior involves not going on a journey 'to do your business (עשות חפציך)';[and] 'not making' (עשות) a trip, nor engaging in business (חפצך) nor arranging deals (דבר דבר)'. Couched in the language of Mikra, the sectarian rules seem only loosely to be derived from it. Further attention to the phrase דבר דבר suggests that the legist has exegetically generated his specific new rules on the basis of the principle of *gezera shawa*. For just as דבר is used in Deut 32:47 with ריק ('empty word'), and in Deut 15:2 with ישה ('lend'), and in Deut 17:2 with משפט ('judgement'), so are these three terms found in *CD* 10:17 as well.[73] In this way, the explicit uses of these terms in Deuteronomy serve to extend the sense of the phrase דבר דבר in Isa 58:13 and thereby generate new Sabbath rules.[74]

3. *Topical specification or restriction.* Exegetical concerns to restrict or more carefully delineate an older rule may be found both in the stylistic structure of sectarian rule formation and in the way Mikra rules have been reformulated. The formulation of the law in *CD* 9:17-22, dealing with the witnesses, may exemplify the first category. Here we find an opening statement made in

---

[73] See also Slomovic, 'Understanding' 9-10.
[74] For the technical terms of Isa 58:13, see Fishbane, *Biblical Interpretation*, 304n. 31; and for inner-biblical reuse of Isa 58:13-14, ib., 478f.

generalizing terms ('*[In] any matter* concerning which a person might transgress against the Tora, and his neighbour, alone, witnesses [it]'), followed by a specification of the type of delict ('if it is a capital case'), along with subsidiary considerations (including such a transgression before two witnesses), and then a further specification of the delict ('[whereas'] concerning property [cases]'), along with subsidiary considerations (including the number of witnesses).[75] The development is thus from the general to the specific; or, in rabbinic terms, from *kelal* to *perat*.

With respect to the formulation of the laws themselves, we noted earlier that *11QTemp* 17:6-9, dealing with the rules of the paschal-sacrifice, the generalizing formulation of this practice in Exod 12:47 (addressed to 'the *entire* congregation of Israel') has been restricted to persons 'twenty years of age and older'. Such a 'delimitation', or *mi'uta'*, is presumably supported by the use of the identical phrase (יעשו אותו, 'they shall do it') in both cases. The exegetical logic would thus be as follows: just as in the citation from *11QTemp* the phrase יעשו אותו serves to restrict cultic practice, so must this sense be inferred in the first case as well. By writing the restriction into the formulation of the law, the sectarian legist merely makes this hermeneutical technique explicit. In other instances, the exegetical qualification is not based on linguistic correlations *between* Mikra citations, but on conceptual restrictions, not specified in Mikra but now introduced *into* the new formulation. The insertion of the explication 'and she is permitted to him according to the law' in *11QTemp* 66:8-11, noted earlier in connection with the anthological conflation there of Exod 22:15-16 and Deut 22:28-29 (dealing with marriage after seduction and rape), is a case in point.[76]

HOMILETICAL EXEGESIS

In the category of 'homiletical exegesis' we shall by-pass those exegetical features which do not pertain to eschatology *per se*, and focus on nonlegal exegesis which occurs either within nonlegal discourses or serves to justify legal matters.[77]

1. *Nonlegal justifications.* Earlier, *1QS* 5:7-6:1 was referred to in connection with citations used to justify restrictive contact between sectarians and non-sectarians. Two nonlegal sources are adduced. In the first case, Exod 22:7 (admonishing judges to refrain from 'any manner [כל דבר] of falsehood') was cited to support the rule to keep apart from nonsectarians 'in every matter (כל דבר; 5:15); in the second Isa 2:22 (admonishing hearers to keep apart from 'mankind' for it is of no 'account (נחשב)' is cited to support separation from

---

[75] See the similar translation and remarks of Levine, 'Damascus Document' 195f.

[76] For other instances of legal clarification, see *11QTemp* 43:12, and 60:4-8.

[77] For this phenomenon of 'aggadic' exegesis in the Hebrew Bible, see Fishbane, Biblical Interpretation, Part 3.

those not 'accounted (נחשבו)' among the sectarians (5:11, 17-18). Notably, both legal admonitions are justified by manifestly nonlegal statements. More-over, the terminological links between each rule and citation are conceptually unrelated; so that it is only on the basis of their exegetical extension that they serve their new purpose. Other instances of this phenomenon, e.g., *CD* 9:2-5 (discussed earlier) and 11:18-21, are no less striking from a hermeneutical point of view. Presumably, these are all cases of exegetical justification *ex post facto*, and are not indicative of the exegetical derivation of laws from nonlegal sources by sectarian legists. This latter practice was forbidden by the rabbis.

2. *Paraenetic or liturgical reapplications.* Among the sources treated earlier, three types may be recalled here. The first type involves the theological reuse of the Priestly Blessing in *1QS* 2:2-10. There the liturgical language of Num 6:24-26 was cited and reapplied in light of the sect's theology. The result is a new prayer achieved by means of covert exegesis. The lemmata and theological attributions are stylistically integrated in this new recitation, with no attempt to distinguish the one from the other. Moreover, the relationships between the lemmata (e.g., 'May He [the Lord] bless you') and their extensions (here: 'with every good') are simply introduced dogmatically. No philological relationships connect them. The same structure is also characteristic of exegetical reuses of the Priestly Blessing in Mikra and rabbinic literature.[78]

In two other instances, more subtle techniques of interpretation are involved. The first of these, *CD* 8:14-18, is part of a hortatory reprise from Deut 9:5a and 7:8a. As indicated earlier, the way Mikra has been cited, abbreviated, and blended here thoroughly transforms the force and application of the paraenesis. The ancient divine words are now transferred from the generation of the first conquest to the sectarians themselves: the new Israel. In this way, the older text which stated that the land was inherited as a result of God's love for the Patriarchs, and His promise to them, is also changed. It is now because of the penitent faithfulness of an earlier generation of Jews that God determines to extend His love to their sectarian successors. The old Deuteronomic sermon has thus been exegetically redirected to contemporary times.

In another instance, Deut 1:13 has been recited and exegetically reworked in *CD* 6:2-3 in order to justify the sectarian's arrangement of courts and councils. The original Deuteronomic reference to the appointment of 'men of under-standing' and 'men of wisdom' as judges is now formulated so that such persons portrayed as coming from the Aaronids and Israelites, respectively. In addi-tion, the men are not chosen by other men, as in the Mikra, but are 'raised up' by God Himself; and these delegates are not inferior to some superior judge, like Moses in Deut 1:7, who alone will be 'informed' (lit., 'I [God] will make him understand [ושמעתיו]') of the verdict, but they will themselves be 'informed' (lit. 'made to understand [וישמיעם]') the divine will. Even more significantly, the subsequent lines make clear that such divine inspiration leads

---

[78] See above n. 43.

men to the new (sectarian) interpretations of Tora by which they might judge and teach the people. And so, through consummate exegetical dexterity, an entirely different model of leadership and judgement is presented: not one accomplished by wise and discerning men, with divine oracular intervention in rare instances; but one accomplished by *interpreters of the Tora*, with continuous divine inspiration through them.[79]

PROPHETIC EXEGESIS

The reinterpretation of prophecy is a major exegetical feature of the Qumran scrolls, and is represented in a wide variety of genres: the *War Scroll*; the *Damascus Document*; the *(11Q) Melchizedek* and *(4Q174) Florilegium* anthologies; and, of course, in the *pesher*-literature.[80] Naturally, the style of interpretation varies in relation to the genre used. Thus in *1QM*, single verses from Mikra are reapplied globally to a new situation; in *11QMelch* and *4QFlor*, multiple verses from Mikra are grouped together and reapplied to specific topics on the basis of related thematics; and in the *pesher*-literature and pesherite comments in *CD*, successive verses from one bok of Mikra (the prophets or psalms), or single verses from one book, are atomized into their verbal components and successively reapplied to a new situation.[81] But it should also be noted that the methods of interpretation used overlap these genres, and present a more unified picture. Thus the terminology (פשרו, 'its interpretation is', and variants) and atomizing style of the *pesher*-literature are also found in *4QFlor*, even as this structural form occurs with different technical terms (e.g., הוא, 'it means') to link lemmata to interpretations in the pesherite comments in *CD*.[82] In addition, many of the exegetical techniques employed in prophetic reinterpretations occur in legal and homiletical contexts. Withal, the types of verbal exegesis used in the prophetic reinterpretation of Mikra do have a distinctive character. As most of these latter go against the plain-sense of the passage at hand, it is reasonable to assume that they have been developed in order to understand the true (viz., contemporary) intent of the ancient oracles, meanings which the interpreter of Habakkuk actually claims to have been unknown even to their original speakers (*1QpHab* 7:1-2). For the sectarians, both the techniques and the meanings derived thereby originate with the inspired tutelege of the Teacher of Righteousness. Indeed, their knowledge of them constitutes their hope in imminent divine vindication.

1. *Dogmatic links between lemma and interpretation.* Hereby, the claim is simply asserted that a certain contemporary event was alluded to by the ancient

---

[79] The institution in Deut 1:17 is itself a reinterpretation of older texts; see Fishbane, *Biblical Interpretation*, 245.
[80] On this phenomenon in the Hebrew Bible see ibid., Part 4.
[81] For the techniques and terms, see Fishbane, 'Qumran Pesher'; and now also Horgan, *Pesharim*, Part 2, *passim*.
[82] Examples related to these assertions will be given below.

prophets, or that the meaning of a prophetic text is this or that. For example, Num 24:17-19, which promises that a star shall come forth from Jacob who will defeat Israel's enemy, is cited in *1QM* 11:6-7; and Isa 31:8, which announces that Asshur shall 'fall with the sword not of man', is cited in *1QM* 11:11-12, both times in connection with contemporary events; but in neither case is any verbal or textual justification for such reapplication provided. Presumably, such reuse derives from inspiration. Similarly, in the course of interpreting Amos 5:26-27, it is simply asserted that 'the king' (in the phrase '*sikkut* your king') *is* (הוא) 'the congregation', and that 'the *kiyyun* of the images' *are* (הם) 'the books of the prophets'. To be sure, the basis for this reinterpretation is the larger interpretative context of *CD* 7:10ff.; but, again, no ostensible textual basis for these rereadings is provided.

2. *Direct verbal links between lemma and interpretation.* In the course of reapplying a lemma to a new context, the interpreter may repeat a key word from the lemma (sometimes even retaining its grammatical form). Thus, in Hab 1:5, the prophet encourages the ancient Israelites with the pronouncement that God will soon do wonders for them, which 'you will not believe (לא תאמינו) when it will be told (יסּפר)'; while in *1QpHab* 2:3-10 this very same verse is utilized to criticize those Jews who do 'not believe (לא האמינו) in the covenant of God' or the prophetic words which God has 'foretold (ספר)'. In other cases, a repeated word can serve as the basis for a paraphrastic expansion and reapplication of the lemma (e.g., 3:7-10); or repeated words can link several citations which are used to support a given theme (e.g., the common verb נטע serves to link the citations from 2 Sam 7:10-11 and Exod 15:17-18 anent a new Temple in *4QFlor* 1:2-7; and the common nouns דרך in Ps 1:1 and Isa 8:11, and מושב in Ps 1:1 and Ezek 37:23, serve to link these passages on the topic of sectarian separateness in *4QFlor* 1:14ff.). The exegetical dynamics of the latter have some resemblence to the *gezera shawa* technique, considered earlier. Of related interest is the exegetical use here of one Scriptural lemma to explain another.[83]

3. *Transformed verbal links between lemma and interpretation.* After Amos 5:26-27 is cited in *CD* 7:14-15 ('and I have exiled the *sikkut* [סכות] of your king . . . from My tent [מאהלי] to Damascus') to support a statement of an exile northward (itself justified by a citation from Isa 7:17), the text abruptly continues with a pun on the pagan object *sikkut*, when stating that 'the books of the Tora are the Tabernacle (*sukkat* [סוכת]) of the King.' This reinterpretation is itself immediately justified by a citation from Amos 9:11: 'as He (God) said: "I will raise up the tabernacle (סוכת) of David that is fallen".' Once again, one Scriptural passage is adduced to support another; though it will be clear that in this case the intertextual chain becomes conceptually more torturous. For one thing, the pagan objects are reinterpreted as the Tora, and an image of exile is

---

[83] On this text, see the exegetical comments of Slomovic, 'Understanding', 7f; and Brooke, *Exegesis at Qumran, passim.*

reinterpreted by one of eschatological hope; for another, the pagan object of a 'star' (in Amos 5:26, though not explicitly cited in *CD* 7:18-20)[84] is reinterpreted as the Teacher of Righteousness, and this last on the basis of a citation from Num 24:17! The tendentious proofs notwithstanding, Scriptural texts have hereby become pretexts for new ideological agenda. The verbal puns powerfully serve to carry the logic of rhetoric forward to these goals.

In addition to puns, which fairly abound as a hermeneutical technique, a more radical use of the letters of the lemmata can be found. Here we may call attention to what the rabbis called *serus*, or the 'rearrangement' of letters in order to achieve new applications of Mikra. For example, in *1QpHab* 2:5-6 the word עמל ('work') in the lemma is transposed as מעל ('transgression') in the *pesher*. In this light, we may now add that the aforecited passage from Amos 5:27 ('from My tent [מאהלי] to Damascus' does *not* conform to the Mikra itself (which reads: 'from beyond [מהלאה] Damascus'), so that the purported lemma is actually a reinterpretation of the passage on the basis of a hermeneutical rearrangement of the letters. One can only marvel at the exegetical *tour de force* involved, and the exegetical confidence of the new readings, even to the extent of introducing the citation from Amos 5:26-27 (a 1st person divine pronouncement with the formulaic introit: '*as* He said'.

4. *Typological reinterpretations.* In *1QM* 11:11-12, noted above, a passage from Isa 31:8 was adduced to support sectarian hope in a victorious eschatological war. Quite clearly, the appearance of Asshur in Mikra is now understood as a cipher for contemporary enemies of the covenanteers. In a similar vein, it is generally agreed that references to the Kittim in *pesher Nahum* refer to the Romans; and that, in the same text, 'Judah' = the sectarians, 'Menasseh' = the Sadducees, the 'Deceiving Interpreters' = the Pharisees, and the 'lion' = Alexander Jannaeus.[85] These and other examples thus combine to suggest that the sectarians also read Mikra with an eye to deciphering its tribal and other references in terms of the groups and figures of the day, and that they further believed that these meanings were part of the divine intention regarding them from the beginning, only now correctly decoded.

Conclusion

In the scrolls from Qumran and its environs which we have analyzed in the preceding pages, Mikra is the literary expression of divine Truth: at once the unique resource of past revelations, and the mediating source of all subsequent ones. As found in Mikra, God's Word is an illimitable Word of Truth: for the ancestors of ancient Israel, as well as for their legitimate inheritors, the Qumran covenanteers, who *alone* understand it rightly. There is thus Mikra *and* its

---

[84] The explicit interpretation is based on the second half of the verse, as commonly in rabbinic midrash.

[85] On this, see Flusser, 'Pharisees, Sadducees, and Essenes'.

Interpretation. We may understand this conjunction in two ways: as continuity and as correlation. As a matter of continuity, Mikra is succeeded by the interpretations of it. In this regard, the Qumran covenanteers are both the heirs of ancient Israel and progenerators of the great culture of biblical interpretation which (in large part) constitutes Judaism. Like the former, the Israelites of old, the sectarians interpreted 'biblical' traditions (laws, theology, prophecies) in sophisticated ways, with technical terms and procedures.[86] But unlike this earlier 'biblical' interpretation in ancient Israel, which was incorporated into Mikra itself, and as part of the older genres of composition, the sectarians, similar to early Jewish practice, further developed exegetical techniques and terms, produced new 'nonbiblical' genres within which Mikra was interpreted (including rewriting the Pentateuch, as in *11QTemp*), and looked to Mikra as an authoritative collection of completed books whose contents were recurrently cited.[87] However, unlike their ancestors and contemporaries, the sectarians viewed the relationship between Mikra and Interpretation as a continuity of divine revelations; viz. the revelations to Moses and the prophets were succeeded by *exegetical revelations* to the authoritative teachers of the sect. Thus, for the covenanteers, each period had its teachers and its books: ancient Israel had the teachings of Moses and the prophets, preserved in Mikra; and they had the inspired teachings of the Teacher and Seeker, and various new works. As the discourse on new interpretation in *CD* 7 makes clear, God produces 'an instrument for His [ongoing] work.'

Turning, in conclusion, to Mikra and its Interpretation as a matter of correlation, the preceding perspective is reinforced. For the sectarians, as for contemporary Judaism, generally, there is no Mikra *without* its interpretation; indeed, there is only the Mikra *through* its *legitimate* and *proper* interpretation. On this point everything hinged. For to practice the word and will of God in society, one had first properly to understand it; and to know the plan and purpose of God in history one also had first properly to understand it. The Interpreter of the Tora and the Teacher of Righteousness, as well as all their subsequent delegates and followers, safeguarded these true understandings, the 'hidden things' of the Law and the 'mysteries' of the prophets, and gave the Qumran fellowship definition and distinction. The *yaḥad*, or 'community', was thus a community by virtue of its style of 'biblical' interpretation – *and the practical consequences derived therefrom*. Further, the members constituted a true community, to be vindicated by God in the End to Come, also only by virtue of their 'biblical' interpretation, *and the practical consequences derived therefrom*. For the sectarians, then, all others practiced and hoped in vain, because their interpretation of Mikra was itself vanity: without authority in technique, and so without

---

[86] See Fishbane, *Biblical Interpretation, passim.*
[87] Only in a limited way, and only in late books were texts cited and reinterpreted in Mikra; see ibid., 106-29.

authority in result. Fatefully, the sectarians believed that outside their authoritative use and interpretation of Mikra there was no salvation.

Bibliography

For survey and annotation of texts, together with listings of major publications and pertinent studies, the reader is referred to the study of DIMANT, 'Qumran Sectarian Literature', in *Compendia* II/2, 483-550. For more specific analyses, relative to the topics and texts treated in the present study, the following selection is offered:

BETZ, *Offenbarung und Schriftforschung*; BLOCH, 'Midrash'; BROOKE, *Exegesis at Qumran*; BRUCE, *Biblical Exegesis*; FISHBANE, *Biblical Interpretation*; GABRION, 'L'interprétation de l'Ecriture'; HORGAN, *Pesharim*; PATTE, *Early Jewish Hermeneutic*.

Chapter Eleven

Use and Interpretation of Mikra in the Apocrypha and Pseudepigrapha

Devorah Dimant

Introduction

STATEMENT OF THE PROBLEM

The corpus designated as the Apocrypha and Pseudepigrapha of the Old Testament includes various Jewish writings of different origin and character,[1] that have, nevertheless, certain common features which distinguish them from other contemporary bodies of literature such as the Ancient Versions, the rabbinic midrashim, the Qumran sectarian writings and some of the Jewish Hellenistic works.[2] One of these is the extensive use made of biblical language, style and literary genres in a specific way. For unlike most of the writings of other corpora, the Apocryphal and Pseudepigraphic compositions take up styles and forms of the biblical literature. They may, therefore, be seen as aiming to *recreate* the biblical world, while other literatures, inasmuch as they employ biblical materials, usually aim at interpreting it. But while specific aims and literary forms vary, all post-biblical writings draw upon the biblical tradition and interpret it in various ways. The numerous exegetical affinities between these writings show that they share a common exegetical tradition and this fact ought to be taken into account in any research on the subject.[3]

---

[1] Cf. Nickelsburg, 'Stories', 35-84; *ibid.* 'Bible Rewritten', 89-152; Attridge, 'Historiography', 157-60, 171-83; Gilbert, 'Wisdom Literature', 290-312, 316-19; Collins, 'Testaments', 331-53; *ibid.* 'Sybilline Oracles', 357-76; Stone, 'Apocalyptic Literature', 383-433.

[2] In fact, many works traditionally not included in the corpus belong there by virtue of their literary character. Thus, for instance, a non-sectarian work found at Qumran which properly belongs to the Pseudepigrapha, namely the *Genesis Apocryphon* (cf. below), was included in two recent selections of Qumranic, chiefly sectarian, literature, see Dupont-Sommer (ed), *Écrits Intertestamentaires*, 383-99, and Knibb (ed.), *Qumran Community*, 183-202.

[3] This conclusion was forcefully stated by Vermes, 'Qumran Interpretation', 49. He well illustrates this principle by his own investigations. But here lies another pitfall; to set out from unresolved difficulties of a given biblical episode in order to review the solutions offered to them in later writings is to look for common interpretative aims. Such an investigation usually entails playing down or disregarding the specific function of a biblical text in individual compositions. Cf. Vermes's approach in 'Bible and Midrash', 59-91.

Yet while biblical elements in other bodies of literature have received more attention,[4] little has been done on the Apocrypha and Pseudepigrapha. Apart from scattered comments in monographs, commentaries and various articles,[5] few works have been devoted entirely to this aspect in the literature under discussion.[6] Much pertinent material may be found in various studies, but they have never been assembled and systematized.

DEFINITIONS AND METHOD

Every systematic treatment of the subject must tackle the problem of methodology. Until recently the work done on the Apocrypha and Pseudepigrapha was mostly concerned with identifying and analysing diverse biblical elements.[7] Studies of the wider functional contexts of such elements are only gradually beginning to be published.[8] But such studies are few and of limited scope and methodology, with only occasional comparisons with other bodies of literature.[9] This only enhances the need for a more rigorous and comprehensive methodology which takes into account both the general and specific literary features of the Apocrypha and Pseudepigrapha.

One of the major weaknesses of previous investigations is their inductive approach, method and definitions being generalized from a close analysis of

[4] This is especially true of expositional genres, such as the midrash, the pesharim and Philo's commentaries. Understandably, research on these works has tended to concentrate on the exegetical implications of the use of Mikra, and less on its function within the structure of the work. A change in this orientation has recently been seen in works such as Nikiprowetzky, *Commentaire*; Cazeaux, *La Trame*. For the pesharim cf. the older works of Elliger, *Studien*; Bruce, *Biblical Exegesis*, and more recently Brownlee, *Pesher of Habakkuk*, 23-36; Horgan, *Pesharim*, 229-59; Nitzan, *Pesher Habakkuk*, 29-79; cf., Dimant, 'Qumran Sectarian Literature', 504-08. The non-expositional literature most extensively researched is the NT. Cf. the reviews by Kaiser, *Use of the Old Testament*, and Moody Smith, 'Use of the Old Testament'.

[5] Much material may be found in the volumes of the series *Jüdische Schriften aus hellenistisch-römischer Zeit (JSHRZ)* and the *Anchor Bible – Apocrypha*. Various monographs and articles on individual issues will be referred to throughout the chapter.

[6] Some of the materials were assembled by Zink, *Use of the Old Testament*. The work is hampered by a confused methodology. Of much relevance to the present enquiry is the recent survey by Fishbane, *Biblical Interpretation*, which concerns inner-biblical interpretation. The author has assembled an impressive amount of data and provides many new insights into them. The weakness of the work lies in the absence of an overall comprehensive formal framework. It seems to me that the selection of the pair *traditio/traditum* as the operative terms of analysis is unfortunate; for they introduce socio-historical criteria instead of formal ones. Cf. also the review of Greenberg in *Numen* 34 (1987) 128-30.

[7] This is the typical attitude of the current commentaries, even the most recent ones (cf. n. 5).

[8] Cf. e.g. the studies of Hartman, *Asking for a Meaning*, on *1 Enoch*, and Sheppard, *Wisdom*, on Ben Sira and Baruch.

[9] This is typically the situation in NT studies. Cf. e.g. monographs such as Gundry, *Use of the Old Testament*; Freed, *Old Testament*. See also n. 4. Thus, for instance, much was made of the affinity of the so-called Formula Quotations in the Gospel of Matthew to the Qumranic Pesharim. Cf. the influential monograph by Stendahl, *School of St. Matthew*, esp. pp. 183-202; cf. Ellis, below, pp. 692ff.

specific individual cases. Such an approach tends to concentrate on elements of content at the expense of the formal and functional. The result is a limited and fragmentary methodological framework, which has to be modified with each new text.[10] The present chapter is based on the fundamental characteristics of the literature under discussion and its use of biblical elements. The definitions and method proposed here are all derived from these fundamental notions.

Thus, instead of defining only *what* a certain biblical element implies in a given context, the stress will be on *how* it is said and *why*. Our approach will be to outline the architecture and structural patterns, and the compositional techniques, inasmuch as they help to identify biblical elements and define their functions.[11] Such a functional approach is especially helpful when analysing the works of composite literary character which make up the bulk of the corpus.[12]

The functional-structural form of analysis also suites the character of the Apocrypha and Pseudepigrapha as written compositions. Unlike early biblical literature, these works were composed mostly by individual authors, as is evident from their unified plan and purpose. To a large extent, this is true even of writings with a complex literary history, such as the *Testaments of the Twelve Patriarchs*; for even in such cases we are dealing with a history of written documents.[13] It is clear that these works were conceived as written compositions, and were produced in a literate milieu. As a rule they have no oral prehistory, a stage assumed for many of the biblical literary complexes.

PURPOSE OF THE PRESENT STUDY

A thorough and systematic application of the functional analysis outlined above would demand a full understanding of the literary genres and forms employed, and their social and historical background. Such a task, however, is far beyond the size and scope of the present chapter. It would also demand a summary of results of research hardly yet begun. The present survey, therefore, cannot pretend to be more than programmatic and suggestive. It will not be able to go

[10] Cf. for instance the attempts to define the genre 'midrash', as represented by Bloch, 'Midrash' and Wright, *Literary Genre*.

[11] Elements proposed by Hartman ('Survey', 333-34) for the definition of the apocalyptic genre are also relevant for the present discussion. Hartmann stresses that the constituents of a genre are not only linguistic (style, vocabulary and phraseology) or propositional (typical themes and motifs and their structure of presentation), but also 'the functional relations between the elements'.

[12] Cf. the comments on the apocalyptic genre by Koch, *Rediscovery*, ET, 23-28 (esp. 27f.). Many works, such as testaments, narratives or wisdom discourses, interweave smaller units of different forms into their framework: thus we find prayers and testaments in narrative works (cf. e.g. Tobit 3-4, 12-13 and 1 Macc 1-2) or in wisdom discourses (cf. e.g. Wis 7-9), and autobiographical accounts in apocalyptic works (cf. 1 Enoch 83). There is also an inverse phenomenon: testaments include wisdom discourses or apocalyptic predictions, and are framed in a narrative. In fact, the tendency to create complex literary forms is operative in the biblical literature itself. Cf. Fishbane, *Biblical Interpretation*, 271-73, who notes the similar phenomenon of *Mischgattung* in the biblical law.

[13] On the composition of the *Testaments* cf. Collins, 'Testaments', 331-32. See now the opinion of Hollander-de Jonge, *Testaments*, 27ff.

into the social and historical background of various usages of Mikra, nor to embark upon investigation of the literary genres involved.[14] As a rule, genres will be treated within the generally accepted terms, and only inasmuch as they clarify a specific use of biblical elements in a given context. Due to limitations of scope and space, matters of language, style and theology cannot be treated independently, but only as far as they are relevant to the functional analysis.[15]

In spite of these limitations the present contribution will attempt to outline a wider methodological framework, into which observations relevant to the use of biblical elements may be organized. After a short description of the suggested approach, an example will illustrate each of the methodological elements proposed.

The application of the functional approach to the use of biblical elements in post-biblical literature reveals two broad, formally distinct, categories: one evincing a *compositional* and the other an *expositional* use of biblical elements.[16] In compositional use biblical elements are interwoven into the work without external formal markers; in expositional use they are presented explicitly as such, with a clear external marker. These two distinctive functions have different aims. In the exposition the divine word is introduced in order to interpret it as such, while the composition is employed when the biblical element is subservient to the independent aim and structure of its new context.[17]

These two fundamentally different attitudes to the biblical material find expression in corresponding different literary genres and styles. Thus, we find literary genres in which the exposition predominates, while others prefer a composition. In the first type, the aim is to explain the biblical text. This usually involves a fixed terminology and special syntactical patterns, in order to separate the biblical elements from their exposition. Thus one often finds the biblical materials presented in lemmata, clearly distinct from the expositional

---

[14] For the present, there exist systematic attempts to define literary genres only of the genre 'testament' and the genre used by the apocalyptic literature. Cf. von Nordheim, *Die Lehre der Alten* 1; Collins, 'Jewish Apocalypses'. See also Hartman, 'Survey'.

[15] As theological elements received most of the scholarly attention, the reader may be referred to current commentaries. Problems of style and phraseology need a separate study, which would involve, among other things, complex textual investigations which cannot be embarked upon here.

[16] A similar distinction between 'creative description' and 'creative exposition' was advanced by Heinemann, *Darkhei ha-Aggada*, 163-64, 176. Another distinction along similar lines, between *texte expliqué* and *texte continué* was suggested by Perrot in discussing the literary genre of the *Biblical Antiquities*. Cf. Perrot (ed.) *Pseudo-Philon*, 2, 24-27.

[17] The distinction between expositional and compositional genres permits a better appreciation of the distinctive character of the midrashic texts and the compositional texts. Thus, for instance, the *Genesis Apocryphon*, which was judged by many to be a targum or a midrash (cf. the survey of scholarly opinions by Fitzmyer, *Genesis Apocryphon*, 7-11), is clearly a narrative composition utilizing the biblical text as part of its own running story, and not a midrash or a targum. To apply the term 'midrash' to works of the type 'rewritten Bible' (as done by Wright, *Genre Midrash*, 52ff. and Vermes, *Scripture and Tradition*, 67-126) is misleading.

part. To this category belong the rabbinic midrash, the Qumranic pesher, the commentaries on the Tora by Philo and certain types of quotations in the NT.[18]

Another use of biblical elements may be defined as a middle type between expositional and compositional. Here, a divine word or action is represented in order to extract a lesson from it. Divine speeches, either direct or through a prophet, are usually quoted explicitly, and occur mostly in a discourse. Here, too, the biblical elements are distinguished by external markers, but the formal exposition is absent. The dominant interpretative principle here is actualization of a divine utterance, as expressed in a given biblical text (law, promise, prophecy). Divine acts, on the other hand, are usually referred to in short narrative summaries mentioning biblical events or characters. These are always introduced by explicit names or clear allusions to the original context, but never in precise quotations. This usage figures in rhetorical contexts as well as in narratives proper. As in the previous type, the exposition is not formally introduced, but is expressed by the rhetorical or narrative use of the biblical elements.

In contradistinction to the above types, the genres employing biblical elements in compositional use do not have the same exegetical or rhetorical aims, but create a new and independent text. Biblical material becomes part of their own texture. Typical compositional genres are narratives, psalms, testaments, and wisdom discourses, which use biblical elements for their own patterns, style and terminology. Accordingly, and unlike expositional genres, the compositional works do not introduce the biblical elements by formal terms, but weave them unobtrusively into their own fabric. In the Apocrypha and Pseudepigrapha, as stated already, the genres evincing such use predominate; and this is why biblical elements used in an expositional way are scarce in these works, while in compositional work they are used abundantly.

The distinction between exposition and composition helps us better to define the different types of biblical interpretation involved. In fact, unless they appear in purely stylistic or linguistic functions,[19] biblical materials are always interpreted. Yet there is a difference between interpretations conveyed by exposition and those implied by the composition. In order to facilitate this distinction, different terms will be employed below. The term 'interpretation' will be reserved for the understanding of a biblical element used in compositional or rhetorical way, while the term 'exegesis' will be employed for its use in an expositional context.

---

[18] The lemma-and-comment form was widespread in the Ancient East in interpreting dreams and omens, and was adopted by apocalyptic literature as exemplified by the Book of Daniel (Cf. Fishbane, *Biblical Interpretation*, 446-57) and the Qumranic Pesharim (cf. Horgan, *Pesharim*, 230-37, 244-45). Alexander, 'Rabbinic Rules', compares the lemmatic structure of the rabbinic midrash with the literary structure of the paraphrastic Aramaic targums. He rightly stresses their distinct literary character, inspite of their similarity. Cf. above, ch. 6.

[19] In current literature the use of biblical elements in stylistic functions are not sufficiently differentiated from other types of uses.

Likewise, for procedures employed in explicit exposition we shall use the current 'hermeneutical rules', such as those used in the rabbinic midrash and the Qumran pesharim.[20] Philo utilized other 'hermeneutical rules', mainly the allegory, which was borrowed from the Hellenistic philosophical exposition of Homer. The use made of biblical elements in rhetorical as well as in compositional contexts involves a variety of exegetical techniques which have not been properly studied until now. In the present discussion the techniques involved in rehtorical use will be termed 'exegetical procedures', while those used in compositions will be termed 'interpretative procedures'.

Another helpful distinction is that between narrative and discourse as genres or literary forms. One of the results of the present study is a clear distinction between how biblical elements work in narrative and in discourse. From this perspective it does not matter whether the discourse or the narrative operates as the main or the subservient genre.[21] We will often find, for example, that biblical elements function in the same way in the testament genre, be it a large testament comprising an entire work or a small one forming only a subordinate unit in a larger work of a different genre.

Finally, these definitions are offered as a framework for the analysis of specific texts. But as the literature under discussion rarely includes pure exposition, the latter will not be discussed. The chapter will be devoted mainly to the use of biblical elements in compositional use, either in rhetorical or other contexts.

Explicit Use of Mikra

The explicit use of Mikra in our literature means that the biblical elements are introduced with an explicit reference to their source. Such a use consists mostly of explicit biblical quotations, or references to biblical personalities and circumstances. Both types are made explicit by overt references: either by naming the biblical source of the quotation or by mentioning a name or circumstances taken from a specific and recognizable context. Both types use special stylistic devices in order to refer the reader to the function and meaning intended.

A survey of the available material reveals that these usages often occur in discourses in order to illustrate and prove a point as a part of a rhetorical argument.[22] In these contexts the expositional function of the biblical quotation

[20] On the use in the pesharim of hermeneutical rules similar to the ones used by the rabbinic midrashim cf. Dimant, 'Qumran Sectarian Writings' 505-07; Brooke, *Exegesis*, 8-79. Patte, *Early Jewish Hermeneutic*, 139-208 offers a collection of disparate materials with no conceptual framework.

[21] This similarity comes out well when comparing biblical elements in units of different size but of the same genre.

[22] The commonest of these arguments is the so-called Rule of Justice, that is 'identical treatment of beings or situations which can be integrated in the same category'. Cf. Perelman-Olbrechts-Tyteca, *Traité de l'Argumentation*, 294-95.

or reference, as well as its exegetical contents, form part of rhetorical argumentation.

Explicit quotations are biblical phrases of at least three words, more or less accurately reproduced, and introduced by special terms and explicit references to the source. In our literature such quotations are relatively few and occur mainly in the non-biblical narrative, for the literary character of the pseudepigraphic or biblical narrative excludes such quotations (cf. below). Typical cases are to be found in what may be termed 'free narrative', namely, narrative which does not rework a biblical story. In the literature at hand such are most of the narrative books of the Apocrypha, fictional as well as historical.[23]

The following is a list of explicit quotations in the Apocryphal narrative books:[24]

Pentateuch

Gen 2:18	Tobit 8:6	(in prayer)
Gen 34:7	Judith 9:2	(in prayer)
Gen 49:7	4 Macc 2:19	(in discourse)
Exod 15:17	2 Macc 1:29	(in prayer)
Exod 20:17	4 Macc 2:5	(in discourse)
Exod 23:7	Susanna 53	(in admonition)
Exod 23:22	2 Macc 10:26	(in summarized prayer)
Lev 26:44	3 Macc 6:15	(in prayer)
Lev 26:29	Bar 2:2	(in discourse)
Deut 30:20	4 Macc 18:19	(in discourse)
Deut 32:39	4 Macc 18:18	(in discourse)
Deut 32:36	2 Macc 7:6	(in prayer)
Deut 33:3	4 Macc 17:19	(in discourse)

Prophets

Amos 8:10	Tobit 2:6	(autobiographical story)
Isa 43:2	4 Macc 18:14	(in discourse)
Ezek 37:3	4 Macc 18:17	(in discourse)

Psalms

Ps 79:2-3	1 Macc 7:16-17	(comment on events in narrative)
Ps 34:20	4 Macc 18:15	(in discourse)

Writings

Prov 3:18	4 Macc 18:16	(in discourse)

---

[23] On the basic structural identity of historical and fictional narratives cf. Ricoeur, 'Narrative Function'. A comparison between the narrative function of books considered historical, as 1 Macc and 2 Macc, and that of historical novellae such as Tobit and Judith, should be made the subject of an illuminating study.

[24] 2 Macc 7:6 was analyzed in Dimant, 'The Problem of a Non-Translated Biblical Greek'.

The picture emerging from these instances[25] may be summarized as follows:

a. All explicit quotations from the Tora are used in discourses of various types. Two of the quotations from the Prophets and Psalms appear in narratives.

b. The explicit quotations from the Tora always cite a real speech in the original, made either by God[26] or by Moses, and one by Jacob (4 Macc. 2:19). Accordingly they are introduced by formulae including verbs of saying or speaking.[27]

c. The Tora quotations cite laws (Tob 8:6, Sus 53, 4 Macc 2:5) or divine promises. In fact, in their manner of introducing explicit quotations the Apocrypha books follow closely the biblical books themselves.[28]

While the general character of the quotations in our literature is still close to biblical usage,[29] 4 Macc is different. This work is not a proper narrative, but a philosophical encomium, which uses the story of the Jewish martyrs in the time of Antiochus IV to illustrate a philosophical principle, namely, that reason should govern emotions.[30] Most of the quotations from the Pentateuch follow the pattern of explicit citations in other works. They use similar terminology of introduction and they occur in discourse as part of the argument. But 4 Macc employs the quotations in a deliberative discourse, and it evokes the biblical text not in order to demand the fulfilment of the Law or a divine promise, but in order to interpret it in the light of certain philosophical ideas.

A special case is presented by the catalogue of references and quotations in the final speech of the mother, in which she evokes the education of her children by their dead father (ch. 18). The quotations are from the Tora, the Prophets and the Writings (Proverbs), and used as scriptural proof of the ethical religious principles of the father. Both the exegetical purpose and the form of the

[25] Judith 9:2 is analyzed in detail below, p. 397.

[26] In biblical literature, too, divine speech is quoted in various prayers, cf. e.g. Gen 32:10, 13, Exod 33:12, Num 11:21, Jer 32:25.

[27] 'Say' (εἰπεῖν) in Tob 8:6, Jdt 9:2, 3 Macc 6:15, referring to a divine speech, and 2 Macc 1:29 referring to Moses. Cf. also Tob 2:6 referring to the prophet Amos. The word 'explain' (διασαφεῖν) is used in 2 Macc 7:6, 10:26 of the Tora and of Moses.

[28] Explicit quotations of the Tora are rare in biblical literature. There is only one case which conforms to the criteria defined above, namely 2 Kgs 14:6 (= 2 Chr 25:4), citing Deut 24:16.

[29] Another type of scriptural reference does not involve a quotation in the sense defined above, but serves as a scriptural support for a particular deed, and is accompanied by the expression 'according to the Tora of Moses'. Cf. 1 Kgs 2:3, 2 Kgs 23:21, Ezra 3:4, Neh 10:35, 2 Chr 30:5, 18; 31:3, 34:21, 35:12. In some cases the verse adduces scriptural support and then goes on to employ it in a composition. In this way the verse indicates the conformity of an action to the Tora by referring to the pertinent verse, and using its wording. Cf. e.g. Josh 8:31 using Deut 27:5-7. Neh 8:14 presents an interesting case, for it employs all the relevant verses (Lev 23:34, 39 + Deut 16:13) in an abbreviated way. The same technical term for scriptural support occurs also in the Apocrypha. Cf. e.g. Tob 1:8, 7:13, 1 Macc 3:56, 4:47, 53.

[30] A major Stoic tenet. The definition of the literary form of the work is debated. The earlier view defined it as a philosophical diatribe of which the second part is an encomium for the martyrs. Cf. the formulation of Lebram, 'Die literarische Form'; Gilbert, 'Wisdom Literature', 317. Redditt, 'Concept' proposes to see it as a funerary discourse (epithaphios). Sigal, 'Manifestations', 167 suggests 'a didactic commemorative panegyric sermon'.

quotations differ from other books and closely resemble the types of quotations most frequent in expositional genres such as the rabbinic midrash.[31] This may reflect a later usage more frequent at the time of the composition of 4 Macc, during the first century C.E.[32]

In our literature the paucity of explicit quotations from books other than the Tora is striking compared with the profusion of implicit quotations and allusions from almost all the biblical books. This may be explained by the different usages involved: the explicit quotations presents the sacred word as such, while the implicit quotation is just one of the elements of the literary composition. A similar situation is to be observed in the biblical literature itself: explicit quotations are rare and appear chiefly in late biblical books, while implicit quotations in compositional use are current in most of the later biblical writings.[33]

EXAMPLES

Tobit 8:6 (= Gen 2:18)
Text[34]
G[II]: σὺ ἐποίησας τὸν Ἀδὰμ καὶ ἐποίησας (ἔδωκας) αὐτῷ βοηθὸν στήριγμα Εὔαν τὴν γυναῖκα αὐτοῦ, καὶ ἐξ ἀμφοτέρων ἐγενήθη τὸ σπέρμα τῶν ἀνθρώπων· καὶ σὺ εἶπας ὅτι Οὐ καλὸν εἶναι τὸν ἄνθρωπον μόνον, ποιήσωμεν[35] αὐτῷ βοηθὸν ὅμοιον[36]αὐτῷ.

Translation[37]

> You made Adam and made (vr: gave) for him a helper and a support, Eve his wife; of them both there came the seed of men; and You said: 'It is not good for the man to be alone; let us make him a helper[38] like him'.

---

[31] It should be noted in this context that 4 Macc already employs the term *nomos* in the late sense as a technical name for the Pentateuch. Cf. Redditt, 'Concept', 251.

[32] Cf. Gilbert, 'Wisdom Literature', 318. For a mid-first century date cf. Bickermann, *Studies* 1, 276-77; Anderson '4 Maccabees' 534; Schürer, rev. ed. 3.1, 591. The rhetorical Asian style of the work also points to the first or second centuries. Cf. Dupont-Sommer, *Quatrieme Livre*; Breitenstein, *Beobachtungen*, 178-79.

[33] Fishbane's collection of data in *Biblical Interpretation* is a mine of examples for the use of previous biblical books by later ones, though his method of classification is different. Cf. pp. 109-12 for explicit quotations, 307-14 for implicit quotations and pp. 138-43 for allusions.

[34] Text following Hanhart, ed. *Tobit*.

[35] As the reading of the Septuagint and *Jub*. 3:4. Cf. Gen 11:7 (note 3:22).

[36] This is also the reading of the Palestinian Targums, the Syriac and the Vulgate, and also *Jubilees*, ibid. Apparently no Hebrew variant lies behind the translation, but a common exegetical tradition of a difficult word in the masoretic text (כנגדו). On the difference between the rendering here and that of the received text of the Septuagint cf. Hanhart, *Text...Tobit*, 34-35, n. 5.

[37] Mainly following the rendering of Zimmerman, *Book of Tobit*, 93, 95.

[38] The translation follows the interpretative rendering, but does not reconstruct a *Vorlage*. Cf. n. 36.

This is taken from the prayer of Tobias, son of Tobit, uttered just after his exorcising the demon from his bride Sara, and before the consummation of the marriage. The prayer apparently functions in the story as a Blessing of the Bridegroom's, as it was probably practised in Israel during the Second Commonwealth.[39]

The prayer consists of four parts:[40]

(a) 8:5 – An opening address of praise to God.
(b) 8:6 – Evoking the creation of Adam and Eve (quotation).
(c) 8:7a – Statement of deeds and intentions of Tobias and Sara.
(d) 8:7b – Request for long life together.

The prayer forms a carefully constructed argument: first, Tobias affirms the sovereignty of God over the created world by referring to the praise offered him by the entire creation. Then Tobias evokes particular divine acts of creation, the creation of Adam and Eve. He goes on to quote the divine words which give the reason for the creation of the woman. By evoking these acts Tobias points to the laws governing human existence as laid down by the creative acts and sanctioned by God. These laws prescribe that human beings should live in couples in order to support each other and procreate. Tobias then states that his marriage conforms with the divine law that man should live with a wife, as expressed in Gen 2:18. Tobias terminates his prayer by a request for long life together, for obedience to the law.[41]

A closer look at the function of biblical elements in the prayer reveals some significant features: the prayer refers to the divine actions and divine speech by using the same biblical verse, Gen 2:18, but in each case it is employed differently: in depicting the action the biblical textual elements are introduced in an implicit manner, while the speech is introduced through an explicit and accurate quotation. One may wonder what is the precise function of the quotation as distinct from the depiction. The answer may lie in the understanding of the speech as a divine commandment, distinct from the act of creation. Tobias is thus saying that his conduct agrees with what was laid down by the creative deed as well as with an express command of God. In this way the understanding of the biblical verse as a divine command becomes part of the entire argument.

---

[39] A papyrus scroll discovered at Qumran *(4Q502)* contains various blessings, among which there is a Blessing of the Bridegrooms strikingly resembling the prayer of Tobias. Note especially *4Q502* 1:1-2 lines 3-7. The resemblance was noticed by the editor, M. Baillet *(Qûmran Grotte 4-III*, 81-82). The version of the Blessing of the Bridegrooms attested by rabbinic sources also alludes to the creation of Eve (Gen 2:22 and 1:27; cf. *B.T. Ketubbot* 8a).

[40] The prayer occupies a central place in the chiastic-concentric structure of the Book of Tobit. By virtue of this position the quotation also acquires a central place in the work.

[41] The request expressed in the prayer involves several rhetorical arguments such as that of the part and the whole (for establishing the identity of Tobias and Sara with Adam and Eve), and the Rule of Justice (to request an equal treatment for Tobias and Sara as for Adam and Eve). For these arguments cf. Perelman-Olbrechts-Tyteca, *Traité de l'Argumentation*, 294-97, 311-15.

3 Macc 6:15 (= Lev 26:24)
Text[42]

δειχθήτω πᾶσιν ἔθνεσιν ὅπι μεθ' ἡμῶν εἶ κύριε, καὶ οὐκ ἀπέστρεψας τὸ πρόσωπόν σου ἀφ' ἡμῶν ἀλλά καθὼς εἶπας ὅπι Οὐδὲ ἐν τῇ γῇ τῶν ἐχθρῶν αὐτῶν ὄντων ὑπερεῖδον αὐτούς, οὕτως ἐπιτέλεσον, κύριε.

Translation[43]

> Let it be shown to all the heathen that You are with us, Lord, and have not turned your face away from us; but, as You have said: 'Not even when they were in the land of their enemies have I forgotten them', so bring it to pass, O Lord.

This is from the prayer of Eleazar the priest, uttered just before the elephants were to be let loose on the Jews of Alexandria. As a prayer at a time of distress, it consists of an opening address to God (6:2-3), with a list of historical precedents of the punishment of wicked gentiles and the rescue of righteous Jews (6:4-8). The last part consists of specific requests (6:9-15). Our quotation forms part of the final plea, summarizing the central theme: a request for deliverance so that the Gentiles should witness that Israel is still protected by God. This would serve both as punishment for the vanity expressed by the foreign king, and as deliverance of the blameless Jewish community. The argument is reinforced by an additional claim: the Jews ought to be rescued because of the promise of salvation made to Israel as part of the covenant. The promise is given in an explicit quotation from Leviticus, which actually cites a divine speech. Eleazar thus shows that he equates the situation of the Jews in Alexandria with that of the people of Israel in the wilderness of Sinai. The exegetical procedure by which this is effected, is the equation of the terms in the quotation with contemporary ones.
This technique of equation is the most frequent means of effecting actualization, as is the case here.[44]

---

[42] Text following Hanhart, ed. *Maccabaeorum Liber III*.
[43] Following mainly Hadas, *Third and Fourth Books*, 73.
[44] This technique is also common in the Qumranic pesharim. Cf. my analysis in '*4QFlorilegium*', 172ff. Interestingly, such a technique often uses atomization as an exegetical procedure; atomization turns up as one of the techniques used by the early Bible translators. Brock, 'Aspects', 69-79 has shown that this method corresponds to the mode of literal translation prevalent in the Greco-Roman world.

Tob 2:6 (= Amos 8:10)
Text[45]

G¹: καὶ ἐμνήσθην τῆς προφητείας ᾽Αμώς καθὼς εἶπεν Στραφήσονται αἱ
ἑορταὶ ὑμῶν εἰς πένθος, καὶ πᾶσαι αἱ εὐφροσύναι[46] ὑμῶν εἰς θρῆνον καὶ
ἔκλαυσα.

Translation[47]

> And I recalled the prophet Amos, as he said:
> 'Your feasts shall be turned into mourning
> and all your joys into lamentation',
> (and I wept.)

The quotation occurs at the end of the episode in which Tobit tells how on the
eve of the Feast of Shavuot he has buried a Jew left dead in the market. The
quotation is introduced by the term 'recall' (ἐμνήσθην), which equates the
verse with the preceding situation. This is also indicated by the terms used: the
'feasts' of the verse are identical with the feast in the story, and the mourning of
the prophet is equated with the weeping of Tobit. Thus Tobit is made to read his
own situation into the prophecy of Amos, and sees in his own circumstances its
fulfilment.

This is another example of the use of actualization as an exegetical principle,
here applied to a prophecy.

1 Macc 7:16-17 (=Ps 79:2-3)
Text[48]
καὶ ἐνεπίστευσαν αὐτῷ, καὶ συνέλαβεν ἐξ αὐτῶν ἑξήκοντα ἄνδρας καὶ
ἀπέκτεινεν αὐτοὺς ἐν ἡμέρᾳ μιᾷ κατὰ τὸν λόγον, ὃν ἔγραψεν αὐτόν κρέας
ὁσίων σου καὶ αἷμα αὐτῶν ἐξέχεαν κύκλῳ Ιερόυσαλημ, καὶ οὐκ ἦν αὐτοῖς ὁ
θαπτων.

Translation[49]

> And they believed him; but he arrested sixty of them and put them to
> death in a single day, in accordance with what he wrote: 'The flesh of
> Your *Hasidim* and their blood
> They did shed around Jerusalem,
> And there was no one to bury them'.

---

[45] Text following Hanhart, ed. *Tobit*.
[46] For textual variants of the Septuagint cf. Hanhart, *Text*, 35.
[47] Mainly following Zimmerman, *Book of Tobit*.
[48] Text following Kappler, ed. *Maccabaeorum Liber I*.
[49] Translation following Goldstein, *I Maccabees*. For a detailed literary analysis cf. recently
Martola, *Capture and Liberation*, 47-48, 259-67.

This verse offers another example of the exegetical procedure of actualization. But in this case the quotation is taken from a psalm and is applied to a real historical event. The introductory formula 'in accordance with' establishes a relationship between the written word and the historical event. Such relationship rests primarily on an exegetical equation between the *Hasidim* mentioned in the psalm with the historical Asideans. As a result, also the contemporary situation is read into the psalm, which is apparently considered as a prophecy.[50] In both purpose and method this quotation is strikingly reminiscent of the Qumranic pesharim.[51]

It is also noteworthy that in the above instances the quotations occur in narratives. Yet they obviously do not belong to the plot. The quotations express, in fact, reflections on the events taking place in the plot, put either in the mouth of one of the protagonists, or, as is the case in 1 Macc, expressed by the author himself. In this sense they may be viewed as belonging to a discourse, and not to the narrative.

Another point of interest is the fact that the quotation of Psalm 79 is slightly curtailed, omitting some details. Yet it functions precisely as do exact quotations. This shows that a precise reproduction of the text cited was not imperative; it was enough to quote the essentials, and sometimes it was deemed necessary to alter some details in accordance with the context.[52]

EXPLICIT MENTION OF PERSONS AND CIRCUMSTANCES

The use of biblical elements includes mention of persons and circumstances. Such cases serve as markers announcing a biblical context. Although this type of biblical reference is not followed by a formalized exegesis, the exegesis is present, embedded in the rhetorical context.

Of this there are mainly two types in the Apocrypha and Pseudepigrapha: catalogues of biblical persons, and isolated references to persons or circumstances. These two types often occur in 'free narrative'. A third type of explicit mention of biblical persons or circumstances occurs in genres such as 'rewritten Bible' and pseudepigraphic biographies, and will be discussed below.

---

[50] In the Psalms scroll from Qumran *11QPs*[a] 27:11 David is considered a prophet who composed the psalms under divine inspiration. This explains why the Qumranites wrote pesher-like commentaries on the biblical prophecies as well as on psalms. David may have be seen as a prophet already by the Chronicler and Nehemiah, both giving him the prophetic title 'the Man of God' (2 Chr 8:14; Neh 12:24, 36).

[51] Cf. similarly Bar 2:2. On the exegetical methods of the pesharim cf. Horgan, *Pesharim*, 244-48; Nitzan, *Pesher Habakkuk*, 29-79. Cf. my comments in a review of Nitzan, *RQ* 48 (1987) 599-600.

[52] Note e.g. 2 Macc 10:26 where the quotation is put into indirect speech. This procedure is also found in implicit quotations.

1. List of historical examples

The lists under discussion are known as 'lists of examples' or 'catalogues of paradigms'.[53] These are concise references to historical precedents grouped in a sequence of examples in a special literary structure, which is usually considered a distinct literary form. Seven such lists occur in our literature:[54]

1 Macc	2:49-64	(in exhortation within testament)
3 Macc	2:1-8; 6:4-8	(in prayers)
4 Macc	16:18-23; (18:11-13)	(in admonition)
Wis	10:1-21	(in hortatory sapiental diatribe)
Sir	16:6-10	(in sapiental exhortation)
4 Ezra	7:106-110	(in polemical dialogue)
(Test. Naphtali 3)		(in hortatory testament)[55]

The rhetorical nature of these lists comes through clearly in their function, structure and form. Such lists always occur in discourses. Most of the examples are found in exhortations, and are tinged with sapiental elements and terminology.[56] Only two of the examples, both figuring in 3 Macc, occur in prayers. As a rule, such lists are introduced by a concise formulation of the central idea dominating the list. Then follow historical figures arranged in chronological order; each characterized by the facet of its career, relevant to the principle given in the introduction. Often introduction and examples are linked by terminology and structure.[57]

[53] Also known as *Beispielreihen*. Cf. Lampe, 'Exemplum'; Berger, 'Gattungen' 1147-48. On this point Berger bases himself almost exclusively on the analysis of Schmitt, 'Struktur'. Schmitt concluded for Wis that the list in question is modelled after the catalogues of historical examples in Greek and Hellenistic literature. This conclusion is fully adopted by Berger and applied to the genre in general. A similar argument was recently advanced in connection with Sir 44-50 by Lee, *Studies*, 29-48, 241-45. Yet it should be noted that Wis is the exception to the rule, being a Greek work, and overtly drawing upon Hellenistic rhetorics and philosophy. This is by no means the case for other works of this form.

[54] Berger, *ibid.* adds to the lists also *ApZeph* 9:4 (in the enumeration of Wintermute, 'Apocalypse of Zephaniah', 514). But it is questionable whether this list belongs to the present literary from, as it lacks the fundamental structure and rhetorical purpose common to all the other lists. For similar reasons the catalogue of the Praise of the Fathers in Sir 44-50 should not be included here (cf. Schmitt, 'Struktur' 1, n. 1) despite the arguments of Lee, *Studies*, 29-48.

[55] Although not included in our literature, the list in *CD* 2:14-21 contains all the features of the genre, and should in fact, be discussed with them. The same is true of Heb 11 and *1 Clement* 4:5-6, 9:2-12:8 adduced by Berger, 'Gattungen'. Of special note is the affinity between the lists in Sir 16:1-12 and *CD* 2-3. I have discussed it in detail in my dissertation *Fallen Angels*, 146-51. Berger has compared the two lists in respect to the use of the term 'stubbornness of heart'. Cf. Berger, 'Hartherzigkeit'. See also the comments on the literary structure of the lists by Lee, *Studies*, 29-48.

[56] The character of the lists as examples of conduct makes them suitable for sapiential admonitions; cf. Berger, 'Gattungen', 1146.

[57] Cf. the analysis of Wis 10 by Schmitt, 'Struktur', 13-19, which is valid for the remaining lists.

Each of these lists gives examples to butress the argument presented in the larger discourse. The role of the historical or mythical example in rhetorical argument was well-known in the ancient world, and was used extensively in biblical as well as in classical literature.[58] This role consists of three functions: the example establishes a general rule, or illustrates a rule already in force, or is a model or anti-model in order to recommend or condemn a certain type or behaviour.[59] Our lists use examples in the second and third functions, usually combined. Such a combination is to be found mostly in discourses of a hortatory nature, whereas in prayers the examples are used only as illustrations.

In the hortatory and liturgical contexts of our lists we find that the principle most frequently advocated is that of divine justice, as expressed in reward and punishment. This is the subject of the lists in 1 Macc 2:49-64, 3 Macc 2:1-8, 6:4-8 and Sir 16:6-10 (Compare *CD* 2:14-3:12).

A closely related theme is the one recommending pious action found in 1 Macc 2:49-64, 4 Macc 16:18-23 and Sir 16:6-10. Wis 10:1-21 propounds a similar rule, when it equates wisdom with justice and urges the adoption of wise action. Only *4 Ezra* 7:106-10 stands apart in that its list may be seen as an illustration of the Prayer of the Righteous, and not as a model of them.

An interesting feature of these lists is that they include both wicked and righteous figures. Thus 1 Macc 2, 4 Macc 16 and *4 Ezra* 7 produce lists of righteous figures, while 3 Macc 2 and Sir 16 (and also *CD* 2-3) present lists of the Wicked. In both cases the rhetorical result is to illustrate divine justice and pious conduct by either adhering to the model merits of the Righteous in order to receive their recompense, or by shunning the sins of the Wicked for fear of punishment. In two cases we even have a combined list: in 3 Macc 6:4-8 the wicked gentile rulers Pharaoh and Sanherib and their respective punishments are contrasted with the suffering righteous who were miraculously saved – Daniel and his three friends, and Jonah. In Wis 10:1-21 the list achieves a perfect symmetry by matching seven righteous alternating with seven wicked.[60]

---

[58] For biblical literature cf. the list in Pss 78, 105, 106, 136. Schmitt, 'Struktur', does not deny the similarity of structure between these psalms and the list of Wis, yet discards them as a possible source of inspiration for Wis. While such a claim can, perhaps, be argued for Wis, it cannot be asserted with the same certainty for other lists.

[59] For the rhetorical definitions cf. Perelman-Olbrechts-Tyteca, *Traité de l'Argumentation*, 471-99.

[60] Schmitt, 'Struktur', following others, suggests that the series of oppositions between Just and Wicked is modelled after the Greek rhetorical device of *synkrisis*. Cf. also Winston, *Wisdom*, 212. This may be true for Wis, but not necessarily for other lists. The fact that both Just and Wicked figure in other lists may point to a different origin of the idea. It should be noted that alternating Just and Wicked persons in history appear in other literary contexts such as the *Apocalypse of Weeks* (1 Enoch 93:1-10; 91:12-16), *CD* 2-3 and *2 Apoc. Bar.* 53, 57-68. Perhaps this is also the case in the Qumranic work known as 'The Pesher on the Periods' *(4Q180)*. Cf. my analysis in 'Pesher on the Periods' 98ff.

1 Macc 2:49-64[61]

The long list of biblical precedents forms the major part of Mattathias' testament on his deathbed: After a narrative introduction modelled on the Testament of Jacob (Gen 49),[62] Mattathias depicts the difficult circumstances. He admonishes his sons to be zealous for the Tora (ζηλώσατε τῷ νόμῳ) and to keep the Covenant of the fathers. Then follow figures from biblical history whose lives attest to their zeal and their recompense. Thus the list illustrates the principle, and serves as its model. The catalogue of various traditional merits can be viewed as exemplifying the principle 'be zealous for the Tora'. Clearly the author conceives the good deeds enumerated in his sequence as zeal for the Tora. Thus the term 'zeal', central to the religious ethos of this passage (cf. at the end of the testament 2:58 ζηλῶσαι ζῆλον and in 2:24, 26-27 ἐζήλωσε τῷ νόμῳ) covers a wider range of acts and gives the term a large and comprehensive meaning.[63]

The actual list is introduced by the phrase: 'remember the deeds of our fathers,[64] a typical way of introducing historical precedents. The examples are all structured in the same way: the merits of the heroes on one hand, and their recompense on the other. Each good act is introduced by the preposition ἐν and a substantive standing in the dative, while the recompense is usually indicated by a finite verb. All the good deeds are models of the rule at the beginning of the list and winding it up (*inclusio* τῷ νόμῳ / τοῦ νόμου in vv. 50, 68).

Although the examples use biblical elements, they seldom use quotations but prefer to reformulate the biblical circumstances. Yet in addition to the names, the author gives one or two terms, taken from the original biblical text, as shown in the following list:

Abraham – 'found faithful when tested' – the formula is used of Abraham also in Sir 44:20 LXX, and is composed of an allusion to Gen 22:1 'God tested' (LXX: ἐπείραζεν), and to Neh 9:8 'you have found his heart faithful to you'. The second part of the verse is a slightly altered reproduction of Gen 15:6 (influenced by the formula applied to Phineas in Ps 106:31).

Joseph – 'lord of Egypt' – Cf. Ps 105:21 LXX (κύριον) summarizing Gen 41:40-44.

---

[61] Text according to Kappler, ed. *Maccabaeorum Liber I* For translation cf. Goldstein, *I Maccabees*.
[62] For the testament form of this passage cf. the analysis of von Nordheim, *Die Lehre der Alten* 2, 5-8.
[63] For a detailed analysis of the motif of zeal in Num and in 1 Macc cf. Martola, *Capture and Liberation*, 208-21.
[64] μνήσθητε τῶν πατέρων ἡμῶν τὰ ἔργα. It is similar to the opening of the Praise of the Fathers in Sir 44:1-16. Lee, *Studies*, 47-48 notes the use of catch-words in certain lists: Sir 44-50; 1 Macc 2; 3 Macc 2, 6 and 4 Macc 16, 18.

Phineas – 'zeal' – the Greek here reproduces the Hebrew usage of קנא (לאלהיו) said of Phineas in Num 25:13. (The expression 'a Covenant of Priesthood forever' is also taken from Num.) The same expression is used of Elijah and Mattathias himself (2:26). It is also used of the chief virtue which Mattathias recommends to his sons at the beginning of his testament.

Caleb – 'the congregation' (ἐκκλησία) – cf. Num 14:1ff.[65] 'inheritance' (κληρο-νομίαν) cf. Josh 14:13-14 (note Sir 46:5-9).

David – 'the throne of kingdom forever' – cf. 2 Sam 7:13 MT.

Elijah – 'zeal' – cf. 1 Kgs 19:10. Interestingly, the author here adds 'for the Tora', not found in the biblical parlance, but typical of our work. 'was taken up as if into heaven' (ἀνελήμφθη ὡς εἰς τὸν οὐρανόν), a precise reproduction of the LXX to 2 Kgs 2:11 (καὶ ἀνελήμφθη Ηλιου...ὡς εἰς τὸν οὐρανόν; compare Sir 48:9 ὁ ἀναλημφθείς).

Hananiah, Azariah, Mishael – 'maintained their faith', 'were saved' – cf. Dan 3:23 MT.

Daniel – 'the mouth of lions' – cf. Dan 6:23.

The techniques of evoking biblical circumstances, as used in this type of literary form, may be described as introducing an explicit element, a name of a biblical figure, summarizing the most typical aspect of its life, and finally sprinkling it with terms taken from the original source.

A comparison between the lists of examples and the explicit quotations brings out their differences and similarities: while quotations are made explicit by an introductory formula, the lists are made explicit by details from the biblical materials, such as names or characteristic features, and often both. In addition, such lists use terms from the original contexts, and though they are not proper quotations, they evoke the biblical text.

The exegetical purpose of such lists is clear from the rhetorical use of the lists. It always involves the actualization of major biblical tenets within an argument, serving the aim of a larger literary unit, such as prayer or admonition.

2. Isolated References

The use of biblical circumstances as examples is not limited to lists, but is also found in isolated instances. Such cases are very similar to the lists of historical examples, and they often appear in prayers or discourses.

---

[65] The Greek of 1 Macc uses here the term ἐκκλησία which regularly translates the Hebrew קהל, while the story of Num 14 employs the term עדה, normally translated in the LXX by συναγωγή. But undoubtedly 1 Macc had in mind the story of Num.

EXAMPLE

The Rape of Dinah (Gen 34)

The story of the Rape of Dinah (Gen 34) offers a good example of a whole biblical context in a rhetorical function. It is used in three texts: Judith 9:2-4, *Jub* 30 and *Test. Levi* 2:1-2; 5-7.[66]

In all three instances the original biblical episode is evoked by the same technique: by introducing names and events of the original story, and by re-employing elements of style and terminology. Of special interest is the fact that all three make reference to the four central terms; two are taken from the biblical context: the defilement (of Dinah)[67] and the sword (by which the sons of Jacob killed the Shechemites).[68] Two additional ones, vengeance and zeal,[69] do not occur in the original Dinah story but refer to other biblical contexts, and are essential to the interpretation of Gen 34 in these writings. At the same time the writings differ both in treatment and in presentation because of different literary forms and ideological interests. All three adduce the story of Dinah in discourses and make a rhetorical use of it. But there are important differences between *Jub* and Judith and *Test. Levi*. Judith is a 'free narrative' and therefore the choice of biblical elements is in itself revealing. *Test. Levi* is a pseudepigraphon attributed to the biblical figure of Levi, and therefore is more closely bound with the biblical narrative, but it still has a considerable freedom in reworking biblical materials. Whereas *Jub* systematically reworks the narrative of Genesis. The author is, therefore, working within the framework of the Genesis stories. Consequently the message of *Jub* is conveyed more by rework-

---

[66] The Rape of Dinah is mentioned by other contemporary authors: it is briefly related by *LAB* 8:7, and retold in more detail by Josephus, *Ant.* 1:337-40 (cf. the discussion of Franxman, *Genesis*, 206-08). The Jewish epic poet Theodotus devoted a detailed discussion to Gen 34 in his lost writing *On the Jews*. Cf. the recent translation and discussions: Fallon, 'Theodotus', 785-89, esp. 786; Walter, *Poetische Schriften*, 154-71, esp. 159-61. Cf. van der Horst, below pp. 526-28; Pummer, 'Genesis 34', 177-88. A review of the sources mentioning Gen 34 is found in Gutman, *Beginnings* 1, 251-55.

[67] Cf. the masoretic text of Gen 34:5, 13, 27 טמא in the rendering of the LXX μιαίνειν; it is taken up by *Test. Levi* 7:3 (cf. de Jonge, ed. *Testaments*, 32) and also by the term βδέλυγμα (6:3). Cf. the notes ad loc. by Hollander-de Jonge, *Testaments*, 147. The term occurs also in *Jub* 30:2, 4, 6, 13, 14 (cf. the Latin *polluere* and the Ethiopic ለ ৫ *ঌ* and *१*(Charles, *Ethiopic Version*, 110-13; see the Vulgate and the Ethiopic version to Gen ad loc.) Judith 9:2 echoes the motif with three similar terms: μίασμα, αἰσχύνην and ἐβεβήλωσαν. Note also the occurrence of the term 'shame' (חרפה) in Gen 34:14, rendered by ὄνειδος in the LXX and reproduced by Jdt 9:2 and *Jub.* 30:12-13.

[68] Compare Gen 34:25-26 with Jdt 9:12. *Test. Levi* 5:3, 6:1,5 and *Jub.* 30:5. Death by the sword is often considered a divine punishment. Cf. Lev 26:25, 33, 37; 2 Sam 12:10; Isa 1:20, 34:6; Jer 12:12, 47:6; Ezek 6:3, 11:8, 29:8. Note *1 Enoch* 14:6 where the Giants are to be annihilated by the sword. This form of death is prescribed also for the Wicked on the Day of Judgment (e.g. *1 Enoch* 91:12, 99:16).

[69] Cf. Jdt 9:2 and *Test. Levi* 5:3 using ῥομφία, ἐκδίκησις. Compare *Jub.* 30:16, 23. Note the influence of Ps 149:7 לעשות נקמה בגוים rendered by the LXX τοῦ ποιῆσαι ἐκδίκησιν ἐν τοῖσ ἔθνεσιν. As for the term 'zeal' cf. the use of the verb ζηλοῦν in Jdt 9:4, *Test. Levi* 6:3 and *Jub.* 30:18.

ing the biblical text than by a free selection of biblical materials.[70] At the same time the author of *Jub* also has recourse to biblical episodes outside the main sequence of his story in order to express some of his particular views. This is also the case in reworking Gen 34.

Judith 9:2-4

The passage forms the opening part of Judith's prayer.[71] It summarizes poetically the biblical episode, as part of the argument advanced by the prayer. In this argument Dinah's rape functions as the historical precedent, and as such forms part of the justification for the request addressed by Judith to God. The prayer retains the biblical emphasis on the violation of an Israelite virgin and her ensuing defilement, but omits the name of Dinah. The crime is ascribed to all the Shechemites (a view taken also by *Jub* 30 and *Test.Levi*)[72], instead of Shechem alone. Such a sin is presented as a transgression of divine interdiction, read into the phrase 'And this shall not be done' (Gen 34:7).[73] Consequently, the killing of the Shechemites by the sword of the sons of Jacob is seen as a just punishment prescribed by God. Moreover, the vengeance is represented as an act of piety and zeal for God.

Hence the interdiction as a divine utterance carries the main burden of proof, and this is why it is presented by an explicit quotation, though not in the literal sense of the Hebrew. The prayer makes use of the so-called Rule of Justice by showing that the Rape of Dinah is analogous to the situation of Judith and the Jews of Betulia, threatened by the Assyrian army. When going to the Assyrian camp, Judith exposes herself to a double danger, as Jew and as a woman, just like Dinah. The author is clearly playing on the analogy between the temple of Israel violated by a gentile army and a woman violated by a man.[74] When Judith prays she identifies her own situation both with the victim Dinah and the avenger Simeon, her forefather.

The prayer is concerned only with the analogy between the biblical episode and the heroine's own fortunes. Other details are omitted: Simeon as Judith's ancestor becomes the main hero, Levi is not mentioned. Dinah is 'a virgin', and the inhabitants of Shechem are 'foreigners'. Other details are left out: the circumcision of the Shechemites and Jacob's reproach to his sons.

---

[70] For the literary methods of *Jub.* in particular cases cf. recently Endres, *Biblical Interpretation*. The methodological introduction on pp. 15-17 is disappointing.
[71] Cf. the discussion on explicit quotations above. For text see Hanhart, ed. *Iudith*. A new translation has been made by Moore, *Judith*.
[72] Cf. the comments of Haag, *Studien*, 44-45, Enslin, *Book of Judith*, 122.
[73] Οὐχ οὕτως ἔσται. Quoted in the LXX. Cf. Hanhart, *Text...Judith*, 83-84, 98-99 n. 2.
[74] βεβηλοῦν in 9:2 applied to Dinah and in 9:8 to the Temple. Cf. 4:3, 12; 8:21. See the observations of Zenger, *Judith*, 493. Note also the use of the word στρωμνή, 'couch', in 9:3 and in 13:9 (cf. Zenger, *Judith*, 508).

Jubilees 30

In *Jubilees*[75] the Rape of Dinah is in the main narrative taken over from Genesis. Like the entire narrative, it forms part of the angel's revelation to Moses on Mount Sinai. The main features of the episode are briefly related, accentuating the role of Levi and playing down that of Simeon, in line with the general priestly tendencies of the work. But the true significance of the episode is revealed in one of the additions of the angel. He explains that the story of Dinah was included as example of the rule prohibiting mixed marriage between Israelites and gentiles (*Jub* 30:12, 21).[76] This rule is read into Lev 18:21, which prohibits an Israelite to offer his offspring to Moloch.[77] Although the author of *Jub* quotes Lev, he is prevented from stating so explicitly because the pseudepigraphic framework situates the story at a point before the Tora was written. The quotation is, then, said to come from the Heavenly Tablets (*Jub* 30:8-10).[78] The story of Dinah at once illustrates the rule, exemplifies transgression of it and shows its punishment. Here too, the wording of Gen 34:7 'and this shall not be done', is seen as a reaffirmation of the rule and its validity for the future, but it is not explicitly quoted, due to the peculiar literary form.[79] The avengers, Simeon and especially Levi, are seen as righteous and zealous for God when they took vengeance on behalf of their sister (30:23). As a reward for such zeal, Levi receives the Priesthood for his offspring (30:18-19).

The Testament of Levi 2:1-2.5-7

In this work the episode of Dinah is mentioned in a narrative section in which Levi tells his sons of his youth. The story of Dinah is evoked by the names and circumstances of the protagonists (2:1-2; 5:3-4; 6:3-11). The story is linked to the promise of priesthood to Levi (5:2), as is clear from the sequence of the episodes. Levi officiates as priest only after killing the Shechemites, which indicates the motif of the priesthood as a reward for Levi's zeal. These motifs are also indicated by the verb 'to be zealous' (ζηλόω) which is said of Levi (6:3).

---

[75] For Ethiopic and Latin texts see Charles, *Ethiopic Version*. Several new translations were recently published. Cf. the translation with judicious comments by Caquot, 'Jubiles'; Rabin revised R.H. Charles' translation in Sparks ed. *The Apocryphal Old Testament*, 10-139 and Wintermute in Charlesworth, *OTP* 2, 52-142. For general comments cf. Berger, *Jubiläen*, 469-70.

[76] Note the change of style in Jub 30:12, 21 where the speaker, the Angel of the Face, specifies his reasons for relating the episode.

[77] The same interpretation is attested by the Peshitta, Targum Pseudo-Yonatan and the margins of Targum Neofiti on the above verse. Cf. *M. Megilla* 4:9. See the comments of Alon, *Studies* 1, 101-04.

[78] Most of the Tora laws cited in *Jub.* are said to be derived from the Heavenly Tablets. This is an interesting example showing how pseudepigraphic framework expresses a particular ideology: in this case, the idea that the laws were inscribed on the Heavenly Tablets. The Tablets are also mentioned in *1 Enoch* (81:1-2; 93:2; 103:2; 106:19) and the *Testaments of the Twelve Patriarchs* (*Test.Levi* 5:4; *Test.Asher* 2:10, 7:5).

[79] Endres, *Biblical Interpretation*, shows that verse 30:5-6 are arranged in a chiastic structure, but he did not mention that the beginning and end of the chiasm are in fact formed by implicit quotations of Gen 34:7c. So the quotation forms a kind of *inclusio* indicating a well-defined unit.

The events connected with the Rape are mentioned only in passing, and only as far as they are relevant to the life and mission of Levi.[80]

Summary – Comparison of the three
The comparison between the three texts shows that the same technique of reference was employed in different contexts and for different purposes: all three summarize some of the essential events of the episode, selected according to the aim of each work. In *Judith* it serves to build an analogy between Dinah and Judith; in *Jub* the biblical story serves as an admonition against mixed marriage, while in *Test.Levi* it is adduced in order to enhance the merits of Levi.

These common traits show that all three have recourse to the basic biblical tradition of the defilement of Dinah the Israelite by gentiles. All three turn the crime of Shechem into the sin of all the inhabitants of Shechem. All three omit *(Judith, Jub)* or play down *(Test.Levi)* the circumcision of the Shechemites related in *Genesis*;[81] *Jub* and *Test.Levi* render the crime even graver by making Dinah a girl of twelve. Finally, all three play to various degrees on the analogy of the story to the episode of the sinful association of Israelites with the Midianite women, and the zealousness of Phineas on this occasion, which earned him the High Priesthood for eternity.[82] Though this episode is not mentioned explicitly, the thematic and terminological allusions to it are clear: the context of illicit sexual intercourse between Israelite and a gentile, the immediate act of vengeance by killing by the sword, and the definition of the vengeance as an act of zeal for God. But while *Jub* and *Test.Levi* associate the motif of sexual offence and the zeal for God with Levi and the priesthood, *Judith* connects it with Simeon and a military victory. Interestingly, 1 Macc 2 uses the same analogy with Phineas, but without apparent connection to sexual abuses. It shows that the motif of zeal was also used independently of the sexual motif.[83]

Finally, it should be noted that the context of Phineas is alluded to here in a way characteristic of allusion in general (cf. below). It consists of using typical motifs together with typical terms belonging to these motifs in their original context. It is important to note here that this device is employed by both explicit and implicit usages of biblical elements.

---

[80]   The materials about Levi and his role in the story of Dinah are taken from the biographical part of the *Testament*. Hollander-de Jonge, *Testaments*, 131 see chapters 2-7 as an independent source used by the redactor of *Test.Levi*.
[81]   Much was made of this omission by scholars who wished to see in the use of Gen 34 in the present works an anti-Samaritan polemic. Cf. most recently Coggins, *Samaritans*, 88-93. For older literature cf. Pummer, 'Genesis 34', 177. But the evidence for such an interpretation is meagre. More plausible is to see it as a polemic against contact with gentiles in general, as argued by Collins, 'Epic' 99.
[82]   For the entire issue cf. the discussion of Hengel, *Die Zeloten*, 151-59, 181-88.
[83]   Apparently 1 Macc 2 combines the models of Phineas and Elijah, both of whom are zealous for God (cf. above).

The aim of the above review was to analyse the explicit usages of biblical elements. It was shown that in our literature such explicit usages always occur in rhetorical contexts and are of two types:

a. quotations and

b. mention of biblical persons and events.

Both types are introduced in a formal way, thus referring the reader to their scriptural source and the authoritative nature of its contents. In quotations it is the divine word which is evoked, and therefore the quotation actually stands for the divine speech. In explicit mention of biblical persons or circumstances it is the event or deed which is evoked, and therefore the reference stands for the divine action. Accordingly, the divine speech is represented with a quotation, while the divine action is represented with the depiction of an event.

The usages described above are not identical to the use of biblical elements in an expositional role, such as, for instance, the explicit quotations in the pesharim or in rabbinic midrash. But the two clearly have close affinity: both functions present biblical materials as authoritative, and in an explicit, formal way, and both involve an intended and explicit exegesis of the passage quoted. In this both usages differ radically from the implicit usages of Mikra.

Implicit Use of Mikra – Composition

While explicit use of Mikra is relatively rare in the Apocryphal and Pseudepigraphal writings, the use of biblical elements in compositions is most extensive and varied. In fact, it is through such usage that this literature aquires its characteristic style and flavour.

Biblical elements are used in compositions when they are integrated into the structure and style of a different work. Unlike elements in exposition, they are not presented in order to be interpreted, nor are they adduced as representing divine speech or action. Accordingly, their presence is not indicated by explicit formal markers. Their identification depends on the ability of the reader to recognize the biblical elements and to see their meaning in the new writing. In order to build up the intended meaning, and to refer the reader to the underlying biblical source, various techniques are employed in our literature. Three ways of using biblical elements in composition may be discerned: *a.* implicit quotations; *b.* allusions; *c.* motifs and models. The two first types involve textual elements, while the last involves thematic elements. Often two or three types of functioning are combined to refer to one biblical context. Also, these types are exploited by various literary procedures and forms, and to various purposes.

IMPLICIT QUOTATIONS

The implicit quotation is one of the most characteristic features of the narrative works in the Apocrypha and Pseudepigrapha. It may be defined as a phrase of at least three words, which stems from a specific recognizable biblical context.[84] When used in compositions these quotations are not introduced formally, but are interwoven into the new text. The manner and frequency with which such quotations are used are conditioned by the literary form, aims and techniques of individual writers.

IMPLICIT QUOTATIONS IN NARRATIVES

In our literature there are three kinds of narratives: the dominant form in the Apocrypha is the 'free narrative', created mainly of non-biblical materials.[85] In such narratives non-explicit quotations are used to lend a biblical character to an episode.

Two additional forms of narrative may be discerned: the Biblical Expansion and the Pseudepigraphic Biography. The Biblical Expansion consists of retelling a story by borrowing from the original text and expanding it in various ways. There are at least two variations of the Biblical Expansion: one is a narrative which follows closely the sequence and the text of a given biblical episode, using large segments of the actual biblical text. This form, termed as 'Rewritten Bible', is adopted by works such as *Jubilees*, *The Biblical Antiquities*, the *Genesis Apocryphon* and *1 Enoch* 6-11.[86] Another variation of the Biblical Expansion is freer in the adaptation of the biblical text. It usually takes up the main lines of a biblical story, and embellishes it with large aggadic expansions and other additions, sprinkled with occasional implicit quotations from the

---

[84] The implicit quotation presents a major problem of definition. Especially thorny is the problem of making a distinction between quotation and a biblical collocation (An analogous problem is presented by the distinction between allusion and reminiscence). Here a quotation or allusion is recognized by its inclusion of specific elements which refer to a particular source, while the collocation or locution is always general and occurs in more than one instance.

[85] For a similar distinction on different grounds cf. Nickelsburg, 'Bible Rewritten' 89. In Charlesworth's edition of the Pseudepigrapha these works are termed 'Expansions of the "Old Testament" and Legends' (*OTP* 2, 5-475) and the editor had clearly in mind a narrative genre.

[86] In Charlesworth's collection additional works are included, such as the *Lives of the Prophets*. In narrative techniques and interpretative use of biblical materials Josephus's *Jewish Antiquities* shares numerous features with the 'Biblical Story' and some scholars define it as 'rewritten Bible'. Cf. for instance, Harrington, 'Palestinian Adaptations' 239-40. But see the analysis of Attridge, *Interpretation*.

original context. Such a form is adopted by works like the *Life of Adam and Eve* and *Joseph and Aseneth*.[87]

A third type of narrative may be called Pseudepigraphic Biography. It appears mostly in pseudepigraphic works, from revelations to testaments and wisdom discourses.[88] As a rule, pseudepigraphic works consist of discourses of various types, pronounced by the chief protagonist, set in a narrative framework. As the works of our literature are usually attributed to biblical figures, the biographical frameworks constitute biblical stories of a special kind.[89]

IMPLICIT QUOTATIONS IN BIBLICAL EXPANSION ('Rewritten Bible')

Since the term 'rewritten Bible' was coined by Geza Vermes more than two decades ago,[90] there has been a growing tendency to group under this heading an ever increasing number of works, narrative as well as others.[91] This results in a blurring of the specific literary character of the individual works grouped under this heading, and of their specific methods of rewriting biblical materials. Thus, works such as *Jubilees*, *LAB*, *the Genesis Apocryphon* and *1 Enoch* 6-11, are sufficiently distinctive to be included in a special category. But in order to create more precise terms of reference, a more restrictive definition of the term 'rewritten Bible' will be adopted here,[92] to include only narrative works.[93]

---

[87] Perhaps the variations of form are due to historical development. Works reworking the Hebrew Bible more closely are on the whole earlier than those freer in their adaptations. But this may also be accidental, and perhaps the apocryphal works from Qumran, still unpublished, will shed light on the question. Works of the type rewritten Bible were continued to be composed into the Middle Ages, cf. the midrash *Sefer Ha-Yashar*. Cf. Vermes, *Scripture and Tradition*, 67-126. Characteristically, Vermes discusses 'rewritten Bible' works as part of the aggada (cf. most recently in Schürer, *History*, rev. ed. 2, 346ff.), thus indicating their common exegetical traditions, but blurring their distinct literary and historical origins.

[88] Cf. the recent discussion on pseudonimity by Meade, *Pseudonimity*.

[89] For an illustration of the method and form of pseudepigraphic biography cf. my analysis of the framework of *1 Enoch* in 'Biography of Enoch'.

[90] Vermes, *Scripture and Tradition*, 95, 124-26. Cf. also his comments on the exegetical purposes of the form in 'Bible and Midrash' 67ff.

[91] Cf. Nickelsburg, 'Bible Rewritten' 113-18; Charlesworth, *OTP* 2, and Harrington, 'Palestinian Adaptations' 238-43. Harrington, *ibid.* 243 tries to resolve this difficulty of definition by suggesting that the 'rewritten Bible' should be viewed as a process or activity, but this is entirely irrelevant to an obvious generic term.

[92] The imprecision of the definition arises from a failure to distinguish between literary techniques and literary genres. For in itself, adapting or rewriting biblical materials does not constitute a genre, but a technique used in different genres. The *Temple Scroll* offers an excellent example of the technique of rewriting legal and non-narrative biblical sections. Cf. Brin, 'Bible', and Kaufman, 'Temple Scroll'. Kaufman discerns six 'compositional patterns', which may be reduced to three: 1) original composition; 2) conflations of the biblical text; 3) quotations. All these procedures are found in biblical as well as apocryphal literature. Biblical examples are given by Fishbane, *Biblical Interpretation*, 117, 154-60, 164ff. etc.

[93] Cf. the observations made on specific works: for *Jub.* see Endres, *Biblical Interpretation*, 14-15. For *LAB* cf. Perrot-Bogaert, eds. *Pseudo-Philon* 2, 229-30. For the *GenApoc* cf. Fitzmyer, *Genesis Apocryphon*, 6-14.

The functions of the biblical materials in works considered as 'rewritten Bible', are defined in relation to their role within the compositional structure. Thus, a distinction should be made between materials used for the narrative sequence and the axis of the main plot, and those used in digressions of various types. In choosing to write a Biblical Expansion the author adopts the position of the original biblical writer. He is thus prevented from presenting biblical quotations as such, especially if the quotations are taken from the main sequence of his own rewritten biblical story. Instead, he interweaves the quotations into his own text, and the contents themselves refer the reader to the source. But in digressions from the main plot, sometimes the need arises for a quotation from other biblical contexts. In such cases authors have recourse to various manners of presentation. In *Jub*, for instance, the author introduces formal quotations of the Tora as quotations of what is written on the Heavenly Tablets or what is said by the angels.[94] The *LAB* employs another device, putting the quotations in the mouth of one of the protagonists.[95]

Implicit quotations are usually accompanied by biblical elements used in other ways, such as allusions and motifs. Together, and in addition to various aggadic expansions, embellishments and interpretative supplements, they create the stylistic mixture of biblical elements so typical of the Biblical Expansion.[96]

EXAMPLE

1 Enoch 6-11

1 Enoch is a collection of five writings ascribed to the biblical patriarch Enoch. Literary analysis shows that these five are independent compositions, though they draw on common aggadic traditions on Enoch.[97] The writings are assembled and arranged into one collection so as to reflect the legendary biography of Enoch: his youth, his exploits with the angels, and his final translation into Paradise.[98] The first piece, the so-called *Book of the Watchers*,[99] relates events belonging to Enoch's life. This part in itself is a compilation of disparate

---

[94] Cf. e.g. *Jub.* 16:29 citing Lev 23:42, *Jub.* 30:9-10 citing Lev 20:2. *Jub.* uses other formulae, like citing the books of the forefathers. Cf. *Jub.* 21:7-10 citing various verses from Lev.

[95] Cf. e.g. *LAB* 9:3, 5 where Amram quotes God's promise to Abraham (Gen 15:13), and Tamar's words (Gen 38:25); or *LAB* 9:8 where God cites his previous judgement on men (Gen 6:3).

[96] A current definition for this kind of mixture is 'the anthological style', as described by Robert, 'Littéraires (Genres)' and Bloch, 'Midrash', esp. 1269ff. It is still used by as recent a study as Sheppard, *Wisdom*, 103. Such a definition is too descriptive and vague, and disregards aspects of functionality.

[97] Cf. Stone, Apocalyptic Literature', 396: The independent character of the five texts was already shown by scholars like Beer and Charles. Cf. Beer, 'Das Buch Henoch', 220-21; Charles, *Book of Enoch*, XLVI-LVI.

[98] Cf. in detail in my 'Biography of Enoch'. Meade, *Pseudonimity*, 100-01 rightly stresses the interpretive over the literary nature of the pseudepigraphic attributions.

[99] Stone, 'Apocalyptic Literature' 396-401.

403

literary pieces, arranged again, according to the sequence of Enoch's biography: 1-5 is an introductory discourse on the End of Days,[100] 6-11 relates the story of the Fallen Angels, 12-16 concerns Enoch's dealings with the Fallen Angels, and 17-36 consists of two voyages in the universe which Enoch makes in the company of the angels (17-19; 20-36).[101] It has been observed that chapters 6-11 stand out both in content and form. Unlike the other units of the *Book of the Watchers*, they are not written as a biographical narrative told by Enoch in the first person, but as a third-person narrative with no mention of Enoch. Instead, Noah is the hero of this little piece. This led scholars like R.H. Charles to attribute these chapters, together with additional sections, to a lost *Book of Noah*.[102] In any case, the section stands out as a fragment of an ancient Biblical Expansion of the type of 'rewritten Bible'.[103]

The story told in 6-11 is based on Gen 6:1-4[104] by quotations not given *en bloc*, but distributed among large aggadic and interpretative expansions. Each implicit quotation initiates a new development in the story. Thus, chapter 6 depicts the circumstances and intentions of the protagonists, while chapter 7 relates their deeds and the results.

6:1-2 – The initial quotation of Gen 6:1-2a sets the scene: the birth of beautiful women and the Angels' lust.

---

[100] For a detailed analysis of the nature of these chapters as introduction, cf. Hartman, *Asking for a Meaning*, 138-45.

[101] Stone, 'Apocalyptic Literature', 396-401. In spite of the many discussions recently published on these chapters there is very little on its literary form. They are particularly suited for a comparative study, as they are extent in two Greek versions in addition to the Ethiopic one. For texts cf. Black, *Apocalypsis Henochi Graece*, together with additions and corrections in idem, *The Book of Enoch*, 419-22. Full textual information may be found in two recent translations of the book: Knibb, *Ethiopic Book*; Uhlig, *Henochbuch*. For a detailed discussion of *1 Enoch* 6-11 cf. my dissertation *Fallen Angels*, 21-72 and the literature cited in Stone, 'Apocalyptic Literature', 395ff.

[102] Argued most thoroughly by Charles, *Book of Enoch*, XLVI-XLVII. On literary grounds I have argued against ascribing chapters 6-11 to the Book of Noah in my dissertation *Fallen Angels*, p. 125ff. I have postulated the existence of 'an independent midrashic source' from which these chapters derive. Cf. my discussion '1 Enoch 6-11', 323. I still stand behind this suggestion, but would rather define the source as 'a biblical expanded story'.

[103] Note Nickelsburg, *Bible Rewritten*, 90-92; Hanson defined these chapters as 'expositionary narrative', a term too vague to be helpful. Cf. his discussion in 'Rebellion in Heaven', 196. In a recent article by le Roux entitled 'Use of Scripture', 28-38 only the thematic biblical elements are discussed. Another recent publication is the monograph by Rubinkiewicz, *Die Eschatologie*. One is surprised to discover an entire monograph based on separating chapters 9-11 from chapters 6-8, which goes against all the literary and thematic logic of the story. Taking up the suggestion of Milik, *Books of Enoch*, 25, Newsom, 'Development', advances another questionable entity, *1 Enoch* 6-19. No satisfactory justification is given for the separation of *1 Enoch* 17-19 from the similar chapters 20-35, or to the attachment of 6-16 to 17-19.

[104] Milik, *Books of Enoch*, 31-32 argues that it is Gen 6:1-4 which refers to *1 Enoch* 6-7. This is unacceptable on historical as well as literary grounds. Cf. the criticism of VanderKam, *Enoch*, 113-14. But the comparitive table Milik adduces (p. 32) of the masoretic text and *1 Enoch* 6-7 shows well the literary method applied by *1 Enoch* of rewriting, expounding and supplementing the biblical text.

6:3-6 – An expansion, the deliberations of the angels. It makes clear their intentions and shows that their leader Shemiahaza instigated the Angels to swear to carry out their intention.

6:7 – A list of the twenty heads of the angels winds up this section.

7:1 – Another implicit quotation of Gen 6:4 opens the second stage of the plot, the deeds and their consequences. The quotation gives only the intercourse of the Angels with the women. The expansion added here tells of the magic which the Angels taught the women.

7:2 – A further quotation from Gen 6:4 relates the birth of the Giants, the offspring of the unlawful union.

7:3-6 – The next section is an expansion describing the iniquity of the Giants and the ensuing suffering of men.

8 – Two parallel versions of the Angels' teachings to the women and the ensuing corruption of mankind give the outcome of the Angel's intercourse.[105]

9-11 – The remaining portions are expansions depicting the judgements on the Angels and their offspring. Though this part of the story does not use actual quotations, it alludes to Noah and his role in this context (10:1-3; cf. Gen 6:13ff.) in a succinct mention of the 'son of Lemech', and the approaching flood. The technique is identical with the mention of historical events discussed above.

The foregoing summary brings out clearly the technique of the Biblical Expansions, as it is practised in the present story. The biblical quotations set the narrative framework, the characters and the plot. The expansions provide motives, explanations and embellishments to the actions and events. Sometimes, as here, there are additional figures and actions, subservient to the main plot.

Although the quotations and the expansions are combined in a single text, they differ in their relation to the biblical source and employ different methods of adaptation. The implicit quotations use mainly two techniques: exegetical substitutions and slight editorial alterations. In 6-11 there are two typical examples of exegetical substitutions: the Angels and the Giants. Neither is mentioned in the original biblical story, but at a stage as early as our story[106] the Sons of God were identified as the Angels, while the offspring of the Angels and the women, the Heroes, were identified with the Giants.[107] The Enoch story thus gives the original story a new, more explicit meaning. Such explicitness is achieved also by slight manipulations of the quotation itself. Our author, for instance, emphasizes the temptation presented by the women, so he has accen-

---

[105] For the different traditions combined in these chapters cf. my dissertation, *Fallen Angels*, 23-72 and Nickelsburg, 'Bible Rewritten', 90-92.

[106] The story of chapters 6-11 must be at least as old as the compilation of the *Book of Watchers*, namely the third century B.C.E. but possibly even older, for already chapters 12-16 build on the traditions of 6-11. Cf. Stone, 'Book of Enoch', 404.

[107] These two exegetical identifications are attested by the oldest witnesses. Cf. the LXX to Gen 6:4; CD 2:18-21; Sir 16:7. Note the polemical formulation of *Gen. Rabba* 26:5 (p. 247ff.).

tuated their beauty by advancing the relevant adjective from the quotation of the second biblical verse to the quotation of the first verse, and by adding another adjective to the same effect.

While the implicit quotations are reworked in a way as to preserve their essential lexical and syntactical structure, in the expansions the author is free to shape them according to the narrative plot and his own aims. It is often done by adding details to a general picture or group which figured in the original context. A good example of this method is offered by the personality of Shemiahaza and his role in establishing the deliberate nature of the crime.[108] Shemiahaza is not entirely invented, for he could be considered as one of the Angels referred to in the bible as 'the Sons of God'. The actual expansion on the teachings of the Angels provides motives for the corruption of mankind before the flood. The other long expansion in the second part of the story makes more explicit the theme of divine providence, and shows that the flood fits into a system of punishments for each of the crimes mentioned.[109]

IMPLICIT QUOTATIONS IN 'FREE NARRATIVE'

While in Biblical Expansions the implicit quotations rework the main biblical text, in the 'free narrative' implicit quotations are used to imitate biblical styles and forms. This technique is characteristic of Apocryphal works translated from Hebrew or Aramaic, and it was probably at home in the cultural and literary milieu of Israel, where the traditions of the biblical narrative were still alive.[110] Such a technique is used when the author wishes to draw an analogy between his story and a biblical one. Many examples of this are found in works such as Tobit, Judith, Susana and 1 Macc, all of which stem from a semitic óriginal.[111] This characteristic is especially clear when the Greek 2 Macc, using a Hellenistic model of historical writing, is compared to 1 Macc, using a biblical model.[112] 1 Macc emerges as particularly rich in implicit quotations and biblical allusions.[113] The example chosen below will illustrate a quotation of a special type, which may be termed a conflated quotation.

---

[108] In legal terms the crime was committed intentionally ('bemēzid').

[109] This is not, then, a story on the origin of evil, as most scholars would have it, but on the primordial sinners and their punishment.

[110] This is why the true nature of such a style comes out in reconstructions of the Hebrew originals. For such attempts cf. e.g. Grintz, Book of Judith; Neuhaus, Studien, 40-75. In this respect, of interest are also the Hebrew translations of the Apocrypha and Pseudepigrapha found in the edition of A. Kahana (1937).

[111] See the detailed analysis in my 'The Problem of a Non-Translated Biblical Greek'.

[112] In itself the use of Hellenistic models should not hinder the author from employing biblical quotations, usually in the Septuagint version. This is well illustrated by the Wisdom of Solomon, 4 Maccabees and Joseph and Aseneth.

[113] This is revealed through the Hebrew retroversions, as made by Neuhaus, Studien. The same phenomenon can be observed in the poetic passages of 2 Macc.

1 Macc 5:48[114]
καὶ ἀπέστειλεν πρὸς αὐτοὺς Ιουδας λόγοις εἰρηνικοῖς λέγων Διελευ-
σόμεθα διὰ τῆς γῆς σου τοῦ ἀπελθεῖν εἰς τὴν γῆν ἡμῶν, καὶ οὐδεὶς κακο-
ποιήσει ὑμᾶς, πλὴν τοῖς ποσὶν παρελευσόμεθα. καὶ οὐκ ἠβούλοντο
ἀνοῖξαι αὐτῷ.

Translation[115]

> And Judas sent them a peaceable message, as follows: 'Let us pass
> through your territory on our way back to our own. No one shall harm
> you. We shall pass through on foot'. However, the inhabitants of the city
> refused to open their gates to him.

This is taken from the episode relating the successful campaign of Judas to
Gilead. Having defeated Timotheus' army, Judas makes his way to Judaea with
his army and the evacuated Jews of Gilead. On their way, and before crossing
the Jordan near Beit-Shean, they had to pass through the city of Ephron, but
were refused passage, in spite of the peaceful request of Judas. The situation is
modelled on the biblical story of the Israelites passing through the land of the
Edomite and Amorite kings, just before crossing the Jordan to Canaan, as
related in Num 20:17-20, 21:22. The analogy between the two events is obvious
by the similarity of the circumstances. But in addition to the similarity of motifs,
1 Macc actually interweaves the pertinent biblical text into its own story. In fact
it creates a quotation combined from the existing biblical accounts. The most
succinct version of Deut 2:26-29 serves as basis, with small omissions. One
detail is taken over from Judg 11:19 (Jephthah's: 'to our place'), and finally the
first person plural of the Num 21:22 version replaces the first person singular of
Deut. This formulation is put into the mouth of Judas, addressing the inhabitants, just as Moses did in the Deut version. The result achieved is a speech of
Judas formulated in the words uttered by the biblical Israelites to the Amorites.
The refusal of the inhabitants of Ephron, though not a precise quotation,
echoes the refusal of the Amorites in Deut 2:30. In this manner the author of 1
Macc implies that Judas was enacting the patterns of the biblical history.[116]
Interweaving implicit biblical quotations is one of the techniques by which this
view is expressed. Technically the author is not using one quotation, but a kind
of *topos* of the event, represented by a conflated quotation.

IMPLICIT QUOTATIONS IN DISCOURSES

While examples of implicit quotations in narrative usually refer to narrative
episodes, and are therefore tied up with a plot or a sequence of events,

---

[114] Text following the edition of Kappler, *Maccabaeorum Liber I.*
[115] Translation following Goldstein, *I Maccabees.*
[116] Cf. the qualification of Neuhaus, *Studien*, 180 of the writer as deeply versed in the Hebrew Bible.

quotations in discourses can originate from almost every possible biblical context. Two examples will be given below, one taken from a prophetic discourse, the other from wisdom proverbs.

EXAMPLE

Judith 8:16 (= Num 23:19)
ὑμεῖς δὲ μὴ ἐνεχυράζετε τὰς βουλὰς κυρίου τοῦ θεοῦ ἡμῶν, ὅτι οὐχ ὡς ἄνθρωπος ὁ θεὸς ἀπειληθῆναι οὐδὲ ὡς υἱὸς ἀνθρώπου διαιτηθῆναι.

Translation[117]
> But as for you, cease speaking to force the councels of the Lord our God; for God is not as a man to be threatened nor as a son of man to be cajoled.[118]

The example is from Judith's address to the elders of Bethulia. The speech aims at persuading them to change their course of action. The address may be divided into six parts:

a. Judith contests the deeds of the elders – 8:11.
b. It is not fitting, she argues, for frail and ignorant humans to impose conditions on their creator (8:12-14).
c. Rejecting the elders' course of action Judith recommends trust in God, for He is not influenced by lies or entreaties (quotation from Num 23:19 in the LXX version) (8:14c-17).
d. Unlike their ancestors, contemporary Israelites are faithful to the Tora, and consequently the danger of exile and desecration of the Temple by the Assyrians should not be seen as punishment but as a test. Therefore God is to be trusted (8:18-25).
e. Historical precedents show that the Just were put to test in a similar way (the three patriarchs) (8:26).
f. Conclusion: God teaches through test, and therefore the present danger is only a test from which God will rescue those who trust him (8:27).[119]

This short outline shows that implicit quotation is placed in a crucial point of the argument. On its authority rests the central statement about the nature of God as immovable and uninfluenced like humans. This same statement serves in turn as a basis for proving the consistency of divine action, and the appeal to

---

[117] Text cf. Hanhart, ed. *Iudith*. The translation is basically that of Enslin, *Book of Judith*, with some details from the translation of Moore, *Judith*.
[118] The quotation is reproduced from the Septuagint with a slight lexical variation. The translation of Judith interchanges the verbs of the two strophes, ἀπειληθῆναι and διαιτηθῆναι. Hanhart, *Text...Judith*, 84-85 estimates that the substitution διαιτηθῆναι (= 'to turn by entreaty'; Lidell-Scott, *Lexicon*, 396), replacing in Judith the verb διαρτηθῆναι of Num, suits the context and is therefore original.
[119] For a structural analysis of the passage from a different perspective cf. Craven, *Artistery*, 86-89.

trust Providence. Significantly, the quotation is not formally presented as such, and therefore its biblical source is not explicitly referred to. This may be due to the fact that the quotation does not stem from an actual divine speech, and therefore it is quoted as a general truth.[120] The reader was probably able to recognize its scriptural source and attribute to it the proper authority. Thus, the manner of quotation may depend on the content and context of the text cited.

Implicit quotations are often employed to create a text in a biblical style. An example is offered by the sapiential proverbs in the farewell discourse of Tobit to his son Tobias, in the Book of Tobit, chapter 4. This chapter is written as a testament, a typical context for sapiential instructions.[121] Not surprisingly *Tobit* employs a Proverbs-like style and a number of quotations from the Proverbs,[122] as well as from other books.[123] The technique of implicit quotations is extensively used in creating other biblical genres too, such as sapiental works[124], prayers, psalms and testaments.

The foregoing discussion offers only a sketch of a rich and varied phenomenon. As a major literary technique of post-biblical literature, it merits separate study.[125] However, one of the difficulties of such a study is the need of a clear definition, to distinguish implicit quotation from biblical allusion[126] or locution.

ALLUSIONS

A similar difficulty of definition is involved in any discussion of the role of biblical allusions in our literature. Allusions are notoriously difficult to define and little investigated.[127] For the purpose of the present discussion allusion will

---

[120] The introductory term of the quotation ὅτι is ambiguous. It can serve as opening a quotation or as a causual proposition. The author may be playing on both senses here.

[121] On the form of testament here cf. the comments of von Nordheim, *Die Lehre der Alten* 2, 10-12. He rightly observed that the author employs the testament form as a literary device to stress Tobit's conviction that he was about to die, while in fact this was not the case.

[122] Cf. e.g. 4:10 citing Prov 10:2, 11:4; 4:15 citing Prov 23:20-21, 29. For quotations from the Tora cf. e.g. 4:3 quotating Exod 19:11, 4:14 citing Lev 19:3. In 4:17 *Ahikar* 13 (Syriac) is quoted.

[123] In Tobit 4:17 the author quotes the pagan wisdom work known as the *Wisdom of Ahikar* (Syriac version 13). Cf. Küchler, *Weisheitstraditionen*, 374-79. For general information cf. Lindenberger, 'Ahiqar'.

[124] Cf. the interesting instance in Sir 24:23, where the author quotes implicitly Deut 33:4. The context is a sapiential discourse depicting Wisdom, and the quotation from the Song of Moses functions as a definition of the preceding term 'the Book of the Covenant of God the most high'. This is one of the passages where Ben Sira clearly identifies Wisdom with the Tora, and therefore the use of the quotation carries special weight. In recent discussion this formal aspect is usually lost. Cf. e.g. Stadelmann, *Ben Sira*, 250-51. More refined is Sheppard, 'Wisdom and Torah' 166-76, and *idem*, *Wisdom*, 60-63.

[125] Biblical allusions in the post-biblical literature are usually studied as specific cases. Future study will have to tackle the more basic problems of definition and categorization.

[126] Cf. for instance, the uncertainties in locating quotations in Ben Sira, as reflected in the works cited in n. 124.

[127] Cf. the qualifications of Ben-Porat, 'Poetics', 105-07.

be defined as a device for the simultaneous activation of two texts, using a special signal referring to the independent external text. These signals may consist of isolated terms, patterns and motifs taken from the independent text alluded to.[128]

The technical procedure by which the allusion is triggered is similar in all types of allusions. It consists of interweaving into a new composition motifs, key-terms and small phrases from a specific and recognizable biblical passage. The reader is referred back to the original context by the combinations of these elements, even though no explicit mention ofthe original context is actually made. In our literature there are two types of allusion: allusion to isolated verses, and allusion to one ortwo running biblical texts.[129]

EXAMPLES

Isolated allusions
The Wisdom of Solomon 1:1-6:21[130]
The Wisdom of Solomon is a work originally written in Greek: by a Jew in Alexandria, perhaps active in the second half of the first century B.E.C.[131] It appears as a discourse of king Solomon,[132] centring upon divine justice, the fate of the Just and the Wicked, and the role of wisdom and divine justice in the life of Solomon and in the history of Israel. The work consists of three parts, forming a tightly knit unity:

1:1-6:21 – an exhortation to the rulers of the world;
6:22-10:21 – Solomon's prayers for wisdom and wisdom as the saviour of the Just;
11-19 – God dispenses justice to wards the Israelites and the Egyptians during the Exodus.[133]

The composition combines the refinement of a Hellenistic rhetor and the acumen of a biblical exegete, and serves as an excellent illustration forthe use and influence of both biblical and Hellenistic literary traditions. The traces of biblical modes of expression are especially apparatent in the two first parts,

---

[128] A slightly adapted version of the definition of allusion is proposed by Ben-Porat, 'Poetics', 107-08.
[129] Cf. below. The *Temple Scroll* provides an interesting illustration of the technique of reworking or alluding to one or two major biblical texts.
[130] For text cf. Ziegler, ed. *Sapientia Salomonis*. For translation cf. Winston, *Wisdom of Solomon*.
[131] For the problems involved in dating the book cf. Winston, *Wisdom of Solomon*, pp. 20-25. Winston himself opts for the reign of Caligula (37-41 c.e.) on the basis of the occurrence of terms from that period.
[132] On the pseudepigraphic form of the book as a discourse of Solomon cf. my analysis in 'Pseudonimity'. Cf. also Meade, *Pseudonimity*, 62-66.
[133] On the last section of the book cf. Gilbert, *La critique des dieux*. For the unity of the book cf. Wright 'Structure'; Winston, *Wisdom*, 9-14; Larcher, *Livre de la Sagesse* 1, 100-07. In the book's overall framework, chapter 10 forms a separate unit consisting of a list of Just saved by Wisdom. It bridges the second and third parts of the work.

which are in fact modelled on specific biblical traditions.[134] For the purposes of the present discussion the first part is of special interest, for it employs a peculiar system of biblical references closely connected with its form and ideas.

The Exhortation is built in a concentric chiasmus, each part of which is defined by an *inclusion*:

a. 1:1-15 – Exhortation to the judges to seek justice and wisdom;
b. 1:16-2:24 – The blasphemous speech of the Wicked;
c. 3;
c'. 4 – Reward for the Just and punishment for the Wicked;
b'. 5:1-23 – The remorse of the Wicked;
a'. 6:1-21 – Exhortation to kings to seek justice and wisdom.[135]

The chiasmus is clearly indicated both by the formal *inclusio* and the contents. In addition, a special system of inner cross-references is created by the use of identical or similar terms in parallel units of the chiasmus. It establishes close interlinks between the sections and weaves a subtle and ironical play of inversions. Inversion also operates on the level of the biblical allusions.

Allusions in 1:1-15, 6:1-21

The opening verses of these two sections provide a good illustration of the author's technique. They are linked by style, words and subject. They exhort 'the judges of the earth' (1:1a) and 'the judges of the ends of the earth' (6:1b) to exercise justice and wisdom. The address to the rulers is echoed by words like 'kings' (βασιλεῖς – 6:1), 'the mighty' (κρατοῦντρς – 6:2a: δυνατοί – 6:6b) and 'tyrants' (τύραννοι – 6:9a). The two verses are further linked by biblical allusions. Both verses include words from Ps 2:10 (LXX.[136] Thus the text of Wis alludes to Ps 2, integrating it and commenting upon it. Ps 2 is selected apparently because it urges kings and judges to exercise wisdom. The address to rulers as a literary model may be explained also by an indirect polemic against Hellenis-

---

[134] On the use of Mikra in Wis cf. Fichtner, 'AT-Text'; Skehan, *Studies*. For the second part see Gilbert, 'La Structure'. For general comments on the use of biblical books by Wis cf. most recently Larcher, *Études*, 83-103. On the use of Isa 52-53 by Wis 2:4-5 cf. also Nickelsburg, *Resurrection*, 62-66.

[135] For details the reader is referred to the thorough analysis of this system and the structure of the first part by Perrenchio (who does not concern himself with biblical allusions). Cf. *idem*, 'Struttura-...di Sapienza 1,1-15' and 'Struttura...di Sapienza 1,16-2,24 e 5,1-23'. Cf. also Bizetti, *Libro della Sapienza*, 51-67, especially for additional lexical interlinks within the units of the chiastic framework.

[136] Compare Ps 2:10a-b καὶ νῦν, βασιλεῖς, σύνετε / παιδεύθητε, πάντες οἱ κρίνοντες τὴν γῆν with Wis 6:1a-b Ἀκούσατε οὖν, βασιλεῖς, καὶ σύνετε / μάθετε . . . The expression οἱ κρίνοντες τὴν γῆν figures in Ps 2:10b and Wis 1:1a. The form παιδεύθητε in Ps 2:10b is echoed in Wis 6:11b παιδευθήσεσθε. Wis 1:1 echoes also Ps 45:8 (LXX) and other verses. These affinities were observed by most commentators, and in special detail by Skehan, *Studies*, 149ff. In my judgement this type of allusion should not be termed 'midrash', as is done by Schaberg, 'Midrashic Traditions', 76.

tic theories of kingship. The author of Wis betrays knowledge of such theories on more than one occasion.[137]

While the allusion to Ps 2:10 is articulate, others are hinted at in a more discrete way. Thus, an allusion to Prov 8:15 is suggested by the similarity of ideas, style and general tenor. In Prov 8:15 Wisdom asserts that through her kings rule and judges do justice. If forms part of a larger Wisdom discourse, included in the series of sapiential addresses of Prov 1-9. This verse thus converges with the style and themes of the opening diatribe in Wis. Actually, most of the words of Prov 8:15 are spread over Wis 1:1 and 6:1, 6.[138] In a general way, the first chapters of Wis are clearly inspired by Prov 1-9 and incorporate many of their elements.[139]

These verses illustrate two procedures of biblical allusion: one employs a specific and characteristic phrase from the original in addition to the affinity of context, while the second method plays on accumulating less defined elements reminiscent of the original.

Another interesting allusion is contained in the second part of Wis 1:1, which urges the reader to seek God with 'simplicity of heart'. The Greek ἐν ἁπλότητι καρδίας is found in the LXX only once more, in describing the attitude of David towards the building of the temple (1 Chr 29:17 LXX). The author of Wis adds another allusion by combining the 'simplicity of heart' with 'love if righteousness', a combination only found in the speech of David in 1 Chr 29:17 (LXX).[140] This is another example of the first method described above. It exemplifies the relation which the allusion establishes between the old and the new texts, and which is one of both dependence and innovation.[141]

From the same context comes another allusion made by Wis 1:1, namely 1 Chr 28:9 (LXX). In this verse David instructs his son Solomon to seek God, so that

---

[137] Cf. for instance, the use of the characteristic 'kingship' term φιλάνθρωπος in 1:6 and elsewhere in Wis. For the connection of Wis to Hellenistic theories of kingship cf. Reese, *Hellenistic Influence*, 71-80. Cf. my comments in 'Pseudepigraphy', 249 n. 102 and Meade, *Pseudepigraphy*, 64-65, n. 87.

[138] Cf. Prov. 8:15 (LXX): δι' ἐμοῦ βασιλεῖς βασιλεύουσιν / καὶ οἱ δυνάσται γράφουσιν δικαιοσύνην. Note Wis 6:1 βασιλεῖς, 6:6 δυνατοί, 1:1 κρίνοντες.

[139] Cf. the list of elements shared by Prov and Wis in my 'Pseudonimity', 251-52 and my comments on pp. 247-58. Cf. also Skehan, *Studies*, 172.

[140] Cf. the LXX: καὶ ἔγνων, κύριε, ὅτι σὺ εἶ ὁ ἐτάζων καρδίας καὶ δικαιοσύνην ἀγαπᾷς / ἐν ἁπλότητι καρδίας προεθυμήθην πάντα ταῦτα . . . The Septuagint for the present verse and Ps 2:10 differs from the Masoretic Text, so that the author of Wis must have known them in their Greek form. Another example is offered by 1:12 alluding to Isa 5:18 (LXX). For this and other references to Isa 5 and 28 cf. Amir 'Figure of Death'. For the more general use of Isa in Wis see Skehan, 'Isaias', 163-71. On the use of Isa 44 cf. Gilbert, *La critique des dieux*, 64-75, 210-11. Other indications show that the author had recourse also to the Hebrew text of various biblical books, cf. Larcher, *Études*.

[141] A description of the same phenomenon in Mikra offered by Skehan may be applied equally well to the literature under discussion: 'It is of course a familiar fact that the later Old Testament writings in several instances draw much of their message from an appeal to the acknowledged sacred authority of the earlier inspired books. This appeal is rarely a matter of formal quotation, but is made by means of allusions, reworkings of the material found in the older books, inferences and examples drawn from the same sources' (*Studies*, 163).

God may be found by him. In this he offers his own formulation for a basic biblical tenet, namely that God is found only when sought in earnest. This rule is expressed in biblical parlance by the pair 'seek/find' God, and occurs in various formulations.[142] In Wis the formulaation of the Chronicles is taken up, as is clear from the association of 'love of righteousness' with 'simplicity of heart' (Wis 1:1c-2a). Again, the relation between the two verses is explained by the association of motifs: David's admonition to his wise son is a context which suits well the author of a pseudephigraphic diatribe of Solomon.[143]

Allusions in 1:16-2:24 and 5:1-23

These two sections form two discourses of the Wicked. The first gives the philosophy of the Wicked by which they justify their way, the second represents their repentence and admission of their error. Here the author achieves a particular vividness both by the discourse form and by a subtle and ironic play of cross-references and allusions.[144] A striking example of this is the depiction of man by the Wicked. In the first speech man is said to consist of three elements, corresponding to natural ones: the breath (πνοή) of the nostrils is like msoke (καπνός); the reason (λόγος) ressembles a spark (σπινθήρ), setting in motion the heart, which being extinguished, the body turns into ashes; and finally the spirit (πνεῦμα),[145] which is dispersed like air (ἀήρ) (2:2-3).

The breath, reason and spirit are a mixture of biblical and Hellenistic elements, characteristic of Wis. The breath in the nostrils is taken from biblical description of the creation of man.[146] The *logos* as a spark setting the body in motion and the spirit animating it, are taken from a popular version of Stoic ideas.[147] But the main targets for the irony of the author are the images of smoke, spark and air. In the first speech they emphasize the brevity of human existence in order to justify a life of self-indulgence. In the speech of penitance each is turned into an image of brevity for the life and hope of the Wicked. Moreover, in an ironic twist the three images are combined into suggesting a

---

[142] Cf. e.g. Deut 4:29; Isa 55:6; Jer 36 (29):13; 1 Chr 28:9. Cf. Georgi, *Weisheit Salomos*, 402-03 n. 2a.

[143] On the attribution of Wis to Solomon cf. my discussion in 'Pseudonimity' and the comments of Meade, *Pseudonimity*, 62-65. Cf. also Gilbert, 'La Structure'.

[144] The use of a discourse put in the mouth of fictitious opponents in order to refute it is a well-known rhetorical procedure, cf. e.g. the Wicked's words in Isa 5:19, 28:15; Ps 10:6, 12:5; Prov 1:11-14; Job 21:14-15, all of which are used by the author of Wis. On the use of the same device in the Hellenistic diatribe cf. Capelle-Marrou, 'Diatribe' and the review of Stowers, *Diatribe*, 72-77. Cf. Winston, *Wisdom*, 114ff. A full and detailed analysis of our sections is found in Perrenchio, 'Struttura...di Sapienza 1,16-2,24 e 5,1-23', 2-43, esp. 33.

[145] The general context shows that here πνεῦμα is used in a concrete sense, and in fact reproducing Stoic terminology for the heat-generating spirit which animates the body. Cf. Winston, *Wisdom*, 117; Larcher, *Livre de la Sagesse* 1, 217ff. At the same time the author is playing on the biblical terminology חיים נשמת (Gen 2:7, rendered in the LXX by πνοή and used by Wis in 2:2), as well as on the image of the air (ἀήρ) used by the Wicked.

[146] Cf. Gen 2:7 LXX: καὶ ἐνεφύσησεν εἰς τό πρόσωπον αὐτοῦ πνοὴν ζωῆς . . .

[147] Cf. Winston, *Wisdom*; Larcher, *Sagesse*.

burning fire: the smoke dispersing in the air and the spark produced by the blaze. Finally, the ashes of the body are all that remains. In fact, without being aware of it, the Wicked are drawing a picture oftheir own doom in fire, instead of their self-image as prosperous. This is not only an ironical inversion of the Wicked's own words, but also of the later depiction of the Just as eternally shining.

Inversion is also achieved by playing on biblical allusions in a peculiarway. Thus, the image of smoke for the brevity of human life already occurs in the biblical sources.[148] But it is taken up in Wis 5:14c to describe the Wicked's hopewhich is 'dispersed like msoke by the wind'. The Wicked intended to speak of the breath of life as smoke, but it is their own hope which was dispersed like smoke. Moreover, in structure and words Wis 5:14c parallels another description of the Wicked's hope, which will be 'like chaff carried in the wind' (Wis 5:14a). Both share the word 'wind' (ἄνεμος), which is an ironic punreflecting both on the terms 'air', 'breath' and 'spirit' in Wis 2:2c, 2:3b and their inversions in Wis 5:11a, c; 5:12a. The image of chaff in the wind is used in biblical passages as a metaphor for the fate of the Wicked (Ps 1:4 (LXX), Isa 5:24 (LXX).[149] By using similar words and structure forthe chaff and the smoke, the author of Wis equates the two; in this way he forms new interpretative links between thetwo biblical pictures.[150]

Allusions in 3-4

The next example continues the picture of fire, which is carried through into the central sections of the chiastic structure, chapters 3-4. These chapters depict the contrasting behaviour and fate of the Just and the Wicked. The example analysed here is taken from 3:7: 'And in the time of their visitation[151] they shall shine (burn/radiate), and as sparks (σπινζῆρες) in the stubble they will run to and fro'.[152]

The term 'spark' makes here its second appearance; see 2:1f. above. In both instances it is used figuratively. The Wicked employ it as an image for the *logos* as the cause for the movement of the hearth; while in 3:7 it is an image of the brilliance of the souls of the Just in their blissful state at the time of recompense.[153] Evidently, the author plays again an ironic turn on the Wicked. The Wicked see themselves as moved by the *logos* like a spark, which in fact will

[148] Cf. Ps 102:4 (LXX) and of the quick disappearance of the Wicked Hos 13:3; Ps 37:20, 68:3.
[149] The image is biblical, said of enemies (Isa 17:13, 29:5; Ps 18:43, 35:5, 83:14) or the Wicked (Hos 13:3, Ps 1:4; Job 21:18). Wis combines the Greek of Isa 29:5 and Ps 1:4.
[150] Note in this connection Hos 13:3, which assembles at least three of the elements appearing in the Wicked's speech: cloud, chaff and smoke, all of which refer to the short existence of sinners.
[151] The term employed is ἐπισκοπή, which translates the Hebrew פקודה in the sense of recompense in general and the final recompense in particular. Cf. e.g. Isa 10:3; Jer 8:12, 10:15; Hos 9:7. Note the similar term of the Sectarian scrolls פקודה, מועד פקודה e.g. *IQS* 4:19; *CD* 7:21.
[152] καὶ ἐν καιρῷ ἐπισκοπῆς αὐτῶν ἀναλάμψουσιν καὶ ὡς σπινθῆρες ἐν καλάμῃ διαδραμοῦνται.
[153] It is not clear when this will happen. Some would understand it as taking place after a bodily resurrection. Cf. Larcher, *Etudes*, 322-23.

burn until they are consumed, but the Just will shine eternally in an everlasting radiance in the presence of God. The image previously used of ephemeral physical existence, is now used for eternal existence of light and splendour.[154] The idea of the brilliance of the Just at the End of Days is common in the writings of the Second Common-wealth Period, but the formulation here may have well been influenced by the classical verse of Dan 12:3,[155] where the future existence of the Wise is described as 'they will shine like the radiance of heaven'.[156] Wis associates this picture with the biblical image of sparks moving in stubble. Interestingly, in biblical imagery sparks in the stubble are used infavourable. They depict the end of enemies or of the Wicked.[157]

Significantly, very few allusions in Wis employ the device so common in other works, namely, the patterning of the new text on the syntactical structure of the old.[158] This may be due to the fact that Wis leans heavily on Greek stylistic models. Another aspect of the biblical allusions in Wis 1-6 is that they are usually taken from different contexts, and are interwoven into one unity by virtue of the work itself.

Finally, a distinction should be made between the technical setting of the allusion, and its actual functioning within a given context. For the same allusion may be used in different contexts for different purposes.[159]

Allusions to a running text
Another type of procedure interweaves running allusions to one or two biblical texts into the fabric of a new text. Such a procedure usually serves when the new text is modeleld on the biblical one. Such modelling is done by adopting the original motif and by borrowing terms and small phrases from the source. In

---

[154] The Greek verb διαδραμοῦνται should be seen in the light of the picture in Nah 2:5 (LXX) where the similar Greek verb διατρέχουσαι renders the form יְרוֹצֵצוּ, a *pi'el* form of רוץ describing the movement of lightnings, in parallelism to torches. Wis alludes to the quick movement of the sparks. Cf. Larcher, *Livre de la Sagesse*, 1, 286. Perhaps this is an ironic reverse of *logos* as spark in the movement (ἐν κινήσει) of the heart (2:2d).

[155] Cf. Dan 12:3 (Th): καὶ οἱ συνιέντες ἐκλάμψουσιν ὡς ἡ λαμπρότης τοῦ στερεώματος . . .

[156] The notion of the brilliance of the Just in the future is common in post-biblical literature. Cf. *1 Enoch* 104:2; *4 Ezra* 7:97; *2 Bar* 51:10; 4 Macc 17:5. Cf. Winston, *Wisdom*, 128; Larcher, *Livre de la Sagesse* 1, 285-86. Cf. also Nickelsburg, *Resurrection*, 60-61. Against this background, and in the light of the play on biblical allusions, Wis 3:7 should be understood in this context, rather than as reflecting Hellenistic ideas, as was suggested by some scholars (Cf. Reese, *Hellenistic Influence*, 79 n. 212).

[157] Cf. Isa 1:31 (LXX), 5:24 (LXX), which must have both inspired the authors of Wis. Joel 2:5 and Zech 12:6 use similar images of enemies.

[158] Yet even behind a section as intricate as Wis 1-6, a systematic interpretation of certain biblical passages such as Isa 5 and 28 and Prov 1-9 may be discerned.

[159] The failure to make a clear distinction between the formal procedure of allusion and its exegetical contents is one of the weaknesses of Sheppard's analysis of Sir 24:3-29, 16:24-17:14 and Bar 3:9-4:4 in *Wisdom*.

such allusionsthe context itself often provides an explicit reference to the source.[160]

Allusions to disparate biblical contexts as well as to one running biblical text are to be found in narrative as well as paraenetic discourses of various kinds. In fact, these allusions often serve wider literary purposes. Thus, for instance, a pseudonymic attribution can be, and is, established with the aid of systematic allusions to the biblical accounts of the pseudepigraphic personage, and often involves a re-interpretation of the biblical material. A system of allusions is often used to introduce an analogy with a pattern of biblical motifs (cf. the case of Tobit below). And finally, allusions to and reworking of a biblical text is thep rocedure by which the author of the new text expresses his dependence on tradition.[161]

Here the difference should be noted between imitating biblical style for literary or for exegetical purposes. In purely stylistic usages biblical elements usually retain only general characteristics and cannot be recognized as pointing to one specific context, while elements used for exegetical purposes are always anchored in specific contexts.

Allusions to one text

This mode of using allusions consists of drawing mainly from one or two texts and is often used to create a new text in biblical forms and genres. Thus, for instance, most of thep rayers and hymns of the Second Temple Period take biblical prayers and the Psalms as models.[162] In the same way most of the compositions written as testaments employ the patterns of the biblical testaments of Jacob (Gen 49) and Moses (Deut 31-34).[163] A similar phenomenon is to be observed in narrative compositions, either of the type 'rewritten Bible' or

---

[160]   For example cf. below, the analysis of Tobit.

[161]   Cf. the discussions of Robert and Bloch on anthological style: Robert, 'Littéraires (Genres)'; Bloch, 'Midrash'.

[162]   This is true of many of the prayers and hymns in the Apocrypha and Pseudepigrapha. Cf. e.g. Tobit 12; Judith 17; 2 Macc 1:24-29; 3 Macc 2:1-20; Dan 3:24ff. (LXX) and the collection known as the *Psalms of Solomon*. Similar methods can be detected in psalmodic compositions at Qumran such as the *Hodayot* and the apocryphal psalms. Cf. most recently the comments of Schuller, *Non-Canonical Psalms*, 32-38.

[163]   For the influence of Gen 49-50 cf. the discussions on the *Testaments of the Twelve Patriarchs* by von Nordheim, *Die Lehre der Alten* 1, 12-106. But see Hollander, *Joseph*, 1-6. He rightly stresses the role of the biblical testaments as models in later post-biblical literature (cf. esp. p. 4 n. 15). See also Hollander-de Jonge, *Testaments*, 29-33 and the review of von Nordheim's first volume by de Jonge in *JSJ* 12 (1981) 112-17. For the *Testament of Moses* cf. Harrington, 'Interpretation', 59-68; von Nordheim, *ibid.*, 1, 206.

of the type 'free narrative', where various biblical stories serve as models. Other examples are offered by works written as prophetic visions.[164]

In all these cases the adherence to a certain text proves to be linked with the nature of the work and its affinity with certain biblical themes or figures. Not surprisingly, this type of allusion is revealed as one of the main literary vehicles for building up pseudepigraphic frameworks.[165]

MODELS AND MOTIFS

The referential value of the motifs in the functioning of allusions has already been pointed out. In itself, a term taken out from its original context is deprived of its power of reference without the support of a relevant context or motif. But the relationship between the motif and the specific terminology belonging to it can be reversed: the motif is carried out and articulated by certain terminology and phraseology belonging to it. This phenomenon is especially clear in a cluster of motifs which are organized to form a model.

In the literature under discussion motifs are used with or without their characteristic phraseology. Often such phraseology is used to enhance the referential value of the motif.

EXAMPLE

The model of Job in Tobit

The Book of Tobit offers a good example of reworking biblical narrative models and motifs. It has often been observed that the author of this work attempts to re-create the religious ethos and atmosphere of the patriarchal narratives by evoking various motifs of the Genesis stories.[166] In this context he also exploits the narrative elements of the book of Job, perhaps placing him too in ancient patriarchal times.[167]

That Job is a model is indicated first of all by the similarity of the main motifs

---

[164] Cf. Kvanvig, 'Henoch', Kvanvig has shown that *1 Enoch* 14 depends on Ezek 1. It is certainly related also to the Trone vision in Dan 7, as may be clearly seen from the analysis of Kvanvig, but it is less clear in what way. One cannot argue any more for a simple dependence of *1 Enoch* on Dan 7, for the Qumran Aramaic fragments of *1 Enoch* suggest that *1 Enoch* 14 may be earlier than Dan 7. This was the position of Glasson, re-formulated in 'Son of Man Imagery'; Kvanvig, *ibid.* 119-30 reaches the same conclusion. Emerton, 'The origin' 229-30, following others, suggests that the two drew upon a common source.

[165] An illustration of this procedure is offered by the way Wis attributes its discourses to Solomon. Cf. my discussion in 'Pseudonimity'.

[166] For the use made by Tobit of Gen 24 cf. the discussion of Deselaers, *Das Buch Tobit*, 292-302.

[167] This view is already attested in the Septuagint version of Job, according to which he is identified with Jobab, the Edomite king, one of the descendents of Abraham (Gen 36:33-34; cf. the final section of the Greek Job). The rabbis variously placed Job in the days of Abraham, of Jacob or of Moses. Cf. *P.T. Sota* 5 (20c) and *B.T. Bava Batra* 15a.

attached to Tobit and Job. The author of *Tobit* follows both the contents and sequence of the motifs of the Book of Job:

Motifs	Job	Tobit
The hero is pious and righteous	1:1, 8	1:6-12, 16-17
	2:3	2:2-5
He is prosperous	1:2-3	1:13
He is deprived of his possessions	1:14-19	1:15-20
He is crippled by illness	2:7-8	2:9-10
His wife works for others	31:10	2:11-14
	2:9 (LXX)	
He is provoked by his wife	2:9	2:14
	(note LXX)	
He prays and wishes to die	3 *et passim*	2:1-6
His final vindication and restitution of health and wealth	42:11-15	14:2-3
He dies in old age, blessed with offspring and wealth	42:16-17	14:11-12

In addition to similarity of contents, the author sometimes interweaves details from the actual text of Job. A striking example is provided by Tobit's conversation with his wife. This episode follows the impoverishment and illness of Tobit, just as the dialogue of Job and his wife occurs after the loss of his children, fortune and health. Moreover, *Tobit* models his episode on the Greek version of Job, not on the Hebrew. This is clear from additions in Tobit and Septuagint of Job 2:9a, but absent from the Hebrew. The Septuagint quotes Job's wife as complaining that she is forced to work as a servant in other houses. This detail, probably based on the Hebrew of Job 31:10, is taken up by Tobit 2:11, where it is stated that Tobit's wife was hired as a servant in other houses.[168] The entire scene between Tobit and his wife takes place against this background: Tobit's wife receives a kid as a gift from her masters, without telling her husband. Tobit discovers the kid and doubts his wife's explanation. His disbelief provokes a sharp rebuke from his wife, echoing the rebuke of Job's wife.[169] This throws Tobit into profound despair, leading him to wish for death, a wish which he expresses in his prayer, echoing the discourse in Job 3.

---

[168] Compare the term λάτρις (= 'labourer, maidservant'; Lidell-Scott, *Lexicon,* 1032) used by Job 2:9d of Job's wife with the term employed by Tobit 2:11 of Tobit's wife: ἠριθεύετο (= 'was hired to work', 'served'; Lidell-Scott, *Lexicon*, 688). The entire verse runs as follows: 'Now at that time Anna my wife was hired to work in women's quarters (thus G1; cf. Lidell-Scott, *Lexicon*, 363 for 'quarters'; G2 reads 'in women's works'). For text cf. Hanhart, *Tobit*.

[169] In the original Hebrew Job's wife scolds her husband (2:9): 'Are you still holding fast your integrity? Curse God and die!' These words are echoed in the retort of Tobit's wife (2:14); 'And where are your acts of kindness? Where are you righteous deeds? Behold, your humiliation is well-known'. These words could have been uttered by Job's own wife.

The episode in *Tobit* may be seen as an elaboration of Job's story. It is as if the author of Tobit renders explicit elements hinted at in *Job*, or even in the LXX. Thus, in *Tobit* the whole story about the kid is incomprehensible without attributing to it sexual overtones. This is implied not only by context of a woman working in other houses (cf. Job 31:10), but also by introducing the kid, which brings to mind the kid given by Judah to Tamar as a harlot's pay (Gen 34:17, 20).[170]

These affinities with the story of Job are notable because they are present without any explicit reference to Job or the Book of Job. Moreover, the materials of the plot are not taken from Job or a similar biblical figure, but are independent of them. The use made by *Tobit* of biblical motifs differs, then, in purpose and form from that of narratives of the rewritten Bible or pseudepigraphic biography type. In the case of a 'free narrative' like *Tobit*, the author achieves a Job-like plot. The referential value lies in the coincidence of motifs and some of the terms, but it leads to a comparison between the new and old texts, and not to an integration of the old in the new, as was the case in the pseudepigraphic or 'rewritten Bible' narratives.

Summary and Conclusions

We have attempted to describe use of biblical elements in the Apocrypha and Pseudepigrapha. The method of presentation consisted of a general definition and categorization, each category illustrated by specific cases. After a general distinction between biblical elements used in expositional and compositional functions, the discussion centred upon the various types of compositions in our literature. These were found to be of two major types: biblical elements used in explicit or implicit ways. The explicit uses were employed in rhetorical contexts, namely in various types of discourse, and for various rhetorical purposes. The uses in compositional functions occur in all types of contexts and genres. In explicit rhetorical uses the biblical elements stand for the divine authority and are presented as such. In implicit compositional uses biblical elements are part of the materials forming the texture of the composition. Authors employing biblical elements in this way aim at re-creating the biblical models and atmosphere, and identify themselves with the biblical authors.

These two modes of approach to biblical elements are not incompatible. They exist side by side in the various types of literature composed during the Second Temple Period.

---

[170] Cf. the expression ἔριφος ἐξ αἰγῶν in Gen 38:20 and Tobit 2:12 (G2).

Chapter Twelve

Authority and Interpretation of Scripture in the Writings of Philo

Yehoshua Amir

Introduction

In the present study we are concerned with the specific question of the place and treatment of Mikra within Philo's extensive oeuvre. General questions on the understanding of Philo will be touched upon only insofar they seem inescapably relevant to the difficult subject of Philo's views on Scripture.[1]

We shall in this essay leave open the question whether Philo is to be regarded primarily as a philosopher, who uses the Bible as a vehicle[2] for a religious philosophy, nourished by Stoicism and Plato, which may be characterized as late Stoic[3] or middle Platonic,[4] or whether, on the contrary, he is to be seen as a Bible exegete who places both his general education[5] and the entire mass of contemporary thought in the service of the absolutely true doctrine of Divine revelation, set down above all by Moses in the Pentateuch.[6] To take these two possibilities as alternatives is, I think, to pose the question in a wrong way. Both ways of looking at the problem have their own inner justifications, and each complements the other. The truth is surely that Philo's thought-process oscillates between the two foci which were given him at the outset, namely the reliability of the word of Divine revelation as formulated by Moses, and the convincingness of the doctrine which emerged from the philosophical dis-

---

[1] A good survey of Philo's activity as a writer and a look into the world of his thought, can be found in Borgen, 'Philo of Alexandria'.

[2] Since the 19th century there has been a widespread notion among scholars, though as time goes on it takes milder and milder forms, that Philo was only using the biblical text as a pretext in order to pass Greek philosophical doctrines off as Jewish with the help of an artificial exegesis. His purpose has been variously fathomed as a wish to give the despised Jewish religion a little philosophical prestige in the eyes of a Hellenistic audience (Schwartz, in 'Aporien im 4. Evangelium', advocates this view in especially provocative form), or, on the contrary, as an attempt to make acceptable to a Jewish audience the suspect philosophy, and more than suspect mysticism, of the Hellenistic milieu (a position last taken by Goodenough in *By Light, Light*).

[3] This classification is seen as the essential one by, e.g. I. Heinemann, *Philons griechische und jüdische Bildung*.

[4] This view has been emphatically followed through by Dillon, *The Middle Platonists*.

[5] On this subject see Mendelson, *Secular Education*.

[6] Wolfson, *Philo*, may be regarded as the most prominent representative of this view. The same orientation is demanded by Völker, *Fortschritt und Vollendung*, and worked out with strict consequence by Nikiprowetzky, *Le commentaire*.

cussions of his time. The movement between these two positions, neither of which is static – the biblical word is enigmatic and its meaning is yet to be found out, while philosophical discussion is still in flux – keeps his thought in perpetual suspense. A faithful retracing of Philo's thought process would have to show on the one hand how motifs which his exegetical method justify him in extracting from the biblical word, enrich his philosophically grounded mysticism and give it new shades of meaning, and how on the other hand in his interpretation of the biblical text he is guided by his philosophical-mystical commitment. If in the following treatment the first standpoint is somewhat obscured by the second, this is due solely to the limited task we have assumed here, namely to show how Philo deals with the biblical word.

Use of Mikra

THE DISTRIBUTION OF QUOTATIONS OVER THE BIBLICAL BOOKS

To find out how Philo employs quotations from Scripture in the Greek texts that have come down to us, we need only consult the Scripture Index contained in the edition of the text with English translation.[7] A casual glance at the Index reveals the remarkable fact that while quotations from the Pentateuch alone fill 65 pages, only five pages suffice for the listing of quotations from all other parts of the OT, and there are no quotations whatever from the Apocrypha and the Pseudepigrapha.[8] This disproportion will increase when in the following pages we see what familiarity with the exact phrasing of the Pentateuch Philo assumes on the reader's part in certain parts of his writings. When this is taken into account, the preponderance of the Pentateuch in Philo's use of the Bible becomes downright overwhelming.

Yet it would not be accurate to say that Philo completely dismisses the other parts of Scripture, or fails to regard them as holy books. Philo's concept of the Bible is clearly not that of the Samaritans, for whom only the Pentateuch is holy; at times he does make use of the Prophets and the Psalms as authorities. And while we have only a single quotation from the book of Job,[9] his manner of quoting it leaves no doubt that he took his readers' knowledge and recognition of the book of Job for granted. Without committing ourselves on the subject of the 'canon', for which concept as such we have no evidence among Jews, it is

---

[7] All references to Philonic texts are taken from the *LCL* edition, of which the 10 volumes by Colson and Whitaker in the years 1919-1962 include all the Greek texts that have been preserved, together with English translations, while the supplement volumes, edited by R. Marcus, 1953, contain the English translations of works which were preserved only in Armenian. The Scripture Index is in *LCL* 10, 189-268.

[8] The index references to these books refer not to Philo's text, but to Colson's notes.

[9] *Mut.* 48f quotes Job 14:4 (all other references are to Colson's notes).

safe to say that books belonging to the Prophets and Hagiographa were regarded by Philo as holy books, to be quoted as such.

What is not clear is why Philo so seldom quotes these books, and in particular why he fails to quote them in passages where a quotation from one of these sources would have fitted into Philo's train of thought better than the Pentateuch verses which he has to subject to a very cumbersome method of interpretation before they will serve his turn. Obviously the Prophets and Hagiographa have not the same status for him as the the Pentateuch. But the same is true for the Rabbis, who nonetheless did not hesitate to make extensive use of these books, and particularly in their interpretation of the Pentateuch. Heinemann gives a possible answer to the question: 'The reason is not that the other books were not yet all translated, or all recognized. (. . .) The scattered quotations which we do find show that such was not the case. Rather, Philo knows the Bible only from the worship service and from occasionally looking things up.'[10] Now, this conclusion is based on circular reasoning, for Heinemann's conjecture as to the source of Philo's knowledge of these books is derived from Philo's sparse use of them. Still, he may have hit on the truth. In such a case we should also have to assume that in the Alexandrian synagogue no portions of the Prophets were read, which is by no means certain. The question whether Philo was able to read the books of the Bible otherwise than in Greek translation is likewise moot.

If we do not accept Heinemann's explanation, we may call to mind that in Hellenistic Judaism – to judge by the texts it has left behind – the figure of Moses was even more central than in the motherland. Evidence of this in Philo is the fact that although he is acquainted with other prophetic figures, when he deals with the concept of the prophet or friend of God he thinks first, and almost exclusively, of Moses. Thus wherever a word can be traced back to him he does so, bypassing all other sanctified words.

Use of Mikra in the Different Categories of Writings

The way in which Philo treats Mikra in one category of writings is not necessarily the way he treats it in another; we must therefore consider them separately.

(1) *Books not concerned with the Bible*
Only a few of the writings by Philo that have come down to us are not directly related to the Bible.[11] Even these writings are not completely devoid of biblical references. Thus even in a purely academic discussion of the doctrines held by various philosophical schools concerning the indestructibility of the world, there is a reference to 'Moses the Lawgiver of the Jews' who in Genesis, the first

---

[10] Heinemann, *Philons griechische und jüdische Bildung*, 527, n. 4.
[11] All Philo's writings on subjects other than Scripture which have been preserved in Greek are contained in *LCL* 9-10.

of his five holy books, taught that the world is imperishable; in support of this the first two verses of the Bible are quoted word for word.[12] In another treatise, written in the spirit of Cynic or Stoic ethics, he praises the Sage's unshakeable strength of character, citing as a reference the 'lawgiver of the Jews', concerning whom it is written: 'The hands of Moses were heavy'.[13] On the other hand one is struck by the fact that when describing contemporary Jewish trends and conditions Philo gives expression to a strong Jewish religiosity yet does not refer to specific biblical sayings, even when describing the Therapeutic sect, whose members dedicated their entire lives to the study of the books of the Bible.[14]

All of Philo's other writings refer in various ways to Mikra. They fall into three groups, which we shall consider in turn.

(2) The Exposition of the Law[15]

The 'Exposition of the Law' reads the Pentateuch as Moses' book of law. Such an approach compels Philo to ask a preliminary question which he, as a Greek writer, could not evade: is a conception of the book as a law-code possible, from the literary-critical point of view?

The question occurs with regard to Genesis, beginning with the first chapter. Do such non-legislative elements have a legitimate place in a lawbook? Here Philo recurs to Plato's statement that a law needs a *proem*.[16] As such a *proem* Moses placed his philosophy concerning the creation of the world at the entrance to his legislation, in order to make clear that what follows is not merely one among innumerable territorial law-codes, but rather that 'natural law', that 'law of the cosmos' which, according to the Stoic view, stands *idealiter* behind all local laws.[17]

A similar question confronts Philo when he comes to the stories of the Patriarchs. These he integrates into the law code with the help of the concept of 'unwritten law',[18] which, according to a Hellenistic theory, is present as 'embodied law'[19] in a perfect human being and precedes the written law as its archetype. As such, the figures of the Patriarchs are an integral part of the law itself.

[12] *Aet.* 19.
[13] *Prob.* 29, after Exod 17:12.
[14] *LCL* 9, pp. 103-69.
[15] Borgen, 'Philo of Alexandria', 233-43: Exposition of the Law. Texts *LCL* 6-8; and additionally 1:1-137.
[16] Plato, *Leges* 4, 723a; cf. Pfister, 'Die Prooimia'.
[17] *Op.* 3. Here and in the following pages the reader will easily recognize that I differ with Borgen's ('Philo of Alexandria') view of Philo's basic tendency. In the cosmopolitanization of the concept of law I see rather a tendency to derealization of the concrete concept of the nation. This is not the place to explore this difference.
[18] *Abr.* 267; on the history of this concept see Hirzel, 'Agraphos Nomos', 1ff. Whoever reads here that Abraham was not only 'one who obeyed the Law' but 'himself a law and an inwritten Statute', will agree with Heinemann, *Philons griechische und jüdische Bildung*, 10, who insists that Philo has in mind here a different concept from the rabbinic Oral Tora, which one can *keep*, but not *be*.
[19] *Abr.* 5. The passage continues: 'The enacted laws are nothing else than memorials of the life of the ancients', a notion which could scarcely be farther from the rabbinic conception.

The function of the biographies of the Patriarchs, as well as the loosely inserted treatise on Moses in two books,[20] is thus to depict ideal figures. In their organization they do not follow the pace and sequence of the biblical narratives; instead the material is arranged under several headings and represents a deliberate selection. In the biography of Moses the episode of Moses' sin is omitted, and of the numerous stories of the sins of the people in the desert, only the story of the spies is included in Philo's account.

The same is true for those portions of the series which are devoted to the laws proper. Philo does not attempt a complete presentation of the laws of the Pentateuch. The absence of some particular by no means justifies the conclusion that Philo forgot about it or overlooked it. For instance, when he deals with the Sabbath laws as a whole,[21] he omits certain regulations which he mentions in other contexts, so that we cannot assume he did not knew them. But a presentation without gaps is not what he is aiming for. Rather he is concerned with proving in detail that the law of Moses is perfect in itself and therefore identical with the law of the cosmos, the absolute Logos.

A law which is equivalent to the 'Logos' has to be built up 'logically', i.e. systematically. This is the reason for the arrangement of the entire, immense mass of legislation under the rubrics of the Ten Commandments, whose number corresponds to the number of categories in Aristotelian logic.[22]

This attempt at systematization, which incidentally has no complete parallel in the rabbinic tradition,[23] naturally compels Philo to take considerable liberties in regrouping his material, bringing together statements on related matters from widely-scattered contexts and adding interpretations of his own to emphasize the excellence of these laws, sometimes by comparison with those of other peoples.[24] Only in one instance does he make an exception to the systematic arrangement of his material: when he begins his treatment of individual laws with circumcision[25] because it is, as he says, 'an object of ridicule among many people'. The apologetic sense of the arrangement is clear: it is no use trying to place the other commandments in the correct perspective until he has disposed of a prejudice which might so repeal the (non-Jewish) reader as to prevent him from giving a fair hearing to the rest of his presentation.

Not much can be gleaned from this series in the way of direct textual exegesis. The Bible is presented, both narrative and legislation, mostly in free paraphrase; only rarely is it quoted verbatim. Heinemann,[26] at several points in his treatment of Philo's presentation of the law, calls attention to the fact that

[20] See Borgen, 'Philo of Alexandria', 234 n. 6.
[21] *Spec.* 2:56-70. But cf. *Mig.* 91.
[22] *Decal.* 30.
[23] See Urbach, *Sages* 1, 360ff.
[24] See esp. *Jos.* 42f. on the strictness of Jewish sexual morality in comparison with the Hellenic.
[25] *Spec.* 11:2ff.
[26] Heinemann, *Philons griechische und jüdische Bildung* 421, the distinction between theft and robbery.

Philo's exposition implies certain definite interpretations of the legal concepts in the Pentateuch; but it does not inquire explicitly into the precise meaning of this or that legal concept. Verbatim quotations from the Bible and linguistic explication of these quotations occupy more space in the treatise 'On the Account of the World's Creation'[27] than in other parts of this series. This may be attributed to the fact that this treatise may also be regarded as the first part of another series, with which we shall deal presently.

A peculiarity of the series on legal exposition is that the reflections, which are generally guided by pragmatic considerations, are frequently interrupted by allegorical disquisitions which, while profound in themselves, could be omitted without prejudice to the general coherency. If anything these disquisitions detract from the coherency because in allegory the personality of the hero is lost, and it is precisely on the *personality* of the forefathers that their claim to be regarded as 'embodied law' rests! The inclusion of such passages leads us to suspect that the aspect under which the work of Moses is considered in this series is only of secondary importance to Philo, since even here he cannot refrain from pursuing the kind of thoughts that represent his essential nature.

(3) Allegorical Commentary

In this series the text of Mikra is treated quite differently. It is Philo's vast allegorical commentary, which despite its volume[28] accompanies only a part of Genesis with its explications. This time the character of the Pentateuch as law code is simply ignored. It is a legal document only in its literal meaning, which this second series leaves far behind. The subject here is not Mosaic legislation, but Mosaic philosophy.

The main effort of this philosophy is devoted to revealing the essential, 'spiritual' meaning behind the 'sensible'. The act of allegorization, which purports to bring out the meaning really intended by Moses, consists of divesting the thing named by the word of its concreteness, leaving an intrinsic meaning which is conceptual, abstracted from all spatial-temporal being, absolutely valid, eternal. Where the living human beings of biblical narrative are concerned, it is precisely their personality which must be eliminated: 'Now probably there was an actual man called Samuel; but we conceive of the Samuel of the Scripture, not as a living compound of soul and body, but as a mind which rejoices in the service and worship of God'.[29] Allegory can take the biblical

---

[27] Thus he deduces (*Op.*. 15) from the use of the word μια and not πρώτη for the first day of Creation (Gen 1:5) that this day has a special status in relation to the following 5; thus he concludes, on the basis of an eccentric interpretation (*Op.* 25) of κατ 'εἰκόνα (Gen 1:17), which he takes to mean 'in conformity to a similitude', i.e. a similitude once removed, that man (and *a potiori* the rest of creation) is not the image of God, but only the image of that image, i.e. of the Logos; and thus he insists (*Op.* 26) that 'beginning' in the first verse of the Bible is to be understood 'not in a chronological sense'.

[28] In *LCL* it takes up vols. 1-5. See Borgen, 'Philo of Alexandira', 243-45, who lists some further parts of this series which have not been preserved.

[29] *Ebr.* 144.

personalities only as sensible representations of certain spritual types. On this level of Bible interpretation it is irrelevant whether and when, historically speaking, a man called Samuel lived. It is quite possible for a certain type to appear in the Bible as Laban, and then again as Jethro.[30] Allegorical interpretation treats these figures as identical.

This explains the diffuse compositional character of this series. Nearly every treatise begins with one or more biblical verses, which are given in the Septuagint version.[31] But the text itself is only a point of departure for a lengthy symbolic exegesis. As we have seen, this entails finding the announced theme in all kinds of different, widely separated biblical contexts. The disjointed thought-process which makes the reading of these works so laborious, is thus a necessary consequence of the inner presuppositions of the way of thinking that prompted this exegesis. The weight of symbolic meaning is borne by the isolate word, so that the exact wording of the text to be interpreted must be punctiliously attended to. In these works, then, Philo is addressing a reader who has in his head not only the law or the narrative in general, but the exact wording of the biblical text. Practically, only a Jewish reader would be able to follow the arbitrary stringing-together of biblical passages from widely varying contexts, without losing the thread.

With this method a single verse suffices to set the theme for an entire treatise; indeed the brief verse Gen 9:20 provides material for two treatises.[32] In 'On Flight and Finding' the short story of Hagar in the desert[33] becomes the starting-point for the development of the deepest motif in Philo's conception of the human being.

Thus the verse is only the point of departure for an often widely-ramified train of thought which sometimes loses sight of the verse and does not come back to it.

(4) Questions and Answers

In the third series of his writings on the Bible, 'Questions and Answers',[34] Philo adopts the opposite procedure, keeping strictly to the form of the running commentary. The verses are discussed in biblical sequence, the discussion opening each time with questions that usually begin with 'Why does he say . . .' or 'What does he mean by . . .' Here Philo limits himself in his answer to the verse under discussion and refrains from adducing further parallels. Most of the

---

[30]   Ebr. 36ff. Jethro 36-45, and immediately afterward Laban 46-53.

[31]   Katz, Philo's Bible, has established that those Bible texts which deviate from the Septuagint as handed down to us – particularly in the lemmata at the beginnings of treatises, which we find in some Philo manuscripts – do not go back to Philo himself, but were inserted into the text by later copyists.

[32]   Agr. and Plant., both in LCL 3.

[33]   Gen 16:11-12, treated in Fug., LCL 5.

[34]   LCL Suppl 1-2. Cf. Borgen, 'Philo of Alexandria', 241-42. The text has been preserved only in an Armenian translation which is itself fragmentary. The supplement volumes contain R. Marcus' English translations of these texts without the Armenian, but with the addition of the few fragments of the Greek originals which have been preserved.

answers can be divided into two parts: in the first he gives the literal meaning of the verse, in the second he interprets it allegorically. In keeping with his basic attitude as exegete, Philo usually disposes of the literal meaning in a few words, while the allegorical interpretation may go on for several pages.

Here, then – in contrast to the great allegorical commentary – Philo has doubtless subordinated his own religious-philosophical thinking to his task as Bible exegete. It must be stated, however, that it is not the 'Questions and Answers' that define Philo as a Bible commentator, but rather the great 'Allegorical Commentary', in which his hermeneutic genius celebrates its most impressive triumph.

Authority of Mikra

MIKRA MORE THAN LITERATURE

We shall have to deal with the question of the degree to which Philo's allegorical Bible interpretation is indebted to the Homeric allegory which originated in his native Alexandria. This way of interpreting the poet, which developed in close connection with Alexandrian philology, is a branch of that literary scholarship which regarded Homer as the perfect poet, learned both in science and in philosophy.[35] The task of the allegorist was to extract evidence for this from Homer's text.

Although, as we shall see, Philo pursues the deeper mysteries of the biblical text with similar methods, he is still far from naming the work of Moses in the same breath with the Homeric epics. With a decisiveness whose pathos derives from the critique of poetry in Platon's *Politeia*,[36] he draws a sharp distinction between Moses and poetry: art, like the Sophists, is concerned with seeming, Moses with being.[37] True, Philo thereby loses all sense of the aesthetic standard of biblical poetry; but that is only the lamentable reverse side of his philosophical sense of superiority.[38]

Thus it is certainly no literary interest that leads Philo to devote almost his entire activity as a writer to Mikra. He regarded literature, which for the consciousness of that time also included historiography, as belonging to the preliminary studies[39] whose worth is only relative, in contrast to the study of absolute truth:

---

[35] On the interpretation, especially the allegorical interpretation, of Homer, see Buffière, *Les mythes d'Homère* and Pépin, *Mythe et allégorie*.

[36] See Pépin, *ibid.* ch. 5: La réaction platonicienne, 112-24. Plato's critique of Homer is in the *Politeia*, Books 2 and 3, and esp. book 10.

[37] For instance *Sac.* 12; *Det.* 38.

[38] I have noted an example of this in my *Studien*, 84 n. 4.

[39] To which the treatise *Cong.*, LCL 4, is devoted.

428

Nou doubt it is profitable, if not for the acquisition of perfect virtue, at least for the life of civic virtue, to feed the mind on ancient and time honoured thoughts, to trace the venerable tradition of noble deeds, which historians and all the family of poets have handed down to the memory of their own and future generations. But when, unforeseen and unhoped for, the sudden beam of self-inspired wisdom has shone upon us, when that wisdom has opened the closed eye of the soul (. . .) then it is idle any longer to exercise the ear with words (. . .) For truly it is sweet to leave nothing unknown. Yet when God causes the young shoots of self-inspired wisdom to spring up within the soul, the knowledge that comes from teaching must straightway be abolished and swept off. (. . .) God's scholar, God's pupil, God's disciple (. . .) can not any more suffer the guidance of men.[40]

Thus science and art can form only an intermediate stage on the road to absolute truth. That is the subject of Philo's exegesis of the story of the slave Hagar, who gives birth for her mistress Sara.[41] In his exegesis Philo speaks in the first person and says that he has learned this and that science, 'yet I took none of her children for my private use, but brought them as a gift to the lawful wife',[42] the mistress, who stands allegorically for Wisdom.

Mikra, then, must belong to the sphere of this wisdom, although simply to equate them, as some Philo commentators have done,[43] is to reckon without the fundamental non-concreteness of his thinking. We shall also have to deal with the question of how, in the above quotation, it can be taught both that wisdom is of God (and not of man) and that it is self-inspired.

It is in any case clear that the biblical word, in contrast to the irresponsible productions of poetic fancy, has authority. As to the source of this authority, this is not quite so transparent in Philo as in rabbinic Judaism. Wherever interpreters have tried simply to apply the categories of rabbinic Judaism to Philo, they have either left part of his statements out of consideration or have robbed them of meaning by refusing to take them literally. This was possible because Philo's work contains unambiguous proof that he regarded the biblical word as of Divine origin; this seemed to ensure the identity of his views with those of the rabbis.

If we wish to reopen this question, we must begin by reexamining some of Philo's statements on the Divine origin of the biblical word.

THE BIBLICAL WORD AS ORACLE

On what, according to Philo, is the authority of the biblical word founded? A

---

[40] Sac. 78.
[41] Gen. 16:1-2.
[42] Cong. 75.
[43] This is the view of Wolfson, Philo 1, 87ff. in his chapter, 'Handmaid of Scripture'.

first answer to this question is provided by his designations for the biblical verse: he calls it an 'oracle'[44] or a 'logion';[45] the two in his usage are synonymous.[46] Both designations are derived from the language of Greek oracular institutions. In order to evaluate this usage correctly, we have to take into consideration that we do not find in Philo that avoidance of pagan vocabulary which marks both the Septuagint and other Jewish-Hellenistic literature; thus he does not hesitate to extol an overwhelming love of God as 'Olympian'.[47] This insouciance must be attributed to the need to place the most resonant expressive resources of the Greek tongue at the service of religious fact and feeling; these resources are naturally most intimately bound up with paganism.

If we compare Philo with Josephus in this respect, we find that the latter uses the word 'oracle' 7 (8) times.[48] Four of the passages speak of pagans consulting the oracle. In one passage he tells of an oracular saying which became current, and which the Jews trusted so far as to wage war on Rome because of it.[49] In one (uncertain) passage Moses perhaps expects to bring word from God down from Mount Sinai.[50] But in the only two passages which are of interest for our discussion,[51] biblical prophetic sayings, as such, are designated as oracles. These two sayings are naturally marked in the biblical original as words coming directly from God.

Philo, too, likes to speak of 'oracles' in connection with Bible texts where God is actually the speaker. Thus he enumerates four laws which, according to biblical report, came into being when Moses asked God and God gave him an answer via an 'oracle'.[52] When Moses asked to see God, he received an 'oracle' whose content corresponds to what is introduced in Exod 33:21 with the words: 'Thus spoke the Lord'.[53] Moses is commanded to tell Pharaoh: 'The people has received an oracle from Me',[54] meaning the command reported in Exod 3:18. Moreover, when he describes the giving of the oracle, Philo makes liberal use of the hieratic terminology of the Delphic Oracle: 'an oracle falls out'[55] for Moses, harking back to the archaic technique of drawing the oracle by lot; and Abraham 'is smitten by an oracle',[56] as in the ecstatic states of the Delphic Pythia.

---

[44] χρησμός; see on this Mayer, *Index Philoneus*, s.v.

[45] Both words are used synonymously in close proximity to each other, e.g. *Mos.* 1:57. *Spec.* 1:315. Another synonym is θεοπρόπιον.

[46] λόγιον; see *Index Philoneus*, s.v.

[47] ὀλύμπιος; see *Index Philoneus*, s.v.

[48] In one of the passages (*Ant.* 3:75) the manuscript versions give both χρησμόι and χρήσιμοι; the second reading is preferable.

[49] *War* 6:109.

[50] See n. 48.

[51] Applied to biblical texts only in *War* 4:386; 6:109.

[52] *Mos.* 2:192.

[53] *Post.* 169.

[54] *Mos.* 1:73.

[55] *Post.* 69.

[56] *Abr.* 62.

Thus Colson is not quite methodically sound in frequently translating the Greek word not by 'oracle' but merely by 'command'.

But Philo is not always speaking of a word from God reported in the Bible, when he uses the word 'oracle'. When Philo speaks of the loaves of showbread in the sanctuary as 'arranged by oracle',[57] we may still take this as an exalted way of speaking of the Divine directions so prosaically set forth in Exod 29:29; but when he has a 'logion' tell us that on the way to the sacrifice Abraham and Isaac walked together,[58] or that Aaron's rod swallowed up the others,[59] we are dealing with passages where God is not introduced as speaker. They can be called logia only because they are in the Bible; the logion, then, is the biblical verse as such. The fact of being written in the Bible suffices, according to Philo, to give a saying oracular status. 'The Divine oracles'[60] – i.e. the report in Exod 20:21 – 'say' that Moses entered into the mysterious darkness of the Godhead. Nevertheless the fact that he speaks of 'oracles' here in the plural may be taken as evidence of a reluctance on Philo's part to allow the word 'oracle' to rigidify into a simple synonym for 'Bible verse'. The word 'oracles' in the last-quoted example is applied to a single verse;[61] in such cases 'the oracles' may be taken to mean the Bible as a whole.[62] The use of the word 'oracle' in this paler sense, which had established itself in his writing, seems to have been what prompted Philo, in passages where the actual word of God is the subject, to redundancies like 'proclaimed oracles'[63] or even an 'oracle proclaimed (by God) in person'.[64] Such words from God are proclaimed not only by Moses, i.e. in the Tora, but also by prophets.[65] The verbs that designate the act of proclamation are applied both to the Godhead and to earthly proclaimers;[66] the latter is thus both a receiver and a transmitter of oracles. How both sides of his function belong together is stated in the simplest possible way: 'Moses himself learnt it by an

---

[57] Cong. 168: χρησμοῖς προστέτακται.

[58] Mig. 166; the same goes for Ebr. 82, where the verse cited immediately afterward is introduced as 'the oracles'.

[59] Mig. 85.

[60] Mut. 7.

[61] E.g. Mig. 60, 108; Heres 21; Fug. 50.

[62] This is especially evident in Sobr. 17, where οἱ χρησμοί repeats what had just been called αἱ ἱερώταται βίβλοι.

[63] χρησθὲν λόγιον, e.g. Det. 48; χρησθὲν θεοπρόπιον, e.g. Som 1:148 or λόγιον θεσπισθέν Mut. 13. If Mut. 34 speaks of a χρησθέν ἐπί τοῦ Ἐνὼχ λόγιον and Som. 1:64 of a λόγιον χρησθὲν ἐπὶ Αβρααμ, neither of which is the word of God in the text, then χρησθέν is here used not attributively, as an appositive, but predicatively, as a qualifier.

[64] Mut. 13.

[65] Of these Jeremiah (Cher. 49) is referred to by name; without naming them he also cites sayings of Hosea (Mut. 139), Isaiah (Mut. 169), and Zechariah (Conf. 62). It is worth noting that in the passage (Cher. 49) where he is named Jeremiah is called prophet, authorized hierophant, and one filled with God, so that he receives practically the same distinctions as Moses.

[66] On Moses as receiver of oracles see Mos. 2:176; L.A. 3:142; Som. 2:227; Virt. 63; on Moses as giver of oracles see Fug. 138; Mos. 2:269.

oracle and has taught us how it was'.[67] But it is not only Moses who exercises this double function. Concerning Jeremiah, Philo writes: 'I myself was initiated under Moses the God-beloved into his greater mysteries, yet when I saw the prophet Jeremiah and knew him not only a *mystes* but a worthy *hierophantes*, I was not slow to become his disciple'.[68]

The title 'hierophant', here applied to Jeremiah, is one of Philo's standard designations for Moses. In Hellas this term referred to 'the foremost cult official in the Eleusinian rites',[69] i.e. the rites of the Attic mystery cult. Philo alternates this title with another which had been used since Homer for the priest of the oracle.[70] In examining Philo's conception of Moses, we shall have to come back to these pagan associations.

After all that has been said, it is almost self-understood that Philo consistently speaks of Mikra as 'holy Scripture', the 'holy books', and the like.[71] It has been rightly pointed out that such terms were widespread in Hebrew usage, and probably had been since much earlier times; probably they had come with the Egyptian Jews from the motherland.[72] What we have yet to do is to show how the particular nuance of this holiness in Philo differs from that in other views.

It is first to be said in any case that for Philo the fact that something is stated in Mikra is sufficient proof that it is so. After allegorically extracting a Stoic proposition from a Bible verse, he says, 'This is no invention of mine, but a statement made by the holy oracles'.[73] In another passage he writes that when the soul frees herself from all earthly things and clings only to God, then God grants her himself: 'This my affirmation is warranted by the oracle which says, "The Lord Himself is his portion" '.[74] The fact that the statement is made in a Bible verse guarantees its truth. Again and again a Bible verse is called to 'witness' for a claim.[75] This is most impressively stated when Philo explains that for God's ownership of the universe 'the oracle is a true witness in these words; "and the land shall not be sold in perpetuity, for all the land is mine . . ", a clear proof surely that in possession all things are God's, and only as a loan do they belong to created beings'.[76] He returns to this in summing up: 'All things are God's possessions on the strength of true reasonings and testimonies which none may convict of false witness, for our witnesses are the oracles which Moses wrote in the sacred books'.[77] Since Moses wrote it in the sacred books, any objection would be absurd.

---

[67] *Det.* 86.
[68] *Cher.* 49.
[69] *PW* 2, 2 p. 1581.
[70] θεοπρόπος, see *Index Philoneus*, s.v.
[71] See *Index Philoneus*, s.v. ἱερός.
[72] Cf. *M. Shabbat* 16:1; *M. Yadayim* 3:5.
[73] *Mut.* 152.
[74] *Cong.* 134.
[75] Thus *Det.* 166; *Conf.* 94; *Fug.* 178; *Mut.* 39; *Som.* 1:231; *Som.* 2:220.
[76] *Cher.* 108f.
[77] *Cher.* 124.

In these last words, however, there is something that has a foreign sound for the reader versed in the writings of the Rabbis. Of course, the Rabbis too speak of the Tora as written by Moses. But its irrefutable truth does not rest for them on the fact that he wrote it. He was only permitted to write what God made him write, even when he himself rebelled against it.[78] And only because he submitted to this condition is the Tora unconditionally true for the Rabbis. Philo sees the role of Moses in relation to the Tora in a fundamentally different light.[79] In all the writings he devotes to Scripture, he treats Moses as the author. When he quotes a Bible verse, he says: Moses says. And that this saying does not only mean the obedient writer who has to write what he is told whether he accepts it or rebels against it, becomes evident when, concerning a passage which speaks of an oath taken by God, Philo asks: 'Why did it seem well to the prophet and revealer to represent God as binding himself by an oath?'[80] Thus when the biblical narrative poses a problem for Philo, he formulates his astonished question in the form: 'what was Moses thinking of, when he said this or that of God?' Such a question can obviously be asked only of an author who can determine how God is to be spoken of in this text.

How did Philo understand Moses' personal role as writer? We can gain some light on this matter from a remarkable exposition called forth by the verse 'And Abel became a shepherd of sheep, but Cain was a tiller of the ground'.[81] Philo is struck by the sequence, as the younger Abel must have chosen his occupation after his brother. This is a violation of logic, 'But Moses sets no value on probabilities and plausibilities, but follows after truth in its purity'.[82] This opposition between probability/plausibility and truth is of course a late echo of Socrates' debate with the Sophists in Plato's *Apologia*. What motive of truth it was that prompted Moses to dispense with plausibility, becomes understandable only from Philo's allegorical interpretation of the verses, which we need not go into. What is important for our purposes is the continuation of this sentence in Philo: 'And when he comes to God apart from all, he frankly says that he is not eloquent (here Philo uses a Greek word[83] which may also mean: plausible, standing to reason)'. The last sentence of course alludes to Moses' answer at the thornbush: 'I am not a man of words',[84] which is translated by the Septuagint, in one variant which Philo was evidently using, with this Greek

---

[78] *Gen. Rabba* 8:8, p. 61-62.
[79] See on the following the essay 'Moses als Verfasser der Tora bei Philon' in my book *Die hellenistische Gestalt*, 77-106.
[80] *Sac.* 94.
[81] Gen 4:2.
[82] *Sac.* 12.
[83] εὔλογος.
[84] Apparently Philo's copy of the Septuagint had in this passage the variant εὔλογος, which is found in some Septuagint manuscripts. This reading was also used by the tragic poet Ezekiel, as we see from v. 113 of the fragments of his tragedy.

word, so that the answer can read either 'I am not eloquent' or 'I do not speak plausibly'. Here not only is Moses named as the author of the Tora, but a stylistic peculiarity of the Tora text as we have it is causally connected with Moses as we know him through the Bible narrative itself. The authorship of the Moses we know is taken as an explanation for a certain trait that characterizes the style of the Bible.

Anyone acquainted with rabbinic Bible exegesis will immediately see that nothing could be more alien to the rabbis than this way of thinking. But still more immediately, we are faced with the question: how does the authorship of Moses,[85] which Philo assumes as a thing self-understood, consort with Philo's own view of the biblical word as 'oracle', for which we have just presented detailed evidence? In one of the passages quoted above, Philo himself drew a sharp distinction between instruction by God and instruction by human beings.[86] Does not Moses' authorship imply a human, that is, if we maintain the sharpness of the alternative, a non-divine status for Mikra?

Here we find ourselves in a blind alley, from which we can exit only by seeing through the hasty conclusion which we drew by equating Mikra too directly with the Divine instruction which Philo enthusiastically praises. In the above quotation[86] the opposition between human and Divine teaching was accented in a very particular fashion:

> When (. . .) the sudden beam of self-inspired wisdom has shone upon us, when that wisdom has opened the closed eye of the soul and made us spectators rather than hearers of knowledge, and substituted in our minds sight, the swiftest of senses, for the slower sense of hearing, then it is idle any longer to exercise the ear with words.

Here Philo distinguishes between human instruction, which is absorbed through the ear, and Divine instruction, which appears to the eye.[87] Divine wisdom as a ray of light perceived only by the eye rather than the ear preoccupies Philo quite intensively, especially in connection with the revelation at Sinai, where 'All the people saw the voice'.[88] In his allegorical commentary Philo writes of this verse:

> The writer distinguishes things heard from things seen and hearing from sight, (. . .) making a very subtle distinction, for the voice dividing itself into noun and verb and parts of speech he naturally spoke of as "audible", for it comes to the test of hearing; but the voice of sound that was

---

[85] In my essay cited in note 79 I have adduced a large amount of further evidence for this view in Philo.

[86] In the quotation given above, n. 40, from *Sac.* 78.

[87] See my book, *Die hellenistische Gestalt*, 143-53, where I examine the notion of the visible voice in connection with the Sinaitic revelation.

[88] Exod 20:15, translated according to the text of the Septuagint.

not that of verbs and nouns but of God, seen by the eye of the soul, he rightly represents as "visible".[89]

Thus for Philo the language of Divine revelation is not that which is articulate and can be grasped in the grammatical categories of verb and noun. To facilely equate what 'God's scholar, God's pupil, God's disciple'[90] experienced with Mikra is to miss this dialectic between the audible and the visible word. In order to understand the precise nature of the holiness of Mikra in Philo, we must be very careful in our use of statements of this kind.

On what sources, then, shall we rely? First we must again recall that Philo, alone among Hellenistic Jewish writers, makes free use of pagan cult terminology. Not only does he designate the biblical word as an 'oracle', he also speaks of its proclamation as 'soothsaying',[91] and of its human carrier as hierophant, priest of the oracle, and prophet.[92] We would do well, then, to cast a brief sidelong glance at certain views held in the pagan milieu concerning these phenomena of its religious life.

The main line of Plato's view of prophecy,[93] which Philo adopts to a considerable extent in his own prophetology,[94] seems to me less fruitful for the understanding of Philo's concept of Scriptural authority than the treatment of mantic utterance in the *Timaios*,[95] which in many respects contradicts Plato's other statements. Here, apparently following the practice of the Delphic oracle of his time, he makes a sharp distinction between the soothsayer who, in the grip of the god, can only utter incomprehensible sounds, and the insightful prophet, who, using his reason to the fullest, 'critically judges'[96] these sounds and extracts a reasonable meaning from them.

There is a passage in Plutarch[97] which points in somewhat the same direction. True, Plutarch lived two generations after Philo, but the thought which his work incorporates is partly of a much older date. Plutarch has one of the participants in his dialogue explain why the oracles assume an artless form which is unworthy of the god: this is because the oracles are formulated by the soothsaying priestess, who is a simple woman of the people: 'The voice is not that of a god, nor the utterance of it, (. . .) but all these are the woman's; he puts into her mind only the visions, and creates a light in her soul in regard to the future; for inspiration is precisely this'.

---

[89] *Mig.* 48.
[90] *Sac.* 79.
[91] θεσπίζειν, see *Index Philoneus*, s.v.
[92] On προφήτης cf. Fascher, *ΠΡΟΦΗΤΗΣ*. Even the Septuagint could not manage without this word taken from the terminology of pagan cults.
[93] Fascher, *ibid.*, pp. 17-20, 66-70.
[94] Fascher, *ibid.*, 152-60.
[95] Plato, *Timaeus* 72ab.
[96] κρίνει.
[97] Plutarch, *De Pythiae Oraculis*, 397c.

Though their accounts differ in many respects, Plato and Plutarch concur on one point: they show that the concept of inspiration, as understood at many points in Philo's spiritual milieu, left room for autonomous linguistic activity on the part of the human being. Both authors assume that such autonomous activity does not detract from the authenticity of the Divine word which finds expression in the saying.

What is true of the oracle-priest would seem to apply with even greater force to the mystery priest, i.e. the hierophant. The hierophant is considered as the human representative of his god. As such, his task is to initiate those who approach into the mysteries of his God. Thus it is perfectly appropriate for Philo to invoke Moses as hierophant and to beg of him: 'Be our prompter and preside over our steps and never tire of anointing our eyes, until conducting us to the hidden light of hallowed words thou display to us the fast-locked lovelinesses invisible to the uninitiate'.[98]

Elsewhere we are urged to call on Moses for help in order that 'as he learned when he did not know, he may teach us too'.[99]

Moses, then, can assist us in fathoming the holy words, because they were given to him. He is both receiver and transmitter of the Divine teaching. As receiver he not only receives a knowledge of Divine teaching from without; he also receives from within a share of the Divine being, as Philo likes to explain in connection with the verse 'Stand thou here with Me'.[100] Thus for Philo the word of Mikra can be a word that comes to Moses and a word that proceeds from him, at one and the same time. Even the fact that in two passages[101] the Tora conditionally refers to Moses as 'God' – a fact that the rabbis did their best to explain away[102] – is enthusiastically welcomed by Philo.[103]

This being so, what does Philo have to tell us about the Mosaic origin of the Pentateuch? The answer is to be found in the second book of his 'Life of Moses', where he describes Moses' personality under three headings: Moses as law-giver, priest and prophet. In the first part Moses is treated without reservation as the author of the law, with the excellence of the laws serving as proof of their author's outstanding human qualities. For the non-Jewish reader, to whom this treatise is primarily addressed,[104] such a line of reasoning would have seemed logical and quite sufficient; he had met with it in the biographies of other great lawgivers. But for us the critical point is reached only in the section on Moses as prophet, where Philo recurs to this theme. We approach this section with the question: is Philo going to present the Tora as a whole as a revelation which came to Moses and which he now has to interpret as prophet? If so, how is he

---

98   *Som.* 1:164.
99   *Som.* 2:1.
100 Deut 5:31, e.g. *Som.* 2:227. This thought is clearly formulated in *Mos.* 2:190.
101 Exod 4:6; 7:1.
102 See for instance Targum Onkelos on both verses.
103 See the Scripture Index to both verses, *LCL* 10.
104 Cf. Borgen, 'Philo of Alexandria', 235.

going to reconcile this depiction with the first part's view that the lawgiver was able to devise so excellent a constitution for the people because of his own excellent character? Our questions are answered by the first sentence of this section: 'Now I am fully aware that all things written in the sacred books are oracles delivered through Moses; but I will confine myself to those which are more especially his'.[105] That is to say: If I were to take the title 'Moses as Prophet' in the broadest sense, I would really have (again) to discuss the Tora as a whole. But I shall limit myself here to those expressions of Moses' prophecy which belong here in an eminent sense. In order to understand this decision (which we find disappointing), we need a scheme of distinctions among prophetic experiences, which Philo promptly undertakes to supply.

There are, he says, three kinds of prophecy, the first of which he does not wish to discuss here. The first is undoubtedly the one which gives all the verses of the Tora the character of oracles; Philo defines it as an utterance 'spoken by God in His own person with His prophet for interpreter'.[105] Perhaps because Philo is not concerned here with this first category, but wants to get on to the third, he seems to have been somewhat careless in his definition; for if it is supposed to include the entire content of Mikra, we might object that God does not speak in the first person throughout the Bible.[106] More important, however, are the reasons he gives for skipping over this category:

> The first kind must be left out of the discussion. They are too great to be lauded by human lips; scarcely indeed could heaven and the world and the whole existing universe worthily sing their praises. Besides, they are delivered through an interpreter, and interpretation and prophecy are not the same thing.[107]

The praise and exaltation cannot conceal the fact that here Philo finds himself short of concepts adequate to his subject. According to the outline it is supposed to be one of the three kinds of prophecy; yet for the role attributed to Moses in this process, and called interpretation as a stopgap, 'prophecy' is not quite the right word.

But it is hardly possible to reduce the duality of Moses' position as receiver and author of the law to an exact formula. If the statement that all the words of the Tora are oracles really said all that is to be said, there would be no insuperable obstacles to describing how the Tora is received. But the truth is that the relationship between what comes to Moses and what he gives out cannot be disentangled. There is more of Moses' own personality in the Tora than the concept of him as interpreter can cover.

---

[105] *Mos.* 2:188.
[106] Philo here ignores the distinction which he himself makes (*Decal.* 18) between the Ten Commandments, which God proclaimed in person, and the other commandments, for which He used a prophet as interpreter. The two alternatives are here grouped rather carelessly together.
[107] *Mos.* 2:191.

Thus the biblical creation story is not simply a communication from God through Moses about what He did in the six days of Creation; rather it is an 'exalted theology'[108] formulated by Moses about the Creation. In order to understand it[109] we must, for instance, retrace the line of reasoning that led Moses to set a time of six days for the creation of the world, an act which in truth occurs outside the dimension of time.[110] Moses was capable of this outstanding philosophical accomplishment 'both because he had attained the very summit of philosophy, and because he had been instructed by oracles in (. . .) Nature's lore'.[111] These two reasons, which Philo gives in paratactically juxtaposed clauses, can hardly have been intended by him to mean two separate processes; but he had no better linguistic means of conflating the intrahuman and the suprahuman aspects. This double determination of Moses' position makes it impossible for us to regard Philo as representing a clear-cut dichotomy which would place Moses, as the possesser of Divine wisdom, in opposition to the philosophers, who are dependent on human wisdom alone. Moses is for him *both* the receiver of Divinely proclaimed truth *and* a member of the philosophic gild. In a wide-ranging disquisition on the merits and demerits of drunkenness, Philo first gives the opinions of 'the other philosophers'[112] and then that of Moses. To be sure, Moses is of all philosophers the one who reached the peak of philosophy, and Philo will pronounce him right in any dispute with the rest. But this does not take Moses out of the category of philosophers.

He remains, similarly, in the category of lawgivers. Philo's whole *Exposition of the Laws* is dedicated to the proposition that the laws of Moses are the most excellent ever conceived by the human mind. If he speaks of them as laws 'which could not possibly have been conceived by the human mind without divine inspiration',[113] this is not to deny that they were conceived by a human mind, only that this could have occurred without divine inspiration.[114] Divine inspiration stands behind human thought, but does not replace it. The idea of friendship with God, whose content is the gift of participation in Divine being, is the connecting link. This alone makes it possible to understand how Philo can say in one breath, 'Oracles which are both words of God and laws given by men

---

[108] *Op.* 12.

[109] To which the treatise *De Opificio Mundi* is devoted.

[110] *Op.* 13f.

[111] *Op.* 8.

[112] *Ebr.* 1; the same combination of words is to be found in *Gig.* 1; *Som.* 1:141. In *Abr.* 13: 'In the other philosophers and especially in the all-wise Moses' the philosophers and Moses are not contrasted but associated.

[113] *Prob.* 80; note that the expression is modeled on Plato, *Leges* 7, 811c, where the legislating elders say of their own philosophical conversations that they were probably held 'not without inspiration from the gods'.

[114] Similarly the legislative ideas of the elders in Plato (see preceding note) were considered human, despite the divine inspiration.

who are friends of God'.[115] The words of God and the laws of friends of God, i.e. of Moses, are identical. They represent two ways of looking at the same thing. Whether I choose one formula or the other, the authority, the unimpeachable validity of the laws is guaranteed. The same goes for the doctrinal aspect of Mikra: whether I speak of the philosophy of Moses or simply of oracles, both are legitimate ways of confirming the authority of the word of Mikra.

What has led many scholars to portray Philo as the advocate of a fundamental dichotomy between (human) philosophical knowledge and (Divine) communication of absolute truth, is a line of thought most clearly expressed in the allegory of Hagar and Sara.[116] In general this allegory is said to mean the subordination of general education to philosophy, but in one passage[117] it is taken to mean, on a higher level, the subservience of *philosophia* itself to *sophia*. Moreover, sophia and philosophia (which means literally love of sophia or striving for sophia) are furnished with definitions familiar from Stoic teaching. If one then maintains the association of sophia with the figure of *Ḥokhma* (Wisdom) from the Hebrew Bible – a figure which since the book of Ben-Sira,[118] as throughout rabbinic literature, had been identified with the Tora – then it is possible to read into Philo's allegory the doctrine of philosophy as 'handmaid of Scripture',[119] in analogy to the famous formula of philosophy as 'ancilla theologiae' which was later developed by Christian theologians.

Tempting as this combination is, there are objections to it.[120] The concrete, mythologically-coloured figure of 'Tora', such as we find in rabbinic Judaism, is nowhere to be found in Philo and seems to me incompatible with a way of thinking which attributes only superficial importance to the concrete. But if this figure is missing, there is nothing on which to base the identification of Tora with 'Wisdom'.

On the other hand, Leisegang has shown[121] that in Philo the attainment of *sophia* acquires for the first time the ecstatic meaning that reaches its highest expression in the philosophy of Plotinus. But from this ecstatic view which permeates his depiction of Moses as prophet, Philo, as we have seen, *excludes* the reception of the Tora, even though the Tora as a whole could be called an 'oracle', by distinguishing prophecy in the narrower sense from Tora. What the soul receives directly from God, that before which all human instruction must fall silent, is no longer a 'hearing' but a 'seeing', a 'light' which may be called a 'voice', but a voice which does not express itself in 'verbs and nouns' and so

---

[115] *Det.* 13: τοὺς ἱεροφανθέντας λόγους μὲν θεοῦ, νόμους δὲ ἀνθρώπων θεοφιλῶν. Note that the two nouns λόγους and νόμους are covered by the one article τούς and therefore must denote the same quantity.

[116] To which the treatise *De Congressu Eruditionis Gratia* is devoted.

[117] *Cong.* 79.

[118] Sir 24:23.

[119] Thus Wolfson, *Philo*, 1, 87ff.

[120] Cf. my book, *Die hellenistische Gestalt*, 185.

[121] Cf. Leisegang, 'Sophia', 1025.

cannot be received discursively, still less written down as a text.[122] As to how the gulf between an inspiration sublimed beyond the word and the nevertheless available and interpretable text is to be bridged, Philo himself refrains from all speculation. He offers us no theory to explain how words that are really 'all oracles' can at the same time express the opinions and wisdom of the 'all-wise'[123] Moses himself. But it is methodically unsound to establish a harmony between the two positions by interpreting one of them away with inadequate means.

PHILO'S AUTHORITY: THE GREEK TEXT

Philo's appeal to the authority of Mikra contains yet a further complication with which we must deal in closing: the text from which he takes the truth imparted or mediated by Moses is not the Hebrew text of Moses himself, but its Greek translation. From a purely technical point of view this is to be expected of any author who writes in Greek; Josephus too always gives his Bible quotations in the Septuagint translation, though it goes without saying that, as a priest from Jerusalem, he has read the Hebrew original.

Nonetheless, Philo's situation is fundamentally different. Even if we assume that he knew enough Hebrew to consult the original – a question which is highly controversial[124] – he can have done so only very seldom. And this, given the kind of questions he asks of the text, is a far more serious matter for him than for Josephus. Josephus is concerned only with the content of the biblical stories, whereas Philo's allegorical commentary is, as we have seen, entirely founded on a sensitive investigation of the verbal formulations, of whose precise and deliberately-chosen rightness the interpreter is convinced, and whose fine nuances often have far-reaching exegetical consequences.

One example will suffice to illustrate how important the differences between linguistic versions can be for such interpretations. In the treatise 'Who is the Heir of Divine Things' there is[125] an exposition of the concept of 'ecstasy', an extremely important key concept for Philo. The interpretation starts from a verse which in the Septuagint reads: 'About sunset an "ecstasy" fell upon Abraham and lo a great dark terror falls upon him'.[126] This word 'ecstasy', Philo tells us, has various meanings in Moses' work:

> Sometimes it is a mad fury producing mental delusion due to old age or melancholy or other similar cause. Sometimes it is extreme amazement at the events which so often happen suddenly and unexpectedly. Sometimes

---

[122] See n. 86.
[123] πάνσοφος, e.g. *Abr.* 13.
[124] Wolfson's confident assertion (*Philo*, 1, 88); 'His knowledge of Hebrew was such that he could himself without too much effort provide his own translation' is shared by few. The latest discussion on the question: Sandmel, Philo's Knowledge of Hebrew'.
[125] *Heres* 249ff.
[126] Gen 15:12.

it is passivity of mind, if indeed the mind can ever be at rest; and the best form of all is the divine possession of frenzy to which the prophets as a class are subject.

Philo gives examples for each of these six meanings, taken from widely-differing Pentateuch verses in which 'Moses' uses the word 'ecstasis'. The last-named meaning is the one supposedly represented in the verse from Genesis on which he is commenting. How important this compilation is for Philo becomes evident when we realize that he is here using the famous Platonic depiction of the different kinds of 'mania'[127] as a model. But when we consult the Hebrew text we see that in the passages[128] quoted by Philo the word 'ecstasy' represents not one but five different words. Thus all this lofty train of thought is quite devoid of any 'Mosaic' textual basis.

Such examples could be multiplied ad lubitum. They show that Philo uncritically accepted the Septuagint text he had before him[129] as identical with the Hebrew Bible. Otherwise he could not have extracted from it the deeper layers of Mosaic wisdom supposedly hidden in every fine nuance of word-choice.

This would make Philo the only interpreter in the two-thousand-year history of Jewish Bible exegesis whose hermeneutics were not – or at the very least not consistently – based on the Hebrew text. This makes him an exceptional and problematic figure for anyone who is at home in rabbinic literature, in the medieval commentaries, in the textual interpretations of the philosophers and kabbalists, or even in modern Jewish Bible scholarship. For the Jewish traditional consciousnesses 'Tora study' starts, by definition, from the masoretic text. No wonder, then, that Jewish scholars have tried again and again at least to soften Philo's position as an outsider, by showing that certain of Philo's interpretations make use of the Hebrew original and then going on to assume that it was always possible for Philo to refer to the Hebrew original, but that he had in general kept to the Septuagint out of consideration for his readers who did not know Hebrew. In the light of the above example we must approach such theses with skepticism.

In order to understand the trust Philo places in the Septuagint version, we must briefly consider:
1. the status of the Septuagint in Hellenistic Judaism generally;
2. Philo's own evaluation of the Septuaginta.

(1) The status of the Septuagint among Hellenistic Jews may best be illumined by a comparison with the status of the Aramaic targum in the motherland. The name 'Septuagint' by which the Greek translation is conventionally designated goes back to a story which has come down to us in several versions,[130] according

---

[127] Plato, *Phaedrus* 244a ff.
[128] Gen 15:12; Deut 28:28f.; Gen 27:33; Gen 45:26; Exod 19:18; Lev 9:24.
[129] See above n. 31.
[130] The Jewish versions are: the *Letter of Aristeas*, Philo, *Mos.* 2:25-44; Jos. *Ant.* 12:11-118.

to which this version is the work of 70, or more precisely 72, translators who traveled from Jerusalem to Egypt in order to translate the Pentateuch into Greek.[131] Whether or not the main features of this story correspond to some historical event, all of its literary versions contain a liberal share of miraculous elements. We shall not attempt to settle the question whether the whole story should be dismissed as mere invention because of these elements. But one thing which has so far not been sufficiently considered in the discussion of this question, is that a story which seems to be essentially mythical gives an indication of certain dynamics behind the making of the myth. The Rabbis have no such myth to relate concerning Onkelos or the author of any other targum. The mere existence of this Hellenistic saga, adorned as it is with elaborate and picturesque detail, is evidence of the extraordinary importance with Greek-speaking Jews attached to their work of translation. Indeed, Philo[132] tells us of a yearly festival with which the Jews of Alexandria commemorated the day on which, according to tradition, the translation was presented to King Ptolemy II.[133] For them, then, the publication of the Septuagint was a major historical event. Again we may compare this with the sparse information which we have on the making of the Aramaic targums.

Thus the Hellenistic Jews saw the Greek Bible not as an unfortunately indispensable aid to the understanding of the Hebrew Tora, but a treasure and source of pride in its own right. And this is not surprising, given the fact that Hellenistic society as a whole accorded to books (which meant, practically speaking, books in Greek) a prestige unprecedented in any earlier society. With their own book in hand, the Jews could move up to a respected position in this milieu; they now had a share in Greek literature which in the Hellenistic world meant world literature. This, at least, is how the Jews saw it, and the saga of a Bible translation commission led by a Hellenistic king is simply a palpable expression of this self-evaluation.

(2) Let us now turn to Philo's own account, in *Life of Moses*, 2: 26-44,[134] of how the Bible was translated into Greek. The account begins with the following curious remark:

[131] For further details see Tov, above, pp. 164-65.

[132] *Mos.* 2:41-44.

[133] In all probability this yearly celebration took place on the 8th of Tevet. In an undatable supplement to *Megillat Taanit* this date is included in a list of days on which one should fast, for on this day 'the Tora was translated into Greek in the days of King Ptolemy, and darkness came over the world for the space of three days.' This late tradition is in the spirit of the Rabbis, who regarded the Greek translation as a disaster; but it is likely that the calender date we have here comes from an ancient tradition and designates the day which for Philo and his Alexandrian contemporaries was a day of rejoicing. Cf. *Megillat Taanit*, p. 201.

[134] This section has been closely analysed by Otte, *Das Sprachverständnis*, 32-43, in which, however, by a tricky way of translating, he burdens Philo with dimensions of existential philosophy of language, which the unprejudiced reader will hardly find in him.

> In ancient times the laws were written in the Chaldaean tongue, and remained in that form for many years, without any change of language, so long as they had not yet revealed their beauty to the rest of mankind.

Our own logic would lead us to expect something like 'remained restricted to that language'. But the word-for-word meaning of Philo's sentence is that the language of the book *was* originally Hebrew (or as Philo likes to say, 'Chaldaean'), but *is* Hebrew no longer. Of course he knows that the original text continues to exist – later he refers to it – but now that the law of Moses can reveal its beauty to all humankind in the garment of the Greek language, the Hebrew is of no importance. He could hardly have expressed this estimate more bluntly than in the grotesque sentence we have just read. Only in the Greek version can the law become available to all of humanity and thus assume the position to which its excellence entitles it. Hence the 'importance and public utility of the task'[135] of translation. A great king undertakes the work,[136] and the high priest with whom he consults also favours the plan, reflecting that 'the King would not have taken on such a task without God's guiding care'.[137]

Finally Philo comes to the work of the translators themselves, who are conscious of their mission to 'translate laws which were soothsaid in oracles'.[138] They concentrate utterly on 'bringing the soul alone into contact with the laws alone'.[139] Their activity is designated by verbs derived from 'prophet', 'hierophant', and 'enthusiasmos', the same words which Philo uses elsewhere in connection with Moses himself. In their choice of words, he tells us, they did not let themselves be led astray by the Greek language's wealth of synonyms; rather they found each time the one word that was equivalent to the Hebrew word, exercising a linguistic stringency which Philo equates with the umambiguous terminology of geometry or dialectics. That, in his view, is the explanation for the famous linguistic miracle: the versions of all 72 translators corresponded word for word, although they had worked independently of one another!

> The clearest proof of this is that, if Chaldeans have learned Greek, or Greeks Chaldean, and read both versions, the Chaldean and the translation, they regard them with awe and reverence as sisters, or rather one and the same, both in matter and words, and speak of the authors not as translators but as prophets and priests of the mysteries, whose sincerity and singleness of thought has enabled them to go hand in hand with the purest of spirits, the spirit of Moses.[140]

---

[135] *Mos.* 2:28.
[136] *Mos.* 2:28-30.
[137] *Mos.* 2:32.
[138] *Mos.* 2:34.
[139] *Mos.* 2:36.
[140] *Mos.* 2:40.

It is scarcely conceivable that Philo would have maintained this extravagant opinion if he had had sufficient linguistic knowledge to compare the two texts in detail. What guarantees for him the congruence of the Septuagint with the Hebrew original, is the miracle of the different translators' word-for-word agreement.[141] We must understand that this was no rhetorical exaggeration, but represents Philo's serious belief in the quality of this translation, however little our own critical judgment agrees with him; for this is the inner justification for Philo's use of the Septuagint. Of course, the Holy Scriptures were originally given in Hebrew; but now they are (also) available in Greek, and in the making of the Greek version the same prophetic forces were at work as in the Hebrew text. In the Greek version, too, every word was chosen with Divinely inspired accuracy, so that the exegete, probing the depths of meaning in every Greek word, has the same chance as the Hebrew exegete of arriving at the original truth which dictated the word.

With this the question whether Philo could read the Hebrew original becomes theologically irrelevant. Even supposing him capable – as some have[142] – of offering his own translations rather than relying on the Septuagint 'out of consideration for his Greek-speaking readers', he would have had to refrain from so doing, unless he wanted to lay claim to the same supernatural gifts which, in his view, made the Septuagint possible.

Finally we may draw attention to the last words of the above quotation, which epitomize Philo's particular view of Scriptural authority. In certifying that the translators have adequately rendered the content of Mikra, he does not say that they have captured 'the word of God' but that they captured 'the spirit of Moses'. If all the words of the Bible may be called 'oracles', then certainly they must be the word of God; but to attribute them to 'the spirit of Moses' is also to do justice to them.

Exegesis of Mikra

PHILO'S BATTLE ON TWO FRONTS

We have already stated that Philo's exegesis is fundamentally double-tracked. Everything in the Bible is capable of, and indeed requires, both a literal[143] and

---

[141] Scholars have pointed out that the story of the linguistic miracle is also found in the writings of the Rabbis, but it has not been noted that here the tables are turned. Thus in *Massekhet Soferim* 1:9 it is said of the sages who 'translated the Tora for king Ptolemy' that 'God put a counsel into the heart of each of them; they agreed together in one opinion and wrote the Tora for him, each one apart, and changed 13 passages in it', which the Rabbis then enumerate, pointing out where they deviate from the original (which for the Rabbis of course means the masoretic) text. Thus the Rabbis are aware of the linguistic miracle reported in the Greek sources, but they use it to point out not the congruence but the incongruence of the Greek with the Hebrew text.

[142] See n. 124.

[143] ῥητόν.

an allegorical[144] interpretation. In general[145] these two modes of interpretation are kept strictly separate; in innumerable instances, Philo tells us exactly when he leaves the ground of literal interpretation and ventures into allegory. Both ways of looking at Mikra are justified and necessary, and even where Philo is dissatisfied with the literal sense of a passage, he feels obliged to begin by conveying it.

In the literal sense the book of Moses, as we have seen,[146] is a book of laws, with narrative appendages. In the allegorical meaning it reveals itself as the teaching of God's transcendant being and of the soul's distance from and nearness to God. From the foregoing analysis it will be clear that both ways of interpretation are legitimate in his eyes, but that the two are not in balance. Philo repeatedly makes it clear that Moses' deepest concern was his religious-philosophical doctrine, which may be arrived at by allegorical interpretation.

Thus Philo as interpreter of the Bible is fighting, as it were, on two fronts: against the extreme allegorists who abolish the literal meaning of Mikra, and against the literalists, who do not want to go beyond the literal sense. Both these extremes he rejects, but given the predominance of allegorical interpretation in his thinking, we may expect him to take a more resolute position on the second front than on the first. Let us look at his confrontations with both extremes:

(1) Philo confronts the extreme allegorists explicitly in one passage. Characteristically, what is in question here is the literal meaning, not of the biblical narratives, but of the biblical laws. Let us see how the battle is conducted.

In the discussion of the promises God makes to Abraham when He commands him to leave his birthplace,[147] Philo comes to the words: 'I will make thy name great'.[148] On this he comments that while the name a person has, i.e. the good reputation he enjoys in society, is less important than his real moral standard, still it is 'a great matter and of much advantage to the life which we live in the body'. The way to preserve one's good name is to keep strictly to the way of life inherited from the fathers. However, 'there are some who, regarding laws in their literal sense in the light of symbols of matters belonging to the intellect, are overpunctilious about the latter, while treating the former with easygoing neglect (. . .) They ought to have given careful attention to both aims'. Philo chides them for behaving 'as though they were living alone by themselves in a wilderness, or as though they had become disembodied souls' and human society, in which they after all live, did not exist. 'These men are

---

[144] Especially ἀλληγορία and ὑπόνοια, see *Index Philoneus*, s.v.; of the rich literature on Philo's allegory we cite Stein, *Die allegorische Exegese*; Christiansen, *Die Technik*; Sowers, *Hermeneutics*; Heinisch, *Der Einfluss*, as well as the articles in the pertinent encyclopaedias.

[145] Only for the treatise *De Opificio Mundi* is this clear distinction not valid; this treatise was apparently written as the first piece both of the Exposition of the Laws and of the Allegorical Commentary. But the relation of literal and allegorical interpretation in this work would require a study to itself.

[146] See n. 15.

[147] *Mig.* 88-92.

[148] Gen 12:2.

taught by the sacred word to have thought of good repute, and to let go nothing that is part of the customs fixed by divinely empowered men greater than those of our time'. As examples of what he means, he mentions the Sabbath, the holidays, circumcision and the Temple service. Of the Sabbath he says: 'It is quite true that the Seventh Day is meant to teach the power of the Unoriginate and the non-action of created beings. But let us not for this reason abrogate the laws laid down for its observance, and light fires or till the ground or carry loads or institute proceedings in court', etc. 'We should look on all these outward observances as resembling the body, and their inner meanings as resembling the soul. (. . .) If we keep and observe these, we shall gain a clearer conception of those things of which these are the symbols; and besides that we shall not incur the censure of the many and the charges they are sure to bring against us'.

Thus Philo does *not* say: these are the commandments, in black and white, this is what God has ordered you to do; you have broken the Law, therefore you are a sinner. Rather he says: Of course what is really commanded is in the realm of religious knowledge, and this you are following very well; all the same, you ought not simply to shrug off what has literally been said. Why not? We have heard two answers. First, by corporeally fulfilling the symbolic commandment you also come to a clearer understanding of it. This is an answer which, pursued to extraordinary depths, reverberates again and again through the history of Jewish thinking on the problem. But in Philo it is only a momentary idea, which receives no further development in his writings and indeed is not in consonance with his views on the relation between body and soul. Much more solidly anchored in his argumentation is the second answer: If you disregard the outward forms, you will acquire a bad reputation in the community to which you belong and want to belong. One must say that, coming from a thinker so imbued with the Stoic pride in the asocial self-reliance of virtues and the Socratic pathos of the opposition between being and seeming, such arguments make a very feeble impression. He 'censures' the radical allegorists, but his rebuke does not have much substance.

(2) On the other hand, his dispute with the literalists is scattered all over his oeuvre and surfaces on many occasions. A typical epithet for them is 'Micropol-itans',[149] or 'men of narrow citizenship', to whom he contrasts 'those who are on the roll of a greater country, even this whole world'. Their narrowmindedness is opposed by the Stoic doctrine of the cosmos as the only true home of the sage. Here Philo contents himself with claiming that the literal sense is insufficient; elsewhere he goes so far as to say that the idea that God literally planted a garden in Eden is irreligious,[150] 'as though God tills the ground and plants pleasances'.[151] Relations with the literal meaning become especially tense

---

[149] μικροπολῖται *Som.* 1:39.
[150] Gen 2:8.
[151] *L.A.* 1:43. Other passages of this kind, whose literal interpretations Philo rejects, are listed by Shoyer, 'Alexandrian Jewish Literalists' 272.

whenever God is spoken of in anthropomorphic terms. Moses, according to Philo, has two ways of talking about God, as he informs us in two contradictory verses,[152] 'two leading statements about the Cause (= God), one that "God is not as a man"; the other that "He is as a man" '. Of these two statements only the first, naturally, is correct; the second is 'introduced for the instruction of the many', who can only be induced to follow the law through fear of an anthropomorphic God. One naturally acquires such a conception of God if one gives the literal meaning to many biblical statements on God, of which Philo cites examples. The literal meaning of these verses is thus not true, still there is a point to it: 'All such may learn the untruth, which will benefit them, if they cannot be brought to wisdom by truth'.[153] Here, then, the literal meaning is insufficient, even wrong; and yet it is not a simple misunderstanding of the text.[154] Those who do not go beyond it remain caught in a baseless mythological fiction, and that is irreligious.

The representatives of literal meaning do not always come off quite so badly. Thus if someone reads the story of the Tower of Babel as an account of the origin of different languages, 'I would not censure such persons, for perhaps[155] the truth is with them also. Still I would exhort them not to halt there, but to press on to allegorical interpretations'.[156] To the story of Jacob's placing a stone under his head[157] he responds – an exceptional thing for him – with a full appreciation of the literal content, before getting on with the allegorical interpretation: 'Our admiration is extorted', he writes, not only by the deeper meaning but also 'by the way in which the literal narrative inculcates (. . .) endurance'.[158]

But the literal meaning as such cannot always be retained. The verse 'The strong current of the river makes glad the city of God'[159] cannot refer to the concrete city, for Jerusalem lies neither on the sea nor on a river.[160] 'Cain went out from the face of God'[161] cannot be understood literally, since, first, God has no face, and, second, no one can escape his field of vision.[162]

From here it is not far to cases where Philo destroys the possibility of literal comprehension in order to prove the rightness of allegory. Thus various motifs of the story of Paradise – the planting of the garden,[163] the creation of Eve from

---

[152] *Deus* 52.
[153] *Deus* 64.
[154] The pragmatic justification of untrue statements is modeled on Plato, *Republic* 389b.
[155] Wolfson, *Philo* 1, 125 translates here not *perhaps* but *probably*, which is linguistically quite possible.
[156] *Conf.* 190.
[157] Gen 28:11.
[158] *Som.* 1:120ff.
[159] Thus Psalm 46:5 in the Septuagint translation.
[160] *Som.* 2:246.
[161] Gen 4:16.
[162] *Post.* 1ff.
[163] *L.A.* 1:43; *Plant.* 32.

a rib,[164] the speech of the serpent[165] – are shunted off into the realm of fable, to leave room for their allegorical interpretation. Yet such rebellions against the simple meaning are after all not to be taken seriously, as we can see by comparing such passages with the 'Questions and Answers on Genesis'[166] in which these motifs are allowed their literal validity. At times Philo brings a Sophistic-sounding rhetoric into play even against legal prescriptions; but in the Exposition of the Laws these prescriptions are upheld, and sometimes even praised for their rational character.[167]

We may conclude, then, that on the whole, despite certain escapades, Philo recognizes a dual meaning in Scripture, neither sacrificing the literal meaning to the allegorists, nor allowing the literalists to contest his right to allegorize.

THE RELATION BETWEEN THE TWO LAYERS OF MEANING

This brings us to the question how the two layers of meaning in Mikra relate to each other according to Philo.

First let us see how Philo expressed himself on the subject. When he writes of the Therapeutic sect, 'To these people the whole law book seems to resemble a living creature with the literal ordinances for its body and for its soul the invisible mind laid up in this wording', he is basically describing his own position.[168] As we saw, he himself used the same image, when he admonished the radical allegorists to see the relation between the holiday and its concrete prescriptions as a relation between body and soul.[169] As a Platonist he of course attached a vastly greater importance to the soul than to the body.

In the account of the Therapeuts this image is followed by another: 'Looking through the words as through a mirror the rational soul beholds the marvellous beauties of the concepts'.[168] The mirror is only an instrument for the perception of the object. This image suggests that the literal meaning is of no importance in itself, it is only intermediate to the perception of the one thing which is to be seen.

Elsewhere[170] the relationship between the two is likened to that between an object and the shadow it casts. A shadow is not even an instrument which helps me to examine the object; it is merely an indication of the object's being there.

---

[164] L.A. 2:19.
[165] Agr. 97.
[166] Q.G. 1:14; 20-22; 32.
[167] In Fug. 108 he denounces the law of negligent homicide for inner lack of logic, yet in Spec. 3:131ff. this same prescription is demonstrated to be reasonable. The freeing of certain categories of soldiers before the battle (Deut 20:5-8) is extensively citicized in Agr. 148-156 as senseless and immoral; in Virt. 28-31 it is explicitly praised as reasonable.
[168] Cont. 78. On the question of the reliability of Philo's report on this sect in Cont. see the critical article of I. Heinemann, 'Therapeutai'. The very objections angast the reliability of his description reinforce the value of Philo's explanations as evidence of his own attitudes.
[169] See above n. 148, Migr. 93.
[170] Conf. 190.

There is food for reflection in the fact that this image is used precisely in the passage where a literalist interpretation (of the Tower of Babel story as an explanation of linguistic difference) is recognized as correct as far as it goes.

In still another passage[171] a biblical report of a dream is first presented as a 'foundation'; then comes the 'wise builder', namely Allegory, to erect the building on it. Here the literal meaning is treated as the precondition.[172]

We see that these different images do not quite add up to the same notion of the relation between the two modes of exegesis. But all of them do suggest that Philo thought he could capture some kind of communication between the two methods he practiced. If we are right in this surmise, the next question would be to what extent his own work fulfills this notion.

It seems to us that it does so only vere partially. True, it has been demonstrated that the Abraham of his Exposition of the Laws is the same Abraham whom we meet in his allegorical writings.[173] But this conclusion cannot be generalized. The Joseph of the allegorical writings is a problematic character, who is always in the wrong in the confrontation with his brothers; the Joseph of the biography of the Patriarchs is an ideal ruler.[174] The story of Cain, which provided material for four allegorical treatises,[175] is completely omitted from the Exposition of the Laws. Likewise in the latter Noah is dealt with, but only in connection with the Deluge,[176] which is not mentioned in the four allegorical treatises on Noah. On the other hand, Enoch figures in the biography of the Patriarchs,[177] but is completely forgotten in 'The Posterity and Exile of Cain'. Thus it would hardly seem that the two ways in which Philo worked were coordinated with each other. We saw that when Philo cites a law in one of his allegorical works,[178] he does not base his speculations on its literal meaning; on the contrary, he has to dispose of the literal meaning before he feels he can use the text allegorically. The same goes for the narrative parts of Mikra: 'Probably there was an actual man called Samuel; but we conceive of Samuel (. . .) not as a living compound of soul and body, but as a mind (. . .)'[179] Once we have scaled the heights of allegory – or in Platonic terms, of the idea – we are no longer dealing with a man named Samuel, but only with the species of soul-being which is meant by this figure. We need not deny the historical Samuel, but he is now irrelevant.

---

[171] *Som.* 2:8.
[172] This thesis follows in its essentials the contribution of Pépin, 'Remarques', 139.
[173] This thesis is worked out in Sandmel, *Philo's Place*.
[174] This is shown in detail in Goodenough, *Politics*. The disputed political explanation which the author gives to the phenomenon need not concern us here.
[175] All contained in *LCL* 2.
[176] *Abr.* 27-47.
[177] *Abr.* 17-26.
[178] See above n. 167.
[179] *Ebr.*, 144; similarly on Terah *Som.* 1:58, on Isaac *Fug.* 167.

If I am seeing rightly, the same goes, as far as Philo is concerned, for Israel. Of course Israel is first of all the chosen people to whom he belongs. But Israel means 'beholding God'. Once we have reached the summit of religion and philosophy, Israel as a concrete reality becomes, in a manner with which existentialist thinking cannot sympathize, irrelevant in the face of the eternal reality symbolized by Israel, namely the contemplation of God.

THE CHARACTER OF PHILONIC ALLEGORY

Philo's trust in the allegorical method rests on a certain assumption concerning the possible content of the 'all-wise' Moses' divinely inspired wisdom. For a thinker of Platonic orientation such wisdom would have to transcend the world of the senses, ascend to the world of ideas, and, passing beyond even that, bring the mind in contact with the absolute God Who is exalted even above the world of ideas.[180] The literal sense of Mikra, with its earthbound stories and commandments, could not do this; therefore the teaching of the all-wise Moses must be something more than this. The text must be 'saying something else' (the meaning of the Greek words *alla agoreuein*), beyond the meaning comprehensible to everyone.

It was this assumption, no doubt, that set Philo on the way to *all-egory*, just as, some hundred years before, it had been developed by the Greeks for the reinterpretation of their mythological traditions.[181] A few Jews had begun in recent years to apply the method to Mikra.[182] The influence of the Greek exegetical tradition is particularly obvious where Philo simply takes motifs familiar from the interpretation of Homer and applies them to biblical motifs.[183] Nor is there anything contradictory in his also taking over many midrashic motifs from the motherland.[184] It has been shown that he occasionally also employs the rabbinic rules of interpretation; however, one should not forget that these rules themselves owe a great deal to Greek rhetoric.[185]

The Stoic allegorists of Philo's time had a strong tendency to explain away whatever they found morally or religiously offensive in the old songs.[186] This tendency rubs off on Philo's way of thinking only occasionally, as when he writes, 'We shall avoid that which is unanswerable . . ., and for which we should not like to be held accountable, if we attempt to get at the secret physical

[180] Philo thus outdoes the Platonic ascent of Eros into the world of ideas by 'another yearning' which draws the soul above and beyond the world of ideas 'to the Great King Himself', see for instance *Op.* 71.

[181] On the history of the Greek mythological allegory see, besides the books named in n. 35, Tate, 'History of Allegorism'.

[182] On Philo's predecessors in the field of Jewish allegory see Haye, 'Philo's Reference'.

[183] On this see my book, *Die hellenistische Gestalt*, 119-28.

[184] Cf. Stein, *Philo und der Midrash*.

[185] Cf. Daube, 'Rabbinic Methods'.

[186] The leading Homeric allegorist Heraclitus, *Quaestiones Homericae*, 1, formulates this apologetic line: 'He would be entirely irreligious if he had said nothing in an allegorical way'.

meaning'.[187] What Philo here and in many places calls 'physical' was a direction in Homeric allegory which had originally attempted to read knowledge of modern physical science into the poets' words, but which in recent times had shifted to the final, supramundane ground of being. Hence Philo too calls the search for divine mysteries in the biblical word 'physical'. Whenever Philo takes issue with earlier Jewish allegories, it is invariably in order to fathom more deeply the 'physical' in this sense.

For instance, he tells us[188] that according to some the tree of life in Paradise means the human heart, 'since it is the cause of life and has been allotted the central place in the body'. That is why the tree stands 'in the middle of the garden'.[189] 'But these people should remember that they are setting forth a medical interpretation, not a physical one'. Instead he considers the central essence represented by the tree to be virtue. Again we clearly see the logic of his thought: an interpretation leading only to a piece of 'medical' information cannot represent the real meaning of the all-wise Moses' utterance, or of an oracle entrusted to him.

When at Abraham's death he is said to have been gathered to his 'fathers',[190] others take the 'fathers' to mean the four elements into which the dead body decomposes; but Philo tells us that the fathers are 'the incorporeal Logoi of the Divine world, whom elsewhere it is accustomed to call "angels" '.[191] Here the exegesis of the biblical word has led Philo into the seldom-trodden territory of belief in immortality, since a purely physical process would not suffice to constitute what Philo calls a 'physical' teaching.

Philo is convinced that in such cases he is offering not only a deeper interpretation, but thereby necessarily a more correct one. Only when he has arrived at the real grounds of being can he be satisfied that he has indeed completed his methodological task, brought to light what Moses, the perfect philosopher, really meant. In this sense he feels indebted to science with its strict method, and speaks of the 'rules of the art'[192] of allegory.

Still and all, his allegorical method never became a system of rules to be routinely applied. Occasionally he presents an interpretation in a tone which tells us that it came to him as a religious experience. In speaking of the two Cherubim which stand in the Holy of Holies of the Tabernacle,[193] he first interprets them cosmologically as the two hemispheres of the sky. But then he continues:

[187] *Fug.* 106.
[188] *L.A.* 1:59.
[189] Gen 3:3.
[190] Gen 15:15.
[191] *Heres* 281ff.; Q.G. 3:11.
[192] οἱ τῆς ἀλληγορίας κανόνες, *Som.* 1:73.
[193] Exod 18:19f.

But there is a higher thought than these. It comes from a voice in my own soul, which oftentimes is god-possessed and divines where it does not kwow. This thought I will record in words if I can.[194]

After this unusual prologue he then presents an interpretation which indeed leads us into the core of his religious thought. The Godhead is flanked by its two highest potencies, which are called *sovereignty and goodness*. These two are what the two Cherubim in the Holy of Holies represent.

This is not the place to discuss Philo's doctrine of the two highest potencies, or its obvious connection with the rabbinic doctrine of God's two aspects;[195] we are concerned only with the profoundly moving way in which this doctrine comes to him through exegesis, or goes into it. This is not the only passage, though it is the most impressive, in which he speaks of such an exegetical inspriation. But we must not lose sight of the fact that even in such exalted moments Philo feels his allegorical interpretation to be bound by a strict discipline which leaves no room for what is merely arbitrary and subjective.

Bibliography

A general bibliography on Philo is appended to BORGEN, 'Philo of Alexandria' in *Compendia* II/2 (pp. 280-82).

As to the status of *Mikra* in Philo's work, WOLFSON, *Philo*, in his chapter 'Handmaid of Scripture' (1, 87-163) pleaded for an absolute opposition between the Bible as God's word and philosophy as a purely human endeavour. For restrictions against his view see AMIR, *Die hellenistische Gestalt*, 77-106. For a detailed study of the interrelation between the divine and the human aspect in the authorship of Mikra, the present writer could not rely on any previous research.

As to Philo's reliance on the *Greek* text of Mikra, see the diligent analysis of OTTE, *Das Sprachverständnis*. KATZ's book *(Philo's Bible)* has a misleading title; it has no relevance to our subject.

The most comprehensive survey of Philo's *exegetics* was presented already by SIEGFRIED, *Philo von Alexandria als Ausleger*, complemented by his *Studien*. For Philo's versatility in the various parts of Mikra HEINEMANN, *Philons griechische und jüdische Bildung*, made valuable observations. His relation to rabbinic midrash has been studied by STEIN, *Philo und der Midrasch*.

As to *allegorical* interpretation, for the Greek background the reader may be referred to BUFFIÈRE, *Les mythes d'Homère* and PÉPIN, *Mythe et allégorie*. For Philo's connection with this background, see AMIR, *Die hellenistische Gestalt*, 119-28. His place in this Greek tradition is aptly formulated by LEISEGANG, *Der heilige Geist*, 160. His handling of this kind of exegesis is presented by STEIN, *Die*

---

[194]   *Cher.* 27.
[195]   Hebrew: מדת הדין ומדת הרחמים.

allegorische Exegese. CHRISTIANSEN, *Die Technik* delved into the philosophical presuppositions of this endeavour, found by her in Middle Platonism. For the room left by Philo for literal exegesis, see SHOYER, 'Alexandrian Jewish Literalists'.

Chapter Thirteen

Use, Authority and Exegesis of Mikra in the Writings of Josephus

Louis H. Feldman

Josephus' Biblical Text

Second only perhaps to his significance as a historian[1] is Josephus' importance for our knowledge of the text and interpretation of the Bible in the first century. The question as to which biblical text or texts he had before him is complex, however, since there seems good reason to believe that he had access to three texts, one in Hebrew, one in Greek, and one in Aramaic; and his use of one or more of these texts appears to have varied from book to book in his paraphrase of the Bible in the first half of the *Antiquities*. The fact, moreover, that in Rome, where Josephus composed his *Antiquities*, Jews had settled in large numbers from all over the Roman Empire meant that Josephus, if he had any contact at all with these Jews, was brought in touch with various texts, at least in Greek, and diverse periphrases of these texts.

Strangely, despite Josephus' importance for the biblical text, no systematic study of Josephus' biblical *Vorlage* has been made, with the exception of Mez's study for Joshua, Judges, and Samuel. Assertions range from the statement of Tachauer that Josephus employed only a Hebrew text to that of Schalit[2] that Josephus used only the Greek Bible. The overwhelming majority of scholars,[3] however, have taken an intermediate position, suggesting that Josephus used both, in addition to, perhaps, an Aramaic targum. What complicates the matter is that apparently at the time of Josephus there were a number of divergent Greek and Hebrew texts of the Bible; and the presence of proto-Lucianic readings in the Dead Sea fragments of Samuel, in Josephus, and in his presumed contemporary Pseudo-Philo, would seem to confirm this situation.

The only published attempt to study this question for even a portion of the Pentateuch is Shutt's examination[4] of the biblical names in Josephus' version of Genesis. He notes that in four cases Josephus' names follow the Hebrew text

---

[1] See Attridge, 'Josephus and His Works' 185-232.

[2] Mez, *Die Bibel*; Tachauer, *Verhältniss*; Schalit, *Namenwörterbuch*, 108. S. Cohen, *Josephus in Galilee and Rome*, 36, n. 45, concludes that of the twenty proofs cited by Schalit, 'Introduction', xxvii-xxxv, for Josephus' use of the Septuagint, only four are more than conjecture.

[3] E.g., H. Bloch, *Quellen*; Schürer, *Geschichte* 1, 80; Rahlfs, *Septuagintastudien*, 3, 80; Thackeray, *Josephus*, 81.

[4] Shutt, 'Biblical Names', 167-82.

rather than the Septuagint, in twenty-five cases he follows the Septuagint rather than the Hebrew, in six cases his discussions or interpretations of names follow the Hebrew rather than the Septuagint, in fourteen cases his discussions follow the Septuagint rather than the Hebrew, in twenty cases Josephus is independent of both, and in sixteen other cases he is apparently independent. This would hardly support the conclusion of Schalit[5] that Josephus used only the Greek Bible. Moreover, Shutt inexplicably does not consider systematically the various manuscripts of the Septuagint or the possibility that the gap between the Septuagint and the Hebrew text may not, to judge from the Dead Sea fragments, have been so great in Josephus' day as in our own. Furthermore, we may suggest that a Greek form in proper names may reflect the fact that Josephus is writing in Greek or that he or his alleged literary assistants Hellenized the form of Hebrew proper names. Just as the Latin Josephus, despite the fact that it is approximately half a millennium older than our earliest extant Greek manuscript, is virtually valueless for names, as Rahlfs[6] has correctly noted, since it often adopts forms in current usage, so the choice of proper names as a litmus paper test of the text employed by Josephus is particularly unfortunate; such names, as we may see in the text of Philo as well, have often been modified by later copyists in order to conform with their own text of the Septuagint.

KNOWLEDGE OF A HEBREW TEXT

One would assume that since Josephus was born and brought up in Jerusalem (*Life* 7-8) and since at an early age he made such great progress in his education (*Life* 8) that he far excelled his compatriots in Jewish learning (which was presumably centered on knowledge of the Tora in Hebrew; cf. *Ant.* 20:263), he knew well the Hebrew text, which he regarded as having been fixed unalterably (*Ag.Ap.* 1:42) long before. The fact, however, that the *Letter of Aristeas* (30) seems to refer to corrupt Hebrew manuscripts of the Pentateuch and that the Dead Sea fragments from the Pentateuch do not seldom disagree with the so-called Masoretic Text may indicate that the Hebrew text available to Josephus was different from ours. Be that as it may, according to Josephus (*Ag.Ap.* 2:178), any Jew – and this obviously included Josephus himself –, if asked about the laws, would repeat them all more readily than his own name. Every week, he says (*Ag.Ap.* 2:175), Jews – and this again must have included Josephus – assemble to listen to a portion of the Law. Moreover, Josephus received from Titus (*Life* 418) a gift of sacred books, presumably a Tora scroll; and he may have had this with him in Rome when he wrote the *Antiquities*. Hence Josephus would have had an advantage over Paul, who often cites the Bible but with no manuscript at hand (cf. 2 Tim 4:13). It is hard, however, to prove at any given point what text Josephus is relying upon, inasmuch as he is

---

[5] Cf. Schalit, *Namenwörterbuch*.
[6] Rahlfs, *Septuagintastudien* 3, 91, n. 1.

usually paraphrasing rather than translating and since he is elaborating as well.[7] We must not discount the possiblity that Josephus is perhaps following a Jewish tradition independent of both the Masoretic Text and the Septuagint, as we may infer from his agreement with Pseudo-Philo even in some places where their views are found neither in the Masoretic Text nor in the Septuagint.

USE OF A GREEK TEXT

As to the likelihood that Josephus would use a Greek text of the Bible, there would naturally be an attraction in doing so because he is writing in Greek; but one would expect, *a priori*, that Josephus would shy away from employing the Septuagint because, despite Pseudo-Longinus' compliment in his *On the Sublime* (9:9), it is stylistically inferior to the classical authors whom Josephus quite obviously preferred and because it would be readily understood only by those who already were acquainted with the Bible in its original language. Indeed, Kennedy[8] has remarked that Josephus is more persistent that any other writer of Hellenistic Greek in his use of classical Greek words, particularly from Herodotus, the tragedians, Plato, Xenophon, Aristotle, and, above all, Thucydides, even to the extent of using rare words employed by these authors. The very fact, we may add, that Josephus sought assistants (*Ag.Ap.* 1:50) to help him with his Greek style and that he declares (*Ant.* 20:263) that he laboured strenuously to partake of the realm of Greek prose and poetry, would make him hesitant to use the Septuagint as a source, especially since he was trying, quite obviously, in his *Antiquities* to reach a cultured Greek audience and to render the biblical narrative respectable in their eyes. Moreover, the very fact that he is paraphrasing the Bible in Greek would seem to indicate that he hoped to improve on that rendering; otherwise there would hardly have been much point in a new version. Hence, it is only where the style of the Septuagint is more polished, as in the additions to Esther or in 1 Esdras, that one would expect him to adhere to its text.

And yet, the very fact that Josephus cites the Septuagint (*Ant.* 1:10-12) as a precedent (it really was not a very good precedent, inasmuch as it had been done upon demand of a head of state rather than for non-Jews generally) for presenting the history of the Jews to the non-Jewish Greek world and that he devotes so much space (*Ant.* 12:11-118) to his paraphrase of the account in the *Letter of Aristeas* pertaining to the Septuagint would indicate its importance to him, especially since one would hardly have expected, *a priori*, that Josephus, in a work emphasizing the political and military history of the Jews, would give

---

[7] Thus, for Ginzberg, *Legends* 6, 130, n. 764, to assert that he has proof that Josephus was definitely relying upon a Hebrew text because Josephus declares (*Ant.* 4:125) that Balaam fell upon his face (πεσὼν δ' ἐπὶ στόμα), where the Hebrew of Num 24:4 and 16 has *nofel* ('falling'), whereas the Septuagint on these passages speaks of Balaam as having a vision of God in his sleep, is unwarranted, since it is not clear that Josephus is, in fact, here expounding this verse.

[8] Kennedy, *Sources*, 56-57.

so much attention to a subject which, strictly speaking, belongs in cultural and religious history. And yet, if he had ignored the Septuagint it would have been viewed as an indication that he was trying to hide something because of the tremendous regard in which that version was held. However, even when Josephus agrees with the Septuagint, there is no guarantee that this is because he had the text of the Septuagint before him, since such an agreement might well be due to an exegetical tradition which he happened to know and which had been incorporated earlier by the translators of the Septuagint. Moreover, of the thirteen changes listed by the rabbis (*B.T. Megilla* 9a, *Soferim* 1:8) as having been made deliberately by the translators when they rendered the text into Greek, only four can be found in any current manuscript of the Septuagint. This would seem to imply that Josephus might well have had a text different from any of the two thousand manuscripts of the Septuagint that we now have. Finally, the biblical texts discovered at Qumran indicate that the differences between the Septuagint and the Hebrew text were not as great as we had previously supposed, even in sectarian circles. It is generally difficult, we may add, because Josephus is usually not translating but paraphrasing, to discover which manuscript tradition of the Septuagint he is following. Thackeray[9] has noted that of the thirteen instances where we can determine which manuscript he followed, he adheres to the Alexandrinus ten times and the Vaticanus three times; this, we may comment, would seem to indicate that the manuscript before him was the direct ancestor of neither but rather belonged to a still different tradition.

USE OF AN ARAMAIC TARGUM

A third possible source for Josephus's paraphrase was the Aramaic targum. Aramaic was, after all, Josephus' primary language, as it was for the Jews generally in Palestine at his time. While it is true that the earliest extant targum for the Pentateuch, that of Onkelos, dates from the second century C.E., there can be little doubt that the practice of translating the Bible into the Aramaic vernacular in the synagogue is much older; and the fact that its origin is attributed to Ezra (fifth century B.C.E.) by Rav (third century C.E., *B.T. Megilla* 3a) meant that it had the sanctity and authority associated with the great name of Ezra. Indeed, if we may judge from Philo (*Life of Moses* 2:5, 26), the Septuagint was translated from 'Chaldean', that is Aramaic (though admittedly most scholars understand this to refer to Hebrew); and it is thus that Azariah dei Rossi, in his sixteenth-century masterwork *Me'or 'Einayim*, explains the 'errors' of the Septuagint. The very fact, moreover, that the targumim permit themselves considerable latitude in paraphrasing and expounding the text must have attracted them to Josephus in his task of rephrasing the Bible for his Greek audience. If, indeed, as N. Cohen[10] has remarked, Josephus is much freer in

---

[9] Thackeray, 'Josephus', 461-73.
[10] N. Cohen, 'Josephus and Scripture', 311-32.

vocabulary, style, order, and content in his rendering of biblical material in the first five books of the *Antiquities* as against Books 6-11, it may well be that a reason for this is the availability of targumim for these earlier books. The same phenomenon of greater freedom in paraphrasing and commenting on the Tora may be remarked in Philo and in rabbinic literature, presumably because it was the Tora which was read and expounded each week in the synagogue. Indeed, R. Bloch[11] has even gone so far as to declare that the aggadic source for Josephus' paraphrase of the Bible was an Aramaic translation; but we may object that this theory will hardly account for such vast expansions of the biblical material as Josephus' account of Moses campaign in Ethiopia (*Ant.* 2:238-253).

The examples cited by those who postulate the use of a targum by Josephus usually center on names and etymologies.[12] Thus, for the name Reuben Josephus has 'Ρουβῆλος,[13] reflecting the spelling of the Syriac (which is closely akin to Aramaic). Such a coincidence is admittedly not likely to be due to the fact that Josephus spoke Aramaic, because if so, we may ask, why is it so relatively rare? Moreover, the spelling 'Ρουβῆλος may be due simply to a scribal error, with *lambda* substituted for *nu*, which in uncials has only one extra stroke. As to etymologies, they were probably popular lore and well known and hence of no real significance, or they may be derived from the kind of onomasticon such as Rokeah[14] believes was the source of Philo's etymologies. As to Aramaic transliterations, such as σάββατα (*Ant.* 1:33), πάσχα (Ant. 2:313), and ἀσαρθά (*Ant.* 3:252), these are merely indications that Josephus spoke Aramaic. Moreover, despite the importance of geography for Josephus' work, he seems to have been unaware, as Epstein[15] has noted, of the extensive geographical knowledge embodied in the Targum of Pseudo-Yonatan, which, to be sure, though written down later, was probably extant, at least in part, in oral form at a much earlier period.

There are a number of individual passages which seem to point to a targumic source:

1) the change, for example, from 'spirit of God' (Gen 1:2) to 'a breath from above' (*Ant.* 1:27), presumably to avoid the anthropomorphism;
2) the delay in Cain's punishment (Gen 4:13) as a reward for his sacrifice and prayer (*Ant.* 1:58);
3) the insertion of the phrase 'at the beginning' (*Ant.* 1:110) parallel to Targum Onkelos on Gen 11:2;

---

[11] R. Bloch, 'Note méthodologique', 194-227.

[12] See Thackeray, *Josephus*, 81-82, Rappaport, *Agada und Exegese*, xxi-xxiv; and Schalit, 'Introduction' xxxi-xxxii.

[13] See Thackeray, *Josephus*, 78; and N. Cohen, *Jewish Names*, 89-94.

[14] Rokeah, 'A New Onomasticon Fragment', 70-82. Rajak, *Flavius Josephus*, 240, notes that Jerome, in his *Liber Interpretationis Hebraicorum Nominum*, speaks of a Greek predecessor (which he ascribes to Philo) in his preface.

[15] See Epstein, 'Les Chamites', 82-98.

4) the identification of Iscah with Sarai (Targum Pseudo-Yonatan on Gen 11:29; *Ant.* 1:151;

5) the placement of the king of Elam at the head of the coalition in first rather than in third place (*Genesis Apocryphon* 21:23; *Ant.* 1:171-72);

6) the stress on Isaac's merit and on his voluntary self-sacrifice (*Ant.* 1:222-36);

7) the immediate information (*Ant.* 2:2 and Targum Pseudo-Yonatan and Neofiti), rather than its postponement, (Gen 25:34) that Jacob was preparing a dish of lentils;

8) the chronology of the death of Rebecca (*Ant.* 1:345; Targum Pseudo-Yonatan on Gen 35:8);

9) the comparison of the children of Jacob to the stars of heaven (*Ant.* 4:115-17; Fragmentary Targum on Num 23:10);[16]

10) the description of the manna[17] as being 'sent down' (*Ant.* 3:26, 31, 32; Targum Pseudo-Yonatan on Exod 16:13ff.) and the complaint of the Israelites about the manna (*Ant.* 3:296; Targum Pseudo-Yonatan on Num 11:7);

11) King Ahab's going with bare feet (*Ant.* 8:362; targum on 1 Kgs 21:27); and

12) Jehu's quiet driving (*Ant.* 9:117; targum on 2 Kgs 9:20).[18]

The number of such instances is not great, however, and may reflect a Greek version which is now lost to us, parallel to that alluded to by the rabbis (*B.T. Megilla* 9a, *Soferim* 1:8).[19]

<h3 style="text-align:center">JOSEPHUS' SOURCES FOR THE VARIOUS BOOKS OF THE BIBLE</h3>

If we now turn to the evidence for Josephus' biblical text for the various books of the Bible, there seems to be strong evidence that Josephus' main source for the Pentateuch was a Hebrew text and/or a targumic paraphrase in Aramaic.[20] This is what we would expect in view of the fact that in the synagogue Josephus would have heard the Hebrew text with, in all probability, an accompanying targum. There is, however, a greater degree of agreement between the Hebrew and Greek texts for the Pentateuch than for other books of the Bible, on the one hand, while Josephus himself is freer in his paraphrase of the Pentateuch than he is of the later books of the Bible, on the other hand; and hence it is difficult to be sure whether he is using a Hebrew or a Greek text at any given point. While it is true that in Genesis there appear to be more instances where Josephus seems to be following the Septuagint rather than a Hebrew text, in some cases these are proper names, where, as we have noted, corruption could most readily have

<hr>

16   See Vermes, *Scripture and Tradition*, 147.

17   See Malina, *Palestinian Manna Tradition*, 54-55.

18   Thackeray, *Josephus*, 82.

19   Gaster, *Asatir*, 61-80. As Rappaport, *Agada und Exegese*, xi, n. 3, has pointed out, many of the alleged parallels are far-fetched, and some of them are also to be found in rabbinic midrashim.

20   For a different position, see Attridge, 'Josephus and His Works', 211.

taken place, in view of the well-known tendency of copyists to bring the text into consonance with the Septuagint.[21] Alternatively, he may actually be adopting the language of Philo, as we see in his paraphrase of the creation chapter, where he closely follows Philo's *On the Creation*, which, to be sure, is clearly indebted to the Septuagint;[22] or he may be indebted to a *glossary of terms*, such as we know from papyri existed; or he may be reflecting a Palestinian tradition which the translators, who allegedly came from Palestine, had incorporated into their version and which Josephus knew independently; or he may have independently adopted some incorrect translation of a Hebrew term;[23] or, he may have arrived at a given translation into Greek because the Greek word was really the best way to render a given term;[24] or the apparent dependence may be due to a scribal error.[25] On the other hand, when he seems to be following the Hebrew, the renderings may simply be synonyms for the Septuagint's words (and Josephus, as we can see from his paraphrase of the *Letter of Aristeas*, is almost pathological about avoiding the usage of the same word as that found in his source); or he may be using words that are more classical. In any case, that Josephus is not following the Septuagint (or, at least, our Septuagint) blindly is clear from the fact that where (*Ant.* 4:274) he renders Deut 22:1, he definitely disagrees with the Septuagint's version that declares that a domesticated animal which is found wandering on the road is considered a lost object, whereas Josephus and the Mishna (*Bava Metsia* 2:9) assert that it is not.

Rajak's collection[26] of the instances for the book of Exodus (*Ant.* 2:206-3:207) where we can apparently see whether Josephus used a Hebrew or a

---

[21] Hence, the finding of Shutt, 'Biblical Names', 169, that in four instances Josephus follows the Masoretic Text, whereas in twenty-five cases he follows the Septuagint for names is of questionable significance, especially when we consider that in twenty cases his spelling of the names is independent of both the Masoretic Text and the Septuagint. Similarly, the fact that in six cases Josephus appears to follow the Masoretic Text in his statements and interpretations of names, whereas in fourteen instances he is following the Septuagint, has doubtful significance, since there are sixteen cases where his statements are independent of both. In any case, the fact that Josephus is writing in Greek and that he generally hellenizes proper names may account for some of these.

[22] Hence, the fact that Josephus (*Ant.* 1:27) writes, ἐν ἀρχῇ ἔκτισεν ὁ θεὸς τὸν οὐρανὸν καὶ τὴν γῆν, which seems to be derived from the Septuagint's version of Gen 1:1, may actually, in view of the obvious debt of Josephus to this tractate of Philo for his account of creation, be derived from Philo, *Op.* 26.

[23] Rajak, *Flavius Josephus*, 232, cites as an example the rendering of *sar ha-tabahim* (Gen 39:1) as ἀρχιμάγειρος ('chief cook') by the Septuagint and ἐπὶ τῶν . . . μαγείρων ('chief of the cooks') by Josephus (*Ant.* 2:39) as an instance when both may have independently rendered the original Hebrew in an incorrect, though literal, interpretation, a mistake also made by the Samaritan version.

[24] Cf. Rajak, *Flavius Josephus*, 237. S. Cohen, *Josephus in Galilee and Rome*, 36, notes that Hölscher, 'Josephus', in his collection, cols. 1953-54, of verbal coincidences between the first book of the *Antiquities* and the Septuagint is remarkable for the paucity and insignificance of the list.

[25] E.g., as noted by Franxman, *Genesis*, 87, n. 45, Josephus' θαλλὸν ἐλαίας, 'branch of olive' (*Ant.* 1:92), which seems to be dependent upon the Septuagint's φύλλον ἐλαίας κάρφος, 'a leaf of olive, a twig', against the Masoretic Text's 'olive leaf' (Gen 8:11), may actually be due to a scribal error of θαλλόν for φύλλον.

[26] Rajak, *Flavius Josephus*, 238, and her Appendix V.

Greek *Vorlage* yields similarly inconclusive results. If we compare, as I[27] have done, the names and the order of the stones on the breastplate of the high priest (Exod 28:17-20) with Josephus' two versions (*War* 5:234 and *Ant.* 3:168), we find that the two versions agree with the names in the Hebrew in nine or possibly ten out of twelve instances, and with the Septuagint in all twelve instances; and when it comes to the order of the stones, Josephus agrees with the Masoretic Text in only four instances in the *War* and in only five or possibly six cases in the *Antiquities*, whereas he agrees with the Septuagint's order in five instances in the *War* and in five or six cases in the *Antiquities*. What is, however, most significant is that Josephus disagrees with both the Masoretic Text and the Septuagint in the order of five of the stones. Hence, Josephus, who was himself a priest, may well have had a text different from both, or he may have used a glossary, or he may be writing from memory, or he may be paraphrasing freely.[28] Again, as in *Ant.* 3:102, where his interpretation of *shittim* (Exod 25:5) coincides with the Septuagint's ἄσηπτα ('not liable to decay'), the explanation may be that he had access to a glossary or that he knew a tradition that this was the meaning of the term; or he may have asked one of the rabbis who constantly visited Rome to ask favours of the Emperor.[29]

Whereas for Joshua Josephus seems to be closer to the Masoretic Text, in Judges and Ruth he is quite free in his rendering of the biblical text, perhaps, as Thackeray and others[30] have suggested, because he was using a targum. In Samuel, according to Mez and Thackeray,[31] he is generally aligned with the Septuagint in the proto-Lucianic version, against the Masoretic Text, though Thackeray[32] also postulates that he employed a Semitic text as a collateral source, as one can see, for example, in Josephus' rendering (*Ant.* 6:330) of Endor (1 Sam 28:7) as the city of Dor, a reading apparently due to a text that mistakenly had *'irdōr* for *'endōr*,[33] and in Josephus' εἰς ῾Ρεγάν (*Ant.* 6:325) for the Hebrew *Yisra'el*, which was presumably corrupted into IECPAEΛAN and then into EIC PAEΛAN and finally into EIC PEΓAN, as Rajak[34] has suggest-

[27] Feldman, 'Prolegomenon', cxii-cxiv.

[28] It is perhaps significant, as I, 'Prolegomenon', cxiii-cxiv, note, that in the one place where Pseudo-Philo (26:10-11) in his list of stones does not agree with the Septuagint in the order of the stones, he is in agreement with Josephus' *Antiquities*, which is a later version than the list in the *War*, and presumably a correction. Hence, this may reflect the Hebrew or Greek biblical text available to both Josephus and Pseudo-Philo, a text which differed from both the Masoretic Text and the Septuagint as we have them.

[29] It has been conjectured that the nameless philosopher whom four great Sages visited in Rome toward the end of Domitian's reign was Josephus, since he was the one Jew who continued to have influence during Domitian's reign. See Feldman, *Josephus*, 77-78.

[30] Thackeray, *Josephus*, 81; Rappaport, *Agada und Exegese*, xxi-xxiv; Schalit, 'Introduction', xxxi-xxxii.

[31] Mez, *Die Bibel*; Thackeray, *Josephus*, 83-89.

[32] Thackeray, 'Note', ix.

[33] Thackeray, *Josephus*, 82.

[34] Rajak, *Flavius Josephus*, 250.

ed. Rahlfs, Moore, Brock, and Rajak[35] have contested the thesis of Mez and Thackeray; and Brock has argued that of the mere thirty examples adduced by Mez in support of his theory, only nine are actually valid, noting that in many places where Josephus supposedly agrees with Lucian against the Septuagint this is simply due to his attempt to make better sense. The fact, we may add, that most of Mez's evidence is from Josephus' spelling of proper names and from the numbers that he cites weakens his case immeasurably, because it is precisely in such details that copyists are most likely to make corrections to bring a text into accord with their preconceived data. Mez conveniently does not note the degree to which Josephus disagrees with Lucian or agrees with the Masoretic Text or is unique in agreeing with no text, though we must admit that Schalit[36] has hardly established a case for Josephus' use of a Hebrew text for Samuel, inasmuch as his chief arguments are that there are a number of instances where Josephus is not paralleled by the Greek text and that in the names of Solomon's provincial governors – an instance where, as we have noted, corruption is most likely to take place – Josephus (*Ant.* 8:35-38) is closer to the Masoretic Text (1 Kgs 4:7-19) than to the Septuagint.[37] Kahle,[38] while ready to grant that Josephus' text does agree with Lucian, explains this phenomenon as due to Christian copyists, just as Katz contends that Philo's quotations from the Bible, which so often do not agree with our text of the Septuagint, represent corrections reflecting a late recension of the Septuagint inspired by Aquila's version.

Ulrich[39] offers a number of examples to prove that Josephus used a Greek rather than a Hebrew text for 1 and 2 Samuel, the most convincing of which[40] are 2 Sam 6:8 (*Ant.* 7:82) and 2 Sam 6:19 (*Ant.* 7:86), where the Greek words are very rare in the Septuagint.[41] He has gone so far as to conclude that Josephus used only a Greek text for Samuel, and that this Greek text, as Cross[42] has

---

[35]   Rahlfs, *Septuagintastudien*, 3, 92-111; Moore, 'Antiochian Recension'; Brock, *Recensions*, 207-21; Rajak, *Flavius Josephus*, 232. Rahlfs, we may note, after making a study of biblical quotations in early Church Fathers, through the end of the third century, concludes that it is not possible to isolate 'Lucianic' texts as such, since we may find 'Lucianic' readings scattered everywhere and often combined with non-Lucianic readings. Brock argues that agreements between Josephus and Lucian may often be due to Josephus' desire to make sense of a given context.

[36]   Schalit, 'Introduction', xxvii-xxxi.

[37]   We may suggest that one reason why Josephus is closer here to the Hebrew text is that this passage is part of the Haftara (2 Kgs 4:1-37, or 23 in the Sephardic rite) that is read in the synagogue after the Tora portion of *Wayera* (Gen 18:1-22:24), and that Josephus may well have heard it therefore in the synagogue year after year.

[38]   Kahle, *Cairo Geniza*, 233-34.

[39]   Ulrich, *Qumran Text*. Howard, 'Kaige Readings', theorizes that Josephus relied upon two types of the Greek Bible, a proto-Lucianic text (manuscripts boc_2e_2), identified by Barthélemy, *Devanciers*, with the old Septuagint, and a *kaige* recension, which is the basis of Aquila's version. One may just as easily, however, postulate that Josephus' two texts were a Greek text of the boc_2e_2 type and a Hebrew text which was the basis of Aquila's version.

[40]   See Tov, 'Textual Affiliations'.

[41]   See Ulrich, *Qumran Text*, 210 and 211.

[42]   Cross, 'History'; 'Contribution'; and 'Evolution'.

suggested, was revised so as to conform to the Hebrew text as found in the Dead Sea fragments, resulting in a 'Palestinian' text as found in the Chronicler, Josephus, Pseudo-Philo,[43] Lucian, and the sixth column of Origen's Hexapla.[44] The Rylands Greek Papyrus 458, our oldest extant papyrus of the Greek Bible, indicates that, at least for the portions of Deut 23-28 that we have, Lucianic readings appear already in the second century B.C.E.

It does seem hard, however, to believe that Josephus would have ceased to consult the Hebrew text so suddenly and so utterly, especially since he must have heard portions from Samuel (seven selections from which are included in the Annual Cycle) in the synagogue on Sabbaths and holy days during readings of the *haftarot*. Moreover, in an instance such as 2 Sam 11:3, where Josephus (*Ant.* 7:131) agrees with the Dead Sea manuscript *4QSam*[a] in calling Uriah Joab's armor-bearer, this does not prove that Josephus was dependent upon a Greek *Vorlage*, since we have no Greek manuscript which has this reading. In addition, Muraoka has indicated at least one case (2 Sam 11:8) where Josephus (*Ant.* 7:132) is not dependent upon the Greek text.[45]

For the period of Ezra, Josephus' chief source, to judge from verbal similarities,[46] was, it would seem, the apocryphal Greek book of Esdras (1 or 3 Esdras), rather than the Hebrew or the Septuagintal text, apparently because he was attracted by its superior Greek style,[47] its elimination of some chronological difficulties, and, perhaps most of all, the highlighting of romantic interest in the debate, so reminiscent of Herodotus (*Historiae* 3:80-84), as to whether wine, the king, or a woman is the most powerful. And yet, there is reason to think that here, too, as in his version of other books of the Bible, Josephus was aware of both a Hebrew text and the Septuagint. The fact that he diverges so widely from the Masoretic Text, the Septuagint, and the Apocryphal text is for

---

[43] Harrington, 'Biblical Text', 1-17, has shown that Pseudo-Philo's biblical text generally agrees with that of Josephus as against the Masoretic Text and the Septuagint, and that especially in 1 Samuel his readings agree with the Lucianic text.

[44] There is no basis for the assertion of Jellicoe, 'Occasion', 144-50, that the presence of proto-Lucianic readings in Josephus and at Qumran shows that there was recensional activity at Leontopolis.

[45] Muraoka, 'Greek Text'. N. Cohen, 'Josephus and Scripture', 311-32, does, however, note evidence of a remarkable shift in diction between the first five books of the *Antiquities* covering the Pentateuch, Joshua, Judges, and Ruth, and Books 6-11, covering the rest of his paraphrase of the Bible. For example, she remarks that the word ἑκατοντάρχης (ἑκατόναρχος), 'captain of a hundred', does not appear at all in the first five books of Josephus, despite the fact that it is found in the Septuagint seven times, but that it is used nine times, all of them paralleled by the Septuagint, in the next five books. This would seem to show that Josephus used the Hebrew text for his first five books and the Septuagint for the next five; but the matter must remain *sub judice* since there is some reason to believe that Josephus' Hebrew text, starting with the books of Samuel, was closer to our present Greek (or proto-Lucianic) text.

[46] See H. Bloch, *Quellen*, 69-77, for a list of these parallels.

[47] Jellicoe, *Septuagint*, 294, has remarked that Josephus' decision to follow the Greek Esdras was determined chiefly by its style, especially if it is true that the Atticizing reaction against the *koinē* Greek actually began not in the second century in the age of Lucian but a century earlier.

Rudolph[48] evidence of the validity of Hölscher's thesis,[49] that for the *Antiquities* Josephus employed neither a Hebrew nor a Greek biblical text but rather a paraphrase written by a Jewish Hellenist. Ararat[50] postulates a 'Comprehensive Chronicle' as the source of the Hebrew and Greek Ezra, the Apocryphal 1 Esdras, Josephus' account of Ezra, and the legends in rabbinic literature pertaining to this era. There is not a single fragment in existence, however, from the work postulated by either Hölscher or Ararat; and it seems most reasonable to assume that Josephus proceeded here as apparently elsewhere with the three texts before him that are before us.[51]

For the book of Esther Josephus clearly used a Greek text, presumably because he found it to be stylistically on a more polished level than the rest of the Greek Bible. Motzo[52] notes evidence in Josephus' text of kinship (though not identity) with the major groups of manuscripts of the Septuagint. There can be no doubt that for the additions to the Book of Esther Josephus used a Greek version, since his paraphrase of four of the six additions is often very close, presumably because he found the romantic spirit of such a passage as Addition D very much to his liking. One would assume, however, that although the third-century rabbis Rav and Samuel grudgingly permitted the Book of Esther to be read in Greek on Purim (*B.T. Megilla* 18a), Josephus, as one who knew Hebrew, would have heard it twice each year in the original Hebrew. Bickerman,[53] noting evidence that seems to point to Josephus' access to various texts now extant, prefers to postulate that Josephus is following a particular recension of the Greek Esther, namely the one that was popular among the Jews of Rome, but that this version is now lost. Such a theory can hardly be proven, inasmuch as this version is no longer to be found. Faced with this problem, Hölscher[54] postulates a single source for Josephus, namely Alexander Polyhistor's *On the Jews*; but inasmuch as we have not a single fragment of Alexander's work that deals with the story of Esther, it is difficult to accept such a hypothesis. Another possibility is that Josephus may have had access to an Aramaic targum; but Seyberlich, who notes that the second edict of King Ahasuerus is found only in Josephus (*Ant.* 11:273-83) and in the Targum Sheni 8:12,[55]

[48] Rudolph, *Esra und Nehemia*, xvii and 107.

[49] Hölscher, 'Josephus', 1955-60.

[50] Ararat, *Ezra*.

[51] The same propensity for using both a Hebrew original and a Greek translation may be seen in Josephus' version of 1 Maccabees, as Melamed, 'Josephus and Maccabees I', 122-30, has shown through a comparison of nineteen passages.

[52] Motzo, 'Il testo di Ester', 84-105.

[53] Bickerman, 'Notes', 104.

[54] Hölscher, *Die Quellen*, 52.

[55] Seyberlich, 'Esther', 363-66. Rajak, *Flavius Josephus*, 228, noting the presence of many Greek words in *Targum Sheni*, suggests that Josephus may have consulted in a Greek version the material which is there embodied; but we may note that on this basis one might postulate a Greek source for the rabbinic midrashim generally, which contain such a high percentage of Greek words that some have spoken of its Aramaic as a kind of Graeco-Aramaic.

dismisses this theory as improbable because Josephus had been living in Rome for twenty years at the time of the completion of the *Antiquities* and had presumably lost contact with targumim; instead she postulates that Josephus had recalled some details of Pharisaic midrashim that he had heard in his earlier years. We may, however, comment that it seems likely that a large portion of the Roman Jewish community had originated from Palestine and presumably was Aramaic-speaking, at least in the generation when Josephus was living in Rome; and contacts between the Jewish communities of Palestine and Rome continued to be close throughout this period. In any case, if Josephus had lost contact with his Aramaic mother tongue, it seems even more far-fetched that he would remember midrashim that he had heard decades before. We may not go so far as Torrey,[56] who postulates that Josephus used only the Aramaic version in a Greek translation and did not know the Hebrew text of Esther, which he regards as an abbreviated translation of an Aramaic original, but it seems likely that for Esther, too, as elsewhere, Josephus availed himself of his trilingual competence in consulting the Hebrew, Greek, and Aramaic versions.

Josephus' Promise Not to Modify the Scriptures

In the introduction to his *Antiquities* (*Ant.* 1:5) Josephus proclaims that his work (or, at any rate, the portion dealing with the biblical period) will embrace the entire ancient history (ἀρχαιολογίαν) and political constitution (διάτα-ξιν τοῦ πολιτεύματος) of the Jews, translated from Hebrew records (ἐκ τῶν Ἑβραϊκῶν μεθηρμηνευμένην γραμμάτων). Josephus promises his readers (*Ant.* 1:17) that he will throughout his work set forth the precise details of the Scriptures (τὰ μὲν οὖν ἀκριβῆ τῶν ἐν ταῖς ἀναγραφαῖς), each in its place (κατὰ τὴν οἰκείαν τάξιν), neither adding nor omitting anything (οὐδὲν προσθεὶς οὐδ' αὖ παραλιπών). At the conclusion of his history (*Ant.* 20:260) Josephus notes that he has told the whole story of the Jewish people in full and accurate detail, reminding the reader (*Ant.* 20:261) that this is what he had promised to do at the beginning of his history. He declares (*Ag.Ap.* 1:42), moreover, that not only he but no one else has for long ages past ventured to add or to remove or to alter a syllable (προσθεῖναί τις οὐδὲν οὔτε ἀφελεῖν αὐτῶν οὔτε μεταθεῖναι) of the Scriptures. And yet, as we shall note, Josephus has added numerous details and even whole episodes, while omitting such passages as the cunning of Jacob in connection with Jacob's flock (Gen 30:37-38), the Judah-Tamar episode (Gen 38), Moses' slaying of the Egyptian (Exod 2:12), the building of the golden calf (Exod 32), the grumbling and doubting before the second miraculous feast of quails (Num 11:11-23), Miriam's leprosy (Num 12), the story of Moses' striking the rock to bring forth water which speaks of Moses' disgrace (Num 20:10-12), and the story of the brazen serpent (Num 21:4-9) whereby Moses cured those who had been bitten by the fiery

---

[56] Torrey, 'Older Book of Esther', 1-40.

serpents, the account of Gideon's smashing of the Baal altar (Judg 6:25-32), and the story of Micah and his idolatry (Judg 17-18).

A number of attempts have been made to resolve the apparent failure of Josephus to live up to his promise. One approach is to declare[57] that Josephus depends upon the ignorance of his readers, knowing full well how difficult it was for most of them to acquire a manuscript, let alone to look up a particular passage without benefit of an index. But to this we may counter that Josephus was certainly not the only Jew in Palestine who knew Greek, and that his rival, Justus of Tiberias, at the very least, was in a position to read – and criticize – Josephus' work, especially since we know (Photius, *Bibliotheca*, 33, p. 6b23-7a5 = Jacoby, *FGH* 734 T2) that Justus composed *A Chronicle of the Jewish Kings*, which apparently covered the period from Moses until the death of Agrippa II, thus more or less duplicating the coverage of Josephus' *Antiquities*, even if Photius describes it as 'very scanty in detail'. Moreover, there were surely many Jews in the Diaspora who were in a position to check on his statements through consulting the Septuagint. Indeed, Pseudo-Longinus' (*De Sublimitate* 9:9) highly laudatory paraphrase of Gen 1:3, 9, 10, in a work of literary criticism dating presumably from the first century C.E. shows that the Septuagint was well known.

A second approach taken by a number of scholars[58] is to remark that the phrase 'neither adding nor omitting anything' is a stock and essentially mean-ingless formula for affirming one's accuracy, as may be seen by its use in the first century B.C.E. Greek Dionysius of Halicarnassus' *Thucydides* 5 and 8, in the second century C.E. Lucian's *Quomodo Historia Conscribenda Sit* 47, and in the Roman pseudo-Cornelius Nepos (allegedly first century B.C.E.) in the introduction of *Dares Phrygius*. As S. Cohen[59] has remarked, it was customary for the writer to insist that his account was merely a translation from sacred texts; and such a statement will be found in the works of other Hellenized Orientals, similar to Josephus, such as Berossus (ca. 300 B.C.E.), Manetho (third century B.C.E.), and Philo of Byblus (first-second century C.E.), as well as in the works of such Greeks as Ctesias (fifth-fourth century B.C.E.) (*ap.* Diodorus Siculus, *Bibl. Hist.* 2:32.4) and Hecataeus of Abdera (ca. 300 B.C.E.) (*ap.* Diodorus, *Bibl. Hist.* 1:69.7). That Josephus' phrase is not necessarily to be taken literally would seem to be indicated by the fact that Matthew (5:17-18) uses similar language: 'Think not that I have come to abolish the law and the prophets; I have come not to abolish but to fulfill them. For truly I say to you, till heaven and earth pass away, not an iota, not a dot will pass from the law until all be accomplished'. It would seem that portions, at least, of the law were abolished by Jesus' disciples in his own lifetime (for example, with regard to the Sabbath and the dietary laws); and the apparent inconsistency was pointed out

---

[57] Siegfried, 'Die hebräischen Worterklärungen', 32-33, n. 3.

[58] Avenarius, *Lukians Schrift*; Attridge, *Interpretation*; and S. Cohen, *Josephus*, 25-28.

[59] S. Cohen, *Josephus*, 27.

to a judge (or philosopher) who, according to the Talmud (*B.T. Shabbat* 116b) had quoted from a nameless book, presumably a Gospel, 'I came not to destroy the Law of Moses nor to add to the Law of Moses'.

Moreover, there would seem to be a precedent for modifying the sacred text, namely the very work, the Septuagint, which Josephus cites (*Ant.* 1:10) as justifying his presentation of biblical history to Gentiles. The Septuagint, despite the fact that the translation was apparently divinely inspired (*Letter of Aristeas* 306), and though the work of translation had been carried on with the greatest of accuracy, inasmuch as a curse was pronounced upon anyone who ventured to add or transpose or remove anything (προστιθεὶς ἢ μεταφέρων τι ... ἢ ποιούμενος ἀφαίρεσιν), yet contains numerous modifications of the original. In fact, the rabbis, who (*B.T. Megilla* 9a), with obvious approval, refer to the miraculous manner in which the seventy-two translators had been placed in seventy-two separate rooms and yet had emerged with identical translations because of Divine inspiration, mention, nevertheless, certain deliberate changes which they had all made in the process of translating the sacred text. The fact that, despite the ban on any modification of the Septuagint, three major recensions had emerged by the time of Jerome,[59a] shows that the curse was not taken too seriously. The fact is, moreover, that the rabbis themselves sanctioned (*B.T. Megilla* 25a-b) the omission of the translation of certain biblical passages when they read the Bible in the synagogue, presumably because of the embarrassment involved.[60]

When we examine the words which Josephus uses for 'translate', we shall find that they are all ambiguous and seem to include paraphrasing and amplifying. When he declares (*Ant.* 1:5) that his work has been translated from the Hebrew records he employs the verb μεθερμηνεύω for 'translate'. Josephus uses the same verb (*Ant.* 12:20 and 48) in speaking of the 'translation' of the Pentateuch known as the Septuagint; but inasmuch as this was hardly a literal translation, as we have noted, and indeed took considerable liberties, it will hardly buttress the meaning of 'translate', but rather seems to signify 'interpret'. Indeed, in one of these passages we hear that the translators of the Pentateuch not merely translated (μεταγράφαι 'transcribe') but also interpreted (μεθερμηνεῦσαι) the Law for Ptolemy's pleasure. There would hardly be much point in transcribing the Law for Ptolemy; there would be a point in translating and elucidating it, and it would be this latter act that would bring pleasure to Ptolemy; hence the word μεθερμηνεύω seems to imply much more than mere translation. Elsewhere (*Ant.* 1:52 and 8:142) it seems to refer not to the translation but to the etymology of words. There are at least two instances (*War* 5:151 and *Ag.Ap.* 1:167) where the meaning is not 'to translate' but rather 'to signify'. In one important passage (*Ag.Ap.* 1:54) Josephus remarks that he has, in his *Antiquities*, given a translation (or interpretation, μεθηρμήνευκα) of the Bible, being

[59a] Preface to the Book of Chronicles, in Migne, *PL*, 28, 1324-25.
[60] The list does not completely coincide with Josephus'. See my 'Hellenizations in Josephus' Portrayal of Man's Decline', 337-38.

(γεγονώς) a priest and of priestly ancestry and being well versed (μετεσχηκώς) in the philosophy (φιλοσοφίας) of those writings. Since the participles used show that the clauses are directly connected with the first part of the sentence, it would appear that Josephus' qualifications as a 'translator' were enhanced by the fact that he was a priest and by his knowledge of the philosophy, that is, scientific, systematic, and methodical study of the Bible. Clearly, to be a good 'translator' required more than the mechanical knowledge of language. In fact, there is only one passage (*War* 4:11) of the nine occurrences of this verb in Josephus where the meaning is unambiguously 'to translate'.

As to the uncompounded verb, ἑρμηνεύω, its meaning (*War* 5:182, 5:393, 7:455; *Ant.* 6:230) seems to be 'describe', 'explain', 'render', 'express'; and only once (*Ant.* 6:156) does it unequivocally mean 'to translate'. In particular, in the statement (*Ant.* 20:264) that Jews 'give credit for wisdom to those alone who have an exact knowledge of the law and who are capable of interpreting (ἑρμηνεῦσαι) the meaning of the Holy Scriptures', the meaning is not to 'translate', since that would be too mechanical an art to ascribe wisdom to its practitioners.

With regard to other words that are used with reference to the translation known as the Septuagint, whether the word μεταβάλλω (*Ant.* 1:10, 12:14, 12:15, 12:107) means 'translate' in the narrow sense or includes interpretation in the broader sense is not apparent from the context; but Thackeray[61] makes an interesting point when he remarks that the word must have been used loosely, since Josephus (*War* 1:3) employs it with reference to his own translation of the *War* from it original Aramaic into Greek; and that translation was hardly literal, inasmuch as our version of the *War* shows no trace of Semitic parentage (but this may be due to the assistants who aided him in the composition of that work). Hence, we may conclude that since Josephus viewed himself as carrying on the tradition of the Septuagint in rendering the Bible for Gentiles, he conceived of his task as not merely translating but as also interpreting the Scriptures, and therefore he did not conceive himself as adding or subtracting anything if he continued their tradition of liberal clarification.

Another possibility is that Josephus understood the phrase 'neither adding nor omitting anything' as referring to the commandment (Deut 4:2 and 13:1) that one may not add to or subtract from the commandments of the Tora, since the Septuagint, indeed, does render this clause in a way (οὐ προσθήσετε, οὐκ ἀφελεῖτε) that combines the language of *Ant.* 1:5 and *Ag.Ap.* 1:42. Hence, the meaning may be that one is not permitted to alter Jewish law by adding to or subtracting from the commandments, whereas Josephus' changes are, at least primarily, in the realm of aggadic material.

Albrektson[62] interprets Josephus' statement (*Ag.Ap.* 1:42) that for long ages past no one has ventured either to add to or subtract from the Bible to mean that

---

[61]   Thackeray, *Josephus*, 34.
[62]   Albrektson, 'Josefus', 201-15.

it is prohibited to add to the content of the Bible but that it is not forbidden to modify the actual consonantal text. But if so, this would make it difficult to understand the statement in the Letter of Aristeas (30) that the Tora had been committed to writing somewhat carelessly (ἀμελέστερον) and would certainly go against the very stringent laws embodied in the talmudic literature pertaining to the writing of a Tora scroll. The fact that there were proofreaders in Jerusalem who were paid from Temple funds during the period of the Second Temple(*B.T. Ketubbot* 106a) again indicates the premium placed upon the exact spelling of words in the Tora.

Finally, when Josephus says that he has set forth the precise details of the Scriptures (ἀναγραφαῖς), he may mean not only the written Bble but also Jewish tradition generally. If the objection is offered that aggadic material had not been reduced to writing by the time of Josephus, the answer is that we do have midrashim embodied in such Hellenistic Jewish writers as Artapanus, Eupolemus, Ezekiel the tragedian, and Philo, as well as in such Palestinian writings as the *Genesis Apocryphon* and Pseudo-Philo's *Biblical Antiquities*. In fact, as R. Bloch[63] brilliantly pointed out, the origins of midrash are to be found in the Bible itself. The fact that Josephus (*Ag.Ap.* 1:43) declares that Jews do not utter a single word against the laws (νόμους) and the allied writings (τὰς μετὰ τούτων ἀναγραφάς) indicates, despite S. Cohen,[64] that he perceives a distinction between the laws (νόμοι) and the Scriptures (ἀναγραφαί), the latter of which presumably included more than written law.

Josephus as an Interpreter of Biblical Narrative

JOSEPHUS' AUDIENCE

To understand what Josephus has done with the biblical narrative in the *Antiquities* we must first ask for whom the work is intended. It would seem that Josephus actually had two audiences in mind. On the one hand, the very fact that in his prooemium he cites (*Ant.* 1:10) as a precedent for his work the translation of the Tora into Greek for King Ptolemy Philadelphus is clearly designed as a justification for his directing his work to Gentiles with apologetic intent, inasmuch as he apparently realized that normally it is prohibited to teach the Tora to Gentiles (*B.T. Hagiga* 13a, *B.T. Sanhedrin* 59a). Indeed, he inquires (*Ant.* 1:9) whether Jews have been willing to communicate such information to Gentiles. The fact that he asks (*Ant.* 1:9) whether any of the Greeks have been curious to learn 'our' history and that he specifically declares (*Ant.* 1:5) that his work was undertaken in the belief that the whole Greek world would find it worthy of attention indicates that he was directing the

[63] R. Bloch, 'Midrash'.
[64] S. Cohen, *Josephus*, 24-25.

Antiquities to pagans. Again, the fact that at the end of the work (*Ant.* 20:262) he boasts that no one else would have been equal to the task of issuing so accurate a treatise for the Greeks (εἰς "Ελληνας) indicates that he directed the work to the non-Jewish world, since the term 'Greeks' for Josephus is used in contrast to Jews.

That, however, Josephus is also directing his work to Jews seems clear from the statement (*Ant.* 1:14) that 'the main lesson to be learnt from this history by those who care to peruse it' is that God rewards those who obey His laws and punishes those who do not. Josephus, of course, realized that Gentiles are obligated to obey only the seven Noachian commandments, whereas Jews are required to obey 613 commandments; and it would seem that his statement is here directed to his fellow-Jews, since he gives no indication that when he speaks of 'laws' he is distinguishing between Noachian and other commandments. Moreover, his highlighting of certain episodes, notably the incident of Israel's sin with the Midianite women (Num 25:1-9; *Ant.* 4:131-55; Josephus expands it from nine verses to twenty-five paragraphs) and Samson's relations with alien women (Judg 14:1-16.31; *Ant.* 5:286-317), is directed, apparently, to those Jews who sought assimilation with Gentiles.[65] Josephus (*Ant.* 4:150-51) vehemently condemns Zambrias (Zimri) and bestows exalted praise upon Phinehas, 'a man superior in every way to the rest of the youth' (*Ant.* 4:152), who, after all, might well have been condemned for taking the law into his own hands in putting Zambrias to death without a trial. He likewise condemns Samson (*Ant.* 5:306) for transgressing the laws of his forefathers and debasing (παρεχάρασσεν, used with reference to coins) his own rule of life by imitation of foreign usages, which, he says, proved the beginning of his disaster. Moreover, we may note, Josephus makes a point of stressing that the fortunes of Anilaeus and Asinaeus, the robber-barons who established an independent Jewish state in Mesopotamia, began to deteriorate at the very peak of their success because Anilaeus plunged into lawlessness (*Ant.* 18:340) 'in violation of the Jewish code at the bidding of lust and self-indulgence'.

That, however, Jews were not Josephus' main audience seems evident from his remark (*Ant.* 4:197) that he has deemed it necessary to state that he has merely reclassified the laws without actually modifying them at all, 'lest perchance any of my countrymen who chance upon (ἐντυγχανόντων) this work should reproach me at all for having gone astray'. Evidently he expected that his fellow-Jews would read his book only by chance.

JOSEPHUS' SOURCES

We may next consider what Josephus' sources – midrashic, Hellenistic Jewish,

---

[65] Cf. Van Unnik, 'Josephus' Account', 259: 'It is hardly conceivable that the words of this remarkable speech [Zambrias' defense of his apostasy: *Ant.* 4:145-49] arose out of Josephus' own imagination. They are the expression of what was thought by his contemporaries who broke away from the ancestral religion and gave these reasons for doing so'.

and personal – were for the changes that he introduces into the biblical narrative. In the first place, there was the Jewish midrashic tradition, which, though it had not yet been written down for the most part, contained many of the aggadic traditions found in Josephus.[66] Schalit[67] has even gone so far as to suggest that while he was living in Rome Josephus had an opportunity to deepen his knowledge of the Jewish tradition; but this seems unlikely in view of the fact that he was looked upon with disdain and bitterness by the Jewish community generally because of what they regarded as his traitorous behaviour in the war against the Romans, unless some of the rabbis, in their constant visits to Rome, chose to see him (though there is no reference to him in the entire talmudic corpus) in the hope of gaining his intercession with the Roman Emperor, the infamous Domitian, with whom he, almost alone, remained on good terms.[68]

There has been much debate as to whether Josephus depended primarily upon written or upon oral sources for midrashic traditions. Schalit[69] believes that details which involve exposition of specific verses derive from oral traditions, since this is the midrashic style as it was eventually recorded, whereas longer additions, such as the account of Moses' campaign against the Ethiopians, are taken from written sources. Since the overwhelming majority of Josephus' changes are, indeed, minor modifications of individual verses, this would indicate the paramount importance of oral sources. Rappaport,[70] on the other hand, believes that Josephus was dependent upon written sources exclusively. The fact, we may add, that there are numerous details which Josephus shares with his presumed contemporary, Pseudo-Philo,[71] would seem to indicate a common source. It is impossible to identify this or any other midrashic source, though it is perfectly possible that Josephus did have access to written midrashic sources akin to the *Genesis Apocryphon*. The important point to be discerned is Josephus' choice of certain midrashic details from whatever source and his reasons for such a choice.

We may guess that Josephus' propensity for giving specific names or other such data for vague biblical references – for example, the name of the man who inspired the building of the Tower of Babel, Nimrod (*Ant.* 1:113); the name of Pharaoh's daughter who adopted Moses, Thermuthis (*Ant.* 2:224); the name of the prophet who rebuked Ahab for releasing Ben-hadad, Micaiah (*Ant.* 8:389)

---

[66] Rappaport, *Agada und Exegese*, xx-xxiii, concludes that Josephus had a written source for aggadic traditions.

[67] Schalit, 'Introduction', xxxv.

[68] See Feldman, *Josephus*, 127.

[69] Schalit, 'Introduction', xxxix-xli.

[70] Rappaport, *Agada und Exegese*, xv.

[71] See Feldman, 'Prolegomenon', lviii-lxvi, and 'Epilegomenon', 306-07. I have noted thirty parallels between Josephus and Pseudo-Philo (Zeron, 'Erwägungen', 45, n. 43, has added another) that are to be found in no other work that has come down to us and fifteen cases where Josephus is not alone in agreeing with Pseudo-Philo but where both may reflect a common tradition. That, however, the relationship between Josephus and Pseudo-Philo is not a simple matter may be deduced from the fact that I have noted thirty-six instances where they disagree.

– is due to rabbinic midrashim. But the fact that such details are found in such pseudepigraphic works as Jubilees[72] or in Pseudo-Philo's *Biblical Antiquities* or in sectarian works such as the Dead Sea Scrolls' *Genesis Apocryphon* or in the Samaritan *Asatir*[73] would seem to indicate that we are dealing with a Palestinian and not merely rabbinic tradition.

A second source that Josephus might have employed is the Hellenistic Jewish tradition. In particular, the Hellenistic Jewish writers might have provided him with an excellent precedent and a stylistic model. This would have been especially true of Philo, who writes such excellent Greek. The fact, however, that Josephus mentions Philo on only one occasion (*Ant.* 18:259-60), that he refers to other Hellenistic Jewish writers on only one other occasion (*Ag.Ap.* 1:218), that he there speaks of them as if they are pagan (he notes their inability to follow accurately the meaning of 'our' records), and that he confuses Demetrius the historian with Demetrius of Phalerum would indicate that he made minimal use of them.[74] Evidence that Josephus could not have read Eupolemus very closely may be deduced from the fact that he declares (*Ag.Ap.* 1:218) that Eupolemus did not deviate far from the truth, when, in fact, Eupolemus commits such 'howlers' as his statements that David was Saul's son (*ap.* Eusebius, *Praeparatio Evangelica* 9:30,3) that Eli was the high priest at the time when Solomon became king (*ap.* Eusebius, *Praeparatio Evangelica* 9:30,8), and (unless this is part of the work of Pseudo-Eupolemus) that Enoch is to be identified with the Greek mythical Atlas (*ap.* Eusebius, *Praeparatio Evangelica* 9:17,9). We may also suggest that if, indeed, Josephus had used these Hellenistic Jewish historians he would have cited them as a precedent for his own work, whereas in the preface to the *Antiquities* (1:9-12), he seems to be groping for a justification for presenting his paraphrase of the Bible to a non-Jewish audience, and he is able to cite only the Septuagint as such a precedent. Hölscher,[75] as we have noted above, presents a hypothesis that Josephus' source was a Hellenistic Jewish midrash, but he has no trace at all of such a work. Wacholder[76] has theorized that Josephus might have derived his extra-biblical material from the *Chronicle of the Jewish Kings* of his rival, the Jewish historian Justus of

---

[72] For parallels between Josephus and Jubilees (particularly in geographical details) see Rappaport, *Agada und Exegese*, xix-xx; Thackeray, *Josephus*, 92; and Franxman, *Genesis*, 98. One of these parallels is in the name of Pharaoh's daughter, Thermuthis, which is also found in Jubilees 47:5 as Tharmuth. That Josephus did not derive this extended addition from Artapanus would seem to be indicated by the fact that in Artapanus (*ap.* Eusebius, *Praeparatio Evangelica*, 9:27, 3) her name is Merris.

[73] For parallels between Josephus and *Asatir* see Gaster, *Asatir*, 65-79, who has, however, stretched the evidence.

[74] Freudenthal, *Hellenistische Studien*, asserts that Josephus knew these Hellenistic Jewish writers primarily through the work *On the Jews* by the pagan Alexander Polyhistor, who wrote in the middle of the first century B.C.E. and who is later quoted by Eusebius in his *Praeparatio Evangelica*, Book 9. Cf. van der Horst, below, pp. 519-20.

[75] Hölscher, 'Josephus', 1955-60.

[76] Wacholder, *Eupolemus*, 56-57.

Tiberias; but in view of Photius' remark which we have noted above, that it was 'very scanty in detail', this seems unlikely. Sprödowsky[77] has suggested that for the story of Joseph in Egypt Josephus has drawn upon an Alexandrian-Jewish tradition; and Rajak[78] has similarly argued that the story of Moses' campaign on behalf of the Egyptian pharaoh against the Ethiopians must have arisen in Egypt, presumably in Alexandria, for the same reason, namely, that the setting indicates that it would have been of particular interest to Egyptians. But Rajak herself is forced to admit that Josephus has a number of details which are not found in Artapanus' version of the Moses story; and she, like Freudenthal and Gaster,[79] concludes that they both drew upon a common source. As to Ezekiel the tragedian, Jacobson[80] has argued that the absence of Ezekiel from the list of Hellenistic writers mentioned by Josephus (*Ag.Ap.* 1:218) does not prove that Josephus did not know Ezekiel's work, and that Josephus' acount of the crossing of the Red Sea, particularly the depiction of the Egyptians as lacking weapons (*Ant.* 2:321, 326; Ezekiel, 210), Moses' striking of the sea with his staff (*Ant.* 2:338; Ezekiel, 227), the postponement of battle by the Egyptians (*Ant.* 2:334; Ezekiel, 218), the energetic entry of the Israelites into the sea (*Ant.* 2:340; Ezekiel, 228-29), and the darkness which overcame the Egyptians (*Ant.* 2:344; Ezekiel, 237), indicates such knowledge.

Furthermore, there seems good reason to believe that Josephus drew upon the work of Philo, particularly for the preface to the *Antiquities* (compare *Ant.* 1:21 and Philo's *On the Creation* 1-3 on the question as to why the Tora begins with creation rather than with a statement of the laws), for the close correspondence[81] in phraseology between Philo (*On Abraham* 40:233-34) and Josephus (*Ant.* 1:177) in their description of Abraham's attack upon the Assyrians, for similar interpretations of the names Abel (*Ant.* 1:52; Philo, *On the Migration of Abraham* 13:74) and Ishmael (*Ant.* 1:190; Philo, *On the Change of Names* 37:202) (though this may be due to mutual dependence upon onomastica such as have been found on papyri in Egypt), and for the allegorical method, particularly the symbolism of the tabernacle and the clothing of the high priest (*Ant.* 3:179-87; cf. Philo, *Life of Moses* 2:18, 88; 2:21, 101-2:24, 126, *On the Special Laws* 1:172, *Who Is the Heir* 45-46, *Questions and Answers on Exodus* 2:73, 75, 85, 112-14, 117-20).[82] We may comment that though there are some

---

[77] Sprödowsky, *Hellenisierung*.

[78] Rajak, 'Moses in Ethiopia', 114. Most recently Runnalls, 'Moses' Ethiopian Campaign', has argued that Josephus' version of Moses' campaign against the Ethiopians is a polemic written against the Hellenistic version of Artapanus and that the core of the story probably dates from the Persian era. See also Attridge, 'Historiography', 166-67.

[79] Freudenthal, *Hellenistische Studien*, 170; Gaster, *Asatir*, 72.

[80] Jacobson, *Exagoge*, 37-39.

[81] Sandmel, *Philo's Place*, 64, has, however, noted differences in detail.

[82] For further parallels see Schalit, 'Introduction', xli-xliii. On the whole question of Josephus' dependence upon Philo see my *Josephus*, 410-18. For Genesis the most systematic comparison is that of Franxman, *Genesis*. For a differing view see Attridge, *Interpretation*, 36 and 'Josephus and His Works', 211.

striking points of agreement, the details in which they disagree are also so numerous that we must postulate an additional or a common source. As to the symbolism, the fact that similar interpretations are to be found in rabbinic midrashim indicates that it is not personal but widely current. Moreover, such a conception, shared by Philo and Josephus, as that the whole cosmos is the robe of God (*Ant.* 3:184; Philo *Life of Moses* 2:24, 117) is at least as much Platonic or Stoic as it is distinctively Jewish.

Finally, we must not exclude the possibility that Josephus introduced details of his own, particularly for apologetic reasons. The very fact that his portraits of biblical personalities are consistent in emphasizing the cardinal virtues, as well as dramatic and erotic elements, and in de-emphasizing theological and magical elements, is indicative of a personal imprint, rather than, as Vermes[83] has suggested, that Josephus represents a stage in the historical development of the midrashic tradition. Furthermore, in language and in style there are important links between the *War* and the *Antiquities*. In view of his slow rate of composition (about ten lines of Greek a day)[84] we would, indeed, expect not only a careful and consistent work but also one which carries Josephus' personal imprint.

In particular, we may note the influence of contemporary events, especially those of Josephus' own life, upon his biblical interpretation. Thus, his elaboration of the sacrifice of Isaac was perhaps influenced by later events, namely by the martyrdom in the days of the Maccabees and by the mass suicides at Jotapata and at Masada in Josephus' own day. Inasmuch as he himself had declined to allow his life to be taken at Jotapata, Josephus had to be careful to explain how God could have commanded the sacrifice of Isaac's life. Daube[85] has suggested that Josephus identified himself, in particular, with Joseph, who likewise was accused falsely; with Jeremiah, who was a prophet (as Josephus conceived himself because of his accurate prediction that Vespasian would become emperor) and who likewise suffered at the hands of his fellow-Jews; Daniel, who likewise suffered for his convictions; Esther and Mordecai, who suffered gladly in order to help their people.[86] To this list we may add Josephus' identification with Saul, whom he viewed as a martyred general like himself. In addition, as van Unnik[87] remarks, the very fact that Josephus omits the name of Shittim (Num 25:1) and Ba'al Pe'or (Num 25:3) means that the story of Israel's sin with the Midianite women is no longer dated but takes on a universal

---

[83] Vermes, *Scripture and Tradition*.

[84] Feldman, 'Josephus' Portrait of Saul', 97.

[85] Daube, 'Typology', 18-31. For a similar theme, that Josephus' aggadic remarks are based on his personal background, see also Heller, 'Grundzüge, 237-46, 363.

[86] Daube, 'Typology', 18-31, remarks that Josephus probably saw the scene of Esther before Ahasuerus as a prefiguration of his own experience before Vespasian. In particular, he suggests that the picture of Ahasuerus as attended by bodyguards with axes is not based on the Bible or on the Apocryphal additions to Esther but rather on the fact that Vespasian had such guards.

[87] Van Unnik, 'Josephus' Account of the Story of Israel's Sin', 241-61.

flavour, with contemporary warning to Jewish youth who may be tempted to succumb to sensual temptations.[88]

STYLISTIC CHANGES

In view of his intended audience, Josephus sought both to impose upon the style of his source[89] and to highlight certain subject matter which he felt would answer the charges of anti-Semites. As to the first, Josephus (*Ant.* 1:17) stresses that the proposes to set forth the details in accordance with their proper order (κατὰ τὴν οἰκείαν τάξιν), using the military term τάξις (arrangement or order of troops, battle array or order of battle), as if he were in literature the general that he was in the field during the war against the Romans. Similarly, at the end of his summary of the laws, he declares (*Ant.* 4:197) apologetically that he has added nothing for the sake of embellishment but that his one innovation has been to classify (τάξαι) the subjects; again the verb which he uses has military connotations, signifying drawing up troops in order of battle. The very fact that Josephus uses the word τάξις and its related verb τάττω indicates that he conceived of his task as being the careful marshalling of his data. In a revealing remark, he states (*Ant.* 4:197) that Moses left his writings in disarray (σποράδην, scattered like seed), just as he had received them from God. He thus rearranged the biblical material in accordance with the 'thematic' school followed by a number of Hellenistic historians, as remarked by Avenarius and Cohen,[90] whereby he brings into juxtaposition those items which belong together on the basis of subject, regardless of chronology or source. Thus, whereas the Bible first has the story of Noah's drunkenness and his cursing of Canaan, the son of Ham (Gen 9:20-25), and then has the detailed genealogies of all of Noah's sons, Josephus presents in juxtaposition the genealogy of Ham's sons, including Canaan (*Ant.* 1:130-39), and the account of Noah's curse upon Canaan (*Ant.* 1:140-42).

Moreover, in his recasting of the narrative, Josephus seeks *to resolve theological problems and contradictions* in the text. Thus he substitutes (*Ant.* 1:27) the verb ἔκτισεν, 'founded', for the Septuagint's ἐποίησεν, 'made', his purpose being, presumably, to avoid the inference that God had created the world out of pre-existing matter, since that would be implied in the use of the verb ποιέω. That this is a deliberate change seems clear, since Josephus' language, including

---

[88] Gafni, 'Use of I Maccabees', 81-95, notes that Josephus, as compared with his source, 1 Maccabees, stresses the virtue of martyrdom for the cause of religious freedom rather than engaging in active resistance, again reflecting Josephus' own view in the war against the Romans, in which he had participated, that the aims and behaviour of the Zealots were not justified.

[89] Downing, 'Redaction Criticism', 46-65, has noted that Josephus' reworking of the Bible is similar to the method adopted by the authors of the Gospels, notably Luke, in removing discrepancies, duplications, interruptions, miracles, magic, inappropriate theology, and the apologetically awkward, and in adding harmony and continuity, providence and prophecy, piety and moral uplift, interest and clarity, and apologetics.

[90] Avenarius, *Lukians Schrift*, 119-27; S. Cohen, *Josephus*, 39-42.

word order, is exactly the same as it is in the Septuagint (and Philo)– except for this one word. Again, there is a genuine theological problem (Gen 1:26) in the use of the plural 'Let us make man in our image', as if God had collaborators in His creation of man or as if God were Himself a plurality of forces, such as a Trinity. Indeed, according to the rabbis (*B. T. Megilla* 9a), the translators of the Tora into Greek changed the verse to read 'I shall make man'. Josephus himself (*Ag.Ap.* 2:192) – perhaps in answer to Plato (*Timaeus* 41C, 42E) and Philo (*On the Creation* 72), who had asserted that God had employed collaborators – specifically stresses that God performed his creation 'not with assistants, of whom He had no need'. Josephus, in his paraphrase of Genesis, resolves this problem by asserting (*Ant.* 1:32) merely that 'on this day also He formed man', omitting also the troublesome phrase 'in His image', presumably because it raised problems of anthropomorphism. Again, the Bible (Gen 2:17) declares that God told Adam that he would die on the day that he would eat from the tree of knowledge. The fact, of course, is that not only did Adam not die but he lived until the age of 930. Josephus (*Ant.* 1:40) resolves the problem by omitting the phrase 'on the day' and by generalizing that if they touched the tree it would prove the destruction of Adam and of Eve.

Another reason for recasting the narrative is *to remove chronological difficulties*. Thus, in dealing with the problem of the unusual longevity of the patriarchs, Josephus has a three-fold approach. In the first place, he cites (*Ant.* 1:107-08) the evidence of Greek poets and historians, from the revered Hesiod down to the learned Nicolaus of Damascus, that the ancients had a lifespan of up to a thousand years, just as did the patriarchs; and he also cites a number of non-Greek historians to a similar effect. In the second place, Josephus tries to rationalize by noting (*Ant.* 1:106) four factors that help to explain their longevity: they were dear to God, they had a diet (τροφάς), presumably because they were vegetarians more suitable for long life, they possessed merit (ἀρετήν), and they had to live long lives in order to promote the utility of their discoveries in astronomy and geometry, since they could not have predicted anything with certainty if they had not lived for six hundred years.[91] Finally, Josephus closes with his familiar formula (*Ant.* 1:108): 'On these matters let everyone decide according to his fancy'.

Sometimes Josephus in his paraphrase *seeks to avoid anthropomorphisms*. Thus in Gen 1:2 there is an anthropomorphism implied in the word מרחפת, which indicates not merely hovering but also brooding, as over a world-egg, a concept familiar from the Orphic theogony. The Septuagint partly avoids this problem by asserting that 'the spirit of God was borne' above the water, but even this does not completely avoid the anthropomorphism. Josephus (*Ant.* 1:27) resolves the difficulty by asserting that 'a breath from above sped', thus referring to something distinct from God Himself. Similarly, to speak of God,

---

[91]   One is reminded of the discussion of diet as the factor responsible for the length of the lives of the Ethiopians (Herodotus, *Historiae* 3:23).

as does Gen 2:7, as breathing the breath of life into man's nostrils must have seemed a grotesque anthropomorphism to Josephus, and so he says simply that God instilled (ἐνῆκεν) into man spirit and soul.

Besides, Josephus seeks in his paraphrase *to provide better motivation and to increase the plausibility of events*. Thus, whereas Manoah's desire in the Bible (Judg 13:8) to recall the angel is not well motivated, Josephus' elaboration (*Ant.* 5:280) makes it more plausible, for he has Manoah's wife entreat God to send the angel again so that her husband may see him and thus allay the suspicions arising from his jealousy of the angel. Similarly, in order to remove the implausibility of the narrative, Delilah in Josephus (*Ant.* 5:310), full of feminine wiles, uses Samson's love for her as a weapon against him: thus she keeps saying to him that she takes it ill that he has so little confidence in her affection for him as to withhold from her what she desired to know, 'as though', she adds, with typical strategy, 'she would not conceal what she knew must in his interests not be divulged'. Again, the reader of the biblical narrative might well ask how Mordecai was able to discover the conspiracy of Bigthan and Teresh against King Ahasuerus (Esther 2:22). Josephus (*Ant.* 11:207) has a plausible explanation which is found in no other source, namely, that the plot was discovered by a certain Jew, Barnabazos, the servant of one of the eunuchs, who, in turn, revealed it to Mordecai. Furthermore, the reader might well ask how Harbonah was able to learn (Esther 7:9) about the gallows which Haman had prepared for Mordecai. Josephus (*Ant.* 11:261 and 266) explains this by noting that he had learned this from one of Haman's servants when Harbonah had gone to summon him to Esther's second banquet.

Furthermore, Josephus seeks to *clear up an obscurity in the text*. Thus it is by no means clear what God means when He says (Gen 1:6), 'Let there be a firmament in the midst of the waters, and let it divide the waters from the waters'. Josephus (*Ant.* 1:30) clarifies the matter by noting that what God did was to set the heaven above the universe and to congeal ice around it, thus explaining, as the Bible does not, the origin of rain. Another obscurity which Josephus clarifies is the 'strange' fire (Lev 10:1) which Nadab and Abihu, the sons of Aaron, offered and on account of which they suffered death. The rabbis (*Lev. Rabba* 20:8-9, pp. 461-64), noting the juxtaposition in the Bible of the warning to priests not to partake of wine and strong drink before entering the sanctuary (Lev 10:9), suggest that they were intoxicated when they offered the fire. Josephus is unique in presenting the rationalization that they brought on the altar not the incense which Moses had commanded but what they had used previously.[92]

Another goal of Josephus in his adaptation of the biblical narrative was *to have his work appeal to those who appreciated Hellenistic rhetoric*. Indeed, as I[93] have noted, Abraham's speech to Isaac (*Ant.* 1:228-31) is an example of a

---

[92] See Shinan, 'Sins', 201-14.
[93] Feldman, 'Aqedah', n. 74.

progymnasmatic (preparatory) exercise called *ethopoeia*. Cicero (*De Legibus* 1:5) had already noted that history is an *opus . . . . unum oratorium maxime*;[94] and the rhetorician Theon[95] (apparently a younger contemporary of Josephus) had remarked on the utility of rhetorical exercises for the writing of history.

In his rewriting of his source, Josephus, like the rhetorician, is constantly concerned with how his work will sound to the ear. Thus he declares (*Ant.* 2:176-77) that he is inclined to omit, because of their strangeness to a Greek ear, the names of the seventy descendants of Jacob who went down to Egypt ; but he inserts the names only to refute those anti-Semites who had contended that the Jews were of Egyptian rather than of Mesopotamian origin. On the other hand, he omits (*Ant.* 11:68) the names of the families that returned to Jerusalem from Babylonian captivity, the names of those Jews who sent away their foreign wives at the request of Ezra (*Ant.* 11:152), and the names of King Ahasuerus' seven chamberlains (Esther 1:10), of his seven counsellors (Esther 1:14), and of Haman's ten sons (*Ant.* 11:289; Esther 9:7-9).

In any case, to judge from Josephus' method of paraphrasing the *Letter of Aristeas* (*Ant.* 12:12-118),[96] aside from a single broken sequence of twelve words and another of ten words, Josephus has deliberately varied the language of his source, even going so far as to substitute synonyms for individual words, altering the prefixes in his verbs, and varying the syntax, though he sticks to the sequence of events in the original. In this avoidance of copying the language of his source, Josephus, as Cohen[97] has remarked, is following in the footsteps of Aeschines (2:172-76) in his paraphrase of Andocides (3:3-12), as well as of Livy's paraphrase (7:9,6-10,14) of Claudius Quadrigarius, Livy's version of Polybius, Diodorus' version of Agatharchides, and Plutarch's paraphrase (in his life of Coriolanus) of Dionysius of Halicarnassus. Apparently there was always the fear of the dreaded accusation of plagiarism.

Another factor in Josephus' rewriting of the Bible is his desire to *enhance the sense of drama*. Thus, for example, the drama of Saul's selection by God is increased because it is at night (*Ant.* 6:37-40) and not during the day (1 Sam 9:15) and while Samuel is tossing with sleeplessness that God instructs him to choose the king whom He will point out. This dramatic element is augmented still more by the fact that on the day before Saul's arrival God had declared that at precisely that hour on the following day Saul would arrive, whereas the Hebrew does not indicate the precise hour but merely declares that it will be 'tomorrow about this time', and the Septuagint does not mention the hour at all.

Still another factor in Josephus' mind is *to increase the irony*. Thus, the fact that Josephus in the brief pericope in which he paraphrases Abraham's intended sacrifice of Isaac (*Ant.* 1:222-36) on five occasions uses a word for happiness, stresses on the one hand how much happiness meant to Abraham,

---

[94] See Feldman, *Cicero's Conception of Historiography*, 149-69.
[95] See Feldman, 'Aqedah', n. 74.
[96] Pelletier, *Flavius Josèphe*.
[97] S. Cohen, *Josephus in Galilee and Rome*, 29-31.

and on the other hand how ready he was to forego that happiness because of his faith in God. In particular, the irony is increased by Josephus' statement (*Ant.* 1:223) that Abraham sought to leave his son ἀπαθῆ, a word which has two very different meanings, both of which are here applicable: 'unscathed', in the sense that in the end Isaac will be unharmed, and 'emotionless', in the sense that Isaac will actually welcome his being sacrificed. Likewise, Josephus increases the irony in his version of the Esther narrative by introducing God's ironic laughter at Haman's hopes just before the περιπέτεια. Again, whereas in the Bible (Esther 6:6) Ahasuerus asks Haman what should be done for the man whom the king wishes to honor, Josephus' Ahasuerus (*Ant.* 11:252) adds to the irony by declaring that he knows that Haman is the only friend loyal to him. Furthermore, the irony is increased, for whereas the Bible (Esther 6:11) declares that Haman took the apparel and the horse and arrayed Mordecai, Josephus (*Ant.* 11:256) stresses the contrast between Mordecai clothed in sackcloth and the new purple robe which he is now told by Haman to put on. Finally, Josephus (*Ant.* 11:267-68) stresses the supreme irony in the fact that Haman was hanged on the very same gallows that he had prepared for Mordecai: he thus marvels at God's wisdom and justice in bringing about the result, and adds to the drama of the scene by having Queen Esther show the king the letter which Haman had written in which he had ordered the destruction of all the Jews.

One device which Josephus resorts to only rarely (perhaps in reaction against Philo) in solving difficulties is the *use of allegory*, though he admits (*Ant.* 1:24) that one of the methods of the Tora is solemn allegorizing, and though this pattern had been employed by Stoics in interpreting Homer's and Hesiod's references to the obscenities of the gods.[98] Indeed, Josephus (*Ag.Ap.* 2:255) speaks sneeringly of the 'frigid subterfuges' (ψυχρὰς προφάσεις) of the allegorists. Nonetheless, Josephus does resort to allegory in explaining the tabernacle as symbolic of the earth and the sea (*Ant.* 3:181), the twelve loaves upon the table as the twelve months, the candelabrum with its seven lamps as the seven planets, the tapestries of four materials denoting the four elements, and the high priest's garments signifying the parts of the universe.[99] Thus the Jews' seemingly irrational rules with regard to the Temple and its cult would seem to accord with the nature of the cosmos.

In addition, Josephus gave added coherence to his narrative by subscribing to the 'great-man' theory of history and by thus *focussing upon certain key personalities* in his narrative. Thus, as I[100] have suggested, Josephus presents a coherent portrait of Abraham as a typical national hero such as was popular in Hellenistic times, with emphasis on his qualities as a philosopher-king, scien-

---

[98] See Wolfson, *Philo* 1, 132-33.

[99] Josephus' allegory bears a number of similarities to that of Philo, *Moses* 2:18, 88 and 2:24, 117-27; but inasmuch as these allegories are also, to some degree, paralleled in rabbinic midrashim, the most likely explanation is that both Philo and the rabbis in their allegorization go back to a common tradition. See Holladay, *Theios Aner*, 83-86.

[100] Feldman, 'Abraham', 143-56.

tist, rhetorician-logician, and romantic hero. Indeed, despite the contention of Sandmel[101] that Josephus' account of Abraham, at any rate, lacks any striking, unified, and coherent conception, and that of Cohen,[102] who even goes so far as to accuse Josephus of sloppiness, inconsistency, and capriciousness, Attridge[103] has remarked on Josephus' internal consistency; Holladay[104] has commented on the strikingly uniform mold into which Josephus has cast his major heroes – Abraham, Joseph, Moses, David, and Solomon –, transforming them into a reflection of the Hellenistic ideal of the virtuous wise man, especially as seen in the popular ethics of the first-century Graeco-Roman world; Franxman[105] has noted that beneath the surface lies a careful author; and I[106] have remarked on the unity in his portrait of Saul, noting that we should expect a careful product from a gifted historian who spent at least a dozen years writing the *Antiquities*, while living on an imperial pension and without any additional duties, composing no more than an average of about ten lines of Greek per day.

JOSEPHUS' AIMS: APOLOGETICS

HELLENIZATIONS IN JOSEPHUS. Two major goals have been presented as motivating Josephus' modifications, to defend the Jewish people against anti-Semitic attacks and to present a religious interpretation of history. I[107] have stressed the apologetic aim of Josephus, which may be seen in the Hellenization of his narrative, both in language and in ideas, so as to appeal to his Greek-educated readers and in the glorification of his heroes.

As to the Hellenization of his account, the very fact that Josephus mentions by name no fewer than fifty-five Greek authors, even if many of these names may simply be copied from second-hand sources,[108] is an indication that he was out to impress his readers with his knowledge of Greek literature. In particular, we may note his debt to Homer, Aeschylus, Sophocles, Euripides, Herodotus, Thucydides, and Plato.

Josephus himself (*Ag.Ap.* 1:50) admits that, despite the fact that he had every material (πραγματείας, 'treatment', 'treatise') at his disposal, he employed assistants (συνεργοῖς) for the sake of the Greek language (πρὸς τὴν

---

[101] Sandmel, *Philo's Place in Judaism*, 75.
[102] S. Cohen, *Josephus in Galilee and Rome*, 38-39.
[103] Attridge, *Interpretation*, 182.
[104] Holladay, *Theios Aner*, 67-78.
[105] Franxman, *Genesis*, 285-89.
[106] Feldman, 'Josephus' Portrait of Saul', 97-99.
[107] Feldman, 'Josephus' Commentary on Genesis', 121-31; 'Hellenizations in Josephus' Portrayal of Man's Decline', 336-53; 'Abraham' 143-56; 'Aqedah'; 'Saul', 45-99; 'Solomon', 69-98; 'Esther', 143-70.
[108] As I, *Josephus*, 177, have remarked, the fact that on two occasions (*Ant.* 10:219-28 and *Ag.Ap.* 1:134-44) Josephus cites the same passage about Nebuchadnezzar from Berossus, together with precisely the same confirmatory references from Philostratus and Megasthenes would indicate that there, at least, he was using a handbook.

Ἑλληνίδα φωνήν) when he composed his account of the *Jewish War*. Whether, however, Josephus had assistants to help him with the Greek when he wrote the *Antiquities* during the next dozen years has been debated. There are those, such as Thackeray,[109] who devised a kind of documentary hypothesis for the later books of the *Antiquities*, indicating, on the basis of a close study of Josephus' vocabulary and style, that he had for Books 15 and 16 an assistant who had a particular love of Greek poetry, especially Sophocles, and that for Books 17 through 19 he had an assistant who was particularly fond of Thucydides. But, as I[110] have noted, it is ironic that Thackeray cannot pinpoint the nature and extent of the help of the assistants for the *War*, where Josephus admits he had assistants, whereas for the *Antiquities*, about which Josephus says nothing concerning assistants, Thackeray claims that there is evidence. Moreover, there are Sophoclean elements not only in Books 15 and 16 but also in the earlier books of the *Antiquities*, as Thackeray[111] himself admits. In addition, many of the Sophoclean and Thucydidean phrases occur in other Greek works of the period, particularly Dionysius of Halicarnassus, and hence may have come to Josephus through such sources. Finally, inasmuch as Josephus completed his *Antiquities* in Rome after a twenty years' stay (while working at nothing else so far as we know), it seems hardly likely that he would have needed as much assistance as he did for the *War*, which he wrote relatively early in his career.

Josephus' Hellenization of the Bible may be seen most readily in his adoption of distinctive phraseology and concepts from classical Greek authors. Thus, to give a few illustrations, as we follow the order of Josephus' narrative, the phrase (*Ant.* 1:14) ἄπορα μὲν γίνεται τὰ πόριμα ('the practicable things become impracticable') is clearly reminiscent of the very reverse in the choral passage in Aeschylus (*Prometheus Bound* 904): ἄπορα πόριμος ('making possible the impossible'), the only other extant author who has these two words thus in paradoxical juxtaposition. Again, as I[112] have noted, Josephus (*Ant.* 1:46), in his developed picture of the original bliss of mankind, which has no parallel in the Bible, is following a tradition which appears in many pagan authors from Hesiod on. In particular, the idea (*Ant.* 1:46, 48, 54) of food arising spontaneously, which appears in Josephus' description of the Golden Age, is also found in Homer's description of the Cyclopes (*Odyssey* 9:109). Likewise, his condemnation (*Ant.* 1:61) of Cain for putting an end to the guileless and generous simplicity and ignorance in which men had previously lived and converting them to a life of knavery is in line with classical portrayals of the primitive age of

---

[109] Thackeray, *Josephus*, 107-18.
[110] Feldman, *Josephus*, 828-29.
[111] Thackeray, trans. of Josephus, vol. 4, p. xv, cites, as examples of passages that reveal the style of the Sophoclean assistant, Josephus' proem (*Ant.* 1:1-26), the wooing of Rebecca (*Ant.* 1:242-55), the temptation of Joseph by Potiphar's wife (*Ant.* 2:39-59), the exodus and the passage of the Red Sea (*Ant.* 2:315-49), the rebellion of Korah (*Ant.* 4:11-66), the story of Balaam (*Ant.* 4:102-30), and the death of Moses (*Ant.* 4:323-31).
[112] Feldman, 'Hellenizations in Josephus' Portrayal of Man's Decline', 341.

simplicity in Homer, Plato, Virgil, and Ovid. Again the idea of a periodic destruction of the earth by fire and water alternately (*Ant.* 1:70-71), while it is, to be sure, to be found also in the Pseudepigraphic *Vita Adae et Evae* 49:3-50:2, would be recognized by the reader of Josephus as being parallel to the statement in Plato (*Timaeus* 22C) that there have been many and diverse destructions of mankind, the greatest by fire and water.[113]

Despite the fact that Josephus assures the reader in his proem (*Ant.* 1:15) that Moses has kept his remarks about God pure of that shameless mythology (ἀσχήμονος μυθολογίας) found among others, he does occasionally make such comparisons, as, for example (*Ant.* 1:73), when he compares the deeds of the sons of the angels of God (Gen 6:4) to the exploits ascribed to the Giants of Greek mythology. Similarly, there is an implied comparison between Noah's flood and that of Deucalion, for Josephus (*Ant.* 1:76) declares that God put into Noah's mind (ὑποθεμένου) the means of salvation, using language very similar to that of Apollodorus (1:7, 2), who states that Deucalion constructed his boat upon the advice (ὑποθεμένου) of Prometheus. The very fact that the word which Josephus uses for Noah's ark is λάρναξ (*Ant.* 1:77), precisely the word used for Deucalion's ark by Apollodorus and apparently adopted by Nicolaus of Damascus, whom he later quotes (*Ant.* 1:94-95), rather than the Septuagint's word, κιβωτός, would seem to corroborate this implied comparison.

Again, in describing Ishmael's dying state, Josephus (*Ant.* 1:218) employs the same rare word for expiring, ψυχορραγοῦν, literally 'letting the soul break loose', which Euripides uses (*Alcestis* 20 and *Hercules Furens* 123, 324, the latter in precisely this form). In fact, as I have tried to indicate,[114] there are several striking parallels between Isaac and Iphigenia, notably in the enthusiasm with which they both approach the sacrifice, and, in particular, in such a

---

[113]   Josephus shows knowledge of Plato in a number of places: 1) He borrows (*Ag.Ap.* 1:7), without specifically mentioning it, from the *Timaeus* (22B-C) the idea that 'in the Greek world everything will be found to be modern and dating, so to speak, from yesterday or the day before'; 2) he correctly remarks (*Ag.Ap.* 2:168-69) that the philosophy of Plato is addressed only to the few, whereas the Tora's teachings are intended for the many; 3) he deliberately (*Ag.Ap.* 2:192), as we have noted above, combats the idea that God had collaborators in the work of creation, a view held by Plato and by Philo; 4) he cites Plato by name (*Ag.Ap.* 2:223) as one admired by the Greeks for his dignity of character and persuasive eloquence but who is ridiculed by self-styled expert statesmen; 5) he remarks (*Ag.Ap.* 2:224) that if one examines Plato's laws, they will be found frequently easier than the Jewish code and more closely approximating the practice of the masses; 6) he remarks (*ibid.*) that Plato himself (*Timaeus* 28C) has admitted that it is not safe to express the true opinion about God to the ignorant masses; 7) he cites the opinion (*Ag.Ap.* 2:225) of those who regard Plato's discourses as brilliant but empty; 8) he is aware (*Ag.Ap.* 2:256) that Plato banishes the poets, including Homer, from the ideal state in order to prevent them from obscuring with their fables the correct doctrine about God; 9) he declares (*Ag.Ap.* 2:257) that Plato followed Moses in prescribing that the citizens must all study the laws and learn them verbatim, and that foreigners must not be permitted to mix at random with the citizens; 10) there is evidence of the influence of Plato upon the speeches of Eleazar ben Jair at Masada (*War* 7:323-36, 341-88), as noted by Ladouceur, 'Masada', 250-51. For further indications of Josephus' indebtedness to Plato see Brüne, *Flavius Josephus*, 194-98.

[114]   Feldman, 'Aqedah'.

statement as Isaac's (*Ant.* 1:232) that he could not even consider rejecting the decision of God and Iphigenia's (*Iphigenia at Aulis* 396) that she, a mortal woman, could not stand in the way of the goddess. We may also note the pathetic irony of the fact that Abraham seeks happiness only through his son, who paradoxically, is about to be sacrificed, just as there is irony in the chorus' ode (*Iphigenia at Aulis* 590-91). that begins, 'Oh! oh! great happiness of the great!' One may also note the remarkable addition (*Ant.* 1:233) to the biblical narrative in which God declares that He gave His order to Abraham 'from no craving for human blood', which is clearly in contrast to the statement of Artemis (*Iphigenia at Aulis* 1524-25), who rejoices in human sacrifices.[115]

Likewise, Josephus uses a phrase clearly reminiscent of Homer when he declares (*Ant.* 1:222) that Isaac was born on the threshold of old age (ἐπὶ γήρως οὐδῷ) of Abraham. The fact that this phrase occurs in the *Iliad* (22:60) in connection with Priam, who addresses his son Hector before the latter goes off to his last fateful battle with Achilles makes its use in the context of the Akeda all the more poignant and pathetic because of the parallels between the aged fathers, Abraham and Priam, and between the promising sons, who are apparently about to die in the flower of youth.[116] Indeed, as I have tried to indicate,[117] Josephus has Hellenized the biblical narrative of the Akeda so that it acquires precisely those qualities that are missing in the Bible: clarity, uniform illumination, and lack of suspense. By eliminating the direct command of God to Abraham, as well as Abraham's laconic response, 'Here I am', and by putting the whole scene in indirect discourse, Josephus removes the suspense and indicates that Abraham took all this in his stride.

Josephus shows his indebtedness to Herodotus[118] in numerous places, particularly in his description of Moses' march during his campaign against the Ethiopians, where he gives details about the winged serpents which he put to flight with ibises, a passage which would remind the reader of Herodotus' story (*Historiae* 2:75) of the winged snakes which comes flying every spring from Arabia towards Egypt and are stopped by ibises, which destroy them all. Indeed, Josephus (*Ant.* 2:247) would seem to be alluding to the passage when

---

[115] For other indications of Josephus' debt to Euripides see my 'Aqedah'.

[116] Josephus shows knowledge of Homer in several other places: 1) he (*Ag.Ap.* 1:12) mentions Homer as an oral poet, noting his numerous inconsistencies; 2) he (*Ag.Ap.* 2:155) realizes that Homer nowhere employs the word νόμος ('law', 'custom'); 3) he quotes (*Ant.* 19:92) Homer's *Iliad* (14:90-91) when discussing the conspiracy to assassinate Caligula; 4) he shows a fondness for epithets which are distinctively associated with Homer, in particular πολύτροπος ('manifold', 'versatile') (*War* 1:347, 7:272, 7:451; *Ant.* 1:8, 2:303, 10:142, 15:179, 15:416, 17:125); 5) he shows a fondness for other Homeric expressions, for example, ἀνέτλη ('endured') (*Ant.* 19:321; cf. *Odyssey* 3:104, 10:327, 14:47), τλημονεστάτη ('most wretched') (*War* 5:19; cf. *Iliad* 10:231, 10:498, 21:430, normally used only in poetry in later Greek literature) and χῶρος ('place') (*War* 5:19; cf. *Iliad* 3:315, 3:344, 8:491, 10:520, 13:474; *Odyssey* 11:94, 14:2, normally used only in poetry).

[117] Feldman, 'Aqedah'.

[118] On Josephus' indebtedness to Herodotus see Brüne, *Flavius Josephus*, 164-68, and my 'Aqedah', n. 38.

he remarks that he will refrain from saying more about the ibises and snakes, 'for Greeks are not unacquainted with the nature of the ibis'.

Josephus' debt to Sophocles is seen particularly in his account of Solomon,[119] where he exaggerates Solomon's wisdom by stating (*Ant.* 8:30) that when no one could see what judgement to give, but all were mentally blinded (τῇ διανοίᾳ τετυφλωμένων), as by a riddle (αἰνίγματι), in finding a solution, the king alone devised a plan to discover the real mother in the dispute of the two harlots about the infants (1 Kgs 3:16). The addition about the mental blindness would remind the reader of the ironic fact that in Sophocles' *Oedipus the King* it is Oedipus who is mentally blinded but has physical sight at the beginning of the play, while the reverse is true for Teiresias the prophet, whereas at the end of the play the roles are reversed. The riddle would, of course, remind the reader of the fact that whereas others had failed to solve the riddle of the Sphinx, it was Oedipus who had succeeded in doing so.

THE QUALITIES OF BIBLICAL HEROES. The very fact that Josephus centers his narrative around great heroes, such as Abraham, Moses, Saul, David and Solomon, would defend the Jews against the charge (*Ag.Ap.* 2:135) that they had failed to produce marvelous (θαυμαστούς) men, such as inventors of the arts or outstandingly wise men. Hence, Josephus determined to follow the Peripatetic tradition[120] (his chief source for the last half of the *Antiquities* was, it appears, Nicolaus of Damascus, a well-known Peripatetic) and to stress the role of great men in history; and in his great apologetic work, *Against Apion* (2:136), he refers the reader to this goal of the *Antiquities* when he declares that 'our own famous men are deserving of winning no less praise than the Greek wise men and are familiar to readers of our *Antiquities*'. Indeed, the chief questions in his history are designed to ascertain the human motives of his heroes, whereas Scripture more often stresses the role of God as directing human actions.[121]

We may note, furthermore, that this same tendency to build up Jewish biblical heroes, notably Moses, is to be found in such Hellenistic Jewish writers as Aristeas (in his *Letter*), Artapanus, Ezekiel the tragedian, Philo the Elder, and Philo the philosopher. If we ask why a figure such as Ruth is not built up, the answer would seem to be that she was hardly a major historical figure and hence hardly a model for the range of virtues to be emulated by Josephus' Greek readers, and that she, as a woman, was subject to Josephus' patent misogyny, as seen, for example, in his snide remark (*War* 7:399) about the woman at Masada who was 'superior in sagacity and training to most of her sex'. On the other hand, it is interesting to note, as I[122] have remarked, that Josephus devotes approximately three times as much space to his encomium of Saul (*Ant.* 6:343-50) as to his eulogy of Moses (*Ant.* 4:328-31), or David (*Ant.* 7:390-91),

[119] See my 'Solomon', 82-84, 88-89.
[120] See my 'Saul', 46-48.
[121] See Heinemann, 'Josephus' Method', 185; and Lowy, *Principles*, 482.
[122] Feldman, 'Saul', 52.

four times as much as to his encomium of Samuel (*Ant.* 6:292-94), and approximately ten times as much as to his encomia of Isaac (*Ant.* 1:346), Jacob (*Ant.* 2:196), Joseph (*Ant.* 2:198), Joshua (*Ant.* 5:118), Samson (*Ant.* 5:317), and Solomon (*Ant.* 8:211). From this we may deduce that Josephus identified himself with Saul, who, like him, was a general, and looked upon him as a foremost paradigm in expressing the goals of his work, in terms of his specific apologetic aims.

If we examine such key figures in Josephus' narrative as Abraham, Joseph, Moses, Samson, Saul, David, Solomon, and Esther, we shall see that stress is generally placed on the external qualities of good birth and handsome stature, the four cardinal virtues of character – wisdom, courage, temperance, and justice – and the spiritual attribute of piety.[123] The Jewish hero must be, in effect, a Platonic-like philosopher-king, a high priest, and a prophet, all in one. The recitation of his virtues is a veritable aretalogy, such as was popular in Hellenistic times.

(a) *Genealogy and Handsomeness*

With regard to genealogy, the first of the thirty-six stages, according to the Greek rhetorician Theon, when praising a person, was to laud his ancestry. Thus, in the case of Abraham, Josephus tells us that Abraham was the tenth generation after Noah (Scripture simply enumerates his ancestors), and adds to his antiquity by remarking (*Ant.* 1:148) that he was born 992 years after the flood, thus increasing by some 701 years the interval between the flood and the birth of Abraham. Josephus would thus seem to be answering such anti-Semites as Apollonius Molon (*ap.* Eusebius, *Praeparatio Evangelica* 9:19, 2-3), who had declared that Abraham was born only three generations after Noah. In this connection, one recalls the remark (Plato, *Timaeus*, 22B) of the aged Egyptian priest to Solon, 'You Greeks are always children; in Greece there is no such thing as an old man'. In particular, the Egyptian sneers (*Timaeus*, 23B) at the genealogies of the Greeks, which, he says, are little better than nursery tales. As to Joseph, Josephus, in explaining why Jacob loved him more than his brothers, adds the extra-biblical explanation (*Ant.* 2:9) that he did so because of the beauty of person that he owed not only to his excellence of character but also to his good birth (εὐγένειαν), that is, the fact that his mother Rachel was exceptionally beautiful. Again, Amram, Moses' father, is described (*Ant.* 2:210) as of noble birth (εὖ γεγονότων), whereas the Bible (Exod 2:1) simply describes him as 'a man from the house of Levi'.

In addition, the great leader must be precocious as a child and unusually handsome. Thus Josephus (*Ant.* 2:230) remarks that Moses' growth in understanding (σύνεσις) far outstripped his physical growth, and that even in his

---

[123] See my 'Saul', 59-93. We may note that King David is praised for the same virtues (*Ant.* 7:390-91): wisdom (σώφρων), courage (ἀνδρεῖος), temperance (ἐπιεικής), and justice (δίκαιος), to which the quality of piety (εὐσέβεια) is also added (*Ant.* 6:160).

games he displayed his superiority (περιουσίαν), so that his achievements even at that tender age gave promise of greater deeds yet to come.[124] Such a picture is reminiscent of that of the ten-year-old future Persian king Cyrus, whose parentage was discovered through an incident which occurred while he was playing with the village boys, during which he ordered one of them to be beaten because he had disobeyed his command.

That the hero must be handsome may be perceived in the description of Jacobs' sons (*Ant.* 2:98), of whom Josephus says that it was impossible for any commoner to have reared any such with figures (μορφάς) so distinguished when even kings found it hard to raise the like. The same quality is stressed by Pharaoh's daughter Thermuthis when she first beholds (*Ant.* 2:224) the infant Moses and is enchanted by his size (μεγέθους) and beauty (κάλλους). Likewise, she speaks (*Ant.* 2:232) of both his divine beauty (μορφῇ τε θεῖον) and outstanding intellect (φρονήματι γενναῖον), the very nouns which are used by Dionysius of Halicarnassus (1:79, 10) in indicating the excellence of Romulus and Remus. Josephus (*Ant.* 2:230) adds that when Moses was three years old, God gave wondrous increase to his stature,[125] so that passers-by could not avoid being amazed at his beauty of form (εὐμορφίας) when they beheld him. Indeed, we are told (*Ant.* 2:231) that it often happened that persons meeting him as he was borne along the road turned (ἐπιστρέφεσθαι), being attracted by the appearance of the child, and neglected their serious affairs in order to give their time to gazing at him, so that he held his beholders spellbound with his bountiful and undiluted childish charm (χάρις ἡ παιδικὴ πολλὴ καὶ ἄκρατος).[126] Again, this seems to be a stock remark about the future great man, as we see, for example, in the statement of Apollonius-Iamblichus (10, p. 11, lines 6-7; cf. Apuleius, *Florida*) that everyone turned (ἐπέστρεφε) to look at the small Pythagoras; indeed, the verb which he uses for those who gazed is the same as that employed by Josephus.[127] Moreover, Josephus' version (*Ant.* 6:45) of 1 Sam 9:2 adds considerably to the picture of Saul, for he is not only young and tall but also best in shape (μορφὴν ἄριστος). Similarly, Josephus stresses (*Ant.* 6:164) David's handsomeness, particularly his ruddy colour and his piercing eyes. Furthermore, Josephus emphasizes (*Ant.* 7:189) Absalom's handsomeness when he adds that 'he had not suffered any loss of beauty

---

[124] To be sure, Moses' precocity is also recognized by Philo (*Moses* 1:5, 20), who notes that the young Moses did not engage in fun, frolic, and sport like an infant, even though his guardians were utterly lenient, but 'applied himself to learning and seeing what was sure to perfect the soul'. This precocity is also recognized in rabbinic literature (*Cant. Rabba* 1:26).

[125] The rabbinic tradition (*Yalkut Shimoni, Shemot*, 1:166) remarks that at the age of five Moses appeared grown both in stature and intelligence. On Moses' extraordinary growth see *Tanḥuma Shemot* 9, *B.T. Berakhot* 54b, and *B.T. Bekhorot* 44a, the last of which notes that Moses grew to be ten cubits (about fifteen feet) tall.

[126] Philo (*Moses* 2:70) similarly notes Moses' effect upon onlookers after his descent from Mount Sinai: 'He descended with a countenance far more beautiful than when he ascended, so that those who saw him were filled with awe and amazement'.

[127] Cited by Lévy, *Légende de Pythagore*, 141.

through sorrow or lack of care proper to a king's son, but was still remarkable and distinguished among all for his looks and bodily stature, and surpassed even those who lived in great luxury'. This stress on the importance of physical beauty reminds one of Plato's remark (*Republic* 7:535 A11-12) that the philosopher-kings should be, so far as possible, the most handsome (εὐειδεστάτους) persons. Indeed, in the very earliest of biographies, Isocrates' *Evagoras* (22-23), we find the qualities of beauty and bodily strength as the *sine qua non* for the hero.

(b) *The Cardinal Virtues*

The great hero, as we see particularly in the portraits of Abraham,[128] Moses, Saul, and David, must, like Plato's philosopher-king, possess the four cardinal virtues of wisdom, courage, temperance, and justice, plus the virtue of piety, which Plato (*Protagoras* 349B) already counts as the fifth of the virtues. Again, like Thucydides' ideal statesman (2:60-65), he must excel in ability to persuade, must be beyond corruption, and must put the nation above his own needs.

As to *wisdom*, Abraham is portrayed as a philosopher whose logic is impeccable (*Ant.* 1:154), who is clever in understanding (*Ant.* 1:154) (δεινὸς ὢν συνιέναι, a phrase reminiscent of Oedipus, φρονεῖν . . . δεινόν, Sophocles, *Oedipus Tyrannus* 316), who is able to arrive at an original and unique proof of the existence of God (*Ant.* 1:156)[129] from the irregularity of heavenly phenomena, in a form promulgated by the Greek philosophical schools, notably the Stoics. Indeed, his hearers are termed ἀκροωμένοις (*Ant.* 1:154), a word used especially of those who listen to lectures in the philosophical schools. Likewise, Isaac is praised (*Ant.* 1:261) for the reasonable calculation (εὐγνώμονι λογισμῷ) which he exhibited in settling the dispute over wells with Abimelech's shepherds. Jacob exercises wisdom (σοφίας) and intelligence (διανοίᾳ) in understanding the meaning of Joseph's dreams (*Ant.* 2:15). In turn, Josephus' tremendous understanding (σύνεσιν ἱκανώτατος, *Ant.* 2:80) recommends him to Pharaoh; and, in view of his incredible intelligence (πρὸς τὸ παράδοξον τῆς συνέσεως *Ant.* 2:91), he is given a name by Pharaoh signifying 'Discoverer of Secrets'. Moses (*Ant.* 4:328) likewise is eulogized as having surpassed in understanding (συνέσει) all men who have ever lived. The fact that Josephus uses the term 'lawgiver' (νομοθέτης) sixteen times in the first four books with regard to Moses, referring to him usually merely as 'the lawgiver', without explicitly naming him as Moses (just as Pseudo-Longinus 9:9 refers to him as θεσμοθέτης 'lawgiver', without deeming it necessary to name him), is an indication that to Josephus Moses is *the* wise man *par excellence*, to be bracketed with the Spartan Lycurgus, the Athenian Solon, and the Roman Numa Pompilius, even though,

---

[128] In connection with Abraham, in particular, Josephus seems to be trying to answer the charge, reported and refuted by Philo (*On Abraham* 33:178), that Abraham did not do anything unique or remarkable.

[129] See my 'Abraham', 145-50.

strictly speaking, it is God alone Who is the lawgiver.[130] His wisdom as a legislator is to be seen in the fact, noted by Josephus (*Ant.* 3:317), that although it is possible for violators to escape detection, there is no Jew who does not obey his ordinances, as if he were present to punish any breach of discipline.

Even in the case of Samson, where many commentators have remarked that he appears rather foolish, since he could not reasonably have expected anyone to solve his riddle (Judg 14:22), inasmuch as it was based on an incident which no one had witnessed, in Josephus (*Ant.* 5:290) Samson's reputation for wisdom is not damaged, since Josephus converts the riddle into a story (λόγον), which is exactly what it is. Moreover, by introducing the non-biblical statement that the Philistines at the wedding feast at Timnah were ambitious to win renown for sagacity (συνέσεως) in explaining his story, Josephus (*Ant.* 5:290) stresses Samson's own sagacity.

Likewise, as Satran[131] has pointed out, the disciplined pursuit of purification has brought Daniel in Josephus to the supreme achievement of the Graeco-Roman sage, of the type found in Philostratus' *Life of Apollonius of Tyana*, the movement from human to divine wisdom.

Connected with the virtue of wisdom is *excellence in the sciences*, a field which had become increasingly important in the Hellenistic period. Thus Josephus (*Ant.* 1:106) explains the longevity of the early patriarchs by declaring that God rewarded them with long life not only for their virtue (ἀρετήν) but also in order to promote the utility of their discoveries in astronomy and geometry. Again, Josephus (*Ant.* 1:167) adds to the biblical narrative that Abraham graciously taught (χαρίζεται) the Egyptians arithmetic (the study of which had been stressed by both Plato and Isocrates, the founders of the two leading schools of education in the fourth century B.C.E.) and astronomy (which was to become the most popular of the four branches of mathematics in Hellenistic times),[132] two sciences, according to Josephus (*Ant.* 1:168), of which the Egyptians had previously been ignorant.[133]

Moreover, the true scientist must show his open-mindedness by being willing to change his mind if honestly convinced by others.[134] Such a quality is exhibited by Abraham (*Ant.* 1:161), who visits Egypt, not merely, as indicated in the

[130] On Josephus' portrait of Moses, particularly as the virtuous lawgiver, see Graf, *Hellenization*, 131-44.

[131] Satran, 'Daniel', 33-48.

[132] Marrou, *History*, 182.

[133] We may note that whereas Artapanus, the Hellenistic Jewish historian (ca. 100 B.C.E.) says (*ap.* Eusebius, *Praeparatio Evangelica* 9:18, 1) that Abraham taught astrology to the Egyptian pharaoh, Josephus elevates Abraham by declaring that he consorted with the most learned of the Egyptians. Cf. Attridge, 'Historiography', 165-67.

[134] Cf. Apollonius, Josephus' contemporary, who similarly visits the Magi, the Indians, and the Egyptians (*ap.* Philostratus, *Vita Apollonii*, 1:26, 3:16ff., 6:10ff.). Josephus himself (*Ag.Ap.* 1:176-82) tells of a learned Jew who visited Aristotle to converse with him and to test his learning but who, in the end, imparted to Aristotle something of his own.

Bible (Gen 12:10), in order to obtain food because of the famine in Canaan, but also to hear what the famed Egyptian priests said about their gods, with the intention, characteristic of true wise men, either of adopting their views if he found them more excellent than his own or of converting them if his views should prove superior. The picture, as I[135] have suggested, is reminiscent of Solon the wise Athenian (Plato, *Timaeus* 22A), who discovered, when he visited Egypt, that neither he nor any other Greek had any knowledge of antiquity worth speaking of, and of the pre-Socratic philosophers, such as Pythagoras, who allegedly visited Egypt to become acquainted with the science and the other esoteric lore of the Egyptians.

Another attribute connected with wisdom, as we may see in Thucydides' (2:60) portrait of the ideal statesman, is *the ability to persuade the people*. Thus Josephus remarks (*Ant.* 1:154) that Abraham was persuasive (πιθανός) with his hearers (ἀκροωμένοις, a word used especially of students who listen to lectures in the philosophical schools)[136] and was not mistaken in his inferences. His power of persuasion is seen particularly in his ability to convince the Egyptians (*Ant.* 1:167) on any subject which he undertook to teach. As to Moses, it is nothing short of amazing that Josephus is able to praise his extraordinary ability in addressing a crowd (*Ant.* 3:13, 4:328), despite the fact that the Bible declares that he had a speech impediment (Exod 6:12). Likewise, Joshua is termed highly gifted in speech (*Ant.* 3:49) and supremely skilled in expounding his ideas clearly to the multitude (*Ant.* 5:118). Again, Nehemiah, before approaching the king for permission to go to Jerusalem, prays (*Ant.* 11:165) to God to give his words some measure of grace and persuasion (πειθώ).

The second of the cardinal virtues, *courage and skill in battle*, is stressed by Josephus in a number of additions to the biblical narrative, especially since the Jews had been reproached with cowardice by such anti-Semites as Apollonius Molon (*Ag.Ap.* 2:148). Moreover, Josephus himself had been subjected to such a charge (*War* 3:358). Thus, whereas the rabbis (*B.T. Sanhedrin* 96a) stress the miraculous help which Abraham received from an angel named Night in attacking the Assyrians, Josephus adds a number of details to enhance Abraham's military prowess, notably that the battle was a stubborn contest (*Ant.* 1:172), that Abraham (*Ant.* 1:177) determined to help the Sodomites without delay, that he surprised them before they had time to arm, and that he slew some in their beds, while others who were drunk took to flight. This military tradition is continued, according to Josephus (*Ant.* 1:240-41), who quotes a certain Cleodemus-Malchus, by two of Abraham's sons of Keturah, who joined Heracles, the most famous of the Greek legendary heroes, in his campaign against Libya and

---

[135] Feldman, 'Abraham', 151-52.
[136] Cf. Xenophon, *Symposium* 3:6.

Antaeus, the giant son of Earth. Josephus, who normally, as we shall see, inveighs bitterly against intermarriage, here seems to record proudly the fact that Heracles married the daughter of one of them. Moreover, Jacobs' sons are described (*Ant.* 2:7) as courageous for much labour and endurance of toil (πρὸς ἔργα χειρῶν καὶ πόνων ὑπομονὴν ἦσαν εὔψυχοι).

The supreme example of military acumen and courage is Moses, who (*Ant.* 2:238-51), is depicted as the conqueror of Ethiopia, a land that had successfully resisted invasion by generals of the caliber of Cambyses (Herodotus, *Historiae* 3:17-25) and Alexander the Great. As Holladay[137] has noted, Moses is never called στρατηγός or even ἡγεμών in the Septuagint, whereas in Josephus these are frequently used, particularly to describe Moses' role in the wilderness, where he is the model general, unperturbed despite great difficulties, unconcerned about his own safety despite grave threats to his life, always encouraging his troops, and admired by his father-in-law Raguel (*Ant.* 3:65) for his gallantry (ἀνδραγαθίας) which he had devoted to the salvation of his friends. Moses (*Ant.* 3:42) shows his ability in his excellent strategy in attacking the Amalekites before they were too strong, in exhorting his men (*Ant.* 3:47), in his preparations for the battle (*Ant.* 3:5), and even in his ability to lead a retreat (*Ant.* 4:9). Indeed, in summarizing his career (*Ant.* 4:329), Josephus selects two traits in which Moses particularly excelled, his ability as a general, where he had few to equal him, and his role as a prophet, where he was unique.[138] Again, one of the principal factors leading to Moses' choice of Joshua (*Ant.* 3:49) to lead his army is that he is extremely courageous (ἀνδρειότατον) and valiant in enduring toil (πόνους ὑποστῆναι γενναῖον). Joshua is later (*Ant.* 5:118) eulogized as stout-hearted (εὔψυχος) and greatly daring (μεγαλότολμος).

Moreover, Josephus omits details that would detract from the heroic stature of his biblical personalities. Hence, since the Greeks generally had contempt for menial labour, and since the toil of working at the mill was a common and much-dreaded punishment of slaves often referred to in the comic poets, Josephus is careful to omit the fact (Judg 16:21) that Samson 'did grind in the prison house'.

Likewise, in his long appreciation of Saul's character, Josephus (*Ant.* 6:347) declares categorically that the terms 'stout-hearted' (εὔψυχος), 'greatly daring' (μεγαλότολμος), and 'contemptuous of danger' (τῶν δεινῶν καταφρονητής) can be justly applied only to such as have emulated Saul, since he engaged in his exploits knowing beforehand that he was destined to die.[139]

The third of the cardinal virtues, *temperance*, is likewise a recurring theme in Josephus, who identifies it (*Ant.* 6:63) with *modesty*. Just as the Greeks had to

---

[137]   Holladay, *Theios Aner*, 69.
[138]   Josephus (*Ant.* 3:265-68) also replies to the charge (for example, by Manetho, *ap. Ag.Ap.* 1:279) that Moses was a leper by declaring that this could hardly have been so in view of the laws that he promulgated on leprosy.
[139]   On the build-up of Saul's quality of courage by Josephus see my 'Saul', 66-79.

be constantly reminded of this virtue through the motto at Delphi, μηδὲν ἄγαν, so the Israelites had to be exhorted (*Ant.* 4:189) by Moses before his death to learn moderation (σωφρονήσειν); and he notes that he himself had refrained from wrath at the moment that he felt most aggrieved by them. Moses' own modesty is shown (*Ant.* 3:74) by the fact that he was willing to take advice from his father-in-law and that he acknowledged this assistance. Likewise (*Ant.* 4:157), Moses modestly recorded the prophecies of Balaam, though he could easily have appropriated them for himself, since there was no witness to convict him. Thus Moses was not guilty of the sin of plagiarism so frequently practiced in antiquity.[140] Indeed, in his final encomium of Moses, Josephus (*Ant.* 4:328) singles out his thorough command (αὐτοκράτωρ), a term indicating that he was commander-in-chief, so to speak, of the passions. Similarly, Samson shows the quality of humility in acknowledging (*Ant.* 5:302), after he had been seized by a mighty thirst, that human virtue (ἀρετή) is nothing, since all is attributable to God.

The fourth of the cardinal virtues, *justice*, is displayed by Abraham (*Ant.* 1:158), who is termed a just (δίκαιος) man in a passage which Josephus quotes from the Babylonian historian Berossus. We read (*Ant.* 3:66) that everyone came to Moses, thinking that only thus would they obtain justice (τοῦ δικαίου), so that (*Ant.* 3:67) even those who lost their cases were convinced that it was justice (δικαιοσύνην) rather than cupidity that determined their fate. To parallel the embezzlement charge against Pericles (Plato, *Gorgias* 516A), Josephus elaborates (*Ant.* 4:46) the point that Moses did not accept a present from a single Hebrew to pervert justice, so that we see that Moses possesses one of the qualities of the ideal statesman, who, according to Thucydides (2:60, 5) must be able to resist a bribe. Again, when the people demand that Samuel name a king for them, he (*Ant.* 6:36) is sorely aggrieved because of his innate sense of justice; and in his eulogy of him Josephus (*Ant.* 6:294) describes him as a just (δίκαιος) and kindly man. Similarly, when Jonathan (*Ant.* 6:212) appeals to Saul, Josephus declares that thus a just cause (δίκαιος λόγος) prevailed over anger and fear. Again, one of the qualities which God declares (*Ant.* 6:160) that Samuel is to look for when he is about to select David as king is justice. Indeed, when David spares Saul's life, the latter compliments him (*Ant.* 6:290) for having shown the righteousness (δικαιοσύνην) of the ancients. Josephus likewise editorializes (*Ant.* 7:110) in declaring that David was just (δίκαιος) by nature and that he looked only toward the truth in giving judgment; and in his final eulogy one of his qualities singled out for praise (*Ant.* 7:391) is that he was just. Solomon, Josephus (*Ant.* 8:21) declares, was not hindered by his youth from dispensing justice (δικαιοσύνην); and God, in His turn, promises to

---

[140] For examples of plagiarism see Aristophanes' accusation of Eupolis (*Clouds* 553-54) and Eupolis' of Aristophanes (frag. 78 Kock). Plato was accused of deriving the idea of the *Republic* from the Sophist Protagoras. In Hellenistic Alexandria investigations of plagiarism were apparently frequent.

preserve the kingdom for his descendants if he continues to be righteous (δίκαιος).

Connected with the virtue of justice is the enormous responsibility to tell the *truth*. That the Greeks realized its importance is to be seen in the fact that Herodotus quite obviously admires the fact that Persian sons are carefully instructed to speak the truth (*Historiae* 1:136) and that they regard it as the most disgraceful thing in the world to tell a lie (*Historiae* 1:139), this in contrast to the reputation that the Greeks themselves had, from the figure of Odysseus on down, for cleverness in lying. Hence, Josephus takes pains and explains (*Ant.* 1:162, 1:207) why Abraham has to devise a lying scheme when he comes to Egypt and to Abimelech with his wife Sarah; and he omits (*Ant.* 1:209) the passage (Gen 20:9) in which Abimelech rebukes Abraham for his deceit. Moreover, he describes Moses (*Ant.* 4:303) as one who had in no respect deviated from the truth. Likewise, Josephus (*Ant.* 7:110) remarks that David was of just nature and that when he gave judgment he considered only the truth. Again, Mephibosheth declares his confidence that no calumny enters David's mind, 'for it is just and loves the truth' (*Ant.* 7:269).

Likewise, coupled with justice is the virtue of *humanity* (φιλανθρωπία), as we see in Philo,[141] just as its Latin equivalent, *humanitas*, is likewise connected with the virtue of justice.[142] In particular, Reuben, in his speech to Joseph (*Ant.* 2:101), declares his confidence in his humanity (φιλανθρωπίαν). Moreover, in his final eulogy of David's character, Josephus (*Ant.* 7:391) stresses, among other qualities, that he was just and humane (φιλάνθρωπος), 'qualities which are especially applicable to kings'. Here again Josephus seems to be answering such anti-Semites as Apollonius Molon and Lysimachus (*Ag.Ap.* 2:145), who had charged the Jews with hatred of mankind, as repeated somewhat later also in Tacitus *Histories* 5:5.1, who refers to the Jews' hatred of the human race *(adversus omnes alios hostile odium)*, whereas, in fact, says Josephus (*Ag.Ap.* 2:146), humanity is one of the qualities especially fostered by the law code of the Jews.

Finally, that *piety*[143] is coupled with the other virtues is clear from Josephus' statement (*Ant.* 1:6) that it was under the great lawgiver Moses that the Israelites were trained in piety (εὐσέβειαν) and the exercise of the other virtues. Furthermore, he indicates the importance of piety when he declares (*Ant.* 1:21) that when once Moses had won the obedience of the Israelites to the dictates of piety he had no further difficulty in persuading them of all the remaining virtues. Indeed, it is the piety of Abraham and Isaac that Josephus stresses in his account of the readiness of Abraham to sacrifice his son (*Ant.*

---

[141] Philo, *On the Change of Names* 40:225; *Moses* 2:2,9; *On the Decalogue* 30:164. See the discussion by Wolfson, *Philo*, 2:218-20.

[142] Cf. Macrobius on Cicero's *Somnium Scipionis* 1:8, cited by Wolfson, *Philo* 2, 220, n. 146.

[143] Cf. Aristotle, *De Virtutibus et Vitiis* 5, 1250b22-23, who defines piety as either a part of justice or an accompaniment of it.

1:222-36).[144] Again, in his one-sentence eulogy of Jacob (*Ant.* 2:190), the sole virtue which he mentions is his piety, in which quality he is said to have been second to none of the forefathers. Furthermore, when describing (*Ant.* 3:491) the qualities of Joshua, he notes the singular piety which he had learned from his mentor Moses. Again, in singling out the qualities which Samuel is to look for in a king, God first mentions (*Ant.* 6:160) piety (εὐσεβείᾳ) and only then mentions the virtues of justice, bravery, and obedience, declaring that these are the qualities of which beauty of soul consists. As to Saul's piety, Josephus (*Ant.* 6:124) stresses his respect for an oath, a matter which was so important to the Romans, as we see in Cicero (*De Officiis* 1:7, 1, 10); and, indeed, when Jonathan faces death at the hands of his father because of his vow, he declares that he would be very glad to undergo death for the sake of his piety (εὐσεβείας, *Ant.* 6:127). Even when the Bible (1 Sam 13:8-14) exhibits Saul's lack of piety in offering a sacrifice before waiting for Samuel, Josephus (*Ant.* 6:103) offers an excuse, namely that he did so out of necessity because of the desertion of his frightened troops.[145] Similar attributions of piety are to be found in the case of David (*Ant.* 6:160, 7:130, 8:196, 8:315), Solomon (*Ant.* 8:13, 9:22), and the later kings, notably Hezekiah (*Ant.* 9:260, 9:276) and Josiah (*Ant.* 10:50, 10:51, 10:56).[146]

ANSWERS TO ANTI-SEMITIC CHARGES. In addition to answering the anti-Semitic contention that the Jews had produced no great men, Josephus seeks to answer other charges. Living in Rome during the period from 70 to the end of the century, Josephus may have had contact with the writings,[147] or at least the ideas, of such vicious anti-Semites as Quintilian and Martial, and perhaps Tacitus and Juvenal. As to the charge of misanthropy, even Hecataeus (*ap.* Diodorus, *Bibl. Hist.* 40:3, 4), who is otherwise well disposed toward the Jews, describes the Jewish way of life as 'somewhat unsocial' (ἀπάνθρωπόν τινα) and hostile to foreigners (μισόξενον). The Alexandrian Lysimachus (probably first century B.C.E.) reflects such a charge when he says (*ap.* Josephus, *Ag.Ap.* 1:309) that Moses instructed the Israelites 'to show goodwill to no man, to offer

---

[144] The striking omission from Josephus' account of the word which the rabbis regarded as the single most important word in it, 'aqad, 'bound', (Gen 22:9) and its replacement by a homily delivered by Abraham to Isaac is due, it would seem, to the fact that the physical binding of Isaac would probably have been too much for a Greek audience and would have been incriminating toward Abraham, as well as toward Isaac (since it would have implied that it was necessary thus to prevent him from trying to escape). Josephus deliberately heightens the heroic faith of Isaac in depicting him as rushing (*Ant.* 1:232) upon the altar.

[145] On Saul's piety see my 'Saul', 83-93.

[146] Attridge, *Interpretation*, 183, denies that the Hellenistic historians stressed the importance of the specifically religious response (εὐσέβεια) to the facts of providence. But, we may note, Dionysius of Halicarnassus (4:778) praises Xenophon for displaying, first of all, the virtue of piety. Moreover, Diodorus (1:22), in his prologue, likewise stresses piety and justice as the two virtues which historians extol in their heroes.

[147] On the question of Josephus' knowledge of Latin see Thackeray, *Josephus*, 119-20; Daube, 'Three Legal Notes', 191-94; and my comments thereon, *Josephus*, 836.

not the best but the worst advice and to overthrow any temples and altars of gods which they found'. Tacitus (*Histories* 5:1) remarks that while the Jews are extremely loyal to one another and always ready to show compassion to compatriots alone, they feel only hate and enmity toward all other peoples. Juvenal (*Satires* 14:103-104) goes so far as to attack the Jews for not showing the way or a fountain spring to any but fellow-Jews. Haman, we may note, according to Josephus (*Ant.* 11:212) charges that the Jews refuse to mingle with others (ἄμικτον, a term used of the Centaurs in Sophocles, *Trachiniae* 1095, and of the Cyclopes in Euripides, *Cyclops* 429), are unsocial (ἀσύμφυλον, 'not akin', 'incompatible', 'unsuitable'), and are in customs and practices the enemy both of the Persians and, indeed, of all mankind.

In answer to such charges, and particularly of the Alexandrian anti-Semites, Josephus (*Ant.* 1:166) declares, in his narrative of Abraham's visit to Egypt, that it is the Egyptians who disparaged one another's practices and were consequently at enmity with one another, in contrast to Abraham, who patiently conferred with each party and pointed out the flaws in their arguments. In addition, Abraham is depicted (*Ant.* 1:181) as graciously reciprocating Melchizedek's lavish hospitality with a more gracious offer of a tithe of all the spoil which he had taken in the campaign against the Syrians, whereas in the Bible (Gen 14:20) it is not clear whether Abraham gave a tithe or received it. Moreover, it is in answer to such a charge as that repeated by Tacitus that Jews were devoid of pity for anyone who was not of their religion that Josephus' Abraham (*Ant.* 1:199) shows pity for his friends the Sodomites.[148] The fact, we may add, that the Sodomites are depicted in even blacker colours in Josephus than in the Bible glorifies still more the figure of Abraham for showing pity toward them and for praying in their behalf. Moreover, Josephus (*Ant.* 1:200) remarks that Lot had acquired the lesson of hospitality from Abraham; but the rabbis speak in general terms, whereas Josephus declares that Lot learned to be φιλάνθρωπος, thus answering those critics who claimed that the Jews were misanthropes. Likewise, Abraham (*Ant.* 1:211) shows devotion and kindness to Abimelech in order to demonstrate that he was in no way responsible for the king's illness but eager for his recovery. Furthermore, Josephus (*Ant.* 1:218) completely omits the pathetic scene (Gen 21:16) in which Hagar weeps when cast out into the wilderness by Sarah, since this might cast an unfavourable reflection upon Abraham as pitiless.

Again, whereas the Jews had been accused of a blood libel by Apion (*ap.* Josephus, *Ag.Ap.* 2:91-96) and by Damocritus (*ap.* Suidas, *s.v.*), Josephus (*Ant.* 1:233) stresses, as we have noted,[149] the contrast between the sacrifice of Isaac, which was not consummated, and that of Iphigenia, which was actually carried out. In particular, he puts a speech (*Ant.* 1:233-36) into the mouth of

---

[148] We may remark that it is only in the Zohar (1:112b), which was codified in the thirteenth century, that we hear of Abraham's friendship with the Sodomites.

[149] Feldman, 'Aqedah'.

God, rather than of an angel as in Gen 22:11, that He does not crave human blood and that He is not capricious in taking away what He has given. This is, as we have noted, in direct contrast to Artemis, who (Euripides, *Iphigenia at Aulis* 1524-25) 'rejoices in human sacrifices'.

David (*Ant.* 7:391), far from being a misanthrope, is described as φιλάνθρωπος, 'humane', the very opposite of ἀπάνθρωπος. Josephus, moreover, in the spirit of tolerance, follows the Septuagint (Exod 22:28) in declaring that the Jews are forbidden to blaspheme the gods of others (*Ant.* 4:207 and *Ag.Ap.* 2:237) out of respect for the very word 'god'. Likewise, for the same reason, presumably, he omits (*Ant.* 9:138) the conversion of the temple of Baal into a latrine (2 Kgs 10:27). Moreover, significantly, though he generally follows closely the Apocryphal Addition C, which contains Esther's prayer to God, Josephus omits the detestation of non-Jews expressed by Esther (C26-27). Likewise, though Additions A and F were available to Josephus,[150] he omits them, presumably because in them the struggle between Haman and Mordecai is viewed not as a personal one but as part of the eternal conflict between Jew and non-Jew. In answer to the same charge of misanthropy, Josephus' King Solomon (*Ant.* 8:117), in his prayer at the dedication of the Temple, specifically denies that the Jews are inhuman (ἀπάνθρωποι) by nature or unfriendly to non-Jews, and expresses the wish that all men equally may receive aid from God and enjoy His blessings.

APPEAL TO POLITICAL, MILITARY AND GEOGRAPHIC INTERESTS. To further appeal to the non-Jews and secularly educated Jews in his audience, Josephus catered to their political, military and geographic interests.

Thus, in his prooemium, Josephus (*Ant.* 1:5) sets forth as the goal of his work that it should embrace not only the entire ancient history of the Jews but also an evaluation of their *political constitution* (διάταξιν τοῦ πολιτεύματος). He appeals to his politically-minded audience by stressing the theme of civil strife (στάσις) so familiar to readers of Thucydides' description (3:82-84) of revolution at Corcyra. Thus he portrays (*Ant.* 1:117) the punishment inflicted by God upon the builders of the Tower of Babel as discord (στάσις, a word not found in the Septuagint version, Gen 11:9), created by having them speak various languages. Again, according to Josephus' addition (*Ant.* 1:164), God thwarted Pharaoh's unjust passion toward Sarah by bringing about an outbreak of disease and of political strife (στάσει τῶν πραγμάτων). Similarly, in his treatment of the rebellion of Korah, Josephus (*Ant.* 4:12) remarks that it was a sedition (στάσις) 'for which we know of no parallel, whether among Greeks or barbarians', clearly implying that information about seditions was familiar to his readers. Likewise, in discussing the consequences of the seduction of the Hebrew youth by the Midianite women, Josephus (*Ant.* 4:140) remarks that the whole army was soon permeated by a sedition far worse than that of Korah.

[150] See Feldman, 'Esther', 164.

Indeed, a good portion of Book 4 (11-66, 141-55) of the *Antiquities* is devoted to accounts that illustrated the degree to which στάσις is the mortal enemy of political states, a subject particularly stressed by Josephus as a comment on the warring factions among his contemporary Jews during the war against the Romans.

Josephus' acquaintance with the terminology of politics is especially manifest in his graphic description (*Ant.* 5:132-35) of the results of the peace which the Israelites established with the Canaanites after their initial entry into Canaan. The sequence of luxury (τρυφῆς)[151] and voluptuousness (ἡδονῆς) and pleasure of lucre (ἡδονῇ τοῦ κερδαίνειν) and gross recklessness (ἄδειαν, 'lack of scruple', 'lack of restraint'), leading to disdain for the order (κόσμου) of the constitution (πολιτείας) and for the laws (νόμων) and to grave sedition (στάσις . . . δεινή), thus corrupting the aristocracy (ἀριστοκρατίαν), is familiar to readers of the Greek and Roman orators and historians.[152] Furthermore, Josephus (*Ant.* 4:297) declares, in a passage imitating Thucydides (6:72), that divided control (πολυαρχία) makes prompt governmental action impossible and thus injures those who practice it. There is a further purpose in such a discussion in that one of the charges made by the anti-Semite Apion (*Ag.Ap.* 2:68) is that of fomenting sedition *(seditionis)* in Alexandria; and Josephus stresses throughout that the Israelites are conspicuously well aware of the dangers of such strife, and that it is the enemies of the Jews (namely the Egyptians) who are the real promotors of sedition, whereas the Jews are noted for their concord.

Josephus also appealed to his educated readers by his interest in the question of the ideal form of government. Like Plato, with whom, as we have seen, he was clearly acquainted, he was filled with contempt for the masses. Thus he adds a snide remark (*Ant.* 3:5), directed against the rabble (ὄχλος) of women and children, who, he says, were responsible for vitiating the nobler instincts of the Israelites in the desert. He describes (*Ant.* 4:36-37) the rebellious Israelite assembly in terms familiar from Plato (*Laws*, 2:671A), as a tumultuous (θορυβώδη) mass (ὅμιλος), with its innate delight in decrying those in authority and ready to be swayed by what anyone said. He returns to the theme of the fickleness of the mob when he speaks sneeringly (*Ant.* 6:81) of 'all that a crowd, elated by success, is wont to utter against those who were of late disparaging the authors of it'. Indeed, in his summary (*Ant.* 4:223) of the Mosaic Code, Josephus declares that aristocracy is the best form of government; and, in fact,

---

[151] A similar condemnation of luxury (τρυφᾶν) and lack of exertion (ἀπόνως) is to be found in Moses' condemnation (*Ant.* 4:167) of the tribes of Gad, Reuben, and half the tribe of Manasseh for requesting the recently won Amorite land for their flocks. Likewise, Samuel's sons are condemned (*Ant.* 6:34) for abandoning themselves to luxury (τρυφήν), thereby acting in defiance of God. On the contrary, when David (*Ant.* 7:96) refuses to succumb to idleness or slackness (μηδὲν ἀργὸν μηδὲ ῥάθυμον) this leads to victory over the Philistines and his other enemies.

[152] Cf. Polybius, *Historiae* 6:57, and Livy, *Praefatio*, for the political effects of prosperity and luxury.

when the Israelites demand a king, Samuel expresses (*Ant.* 6:36) his keen preference for an aristocratic government, 'accounting it divine and productive of bliss to those who adopted it'.

On the other hand, the worst form of government, as in Plato (*Republic* 566C-580B) is tyranny. Thus Josephus (*Ant.* 1:114) declares that the rebel Nimrod gradually transformed his state into a tyranny, completely dependent upon his own power. Again, when Zambrias (Zimri) attacks Moses (*Ant.* 4:146) it is for acting tyrannically (τυραννικῶς) under pretext of laws but actually robbing the Israelites of the sweet things of life and of self-determination (αὐτεξούσιον).[153] Moreover, Josephus (*Ant.* 5:234) attacks Abimelech for transforming the government into a tyranny, acting in defiance of the laws and of the principles of justice. Likewise, the behaviour of the sons of the high priest Eli (*Ant.* 5:339) is said to differ not at all from a tyranny in their violation of all the laws.

Josephus' highlighting of the *military context* of the Bible is to be expected in view of his own experience as a general. This is particularly to be seen in his paraphrase of the story of Balaam, where Josephus (*Ant.* 4:100) has inserted the extra-biblical theme of the Israelites' desire for war and has connected the episode of the war against Sihon and Og with the Balaam incident that follows. Furthermore, Josephus (*Ant.* 4:156) looks upon the Balaam episode as the preliminary to the war against the Midianites.

As to *geography*, the advances in scientific geography made by figures such as Eratosthenes during the Hellenistic period led to renewed interest on the part of historians such as Polybius and Strabo in descriptive geography. In line with this trend, Josephus (*Ant.* 1:38) introduces the conception, well known to his Greek audience, of a stream encircling the entire earth. In particular, he expands very considerably (*Ant.* 1:122-47) the biblical account of the table of nations descended from Noah's sons (Gen 10), as well as of Abraham's sons by Keturah (*Ant.* 1:238-41) and of the sons of Esau (*Ant.* 2:4-6). He is particularly interested in identifying the various peoples mentioned by the Bible.

APPEAL TO PHILOSOPHIC INTEREST. The very fact that Josephus compares the religious groupings of the Jews to the Greek philosophical schools, asserting (*Life* 12) that the Pharisees are a sect very similar to the Stoic school (implying that the Sadducees are comparable to the Epicureans, and that the Essenes [*Ant.* 15:371] follow the Pythagorean way of life), is an indication of the philosophical interests that he expected his audience to have, especially since such comparisons would hardly appear to be central to one who viewed the religious dimensions of these groups. Inasmuch as Stoicism was the favourite

---

[153] Cf. Van Unnik, 'Josephus' Account', 255-56, who notes the philosophico-ethical context in which this word occurs in Epictetus (*Diss.* 4:1, 62 and 4:1, 68), Diogenianus Epic. (frag. 3, *ap.* Eusebius, *Praeparatio Evangelica* 6:8, 36) and Clement of Alexandria (*Quis Dives Salvetur* 10:1). On the other hand, Moses is praised (*Ag.Ap.* 2:173) for leaving nothing, however insignificant, to the individual discretion (αὐτεξούσιον).

philosophy of Hellenistic intellectuals,[154] it is not surprising that he should attempt to appeal particularly to them in his recasting of the biblical narrative. Indeed, at the very beginning of his account, Josephus employs Stoic terminology in his extra-biblical statement (*Ant.* 1:46) that God had decreed for Adam and Eve a life of happiness unmolested (ἀπαθῆ) by all ill. We should note that the term ἀπαθής, as well as the corresponding noun ἀπάθεια (freedom from emotional disturbance), is a common Stoic term with reference to freedom from emotion.[155] That Stoic influence is at work here is indicated by the fact that Josephus does not in either passage employ the synonymous word ἀβλαβής, which means 'unharmed' and which he uses on six occasions in the first half of the *Antiquities*.

Another Stoic term, πρόνοια, appears no fewer than seventy-four times in the first half of the *Antiquities*. Thus, in the primitive utopia (*Ant.* 1:461), all things that contribute to enjoyment are said to spring up spontaneously through God's providence (πρόνοιαν). Likewise, as I[156] have endeavoured to show, Abraham's teleological proof for the existence of God (*Ant.* 1:156) from the irregularities of the heavenly bodies is in the form of the proofs promulgated by the Greek philosophical schools, notably the Stoics, as we can see from several favourite Stoic words (προνοῆσαι, εὐταξία, τοῦ κελεύοντος). It is, moreover, significant that in the very next sentence after this proof, Josephus refers to the Chaldeans, to whom, as Wolfson[157] has astutely remarked, Philo (*On the Migration of Abraham* 32:179) imputes certain conceptions of God which are definitely Stoic. Likewise, in his version of Abraham's readiness to sacrifice his son Isaac, Josephus, realizing that to present Abraham as being motivated by mere blind faith would have proven unsatisfactory to his cultured Greek readers, depicts him (*Ant.* 1:225) in the guise of a kind of Stoic philosopher, reasoning that 'all that befell His favoured ones' was ordained by His providence (προνοίας). Likewise, Moses is presented (*Ant.* 2:229) as a Stoic sage, remarkable for his contempt for toils (πόνων καταφρονήσει), a typically Stoic phrase. Furthermore, as Holladay[158] has remarked, Moses' emphasis on Law (νόμος) is in accord with the Stoic view that regarded νόμος as the expression of the cosmos and that viewed man as a κοσμοπολίτης who must arrange his life in accordance with universal law; hence, by allegorically imputing cosmic significance (*Ant.* 3:181-87) to the tabernacle, the twelve loaves, the candelabrum, the tapestries, and the high priest's garments, Josephus was appealing to the Stoic view that law must have a cosmic dimension. Furthermore, Josephus (*Ant.* 10:278) goes out of his way in his paraphrase of the book of Daniel to note how mistaken are the Epicureans who exclude Providence (πρόνοιαν) from

---

[154] See Tarn and Griffith, *Hellenistic Civilisation*, 325; Martin, 'Josephus' Use of *Heimarmene*', 127-37.
[155] See Feldman, 'Aqedah', notes 30 and 36.
[156] Feldman, 'Abraham', 146-50.
[157] Wolfson, *Philo* 1, 176-77 and 2, 78.
[158] Holladay, *Theios Aner*, 102.

human life.[159] Josephus even goes so far as to introduce (*Ant.* 6:296) a reference to the philosophical school of Cynics where Nabal is described as a hard man and of bad character, who lived according to the practices of the Cynics, whereas the Hebrew original reads that 'he was a Calebite' and the Septuagint, understanding this word to come from the Hebrew word for dog, *kelev*, read κυνικός('churlish').

DRAMATIC MOTIFS AND LANGUAGE. Josephus, as we have noted, has Hellenized his narrative by including many phrases from Aeschylus, Sophocles, and Euripides. In addition, he also seeks to win his intellectual audience by presenting them with themes familiar to them from the tragedians. Thus we find the motif of ὕβρις and its consequences introduced at many points. For example, whereas the Bible (Gen 6:5) speaks merely of the wickedness and the evil thoughts of the sons of the angels, Josephus (*Ant.* 1:73) converts this into the language of Greek tragedy by remarking that they were overbearing (ὑβριστάς) and disdainful (ὑπερόπτας) of every virtue, being over-confident of their strength. Likewise, when the Bible (Gen 6:11-13) declares that God decided to destroy the human race because the earth was corrupt and filled with violence, Josephus (*Ant.* 1:100) again, employing the language of tragedy, says that he did so because of the outrages (ἐξύβριζον) with which mankind met God's reverent regard and goodness. Likewise, Josephus (*Ant.* 1:113) describes the generation of the Tower of Babel in terms of the typical tragic sequence of prosperity (εὐδαιμονεῖν), insolence (ὕβρις) and punishment. Josephus dwells (*Ant.* 1:110) on the wilful blindness (ἀμαθίας, 'ignorance', 'stupidity') of the generation of the Tower of Babel in refusing to listen to God's advice to found colonies (an addition that the Greeks, so renowned for the foundation of colonies in the seventh and sixth centuries B.C.E. would surely have appreciated) and in failing, due to their insolent pride, to perceive (*Ant.* 1:111) that their blessings were due to God's benevolence and that their felicity was not due to their own might.

Another scene reminiscent of Greek tragedy is that in which God (*Ant.* 1:164) thwarts Pharaoh's criminal passion toward Sarah by causing an outbreak of disease, which is reminiscent of the plague inflicted upon Thebes because of Oedipus' incest. Indeed, in order to find a remedy for the plague, Pharaoh, like Oedipus, consults priests (ἱερεῖς), who declare that the calamity is due to the wrath of God because Pharaoh had wished to outrage (ὑβρῖσαι) the stranger's wife.

The idea of *fate*, which is so prominent to Greek tragedy, is likewise introduced by Josephus in several extra-biblical additions. Thus, we read (*Ant.* 5:312) that it was necessary (ἔδει) for Samson to fall a victim to calamity.

[159] That Josephus did have regard for possible criticism by Epicureans among his readers may be seen from the fact that he has God, not Adam, name the animals, since the Epicureans had specifically declared that it was naive and ridiculous to think that one man had assigned names by his spontaneous declaration. See my 'Josephus' Commentary on Genesis', 124-25.

Likewise, fate (χρεών) prevails and causes the false prophet Zedekiah to appear more convincing than the true prophet Micaiah to Ahab, in order to hasten Ahab's end (*Ant.* 8:409). Again, after Ahab takes off his royal garments and Jehoshaphat puts on Ahab's garments in order to escape the fate foretold by Micaiah, fate (χρεών), we are told (*Ant.* 8:412), was not deceived. The moral of the tale, indeed, as Josephus (*Ant.* 8:419) puts it, is that 'it behoves us to reflect on the power of fate (χρεών), and see that not even with foreknowledge is it possible to escape it'. Finally, Josephus (*Ant.* 10:76) explains the death of Josiah by remarking that it was destiny (πεπρωμένης) that led Josiah to ignore the request of King Necho of Egypt so as to have a pretext for destroying him.

That Josephus is, indeed, thinking in terms of tragedy may be seen by his use of the word προσωπεῖα ('stage-masks'), where, in commenting on Saul's cruelty in slaughtering the priests of Nob, he reflects (*Ant.* 6:264) that it is characteristic of human nature when men attain to power to lay aside their moderate and just ways 'as if they were stage masks', and instead assume an attitude of audacity, recklessness, and contempt for things human and divine.[160]

ROMANTIC MOTIFS. Finally, Josephus has made his narrative more appealing to his Greek readers by introducing romantic motifs reminiscent of Homer, Herodotus' account (*Historiae* 1:8-12) of Candaules' wife and Gyges, Xenophon's *Cyropaedia*, and Hellenistic novels.[161] Thus, in an extra-biblical comment which has no rabbinic parallel, Josephus (*Ant.* 1:162) mentions the Egyptians' frenzy for women and Abram's fear that the Pharaoh would put him to death so that he might have her. The erotic motif is further developed in Pharaoh's meeting with Sarah (*Ant.* 1:165), where, in terror, he asks who she is and who the man is who has accompanied her. The *Genesis Apocryphon* (col. 20), on the other hand, emphasizes not Pharaoh's terror but Abram's grief. Again, there is more romance in Josephus (*Ant.* 1:165) than in the Bible (Gen 12:19) in Pharaoh's statement that he had set his affections on Sarah because he had believed that she was Abram's sister, and he had hoped to marry her rather than to outrage (ἐξυβρίσαι) her in a transport of passion (κατ' ἐπιθυμίαν ὡρμημένος, i.e., 'having rushed headlong into passion').

There is likewise an added romantic flavour in Josephus' treatment of the episode of Eliezer's search for a wife for Isaac. Thus, in an extra-biblical

---

[160] On Josephus' use of the language of stage production see his remark (*War* 1:471) that Antipater, with a careful eye to every detail in the staging of the play (δραματουργῶν), assumed the stage mask (προσωπεῖον) of a devoted brother and left that of informer to others. Again, Josephus (*War* 1:530) speaks of Eurycles, Antipater's assistant in his intrigues against Alexander, as the 'stage-manager' (δραματουργόν) of the whole abominable business. Likewise, he adopts the language of tragedy when, in speaking of the trial of Herod's sons (*War* 1:543), he says that all Syria and Jewry were in suspense anxiously awaiting the last act of the drama (for a similar phrase see *Ant.* 19:199). Again, he presents (*War* 4:156) the picture of the high priest Phanni, who had been chosen by lot, as being dressed up with another's stage-mask (προσωπείῳ), as if on a stage (σκηνῆς).

[161] See my 'Esther', 143-70.

touch that is reminiscent of Hellenistic novels, Josephus (*Ant.* 1:244) emphasizes the difficulty of his journey, in that he must pass through a country that is muddy in winter and parched by drought in summer and that is infested by brigands. Furthermore, when he arrives, the other maidens (*Ant.* 1:245), just as in Homer's *Odyssey* (6:137-41), except for Rebecca, refuse to show him hospitality. Likewise, Rebecca rebukes the other maidens (*Ant.* 1:246) in terms reminiscent of Nausicaa to her companions (*Odyssey* 6:198-210). Thereupon, Eliezer (*Ant.* 1:247), in a remark that reminds the reader of Odysseus' reaction to Nausicaa's hospitality, declares that the parents of such a child should be congratulated and that she deserves to be married to the son of his master.

Josephus introduces a number of other romantic elements in his accounts of Abimelech's attempted seduction of Sarah (*Ant.* 1:208); Jacob's falling in love with Rachel at first sight (*Ant.* 1:288) and the protracted negotiations between Jacob and Laban in order to emphasize their love (*Ant.* 1:298); Dinah's seduction at a festival (*Ant.* 1:337) and Hamor's request that Dinah be given to Shechem (*Ant.* 1:338); the infatuation of Potiphar's wife with Joseph (*Ant.* 2:41-59); Moses' marriage with the Ethiopian princess Tharbis (*Ant.* 2:252-53, perhaps based on the Scylla legend);[162] the connection with the story of Balaam of the seductive words of the Midianite women to the Israelite youths, the leit-motif being how to subvert one's enemy by sex (*Ant.* 4:129);[163] the failure of the Levite concubine to return the love of her husband (*Ant.* 5:136-37); the apology offered for the rape of the women of Shiloh by the Benjaminites, namely the failure of the people of Shiloh to protect their daughters (*Ant.* 5:171), and the actual seizure of the women of Shiloh by the Benjaminites in a manner reminiscent of the rape of the Sabine women by the Romans (*Ant.* 5:172-73); Manoah's mad love for his wife and consequently his inordinate (ἀκρατῶς, i.e. 'without command over oneself or one's passion', 'incontinent', 'immoderate', 'intemperate') jealousy (ζηλότυπος, *Ant.* 5:277); the enhancement (*Ant.* 5:287) of the romantic aspect in the episode of Samson and the Timnite woman by Josephus' statement that it was in the course of his constant visits to her home that he performed his first great exploit, strangling the lion; the exaggeration of the melodrama in Josephus' version (*Ant.* 5:292) of the scene in which Samson's wife begs her, bursting (προπιπτούσης, 'rushing headlong') into tears, to reveal the answer to the riddle; the description (*Ant.* 5:306) of Delilah as a courtesan (ἑταιριζομένης) reminiscent of those for which the Greeks were famous, rather than as a harlot (πόρνη), as in the Septuagint (Judg 16:1); the dishonouring (*Ant.* 5:339) by the sons of Eli the high priest of the women who came to worship; the fact (*Ant.* 6:193) that David's exploits are celebrated by maidens, whereas Saul's are by older women; the fact

---

[162] See Braun, *History and Romance*, 97ff.

[163] Van Unnik, 'Josephus' Account', 243, notes the significant fact that Josephus expands at great length (*Ant.* 4:126-51) the story of the seduction of the Israelite youths by the Midianite women, whereas he deals only briefly with the Phinehas episode (*Ant.* 4:152-55), even though they are of approximately equal length in the Bible (Num 25:1-5 and 6-13).

that Saul's daughter Michal (*Ant.* 6:196, 6:215) has such a great passion for David that it betrays her; the fact that David's love, in return, for Michal is so great (*Ant.* 6:203) that he proceeds to fulfill Saul's demand for six hundred Philistine heads as a dowry without stopping to consider whether the proposed enterprise was possible; the love-sickness (*Ant.* 7:164) of Amnon, David's son, because of his infatuation with his sister Tamar, whom he rapes; the amplification (*Ant.* 7:130-53) of David's affair with Bath-sheba; Ahasuerus' world-wide search for beauties (*Ant.* 11:196) throughout the entire habitable (οἰκουμένη) world, in contrast to the Bible (Esther 2:2), where his resolve to find a replacement for the deposed queen Vashti is a political decision coming from the king's servants who ministered to him; the fact that Josephus (*Ant.* 11:200) gives the exact number of maidens (400) in Ahasuerus' harem, just as the Hellenistic novels are addicted to presenting exact data about erotic matters; the more explicit reference (in connection with Ahasuerus' search for a replacement for Queen Vashti) to sexual intercourse (*Ant.* 11:201);[164] Ahasuerus' actually falling in love with Esther (*Ant.* 11:202); and Josephus' exaggeration of the beauty of a number of women: Rachel (*Ant.* 1:288), Samson's mother (*Ant.* 5:276), Bath-sheba (*Ant.* 7:130), David's daughter Tamar (*Ant.* 7:162), Vashti (*Ant.* 11:190), and Esther (*Ant.* 11:199), though the last was, according to the rabbis, a seventy-five-year-old woman.[165]

JOSEPHUS' AIMS: THEOLOGIZING

In addition to the apologetic aim, a second major goal to explain Josephus' modification of the Bible has been stressed by Attridge,[166] namely, to present a consistent and profoundly religious and Jewish interpretation of history. This would seem to be in line with Josephus' own statement (*Ant.* 1:14) that the main lesson to be derived from a perusal of his history is that God rewards those who obey His laws and punishes those who do not. And yet, despite such moralizing, Josephus, in point of fact, prefers to approach the Bible as history rather than as theology, as is clear from a number of references in the *Antiquities* that he intends to discuss *elsewhere* such theological matters as the reasons for the

---

[164] If Josephus omits (*Ant.* 11:204), as he does, the second gathering of the virgins (Esther 2:19), which does have erotic interest, it is, it would seem, because in immediate juxtaposition is the statement that Mordecai sat in the king's gate. To say that Mordecai had charge of the reception of the virgins would be to ascribe something unbecoming to Mordecai.

[165] If Josephus, in his paraphrase of the story of Ruth (*Ant.* 5:318-37), compresses, rather than expands, as one might expect in view of what we have noted above, the potentially sexually charged scene at the threshing floor, this may be due not to Josephus' failure to realize the erotic potential of this scene, but to the fact that he apologetically sought to avoid suspicion of immoral behaviour on the part of the ancestors of King David. Moreover, to have expanded on such an episode would have diverted the reader's attention from the main historical trend of his narrative, since the whole story of Ruth is really secondary to Josephus' main interest in the history of the Jewish people, and her story is told only because of the facet that she is the great-grandmother of David.

[166] Attridge, *Interpretation*. See also his remarks in 'Josephus and His Works', 218-19.

503

commandments generally (*Ant.* 1:25), the reasons for the practice of circumcision (*Ant.* 1:192), the major portion of the laws (*Ant.* 3:94), the reason for the shewbread (*Ant.* 3:143), the laws concerning mutual relations (*Ant.* 4:198), the Jewish belief concerning God and His essence and the reasons for the commandments (*Ant.* 20:268). In other words, it is not that Josephus was unacquainted with such matters: the projected work *On Customs and Causes* had apparently taken a very definite shape in Josephus' mind, since he even indicates (*Ant.* 20:268) that it will be in four books. Rather, it is that Josephus regarded his history as an inappropriate place for such discussions, at least at any length. It is ironic that in the *War*, which has, especially as seen in the speeches,[167] a clear theological lesson, Josephus says nothing in his preface as to what lesson the reader is to derive, whereas in the *Antiquities*, where, as we shall see, the theological element is played down, Josephus proclaims his theologizing and moralizing purpose in his preface. The explanation, it would seem, is that Josephus in the *Antiquities* is presenting an apologetic for the Bible and consequently for God's deeds, but that he does so not as a theologian but as a historian, noting the consequences of the actions of his most important *human* characters.

Thus we see that Josephus stresses Abraham's address to Isaac (*Ant.* 1:228-31) and omits any appeal to God, fraught as it is with the problem of theodicy, in contrast to the rabbinic emphasis on Abraham's address to God, in which he contends that though he might have argued against the Divine decree he did not do so. Likewise, the fact that Abraham makes no appeal to Isaac to sacrifice himself altruistically for the sake of his descendants and for the sanctification of God's name, such as we find in rabbinic literature, removes the theological dimension and concentrates on the character of Isaac himself. Finally, the most important difference between Josephus and the other Jewish sources with regard to the Akeda is that Josephus omits the concept that God tested both Abraham and Isaac, a motive that is crucial for the understanding of theodicy.

We may also note that Josephus (*Ant.* 1:305) omits Jacob's angry exchange with Rachel (Gen 30:1-2), in which, in the biblical version, he says, 'Am I in God's stead, Who hath withheld from thee the fruit of the womb?' Josephus omits the connection of her lack of fecundity with God and instead restricts himself to the human dimension as he psychologizes in his statement that Rachel fears that her sister's fecundity will lessen her own share in her husband's affections. Again, when Rachel gives birth to Joseph, Josephus (*Ant.* 1:308) does not repeat the reference to God found in both the Hebrew and the Septuagint versions (Gen 30:23) that 'God hath taken away my reproach'.

There is likewise a de-emphasis of the role of God in the story of Joseph and Potiphar's wife. Whereas the Bible (Gen 39:9), in response to the latter's invitation to Joseph to have relations with her, has Joseph call out, 'How, then, can I do this great wickedness and sin against God', Josephus' Joseph (unlike

---

[167] See Bomstad, *Governing Ideas*, and Thérond, *Le discours*.

Philo's *On Joseph*, 9:48, of which Josephus seems to have been aware)[168] says nothing about God and only later mentions God when he appeals (*Ant.* 2:51-52) dramatically to her conscience.

To be sure, in his account of Moses, Josephus does not de-emphasize the role of God. Thus (*Ant.* 2:222-23), he comments that the miraculous way in which Moses was saved after he had been placed in the ark after birth shows plainly that human intelligence is of no worth and that God accomplished whatever He intends to do. Again, at the burning bush (*Ant.* 2:272) it is God who exhorts Moses to have confidence, and not, as in Artapanus (*ap.* Eusebius, *Praeparatio Evangelica* 9:27, 22), Moses himself who took courage. Similarly, when Moses returns to Egypt from Midian, the Hebrews, we are told (*Ant.* 2:280), were hopeful that all would be well, 'since God was taking forethought (προνοου-μένου) for their safety'. Likewise, Josephus (*Ant.* 2:293) declares that one of the reasons why he has chosen to mention all of the plagues that afflicted the Egyptians is that one should learn thereby the lesson that those who provoke God's wrath are punished. Again, at the Red Sea, where all hope seemed lost, Moses (*Ant.* 2:332) encourages the Israelites by remarking that God helps people precisely at the time when He sees that they have lost all hope. This emphasis, however, on God and on His providence is the exception in Josephus' history and may be explained by the fact that since the Greeks believed that great leaders, such as a Lycurgus, had to be divinely directed, so Josephus, for apologetic reasons, inasmuch as he knew that Moses would be compared with other lawgivers and formulators of constitutions actual or ideal,[169] similarly emphasized that Moses had been directed by God's providence (*Ant.* 2:329, 331, 335). That, indeed, Josephus is actually de-emphasizing the role of God may be seen by the fact that whereas the Dead Sea *Temple Scroll*, for example, excludes Moses entirely in its statement of the laws and instead ascribes them directly to God, Josephus mentions Moses by name constantly as the author of these laws, identifies the virtue of his constitution with his own virtue (*Ant.* 1:20), and nowhere quotes God directly in his citation of legal materials.[170]

Perhaps the most striking example of the diminution by Josephus in the role of God is in the Ruth pericope. Despite the fact that at the end of the narrative (*Ant.* 5:337) Josephus explains that he was constrained to relate it in order to demonstrate the power of God and how easy it is for Him to raise ordinary people to illustrious rank, Josephus nowhere, in the entire episode (*Ant.* 5:318-36) mentions God, despite the fact that the biblical account refers to the

---

[168]   Thackeray, trans. of Josephus, 4:187, notes words and phrases in Josephus that seem to have been taken from Philo.
[169]   Cf., e.g. Strabo (*Geography*, 16:2, 38-39, 762), who makes Moses parallel to the revered Cretan king and lawgiver Minos and to the similarly revered Spartan king and lawgiver Lycurgus as a lawgiver who claimed Divine sanction for his laws. Cf. also Numenius (*ap.* Clement of Alexandria, *Stromata* 1:22, 150, 4), who compares Moses with Plato: 'For what is Plato but Moses speaking in Attic?'
[170]   See Altshuler, 'On the Classification', 11.

Him seventeen times. If, then, he does mention God at the very end of the pericope, it is perhaps because he feels that he ought to connect Ruth's descendant David, whom he has just mentioned (*Ant.*. 5:336), with the Divine will.

In the case of the Book of Esther, the reverse is the case, for in the biblical book there is not a single mention of God; and the Septuagint and Josephus, for apologetic reasons, attempt to remedy this in several places. Thus, when there is an obvious suppression of God's name in the passage (Esther 4:14) where Mordecai tells Esther that if she does not speak to the king, deliverance will come to the Jews 'from another place', the Lucianic version and Josephus specify that this relief will come from God. Yet, Josephus tones down Divine intervention; for where the Apocryphal Addition (D 8) declares that God changed the spirit of Ahasuerus into mildness, Josephus (*Ant.* 11:237) qualifies this by the phrase 'I believe' (οἶμαι). Again, where the Apocryphal Addition (D 13) reports that Esther explains that she had fainted when she had seen Ahasuerus as an angel of God, Josephus (*Ant.* 11:240), seeking to diminish the supernatural, says that she fainted when she saw him 'looking so great and handsome and terrible'.

Similarly, with miracles, Josephus frequently (for example, *Ant.* 1:108, 3:81, 4:158, 10:281) employs the time-honoured formula, found not merely in Dionysius of Halicarnassus (*Roman Antiquities* 1:48.1, 1:48.4, 2:40.3, 2:74.5, 3:36.5), Lucian (*How to Write History* 10), and Pliny (*Hist. Nat.* 9:18), but also earlier in Herodotus and Thucydides, allowing the reader to make up his mind, which, as Delling and MacRae[171] have remarked, is an expression of courtesy to his pagan readers more than a confession of his own doubt about the veracity of these accounts. Thus the prediction (Gen 18:10) that the angel will return and that Sarah will bear a son 'according to this season of life', that is a year from then, is toned down in Josephus, so that we have merely the statement (*Ant.* 1:197) that one of the angels will return some day in the future. Then, when the birth does occur, Josephus (*Ant.* 1:214) says simply that it occurred during the following year. Again, the scene of the ram being caught in a thicket by its horns (Gen 22:13) may have seemed grotesque and too much of a miracle for a rationalizing Greek intellectual. Hence, Josephus omits it and says merely that God brought the ram from obscurity into view, implying that it had always been there. Moreover, Josephus does not state explicitly, as does the Bible (Gen 22:13), that Abraham offered the ram in place of his son, presumably because he wished to avoid the theological implication that it was a substitute for the sins of man.

Again, Josephus, much as he might have liked to exaggerate Samson's exploits in order to build up his stature as a hero, is careful to omit miraculous and magical elements. Thus, whereas the Bible (Judg 16:9) declares that Samson broke the bowstrings binding him, 'as a string of tow snaps when it touches the fire', Josephus' Samson omits the miraculous element, and we are

---

[171] Delling, 'Josephus', 291-309; and MacRae, 'Miracle', 136-42.

left with the statement (*Ant.* 5:310) that he burst the shoots asunder. Again, the Bible (Judg 16:12) remarks that Samson snapped the ropes off his arms as if they were a thread, but Josephus (*Ant.* 5:311) states merely that Delilah's device met with no success.

Josephus as an Interpreter of Biblical Law

Josephus (*Ag.Ap.* 2:178) would have us believe that every Jew was exceedingly well versed in the laws, so that he could 'repeat them all more readily than his own name'. The fact that Josephus boasts (*Life* 9) that, while a mere lad (ἀντίπαις) of fourteen, the chief priests and the leading men of the great city of Jerusalem used to come to him constantly for information on particular laws shows that he regarded himself as eminently well qualified to comment on the legal code. Again, when a delegation of learned Pharisees is sent to expel Josephus from his command in Galilee they were to say, according to Josephus (*Life* 198), that if the Galileans' devotion to him was due to his expert knowledge of the Pharisaic laws, they, too, were learned, the implication being that Josephus' own extensive learning could not be denied. Indeed, he boasts (*Ant.* 20:263) that his compatriots admit that in Jewish learning – which certainly puts the stress on law – he far excelled them. Moreover, the very fact, mentioned in several places, notably at the very end of the *Antiquities* (20:268), that he announces his plans to write a work on the laws, obviously more extensive than his summary treatment in Books 3 and 4 of the *Antiquities* or his succinct résumé in *Against Apion* (2:190-219), is further indication that he regarded himself as eminently qualified to write such a work. And yet, if Josephus' promise (*Ant.* 1:17) not to add to or to subtract from Scripture applied to aggada, his failure to comply with it did not seriously threaten the fabric of Jewish religious beliefs and practices; but if he did not abide by it when it came to halakha, his failure had truly serious consequences.

There are a number of respects (certainly no more than ten per cent of the whole) in which Josephus' interpretation of Biblical law does not agree with that of the rabbis, who claim to be codifying the oral law as Moses received it on Sinai; and this gives rise to the question as to whether Josephus may not represent an earlier version of the oral law:

(1) He identifies (*Ant.* 3:245) 'the fruit of goodly trees' (Lev 23:40) as the persea (περσέας), a fleshy one-seeded fruit of the laurel family, the most common member of which is the avocado, though elsewhere (*Ant.* 13:372) he refers to it as a citron (κιτρίοις), whereas the rabbis (*B.T. Sukka* 35a) identify it as a citron.

(2) He declares (*Ant.* 3:282) that debtors are absolved from debts in the Jubilee year, whereas the biblical text (Deut 15:1-11) speaks of the remission of debts in the seventh or sabbatical year.

(3) Josephus (*Ant.* 4:175) understands the Bible (Num 36:3) literally when it declares that if a daughter marries into another tribe the inheritance

remains in her father's tribe, whereas the rabbis (*B.T. Bava Batra* 112b, *Sifrei Numbers* 134, p. 178ff.) declare that the inheritance is transferred.

(4) He says (*Ant.* 4:207), following the Septuagint's understanding of Exod 22:27,[172] that it is forbidden to blaspheme the gods which other people revere, whereas Deut 7:25 mandates the destruction by fire of the graven images of the heathen.

(5) Josephus (*Ant.* 4:209) says that the high priest is to read the laws every seven years, whereas Scripture (Deut 31:10-13) does not specify who is to read them, and the Mishna (*Sota* 7:9) states that it is the king who reads the passage.

(6) He speaks (*Ant.* 4:240) of a third tithe (Deut 14:28-29) for the poor, whereas the rabbis understand this as taking the place of the second tithe in the third and sixth years of the Sabbatical period.

(7) He states (*Ant.* 4:248) that if a man betroths a bride in the belief that she is a virgin and it turns out that she is not, she is to be stoned if not of priestly parentage but burnt alive if she is of priestly stock, whereas the Bible (Deut 22:21) prescribes stoning for all cases.

(8) According to Josephus (*Ant.* 4:254) the child born of a levirate marriage (Deut 25:5-10) is the heir to the estate, but the rabbis (*M. Yevamot* 4:7) declare that the *levir* himself is the heir.

(9) Josephus (*Ant.* 4:263) says that the law of the rebellious child applies to sons and daughters, and he does not mention the necessity of bringing the child to be judged by a court, as prescribed by Scripture (Deut 21:19), whereas the Bible itself (Deut 21:18) and the rabbis (*M. Sanhedrin* 8:1) restrict the law to sons alone.

(10) He likewise requires (*Ant.* 4:264) the condemned child to be exposed for a day after he has been stoned to death, whereas there is no such statement in the Bible (Deut 21:21).

(11) Josephus (*Ant.* 4:273) declares that a slave woman and her children go free with her in the Jubilee year, but the rabbis affirm that the children of a Canaanite slave woman are like herself in all respects (*B.T. Kiddushin* 68b-69a) and that they are regarded as property (*B.T. Megilla* 23b).

(12) Josephus (*Ant.* 4:278) says that if a man kicks a woman and causes her to have a miscarriage, he is to be fined by the judge and a further sum is to be given to her husband, whereas Scripture (Exod 21:22) speaks of one fine only to be determined by the judge.

(13) Josephus (*Ag.Ap.* 2:199) says that the sole purpose of sexual relations in marriage is to have children, whereas the rabbis permit such relations during pregnancy, for example (*B.T. Yevamot* 12b), and they permit (*M. Yevamot* 6:6) a man to marry a woman incapable of bearing children if he has already fulfilled the commandment 'Be fruitful and multiply'.

---

[172] So also Philo, *Moses* 2:26, 205, and *On the Special Laws* 1:7, 52. Josephus himself (*Ag.Ap.* 2:237) gives the same reason for this tolerance, namely out of reverence for the very word 'God'.

(14) Josephus (*Ag.Ap.* 2:202) declares, without qualification, that a woman is forbidden to have an abortion, whereas the rabbis (*B.T. Sanhedrin* 72b) state that an abortion is permissible if the fetus is endangering the life of the mother.

(15) Josephus (*Ag.Ap.* 2:207) indicates that for a judge to accept bribes is a capital crime, but there is no such law in the Talmud.

(16) Josephus (*Ag.Ap.* 2:215) declares that violating an unmarried woman is a capital crime, without indicating (Deut 22:23-24) the crucial proviso that this applies only to a betrothed woman.

(17) Josephus (*Ag.Ap.* 2:271) maintains that maltreatment (presumably castration) of a brute beast is a capital crime, but there is no such penalty specified in the Bible (Lev 22:24) or in the Talmud (*B.T. Hagiga* 14b).

(18) Josephus (*Life* 65) says that representation of animals is forbidden by Jewish law, and he declares (*Ant.* 8:195) that Solomon violated the Law in making images of bulls under the sea which he had set up as an offering and of lions around his own throne, but the Talmud (*B.T. Avoda Zara* 43b) declares that only a human shape is halakhically forbidden.

On the other hand, there are many cases where Josephus seems to be in accordance with the oral tradition as we know it from the talmudic corpus, for example:

(1) He notes (*Ant.* 3:226) that a lamb that is offered for sacrifice is to be one year old, as specified also in the Mishna (*Para* 5:3).

(2) He declares (*Ant.* 3:261) that a menstruating woman is removed from pure things and is separated from the public on account of uncleanness, just as the rabbinic tradition states (*Seder Eliyahu Rabba* 16, pp. 75-76).

(3) Josephus (*Ant.* 4:202), like the Mishna (*Sanhedrin* 6:4) indicates that blasphemers are stoned and hanged, whereas the Tora (Lev 24:14-16) specifies only stoning.

(4) He, like the rabbis (*B.T. Berakhot* 27b), speaks (*Ant.* 4:212) of two statutory prayers daily.

(5) He mentions (*Ant.* 4:214), as does the Talmud (*B.T. Megilla* 26a) that civic bodies are to have seven members.

(6) He states (*Ant.* 4:219), as do the rabbis (*Sifrei* 190, p. 230) that the evidence of women is not acceptable.

(7) He declares (*Ant.* 4:224), as does the Talmud (*B.T. Sanhedrin* 2a, 20b), that a king is to consult the Sanhedrin of Seventy-one before engaging in a voluntary war.

(8) He reduces (*Ant.* 4:238), as do the rabbis (*B.T. Makkot* 22a), the number of lashes inflicted in the penalty of scourging from forty to thirty-nine.

(9) Josephus (*Ant.* 4:253), like the school of Hillel, which prevails in rabbinic law (*B.T. Gittin* 90a), permits divorce for any reason whatsoever.

(10) The penalty of paying double in the case of theft, according to Josephus (*Ant.* 4:271), applies not only if one steals animals, as in the Bible (Exod

22:3), but also if one steals money, a provision paralleled in the Talmud (*B.T. Bava Kamma* 64b).

(11)   Josephus (*Ant.* 4:274), like the rabbinic tradition (*T. Bava Metsia* 2:19), in discussing the law of the restitution of lost property, differentiates on the basis of where the object was found, whereas the Bible (Deut 22:1-3) makes no such distinction, and likewise he mentions (*Ant.* 4:274) public proclamation of the place where it was found, as does the oral tradition (*Mishna, Bava Metsia* 2:1), though it is only in the fourth century that we hear of a rabbi (Rava, in *B.T. Bava Metsia* 22b) who holds this view.

(12)   Josephus (*Ant.* 4:276), as pointed out by Goldenberg,[173] agrees with the oral tradition (*T. Bava Metsia* 2:29) in placing the law of pointing out the road to one who has lost his way immediately after the law of lost objects.

(13)   Josephus (*Ant.* 4:277), like the rabbinic Tosefta (*Bava Kamma* 9:5-6), declares that one is not punished if the person whom he has struck remains alive several days before dying.

(14)   In his interpretation of the *lex talionis* (Exod 21:24), Josephus (*Ant.* 4:280) gives the victim the choice of accepting a monetary settlement, similar to the rabbis (*B.T. Bava Kamma* 83b), who, to be sure, prescribe a monetary penalty and declare that the amount is to be fixed by a court.

(15)   Josephus (*Ag.Ap.* 1:31), in declaring that a priest must marry a woman of his own race, that is not a proselyte, is in accord with the Mishna (*Yevamot* 6:5), which equates a proselyte and a prostitute, whereas the Tora itself (Lev 21:7) says merely that a priest may not marry a prostitute.

(16)   Like the Talmud (*B.T. Moed Katan* 27b, *Ketubbot* 8b), Josephus (*Ag.Ap.* 2:205) indicates opposition to costly shrouds.

(17)   In saying that Jews do not erect conspicuous monuments to the dead, Josephus (*Ag.Ap.* 2:205) is in agreement with the Palestinian Talmud (*Shekalim* 2:7, 47a).

(18)   If the reading of Eusebius (*Praeparatio Evangelica* 8:8, 36) is correct, Josephus (*Ag.Ap.* 2:205) agrees with the rabbinic tradition (*B.T. Ketubbot* 17a, *Megilla* 29a) in declaring that all who pass by a funeral procession must join it.

How can we explain this checkered picture of Josephus' relationship to the rabbis? To answer this, perhaps we should first ask why Josephus includes a survey of the laws, whereas other historians, such as Dionysius of Halicarnassus and Livy, in their histories of Rome, do not. We may remark, in reply, that Josephus, indeed, realizes that a survey of laws does not really belong in a history. He is clearly self-conscious when introducing his survey of the regulations concerning purity laws. 'I cease', he says (*Ant.* 3:223), before giving a brief survey (*Ant.* 3:224-86), 'to speak about these (laws), having resolved to compose another treatise about the laws'. Moreover, when he gives his more

---

[173]   Goldenberg, *Halakhah*, 118.

extensive survey of the laws, he is again self-conscious and offers (*Ant.* 4:196) two reasons for the digression:

1) it is consonant with the reputation for virtue (ἀρετῆς) of Moses; that is, by implication at least, Josephus is presenting an apologetic work, since Moses is *the* greatest Jewish hero, and whatever redounds to his credit will redound to the credit of the Jewish people;

2) it will enable those who will read (ἐντευξομένοις), 'chance upon') his book to learn what was the nature of the laws from the beginning, thus directing the digression to his non-Jewish readers, presumably for apologetic reasons. Josephus (*Ant.* 4:198) says that he will restrict himself to those laws pertaining to the Jewish polity (πολιτείαν), reserving for his projected treatise those pertaining to the mutual (private) relations (πρὸς ἀλλήλους) of man and man, though he seems to include some of these in his survey as well.

What are Josephus' sources, in addition to the Bible in the Hebrew and Septuagint versions, for his account of Jewish law? Could he have had a written source for his version of the Oral Law when the rabbinic version was not written down until the end of the second century by Rabbi Yehuda the Patriarch? In the first place, we may note our suspicion, though admittedly without concrete evidence, that Josephus has a written source for his extensive digressions, such as the out-sized passages concerning the Essenes (*War* 2:119-61), the robber-barons Asinaeus and Anilaeus (*Ant.* 18:310-70), the assassination of Caligula and the accession of Claudius (*Ant.* 19:1-273), and the conversion of Izates, the king of Adiabene (*Ant.* 20:17-96). The very fact that Philo (*On the Special Laws*), as well as the Dead Sea *Damascus Covenant* and the *Temple Scroll* and Josephus, do record the laws, including much oral law, in a systematic way should lead us to think that perhaps there was such a written compendium available to Josephus. Indeed, Hölscher[174] has theorized that Josephus not only had a written source book for his aggadic passages but that he had a Hellenistic Jewish composition, developed over the centuries from notes taken in Jewish schools, for the legal portions of his history as well; but we have not a single fragment of such a document, and it would seem strange that Josephus, a very learned Palestinian Jew, educated in halakha in Jerusalem, should have turned to Alexandrian sources for his knowledge of the Oral Law. Kohler[175] postulates a priestly document, such as the *Damascus Covenant* of the Dead Sea Sect; but in an age that was sensitive to charges of sectarian heresy, it would seem unlikely that Josephus, a Pharisee, would have turned to such an extremist group. In any case, we have not a single fragment of such a document.

If Josephus did have a written source, the most likely hypothesis would appear to be that he had a rabbinic document or a written targum (as Olitzki[176] has suggested). As Goldenberg[177] has noted, we do have evidence that the oral

---

[174] Hölscher, 'Josephus', 1953-67.
[175] Kohler, 'Halakik Portions', 69.
[176] Olitzki, *Flavius Josephus*, 27, n. 36.
[177] Goldenberg, *Halakhah*, 18.

law was put into writing in the Tannaic period, roughly contemporary with Josephus; and a newly discovered manuscript of the Talmud (*B.T. Avoda Zara* 8b, MS. Marx-Abramson) declares that Rabbi Yehuda ben Bava, a younger contemporary of Josephus, recorded laws of fines. Indeed, Goldenberg[178] has astutely comented that the breakdown of each biblical law into more precisely defined cases is precisely the kind of structure which one would find in a legal code, though, of course, admittedly this might have been in an oral state at the time when Josephus studied it.

If the code was not in written form, might Josephus have remembered it several decades after he had learned it, even if memories were cultivated in those days and even if Josephus was outstanding in this regard? We must recall that writing in Rome Josephus was far removed from the Palestinian rabbis whom he might have consulted in matters of doubt. Indeed, there are those[179] who say that Josephus' deviations from rabbinic law are due precisely to the fact that he had forgotten what he had learned long before in Jerusalem.

One point that we must emphasize is that Josephus is writing a work of history and not a legal treatise. Thus, if he states a law without giving its conditions, we must remember that he is not here presenting a legal code and that he had hoped to do so in a separate treatise.

Rejecting completely the influence of oral law upon Josephus, Altshuler[180] has taken the extreme position that Josephus' only source was the Bible, and that his deviations from Scripture, as well as his selection from and organization of the Laws may all be ascribed to his desire to defend Judaism. He notes Josephus' frequent use, clearly for apologetic reasons, of the words 'good' (καλόν, καλῶς, *Ant.* 4:204, 210, 239, 258) and 'just' (δίκαιον, *Ant.* 3:250, 4:205, 212, 233, 258, 266) in characterizing the laws. Tachauer, Olitzki, and Riskin,[181] more plausibly in view of clear evidence of knowledge of the oral law in such biblical books as Ruth and in such works as the Septuagint, as well as in various books of the Apocrypha, argue that Josephus was acquainted with the oral law as later codified by the rabbis, but that where he deviates from it he does so for apologetic reasons.

A good example of Josephus' recasting of biblical law for apologetic reasons is to be seen in his extension (*Ant.* 4:276) of the injunction against putting a stumbling block in front of the blind (Lev 19:14, Deut 27:18) into a law that one must point out the road to those who are ignorant of it. This would seem to be a direct refutation of the bitter anti-Semitic satirist Juvenal who declares (*Satires* 14:103) that Jews do not point out the road except to those who practice the same rites. Josephus likewises declares (*Ant.* 4:283) that those who dig wells are required to keep them covered not in order to keep others from drawing water from them but rather to protect passers-by from falling into them. Here, too, he

---

[178] Goldenberg, *Halakhah*, 206-07.
[179] E.g., Revel, 'Some Anti-Traditional Laws', 293-301.
[180] Altshuler, *Descriptions*.
[181] Tachauer, *Verhältniss*, 34-46; Olitzki, *Flavius Josephus*; and Riskin, *Halakhah*.

seems to be answering Juvenal's charge (*Satires* 14:104) that Jews conduct 'none but the circumcised to the desired fountain'.

Sometimes Josephus seems to have reformulated the law in order to avoid embarrassment in comparison with non-Jewish law. Thus, in equating abortion with infanticide (*Ag.Ap.* 2:202), Josephus, as Riskin[182] has remarked, did not want to have it appear that Jewish law was more lenient than the Noahide law that is applicable to non-Jews, inasmuch as, according to the Talmud (*B.T. Sanhedrin* 57b), Noahide law forbids killing a foetus in the womb of its mother on the basis of an interpretation of Gen 9:6. Moreover, Josephus apparently felt uneasy that Jewish law on this topic was more lenient than that of Plato (*ap.* (Plutarch, *De Placitis Philosophorum* 5:15), who declares that a foetus is a living being.

Again, as Cohn[183] has pointed out, according to the earlier Roman law (*Lex Cornelia testamentaria*) of 81 B.C.E., the penalty inflicted upon a judge for accepting a bribe was exile, the death penalty not being imposed until 392 C.E.. Josephus (*Ag.Ap.* 2:207), eager that it should not appear that Jewish law was less stringent than that of the Gentiles in such a sensitive area, declares that a judge who accepts bribes suffers capital punishment. Here again, Noachian law did require a death penalty, and Josephus did not want to have it appear that he was less severe.

Moreover, Josephus' omission of the prohibition of converting to Judaism the Ammonites and Moabites until the tenth generation (Deut 23:4) and the Edomites and the Egyptians until the third generation (Deut 23:9) seems to be actuated by the eagerness to answer the charge that the Jews are exclusivistic and haters of mankind. This apology was particularly important because the Jewish proselyting activities, so enormously successful during this period, depended upon making it clear to all that Jews welcomed all those who come to them in true sincerity.

Goldenberg[184] has systematically challenged the thesis that Josephus' goal in his formulation of Jewish law was apologetic by noting, for example, that his omission of child sacrifice to Molech (Lev 18:21) was far from being due to apologetic purposes, since if Josephus was interested in showing the humanity of Judaism a prohibition against child sacrifice was certainly one law not to omit. He likewise notes[185] that if it were for apologetic reasons that Josephus omitted the prohibition of setting up an ashera tree or a pillar (Deut 16:21-22), Josephus should also have omitted the prohibition against graven images, which he does mention (*Ant.* 3:91; *Ag.Ap.* 2:191) and even emphasizes, as we shall see. Likewise, if it is for apologetic reasons that Josephus omits the reference to sacrifices to foreign gods (Exod 22:19), Josephus should not have expanded (*Ant.* 4:126-49) the incident of the fornication with the Midianite

---

182 Riskin, *Halakhah*.
183 Cohn, 'Flavius Josephus'.
184 Goldenberg, *Halakhah*, 218-35.
185 Goldenberg, *Halakhah*, 226.

women. Similarly, the omission of the prohibition (Deut 18:10-11) against consulting a soothsayer, a sorcerer, or a necromancer is inconsistent with Josephus' anecdote (*Ag.Ap.* 1:200-04) of the Jewish soldier Mosollamus, who shot and killed a bird that a seer was observing and who sneeringly asked how any sound information could come from a creature that could not provide for its own safety. Again, the mention of the prohibition of the use of non-Jewish oil (*Life* 74) would seem to play into the hands of those who charged that Jews were haters of mankind. Likewise, Josephus (*Ant.* 4:266) has not omitted what would seem to be the embarrassing law (Deut 23:21) that one may charge interest from a non-Jew but not from a Jew, to which Josephus adds as a reason, 'for it is not just to draw a revenue from the misfortunes of a fellow-country-man'. To these objections we may remark that the *argumentum ex silentio* is particularly dangerous, since Josephus is not presenting a systematic code of law and that he is not merely seeking to defend Jews against the charges of anti-Semites but that he is also eager to attract non-Jews to Judaism, hence the statement about interest-free loans, which might well prove to be a major attraction in winning proselytes.

If Josephus does differ in some points from the rabbinic code, we would comment, in the first place, that Josephus, who was under constant attack from his fellow Jews, would hardly have dared to present such deviations unless he had solid ground for his interpretations. We may explain his deviations by stating either that he is merely paraphrasing biblical law or that he reflects the law in force in his own day (in which case Josephus, like Philo presumably, would be very important as a stage in halakhic development prior to the codification of halakha in the Mishna), or that he reflects sectarian law, or that he is influenced by Philo or by Roman law or that he is more strict than the rabbinic law or that he is presenting merely good advice rather than legal prescriptions or that he reflects the law that he believes will take force in the Messianic future. As to the first possibility, the statement (*Ant.* 4:175) that the heritage of Zelophehad's daughters should remain in the tribe is merely a restatement of the Bible (Num 36:8), whereas the rabbis (*Sifra Emor*, p. 96a on Lev 22:3) declare that the law was in force only when the land was divided according to tribes.

In explaining these discrepancies, we may cite a parallel in the differences between Josephus' description (*Ant.* 15:410-11) of the Temple as against that of the Mishna in the tractate *Middot*,[186] which may be explained by the hypothesis that the Mishna represents the period before, whereas Josephus depicts the period after Herod, or that the Mishna may be setting forth the ideal, if ever the Temple is to be rebuilt in the future, for surely Josephus, who himself was a priest and of the most eminent of all the priestly families (*Life* 2), should have had an intimate acquaintance with the Temple's dimensions and description.

---

[186] See my discussion, *Josephus*, 438-44.

As to Josephus' indication (*Ant.* 4:264-65) that the rebellious son is to be exposed for a day after he has been stoned to death and then is to be buried at night, this law is, indeed, unparalleled in halakha and may reflect the practice in Josephus' own day. Again, the fact that there is no Tannaic parallel to Josephus' statement (*Ant.* 4:274) that the finder of a lost object is to proclaim the place where he found it would suggest that Josephus is reflecting contemporary practice. All attempts, such as Riskin's and Goldenberg's,[187] to explain away Josephus' divergences from the rabbinic code fail to give sufficient weight to the artistic evidence compiled by Goodenough,[188] the evidence of papyri and inscriptions in Egypt which I[189] have discussed, and the evidence from Philo, which even Belkin,[190] with all his ingenuity, must admit disagrees in a number of instances from rabbinic law. The picture, we may suggest, that emerges is of a Judaism that is not as monolithic or as normative as Moore[191] has described, but rather of a religion where the authority of the rabbis was not as pervasive as we have been led to believe by such writers as Josephus himself (*Ant.* 18:15).

Kohler[192] has suggested that Josephus' source for his paraphrase of the laws was an older priestly document similar to the *Zadokite (Damascus) Document* originally discovered by Solomon Schechter (and later found also in the Qumran caves) and that Josephus' legal material actually represents an older stage of halakha, midway between Sadduceeism and Pharisaism. As evidence he cites Josephus' statement (*Ant.* 4:248) of the law that a bride of priestly parentage is burnt alive if it turns out that she is not a virgin when her husband is led to believe that she was. Elazar ben Zadok mentions that he witnessed the burning of such a woman, and the rabbis (*B.T. Sanhedrin* 52b) explain that it must have been a Sadducean *beit din* that imposed such a punishment. Josephus, however, has very negative comments about the Sadducees, namely, that in their relations with their peers they are as rude as with aliens (*War* 2:166), that they accomplish practically nothing (*Ant.* 18:17), and that they are tolerated by the masses only because they submit to the formulas of the Pharisees (*ibid.*). It seems hard to believe, in view of the bitter antagonism between the Sadducees and the Pharisees, with whom Josephus identified himself (*Life* 12), that Josephus would be influenced in his interpretation of law by such a group.

Yadin[193] has noted that there are parallels between Josephus' classification of the laws and that of the author of the *Temple Scroll* from Qumran and has suggested that Josephus may have been influenced by the years (*Life* 9-12) that he spent with the Essenes and with the hermit Bannus. Moreover, there are even parallels in points of detail: e.g., both the *Temple Scroll* (63:5) and

[187] Riskin, *Halakhah*; Goldenberg, *Halakhah*.
[188] Goodenough, *Jewish Symbols*.
[189] Feldman, 'Orthodoxy', 215-37.
[190] Belkin, *Philo*.
[191] Moore, *Judaism*.
[192] Kohler, 'Halakik Portions', 74.
[193] Yadin, *Temple Scroll* 1. 62, 93-94, 305.

Josephus (*Ant.* 4:222) state that the public officers of the nearest town are to wash their hands in holy water over the head of a heifer in expiation for an undetected murderer, whereas the Bible (Deut 21:6) states that they are to wash their hands over the heifer, without specifying the head. In addition, Ginzberg[194] has concluded from the fact that whereas according to both the Hebrew Bible (1 Kgs 21:13) and the Septuagint (1 Kgs 20:13) there were two false witnesses against Naboth while Josephus (*Ant.* 8:358) speaks of three, that Josephus is following an earlier halakha, which required three witnesses (that is, one accuser and two witnesses) in cases of capital punishment, and notes that the *Damascus Covenant* (9:17, 22) similarly requires three witnesses in capital cases. Altshuler,[195] however, has shown that the parallels in classification, purpose, program, and structure with the *Temple Scroll* are few and superficial, and that the differences are major. As to the procedure in the case of the undetected murderer, Josephus may simply be following the Septuagint, which reads 'over the head', or he may reflect the actual practice, since the Bible does not specify over which part of the heifer the elders are to wash their hands. Finally, with regard to the number of witnesses, the Bible itself (Deut 19:15) declares that a matter shall be established through two or three witnesses; and Josephus may reflect a divergent understanding of this peculiar prescription, namely that in civil cases the murder of witnesses required is two, whereas for capital cases three witnesses are needed. Or, alternatively, Josephus may simply be describing the fact that three men rose in witness against Naboth, without any indication that evidence from three witnesses is required in such a case.

We have already noted indications, particularly in his symbolism, of Josephus' probable indebtedness to Philo. Belkin[196] cites support for his startling statement that Philo, an Alexandrian, knew more about Palestinian law than did Josephus, the Judean; and we may guess that Josephus, who shared Philo's apologetic motive, was not unaware of Philo's knowledge in this area. In particular, there are four instances where Josephus' interpretation of law agrees with Philo's *Hypothetica*: the public reading of the Tora on the Sabbath (*Ag.Ap. 2:175*), the death penalty for abortion (*Ag.Ap.* 2:202), the prohibition of concealing anything from friends (*Ag.Ap.* 2:207), and the prohibition to kill animals that have taken refuge in one's home (*Ag.Ap.* 2:213). While it is true that these are also paralleled in rabbinic sources, the rabbinic parallels are not quite as precise as those in Philo. In particular, we may note the striking parallel in language between Philo (*Hypothetica* 7:9) and Josephus (*Ag.Ap.* 2:213) in connection with the animal that has taken refuge in one's house as a suppliant. To this we may add that Josephus' statement (*Ag.Ap.* 2:199) that sexual intercourse is permitted only if intended for procreation may have been influen-

---

[194] Ginzberg, *Legends* 6, 312, n. 39.
[195] Altshuler, 'On the Classification', 1-14.
[196] Belkin, *Philo*, 22-23.

ced by the practice of the Essenes (*War* 2:161) or by Philo's remark (*Moses* 1:6, 28) that Moses had sexual relations solely in order to beget children. Moreover, while it is true that the Septuagint also interprets Exod 22:27 (28) as forbidding the blasphemy of other people's gods, Josephus' reason (*Ag.Ap.* 2:237) agrees with that of Philo (*Moses* 2:38, 205), namely, that this is forbidden out of respect for the very name 'God'. Moreover, Josephus' presentation (*Ant.* 4:285-86) of the law of deposits has some similarities in language to that of Philo (*On the Special Laws* 4:7, 30-31), so that a hypothesis of borrowing or of a common source is plausible, as Ehrhardt[197] has suggested.

The thesis that Josephus was influenced by Roman law has been broached by a number of scholars: Weyl, Cohen, and Jackson.[198] Cohen, commenting on Josephus' statement (*Ant.* 4:272) that if a thief is unable to defray the penalty imposed upon him, he is to become the slave of the aggrieved party, notes that there is no parallel in either the Bible or the Talmud but that there is in Roman law. Jackson has suggested that Josephus' aim in accommodating Jewish to Roman law may have been to smooth his way with his Roman audience. We may reply, however, that Josephus nowhere indicates that he had studied or admired Roman law (and modesty is not one of his virtues, and he did seek to ingratiate himself with the Roman imperial family at least); and, on the contrary, he insists on the unique excellence of Jewish law (*Ant.* 1:22-23; *Ag.Ap.* 2:163).

Josephus is at times more strict than the rabbis in his interpretation of law, as notably in the case of artistic representation, where, for example (*Life* 65), he indicates to the Jews of Galilee that he will lead them to destroy Herod the Tetrarch's palace because it had been decorated with images of animals, and when he condemns (*Ant.* 8:195) King Solomon for breaking the Second Commandment in putting the images of bulls and lions in the Temple, whereas the Bible (1 Kgs 7:25, 10:20) has no such rebuke. The rabbis (*B.T. Avoda Zara* 43b), in contrast, declare that all faces are permissible except that of a human. Avi-Yonah[199] attempts to explain the discrepancy by suggesting that Josephus is reflecting the view of the Pharisees and of the masses, whereas the art that has come down to us is that of Sadducean aristocrats; but this is an unlikely hypothesis, since the Sadducees were so few in number (*Ant.* 18:17), were literalists in their interpretation of the Bible, and apparently disappeared with the destruction of the Temple, whereas the 'liberal' approach to images in art continues. A more likely explanation for the rabbis' liberalism is that the masses of the people were liberal in matters of artistic representation despite all rulings, and that the rabbis were realistic enough to recognize this, as they were in their attitude toward magic and charms, which are clearly forbidden in the

---

[197] Ehrhardt, 'Parakatatheke', 32-90.
[198] Weyl, *Jüdische Strafgesetze*; Cohen, 'Civil Bondage', 113-32; Jackson, *Essays*, 3-4. On the question as to whether Josephus knew enough Latin to be able to follow discussions of Roman law see above, n. 147.
[199] Avi-Yonah, *Oriental Art*, 23-27.

Bible (Deut 18:10-11) and which yet are tolerated (e.g. *B. T. Sanhedrin* 68a and *B. T. Shabbat* 62a). Josephus, on the other hand, had no 'constituency' and could afford to maintain an unyielding posture.

Wacholder[200] has presented the revolutionary suggestion that the Mishna does not present the halakha current in the Second Temple period but rather the law that would take force when the Messiah would come and would rebuild the Temple; and we may be tempted to suggest that the same may be true of Josephus' summary of the law. But the patently apologetic nature of the *Antiquities* and especially of the treatise *Against Apion*, which contain compendia of the legal code, would militate against such a theory; for apology, we may remark, has force only when it is supported by reality.

Bibliography

For an annotated, critical bibliography see FELDMAN, *Josephus and Modern Scholarship* 1937-1980, pp. 121-91 and 492-527.

On Josephus' biblical text the sole systematic work remains that of MEZ, *Die Bibel*, who restricts himself to *Antiquities*, Books 5-7, and whose work is now viewed in the light of the Dead Sea manuscript of Samuel by ULRICH, *Qumran Text*.

For Josephus' reworking of the biblical narrative see RAPPAPORT, *Agada und Exegese*, who often stretches the evidence in noting parallels with rabbinic midrashim; BRAUN, *History and Romance*, who stresses Josephus' use of erotic and romantic motifs; ATTRIDGE, *Interpretation*, who has the closest to a comprehensive treatment of the whole subject and who emphasizes theological motifs; and the essays on individual biblical episodes and figures by FELDMAN, who highlights Josephus' debt to classical Greek authors and motifs. The only biblical book which has been systematically analyzed (though with a number of omissions) for its sources is in FRANXMAN, *Genesis*. On individual passages in Josephus, the rich notes in GINZBERG, *Legends*, are most useful in noting parallels with Philo, Pseudo-Philo, rabbinic midrashim, and Church Fathers.

For Josephus' paraphrase of the legal portions of the Pentateuch and his relationship to rabbinic law the sole work which approaches comprehensiveness is the unpublished doctoral dissertation by GOLDENBERG, *Halakhah*.

---

[200] Wacholder, *Messianism*.

Chapter Fourteen

The Interpretation of the Bible by the Minor Hellenistic Jewish Authors

Pieter W. van der Horst

Introduction

In this contribution, not all minor Hellenistic Jewish authors will be dealt with. Excluded are all pseudepigrapha because they constitute a class of their own and are discussed elsewhere in this volume, as is also Aristobulus.[1] Some borderline cases, like Thallus and Theophilus, have also been omitted either because their Jewish identity is uncertain or because their tiny fragments do not yield much of importance. We have restricted ourselves to the nine authors from whom quotations or excerpts have been preserved via Alexander Polyhistor in the ninth book of bishop Eusebius' *Praeparatio Evangelica* (henceforth *PE*), written in the first quarter of the fourth century C.E.[2]

Alexander Polyhistor[3] was a prolific writer in the genre of geographical-historical periegesis. According to the Suda (*s.v.* Ἀλέξανδρος ὁ Μιλήσιος, ed. Adler 1, p. 104) he was brought as a captive from Miletus to Rome in the time of Sulla, but regained his liberty in 82 B.C.E.; he died in Italy as an aged man somewhere after 40 B.C.E.[4] Innumerable books came from his pen (συνέγραψε βίβλους ἀριθμοῦ κρείττους, Suda *s.v.*), e.g. on the history of Egypt, Babylonia, India, Crete, Libya, Phrygia, Lycia (Αἰγυπτιακά, Χαλδαϊκά, Ἰνδικά, Κρητικά, Λιβυκά, Περὶ Φρυγίας, Περὶ Λυκίας), etc.[5] He was not an original and independent author, for most of his work seems to have consisted of

---

[1] On Aristobulus see Borgen, 'Philo of Alexandria', 274-79 (Philo and His Predecessor Aristobulus).

[2] Some fragments or parts of them are quoted also in Clemens Alexandrinus' *Stromateis*. The texts are most conveniently accessible in Denis, *Fragmenta*, 175-228 (Denis prints the text from Mras' edition of Eusebius' *PE* in *GCS* 43, 1, Berlin 1954, but without app. crit.). The historians can now best be consulted in Holladay, *Fragments* 1.

[3] On Alexander Polyhistor see Freudenthal, *Hellenistische Studien*; Susemihl, *Geschichte* 2, 356-64; Christ-Schmid-Stählin, *Geschichte der griechischen Litteratur* 2/1, 400-01; Lesky, *Geschichte*, 873; Stern, *GLAJJ* 1, 157ff.; *Der Kleine Pauly* s.v. 1, 252. The fragments of his historical work have been collected in Jacoby, *FGH* 3 A no. 273.

[4] His pupil, the grammarian Hyginus, had his *floruit* during Augustus' reign. Alexander must have lived from ca. 110/105 to ca. 35/30 B.C.E.. See Unger, 'Wann schrieb Alexander Polyhistor?', and the same, 'Die Blüthezeit'.

[5] He also wrote some works in the field of the history of philosophy and grammar; see Christ-Schmid-Stählin, *Geschichte der griechischen Litteratur* 2/1, 401.

excerpts and quotations from other authors. But in this manner he became one of the most important mediators of knowledge of the history of oriental peoples to later Greek and Latin authors in the West. For us he is most interesting as the author of a work *On the Jews* (Περὶ Ἰουδαίων), which is unfortunately lost, but part of which has been preserved in the quotations made from it by Eusebius of Caesarea in his *PE*. As in his other works, here too Alexander gives quotations (sometimes lengthy) from or summaries of the works of other authors, in this case Jewish ones.

The question of trustworthiness need not be raised when Alexander is quoting poetry; he probably does not alter metrical texts. But when he paraphrases or summarizes prose texts, how reliable is he? The impression is that he has sometimes misunderstood his sources (so that, for example, he makes David the son of Saul), but that in general he has been quite faithful to them.[6] However, it should be borne in mind that in the present case there have been at least five stages of possible corruption of the texts concerned:

1. The transmission of the texts between the autographs and their arrival on Alexander's desk.
2. Alexander's partial rewording or rephrasing of them.
3. The transmission of Alexander's text until it arrived in Eusebius' hands.
4. Eusebius' partial rewording or rephrasing of Alexander's text.
5. The transmission of Eusebius' text through the ages during which it underwent manifold corruption.[7]

These factors should make us somewhat diffident and prevent us from making too apodictic or definitive statements on the material under discussion (especially as to numbers and dates).

Problems of dating and provenance will not be discussed. For most of the authors concerned one could say that their dates cannot be fixed exactly. At any rate it is clear that all of them wrote before Alexander Polyhistor compiled his work *On the Jews* and after the translation of the Pentateuch into Greek. That is to say, they worked somewhere between, say, 250 and 50 B.C.E., most of them probably in the second cent. B.C.E.[8] Their provenance probably was often Alexandria, sometimes Palestine, but certainty is impossible in many cases.[9]

---

[6] See Freudenthal, *Hellenistische Studien*, 16-35.
[7] See for the textual history of *PE* the introduction to Mras' edition, vol. 1, XIII-LIV, and Holladay, *Fragments* 1, 9-13.
[8] See Holladay, *Fragments* 1, 4.
[9] On Jewish Greek literature in Palestine, see Hengel, *Judentum und Hellenismus*, 161-90 (ET 1, 88-102; 2, 59-71).

Poets

EZEKIEL THE DRAMATIST

Ezekiel[10] is the only Jewish playwright known to us from antiquity. He is an important and characteristic example of what could happen when biblical tradition and Greek literary form merged: the content is scriptural story, but the genre is Hellenistic drama.[11] Although he probably wrote more pieces (Clement of Alexandria, *Strom.* 1:23, 155 calls him 'the writer of Jewish tragedies'), portions (which total only 269 iambic trimeters) have been preserved from only one play. It is titled *Exagoge* ('Εξαγωγή) and deals with the exodus story. The LXX text of Exodus 1-15 is followed fairly closely, sometimes almost literally, but there are some significant deviations, varying from minor details to whole non-biblical scenes. In several of these passages one can easily see motifs that recur in later aggadic literature as well, and it is often difficult to say whether Ezekiel depends upon the same sources as the later aggada or that the later aggadists depend upon Ezekiel, the latter being a possibility that one should not dismiss too quickly.[12]

A few of the minor variations will illustrate this point. In the Prologue (vv. 1-65) Moses summarizes the events of Exod 1-2. In v. 21 he says that when the Egyptian princess noticed Moses' basket, she immediately took hold of the child. The biblical text, both the Hebrew and the Greek, have her send her maidservant to fetch it (Exod 2:5). In the Talmud, however, there is a discussion on the question of whether it was the princess herself or one of her maids who took up the child (*B.T. Sota* 12b). And, indeed, the targums Onkelos and Pseudo-Yonatan have the princess do it herself, as does one of the paintings in the Dura-Europos synagogue as well.[13] Ezekiel is our earliest witness to this tradition.

In vv. 60-62 Zippora, a daughter of one of the local rulers, tells Moses that he is in Libya where the black Ethiopians live.[14] So, Zippora is supposed to be an Ethiopian woman. Here, again, Ezekiel works within the framework of Jewish exegesis. In Num 12:1 it is said that Moses had an Ethiopian wife. Targum

---

[10] See Nickelsburg, 'Bible Rewritten', 125-30 (Ezekiel the Tragedian); Robertson in Charlesworth, *OTP* 2, 803-19. Schürer, *History* (rev. ed.) 3/1, 563-65.

[11] Ezekiel's play happens to be the only dramatic piece of the Hellenistic period of which substantial portions have been preserved; everything else is lost except for tiny fragments. Although Ezekiel is heavily influenced by the classical tragedians Aeschylus, Sophocles, and Euripides, his play has several Hellenistic features, e.g. the total abandonment of the unity of time and place. The play probably was divided into five acts, each of which had a different setting. See Jacobson, *Exagoge*, 28-36, and the older literature mentioned in his 'Two Studies' 167, notes.

[12] It is very significant, for instance, that the major non-biblical scene, vv. 68-89, occurs in a Hebrew translation in the aggadic collection of Jellinek, *Bet ha-Midrasch* 5, 159.

[13] See Vermes, 'Bible and Midrash', 90-91; Jacobson, *Exagoge*, 76.

[14] On this apparent geographical oddity see my 'De joodse toneelschrijver', 99; Jacobson, *Exagoge*, 85f.

Neofiti 1 explicitly says there: this Ethiopian woman is no one else than Zippora. The same tradition is found in Demetrius (*PE* 9:29, 1-3) and elsewhere, and it seems to be connected with the legend found in Artapanus and Josephus that Moses stayed for some time in Ethiopia.[15] The apologetic motive is, of course, to avoid the idea that Moses was polygamous.

In vv. 165-66 it is said that the gold, silver and garments that the Jews received from the Egyptians (Exod 11:2; 12:35) are given as payment for all the work the Jews had done for the Egyptians. This apologetic expansion of the scriptural text is also frequently found in rabbinic literature. Obviously, the biblical text was embarrassing to the Jews since it seemed to imply that the Jews borrowed or stole things from the Egyptians without ever returning them. There is evidence that on the basis of this report in Exodus pagans accused the Jews of theft.[16] In the Talmud (*B. T. Sanhedrin* 91a) we read: 'The Egyptians came in a lawsuit against the Jews before Alexander of Macedon. They pleaded thus: Is it not written "And the Lord gave the people favour in the sight of the Egyptians and they lent them gold, etc." (Exod 12:36)? Then return us the gold and silver which you took'. In the ensuing debate between them and Gebiha ben Pesisa the latter refuted them on the basis of Exod 12:40 ('the sojourning of the children of Israel who dwelt in Egypt was 430 years') and said: 'Pay us for the toil of 600.000 men whom you enslaved for 430 years!'. The same anti-Jewish (Egyptian) interpretation of Exod 11:2; 12:35-36 is also reflected in *Esther Rabba* 7:13.[17] 'One can readily understand Ezekiel's introduction of this *apologia* since his Greek audience might well have been regularly subjected to this argument by anti-Semitic native Egyptians'.[18] Here, as elsewhere, Ezekiel avoids or omits all incidents that might cast a bad light on the Jews or Moses.

Now we turn to the most puzzling passage of the preserved fragments, the most extensive non-biblical scene, vv. 68-89. Here Moses says that he dreamt about a great throne on the top of mount Sinai, whereupon a noble man (*i.e.* God) was seated with a crown on his head and a sceptre in his left hand. He beckoned Moses with his right hand, gave the crown and sceptre to him, and summoned him to sit on the great throne which He himself left. From God's throne Moses saw all of heaven and earth, and all the heavenly bodies made obeisance to him. Then he awoke. Moses' father-in-law, Raguel, interprets the dream as predicting that Moses will establish a great throne and become a leader of men, and that he will be able to see 'what is, what was, and what will be'.

---

[15] Jacobson, *Exagoge*, 86ff.; Levy, 'Moïse en Éthiopie', 201-11; Vermes, 'La figure de Moïse', 74; Ginzberg, *Legends* 6, 90 n. 488; Rajak, 'Moses in Ethiopia'; Runnals, 'Moses' Ethiopian Campaign'.

[16] Jacobson, *Exagoge*, 126ff.

[17] Cf. further, *Jub.* 48:18-19; Philo, *Mos.* 1:141-42; *Avot de-R. Natan* A 41, p. 132-33; perhaps Wisdom 10:17?

[18] Jacobson, *Exagoge*, 127. See also Le Déaut, *Targum du Pentateuque* 2, 30 n. 92; Ginzberg, *Legends*, 5, 436-37 n. 233.

This scene has been explained in very divergent ways, I will mention only two important recent opinions which are very opposed to one another. The first one[19] sees in this scene a polemic against notions of Moses' divinization and cosmic kingship, and against throne-mysticism. Consequently, it represents, according to this interpretation, a playing down of anything supernatural in Moses. Many other stories of heavenly ascension by Moses speak of a real ascension, not a visionary one nor in a dream. 'Ezekiel deliberately chose to portray the "ascension" as an imaginary event'.[20] The reason for this conscious rejection of the legend that Moses actually ascended to heaven and beheld God is to be found in the Bible itself. In Num 12:6-8 God says: 'If there is a prophet among you, I the Lord make myself known to him in a vision, I speak with him in a dream. Not so with my servant Moses; he is entrusted with all my house. With him I speak mouth to mouth, clearly, and not in dark speech; and he beholds the form of the Lord'. The fact that in Ezekiel's text God does make himself known to Moses in a vision and speaks to him in a dream makes all this an irrelevant event.

Whereas according to this interpretation Ezekiel is critical of traditions concerning Moses' exaltation, the other interpretation[21] maintains that it is precisely Ezekiel who is one of the earliest champions of such traditions exalting Moses. This interpretation regards the scene not only as one of the earliest post-biblical *merkava* – visions, of which there are so many in the later *hekhalot* – literature (based on Ezek 1), but also as one of the earliest examples of the post-biblical Jewish idea of a vice-regent or plenipotentiary of God: the Old Testament figure of 'the angel of the Lord' could become identified with a human being who achieved a divine status and became God's helper or the mediator between God and men or the highest angel. This person received charge over the world and came close to being an anthropomorphic hypostasis of God himself. That Moses was qualified for such a position was suggested, *inter alia*, by the fact that he is twice called 'god' in Exodus (4:16 and 7:1), and that by God himself. Another serious candidate was, of course, Enoch (Gen 5:24: 'Enoch walked with God. Then he vanished because God took him away'). Hence the most striking parallels to this scene are found in the Enochic literature, especially in the Hebrew Book of Enoch *(3 Enoch)* where Enoch is identified with the highest angel, Metatron (*i.e.*, probably, 'he with whom God shares His throne'). Metatron is called 'the little YHWH' (12:5), which is exactly what Moses is in Ezekiel's play.[22] There probably was even a certain rivalry between Moses and Enoch in this function, but it should be added that they were not the only ones who were identified with the angel of the Lord. The

[19] Jacobson, 'Mysticism and Apocalyptic', and *Exagoge*, 89-97.

[20] Jacobson, 'Mysticism and Apocalyptic', 277.

[21] Van der Horst, 'De joodse toneelschrijver'; 'Moses' Throne-Vision'; 'Some Notes'. Now also Rowland, *Christian Origins* 37, and Fossum, *Name of God*, 191 n. 348.

[22] It should be remembered that in Exod 23:21 God says of the 'angel of the Lord': 'My Name is in Him'.

theme of Moses' divine kingship over the universe is also found elsewhere, in Philo in such a pronounced way that 'the analogy between Moses and God (. . .) approaches consubstantiality'.[23] (Naturally, all this is an important chapter in the prehistory of christology.) The implication of this interpretation is that, for Ezekiel, Moses still is 'an active and present power'[24] who rules the world in God's name, as his plenipotentiary. This is boldly expressed by making God leave his throne, giving it to Moses.[25]

The first mentioned interpretation cannot be entirely ruled out, but the problem is that the play itself does not give any indication that this scene should be so interpreted. The supposed subtle reference to Num 12:6-8 could not have been understood by his Greek audience (and hardly by his Jewish), and since the play drew its biblical material only from Exod 1-15, it is difficult to imagine how Num 12:6-8 could have been brought in somewhere. Moreover, Ezekiel would completely overshoot his mark if he represented the hero of his play as a kind of megalomaniac dreaming about his exaltation to divine cosmic kingship. If that was what Ezekiel wanted to say, he could have made the point by having Raguel say so in his interpretation of the dream. But, on the contrary, Raguel says that Moses will establish a great throne and be a great prophet (thereby indicating, incidentally, that he has not yet grasped the full meaning of the vision, a well-known literary device). Just as the prohibition of animal-worship in Exod 20:4-5 did not inhibit Ezekiel's contemporary Artapanus from presenting Moses as the founder of the Egyptian animal cult, so Num 12:6-8 did not prevent Ezekiel from giving his view of Moses in the form of a dream-vision (thus using a dramatic form well-known from his classical predecessors).[26]

The other great non-biblical scene, depicting the appearance of a phoenix at the exodus, can only be dealt with very briefly.[27] Recent study of the myth of the phoenix has shown that the common element in stories about the appearances of this miraculous bird is that it indicates an important turning-point in history.[28] The accent always falls on the symbolism of the phoenix as inaugurator of a new era. In a sixth cent. C.E. Coptic sermon (which contains much older tradition) it is also reported that 'at the time that God brought the children of Israel out of Egypt by the hand of Moses, the phoenix showed itself on the temple of On, the

---

[23] Meeks, *Prophet-King*, 104f. The above-said is based upon Meeks' *Prophet-King*, his article 'Moses as God and King'; Segal's *Two Powers in Heaven*, and his article 'Ruler of this World'; and upon Fossum, *Name of God*. Detailed evidence can be found in my three articles mentioned in n. 21.

[24] The phrase is Goodenough's who uses it for Philo's view of Moses (*By Light, Light*, 233).

[25] What is meant here is the same as what Jesus says in Matt 28:18 ἐδόθη μοι πᾶσα ἐξουσία ἐν οὐρανῷ καὶ ἐπὶ γῆς.

[26] See Kappelmacher, 'Zur Tragoedie', 78-80; Starobinski-Safran, 'Un Poète', 220; Snell, *Szenen*, 170ff.

[27] See my 'De Joodse toneelschrijver', 110-12; Jacobson, *Exagoge*, 157-66.

[28] See Van den Broek, *The Myth of the Phoenix*. Collins (*Athens*, 209f.) misses the point because he does not know Van den Broek's work.

city of the sun'.[29] The exodus is the beginning of a new era in world-history, marked by the manifestation of the fabulous phoenix.

It is clear from all this that Ezekiel's deviations from the biblical text serve one purpose: the glorification of Moses and of the people and Israel. Detractions by anti-Semitic propaganda probably inspired him to emphasize the nobility of this people and its first leader, even the divine status of the latter, whose heavenly enthronement validates the nation of the Jews as divinely established.[30]

PHILO THE EPIC POET

This author[31] wrote a lengthy epic of at least 14 (or 4?) books, *On Jerusalem*, in what is sometimes almost unintelligible Greek. This obscurity may be due partly to the author's own tortuous style and diction,[32] partly to faulty transmission of the text. Only 24 lines (hexameters) are extant. The first fragment deals with the binding of Isaac, the second with Joseph's rule over Egypt, the third with the water-supply of Jerusalem. This time not drama but epic, more exactly epic on the history of a city,[33] is the Greek genre used to convey the biblical story.

It is important to notice that in the first book of this poem on the history of Jerusalem the story of Gen 22 is dealt with, since this implies the equation of the *land* Moriah (Gen 22:2) with the *mount* Moriah, probably already hinted at in 2 Chr 3:1,[34] and explicitly stated in later tradition, e.g. *Jub.* 18:13; Josephus, *Ant.* 1:226, 7:333; targums Onkelos and Ps.-Yonatan *ad* Gen 22:2; *Gen. Rabba* 55:7 (p. 591-92); etc.[35] According to current opinion, it is only in vv. 8-10 that the *Akeda* is mentioned.[36] However, I believe that already in v. 2, where Abraham is said to be 'famous especially by reason of the knot of the bonds' ('Αβραὰμ

---

[29] Van den Broek, *The Myth of the Phoenix*, 47. In Ezekiel the bird appears at Elim (Exod 15:27); so probably the Coptic sermon does not derive the motif from Ezekiel.

[30] See Fallon, *The Enthronement*, 48. It has to be emphasized here that since Manetho (beginning of the third cent. B.C.E.; see Stern, *GLAJJ*, 1, 62ff.) there was a continous tradition of anti-Semitic versions of the exodus story; see Gager, *Moses* 113-33, and my *Chaeremon*, 49f.

[31] See Nickelsburg, 'Bible Rewritten', 118-21; Attridge in Charlesworth, *OTP* 2, 781-84. Probably he is not identical with Philo the Elder (mentioned by Josephus, *Ag. Ap.* 1:218, and Clemens Alexandrinus, *Strom.* 1:141, 3); see Walter 'Philon der Epiker'; Wacholder, 'Philo (the Elder)'; Schürer, *History* (rev. ed.) 3/1, 559-61. Unfortunately, about another Jewish epic poet, Sosates, called the 'Jewish Homer', we know next to nothing; see Cohen, 'Sosates, the Jewish Homer', and Van der Horst, 'Korte notities' 102-03.

[32] Schürer, *Geschichte* 3:498 'bis zur Unverständlichkeit schwülstig und geschraubt'. Walter, 'Philon, der Epiker', 141 refers to an unpublished paper by J. Atwell and J. Hanson who compare Philo's style to that of Apollonius Rhodius' *Argonautica* and Rhianus' *Messeniaca*, both third cent. B.C.E. epics; see already Gutman, 'Philo the Epic Poet', 60-63.

[33] On this genre see Ziegler, *Das hellenistische Epos*, 18ff.; Gutman, 'Philo the Epic Poet' 38f., 59ff.

[34] See Williamson, *1 and 2 Chronicles*, 203f.

[35] See Fohrer, 'Morija', 1239; Barrois, 'Moriah', 438f.; Bowker, *Targums*, 230.

[36] See e.g., most recently, Walter, 'Philon der Epiker', 149.

κλυτοηχὲς ὑπέρτερον ἅμματι δεσμῶν), reference is made to the *Akeda* (rather than to the making of the covenant in Gen 17).[37] Vv. 5-7 fit in well with this interpretation: 'with a loud voice the Blessed One stopped the kindling (of the wood) and made his (Abraham's) fame immortal' (ἔκκαυμα βριήπυος αἰνετὸς ἴσχων / ἀθάνατον ποίησεν ἐὴν φάτιν). These lines are best explained as a free rendering of Gen 22:11-12. 16-18, comparable with the later aggadic accounts as reflected in the targums *ad loc.* and *Gen. Rabba* 56:7ff. (p. 602ff.).

Aggadic elements come to the fore even more clearly in the description of Abraham as the one who left the splendid enclosure of the giants (4-5 λιπόντι . . . ἀγλαὸν ἕρκος αἰνοφύτων).[38] This most probably refers to the equation of the giants of Gen 6:4 with the rulers of Babel who planned and executed the building of the tower under Nimrod (Gen 10:8-12 combined with 11:1-9) and who tried to coerce Abraham to join in their enterprise; see for instance *Jub.* 10; Josephus, *Ant.* 1:113-14; Ps-Eupolemus, fragm. 1; Ps-Philo, *LAB* 6; *B.T. Pesahim* 118a; *PRE* 24.[39]

The second short fragment, on Joseph as ruler of Egypt, does not exhibit specific aggadic traits,[40] unless they are hidden in the very obscure 5th line in which Joseph is said to be δινεύσας λαθραῖα χρόνου πλημμυρίδι μοίρης ('unraveling the secrets of fate in the flood of time'?), perhaps a reference to his onirocritic activities in Gen 40 and 41.

The third fragment contains a rather unclear description of a part of the water supply system of Jerusalem.[41] Its astonishing features are emphasized (vv. 1 and 7). A comparable enthusiasm for this system is also reflected in Sir 50:3 and especially in *Ep. Arist.* 89-91.[42] As this account is not based on the text of the Bible, it may be an eye-witness account, but it may also derive from literary sources similar to (those of) *Ep. Arist.* The tendency to underline the magnificence of Jerusalem and to eulogize Abraham is similar to the one manifesting itself in Ezekiel's picture of Moses and Israel.

THEODOTUS

Like Philo, Theodotus wrote an epic about the history of a city, Shechem. Because of this theme and because the author calls Shechem 'a holy city' (ἱερὸν

---

[37] See also Collins, *Athens*, 45, and Attridge in Charlesworth, *OTP* 2, 783.

[38] For this translation of αἰνόφυτοι see Mras *ad loc.* and Walter, 'Philon der Epiker', 149.

[39] Other rabbinic texts in Strack-Billerbeck, *Kommentar* 2, 95; 3, 34-35. Walter, *ibid.*; Holladay, *Fragments* 1, 178 n. 5. See also below, n. 120.

[40] The theory of Dalbert (*Theologie*, 34-35) and Gutman ('Philo the Epic Poet', 59) that Joseph is described here as a god is rightly refuted by Walter, *ibid.* 150 n. c.

[41] On this system see Kosmala, 'Jerusalem' 825-27, and Jeremias, *Rediscovery of Bethesda* (non vidi); also Amiran, 'Water Supply' and Mazar, 'Aquaducts'.

[42] Walter, *ibid.*, 142-43. A remote pagan parallel is Frontinus' *De aquis urbis Romae*.

ἄστυ, fragm. 1) he has often been held to be a Samaritan.[43] But nowadays there is a growing consensus that he was not: there is no clear pro-Samaritan tendency in the poem; Garizim is not mentioned; and the murder of the Shechemites by Jacob's sons (Gen 34) is not condemned (as in Gen 49:5-7) but viewed as an act commanded by God against the godless (ἀσεβεῖς, fragm. 5) inhabitants of Shechem; and 'holy city' is a traditional Homeric expression.[44] But these facts do not disprove that Theodotus was a Samaritan. Against the consensus it may be argued that the Samaritans of Theodotus' time, as Pentateuchal Jews, did not claim to be descendants of the Shechemites (who were all murdered), but of the Israelites left in the land at the time of the Assyrian exile, and of the priests who came back to teach the Assyrian colonists to worship the God of Israel (2 Kings 17). The Jews partly accepted these claims. The Shechemites of Hellenistic times can, therefore, easily be supposed to praise Simeon and Levi and to represent them as heroes who by their violent deed liberated the 'holy city' from its former wicked inhabitants. So Theodotus may have been a Samaritan author after all.[45]

The 47 lines that are extant (*PE* 9:22, 1-11) are partly a description of Shechem's surroundings and a summary of Jacob's history, especially with Laban (Gen 29-30, without aggadic embellishments: fragm. 1-3), and partly a free poetic rendering of Gen 34 (fragm. 4-6) in Homeric style. There are some interesting agreements with Josephus' presentation of the same story in *Ant.* 1:337-41,[46] and also with *Jub.* 30, Judith 9:2-4, *Test. Levi* 5-7. For example, Dina is said to have gone to Shechem because there was a festival (fragm. 4 – *Ant.* 1:337). It is not both Simeon and Levi who thought out their murderous plan, but only Simeon (fragm. 4 – Judith 9:2), as in *Test. Levi* 5 it is only Levi. In fragm. 5 their act is justified as being in accordance with God's will, just as in *Jub.* 30:23-25 it is counted to them as righteousness; also in *Test. Levi* 5:3-4; 6:8; Josephus, *Ant.* 1:341, and *Jos.As.* 23:14, we find attempts to unburden the two brothers. Philo praises their role in *On the Migration of Abraham* 224 and *On the Change of Names* 195 and 200. Cf. also *Gen. Rabba* 80:8. 10 (p. 960-61, 964-66); 97 (p. 1206-07). In fragm. 6 it is not only said *that* they killed Hamor and Shechem, which is the only thing mentioned in Gen 34:26, but *how* they killed them is also described, and who killed whom: Simeon kills Hamor, Levi kills Shechem; in *Test. Levi* 6:4 first Levi kills Shechem, then Simeon kills Hamor. It is also noteworthy that, whereas Gen 34 only states that the brothers say: 'We cannot give our sister to a man who is uncircumcised', Theodotus has

---

[43] Freudenthal, *Hellenistische Studien*, 99f. Schürer, *Geschichte* 3:499f. But see now, Schürer, *History* (rev.ed.) 3/1, 561-63; since then many other scholars, see Walter, 'Theodotus der Epiker' 158 nn. 24, 25; Pummer, 'Genesis 34', 177 n. 2; Fallon in Charlesworth, *OTP* 2, 785ff.

[44] Kippenberg, *Garizim*, 83f.; Collins, 'The Epic of Theodotus', 91ff.; Walter, *ibid.* 157-61. Cf. e.g. Homer, *Odyssey* 1:2.

[45] See M. Smith, *Palestinian Parties*, 188-89 (with nn. 207-17). For this paragraph I owe several important hints to Prof. Morton Smith, for which I am very grateful.

[46] Josephus may have known Theodotus' work, however.

Jacob say: 'It is not allowed (οὐ θεμιτόν) to the Hebrews to marry sons or daughters from elsewhere, but only such ones as declare to belong to the same people'. This wording, especially οὐ θεμιτόν, is reminiscent of a similar addition to the text that targums Neofiti, Onkelos and Ps.-Yonatan make in v. 7 (in a comparable context): it is לא כשר, 'not allowed', to do such a thing. The poem evidently insists on the prohibition of mixed marriages with the uncircumcised Gentiles.

The poem is often thought to be a piece of ideological justification of the anti-Samaritan policy of John Hyrcanus I (135-104 B.C.E.)[47] – this ruler destroyed the temple on mount Garizim in 129 and devastated Shechem in 109 B.C.E. –, since an anti-Samaritan interpretation of the story of Gen 34 could be very helpful in justifying his acts of violence against the Samaritans.[48] Indeed, the procedure to re-interpret biblical texts in an anti-Samaritan way is also used elsewhere: It has been demonstrated that in the course of the textual transmission of the Hebrew Bible, scribes made subtle changes in several texts so that they received an anti-Samaritan edge.[49] But if, as has been argued above, the consensus that Theodotus was not a Samaritan author is wrong, the poem should be read as a piece of Samaritan propaganda, in which the author presents the ancestors of the Samaritans as zealous Jews.[50] Theodotus had an obvious desire to purge the character of these forefathers from negative traits.[51]

Historians

DEMETRIUS

Demetrius, the so-called chronographer, is almost certainly the earliest Jewish author we know to have written in Greek.[52] He is interesting in that he tries to mould biblical material into both the Hellenistic genre of the description of the history of a non-Greek people by one of its members in a way that could meet

---

[47] Walter, 'Theodotus der Epiker', 159-61; Collins, *Athens*, 48; Collins, 'The Epic of Theodotus'. Pummer, 'Genesis 34' rightly emphasizes that not every treatment of Gen 34 with a positive valuation of the patriarchs' deed is *per se* anti-Samaritan polemic.

[48] Kippenberg, *Garizim*, 85-87, 93.

[49] Tournay, 'Quelques relectures'. Tournay dates most of the examples of 'relectures antisamaritaines' to the 2nd cent. B.C.E. A relatively simple instance is, e.g., Hosea 14:9 where MT has אפרים מה לי עוד לעצבים, LXX τῷ Ἐφραιμ τί αὐτῷ ἔτι καὶ εἰδώλοις; Here LXX's αὐτῷ = לו is original, MT's לי is an anti-Samaritan correction. For the reverse process cf. Joshua 24:1 in Mt and LXX.

[50] Smith, *Palestinian Parties*, 189. Van der Horst, 'Korte notities' has to be corrected on this point.

[51] Pummer, 'Genesis 34', 180. The same tendency is also noticeable in Artapanus' account (fragm. 2) of Joseph's move to Egypt: he is not sold by his brothers, but goes of his own accord.

[52] Walter, 'Demetrios', 282. He worked in the last half or quarter of the third cent. B.C.E. For literature on Demetrius see Holladay, *Fragments* 1:57f. J. Hanson in Charlesworth, *OTP* 2:846-47; Attridge, 'Historiography' 161-62; Schürer, *History* (rev. ed.) 3/1, 513-17. On Demetrius, Artapanus and Eupolemus, see Van der Horst, 'Schriftgebruik'.

528

scientific criticism and into the genre of *erotapokriseis*. The somewhat unwieldy definition of the first-mentioned genre refers to the works of people like the Egyptian Manetho, the Babylonian Berossus, the Roman Fabius Pictor (and, from a later period, the Phoenician Philo of Byblos and the Jew Josephus), and others. When at the beginning of the Hellenistic era new, especially oriental, peoples came within the horizon of the Greeks, these peoples competed with one another in trying to win the ear of their Hellenistic masters. Adopting Greek modes of reasoning, they tried to remedy the ignorance of the Greeks concerning their respective peoples, their history, wisdom, and especially their antiquity. They tried to trace their own origin back to remotest antiquity in order not to appear to be the imitators of other people.[53] Proudly aware of the greater antiquity of their people over against the Greeks (the implication being that Greek culture was dependent upon theirs), they made various chronological calculations (and exaggerations) when presenting their respective national histories, thereby using Greek forms of historical thinking, but following their national sources. This is the cultural framework in which the Jewish historian Demetrius' work *On the Kings of Judaea* (if that was its title, which is uncertain)[54] has to be placed.[55] An additional factor in this case may have been a growing critical attitude of some hellenized Jews themselves towards their Bible. Over against that, the credibility of the biblical record had to be defended and established.[56] As Berossus and Manetho did for their peoples, so Demetrius gave a matter-of-fact abridgement of the biblical materials from Abraham (or Adam?) to at least the end of the kingdom of Juda (in 586 B.C.E.), skilfully placing everything in an accurate chronological framework. *Mutatis mutandis* one may compare this also with works like *Jubilees* and *Seder Olam Rabba* where similar calculations occur.[57]

The second-mentioned genre is the *erotapokriseis*.[58] This is a literary style in which the theme is dealt with in the form of questions and answers (κατὰ πεῦσιν καὶ ἀπόκρισιν; also called ἀπορίαι καὶ λύσεις or ζητήματα καὶ λύσεις, 'problems and solutions'). This form was applied especially in scientific literature, particularly in the exegesis of Homer. Demetrius uses it in a rather loose, unsystematic way.[59] Not much of his materials are dealt with in this way, but occasionally problems created by the biblical accounts are introduced

---

[53] See Bickerman, 'The Jewish Historian Demetrios'. A later Jewish example is Justus of Tiberias, fragm. 2 (Holladay, *Fragments* 1:383).

[54] See Walter, 'Demetrios', 280.

[55] See Fraser, *Ptolemaic Alexandria* 1:690-94, esp. 693.

[56] Collins, *Athens*, 29.

[57] See M. Gaster, 'Demetrius and Seder Olam'. On Hellenistic biblical chronologies see Wacholder, *Eupolemus*, 97ff.

[58] Dörrie – Dörries, 'Erotapokriseis'.

[59] On the unsystematic use of *erotapokriseis* see Dörrie – Dörries, *ibid.*, 343-45; they also refer to Philo's *Quaestiones in Genesim et Exodum*.

in question-and-answer form (fragm. 2, 3, and 5; see below). Polyhistor's abridgement may of course have erased other examples of this form.

The substantial fragm. 2 (*PE* 9:21, 1-19)[60] first gives a discussion of Jacob's age when he left for Haran (comparable with *B.T. Megilla* 17a) and (omitting Gen 28-29) then presents the exact dates and chronological sequence of the births of Jacob's sons (each ten months after the other or simultaneously from both mothers or maidservants). Then he mentions Jacob's struggle with an 'angel', whereas both the Hebrew and the Greek ot (Gen 32:25) have just 'man'. This modification, which occurs here for the first time, is current in all later aggadic literature: Targum Ps.-Yonatan says it was an angel in the shape of a man, targum Neofiti says it was Sariel with the appearance of a man, *Gen. Rabba* 77:2 (p. 910-12) and 78:1 (p. 916-18) says it was Michael or Gabriel.[61] The influence of post-biblical angelology is noticeable here. There follows a short account of Simeon's and Levi's revenge for the raping of Dina by Shechem (Gen 34), unlike Theodotus without any embellishments, but with the exact ages of all persons concerned indicated: Dinah 16 years and 4 months, Levi 20 years and 6 months, Simeon 21 years and 4 months, and Jacob 107 years. This again shows his almost grotesque preoccupation with chronology.

When dealing with the Joseph story in Gen 37-50, Demetrius again omits many scenes, so that it becomes no more than a series of disconnected events.[62] He raises two questions. First, why did it take 9 years before Joseph, who lived in wealthy circumstances in Egypt, sought to rescue his father from the famine-ridden Canaan to Egypt? The answer is: 'Because Jacob was a shepherd, as were Joseph's brothers too. But being a shepherd is considered something disgraceful by the Egyptians. That it was for this reason that he did not send for his father is made clear by himself. For when his relatives came to him, he said to them that if the king would invite them and ask them what kind of work they did, they were to say that they were cattle-keepers' (fragm. 2; *PE* 9:21, 13). Obviously Demetrius interpreted, in an almost rabbinic fashion, the lxx text of Gen 46:31-34 in such a way as if it meant to say that shepherd (ποιμήν) and cattle-keeper (κτηνοτρόφος) indicate different kinds of work. The second question raised is: why did Joseph give Benjamin at dinner five times as much as to his other brothers (Gen 43:34), whereas obviously Benjamin could never consume so much meat? The answer is: 'He did this because six (mss: seven)[63] sons had been born to his father by Leah and only two by Rachel, his mother. Therefore he gave Benjamin five portions and he himself took one: together

---

[60] Fragm. 1 is not dealth with, not only since the attribution to Demetrius by Freudenthal (*Hellenistische Studien*, 14f., 36) is very uncertain – it is quoted anonymously in *PE* 9:19,4 –, but also because it is nothing but a very short summary of Gen 22 without any aggada, contrary to Philo the epic poet and all later *akeda* literature.

[61] See also *PRE* 37; for other instances Ginzberg, *Legends* 1:384ff., 5:305; Vermes, 'The Archangel'. Josephus, *Ant.* 1:331-34, has φάντασμα in 331 and 334, ἄγγελος in 333.

[62] But how much of this is due to Polyhistor? See Fraser, *Ptolemaic Alexandria* 1:691.

[63] On this text-critical problem see Holladay, *Fragments* 1, 84-85 nn. 34-37.

that was six (MSS: seven)[64] portions, just as many as Leah's sons had got. (. . .) So the house of his mother was put on a par (with Leah's house)' (*ibid.* 14-15). Compare another solution in *Gen. Rabba* 92:5 (p. 1143).

The fragment closes with a computation of the number of years from the creation till Jacob's arrival in Egypt (3624 years), a genealogy from Jacob to Moses, and a calculation of the length of Israel's sojourn in Egypt (215 years) and of the time-lapse from Abraham's departure from Ur till the exodus (430 years). This last number (430) is given in the Hebrew text of Exod 12:40 as the time of Israel's stay in Egypt, in the LXX however as the time of Israel's stay in Egypt and Canaan. The latter reading is presupposed non only by Demetrius but also by the apostle Paul (Gal 3:17) and *Seder Olam Rabba* 3; Josephus has 215 years in *Ant.* 2:318, but in 2:204 he speaks of 400 years of oppression of the Israelites in Egypt (from Gen 15:13), thus indicating how the biblical texts created chronological problems to the Jews. This becomes still more apparent in *Mekhilta de-Rabbi Yishmael, Pisha* 14, p. 50 (*ad* 12:40) where both biblical passages, Exod 12:40 and Gen 15:13, are quoted and opposed and where it is asked, 'How can both these passages be maintained?'. *Exod. Rabba* 18:11 (*ad* 12:40) says about the 430 years: 'that is from the time that the decree was pronounced (*sc.* Gen 15), for they were only 210 years in Egypt'.[65] Again we see how Demetrius, sensitive as he was to the requirements of scientific historiography, attempted to solve problems of biblical chronology which could undermine faith in the reliability of the Scriptures.

Similar problems are treated in Fragm. 3 (*PE* 9:29,1-3). In fragm. 2 Moses' genealogy was presented as: Abraham – Isaac – Jacob – Levi – Kehat – Amram – Moses (Moses being the seventh in that line); in fragm. 3, however, the genealogy of Moses' wife, Zippora, is: Abraham and Keturah – Jokshan – Dedan – Raguel – Jethro – Zippora (the LXX inserted Raguel into the text of Gen 25:1-4, and Demetrius took him to be the father of Jethro),[66] and here Zippora is the sixth in the line. How she could be a contemporary of Moses, is the problem. The solution given is that Abraham begat Isaac when he was 100 years, and Jokshan when he was 142 years; this time-gap being a generation, Zippora could be Moses' contemporary. The fragment continues by stating that, since Abraham sent the sons of his concubines to the East (Gen 25:6), Aaron and Miriam could say that Moses had taken an Ethiopian wife (Num 12:1), the implication being that Ethiopia lies in the East[67] and that Zippora is identical with Moses' Ethiopian wife, a motif we have already met in Ezekiel the dramatist. No doubt Demetrius' concern was to show that Moses was not

---

[64] On this text-critical problem see Holladay, *Fragments* 1, 84-85 nn. 34-37.
[65] See Heinemann, '210 Years of Egyptian Exile'.
[66] Freudenthal, *Hellenistische Studien* 42-44; Fraser, *Ptolemaic Alexandria* 3, 960 n. 91.
[67] Cf. Gen 2:13. The ancients often located Ethiopia in the East, even as far as India; see *OCD s.v.* Ethiopia, and above, n. 14.

polygamous and did not marry outside his own people (cf. Theodotus, fragm. 4, *PE* 22, 6), a relevant issue in diaspora-Judaism.[68]

Fragments 4-6 are very brief, fragm. 5 (*PE* 9:29, 16) being especially worth mentioning in the present context.[69] There the question is raised how the Israelites could have weapons (implied, e.g., in Exod 17:8-13), whereas they left Egypt unarmed. The answer is: probably they took arms from the drowned Egyptians who drifted ashore. Ezekiel, *Exagoge* 210, and Josephus, *Ant.* 2:321, also say that the Israelites were unarmed, Josephus adding later (2:349) that they got their weapons from the dead Egyptians. Exod 13:18 says that the Israelites left Egypt חמושים. This is often translated 'armed, equipped for battle', but the exact meaning is quite uncertain. Although most ancient versions take it to mean 'armed' here, the LXX read 'the fifth generation', obviously deriving it from חמש, 'five'. This may have induced Demetrius, Ezekiel, Josephus and others to deny the Jews weapons, thus causing the problem discussed here by Demetrius.[70] Discussion of the meaning of the word is still visible in *Mekhilta, Beshallah* 1, p. 77-78.[71]

Compared to other, later Jewish Hellenistic historians (Eupolemus, Artapanus, etc.) Demetrius is remarkably sober in his descriptions of biblical personalities. No exaltation of Moses, no glorification of Abraham or such like is to be expected from him. 'There is a dryness and lack of adornment of substance and style which is in marked contrast to all other Jewish historiography, in which the figures of early biblical history take on some of the wondrous qualities bestowed on non-biblical figures in the contemporary world'.[72] There is also no evidence of the tendency towards syncretism which we will meet in his successors. The main emphasis is on the credibility of the Bible as a historical record, although he was not a literalist and did not hesitate to modify the text when a passage contradicted his chronological schemes.[73]

ARTAPANUS

A striking contrast with the academic chronographer Demetrius is formed by the 'historian' Artapanus.[74] His Persian name suggests that he was a Jew of

---

[68] Collins, *Athens*, 28.
[69] Although being quoted anonymously, like fragm. 1, it almost certainly is from Demetrius. On fragm. 6 and rabbinic parallels see Wacholder, *Eupolemus* 101 with n. 17, and the notes by Holladay, *Fragments* 1, 90-91 nn. 92-97.
[70] See Jacobson, *Exagoge*, 216 n. 53; Holladay, *Fragments* 1, 89 n. 88; and my 'Some Notes'.
[71] See the excellent examination of the problem by Le Déaut, 'A propos'.
[72] Fraser, *Ptolemaic Alexandria* 1, 693; cf. also Dalbert, *Theologie*, 27.
[73] Wacholder, *Eupolemus*, 103 n. 25 says that 'the idea that the non-legal texts (even the Pentateuch) of Scripture were authoritative and unalterable is evidently post-Maccabean'.
[74] Literature on Artapanus in Fraser, *Ptolemaic Alexandria* 2, 983 n. 177; Walter, 'Artapanos', 126; Holladay, *Fragments* 1:199-201; J.J. Collins in Charlesworth, *OTP* 2:896; add: Droge, 'Interpretation' 151-57; Attridge, 'Historiography' 166-68.

mixed descent or a proselyte.[75] The longest and most important of the three fragments preserved (fragm. 3 = *PE* 9:27, 1-37) is a kind of 'Life of Moses',[76] running from his birth to the exodus (Exod 2-16). Two shorter fragments deal with Abraham (fragm. 1) and Joseph (fragm. 2). The most striking thing about these three fragments is that they deviate from the biblical accounts much farther than those of other Jewish historiographers and that most of the aggadic embellishments do not have exact parallels in contemporary or later Jewish midrashic literature. To be sure, fragm. 1 (*PE* 9:18, 1) has an aggadic element that does have parallels: Abraham came to Egypt, remained there twenty years,[77] and taught the pharao astrology. So, contrary to what was often asserted in antiquity, this important science was originally a Jewish, not an Egyptian invention. Also Ps-Eupolemus (fragm. 1 = *PE* 9:17, 3-4) makes Abraham the inventor of astrology, and Ps-Hecataeus (ii), fragm. 1 (= Josephus, *Ant.* 1:167), again makes him the teacher of this 'Chaldaean art' to the Egyptians. These traditions were probably based upon Gen 15:5. In some Jewish circles Abraham's astrological knowledge was considered a mark of his greatness, especially among syncretistic Jews, but in more conservative circles this idea was so scandalous that they presented it as a pre-conversion practice, which he later abandoned; see e.g. *Jub.* 12:16ff.; Philo, *On Abraham* 68-71 and 81-83; *Sib. Or.* 3:221-30.[78]

The second fragment (*PE* 9:23,1-4) presents Joseph, who after his voluntary (!) voyage to Egypt became right away its administrator or governor, as an organizer of a radical landreform on behalf of the weak and the poor (contrary to Gen 47). So he, too, like Abraham, is a benefactor of the Egyptian people.[79]

The third fragment is too long to be summarized here. The first half (*PE* 9:27,1-20) is an almost wholly non-biblical account of Moses' deeds in Egypt. Artapanus calls him Μώϋσος (instead of Μωϋσῆς) and says that the Greeks called him Mousaios, the mythical Greek poet and teacher of Orpheus.[80] Since according to tradition Orpheus brought culture and religion from Egypt to Greece (e.g. Hecataeus of Abdera *apud* Diodorus Siculus 1:96, 4ff.), the

---

[75] On other Jews with Persian names see Mussies, 'The interpretatio judaica of Thot-Hermes' 92.

[76] The real title of the work probably was *On the Jews*; see Fraser, *Ptolemaic Alexandria* 1, 704 with n. 177, and esp.: Holladay, *Theios Aner*, 215-16 n. 98.

[77] On the midrashic chronology implied here see Wacholder, 'How long did Abraham stay in Egypt?'; he refers to several other calculations in early Jewish literature (*Jub.* 13:11; *1QGenAp* 20:18; *Seder Olam Rabba* 1).

[78] Knox, 'Abraham'; Vermes, 'Life of Abraham', 79ff.; Collins, *Athens*, 35; Walter, 'Pseudo-Orpheus', 225 n. 47; Mayer, 'Aspekte' 123ff.; Mayer says: 'Der Topos "Abraham als Astrolog" lebt von der Authorität, die die populäre wie die wissenschaftliche Astrologie bzw. Astronomie im zweiten vorchristlichen Jahrhundert besonders in Ägypten genossen'. Cf. Georgi, *Gegner*, 67-73.

[79] Similar land reforms are attributed to Sesostris, Isis and Osiris in Diodorus Siculus 1; see Holladay, *Fragments* 1, 228 n. 18.

[80] Usually Musaeus is Orpheus' disciple, but Artapanus reverses the relation; see Kern, *Orphicorum fragmenta*, 50-51; Denis, *Introduction*, 255 n. 43; West, *Orphic Poems*, 39-40.

implication is that Moses is the ultimate source of Greek culture.[81] But there is more: Moses appears to be the inventor of 'many useful things': ships, instruments for quarrying, hydraulic machinery, weapons of war, hieroglyphs, philosophy; he divides the country into 36 districts and assigns to each district its titulary deity (cats, dogs, ibises, etc.). All this made him a favourite among the people (cf. Exod 11:3), especially among the priests who honoured him as a god and called him Hermes, the Greek name of the Egyptian god Thoth. Then follows a long story of pharao's jealousy of Moses' popularity and the ambushes he lays to put Moses out of the way, all of them unsuccesful.[82] (In one of the attacks on him, Moses kills his assailant out of self-defence, clearly a favourable rendering of the story in Exod 2:12, more or less comparable to *Exod. Rabba* 1:29, where the same embarrassment is perceivable. Josephus, *Ant.* 2:254ff., simply omits the story). When Moses is put into jail by the pharao, the doors open of their own accord to set Moses free. He enters the palace, wakes up the king, and when thereupon the kings asks him to tell him the name of his God, Moses whispers the holy Name into the ear of the pharao who collapses consequently. An Egyptian priest who scorns the Name dies. The rest of the story more closely follows the biblical text, although not without many minor midrashic additions (e.g. Moses' staff plays a much greater role than in Exodus).[83]

Several remarks are in order here. First, Artapanus' remarkably great freedom in dealing with the biblical tradition probably is inspired partly by his desire to present Moses in a way that is in direct opposition to the account of Moses given by Manetho (or similar anti-Semitic Greco-Egyptian writers), who present(s) the Jewish leader as the embodiment of hostility to Egypt who attacks their temples and homes, etc. Artapanus' picture of Moses is that of a great teacher to whom the Egyptians owe their culture, their religion, the arts of war and peace, and the basic economy of the country.[84] 'By demonstrating the dependence of Egyptian culture on the Jews, he not only establishes the priority of the latter, but at the same time proves their benevolent as opposed to their malevolent posture'.[85] It is this concern which makes him go even as far as attributing to Moses the establishment of the Egyptian animal-cult, in spite of

---

[81] Collins, *Athens* 34; Holladay, *Fragments* 1, 232 n. 45; Schalit, 'Artapanus' 646: 'In view of the fact that, like Herodotus and Plato, Artapanus sees in Egyptian civilization the origin of all civilization, it may be said that he regards Moses as the father of universal civilization'.

[82] In this context Artapanus reports Moses' war with the Ethiopians and his prolongued stay in Ethiopia, a motif which occurs with many variations in several other sources; see above n. 15.

[83] See Tiede, *Charismatic Figure*, 170ff. It should also be noted that pharao, the Egyptian princess and many other persons, the names of which are not given in the Bible, receive a name here. On this well-known process see Heller, 'Die Scheu vor Unbekanntem'; for the NT Metzger, 'Names for the Nameless'.

[84] Fraser, *Ptolemaic Alexandria* 1, 705.

[85] Holladay, *Theios Aner*, 217.

Exod 20:4-5.[86] It should also be borne in mind that the claim that someone was a 'first inventor' (πρῶτος εὑρετής) was very prestigious in antiquity.[87] In this case it certainly helped to serve the glorification of the Jewish people and its history.

Moses is identified with Thoth-Hermes, the Egyptian god of science and culture. True, the identification is explicitly said to have been made by the Egyptian priests (just as the equation with Musaeus is made by the Greeks) and it has a strong Euhemeristic ring about it[88] which relativizes Egyptian religion, but one cannot say that Artapanus distances himself from this divinization of Moses.[89] As we have seen before, in 'heterodox' circles divinization of Moses did occur (see above on Ezekiel Tragicus); and we also know of Rabbinic speculations regarding the identity of Joseph and the Egyptian god Sarapis[90] (compare Ps-Eupolemus' equation of Enoch and Atlas, *PE* 9:17, 9). The equation of Moses and Thoth-Hermes was possible because there were several contact-points between the two: Thoth as architect of temples – Moses as the one who passed on God's instructions for the making of the Tabernacle; Thoth as giver of laws and as judge – Moses as lawgiver and judge; Thoth as the founder of (local) cults – Moses as the giver of cultic prescriptions; Thoth as the inventor of language and writing and as scribe of the gods – Moses as the first man in the Bible who is said to have written and who was called 'scribe' (*sc.* of God) in later tradition; Thoth's holy bird is the ibis – ibises help Moses during his Ethiopian campaign (Josephus, *Ant.* 2:246ff.); Thoth as a great magician – Moses as a great magician (according to pagan tradition); etc.[91] Besides these parallels with Thoth there are other ones with traditional Egyptian benefactors who gained immortality and divine status because of their benefits to men, especially Sesostris (Hecataeus in Diodorus Siculus 1:53-58), but also Isis and Osiris.[92] The equation of Moses with Egyptian divine personalities shows that, as so often, here too the lines between what is Jewish or Jewish syncretistic and pagan are not easily drawn.[93]

---

[86] That Jews abhorred the cult of animals needs no further documentation; see Holladay, *Fragments* 1, 234 n. 51. N.B.: the LXX inserted the Egyptian sacred bird, the ibis, into the lists of unclean birds in Lev 11:17 and Deut 14:16. Contrast Artapanus in *PE* 9:27, 4.

[87] Thraede, 'Erfinder'.

[88] Euhemerus (± 300 B.C.E.) developed the theory that the gods had originally been great leaders or kings to whom mankind had shown their gratitude for their helpful deeds by worshipping them as gods.

[89] Here I disagree somewhat with Holladay, *Theios Aner*, 227.

[90] See Mussies, 'The interpretatio judaica of Sarapis'.

[91] Detailed evidence in Mussies, 'The interpretatio judaica of Thot-Hermes'.

[92] Tiede, *Charismatic Figure*, 146-77; Holladay, *Theios Aner*, 209ff.; idem, *Fragments* 1, 232-33 n. 46. See above n. 78.

[93] See Tiede, *Charismatic Figure*, 105ff. Freudenthal's theory (*Hellenistische Studien*, 146ff., 162ff.) – based on the half-Jewish half-pagan character of these fragments – that Artapanus' work was a 'Trugschrift' and that he was identical with Ps-Aristeas and Ps-Hecataeus, has been effectively refuted; see e.g. Fraser, *Ptolemaic Alexandria* 2, 983 n. 179.

Many elements still ask for some comment, but I single out the 'Türöffnungs-wunder' and the tremendous power of the holy Name. Doors opening of their own accord (αὐτομάτως) is a motif found in Greek literature from Homer onwards; when opening in order to liberate someone from prison, Euripides' *Bacchae* is our earliest instance.[94] Well-known are the stories of such liberation miracles in the Acts of the Apostles (5:17ff; 12:6ff; 16:25ff).[95] In Jewish litera-ture there are instances of doors opening automatically, but none of them in order to liberate someone. Josephus relates, among several prodigia preceding the destruction of the temple, that its doors opened of their own accord in the middle of the night (*War* 6:293; it is also reported by Tacitus, *Hist.* 5:13),[96] and there are other stories about spontaneous opening of the temple doors in rabbinic literature, but none of these in the context of a liberation (not even the story about the opening of Akiva's prison-gates in *Midrash Prov.* 9:2, p. 31a/b).[97] The fact that the Greek stories of liberations by automatical opening of doors often occur in a Dionysiac context (in the *Bacchae* it is Dionysus who is so liberated) might suggest that Artapanus' story has a point directed against the Dionysus cult in Alexandria.[98] Alongside this typically Greek motif, the next paragraph in the story has a more typically Jewish motif in that it relates the destructive power depending upon the use or abuse of the tetragrammaton. Not only pharao lost consciousness (or died?; the text is unclear) when he heard the Name, but the priest who treated contemptuously the tablet upon which Moses (or pharao) wrote this Name, died a terrible death. 'The Name was endowed with power. The Name and the Power were synonyms'.[99] Acts 4:7 says: 'By what *power* or by what *Name* have you done this?' The *shem ha-meforash* was believed to be extremely powerful and effective both *in bonam* and *in malam partem*. *Exod. Rabba* 1:29-30 (*ad* 1:12 and 14) raises the question, 'with what did Moses slay the Egyptian' (. . .)? The Rabbis say that he pronounced God's name against him and thus slew him' (a tradition also reported by Clemens Alexandrinus, *Strom.* 1:154,1: 'the initiated say that Moses killed him by only a word'). In *1 Enoch* 69:14 the angel requests Michael 'to show him the hidden Name in order that he might enunciate it in the oath so that those might quake before that Name and oath'. In *B.T. Bava Batra* 73a Rabba says that seafarers told him that a stormy sea can be subsided by beating it with clubs on which is engraven: 'I am that I am, Yah, the Lord of Hosts, Amen'. People frequently used the Name on amulets and for incantations, as the Greek magical papyri amply demonstrate, and it does not matter whether the Name is pronounced by

---

[94] See Weinreich, 'Türöffnung' 45ff., 118ff.
[95] Discussed in Weinreich, 'Türöffnung' 147ff.
[96] Weinreich, 'Türöffnung' 109ff.
[97] Strack-Billerbeck, *Kommentar* 2, 707.
[98] On which see Fraser, *Ptolemaic Alexandria* 1, 201-12.
[99] Urbach, *The Sages* 1:124.

a Jew or by a heathen because the effective power lies in the Name itself.[100] Hence the Rabbis developed halakha for the use of the Name in writing and speaking.[101]

So we see how Artapanus uses side by side typically Greek and typically Jewish elements in order to emphasize the superiority of Moses and of Moses' religion. In the anti-Semitic atmosphere of Ptolemaic Egypt, where people like Manetho were no exception, this Jewish writer felt free to embellish and enrich the biblical story drastically with motives that were designed to enhance the prestige of his people and to bolster their ethnic pride.

EUPOLEMUS

Eupolemus[102] is a fascinating example of how a mid-2nd cent. B.C.E. member of an influential priestly family in Jerusalem could be critical of the biblical traditions and rewrite them in order to magnify the great figures of Israel's past, especially Solomon. Eupolemus is probably identical with the Eupolemus, son of John, mentioned in 1 Macc 8:17f. (cf. 2 Macc 4:11) as the man whom Judas Maccabee sent as an ambassador to Rome in order to conclude a Roman-Jewish friendship-treaty, in 161 B.C.E..[103] His work *On the Kings in Judaea* was written in Greek, a fact that demonstrates that being an adherent to the Maccabees need not be identical with being anti-Greek.[104]

In the first fragment (*PE* 9:26,1) Eupolemus says that Moses was the first wise man, that he gave the alphabet to the Jews and that the Phoenicians received it from the Jews and the Greeks from the Phoenicians.[105] Moses was also the first lawgiver. This picture of Moses as cultural benefactor and founder of civilization is reminiscent of Artapanus and is found, *mutatis mutandis*, also in Philo's *Life of Moses* 2:1ff. and Josephus' *Ag.Ap.* 2:154ff.

The long second fragment (*PE* 9:30, 1-34, 18) first summarizes Jewish history from Moses to Saul[106] but then focuses on David and especially on Solomon. The territory conquered by David, according to Eupolemus, not only exceeds the biblical account but is also anachronistic (e.g. the country of the Nabataeans is mentioned) and probably reflects the political situation during the Maccabees; the description of the land promised to Abraham's descendants in *Genesis*

---

[100] See e.g. *P.T. Yoma* 3:7, 40d: 'Samuel once heard, as he was passing, a Persian cursing his son by the Name and he died'.

[101] See esp. Urbach, *The Sages* 1, 124-34, 2, 733-40; and Fossum, *Name of God*, ch. 3.

[102] Bibliography in Holladay, *Fragments* 1:105-07; Fallon in Charlesworth, *OTP* 2:864. Add: Bartlett, *Jews* 56-71, and Attridge, 'Historiography', 162-65.

[103] Wacholder, *Eupolemus*, 4-21.

[104] For other instances of Jerusalem priests writing in Greek see Wacholder, *Eupolemus*. 274ff. and Van der Kooij, 'On the Place of Origin'.

[105] The origin of the alphabet was a much-discussed theme in antiquity; see Wacholder, *Eupolemus*, 81f., and Droge, 'Interpretation' 142-43.

[106] This summary omits the period of the judges (contrast Ps-Philo, *LAB*!) and calls Saul David's father; both the omission and the mistake may be due to Alexander Polyhistor, however.

Apocryphon 21:8-29 roughly reflects 'the utopian borders of the Davidic empire as reported by Eupolemus'.[107] These descriptions reflect a midrashic version of Israel's early history in the light of the situation under the Maccabees. David also subdues Suron, *i.e.* Hiram,[108] and concludes a pact of friendship with Ouaphres, the Egyptian pharao, both non-biblical episodes – maybe Eupolemus derived the name Ouaphres from Jer 51:30 LXX (MT 44:30) where a pharao Ouaphre is mentioned who lived at least 4 centuries after David.[109] Both Suron and Ouaphres play an important role in the then following account of the building of the temple by Solomon. After a peaceful (!) transfer of David's kingship to Solomon when the latter is twelve – see 1 Kgs 2:12 LXX cod. A; *Seder Olam Rabba* 14; *Sifrei Deut.* 357 (p. 426) – the building activities begin when Solomon is thirteen (*bar mitswa*?).[110] The first thing he does is to write letters to Suron (cf. 1 Kgs 5:2-6 and 2 Chr 2:2-9) and to Ouaphres in order to procure enough manpower for the task. These letters and the replies by both kings are fully quoted by Eupolemus, as if from an archival document.[111] Solom writes severely, as if to client kings, the others submissively, to 'the great king' (they themselves are addressed as just kings), as if Solomon were an emperor with subordinate vassal-kings. Then follows a remarkably detailed description of the construction of the temple that deviates from the biblical account in many respects. E.g., the dimensions of the sanctuary are larger than in 1 Kgs and 2 Chr (neither do they fit in with those in Ezekiel, the *Temple Scroll* from Qumran, Josephus, or the Mishna treatise *Middot*); the amount of gold and silver spent in the interior is so fantastically exaggerated (4.600.000 talents) that even the high figures of 1 Chr are left far behind (e.g., the two bronze pillars are gilded with pure gold a finger thick, 34:7); also measures of items of furniture and tools in the temple (altar, laver, king's podium) are modified or aggrandized; new items are added, e.g. an elaborate 'scare-crow system' for protecting the temple from defilement by birds: here, as elsewhere, he retrojects elements from the temple of Zerubbabel or Herod (see *Temple Scroll* 46:1-4; Josephus, *War* 5:224; *M. Middot* 4:6) into Solomon's time. But other elements have been

---

[107] Wacholder, *Eupolemus*, 138; Hengel, *Judentum und Hellenismus*, 172. n. 274 (ET 2, 64 n. 282); Fitzmyer, *The Genesis Apocryphon*, 146ff. Note also that David's major enemies, the Philistines, are not mentioned by Eupolemus; in the second cent. B.C.E. they were non-existent.

[108] On this curious transcription see Wacholder, *Eupolemus*, 135ff.

[109] Holladay, *Fragments* 1, 141 n. 23.

[110] Wacholder, *Eupolemus*, 155. The Bible says: in his *fourth* year (1 Kgs 6:1; 2 Chr 3:2), which is clearly corrected by Eupolemus. Josephus, *Ant.* 8:211, makes him fourteen years.

[111] On these letters Wacholder, *Eupolemus*, 155ff. Josephus, *Ant.* 8:55, says that the Solomon – Hiram correspondence was still extant in his days in a Tyrian archive. There is a rabbinic tradition that Solomon wrote to pharao Necho for men to assist with the temple building. Necho sent men that he knew would die within a year. By the Holy Spirit Solomon recognized the trick and sent them back immediately (*Num. Rabba* 19:3; *Eccles. Rabba* 7:23, 1). Whether this is an independent tradition or meant to satirize Eupolemus is uncertain; see Wacholder, *Eupolemus*, 168. Very probably Eupolemus invented the correspondence with the Pharao. 'His aim is to demonstrate to his second century B.C. readers that the ancestors of the Ptolemaic and Seleucid kingdom were respectively friendly and subservient to the interests of Jerusalem' (Bartlett, *Jews*, 68).

brought into conformity with the Tabernacle, obviously because he felt a need for harmonization between these. In fact, however, Eupolemus may have been describing neither Solomon's temple nor Moses' Tabernacle nor Zerubbabel's or Herod's temple, but a futuristic temple, out of dissatisfaction with the contemporary one.[112] Curiously enough, when describing the size of the offerings at the dedication of the temple, his figures are considerably smaller than the biblical ones (compare 34:16 with 1 Kgs 8:62, 2 Chr 7:4). In general it can be said that if Eupolemus follows the biblical data at all, he either prefers Chr or (less frequently) he harmonizes Chr and Kgs. But more often he either abbreviates or expands by adding from other sources (or his own imagination), thus treating the biblical text as 'a mere starting point rather than as an authoritative history'.[113] In the same period we can see a similar procedure in the book of *Jubilees*, also 'rewritten Bible' in accordance with the contemporary religious outlook. In Eupolemus' case, this outlook is clearly a priestly one. The temple is the focus of Jewish history; it is the religious, economic and political centre of the people; and its fabulous wealth serves to underline its spiritual value.

A short glance at fragments 4 and 5. Fragm. 4 (*PE* 9:39,1-5) reports, *inter alia*, that Jeremiah saved the ark and the two tablets it contained from being transported to Babylon. Almost the same tradition is found in 2 Macc 2 and *Lifes of the Prophets*, Jer 9-10; and also, although without mentioning Jeremiah, in *M. Shekalim* 6:1, *T. Shekalim* 2:18, *B.T. Yoma* 53b; and in *Para. Ier.* 3:8-20, albeit there without explicit mention of the ark. Here again the concern for the temple, especially for its holiest object, is apparent. It is not impossible that Eupolemus is the originator of this tradition concerning Jeremiah. His purpose 'seems to be to indicate that in spite of the destruction of the Temple in 587 B.C.E., continuity was assured by the secret preservation of the Ark and of the commandments'.[114]

The fifth fragment (*Strom.* 1:21, 141, 4-5) is very much like Demetrius' chronography. It calculates the time from Adam to 158/157 B.C.E. as 5.149 years (*i.e.*, the creation took place ca. 5.307 B.C.E.) and from the exodus to 158/157 as 2.580 years (*i.e.*, the exodus took place ca. 2.738 B.C.E.[115] These numbers neither agree with MT nor with LXX. They also disagree with Demetrius, and it is unknown how Eupolemus came to this calculation. There were of course more than one exegetical and chronological systems in this period, as is attested by a remark in Clement of Alexandria, *Strom.* 1:141, 1-2 (immediately preceding

---

[112] Wacholder, *Eupolemus*, 196-201. Josephus' description of Solomon's temple sticks much closer to the biblical data; see Faber van der Meulen, *Das Salomobild*, 122-47.

[113] Wacholder, *Eupolemus*, 250.

[114] Bartlett, *Jews*, 71.

[115] Wacholder, *Eupolemus*, 111ff. There have been several attempts at emendation of these numbers in order to get them in more accordance with either LXX or MT, without much success; see also Holladay, *Fragments* 1, 154f. nn. 118-20.

this excerpt from Eupolemus). The tendency to make the Jewish people older than the Greeks – and hence more venerable – is the same as in Demetrius.[116]

PSEUDO-EUPOLEMUS

'Pseudo-Eupolemus'[117] is a misleading designation since one of the two fragments has been attributed erroneously to Eupolemus by Alexander Polyhistor (*PE* 9:17, 1-9), and the other has been transmitted anonymously (*PE* 9:18, 2); so they are no pseudepigrapha *stricto sensu*.[118] Both deal primarily with Abraham. Ps-Eupolemus uses not only biblical but also aggadic traditions and Greek and Babylonian mythological traditions as well, and interweaves these. Hesiod, Berossus and the Bible are intermixed, with some Samaritan elements added. Kronos and Asbolus are incorporated into the genealogy of Gen 10 as is also the Babylonian Belus (= Bel); Enoch is identified with Atlas; and Abraham is received as a guest at mount Garizim ('Αργαριζίν), which is interpreted as 'mount of the Most High'. This syncretistic concoction cannot derive from the real Eupolemus for whom the Jerusalem temple was of such a central importance. If the author was a Samaritan, he is important as representing Samaritan midrashic traditions from a period much earlier than most of the other Samaritan literature (which is of the fourth cent. C.E. and later). It points to an open-minded and universalist attitude among (at least some) early Samaritans, who, like other Hellenistic Jews, tried to heighten their own tradition by establishing kinship with other nations of great distinction.[119]

Fragm. 1 states that the tower of Babel was built by the giants who were saved from the flood, a theory based upon a combination of LXX Gen 6:4; 10:8; 10:10 and 11:1ff. that we already met in Philo the epic poet.[120] Like Artapanus, Ps-Eupolemus claims Abraham to be the inventor of astrology, but the Patriarch seems to share this distinction with Enoch, of whom, curiously enough, in the same fragment Abraham says that he was the discoverer of that science and that he, Abraham, received it from him. In *Jub.* 4:17 the discovery of astronomy is attributed to Enoch; his knowledge of the heavenly bodies is stressed in *1*

---

[116] Wacholder, *Eupolemus*, 243-46, presents a convenient synopsis of Eupolemus and OT passages, showing where Eupolemus is original and introduces new elements.

[117] Bibliography in Holladay, *Fragments* 1, 166-67; R. Doran in Charlesworth, *OTP* 2:879; add: Droge, 'Interpretation' 146-51, and Prato, 'Babilonia'.

[118] Some scholars doubt whether the two fragments come from the same author; see Doran in Charlesworth, *OTP* 2:874. Doran even believes that fragm. 1 is from the real Eupolemus.

[119] See Wacholder, 'Pseudo-Eupolemus'; Hengel, *Judentum und Hellenismus* 162-69 (ET 1:88-92, 2:59-63); Walter 'Pseudo-Eupolemos' 137-40; Holladay, *Fragments* 1:158-65. On the Hellenistic elements see esp. Prato, 'Babilonia'.

[120] See above p. 526 with n. 39. Cf. also Josephus, *Ant.* 1:113ff.; Ps-Philo, *LAB* 6:3ff., and some rabbinic parallels noted by Wacholder, 'Pseudo-Eupolemus' 89 n. 45, and by Ginzberg, *Legends* 1:179, 5:198, 201, 213.

Enoch (43-44; 72-82) and *2 Enoch* (11-17).[121] The borderline between astronomy and astrology was always fluid in antiquity (the distinction, if existent at all, was mostly no more than that between theoretical and applied science), and although most Jewish authors from antiquity reject astrology, there certainly was great interest and even the practice of it in some circles[122] who justified their stance by retrojecting this practice onto the great heroes of the past (cf. Artapanus, fragm. 1; Ps-Hecataeus (II) *apud* Josephus, *Ant.* 1:167). In our fragment Abraham teaches astrology to the Phoenicians and Egyptians, who are grateful for it. Skipping his presentation of the war of the kings in Gen 14, I mention Abraham's reception into the temple of mount Garizim, translated as 'mountain of God Most High' (ὄρος ὑψίστου), clearly intended to legitimize the Samaritan cult near Shechem.[123] The following line probably says that it was there, not in Jerusalem, that Abraham received gifts from Melchisedek. Only after this scene Ps-Eupolemus tells the story of Gen 12 with the typically aggadic emphasis on the miraculous protection of Sarah's chastity ('the king was unable to have intercourse with her') also found in *Genesis Apocryphon* 20:1-32; Josephus, *Ant.* 1:162-65; Philo, *On Abraham* 96-98; *Gen. Rabba* 40:2 (p. 388-90); etc.[124] Then follows the genealogy in which Bel (identified with Kronos)[125] is the father of Canaan, who is the father of Cush (identified with Asbolus, see Hesiod, *Scutum* 185), who is the brother of Mizraim, the father of the Egyptians. This same Bel is said (in fragm. 2) to have escaped the flood (= Noah) and to have built the tower of Babel as one of the giants (= Nimrod). Here either two different traditions with different identifications are combined (although the extreme brevity of the account suggests that Alexander Polyhistor may have misunderstood things when abbreviating the text of the anonymous author) or we have to assume that Ps-Eupolemus indeed made the striking identification of Noah and Nimrod. Texts like *Genesis Apocryphon* 2:1ff. and *1 Enoch* 106:8ff. at least seem to imply that there were Jews who believed that Noah was a child of the antediluvian giants.[126] In any event, the text shows that early Samaritan aggada went very far in combining pagan

[121] All this and much more was derived from the intriguing Gen 5:24 ('Enoch walked with God, and he was no more, for God took him away'). For further aggadic developments see Kasher, *Encyclopedia* 1, 174-7; Ginzberg, *Legends* 1:125-42, 5:152-66; Milik's Introduction to his *The Books of Enoch* (1976). The basis of his identification with Atlas was the Greek tradition about Atlas as the discoverer of astrology; see Wacholder, 'Ps-Eupolemus' 96 n. 83.

[122] Hengel, *Judentum und Hellenismus* 432-38 (ET 1, 236-39 2, 159-61); Wächter, 'Astrologie'; Charlesworth, 'Jewish Astrology'. On this passage see Droge, 'Interpretation', 149f.

[123] Kippenberg, *Garizim*, 83: 'Dieses Heiligtum ist nicht etwa erst 150 Jahre alt, sondern schon Abraham fand es in Phoenizien vor'.

[124] Holladay, *Fragments* 1, 184 n. 24; Hengel, *Judentum und Hellenismus*, 165 n. 248 (ET 2, 61 n. 256).

[125] On the reasons for this identification see Wacholder, 'Ps-Eupolemus' 90f.

[126] Wacholder, 'Ps-Eupolemus' 94 distinguishes between two giants, Belus I – Kronos – Noah, and Belus II – Nimrod. *Ibid.* 99 Wacholder discusses the possibility that there has been a belief that Noah was the offspring of the 'sons of God' of Gen 6:1-4. Hengel, *Judentum und Hellenismus*, 163 with n. 237 (ET 1, 89; 2, 60 n. 244), says that Noah = Nimrod here.

mythology with biblical traditions, but that in Euhemeristic fashion. This religious outlook is close to that of Artapanus and Cleodemus-Malchus. 'It finds its identity in a glorified tradition, but one that is placed in a cosmopolitan, syncretistic setting'.[127]

CLEODEMUS – MALCHUS

The only surviving fragment of the work of this historian[128] (*PE* 9:20, 3-4 = Josephus, *Ant.* 1:240-41) deals primarily with Abraham's descendants through Keturah. The genealogical data of Gen 25:1-6 are reshuffled and expanded somewhat. Three grandsons of Abraham, Asshurim, Epha, and Epher (so MT) are promoted to the status of sons, now called Assouri, Apher, and Aphras.[129] The first of course is the ancestor of the Assyrians, the other two of the Africans. Apher and Aphras join Heracles in his battle against the Libyan giant Antaeus.[130] Heracles then marries Aphras' daughter. Their son, Diodorus, is the father of Sophon, ancestor of the Sophakes and king of Libya.[131] The most striking feature is the attempt to forge a genealogical link between Abraham and the Greek mythological hero Heracles; in Cleodemus' version Heracles marries Abraham's granddaughter.[132] There is also a clear tendency to make several peoples descend from Abraham and so to create kinship between the Jews and other peoples. This trend also comes to the fore in the well-known letter supposedly sent by the Spartan king to the Jerusalem highpriest stating that a document has come to light which shows that Spartans and Jews are kinsmen, descended alike from Abraham (1 Macc 12:21).[133] By this device the diaspora Jews wanted to make clear to the native inhabitants of the countries where they lived as 'guests' that they were their equals.[134] Here again, as in Artapanus and Ps-Eupolemus (although Artapanus lacks the genealogical element), we observe the free and unconcerned interweaving of pagan mythology

---

[127] Collins, *Athens*, 39. Note the contrast to Theodotus.

[128] Bibliography in Holladay, *Fragments* 1, 250; Doran in Charlesworth, *OTP* 2, 886.

[129] There are numerous orthographical variants of these names, both in Josephus and in Eusebius.

[130] See Diodorus Siculus 4:17, 4-5 and many other passages collected by J.G. Frazer in his *LCL* edition of Apollodorus' *Bibliotheca*, vol. 1, p. 222f. n. 2.

[131] The line Heracles – Sophax – Diodorus (in this order!) occurs also in a book by the first cent. B.C.E./C.E. historian-king Juba of Mauretania; see *FGH* 275T10 (= Plutarch, *Sertorius* 9:8).

[132] A comparable idea is reported by Epiphanius, *Panarion* 55:2, 1, where he states that some (Jews?) say that Heracles is the father of Melchisedek.

[133] Cf. Josephus, *Ant.* 12:226 and 13:164. See Cardauns, 'Juden und Spartaner'; older literature in the *LCL* edition of Josephus, vol. 7, p. 769 (App. F).

[134] Walter, 'Kleodemos Malchas' 116f. does the attractive suggestion that the prominence of Africa/Libya in the fragment may indicate that the author lived in or near Carthago. On the North-African Diaspora see Stern, 'The Jewish Diaspora' 133-37. It is interesting to note that Ezekiel the dramatist identifies Midian and Libya and Ethiopia (*Exagoge*, 60-62) and that in Gen 25:4 the two sons mentioned by Cleodemus as the ancestors of the Libyans are the sons of Midian. This can hardly be accidental.

and biblical tradition in order to posit Abraham as a kind of universal ancestor and so to trace other cultures to Jewish origins.[135]

Only one short fragment of Aristeas' work *On the Jews*[136] is extant (*PE* 9:25, 1-4). It summarizes in a few lines the story of Job, following the LXX including the epilogue to this translation (42:17b-e).[137] There are only a few aggadic elements. The fragment begins by saying that Esau married Bassara and fathered a son Job, who was first called Jobab. Jobab is an Edomite king from Bozrah, mentioned in Gen 36:33, and Aristeas certainly mistook the LXX's ἐκ Βοσορρας for the name of his mother, Basarra. The same name of the mother is also mentioned in LXX Job 42:17b where the identification of Job with the Edomite king Jobab is also explicitly stated;[138] but there Esau is not Job's father, but grandfather. It should also be noted that Job is thus placed in the patriarchal period, a tradition also found in Ps-Philo, *LAB* 8:8 and *Test. Job* 1:6. Finally it is said that God admired his imperturbability or fortitude (ἀγασθέντα τὴν εὐψυχίαν αὐτοῦ).[139] This non-biblical element can be compared to *11QtargJob* 38:3 where it is said that God turned to Job in love for his attitude in his misfortunes.[140] We see here the beginnings of the post-biblical Job tradition which is more elaborated in the *Testament of Job* and (in a lesser degree) in *11QtargJob*.[141]

Conclusions

For reasons of space the present survey had to be a selection in more than one sense. First, not all (not even all minor) Hellenistic Jewish authors have been dealt with. Second, from these authors only a selection of the motifs and elements relevant to the study of their use of Scripture has been presented, and very briefly at that. One hopes that it was enough to get a clear idea of the fascinating variety of ways in which they appropriated the biblical traditions and tried to reshape them in Greek literary modes. There has been much complaint about the low literary level of these attempts, but one should not underestimate

---

[135] Holladay, *Fragments* 1, 246f. Sandmel, *Philo's Place*, 56, says: 'Insofar as one can see, there are no specifically 'Jewish' qualities to Abraham'.
[136] Bibliography in Holladay, *Fragments* 1, 265; Doran in Charlesworth, *OTP* 2, 858.
[137] Unless the author of the epilogue used Aristeas' work, which would seem to be less probable since he says that he translated the epilogue from the Syriac book (ἑρμηνεύεται ἐκ τῆς Συριακῆς βίβλου), a targum?; see Fitzmyer, *Wandering Aramean* 167; contra Walter, 'Aristeas', 293.
[138] This identification is also found in the later *Testament of Job* 1:1.
[139] Dalbert, *Theologie*, 67-70; Collins, *Athens*, 31.
[140] Fitzmyer, *Wandering Aramean*, 177, n. 16.
[141] Aristeas presents Job more as a patient sufferer than as a critical questioner.

how great and many the problems were that had to be solved by these pioneers.[142]

The variety not only of literary forms but also of religious outlooks of these hellenized Jews is so great that they can hardly be reduced to a common denominator. Nevertheless it is possible to sketch some motives that were common to several or most of them in their use of biblical traditions. It can be said that it was a special concern to strengthen the Jewish self-consciousness by repeated assertions that several inventions of major cultural importance, e.g. astrology or the art of writing (be it in hieroglyphs or in alphabet), were made by Abraham and/or Moses and were therefore in fact Jewish discoveries. Because Moses was regarded as the author of the Tora, and his books were the oldest and hence most prestigious of all books, many cultures, including Greek civilization, were regarded as ultimately dependent upon Moses. In authors not discussed here, it is sometimes more explicitly stated that the great Greek philosophers drew all their wisdom from the books of Moses (Aristobulus, fragm. 3 = *PE* 13:12, 1, and *Aristeas to Philocrates* 30 and 313-16, go so far as to postulate the existence of an early pre-LXX translation of the Pentateuch in order to substantiate this claim).[143] In view of this idea it is all the more conspicuous that in none of the fragments we find any emphasis on the central significance of the Tora as a book of commandments and laws. Moses is *not* presented as the man to whom God has revealed all these commandments and prohibitions on Sinai; he is presented as the first wise man or the wise man par excellence, as an inventor, as a cultural benefactor, as a great king, even as a cosmic ruler with divine status, but hardly as a lawgiver. The striking absence of a central role of the Tora is one of the most notable features of this literature and gives an impression of a world that is entirely different from the early rabbinic world. Early Hellenistic Jewish literature and early rabbinic literature are worlds apart, connected by nothing but the wish to be Jewish and to remain so. The ways in which this wish took shape show a high degree of discrepancy. Illustrative is the fact that, as far as we can judge from these few fragments and as far as the Pentateuch is concerned, these writers concentrated on the non-halakhic parts of the Tora, Genesis and the first half of Exodus, whereas the early rabbinic literature (e.g. the Tannaic midrashim *Mekhilta, Sifra, Sifrei*) focused exactly on the other parts of the Pentateuch. Even when compared to Philo and Josephus, these earlier authors show a significant lack of interest in halakhic matters. Again, however, it should be remembered that this might just be a distorted picture because Alexander Polyhistor may have left out such

---

[142]   See Amir, 'Wie verarbeitete das Judentum' 153.
[143]   See the discussion of these passages by Fraser, *Ptolemaic Alexandria* 2, 956. n. 72.

matters. In view of the whole atmosphere of the fragments, however, that would seem to me to be less likely.[144]

In spite of the above-said, we have seen that many of the fragments exhibit aggadic traits and elements that occur also in later midrashim or aggadic passages of the halakhic literature. It has often been too easily assumed that the Hellenistic Jewish authors are in such cases dependent upon early aggadic traditions as reflected in these later sources. That may be correct in some cases, but, as already said, we should not deny the possibility that many motifs in later aggada derive from these Hellenistic authors. This has to be decided from case to case, although often a decision will not be possible. Much work remains to be done here.

The Greeks were aware that oriental historians writing in Greek tried to glorify their respective peoples.[145] That is certainly true of our authors. The glorification of Israel's past, of its heroes and their achievements, is the most conspicuous trait of this literature. No doubt, this has to be seen against the background of anti-Jewish sentiments, especially in Alexandria but also elsewhere.[146] But it was not only as a corrective of and *apologia* against anti-Semitic stories about Moses and others[147] that they wrote their versions, but also as a means to prevent strongly hellenized co-religionists from giving up Judaism altogether. They tried to do this by showing that it is worthwile to be a member of the people of Abraham and Moses since these were the founders of human culture. Whether they ever convinced a pagan, or a Jew on the verge of apostasy, remains unknown.[148] At any rate, later Church Fathers were happy to have these writings at their disposal which could serve their own apologetical purposes. Thanks to these learned Christians we can now catch glimpses of the free and creative ways in which these Jewish pioneers (Samaritans included) used and even rewrote their Bible in an attempt to respond to the changed political, social, and religious situation of their times.

Bibliography

The fundamental work on Alexander Polyhistor and our authors (although mainly dealing with historians, not with the poets) still is FREUDENTHAL, *Helle-*

---

[144] Collins, *Athens* 51: 'We must emphasize that a significant segment of Hellenistic Judaism did not think primarily in terms of the law or ethical practices, but found its identity in the often fantastic stories of ancestral heroes who outshone the best of the Greeks, Babylonians, and Egyptians'. On the gradually increasing importance of the Mosaic laws in Hellenistic Judaism see Mack, 'Under the Shadow of Moses', esp. 310f.

[145] *FGH* 609T11 . . . τὸ ἴδιον ἔθνος θελόντων δοξάσαι . . . Georgi, *Gegner* 139, rightly says 'dasz das Selbstbewusztsein der Apologeten, das auf die Fragen der hellenistischen Welt eine Antwort zu haben meint, nicht einfach mit billiger Aufschneiderei verwechselt werden darf'.

[146] See Sevenster, *The Roots of Pagan Anti-Semitism*, with the corrections by Gager, *Origins*.

[147] Gager, *Moses*, 113-33; Stern, *GLAJJ*, *passim*.

[148] That educated Greeks and Romans were highly critical of Oriental claims to great antiquity for their cultures can be seen in Cicero, *De Divinatione* 1:19, 36.

nistische Studien 1-2. Good general introductions are (in chronological order): SUSEMIHL, *Geschichte* 2, 644-56; SCHÜRER, *Geschichte* 3, 468-82, 497-503, 512-22 (see now the revised English edition by VERMES-MILLAR-GOODMAN: *History* 3/1, 513-31, 559-66); VON CHRIST-SCHMID-STAEHLIN, *Geschichte der griechischen Litteratur* 2/1, 588-608; GUTMAN, *Beginnings, passim*; DENIS, *Introduction*, 239-83; HENGEL, 'Anonymität', 234-44; CHARLESWORTH, *The Pseudepigrapha and Modern Research, passim*; COLLINS, *Athens*, 27-51; DROGE, 'Interpretation', 135-59.

The only complete edition of our authors is found in MRAS (ed.), *Eusebius' Werke*, 8/1. Mras' text is conveniently reprinted (but without app. crit.) in DENIS (ed.), *Fragmenta*, 175-228. The historians are now available in HOLLADAY, *Fragments, 1: The Historians*, an excellent edition with app. crit., English translation, introduction and explanatory notes; Vol. 2, with poets, philosophers, etc. is soon to be published. For Ezekiel we now have the fine new edition by SNELL in his *Tragicorum graecorum fragmenta* 1, 288-301. Poets and historians alike are now available in English translation in the various contributions to CHARLESWORTH, OTP 2, 775-920.

Ezekiel: There are three commentaries on Ezekiel, all of them with edition of the Greek text: WIENEKE, *Ezechielis Iudaei poetae Alexandrini fabulae*; FORNARO, *La voce fuori scena*; JACOBSON, *The Exagoge of Ezekiel*. Wieneke and Fornaro are useful for text-critical and grammatical points, but Jacobson was the first to interpret the play against its aggadic background (for some corrections and additions see VAN DER HORST, 'Some Notes').

Philo Epicus: basic discussions can be found in GUTMAN, 'Philo the Epic Poet' and WALTER, 'Philon der Epiker', with some corrections on Gutman.

Theodotus: relevant is the discussion between COLLINS, 'The Epic of Theodotus', and PUMMER, 'Genesis 34'. For a good survey see WALTER, 'Theodotus der Epiker'.

Demetrius: important discussions are FRASER, *Ptolemaic Alexandria*, 1, 690-94; 2, 958-63 (notes); BICKERMANN, 'The Jewish Historian Demetrios'; further WALTER, 'Demetrios'; HOLLADAY, *Fragments* 1, 51-91.

Artapanus: the only monograph on Artapanus is MERENTITIS, Ὁ Ἰουδαῖος λόγιος Ἀρτάπανος καὶ τὸ ᾽έργον αὐτοῦ, (*non vidi*, but see Walter's very critical review in *Helikon* 3 [1963] 789-92); good discussions are WALTER, 'Artapanos', and HOLLADAY, *Fragments* 1, 189-243.

Eupolemus: The standard work on Eupolemus is WACHOLDER, *Eupolemus*. See further especially HOLLADAY, *Fragments* 1, 93-156; also BARTLETT, *Jews in the Hellenistic World* 56-71.

Pseudo-Eupolemus: again the standard discussion is by WACHOLDER, 'Pseudo-Eupolemus'; but cf. the corrections by WALTER, 'Zu Pseudo-Eupolemos'. See further especially HOLLADAY, *Fragments* 1, 157-87.

Aristeas: the best studies are WALTER, 'Aristeas', and HOLLADAY, *Fragments* 1, 261-75.

Cleodemus-Malchus: again the reader is best referred to WALTER, 'Kleodemos-Malchas', and HOLLADAY, *Fragments* 1, 245-59.

Chapter Fifteen

The Interpretation of Scripture in Rabbinic Literature

Rimon Kasher

Introduction

PURPOSES AND METHODOLOGY

The Bible is unquestionably the central literary work in the life of the Jew of the Second Temple Period and the first centuries of the Common Era. In school, small children began their studies with the Tora and the Prophets,[1] in the synagogues, the public reading of the Tora was completed about once every three years; these readings were accompanied by reading of the Haftara sections from the Prophets.[2] Bible study in the schools included an accompanying translation in Aramaic (the targum),[3] while in the synagogues more elaborate Aramaic explanations were given. Occasionally, the readings were accompanied by long homiletic discourses, either in Hebrew or in Aramaic.[4] Small wonder, then, that a wide-ranging literature of interpretation of the Bible came into existence.

This literature is multi-faceted. Besides the Aramaic targumim, which reflect the way Scripture was studied in the schools and synagogues, there are other literary works, which were also edited and arranged in the order of the biblical verses. For example, the books of *Midrash Rabba* on Genesis, Exodus and the Five *Megillot* are a collection of expositions of an aggadic-exegetical nature on almost every single verse of those books. By contrast, other collections, like the *Mekhiltot* on Exodus, the *Sifra* on Leviticus or the *Sifrei* on Numbers and Deuteronomy, which also form a running commentary on almost every verse of those books, are primarily halakhic in nature. Furthermore we also find interpretation of the Bible in other collections whose primary purpose is not commentary, such as the Mishna, Tosefta and the Babylonian and Palestinian Talmuds.

---

[1] See Safrai, 'Education', 950-58.
[2] Cf. Heinemann, 'Triennial Cycle', 41-48; Perrot, above pp. 138ff.
[3] On the use of the Aramaic targums in the school see York, 'The Targum', 81-86; Alexander, 'Rabbinic Rules', 22-23; Alexander, above pp. 238-41.
[4] Heinemann, *Public Sermons*, 7-11; Safrai, 'Education', 966-69.

The wide range of these compositions, their varied literary styles and the multiplicity of subjects treated in them, make any definitive description of the Sages' exegetical work, even over the limited time period of three hundred years, exceedingly difficult. Furthermore, this literature contains not only a minimum of explicit methodological principles and exegetical guidelines but also an extremely wide variety of concepts, opinions and also of basic assumptions. Even where we can identify different schools of interpretation, it is doubtful whether those schools existed for more than a single generation. Our main concern will be to identify basic principles, to analyse the different exegetical approaches and to investigate the exegetical categories employed by the rabbis.

SCRIPTURE AS VIEWED BY THE RABBIS

Before we can understand the centrality of Scripture in the Jewish world and the motivations for the creation of this extensive literature of interpretation, we must acquaint ourselves with the basic assumptions regarding the nature of Scripture as expressed by the Sages of the period we are discussing.

(a) First of all the common title *Kitvei (ha-)Kodesh* can teach us a great deal about the Rabbis' concept of Scripture. This expression already appears in Tannaic literature,[5] though its exact meaning is unclear. Some view the word *Kodesh* in the phrase as a name for God, thus *Kitvei ha-Kodesh* would mean: 'the writings of God'.[6] Others, though, explain the word *Kodesh* as meaning 'holy'; thus the phrase would have the meaning 'sanctified or sacred writings' as opposed to profane literature.[7] In either case, the Scriptures are associated with the realm of holiness and are clearly distinguished from all other compositions. This concept is expressed concisely by Rabbi Akiva in his discussion of the Song of Songs: 'For all the Writings are holy, but the Song of Songs is the Holy of Holies'.[8]

(b) The Holy Scriptures were accorded a special status by Tannaic halakha. For example, the halakha determines that on the Sabbath 'one is required to save all Holy Scriptures from the fire';[9] likewise it states that 'all Holy Scriptures render the hands impure'.[10]

(c) The books of the Bible were considered as dictated, written and edited with divine inspiration, that is, through the 'holy spirit'. In the words of

---

[5] E.g. *M. Shabbat* 16:1; *M. Yadayim* 3:2; *T. Yadayim* 2:19; 14:6; for references in Philo, Josephus, NT and Patristic literature, see Beckwith, above, p. 39.

[6] Blau, *Zur Einleitung*, 12-16.

[7] Bacher, *Exegetische Terminologie*, 1, 89-90; 168-70; Urbach; *The Sages*, 78.

[8] *M. Yadayim* 3:5.

[9] *M. Shabbat* 16:1; *T. Shabbat* 14:6.

[10] *M. Yadayim* 3:5; 4:6; *T. Yadayim* 2:19; on the various opinions concerning the 'books that defile the hands' see Leiman, *Canonization*, 102-20.

Moore,[11] they 'were written by prophets, that is, by men who had the holy spirit'. By this, the Sages sought to distinguish them from books written after the cessation of prophecy. Thus Rabbi Akiva did not ban the – private? – reading of books 'that were written down *beyond that*'[12] that is *beyond Scripture* or *after the cessation of prophecy.*[13]

(d) The special status of the biblical books is attested to by a *baraita* in *B.T. Bava Batra* 14a-15b, which discusses the order of the biblical books, their authors and dates of composition.[14] In response to the question 'and who wrote them?' (that is, who authored, wrote down, published or edited the biblical books) the *baraita* names a long list of principal persons and institutions: Moses, Joshua, Samuel, David, Jeremiah, Hezekiah (in some versions: Isaiah) and his party, the men of the Great Assembly, Ezra and Nehemiah. This list was meant to convey to us that the composition of the Bible, in all its aspects, was the work of prophets and outstanding authorities.

(e) Among the books of the Bible, the first part – the Pentateuch – occupies a special position. According to an early aggada[15] the Tora preceded creation and God created the world by means of the Tora. This comes to teach us that the Tora, in its entirety, was viewed as an independent creation, beyond space and time.

(f) Another expression of the uniqueness of the Tora is the affirmation that the Tora is 'from heaven'. This affirmation, which indicates that the entire Tora is the word of God, is, apparently, among the most accepted and widespread basic assumptions. This notion is employed by a well-known *mishna*, directed against those 'sectarians' who reject certain truths: 'These have no part in the world to come: He who says there is no resurrection of the dead and no Tora from heaven . . .'[16] In another text we learn that whoever, although admitting that 'the entire Tora comes from the mouth of the Holy One', maintains that a certain verse, or even a part of it, should not be attributed to God but to 'Moses (who) said it on his own authority', is to be considered as one 'who has despised the word of the Lord' (Num 15:31).[17] The various extant sources mention a disagreement as to the identity of the authors of two sections of the Tora: the last eight verses of the book of Deuteronomy (34:5-12) describing the death and burial of Moses[18] and the section concerning the cities of refuge (Deut 4:41-

[11] Moore, *Judaism* 1, 238.

[12] P.T. Sanhedrin 10:1, 28a. On the exact meaning of 'beyond that' see Lieberman, *Hellenism*, 109 n. 60.

[13] On the cessation of the prophecy, that is of the production of inspired writings, see Leiman, *Canonization*, 129-30.

[14] On this baraita, see Sarna, 'Order of the Books', 407-13; Ellis, below, p. 660.

[15] *M. Avot* 3:14; *Sifrei Deut.* 37, p. 70; 48, p. 114; *Avot de-R. Natan* A 39, p. 118; *ibid.* B 44, p. 124; *B.T. Pesahim* 54a; *B.T. Nedarim* 39b.

[16] *M. Sanhedrin* 10:1; cf. Urbach, *The Sages*, 652-53.

[17] Cf. *B.T. Sanhedrin* 99a.

[18] *Sifrei Deut.* 357, p. 427; *B.T. Bava Batra* 15a.

43).[19] But no one questioned the ascription of the Tora as a whole to the prophet Moses. Furthermore, even the authorship of these two sections of Deuteronomy was attributed by some scholars to Moses, rather than to Joshua, so deeply ingrained was the idea of the divine or prophetic origin of the Tora.[20] By contrast, doubts are expressed in the literature as to the canonicity of some of the books of the Writings.[21]

(g) The high status of the Tora is also attested to by the early halakhic discussion as to whether it was permissible to combine the different parts of Scripture (Tora, Prophets and Writings) into one unit. Rabbi Yehuda's opinion was 'the Tora by itself, the Prophets by themselves and the Writings by themselves', while Rabbi Meir was of the opinion that 'one could bind the Tora, the Prophets and the Writings into one whole'.[22] The precise background of this controversy is unclear: were there different fundamental approaches to the holiness of the various biblical books, or are we to understand the dispute as part of a polemic against certain sects?[23] In any case, we may learn from this that at least some people were of the opinion that the Tora (Pentateuch) enjoyed a status superior to the other portions of the Bible.

THE AUTHORITY OF THE ORAL TORA

The term 'Oral Tora (*Tora she-be'al-pe*'[24]) is not an ancient one; it reflects the linguistic usage of the Amoraim of Babylonia.[25] But the basic idea that Israel was given two *Torot* is already expressed in early Tannaic traditions. In the famous story of Hillel and Shammai and the proselyte who wished only to accept the Written Tora, the aggada has the gentile ask 'how many *Torot* were given from heaven?', and the aggada has Shammai answer 'one written and one oral'.[26] Similarly it is related that 'Agnitus,[27] the consul, queried Rabbi Gamliel, saying: how many *Torot* were given to Israel?[28] He (Rabbi Gamliel) said: Two, one oral and one written'.[29]

This fundamental concept is also expressed in the *Sifra* on Lev 26:46,[30] ' "These are the statutes and the ordinances and the laws *(Torot)* which the

[19] *B.T. Makkot* 11a.
[20] Jacobs, *Principles*, 221.
[21] See Beckwith, above pp. 61-73.
[22] *B.T. Bava Batra* 13b. On the various formulations of these opinions, see *P.T. Megilla* 3:1, 73b-74a; *Massekhet Soferim* 3:1.
[23] On this passage see Leimann, *Canonization*, 60-61, 202.
[24] On the term Oral Tora see Safrai, 'Oral Tora', 42-45.
[25] See Blidstein, 'A Note', 496-98.
[26] *B.T. Shabbat* 31a.
[27] Urbach, *The Sages*, 815 n. 20 suggests that we read 'Antonius'. *Midrash Tannaim*, p. 215 reads: 'Agrippa, the general, asked Rabban Yohanan ben Zakkai'.
[28] In *Midrash Tannaim*, ibid. the question is 'How many *Torot* did you receive from Heaven'?
[29] *Sifrei Deut.* 351, p. 408.
[30] *Sifra, Behukotai* 2, 112c.

Lord made between him and the people of Israel on Mount Sinai by Moses" . . . "and the *Torot*" – this teaches us that two *Torot* were given to Israel: one written and one oral'. In *Pesikta de-Rav Kahana* this opinion is attributed to Rabbi Yehuda bar Ilai, explaining the word *pifiyot* in Ps 149:6 ' "Let the high praises of God be in their throats and two-edged (*pifiyot*, lit. two-mouthed) swords in their hands" – two mouthed: the Written and the Oral Tora'.[31]

These traditions attest to the existence of an Oral Tora alongside the written one. Both were considered 'Tora'; neither took precedence over the other.[32] Moreover, we sometimes encounter the slightly different notion attributed to Rabbi Akiva that the Written Tora and the Oral Tora were one. In response to the midrash on Lev 26:46 cited above, according to which Israel has two *Torot*, he declares:

> 'This is the Tora of the burnt-offering' (Lev 6:2; 6:8), 'this is the Tora of the cereal offering' (Lev 6:7; 6:14) . . . This teaches us that the Tora, its laws, its details and its explanations, were given by Moses from Sinai.

We may reasonably assume that this concept is taken for granted by the first mishna in the tractate *Avot*: 'Moses received the Tora on Mount Sinai and transmitted it to the men of the Great Assembly'.[33] It may be that in its use of the word 'Tora' this mishna intends to refer to both the Oral and the Written Tora,[34] rather than to the Oral Tora alone.[35] But even then, this passage shows that the Oral Tora was seen as part of the divine revelation given to Moses.

What is the exact meaning of the term *Tora she-be'al-pe?* On the basis of the traditions discussed above and their contexts, we might say that the term means 'all of Hebrew law (halakha) not explicitly mentioned in the Written Tora'.[36] But there is some support for the theory that the entire exegetical tradition developed and orally transmitted by the Rabbis, both halakhic and midrashic might come under the category *Tora she-be'al-pe.*

What then was the source of the Rabbis' authority? For the purposes of our brief discussion, we must emphasize that, first and foremost, the Rabbis' authority stemmed from their belief in the extreme antiquity of the oral tradition, whether it was seen as accompanying the Written Tora or as an inseparable part of that Tora. But, in addition, sometimes the source of the Sages' authority was based, paradoxically, on the Written Tora, particularly their explanation of the verse in Deut 17:11 'You shall not turn aside from the verdict that they declare to you, either to the right hand or to the left'.[37] Moreover,

---

[31] *Pesikta de-R. Kahana, Bahodesh* 5, p. 207.
[32] Urbach, *The Sages*, p. 290.
[33] *M. Avot* 1:1.
[34] Elon, *Jewish Law*, 1, 182.
[35] Elon, *ibid.*, 182 n. 7.
[36] Elon, *ibid..*, 1, 181.
[37] *Sifrei Deut.* 154, p. 207. The same verse is used to arrive at a contradictory conclusion, see *P.T. Horayot* 1:1, 45d.

while the Oral Tora derives its authority from its sharing in the divine revelation, its power was given to mankind alone. The Sages of the halakha viewed themselves as the heirs of the Priests and the Levites, the teachers of the Law in the biblical period.[38] They even usurped the prophets' authority to intervene in questions of halakha: 'Henceforth, a prophet may not introduce innovations'[39] An outstanding expression of the authority of the rabbis on the one hand, and the lack of any supernatural influence in the determination of the halakha on the other, can be found in the famous aggadic story of the oven of Akhnai. The practical conclusion of this story is that the Tora, once it was given to man 'is not in the heavens'[40] any longer. This concept is probably taken for granted by the author of the statement in the Sifrei: 'The Tora gave wisdom to the Sages to expound and say . . .'[41]

We should note, however, that some Sages did indeed accept supernatural forces as an influence in determining the halakha, both in their reliance on the earlier traditions of the prophets and in their acceptance of heavenly voices as a means of determining the law.[42]

Systems of Interpretation

TERMINOLOGY

Investigation of rabbinic literature shows that the roots פשט *(Peshat)* and דרש *(Derash)*, whether used as verbs or nouns, do not appear in every textual stratum of this literature; neither is their context or their meaning uniform. *Peshat*, meaning an exegetical activity, can be found only in Amoraic literature. Its best-known usage is in the statement אין מקרא יוצא מידי פשוטו 'A biblical verse never departs from its plain meaning'.[43] By contrast, Tannaic literature makes intensive use of the root דרש, in its general sense, meaning explanation of a text and investigation of its contents and intent, rather than in its general sense, referring exclusively to explanation of the biblical text.[44] Even if we assume that *derash* is a technical term referring to the act of commentary, it is doubtful whether that can offer us any clues as to the exegetical method used by the *doresh* (commentator).[45] In other words, while in later periods the

---

[38] *Sifrei Deut.* 153, p. 206.
[39] *Sifra, Behukotai* 5, p. 115d.
[40] *B.T. Bava Metsia* 59b; *P.T. Moed Katan* 3:1, 81d.
[41] Cf. Safrai, 'Halakha', 162.
[42] See Urbach, 'Law and Prophecy'; idem, *The Halakha*, 171-73.
[43] *B.T. Yevamot* 11b, 24a; *B.T. Shabbat* 63a. Cf. Greenberg, 'Rabbinic Exegesis', 6-7.
[44] On the use of *darash* in early sources see Bacher, *Exegetische Terminologie*, 1, 25-27; Heinemann, 'Technical Terms', 182-89; Lieberman, *Hellenism*, 47-48; Epstein, *Introduction*, 501-05; Margalioth, 'The Term "DRŠ" ', 50-61; Gertner, 'Terms of Interpretation', 4-14; Elon, *Jewish Law*, 1, 239; Porton, 'Midrash', 105-09; Urbach, *The Halakha*, 70.
[45] Heinemann, 'Technical Terms', 187; Margalioth, 'The Term "DRŠ" ', 54-56.

terms *peshat* and *derash* signified vastly different methods of exegesis, early rabbinic literature makes no methodological distinctions between the two. This fact will preclude any use of the terms in determining the nature of the different methods of explanation in that literature. However, it is certain that later distinctions between *peshat* and *derash* existed earlier and can be found in Tannaic literature, even if they are not always referred to by fixed terms.

PESHAT

If we define *peshat* as an exegetical method that seeks *to expose the meaning of scripture by considering its context, using philological insights and with historical 'awareness'*, then the foundations of this method are to be found in rabbinic literature. These foundations appear on two different levels:

1. In the exegetical conclusions: The commentary itself fits the requirements of *peshat*.
2. In the exegetical questions – here, not the explanation, but rather the way the exegetical problem is posed, or the method guiding the commentator in answering the problem, demonstrates instances of *peshat*.

Besides the positive definition given above, we can also characterize *peshat* in opposition to other exegetical methods. Those methods, defined as *derash*, are cited more than once in rabbinic literature in contrast to the *peshat* method. Thus we have another, and perhaps more important, means of identifying the characteristics of *peshat*.

In this way we may recognize the following features of the *peshat* method:

(1) Literalness

In many cases we do find explicitly literal explanations which are opposed to midrashic (metaphorical) explanations. The literal exegesis of scriptural verses is often referred to by terms like כשמעו/כמשמעו, 'as it founds, as is implied',[46] דברים ככתבם, 'the words are as they are written',[47] ודיי, 'certainly',[48] ממש, 'actually'.[49] Thus, for example, the word 'water' in Exod 16:22 is interpreted by Rabbi Yehoshua (ben Hananya) כשמועו, 'as it sounds', while the *doreshe reshumot* (those who interpret metaphorically)[50] expounded: 'the words of the Tora which are likened unto water'.[51] The same Tanna explains the war between Israel and Amalek in its literal sense (Exod 17:8-16). Among other things, in referring to verse 9 'tomorrow I will stand on the top of the hill', Rabbi Yehoshua comments: כשמועו/כמשמעו, 'as it sounds, as is implied', while Rabbi Elazar ha-Modai expands the verse in a metaphorical, midrashic fashion:

---

[46] Bacher, *Exegetische Terminologie*, 1, 190-92.
[47] Bacher, *ibid.* 1, 89-90.
[48] Bacher, *ibid.* 1, 48-49.
[49] Bacher, *ibid.* 1, 105.
[50] On this term, see below, p. 564.
[51] *Mekhilta, Wayassa* 1, p. 154.

553

'tomorrow we shall declare a fast and be ready, relying on the deeds of the patriarchs. "Top" – these are the deeds of the patriarchs; "the hill" – these are the deeds of the matriarchs'.[52]

Another exegetical dispute can be found in *Sifrei* on Deut 22:17 regarding the interpretation of the phrase 'and they shall spread out the cloth', in the case of a husband's suit claiming that his bride had previously lost her virginity. The phrase is interpreted metaphorically: 'the witnesses for each party shall come and speak their cases before the elders of the city', so that 'the matters shall become as clear as a sheet'.[53] Rabbi Eliezer ben Yaakov counters: דברים ככתבם , 'the words are as they are written', meaning that the verse reflects the custom of preserving the dress-sheet with the stains of virginal blood.[54]

The term ודיי, 'certainly', also serves as one of the names for the literal interpretation. For example, the statement that God 'tested (נסה) Abraham' (Gen 22:1) is interpreted by Rabbi Yose ha-Gelili not according to its literal meaning, but rather 'God lifted him up like the flag (נס) of a ship', meaning that God made Abraham's name known to all. By contrast, Rabbi Akiva sticks to the literal interpretation: 'God tested him בודיי, in reality, that people might not say that he confused and perplexed him so that he did not know what to do'.[55] On the other hand, in Deut 21:13 part of a section dealing with a beautiful woman taken captive, the verse 'and she shall bewail her father and her mother a full month' is interpreted by Rabbi Akiva in a non-literal manner: 'her father and her mother meaning idolatry', whereas Rabbi Eliezer says: 'her father and her mother literally (ממש)'.[56]

These examples lead us to conclude that in the first and second centuries of the Common Era there was a literal apporach to interpretation of the biblical text in use. This approach is not particular to any specific group of rabbis; some of them employ literal interpretations for one verse and allegorical ones for others (e.g. Rabbi Eliezer ben Yaakov, Rabbi Elazar ha-Modai and Rabbi Akiva). Thus, it is unlikely that we can isolate any general hermeneutic intentions guiding these literal interpretations. We ought to note, however, that in many of the examples we find the literal approach juxtaposed to a conflicting allegorical approach; it is entirely possible that this phenomenon may provide a clue as to the *raison d'être* for the literal interpretation.

Although on the one hand the *peshat* interpretation is based on the literal meaning of scriptures, on the other it sometimes rejects literalism as the absolute standard for all interpretation. This rejection of the literal meaning of

---

[52] *Mekhilta, Amalek* 1, p. 179. On the background of these interpretations, see now Elbaum, 'Amalek Pericope' 116-99.

[53] *Sifrei Deut.* 237, p. 269-70; *Mekhilta de-R. Yishmael, Nezikin* 6, p. 270; *ibid.* 13, p. 293. See below p. 578.

[54] On this custom, see Tsevat, *'Betula'* 342.

[55] *Gen. Rabba* 55:6, pp. 588-89.

[56] *Sifrei Deut.* 213, p. 246. On this passage, cf. Safrai, 'Halakha', 199.

a text is one of the hallmarks of halakhic interpretation, as we shall see later, but it appears in non-halakhic contexts as well. For example, the term לשון הביי, 'exaggeration', is used in explaining expressions which are obvious exaggerations. In commenting on the verse 'cities great and fortified up to heaven' (Deut 1:28) Rabban Shimon ben Gamliel says 'The Scriptures used (or in another version: the Tora used the language of . . .) לשון הביי, words of exaggeration'. He even provides an additional example from Deut 9:1 'Hear O Israel, you are to pass over the Jordan *this day*'.[57] We should note, though, that Tannaic and even Amoraic[58] literature makes very rare use of this term. Perhaps the term לשון הביי was seen as providing a toehold for unrestrained allegorical interpretation.

Another example of the rejection of the literal interpretation is Rabbi Yishmael's explanation of Josh 1:8 ('This book of the law shall not depart of your mouth'): ' "and you shall gather in your grain" (Deut 11:14) – why was this written? For it is written "this book of the law shall not depart out of your mouth". I might understand the verse according to its literal meaning; therefore the scripture says "and you shall gather your grain . . .". The Tora spoke in common parlance'.[59] In other words, the passage in Joshua cannot be interpreted literally since such an interpretation would conflict with the daily reality of the working man.

Unlike the tendency guiding the explanations discussed above, which render the primary and obvious meaning of the text through literal interpretation, occasionally literal explanation of the words does not necessarily reflect the text's simple meaning. For example, the places named 'Sukkot' in Gen 33:17 and Exod 12:37 are explained by the Sages as such ('Sukkot is merely the name of a place'). Rabbi Eliezer renders the name in its simple meaning: ' "To Sukkot" – to the place where they actually (ממש) put up booths'.[60]

(2) Consideration of biblical language
A feeling for biblical language is evident in many of the explanations of Bible passages which use other passages as supporting evidence for a particular exegesis. One could argue that referring to other verses for supporting evidence indicates a fundamentally literal, *peshat* approach to the text. However, the widespread use of biblical verses does not necessarily bear out this argument, as the evidence brought from other passages does not necessarily fit criteria for *peshat* interpretations. We do, however, find several instances with demonstrate sensitivity to biblical language and the use of purely philological tools of interpretation. For example, we find in the *Mekhilta* on Exod 15:25 disagreement as to the meaning of the word *nisahu* (נסהו):

[57] *Sifrei Deut.* 25, p. 35.
[58] Cf. *B.T. Hullin* 90b; Bacher, *Exegetische Terminologie*, 2, 43-44.
[59] *Sifrei Deut.* 42, p. 90. Rabbi Shimon ben Yohai explains this verse literally.
[60] *Mekhilta de-Rabbi Yishmael*, Pisha 14, p. 48. Cf. the reading in *Mekhilta de-R. Shimon ben Yohai*, p. 33.

there he raised (נשא) him up to greatness, so says Rabbi Yehoshua as it is written 'Evil-Merodach . . . did raise up (נשא) the head of Jehoiachin king of Judah' (2 Kgs 25:27) and it says: 'Raise up the heads of the sons of Gershon' (Num 4:22). Rabbi Elazar ha-Modai said to him: But this interpretation – greatness – requires the letter *sin* (of the word נשא), whereas here the word is spelled with a *samekh* (נסה). What do the words ושם נסהו como to teach us? That there God tested Israel.[61]

Elazar ha-Modai rejects the midrashic interpretation of Rabbi Yehoshua on grammatical-orthographic grounds, as we never find the verbal root נשא meaning 'greatness' spelled with a *samekh* anywhere in the Bible.

Another, philological aspect of the *peshat* approach derives from the multiplicity of meanings for a given word or 'phrase'. For example: the *Mekhilta* on Exod 13:14 distinguishes between 'tomorrow' meaning the next day and 'tomorrow' meaning later on, not specifically the coming day.[62] Again, the expression אז (then) + imperfect is explained in more than one way in the *Mekhilta* on Exod 15:1: 'In some places אז refers to the past and in others אז refers to the future'.[63] It seems that the different meanings are determined by the context.

Similarly, Rabbi Elazar ben Yaakov suggests three different meanings for the word תשואה, 'uproar, shoutings(?)' in Isa 22:2 ('you who are full of shoutings'): 'Rabbi Elazar ben Yaakov said: The word (rendered "uproar") is used in three senses, viz. troubles, disorders, and darkness'. So, too, Rabbi Meir, in explaining the phrase אשא דעי, 'I will fetch my knowledge' in Job 36:3 suggests that 'this term is used in two connections – with song and with speech; in connection with song it is applied to the praise of the righteous, and in connection with speech to the downfall of the wicked'.[64]

(3) Literary-stylistic aspects

Another aspect of the *peshat* interpretation is the recognition of synonyms in Scripture. For example, in *Sifrei Numbers* 23, p. 27 on Num 6:3 'He shall separate himself from wine and strong drink', the *Sifrei* assumes 'but יין (wine) is שכר (strong drink) and שכר is יין', leading to the important conclusion of the principle that 'the Tora employed two different words'.[65] This conclusion is supported by several other examples of pairs of synonyms. Even if all the

---

[61] *Mekhilta de-R. Yishmael, Wayassa* 1, p. 156-57; see also *Mekhilta de-R. Shimon ben Yohai*, p. 104-05.

[62] *Mekhilta de-R. Yishmael, Pisha* 18, p. 73. The examples given by the *Mekhilta* for the first meaning are Exod 8:19; 17:9; the example for the second meaning: Josh 22:24. See Dobschütz, *Einfache Bibelexegese*, 27-28.

[63] *Mekhilta de-R. Yishmael, Shirta* 1, p. 116.

[64] *Lev. Rabba* 14:2, p. 299.

[65] According to Rabbi Elazar ha-Kappar there is a difference between the two words: יין is wine mixed with water, while שכר is a pure wine.

examples do not fit the definition of *peshat* commentary,[66] the very acceptance of repetitions in the Bible that neither add to nor detract from the meaning of the text indicates a heightened sensitivity to the *peshat* of the text. This sensitivity is also in evidence in halakhic exegesis, as we shall see later.

There is another feature of this conception which may be derived from the statement, attributed to Rabbi Yishmael and his students, that some of the concluding verses of Tora sections are merely 'sealing' verses. For example, Rabbi Yonatan, the student of Rabbi Yishmael, understands verses such as 'This is the law in cases of jealousy' (Num 5:29) or 'And this is the law for the Nazarite' (Num 6:13) as sealing verses, or in his words 'as the seal of the words (כחותם הדברים)'.[67] These explanations are not different, in principle, from other cases in which Rabbi Yishmael regards certain words as semantically superfluous but present for stylistic reasons. For example, Rabbi Yishmael interprets Num 29:39-30:1 as verses that separate one topic from another: the section dealing with daily-offerings and additional offerings (chap. 28 and 29) from the section dealing with vows (30:2ff.); in his own words: להפסיק העניין, 'to separate the subject'.[68] Similarly, Rabbi Yishmael interprets the words 'and kill every woman who has known man by lying with him' (Num 31:17) as a mere interruption of the flow of the text.[69]

The stylistic-literary approach using the term 'to separate the subject' serves Rabbi Yose ha-Gelili in his explanation of biblical verses with words such as אך, 'only, but' or רק, 'only, except'. In contrast to the midrashic interpretation which seeks somehow to derive new content from these connecting words, Rabbi Yose, using the *peshat* approach, considers sentences beginning with אך or רק as restrictive clauses, and explains the scriptures in Exod 12:16, Josh 11:22 and 1 Kgs 8:9; 15:4; 22:16 accordingly.[70].

(4) The critical approach

One of the characteristics of the *peshat* system of interpretation is the critical view of those who raise questions about Scripture and its interpretations, and who cast coubts on the veracity of the text and its explanations. We ought to specify immediately that in the rabbinic literature under discussion we will find no doubts as to the historical authenticity of the biblical stories and descriptions. In this respect, rabbinic literature clearly differs from modern biblical criticism (beginning with Spinoza). Rabbinic literature does, however, subject basis principles to criticism, drawing interesting and important conclusions from its analysis. The critical approach is most prominently expressed in the Rabbis' recognition of contradictions among texts, be they in a single biblical

---

[66] E.g. יין ושכר. But cf. Num 28:7.
[67] *Sifrei Numbers* 20, p. 24; 38; p. 41.
[68] *Sifrei Numbers* 152, p. 197.
[69] *Sifrei Numbers* 157, p. 212. See also *Mekhilta de-R. Yishmael, Pisha* 3, p. 10.
[70] *Mekhilta de-R. Shimon ben Yohai* on Exod 12:16, p. 20. On another use of the phrase הפסיק העניין, see Epstein, *Introduction*, 535 n. 164.

book or in several different compositions.[71] While the Sages' resolutions of contradictions in the realm of halakha are of a strictly harmonizing nature, in the narrative field several types of resolutions may be discerned. The vast majority of these are based on the assumption discussed above that the biblical books are the word of God, and that the contradictions in Scripture do not indicate different conceptions or changes of opinion. Thus, we are presented with an interpretative approach which is only partially *peshat*: whereas the act of recognition of contradictions points naturally to a *peshat* approach, the hermeneutic solutions are generally midrashic.

Sometimes the critical approach leads rabbinic scholars to the conclusion that contradictory passages in Scripture have to be attributed to different speakers. In some Tannaic sources[72] we find lists of adjacent verses which are attributed to different speakers, subjects or objects.[73] While not all of the examples can be considered *peshat*, some of them do accord with the characteristics of the *peshat* method. Three outstanding examples are in the *Tosefta, Sota* 9:5ff. (p. 211ff.), all of which are summarized by the formula 'the entire chapter is a melange of utterances; whoever said the one did not say the other'. Thus, the passage in Jer 26:18-23 is attributed to two different parties: the first, verses 18 to 19 'were spoken by the righteous among them', that is, those who wished to protect and save Jeremiah; the second part, verses 20-23 'was spoken by the wicked among them'. A similar approach is used in explaining the first verses of the prophecy of Nahum (1:1-4), which list various conflicting attributes of God side by side; so, too verses 1-4 in Ps 58.[74]

Occasionally, a critical *peshat* approach to the text results from a conflict between Scripture and reason. For example, the statement in Exod 16:20, referring to the manna that it 'bred worms and became foul' contradicts reality according to the Sages. They said: 'First it becomes foul, and then it breeds worms'.[75] Therefore, the conclusion is that 'the order of the text is transposed';[76] in other words, we ought to read the verse as though it said 'and it became foul and bred worms'.[77] Although other verses are also explained, using the method of transposition of the word-order of a verse,[78] the suggested interpretations are usually responses to questions which have little to do with the *peshat* of the verse.

Another facet of the lack of consideration for the order of the sayings of Scripture is demonstrated by the Sages' attempt to resolve the difficulties that

[71] A comprehensive list of such verses is found in Melamed, *Bible Commentators*, 1, 76-89.
[72] *T. Sota* 9:2-8; *Sifrei Num.* 88, pp. 87-88; *Sifrei Zutta*, p. 269; *P.T. Sota* 9:7, 23d.
[73] The lists contain Gen 38:25-26; Num 11:6-7; 13:27-30; Deut 21:7-8; 25:18; Judg 5:28-31; 1 Sam 4:8-9; Jer 26:18-24; Nah 1:1-4; Ps 58:1-4; Cant 8:5-6; Ruth 3:13.
[74] The two final examples are quite difficult to explain.
[75] See Exod 16:24.
[76] *Mekhilta de-R. Yishamel, Wayassa* 4, p. 167.
[77] ויבאש can mean 'stank', or we can explain the ו in ויבאש as a pluperfect.
[78] See Bacher, *Exegetische Terminologie*, 1, 136-37.

arise from the chronological order in the text. In *Mekhilta* on Exod 15:9[79] we have a long list of verses which were considered as introductory verses to chapters or books, even though they are not found at the beginning of those chapters and books in the Bible. This list includes the following verses: Exod 15:8 is considered the introduction to the Song of the Sea (Exod 15:1-19); the following verses were seen as to be the opening verses of biblical books: Lev 9:1; Isa 6:1; Ezek 2:1 or 17:2; Jer 2:2; Hos 10:1 and Eccl 1:12. The midrash *Ecclesiastes Rabba* 1:2 cites additional examples: Deut 29:9; Josh 3:7; Ps 73:22 as the introductory verses of books, and Judg 5:3 as the opening verse to the Song of Deborah. What is the meaning of such statements? The text in *Eccl. Rabba* 'this is fit to the beginning of the song/book' makes it clear that we are dealing, not with the redaction process, but simply with the recognition that certain passages are not arranged according to their proper chronological order. The formulation of the *Mekhiltot* on the other hand, 'this was the beginning of the section', may support another interpretation: a critical-redaction approach, whereby at some previous stage of textual development the verses did serve as the introduction to songs or books, but at a later stage (of literary development?) the original order was changed. In either case, the statements are a recognition of the fact that the books of the Bible are not written and edited according to chronological order (of description of events and saying). This recognition is summarized by the term, mentioned in the text cited above 'there is no "earlier" or "later" in the Tora'. We also find this expressed in other places. For example, the Sages saw that the date at the beginning of the book of Numbers (1:1) 'On the first day of the second month, in the second year' is later than the date mentioned further on, in Num 9:1, 'in the first month of the second year'.[80] Also, both verses in Num 10:35-36 are seen as not being in their proper places: 'the phrase ויהי בנסוע הארון ("and whenever the ark set out") is marked with dots above and below,[81] as it is not in its proper place . . . Rabbi Shimon says: it is punctuated above and below to indicate that it is not in its proper place . . '.[82] It should, then, come as no surprise that the achronological conception of the Bible gave rise to the statement, attributed to Rabbi Yehuda (bar Ilai) or to Rabbi Meir, that 'many topics that adjoin each other in the text are as distant from one another as East and West'.[83]

This conception of the order of passages and verses in Scripture is apparently based on the assumption formulated by one of the last of the Tannaim in the phrase 'The Tora was transmitted in separate scrolls' (*B.T. Gittin* 60a, Rabbi

[79] *Mekhilta de-R. Yishmael, Shirta* 7, p. 139 = *Mekhilta de-R. Shimon ben Yohai, Beshallah* 15:9, p. 88.
[80] *Sifrei Numbers* 64, p. 61.
[81] On the function of the dot as a mark of textual doubt, see Butin, *Ten Nequdoth*; Lieberman, *Hellenism*, 43-46.
[82] *Sifrei Numbers* 84, p. 80.
[83] *Sifrei Numbers* 131, p. 169. See below, p. 591.

Yohanan in the name of Rabbi Benaa).[84] In other words, the Tora was not given as a single unit; each topic was written down at a different time, and only at a later stage were they combined by Moses into a single continuous composition, the Pentateuch. It is entirely possible, then, that the scrolls were not arranged in chronological order; perhaps other criteria determined the final redaction.

DERASH

Defining the method of midrashic interpretation – that of the *midrash* or *derash* – is a most difficult task. A cursory glance at the scholarly research on midrashic literature suffices to indicate the incredible number of conceptions, definitions and characterizations. Some emphasize the purpose (religious, educational or social), some focus on the function of midrashic literature in Jewish society, others attempt to characterize the midrash by its literary genre, while still others emphasize techniques and methods.[85] It seems to me that we ought to define midrashic interpretation by referring to the definition of *peshat*. In other words, an interpretation which does not fit the criteria for *peshat* will be considered as *misdrash/derash*.

Peshat consists of two principal elements: 1. Exposing the original or contextual meaning of the text through a historical awareness and 2. use of methods based mainly on context and philology. Thus, a *midrash* does not always fulfil both requirements: it does not always seek to reveal the original or contextual meaning of scripture, nor is it always a response to legitimate problems of interpretation. Moreover, even when the *midrash* does answer to the first requirements of *peshat*, the difference between the method of the midrash and that of the peshat is particularly striking. *The midrash completely ignores both the context and the rules of biblical language.*

The advantage of this formalistic definition is that it allows us to include different literary types, different and sometimes contradictory goals and a wide variety of motivations under the heading of 'midrash'. We can thus apply the title 'midrash' to interpretations in many different works, such as halakhic and aggadic midrashim, targumim, pesharim, rewritten biblical literature, etc. . . .

It was undoubtedly the assumption that biblical literature was divine in origin that made the rise of midrashic commentary possible. This assumption led to many important conclusions. For example, assigning an eternal meaning to the biblical text: that every expression, word and even letter of every sentence is significant; that there are no contradictions between passages of Scripture; that there are no superfluous trivial details.[86] Awareness of these conclusions can

---

[84]   Heschel, *Theology* 2, 405.
[85]   On the various conceptions of *midrash*, see Le Déaut, 'Définition', 262-82; Miller, 'Targum Midrash', 43-48; Porton, 'Midrash' 109-12. An interesting definition of *midrash* was offered recently by Shinan and Zakovitch in their article 'Midrash on Scripture', 258ff.
[86]   Heinemann, *Darkhei ha-Aggada*, 96-107.

allow us to understand many of the midrashic explanations which seem so far from the simple meaning of the text.

The assumption of the divine origin of Scripture results in the conclusion that the Bible retains its relevance and meaning. This view allowed the Sages to adapt the Bible to their needs; thus, the Sages add their own opinions on various issues to the Bible. The midrashic commentaries do not always stem from textual and exegetical needs, but (and this is true for the vast majority of the material) they often reflect the contemporary needs of a particular Sage, who seeks to ground his decisions in the Sacred Scriptures.

The many attempts to resolve the textual problems at all costs, while subjugating biblical belief to later conceptions, necessarily resulted in development of a wide variety of exegetical techniques. As Lieberman[87] has shown, certain techniques of non-halakhic commentary are similar to mantic methods of interpretation. That is, the techniques used in antiquity to interpret dreams, prophecy or esoteric texts probably influenced the Sages in their commentaries on the Bible and their derivation of certain specific ideas from the text. On the other hand, only a restricted number of exegetical techniques were adapted in interpreting legal texts. These were known as *middot*,[88] and they alone were used by the Sages in explaining biblical law.

The great quantity and complexity of material dealing with *derash* interpretation make any definitive conclusions difficult. Among the many questions is the 'interpretative' one: to what extent does a specific midrashic explanation attempt to resolve exegetical problems and to what degree is the scriptural passage merely an *asmakhta*, 'a pig', a text cited (sometimes out of context) to support an already held view? This question is applicable to both halakhic as well as non-halakhic midrashim[89] and in many cases the answer is not at all obvious. Let us now examine some of the outstanding characteristics of the *derash* as it appears in midrashic literature.

(1) The non-literal interpretation and its relation to the literal approach
In our discussion of the *peshat* we identified several cases in which the *peshat* explanation is opposed to a midrashic one which deviates from the literal meaning of the text. Indeed, many midrashim explain the Bible using an entirely non-literal approach, completely[90] ignoring the literal meaning of Scripture. The following are some of the main motivations for the non-literal approach:

A. *Hapax legomena* – The assumption that biblical literature must be interpreted on internal evidence alone sometimes leads the Sages to reject the

---

[87] Lieberman, *Hellenism*, 70-79; see also Tigay, 'Aggadic Exegesis', 170-81.
[88] See below, pp. 584-94.
[89] See also pp. 566, 578-79.
[90] Heinemann, *Darkhei ha-Aggada*, 153-57.

peshat approach. In explaining the word לאט in Isa 8:6[91] the *Pesikta Rabbati* 16 (p. 82b) says: 'We went through the entire bible and found no mention of a place named לאט'. This led Bar Kappara[92] to conclude that לאט must be the number 40 according to *gematria* (the numerical value of the Hebrew letters of the word) and the verse must refer to the forty *se'a* of water in the *mikwe* (ritual bath) used for purification of the ritually impure. Similarly, Rabbi Yishmael (in the name of Rabbi Yosse?) says of the place-names 'Tophel' and 'Laban' mentioned in Deut 1:1: 'We examined the list of all the encampments in the desert and we found no place called "Tophel" (תפל) or "Laban" (לבן).[93] As a result, other Sages interpret these names not according to their literal meaning but as words referring to the manna, which the people slandered (תפלו) with frivolous, indecent words (דברי תפלות), with its white (לבן) colour.[94] Wherever we find hapax legomena in the text we find explanations based on purely midrashic techniques.[95]

B. *Anthropomorphism and Anthropopathism* – The Sages' theological conception, which denied God physical form or human attributes, gave rise to a special interpretative approach to verses of Scripture that describe God in material terms. The material descriptions in the Bible were used, they said, only to make things easier for men to understand. Thus the images describing God's revelation as 'a kiln' (Exod 19:18), 'a roaring lion' (Amos 3:8), 'many waters' (Ezek 43:2), are man's attempt at description of his God. 'For we name him by means of his creatures to make things easier for the ear to comprehend'.[96] The Sages' opposition to material description of God often leads to explanations that deviate greatly from the literal or *peshat* meaning. For example ועברתי, 'For I will pass (through the land of Egypt)' in Exod 12:12 is rendered as 'I shall become angry', based on the word עברה, 'anger'.[97] In Exod 12:13 וראיתי 'And I shall see the blood' and Exod 12:23 וראה 'and He shall see the blood' the word ראה 'to see' is interpreted in the sense of *knowing*.[98] The commandment 'to cleave unto Him' (Deut 11:22) is interpreted as 'cleave unto the Sages and their disciples' or 'learn *aggada* so that you come to recognize Him who created the world through His word and cleave unto His ways'.[99]

The gap between the literal meaning of the text and the theological conceptions of the Sages sometimes leads a Rabbi to determine that the text transmits

---

[91] The word לאט does not occur in rabbinic literature.
[92] According to the *Arukh*, s.v. לאט, one has to read Rabbi Shimon ben Lakish (250 C.E.).
[93] *Midrash Tannaim* p. 2.
[94] *Sifrei Deut.* 1, p. 5; *Midrash Tannaim* p. 2.
[95] See Vermes, 'Bible and Midrash', 203-05.
[96] *Mekhilta de-R. Yishmael, Bahodesh* 4, p. 215. *Mekhilta de-R. Shimon ben Yohai*, p. 144 refers to Ps 24:8 as well; *Avot de-R. Natan* A2, p. 13 adds Isa 42:13; *ibid.* B3, p. 13 adds Deut 4:11.
[97] *Mekhilta de-R. Yishmael, Pisha* 7, p. 23; *Mekhilta de-R. Shimon ben Yohai*, p. 14.
[98] *Mekhilta de-R. Yishmael, Pisha* 7, p. 24; 11, p. 38-39.
[99] *Sifrei Deut.* 49, pp. 114-15; cf. Heschel, *Theology* 1, 183-98.

no information about God whatsoever. For example on the scripture 'And He rested on the seventh day' (Exod 20:11) the *Mekhilta*[100] says: 'And does weariness apply to God? . . . How then can Scripture say: "And rested on the seventh day?" But God allowed it to be written about Himself, so to speak (כביכול), that He created the world in six days and He rested on the seventh . . .'. Using the term כביכול, 'so to speak'[101] the rabbinic interpreters reject the literal meaning of Scripture and, in some cases, change the meaning of Scripture from being a description of God into a didactic instruction.

It is entirely possible that one of the motivations for Rabbi Yishmael's interpretation of the word אתו in Deut 34:6 'and He (God) buried him (אתו) in the valley' as 'and he (Moses) buried *himself*'[102] may be the desire to avoid material descriptions of God. Rabbi Yishmael here fails to conform to his system of interpretation in order to avoid a blatantly anthropomorphic statement. According to Rabbi Yehuda bar Ilai the desire to uphold God's honour is already evident in the biblical text. Thus, in places where the original text sounded offensive 'Scripture called it otherwise'. In this way Zech 2:12 'for he who touches you touches the apple of *his eye*' is explained as follows: 'It does not say here "the apple of the eye", referring, so to speak, to the One above. Scripture, however, called it otherwise'.[103] In other words, we are to understand the verse as if 'My eye' were written there, but the Bible used the word 'his eye' in order to uphold God's honour and avoid any explicit attribution of an eye to God. Rabbi Yehuda uses a similar approach in explaining other verses in the Pentateuch (Num 11:15; 12:12) and in the Prophets (1 Sam 3:13, 1 Kgs 12:16, Jer 2:11, Ezek 8:17, Hab 1:12, Mal 1:13) and the Writings (Ps 106:20, Job 7:20). With the exception of Num 12:12 all the other verses belong to the same category; they result from the desire to uphold God's honour. Note that in the Amoraic period all these cases are considered to be 'emendations of the Scribes' *(Tikkunei Soferim)*,[104] changes introduced into the biblical text by the Scribes (early Second Temple Period?). However, Rabbi Yehuda's use of the term 'Scripture called it otherwise' leaves no doubt that he considered the text original, and not a later emendation.

C. *Trivial verses* – Sometimes the Sages consider a verse superfluous, if interpreted literally. For example, the statement in Eccl 9:8 'Let your garments be always white' was considered by Rabbi Yohanan ben Zakkai to be meaningless: 'If Scripture is referring to white garments, don't the nations of the world have many white garments?' Thus, he interprets the verse allegorically: 'Surely, the Scripture must be referring to commandments, good deeds and Tora' (*Eccl. Rabba* on that verse).

---

[100] *Mekhilta de-R. Yishmael, Bahodesh* 7, p. 230.
[101] Bacher, *Exegetische Terminologie*, 1, 72-73.
[102] *Sifrei Num.* 32, p. 38-39.
[103] *Mekhilta de-R. Yishmael, Shira* 6, p. 135; *Sifrei Num.* 84, p. 81.
[104] Cf. Mulder, above pp. 92-93.

I remarked earlier, in my description of the *peshat* approach (as opposed to the *midrash*), that the accounts of the history of Israel in the desert were interpreted allegorically. These verses, mostly attributed to the *doreshe reshumot* (those who interpret metaphorically),[105] may be based on the assumption that the Bible does not aim to describe historical events and that knowledge of the past is worthless.

The allegorical approach is most clearly expressed in the commentary on the Song of Songs. In an early mishna (*Taanit* 4:8) we still find a verse of the Song of Songs in the context of a love song:

> Rabban Shimon ben Gamliel said: There were no happier days for Israel than the 15th of Av and the Day of Atonement, for on them the daughters of Jerusalem used to go forth in white raiments . . . And the daughters of Jerusalem went forth to dance in the vineyards. And what did they say? 'Young man, lift up thine eyes and see what thou wouldest choose for thyself: set not thine eyes on beauty, but set thine eyes on family'; for . . . "Go forth ye daughters of Sion, and behold king Solomon with the crown wherewith his mother hath crowned him . . ." (Cant 3:11)

Rabbi Hananya, the adjutant of the High Priest, however, interprets Cant 1:6 as hinting at contemporary events.[106] Rabbi Yohanan ben Zakkai, too, interprets Cant 1:8 as referring to the events of his days.[107] The most extreme allegorical interpretation of the Song of Songs is expressed by Rabbi Akiva's attitude, forbidding any consideration of the book as 'a kind of song',[108] opposing its secular use at banquets and other festivities and regarding it as 'the Holy of Holies'.[109] We still have many midrashim written by Akiva and his contemporaries in which the book of the Song of Songs is interpreted as a love songe between the soul and God, between the individual Jew and his Creator and between the congregation of Israel and her God.[110] It was, unquestionably, the decisive approach of Rabbi Akiva that resulted in the acceptance of an allegorical approach to the Song of Songs for many generations to come.[111]

The allegorical approach finds expression in both halakhic contexts and in aggadic statements. For example, a statement attributed to Rabbi Yishmael says that three verses should not be understood literally but כמין משל 'as metaphors'. The words על משענתו, 'upon his staff', in Exod 21:19 are interpreted in the sense of על בוריו, that is 'restored to his health or strength';

---

[105]   Cf. Lauterbach, 'Jewish Allegorists', 291-333; ibid. 503-531 on the so-called דורשי חמורות.
[106]   *Avot de-Rabbi Natan*, A20, p. 72.
[107]   *Mekhilta de-R. Yishmael, Bahodesh* 1, p. 203.
[108]   *T. Sanhedrin* 12:10, cf. *B.T. Sanhedrin* 101a.
[109]   *M. Yadayim* 3:5.
[110]   Bacher, *Aggada der Tannaiten* 1, 310-13; Urbach, 'Song of Songs', 149-70.
[111]   Other passages were interpreted allegorically too. Cf. Ginzberg, 'Allegorical Interpretation', 405-06.

the words 'if the sun has risen upon him' in Exod 22:2 are understood as hinting at the non-violent intentions of the thief ('sun' = peace):

> 'If the sun has risen upon him' – But does the sun rise upon him alone? Does it not rise upon the whole world? It simply means this: What does the sun signify to the world? – Peace. So, then, if it is known that this burglar would have left the owner in peace, and yet the latter killed him he is guilty of murder.

The passage in Deut 22:17 'and they shall spread the garment' is interpreted as 'matters will become as clear as a white sheet'.[112] The allegorical method is also used by other Sages in interpreting halakhic passages. To give a few examples:
- Deut 24:6 'No man shall take a mill or an upper-millstone in pledge' is interpreted by Rabbi Yose ha-Gelili as referring to marital relations (*Genesis Rabba* 20:7, p. 191).[113]
- Deut 21:13 'and she shall bewail her father and her mother' is interpreted by Rabbi Akiva as referring to idolatry (*Sifrei Deut* 213, p. 246).
- Rabbi Elazar ben Azaria explains Deut 25:4 'You shall not muzzle an ox when it treads out the grain' as referring to the law that we cannot force a widow to marry her brother-in-law in levirate marriage if he is afflicted with boils (*B.T. Yevamot* 4a).

D. *Contradictions between halakhic texts* – occasionally the rejection of the literal meaning of the text is brought about by the need to resolve contradictions among several legal texts. For example, verses 4 and 5 in Exod 23 were seen as mutually contradictory: whereas verse 4 says 'if you *meet* (תפגע) your enemy's ox or his ass', indicating a physical encounter, verse 5 'if you *see* the ass of one who hates you' seems to indicate that seeing, even without physical proximity, is sufficient. The word תפגע, 'meet', is not taken literally, but in the sense of relative proximity, a distance fixed by the Sages at two fifteenths of a mile.[114] Similarly, the contradiction between Exod 12:19, which prohibits leaven in houses on the Passover, and Exod 13:7, in which the prohibition applies to the entire territory, is resolved by interpreting the word בבתיכם, 'in your houses', in Exod 12:19 in the sense of 'property', rather than taking it literally.[115] Similarly, in Exod 12:6, the text fixes the hour of the slaughter of the Passover sacrifice as 'between the two evenings', whereas Deut 16:6 says 'in the evening at the going down of the sun'. The description in Deut is not understood literally ('I might understand it literally') but is linked to the second part of the verse

---

[112] *Mekhilta de-R. Yishmael, Nezikin* 6, p. 270; *Sifrei Deut.* 237, pp. 269-70.
[113] This interpretation may be based on the connection between this verse and the preceding one (verse 5).
[114] *Mekhilta de-R. Yishmael, Kaspa* 2, pp. 323, 325.
[115] *Mekhilta de-R. Yishmael, Pisha* 10, p. 34; *Pisha* 17, p. 66.

which fixes the time of the sacrifice as 'at the time you came out of Egypt', which is understood, correctly, as the sixth hour of the day.[116]

E. *Contradictions between the literal meaning of the text and the accepted halakha* – Sometimes the literal meaning of Scripture does not accord with the tradition of halakhic interpretation. In such cases the verse is interpretated in accordance with the halakhic tradition and the literal meaning is rejected. For example, the literal interpretation of the word לְעוֹלָם, 'forever', in Exod 21:6 is rejected in favour of the halakhic explanation that לְעוֹלָם means 'until the Jubilee year'.[117] The statement 'an eye for an eye' in the context of bodily injuries (Exod 21:24) is explained in the sense of monetary compensation and not as an actual eye.[118]

F. *The law is no longer relevant* – Sometimes the formulation of a law in the Tora is closely tied to the time in which the law was given and the surrounding contemporary culture. Drastic changes in cultural conditions may void the law of its contents or original intent. For example, we read in Lev 18:21 (= 20:2) 'You shall not give any of your children to devote them to Molech'. This law was, apparently, irrelevant in the period under discussion. As a result, it was given a more general interpretation:

> Rabbi Hananya ben Antigonos says: the language used by the Tora to refer to Molekh (מֶלֶךְ) applies equally to anything that you accept sovereign (מֶלֶךְ) above you, even if it be a mote of wood or a shard.[119]

Thus 'Molekh' no longer refers to a specific form of idolatry, but to any foreign religion. Other Sages interpreted 'Molekh' in a general sense, not as referring to idolatry, but to Gentiles:

> The school of Rabbi Yishmael learned: the Scripture refers to any Jew who had intercourse with a gentile woman and conceived a son for idolatry.[120]

While the midrash often employs a non-literal approach to Scripture, we sometimes find midrashic interpretations that are *excessively literal*. These explanations are based on the widely-held axiom that every expression and phrase of the biblical text is significant. For example, the demonstrative pronoun זֶה or זֹאת, 'this', often appears in the text without referring to any specific object. The midrashic approach, however, is based on the functioning of these pronouns in a strictly demonstrative way. The verse 'This month (הַחֹדֶשׁ

---

[116] *Mekhilta de-R. Yishmael*, Pisha 5, p. 17. For other examples of the expression שומע אני כשמועו, see *Mekhilta de-R. Yishmael*, Pisha 17, p. 67; *Nezikin* 7, p. 274.

[117] *Mekhilta de-R. Yishmael*, Nezikin 2, p. 254.

[118] *Mekhilta de-R. Yishmael*, Nezikin 8, p. 277. Cf. also below.

[119] *Mekhilta de-R. Yishmael*, Bahodesh 6, p. 224.

[120] *B.T. Megilla* 25a. On this verse see Vermes, 'Leviticus 18:21', 108-24.

הזה) shall be for you the beginning of months; it shall be the first month of the year for you' (Exod 12:2) is interpreted both by Rabbi Yishmael and by Rabbi Akiva as referring to a specific object (החדש = the new moon at the beginning of the month). According to Rabbi Yishmael 'Moses showed the new moon to Israel' in order to teach them how to 'observe the new moon and to fix the beginning of the month'. According to Rabbi Akiva, the pronoun הזה hints that Moses had difficulty in fixing the time of the new moon and so the Holy One Blessed Be He showed him the actual form of the moon.[121] Rabbi Akiva interpreted other verses similarly: Lev 11:29 'And *this* (וזה) is unclean to you among the swarming things that warm upon the earth' and Num 8:4 'And *this* (וזה) was the workmanship of the lampstand' (*Mekhilta*, ibid.).[122] Deut 34:4 'And the Lord said to him: *this* (זאת) is the land of which I swore to Abraham, to Isaac and to Jacob . . .' is also interpreted literally by Rabbi Akiva: 'Scripture tells us that God showed Moses all the hidden places of the land of Israel as if it were a set table'.[123] Another example of such a midrashic-literal interpretation is attributed to the school of Rabbi Yishmael. The *derash* exegesis of Exod 24:6 'And Moses took *half* of the blood . . .' says that Moses actually divided the blood into two equal portions.[124]

The literal-midrashic approach is most strikingly expressed in verses with personified descriptions of God. Whereas some of the Sages cannot accept the literal meaning of the text – 'and is such an explanation possible?!' – others affirm the literal meaning of the text. Sometimes the acceptance of the literal meaning is stated as a universal principle, such as: 'Had it not been written, we could never have said it'. In other words, since the biblical text is formulated in a certain way, we must take it literally. For example, the description of God during the smiting of the first born in Exod 12:13 'I will pass over you' is understood literally by Rabbi Eliezer: 'had it not been written, I could never have said it; "and I will pass over you . . ." – like a father who brings something to his son'.[125] The verse 'And the Lord went before them by day in a pillar of cloud to lead them along the way' (Exod 13:21) is explained by Rabbi Yose ha-Gelili in the same wording: 'Had it not been written in the Bible, we could never have said it; like a father who carries a torch before his son . . .'.[126] Similarly, the description of God in Isa 31:5 'Like birds hovering, so the Lord of hosts will protect Jerusalem' is explained literally in the *Mekhilta de-R. Shimon ben Yohai, Bo* 12:27, p. 27: 'Had it not been written, we could never have said it; like an animal that hovers over her young and gives her suck'. But the most extreme formulation of this approach can be found in *Mekhilta de-R. Shimon*

---

[121] *Mekhilta de-R. Yishmael, Pisha* 1, p. 6.
[122] Cf. *Sifrei Num.* 61, p. 58-59.
[123] *Sifrei Num.* 136, p. 182.
[124] *Lev. Rabba* 6:5, p. 138. In *Midrash Tannaim*, p. 57 this idea is ascribed to R. Yishmael and to two other persons as well.
[125] *Mekhilta de-R. Shimon ben Yohai, Bo* 12:13, p. 16.
[126] *Mekhilta de-R. Shimon ben Yohai, Beshallah* 13:21, p. 47.

ben Yohai, Beshallah 15:11, p. 92, in a passage that compares God to the Gods of the nations:

> 'They have eyes, but do not see' (Ps 115:5) – but He who created the world by His word is not like that: 'For the eyes of the Lord run to and fro throughout the whole earth' (2 Chr 16:9)
>
> 'They have ears, but do not hear' (Ps 115:6) – but He who created the world by his word is not like that, for 'Thou who hearest prayer, to thee shal all flesh come' (Ps 65:3)
>
> 'They have noses, but do not smell' (Ps 115:6) – but He who created the world by His word is not like that, for 'the Lord smelled the pleasing odour' (Gen 8:21)
>
> 'They have hands, but do not feel' (Ps 115:7) - But He who created the world by His word is not like that, for 'my hand laid the foundation of the earth' (Isa 48:13)
>
> 'They have feet, but do not walk' (Ps 115:7) – but He who created the world by His word is not like that . . . rather, 'on that day His feet shall stand' (Zech 14:4)
>
> 'They do not make a sound in their throat' (Ps 115:7) - but He who created the world by His word is not like that, for 'his speech is most sweet' (Cant 5:16) and it is written 'the rumbling comes from his mouth' (Job 37:2)

These examples and others led Heschel to conclude, correctly, that this style of literal interpretation is characteristic of the school of Rabbi Akiva, as opposed to the school of Rabbi Yishmael, which refused to interpret those scriptures literally.[127]

(2) Significance of each and every detail

While the *peshat* interpretation recognized the possibility of interpreting Scripture using conventional literary means, the *derash* interpretation assigned meanings to even the tiniest unit of language, the letter.[128] Furthermore, as Scripture in its entirety was considered the word of God, its interpretation assigned meaning to the form of the text, as well as to its content. Thus, not only the details, but also the order in which they appear were considered significant.

This style of interpretation is particularly characteristic of Rabbi Akiva, who, according to the tradition, was a disciple of Nahum of Gamzu (also called Nahum ha-Amsoni). It was said of Nahum of Gamzu that he could explain every particle אֶת, the *nota accusativi*, in the biblical text as intending some new meaning. The story which is told in a baraita[129] about his inability to interpret thus the particle אֶת in the phrase 'You shall fear the Lord, your God' (Deut

---

[127] Heschel, *Theology*, 1, 183-98.
[128] Heinemann, *Darkhei ha-Aggada*, 103-29.
[129] *B.T. Bava Kamma* 41b; *B.T. Pesahim* 22b.

6:13; 10:20) leads us to conclude that later on he may have abandoned this way of interpreting every particle את.

However, the same story tells us that Rabbi Akiva found an interpretation even for the word את in that verse. את ה' אלהיך תירא, "You shall fear the Lord your God" is written to include the Tora scholars'. Rabbi Akiva and his disciples expounded not only the word את, but other particles as well, thus following the approach of his teacher, Nahum of Gamzu, who, we are told, expounded each appearance of the words אך or רק, 'but', as restrictive, and each את or גם as inclusive.[130] Thus, we find Rabbi Akiva (often in opposition to Rabbi Yishmael) explaining every word and letter. For example, we have a halakhic discussion on the punishment for a priest's daughter who has fornicated, as to whether she should be sentenced to death by burning or by strangulation (as in the case of other women convicted of fornication). According to Rabbi Yishmael the sentence for a priest's daughter guilty of fornication is the same as that of any married woman, that is: strangulation, whereas Rabbi Akiva derives from the verse Lev 21:9 that she is to be killed by burning. He expounds the word ובת, 'and the daughter', in Lev 21:9 'And the daughter of any priest, if she profanes herself by playing the harlot . . shall be burned with fire', saying 'I expound both the word בת, "daughter", and the word ובת, "and the daughter".' The additional letter ו in the word comes to teach us that the verse applies to the married daughter of a priest as well as to one engaged'.[131]

The approach of Rabbi Akiva is not limited to halakhic contexts, but appears in literary sections as well: the word את which appears twice in the phrase את השמים ואת הארץ, 'the heavens and the earth' (Gen 1:1), comes to include the stars, on the one hand, and the plants, on the other (Gen. Rabba 1:14, p. 12). The same particle in the phrase 'קניתי איש את ה', 'I have gotten a man with the help of the Lord' (Gen 4:1), is interpreted in the sense of 'with', signifying that the affection between partners in a married couple depends on the Divine Presence.[132] In the sentence ויהי אלהים את הנער, 'And God was with the lad', (Gen 21:20) the word את comes to include Ishmael's property and household, which received the Lord's blessing.[133]

Rabbi Akiva uses a similar method in interpreting biblical phrases which Rabbi Yishmael explains by the category 'the Tora spoke in common parlance'. Thus Rabbi Akiva explains duplications of nouns such as איש איש, 'every man', or duplications of verbs such as המול ימול, הכרת תכרת, ידור נדר etc. We often find this exacting type of interpretation in halakhic midrashim issuing from the school of Rabbi Akiva, especially in the Sifra.[134] Other Sages use a similar method in explaining a word which appears more than once in a given verse or section. For example, the word היום, 'this day', appears three

130 P.T. Sota 5:7, 20c; Gen. Rabba 1:14, p. 12; 22:2, p. 206; 53:15, p. 574.
131 B.T. Sanhedrin 51b.
132 Gen. Rabba 22:2, p. 206.
133 Gen. Rabba 53: 15, p. 574.
134 See Epstein, Introduction, 521-22.

times in Exod 16:25. The *Mekhilta de-R. Yishmael* offers several midrashim based on this repetition:

> 'And Moses said: Eat it today, for today is a sabbath to the Lord; today you will not find it in the field' – Rabbi Zereka says: From this we learn that one should have three meals on the Sabbath . . . Rabbi Eliezer (ben Hyrcanus) says: If you become worthy, by keeping the Sabbath, you will be saved from three misfortunes – from the day of Gog (and Magog), from the birth pangs of the Messiah and from the day of the Final Judgement (*Mekhilta de-R. Yishmael, Wayassa* 4, pp. 168-69).

The appearance of the word עדה, 'congregation', three times in Num 35:24-25 is understood as hinting at the legal procedure for capital cases, which must be tried before a count of thirty judges (עדה = ten men).[135]

The Sages' sense of the need to interpret the meaning of each and every expression of Scripture is also revealed in their attempt to explain proper names. For example, Rabbi Meir interpreted the names of the kings of Sodom and its neighbouring cities:

> Bera – for he was a son of evil *(Ben ra')*
> Bersha – for he was a son of wickedness *(ben resha)*
> Shinav – for he would suck up money *(shoēv mammon)*
> Shemabar – for he took wings *(sām ēver)* to fly and obtain wealth
> Bela – whose inhabitants were swallowed up (derivation of the verb *bela')*
> (*Genesis Rabba* 41:5, pp. 409-10).

Similarly, Rabbi Meir and his colleague, Rabbi Yoshua ben Karha, interpreted the names of the princes of the tribes of Ephraim and Menasseh (Num 1:10), the names mentioned in the book of Ruth and other names mentioned in the Bible.[136]

Thus we can understand the Rabbis' puzzlement over the many names used by different nations for Mount Hermon in Deut 3:9 'The Sidonians call Hermon Sirion, while the Amorites call it Senir' or in Deut 4:48 'until Mount Sirion that is Hermon'. These verses prompted the question 'What need do the peoples of the world have of this?' The answer given is that the mention of the names serves as praise for the Land of Israel.[137] Similarly, the Rabbis wonder at the three names given to Mount Nebo (Deut 3:27; 32:49) and the three names given to Debir (Josh 15:15, 49). The answer, there too, is that the multiplicity of names is in praise of the Land of Israel (*Sifrei*, ibid.).

It should not surprise us, then, that the Rabbis took a dim view of anyone who mocked the Bible's inclusion of seemingly irrelevant texts. Thus, they censured

---

[135] *Sifrei Num.* 160, p. 220.
[136] Bacher, *Agada der Tannaiten*, 2, 38-39.
[137] *Sifrei Deut.* 37, pp. 71-72.

Menasseh, son of Hezekiah, King of Judah 'who would expound an aggada slandering God, saying, had God nothing better write in the Tora than "In the days of the wheat harvest Reuben went . . ." (Gen 30:14) or "and Lotan's sister was Timna" (Gen 36:22)!'[138]

The importance attached to each and every letter is also expressed through the Rabbis' use of *notarikon* (= νοταρικόν – shorthand, the method of *notarii*). Either each letter of a word is interpreted as the beginning of a word, so that a word is a string of first initials, or a word is seen as composed of two separate words.[139] Thus the word לשד, 'dainty' in Num 11:8 is understood as the first letters of the words ליש, 'dough', שמן 'oil', and דבש, 'honey'.[140] Similarly, the word אברך (the meaning of the word is unclear) in Gen 41:43 is explained as a combination of two words, אב and רך, 'this is Joseph who was a *father* in wisdom, but *tender* of years'.[141]

The use of *gematria* (γεωμετρία?), a system whereby the numerical values of words are computed based on an assignment of a number to each Hebrew letter, may be another manifestation of the Sages' wish to assign meaning to each and every letter. We should note, however, that gematria hardly exists in Tannaic sources. In Amoraic sources we find a midrashic explanation attributed to Bar Kappara, whereby the 318 members of Abraham's household mentioned in Gen 14:14 referred to Eliezer alone, whose name has the numerical value 318, according to the gematria system.[142]

I mentioned that the attribution of meaning to every single detail explains the form as well as the content of the text. It should come as no surprise, then, that it is Rabbi Akiva who considers the proximity of certain verses to each other as intentional, and thus, as requiring interpretation.[143] We encounter this method of interpretation more than once in Tannaic literature. For example, in an interpretation attributed to the *'doreshe reshumot'* ('those who interpret metaphorically')[144] we find an explanation of the connection between Exod 22:27 'You shall not revile God' and Exod 22:28 'You shall not delay to offer from the fullness of your harvest and from the outflow of your presses': For if you cursed a judge (= God), you will ruin your harvest.[145]

---

[138] *Sifrei Num.* 112, p. 120; *B.T. Sanhedrin* 99b.
[139] Bacher, *Exegetische Terminologie*, 1, 125-27; Heinemann, *Darkhei ha-Aggada*, 104-05; Lieberman, *Hellenism*, 69.
[140] *Sifrei Num* 89, p. 89.
[141] *Sifrei Deut* 1, p. 8.
[142] *Gen. Rabba* 44:9, pp. 431-32. On the polemical background of this interpretation, see Urbach, 'Song of Songs', 169 n. 77. For a different opinion see Hallewy, *Erkhei ha-Aggadah*, 168.
[143] *Sifrei Num.* 131, p. 169.
[144] See note 105.
[145] *Mekhilta de-R. Shimon ben Yohai*, ed. Hoffmann, p. 153.

(3) The multiplicity of meanings in Scripture

While the *peshat* approach seeks to divulge the original meaning of the text, taking into account the context and assuming that each verse or sentence has only one immediate meaning, the *midrashic* approach assumes that the Bible may contain many different levels of meaning. The combination of this assumption with the one discussed previously, that each expression is significant, yielded many midrashic explanations reflecting the meanings assigned to each individual word or phrase. This applies both to the literary as well as the legal sections of the Bible. For example the form יטמא, 'shall defile', in Lev 11:33 is interpreted by Rabbi Akiva as meaning 'to defile others'.[146] In other words, the unvocalized word יטמא may be read in several ways; therefore, a halakha should be deduced from the word.[147] Similarly, the form יֵאָכֵל, 'shall be eaten', in Exod 13:3 is explained by the *Mekhilta* as an indication that the prohibition applies both to one who eats (יֹאכַל) and one who feeds another (יַאֲכִל).[148]

Apparently, the many midrashim of the אל תקרי (*al tiqrei* – read the word not as X, but rather as Y) type assume that a single text may have many meanings. This phenomenon, which has been accounted for in different ways,[149] does not really aim at explaining the text, since the *al tiqrei* midrashim are not found in cases of difficult words or forms. Furthermore, even in the rare cases where alternative readings which do not occur in the masoretic text, support the *al tiqrei* midrashim,[150] it seems that these midrashim serve only as a very loose way of connecting certain ideas and opinions with the biblical text. For example, the Tanna Rabbi Elazar the son of Rabbi Yehuda sought to emphasize the commandment of the separation of חלה (*halla* – a portion of dough): 'Because of the sin of not observing the commandment of *halla*, there is no blessing on what is gathered in . . . as it is written: "I wil appoint over you sudden terror (בהלה) . . ." (Lev 26:16). Don't read בהלה, but rather בחלה, for *halla*'.[151] Similarly, Bar Kappara, interpreting Deut 23:14 'and you shall have a stick with your weapons (אֲזֶנֶךָ)' said: 'Don't read (*al tiqrei*) אֲזֶנֶךָ, 'your weapons', but rather אָזְנֶיךָ, 'your ears', – that if a man hears something improper let him stick his finger in his ear'.[152] The verse is interpreted as prohibiting gossip. Similarly, Rabbi Yoshiya wanted to encourage people to observe the commandments; he thus expounded Exod 12:17 ' "and you shall observe the unleavened bread (מצות)". Do not read the verse as such, rather read "and you shall observe the commandments (המצוות)". Just as we do not allow the unleavened bread to remain idle and become leavened, so you should

---

[146] *M. Sota* 5:2.

[147] See also Akiva's interpretation on Lev 18:22 'תשכב' in *Sifra Kedoshim* 9, 92b; *P.T. Sanhedrin* 7:9, 25a.

[148] *Mekhilta de-R. Yishmael*, Pisha 16, p. 61-62. Berliner, *Beiträge*, 45.

[149] The most comprehensive list, including many similar phenomena, was published by Woldberg, *Sefer Darkhei Hashinuiim*. See also the list in *JE* 2, 77-86.

[150] Cf. Talmon, 'Textual Transmission', 126-28.

[151] *B.T. Shabbat* 32b.

[152] *B.T. Ketubbot* 5a/b.

not neglect the commandments. Rather, if you are given the opportunity to perform a commandment, do it immediately'.[153]

An outstanding example of a midrash that serves contemporary needs and interests is the midrash applied to Bar-Kokhba: 'Rabbi Shimon ben Yohai said: Rabbi Akiva, my teacher used to explain the passage "A star *(kokhab)* shall come forth out of Jacob" (Num 24:17) thus: Koziba (= Bar Kosiba) shall come forth out of Jacob'.[154] The wide diffusion of *al tiqrei* midrashim in Tannaic sources indicates the tendency of the Sages to associate outside events and factors with the interpretation of the Bible, in both the aggadic and halakhic realms.

The multiplicity of meanings of the biblical text allowed the Sages to explain unusual word-spellings or word-forms which are written one way *(ketiv)* and read another *(qere)*. For example, the form לוא which may mean either לא, 'not' or לו 'to him' may be interpreted in both senses. Thus in Lev 25:30 the phrase אשר לוא חומה, 'that is walled', is interpreted by Rabbi Elazar bar Yose 'even though it now has no (לא) wall, but it had one (לו) previously'.[155] Similarly, the words of Job הן יקטלני לו אייחל (Job 13:14) are explained by Rabbi Yoshua ben Hananya in two senses:

> That same day Rabbi Yoshua ben Hananya expounded: Job served the Holy One, blessed be He, only from love, as it is written 'Though he slay me yet will I wait for him'. Thus far the matter rests in doubt (whether it means) 'I will wait for him (לו)' or 'I will not (לא) wait' . . . (*M. Sota* 5:5).[156]

(4) Lack of consideration for biblical language

While the *peshat* approach is based on philological-contextual axioms, *derash* takes a completely free approach to the biblical text. Grammatical forms are interpreted without relating them to their context; the syntactical structure of verses is destroyed; the meaning of words is established based on rather tenuous comparisons; linguistically late terms are projected back into the Bible, etc. . . For example, the Sages wished to find hints of the belief in resurrection of the dead in the Bible and interpreted several scriptures accordingly: the words אז ישיר, 'Then Moses sang', in Exod 15:1 were seen as evidence for the resurrection, since the verb was not used in the past tense – אז שר 'Moses sang', but in the future tense אז ישיר 'Moses shall sing', and so it refers to what is to come in the future.[157]

Likewise the school of Hillel interpreted Job 10:10-11 where we find the verbs in the future tense:

---

153 *Mekhilta de-R. Yishmael*, Pisha 9; p. 33.
154 *P.T. Taaniyot* 4:8, 68d. Cf. *Lam. Rabba* 2:2 'Do not read Kokhab (Star) but Kozeb (Liar)'
155 *B.T. Megilla* 3b.
156 On this verse, see Rosenthal, 'Textual Variants', 406-07.
157 *Mekhilta de-R. Yishmael*, Shira 1, p. 116.

The school of Hillel says that just as (man) was created in this world, so he will be created in the world to come . . . in the future God will begin with flesh and skin and finish with sinews and bones, as Job said: 'For you *shall* pour me out like milk . . .' It is not written 'You *have* poured me out . . . you *have* curdled me', but rather 'you *shall* pour me out . . . you *shall* curdle me'.
(Genesis Rabba 14:5, p. 129).

The Sages were so interested in finding references to the resurrection of the dead that they distorted the syntax of a perfectly straightforward verse, Deut 31:16, in order to obtain the desired result:

Issi ben Yehuda says: These are the five expressions in the Tora whose syntactical construction is not certain . . . The passage where it is said 'And this people will rise up and go astray' (Deut 31:16) could also be construed to read: 'Behold, thou art about to sleep with thy fathers, but shall rise.'
(Mekhilta de-R. Yishmael, Amalek 1, p. 179).

Halakhic interpretation may distort biblical syntax as well. For example, the Rabbis understood Exod 12:6 as hinting at the law that the Passover lamb was brought in three shifts: ' "the whole assembly of the congregation of Israel shall kill their lambs" – the assembly, the congregation and Israel'.[158] Here, a construct state is split up into three separate subjects.

The most salient expression of the disregard for biblical language is the Rabbis' interpretation of biblical words based on their usage in rabbinic language.[159] For example, the word *makom*, used by the Rabbis as a name for God, is a late linguistic development.[160] But the Rabbis interpret Isa 28:8 'For all tables are full of vomit, and filthiness without a place *(makom)*', as referring to God:

Rabbi Shimon said: If three have eaten at one table and have not spoken over it words of Tora, it is as though they had eaten of the sacrifices of the dead, for it is written: 'For all tables are full of vomit and filthiness without *God*'. But if three have eaten at one table and have spoken over it words of Tora, it is as if they had eaten from the table of God, for it is written: 'And he said unto me, This is the table that is before the Lord' (Ezek 41:22).
(M. Avot 3:3)

Also, whereas the word *ger* in the Bible refers to a foreigner who dwells among the people of Israel in their land, the Sages use it to refer to a gentile who accepted the Jewish religion (proselyte). Thus, it should come as no surprise

---

[158] *M. Pesahim* 5:5.
[159] Heinemann, *Darkhei ha-Aggada* 112-16; Melammed, *Bible Commentators*, 1, 100-03.
[160] Urbach, *The Sages*, 66-69.

that every scripture mentioning the *ger* is interpreted by the Sages as referring to the righteous proselyte:

> 'Nor thy stranger' (Exod 20:10) – Meaning the righteous proselyte. Perhaps this is not so, but means the resident alien? When it says 'And the stranger' (Exod 32:12), behold, it speaks there of the resident alien. Hence what does it mean by saying here: 'Thy stranger?' The righteous proselyte.
> (*Mekhilta de-R. Yishmael, Bahodesh* 7, p. 230)

(5) The totalistic approach

Whereas the *peshat* method examines the context, making careful and restricted use of analogies (most of them of a philological nature), *derash* interpretation considers the Bible as a single monolithic unit. This assumption is reflected in many ways. For example, the attempt to resolve inconsistencies is guided by the assumption that the Bible, as a divine composition, cannot contradict itself. There are several ways of resolving these contradictory statements. In *T. Sota* 11-12 and *Sifrei Num.* 42, p. 45-48 on Num 6:26 we find a long list of contradictions among verses and their resolutions. The *Sifrei* has two lists, one of eight contradictory passages, and another of five. Most attempts to resolve them are based on harmonization, that is, demonstrating that each verse deals with a different case and that the inconsistency is only apparent. Thus, the contradiction between 2 Sam 24:24, which states the price David paid for the threshing floor of Araunah the Jebusite as fifty shekels of silver, while 1 Chr 21:25 mentions a price of 600 shekels of gold, is resolved by explaining that, whereas the Book of Samuel referes to the site of the altar alone, Chronicles refers to the price of the entire threshing floor. The *Tosefta*, which lists over eight instances of contradictions between scriptures, resolves the problem not through harmonization but by giving an unlikely explanation to one of the passages. For example, according to 2 Sam 21:8, Michal, the daughter of Saul, had five sons; according to 2 Sam 6:23 Michal died without having given birth to any male offspring. This blatant contradiction is explained away by saying that the sons attributed to Michal (in 2 Sam) were actually sons of her sister Merav that Michal raised.

In halakhic contexts, too, we find attempts to solve the contradictions in Scripture. The most common resolution is by adducing a 'third scripture'. In other words, annulments of one of the two conflicting verses by a third verse. For example, in Exod 12:5 Israel is ordered to bring the Passover sacrifice 'from the sheep or from the goats' – of the flock alone – whereas in Deut 16:2 one may bring the sacrifice 'from the flock or the herd'. This contradiction is resolved by Rabbi Akiva by adducing a 'third scripture':

> How can both these verses be maintained? You must say: this is one of the rules (*middot*) of the Tora: Two passages opposing one another and

conflicting with one another stand as they are, until a third passage comes and decedes between them.

In this case the third verse is found in Exod 12:21 'Select lambs for yourselves according to your families and kill the Passover lamb', from which we may conclude that the Passover sacrifice may come from the flock only and not from the herd.[161] This solution became a general exegetical category and is included among the *middot* attributed to Rabbi Yishmael (see below).

The device of the 'third scripture' which characterizes mainly the resolution of halakhic contradictions, is sometimes used in non-halakhic contexts as well. For example, Rabbi Yishmael offers a solution for the conflicting passages Exod 20:22 where God says that 'I have talked with you from heaven' and Exod 19:20 which says 'And the Lord came down upon mount Sinai' by adducing a third passage: 'Out of heaven he made thee to hear his voice, that He might instruct thee . . .' (Deut 4:36).[162] The totalistic approach most probably generated the resolution of conflicting statements by means of *gezera shawa* (comparison of equals).[163] This method is already attributed to Hillel and is also one of the rules of interpretation ascribed to Rabbi Yishmael. This rule draws an anology between two scriptures congruous in meaning or language. This rule, too, is used both in halakhic and non-halakhic contexts. For example, the definition of a stubborn and rebellious son, 'a glutton and a drunkard' (Deut 21:20), is explained by referring to Prov 23:20: 'Be not among winebibbers or among gluttonous eaters of meat'. The halakhic conclusion is that 'he cannot be called a stubborn and rebellious son until he eats meat and drinks wine' (*M. Sanhedrin* 8:2). We find another, more daring application of the *gezera shawa* rule in the non-halakhic context of the analogy between Moses and Joshua, according to which the sun stood still for Moses as well as Joshua. This midrashic conclusion is based on a comparison of Deut 2:25: 'This day *I will begin* to put the dread and fear of you upon the peoples. .' with Josh 3:7 'This day *I will begin* to exalt you'. According to Rabbi Elazar, the appearance of the word אחל, 'I will begin', in both passages suffices for construction of a general analogy between the two personalities.[164]

The totalistic approach not only creates analogies between different verses, it sometimes even generates general exegetical rules based on the meaning of a single word in a particular context. This rule is usually formulated as 'wherever is written X (this) means Y' (בכל מקום שנאמר..הרי זה. . .) or 'X is nothing other than Y' (אין..אלא). Thus for example, Rabbi Shimon bar

---

[161] *Mekhilta de-R. Yishmael, Pisha* 4, p. 13.

[162] *Mekhilta de-R. Yishmael, Bahodesh* 9, p. 238. On contradictory passages in Scripture and the way to solve them, see Bacher, *Exegetische Terminologie*, 1, 86-87; Rosenblatt, *Interpretation*, 30-31, 51 n. 7; Hallewy, 'Biblical Midrash', 159-65; Melammed, *Bible Commentators*, 1, 76-89.

[163] Lieberman, *Hellenism*, 59.

[164] *B.T. Taanit* 20a. See also Bacher, *Exegetische Terminologie*, 1, 13-16; Rosenblatt, *Interpretation*, 28-29.

Yohai states that 'wherever we find written נצים, 'strugglers', or נצבים, 'standers', these are none other than Dathan and Abiram'.[165] Elsewhere, answering a question put forward by Rabbi Natan about the meaning of *Elohim* in Exod 14:19 he says: '*Elohim* everywhere means nothing other than a judge. This passage ("Then the angel of God . . . moved and went behind them") therefore tells you that Israel at that moment was being judged whether to be saved or be destroyed with the Egyptians'.[166]

(6) The actualizing approach

The examples discussed above clearly show that the motivations for the majority of midrashic explanations are not purely exegetical, but extra-biblical in nature. Contemporary theological, social, moral, religious and political problems of the Rabbis' time are firmly linked to the biblical text. The assumption that the Bible is, in its entirety, the word of God, gives Scripture eternal meaning; thus, one must seek the meaning of Scripture on all levels and in all its literary genres, for each and every generation and in all situations. Furthermore, since the Bible was considered the word of God, it must impart a religious-moral lesson. Small wonder, then, that people searched in the Bible for solutions to contemporary problems of Jewish society during the Second Temple Period and afterwards.

While the *peshat* approach sought to reconstruct the meaning of the Bible in its time setting, to answer the question of 'what the Bible meant', the *derash* approach poses the question of 'what the Bible means'. As a result the *derash* approach analyses all the expressions and phrases of the Bible, attributing to them meanings that accord with the views of the Sages. While space will not permit me to mention all the contemporary issues which were seen as hinted at in the Scripture, I should note that the actualizing approach may give rise to differing, and even contradictory, interpretations. Even a cursory glance at the midrashic literature reveals that there is hardly a subject that is not reflected by a multiplicity of views. This variety is not always a result of earlier biblical traditions; it may reflect the variety of opinions and beliefs that developed in Second Temple Jewry. Whereas the *peshat* approach emphasizes the differences among the varieties of biblical literature, the *derash* approach subjects the entire Bible to some unified view or another. The interpretative results of the actualizing approach are many, but we can summarize the main points as typology, anachronism and harmonization.[167]

HALAKHIC AND HOMILETIC INTERPRETATION

HALAKHIC INTERPRETATION. So far, I have dealt almost entirely with non-halakh-

---

[165] *B.T. Nedarim* 64b.
[166] *Mekhilta de-R. Yishmael, Wayehi* 4, p. 101. See below.
[167] Heinemann, *Darkhei ha-Aggada*, passim; Panitz, *Textual Exegesis*, 401-03.

ic biblical interpretation, though, occasionally, we have seen examples from Tannaic interpretations of biblical law. This fact hints at the nature of halakhic interpretation and its status within Bible interpretation as a whole. That is, the same methods and techniques are used for both the halakhic and the narrative portions of Scripture. Just as both the *peshat* and the *derash* approaches are applied to the non-halakhic sections, so both can be applied to interpret biblical law. Thus, for example, we find both literal and allegorical approaches in halakhic interpretation. The phrase 'an eye for an eye' (Exod 21:24) is interpreted literally by Rabbi Eliezer ben Hyrcanus (ממש, 'actually'; *B.T. Bava Kamma* 84a);[168] The words 'And they shall spread the garment' (Deut 22:17) are also taken literally by Rabbi Eliezer ben Hyrcanus (other versions read: Eliezer ben Yaakov), whereas Rabbi Yishmael explains this verse as a metaphor, that is 'the matters shall become as clear as a (white) sheet'.[169] But it seems that this last example illustrates a fine distinction between halakhic and non-halakhic interpretation. Whereas the latter does not hesitate to interpret many scriptures allegorically, halakhic interpretation uses this type of explanation in a very limited way: even Rabbi Yishmael only makes use of this method three times.

The self-imposed limitations of halakhic interpretation are most clearly expressed in the attempts to fix a restricted number of exegetical rules. Thus, tradition attributes the formulation and fixing of seven rules of interpretation to Hillel the Elder, whereas thirteen rules are ascribed to Rabbi Yishmael. These rules were undoubtedly formulated in order to limit difficult or aberrant explanations of biblical law. Furthermore, even the application of those rules is restricted, at least as they are employed by some of the Sages. For example, Rabbi Yishmael employs the *gezera shawa* only in cases where the word in the biblical verse on which the analogy is based is superfluous (*mufne*, 'free for interpretation', 'unnecessary for the plain sense', in halakhic terminology). Furthermore, he says that one may not introduce a *gezera shawa* on one's own authority. Another restriction of Rabbi Yishmael is that one cannot be punished for violation of a law that is learned by means of a *gezera shawa*, a *kal wa-homer* (conclusion from a minor to a major case) or a *ma matsinu* (deduction of the type 'just as we found in the case of X so in the case of Y'). We can also say that Rabbi Yishmael's extremely restricted use of the interpretative rule *ribui u-miut* (see below) results from the fear that it might be used to attribute aberrant matters to the biblical text.[170]

Is halakhic interpretation closer to the *peshat* or the *derash* approach? This question may be linked to the fundamental question of the role and status of halakhic interpretation: does it innovate halakha based on biblical study or does

---

[168] On the additional literal interpretation held by the same scholar, see Gilat, *R. Eliezer Ben Hyrcanus*, 68-82.

[169] *Sifrei Deut.* 237, p. 269. On Rabbi Eliezer ben Hyrcanus' literal interpretations in the tradition of *Beit Shammai*, see Safrai, 'Halakha', 198-99.

[170] On the whole subject, see Epstein, *Introduction*, 521-36.

the halakhic midrash seek to link the normative halakha to Scripture. This basic question has been discussed often and in great detail. Some view the halakhic midrash as a linking of the already existing halakha to the biblical text,[171] while others see the halakhic midrash also as the means for deriving new laws from Scripture.[172] It seems that the midrash fulfilled both functions, that is, it was both confirmatory and innovative,[173] and it hardly seems possible to categorize the two functions as belonging to two different periods.[174] On the basis of this we may distinguish between *confirmatory midrashim*, which provide scriptural evidence for existing halakhot, and *creative midrashim* which seek to deduce new laws from Scripture. While the creative midrash usually derives from the literal *peshat* meaning of the text, the confirmatory midrash interprets every word and uses all means possible to find some scriptural base for the halakha.[175] In other words: 'The explanatory and creative midrash remains within the bounds of reason and legal interpretation . . . whereas the midrash written after the halakha was already in existence, seeks only to confirm the halakha and integrate it with a scriptural verse. This type of midrash interprets the letters, jots and tittles of a verse knowing all the while that the halakha does not convey the true meaning of the verse . . . This type of literary-rhetorical device used to serve this purpose, was understood and accepted in the entire cultured world of that period'.[176]

Another aspect of halakhic interpretation as displayed in some halakhic midrashim is its moral conception. The laws concerning a city led astray (Deut 13:13-17), a stubborn and rebellious son (Deut 21:18-21), or the prohibition against accepting proselytes from among the nations (Deut 23:4-7), could have given rise to questions and doubts about the Jew's attitude to gentiles and dissenters. Halakhic interpretation attempted to limit the applicability of these laws as far as possible. The Sages did this through blatant and exaggerated use of literal explanations.[177] For example, the scripture dealing with a town led astray: 'If you hear in one of your cities..' (Deut 13:13) is interpreted in a very restricted way: 'if you heard – but not if you find out on your own' (*Midrash Tannaim*, p. 66). In other words, you have no duty to inquire; the law applies only if you heard a rumour. The same midrash continues: 'your city – one but not three'. In other words, we cannot designate three cities as 'cities gone astray'. The passage 'and you shall burn the city and all its spoil with fire' (Deut

---

[171] E.g. Epstein, *ibid.*, 511.
[172] E.g. Albeck, *Introduction to the Mishna*, 42; Albeck, *Introduction to the Talmud*, 79.
[173] Urbach, 'The Derasha', 166-82; Urbach, *Ha-Halakha*, 69-78; Lieberman, *Hellenism*, 62; Elon, *Jewish Law*, 1, 243-63.
[174] Elon, *Jewish Law*, 1, 245-46.
[175] Elon, *Jewish Law*, 1, 260-62.
[176] Guttmann, *Clavis Talmudis*, 7.
[177] On the examples given below, see Elon, *Jewish Law* 1, 302-09.

13:17) leads Rabbi Eliezer to conclude that 'a city that has even a single *mezuza* cannot become a city led astray,[178] since the *mezuza* cannot be set on fire.

We find a similarly restrictive application of the law to the case of a stubborn and rebellious son. Thus, the word 'son' (Deut 21:18) is interpreted as 'a son and not a daughter, a son and not a man, and a minor is innocent since he has not reached the age where he is obliged to keep the commandments'.[179] The scriptural passage 'then his father and mother shall take hold of him and bring him out . . . and say . . . this our son is stubborn and rebellious..' (Deut 21:19-20) is interpreted very literally:

> 'and his father and his mother shall take hold of him' – this teaches us that he is not guilty unless he has both a father and a mother (living) . . . if one of the parents was missing a hand or lame or mute or blind or deaf, he cannot be considered a stubborn and rebellious son, as it is written 'and they shall take hold of him' – this excludes those missing a hand, 'and they shall bring him out' – this excludes the lame, 'and they shall say' – this excludes the mute, 'this our son' – this excludes the blind, 'he will not hearken unto our voice' – this excludes the deaf
> (*Sifrei Deut.* 219, p. 252).

In relation to the prohibition against accepting an Ammonite or Moabite, Rabbi Yehuda says: '"No Ammonite or Moabite shall enter the assembly of the Lord' – Scripture refers to males and not females: *Ammoni* (male) and not *Ammonit* (female), *Moabi* (male) and not *Moabit* (female)'.[180] Finally, early halakha permitted even male Ammonites to join the assembly of Israel.[181]

The conflict between the word of the Tora and the prevalent moral views and daily realities of the time of the Sages resulted in an interpretation so narrow as to annul the written biblical law: 'There has never been a stubborn and rebellious son and shall never be one. Why then was it written? To teach us: interpret it and you shall receive your reward'.[182] Likewise: 'There has never been a city led astray and there shall never be one. Why then was it written? To teach us: interpret it and you shall receive your reward'.[183]

HOMILETIC INTERPRETATION. The midrashic interpretations on the Bible are arranged in many different ways.[184] Among these there are two which are already clearly expressed in Tannaic literature. The first, the *explanatory midrash*, is arranged according to the order of verses in Scripture, and attempts to explain all or some of the verses in order. The other, the *homiletic midrash* is

---

[178] *B.T. Sanhedrin* 71a, 113a.
[179] *Sifrei Deut.* 218, pp. 250-51.
[180] *Sifrei Deut.* 249, p. 277.
[181] *M. Yadayim* 4:4; *T. Yadayim* 2:17-18.
[182] *T. Sanhedrin* 11:6.
[183] *T. Sanhedrin* 14:1.
[184] See Wright, *Midrash*, 52-59.

not joined to each and every verse, but selects several verses, and discusses a certain topic, using those verses from the Bible. Among the explanatory midrashim we can enumerate the midrashim on Exodus *(Mekhilta de-R. Yishmael* and *Mekhilta de-R. Shimon ben Yohai)*, on *Leviticus (Sifra)*, Numbers *(Sifrei, Sifrei Zuta)* and Deuteronomy *(Sifrei, Midrash Tannaim)*. In these works we find explanations for almost every verse, in the order in which they appear in the Bible.

The homiletic midrash, by contrast, is far less widespread in Tannaic literature. Only occasionally do we find homiletic interpretations embedded in Tannaic midrashim.[185] For example, Heinemann identified several homiletic sermons of the Tannaic period.[186] Among the earliest, he cites the sermon of Rabbi Elazar ben Azaria (end first century c.e.) in *B.T. Hagiga*, 3a/b. This sermon, apparently based on Exod 20:1 deals with the question of the relation of the Tora given on Mount Sinai to the words of the Sages. The thrust of his *derasha* is that the Tora given on Sinai and the Tora of the Sages are one. Thus, this derasha serves as a fitting introduction to the section of the Ten Commandments. Another derasha attributed to Rabbi Akiva, can be found in *Midrash Tannaim* on Deut 21:22. There, Rabbi Akiva develops the idea of 'one sin leads to another', while offering a midrashic explanation linking Deut 21:15ff. with Deut 21:10ff. Other ideas that appear in homiletic midrashim are the close connection between sin, prayer and forgiveness,[187] or the idea that 'the measure a man gives will be measured unto him' which is linked to the granting of rewards in the world to come.[188] Rabbi Yehoshua emphasizes Israel's dependance on the Tora in his derasha on Exod 17:8,[189] interpreting Amalek's attack as a punishment for Israel's abandonment of the Tora. Rabbi Eliezer ben Hyrcanus speaks out against war in his derasha on Gen 14:1.[190]

THE RELATION BETWEEN PESHAT AND DERASH INTERPRETATION

Our investigation of the different methods of interpretation has revealed that often several different explanations for the same text appear alongside each other. While in most cases the interpretations are not presented as reactions to each other, we can safely assume that conflicting interpretations ascribed to two Sages of the same generation do indeed reflect a debate between differing exegetical positions. This view of the facts may lead us to the conclusion that there was a mutual 'tolerance' among interpretations and interpreters, since each side presents its own approach without any attempt at depicting the alternative explanation as incorrect. However, we find in our sources some

---

[185] These mainly serve as proems.
[186] Heinemann, 'The Proem', 100-22; idem, *Sermons*, 31-39, 48-51.
[187] See e.g. *Sifrei Deut.* 26, pp. 38-40.
[188] *Mekhilta de-R. Yishmael, Beshallah, Petihta*, p. 78ff.
[189] *Mekhilta de-R. Yishmael, Amalek* 1, p. 176.
[190] *Gen. Rabba* 41:1, pp. 397-99, *Tanhuma Buber Lekh Lekha* 10, p. 34a-b.

evidence of debates on interpretation in which one side clearly seeks to deny the validity of the other view. Thus, we find in *Sifrei Deut.* 1, pp. 6-7 that Rabbi Yose ben Durmaskit (Durmasek = Damascus) strongly attacks three of Rabbi Yehuda bar Ilai's explanations, claiming that Rabbi Yehuda distorts the scriptures. For example, Rabbi Yose rejects Rabbi Yehuda's interpretation of Zech 9:1 in which the word *Hadrakh* (חדרך) is interpreted as a *notarikon*, hinting at the Messiah 'who is sharp (חד) to the nations but compliant(רך)to Israel'. The wording of Rabbi Yose's statement, rejecting this explanation, is particularly forceful:

> Yehuda be Rabbi, why are you distorting our Scriptures!? I bring heaven and earth as witness that I am from Damascus and there is there a place called Hadrakh . . .[191]

Rabbi Nehemia employs similar language against Rabbi Yehuda bar Ilai in referring to the latter's interpretation of Ps 12:9 'On every side the wicked prowl, as vileness is exalted (כְּרֻם) among the sons of men', in which the verse is seen as describing the wicked in Gehenna around whom walk the righteous in Paradise. These righteous men praise the Holy One Blessed-Be-He in the language of Isa 12:1. The explanation suggests that the Holy One Blessed-Be-He will, in the future, exalt the righteous who suffered in this world as he exalts the despised vineyard (כְּרֶם) i.e. Israel. Against this midrashic interpretation, Rabbi Nehemia counters:

> Be Rabbi, how long will you continue to distort our Scriptures!?

He offers an alternative explanation, whereby the verse describes the wicked who prowl around the righteous who repose tranquilly in Paradise.[192]

This last example shows that the counter-interpretation to a midrashic exegesis need not be a *peshat* explanation. Another comment, less far-fetched or closer in meaning to the words of the text, may be offered as an alternative. Moreover, a Sage may reject a *peshat* interpretation as incompatible with his theological views. Rabbi Akiva interprets the expression לחם אבירים (Ps 78:25) as meaning 'the bread of angels'. This daring *peshat* explanation is rejected by Rabbi Yishmael, in the following words:

> Go forth and tell Akiva that he erred! For do the ministering angels eat bread? Was it not said long ago 'I did neither eat bread nor drink water' (Deut 9:18) How then do I interpret the word אַבִּירִים? Bread that is absorbed by the two hundred and forty eight parts of the body (אִיבְרִים).
>
> (*B.T. Yoma* 75b)

---

[191] The other cases are Gen 41:43 and Deut 1:1.
[192] *Lev. Rabba* 32:1, pp. 734-35.

Another subject that provoked sharp reaction was the Sages' tendency to greatly magnify the miraculous aspect of the wondrous events in the Bible. For example, the *Mekhilta de-R. Yishmael, Wayassa* 3, p. 166 on Exod 16:14 says:

> Once Rabbi Tarfon and the Elders were sitting together and Rabbi Elazar of Modiim was sitting before them. Said to them Rabbi Elazar of Modiim: Sixty cubits high was the manna that came down for Israel. Said they to him: How long will you go on making astonishing statements before us? . . .

Similarly, Rabbi Elazar ben Azaria rejects Rabbi Akiva's explanation of the words 'and the frogs (צפרדע, in the singular) came up' in Exod 8:2 according to which 'there was a single frog that filled the whole land of Egypt'. Rabbi Elazar reacts sharply saying:

> Akiva, what have you to do with Aggada? Take your words and lead them to the laws of leprous wounds and tents! There was but one frog: it whistled to the others and they came.
> (*B.T. Sanhedrin* 67b)

While Rabbi Elazar's explanation is also midrashic, it minimizes the miraculous nature of the event. Rabbi Elazar uses similar language in rejecting Rabbi Akiva's explanation of Dan 7:9 (brought in the name of Rabbi Yose ha-Gelili), according to which the Holy One Blessed-Be-He has two thrones, one for judgement and the other for mercy.[193] In response, Rabbi Elazar says:

> Akiva, what have you to do with Aggada? Better lead your words to the laws of leprous wounds and tents. Rather explain: one is a throne and the other a footstool . . .
> (*B.T. Hagiga* 14a; cf. *B.T. Sanhedrin* 38b)

Rabbi Akiva fiercely rejects the anthropomorphic interpretations of Rabbi Pappias with the words: 'enough, Pappias!'. He does not accept Pappias' explanations of Gen 3:22 'Behold, the man has become like one of us' as 'like one of the ministering angels' and gives his own interpretation of the word *mimmenu*, 'as one of us':

> Said Rabbi Akiva: *Mimennu* does not mean like one of the ministering angels. It only means that God put before him two ways, the way of life and the way of death, and he chose for himself the way of death.
> (*Mekhilta de-R. Yishmael, Beshallah* 6, p. 112)

Likewise he condemns Pappias' interpretation of Job 23:13, Cant 1:9, Ps 106:20 (Ibid. pp.112-113).[194]

---

[193] The former explanation of Akvia was that one chair refers to God and the other to David, the Messiah.

[194] Cf. *Mekhilta de-R. Shimon ben Yohai*, p. 68.

The above-mentioned examples demonstrate that there were different reasons for the rejection of one interpretation in favour of another. Sometimes this was done for exegetical reasons, sometimes for theological reasons and sometimes for reasons connected with the interpreter's conception of miracle.

RULES OF INTERPRETATION

Exegetical-methodological rules in rabbinic literature can be identified either based on explicit statements formulated as rules, or by generalizing from specific rabbinic interpretations. Some of the rules deal solely with the halakhic realm, while others are only applicable in a narrative context. There are categories, however, that are applicable to both the halakhic and the non-halakhic realms.

LISTS OF MIDDOT. Of special status are several of the lists of *middot*,[195] that is, rules of interpretation which form the basis for halakhic interpretation.[196]

(A) The earliest list is attributed to Hillel the Elder (first century B.C.E.) and from the context it seems that Hillel did not invent the rules himself, but only adapted them for his debate with the *Bene Beteira*, when he attempted to establish a law that was not explicitly mentioned in the Tora (i.e. that the Paschal lamb may be slaughtered even on the Sabbat).[197] This list contains seven *middot*, although texts differ in identification of one of the seven rules. According to the *Tosefta (Sanhedrin*, end of chapter 7) and *Avot de-R. Natan* (version A, chapter 37, p. 110) the seven *middot* are:

1. *Kal wa-homer* – an inference from minor to major.
2. *Gezera Shawa* – an inference from analogy of expressions.
3. *Binyan Av* from one scripture – a general law may be derived by induction from different cases which, occurring in *the same* scripture, have yet some feature in common.
4. *Binyan Av* from two scriptures – a general law may be derived by induction from different cases which, occurring in *different* scriptures, have yet some feature in common.
5. *Kelal u-ferat* – a general proposition followed by the enumeration of particulars; and *Perat u-khelal* – an enumeration of particulars followed by a general proposition.
6. *Kayotse bo mi-makom aher* – deducing a law by comparison with a law of the same class.
7. *Davar halamed me-inyano* – the meaning of a passage may be deduced from its context.

[195] On the term *midda*, see Bacher, *Exegetische Terminologie*, 1, 100-03.
[196] Many studies are devoted to these methods. On the terminology, see Lieberman, *Hellenism*, 52-68; On the interpretative aspects, see now Elon, *Jewish Law*, 1, 270-310. Cf. also Mielziner, *Introduction* 117-87; Towner, 'Hermeneutical Systems' 112ff.
[197] Epstein, *Introduction*, 510; Lieberman, *Hellenism*, 54; Elon, *Jewish Law*, 1, 268-69.

According to the *Sifra* (*Petihta* to *Torat Kohanim, Baraita of Rabbi Yishmael*, end of the Baraita) the third *midda* should read *Binyan Av* (as such), whereas the fourth rule should be 'Two scriptures (that contradict each other)'.

(B) The most detailed list is the one attributed to Rabbi Yishmael,[198] who expands the list of his predecessor Hillel. This list in the *Sifra* (ibid.) fixes the number of *middot* as thirteen, although upon examination of its details we find sixteen rules.[199] They are:

1. *Kal wa-homer.*
2. *Gezera Shawa.*
3. *Binyan Av* from one scripture.
4. *Binyan Av* from two scriptures.
5. *Kelal u-ferat.*
6. *Perat u-khelal.*
7. *Kelal u-ferat u-khelal* – two general propositions, separated from each other by an enumeration of particulars, include only such things as are similar to those specified.
8. *Kelal shehu tsarikh li-ferat* – an inference drawn from a general proposition complemented by a particular term.
9. *Perat shehu tsarikh li-khelal* – an inference drawn from a particular term complemented by a general proposition.
10. *Kol davar shehaya bi-khelal . . .* – if anything is included in a general proposition and is then made the subject of a special statement, that which is predicated by it is not to be understood as limited to itself alone, but is to be applied to the whole of the general proposition.
11. *Kol davar shehaya bi-khelal . . .* – if anything is included in a general proposition and is then singled out in order to be made the subject of a special statement, similar to the general proposition, this particularization is intended, so far as its subject is concerned, to lessen and not to add to its restrictions.
12. *Kol davar shehaya bi-khelal . . .* – if anything is included in a general proposition and is then singled out in order to be made the subject of a special statement, not similar to the general proposition, this particularization is intended in some respects to lessen and in others to add to its restrictions.
13. *Kol davar shehaya bi-khelal . . .* – if anything is included in a general proposition and is then made the subject of a fresh statement, the terms of the general proposition will not apply to it, unless the scripture distinctly indicates that they shall apply.
14. *Davar ha-lamed me-inyano* – an interpretation may be deduced from its context.

---

[198] According to Porton, *Legal Traditions*, 429-53 Rabbi Yishmael's exegetical remarks throughout rabbinic literature have little in common with the list.
[199] Porton, *ibid. 431.*

15. *Davar ha-lamed mi-sofo* – the meaning of a passage may be deduced from some subsequent passage.
16. *Shenei ketuvim ha-makhhishim ze et ze* – when two passages are in contra-distinction to each other, the explanation can be determined only when a third text is found, capable of harmonizing the two.

As Elon has shown,[200] these rules can be classified according to their link with two types of halakhic midrash, the explanatory midrash, that clarifies verses in Scripture, which corresponds to the *interpretatio grammatica* of Roman law; and the comparative midrash (= analogy) which compares several cases to each other in order to expand halakhic legislation. This corresponds to the *Analogia* of Roman Law. *Middot* 5-16 belong to the first category, the explanatory midrash, whereas *middot* 1-4 belong to the latter category, the comparative midrash.

As I have mentioned, these *middot* served the Sages in explaining the halakhic sections of the Pentateuch. Occasionally, however, one of these may serve in a non-halakhic context. For example, the last rule, that of two conflicting scriptures, serves as an exegetical means of resolving the conflict between Exod 19:20, according to which God descended on Mount Sinai, and Deut 4:36, according to which God only spoke from heaven. The contradiction is resolved by adducing the 'third scripture', i.e. Exod 20:22 'for I have talked with you from heaven'.[201] This rule is also employed in resolving other contradictions, such as that between Lev 10:1-2 and Lev 16:1 (the reason for the death of Nadab and Abihu the sons of Aaron)[202] and the one between Exod 40:35 and Num 7:89 (how the Lord spoke to Moses).[203]

(C) A third list, the longest of all, is attributed to Rabbi Eliezer,[204] the son of Rabbi Yose ha-Gelili, and it includes thirty two[205] *middot*, which are mainly employed for the aggada rather than the halakha. Bardowicz[206] has already argued that the *Mishna of Rabbi Eliezer* which lists these rules, is a late composition. Both Zucker,[207] who attributes the composition to the Gaon Shmuel ben Hofni,[208] and Halkin[209] (among others) agree with this view. While some of the rules in the list are undoubtedly early, there is ample basis for the view that a significant proportion of these *middot* reflect late interpretations.

[200] Elon, *Jewish Law*, 1, 271.
[201] So in Sifra, *Wayikra, 1, 3a*. In *Mekhilta de R. Yishmael, Bahodesh* 9, p. 238, the contradictory verses are Exod 19:20 and 20:22, while the reconciliatory verse is Deut 4:36. See above, p. 576.
[202] Sifra, *Aharei Mot* 1, 79c.
[203] *Sifrei Zutta*, p. 254.
[204] See the critical edition of Enelow, *The Mishna of Rabbi Eliezer* (1933).
[205] According to Lieberman, *Hellenism*, 68 n. 168 there is a tradition of 36 *middot*.
[206] Bardowicz, *Abfassungszeit*.
[207] Zucker, '*Lamed-Bet Middot*', 1-19; Zucker, *Rav Saadya Gaon's Translation*, 237-60.
[208] But see Greenbaum, *Biblical Commentary*, 93-95.
[209] Halkin, 'Jewish Arabic Exegesis' 21-22.

Thus, I feel justified in omitting the Mishna of Rabbi Eliezer from my survey of biblical interpretation in the Tannaic period.

AKIVA AND YISHMAEL. Were these rules, attributed either to Hillel the Elder or to Rabbi Yishmael, accepted by all the Sages, or did they, perhaps, reflect the views of some particular interpretative-halakhic school? Until very recently, the accepted view was that use of the midda *'Kelal u-ferat'* in its various forms, was characteristic of the Tanna Rabbi Yishmael, while his major disputant, Rabbi Akiva, generally used the midda *'Ribbui u-miut'*.[210] This rule, as used by Rabbi Akiva, expands the meaning of the scripture (*ribbui* – inclusion), restricting its applicability only by the specific things mentioned in the scripture (*miut* – exclusion). The rule employed by Rabbi Yishmael, on the other hand, expands the meaning of the text *(kelal)* only in accordance with the specific detail mentioned in scripture *(perat)*. In the words of the seventh midda in the list attributed to Rabbi Yishmael: 'Two general propositions separated from each other by an enumeration of particulars, include only such things as are similar to those specified.'

For example, Rabbi Yishmael and Rabbi Akiva disagree on the halakhic meaning of Lev 5:4 'Or if any one utters with his lips a rash oath to do evil or to do good, any sort of rash oath that men swear, and it is hidden from him . . .' According to Rabbi Akiva this verse must be interpreted using the midda of *ribbui u-miut*:

> 'if any one utters an oath' – inclusion *(ribba)*; 'to do evil or to do good' – restriction *(mi'et)*; 'any sort of oath that men swear' – repeated inclusion *(ribba)*; inclusion, restriction, inclusion – all is included.
> What is included? All words are included. What is excluded? Oaths to fulfil or violate a commandment are excluded.
> *(B.T. Shevuot* 26a)

In other words: Scripture refers to all oaths except oaths having to do with performance of the commandments. Rabbi Yishmael, on the other hand, interprets this verse using the midda of *Kelal u-ferat*:

> 'or if any one utters with his lips an oath' – general law *(kelal)*; 'to do evil or to do good' – specific detail *(perat)*; 'any sort of oath that men swear' – repeat of general law *(kelal)*; general law, specific detail, general law – the law is determined according to the specific detail. Just as the specific detail speaks of the future, so every case (of oaths) must speak of the future.
> *(ibid.)*

In other words, Scripture speaks only of oaths about events that have not yet occurred.

---

[210] Cf. Epstein, *Introduction*, 527-29.

The view which clearly distinguishes between the methods of interpretation of Rabbi Yishmael and those of Rabbi Akiva is based on evidence in rabbinic literature which contrasts the midrashic methods of these two Sages.[211] The text of the Tosefta, according to the Erfurt manuscript,[212] combined with an investigation of the interpretations of Rabbi Yishmael dispersed throughout midrashic literature, reveals that Rabbi Yishmael used the *ribbui u-miut* method as well. It would appear, though, that Rabbi Akiva made unrestricted us of this method, whereas Rabbi Yishmael was not willing to apply this midda in all cases.[213] Furthermore, the midda of *kelal u-ferat* as used by Rabbi Yishmael is not employed by Rabbi Akiva and is never found in the Sifra or the Sifrei on Deuteronomy, two collections identified with the school of Rabbi Akiva.[214]

THE TORA SPOKE IN COMMON PARLANCE. Another important halakhic-exegetical rule of the school of Rabbi Yishmael was that of דברה תורה כלשון בני אדם 'The Tora spoke in common parlance'. This rule is usually employed when Rabbi Yishmael disagrees with a halakhic explanation of Rabbi Akiva. According to the Palestinian Talmud[215] this rule reflects a general concept, whereby repetitions of words are considered to be of no significance.[216] Moreover, no distinction is made between the halakhic and the narrative portions of the Pentateuch.[217] For example, according to Rabbi Yishmael, there is no halakhic significance attached to the repetition of words in the expression המול ימול, 'they shall be circumcised' (Gen 17:13), since this expression is not different from others that only reflect men's patterns of speech, as we find in Gen 31:30 הלוך הלכת, 'you have gone away', נכסף נכספת, 'you longed greatly' or in Gen 40:15 גנב גנבתי, 'I was indeed stolen (out of the land of the Hebrews)'. This rule, ascribed to Rabbi Yishmael, and sometimes expressed in other words as 'they are merely double expressions, the Tora spoke in the usual way..'[218] is employed by the Babylonian and Palestinian Talmuds in explaining debates between Tannaim.[219] Nevertheless, it is doubtful that other Sages used this category at all. Moreover, Rabbi Akiva's student, Rabbi Yose ben Halafta, applies this category to the repetition in the Tora of similar, though not identical expressions, while changing the meaning of the category:

[211] See *B.T. Shevuot* 26a; *T. Shevuot* 1:7.
[212] See Chernick, '*Ribbuyim* and *Mi'utim*', 97.
[213] Porton, *Legal Traditions*.
[214] Chernick, 'Formal Development', 393.
[215] *P.T. Shabbat* 19, 17a.
[216] Against Rabbi Yishmael's view see Akiva's interpretation of the absolute infinitive combined with finite forms of a verb, as in *B.T. Sanhedrin 64b* (הכרת תכרת) *B.T. Bava Metsia* 31a/b (שלח תשלח, עזב תעזב).
[217] Elon, *Jewish Law*, 1, 311.
[218] See *P.T. Shabbat* 19, 17a; *P.T. Yevamot* 8:1, 8d; *P.T. Sota* 8:1, 22b; *P.T. Nedarim* 1:1, 36c.
[219] Bacher, *Aggada der Tannaiten*, 1, 237.

'Say to the people of Israel' (Lev 20:2), 'and to the people of Israel you shall speak', 'Tell the people of Israel' (Exod 14:2), 'Command the people of Israel' (Lev 24:2), 'And you shall command the people of Israel' (Exod 27:20). Rabbi Yose says: the Tora spoke in the language of men, using many forms of language, and each form must be interpreted. (*Sifra Kedoshim* 10, p. 91b).

In other words Rabbi Yose recognizes that the many styles in the Tora reflect the many styles of speech of people, but whereas Rabbi Yishmael concludes from this that the repetitions have no interpretative significance, Rabbi Yose is of the opinion that one must interpret each and every sentence.[220]

SCRIPTURE SPEAKS OF THE ORDINARY CUSTOM. Another halakhic category of interpretation is דבר הכתוב בהווה, 'Scripture speaks of the ordinary custom'. In other words, the custom of 'the codifier to formulate his words at times using common examples, without intending to limit the law to the explicitly mentioned cases'.[221] The *Mekhilta de-R. Yishmael, Kaspa* 20, pp. 320-21 on Exod 22:30 provides a string of examples:

'(you shall not eat) any flesh that is torn by beasts in the field' – I only learn (that it shall not be eaten) if it is in the field, from where shall I learn (that it shall not be eaten) in the house?
Scripture says: (Lev 22:8) 'That which dies of itself or is torn by beasts (he shall not eat)'. We compare an animal torn by beasts to one that died of itself. Just as in the case of an animal that died of itself, the Tora did not distinguish between an animal in the house or in the field, so too, in the case of an animal torn by beasts, we should not distinguish between the house and the field. What then, does the scripture 'any flesh that is torn by beasts in the field' come to teach us? Scripture speaks of the ordinary custom.

Similarly in the case of Deut 22:27:

'because he came upon her in the fields' – I learn from this only (if he came upon her) in the fields. From where do I learn (of the cases where it occurred) in the house? Scripture speaks only of the ordinary custom.

Similarly, with regard to Deut 20:6.

'What man is there that has planted a vineyard and has not enjoyed its fruit?' – I learn from this only (if he planted) a vineyard. From where do I learn about (the case) of all other fruit trees? Scripture only spoke of the ordinary custom.

---

[220] According to *Mekhilta de-R. Yishmael, Nezikin* 18, p. 313, Rabbi Yishmael does not use this rule in explaining Exod 22:22.
[221] Greenberg, 'Rabbinic Exegesis', 6.

Similarly, with regard to Exod 23:19:

> 'you shall not boil a kid in its mother's milk' – I learn from this only (in the
> case of) a kid. From where do I learn about (the case of) other animals?
> Scripture speaks of the ordinary custom. So, here too, 'any flesh that is
> torn by beasts in the field' – Scripture speaks of the ordinary custom, it
> mentions the place where animals are likely to be torn.

To these examples we should add the case of the *Mekhilta de-R. Yishmael*,
Nezikin 18, p. 313 on Exod 22:21:

> 'You shall not afflict any widow or orphan' – I learn from this only (in the
> case of) a widow or orphan. From where do I learn about other people?
> Scripture says: 'You shall not afflict'. This is the opinion of Rabbi
> Yishmael. Rabbi Akiva says: the widow and the orphan are most often
> afflicted, therefore Scripture mentioned them.

This passage has been interpreted in many ways, as it seems to indicate that it is
specifically Rabbi Akiva who uses the category under discussion. Some have
resolved the problem of this passage and its meaning by referring to a fragment
from the Cairo Geniza which reads as follows:

> 'A widow or an orphan' – I learn from this, only (in the case of) a widow
> or orphan. From where do I learn about other people? Scripture says
> 'Any (כל) . . . you shall not afflict' – These are the words of Rabbi Akiva.
> Rabbi Yishmael says: 'Any widow or orphan' – Scripture mentioned
> those who are most often afflicted.[222]

In other words, according to this fragment, it is Rabbi Yishmael who employs
the category we discussed. We must point out, however, that this category also
appears in *Sifrei Deut* 255, p. 280 on Deut 23:11 in a section of the *Sifrei*
considered to be the writing of the school of Rabbi Akiva. Thus, it seems that
the category 'Scripture speaks of the ordinary custom' was employed by Sages
belonging to several different schools.

THE ORDER OF BIBLICAL BOOKS. There are two categories of interpretation that
relate to the significance of the order of biblical books. The first category is
אין מוקדם ומאוחר בתורה, 'there is nothing earlier or later in the Tora', i.e.
the Scriptures change the chronological order in describing events in certain
cases. Sometimes the chronological order is violated within a single verse, and
sometimes the violation is in the order of arrangement of several different
scriptures.[223] Our sources ascribe this category to the school of Rabbi Yishmael[224] and to Rabbi Meir.[225]

---

[222] Boyarin, 'Hidden Light', 9.
[223] See above, pp. 558-60.
[224] See *Eccl. Rabba* on Eccl. 1:12; cf. the use of this rule in the *Mekhilta, Shira* 7, p. 139.
[225] Cf. *P.T. Shekalim* 6:1, 49d; a variant reads: Rabbi Yehuda.

The second category is attributed to Rabbi Akiva, and apparently, reflects a concept different from the previous one. This category is formulated as 'when any passage adjoins another, we may derive something from it'.[226] That is, there is a meaning to be found in the proximity of scriptural sections, and the interpreter must find the connection and draw conclusions from it. In this way, we learned that the story of the whoring of the Israelites after the Baal of Peor (Num 25:1ff.) was placed next to the section of the Blessing of Balaam in order to teach us that it was he who advised the King of Moab to entice the Israelites to commit prostitution. The proximity of Lev 21:10 to the verse preceding it teaches the halakha that not only a priest's daughter who fornicated is punishable by death by burning (verse 9) but even the priest must be punished by burning. The prophecy of Hosea chapter 2 teaches us that the Holy One Blessed-Be-He reconsidered his intention to expel Israel, as was stated at the end of chapter 1. The link between Hos 14:1 and 14:2 also shows that the first verse is to be understood as a warning rather than as a final decision.

This rule, formulated by Rabbi Akiva met with opposition:

> Rabbi[227] (Yehuda the Patriarch) says: many scriptural sections adjoin one another, yet they are as far from each other as the distance between East and West.
> (*Sifrei Num.* 131, p. 169)

NOT EVERY SCRIPTURE MUST SIGNIFY SOMETHING. Another important rule of exegesis was formulated by Rabbi Yishmael and concerns his general view that 'not every verse of the Bible must signify something. In the *Sifrei* on Num 5:5-6[228] we read:

> This is a *midda* of the Tora: any passage mentioned in one place, but with one thing missing, and repeated somewhere else, was only repeated because of the one thing missing.

That is, we do not need to find interpretations for all of the second passage. It suffices to find a single (halakhically) additional detail. For example, in the *Sifrei* on Deut 14:6[229] the question posed was why the passage on forbidden foods, written in Lev 11, was repeated in Deut 14. The answer is 'The animals – to mention cloven hoofs, the birds – to mention the kite (or in some versions: the buzzard).' Rabbi Akiva, on the other hand, disagrees, and in response, he declares: 'Wherever we find the word לאמר, it must be interpreted'.[230] Perhaps

---

[226] Cf. *Sifrei Num.* 131, p. 169. Bacher, *Aggada der Tannaiten*, 1, 302 n. 2 is right when the claims that Rabbi Akiva does not invent the method but only formulates the rule used by his predecessors, like Rabbi Eliezer ben Hyrcanus and Rabbi Eliezer ben Azaria.

[227] Variant: Rabbi Meir.

[228] *Sifrei Num.* 2, p. 4-5.

[229] *Sifrei Deut.* 101, p. 160-61; see also *B.T. Hullin* 63b.

[230] *Sifrei Num.* 2, p. 5.

we can understand the words of Rabbi Akiva as a generalization, meaning that even the insignificant word לאמר must be interpreted.

A DIFFICULT TEXT CAN BE EXPLAINED BY A MORE EXPLICIT ONE. An additional category of interpretation is ascribed to Rabbi Nehemia:

> 'She is like the ships of the merchant, she brings her food from afar' (Prov 31:14) – words of Tora may be sparse in one place and plentiful in another.
> (*P.T. Rosh Hashana* 3:5, 58d)

The meaning of this category is that we can explain a difficult text using another, more explicit passage. One example of this might be found in the *Mekhiltot*[231] on Exod 15:22 'The Moses led Israel onward from the Red Sea'. Did Moses do what he did following God's command or on his own initiative? According to Rabbi Eliezer Moses led the people according to the word of God: 'They travelled by word of the Almighty. Just as we found in two or three other places in Scripture that they only travelled by word of the Almighty, so, here too, they travelled by word of the Almighty'.

USE OF A GRAMMATICAL RULE. Another rule of *peshat* interpretation is attributed, in several sources to Rabbi Nehemia. This concerns the dative case: 'Instead of prefixing a *lamed* to indicate "to", a *he* is appended at the end of the word'.[232] There are many examples of this grammatical feature to which the Sages pay attention in their explanation.[233]

AUTHORITY OF THE TRADITIONAL READING OF THE BIBLE. Another interesting halakhic rule of interpretation is found only twice in the extant Tannaic literature. This principle is formulated as יש אם למקרא, 'the traditional reading of the Bible (that is according to its established vocalization) has authority'.[234] This rule attempts to link the halakha to the traditional reading of the text. Thus, Rabbi Yehuda ben Ro'ets rejects the possibility of reading the word שבעים (Lev 12:5) as שִׁבְעִים, 'seventy', as contrary to the tradition of vocalization which reads שְׁבָעַיִם, 'two weeks'.[235] Similarly, the Sages dismiss the possibility of reading the word חלב in Exod 23:19, 34:26 and in Deut 14:21 as חֵלֶב, 'fat' rather than the accepted reading which is חָלָב, 'milk'. It may be that in these cases the category was employed to block halakhic interpretations other than the accepted ones. Perhaps this category indicates the tendency, on the part of

[231] *Mekhilta de-R. Yishmael, Wayassa* 1, p. 152 and *Mekhilta de-R. Shimon ben Yohai, Beshallah* 15, p. 101.
[232] *Mekhilta de-R. Shimon ben Yohai, Pisha* 14, p. 48; cf. *B.T. Yevamot 13b*.
[233] See also *Mekhilta de-R. Yishmael*, p. 33; *P.T. Yevamot* 1:6, 3b; *B.T. Yevamot* 13b; *Gen. Rabba* 50:3, p. 518; 68:8, p. 777; 86:2, p. 1053.
[234] See Aminoah, *'Em la-Mikra'*, 43ff.
[235] *Sifra Tazri'a* 2, p. 58d; *B.T. Sanhedrin* 4a.

certain Sages to link the halakhic midrash, or the halakha itself, to the accepted traditional reading of the text.

OTHER RULES. Many rules of interpretation which are midrashic in nature, are scattered throughout rabbinic literature. They mainly relate to specific words or expressions in the Bible. These rules have a standard formulation, such as 'Wherever we find written X, this is nothing but Y' or: 'Wherever it says X, this means Y'. The following are several examples of these rules:

a. Wherever we have found שילוח, 'sending', this means accompanying. (*Mekhilta de-R. Yishmael, Beshallah, Petihta*, p. 75)

b. Wherever we find יציבה, 'standing', this refers to the Holy Spirit (*Mekhilta de-R. Yishmael, Beshallah* 2, p. 94)

c. Wherever we find אלהים, (Elohim) this refers to a judge. (*Mekhilta de-R. Yishmael, Beshallah* 4, p. 101)

d. Wherever we find ישיבה, 'sitting', this refers to sinning (*Sifrei Num.* 131, p. 169)

e. Wherever it says לאמר, 'saying', or ואמרת אליהם, 'and you shall say unto them', this passage is relevant to future generations. Wherever we do not find לאמר or ואמרת אליהם, the passage was for that time only. (*Mekhilta de-R. Yishmael, Beshallah* 1, p. 83)

f. Wherever it says ויסעו ויחנו, 'and they set out and they encamped', they set out in dissension and encamped in dissension. (*Mekhilta de-R. Yishmael, Bahodesh* 1, p. 206)

g. Wherever it says לי, 'to me', it is established for all eternity. (*Sifei Numbers* 92, p. 92)

h. Wherever it says ה:, 'the Lord', this implies God's measure of mercy . . . Wherever it says אלהים (Elohim) this is the measure of justice. (*Sifrei Deut* 26, p. 41)

i. Wherever it says מושבותיכם, 'your dwellings', Scripture speaks of the Land of Israel. (*Sifrei Num.* 107, p. 106).

CONCLUSION. I will conclude my survey of the rules of interpretation with a colourful and interesting literary rule attributed to Rabbi Eliezer, son of Rabbi Yose ha-Gelili: 'First the Holy One Blessed-Be-He places the righteous in doubt and suspense. Only later he explains to them the meaning of the matter'.[236] That is, the Holy One Blessed-Be-He does something perplexing. He gives a command without any reason. Only later does He explain the reason for the command. Thus, for example, we have the unexplained command given to Abraham 'Go . . .to the land that I will show you' (Gen 12:1). Only later on does the reason for this command become clear. Similarly, God commands Abraham to go and sacrifice his son, telling him that He will later reveal him the

---

[236] *Gen. Rabba* 39:9, pp. 372-73; 55:7, p. 592.

mountain that he is to climb – 'upon one of the mountains of which I shall tell you' (Gen 22:2). Similarly, too, in Ezek 3:22 'Arise, go forth into the valley, and there I will speak to you' and in Jonah 3:2 '. . . to proclaim to it the message that I tell you'. The importance of this rule is that it reveals a general biblical style, not restricted to any particular book or collection (such as the Pentateuch), that is characteristic of God's way of revelation.

Selected Bibliography

On rabbinic exegesis see the studies of BONSIRVEN, *Exégèse rabbinique*, 11-259; DOBSCHÜTZ, *Einfache Bibelexegese*; DOEVE, *Jewish Hermeneutics*, 52-90; ELON, *Jewish Law*, 2, 239-320; FRANKEL, *Peshat*; GREENBERG, 'Rabbinic Exegesis'; HALLEWY, *Sharei ha-Aggadah*, 1-112; HEINEMANN, *Darkhei ha-Aggada*; HESCHEL, *Theology*; KADUSHIN, *Rabbinic Mind*, 98-130; LAUTERBACH, 'Jewish Allegorists'; LONGENECKER, *Biblical Exegesis*, 19-50; MELAMMED, *Bible Commentators* 1, 3-128; PATTE, *Early Jewish Hermeneutic*; SEGAL, *Bible Exegesis*, 7-21; STRACK-STEMBERGER, *Einleitung*, 222-56; VERMES, 'Bible and Midrash'.

The following works on the rabbinic terms of interpretation should be mentioned: BACHER, *Exegetische Terminologie*; BLOCH, 'Midrash'; GERTNER, 'Terms of Scriptural Interpretation'; HALLEWY, *Erkhei ha-Aggadah*; HEINEMANN, 'Technical Terms'; LE DEAUT, 'Définition'; LIEBERMANN, *Hellenism*, 47-82; LOEWE, 'The "Plain" Meaning of Scripture'; MARGALIOTH, 'The Term "DRŠ" '; MILLER, 'Targum, Midrash', 43-49; PORTON, 'Midrash'; WRIGHT, *The Literary Genre Midrash*.

Important studies on the hermeneutical rules are: CHERNIK, *Kelal u'ferat*; id., '*Ribbuyim* and *Mi'utim*'; id., '*Derashot*'; id., 'Formal Development'; DAUBE, 'Alexandrian Methods'; id., 'Rabbinic methods'; DOEVE, *Jewish Hermeneutics*, 65-71; ELON, *Jewish Law*, 2, 270-302; EPSTEIN, *Introduction*, 521-36; GOTTLIEB, 'Formula Comparison'; JACOBS, *Talmudic Logic*; LIEBERMAN, *Hellenism*, 53-68; MIELZINER, *Introduction*, 117-87; OSTROWSKY, *Ha-Middot*; SCHWARZ, *Analogie*; id., *Syllogismus*; id., *Induktion*; id., *Antinomie*; id., *Quantitätsrelation*; id., *Kontext*; STRACK-STEMBERGER, *Einleitung*.

Chapter Sixteen

Use, Authority and Exegesis of Mikra in the Samaritan Tradition

Ruairidh Bóid (M.N. Saraf)

General

Scripture for the Samaritans is the Pentateuch. In this they do not differ radically from Jews, who regard the rest of Scripture as having come into existence only because of a general falling away from the teaching of the Tora, only existing for the purpose of leading people back to the knowledge of the Tora, being destined to become largely unnecessary in the ideal future, and being of a decidedly lower level of revelation.[1]

The Samaritans prefer not to call themselves by the name Samaritans, שומרונים. They consider this to be a modification by outsiders of their real name, Shǎmērem, שמרים, 'Guardians', which they explain as meaning those that keep the Tora correctly and guard it.[2]

Use of the Tora

HOW THE TORA IS KNOWN

The written text of the Tora is not fully informative. The Samaritans agree with rabbinic Judaism, against the Qumran Covenanteers and against the Karaites, that there is much not said by the text that could never be derived by exegesis. The classic statement of this principle is an untranslated passage in the *Kitâb aṭ-Ṭubâkh*[3] which deserves to be quoted in full, partly because it is so important for the understanding of the Samaritan theory of the relationship between the

---

[1] The distinction between the Pentateuch and the rest of Scripture (or in other words, the absolute difference between the prophecy of Moses and all other types or instances of revelation) is a fundamental tenet of Judaism. Copious references to the authoritative sources of all periods on this subject can be found in Kaplan, *Handbook*, chs. 7-8. On the ending of the need for all or most of the books of the Prophets and Ketuvim in the future, see *P.T. Megilla* 1:7 (70d, bottom). The opinion is presented as being unopposed in essence.

[2] The Samaritans are *Bǎni Yishrǎ'el ash-Shǎmērem* בני ישראל השמרים. The Jews are *Bǎni Yishrǎ'el ay-Yē'ūdem* בני ישראל היהודים.

[3] For information on the date and authorship of the Samaritan sources in Arabic referred to throughout this article, as well as the mss. available, see the introduction to my *Principles*.

text of the Tora and the tradition that accompanies it, partly because it is such a contradiction to scholarly assumptions,[4] and partly because it has been summarised or referred to before in a misleading way and needs to be made available for independent scrutiny.[5]

> Religious practice *(madhhab)*, by which God is served and by which the permanent benefits, which appear free of all dross, are gained, can be learnt in two ways: the knowledge got from the intimation of the text, and the knowledge got from the testimony of tradition. The second of these is more effective as a guide, because if you have the second one then both are all right. It follows that you need to know the tradition and know the rules for telling a genuine tradition from a defective one.
>
> Let us look into this last point. Tradition can be defined as what is available from a number of people who could not possibly have consulted each other or connived with each other. There are four essential marks of its genuineness.
>
> The first is that it must have been received from a large number of people, right back in the time of the Emissary of God, people who were his contemporaries and received the regulations from him.
>
> The second is that the bearers should be the next generation from them who would then have been supervised by them and must necessarily have been given the information about it.
>
> The third is that they must all agree unanimously on it.
>
> The fourth is that it must not be invalidated, either by reason or by the intimation of the text.
>
> These, then, are the marks of the correctness of tradition, and any information held by the whole of the bearers of tradition, according to all these stipulations, must necessarily be conclusive evidence and decisive

---

[4] There seems to be what could be called a bit of scholarly folklore to the effect that the Samaritans derive their halakha by literalistic exegesis because they have no tradition. The most recent expression of this idea is by Schiffman, *Halakhah*, 17.

[5] I quote from Rylands Samaritan Ms. 9, 151b-153b; Bibliothèque Nationale, Ms. Arabe 4521, 56b-57b. Gaster, *Samaritan Eschatology*, 59-63, was apparently the first to notice this passage. Internal evidence shows that he was working with the Hebrew translation, the text now classified as Rylands Samaritan Ms. 174. His exposition of the passage is useful, but is marred by his failure to register the inter-connection of the ideas in the passage. Halkin, 'Relation', 315-16, has misunderstood the text just as seriously, though less obviously. Briefly, Halkin's attempt at finding an equivalent to the Moslem concept of *sunnah* in this text, which looks convincing in his exposition, is vitiated by the facts of the text, which does not use the term *sunnah*, and which does not make tradition the continuation of the observed practice of Moses. The most serious misunderstanding is in regard to the reason for the introduction of the list of criteria for an adequate tradition. The list is of course modelled on the Moslem requirements for a valid *sunnah*, but the point that the author is making is that by generally accepted criteria the whole nation of Israel have a trustworthy tradition of the whole of the Tora: in other words, both the author and his readers have to use the terminology and categories provided by the environment. (Most attempts at finding Moslem influence on the Samaritans depend on the same fallacy of confusing the vehicle of expression with the message expressed.)

proof. There is no need to scrutinise any information when the essential conditions of tradition are in order and the tradition is sound: scrutiny is only necessary in a case of doubt.

The actual number of the bearers of tradition is irrelevant provided the basic conditions are in order, and the tradition is sound. A fallacy never became the truth through numbers and the truth never became a fallacy through lack of numbers. The nation, and all the experts *('uqalâ')*, will accept a person's declaration, on the strenth of the consensus of the inhabitants of a single village, that Zayd is the son of Khâlid, and on that basis will sort out the details of the inheritance of an estate, making Zayd eligible and disqualifying 'Amr; and they will give a ruling on quite serious questions, by giving permission for a man to marry certain women deemed permissible and disqualifying certain other women. Now if these and other cases can be settled on the basis of the consensus of a single village, then it must be even more right and correct to take the word of the whole nation.

There are some actions that you would never have any knowledge about, and would never know to be all right, without tradition. For instance, take the actions of midwives on Shabbat and festivals, when they perform a delivery: the point here is that the midwives, when they perform a delivery, perform activity that is work, and would not be permissible for anyone else. Then there is the killing of fish, by leaving them in air, so that the life leaves them; or the killing of locusts in hot water.[6] Then there is the question of how to tell the boundaries separating the Qiblah from the profane ground surrounding it on all sides. Then there is the accuracy of the text of the Tora, written down with twenty-two letters, which they witnessed on the Day of Descent.[7] There are plenty of other examples, but there is no room for them in this brief account.

The reason that we know all these details and know they must be right is the tradition received from the nation, who trace it right back to the time of the six hundred thousand that heard the Speech of God, and were alive at the same time as his Prophet, Moses the son of Amram, and received from him. The emissary gives the testimony for tradition and the intimation of the text in the General Speech,[8] where the tradition is given precedence over the intimation of the text. The verse in question is 'My doctrine will pour like rain, my utterance will run down like dew' [Deut 32:2]. He intended these two expressions as a metaphor to teach the

---

[6] Fish and locusts must be killed by an Israelite, and this is done by putting them in an element opposite to their natural one. In this respect the Samaritans partly agree with the Karaites and the Qumran sect against rabbinic Judaism.
[7] The day of the giving of the Tora.
[8] Deut 32.

nation that necessity demands the tradition, just the same as the need for the intimation of the text.

[There follows another example of the correctness and unity of the tradition, the example of the knowledge of the calculation of the calendar by the High Priest, which is the only fully satisfactory calendar].

There can be no doubt that the Samaritans have a theory of a tradition that is essential for the understanding of the text of Scripture. The question then is, to what extent this theory agrees with the rabbinic Jewish view.

The Samaritans know and understand the rabbinic theory of a Written and Oral Tora, and reject the rabbinic concept of Oral Tora explicitly and unequivocally, whenever the matter comes under discussion.[9] The theoretical difference between the rabbinic and Samaritan concepts of tradition is that the Samaritans are not willing to give the tradition the same status as the text. The tradition is the source of knowledge of the intention of the text, but it is not revealed, it is not at the same level of existence as the text. In practice, the Samaritans derive just as much from tradition as the Rabbis do: much more can be learnt from tradition than from reading the text. The tradition gives the necessary additional help needed to understand the text, but most of the time its function is to tell what the text does not even mention.[10] Nevertheless, the information given by the tradition is always ultimately the expression of the intention of the text: the text mentions the existence of a certain area of halakha, and the tradition, by giving the details that are not even hinted at in the text (at least from the point of view of the human mind), only tells us what the text would be saying to us if we could read it on its own level of existence. The tradition does not tell us anything that is not in the text. Everything is in the text, which is a reflection or manifestation of the nature of Creation.[11] Only Moses has ever understood the text fully:[12] ordinary people need to be told what it means, and this is the function of the traditional knowledge.

---

[9] For instance, in the comment of the Commentary on the Tora (*Kâshif al-Ghayâhib*) on Exod 13:9, first noticed by Geiger, *Die gesetzlichen Differenzen*, 318. The passage is in Ms. Petermann I:b of the Prussian State Library, 221a.

[10] Bóid, *Principles*, Conclusions, 345.

[11] The theory on the origin of the Tora that follows could be derived from Marka's major work, the *Mimar Marqâ* (third century C.E.) but the length of this work, and its detail, makes it hard to use as a reference without a previous general familiarity. Besides which, there is no completely satisfactory translation or edition. For practical reasons I therefore give references to the hymns by Marka which are actually often more explicit because of their conciseness. The only trustworthy edition and translation is by Ben-Ḥayyim, *Literary and Oral Tradition* 3b, 214-62. Marka was a younger contemporary of Baba Rabba, which puts him in the third century. See note 33. On the Tora and creation, compare Marka, Hymn 14, lines 7-8: 'Its creator is a consuming fire; it was given from out of the Fire'.

[12] Hymn 14, lines 130-133; 'The gate was opened and Moses went in, and took the Ten Words, and knew how the Universe came about'.

The traditional knowledge ultimately comes from Moses. The source of the Tora is the manifestation of the source of Creation.[13] A description of Creation was fixed in the two tablets.[14] Moses took the tablets, which only he could understand in all their implications, and turned them into the five books of the Tora.[15] This text was still at a level of existence higher than normal objects,[16] or the ordinary level of the human mind, so that only Moses could realise or grasp how much it said. Some aspects were clothed in the garb of ordinary words to the extent of being intelligible (at least at one level) to anyone: but other aspects were not intelligible to anyone except Moses, who had to put their content into form at the level of information that could be grasped by the human mind, so that people would know how to act according to the Tora in all matters, whether or not any given piece of information could be seen by ordinary people in the Tora.[17] The Tora, as the manifestation of the Creative Power, is clearly at a higher level than the information at the level of the human mind that Moses set before Israel so that they would know in practice what was required of them. The tradition, as the transmitted explanatory teaching of Moses, is clearly not equal in status or authority to the book of the Tora.[18]

DIRECT ACCESS TO THE TORA

It would be very misleading to make these comments without adding the other side of the picture, which is that Moses is not, as is often maintained, an intermediary between Israel and the Tora, or between Israel and God. This is made quite clear in the passage from the *Tubâkh* quoted above. The Samaritans

---

[13] Hymn 14, lines 87-89: 'It is said that the King in the Heaven of Heavens came down, though he did not (actually) move'. On the relationship between the various levels of manifestation of the Tora, as the model of existence or creation, see Séd, 'Mēmar samaritain'.

[14] Hymn 14, lines 25-26: 'These were the Ten Words, and from them Creation was filled'. Hymn 14, lines 45-46: 'It is the book of the Standing King, written by the finger of the Living God'. (The reference here is to the two tablets, not the five books.) Hymn 15, lines 10-15: 'It is written by the finger of consuming fire, according to the mind of the Divinity. With fasting and prayers it was received by Moses from out of the flames of fire, from the outstretched arm by which the universe is supported'. (The reference is to the complete scroll of the Tora.)

[15] Hymn 15, lines 38-43: 'Woe on him that does not carry out its commandments. It is the Book of the Tora that Moses the Prophet wrote at the order of his Lord, and put inside (variant 'next to') the Ark, so that the repentant could read it'. Hymn 14, lines 37-42: 'The seed of holiness that Moses brought was sown on the two stones. These were ten specifications (or: details), and from them all the foundations were laid, and from them Moses wrote five books, from which all Israel is nourished'.

[16] Hymn 24, lines 29-30: 'It is the great, pure, and holy book, which came down from the Heaven of Heavens'. (The reference is to the written *Sefer Tora*.)

[17] Hymn 15, lines 35-36: 'The Prophet that was found trustworthy forever taught us everything that is written in it'. Abu 'l-Ḥasan clearly implies this by his insistence that the tradition starts with the people who were present at the giving of the Tora and who were also the contemporaries of Moses. See the quote from the *Kitâb aṭ-Ṭubâkh*, above.

[18] The tradition is explicitly given a completely subsidiary function in the same passage from the *Ṭubâkh*.

agree with the Jewish tradition that the introduction to the Ten Commandments and the first Commandment (which for Jews are the first two Commandments) were heard directly by all six hundred thousand Israelites. They heard
them *mi-pi ha-Gevura (B.T. Makkot* 23b-24a), an expression normally used to
indicate the unique level of the prophecy of Moses, or the level from which the
whole Tora was given to Moses. What appears to be the Samaritan Aramaic
equivalent of the same expression (*băfimme adrēbūte* בפמה דרבותה) occurs in
the same context in the following passage from Marka (Hymn 16, lines 81-85):
'He (God) was speaking to them by the mouth of his (or the) mastery: You shall
have no god (or gods) except for me, for I am the Standing One'. The first half
of this formula is clearly the First Commandment. The second half is an allusion
to the introductory formula of the Ten Commandments (i.e. the First Commandment by the Jewish reckoning.[19] Because they heard them without any
intermediary, all Israel have direct access to the Tora, not just to the book, but
to the unfailing depths of meaning in it. 'He (God) spoke with all Israel, a
speech that can't be repeated (i.e. can't be put in words)' (Marka, Hymn 16,
lines 165-66). 'Each mouth that has the power of speech reads what gives life to
the reader, and his soul is nourished without food. Thus it happened to Moses
the Prophet' (Marka, Hymn 14, lines 99-102). 'The storehouse that nourishes
all that are nourished by it, light and wisdom to those that seek it; the storehouse that enriches every one that desires it' (Marka, Hymn 15, lines 28-31).
This possession of the Tora by all Israel is quite compatible with the need to be
explicitly instructed in it by Moses; compare the following lines, 35-36, of this
hymn (quoted in note 17); and compare the juxtaposition of the two ideas that
all Israel were witnesses of the descent of the Tora, and that Israels' traditional
explanation of the Tora goes back to the time of Moses, in the quote from the
Kitâb at-Ṭubâkh, above.

We now see why the tradition can never over-ride the written Tora. If
information can be taken directly from the Tora, then it must be at a higher level
than information that has been set out by Moses. Nothing can have the same
status as the Tora. The tradition is not, as rabbinic Jews have it, another
manifestation of Tora, but only a help for understanding the Tora.[20]

---

[19] Compare the Samaritan piyyut *The Song of the Precepts*, (ed. Haran), 10 (= p. 183) for an
alternative version of the Samaritan tradition.
[20] Assumed as fundamental by Abu 'l-Ḥasan, above.

The Samaritans are not literalists (in fact, they reproach the Jews with being literalists).[21] Certainly, all halakha and all doctrine must come from the Tora, which for them is the text alone, but the text is not a human book and is not limited like a human book, so it would be futile to try to derive all knowledge from it by logical analysis. The finite does not comprehend the unlimited. It follows that much that is known is not obvious or derivable from the book, as we have seen; and it also follows that the understanding of the book must always be tempered by tradition, lest logic go astray. The three sources of knowledge are the wording of the text, reason, and tradition,[22] but the three items are not equivalent in nature; the relationship is that reason and tradition help in understanding the text, and at the same time, reason and tradition are guided by the text in developing new knowledge, new insights and new solutions.[23] In this way, the written text of Scripture is always the source of new information, without any danger of literalism, and without any danger of finding the information in the text to be inadequate. The comments on Samaritan written and unwritten halakha in *B.T. Hullin* 4a are to be interpreted accordingly, as referring to a Samaritan Oral Tora side by side with the Written Tora. The obscurities in the passage and its context are due to the difference between Samaritan and Jewish theory.

THE TRANSMISSION OF KNOWLEDGE OF TORA

The tradition is not a fixed body of information which could be reduced to writing if enough systematic effort were put into the task. As the bearers of the tradition are the nation as a whole,[24] who live by the Tora, which they have collectively accepted upon themselves at Mt. Sinai and which was in some way revealed to them, it will always be possible for new questions to be solved and for new situations to be handled. The Tora is unlimited, so its application must be unlimited, and because its application is according to a living tradition, new information will appear when necessary. This new information can appear as a result of the argument of learned experts, or can arise as universal popular

---

[21] Munajja bin Ṣadaqah, *Kitâb al-Khilâf*, in a long excursus after chapter 6, on the inadequacies and fallacies of Jewish halakhic exegesis, of which the passage edited in Bóid, *Principles* under the title *Additional Text from the Khilâf* is a part. I quote from Ms. Oriental Quarto 523 of the Prussian State Library, p. 145: 'Because of their reliance on the wording of the passage alone, and their exclusive use in regard to each Scriptural law *(aṣl)* of the details that are written down, they have no conception of details derivable from lay-out [all other mss. are corrupt at this point] or the (main) purpose of the passage or the implications (of the text)'. The concept shows that what is meant is that the fault with Jewish exegesis is that it takes passages in isolation, without comparing related passages, and on a smaller scale it takes the meaning of separate phrases without looking at their place in the structure of the exposition. There is another statement of this complaint on p. 141 of the ms.

[22] Bóid, *Principles*, *Kâfi*, XI, lines 21-32, note; III, lines 31-32, note.

[23] Bóid, *Principles*, Additional Passage from the Khilâf, line 6.

[24] Bóid, *Principles*, Conclusions, *Authority*. See also above, notes 15 and 17.

practice.[25] In both cases the solution is not arbitrary, but the result of the application of a traditional understanding of the intention of the Tora, whether or not formal arguments are used to help reach a decision.

If the bearers of tradition are the nation as a whole, and if the tradition (like the Tora, but not to the same extent or in the same way) is in part beyond the level of verbalisation, if it is living knowledge, then it is possible for different specific solutions to problems to appear, even if the solutions contradict each other.[26] This is not a contradiction or uncertainty within the tradition, but a divergence of manifestation at the most mundane level.

It is, of course, possible to write down the essential facts about an area of halakha. However, the Samaritans have never produced an equivalent of the Mishna, and the halakhic texts that they have produced do not pretend to be complete.[27] It is likely that the explanation for this phenomenon is that no need has ever been felt to write down the halakhic tradition in full. If the tradition is borne by the nation as a whole, then unresolvable contradictions between scholars will not occur, and the situation of necessity, which according to rabbinic tradition produced the Mishna, has never arisen.[28] The 'Oral Tora' is still oral.

The same principle applies to the aggada, at least in the area of doctrine. The source of knowledge of doctrine is the unlimited written Tora, and it would be impossible to fix the possibilities once and for all. It is always possible for a theological writer to develop the message of the text.[29] (In this respect Jews and Samaritans are in the same situation.)

In the area of both halakha and doctrine the written text of Scripture imposes certain constraints. It is not that the text limits development, but it does give a continuous check on the possibility of the adoption of an erroneous practice or concept, when knowledge of the tradition is obscured.[30]

---

[25] Bóid, *Principles*, Marginal Note 2.

[26] Bóid, *Principles*, Conclusions, *Authority*; Id., Conclusions, *Variations within the Samaritan Halachic System*; Id., *Kitâb al-Farâ'iḍ*, lines 97-106.

[27] It is hard to see how the common comparisons of the Samaritan halakhic texts with the *Shulḥan 'Arukh* are arrived at. The only code of laws is the *Kitâb al-Farâ'iḍ*, but even it is not really complete for all details, and anyway, it only survives in fragmentary form, so it could not have been a book generally studied.

[28] A different explanation is given by Crone and Cook, *Hagarism*, 29 and 179. They suggest that halakha is less important or central for Samaritans than Jews. The observation is incorrect, as any acquaintance with Samaritan literature will show. On the other hand, the observation on the less developed state of Samaritan halakhic literature is quite correct, and the fact must be explained. On the production of the Mishna as a remedy for unresolvable and excessive disagreements between scholars which had arisen as a result of the change from transmission of the halakha by the people as a whole to a system of development by academic study and argument, see Ginzberg, *'Significance'* 94-96, and *'Codification'*, 160-61, commenting on *T. Hagiga* 2:9. (Parallels in *T. Sanhedrin* 7:1; *P.T. Sanhedrin* 1:4 (19c, middle); *B.T. Sanhedrin* 88b). But see the remarks of Safrai, 'Oral Tora', 72-74.

[29] The Arabic period is rich in original theological literature.

[30] See note 23.

In short, all areas of halakha and all doctrines are mentioned in the text, and the living national tradition applies them and develops them as necessary.

PRONUNCIATION OF THE TEXT AND TRADITIONAL KNOWLEDGE

Nowhere in the descriptions of the loss of books in the Roman persecutions,[31] and nowhere else in any source before the Mediaeval period, do we find any mention of a written study of Scripture, with the single exception of Marka's book, which is not a formal exegetical study. The first evidence for written notes on halakha is the reference in the preface to the *Kitâb al-Kâfi*[32] to written notes surviving from the obscure past.

A number of questions raise themselves here. Why does no systematic study of Scripture in writing survive from before the Mediaeval period? Why is the surviving literature of the earliest period apparently not concerned with the direct study of Scripture? What is the reason for the existence of a Greek translation and an Aramaic translation of the Tora? What were these translations used for? And most importantly, how was formal study carried on in the absence (perhaps irrelevance) of books?

There is no doubt that systematic-exegetical study of the Tora was widely carried on in the time of Baba Rabba,[33] and as this is the earliest period for which we have any extensive information, we will start there and then see if we can extrapolate backwards. The evidence is set out below in full, so that the probable correctness of the conclusions to be drawn can be gauged by others. The more important pieces have not been translated before.

---

[31] Mainly under Hadrian and Commodus, according to the Chronicles.
[32] Quoted below.
[33] Generally dated in the fourth century c.e., but on inadequate evidence. The correct date is probably the mid third century. On this, see Crown, 'Byzantine Orbit' (forthcoming; I refer to a draft kindly provided by the author).

The first passage is taken from the description by Abu 'l-Fath[34] of the first steps in restoring knowledge and practice after Baba Rabba had taken control.[35]

Baba sent and brought all the Experts *('ulamâ')* in the Tora *(Sharî'ah)*, and the priests *(kahanah)*, from every place, except that not many of the Elders *(mashâyikh)* and Learned Men *(ḥakâkimah* printed text; *ḥukamâ'* recension C)[36] of Israel were to be found . . . He told them: 'Each of you go to his place and be scrupulous, diligent, and clever in teaching all Israel, men, women, and children, the Tora *(Sharî'ah)*, so that they know it by heart *(li-ḥifẓha)* and follow the general commandments *(farâ'iḍ)* and detailed regulations *(aḳhâm*; recension C adds: which are in it) perfectly as your ancestors did and be careful about the correctness of the reading of the Tora *(Tôrâh)'*.

The next passage is taken from the description by Abu 'l-Fath of Baba Rabba's perfected administration.[37]

(Printed Recension)

Baba Rabba said to the Learned Men *(ḥakâkimah)*: 'Reflect and be clever in all that you do and be careful of mistakes and blunders and pay attention to the readers of the Tora and the teachers *(mu'allimîn)'*.

(Recension C)

The Judges *(ḥukkâm)* appointed by Baba Rabba would always be exhorted by him: 'Be extremely pious *('ala ḥadd aṭ-ṭâ'ah)* and reflect and be clever in all that you do, and be careful of mistakes and blunders, and always pay attention to the Tora, because that is the greatest and most important authority *(akbar amr muhimm)*, and talk to the teachers

---

[34] There are two recensions of the *History* of Abu 'l-Fath: the one edited by Vilmar and referred to since then, and translated by Stenhouse; and another so far unpublished and mostly unstudied. As Stenhouse divides the mss. of the better-known version into two groups, I refer to the lesser-known version as recension C, though in actuality the main division is a two-way one, not a three-way one. Recension C is far more accurate than the better-known version, hereafter called the printed text or printed recension, particularly in any technical discussion. I quote the printed recension from Vilmar's edition, corrected against all of Vilmar's mss., which I have re-collated, and a number of other mss. I quote recension C from Ms. Sulzberger 14 of the Jewish Theological Seminary, but its readings have been checked against Ms. Oriental 7927 of the British Library and Ms. Barton 7 of Boston University Library. The text published by Cohen, *A Samaritan Chronicle*, is essentially a Hebrew translation of a part of recension C of Abu 'l-Fath, and as such, is extremely valuable, though it needs to be used with care.

[35] The two recensions are very close in this passage and can be quoted together. Printed recension, ed. Vilmar, 128, lines 9-15 (Stenhouse, 177-78). Recension C, Sulzberger ms., 203b-204a. Some very minor variants are not recorded (Cohen 4:11-13).

[36] The form *ḥukamâ'* is the normal plural of *ḥakîm* (= Hebrew *ḥakham*, Aramaic *ḥakkîm*). The form *ḥakâkimah* is a secondary plural of the same word.

[37] Printed text, ed. Vilmar, 132, lines 2-4 (Stenhouse, 182); recension C, Sulzberger ms., 207a (Cohen 8:1-3). In this case recension C is decidedly superior to the printed text.

(mu'allimîn) about that in regard to their learning by heart *(hifz)* of the reading of the Tora *(Sharî'ah)* according to the Ten Canons *(usûl)* transmitted by tradition from the Seventy Elders of Israel and from the Priests *(a'immah)* who lived at the same time as our Master, the Great Emissary Moses the son of Amram.'

The third passage comes soon after the second, and gives details about the use of the synagogues mentioned in the intervening section.[38]

(Printed Recension)
He built a place for the reading and interpretation *(tafsîr)*, and the hearing of queries, to the south of *(qıbli)* the house of prayer so that anyone that wanted a query answered could ask the Learned Men *(hakâkimah)* about it and they would inform him correctly.

(Recension C)
He also built a central synagogue *(jâmi'an wâsi'an)*, which he assigned for the purpose of the reading and interpretation *(tafsîr)* and the hearing of questions, and set it up opposite *(muqâbil)* the house of prayer he had set up on the lower slopes of Mt. Gerizim, so that anyone that had a query could come there and put his query to the Learned Men *(hukamâ')* and they would inform him what the position was *('an mâ laha)*.

Even on a first reading of these passages, it is obvious that the teaching and study of the text of the Tora is closely connected with the correct reading. Let us examine what is meant by correct reading.

The Ten Canons[39] of reading mentioned in our second passage (in the undamaged recension only) are the ten sets of supra-segmental morphemes that mark the sense divisions, logical inter-connection and sequence of thought, level of reality (statement, question, exhortation, command, warning, speculation, etc.), and emotional content. The system of marking these Canons in a written text was apparently not fully understood by the authors of the extant treatises on the subject. What has been lost is apparently the knowledge of the intonation that is represented by each sign (perhaps as well as the fine points of the rhythm). The principle of marking the text by stress, rhythm, and pitch is still alive, but it is not linked clearly to the written signs. For our present purpose this is not an obstacle, as we can rely on the lists of meanings of the signs (and therefore of the supra-segmental morpheme sets) even if the authors of the lists were a bit uncertain how to link each symbol with the pitch, rhythm, and stress changes used by them on the basis of tradition. The Ten Canons were once applied consciously to the text, and at least the list of meanings of the

[38] Printed text, ed. Vilmar, 132, lines 14-16 (Stenhouse, 183); recension C, Sulzberger ms., 208b (Cohen 9:1-2). Once again, recension C is decidedly superior.
[39] See the excursus by Ben-Hayyim on these Canons and their representation and use in *Literary and Oral Tradition* 1, 53-57.

Canons is in our hands, if not the intonations themselves. The signs for the Canons occur sporadically in the oldest MSS. of the Tora, which indicates that in earlier times their conscious use was part of the study and knowledge of the text.

Aside from the use of the Ten Canons, we can assume that the modern and Mediaeval system of fixing the pronunciation of each single word in the Tora[40] was also practiced in the time of Baba Rabba. This fixed pronunciation has the same functions as the Masora, except that the pronunciation takes precedence over the spelling and has even influenced the spelling in the past.[41]

Correct pronunciation is inextricably linked with correct interpretation in the Samaritan tradition. Correct pronunciation expresses one's knowledge of the etymology and morphology of the word, and one's correct understanding of the syntax of the phrase. To speak about correct reading means in practice to speak about correct pronunciation (the same word is often used for both in the Arabic sources) and to speak about correct pronunciation is to speak about correct understanding of the text, including its implications.[42]

The learning by heart of the Tora referred to by Baba Rabba would then be the acquisition of the knowledge of the application of the Ten Canons to every sense-unit, and the exact pronunciation of every single word. This knowledge would inevitably, given the outlook and assumptions we have described, be acquired along with instruction in the meaning of the text. Those who had obtained this knowledge would then be qualified to teach Scripture, though they would not necessarily be qualified to argue about halakha or doctrine at a scholarly level.

EXPERTS AND LEARNED MEN

Beyond the level of the 'Teachers' is the level of the 'Experts' and 'Learned Men'. It is not entirely clear whether there is a difference in rank or function between the 'Learned Men' *(ḥukamâ)* and 'Experts' *('ulamâ')* in the usage of the Chronicles, but on the whole, when speaking of the work of Baba Rabba, it seems to me that there is a tendency to use the term *'ulamâ'* in the sense of halakhic and doctrinal study of Scripture at an advanced level, and *ḥukamâ'* in the sense of discussion or decision-making where the argument or tradition is more to the fore than the text itself. The 'Judges' *(ḥukkâm)* would be the 'Learned Men' or 'Experts' acting in a specific capacity, probably, if we can go by the analogy of Jewish practice, with some extra training.

The institution for the study of the Tora was apparently concerned with the development of knowledge as well as its transmission. It was concerned with the activity of interpretation *(tafsîr)*, which implies the continued intensive study of

---

[40] Ben-Ḥayyim, *Literary and Oral Tradition* 3a, 27-28.
[41] Ben-Ḥayyim, *Literary and Oral Tradition* 1, 24. On the pointing system, see Ben-Ḥayyim, 5, 4-7.
[42] See note 40. For examples of the relationship between interpretation and pronunciation, see Ben-Ḥayyim, *Literary and Oral Tradition* 1, 22; Halkin, *'Relation'*, 290-91.

the text, as well as the activity of reading, which is an activity that maintains knowledge rather than developing it. From the close connection of the two terms, we can assume that there was a body of established interpretation which was taught and transmitted as an attachment to each word or phrase.

This method of study closely resembles the procedure of the schools of the Tannaim, which produced midrashim that systematically attached traditional halakha and aggada to the text of the Tora, and also recorded the results of intensive study of the text. The Samaritan method of attachment of information to the text could perhaps have resembled that of the *Sifra*.[43] There remains the question of why no written midrashim of the school of Baba Rabba have come down to us. From this period we have Marka's book (which is not a midrash), liturgical compositions, the Targum, and the sources of the extant Chronicles, so obviously texts of midrashim could have been passed on. Part of the answer to this question is provided by the history of the Tannaic midrashim themselves. Although these midrashim were readily available to the Tannaim themselves, the actual books were deposited in the academy in the form of master copies, which were revised over several generations. The midrashim that we have in our hands are not these books: they do not survive. What we have are compilations, each compilation being an edited and abridged version of the midrash of one school, with material from other schools added wherever necessary to produce a satisfactory complete work. Some of the material in our midrashim was not known to the Amoraim and much of the material known to the Amoraim is not in our books. It could be conjectured that Samaritan midrashim would have been even more vulnerable to loss, because of the smaller numbers of the Samaritans, and that they could have perished in the unsettled conditions after the time of Baba Rabba.[44]

Let us see how much of this structure of fact and inference (and, admittedly, some speculation) can be applied to the period of the first and second centuries

---

[43] The format of the *Sifra* is the simplest of all the Tannaic midrashim, particularly in purely halakhic passages.

[44] On these aspects of the history of the Tannaic midrashim, see Albeck, *Mevo ha-Talmudim*, ch. 5, section 3; Melamed, *Pirkei Mavo le-Sifrut ha-Talmud*, part 2, chs. 4, 16, 19. There is an allusion to the establishment of 'the instruction of the synagogues' in what would have been the mid eleventh century (a date that corresponds to the composition of the *Ṭubâkh* and *Kâfi*), in *Chronicle Neubauer*, 448-49. (Compare *Chronicle Neubauer*, 446 and *Chronicle Adler* for the year 5307 on the dating.) This is said to have been the time of the first literary use of Arabic by the Samaritans. It would seem that the disconnected pieces and outlines surviving from the obscure past mentioned by the author of the *Kâfi* in his introduction (see below) must therefore have been written in Hebrew or Aramaic, and that their condition was due to being relics of a period when the study of the Tora was fragmented and disorganised. I suggest that although the early Samaritan midrashim perished, their content survived, both in the form of the disconnected written pieces mentioned above and as traditional knowledge, and that much of the literature of the Arabic period, including quite late works such as the comprehensive commentary on the Tora, the *Kâshif al-Ghayâhib*, contains such material along with much later material.

of the common era. 'Experts' and 'Learned Men' are mentioned frequently in the context of the Roman persecutions.[45] Houses of study *(madâris)* are also mentioned.[46] It is assumed that in normal times most people would know the Tora.[47] If we combine these facts with the mention of 'Informed People' by the *Samareitikon*,[48] we can take it that it is highly probable that Baba Rabba's work was that of restoration, not reformation, as in fact the tenor of the narrative about him indicates. Probably, then, the Samaritan 'Scribes' mentioned in the Jewish sources are the 'Experts' *('ulamâ')* of the Samaritan *Chronicles*; and we actually have one passage that puts these Samaritan scribes or experts in the context of the interpretation of the text of the Tora. This passage is a comment on Numbers 15:31, occurring both in the *Sifrei*[49] and the Babylonian Talmud.[50] The form in the Sifrei is probably more original. The text of the Sifrei reads in this case:

> Rabbi Shimon ben Elazar said: This is how I demonstrated the Samaritans' books to be spurious (זייפתי ספרי כותיים), since they would say: The dead do not revive. I said to them: It says: 'That soul will be absolutely cut off; its fault is in it'. Now the meaning of 'its fault is in it' is that it will have to give account on the Day of Judgement.

It seems surprising to have Samaritans denying the concept of a day of judgement and a general resurrection for the purpose, since this is one of the main items of faith of the Samaritans as we know them. There is also evidence that the Dositheans believed in an individual resurrection, probably not in bodily form.[51] Whether some Samaritans denied any life at all after death is hard to tell from the sources. A denial of resurrection is not the same as a denial of some

[45] Experts *('ulamâ')*: Abu 'l-Fath, ed. Vilmar, 120, line 8 (Stenhouse, 165); 118, line 18 (Stenhouse, 163); *'ulamâ'*, Teachers *(mu'allimîn)*, and *hakâkimah* (Learned Men): 125, lines 3-4 (in recension C, Sulzberger ms. 199b, the form is *hukamâ'* instead of *hakâkimah*). These examples are only representative.

[46] Abu 'l-Fath, ed. Vilmar, 118, line 18 (Stenhouse, 163).

[47] Abu 'l-Fath, ed. Vilmar, 122, lines 3-4: 'No-one taught his child the Tora, except one in a thousand or two in ten thousand, in secrecy' (Stenhouse, 168, has completely misunderstood this). In the Arabic *Book of Joshua*, ch. 48: 'No-one was able to learn the Tora etc.'.

[48] Deut 25:7-8. The significance of this term is discussed below. See note 76 for the reference. The spelling Samareitikon with >ei< representing [i:] corresponds to normal Greek spelling for this period. On Samaritan scribes, see note 80.

[49] *Sifrei Num.* 112 (p. 122).

[50] *B.T. Sanhedrin* 90b.

[51] First example: Abu 'l-Fath, ed. Vilmar, 156, lines 14-15. Vilmar's text is corrupt at this point. Stenhouse, 218 has followed Vilmar's text and not the mss. The actual text (according to the mss.) is: 'They said that the dead would rise soon as the children of Dositheos the prophet (of God)'; or, with Ms. Oriental Quarto 471 of the Prussian State Library: 'They said that the dead would soon rise, thanks to Labi (לוי) and his group, the children of Dositheos the prophet of God'. Second example: Abu 'l-Fath, ed. Vilmar, 155, lines 1-2. Vilmar's text is corrupt again. Stenhouse, 216 admits to being unable to make sense of Vilmar's text, but does not refer at all to the mss. The actual reading of the mss. is 'My faith is in you, Lord, and your servant Dositheos, and his sons and daughters'.

future life. One could, for example, think of re-incarnation, which can be demonstrated from the Tora much more easily that resurrection, individual or collective.[52] Anyway, some form of disagreement on these lines seems to be the explanation of the reading of the Venice edition[53] of the Sifrei of 1546, which assumes the need to specify that not all Samaritans are meant: 'This is how I demonstrated the Samaritans' books (Samaritans that would say . . .) to be spurious'. Rabbi Shimon's proof is in fact one of the standard Samaritan proofs for the concept of a day of judgement.[54]

The Samaritans referred to by R. Shimon rejected the argument quoted just beforehand in the Sifrei, whereby the duplication of the verb for re-inforcement *(hikkaret tikkaret)* to express the idea of absoluteness or completeness is artificially interpreted as a duplication of intended meaning, so that it is taken to mean 'will be cut off and will be cut off', that is, will be cut off in this world and the next, thus proving that there is another world. The rejection of this method of exegesis is fundamental to all known later Samaritan exegesis, and we have here a conclusive example of the continuity of the methodology. Later Samaritan exegesis, which insists on the concept of the Day of Vengeance and Recompense, a concept which is essentially the same as one version of the Jewish concept of the World to Come, continues to reject any special interpretation of the duplication of the verb, and takes the duplication to indicate absoluteness or completeness. Where they find the reference to resurrection is precisely where R. Shimon finds it, in the next phrase, 'its fault is in it', which is taken to indicate that even after death the soul still exists, and is liable to the consequences of its actions.

We learn from this passage that one of the known Samaritan principles of exegesis, the refusal to find special meaning in variants of style, is as old as the time of the Tannaim. We also learn that different Samaritan groups, who disagreed on their theology, still agreed on the methodology of exegesis.

There remains the problem of the mention of Samaritan books by R. Shimon ben Elazar. There is a passage similar in form to this one in *Sifrei Deut* 56 (p.

---

[52] The standard Jewish proof for re-incarnation is from such verses as Exod 20:5-6, where it does not say 'to thousands of generations', but only 'to thousands'; if they are not generations they can only be lifetimes; and the visiting of the sins of the sons on the fathers must have the same meaning, otherwise there would be a denial of justice.

[53] The Venice edition of 1546 is the first printed edition. Its distinctive reading in this place is not a minority reading. Horovitz only had four text-witnesses available for this passage. Of these, two have a secondary reading at this point. This leaves only one ms. (the reading of which I have translated above) and the Venice edition. The reading of the Venice edition is not recorded in Horovitz's edition, and I have consulted the original. This reading would look like a simple dittography if its significance was not appreciated, and would tend to be eliminated by scribes.

[54] This is how the *Kâshif al-Ghayâhib* interprets the verse (Prussian State Library, Ms. Petermann I:c, 307b). The same interpretation is implied by the Samaritan Arabic translation and one version of the Samaritan Targum (the other being inconclusive). A Jewish reading of the verse on the same lines seems to lie behind the translation of the Peshitta, and is conflated with the other interpretation by the Targum Pseudo-Yonatan.

123) on Deuteronomy 11:30, where the Samaritan Tora is said to have been falsified, to be spurious (Cf. *P.T. Sota* 7:3, 21c; *B.T. Sota* 33b; *Sanhedrin* 90b; the phrase is זייפתם את התורה) In that passage, the reference can be explained as being an allusion to the text of the Samaritan Tora, which in this verse has a variant reading which is explicitly quoted. In the passage from the Sifrei on Numbers this explanation will not do. The Samaritan Tora agrees with the Masoretic Text in the verse under discussion, so how can it be said to have been falsified? Besides, all the implication of the wording is that the text was not the issue, but that the text was agreed on and the problem was how to convince the others of its meaning. There are, then, no obvious books that could have been falsified. Geiger[55] suggested reading 'scribes' instead of 'books', an emendation which in Hebrew is very slight, but this will not do, because one does not declare people to be spurious, counterfeit, or forged, which is the range of meanings of the verb. The verb demands the existing reading of 'books'.[56]

I suggest that the books referred to are the Samaritan collections of fixed, official, scriptural exegesis, similar to the Tannaic midrashim, which were being built up at the same time.[57] There is of course the question of how R. Shimon could have been so familiar with Samaritan literature, particularly if we hold to the analogy previously suggested with the Jewish midrashim, which as books were not readily available. It is likely that the solution lies in the fact that the controversy being a major one amongst the Samaritans themselves, one could hardly fail to hear about it and hear the arguments of both sides if one came into social contact or physical proximity to a Samaritan community. Furthermore, the controversy would be one of interest to a Jewish scholar, having a bearing on a disputation between the Pharisees and the Sadducees, and once it came to a Jewish scholar's attention, he would want to pursue the matter till he had uncovered the details. We have evidence from elsewhere of R. Shimon's interest in the arguments of the Samaritans and their practice, an interest for the sake of controversy, but nevertheless much more than a casual interest.[58] Thus his discovery of the standard midrash of one Samaritan group is not unexpected. What R. Shimon quoted against them looks like the standard midrash of another Samaritan group.

We are now in a position to understand why it is that we have a Greek translation of the Tora (or at least, bits of one), and an Aramaic translation of the Tora, from the first centuries C.E., but no equivalent of the Mishna or the Tannaic midrashim. From our description of the probable method of Samaritan

---

[55] *Ha-Mikra ve-Targumav*, 85 (= *Urschrift*, 81).

[56] The impression given by Jastrow's dictionary (p. 389) is misleading. He assigns a certain meaning to this passage, and then derives a meaning of the verb from that.

[57] In which case we should probably take the verb זייף to mean 'to declare false' in agreement with its Syriac cognate.

[58] There is evidence of R. Shimon's strong interest in Samaritan ideas in *P.T. Avoda Zara* 5:4 (44d, middle).

study of halakha, the Mishna form would be very unlikely to be used.[59] As for the midrashim, they have simply perished. The evidence, such as it is, indicates that the content of the midrashim lived on and became incorporated eventually in the Arabic literature. Compare the passage from the *Kâfi* quoted below.

If the books of midrashim, by the nature of their production and use, were vulnerable to loss, the exact opposite must have applied to the translations of the Tora. If all doctrine and halakha had to have some attachment to the text, *if all traditional knowledge was regarded as merely a statement of what to know to understand the text correctly and in detail*,[60] then all study must have been linked to the text (which we have seen to be an attested fact), and a text in the common language would have been absolutely essential. The Hebrew text would have been copied as often as a group of people came together to study or be taught, and would have been the focus of each study group. Attached to this text, not in physical form in writing, *but in the minds of all educated people*, and in this respect that means most people to some extent, was an ever-growing body of interpretation. The Greek translation gave way to the Aramaic, and the Aramaic to the Arabic. (Nowadays most Samaritans would be able to read the Tora in Hebrew.) The text has been re-copied and constantly studied, and the accompanying invisible but real tradition has been passed on with it. The handbooks of faith and practice, and the Scriptural commentaries that were composed in the Middle Ages in Arabic, although to some extent the creation of their authors, and certainly bearing the mark of their personality, are also largely individual selections from this traditional knowledge. This continuous new composition is quite appropriate, since the traditional knowledge, which is the knowledge of the meaning of the Tora, must not only be passed on, but also developed.

Perhaps this is why the Samaritans care so little about identifying the authorship of books, and do not seem to care at all about the distinction between an original book and a revision or adaptation.[61]

KNOWLEDGE RESERVED BY THE PRIESTS

There is a body of traditional knowledge, apparently mystical in nature, and having to do with the meaning of the Tetragrammaton, that is the preserve of the Priests, and in part, the preserve of the High Priest.[62] Obviously such information does not get written down in books for the general reader, and we know nothing about it.

---

[59] Except that there were probably collections of laws as *halakha le-ma'ase* for practical judicial purposes, similar to the Sadducean *Book of Decrees* (see note 130).

[60] See the passage from the *Kitâb aṭ-Ṭubâkh* quoted above.

[61] Gaster, 'Samaritan Literature' 5, column 2. See also Bóid, *Principles*, Introduction, 23-25, on the authorship and recensions of the *Kitâb al-I'tiqâdât*.

[62] Montgomery, *Samaritans*, 213-14.

Some other parts of the mystical tradition are readily available. If we go by the analogy of the Kabbala, which is to be found everywhere in the prayer-book, the traditional Bible commentaries, and many discursive works, without being explicitly labelled as such, we can expect some of the mystical tradition to be alluded to throughout the liturgy. This is in fact the case. The didactic or reflective pieces called *shîrân*[63] in Arabic are quite rich in these ideas. Then there is the material on Moses, which says a lot about the nature of the Tora if read perceptively. Marka's book is only a particularly long prose version of the *shîrân*, or a particularly long version of the prose and verse pieces on Moses, where the real focus is on Moses's function and work, and the purpose behind it. For this reason a study of Marka really belongs with a study of the liturgy, and will not be brought in here. However, for our present purpose it will do as a concentrated example of secret knowledge made public. Much of this material is concerned with the nature of the Tora and the concept of revelation.

The very specific knowledge handed on from one High Priest to another, and not available to other Priests (or said not to be available to them), has to do partly with the actual pronunciation of the Tetragrammaton.[64] The High Priest is also responsible for the calculation of the Calendar.[65] Neither of these matters are directly related to Scriptural exegesis, and they do not concern us here.

The same comment applies to an area of knowledge that was once the exclusive preserve of the Priests but was preserved only in books after the end of the Time of Favour and was lost altogether in the Roman persecutions: the songs for the sacrifices.[66]

In short, there is no area of Scriptural study or interpretation that is the exclusive preserve of the Priests. The only apparent exception is that there was once a difference of opinion on whether the Priests had the exclusive right to make a practical halakhic decision, or decide on the correct pronunciation of a word in the Tora. We will now discuss these questions.

THEORETICAL STUDY BY EXPERTS

As would be expected, there have always been experts in the study and teaching of the Tora. Who these experts are, and how they went about their work, is not entirely clear for all periods, and the evidence is to some extent contradictory. We will start with a discussion of the evidence for the mediaeval period, and try to work backwards to the first centuries C.E.

---

[63] The singular is *shîr*, obviously a borrowing from Hebrew, perhaps by way of Aramaic.
[64] Gaster, *Samaritan Eschatology*, 69.
[65] See ch. 1 of the *Kitâb al-Kâfi*.
[66] Arabic *Book of Joshua*, ch. 47. This was a real loss of knowledge of Tora, as this liturgy theoretically went back to the giving of the Tora and must therefore have been part of the tradition of how to carry out the injunctions of the text in practice. These songs would have been similar in origin and function to the Jewish Psalms.

The most explicit statement on the subject known to me is in the introduction to the *Kitâb al-Kâfi*. The introduction is in flowery and prolix rimed prose. The following mainly gives the gist of the relevant section, but the critical sentences are translated exactly.[67]

[Experts *('ulamâ')* have looked into the details of the Tora and have written their findings down in books containing material derived by investigation *(ma'qûl)*[68] and material known by tradition *(manqûl)*. All sorts of notes *(furû' aqâwîl)* giving information on the practice and details *(sunan wa-aḥkâm)* of certain written laws *(uṣûl)* survive from the obscure past].

Notes *(aqâwîl)* on some matters which are obligatory knowledge for any Israelite have been written up from the outlines *(tasâwîd)* of learned jurisprudents *(fuqahâ')*, each of whom was a leading authority *(sayyid wa-imâm)* in his generation. Some of them were not actually *Imâm* (Priest) by descent and rank, but were *Imâm* (authority) by (religious) standing *(shayâkhah)* and function *(ṭarîqah)*, and any genuine compositions of theirs have validity.[69]

[This book, the *Kitâb al-Kâfi*, has been written up from their statements, which is why it is not always fully systematic in its arrangement. Those who are competent in such questions will be able to sort out the contents and handle the arguments put by each side].

There can be no doubt that the position of Legal Expert *('âlim)* and Jurisprudent *(faqîh)* can be attained by any competent person, Priest or not. The problem lies in reconciling this undeniable fact with the assumption in other places that the Priests have the supreme authority to make decisions.

For the mediaeval period the problem can be solved from a careful reading of the sources. The first chapter of the *Kitâb al-Kâfi* deals with the function and status of the *Imâm* (Priest). The chapter says nothing about their function as jurisprudents. The function given to them in regard to the law is to fix the calendar and regulate the festivals, and read the Tora. In addition, the High Priest has the title of Judge, which significantly is not further defined. Aside from this, any Priest must know and practice the Tora, but this is not because it is his official function to teach the Tora, but rather because the right knowledge and behaviour are necessary prerequisites for such an important position. An ignorant Priest is not allowed to officiate.

This clarifies the practical situation. The theoretical situation is still not entirely clear because there is some evidence that the Priests in general, or perhaps the High Priest, are regarded as the ultimate authorities for any decision on what the law actually is (in Jewish terminology, they are *poskim*).

---

[67] Noja's translation is not precise enough for the present purpose.

[68] Some mss. have *muqawwal* 'stated by the text'.

[69] Noja has exactly reversed the meaning at this point.

The clearest statements on this known to me are both in the *Kitâb aṭ-Ṭubâkh*. The first passage is in the introduction to the book, where the author deals with the question of what happens to the function of Moses after his death. The answer given is that prophecy is not transmitted or inherited, but neither does it disappear with the death of Moses: this would be impossible, because it has permanent validity. It is reserved for the future, for the Day of Judgement, beyond the mundane level of existence. The work and function of Moses is in some respects still necessary, so it is taken over by the High Priest, who then has two functions. We are not told at all how the High Priest takes over the position of Moses, and the rest of the chapter only describes what would be expected as normal priestly functions. The fact that we are not told anything about any activity in regard to the interpretation of Scripture or the study of the halakha, where so much detail in regard to other activities is given, indicates that this is not part of their hereditary function. The solution is probably that ultimate authority lies with the High Priest, but that in practice this only involves making a decree or decision to fix the halakha in case of necessity. This interpretation is confirmed by the description of the function of the Priests in general by the same author in the passage on the Blessing to Levi (Deut 33:8-11). His main concern is with their ritual functions, and the following section on their function as protectors of the Tora and judges has to be read in this context.[70]

> The phrase 'Because they have guarded your utterance' (v.9) refers to their keeping the whole of the assignment that was expressed from God in words by the Emissary, and their actively arguing against the opponents of the religion, as it says: 'and they guard your covenant'. They are the ultimate authorities for the regulations and for the clarification of the details of their real meaning *(wa-'alayhim tantahi al-aḥkâm wa-tubân al-ḥaqâ'iq fîha)*. From them one acquires the legal rulings *(fatâwa)*, statements of forbiddenness or permissibility, uncleanness and cleanness *(wa-'anhum tûkhadh al-fatâwa wa-'l-ḥarâm wa-'l-ḥalâl wa-'ṭ-ṭamâ' wa-'ṭ-ṭuhr)*, as it says: 'They declare judgements to Jacob, and your Tora to Israel' (v. 10). The bit about Jacob refers to the judges *(ḥukkâm)* of Priestly lineage, and the bit about Israel refers to the whole of the nation, whether people occupying special positions or ordinary people, men and women, upon whom they impose the Tora.

We see that one of the main functions of the Priests is to give *fatâwa*, that is, rulings on what the halakha actually is in specific cases of doubt or dispute: the exact equivalent of the Jewish *teshuvot*, except that the decision of the Priest has the authority not only of his learning, but also of his position. The Priest needs skill and understanding so as to reach his decision, and one can assume that ignorant Priests will not be asked for decisions, but the authority of the decision is the authority of the hereditary function of the Priesthood. In this respect they

---

[70] The passage has not been translated before.

are performing the same function as when they decide whether a particular person or object in a particular case is clean or unclean. Their function is to make binding authoritative decisions in particular cases, not to be theoreticians, jurisprudents, collectors of traditions, systematic commentators on Scripture, or authors of handbooks of faith and practice (though any given Priest may well do this in practice). Nevertheless, by giving authoritative decisions on matters of faith or practice or Scriptural interpretation in particular cases, they presumably create a body of case law which becomes a body of authoritative teaching on these matters.

To what extent the Priests actually performed this function in the mediaeval period is not easy to answer. Neither the *Kâfi*, nor the *Ṭubâkh*, nor any other source known to me, actually use such Priestly decisions, and there may well be a discrepancy between theory and practice in this matter.[71] Our main concern here, however, is not the mediaeval period, but the first centuries C.E., and the situation in the mediaeval period is for the present purpose a guide to what to look for at earlier periods. Let us take the rather meagre evidence from the period before Baba Rabba, and then try to see if any of the information about Baba Rabba's work throws light back onto the earlier periods.

Kippenberg[72] has correctly pointed out that the Samaritan Targum translates the term *shūṭǎrem*[73] (commonly taken to mean some kind of administrative officers), as 'scribes'; and that the term 'elders'[74] is translated as 'wise men' or 'learned men'. Now such a translation assumes an identification of administrative function and the knowledge of Scripture and tradition, which indicates that these functions do not belong to the Priests by virtue of their position. It also assumes that the knowledge of the meaning of Scripture was mainly passed down by way of the Seventy Elders, as in fact the text of the Tora[75] implies fairly clearly and as rabbinic Jewish tradition insists. We will see later that there is a strong Samaritan tradition on these lines.

To my knowledge, there is not a single mention in any Jewish source before the Middle Ages of Samaritan Priests in any other connection than their priestly function, i.e. as recipients of tithes and cultic functionaries.

In the one case where the translation of the word *zǎqīnem* (elders) by the *Samareitikon* is known,[76] the word is translated as 'informed men' or 'learned men' *(synetoi)*. This is enough to show that the method of the targum in translating this term (and, presumably, the other term in question) goes back to the method of the *Samareitikon*, and therefore that the concept of learned men,

---

[71] There are in fact collections of priestly *fatâwa*, 'legal rulings', but they are all from the modern period, when the High Priests have a function in practice in deciding the halakha simply by being educated in the Tora.

[72] *Garizim und Synagoge*, 175-76. (See also 180-84.)

[73] The masoretic pronunciation is *shotrim*.

[74] זקנים (the masoretic pronunciation is *zekenim*).

[75] Num 11:25.

[76] Deut 25:7-8, in a fragment published by Glaue and Rahlfs, 'Fragmente'.

not necessarily Priests, who interpret the text and tradition of the Tora, is older than the time of Baba Rabba.[77] A rather slight confirmation, but nevertheless clear in the light of the information so far put forward, is that Josephus refers to the Samaritan administrative council (which could also have been a judicial body) by the term *Boulē*,[78] a term which in the usage of the time means specifically Senate in the Roman sense, or a Council of the Greek type, and would lead the reader away from any thought of the Priesthood. The existence of a Samaritan Patriarch[79] is also attested. Now the term Patriarch (the exact equivalent of the Hebrew term Nasi) is one that in the usage of the time would not be applied to someone holding a Priestly office. It would properly belong to the President of the *Boulē* just mentioned. We also find references to Samaritan scribes, clearly connected with the interpretation of Scripture, in Jewish sources, in passages dealing with the time of the Tannaim.[80]

In the light of this information, we can now put greater reliance on the information in the Samaritan Chronicles on the study of the text and tradition of the Tora before the disruptions caused by the Romans, information which agrees with the evidence put forward so far. A sketch of the evidence will have to suffice here.[81]

(a) There are numerous references to the persecution by the Romans of teachers of the Tora or experts in the Tora, who in some cases are mentioned without any reference to the Priesthood and in some cases are distinguished from the Priesthood.

(b) There are references to the destruction of the houses of study by the Romans, without any indication that these houses of study had any necessary connection with the Priesthood.[82] On the other hand, the Priests are consistently mentioned in connection with the attempt to suppress the synagogue service and destroy the knowledge of liturgy.

(c) When the experts and teachers are mentioned in connection with the synagogues, there is not usually a mention of the synagogue service, and the implication is that the synagogues were also houses of study.

(d) There are places where the experts or teachers are mentioned along with the Priests, and there is a distinction in function.

---

[77] Compare above, in the first quotation from Abu 'l-Fath, the reference to *mashâyikh* and *ḥakâkimah* or *ḥukamâ'* as an institutionalized function before the activity of Baba Rabba.

[78] Josephus, *Ant.* 18:88.

[79] Kippenberg, *Garizim und Synagoge* 139, quoting *Gen. Rabba* 94:7 (p. 1178). The date would be about 150 C.E.

[80] *Sifrei Deut.* 56 (p. 123) on Deut 11:30 (where the interlocutor is R. Elazar ben Yose); *P.T. Avoda Zara* 5:4 (44d, middle), where the interlocutor is R. Shimon ben Elazar. See note 58.

[81] All of what is said here can be verified simply by reading through the relevant sections of Abu'l-Fath and the Arabic *Book of Joshua*.

[82] See above, note 46, for the reference.

(e) It was expected that the Tora would be taught from father to son, which implies that it was common property and therefore accessible at an advanced level to any interested person.[83]

On the other hand, there is some evidence of a viewpoint that ascribed the right to teach the Tora to the Priests, and of an attempt by Baba Rabba to regulate the conduct of the community that held this opinion, an opinion that was once widespread. Whether this opinion had arisen in times of persecution, and the Priesthood was the most stable and visible public office, or whether it is an ancient divergent concept of the teaching of Tora, is not stated by the sources. There is, though, one important piece of indirect evidence that this divergent viewpoint is ancient. We are told that when Baba Rabba took the teaching of the Tora out of the hand of the Priesthood, the ordinary Priests (those not descended from Pinḥas) no longer had any reason to maintain their record of genealogy intact, i.e. back to Levi, and were content to be known as Priests because their immediate ancestors were known to be Priests. Now if the removal of any authoritative function in regard to the Tora could have this effect, it must have been an innovation, otherwise these records would have been abandoned long before.

In view of the importance of this issue, I give here the translation of the relevant passage, taken from the history of Abu 'l-Fath.[84]

> Baba Rabba took seven men out of the best of Israel, men of wealth and learned in the Tora, and honoured them with the title of 'Learned Men' (ḥakâkimah, ḥukamâ). The generality of the Priests (kahanah) were not, however, called Learned Men. Of these seven Learned Men, three were Priests (kahanah) and four were ordinary Israelites. Before this, any of the Priests (kahanah) that was of high authority was called in Israel Chief Priest (Imâm),[85] but from Baba onwards they came to be called Learned Men so as to have a title to call them by.[86] The nomination of the Chief Priests (a'immah) belonged to them and their descendants afterwards.
>
> [Laymen were then put in charge of most of the synagogue service (except for carrying the Sefer Tora) and in charge of circumcision].
>
> From that time onwards the lines of descent of the Priests (kahanah) were lost, and they only traced their descent to their immediate ancestors.[87] None of them cared about the records of the lines of descent, the reason being that Baba Rabba had only bestowed the title of Learned Men on the Experts ('ulamâ'), whether they were Priests (kahanah) or

[83] See above, note 47.
[84] Abu 'l-Fath, ed. Vilmar, 129, line 2, to 130, line 8 (Stenhouse, 178-80); recension C, 204a-205b. Minor differences between the two recensions that do not affect the sense are not recorded. The Hebrew translation (Cohen 5:1-14) has some interesting variants.
[85] So recension C; printed recension Imâm Kabîr.
[86] 'So as to have a title to call them by' (bi-sabab tawqîr man yudda'a minhum ka-dhâlika) only in the printed recension.
[87] This is the situation among Jews at present.

ordinary Israelites. The generality of the Priests were not given the title of either Learned Man or *Imâm* (Chief Priest or eminent person).

[Baba Rabba then gave these men the authority to make decisions].

There is a record of a group called the Sebuaeans (of whom virtually nothing is known) who would not accept the authority of Baba Rabba's appointees as final authorities, but would allow these appointees to make observations and then put a particular case to the High Priest of the Sebuaeans for an authoritative decision. The attitude of this group resembles the theoretical attitude (as opposed to the actual practice) of the mediaeval sources, which, as we have seen, is to allow any learned person to set out his interpretation of the text and tradition, but for the Priests to be the usual experts, and for the High Priest to make the authoritative ruling on any case, if lesser Priests are unable to decide.[88]

The Sebuaeans, however, did not take notice of Baba Rabba and did not accept the Learned Men *(ḥakâkimah)* that he appointed. Instead their Priests *(kahanah)* would give judgement in their villages, and the seven Learned Men *(ḥakâkimah)* appointed by Baba Rabba would travel round all the villages and would leave[89] informants[90] there who would find out if there was any of the Sebuaean Priests there that had made a mistake in a *mitswa (farîḍah)* or Scriptural law *(sharî'ah)* or detail of practice *(ḥukm)*, and would bring the matter before their own *Rabîs*[91] 'Priestly Authority' from their own community *(ar-rabîs alladhi lahum min al-'ashîr)*.

This attitude of the Sebuaeans obviously must have existed before Baba Rabba. Whether it existed before the Roman persecutions is not so obvious. On the whole, however, the evidence seems to point in that direction.

---

[88]   Abu 'l-Fatḥ, ed. Vilmar, 131, line 12, to 132, line 1 (Stenhouse 182); recension C, Sulzberger ms., 206b-207a (Cohen 7:1-6). I quote the printed recension. The only significant difference with recension C is that the wording at the start of the passage implies that the reader might not have heard of the Sebuaeans, which means that it is not possible to speak of them as a numerous group, or as the majority, against a supposed Dosithean Baba Rabba, as is often done.

[89]   Stenhouse follows Vilmar's text against the mss. at this point.

[90]   Stenhouse has failed to recognise an inner-Arabic graphic corruption at this point. The reading *mu'arrifîn* is confirmed by recension C.

[91]   The reference is to the *Rabîs* of the Sebuaeans. Stenhouse has confused the words *rabîs* and *ra'îs* here (as in fact he does throughout his whole translation). On the term *rabîs*, see Ben-Hayyim, *Literary and Oral Tradition* 1, 132-33; 2, 380. The Hebrew and Aramaic equivalent is רבץ or רביס. I suggest that the term is cognate to the Hebrew terms (in Jewish usage) להרביץ תורה and תרבץ. The *Rabîs* is usually the High Priest, but a distinctive community such as the Sebuaeans, or an ordinary community of some size, can have its own *Rabîs*. (On this last point see the reference to *Chronicle Neubauer* by Ben-Hayyim.)

First, as we have seen, the more extreme attitude of the Priests who found Baba Rabba's reforms so traumatic seems to be older than the Roman period, so presumably an attitude lying between this attitude and Baba Rabba's would be at least as old, if the tendency of the times in the Roman period had been in the direction of increasing priestly authority. This argument, although plausible, is not conclusive.

Second, the attitude of the Sebuaeans is echoed in the theoretical statements (as opposed to the actual practice) of the mediaeval sources, and therefore seems to have been one that was not easy to sweep away. This would indicate that the attitude had deep historical and theoretical roots. This argument is not conclusive either, though it adds to the plausibility of the theory.

Third, the Sebuaeans seem to have existed well before the Roman persecutions, so presumably they must have had a distinctive attitude even then.[92]

Fourth, the Sebuaeans seem to have continued to exist as an identifiable group into the Gaonic period.[93] As Baba Rabba's reforms had fallen into abeyance by that time, at least in the matter of the function of the Priesthood, there must have been something that distinguished them even then from other Samaritans. This argument would be stronger if we knew for certain that at that time there were Samaritans that were neither Sebuaean nor Dosithean.[94] In view of the fact that the Sebuaeans are only mentioned once in that period, this is probably the case, but there is no certainty, as they might not have called themselves by that name.

It is to be noticed that the Sebuaeans could not have belonged to a separate sect to Baba Rabba and his officials if their halakha was identical, which it must have been to make the arrangement described workable. This means that the only point of disagreement must have been over the question of ultimate authority on the halakha, as in fact the text fairly clearly implies. If this single point of disagreement was enough to make them a distinctive group, then it must have had much deeper roots than an assumption of authority by the priests

---

[92] The most plausible way of accounting for the names of the two scholars Sabbaios and Theodosios mentioned by Josephus as the Samaritan representatives in the debate before King Ptolemy on the text of the Tora is as names produced by Jewish and Samaritan folklore out of the names of the two most distinctive Samaritan groups of his time, the Sebuaeans and the Dositheans (Josephus, *Ant.* 13:75).

[93] *Halakhot Gedolot, Hilkhot Shiḥrur 'Avadim* (ed. Hildesheimer 2, 522). This passage identifies Cuthaeans, Sebuaeans, and Samaritans, and thus supports the suggestion that the Sebuaeans were a distinctive group rather than a separate sect, since a distinction between Cuthaeans and Samaritans is only one of terminology. (It must be admitted, though, that the main concern in this passage is genealogy, not sectarian divisions.)

[94] This does seem to have been the case in the time of Baba Rabba; see above, note 88. What the anonymous majority might have called themselves is uncertain. I suggest a division as follows: The great majority (probably to be identified with the Gorothenians); a subdivision or distinctive community within this majority, called the Sebuaeans (and possibly the same as the Masbotheans, if the etymology of the two names is the same); and a group with its own organisation, incompatible because of its calendar and halakha, which later produced the Dositheans. The name of the Gorothenians could perhaps be derived from the place-name עורתה.

in a time of turmoil. This argument is probably the strongest of those put forward here.

Perhaps we can approach this problem from another direction. We have seen that there is a discrepancy in the mediaeval sources between theory and practice. Such a situation can be explained as an ancient divergence in the theory of the relative authority of experts in the Tora (who might or might not be Priests) and the Priesthood in regard to ultimate decisions on the interpretation of the Tora. Now in fact there is evidence for such an ancient theoretical divergence. The expression of this theoretical divergence takes the form of a difference of opinion about the relative authority of the Seventy Elders as opposed to the High Priest. Both authorities were constituted by Moses and both were given the Tora to keep. This theoretical divergence is indirectly attested for the period before Baba Rabba.

One version of the theory is given by Abu 'l-Fath just after his description of Baba Rabba's organisation.[95]

> This administration and organisation was not from the Time of Favour. Rather, in the Time of Favour there were Seventy Elders who were honorary agents *(mukhtârîn)* and experts *('ulamâ')* for the population. Twelve of these elders were the chiefs of the tribes. One of the twelve was chief over all of them and was called Leader of the Tribes, and he assisted the most senior of them in adjudicating. [However the Priesthood was autonomous in its internal affairs].

In line with this theory, some sources tell us that the King was appointed by the High Priest and the tribal elders in concert.[96] The tribal elders would be bearers of the type of authority represented by the Seventy Elders.

The other theory expresses itself by having the High Priest choose and appoint the King on his own and by his own authority.[97] It also expresses itself by having Joshua order the King to obey the High Priest,[98] and by deleting the reference to the existence or relevance of the Seventy Elders at the end of the

---

[95] Just before the bit about the Sebuaeans. Abu 'l-Fath, ed. Vilmar, p. 131, lines 2-12 (Stenhouse 181-82); recension C, 206a-206b (Cohen 6:6-8). I translate from the mss. of the printed recension.

[96] Macdonald, *Chronicle II*, 101-02; 104 (three instances); 106-07; 108; 108-09.

[97] *Chronicle Adler*, entries for the years 2844, 2904, 2944, 2994, 3629 (pp. 202-04).

[98] Arabic *Book of Joshua*, ch. 39. A previously unknown text, the Arabic source of the text translated from a Hebrew version by Crown in his doctoral thesis *A Critical Re-evaluation of the Samaritan Sepher Yehoshua* (the first of the two texts translated by him in this study), agrees with the Arabic *Book of Joshua*. (Jewish Theological Seminary, Ms. Adler 1357, 82-83). The Hebrew version translated by Crown omits this whole paragraph and is therefore inconclusive for the present purpose. In the parallel passage, in another Hebrew version (called by Macdonald *Chronicle* II), the injunction for the King to obey the High Priest is omitted (Crown, 192; Macdonald, 99). This agrees with the outlook of this text elsewhere (see note 99), and the alternative tradition.

Time of Favour, when the High Priest Uzzi announces what is starting to happen.[99]

It can be established with a high degree of probability that this divergence in theory existed before Baba Rabba. In regard to the first theory, we have the explicit statement of the source quoted by Abu 'l-Fath, which seems to be a part of his main source on Baba Rabba. This theory is unlikely to have been invented at the time, since it is precisely the theory that explains what seems to have been the actual situation before Baba Rabba, as we have seen. On the other hand, the Sebuaean practice existed before Baba Rabba and must have had a theoretical justification. Such a theory is expressed in the claim of *Chronicle Adler* that the High Priest appointed the King, and this section of the *Chronicle*, in its origins, is probably close to the period of Baba Rabba.

THE AUTHORITY OF PRIESTS AND EXPERTS

As we have seen there are two divergent views on the level of authority of the Priests as compared to people who are expert in the Tora. This divergency has a theoretical foundation, though we do not know whether the theoretical or practical divergence is older. Both views, and both practices, existed in the early centuries c.e., probably before the Roman persecutions. For our present purpose, the main fact is that these two views determined who taught the interpretation of Scripture and who decided doubtful points. It seems that the view that the Priests had the ultimate authority was decidedly the minority view.

The explanation of the origin of this divergence in theory probably lies in seeing it as an expression of two different responses to conditions outside the Time of Favour. One of the institutions that ended with the end of the Time of Favour was that of the Seventy Elders, the direct inheritors of the Seventy Elders commissioned by Moses. The question naturally arises, as to who inherits or takes over their function. Logically, one could argue that as the Elders held their position by virtue of their learning, and represented the whole nation, individual learned men, or the nation as a whole, could take over their function, and the evidence for the mediaeval period shows this to have been the solution in practice at that time. On the other hand, one could argue that the Priests, as the only institutional group founded by Moses still in existence, should take over the functions of the Elders. This concept of inheritance of the Priests (or better, of the High Priests) from the Council of Elders is explicitly attested in the practical and theoretical work on the tradition of pronunciation of the Tora by Ibrâhîm al-'Ayyah.[100]

---

[99] The Seventy Elders are mentioned in Abu 'l-Fath, ed. Vilmar, 40, lines 5-6 (Stenhouse, 50); Jewish Theological Seminary, Ms. Adler 1357, 87; Crown's first text, 87; Macdonald 116. They are omitted in the corresponding passage in the Arabic *Book of Joshua*, ch. 42.

[100] Ben-Hayyim, *Literary and Oral Tradition* 2, 380 and 382.

We now have a historical explanation of the theory put forward in the introduction to the *Kitâb aṭ-Ṭubâkh*,[101] that after the death of Moses, the High Priest inherited his function (but not his prophecy). This is a compressed and rationalised version of the theory that the High Priests took over the function of the Seventy Elders, who were given their function and position by Moses. This explains the apparent artificiality and lack of logical consequence of the theory of a double function of the High Priest. A different rationalisation, one that is logically better, is that both the Elders (presumably as the bearers of knowledge of the practice of the Tora, which includes its pronunciation), and the Priests (presumably as Levites charged with carrying the Ark with its standard *Sefer Tora*), both received the pronunciation from Moses directly. This is the theory of Abu 'l-Fath or one of his sources.[102]

From all that has been said in this section, it seems that the solution to the apparent contradictions in the data on the teaching, study, and use of the Tora, written and traditional, probably lies in distinguishing between ultimate authority in transmitting the secret doctrines and the Calendar, which belongs to the Priests; the authority to read the Tora in the synagogue, which belongs to the Priests; supreme judicial authority or halakhic authority in any particular case, including the pronunciation of a word in the Tora, which belongs to the Priests in one tradition and to experts, Priests or not, in another tradition; the authority to pronounce an opinion on a matter of halakha or doctrine or interpretation of Scripture, which belongs to any expert, Priest or not; the authority to teach the text, pronunciation, and understanding of the Tora, which belongs to any expert; the authority to accept one halakhic opinion as binding and the rest as not binding, which belongs to the people as a whole (though of course some authorities will make their opinion authoritative by their position as recognised experts, just as happens in English law); and the general knowledge of the tradition of the Tora, in regard to both halakha and doctrine which belongs to the people as a whole.

TRAINING

A system of training, taking three full years, probably after a solid general grounding, is attested for the mediaeval period.[103] There was a fixed or formal curriculum, or at least, the recognition of having reached a fixed standard. The training was not intended for the Priests, or was not exclusive to them. One would assume that the knowledge of the meaning of Scripture for doctrine and halakha would be a major component of the requirements. Beyond this nothing is known on the subject.

---

[101] Not translated so far.
[102] In the second passage from Abu 'l-Fath quoted above, according to recension C.
[103] Robertson, *Catalogue* 1, column 383.

Method of Exegesis

There has been no systematic study of the methodology of Samaritan exegesis, of what might be called their *middot*. Part of the reason for this is probably that no large sections of connected text having to do with Scriptural exegesis have been generally accessible.

HERMENEUTIC RULES

There are lists of Samaritan *middot*.[104] The technical meaning of the terms is not yet fully clear, but the overall impression is that they belong to a system of interpreting Scripture on the following assumptions, which are applied as rules:

The text often does not tell you what you need to know and you need traditional knowledge. However, if the text does speak on a topic, it always leads you along if you read with some sensitivity. Reading the text is like reading any human document, except that the Tora is completely consistent. The Tora has its own distinctive manner of expression, which must be studied by systematic perceptive reading, so that the text will be fully intelligible in any particular place. What the text does not say is a source of information, i.e. if in a certain context it could have said something and does not, the omission is deliberate and you can draw an inference, subject to certain limitations. Similar cases have the same regulations, unless you are told otherwise. Terms always have the same meaning, unless you are told otherwise. What a verse means can be determined from its context. General headings or concluding statements make all the cases mentioned in the context share the same rules unless you are told otherwise. If a verse has two possible interpretations, the one that expresses a halakhic statement is the one to be accepted; in other words, meaning is always to be maximised. This can safely be done because the Tora tells you when your natural understanding of a verse would be wrong. The general principle is that the Tora never wastes words. On the other hand, repetitions do not add hidden meanings: the Tora does repeat itself at times. This applies to minor repetitions in a single context; but striking repetitions out of context carry meaning. If two cases share some of their rules, or if they have the same general heading, then what is said about the first applies to the second, and what is said about the second applies to the first, unless you are told otherwise. As the Tora is completely consistent, widely separated passages in the text may be meant to illuminate each other. In such cases the two passages will have one of various types of linkage to show that they are meant to be read together, at least for certain purposes. When you might think that two passages should illuminate

---

[104] Bóid, *Principles, Khilâf*, lines 127-28: *naḥu naṭq; mafhûm; faḥwa; maʿqûl: qiyâs; jâri ʾl-ʿâdât* (this last being a separate source of information). *Khilâf*, excursus at the end of ch. 6 (see above, note 21), Prussian State Library, Ms. Oriental Quarto 523, 145: *naṭq khaṭâb; qiyâs; faḥwa; mafhûm; iʿtibâr ʿâdatuh* (This last corresponds to the last item in the first list). The two lists are the same in content, if *maʿqûl* refers to derivation in general.

each other and they are really different, you will be told this by something in the wording. As well as this, you have to use common sense to tell if two cases are to be treated similarly or not. A vague or non-specific passage is read in the light of a specific passage, if there is one. Any verse means what is says, that is to say, extraneous meanings must not be forced upon the text where such meanings are patently artifical and unnatural, so there is no such thing as an *asmakhta* ('secondary or indirect support'). On the other hand, much that is not said directly is implied by the choice of wording. Tradition clarifies vague or ambiguous expressions. Many an obscurity or ambiguity can be resolved by common sense and general knowledge of realia.

The essential principle behind these rules[105] is that the Tora speaks in the style of a humanly-composed book, and in this principle the Samaritans superficially seem to agree with Rabbi Yishmael. They do agree in rejecting the type of exegesis developed by Rabbi Akiva. Where they would disagree with R. Yishmael in actuality is that they do not accept that there can be special *middot*, rules for reading the Tora, that do not apply to a humanly-composed book. To this last statement, however, there is one fundamental exception that completely transforms the whole system of Samaritan *middot*: the Tora is composed and worded perfectly, and therefore *always leads the reader in the right direction*, if it speaks on the subject at all. It is perfectly cross-referenced, and it is perfect in its choice of what to say and what not to say, its use of terms, the order of material within sections, and the implications of headings and concluding phrases. This means that in practice, the Samaritans are able to apply their rules of exegesis with a degree of finesse equal to that of the Jewish midrashim, if it is considered necessary.

The rules for aggada are as for halakha. One practical consequence of this for the development of Samaritan doctrine is that, just as the halakha is often only known by a tradition that gives the details to be applied to a bare statement in the text, in the same way doctrinal speculation can develop without hindrance provided there is a single phrase to attach the essential concept to. For example, speculation about the Day of Vengeance and Recompense can go on, and ideas can develop, without any need for Scriptural proof, because there is a phrase than can be taken to refer to the existence of the initial concept. Thus sterility is never a danger.[106]

---

[105] All of these items need to be developed in a much more detailed exposition. I hope to bring out a study on the Samaritan *middot* and the general theory that produces them in a separate study. For the moment, the principles extracted empirically from the texts are presented. To see them at work, read through ch. 6 of the Book of Differences *(Kitâb al-Khilâf)*, translated in Bóid, *Principles*. Compare also *Principles, Ṭubâkh*, lines 110-117. Note *P.T. Avoda Zara* 5:4 (44d) on the interpretation of Lev 11:36. Gematria is known and used, but apparently only to confirm what is already known. (Examples in Gaster, *The Samaritans*, 70-71.) The Jewish restriction on Gematria is similar.

[106] The best collection of material on doctrine, showing the development of ideas by speculation and reflection from an initial scriptural concept, is Gaster, *Samaritan Eschatology*.

No application of the principles of exegesis can ignore common-sense or material facts; and observation of facts, and a consideration of the consequences of a given line of interpretation, will determine how to apply the principles of exegesis.[107]

Aberrant Attitudes to Scripture

THE DOSITHEANS

The Dositheans are described by our sources[108] as incompatible with other Samaritans, and are defined as a separate rite; but what eventually definitively and completely estranged them was their veneration of the person of Dositheos himself, who was regarded as actually being able to improve the text of the Tora, and able, by teaching the real meaning and right interpretation of the text, to give his followers, his 'sons and daughters' and his 'children', the knowledge of Tora needed so as to be resurrected after death.[109] Obviously a sect with this basic belief will be very much concerned, one might say obsessed, with the study of the text and interpretation of Scripture; but with its insistence that the text itself had been improved by the prophet Dositheos, and its apparent belief in the authority of Dositheos to interpret the text by his own superhuman insight, it falls right outside any tradition of study and interpretation of Scripture practised by other Samaritans. We must, therefore, distinguish between the practice of the majority of the Samaritans, as represented for example by the anonymous majority in the account of Baba Rabba by Abu 'l-Fath, together with the distinctive but compatible 'community' *('ashîr)*[110] of the Sebuaeans, on the one hand, and the separate rite *(madhhab)*[111] of the Dositheans, on the other hand.

We are only given one certain example in our sources of a textual change by the Dositheans.[112] This is the change of the word *izzob* (אזוב)[113] in Exodus 12:22 to *ṣāttår* (צעתר).[114] This one example is, however, enough to tell us a lot about their reasons for changing the text and how it was done. The *izzob* is a particular plant, used once in Egypt immediately before the Exodus to sprinkle the blood on the door-frames of the Israelites' houses, and permanently after

---

[107] Bóid, *Principles, Khilâf*, lines 122-32.
[108] Abu 'l-Fath is the main source on the Dositheans. The text of the printed recension is translated by Scanlon in Isser, *The Dositheans*, 75-82. It seems that Dositheos took over a movement that already existed, and made it a distinct sect: see below on the evidence of recension C of Abu 'l-Fath.
[109] See above, note 51.
[110] Abu 'l-Fath, 132 line 1 (see above).
[111] Abu 'l-Fath, ed. Vilmar, 82 line 4 (Scanlon 75-76).
[112] Abu 'l-Fath, ed. Vilmar, 155, lines 15-17 (Scanlon, 79).
[113] In the masoretic pronunciation, *ezov*.
[114] In the masoretic pronunciation, *ṣa'atar*.

the Exodus during the Passover ceremony, and also for the purpose of sprinkling the water containing the ashes of the Red Heifer, so as to purify a person contaminated by a corpse, or to sprinkle water to purify a person afflicted with loss of skin pigmentation (צרוע ṣāru). The identification of the exact plant thus has practical significance, and the motivation for the Dositheans' concern with the plant must be seen in these three continuing uses of it, rather than in an antiquarian or theoretical concern with what plant might have been referred to in Exod 12:22 in connection with a unique event.

Now the *izzob* is identified by unanimous Samaritan and Jewish tradition as marjoram. (This is the plant used by the Samaritans to sprinkle or smear the blood from the Passover sacrifice.)[115] The word ṣāttār refers to exactly the same plant. It is well-attested in Jewish usage, and is used in Jewish sources as a more modern or specific Hebrew name for the *izzob*. The word has cognates in Aramaic and Arabic. (In Arabic it refers to both thyme and marjoram.) We see, then, that the Dositheans did not change the meaning when they changed the text in this instance. Why then did they change it? The answer seems to be that the word *izzob* can refer to a number of different plants of related genera, and only has the very specific meaning of ṣāttār, marjoram, in the text of Scripture in this place by virtue of traditional knowledge.[116] Jewish and Samaritan sources agree on this application of tradition to narrow down and define the meaning of the word. What Dositheos did was to put the information carried by tradition into the text itself, so that the text itself would declare its meaning directly. We are not told why he felt the need to make this change, or all the others, but it can be conjectured with a high degree of probability that it was the logical result of his seeing himself as the equivalent of Moses. If he was equivalent to Moses, then he could see directly in the text of the Tora all the information that ordinary people would only be told about by tradition. If his followers were his sons and daughters, they were to be given saving knowledge generation after generation after his translation to a higher realm. This saving knowledge could only be complete insight into the Tora. But how could they acquire such insight? By adapting the text itself so that it said to any ordinary person what it said to Dositheos, by making the text more transparent.[117]

This particular alteration must have had great symbolic significance for both the Dositheans and their opponents, since it is recorded by Abu 'l-Fath as having been used by the Priest Labi (לוי), the great Dosithean martyr, to announce his conversion to Dositheanism.[118] Probably both the term ṣāttār, and the context it appeared in, were significant. If Dositheos was the second Moses,

---

[115] Jewish tradition identifies this plant as Majorana syriaca = Origanum maru (*Leksikon Mikra'i*, article *Ezov*). On the Samaritan practice, see Zohary, *Plants of the Bible*, 97. Zohary uses the botanical term Origanum syriacum.

[116] References as in the previous note; and see the traditional commentators on Exod 12:22. Significantly, many Karaite commentators deny that the plant can be identified by tradition.

[117] Compare John 4:25 and 42, which are utterances attributed to Samaritans.

[118] Abu 'l-Fath, ed. Vilmar, 155-56; Scanlon 79.

it seems natural to connect him with the Exodus, but the connection is not very precise this way. Perhaps the variant זעתר *zāttār* was seen as an anagram of זרעת *zårrēt*, the symbolic name of the Priest that went over to the Dositheans and re-organised them.[119] Recension C of Abu 'l-Fatḥ tells us that the original sect, before the arrival of this Priest, had the same text and pronunciation of the Tora as other Samaritans, and had only separated from them because of their different calendar and incompatible halakha. Rather than multiplying the number of re-organisers with similar backgrounds, it seems reasonable to identify this Priest with Dositheos. Recension C tells us that his original name was זרה (probably = זרע *zēra* 'seed', with a deliberate change in the spelling by his opponents). This name was changed to זרעת *zårrēt*. Both recensions tells us that the name זרעה or זרעת was symbolic of his superior and unequalled knowledge.[120] The bearer of a title like this has identified himself with the supernal Tora, which is the source of all knowledge and wisdom, being the model of Creation. The right or ability to make changes in the text of the book of the Tora would be a natural consequence of this claim. His claim to be superior to other Priests would be based on the idea that they were the guardians of the book, but his knowledge came from the source of the book. He has then put his name in the actual book in the form of an anagram, in the context of the Exodus, in the specific context of the means of salvation from death, and with the implication of the removal of uncleanness caused by contact with corpses, and uncleanness caused by leprosy (צרעת), which according to tradition is the consequence of a deep-seated and stubbornly-held wrong outlook ('sinning'). Labi could hardly have found a more symbolic passage to read. No wonder there was a riot in the synagogue.

Dositheanism is the work of Dositheos, but why Dositheos felt impelled to declare himself, or why anyone should have taken notice of him, we do not

---

[119] Abu 'l-Fatḥ, ed. Vilmar, 83; Scanlon, 76. Recension C, Sulzberger ms., 139b. The printed recension has זרעה, but the form זרעת of recension C is preferable, both because of the general superiority of the text of recension C, and because the secondary change of the form of the name within the textual tradition of the book could only have been from the more difficult to the easier form.

[120] On the concept of the seed, see note 15. One starts to wonder just how much significance the name Dositheos (gift of God) was given by the sectarians. The only objection to all this would be that the term 'the Dositheans' *(ad-Dustân)* is used by Abu 'l-Fatḥ to refer to the sect before this Priest took over. If, however, one reads in context, it seems that the term is a deliberate anachronism so as to have some name for the sect other than 'that lot'. This explanation seems to be almost inevitable in regard to the form of the text of the passage in recension C, in which the name 'Dositheans' is not used till well into the description, where it eventually becomes too awkward to refer to the people under discussion by undefined pronouns. The fact that we are told explicitly that the sect had the same text as other Samaritans, i.e. the text produced by Dositheos was still unknown, right where recension C calls them Dositheans, confirms this interpretation. My analysis of the epithets *zēra* and *zårrēt* is confirmed by the analogy of the sectarian leader Sakta, who is associated with the Dositheans, and whose name is explicitly declared by Abu 'l-Fatḥ to be symbolic, referring to his booth or shelter. Sakta is the correct form: see Bóid, *Principles*, XIII.

know.[121] Perhaps the answer lies in a failure of confidence in the tradition, similar to the one that produced the Qumran sect.[122] It is probably not an accident that an extreme example of the production of a self-styled book of Scripture has turned up at Qumran in the form of the *Temple Scroll*. What this text seems to be is a thoroughgoing example of the writing down of what Scripture ought to say, but does not say, though the information is supplied by tradition and exegesis. What is written in the Temple Scroll is therefore what the Tora actually says if you know how to read it.[123] The Temple Scroll goes far beyond Dositheos's single emendations, but the principle seems to be the same or very similar.

For our present purpose, it is enough to know that Dositheanism is at least as old as the first century C.E.,[124] that it seems to have had a tremendous impact in its time, and that it would be unsound to regard the Samaritans in this period as having a uniform attitude to the study of Scripture that transcended sectarian boundaries. On the contrary, it seems that there was a radical division in this respect between the Dositheans and everyone else. Aside from this, it is likely, from the information we have about the Sebuaeans, that the differences between the various groups that were not Dosithean were largely administrative.[125] If they did affect the interpretation of Scripture, it was more likely over the specific interpretation of single passages, according to differences in theological ideas (perhaps also single details of halakhic practice), and not over the principles and methodology of Scriptural interpretation, which, as we have seen,[126] seem to have been common to groups that disagreed in their theology.

---

[121] We can at this point remove an obstacle from the path of research. Bowman, *Samaritan Researches*, 46-47 argues for a date in the time of John Hyrcanus. His proof is an alleged quote from the *Kitâb al-Kâfi*, as follows: 'When the Temple was destroyed, some people did not see the need to make a pilgrimage to the mountain, or to worship there; they said that to worship in a synagogue was enough'. Bowman gives no reference for this quotation, but it is clear from allusions to it in *Pilgrimage*, 20 and 22, that he is thinking of ch. 17 of the *Kâfi*. The alleged quotation is imaginary. The nearest equivalent in this chapter, or anywhere else in the book, is the following: 'In our time there are some of the inhabitants of the villages and places close to the mountain that do not bother with the pilgrimage and the formal trip *(al-ḥajj wa-'s-sa'i)*, and make out that the formal trip to the synagogue and seeing the Book and the Priest will do instead of the pilgrimage, at least to some extent'. (The Arabic text is quoted by Halkin, 'Polemics', 57 bottom, and discussed briefly by him in section 4 of his article). Furthermore, contrary to what Bowman says in 'Pilgrimage' 22, the discussion is not about sectarianism, but a straightforward halakhic question.

[122] Which seems to have originated for the purpose of recovering the correct knowledge of the Tora. See note 128.

[123] Yadin, *Temple Scroll*, 390-92.

[124] The Christian sources make Dositheos himself a younger contemporary of Jesus and a disciple of John the Baptist. See Kippenberg, *Garizim und Synagoge*, 128-33. This dating is not contradicted by the arrangement of the material on the Dositheans by Abu 'l-Fath, or its place beside other material. There are signs of the use of multiple sources, not always well integrated, in these sections of the book. The original sect, whatever it was called, must have arisen before the Christian era. Compare notes 92 and 120.

[125] See note 94.

[126] In the discussion on the interpretation of Num 15:31, above.

ANTINOMIANISM

Some later developments of the Dosithean movement, or perhaps independent movements that were later ascribed to the Dositheans, were antinomian.[127] The study of those movements must await a detailed investigation of the inter-relationship of the movements with each other and with Dositheanism. Till this is done, any study of these movements is likely to confuse the Samaritan movements of decidedly aberrant character with the Gnostic movements of partly Samaritan or Jewish origin.

The great popularity of Dositheanism, along with related movements that were antinomian or were seen by their opponents as being effectively antinomi-an, would explain many of the hostile references to the Samaritans in rabbinic literature.

The existence of such movements would also account for the favourable reception accorded to Jesus by many Samaritans, and the ready comprehension of his declaration about himself. The authority over the Tora and command-ments claimed by Jesus has no parallel in Judaism or normative Samaritanism, but is only a step beyond the claims of Dositheos. This is not to say that Jesus belonged to the Dosithean sect or any related or similar group: on the contrary, all that we can derive from the evidence available is a congeniality of outlook of some Samaritans with the tenets of Christianity.

Relationship to Jewish Theory

We have seen that the Samaritans accept with complete equanimity the fact that much of the necessary information about the details of the halakha is not derivable from the text of Scripture. In this they differ radically from the Qumran sect and the Karaites, who regard, or regarded, the recovery of the knowledge of halakha, once known by tradition but lost because of certain events, by means of midrash as a necessary task which at the start of both sects was regarded as urgent (though both sects later came to accept the need for the passage of time, as practical experience showed that the process was so difficult and laborious, and the information so hidden and recondite in the text of the Tora, that many generations would be needed to complete the task.).[128] We have also seen that the Samaritans do not accept the rabbinic and Pharisaic theory of two *Torot*, one written and one oral. They also differ from rabbinic Judaism by not being all that interested in establishing the connection between each item of traditional knowledge and the text of the Tora: on the contrary, it is enough to have the information and to know from it how to carry out each item mentioned, however briefly, in the text, without necessarily being able to

---

[127] See Abu 'l-Fath, translated by Scanlon (in Isser, *Dositheans*, 80-81). Not all the sects listed here were antinomian. On Gnostic developments see Fossum, *Name of God*.

[128] For what is said here about the theory of Tora of the Qumran sect and the Karaites I am heavily dependent on Wieder, *Judean Scrolls*, specially ch. 2.

derive the information from the text itself by any kind of formal exegesis. This distinctive theory of the function of tradition, along with the equally distinctive equanimity of outlook, are characteristic of only one Jewish group, the Sadducees.

SAMARITANS AND SADDUCEES

The Talmud, and the Gemara to *Megillat Taanit*,[129] remark on the ineptness of Sadducean proofs from Scripture to support their opinions. What does not seem to have been noticed in the accounts of the Sadducean responses is that most of the Sadducean representatives are unable to offer any proof from Scripture at all, inept or not, which means they did not normally derive halakha by exegesis. The Pharisees accuse them of only being able to offer 'useless talk' instead of the 'perfect Tora' of the Pharisees. In the context, this means that they were only able to offer information about the halakha, but were not able to rely on the union of an oral Tora and a written Tora. In another place, the Gemara to *Megillat Taanit*[130] tells us that they had traditional knowledge of halakha, but that it was not treated by them as equal in status to the text of the Tora. All of this corresponds exactly to the Samaritan outlook.

The resemblance goes deeper. We are told, in the passage just mentioned, how they interpreted the text of Scripture to derive items of halakha. In their method of interpretation, and the theory that is assumed, they agree with the Samaritans. The explanation is provided by means of three examples, which have been consistently misunderstood. We are told that the Boethusians took the expression 'an eye for an eye, a tooth for a tooth' in Exod 21:24 to mean that the same injury had to be inflicted on the perpetrator. Contrary to popular belief, rabbinic exegesis interprets this expression the same way. The reason that monetary compensation can be substituted is that other verses show that the perpetrator is not to bear the consequences that he is actually liable to: instead, strict justice is to be suspended by mercy.[131] The Boethusians, we are told, said that the perpetrator had to be made equal to the injured person. Contrary to popular opinion, this was actually their way of removing any physical penalty from the perpetrator. The Samaritans and some Karaites argue that a physical penalty can never legally be carried out, because no two people are in exactly the same state of health, physical condition, or age, or have

---

[129] Gemara to *Megillat Taanit* 21 (entry for the 27th Marḥeshwan), translated by Le Moyne, *Sadducéens*, 290; *B.T. Bava Batra* 115b-116a, translated by Le Moyne, 300; *B.T. Menahot* 65a, translated by Le Moyne, 184. The first two passages deal with the Sadducees *sensu stricto*, and the third with the Boethusians. In all three the main rabbinic spokesman is Rabban Yohanan ben Zakkai, and in all three there is a similar pattern and similar statements by the protagonists.

[130] Gemara to *Megillat Taanit* 12 (entry for the 4th Tammuz), translated by Le Moyne, *Sadducéens*, 219-20. The reference is to the Sadducean *Book of Decrees*.

[131] There is a masterly exposition of this issue by Halevi in his *Dorot ha-Rishonim*, part 2 or Ic (depending on the edition used), ch. 17.

exactly the same range of normal activities, which means that no physical penalty could ever be exactly appropriate in any case.[132] The Karaite commentators use this legal technicality for the purpose of leniency. On the Samaritan side, see the commentary *Kâshif al-Ghayâhib*[133] on Exod 21:24. If I understand the author correctly he raises the possibility that instead of a monetary fine, or compensation, no penalty at all may be legal. (The Samaritan commentator quotes directly from the Karaite commentary *Keter Tora* in some places in this discussion, but is careful to only quote the arguments on the side that he agrees with.) We conclude that the Samaritan exegesis of the text, and the Samaritan halakha, in this instance, agree with the Boethusian exegesis and halakha.

The third example of Sadducean interpretation is Deut 25:9. The rabbinic comments on the word בפניו try to prove that in this particular instance the word means 'in his presence'. The Sadducees, we are told, took the word literally. It is quite possible that they followed the Samaritan principle that an expression can have more than one literal meaning, but that in any given case you can choose one and reject the other by various criteria. The Samaritans accordingly take 'in his presence' as being the literal meaning of the word in this passage, even if it has a different literal meaning elsewhere. (Compare the Samaritan Targum with the recensions of the Arabic Version.)

It can be conjectured that a similar explanation applies to the second example, Deut 22:17 'And they shall spread the garment before the elders of the city'. The assertion is that the phrase ופרשו השמלה (which would normally mean 'they are to spread the garment') is to be taken literally, presumably in opposition to the usual rabbinic interpretation of it as a metaphor meaning that the matter is to be clarified.[134] There is no extant Samaritan commentary on the whole of Deuteronomy, and I do not know of any discussion of this verse in any Samaritan text. It is perhaps only stating the obvious (though the point seems to have been generally overlooked) to point out that a שמלה is a cloak or shawl, which is not a normal item of bedding and will not get stained with blood, so it is very difficult to make the literal meaning of the verse refer to any actual spreading out of a piece of cloth. (Attempts to make the word mean some specific piece of cloth have been made, notably by the Ramban, but they are artificial and contrived.) It follows that the meaning of 'clarifying the matter' is left as the only possible meaning, and that it is quite reasonable to insist that the metaphorical meaning is in this case the intended literal meaning; or better, to argue that the word שמלה here does not mean 'cloak' but rather 'quality, nature, circumstances' (just as its Arabic cognate has both of these sets of

---

[132] Revel's discussion of this issue ('Karaite Halakah', 56-57) has some value, but his conclusions are vitiated by his failure to see the significance of the requirement of equality in the Boethusian, Karaite, and Samaritan argument, and to understand the rationale of the rabbinic exegesis. (In spite of his reference to Halevi, he has not registered Halevi's main argument).

[133] In the section edited by Klumel, *Mischpâtîm*.

[134] Cf. Kasher, above, pp. 554, 578.

meanings), and that the meaning of 'clarifying the matter' is indeed the literal meaning. I am inclined to think that this is what R. Eliezer ben Yaakov meant by his comment on the verse, as quoted in the *Midrash Tannaim* and *Sifrei*, in opposition to the usual metaphorical interpretation. If this second explanation is correct, then we have another instance of the use of the rule mentioned above, that when a word or phrase can have more than one literal meaning you choose the meaning that is more appropriate in the context.

The application of Samaritan theory seems to work consistently for what else is known of the Sadducaean theory of the interpretation of the Tora. Josephus tells us that the Sadducees would not accept any practice as valid unless it was mentioned in Scripture. The comment refers to popular practices instituted by the Pharisees on the basis of tradition. One thinks of the washing of hands as a possible example. The Sadducees seem to have been following the Samaritan principle that any amount at all of details of halakha can be known by tradition alone, provided there is at least a bare mention of the existence of the whole area of halakha somewhere in the text.[135] We know that this was precisely the objection of the Sadducees to the doctrine of resurrection: that it was not mentioned even briefly in the text, explicitly or implicitly.[136] As we have seen, the debate between different Samaritan groups over resurrection probably took the same form.

It must not be assumed that the agreement in theory and methodology between the Samaritans and the Sadducees necessarily means agreement in the actual details of halakha and theology.[137] It would be reasonable to assume a tendency for such agreement to occur, but in any particular case, the Samaritans and Sadducees could equally well agree or disagree. Besides which, there is extensive disagreement over details within the Samaritan tradition itself, which is at least equal to the amount of disagreement between different Jewish groups.[138]

Bibliography

The number of directly relevant published works is quite limited. Systematic scientific study of the Samaritan use and exegesis of Scripture starts with GEIGER, *Ha-Mikra ve-Targumav* (= *Urschrift*); 'Theologie und Schrifterklärung'; 'Gesetzlichen Differenzen'; 'Neuere Mittheilungen'; and scattered observations. Geiger's findings on the Samaritans are still valid, whether or not his

---

[135] Josephus, *Ant.* 13:297-98. Once again, the evidence, when read in the light of Samaritan principles, does not suggest rigidity or literalism at all on the part of the Sadducees.

[136] See, e.g., *B.T. Sanhedrin* 90b.

[137] Some material on this question was studied by Revel in his 'Karaite Halakah', but his work suffers from inadequate knowledge of Samaritan halakha and a rather uncritical attitude to the common scholarly assumptions about the Sadducees (see above, note 132).

[138] See Bóid, *Principles*, Conclusions, 309-16, for extensive evidence of halakhic disagreement. An example of a major theological disagreement over the question of resurrection was discussed above.

more general theories are accepted. The longest study on the subject since Geiger is LOWY's *Principles*. Unfortunately, most of the examples are not quoted extensively and the book is quite expressly tendentious. All arguments are continually brought back to the theme of a supposed Samaritan rigid literalistic exegesis, combined with arbitrary flights of fancy, which they are supposed to share with all or most Jewish groups except for Pharisaic-rabbinic Judaism.

Examples of aggadic exegesis can be found in GASTER's *Samaritan Eschatology*, or in the *Asâṭîr* (to be read in BEN-HAYYIM's edition or Gaster's translation). See also T.H. GASTER, *Samaritan Poem*. BÓID, *Principles* can be used as a source-book of halakhic exegesis, as well as an exposition of theory. More examples are given by Geiger. BÓID's 'Halakha', in the forthcoming volume on the present state of Samaritan studies mentioned below, can be used as a condensed exposition of some aspects of halakhic exegesis.

On the nature of the Tora the best published source is Marka, to be read in HEIDENHEIM's translation (*Bibliotheca Samaritana*, part 3). A new edition and translation by BEN-HAYYIM is in preparation.

On the Samaritan expression of the religion of Israel in general, see MAC-DONALD's *Theology* (indispensable, but to be used with great care on account of the author's tendency to put incipient Christian ideas into his sources); GASTER, *Samaritan Eschatology* and *The Samaritans* (not to be trusted on details or facts, but full of valuable insights); HALL, *Samaritan Religion* (a good survey of the primary sources); FOSSUM, *Name of God* (relevant for its background information, but not its main theme); BROADIE, *Samaritan Philosophy*. BOW-MAN's translations in his *Samaritan Documents* are untrustworthy. A typical example is discussed in BOID, *Principles*, p. 227. One might also compare his translations of the passages on the Dositheans with SCANLON's (in Isser, *Dositheans*, 75-82).

The fortnightly periodical *Alef-Bet: Hadshot ha-Shomronim* is an indispensable source of all kinds of information. Further references can be got from CROWN, *Bibliography*. A volume of articles on the present state of knowledge of numerous aspects of Samaritan studies, under the general editorship of Professor Crown is to be published in Tübingen.

Chapter Seventeen

Use, Authority and Exegesis of Mikra in Gnostic Literature

Birger A. Pearson

Introduction

It used to be thought that one of the chief characteristics of Gnosticism, as 'the acute hellenization of Christianity,[1] was a rejection of the OT.[2] Even before the publication of the new source material for Gnosticism, such as the Nag Hammadi corpus,[3] this view was hardly tenable, for the ancient heresiologists themselves complained not so much that the Gnostic heretics rejected the OT but that they interpreted it incorrectly.[4] The fact is, the Gnostic interpretation of Mikra is a very complicated matter, and there is great variety in the range of attitudes adopted by Gnostics vis-a-vis the Bible. Now that the new source material is available a comprehensive assessment of the use, authority, and exegesis of Mikra in Gnostic literature is possible.

Unfortunately, no such comprehensive assessment exists,[5] and such a project is beyond the purview of the present study. In this article I shall try instead to summarize the present state of scholarship on this issue, and, concentrating chiefly on some of the new sources from Nag Hammadi, attempt some conclusions of my own.[6]

---

[1] So the famous dictum of Harnack, *History of Dogma* 1, 227. Harnack's position still has its defenders; see e.g. Beltz, 'Gnosis und Altes Testament', 355.
[2] Harnack, ibid., and pp. 169-73; Bauer, *Orthodoxy and Heresy*, 195ff. This view is rightly rejected by Von Campenhausen, *Formation*, 75.
[3] See Robinson, *Nag Hammadi Library*. Unless otherwise indicated, all English translations of the Nag Hammadi Coptic texts in this article are taken from that volume. Citations in each case are according to page and line of the MS. Cf. Robinson, *Facsimile Edition*.
[4] Cf. Von Campenhausen, *Formation*, 76.
[5] A number of articles on the problem have been published. See e.g. Tröger, *Altes Testament*, and esp. the articles in that volume by Haardt ('Schöpfer und Schöpfung'), Nagel ('Auslegung'), Weiss ('Gesetz'), Bethge ('Geschichtstraditionen'), Beltz ('Elia redivivus'), Szabó ('Engelvorstellung'), and Schenk ('Textverarbeitung'). See also Beltz, 'Gnosis und Altes Testament'; Krause, 'Aussagen'; Wilson, 'The Gnostics and the Old Testament', Simonetti, 'Note sull' interpretazione'; Filoramo-Gianotto, 'L'interpretazione gnostica'. Additional studies, such as articles on individual Gnostic tractates, are cited below (passim).
[6] This article can be taken as a companion study to my article in *Compendia* II/2, 443-81 ('Jewish Sources').

Basic Issues

While it is no longer argued by scholars that the Gnostics completely rejected the OT, it is still occasionally stated that they were only concerned with the opening passages of Genesis.[7] Such an assertion is easily refuted. R.M. Wilson has effectively challenged it simply by referring to the index of scripture-citations in the two-volume anthology of Gnostic texts edited by W. Foerster.[8] The statistics he assembles do show a predilection on the part of the Gnostics for the early chapters of Genesis, but most of the other parts of the OT are represented as well, seventeen books in all.[9]

A more complete statistical analysis has recently been put forward by G. Filoramo and C. Gianotto,[10] using a data base that includes all of the heresiological sources as well as the Coptic texts from Nag Hammadi and the other Coptic sources. Around 600 OT references have been assembled. Again, the opening passages of Genesis predominate – 200 of 230 references to Genesis are concentrated on Gen 1-11 – but the other parts of the Bible are represented as well.[11]

More important, of course, is the question as to *how* the OT is utilized and interpreted in the Gnostic literature. It is at this point that the issues become complicated, for there is a bewildering variety of interpretive methods and attitudes displayed in the sources.

Some useful attempts have recently been made to classify the Gnostic use of the OT, with reference to examples drawn from the Gnostic sources. P. Nagel,[12] for example, identifies the following six categories, providing examples for each:[13]

1. Openly disdainful rejection of figures and events from the Old Testament (*NHC* VII, 2: *Treat. Seth*; *NHC* IX, 3: *Testim. Truth*).
2. Exposition in a contrary sense, through changes in roles and functions (*NHC* II, 4: *Hyp. Arch.*; *NHC* II, 5 and XIII, 2: *Orig. World*; *NHC* V, 2: *Apoc. Adam*; the Peratae).
3. Corrective exposition, closely related to group 2 (*NHC* II, 1; III, 1; IV, 1; and *BG*, 2: *Ap. John*; the Ophites).
4. Appropriation of 'neutral' passages by means of allegorical interpretation (Justin, *Baruch*; the Naassenes; *Pistis Sophia*).
5. Eclectic references to individual passages of the OT in support of certain doctrines or cult-practices (the Valentinians; libertine Gnostics).

---

[7] E.g. Betz, 'Am Anfang', 43; Yamauchi, *Pre-Christian Gnosticisim*, 144f.

[8] Wilson, 'The Gnostics and the Old Testament', 165. Cf. Foerster, *Gnosis* 2, 350-52.

[9] Genesis, Exodus, Leviticus, Numbers, Deuteronomy, Joshua, 1 Samuel, 2 Samuel, 1 Kings, Job, Psalms, Proverbs, Isaiah, Jeremiah, Ezekiel, Daniel, and Hosea. See Wilson, ibid.

[10] Filoramo-Gianotto, 'L'interpretazione gnostica'.

[11] Ibid., 55f.

[12] Nagel, 'Auslegung', 51. See also Simonetti, 'Note sull' interpretazione'; and Filoramo-Gianotto, 'L'interpretazione gnostica'.

[13] I use here the standard American sytem of abbreviation of the Nag Hammadi texts.

6. Etiological and typological interpretation of the Old Testament, in part with a soteriological tendency (*NHC* I, 5: *Tri. Trac.*; *NHC* I, 3 and XII, 2: *Gos. Truth*; *NHC* II, 3: *Gos. Phil.*; *NHC* II, 6: *Exeg. Soul*; *Pistis Sophia*).

Nagel points out that there is some overlapping in this classification, and that more than one of these categories can be reflected in a single text. He regards the first three categories as closely related to one another, and sharply distinguishes them from the other three.[14]

It is to be noted that virtually all of the Gnostic texts cited by Nagel as examples of the six categories of OT interpretation, with the arguable exception of the *Apocalypse of Adam*,[15] are Christian Gnostic texts, or at least texts which show Christian influences. The question thus arises as to what role was played by Christian doctrine in the development of Gnostic OT interpretation, as well as the whole issue of the existence of an originally non-Christian *Jewish* Gnosticism.[16] Some of the scholars who have studied the problem of Gnostic OT interpretation have expressed strong scepticism as to the existence of a Jewish Gnosticism and a Gnostic interpretation of the OT unmediated by Christianity. For example, H.-F. Weiss, in his study of the Tora in Gnosticism, suggests that the various Gnostic attitudes adopted toward the Tora all reflect the basic Christian contrast between the Law and the Gospel.[17] H.-G. Bethge, in his study of Gnostic interpretation of the historical traditions in the OT, concludes that Gnostic interpretation of the OT is a feature of Christian Gnosticism, and did not arise in 'heterodox' Judaism.[18]

The strongest stand on this issue has been taken by W. Beltz, in a short article devoted to 'Gnosis and the Old Testament' and the 'question of the Jewish origin of Gnosis'. He states in this article that there are no OT passages used in

---

[14] Nagel, ibid. He goes on in his article to analyze the various Gnostic interpretations of the Paradise narrative in Gen 2-3.

[15] On *Apoc. Adam* as a 'Jewish Gnostic' text see my discussion in 'Jewish Sources', 470-74, and 'Problem', 26-34. *Apoc. Adam* is the only Gnostic text included in the new collection of OT Pseudepigrapha edited by J.H. Charlesworth. See *OTP* 1, 707-19 (translation and introduction by G. MacRae).

[16] For discussion of the problem see e.g. Pearson, 'Jewish Sources', 443-45, 478-80; also 'Problem', 15-19, and Van den Broek, 'Present State', 56-61.

[17] Weiss, 'Gesetz', esp. p. 73. Somewhat anomalously he goes on to acknowledge that Mandaeism, with its negative picture of Moses as the prophet of the wicked *Rūhā*, stands 'outside the scope of early Christian Gnosticism', and cites K. Rudolph's studies on the Jewish origins of Mandaean Gnosticism (ibid., p. 80 and nn. 46-51).

[18] Bethge, 'Geschichtstraditionen', esp. 109. Cf. also Maier, 'Jüdische Faktoren'.

the Gnostic texts from Nag Hammadi which are not already found in the NT.[19] He also argues in support of Harnack's view of Gnosticism as the 'acute hellenization of Christianity' on the grounds that the Church was stronger than Judaism, and the 'anti-Jewish' strain in the Gnostic materials can therefore better be attributed to Christians than to disaffected or heretical Jews.[20]

Both of Beltz's assertions are manifestly wrong, as has been pointed out by W. Schenk. As to the first, it suffices simply to say that the key text from the OT used in the Gnostic parody of the foolish Creator ('I am god and there is no other', Isa 45:22 = 46:9) is absent from the NT. Even if it were there, the important question would be *how* the OT is used in the respective cases.[21] As to the second assertion, it is unlikely that the Christian population in the Roman Empire exceeded that of the Jews until well into the fourth century.[22] But even if the Church were numerically stronger than Judaism much earlier, Beltz's statistical argument is irrelevant to the issue of the existence of a Jewish Gnosticism. After all, Christianity itself began as a 'Jewish heresy'![23]

Three Hermeneutical Presuppositions

In exploring further the question as to how the Gnostics used the OT, it will be useful to set forth the 'hermeneutical presuppositions',[24] or attitudes toward the OT, adopted by the Gnostics. There are three main possibilities, and all of them are found in the sources:
1. a wholly negative view of the OT;
2. a wholly positive view; and
3. intermediate positions.[25]

It will be noted that the question of the methods used in interpreting the OT texts is bound up with these presuppositions, especially the presence or absence of allegorical interpretation and the application or non-application of literal interpretation. Referring to Nagel's six categories of interpretation (discussed above), we can provisionally associate the negative stance with category 1, the

---

[19] Beltz, 'Gnosis und Altes Testament' 355, repeated on p. 356 with reference to the index of biblical passages in the Nestle edition of the Greek NT. Beltz's argument is cited with approval by Yamauchi, 'Jewish Gnosticism', 487. Beltz repeats his assertion as to the Christian mediation of 'Jewish elements' in Gnosticism in 'Elia redivivus' (p. 141, citing his earlier study). In that article he makes much of the absence from the Gnostic material of the Jewish eschatological tradition of the appearance of Elijah and Enoch in the end of days (*Apocalypse of Elijah*, etc.). But this tradition is possibly present in the fragmentary tractate, *Melchizedek* (*NHC* IX, 1), p. 13 of the MS. See Pearson, *Nag Hammadi Codices IX and X*, pp. 25, 63-65.

[20] Beltz, 'Gnosis und Altes Testament' 357.

[21] Schenk, 'Textverarbeitung', 301f. On the 'blasphemy of the Demiurge' see below.

[22] So Schenk, 'Textverarbeitung', 304.

[23] Cf. Pearson, 'Jewish Sources', 479f., where I cite the talmudic saying concerning the 'twenty-four sects of heretics' among the Jews (*P.T. Sanhedrin* 10, 29c).

[24] The term is that of Filoramo and Gianotto, 'L'interpretazione gnostica', 56.

[25] Ibid., 56f. Cf. Krause, 'Aussagen'. Krause cites as examples of the three stances the same three texts from Nag Hammadi discussed in what follows.

positive stance with category 6, and the intermediate positions with categories 2 to 5 (and partially with 6).

While a detailed account is not possible here, I shall treat first the three basic stances with reference to selected examples from Christian Gnostic texts.

WHOLLY NEGATIVE STANCE: THE SECOND TREATISE OF THE GREAT SETH

The Second Treatise of the Great Seth (*NHC* VII, 2)[26] is a revelatory exhortation purportedly addressed to an embattled group of Gnostic Christians by Jesus Christ in an attempt to bolster their steadfastness in the face of persecution by a more powerful group. Strongly polemical, this text attacks adversaries who are easily identifiable as catholic Christians associated with a growing ecclesiastical establishment.[27] As part of its attack, the document advances a radical dualist doctrine of antagonism and separation between the highest God and the Creator, between Christ and the world, and between the true Christians and those who are attached to the OT. This tractate contains the most violent attack against the OT and its heroes that can be imagined:

> Adam was a laughingstock, since he was made a counterfeit type of man by the Hebdomad (= the Creator), as if he had become stronger than I (Christ) and my brothers . . . Abraham and Isaac and Jacob were a laughingstock, since they, the counterfeit fathers, were given a name by the Hebdomad, as if he had become stronger than I and my brothers . . . David was a laughingstock in that his son was named the Son of Man, having been influenced by the hebdomad . . . . Solomon was a laughingstock, since he thought that he was the Christ, having become vain through the Hebdomad . . . . The 12 prophets were laughingstocks, since they have come forth as imitations of the true prophets . . . Moses, a faithful servant, was a laughingstock, having been named 'the Friend', since they perversely bore witness concerning him who never knew me. Neither he nor those before him, from Adam to Moses and John the Baptist, none of them knew me nor my brothers (62, 27-64, 1).

The text goes on to attack the 'doctrine of angels' (= the Tora)[28] associated with these figures, with its 'dietary laws' and 'bitter slavery'. The climax is reached with a virulent attack on the God of the OT:

> for the Archon was a laughingstock because he said, 'I am God, and there is none greater than I. I alone am the Father, the Lord, and there is no

---

[26] For discussions see Krause, 'Aussagen', 450f.; Bethge, 'Geschichtstraditionen', 104-06; Weiss, 'Gesetz', 78f.; Filoramo-Gianotto, 'L'interpretazione gnostica', 59f. The only critical edition of this tractate so far published is Painchaud, *Grand Seth* (with French translation).

[27] Painchaud suggests that it was written in Alexandria at the beginning of the third century; see *Grand Seth*, 6f.

[28] Cf. Gal 3:19.

other beside me. I am a jealous God, who brings the sins of the fathers upon the children for three and four generations'.[29] As if he had become stronger than I and my brothers! But we are innocent with respect to him, in that we have not sinned, since we mastered his teaching. Thus he was in an empty glory. And he does not agree with our Father. And thus through our fellowship we grasped his teaching, since he was vain in an empty glory. And he does not agree with our Father, for he was a laughingstock and judgment and false prophecy (64, 17-65, 2).[30]

Here is a wholesale rejection of the OT: its heroes of faith, its history of salvation, its legal demands, and its God. The text's inclusion of John the Baptist in the list of OT figures serves to strengthen the denial of any suggestion that Christ had any human forerunners at all, much less that he has come in fulfillment of OT prophecy. Yet this text should not be considered necessarily as 'anti-Jewish', for in fact the opponents attacked in it are not Jews but ecclesiastical Christians for whom the OT is still holy scripture.[31]

The closest analogy to this tractate's rejection of the OT in the history of Christian heresy is the attitude adopted by Marcion and his followers.[32] The closest analogy in the history of the Gnostic religion is the Mandaean tradition, for which Moses is the prophet of the evil *Rūhā*, and the Creator of biblical tradition is the chief of the demons.[33] The analogies break down in each case, however. Marcion, though undoubtedly influenced by Gnosticism, was not a Gnostic but a Christian who carried to radical extremes the Pauline doctrine of justification by *faith* (not *gnosis*) apart from the works of the Law.[34] The Mandaeans were both anti-Jewish and anti-Christian, though they probably originated as a splinter-group of Palestinian Judaism,[35] and share a number of traditions with the Gnostics known to us from the Nag Hammadi sources.[36] The community behind *Treat. Seth* was an embattled group of Christian Gnostics (or Gnostic Christians), whose attitude toward the OT was forged out of controversy with other Christians. In their total rejection of the OT they may have been

---

[29] Cf. Isa 45:5, 22; 46:9; Exod 20:5. These passages are part of a Gnostic traditional complex, the 'Blasphemy of the Demiurge'. The author of *Treat. Seth* is probably using the Gnostic tradition, rather than quoting the OT directly, as suggested by Schenk ('Textverarbeitung', 305f.). On the 'Blasphemy of the Demiurge' in Gnostic tradition see below.

[30] For a good commentary on this passage see Painchaud, *Grand Seth*, 128-34.

[31] Bethge, 'Geschichtstraditionen', 106.

[32] On Marcion's rejection of the OT and his role in the development of a NT canon see Von Campenhausen, *Formation*, 148-67.

[33] Weiss, 'Gesetz', 80.

[34] See the classic work of Harnack, *Marcion*, and the recent work by Hoffmann, *Marcion*.

[35] On the Mandaeans see Rudolph, *Gnosis*, 343-66, and literature cited there. For a convenient selection of Mandaean texts in English translation, with valuable discussion by Rudolph, see Foerster, *Gnosis* 2, 121-319.

[36] See e.g. Rudolph, 'Coptica-Mandaica'.

influenced by Marcionites,[37] though, as the Mandaean case shows, their own Gnostic presuppositions could have led them to this stance.

Another Nag Hammadi tractate, *The Testimony of Truth* (*NHC* IX, 3), has been brought into close association with *Treat. Seth* in respect to its aggressive attitude toward the OT.[38] That tractate, too, is a polemical attack on other Christians, in this case not only directed against the ecclesiastical establishment but also against other Gnostics.[39] Its use of the OT is multi-faceted, and while the Law and the OT Creator are vigorously attacked, it is evident that the author looks upon the OT as a source of Gnostic revelation that can be ferreted out by means of allegorical interpretation. *Testim. Truth* is an especially interesting tractate in that it contains two extended 'midrashim', a Gnostic one on the serpent in Paradise (45, 30-46, 2) and one that is not necessarily Gnostic on David and Solomon (69, 32-70, 24). Both midrashim are subjected by the Christian Gnostic author to allegorical interpretation.

I have commented extensively on *Testim. Truth* elsewhere.[40] Suffice it to say here that its use of the OT is not the same as that of *Treat. Seth*.

WHOLLY POSITIVE STANCE: THE EXEGESIS ON THE SOUL

The Exegesis on the Soul (*NHC* II, 6)[41] is devoted to an exposition of the divine origin, fall, and reintegration of the human soul. The doctrine of the descent and ascent of the soul was widespread in the Hellenistic-Roman world, and is part and parcel of the popular Platonism of the period. *Exeg. Soul* presents this doctrine with a Gnostic twist, depicting the (female) soul's descent as a fall into prostitution. Its ascent requires 'repentance' and consists in a restoration of the soul, as a renewed virgin, to her Father's house.

What is of interest to us here is the use made of the OT in this remarkable text. Scriptural passages are cited extensively as 'proof-texts' for the various aspects of the soul's experience, as set forth by the tractate's author.[42] The following examples are taken from the first part of the tractate:

---

[37] Cf. Von Campenhausen, *Formation*, 77.

[38] Nagel, 'Auslegung', 51, and discussion above.

[39] See e.g. Pearson, 'Anti-Heretical Warnings', and Koschorke, *Polemik der Gnostiker*, esp. 91-174.

[40] Pearson, 'Jewish Haggadic Traditions'; *Nag Hammadi Codices IX and X*, esp. 101-203; 'Gnostic Interpretation'; 'Jewish Sources', 457.

[41] For discussion see Krause, 'Aussagen', 452-56; Wilson, 'Old Testament Exegesis'; Kasser, 'Citations'; Nagel, 'Septuaginta-Zitate'; Guillaumont, 'Une citation'. Critical editions of this text so far published are Krause, *Koptische und hermetische Schriften*, 68-87, and Sevrin, *L'Exégèse* (with French translation). See now also the important monograph, with French translation and commentary, by Scopello, *L'Exégèse*.

[42] As Nagel has shown, the LXX text is closely followed in the OT passages quoted in *Exeg. Soul* (Nagel, 'Septuaginta-Zitate'). See also Kasser, 'Citations'. Scopello and Sevrin both argue for the use of an anthology on the part of the author: see Scopello, *L'Exégèse*, 13-44, and Sevrin, *L'Exégèse*, 13.

> Now concerning the prostitution of the soul the Holy Spirit prophesies in many places. For he said in the prophet Jeremiah, 'If the husband divorces his wife and she goes and takes another man . . .' (Jer 3:1-4). Again it is written in the prophet Hosea, 'Come, go to law with your (pl.) mother, for she is not to be a wife to me nor I a husband to her . . .' (Hos 2:2-7).
> Again he said in Ezekiel, 'It came to pass after much depravity, said the Lord . . . You prostituted yourself to the sons of Egypt, those who are your neighbors, men great of flesh' (Ezek 16:23-26) (129, 5-130, 20).

The author is not content simply to cite scriptural proof texts, but he (or she)[43] offers specific interpretive commentary on key words or phrases in the scriptural text, as can be seen in the passage immediately following the material previously quoted:

> But what does 'the sons of Egypt, men great of flesh' mean if not the domain of the flesh and the perceptible realm and the affairs of the earth, by which the soul has become defiled here, receiving bread from them, as well as wine, oil, clothing (cf. Hos 2:5), and other external nonsense surrounding the body in the things she thinks she needs (130, 20-28).

The author then proceeds to fortify his argument with references to, and quotations from, the NT, proceeding subsequently with additional teaching, with scriptural proofs from the Old and New Testaments, and in one case with an apocryphal passage from Ps.-Ezekiel.[44] The author's fund of revelatory scripture is larger than usual, however, for he quotes Homer in the same way that he does the Bible:

> Therefore it is written in the Poet, 'Odysseus sat on the island weeping . . .' (*Odyssey* 1:48-59) (136, 27-35).

This is followed by two quotations from *Odyssey* 4. Our author evidently regards the Bible and 'the Poet' as equal sources of revelation, specifically as allegories of the soul's fall and restoration. His pagan contemporaries were already treating Homer in this way;[45] so it was simply a matter of adding the Christian scriptures to the fund of revelation concerning the nature and destiny

---

[43] *Exeg. Soul* is one of the Nag Hammadi tractates for which a female author could easily be posited. Cf. Scopello's discussion of the role of the feminine in this and other texts (*L'Exégèse*, 49-55). Scopello, however, does not argue for a female author, referring to the author as 'il' (ibid., p. 55). For convenience I also use the masculine gender in what follows, while leaving the question as to the sex of the author completely open.

[44] 135, 31-136, 4. This passage, formerly associated with *1 Clem.* 8:3, was first identified as Ps.-Ezekiel by Guillaumont, 'Une citation'. On Pseudo-Ezekiel see now Schürer, *History* (Rev.ed.) III/2, 793-96.

[45] See esp. Porphyry, *De antro nympharum*, a commentary on *Odyssey* 13:102-12; and Plotinus' interpretation of the flight of Odysseus from Circe and Calypso, *Enn.* 1:6, 8. On the allegorical interpretation of Homer in Hellenistic antiquity see esp. Buffière, *Les mythes d'Homer*.

of the human soul. In the process some new (Gnostic) features were added to the doctrine, including material related to the Valentinian myth of Sophia.

Exeg. Soul is clearly a 'late' product of Christian Gnosticism, as is particularly evident from its eclecticism. Its affinities with Valentinian Gnosticism have been noted.[46] Its affinities with the Naassene Gnostic system are also note-worthy.[47] The Naassenes interpreted Homer in much the same way as the author of *Exeg. Soul*.[48] The OT is also treated in a notably positive way in the Naassene material, with the application of allegorical interpretation.[49] Indeed the Naassene use of the OT is exceedingly sophisticated,[50] ranging from the use of 'proof texts' – for example, Isa 53:8 is quoted with reference to the Divine Man, Adamas[51] – to the poetical elaboration of an OT psalm as an allegory of the soul's salvation as a result of the descent of Jesus the Saviour.

The last-named example deserves further comment, involving as it does one of the most beautiful examples of Gnostic poetry preserved from antiquity. I refer, of course, to the so-called 'Naassene Psalm' (Hippolytus, *Refutatio* 5:10, 2), in which the soul is presented as a 'hind', weeping in her wanderings in the cosmic labyrinth until Jesus asks his Father to send him down to help the soul 'escape the bitter chaos', by transmitting 'the secrets of the holy way . . . Gnosis'.[52] As M. Elze has brilliantly demonstrated, this beautiful poem is a Gnostic interpretation of Psalm 41 (LXX): 'As a hind longs for the springs of the waters, so longs my soul for you, O God . . .'[53]

OT psalms are included among the scriptural passages utilized in *Exeg. Soul*. Psalm 45:10-11 (LXX 44:11-12) is quoted to show the Father's desire for the soul's repentance (133, 15-20). Psalm 103 (102):1-5 is quoted with reference to the ascent of the soul to the Father (134, 16-25). Psalm 6:6-9 (7-10) is quoted at the end of the tractate as part of a final exhortation to repentance (137, 15-22).

---

[46] According to Krause ('Aussagen', 456) it is a Valentinian product; according to Sevrin (*L'Exégè-se*, 58-60) it is pre-Valentinian; according to Scopello (*L'Exégèse*, 48) it relies on Valentinian traditions and much else besides (passim).

[47] Noted by W. Robinson, 'The Exegesis', 116f. For the Naassene material see esp. Foerster, *Gnosis* 1, 261-82, providing a translation of Hippolytus *Refutatio* 5:6, 3-11, 1. See also the important work by Frickel, *Hellenistische Erlösung*. Another Gnostic work preserved by Hippolytus, *Baruch* by the Gnostic Justin, presents an interesting contrast to *Exeg. Soul* in its interpretation of the prophet Hosea, citing Hos 1:2 as referring to the 'mystery' of the ascent of 'Elohim' to 'the Good' (= Priapus!) and his divorce from 'Eden' (*Ref.* 5:27, 4). For a translation of *Baruch*, with discussion by E. Haenchen, see Foerster, *Gnosis* 1, 48-58. Cf. also Batey, 'Jewish Gnosticism', and Kvideland, 'Elohims Himmelfahrt'.

[48] Hippolytus, *Refutatio* 5:7, 30-39 (*Odyssey* 24:1-12); 5:8, 35 (*Odyssey* 4:384f.); 5:7, 36 (*Iliad* 4:350); 5:8, 3 (*Iliad* 15:189).

[49] Cf. Nagel, 'Auslegung', 51, and discussion above.

[50] Unfortunately no extended analysis of the Naassene use of the OT exists, and space does not allow for such an analysis here.

[51] Hippolytus, *Refutatio* 5:7, 2. The passage is introduced with the formula, 'it is written'.

[52] The best edition of the Greek text, with ET and commentary, is Marcovich, 'The Naassene Psalm'. I have used his translation here.

[53] My translation of v. 1. See Elze, 'Häresie und Einheit', 402f.

A similar use of the OT psalms, with the same positive stance toward the scriptural text, is found in *Pistis Sophia*, one of the Coptic Gnostic writings known before the discovery of the Nag Hammadi corpus.[54] In that text the heroine, 'Pistis Sophia', whose mythic fall and restoration are paradigmatic of the fall and restoration of the Gnostic soul, cries out in 'repentance' to the world of light and is ultimately restored by Jesus. There are thirteen such 'repentances', accompanied by extended quotations from the Psalms[55] and the *Odes of Solomon*[56] as 'proof texts' of the experience of salvation. G. Widengren, in an important article, has analysed the use of the OT in *Pistis Sophia*,[57] and I shall therefore forego any further comment here, except to say that the affinities between that text and *Exeg. Soul* are manifest.[58]

INTERMEDIATE POSITIONS: PTOLEMAEUS' LETTER TO FLORA AND OTHER TEXTS

The *Letter to Flora* by the Gnostic teacher Ptolemaeus, a disciple of the famous Valentinus, is one of the few precious Gnostic texts coming down to us from antiquity in its original Greek form (as quoted by Epiphanius).[59] In this letter Ptolemaeus addresses a certain lady, presumably an uninitiated seeker, on the subject of the Law of Moses and the extent of its continuing relevance to the (Gnostic) Christian life. Ptolemaeus' starting point is 'the words of the Saviour' (Jesus), from which it is concluded that the Law is divisible into three parts: a part attributable to God and his legislative activity, a part attributed to Moses himself, and a part added by 'the elders of the people' (4.1-14). The Law of God, in turn, is divided into three parts: The Decalogue, fulfilled by the Saviour, an imperfect part abolished by the Saviour, and a third (cultic) part that must be interpreted 'spiritually', i.e. allegorically (5.1-7.1). Ptolemaeus finally reveals his Gnostic stance by identifying the 'God' who gave the Law as the Demiurge, the Creator of the world, who is actually inferior to the perfect God, the Father (7.2-7). The import of his previous discussion, however, is that the Law is still to some extent authoritative, as defined by 'the words of the Saviour'. Even its cultic legislation contains revelation of value when it is subjected to allegorical interpretation.

---

[54] For the latest edition, with English translation, see MacDermot, *Pistis Sophia*.

[55] Ps 102 (LXX):1-5 is quoted in *Pistis Sophia* 2:75; the same passage is quoted in *Exeg. Soul* (as noted above).

[56] The Coptic translation of parts of Odes 1, 5, 6, 22, and 25 in *Pistis Sophia* was the only version of the *Odes of Solomon* known until the discovery of the Syriac version and then a Greek MS. of Ode 11. The *Odes* are not a Gnostic composition, contrary to the opinion of some scholars. For an English translation, with introduction and bibliography, see Charlesworth, *OTP* 2, 725-71.

[57] Widengren, 'Hymnen'. Cf. also Kragerud, *Hymnen*, and Trautman, 'La citation'.

[58] See esp. Krause, 'Aussagen', 450, 452; Filoramo-Gianotto, 'L'interpretazione gnostica', 65-69.

[59] Epiphanius *Adversus Haereses* 32:3, 1-7, 10. The standard edition is Quispel, *Ptolémée*. For a good English translation, with introduction, see Foerster, *Gnosis*, 1, 154-61. For an important discussion see Von Campenhausen, *Formation* 82-87; cf. also Weiss, 'Gesetz', 82f.

This important text of the Valentinian school, though dealing especially with the Law (i.e. the Pentateuch), can be seen to express the typical Valentinian Gnostic position vis-a-vis the ot as a whole: Even though it is inspired by an inferior deity, the ot contains valuable truth which 'the Saviour' fulfills, or which, when subjected to allegorical interpretation, reveals *gnosis*. The Valentinian use of the ot thus derives not only from Gnostic religious presuppositions (the inferior Creator, etc.) but also from general, non-heretical Christian tradition.

One of the Valentinian texts from Nag Hammadi,[60] *The Tripartite Tractate* (*NHC* I, 5),[61] presents a discussion of the ot prophets comparable to that on the Law in Ptolemaeus' letter. In the framework of a general discussion of various philosophies and theologies existing in the world (108, 13-114,30),[62] the author discusses the various 'heresies' that existed among the Jews as a result of their differing interpretations of scripture (112, 14-113, 1)[63] and offers the following assessment of the prophets:

> The prophets, however, did not say anything of their own accord, but each one of them (spoke) of the things which he had seen and heard through the proclamation of the Saviour. This is what he proclaimed, with the main subject of their proclamation being that which each said concerning the coming of the Saviour, which is this coming. Sometimes the prophets speak about it as if it will be. Sometimes (it is) as if the Saviour speaks from their mouths, saying that the Saviour will come and show favour to those who have not known him. They (the prophets) have not all joined with one another in confessing anything, but each one thinks on the basis of the activity from which he received power to speak about him . . . Not one of them knew whence he would come nor by whom he would be begotten, but he alone is the one of whom it is worthy to speak, the one who will be begotten and who will suffer (113, 5-34).

This passage sounds perfectly 'orthodox', until we realize that, in the context, the 'race of the Hebrews', including the prophets, are 'psychic' people attached to the inferior Creator, who himself is only an 'image of the Father's image' (110, 22-36).

The Valentinians were by no means the only Gnostics who developed this 'intermediate' position vis-a-vis the ot. Another of the Nag Hammadi texts,

---

[60] The other Valentinian texts are: *Pr. Paul* (I, 1); *Gos. Truth* (I, 3 and XII, 2); *Treat. Res.* (I, 4); *Gos. Phil.* (II, 3); *Interp. Know.* (XI, 1); and *Val. Exp.* (XI, 2). Still other Nag Hammadi texts betray Valentinian influences.

[61] There are two critical editions: Kasser et al., *Tractatus Tripartitus*; and Attridge, *Nag Hammadi Codex I* 1, 159-337 + 2, 217-497. For a discussion of its use of the OT see Zandee, 'Alte Testament'.

[62] For an important discussion and commentary see Attridge, ibid., 1, 185f. and 2, 417-35.

[63] On this passage in relation to rabbinic discussions of 'heresy' see Logan, 'Jealousy', 199-200.

The Concept of Our Great Power (*NHC* VI, 4),[64] not a Valentinian text but perhaps influenced by Valentinian Gnosticism, adopts such a stance in presenting a Gnostic-apocalyptic presentation of world history. In this interesting text, which has been referred to as an 'epitome of a Christian Gnostic history of the world,[65] history is divided into three epochs or 'aeons': the 'aeon of the flesh' (38, 13; 41, 2), brought to an end by the Flood; the 'psychic aeon' (39, 16f.; 40, 24f.), during which the Saviour appears and which will end in a conflagration (46, 29f.), and a future 'aeon of beauty' (47, 15f.), which is an 'unchangeable aeon' (48, 13). The Creator is referred to as 'the father of the flesh', who 'avenged himself' by means of the water of the Flood (38, 19-32). Yet, in contrast to most Gnostic treatments, Noah is presented as 'pious and worthy', and a preacher of 'piety' (*eusebeia*, 38, 26).[66]

Many more examples could be cited here, but we can conclude this part of our discussion with the observation that an 'intermediate' stance vis-a-vis the OT is the most characteristic attitude toward the scriptures displayed in the Gnostic sources in general. Scripture is viewed largely as the product of a lower power (or lower powers), but it is nevertheless capable of revealing gnosis so long as the proper exegetical method is adopted. In the case of the Christian Gnostic documents, the proper method involves allegorical exegesis and/or a Christo-centric approach according to which Christ perfects or fulfills the OT or parts thereof.

There remains another set of questions to consider: Does the Christian Gnostic material exhaust our available evidence? That is to say, is there a Gnostic use of Mikra which is not at the same time 'Christian' in some recognizable sense? The Mandaean material already briefly cited[67] suggest that there is.

---

[64] There are two critical editions: Parrott, *Nag Hammadi Codices V, 2-5 and VI*, 291-326; and Cherix, *Le Concept*. For discussions of its use of the Old Testament see Krause, 'Aussagen', 451; Bethge, 'Geschichtstraditionen', 97f.; Filoramo-Gianotto, L'interpretazione gnostica', 60.

[65] Bethge, 'Geschichtstraditionen', 97, crediting H.-M. Schenke.

[66] Cf. Bethge's discussion of the various Gnostic interpretations of Noah and the Flood, 'Geschichtstraditionen', 94-98.

[67] See our discussion of *Treat. Seth*, above.

'Rewritten Scripture'

THE APOCRYPHON OF JOHN AND RELATED LITERATURE

The Apocryphon of John (*NHC* II, 1; III, 1; IV, 1; *BG*, 2)[68] is, in its present form, a Gnostic apocalypse[69] in which the risen Christ transmits revelation of 'mysteries' to his disciple John concerning 'what is and what was and what will come to pass' (II 2, 16-18; cf. 1, 1-2). It is one of the most important of the Gnostic texts that have come down to us, for it contains a Gnostic myth which probably served as the basis for the myth developed by the great Gnostic teacher, Valentinus, and further elaborated by his disciples, especially Ptolemaeus.[70]

Not long after the publication of the Berlin Gnostic Codex in 1955, S. Giversen published a valuable article on the use of the OT (especially Genesis 1-7) in *Ap. John*.[71] Using the *BG* version, Giversen first distinguishes the forms that use of the OT take in the text:

1) actual quotations, with introductory formula (e.g. 'the prophet said');
2) quotations without introductory formula;
3) expressions and phrases clearly derived from the OT text, or sentences recounting events described in the scripture; and
4) use of key words that call for special (allegorical) interpretation.

Instances of the first category also include direct refutation of what 'Moses said'. Among the examples cited by Giversen, the following also illustrates the fourth category, i.e. use of key words:

> 'The Mother (Sophia) now began to be agitated *(epipheresthai)*, knowing her deficiency, since her consort had not concurred with her when she was degraded from her perfection'. But I (John) said, 'Christ, what does "be agitated" *(epipheresthai*, cf. Gen 1:2 LXX) mean?' He smiled and said: 'Do you think that it is as Moses said, "over the waters"?' (Gen 1:2).

---

[68] The following critical editions have been published: of the BG version, Till-Schenke, *Gnostische Schriften*; of the version in NHC II, Giversen, *Apocryphon Johannis*; of all three Nag Hammadi versions, Krause, *Drei Versionen*. The English translation in Robinson, *Nag Hammadi Library* (by F. Wisse) renders the 'long recension' in *NHC* II. For ET of the *BG* version ('short recension'), together with the parallel material in Irenaeus, *Adversus Haereses* 1:29, see Foerster, *Gnosis* 1, 105-20. For discussions of the use of the OT in *Ap. John* see Giversen, 'Apocryphon of John', and Pearson, 'Biblical Exegesis'. See also my analysis of *Ap. John* in 'Jewish Sources', 458-64, 453f.; and 'Problem', 19-26.

[69] For a genre-study of Gnostic apocalypses see Fallon, 'Gnostic Apocalypses', esp. 130f. (on *Ap. John*).

[70] See esp. Quispel, 'Valentinian Gnosis'; Perkins, 'Ireneus', 199-200; and *Gnostic Dialogue*, 79; Jonas, *Gnostic Religion*, 199.

[71] Giversen, 'Apocryphon of John', published originally in Danish in 1957. For a valuable analysis of *Orig. World* (*NHC* II, 5 and XIII, 2) along the same lines see Wintermute, 'Gnostic Exegesis'.

No, but she saw the wickedness and the apostasy which would attach to her son (the Creator). She repented . . .[72]

In discussing the question as to *how* the author of *Ap. John* interprets Genesis, Giversen states that the interpretation is 'largely – but not exclusively – allegorical'.[73] He rightly qualifies this with reference to the basic Gnostic doctrines: phenomena in this world are only likenesses of realities in the world of light; the Creator and his world are evil and inferior to the highest God and the world of light; etc. The attitude taken toward the biblical text is mixed: What 'Moses said' is sometimes flatly rejected, but sometimes the counter interpretation is bolstered by referring to another biblical passage (e.g. the citation of 'the prophet' Isaiah at 59, 1-5). In general, the use of Genesis often involves a 'reverse' interpretation. What is presented in *Ap. John*, finally, does not involve a rejection of Genesis, or a revision of its text, but 'secret doctrine', i.e. 'true knowledge'.[74]

Giversen's discussion is quite sound as far as it goes, i.e. insofar as it takes account of *Ap. John* in its present form as a post-resurrection revelation transmitted by Christ to John and by extension to Christian Gnostic readers. However, formal analysis of the text reveals that it is a composite product, and contains editorial expansions of an earlier stratum of material. The effect of this redactional activity was to create a specifically Christian Gnostic text out of an earlier non-Christian Gnostic revelation. This was done by adding a framework according to which 'Christ' is providing revelation to John, by opening up the text at ten different points so as to create a dialogue between 'Christ' and his

---

[72] *BG* 44, 19-45, 13; ET in Foerster, *Gnosis* 1, 113. See Giversen's discussion (64f.). Giversen (66f.) provides the following table of Genesis passages used in one way or another in *Ap. John*:

Genesis	*Ap. John (BG)*
1:2	45, 1.7.10.19
1:26	48, 10-14
2:9	57, 8-11
2:15-16; 3:23-24	56, 1-10
2:17	57, 12-13
2:21	58, 17-18
2:21-22	59, 18-19
2:24	60, 7-11
3:16	61, 11-12
3:23	61, 19-62,1
4:25	63, 12-14
6:1-4	74, 1-5
6:6	72, 12-14
6:17	72, 14-17
7:7	73, 5-6

Other passages in Genesis could be added to this list. See e.g. my discussion of the 'Blasphemy of the Demiurge' (below); also my discussion of the use of Gen 2:7 in *Ap. John*, in 'Biblical Exegesis'.

[73] Giversen, 'Apocryphon of John', 67.

[74] Ibid., 75f.

interlocutor, John, and by adding a few easily recognizable glosses.[75] That such a procedure was actually carried out with Gnostic texts is indisputably proven in the case of two other Nag Hammadi writings, *Eugnostos* (III, 3 and V, 1) and *the Sophia of Jesus Christ* (III, 4 and *BG*, 3).[76]

The putative Urtext underlying *Ap. John* consists of theosophical revelation (the unknown highest God and the world of light), cosmogony (fall of Sophia, the lower world, and the blasphemy of the Demiurge), and soteriology, in which the primal history in Genesis is retold with the use of other biblical and extra-biblical materials in such a way as to emphasize the saving role of Sophia in behalf of the Gnostic elect, the 'race of Seth'.[77] Such a text can appropriately be labelled 'rewritten scripture'.

The closest analogies to this kind of text are the Jewish pseudepigraphical literature, specifically those writings which fall into the category of 'rewritten scripture', such as portions of *1 Enoch*, *Jubilees*, the *Genesis Apocryphon* from Qumran, the Books of Adam and Eve, and the like.[78] The putative Urtext of *Ap. John* is only one of a number of Gnostic texts that can be classified as 'rewritten scripture'.[79] Such texts, in my opinion, represent the earliest stage of Gnostic literary production, and can be seen as a bi-product of the history of Jewish literature. They are comparable in their method of composition and in their use of biblical texts and extra-biblical traditions to the Jewish pseude-pigrapha. The difference, of course, is in what is conveyed in the respective literatures. If, for example, the *Book of Jubilees* is a rewriting of Genesis 1 – Exodus 14 for the purpose of presenting an alternative sectarian halakha,[80] the Urtext of *Ap. John* is a rewriting and expansion of Genesis 1-7 for the purpose of presenting an alternative, sectarian *myth*, a myth which will serve to reveal saving *gnosis*.[81] The use made of the biblical text in the respective cases are quite comparable both in terms of method and in terms of attitude. That is to say, the biblical text is not rejected out of hand; it is corrected and amplified by the composition of a superior version of the truth.

---

[75] See my discussion in 'Jewish Sources', 458-61, and 'Problem', 19-26, and literature cited there.

[76] *Soph. Jes. Chr.* is a Christian Gnostic 'revelation dialogue' that has been constructed as such using *Eugnostos*, a non-Christian text, as its basic source. See esp. Krause, 'Literarische Verhältnis'; Parrot, 'Religious Syncretism'; and Perkins, *Gnostic Dialogue*, 94-98.

[77] *Ap. John* has rightly been included in the group of texts which belong to 'Sethian' Gnosticism. On the Sethian form of Gnosticism see esp. Schenke, 'Gnostic Sethianism'; Pearson, 'Figure of Seth'; and the other essays in Layton, *Rediscovery* 2. Cf. also Stroumsa, *Another Seed*.

[78] See esp. Nickelsburg, 'Bible Rewritten'.

[79] Cf. Filoramo-Gianotto, 'L'interpretazione gnostica', 69-73, a valuable discussion with the heading, 'Reinterpretazione o rescrittura del racconto biblico'. The following texts attributed to the 'gruppo Sethiano' are discussed under that heading: *Ap. John; Hyp. Arch.* (*NHC* II, 4); and *Orig. World* (*NHC* II, 5 and XIII, 2). Cf. also the extensive discussion by Simonetti of Gnostic reinterpretation of the opening passages in Genesis ('Note sull' interpretazione', 9, 347-59 + 10, 103-26).

[80] Nickelsburg, 'Bible Rewritten', 97-104.

[81] On Gnosticism as a 'mythological phenomenon', see e.g. Stroumsa, *Another Seed*, 1-14; Jonas, 'Gnostic Syndrome', esp. 266-73.

To be sure, there is an observable difference between the Gnostic texts and the Jewish pseudepigrapha, even the most 'non-conformist' or 'sectarian' of them. This difference is so basic that it finally marks Gnosticism off as a new religion altogether, one that has broken through even the widest definable boundaries of what constitutes 'Judaism'. The following passage from *Ap. John* exemplifies this breach:

> And when he saw the creation which surrounds him and the multitude of angels around him which had come forth from him, he said to them, 'I am a jealous God and there is no other God beside me'. But by announcing this he indicated to his angels who attended to him that there exists another God, for if there were no other one, of whom would he be jealous? (*NHC* II, 13, 5-13).

This passage, containing the 'blasphemy of the Demiurge', is found in a number of Gnostic texts, and reflects the Gnostic end product of a discussion in Jewish circles concerning 'two powers in heaven'. The Gnostic conclusion to the debate effectively marks a 'revolution' on the part of Jewish Gnostics against the biblical Creator and a radical alienation from his created order.[82] The text itself is artfully constructed as a rewriting (and re-ordering) of the biblical material in Genesis 1. The Gnostic author indicates that he knows that the 'creation' (Gen 1:1) 'seen' (Gen 1:4, 10, 12, 18, 21, 25) by the Creator is nothing 'good'; rather it is darkness and chaos (Gen 1:2), and the Creator himself is not only arrogant but foolish,[83] not understanding the import of his own vain pronouncements (Isa 45:21; 46:9; Exod 20:5).

The blasphemy of the Demiurge is immediately followed in *Ap. John* by the statement (quoted above) concerning the 'moving to and fro' (= 'repentance') of 'the mother' (= Sophia), a reinterpretation of Genesis 1:2. Following Sophia's repentance a *bat qôl* comes from heaven with the announcement 'Man exists and the son of Man' (14, 14f.). With this revelation we come to know the identity of the highest God whose existence (together with that of his 'son', primal Adam) has been blasphemously denied by the Creator. The highest God is 'Man' (cf. Gen 1:26f.).[84]

The material that follows in the text deals with the creation of earthly man, a composite being whose inner self is akin to 'Man', the highest God. The Gnostic account of the creation of Adam was constructed with the use and reinterpretation of a number of Jewish exegetical traditions, some of which reflect the influence of contemporary Platonism.[85] The import of this Gnostic 're-written scripture' is that the knowledge of God requisite to salvation is really

---

[82] See esp. Dahl, 'Arrogant Archon', and Culianu, 'Angels'.
[83] One of the three names given to the Creator in *Ap. John* is 'Saklas' (Aramaic for 'fool'). The other names are 'Samael', and 'Yaldabaoth'; all three occur together in the text at II 11, 16-18. On these names see Pearson, 'Jewish Haggadic Traditions', 466-68; Barc, 'Samaèl-Saklas-Yaldabaôth'.
[84] See Schenke, *Der Gott 'Mensch'*.
[85] See Pearson, 'Biblical Exegesis', and now esp. Van den Broek, 'Adam's Physic Body'.

knowledge of the awakened self within, a 'man' whose kinship with 'Man' makes him superior to the world and its Creator.

That such a doctrine, so self-evidently alien to the biblical tradition (both Old and New Testaments), was read out of the Bible and given expression in the form of 'rewritten scripture' is one of the fascinating curiosities of ancient Jewish history, indeed, of the history of Hellenistic-Roman religion in general.

While *Ap. John* is arguably the most important Gnostic text for the purposes of this discussion, there are others, too, that fit the category of 'rewritten scripture'. Some of these are closely related to *Ap. John* in terms of structure and content: *The Hypostasis of the Archons* (*NHC* II, 4);[86] *On the Origin of the World* (*NHC* II, 5 and XIII, 2);[87] and the system described by Irenaeus in *Adversus Haereses* 1:30.[88] Like *Ap. John*, these texts have undergone Christianizing redaction. *The Apocalypse of Adam* (*NHC* V, 5) is an especially interesting example of rewritten scripture because of its relation to the Jewish Adam literature.[89] There is no discernible Christian content in *Apoc. Adam*. *The Paraphrase of Shem* (*NHC* VII, 1),[90] another non-Christian text, should probably be included in the category of rewritten scripture, though the divergences from the biblical text are greater in that writing. In addition, the Mandaean anthropogonic myths are clearly related to that of *Ap. John* and other Gnostic texts.[91] Unfortunately, limitations of space prevent us from taking up these materials for discussion here.

Conclusions

The earliest Gnostic literature was heavily indebted to the text of Mikra and biblical exegetical traditions. Though the Gnostics denigrated the biblical Creator by relegating him to an inferior position below a transcendent Deity, they did not reject the Bible itself. On the contrary, they came to their radical theology and worldview in the very process of *interpreting* the scriptural text, the authoritative ('canonical') status of which was self-evident. Their earliest literature took the form of 'rewritten scripture' and resembled in that respect some of the pseudepigraphical literature produced in sectarian Jewish circles.

---

[86] For the most recent editions see Layton, 'Hypostasis', and Barc, *L'Hypostase*. The latter posits several redactional stages in the text's composition, the most primitive of which is a product of Jewish Gnosticism.

[87] The basic edition is still Böhlig, *Schrift ohne Titel*. See Wintermute, 'Gnostic Exegesis', for an analysis of that text's use of the OT.

[88] That system is not labelled by Irenaeus, but scholarly tradition refers to it as 'Ophite'. For ET and discussion see Foerster, *Gnosis* 1, 84-94. For a good discussion of that text's correlation of the biblical prophets with the various archontic powers (1:30, 10-11) see Fallon, 'Prophets'. On the problem of 'Ophite' Gnosticism in general see Kaestli, 'L'interprétation du serpent'.

[89] See my discussion in 'Jewish Sources', 470-74, and 'Problem', 26-34, and literature cited there.

[90] See my discussion in 'Jewish Sources', 475f., and literature cited there, to which should be added Roberge, 'Le rôle du Noûs'.

[91] See esp. Rudolph, 'Grundtyp', and discussion above.

The Gnostic writings were mythological in character, and relied heavily on the primal history of Genesis and current Jewish interpretations thereof. Indeed, there is every reason to believe that the authors of the early Gnostic texts were disaffected Jewish intellectuals open to the various religious and philosophical currents of Hellenistic syncretism.

Early in the history of the Gnostic religion, the Christian mission exerted a profound influence on Gnostic thinking. And, vice-versa, Gnosticism came to play a prominent role in the early development of the Christian religion, particularly as Christianity moved away from its ethnic Jewish matrix and assumed a separate identity as a Hellenistic religion. The coalescence of Gnosticism and Christianity was expressed particularly in making Jesus Christ a Gnostic 'saviour' figure, i.e. a revealer of *gnosis*. The literary manifestation of this trend first takes the form of editorial Christianization of originally non-Christian texts. This was accomplished by attributing the Gnostic myth to Jesus Christ and/or by making him the paradigm of Gnostic salvation. Eventually a new Gnostic Christian literature was created.

The Bible ('Old Testament') was part of the Christian heritage, as it was of the Gnostic heritage. But there was considerable variety in the way in which Gnostic Christians looked upon it. Three basic attitudes emerged:
1) open rejection of the OT; 2) whole-hearted acceptance of it; and 3) an intermediate position according to which the biblical text was inspired by the lower Creator or lesser powers, but nevertheless contained 'spiritual truth' to be ferreted out by means of a spiritual (allegorical) exegesis.

Authorization for this procedure was found in revelation attributed to the Saviour, Jesus Christ, and various of his apostles.

As we have seen, the use and interpretation of Mikra among the various Gnostic groups in antiquity is characterized by a great deal of variety and complexity, thanks to the creative inventiveness of the different Gnostic teachers in their elaboration of Gnostic mythological consciousness. The full story of this process has by no means been told in the present study. It is to be hoped that someone will take up this challenging task in the future.

Bibliography

The standard bibliography on Gnosticism (except Manichaeism and Mandaeism) is SCHOLER, *Nag Hammadi Bibliography*. The best monographic treatments of Gnosticism are JONAS, *Gnostic Religion*; RUDOLPH, *Gnosis*; and FILORAMO, *L'attesa della fine*. The Nag Hammadi texts are available in English translation in a single volume: ROBINSON, *Nag Hammadi Library* (including also the tractates in the Berlin Gnostic Codex). The standard anthology of other Gnostic materials in English translation is FOERSTER, *Gnosis* (2 vols.).

No monograph on the use of Mikra in Gnostic literature exists. A collection of articles on the problem has been published (TRÖGER, *Altes Testament*) as well as individual articles in various journals, Festschriften, etc. (see above, n. 5).

Chapter Eighteen

The Old Testament Canon in the Early Church

E. Earle Ellis

Introduction

The term χανών, from which the English word 'canon' is derived, means 'a measuring stick' and is first used for biblical writings in the fourth or perhaps third century C.E.[1] Cognate forms[2] and similar terms such as 'covenantal books' (ἐνδιαθήκοι βίβλοι)[3] also were employed. At the beginning of the church, however, other terminology was current: Scripture (γραφή),[4] the Law, the Law and the Prophets,[5] the Old Covenant,[6] Moses and all the Prophets,[7] the Law of Moses and the Prophets and Psalms.[8] Or verbal formulas were employed: God said, he says (or said; λέγει, φησίν), Scripture says, Isaiah says, Moses wrote, as it is written.[9] These expressions signified an appeal to divine authority and most, if not all, correspond to designations for the OT that were current in the wider community of Judaism (see Beckwith, above, pp. 39-40).

The attitude of the church is reflected not only by its formulas of quotation but also by its understanding of prophecy. The NT writers consider the prophet to be 'a man of the Spirit' (Hos 9:7; cf. 1 Cor 14:37) and the Holy Spirit to be the

---

[1] Amphilocius, *Iambi ad Seleucum* 319 (*PG* 37, 1598A); Eusebius, *Hist. Eccl.* 6:25, 3; Athanasius, *De Decretis Nicaenae* 18 (*PG* 25, 456A). The expression ὁ λόγος τοῦ προφητικοῦ, often translated 'the doctrine of the prophetic rule', may in the third century (?) Clementine *Homilies* (2:15, end = *PG* 2, 85C) refer to Scripture as such.

[2] Origen, *Prol. in Cant.* 36, end *(canonicus)*; *Comm. in Matt.* on Matt 23:37-39 *(canonizo)* and on Matt 24:23-28 *(canonicus)*. On the term cf. Zahn, *Grundriss*, 1-14; Westcott, *Survey*, 512-19. In the NT χανών is used of a prescribed standard of conduct (2 Cor 10:13, 15f.; cf. Phil 3:16) or belief (Gal 6:16).

[3] Origen, *Comm. in Pss* 1 (Introduction); in Eusebius, *Hist. Eccl.* 6:25, 1; cf. 3:3, 1.

[4] E.g. John 13:18; Gal 3:8. Warfield, 'Scripture', 585 considered the anarthrous use of γραφή to refer to a known, 'unitary written authority', i.e. the Scripture as a whole. Cf. 2 Tim 3:16; 2 Pet 1:20.

[5] E.g. 1 Cor 14:21 (Isa 28:11f.); John 10:34 (Ps 82:6); Matt 7:12.

[6] 2 Cor 3:14f.; cf. 1 Macc 1:56f.: 'the books of the law..(and) a book of the covenant'.

[7] Luke 24:27; cf. John 1:45; Acts 26:22.

[8] Luke 24:44.

[9] E.g. 2 Cor 6:2, 16; Heb 1:5; 8:5, 8; Rom 11:2; 10:20; Mark 12:19; 2 Cor 8:15. On the formulas introducing scriptural citations in the NT cf. Ellis, *Paul's Use*, 22-25, 48f.; Fitzmyer, 'Explicit OT Quotations', 299-305.

spirit of prophecy (Acts 2:17).[10] Thus, they equate the Scriptures, even those specifically classified as 'the Law' or 'the Writings', with 'the Prophets' (Acts 26:27) or with the teaching of prophets and, consequently, regard them as inspired by God. The NT attitude toward the prophetic and, therefore, the divine origin of Scripture is nowhere better summarized than in 2 Tim 3:16 and 2 Pet 1:21:

> All Scripture is inspired by God (γραφὴ θεόπνευστος) and profitable for teaching . . .
> No prophecy was ever produced (ἠνέχθη) by the will of man but, being carried along by the Holy Spirit, men spoke from God.

With variations in nuance this conviction about the prophetic character of Scripture was one with the attitude of Judaism as a whole. Josephus, for example, limits the canon of Scripture not only to prophets but to a particular succession of prophets, and Philo describes the Scripture virtually as an emanation of the prophetic spirit. Similarly, rabbinic writings state that the departure of the Holy Spirit, presumably the spirit of prophecy, brought the giving of canonical prophecy to an end.[11]

Nevertheless, not all prophetic words or writings were included in the received Scriptures. This is recognized in the OT, e.g. 1 Sam 10:10, where certain prophecies remain unrecorded. Josephus regards prophecy as a continuing phenomenon and identifies a number of first-century prophets even though, on principle, he would exclude any writings of such persons from canonical Scripture.[12] Early Christianity also had its writing prophets whose 'scriptures' illumined the church (Rom 16:26) and were sometimes incorporated into the NT canon.[13] But for the most part these inspired writings, including the writings of apostles (1 Cor 5:9), apparently did not enjoy a continuing authoritative use and were allowed to perish. That is, while canonical Scripture was regarded as prophetic, prophetic writing did not necessarily become canonical. This was true both for the prophetic word in ancient Israel and for that in the apostolic church.[14]

The writings to which Jesus and his messianic community appeal as a divine sanction for their message were well-known and evidently recognized by them and their Jewish hearers not only as *divinely inspired* but also as the *continuing, normative authority* for the faith and life of the people of God. It is this twofold

---

[10] Cf. Strack-Billerbeck, *Kommentar* 2, 127-34. For a theory of uninspired 'canonical' books in rabbinic Judaism cf. Leiman, *Canonization*, 127-31.
[11] E.g. *B.T. Sota* 48b; cf. Strack-Billerbeck, *Kommentar* 1, 127; 4, 435-50; cf. Philo, *Mos.* 2, 188-91. See Beckwith, *Old Testament Canon*, 63-71; Leiman, *Canonization*, 30-34, 66, 129ff.
[12] Josephus, *Ant.* 13:311ff.; 15:373-79; *ibid. War* 6:286; 6:300-09.
[13] E.g. 1 Cor 14:33-36, 37; Eph 5:14; 2 Tim 3:1-5; Jas 4:5. Cf. Ellis, 'Pastoral Epistles'.
[14] The same attitude was present in the patristic church. See below.

attribution that can be said to constitute these writings a *canonical authority*.[15] At the same time the NT writers, and Jesus as he is represented by them, not only alter the texts of these canonical books when they cite them[16] but also occasionally quote in the same manner other Jewish writings[17] that were never recognized by the church or the synagogue to have a fixed and abiding, i.e. canonical authority.[18] Thus is posed the problem of the canon in the early church. To address it one must examine (1) the canon of the church in its relationship to the canon of Judaism and (2) the rationale by which canonical and non-canonical writings could be similarly used but nevertheless distinguished.

The Determination of the Canon

WITNESSES: THE FIRST CENTURY AND EARLIER

With its recognition of the books of the NT alongside those of the OT, the church departed decisively from the canon of Judaism.[19] But with regard to the OT it appears to have remained in conscious and intentional accord with the Jewish community.

(1)   Early Christian writings reveal no trace of friction with other Jewish groups about which books carried divine authority. This remains the case in the second century even in Justin's *Dialogue with Trypho the Jew*, where any such divergence might be expected to surface.[20]

(2)   When the later Diaspora, now mainly gentile, church was uncertain about the precise extent of the OT books, it sought an answer from Jewish or Jewish-Christian communities in Palestine.[21]

---

[15] Sanders, *Torah and Canon*, 91; *ibid.* 'Adaptable for Life', 551 somewhat similarly notes the threefold requirement in Judaism for the canonical status of a writing: divine authority, a fixed and invariable acceptance and adaptability. Cf. also Anderson, 'Canonical and Non-canonical', 117f.; Beckwith, *Old Testament Canon*, 63-71.

[16] E.g. Matt 2:23; John 7:38; 1 Cor 2:9; 15:45; Gal 4:22. The citations in Luke 11:49-51, Eph 5:14 and Jas 4:5 (γραφή) appear to be from Christian prophetic writings.

[17] E.g. in Jude 9?, 14f. Regarding the number of apocryphal quotations Oepke, 'κρύπτω', 992 concludes that 'in the New Testament (they) prove to be very small, though one can hardly deny them altogether'.

[18] For the same practices among Jewish and patristic writers see below.

[19] Although dated, Westcott, *Survey* and Zahn, *Geschichte* remain the best and most comprehensive studies. More recently, from a Lutheran perspective, cf. Von Campenhausen, *Formation*. Zahn has much information on the OT canon as well, as does the excellent survey of Westcott, *Bible in the Church*.

[20] The only differences cited are certain passages in the books of the Septuagint said to have been deleted from the Hebrew texts by the rabbis. Cf. Justin, *Dial.* 71-73.

[21] E.g. Melito in the second century, Origen in the third and Jerome in the fourth. See below.

(3) In what has been termed 'the crisis of the Old Testament canon',[22] the second-century church raised questions, in fact, not about the authority of the OT but about its interpretation and

(4) the heretic Marcion, who rejected the OT, represented an aberration in Christian practice that was uncharacteristic even of the heretical movements.[23]

(5) Admittedly, parts of the church later gave canonical status to the OT apocrypha. But this appears to have been the outgrowth of a popular and unreflective use of these writings, a case of custom triumphing over judgment.

These observations must now be supported by a more detailed consideration of the historical witnesses[24] to the canon in the early church and in the Judaism that gave it birth.

JOSEPHUS. Witnesses to the biblical canon at the beginning of the present era appear in Jewish and Christian sources. Most explicit is the Jewish historian Josephus. He identifies twenty-two books[25] 'that are justly accredited (τὰ δικαίως πεπιστευμένα) and contain the record of all time', five of Moses, thirteen of the Prophets 'who wrote the history of the events of their own times', and the remaining four (αἱ λοιπαὶ τέσσαρες) which contain 'hymns to God and precepts for the conduct of human life' (ὕμνους εἰς τὸν θεὸν καὶ τοῖς ἀνθρώποις ὑποθήκας τοῦ βίου). After Artaxerxes (c. 400 B.C.E.) the writings have not been deemed worthy of equal credit because of the failure of 'the exact succession of the prophets' (τὴν τῶν προφητῶν ἀκριβῆ διαδοχήν). Although a long time has passed no one has ventured to add, to remove or to alter by one

---

[22] By Von Campenhausen, *Formation*, 62-102: 'Before Marcion there were hardly any "anti-biblical gnostics" in the strict sense. The view which dominated earlier scholarship, that "the gnosis" had more or less rejected the Old Testament from the start is no longer tenable . . .' (75). 'In general what (the ecclesiastical polemicists) condemn in the gnostics is not the rejection but the arbitrary ǫxegesis of holy scripture . . .' (76).

[23] On Marcion's rejection of the OT cf. Irenaeus, *Haer.* 1:29, 1; 1:27, 2 and Tertullian, *Adv. Marc.* 1:2; 4:1. See Pearson, above, pp. 640-41.

[24] See also Beckwith, above, pp. 51-58 (the Threefold Structure of the Canon).

[25] Probably the books of our present OT: the Pentateuch (5); Joshua, Judges-Ruth, Samuel, Kings, Chronicles, Ezra-Nehemiah, Esther, Isaiah, Jeremiah-Lamentations, Ezekiel, Daniel, the Twelve Minor Prophets, Job (13); Psalms, Proverbs, Ecclesiastes, Song of Songs (4). A couple of passages in Josephus support this reconstruction. In *Ant.* 5:318-37 the story of Ruth follows Judges and is dated on the basis of that combination; in *Ant.* 10:78 Lamentations is regarded as Jeremiah's book; in *Ant.* 10:267f. Daniel is identified as one of the prophets. The same order of the books (5 + 13 + 4) is given by the fourth-century Father, Rufinus (d. 410) in *Exposito Symboli* 35f. Cf. Ryle, *Canon*, 229; see note 86. It is uncertain whether Josephus is referring to Artaxerxes I (d. 425 B.C.E.), Artaxerxes II (d. 359 B.C.E.), or to Xerxes (d. 465 B.C.E.). Like the Septuagint, he (*Ant.* 11:184) also used the name Artaxerxes for Ahasuerus (cf. Esther 1:1). For 4 Ezra (14:45f.; c. 100 C.E.), as for Josephus, writings after the time of Ezra are not placed in the canonical scriptures. Cf. also *T. Sota* 13:3.

syllable[26] those 'laws and allied documents' (νόμους καὶ τὰς μετὰ τούτων ἀναγραφάς). Rather every Jew regards them as 'the decrees of God' (θεοῦ δόγματα) and is willing if need be to die for them.[27]

Such is the view of Josephus. As we hope to show, it represents not just the views of his own religious party, the Pharisees, but the attitude of first-century Judaism as a whole.

PHILO. A second Jewish witness, who wrote in the early part of the first century, is the Alexandrian philosopher Philo. Although he is less specific than Josephus, he is in substantial agreement with him. Of the books of Moses Philo states,

> (The Jews) have not altered even a single word of what had been written by him (who gave them their laws) but would rather endure to die ten thousand times than yield to any persuasion contrary to his laws and customs.[28]

To underscore the Bible-centered character of the Therapeutae, an Essene-like Jewish community in Egypt, Philo comments (*De Vita Contemplativa* 1f., 25):

> (They take into their study rooms nothing) but the Laws, the Oracles uttered by the Prophets, and Hymns and the other (books) (ἀλλὰ νόμους καὶ λόγια θεσπισθέντα διὰ προφητῶν καὶ ὕμνους καὶ τὰ ἄλλα) that foster and perfect knowledge and piety.[29]

That the reference is to the sacred writings commonly received in Judaism and excludes the books of the sect seems to be clear from Philo's following words (28f.): In addition to the Holy Scriptures (τοῖς ἱεροῖς γράμμασι), i.e. the ancestral philosophy (πάτριον φιλοσοφίαν), 'they have writings of men of old, the founders of their way of thinking . . .'[30]

The remarkably similar descriptions of the Scripture in Philo and Josephus are significant. They show that, as far as those two scholars represent them,

[26] Cf. Deut 4:2; Matt 5:17ff.; Rev 22:18f.; *1QS* 1:1-3; 8:22. Like the biblical writers, Josephus is speaking of the divine authority and inviolability of the books and not of the use of other writings nor of translation variants or midrashic elaborations upon or within the received books. Of the latter practices he was not uninformed or disapproving as the proem to his *Antiquities* and his use of 1 Esdras (*Ant.* 10:68-80; 11:33-158) and of Greek additions to Esther show (*Ant.* 11:216-83). But see Swete, *Introduction*, 266f.

[27] Josephus, *Ag.Ap.* 1:38-42, also cited in Eusebius, *Hist. Eccl.* 3:10, 1-5; cf. Josephus, *Ant.* 10:35 where Isaiah and twelve other prophets appear to refer to the thirteen 'prophetic' books.

[28] A fragment from Philo's *Hypothetica* (6:9) preserved in Eusebius, *Praep. Evang.* 8:6f.; 8:11. As is the case with Josephus, the statement is hyperbolic and should not be literally pressed. Nevertheless, it accurately witnesses to the sanctity accorded the Scriptures in first-century Judaism.

[29] In Philo, *De Vita Contemplativa* 1f., 25, there seem to be four divisions of canonical books: laws, oracles, hymns and the rest. But since Josephus subdivides his third division into 'hymns and precepts', the difference may be more apparent than real.

[30] *Ibid.* 28f. But see Colson-Whitaker-Marcus, *Philo 9*, 520; Beckwith, *Old Testament Canon*, 117.

Jewish communities in Palestine, Rome and Alexandria agreed in identifying their sacred writings with a definite number of books, ordered sequentially into three (or four) divisions: Laws, Prophecies or Oracles, Hymns and the rest. A tripartite division of Scripture, not unlike that of Josephus and Philo, is also attributed to Jesus in Luke 24:44: 'the law of Moses and the prophets and psalms'.[31]

BEN SIRA. This tripartite division of the Bible was not the creation of first-century Judaism, for it has a precedent in the prologue attached in Alexandria to the Greek translation (c. 132 BC) of Ben Sira, a Hebrew work originating in Palestine in the early second century B.C.E. The translator observes that

> My grandfather Jesus (devoted himself) to the Law and the Prophets and the other ancestral books (τοῦ νόμου καὶ τῶν προφητῶν καὶ τῶν ἄλλων πατρίων βιβλίων) . . . (In Greek translation) not only this work but even the Law itself and the Prophecies and the rest of the books (αὐτος ὁ νόμος καὶ αἰ προφητεῖαι καὶ τὰ λοιπὰ τῶν βιβλίων) differ not a little (from the original).

As the prologue shows, already in the late second century B.C.E., and probably two generations earlier, certain sacred books had a canonical status. That is, they constituted a definite and identifiable collection with a continuing, normative authority distinguished from that of other religious writings. They had already been translated into Greek and, like the Holy Scriptures known to Philo and Josephus, they were divided into three parts: the Law, the Prophets and the other books. It is possible that, since the individual books are not named, those in the canon of one writer were not identical with those of the others. However, they are designated by very similar expressions and are apparently well-known works requiring no enumeration. In the absence of contrary historical evidence the twenty-two books mentioned by Josephus and perhaps earlier in Jub 2:23 may, with some probability, be presumed to be the sacred books of Philo and Ben Sira as well. Only in the second century C.E., when uncertainty existed about their number or order, are the books of the OT listed by name. We may now turn to these later testimonies.

WITNESSES: THE SECOND AND THIRD CENTURIES

MELITO. The two principal witnesses to the state of the OT canon in the second century are the Babylonian Talmud tractate Bava Batra and Melito, bishop of Sardis. Melito, answering an inquiry concerning the 'number' and the 'order' of

---

[31] Since the Psalms stand at the beginning of the Hagiographa in some Hebrew manuscripts and are a part of the title (ὕμνους καὶ τὰ ἄλλα) of the Hagiographa in Philo, they may represent the third division of the OT canon in Luke. Cf. also Luke 24:27. For a somewhat similar division in a Jewish writing cf. 2 Macc 2:13.

'the old books' (τῶν παλαιῶν βιβλίων), writes the following words (c. 170 C.E.):

> ... when I came to the East and reached the place where these things were preached and done, and learned accurately the books of the Old Testament (τὰ τῆς παλαιᾶς διαθήκης βιβλία), I set down the facts ... These are their names: Of Moses five, Genesis, Exodus, Numbers, Leviticus, Deuteronomy; Joshua son of Nun, Judges, Ruth, four of Kingdoms, two of Chronicles, the Psalms of David, Solomon's Proverbs or Wisdom (ἡ καὶ σοφία), Ecclesiastes, Song of Songs, Job; of the Prophets: Isaiah, Jeremiah, the Twelve (Minor Prophets) in one book, Daniel, Ezekiel, Esdras.[32]

It is apparent in the light of some subsequent catalogues given below, that this enumeration includes Samuel within Kings, Lamentations under Jeremiah and identifies Ezra-Nehemiah as Esdras; Solomon's 'Wisdom' is in all likelihood an alternate designation for Proverbs.[33] If so, this list conforms to the present OT with the exception of Esther, which was apparently omitted, either by accident or by design.[34]

Melito's canon represents the OT as it was received in certain Palestinian Jewish and/or Jewish-Christian circles in the second century. Apart from Esther it presumably contained the same books as the canon of Josephus. It also has three divisions, with the first and third designated 'Of Moses' and 'Of the prophets'. However, it differs in the numbering since Samuel and Kings are counted as four, Judges-Ruth as two, to give a canon of twenty-five books; in this respect, in the books within each division and in sequence it conforms more closely than Josephus to Codex B of the Septuagint: Law (5), Histories (9) and Poetry (5), Prophets (6). It is also closer to the Septuagint in the titles of the books.

Since both the Septuagint (Greek) version of the OT and a Hebrew recension with a Septuagint text-form were already in use in first-century Palestine, the divisions and sequence represented by later codices of the Septuagint may also have been known. At least, Melito's canon, chronologically speaking, has as good a claim to represent an accepted Jewish order as does the rabbinic

---

[32] Eusebius, *Hist. Eccl.* 4:26, 13f. If Melito's reference to a trip was literary convention, as Nock ('Apocryphal Gospels', 63f.) thought, he in any case identifies Palestine as the source of his information.

[33] According to Eusebius (*Hist. Eccl.* 4:22, 9) this designation for Proverbs was common in the second century.

[34] Cf. Ryle, *Canon*, 214-18, 229ff. In other lists 'Εσθήρ follows "Εσδρας and, if this was the case in Melito's catalogue, it may have been omitted by a scribe inadvertently or because of a confusion of names. A parallel for this is offered by Origen's list of OT books which omits the Twelve Minor Prophets. However, of the twenty-two OT books only Esther is lacking at Qumran, and the biblical status of Esther was questioned by some rabbis (cf. Leiman, *Canonization*, 200 n. 634) and by a few Christian writers. Therefore, it is possible if not probable that the book was not recognized as Scripture by Melito's informants. Cf. *B.T. Sanhedrin* 100a.

arrangement that one first encounters also in a second century document, a baraita of the Babylonian Talmud. It is reasonable to suppose that the canonical lists of both the rabbis and of Melito represent revisions of an older order or orders to which Josephus, Philo and Ben Sira bear witness.[35]

BAVA BATRA. A tradition in the Babylonian Talmud tractate Bava Batra (14b) reads:

> Our rabbis taught that the order of the Prophets is Joshua, Judges, Samuel, Kings, Jeremiah, Ezekiel, Isaiah, the Twelve (Minor Prophets). . . . The order of the Hagiographa is Ruth, Psalms, Job, Proverbs, Ecclesiastes, Song of Songs, Lamentations, Daniel, Esther, Ezra, Chronicles.[36]

The section is introduced by the formula, 'our rabbis taught', which identifies it as a baraita and thereby probably dates it before 200 C.E.[37] It appears to represent the accepted limits and divisions of the Sacred Scriptures among (some) second-century rabbinic schools. With some variations in the divisions of the canon and in the sequence of certain books, i.e. Isaiah, Ruth, Song of Songs, Esther, it agrees with the subsequent form of the Hebrew (masoretic) Bible received and used in Judaism. Since the Pentateuch is presupposed, it reflects a canon of twenty-four books:[38] Law or *Tora* (5), Prophets or *Neviim* (8), Writings or *Ketuvim* (11).

It is significant that the baraita is concerned not with the *identity* of the canonical books but with their *order*. That is, it suggests no controversy about the *limits* of the canon, but it may reflect a situation in which there were uncertainties or divergent traditions among the Jews about the sequence and divisions of the canon, e.g. which books belonged among the Prophets and which among the Writings. Just these kinds of variations from the rabbinic order given in the baraita occur in the canons of Josephus and Melito and in the Hebrew Bible known to later Christian writers.

---

[35] On the background of the text-types underlying the Septuagint and masoretic texts cf. Leiman, *Canon and Masorah*, 327-33 (= Albright, 'New Light'), 334-48 (= Cross, 'Contribution'), 833-69 (= Orlinsky, 'Prolegomenon').

[36] The order of the Hagographa is meant to be chronological with the possible exception of Job. Ruth is attributed to Samuel; Proverbs, Ecclesiastes, Song of Songs to Solomon; Lamentations to Jeremiah; Daniel is from the Exile; Esther, Ezra and Chronicles are post-Exilic. Cf. Ginsburg, *Introduction*, 1-8; Strack-Billerbeck, *Kommentar* 4, 415-34.

[37] For the most part the *beraitot* of the Talmuds originated in the Tannaic period (i.e. pre-200 C.E.) but were not included in the Mishna. Cf. De Vries, 'Baraita, Beraitot'.

[38] Cf. The *Gospel of Thomas* 52: 'Twenty-four prophets spoke in Israel and all of them spoke in you'. Some manuscripts of *4 Ezra* 14:44-46 (c. 100 C.E.) may imply a canon of twenty-four books (and seventy apocryphal books), but others give a different numbering. Some manuscripts of the masoretic Bible have four divisions: Pentateuch, Megillot (Ruth, Song of Songs, Lamentations, Ecclesiastes, Esther), Prophets, Hagiographa. Cf. Ryle, *Canon*, 250-61; Ginsburg, *Introduction*, 3. On the possible origins of an 'ordering' of the individual canonical books cf. Leiman, *Canonization*, 162 n. 258, 202 n. 644, and Beckwith, *Old Testament Canon*, 181-234.

ORIGEN. While still at Alexandria, and therefore before 231 C.E., the eminent biblical scholar Origen (c. 185-254 C.E.) wrote an exposition of Psalm 1 in which he included 'a catalogue of the sacred scriptures of the Old Testament' (τῶν ἱερῶν γραφῶν τῆς παλαιᾶς διαθήκης καταλόγου). He comments that 'there are twenty-two canonical books (ἐνδιαθήκους βίβλους) as the Hebrews tradition them, the same as the number of the letters of their alphabet'. He proceeds to give the titles in Greek, followed by a transliteration of the Hebrew names:

> Genesis, Exodus, Leviticus, Numbers, Deuteronomy, Joshua, Judges-Ruth, Kingdoms (1,2) [= Samuel], Kingdoms (3,4), Chronicles (1,2), Esdras (1,2) [= Ezra], Psalms, Proverbs, Ecclesiastes, Song of Songs, Isaiah, Jeremiah-Lamentations-Letter, Daniel, Ezekiel, Job, Esther.

In conclusion Origen states, 'And outside of these are the Maccabees, which are entitled Sarbethsabaniel'.[39]

The account, also preserved by Eusebius (*Hist. Eccl.* 6:24, 2; 6:25, 1f.), gives only twenty-one books, and it is evident that the Twelve (Minor Prophets) has been accidentally omitted by a scribe. Like Melito, Origen employs Septuagint titles and roughly follows the Septuagint sequence of Law, Histories, Poetry and Prophecies. However, he goes beyond Melito in several important respects: He (1) sets the Septuagint titles beside those of the Hebrew books and gives a more specific listing. (2) He considers (elsewhere) the problem of differences between the Hebrew and Septuagint texts and (3) introduces a (?Jewish) practice whereby religious books 'outside of these' canonical writings, but nevertheless useful to the people of God, may be regarded as a kind of appendix to the canon.

1. Origen transcribes the Hebrew names and details those books, usually separated in the Septuagint, that appear 'in one [book]' in the Hebrew canon known to him. Of the six combined books – Samuel, Kings, Chronicles, Judges-Ruth, Jeremiah-Lamentations-Letter, Ezra – the last three are of special interest.

a. As Jerome later states explicitly,[40] the combined and separate disposition of Ruth and Lamentations accounts not only for their different classification, respectively, among the Prophets *(Neviim)* or among the Hagiographa *(Ketuvim)* but also for the different number of books in the Hebrew canon of Josephus, Origen, Epiphanius and Jerome (twenty-two books) and in the list of

---

[39] Eusebius, *Hist- Eccl.* 6:25, 1f. Perhaps, 'the book *(sefer)* of the house *(beit)* of *Sabaniel*, i.e. of the Maccabees. On the problem cf. Abel, *Les Livres des Maccabées*, IVf.; Alon, *Jews, Judaism*, 8f.; Leiman, *Canonization*, 159 n. 229; Attridge, 'Historiography', 171 n. 39.

[40] In *Prologus Galeatus* ('the Helmeted Prologue'), which was the preface to Jerome's Latin translation of the OT. It stands before Samuel and Kings, the first books that Jerome translated, and notes that, while the Jewish canon ordinarily had twenty-two books, some *(nonnulli)* Jews count Ruth and Lamentations separately, giving a canon of twenty-four books. For the text cf. Fischer, *Biblia Sacra* 1, 364ff.; for the ET cf. Schaff-Wace, *Nicene . . . Fathers* 6, 489f. For rabbinic witnesses to a canon of 24 books cf. Leiman, *Canonization*, 53-56.

Bava Batra 14b, other rabbinic traditions and the masoretic Bible (twenty-four books).

b. The 'Letter' attached to Jeremiah in Origen's list refers either to Baruch[41] or to the *Letter of Jeremiah*. While the latter was originally written in Greek, Baruch may have existed in Hebrew and may therefore be the 'Letter' referred to here. In support of this supposition the Greek text of (parts of) Baruch manifests signs of a Hebrew original[42] and, according to the fourth-century *Apostolic Constitutions* (5:20), certain Jews read Baruch on the Day of Atonement. Furthermore a reference to the Letter of Jeremiah is virtually excluded by the following considerations: Origen has the Hebrew Scriptures in his possession and presupposes a knowledge of them in his commentaries and his Hexapla. Even though he defends some Septuagint additions, e.g. to Daniel, he is quite aware of the different readings 'in their [Hebrew] copies' (ἀντιγρά-φοις) and 'in our [Septuagint] books'.[43] It is, therefore, difficult to suppose that Origen has here added a *Septuagint* appendix, whether Baruch or the Letter of Jeremiah, and has then explicitly identified the whole with the *Hebrew* book Jeremiah. Either 'the Letter' is a Baruch appendix to Jeremiah in the Hebrew Bible known and used by Origen, or it is a scribal gloss on Origen's list.

Several items of evidence favour the latter alternative, that is, a scribal gloss as the most satisfactory resolution of the problem. (1) Jerome states that the Hebrews 'neither read nor possess' *(nec legitur, nec habetur)* Baruch, and Epiphanius excludes both Baruch and the *Letter of Jeremiah* from the canon of the Hebrews[44] as does rabbinic tradition. Thus, the isolated comment that certain Jews read Baruch *(Apostolic Constitutions* 5:20) applies at most to a local phenomenon, if it is not completely without historical worth. (2) When other fourth century lists combine either the *Letter of Jeremiah*[45] or both the Letter and Baruch with the book of Jeremiah, they apparently reflect the content of Greek and Latin Bibles currently in use. This usage might have given occasion for a scribe to alter Origen's list accordingly. (3) Scribal 'mending' of texts to conform them to current usage is not unknown elsewhere, and it may well account for the addition of the Letter to Jeremiah-Lamentations.

c. Septuagint manuscripts now extant, all considerably later than Origen, place the Hebrew 'double' book Ezra-Nehemiah in one book under the title 2 Esdras and precede it with a book entitled 1 Esdras, a Greek paraphrase or

[41] So Ryle, *Canon*, 218f.; Wildeboer, *Canon*, 79. Both Baruch and the Letter are referred to as 'epistles' in Epiphanius, *Panarion* 1:1, 5; *De Mens. et Pond.* 5. Cf. the discussion in Sundberg, *Old Testament*, 74-77. See note 67.

[42] Cf. Swete, *Introduction*, 275f. So for Baruch 1:1-3:8, Tov, *Septuagint Translation*, 170.

[43] *Ad Africanum* 5; on different readings cf. *Ad Afr.* 2; 5 (in Daniel); 3f. (in Genesis, Esther, Job, Jeremiah). See note 49. On Origen's possession of Hebrew scriptures cf. Eusebius, *Hist, Eccl.* 6:16, 1.

[44] Jerome's prologue to Jeremiah in his Vulgate; Epiphanius, *De Mens. et Pond.* 5.

[45] Hilary, *Prol. in Libr. Pss.* See note 83.

midrash of parts of Chronicles and Ezra-Nehemiah.[46] In Origen's canon the two Greek books called Esdras are said to be 'in one' book, *viz.* Ezra, in his Hebrew Bible. For reasons given above in the matter of the Letter, Origen's two books of Esdras refer in all likelihood not to the two Septuagint books of those names but to the books of Ezra and Nehemiah, books that were 'one' in the Hebrew Bible but were separated in some Septuagint codices of that period.[47] Readers whose Septuagint copies contained 1 Esdras (alongside Ezra-Nehemiah) may have misunderstood Origen's statement and supposed that 1 Esdras was part of the Hebrew canon. Indeed, this apparent terminological confusion may have promoted the canonical status later accorded 1 Esdras although the major influence to that end seems to have been the inclusion of the work in some early Septuagint codices (e.g. Vaticanus, Alexandrinus). In any case the misunderstanding can hardly be charged to Origen.[48]

2. If the above reasoning is correct, Origen's canon agrees in content with that of *B. T. Bava Batra* (14b) and, with the exception of Esther, of Melito. His defense of the Septuagint additions to Daniel, i.e. Susanna,[49] does not represent a different judgement about *the books* that belong in the canon. Rather, as the context makes evident, it concerns *variant readings and diverse content* within a commonly received book of the Hebrew canon. Like Justin (*Dial.* 71-73), Origen suspects that the texts of the rabbis may have been tampered with. Of course he could not know, as we today know from the library at Qumran, that the Septuagint text-type does have a Hebrew *Vorlage* that in some respects is superior to the masoretic text.[50] He was influenced substantially by a natural preference for the traditional 'Christian' Septuagint Bible. But for him it was a textual and doctrinal rather than a canonical

---

[46] The two books are apparently parallel translations of (Chronicles and) the Hebrew Ezra, Greek 1 Esdras more paraphrastic or midrashic and Ezra-Nehemiah more literal, somewhat analogous to the Septuagintal and Theodotianic translation of Daniel. Cf. Swete, *Introduction*, 265ff.; Jellicoe, *Septuagint and Modern Study*, 290-94. An apocalyptic book, *4 Esdras = 4 Ezra*, is also sometimes called *2 Esdras*.

[47] Jerome, *Prologus in Libro Regum* (= *Prologus Galeatus*). Cf. Fischer, *Biblia Sacra*, 1, 365: . . . 'Ezra is itself similarly divided into two books in the Greek and Latin (Bibles)'.

[48] *Pace* Zahn, *Geschichte* 2, 331.

[49] Origen, *Ad Africanum* 9: The Hebrew copies lack the Septuagint readings because the elders 'hid from the knowledge of the people' passages that might bring discredit on them, e.g. the story of Susanna. Some of the passages 'have been preserved in their non-canonical writings' (ἀποκρύφοις). For an ET of *Ad Africanum* cf. Roberts-Donaldson, *Ante-Nicene Fathers* 4, 386-92.

[50] Cf. Tov, *Septuagint Translation*, 168; Cross, 'Contribution': The biblical manuscripts from Qumran reflect a plurality of text-types including that of the Septuagint. In some instances 'the Septuagint faithfully reflects a conservative Hebrew textual family. On the contrary, the Proto-Massoretic and Massoretic family is marked by editorial reworking and conflation . . .' (82). The (traditional) view that the masoretic text was 'standard' and all others 'vulgar' cannot explain the data (91ff.).

preference and, as his compilation of the Hexapla shows, it was not maintained uncritically.[51]

The canonical list of Origen, which presents the books 'as the Hebrews tradition them', is not inconsistent with his defense of Septuagint text-forms, and it is a most significant witness to the church's canon in the early third century. A hundred years later it is recorded by Eusebius because he, at least, views it as Origen's own conviction about the books that the church should acknowledge. Since Origen's translator and admirer Rufinus endorses a similar list, we may consider it very probable that Eusebius has represented the matter correctly.

3. Like other patristic writers, Origen cites writings outside his 'canonical books' with formulas that also introduce quotations from the canon.[52] He appears to be the first, however, to enunciate a principle to distinguish, in their employment and in their authority, writings that are *canonical* from writings that are *useful* for the church. In his commentary on Matthew he states,

> It is of great virtue to hear and fulfill that which is said, 'Prove all things; hold fast to that which is good' (1 Thess 5:21). Nevertheless, for the sake of those who . . . cannot discern . . . and guard themselves carefully so as to hold that which is true and yet 'avoid every kind of evil' (1 Thess 5:22) no one ought to use for the confirmation of doctrine any books that are outside the canonical Scriptures *(canonizatas scripturas)*.[53]

This distinction, which is elaborated in the following century by a number of Christian writers, is similar to and appears to rest upon earlier Jewish practice.[54] It is implicitly ascribed to the Jews by Origen himself when, in his catalogue, the

---

[51] Cf. Swete, *Introduction*, 480f. for Origen's criticism of certain Septuagint readings. Cf. de Lange, *Origen* 50f.

[52] E.g. *1 Enoch* in *De Principiis* 4:35 ('he says'). In the context Origen, like Jude, views *1 Enoch* as a prophecy. However, in *Contra Celsum* 5:54 he states that *Enoch* does not generally circulate at all (οὐ πάνυ) in the churches as divine (θεῖα). In *Ad Africanum* 13 Origen comments that 'since the churches use Tobit', he can adduce it to rebut an argument of Africanus. But the qualification is hardly an affirmation of the canonicity of Tobit, and it may indicate the opposite. Wiles' conclusion that Origen's usage 'is a case of having it both ways' and of citing the apocryphal writings used by the church 'as authoritatively as any other part of the Old Testament' seems doubtful to me. Cf. Wiles, 'Origen', 456.

[53] Origen, *Comm. in Matt.* 28 (on Matt 23:37-39), extant only in the Latin translation of Rufinus. The reference may be primarily to NT apocrypha, but it is equally applicable to the Old; cf. Westcott, *Survey*, 136f. The Latin *canonizatus* probably translates ἐνδιαθήκος ('covenantal'), a term that Origen uses elsewhere for 'canonical' books. In 117 (on Matt 27:3-10) Origen distinguishes quotations found in a 'standard book' *(regulari libro)* or 'public books' *(publicis libris)* from those in a 'secret book' *(libro secreto)*, i.e. the *Apocalypse of Elijah* and the *Book of Jannes and Jambres*.

[54] When in *Ad Africanum* 13 Origen states that the Jews neither *use* Tobit and Judith nor *have* them in the Hebrew apocrypha (ἀποκρύφοις Ἑβραϊστί), he implies that the Jews had a twofold classification (at least) of religious writings. This seems to be confirmed by the 'kind of intermediate holiness' that is ascribed in rabbinic literature to Ben Sira and, at the same time, the condemnation upon the (?public) reading of 'outside books'; cf. Haran, 'Problems of Canonization', 245; 4 Ezra 14:45f. See also Gilbert, 'Wisdom Literature', 300-01; *M. Sanhedrin* 10:1.

Maccabees are mentioned along with but 'outside of' the canonical books of the Hebrews. It also seems to be presupposed by Josephus, who excluded from the canon writings after Ezra as not 'worthy of equal credit' but nevertheless employed them in constructing his *Antiquities* of the Jews.[55] The distinction is present, moreover, in Philo's comment, given above, on the Holy Scriptures and the sectarian writings of the Therapeutae.

Somewhat different but perhaps not without similarity to Origen's conception are the Qumran writings, Ben Sira and the rabbinic literature. In his prologue the translator of Ben Sira sets his volume apart from writings that had normative authority in Judaism, and yet he clearly regards it as a useful supplement, i.e. 'a further help'. On a different level the rabbis contrast the 'oral law' (*B.T. Shabbat* 31a) or 'traditions of the elders' (cf. Matt 15:2) with the written Tora. But they consider the oral law as embodied in the Talmud to be the authoritative interpretation of the Tora and also cite Ben Sira, a book never received as canonical, with formulas ordinarily used for canonical writings.[56] As we hope to show below, the conception that *Holy Scripture can be supplemented* is significant not only for understanding the patristic church's authoritative use of approved Jewish apocrypha and of post-apostolic Christian writings but also for the process of canonization itself.

THE FOURTH CENTURY: CUSTOM VERSUS JUDGMENT

In the fourth century the canon of the OT posed an increasing problem for the church. Divided by a conscious and widening gap were the scholarly judgments on the canon and the popular usage of the church. The scholarly attitude was often expressed in explicit catalogues and was most clearly defined in the writings of Jerome. The popular conception was reflected in the (greater number of) books contained in many Greek and Latin Bibles and by the quotations of various writers.

There was, moreover, a different perception of the canon in the East and in the West. Especially in Africa, the church appears to have used indiscriminately the additional books of the Old Latin codices that were taken over from the Septuagint. The church in the East was more influenced by leaders who knew the Hebrew Bible (e.g. Origen, Jerome) or at least knew of a Hebrew canon to which their own should be subject.

---

[55] See note 26. Cf. Josephus, *Ant.* 12 and 13 *passim* (1 Macc).

[56] In *B.T. Berakhot* 48a, Sir 11:1 is combined with Prov 4:8 and introduced with the formula, 'as it is written'; in *B.T. Bava Kamma* 92b, Sir 13:15 is introduced with the formula, 'as written in the Hagiographa'. But cf. *T. Yadayim* 2:13 'Ben Sira and all the books written from that time on do not defile the hands', i.e. are not canonical. On the status of Ben Sira in the Pharisaic-rabbinic tradition, see Beckwith, above, pp. 68-73.

CANONICAL LISTS IN THE EASTERN CHURCH. As was true earlier, the compilers of fourth-century canonical lists[57] are for the most part writers of the Eastern church. Early in the century[58] Eusebius (died c. 339 C.E.), bishop of Caesarea, included in his *Church History* the canonical statement of Josephus and the catalogues of Melito and Origen. He thus conveyed his own conviction that the OT to be received by the church was the twenty-two books of the Hebrew Bible. Other fourth-century fathers imply or expressly mention a second order of useful books outside the canonical twenty-two, but they are chiefly concerned to make known the limits of the canon in order to protect the believers from the dangerous influence of heretical writings. Cyril bishop of Jerusalem, writing his *Catechetical Lectures*[59] about the middle of the century, exhorts the catechumens to

> read the divine Scriptures (θείας γραφάς), these twenty-two books of the Old Testament (παλαιᾶς διαθήκης) that were translated by the seventy-two translators (33) . . . (For) the translation of the divine Scriptures that were spoken in the holy Spirit was accomplished through the holy Spirit. Read their twenty-two books but have nothing to do with the apocryphal writings (ἀπόκρυφα). Study diligently only these that we also read with confident authority (μετὰ παρρησίας) in the church. (For) much wiser and holier than you were the apostles and ancient bishops who led the church and handed down these books (34f.).

Cyril proceeds to tabulate the books in three divisions, twelve historical, five poetic and five prophetic.[60] It is not certain whether 1-2 Esdras, 'reckoned [by the Hebrews] as one', refers to Ezra-Nehemiah, as seems probable, or includes 1 Esdras. 'Baruch and Lamentations and Epistle', appended to Jeremiah, clearly represent an accommodation to the contents of (Cyril's) Septuagint; and other books may implicitly comprehend the Septuagint additions. After enumerating the NT books, Cyril concludes:

> Let all the rest be placed outside (the canon) in a second rank[61] (ἐν δευτέρῳ). And whatever books are not read in churches, neither should you read them in private . . . (36).

---

[57] Zahn, *Geschichte* 2, 172-259, gives most of the texts. The lists are conveniently tabulated by Swete, *Introduction*, 203-14, and Sundberg, 'Old Testament', 58f.

[58] The tenth book of his *History*, added in the third edition and dedicated to Paulinus of Tyre (*Hist. Eccl.* 10:1, 2) upon the consecration of the basilica there, can be dated to 317 C.E. Cf. Lake, *Eusebius* 1, XX.

[59] Cyril, *Catech.* 4:33-36, a section with the title, 'Concerning the Divine Scriptures'. For the ET cf. Schaff-Wace, *Nicene . . . Fathers* 7, 26ff.; Zahn, *Geschichte* 2, 172 dates it 348 C.E.

[60] Cyril, *Catech.* 4:35: Genesis, Exodus, Leviticus, Numbers, Deuteronomy, Joshua, Judges-Ruth, Kingdoms (1, 2), Kingdoms (3, 4), Chronicles (1, 2), Esdras (1, 2), Esther; Job, Psalms, Proverbs, Ecclesiastes, Song of Songs; Twelve (Minor Prophets), Isaiah, Jeremiah-Baruch-Lamentations-Epistle, Ezekiel, Daniel.

[61] Cf. Schaff-Wace, *Nicene . . . Fathers*; Westcott, *Survey*, 169.

Cyril makes his strict injunction against reading apocryphal books in the context of opposing the heretical Manicheans.[62] Yet, addressing the same hearers, he himself cites works that he excludes from the canon in a manner somewhat similar to his citations of Scripture.[63] It is probable, then, that in the conclusion quoted above, Cyril has in view three classes of writings, the canonical books, the books of 'second rank' (that also may be read or cited in churches) and the heretical apocrypha.

In his *Easter Letter* (367 C.E.) Athanasius bishop of Alexandria makes this threefold classification explicit: canonical books, books read in church (especially) to catechumens, rejected heretical writings. Like Cyril, Athanasius also writes in the context of opposing the 'apocrypha' that some heretics sought 'to mix . . . with the inspired Scripture' (θεοπνεύστῳ γραφῇ). With respect to approved but non-canonical books, he writes:[64]

> But for the sake of greater exactness I add this also, writing under obligation, as it were. There are other books besides these, indeed not received as canonical but having been appointed (τετυπωμένα) by the Fathers to be read to those just approaching (the faith) and wishing to be instructed in the word of godliness: Wisdom of Solomon, Wisdom of Ben Sira, Esther, Judith, Tobit, the Didache and the Shepherd (of Hermas) Nevertheless, my brothers, neither among those that are received as canonical nor among those that are read is there mention of any of the apocryphal books; they rather are the imagination (ἐπίνοια) of heretics, who indeed write them whenever they wish . . .

---

[62] In *Catech.* 4:36; 6:31 Cyril ascribes the 'pseudepigraphal' *Gospel of Thomas* to the Manicheans; 4:34 appears to have the Marcionites also in view.

[63] Cyril, *Catech.* 9:2; 9:16 (Wisdom of Solomon) and 6:4; 11:19; 22:8 (Ben Sira). However, they are not cited as Scripture or, for the most part, with introductory formulas used to introduce canonical Scripture.

[64] Athanasius, *Easter Letter* 39; ET: Schaff-Wace, *Nicene . . . Fathers* 4, 551f.: Genesis, Exodus, Leviticus, Numbers, Deuteronomy, Joshua, Judges, Ruth, Kingdoms (1, 2), Kingdoms (3, 4), Chronicles (1, 2), Esra (1, 2), Psalms, Proverbs, Ecclesiastes, Song of Songs, Job, Twelve (Minor Prophets), Isaiah, Jeremiah-Baruch-Lamentations-Epistle, Ezekiel, Daniel. Esther is omitted, but by a separation of Judges and Ruth a twenty-two book total is maintained.

Canonical catalogues from Asia Minor during the mid-fourth century[65] show a similar concern to guard the readers from the dangers of 'strange books', and they have virtually the same content as the canons of Cyril and Athanasius.

Epiphanius (d. 404) bishop of Salamis (= Constantia) does not at first impression appear to be a very reliable witness. He is obsessed with number analogies,[66] is incessantly repetitious and rather absent-minded and gives three canonical catalogues that do not entirely agree.[67] However, the differences in the lists are more apparent than real; and the writer's wooden, repetitious style and candid 'after-thought' qualifications suggest a severely honest, if dogmatic temperament.[68] Moreover, Epiphanius has a knowledge of Hebrew and has independent Jewish traditions, i.e. a catalogue of canonical books, that he carefully transliterates for his readers.[69] His comment on the list in *Panarion* (376 c.e.) is, therefore, of considerable importance:

---

[65] (1) Gregory Nazianzus (*Carmen* 1:12) bishop of Constantinople who, like Cyril, follows an arrangement of 12 historical, 5 poetic and 5 prophetic books; he counts Judges and Ruth separately and omits Esther. (2) Amphilochius, cited by Gregory (*Carmen* 2:8, 264-88), indicates no double books and employs no number analogies; he concludes that 'some add Esther'. Both lists, given in verse, are intended to guard the reader from the danger of heretical books. Gregory draws an analogy with the twenty-two letters of the Hebrew alphabet. Neither mentions any books appended to Jeremiah. (3) The synod of Laodicea (c. 360 c.e.), which in its canon 59 restricted readings in church to 'the canonical books of the New and Old Testament', was apparently the first *ecclesiastical* action giving the canonical books a special and exclusive authority. The list of books itself (canon 60), agreeing with Cyril except for the position of Esther and Job, is a later appendage. Cf. Zahn, *Geschichte* 2, 193-202; Swete, *Introduction*, 209.

[66] Epiphanius, *De Mens. et Pond.* 22f. E.g. there are twenty-two generations from Adam to the twelve patriarchs, therefore there are twenty-two Hebrew letters 'from Aleph to Tau'. The Jews have twenty-two canonical books – 'there being twenty-seven but counted as twenty-two' – with five double books, just as there are twenty-two Hebrew letters with five double letters. There are twenty-two works of God in creation and twenty-two sextaria (pints) in a modius (peck), just as there are twenty-two letters and twenty-two sacred books. In *De Mens. et Pond.* 4 he arranges the OT into four pentateuchs – Law, Poets, Holy Writings, Prophets – plus two other books (Ezra, Esther).

[67] In the *Panarion*, i.e. *Haer.* 8:6 (= 1:1, 9 [6]) Epiphanius agrees with Cyril in the content though not in the sequence of books. In *De Mens. et Pond.* 4f. and 22-24, written some fifteen years later, he gives a different sequence and does not mention the additions to Jeremiah. However, Epiphanius (*De Mens. et Pond.* 5) explains that he includes the additions with the book Jeremiah 'though the Epistles (of Baruch and the Letter) are not included by the Hebrews: they join to Jeremiah only the book of Lamentations'.

[68] Zahn, *Geschichte* 2, 222, 224 is certainly mistaken in supposing that Epiphanius wants to 'smuggle in' the Septuagint (apocryphal) books while professing to adhere to the twenty-two books of the Hebrew canon. For Epiphanius is at pains to single out the 'useful and beneficial' apocryphal books of Wisdom and Ben Sira from the canonical twenty-two and to explain that he includes the 'Letters' appended to Jeremiah while the Hebrews do not.

[69] Epiphanius, *De Mens. et Pond.* 23. It is not derived from Origen; Audet, 'Hebrew-Aramaic List', relates it to the list in the Bryennios manuscript (photograph in Lightfoot, *Apostolic Fathers* I/1, 474) whose source he dates to the first or early second century. The 27 books of the Bryennios canon are Genesis, Exodus, Leviticus, Joshua, Deuteronomy, Numbers, Ruth, Job, Judges, Psalms, Kings, (1, 2, 3, 4), Chronicles (1, 2), Proverbs, Ecclesiastes, Song of Songs, Jeremiah, Twelve (Minor Prophets), Isaiah, Ezekiel, Daniel, Esdras (1, 2), Esther.

These are the twenty-seven books given by God to the Jews. But they are to be counted as twenty-two, the number of the Hebrew letters, since ten books are doubled and reckoned as five . . .[70] There are also two other books near to them in substance (ἀμφιλέκτῳ), the Wisdom of Ben Sira and the Wisdom of Solomon, besides some other apocryphal (ἐν-αποκρύφων) books. All these holy books (ἱεραὶ βίβλοι) also taught Judaism the things kept by the law until the coming of our Lord Jesus Christ.

His distinction between the canonical (ῥητά, ἐνδιάθετα) and the apocryphal books is stated more precisely in *De Mensuris et Ponderibus* 4.

In these passages Epiphanius, a disciple of Athanasius, agrees with the Alexandrian in identifying two classes of books that are read in the church. Unlike Athanasius, he names the second class 'apocrypha' and, similar to Augustine (*De Doct. Christ.* 2:12f.), can regard both as 'holy books' or 'divine writings' (*Haer.* 76:1). That the 'apocrypha' have no special connection with his OT is evident also from the fact that he (again like Athanasius) can mention them, *viz.* Wisdom and Ben Sira, after the NT books.

In conclusion, among the fourth-century writers of Asia Minor, Palestine and Egypt[71] the scholarly judgment of the Eastern church is intelligible and relatively consistent, and it rests upon appeal to ancient Christian tradition. It is divided only on the sequence and numbering of the books and on the inclusion of Esther, points at issue already in Judaism. It departs from the rabbinic determinations only with respect to the Septuagint additions to Jeremiah and (apparently) other books, seemingly content to follow the conviction of earlier Christian scholars, e.g. Justin and Origen, that the masoretic rather than the Septuagint text was defective.

At the same time these writers were quite prepared to recognize certain extra-canonical works as a second rank of holy books, to cite them author-

---

[70] From *De Mens. et Pond.* 4 it becomes clear that the double books are Judges-Ruth, 1-2 Chronicles, 1-2 Kingdoms (= Samuel), 3-4 Kingdoms, and 1-2 Esdras which 'also is counted as one'. Jeremiah-Lamentations-Letter-Baruch is counted as one among the twenty-seven and therefore, is not a double book. In *De Mens. et Pond.* 23 Epiphanius is not embarrassed to admit that, beyond the five double books, 'there is also another little book called Kinot' (= Lamentations) joined to Jeremiah. This shows that he is not a prisoner to his number analogies.

[71] The judgement of the fourth-century Syrian church is less clear. The *Apostolic Constitutions* (2:57, 2), extant in Syriac, gives the groupings of OT books without naming them all individually. The Syriac OT, the Peshitta, which may be Jewish in origin (cf. the article of Dirksen, above), apparently contained only the books of the masoretic canon at the beginning. But by the fourth century it, like the Septuagint, had added apocryphal books, books that also were being cited as 'Scripture'. Cf. Jellicoe, *Septuagint and Modern Study*, 246-49; van Puyvelde, 'Versions Syriaques', 836; Zahn, *Geschichte* 2, 227ff.

itatively[72] and to include them in the same volume with canonical scripture.[73] In this matter also they followed ancient practice. However, while they were able to differentiate the two kinds of holy books, the popular mind of the church increasingly mixed and confused them. The popular attitude posed a danger not only for the integrity of the canon received from Judaism but also for the canonical principle itself. It was challenged and resisted by one man above all, who in spite of many faults was 'the great representative of Western learning, its true head and glory, and the rich source from which almost all critical knowledge of Holy Scripture in the Latin Churches was drawn for almost ten centuries'.[74] In his historical knowledge, his scholarship and industry he can be compared in the ancient church only with Origen, and in his judgment on the canon he was unsurpassed. The man was Jerome. He can be best understood in the light of the general situation in the Western church of his time.

THE WESTERN CHURCH: HILARY AND RUFINUS. The church in the West produced no list of OT canonical books before the fourth century. As its Bible it had the Old Latin version(s) and the Septuagint from which it was translated,[75] both of which mixed together rather indiscriminately canonical and other ancient Jewish religious books. The Latin church, which by the fourth century was the church throughout the West, was separated by language and custom, even more than the Greek Church, from its Jewish origins. In its popular expression, at least, it regarded its version of the OT as 'the Bible' and resisted or accepted only reluctantly and gradually even the new Latin translation of Jerome.[76]

---

[72] E.g. Gregory Nazianzus, *Orat.* 29:16f.: 'from the divine oracles', followed by a score of biblical passages and one apocryphal saying (Wisdom 7:26); 45:15: 'the Scripture', referring to phrases from Judith 5:6 and Ps 138:9. Among earlier writers cf. *Barn.* 4:3: 'concerning which it is written, as Enoch says' (1 Enoch?); 16:5: 'the Scripture says' (1 Enoch 89:56?); Hermas, *Vis.* 2:3, 4: 'as it is written in Eldad and Modad'; Clement Alexandrinus, *Strom.* 1:21: 'for it is written in Esdras' (1 Esdras 6-7?); Origen, *Luke: Homily* 3: 'the Scripture promised' (Wisdom 1:2); Cyprian, *Epistulae* 73 (74), 9: 'as it is written' (1 Esdras 4:38-40); Irenaeus, *Haer.* 4:20, 2: 'Well did the Scripture say' (Hermas, *Mand.* 1:1). See notes 63, 100.

[73] The fourth-century Septuagint codices, Sinaiticus and Vaticanus, both contain the apocryphal books of Wisdom, Ben Sira, Tobit and Judith. Vaticanus also has Greek 1 Esdras; Sinaiticus, 1 and 4 Maccabees. The Septuagint apparently had this inclusive character from the beginning of its codex form, i.e. in the second or early third century. Cf. Swete, *Introduction*, 265-88.

[74] Westcott, *Survey*, 180f.

[75] But see Jellicoe, *Septuagint and Modern Study*, 251. Sparks, 'Latin Bible', 102f. calls attention to Jewish (-Christian) influences in the 'haphazard and gradual' process of translation, and Cantera, 'Puntos de contacto', 223-40, finds that the Old Latin has points of contact with the targum and with the Peshitta, and that it probably has a targumic origin. See Kedar, above, pp. 308-11.

[76] For Augustine's reservations cf. *De Civ. Dei* 18:43. See also Augustine, *Epistulae* 71:5 (cf. *DCB* 3, 45), where it is related that a north African congregation loudly corrected its bishop when he, reading Jerome's translation, differed from the traditional wording.

This state of affairs is reflected by the *Mommsen Catalogue*, which was probably composed in north Africa in 359 C.E.[77] In its OT list it numbers the apocryphal books of 1 and 2 Maccabees, Tobit, Judith, and perhaps (under the title 'Solomon') Ben Sira and Wisdom. At the conclusion it compares the twenty-four 'canonical books' with the twenty-four elders of Revelation (4:4). However, the total can be squared with the enumerated books only by arbitrary combinations and appears to be a number, traditional in some circles of the Western church,[78] that has been gratuitously appended to a list with which it has no essential connection. Like certain Greek and Latin biblical codices, the Mommsen Catalogue appears to represent not a critical opinion but a popular usage with which the traditional twenty-four books were then identified. It indicates a changed situation from the early third-century African church where Tertullian (*De Cult. Faem.* 1:3; cf. Epiphanius, *De Mens. et Pond.* 4), in deference to the Hebrew Bible, qualified his use of 1 Enoch with the comment that it was 'not admitted into the Jewish ark'.

Two other sources, that at first look promising, prove to be of little help in determining the canon used in the West. Philaster (d. 397) bishop of Brescia, Italy, states with reference to the OT that 'nothing else ought to be read in the catholic church but the law and the prophets' . . .[79] But he does not identify the books. Equally unhelpful is the *Decretum Gelasianum*,[80] which is usually attributed to Gelasius, bishop of Rome from 492-496 C.E., but in some manuscripts is credited to the Roman bishop Damasus (d. 384). Its second section contains an OT catalogue including apocryphal books that, in the opinion of some scholars, represents a canon promulgated by Damasus at the council of Rome in AD 382. However, Epiphanius, who participated in the council, had only a few years before endorsed a canon limited to the twenty-two books of the Hebrew Bible, and he would not likely have joined in commending as divine Scripture 'which the universal catholic church receives'[81] books that he had earlier set apart as apocrypha. More significantly, the *Decretum* is extant only in a later compilation of mixed vintage, and it is impossible to say what the list may have

---

[77] On the provenance cf. Zahn, *Geschichte* 2, 154f. It is also known as the Cheltenham List from the place where one of the two extant manuscripts was found. It is reproduced and evaluated by Zahn, *Geschichte* 2, 143-56, 1007-12. Cf. also Sanday, 'Cheltenham List', 217-303.

[78] A total of twenty-four books is mentioned also by Hilary (*Prol. in Libr. Pss.*), who compares it to the twenty-four letters of the Greek alphabet; by Victorinus of Pettau (d. 304, *Comm. on Apcl.* 4:6, 8 cited in Zahn, *Geschichte* 2, 338); and by Ps-Tertullian (= ?Commodian, c. 250 C.E.), *Poem against Marcion* 4:251-65 (Roberts-Donaldson, *Ante-Nicene Fathers* 4, 160). Jerome, *Prologus Galeatus*, states that some Jews count twenty-four books in their canon; the twenty-four count in the West also probably has its origin in Jewish tradition or usage.

[79] Philaster, *Treatise on Heresies* 88 (c. 385 C.E.). Cf. Zahn, *Geschichte* 2, 237.

[80] Cf. von Dobschütz, *Das Decretum-Gelasianum*, who gives the text (24-26) and concludes (348-51) that it is a private work, compiled in Italy in the sixth century.

[81] *Decretum Gelasianum* 2, Title: '*quid universalis catholica recipiat ecclesia*'. Cf. Zahn, *Geschichte* 2, 261n.; von Dobschütz, *Das Decretum Gelasianum*, 24. Apocryphal books included in the list are Wisdom, Ben Sira, Tobit, 1 Greek Esdras, Judith, 1-2 Maccabees.

looked like in an original fourth-century document if, in fact, such a document ever existed. The list cannot, therefore, be regarded as a reliable witness to the canon received in the West in the fourth century.[82]

At about the time that the Mommsen Catalogue appeared in north Africa, Hilary (d. 367), bishop of Poitiers in Gaul, published a canon of the OT in the prologue to his commentary on the Psalms.[83] It consists of the twenty-two books of the Hebrew Bible and of our present OT although some books, like Jeremiah, may represent the longer Septuagint text-forms. Apparently influenced by the catalogues of the Greek church, it represents the canon also accepted by some churches and/or teachers in the West. For it concludes with the comment that some 'by adding Tobit and Judith count twenty-four books'. This alludes to a tendency in the West, observable in the Mommsen Catalogue, to accommodate a traditional twenty-four book count to the popular use of apocryphal writings.

Rufinus (d. 410), presbyter of Aquileia in northeast Italy, who had long known Hilary's views,[84] set forth the same canonical standard in that country that Hilary had published in France.[85] He presents a list that in two respects is remarkable. Like the Greek Fathers generally, it limits the OT books to the twenty-two books of the Hebrew canon. But unlike any known Christian catalogue, it follows a sequence like that of Josephus three centuries before: Law (5) + Prophets (13) + Hymns and precepts (4).[86] In this respect he does not follow Origen but, since he appeals to the 'records of the fathers' (*ex patrum monumentis*), he presumably received the sequence from a Christian tradition. Possibly he deduced it from the account of Josephus found in Eusebius, but more likely he found it elsewhere.

Like several Eastern writers, Rufinus distinguishes three classes of 'scriptures': canonical, ecclesiastical and apocryphal. He places the ecclesiastical writ-

---

[82] Otherwise: Schwarz, 'Zum Decretum Gelasianum' 168; Turner, 'Latin Lists', 554f.; Zahn, *Geschichte* 2, 259-67. The supposition of Howorth 'Influence', followed by Sundberg, *Old Testament*, 148f., that Jerome accepted the canonicity of the apocrypha at the Council and later changed his opinion, only adds conjecture to conjecture.

[83] Hilary, *Comm. in Pss.*, Preface 15: Moses (5), Joshua, Judges-Ruth, Kingdoms (1, 2), Kingdoms (3, 4), Chronicles (1, 2), Ezra (= Ezra-Nehemiah), Psalms; Solomon: Proverbs, Ecclesiastes, Song of Songs; Twelve (Minor) Prophets, Isaiah, Jeremiah-Lamentations-Letter, Daniel, Ezekiel, Job, Esther.

[84] Jerome, *Epistulae* 5:2: '(Send) me Hilary's commentary on the Psalms . . . which I copied for (Rufinus) at Trêves . . .'

[85] Rufinus, *Exposito Symboli* 34 (36). Rufinus can elsewhere defend the Septuagint additions, e.g. to Daniel (*Apol.* 2:35). But this is more a textual than a canonical question, as it was also for Origen and for Cyril.

[86] *Ibid.* 35f. (37f.): Five of Moses: Genesis, Exodus, Leviticus, Numbers, Deuteronomy; Joshua, Judges-Ruth, Kingdoms (4) 'which the Hebrew count as two', Chronicles, Esdras (2) 'which (the Hebrews) count as one', Esther; of the Prophets: Isaiah, Jeremiah, Ezekiel, Daniel, Twelve (Minor) Prophets, Job; Psalms, Three of Solomon: Proverbs, Ecclesiastes, Song of Songs. Unlike Josephus, there is no demarcation between a second and third division of the canon. For the text cf. Zahn, *Geschichte* 2, 240-44; for an ET, Kelly, *Rufinus' Commentary*.

ings – Wisdom, Ben Sira, Tobit, Judith, Maccabees – after the list of OT and NT books, thereby avoiding any implication that they belong to his canonical OT and states that they are not to be used as authority 'for the confirmation of doctrine' *(ex his fidei confirmandam)*. He designates as apocrypha those books that are explicitly excluded from the churches' corporate life and worship. His repeated references to 'the fathers' or 'the ancients' as the transmitters of the canon show that he derives his understanding of the matter not from popular usage but from traditional authorities such as Cyril (whom he must have met in Jerusalem), Origen and other Fathers whose writings he had read. Rufinus gives the impression that he is not so much opposing a different canon currently advocated in Italy as he is clarifying uncertain distinctions between canonical and uncanonical books, distinctions that had been preserved among the Greek theologians but were less clearly perceived among the churches of the West.

AUGUSTINE. Of the three Western witnesses to the OT canon discussed above – the Mommsen Catalogue from north Africa, Hilary in Gaul and Rufinus in Italy – only the first identifies apocryphal writings as canonical. These testimonies probably reflect in substantial measure the differing regional attitudes of the Latin church in the latter half of the fourth century. The churches of Italy and Gaul, which had been served by prominent Greek-speaking writers until the beginning of the third century, remained undecided or, at least, of two minds on the question of the canon. On the other hand the churches in north Africa, which from the beginning of the third century exercised an increasingly important role in Western Christianity, had apparently reached a settled acceptance of apocryphal writings and received them at full parity with the other Scriptures.

The north African attitude received an official standing in the canon promulgated at the council of Hippo 393 C.E. and was reaffirmed by two councils at Carthage (397, 419 C.E.).[87] These resolutions, which rested on no appeal to ancient patristic authority and which apparently reflected only the consensus of contemporary usage in Africa, drew no distinction between canonical and ecclesiastical, i.e. apocryphal writings. Both were equated under the dictum 'Nothing shall be read in church under the name of divine Scriptures except canonical Scriptures'.

At these provincial assemblies Augustine bishop of Hippo (d. 430) exercised an influential role, and his name is largely responsible for the far-reaching

---

[87] For the text and the problem of interpolation cf. Zahn, *Geschichte* 2, 246-59. For the OT the councils approved the following 'canonical scriptures': Genesis, Exodus, Leviticus, Numbers, Deuteronomy, Joshua, Judges, Ruth, Kingdoms (4), Chronicles (2), Job, Psalter, Solomon (5), Twelve (Minor) Prophets, Isaiah, Jeremiah, Daniel, Ezekiel, Tobit, Judith, Esther, Esdras (2). A concluding instruction of the Council of 397 C.E. that the transpontine (Roman) church be consulted for a confirmation of the approved canon apparently did not achieve its desired end, for in the renewed affirmation in 419 C.E. the confirmation of Boniface bishop of Rome 'and other bishops of those parts' is again requested.

influence of their decisions.[88] Yet, unlike the councils, the bishop himself did not make an unqualified equation of canonical and apocryphal books. Before his conversion Augustine was for some years an adherent of Manicheism, a sect that was then active in north Africa and that made use of heretical apocrypha to promote its teachings among the Christians. This context best explains both Augustine's concern to circumscribe the writings used in the churches and, at the same time, his relative lack of interest in distinguishing among them the books 'accepted by all catholic churches' from those 'not accepted by all'.[89] In the first half of his treatise *On Christian Doctrine*, written soon after the council of Hippo, he draws this distinction[90] and proceeds to list the 'whole canon of scriptures'. Within the OT section he names a number of apocryphal books with the concluding comment, 'The authority of the Old Testament is restricted *(terminatur)* to these forty-four books'.[91]

Like Epiphanius, Augustine uses the term 'divine scriptures' of a broad category of religious writings of which the 'canonical scriptures' form only a part and, among the canonical, he distinguishes between universally accepted and disputed books.[92] Thus, he appears to recognize a three-fold classification of religious writings common in the East and sometimes known there as canonical, ecclesiastical and apocryphal. But he termed the first two classes 'canonical', apparently held the distinction between them rather lightly and, in any case, failed to impress it upon his readers and upon the north African councils. Furthermore, apparently reluctant to offend popular piety,[93] Augustine preferred to rely on the traditional usage of the churches and on patristic citations to establish the limits of the canon. He shows little knowledge of the Fathers' express canonical statements. For a more acute perception of the issues involved, one must turn to Jerome who, though he lacked the theological creativity of Augustine, was in matters of church history better informed and in spite of a certain narrowness was on this issue gifted with a more critical faculty.

---

[88] As the survey by Westcott (*Survey*, 191-291) shows, even in the Middle Ages the canonical parity of the apocrypha was by no means universally acknowledged.

[89] Cf. Westcott, *Survey*, 185.

[90] Augustine, *De Doct. Chris.* 2:12.

[91] *Ibid.* 2:13: Five of Moses: . . . , Joshua, Judges, Ruth, Kingdoms (4), Chronicles (2), Job, Tobit, Esther, Judith, Maccabees (2), Esdras (2); the Prophets: Psalms, Three of Solomon: Proverbs, Song of Songs, Ecclesiastes; Wisdom, Ecclesiasticus (= Ben Sira); Twelve (Minor) Prophets: Hosea, Joel, Amos, Obadiah, Jonah, Micah, Nahum, Habkkuk, Zephaniah, Haggai, Zechariah, Malachi; Four Major Prophets: Isaiah, Jeremiah, Daniel, Ezekiel.

[92] Cf. Augustine, *De Civ. Dei*: Although 'some writings left by Enoch . . . were divinely inspired . . ., (they) were omitted from the canon of scripture . . . of the Hebrew people' (15:23). 'Three books (of Solomon) . . . are received as of canonical authority, Proverbs, Ecclesiastes and Song of Songs'; two others, Wisdom and Ecclesiasticus, 'are not his but the church of old, especially the Western received them into authority . . .' (17:20). The books of Maccabees are not recognized by the Jews as canonical, but 'the church accepts (them) as canonical because they record the great and heroic sufferings of certain martyrs' (18:36). Cf. Augustine, *On the Soul* 3:2: 'Scripture has spoken' (Wis 1:5).

[93] Cf. Augustine, *Epistulae* 82:35 (end); *De Civ. Dei* 18:43.

JEROME. Jerome of Bethlehem (c. 331-420 C.E.)[94] was born in Dalmatia (= Yugoslavia) near Aquileia in northeast Italy. After his conversion as a student in Rome, he mastered Greek, travelled in Gaul and returned to Aquileia (c. 370 C.E.). In 374 he journeyed to Syria where he adopted a monastic lifestyle, learned Hebrew[95] and was ordained a presbyter. After a brief return to Rome in 382 in the service of the Roman bishop Damasus, he went back to the East and in 386 settled in Bethlehem where until his death he lived in a cell, taught the Scriptures and continually devoted himself to study and to writing.

Jerome began his great work of biblical translation with a Latin rendering from the Septuagint but became convinced, largely by the use of Origen's Hexapla and his own knowledge of Hebrew, that the extant Greek version, no less than the Latin, suffered from many inaccuracies. Like Cyril, he still viewed the original work of the Septuagint as inspired[96] but decided soon after his return to the East to start afresh with a translation directly from the Hebrew text, whose reliability he apparently did not question.

The relationship between Jerome's preference for the Hebrew text and his commitment to the Jewish canon is not entirely clear. The Jewish canon of twenty-two or twenty-four books was observed by some in the West and was known to Jerome very early in his Christian life if not from the beginning:

(1) While in Gaul he copied for Rufinus Hilary's commentary on the Psalms with its canonical catalogue.

(2) He began the study of Hebrew during his first sojourn in the East, some years before his interest in biblical translation.

This indicates an implicit recognition of the priority of the Hebrew Bible, and his translation of certain works of Eusebius and Origen at this time shows the impression that the Greek writers had made upon him. Probably his textual studies, especially his disillusionment with the Septuagint and his use of the Hebrew, sharpened his opinion about the canon but were not the origin of it.

Jerome began his new Latin Bible about 390. In the prologue to the first books translated, Samuel and Kings, and intended as a preface to the whole, he wrote as follows:

> This prologue to the Scriptures may serve as a kind of helmeted preface for all the books that we have rendered from Hebrew into Latin in order that we (all) may know that whatever is outside these is to be set apart among the apocrypha. Accordingly, (the book of) Wisdom, commonly

---

[94] Following Kelly, *Jerome*, 337ff.

[95] Jerome, *Epistulae* 18:10; 125:12. According to Rufinus (*Apol.* 2:9) Jerome also did not know Greek before his conversion.

[96] Cf. the preface to his translation of Chronicles from the Hexaplaric Septuagint (cited by Swete, *Introduction*, 101f.). However, citing Josephus, Jerome appears to restrict the original Septuagint·to the Pentateuch (Preface to the *Book on Hebrew Questions*; cf. *Comm. in Ezek.* 2:5, 12). Cyril restricted it to the twenty-two books of the Hebrew canon. Later (*Apol.* 2:25) Jerome rejected the inspiration of the Seventy.

ascribed to Solomon, and the book of Jesus son of Sirach and Judith and Tobit and the Shepherd are not in the canon.

Apart from the restriction of the OT canon to the Hebrew Bible, the prologue is noteworthy in other respects.

(1) It lists the books of the OT, often with the Hebrew names followed by the Latin, in the masoretic sequence of the Law (5), the Prophets (8) and the Hagiographa (9).[97]

(2) It not only shows an acquaintance with a Hebrew canon of twenty-two books but also explains the origin of the masoretic canon of twenty-four books: some *(nonnulli)* Jews placed Ruth and Lamentations among the Hagiographa, counted them separately and thus obtained a canon corresponding to 'the twenty-four elders of the Apocalypse of John' (cf. Rev. 4:4).[98] The problem of the two different enumerations of the OT books thus appears to be resolved.

(3) The reference to the *helmeted preface*, incorporated into the later title of the prologue, *Prologus Galeatus*, apparently anticipates opposition both to a translation from the Hebrew (rather than from the Septuagint) and to the exclusion from the canon of Septuagint additions. Such opposition was not long in coming, especially from the African church.[99]

(4) The classification 'apocrypha' for non-biblical books used in the church agrees with the terminology of Epiphanius, whom Jerome had known for a decade or more. It also accords with the general attitude of the Greek church although the term 'ecclesiastical' was more often preferred. Like other Christian writers, Jerome introduces apocryphal and canonical citations with similar formulas.[100] But he distinguishes the two kinds of books, in terms reminiscent of Origen and Rufinus, with respect to their authority:

> As the church reads the books of Tobit and Judith and the Maccabees but does not receive them among the canonical scriptures, so also it reads

---

[97] Jerome, *Prol. in Libr. Regum*: Genesis, Exodus, Leviticus, Numbers, Deuteronomy; Joshua, Judges-Ruth, Kingdoms (1, 2), Kingdoms (3, 4), Isaiah, Jeremiah, Ezekiel, Twelve (Minor Prophets); Job, David: Psalms, Solomon: Proverbs, Ecclesiastes, Song of Songs; Daniel, Chronicles (1, 2), Ezra, Esther. 'Ezra' = Ezra-Nehemiah, as the list in his letter to Paulinus shows (see note 98).

[98] A slightly different enumeration is given in a second, annotated catalogue found in Jerome's *Epistulae* 53:8: Genesis, Exodus, Leviticus, Numbers, Deuteronomy, Job, Joshua, Judges, Ruth, Samuel, Kings (1, 2), Twelve Prophets: . . . , Isaiah, Jeremiah, Ezekiel, Daniel, David, Solomon, Esther, Chronicles (1, 2), Ezra-Nehemiah 'in a single book'. The order follows the general sequence of the Hebrew Bible but without the precise sequence or divisions of the Masoretic Text.

[99] Even from Augustine (*Epistulae* 82:35), who was sympathetic to Jerome's intentions. As Swete (*Introduction*, 264-77) rightly observes, the issue was more than translation: much patristic exegesis had been built upon the Septuagint renderings.

[100] E.g. Jerome, *Against the Pelagians* 1:33 (Wis 3:21); Letters 58, 1 (Wis 4:9, 'Solomon says'); 75:2 (Wis 4:11-14, 'as it is written in the book of Wisdom') 66:5 (Sir 3:30, 'it is written'); 77:4 (Bar 5:5, cited as a prophet); *Against Jovianus* 2:3 (Sir 27:5, 'in another place it is written').

676

these two volumes [of Ben Sira and Wisdom] for the edification of the people [but] not as authority for the confirmation of doctrine.[101]

This would perhaps not have been opposed in principle even by Augustine. But Jerome was single-minded and he did not temporize. He never tired of reminding his readers that the Septuagint additions were not part of the canon. Apart from a hasty version of Tobit and Judith, made at the request of friends, and perhaps the additions to Daniel and Esther he declined even to make a translation of books not in the Hebrew canon. He applied the principle in such thoroughgoing fashion probably because he wished to make 'the distinction between the Hebrew canon and the apocrypha as clear in the Latin as it was in the Greek churches'.[102]

CONCLUSIONS

To determine the OT of the early church the above presentation has given priority to explicit canonical affirmations and has interpreted the usage of the writers in the light of them. The opposite approach would infer the canon of the writer from the books that he cites or from the contents of the Septuagint codex that he uses. This not only is a questionable method but also sometimes involves the patristic writer in self-contradictions since he would affirm one canon in his catalogue and reflect another in his citations.

If the approach taken in this essay is correct early Christianity, as it is represented by its writers, received as its OT a collection of twenty-two or, in the later masoretic count, twenty-four books.[103] At the same time many writers quoted authoritatively and occasionally as 'Scripture' documents that they elsewhere explicitly excluded from their canonical catalogues; furthermore, they used a Septuagint that differed in content from their professed canon. How are these discrepancies to be explained?

As we have seen, formulas such as 'Scripture says' or 'it is written' may introduce both express citations of canonical writings and 'rewritten' interpretive renderings of these texts.[104] Equally, they may introduce citations of

---

[101] Jerome, *Prol. in Libr. Sal.*: . . . 'Non ad auctoritatem ecclesiasticorum dogmatum confirmandam' (cf. Fischer, *Biblia Sacra* 2, 957).

[102] Westcott, *Survey*, 182.

[103] On the priority of the twenty-two book arrangement cf. Zahn, *Geschichte*, 2, 336ff.; Hölscher, *Kanonisch und Apokryph*, 25-28; Audet, 'Hebrew-Aramaic List', 145; Katz, 'Old Testament Canon', 199-203. The numerical variation was originally of no consequence for the content of the canon since, as Jerome informs us, it reflects only the arrangement and not the content of the Hebrew Bible. Similarly, Epiphanius, *Panarion* 8:6. Curiously, Beckwith, *Old Testament Canon*, 256-62, thinks that an earlier 24-book enumeration was literally lessened (by merging) to 22 books in order to conform the number of canonical books to the number of letters in the Hebrew alphabet. The earliest reference to a 22-book enumeration appears to be in the first or second century B.C.E.: Jubilees 2:23 (cf. Charles, *Jubilees*, XXXIX-XL, 17f.; Beckwith, *Old Testament Canon*, 235-40).

[104] E.g. 1 Cor 2:9; 2 Cor 6:16-18.

non-canonical documents that are regarded as correct commentary (midrash) on canonical books[105] or as authoritative in some way.[106] Even when they are employed in their technical reference to holy or religious writing, they sometimes have a broader connotation than canonical or covenantal writing.[107] Ordinarily, then, introductory formulas do not in themselves constitute evidence for the canonical authority of the book cited.

The Septuagint originally referred to a Greek version of the Pentateuch translated in Alexandria in the third century B.C.E. and, according to legend, the inspired work of seventy Jewish elders. However, the same name and origin came to be ascribed to the Greek version of the rest of the Hebrew canonical books that by 132 B.C. also existed on Greek scrolls,[108] sometimes with a quite different text-form from the masoretic Bible.[109] Later the name was applied to certain other Jewish religious writings that originated or were translated in Greek.

When the Septuagint was put into codex form, apparently sometime after the mid-second century C.E., it became even more a *corpus mixtum*. In some manuscripts it included two, partially overlapping translations of parts of Chronicles and Ezra-Nehemiah (i.e. 1 Esdras and 2 Esdras) as well as a collection of excerpts from the OT, the Apocrypha and Luke 1-2 (i.e. the Odes). Furthermore, it placed Jewish apocrypha not only among the OT books but also, in one codex, at the end of the NT (the Psalms of Solomon). No two Septuagint codices contain the same apocrypha, and no uniform Septuagint 'Bible' was ever the subject of discussion in the patristic church. In view of these facts the Septuagint codices appear to have been originally intended more as service books than as a defined and normative canon of scripture.[110]

There is no evidence that elements of Diaspora or Palestinian Judaism had an expanded Septuagint canon distinct from the twenty-two book Hebrew canon, and the historical probabilities weigh heavily against such a supposition. There is also no evidence that the ante-Nicene church received or adopted a Septuagint canon although it did apparently consider the Septuagint to be inspired and

---

[105] Jude 14f.; cf. Ellis, *Prophecy*, 225.

[106] E.g. Josh 10:13; 2 Sam 1:18; Eph 5:14; Jas 4:5. See note 52.

[107] E.g. the usage of Gregory, Cyril, Jerome and Augustine noted above, which hardly sprang forth full-grown in the fourth century. For earlier examples cf. Jas 4:5; John 7:38 and probably *Barn.* 16:5 since *1 Enoch* was not in any Septuagint manuscript and, according to Origen, did not circulate in the churches as a 'divine' writing. Beckwith, *Old Testament Canon*, 69-79, 387ff., seems to put too much weight on introductory formulas as an invariable indicator of a reference to canonical authority.

[108] Ben Sira, prologue.

[109] E.g. in Daniel and Esther, which contain considerable additional matter not in the Hebrew text. On the origin of the Septuagint cf. Swete, *Introduction*, 1-28 and Jellicoe, *Septuagint and Modern Study*, 29-73.

[110] The codex gradually replaced the scroll in the early centuries of the Christian era. No codices were found at Qumran (pre-70 C.E.), or Pompeii (pre-79 C.E.). Jerome (d. 420) is said to have been the first scholar to have a library consisting entirely of codices. Cf. Birt, *Buchwesen*, 115; Roberts-Skeat, *Codex*, 61; Paoli, *Rome*, 177f., who dates the first reference to the codex form to 84 C.E.: Martial, *Epigrams* 1:2, 2f. *(libellis)*. See Bar-Ilan, above, pp. 24-25.

its text-forms to be superior to those of the masoretic Bible.[111] Nevertheless, unknowledgeable persons tended to give equal authority to all books used in the church, books that varied from time to time and place to place and that included both apocryphal and other, sometimes heretical books. They were probably confirmed in this attitude by the inclusion of various writings used in church within one or a few codices and tended to equate the resulting volumes with the canonical Bible.

In the face of this situation the fourth century church was compelled to define more clearly the OT canon of the church. The bishops and other writers of the Greek church and, one must assume, the council of Laodicea affirmed on the basis of testimony reaching back to Josephus (96 C.E.) that the twenty-two books of the Hebrew canon and, thus, of the apostles constituted the church's OT. Augustine and the councils of Carthage affirmed as canonical, on the basis of current usage and of citations by the Fathers, an additional number of Jewish apocryphal writings. Even if the north African churches had the theological right to define their canon, the churches of the East, and Jerome as he sharpens and mediates their convictions, had the stronger historical claim to represent the OT canon of Jesus and his apostles. For although the apostolic church left no canonical lists, in all likelihood it agreed with the mainstream of Judaism in this regard. Not without significance for the question is the fact that no explicit quotation from the Septuagintal apocrypha appears in the NT, in Philo or in the literature from Qumran. In its conception of the OT the messianic community of Jesus differed from the mainstream of Judaism not in the content of its Bible but in the interpretive key that it used to open the Bible. Since this key was molded in part by theological conceptions implicit in the process of canonization, it is necessary to consider more closely this aspect of the subject.

The Canon as a Hermeneutical Process

INTRODUCTION

The evidence offered in the preceding section argues that in the first Christian century (Philo, Josephus) and even two centuries earlier (Ben Sira) Judaism possessed a defined and identifiable canon, twenty-two books arranged in three divisions and regarded as an inspired and normative authority for the community. As the church's librarian it preserved and passed on these sacred writings to the Christian community. How the canon of Judaism developed the form and

---

[111] Alexandrian Judaism remained a loyal daughter of Jerusalem even though cultural differences had developed (cf. Feldman, 'Orthodoxy'; Borgen, 'Philo of Alexandria', 257-59). According to Philo, its major spokesman in the first century, it sent tribute (*De Monat.* 2:3) and pilgrims (in Eusebius, *Praep. Evang.* 8:14, 64; cf. Acts 2:10) to Jerusalem. On the status of the apocryphal books in Hellenistic Judaism, see Beckwith, above, pp. 81-84. For a critique of the theory of an Alexandrian canon, Beckwith, *Old Testament Canon*, 382-86.

content in which the apostolic church received and used it requires a further word. First of all, the criteria used in Judaism to set apart the canon from other religious literature are not unimportant for the early church's conception of 'Scripture'. Also, there are scholarly disagreements that need to be evaluated. Finally, the growth of the OT canon involves an interpretive process that continues in the biblical interpretation of Jesus and his apostles and prophets.

THE TRIPARTITE DIVISION OF THE OLD TESTAMENT

THE FAILURE OF THE THREE-STAGE CANONIZATION THEORY. The theory that the three divisions of the Hebrew OT represented three successive acts or stages of canonization was increasingly attractive to nineteenth-century scholars.[112] In its most popular form it postulated the canonization of the Law at the time of Ezra and Nehemiah (Neh 8-10; c.? 400 B.C.E.), the Prophets about 200 B.C.E. and the Hagiographa by the rabbinic academy of Yavne (Jamnia) (c. 90 C.E.).[113] In spite of reservations[114] and opposition[115] it rapidly gained and continues to have a widespread acceptance.[116]

The theory was not unrelated to earlier Roman Catholic hypotheses that, consequent upon the decision of the Council of Trent,[117] sought to show that the

[112] E.g. Westcott, *Survey*, 297-301: 'At the return (from the Exile) a collection of the Prophets was probably made by Ezra and added to the sacred Law. Afterwards the collection of the Hagiographa was . . completed during the period of Persian supremacy' (297).

[113] Graetz (*Kohelet*, 147-73) apparently was the first to attribute to Yavne the role of 'closing' the canon: Both the Law and the Prophets were established by the assembly of Nehemiah since the departure of the Samaritans was occasioned in part by the introduction of readings from the Prophets. The majority of the Hagiographa were confirmed by a rabbinic assembly in c. 65 C.E. and the final two books, Ecclesiastes and Song of Songs, by the school at Yavne. Cf. Beckwith, above, pp. 58-61 (The Date of the Closing of the Canon).

[114] Cf. Smith, *Old Testament*: The work of Graetz is 'a model of confused reasoning' (169). But 'the third collection (of Hagiographa) was formed after the second had been closed' by a sifting process not easily explained (179).

[115] E.g. Beecher, 'Alleged Triple Canon'; Green, *General Introduction*, 19-118, who makes some telling points and shows a commendable caution: 'We have no positive evidence when or by whom the sacred books were collected and arranged' (111). But he offers little evidence for his own hypothesis that the second division of the canon grew with each prophet adding his book until Malachi completed the collection.

[116] Wildeboer, *Canon*, 144; Buhl, *Canon and Text*, 9-12, 25ff.; Ryle, *Canon*, 105, 119: The Tora received its final recognition by the fifth century B.C.E. and the Prophets by 200 B.C.E.; for the Writings 100 C.E. marks an official confirmation that 'had long before been decided by popular use' (133). Cf. Kaiser, *Introduction*, 405-13; Schäfer, 'Die Sogenannte Synode', 54-64, 116-24.

[117] The fourth session (8 April 1546) declared certain apocrypha to be canonical, *viz.* the additions to Esther and Daniel, Ben Sira, Wisdom, Tobit, Judith, 1 and 2 Maccabees. The north African councils were influencial but were not followed precisely. For example, they accepted 1 Esdras (= 3 Esdras) and apparently rejected 2 Maccabees.

Apocrypha had canonical status in first-century Judaism.[118] And it was later adapted to this end.[119] Its popular reception, however, may be largely attributed to the Maccabean (c. 150 B.C.E.) and later dating of certain of the Hagiographa by many scholars of the day. Such dating was incompatible with the older tradition that ascribed the formation of the canon to Ezra and 'the men of the great synagogue' (c. 400-200 B.C.E.),[120] and it produced a pressing need for a new explanation.

The three-stage theory was thought to fill this need, but on several counts it has proved to be unsatisfactory.

(1) It is based not on concrete historical evidence but on inferences, none of which are necessary and some of which are clearly mistaken. Specifically to be faulted is its estimate of the evidence of Josephus, Ben Sira and the academy of Yavne.

(2) For certain books it presupposes a late dating that can no longer be entertained.

a. The testimony of Josephus in c. 96 C.E. to a universal, clearly defined and long settled canon[121] contradicts any theory of an undetermined canon in first-century Judaism. And it cannot easily be set aside. As Thackeray has pointed out, Josephus was writing a closely reasoned polemic against *inter alia* the work of an erudite Alexandrian grammarian,[122] and he could not afford to indulge in careless misstatements that could be thrown back at him. Also, he wrote as a representative of his people and does not transmit only the views peculiar to his own (Pharisaic) religious party or to the Pharisaic-rabbinic traditions:[123]

(1) His canon follows a substantially different arrangement from the rabbis.

(2) He reflects anti-Pharisaic traits elsewhere,[124] and his writings found no apparent acceptance among the rabbis and eventually had to be preserved

---

[118] Genebrard, *Chronographia*, 2, 190 (cited in Cosin, *Scholastic History*, 14): The Hebrew canon was received at the time of Ezra, certain Apocrypha at the translation of the Septuagint (c. 250 B.C.E.) and 1 and 2 Maccabees in the first century C.E. Movers, *Loci Quidam Historiae Canonis*, 20-22: Books peculiar to the Septuagint were at first canonical also in Palestine but were excluded in the second century C.E. in deference to the rabbinic opinion that inspiration ceased with Malachi (*T. Sota* 13:2).

[119] E.g. by Sundberg, *Old Testament*, 108, 126, 129.

[120] Cf. Ryle, *Canon*, 261-83; Graetz, *Kohelet*. Shimon the Just, the last member of the great synagogue according to rabbinic tradition (*M. Avot* 1:2f.), is identified by some with the son of Onias I (c. 300 B.C.E.) and by others with the son of Onias II (c. 200 B.C.E.). See note 149.

[121] Barr, *Holy Scripture*, 49-74, 51, viewing 'canonization' as explicit acts of choosing and listing some books and excluding others, concludes that early Judaism had no 'canon'. He seems to confuse the concept with a particular terminology and process.

[122] Thackeray, *Josephus*, 122f.

[123] *Pace* Meyer, 'Bemerkungen', 298.

[124] Cf. Thackeray, in Thackeray et al., *Josephus* 4, VIII: In the proem to the *Antiquities* Josephus alludes to the legitimacy of paraphrasing the scriptures. In this 'the author is doubtless controverting the views of the contemporary rabbinical schools'.

by the Christians.

Similar to Josephus, and two centuries earlier, the book of Ben Sira also speaks of a tripartite canon of 'the law and the prophets and the rest of the books'. According to the three-stage theory this statement indicates that the law and the prophets were completed collections and 'the rest' or 'the other' books were a less defined miscellany. Apparently the only reason for this odd conclusion is the differing terminology used for the third division. It is scarcely acceptable since even in the first century C.E. the terminology for all three divisions was still flexible: the Psalms could be called 'the law' (John 15:25), 'the law' could be designated 'the writings' (γραφαί, Matt 22:29; cf. Rom 4:3) and 'the law and the prophets' described variously as 'Moses and the prophets' or simply as 'the prophets' (Luke 24:27; Acts 13:27). The statement in Ben Sira mentions each of the three divisions with the same degree of preciseness and, to be meaningful to the reader, it must refer to definite, identifiable books. It could be interpreted otherwise only if one were already convinced that the tripartite canon could not have existed as a subsistent entity at that time.

The rabbinic academy of Yavne affirmed, after discussion, that the Song of Songs and Ecclesiastes 'defiled the hands', that is, were canonical.[125] Such pronouncements were not peculiar to Yavne, resolved nothing and continued into the following centuries.[126] Misunderstanding the proceeding at Yavne as an act of canonization and associating it with other Talmudic discussions addressing quite different questions, advocates of the three-stage theory concluded that the third division of the canon was officially 'closed' at this time. Most likely the questions at Yavne about the Song of Songs and Ecclesiastes had no more to do with the canonization of the OT than the questions of Luther about the letter of James had to do with the canonization of the NT. In so far as they were not discussions of theoretical possibilities, they apparently expressed only a reaffirmation of books long received and now disputed by some.

b. The Qumran library contained all twenty-two books of the Hebrew Bible with the exception of Esther. These books must therefore be dated before 70 C.E. when the community was destroyed, and probably before the accession of Jonathan as high priest in 152 B.C.E., when, apparently, the community separated from the mainstream of Judaism.[127] For books after that time, if written by the other sects, would not likely have found acceptance at Qumran or, if produced by the Qumran sect, would not have been received by the rest of Judaism. Moreover, the textual history of the manuscripts,[128] the dates of

---

[125] M. Eduyot 5:3; T. Eduyot 2:7; M. Yadayim 3:5. Cf. Lewis, 'What Do We Mean'; Newman, 'Council of Jamnia': 'The rabbis seem to be testing a status quo which has existed beyond memory' (349); Schäfer, 'Die sogenannte Synode'.

[126] Jerome, Comm. in Eccl. 12:13f. (c. 390 C.E.); cf. B.T. Megilla 7a (R. Meir, c. 150 C.E.). Cf. Childs, Introduction, 53.

[127] Cf. Beckwith, above, pp. 76-81 (Esther and the Pseudepigrapha in Essenism and the Dead Sea Community).

[128] Cf. Cross, 'Contribution'.

specific scripts and other considerations led W.F. Albright to conclude that, with the exception of Ecclesiastes and Daniel, all of the OT books were written before the end of the Persian period, that is, before 330 B.C.E..[129]

What of Ecclesiastes and Daniel? In the light of Qumran and of other evidence Ecclesiastes cannot have been composed later than the third century B.C.E. and may be considerably earlier.[130] Even Daniel, which in its present form has for the past century usually been assigned to the Maccabean period, viz. 165 B.C.E., must almost certainly have originated before that time.[131] Six manuscript fragments of Daniel reflecting different textual families, one in a script from the second century B.C.E., were found at Qumran.[132] There is also a quotation from Daniel 12:10; 11:32, introduced by the formula, 'As it is written in the book of Daniel the prophet' *(4QFlor* 2:3). As was shown above, introductory formulas are no guarantee of a canonical citation. However, this formula is identical with an earlier one introducing a citation of Isaiah *(4QFlor* 1:15), identifies Daniel as one book (and not a cycle of traditions), and accords with an older division of the Hebrew canon in which Daniel was placed among the Prophets. Customarily today it is supposed that Daniel, originally among the Writings *(Ketuvim)*, was only later placed among the Prophets *(Neviim)*. But the historical evidence, on balance, does not support this view of the matter. The first century witnesses place Daniel among the Prophets. Matthew (24:15) reflects this perspective by its designation of Daniel as 'the prophet'. Josephus (note 25) and the *Bryennios list* (note 69), which J.P. Audet and P. Katz on rather firm grounds date to the late first or early second century, clearly do so.[133] The same is true of the lists of Melito and Origen which illustrate the canon used by certain Palestinian Jews and/or Jewish Christians in the second and early third centuries. Of the early evidence Daniel is counted among the

---

[129] Albright, *Recent Discoveries*, 129; cf. Cross, *Ancient Library*, 165: Qumran supports a dating of the latest canonical Psalms from the Persian period and a *terminus ad quem* for Ecclesiastes in the third century B.C.E.; Williamson, *Israel*, 83-86: the evidence points to the Persian period, i.e. pre-330 B.C.E., for the date of Chronicles.

[130] Cross, 'Contribution'.

[131] For other evidence cf. the form of the Aramaic in Dan 2:4b-7:28, which on balance favours a third-century B.C.E. or earlier date (Albright, 'Date and Personality', 117; Kitchen, 'Aramaic of Daniel', 76, 79); Bate, *Sibylline Oracles*, 64f.: the whole passage (c. 150 B.C.E.) is partly based on Dan 7-9 (65n.). Cf. 1 Macc 1:54; 2:60 with Daniel 11:31; 6:22. Josephus, *Ant.* 11:337, relates a story that Alexander the Great was shown the prophecy of Daniel (8:21) predicting his conquest. Since Josephus (cf. *Ag.Ap.* 1:183-95) used the historian Hecataeus of Abdera (c. 300 B.C.E.) who wrote a book on the relationship of the Jews to Alexander, he presumably found the story there. While he may have elaborated it and perhaps supplied the (obvious) name Daniel, there are no historical reasons to dismiss it as a fiction. Otherwise: Tcherikover, *Hellenistic Civilization*, 42-46.

[132] Cf. Cross, *Ancient Library*, 43, 164n; DiLella, *Daniel*, 72f.

[133] Audet, 'Hebrew-Aramaic List', 145; Katz, 'Old Testament Canon', 196. Otherwise: Beckwith, *Old Testament Canon*, 188, who thinks that the Bryennios list cannot be Jewish 'since it mixes the Prophets and Hagiographa indiscriminately'. But see Orlinsky, 'Prolegomenon', XIX (= Leiman, *Canon and Masorah*, 852): it 'may well be that the Christian, essentially fourfold division of the Bible . . . (is) actually Jewish in origin'.

writings only in *B.T. Bava Batra* 14b, which probably dates (at least) from before the end of the second century. Although *B.T. Bava Batra* 14b may represent an older tradition, it must be judged secondary to the earlier-witnessed and more widely attested order. Qumran, with its reference to 'Daniel the prophet' (*4QFlor* 2:3), lends further weight to this judgment. Given the deep influence of Daniel on the Qumran sect and its known and undisputed canonical standing throughout first-century Judaism, it is altogether likely that at the time the Qumran community became distinct from mainstream Judaism the book was received among them in the canonical collection known in Ben Sira as 'the prophets'.[134]

A Maccabean origin of the Daniel narratives (Dan 1-6) has increasingly given way to the view that they were formed and in use well before the Maccabean period.[135] For a number of reasons the Maccabean origin of the visions (Dan 7-12) is also open to doubt. First of all, (1) it is intrinsically improbable that visions composed as *vaticinia ex eventu* in c. 165 B.C.E. could, within a few decades and without a trace of opposition, be widely and authoritatively received as the revealed word of a sixth century prophet. Also, (2) the theory of the specifically Maccabean origin apparently arose less from historical considerations than from the philosophical assumption that this kind of explicit predictive prophecy was impossible.[136] Furthermore, (3) the theory does not take into account the 'contemporizing' alterations characteristic of the periodic rewriting of biblical books.

To whatever degree the language of Dan 7-12 reflects an origin in the second century B.C.E., it is best explained as a contemporization of an earlier prophecy:[137] (1) The recopying of many OT books was a necessity after the widespread

---

[134] The absence of Daniel in Ben Sira's (48-50) annotations on famous men is no more significant for his canon than is the absence of Ezra or the presence of Enoch. It can also hardly indicate that Ben Sira classified Daniel among the Writings rather than the Prophets since David and Nehemiah, both of whose works were among the Writings, are included.

[135] E.g. Hengel, *Judaism and Hellenism* 1, 113, 29f. ('current . . . in the third century B.C.'). Jepsen, 'Bemerkungen': Apparently there was 'a collection of Daniel narratives and visions already in the time of Alexander' (?chapters 4, 5, 6, 10, 12) supplemented by chapters 2, 7, 8; in the Maccabean period, perhaps, chapters 1, 3 and 4 were added and 7 and 8 elaborated. For an instructive discussion of the date of Daniel cf. Baldwin, *Daniel*, 13-74.

[136] Apparently first made by Porphyry (d. 303). Cf. Archer, *Jerome* (407), 15 Prologue: Porphyry alleged that 'whatever (pseudo-Daniel) spoke of up to the time of Antiochus (Epiphanus) contained authentic history whereas anything that he may have conjectured beyond that point was false, inasmuch as he would not have foreknown the future'.

[137] Cf. Wright, *Daniel*, XIX, 242; Noth, *Gesammelte Studien*, 11-28. Otherwise: Archer, 'Hebrew of Daniel'.

destruction of the Scriptures by Antiochus Epiphanes in c. 169 B.C.E.[138] and such activity, like scribal transmission generally, inevitably included some alterations and also incorporated in greater or lesser degree an 'up-dating' of orthography and terminology along with other explanatory elaboration (midrash). (2) Such elaboration appears earlier in manuscript-transmission and in the translation (as in the Septuagint), revision (as in Esther and Jeremiah) and rewriting (as in Chronicles) of biblical books.[139] (3) Both the Qumran library and the NT make evident that such elaboration was not precluded by the fact that the texts were regarded as canonical scripture and that, on the above analogies, (4) it would very likely have been employed in the transmission of the book of Daniel.

THE CANON AND THE CULT. With the failure of the three-stage canonization theory, at least in its traditional form, the origin and meaning of the tripartite division of the Hebrew Bible remain very open questions.[140] The following suggestions may, it is hoped, contribute to a more satisfactory answer. The tripartite arrangement was, of course, not the only one known in Judaism. The Septuagint preserves a fourfold division – Pentateuch, Historical Writings, Poetic (Wisdom) Literature, Prophets – that is probably pre-Christian,[141] and other sources indicate that a tripartite pattern was not a fixed or necessary conception.[142] The later masoretic Bible in a number of ancient manuscripts shifts to a fourfold division: Pentateuch, Megillot, Prophets, Hagiographa.[143] However, the tripartite scheme, attested by Ben Sira, Josephus and the rabbinic tradition and perhaps by the NT and Philo, was apparently the prevailing usage in first century Judaism. It seems to have arisen from the role of Scripture

---

[138] Cf. 1 Macc 1:56f.; 2 Macc 2:14f.; Josephus, *Ag.Ap.* 1:35f.; Segal, 'Promulgation', 39-45, Cross, 'Contribution', 91. Whether such activity created a standard text (Segal) or one of its forerunners (cf. Cross) need not be discussed here. Beckwith, *Old Testament Canon*, 80-86, 153 argues with some cogency that the standard for canonicity was whether a book was laid up in the Temple and that Judas Maccabaeus was instrumental in regathering the Temple Scriptures after the liberation of Jerusalem in 165 B.C.E. (cf. 2 Macc 2:14), but he is less convincing in his view that Judas also classified and ordered the sacred books in the arrangement later found in *B.T. Bava Batra* 14b.

[139] Cf. Talmon, 'Textual Study'. On the orthographic modernization of transmitted texts cf. Kitchen, 'Aramaic of Daniel', 60-65; Kutscher in 'Current Trends', 399-403.

[140] For an attempt to reconstruct the beginnings of it cf. Freedman, 'Law and Prophets': The Law and Former Prophets (Genesis-2 Kings) were published as one literary unit by 550 B.C.E. and supplemented the Latter Prophets (Isaiah, Jeremiah, Ezekiel, Twelve) before 450 B.C.E.

[141] So, Orlinsky, 'Prolegomenon' XIX-XX. Cf. Swete, *Introduction*, 217ff. It may possibly be reflected by Philo (see note 29).

[142] 'The Law and the Prophets', often used for the whole of Scripture (e.g. in Matt 5:17; 7:12), expresses a twofold division. Cf. 2 Macc 2:13 (c. 100 B.C.E.): Nehemiah 'collected the books about the kings (= ?Samuel-Kings) and the Prophets, the works of David and the letters of Kings concerning sacred offerings' (= ?Ezra 6-7). Although probably traditional idiom, such passages show that the divisions of scripture were not always perceived within a tripartite framework.

[143] Cf. Ryle, *Canon*, 292. The five Megillot together with the Pentateuch also were sometimes transmitted separately.

in the cultus, if the synagogue readings and the activity and traditional picture of Ezra are accurate guides in the matter.

At least from the first century and probably much earlier the Law and the Prophets were read in the synagogue every sabbath on a systematic basis;[144] the Hagiographa, on the other hand, were used only on special occasions or, in the case of the Psalms, for different parts of the service. Certain rabbis rearranged the masoretic Bible into four divisions 'for liturgical or ritual purposes',[145] and others, who at an earlier time transferred two of the Megillot (Ruth, Lamentations) and the book of Daniel from the Prophets to the Hagiographa, may have been motivated by similar considerations.[146] That is, if Ruth, Lamentations and Daniel were excluded from the cycle of weekly readings or were designated for reading only on special occasions, this would on the above analogy have resulted in their transferral to the Hagiographa.

Jewish tradition associates Ezra the priest both with the establishment of the public reading of Scripture and with the ordering of the canon.[147] If it in part represents a later idealized picture, it supports nonetheless an early and close connection between the canon and the cultic usage.[148] It also supports the supposition that between the time of Ezra (c. 400 B.C.E.) and the prologue of Ben Sira (c. 132 B.C.E.), when the tripartite canon is first attested, priestly circles or another body or bodies related to them[149] classified the biblical books to accord with their use in worship. When the use varied, these circles apparently reclassified the affected book within the canonical divisions, a relatively simple procedure before the advent of the codex. They thereby maintained the relationship established by Ezra between the canonical structure and the hermeneutical context.

THE GROWTH OF THE OLD TESTAMENT

TYPOLOGICAL CORRESPONDENCE. The OT displays a hermeneutical progression in

---

[144] Acts 13:15, 27; 15:21; Luke 4:16; cf. Josephus *Ag.Ap.* 2:175; Philo, *De Somn.* 2:127; *M. Megilla* 3:4. Cf. Perrot, above, pp. 149-59.

[145] Ginsburg, *Introduction*, 3.

[146] This was first suggested to me in a lecture of A.A. MacRae, who apparently was following his teacher, R.D. Wilson, *Studies*, 59ff., 64. Cf. also Wilson, 'Book of Daniel', 404 f., 408. Anti-apocalyptic tendencies in post-70 rabbinic Judaism could have occasioned the transfer of Daniel to the Hagiographa and, consequently, its removal from the Haftara readings.

[147] Re the canon cf. *4 Ezra* 14:38-48; *B.T. Bava Batra* 15a; *B.T. Sanhedrin* 21b-22a; Ezra 7:6. Re public reading cf. Neh 8-10; *B.T. Bava kamma* 82a; Perrot, above, pp. 149-50; Elbogen, *Gottesdienst*, 157f. On the problem of dating Ezra's ministry cf. Klein, 'Ezra and Nehemiah', 370ff.; Talmon, 'Ezra and Nehemiah'; Wright, *The Date*.

[148] Cf. Östborn, *Cult and Canon*, 15ff., 96f.

[149] Kuenen, 'Groote Synagoge', showed that most rabbinic references to a 'great synagogue' between Ezra and Shimon the Just are late and confused. But his conclusion (149) that they are based on a fiction created out of Neh 8-10 is doubtful. *M. Avot* 1:1f. and, perhaps, *B.T. Bava Batra* 15a probably preserve traditions of the role (though not the name) of some such body or bodies in the reception and transmission of the canon. See note 120; cf. Bacher, 'Synagogue, The Great'.

which, on the one hand, sacred accounts of God's acts in the past provided models for later accounts of his present and future activity and, on the other hand, the received sacred literature was from time to time conformed to its contemporary or future application and fulfillment. The first aspect of the process is evident in the way in which the prophets 'placed the new historical acts of God . . . in exactly the same category as the old basic events of the canonical history':[150] a new creation,[151] a new Exodus,[152] a new covenant,[153] a new Davidic kingdom,[154] a new Zion or temple.[155] It also is present in those Psalms (e.g. 8, 68, 106, 136) in which the appeal or praise for God's present and future help is keyed to his past acts of redemption. It represents a typological correspondence that is not a mere cyclical repetition but rather a progression in which the new surpasses the old. The process appears to embody a canonical principle as well. That is, inspired prophetic writings are received as normative for the faith and worship of the community as they are recognized to be valid contemporary expressions of and abiding supplements to the ancient election and covenantal traditions. As we hope to show in the following essay, the early Christians' understanding of the OT and its actualization in their own time and community stands within the same perspective.

REWRITING. A second aspect of the hermeneutical process, also to be found later in the NT, likewise involves a contemporization of God's ancient word and work. However, it carries this out in a different way, by a rewriting of the ancient accounts. The process takes several forms: (1) It appears in Deuteronomy (a 'second law') as a reworking and reapplication of Exodus traditions and in Chronicles as a reinterpretation of (mainly) Samuel-Kings. The same procedure is carried further in the non-canonical 1 Esdras, a Greek rewriting of parts of Chronicles and Ezra-Nehemiah.[156] (2) A kind of rewriting also occurs within a book's own manuscript transmission. This has been suggested above in the case of Daniel. On a broader scale it appears to be supported by the textual

---

[150] Von Rad, *Old Testament Theology* 2, 113, cf. 112-19, 272; cf. Goppelt, 'τύπος', 254.

[151] Isa 11:6-9; 51:3; 65:17; 66:22; Ezek 36:35; 47:7-12; cf. Dan 7:13f. with Ps 8:4ff. and Gen 1:26 ('dominion'); Hooker, *Son of Man*, 11-32; Ellis, *Prophecy*, 167.

[152] Jer 16:14f.; Isa 11:15f.; 43:16-21; 48:20f.; 51:9ff.; cf. Ezek 36:8 with 47:13.

[153] Hos 2:18 (20); Jer 31:31f.; Isa 54:10.

[154] Hos 3:5; Amos 9:11; Mic 5:2 (1); Isa 11:1; Ezek 37:24; cf. 2 Sam 7:6-16; Ps 2:7; Ellis, *Prophecy*, 199f.

[155] Isa 2:2ff.; 54:11f.; Ezek 40-48; Amos 9:11.

[156] Cf. the examples in Driver, *Deuteronomy*, VIII-LX; XXXVII-XXXIX; Willi, *Die Chronik*, 48-198; Childs, 'Midrash', 53ff. and the literature cited; Ackroyd, 'The Chronicler'.

history of other biblical books in both their 'creative' and 'recensional' stages.[157] That is, the kind of interpretive alteration usually associated with later scribal activity was in all likelihood made from time to time from the inception of a book. The circles that 'reproduced' the work (with variations) even as they transmitted it thus contributed to its final canonical form. Among other things the alterations involved a reordering and contemporizing of the text, as is evident in the Septuagint and may be inferred at least in some cases for the Hebrew text underlying the Septuagint.[158] (3) Finally, the older writings were likewise brought into the present by the exposition and application of the later canonical writers. For example, Ezek 16 is an allegory built upon themes drawn from earlier books and Ps 132 apparently a 'midrashic reflection' on 2 Sam 7.[159]

The hermeneutical process seen to be unfolding within the OT continued beyond the canonical boundaries. In some circles, for example, Jeremiah, Daniel and Esther were supplemented with material not received as canonical by messianic (i.e. Christian) and rabbinic Judaism and their predecessors. The book of Jubilees provided a rewriting of Genesis, 1 Esdras of Chronicles-Ezra; and in a somewhat different way Qumran's *Temple Scroll* reworked and supplemented parts of the Pentateuch and Ben Sira, along the lines of Proverbs, extended further the re-understanding of the Law in terms of Wisdom. Yet none were received as canonical. And, of course, at some point literary alterations and supplements in the manuscript-transmission were no longer regarded as part and parcel of a canonical book's essential form but as departures from it.

THE LIMITS OF THE CANON. What caused the hermeneutical process characteristic of the canonical progression to cease providing the valid form and continuation of the canon? Our sources provide no clear answer, but they do permit certain

---

[157] Cf. Talmon 'Textual Study': 'It appears that the extant text types must be viewed as the remains of a yet more variegated transmission of the Bible text in the preceding centuries' (325). An 'undetermined percentage of these *variae lectiones* (in biblical manuscripts at Qumran) derive from the ongoing literary processes of an intra-biblical nature . . .' (380). Cf. Gooding, 'Recent Popularization' 130f.; Gordon, 'Septuagint account'. Admittedly, this view of the matter complicates the problem of dating OT books since some internal evidence may reflect the time of a 'revision' and not of the origin of the work.

[158] E.g. Isa 9:11 (LXX: Greeks; MT: Philistines). Cf. Gooding, *Relics*; *idem*, 'Text-sequence'; *idem*, 'Problems of Text and Midrash', 28: The Septuagint 3 Kingdoms 'is quite obviously a commentary on I Kings'. Further cf. Sanders, *Canon and Community*, 22f., 30ff., whose views are both similar to and critiqued by Childs, *Introduction*, 56f., 171ff., 367-70, 434ff. Neither Sanders nor Childs gives sufficient attention to the specific (prophetic disciple-circle) context for the creative rewriting and up-dating of received prophetic books. To my mind a recognized inspired status of the traditioning circles best explains how the 'community', who are the recipients not the makers of books, could accept the rewritten material on a par and in continuity with the prophetic *Vorlage*. Cf. Blenkinsopp, *Prophecy and Canon*, 134-37; Sturdy, 'Authorship', 149f.; Carroll, 'Canonical Criticism'; Foul, 'Canonical Approach'.

[159] Cf. Bloch, 'Midrash', 1271, 1274. For a somewhat different re-use of biblical traditions cf. Nickelsburg, *Resurrection* 82-92.

inferences to be drawn. They do not speak of a 'closing' of the canon, which is apparently a modern conception, but rather of a time after which no subsequent writings were placed on a par with canonical books. Josephus marks this time at the death of Artaxerxes; the rabbis refer to the same general period or, alternatively, to the time of Ben Sira. More significantly, however, both sources also associate the cessation of the growth of the canon with the cessation of a particular kind of prophetic inspiration or succession.[160] That is, the chronological limits of the canon were inextricably combined with convictions about the activity of the prophetic Spirit in the community as well as in the individual writing.

The communities of Qumran and of Jesus, in which prophetic manifestations continue to be quite evident,[161] do not follow the judgement of Josephus and rabbinic Judaism. In their respective ways they continue a canonical progression that resulted *inter alia* in a supplement to the twenty-two book canon received in pre-Maccabean Judaism. They do so not by an undefined 'openness' with regard to the canon but by the recognition of the prophetic inspiration and normative authority of certain of their own books. Although it is difficult to document explicitly, Qumran adherents very probably gave such recognition to the works of their Teacher. The Christian community clearly did so for certain of its writings, not only the NT as it was finally defined but also – from a very early time – individual books and traditions.

The community of Jesus, then, did not differ from other groups in Judaism in the OT canon that it received, but it continued a hermeneutical process that inevitably brought into being a further supplement to the ancient canon. That hermeneutical process also brought about a radically new perception of the OT itself. But this must be considered in a separate essay.

Bibliography

A brief but very useful survey of the canonical lists and the discussions and decisions about the canon in the early church is WESTCOTT's *The Bible in the Church* (1864). Among the older Protestant writings a three-stage canonization theory was championed in the English-speaking world by RYLE's *The Canon* (1892), in the Netherlands by WILDEBOER's *Origin of the Canon* (1889) and in Germany by BUHL's *Canon and Text* (1891). While it was opposed, for example, by GREEN's *General Introduction* (1898), it nevertheless became a dominant

---

[160] Cf. *B.T. Sanhedrin* 11a (= *T. Sota* 13:2); *Seder Olam Rabba* 30, cf. Leiman, *Canonization*, 66.
[161] 1 Thess 2:13; 2 Thess 2:15; Rom 16:26; Eph 3:3-5; Col 4:16; Acts 15:28f.; 2 Pet 3:15f. On prophetic manifestations at Qumran and in the NT cf. Ellis, 'Weisheit' (= Ellis, *Prophecy*, 45-62). Cf. also Yadin, *Temple Scroll* 1, 73-82; 390ff., where *inter alia* YHWH passages in the third person in the OT are shifted to the first person. This suggests a prophetic consciousness on the part of the author and, in Yadin's words, 'the belief that the author . . . construed the Pentateuchal laws correctly' (390). Otherwise: Wacholder, *Dawn of Qumran* 4, 30f., 229, who supposes that the Scroll presents a new and superior Tora to replace the Mosaic Tora.

viewpoint and, with variations, was accepted by some Jewish scholars, for example, MARGOLIS, *The Hebrew Scriptures in the Making*, and ZEITLIN, *An Historical Study*.

Among recent works of significance one may mention SUNDBERG, *The Old Testament of the Early Church* (1964); LEIMAN, *Canonization* (1976); and BECKWITH, *Old Testament Canon* (1985). It was the merit of Sundberg to show the fallacy of the theory that Alexandrian Judaism had a wider canon than that accepted in Palestine. Both Leiman and Beckwith give devastating criticisms of the three-stage canonization theory. Leiman also provides a valuable collection of early Jewish witnesses together with an evaluation of their significance for the canon. Beckwith's book offers the most comprehensive treatment of the subject in this generation and promises to become the standard work from which future discussions will proceed.

Chapter Nineteen

Biblical Interpretation in the New Testament Church

E. Earle Ellis

Introduction

In its interpretation of scripture the community of Jesus is rooted in and remains in continuity with the larger community of religious Judaism. It follows exegetical methods very similar to other groups and is distinguished primarily in the emphasis given to some procedures and in the boldness with which they are applied. In its general conceptual frame of reference it is closest to apocalyptic Judaism and thus, in some respects, to the Qumran community, but here also it is not without affinities with the Pharisaic-rabbinic and Sadducean parties. Jesus and his apostles and prophets, as they are represented by the NT, make their unique contribution to first-century Jewish exposition by their thoroughgoing *reinterpretation of the biblical writings to the person, ministry, death and resurrection of Jesus the Messiah.*

This messianic interpretation of scripture could be understood as a break with Judaism since it involves a new covenant of God (Luke 22:20; Heb 8:8-13) that depicts Israel's preceding institutions and scriptures as an old covenant, i.e. Old Testament, now superceded. However, Jesus and the NT writers present the new covenant as a 'fulfilment' that was prophesied by the OT (Jer 31:31) and that remains in a typological relationship to it (1 Cor 10:1-11). In this way the messianic hermeneutic continues, admittedly in a highly climactic manner, earlier prophetic interpretations of Israel's scriptures in terms of the current acts of God within the nation. And it is employed not only in matters of specific interest to the Christian community, but also in issues of general importance for contemporary Judaism: the Kingdom of God, the Messiah, the role of ritual and the place of the temple, the way to righteousness and to eternal life.

Jesus and the NT church give a prominent place to the OT in the formulation of their teachings. Like other Jewish groups, they concentrate their biblical quotations on certain portions of the Bible, especially the Pentateuch, Isaiah, and the Psalms; and they employ them more in some NT books than in others. In all

691

likelihood this reflects the writers' selected themes, traditions, and interests, and not their limited acquaintance with[1] or regard for the OT.[2]

In their textual form the citations accord with the audience addressed and the argument pursued. They frequently follow the Septuagint, both because this Greek version was used in Palestine and the Diaspora and, at times, because the Septuagint rendering fits the writer's viewpoint.[3] For the same reasons some citations, on occasion against the Septuagint, agree with the Hebrew text (Matt 2:15) or the targum (cf. Eph 4:8). *Ad hoc* renderings usually serve an interpretative interest.[4]

The Bible was the touchstone not only of the NT writers' religious teachings but also of their total life and culture. As might be expected, it was used occasionally for an analogy or illustration or for an expressive idiom.[5] But even in this literary usage it continued to carry theological implications. Similarly, as will be shown below, biblical citations containing widespread variations from the OT text-forms were more often intentional alterations than unintentional lapses.

Exegetical Methods

GENERAL FORM AND USAGE

In many respects NT citations of scripture display methods that are common to all literary quotations: paraphrase, combined citations, alterations in sense and reference.[6] Even when they have special affinity with wider Jewish practice, they often reflect adapted forms of the common usage of the Greco-Roman world.[7] However, some citations display features that, although not unique, do

---

[1] On Jesus' use of selected portions of Scripture cf. France, *Jesus*, 172-226; Grimm, *Die Verkündigung*.

[2] *Pace* v. Harnack, 'Das Alte Testament' 124-41, who thinks that Paul used the OT only as a matter of convenience. Cf. Ellis, *Paul's Use*, 30-33; idem, intr. to the ET of Goppelt, *TYPOS*, IXf.

[3] E.g. in Gen. 12:3; 18:18 the Hebrew may be passive or reflexive ('bless themselves'); the Septuagint is passive and accords with Paul's understanding of the verses (Gal 3:8). On the use of the LXX cf. Swete, *Introduction*, 381-405; Ellis, *Paul's Use*, 11-20.

[4] Cf. Ellis, *Prophecy*, 173-87.

[5] 1 Cor 15:32; Heb 12:14f. (expressive idiom); Rom 10:6-8; Jas 5:11 (illustration); Rom 2:24; Jas 5:17f. (analogy).

[6] For comparisons with secular literature cf. Johnson, *Quotations*. For comparisons with Judaism cf. Ellis, *Paul's Use*, 45ff.; Le Déaut, 'Traditions targumiques'.

[7] Re Hillel's rules cf. Daube, 'Rabbinic Methods'; Kasher, above, pp. 584-85. Certain aspects of the *Yelammedenu* midrash, e.g. the dialogic structure, also may have their background in Hellenistic rhetoric, e.g. Socratic interrogation or the diatribe style; cf. Daube, *New Testament*, 151-57, 161; Bultmann, *Der Stil*, 67, 73f. More generally, Daube, 'Alexandrian Methods': '(The) whole Rabbinic system of exegesis initiated by Hillel about 30 B.C.E. and elaborated by the following generations was essentially Hellenistic . . .' (44).

set forth distinctively Christian conceptions. These features include certain introductory formulas, merged citations and *testimonia*.

(1) *Introductory formulas* often serve to specify the authority of a citation and, for the most part, they are widely used in Judaism.[8] They also may point to the particular context within the Christian movement in which a citation was originally employed. For example, the formula 'have you not read', found in the NT only on the lips of Jesus, usually occurs in debates between Jesus and his religious opposition:

> Have you not read this scripture: 'The stone that the builders rejected, this one has become the head of the corner.'[9]

Two other formulas, 'in order that it might be fulfilled' (ἵνα πληρωθῇ) and 'says the Lord' (λέγει κύριος), apparently were utilized, respectively, by prophetic circles of the Hebraist and of the Hellenist missions. And both introduce quotations whose creatively altered text-forms adapt them to an eschatological, messianic interpretation.[10]

As a formula introducing a biblical citation, ἵνα πληρωθῇ appears only in the Gospels of Matthew and John.[11] Along with other 'fulfilment' formulas, it is favoured by the Hebraist missioners to underscore their perception of salvation history as it is consummated in Jesus:

---

[8] For parallels with formulas in Philo, rabbinic literature and especially at Qumran, e.g. 'as it is written', 'Moses says', 'God said', 'Scripture says' cf. Ryle, *Philo*, XLV; Metzger, 'The Formulas' 297-307; Ellis, *Paul's Use*, 48f.; Fitzmyer, 'Explicit OT Quotations', 299-305.

[9] Mark 12:10. Cf. Matt 12:3, 5; 19:4; 21:16, 42; 22:31. Cf. Luke 10:26. It may imply that the opponent has read but has not understood the passage cited (cf. Daube, *New Testament*, 433). Cf. Justin, *Dial.* 11:3; 29:2; 113:1. On the connection between the Pharisaic opponents of Jesus and the rabbinic circles of Mishna and Talmud, a question which is highly debatable, cf. Bowker, *Jesus and the Pharisees*; Gafni, 'Historical Background', 7-8; Luz, 'Jesus und die Pharisäer'; Sanders, *Palestinian Judaism*, 60-62; Sigal, *Halakhah*, 195ff.

[10] Cf. Ellis, *Prophecy*, 182-87; Freed, *Old Testament Quotations*, 129; Gundry, *Use of the Old Testament*, 89-122; Stendahl, *The School of St. Matthew*, 97-120. Of quotations employing these formulas only Matt 2:15 has a text-form in agreement with the Masoretic Text; only John 12:38 and 19:24 agree with the LXX. On the two-fold mission of the Jewish-Christian church cf. Ellis, *Prophecy*, 101-28, 246: in NT usage (e.g., Acts 6:1) it appears that Hebraists designated those Jews with a strict, ritualistic viewpoint; and Hellenists those with a freer attitude toward the Jewish Law and cultus (Ellis, ' "Those of the Circumcision" ' 392). It is usually supposed that the terms reflect only a difference in language, Hebrew/Aramaic speakers and Greek speakers, but as Schmithals and Ellis have shown, this view cannot explain the NT or wider usage. Cf. Schmithals, *Paul and James*, 16-27.

[11] Matt 1:22; 2:15; 4:14; 12:17; 21:4; cf. 2:23; 8:17; 13:35; John 12:38; 13:18; 15:25 (17:12); 19:24, 36. The formula introduces words of Jesus in John 18:9, 32. It apparently does not occur at Qumran or in rabbinic writings. But see, Fitzmyer, 'Explicit OT Quotations', 303. In the early patristic writings the phrase occurs once (Ignatius, *Ad Smyr.* 1:1) but with a different connotation.

This happened in order to fulfill the word through the prophet saying, 'Say to the daughter of Zion: Behold your king is coming to you . . .'[12]

The λέγει κύριος formula, as an addition to the OT text, appears only in a quotation attributed to Stephen and in the Pauline letters:

For it is written, 'Vengence is mine,
says the Lord, I will repay'.[13]

Elsewhere the phrase is substituted where the OT has φήσι κύριος.[14] The formula is characteristic of OT prophetic proclamation and it, or its equivalent, occasionally appears in the oracles of Christian prophets.[15] For these and other reasons[16] it is probable that the idiom reflects the activity of the prophets, especially those within the Hellenist mission.

The more commonly used formulas, no less than those discussed above, also locate the 'Word of God' character of scripture in the proper interpretation and application of its teaching. Thus, a messianically interpreted summary of OT passages can be introduced with the formula 'God said' (2 Cor 6:16) and those persons who have a wrong understanding of the OT are regarded as 'not knowing the scriptures' (γραφάς, Matt 22:29) or as 'making void the Word of God' (Mark 7:13 = Matt 15:6). What 'is written', i.e. of divine authority, is not the biblical text in the abstract but the text in its meaningfulness for the current situation. The introductory formulas show, in the words of B.B. Warfield, that 'scripture is thought of as the living voice of God speaking in all its parts directly to the reader'.[17] However, to this statement one should add, 'to the reader who has ears to hear' (cf. Matt 11:15). The formulas, then, reveal not only a method of citation but also something of the theological convictions of the NT writers.

(2) *Other exegetical terminology* is also associated with the use of the OT in the New, a small part peculiar to the NT writers and the rest the common property of Jewish exposition.

---

[12] Matt 21:4f. The verb is also used occasionally in the literature of the Hellenist mission as a formula (e.g. Gal 5:14) or otherwise (e.g. Mark 14:49), but not in the same way. The traditional piece in Acts 1:16 is not an exception although Peter may be later associated with the Hellenist mission (cf. 1 Cor 3:22; Gal 2:12; 1 Pet 1:1).

[13] Rom 12:19. Also, Acts 7:49; Rom 14:11; 1 Cor 14:21; 2 Cor 6:17, 18 (Heb 10:30A). Cf. Acts 2:17; 7:7 ('says God', 'God said'). At Isa 66:1f. (= Acts 7:49) and 2 Sam 7:14, 8 (= 2 Cor 6:18) the formula does appear in the immediate context. In Acts 15:16f. it reproduces the OT text. On a few occasions in patristic writings it also occurs within a citation as an addition to the OT text. Cf. Barn. 3:1, 6:8, 14; 9:1; Justin, *Dial.* 136:2.

[14] Heb 8:8-10; 10:16.

[15] Rev 1:8; cf. 2:1, 8, 12, 18; 3:1, 7; Luke 11:49; Acts 21:11.

[16] Detailed in Ellis, *Prophecy*, 186.

[17] Warfield, *Inspiration*, 148; cf. Bloch, 'Midrash', 1266 (ET 33): Scripture 'always concerns a living word addressed personally to the people of God and to each of its members . . .' Cf. Matt 4:4-10; Acts 15:15; Rom 15:4.

(a) One idiom that apparently occurs only in the NT is the formula 'faithful is the word' (πιστὸς ὁ λόγος).[18] Found in the Pastoral letters, it appears to be a favourite idiom of Paul and/or his amanuensis or co-workers at a later stage of his mission. Broadly speaking, it is used to refer to a traditioned teaching-piece of prophets or inspired teachers.[19] But it is also used in connection with their exposition of the OT. For example, in 1 Tim 3:1a the formula appears to conclude the preceding interpretation of Gen 3 that forbids a wife 'to practice teaching' or 'to domineer' over her husband (1 Tim 2:11-15). In Titus 1:9, 14 'the faithful word' is contrasted to the false biblical interpretations of Paul's opponents, and in Titus 3:5f., 8 it appears to refer to a Pentecostal interpretation of Joel 3:1:

> When the goodness and loving kindness of God our Saviour appeared . . ., he saved us by the washing of regeneration and renewal of the Holy Spirit, which he poured out upon us . . . Faithful is the Word.

A more explicit connection with prophecy occurs in a similar formula in Rev 22:6:

> Faithful are these words and true (οὗτοι οἱ λόγοι πιστοὶ καὶ ἀληθινοί), seeing that (καὶ) the Lord God of the spirits of the prophets sent his angel to show his servants what things must shortly come to pass.

The Qumran *Book of Mysteries*, which uses a similar expression with reference to a prophecy, probably represents the Jewish apocalyptic antecedent of the NT idiom:[20]

> Certain is the word to come to pass (נכון הדבר לבוא) and true (אמת) the oracle.

(b) More common is the exegetical usage of such terms as 'this is' (οὗτος ἐστιν), 'learn' (μανθάνειν), 'hear' (ἀκούειν), 'but' (ἀλλά, δέ). In the Greek OT οὗτός ἐστιν translates terms that introduce the explanation of divine revelation through a divine oracle (Isa 9:14f.), parable (Ezek 5:5), vision (Zech 1:10, 19; 5:3, 6), dream (Dan 4:24,[21]) and strange writing (Dan 5:25f.). For example,

> The Lord will cut off from Israel head and tail:
> The elder and the honoured man, this is (הוא) the head,

---

[18] E.g. 1 Tim 1:15; 4:9; 2 Tim 2:11; cf. 1 Cor 1:9; 2 Thess 3:3; see Knight, *Faithful Sayings*. The idiom apparently does not occur elsewhere although similar phrases appear in 2 Clem 11:6 (citing Heb 10:23) and Ignatius, *Tral.* 13:3 and in the Qumran *Book of Mysteries* (see note 20).

[19] Cf. 1 Tim 4:1 ('the Spirit says') with 4:6 ('by the words of the faith'). See also Rev 19:9; 21:5; Ellis, 'Pastoral Epistles'.

[20] *1Q27* 1:8. This work, according to Rabinowitz, 'Authorship' 29, concerns 'the fulfilment of the words of Israel's prophets'. It has another significant parallel with the Pauline literature in the phrase 'mysteries of iniquity' (*1Q27* 1:2 רזי פשע). Cf. 2 Thess 2:7; Dimant, 'Qumran Sectarian Literature' 536 n. 256.

And the prophet who teaches lies, this is (הוא) the tail.

Isa 9:14f.

Again I lifted up my eyes and saw . . . a flying scroll . . .
And [the angel] said to me, 'This is (זאת) the curse . . .'

Zech 5:1,3

In Daniel and at Qumran these terms are used in a similar way in conjunction with or as an equivalent of *pesher* (פשר):[21]

'Because of bloodshed in the city and violence in the land . . .' (Hab 2:17).
It's interpretation (פשרו): 'The *city*', that is (היא) Jerusalem . . .

1QpHab 12:6f.; cf. 12:3ff.

The books of the law, they are (הם) the tabernacle of the King, as he said: 'I will raise up the fallen tabernacle of David that is fallen' (Amos 9:11).

CD 7:15f.

'I will be to him a father and he will be to me a son' (2 Sam 7:14). This is (הואה) the branch of David . . . As it is written, 'I will raise up the tabernacle of David that is fallen' (Amos 9:11). This is (היאה) the fallen tabernacle of David who will arise to save Israel. Exposition (מדרש) of: 'Blessed is the man who does not walk in the counsel of the ungodly' (Ps 1:1). The interpretation (פשר) concerns the backsliders from the way . . .

4QFlor 1:11-14

In the NT οὗτος (ἐστιν) is also employed with the same eschatological orientation and exegetical framework that is found at Qumran. This formula is an equivalent of the Qumran *pesher* and may introduce either an explanation following cited biblical texts or a biblical citation used to explain the described event:[22]

'In Isaac shall your seed be called' (Gen 21:12).
That is (τοῦτ' ἔστιν), not the children of the flesh . . . but the children of the promise . . . For this is (οὗτος) the word of promise, 'About this season I will return and Sarah will have a son' (Gen 18:10).

Rom 9:7-9

---

[21] Cf. also *4QpIsa*[b] 2:6f., 10; *4QpNah* 1:11. The Qumran usage is not restricted to revelations through dreams or visions, as some scholars have supposed, for it is used in the explanation of 'Words of Moses' (*1Q22* 1:3f.) to whom God spoke not in vision but 'mouth to mouth' (Num 12:6-8). For the use of these exegetical formulas in rabbinic writings cf. Silberman, 'Unriddling the Riddle', 326-30; Bonsirven, *Exégèse rabbinique* 42-46; in Gnosticism cf. *Pistis Sophia* 65-67 (131-47); Hippolytus, *Refutatio* 6:14(9).

[22] Cf. also John 6:31, 50; Rom 10:6-8; Heb 7:5; 1 Pet 1:25 and, introducing the citation, Matt 3:3; 11:10; Acts 4:11.

But this is (τοῦτό ἐστιν) that which was spoken by the prophet Joel 'And it shall be in the last days, says God, ...' (Joel 3:1).

Acts 2:16f.

(c) The use of the adversative 'but' (ἀλλά, δέ) in the exposition of scripture also displays a Jewish ancestry. In the NT (1) it may follow a biblical citation or allusion in order to correct, qualify or underscore a particular understanding of it,[23] or (2) it may introduce a citation to correct, qualify or underscore a preceding statement[24] or citation:[25]

> You have heard (ἠκούσατε) that it was said . . .,
> 'You shall not kill' (Exod 20:13) . . .
> But (δέ) I say to you that everyone who is angry . . .
>
> Matt 5:21f.

> I know whom I have chosen.
> But (ἀλλά) that the scriptures might be fulfilled:
> 'He who ate my bread lifted his heel against me' (Ps 41:10)
>
> John 13:18

The usage represents an exegetical technique, a dialectical procedure by which apparent contradictions are resolved and the meaning of scripture is drawn out or more precisely specified. A similar contrast between scripture and scripture or scripture and commentary is observable in rabbinic exposition even though an adversative conjunction may not be used:[26]

> 'And if he smite out his bondsman's tooth' (Exod 21:27) I might under-
> stand (שומע אני) this to mean . . . milk tooth.
> But it also says (תלמוד לומר), 'Eye' (Exod 21:26) . . .
> Just as the eye . . . the tooth must be such as cannot grow back . . .
> *Mekhilta Nezikin* 9 (p. 279) on Exod 21:26f.

> When Scripture says, 'And David . . . wept as he went up' (2 Sam 15:30),
> one might suppose [he lamented].
> But . . . he was composing a Psalm, as it is said,
> 'A Psalm of David, when he fled from Absalom' (Ps 3:1).
> *Midrash Tehillim* 119, 26 (p. 496) on Ps 119:75.

> All shofars are valid save of that of a cow, since it is a horn.
> But are not (והלא) all shofars called . . . 'horn'? For it is written,

---

[23] Cf. also Matt 19:8; Mark 11:17; 14:28f.; Luke 20:37f.; John 6:31f.; Rom 10:15f.; 1 Cor 2:10A, 16; 15:45f.; Gal 4:22f.; Heb 10:37ff.; 12:26f.

[24] Cf. also Acts 2:15f.; Rom 9:7; 15:21; 1 Cor 2:8f.; 10:4f.; Gal 4:30; 3:12; Heb 2:16; 2 Pet 3:12f.

[25] Cf. Acts 7:48f.; Rom 8:37; 10:18f.; 11:2ff.; 12:20; Jude 8ff.

[26] Whether the NT usage is, like the rabbinic, concerned with resolving apparent contradictions in scripture is less certain to me. But see Dahl, *Studies in Paul*, 159-77.

'When they . . . blast with the ram's horn' (Josh 6:5) . . .
'When Moses held up his hand, Israel prevailed' (Exod 17:11).
But (וכי) could the hands of Moses promote the battle? . . .

M. Rosh Hashana 3:2,8

(d) The terms 'hear' (ἀκούειν) and 'learn' (μανθάνειν), appear occasionally in the NT with reference to 'understanding' scripture:

Go learn what it means,
'I will have mercy and not sacrifice' (Hos 6:6).[27]

Matt 9:13

. . . Then 'all the tribes of the land will lament' (cf. Zech 12:12)
And 'shall see the Son of man coming on the clouds of heaven' . . . (Dan 7:13)
And his elect . . . 'from one end of heaven to the other' (Deut 30:4).
From the fig tree learn the mystery (παραβολή) . . .[28]

Matt 24:30ff.

In Matt 21:33 the words, 'Hear another mystery' (παραβολή), like the apparently equivalent phrase, 'Learn the mystery' (Matt 24:32), refer to an exposition of scripture.[29] Also, a biblical exposition may be opened with the words, 'Hear the law', or concluded with the expression, 'He who has ears, let him hear'.[30]

In rabbinic literature the terms 'learn' (למד) and 'hear' (שמע) are similarly employed in formulas coupling biblical texts to commentary upon them.[31]

Behold we have thus learned [from the preceding exposition] that work is forbidden during the intervening days of the festival.

Mekhilta Pisha 9 (p. 30) on Exod 12:16

[27] Cf. also Matt 11:27, 29: '. . . Take my yoke upon you and learn from me'. The 'yoke' implies a 'Law of Christ' that, when followed, brings a knowledge of God. Specifically it is a knowledge of 'the mysteries of the Kingdom of the Heavens' (Matt 13:11 parr) that, along the lines of the book of Daniel, Jesus unveils *exempli gratia* in his exposition of scripture. Cf. Sir 51:23, 26; *M. Avot* 3:5; *M. Berakhot* 2:2; Davies, *The Setting* 94, 214; Cerfaux, 'La connaisance' 244f.

[28] That is, the παραβολή apparently is not only the story of the fig tree (Luke 21:29) but also the 'mystery' (רז) in the scriptures that Jesus has 'interpreted' (פשר). Cf. 1QpHab 7:1-8; Ellis, *Prophecy*, 160ff. For this meaning of παραβολή cf. Jeremias, *Parables*, 16; E. Schweizer, *Das Evangelium*, 51 (ET 92f.) Cf. Matt 13:35 = Ps 78:2; Mark 4:11f.; 7:17f. (cf. ἀσύνετοι); Heb 9:9; John 10:6; 16:25, 29. On the expository, i.e. midrashic origin of Matt 24 = Mark 13 see below. Unlike those of 1 Enoch (e.g. 1:2f.; 37:5; 43:4), Jesus' parables of the kingdom are drawn mostly from daily life (but cf. Matt 25:31-46; Luke 16:19D). However, like the parables of Enoch and other apocalyptic literature (4 Ezra 4:12-22; 7:3-14; 8:41) and unlike those of the rabbis, his are not merely illustrations but are truly 'mysteries', i.e. a hidden eschatological word of revelation, clothed in the form of a story. But see the remark of Gilbert, 'Wisdom Literature' 319.

[29] I.e. Matt 21:33-46.

[30] I.e. Gal 4:21-5:1; Matt 11:7-15. Cf. Rev 1:3; 13:9.

[31] Cf. Bacher, *Exegetische Terminologie* 1, 75, 94f., 189; 2, 220. Le Déaut, 'La tradition juive ancienne' 37. Strack-Billerbeck, *Kommentar* 1, 499, 604.

'She shall go out for nothing'. I might understand (שמע) 'for nothing' to mean without a bill of divorce.

Mekhilta Nezikin 3 (p. 259) on Exod 21:11

(3) *The seven exegetical rules* that, according to later rabbinic tradition, were expounded by the great teacher Hillel represent general hermeneutical principles of inference, analogy and context that were probably in use before that time.[32] They may be derived, as Daube argues, from rules of Hellenistic rhetoric current in Alexandria in the first century B.C.[33] As attributed to Hillel, they were as follows:

1. An inference drawn from a minor premise to a major and vice versa (*Kal wa-homer* = 'light and heavy').
2. An inference drawn from analogy of expressions, that is from similar words and phrases elsewhere (*Gezera Shawa* = 'an equivalent regulation').
3. A general principle established on the basis of a teaching contained in one verse (*Binyan Av mi-katuv 'ehad* - 'constructing a leading rule from one passage').
4. A general principle established on the basis of a teaching contained in two verses (*Binyan Av mi–shenei ketuvim* - 'constructing a leading rule from two passages').
5. An inference drawn from a general principle in the text to a specific example and vice versa (*Kelal u-ferat* = 'general and particular' and *Perat u-khelal*).
6. An inference drawn from an analogous passage elsewhere (*Kayotse bo mi-makom aher* = 'something similar in another passage').
7. An interpretation of a word or passage from its context (*Davar halamed me-inyano* = 'explanation from the context').

For example, a negligent man whose animal kills someone is liable to death, but he may be delivered by the payment of money (Exod 21:29f.); *a fortiori (rule 1)* a man who maims another, a non-capital case, may also compensate by the payment of money and not literally 'eye for eye' (Exod 21:24). It is true that scripture says, 'If a man maims his neighbour . . ., so shall it be done to him' (Lev 24:19); but this *general principle* cannot include more than the following *specific example*, 'eye for eye' (Lev 24:20), which allows monetary compensation *(rule 5)*.[34] A master must free a slave whose eye or tooth he has knocked out (Exod 21:26f.); these two examples establish the general principle *(rule 4)* that a

---

[32] E.g. Prov 11:31; cf. 1 Pet 4:17f. On Hillel see *T. Sanhedrin* 7:11; *Avot de-R. Natan* A37 (p. 110). Danby, *Tractate Sanhedrin*, 76f. See Kasher, above, pp. 584-85.

[33] Daube, 'Rabbinic Methods' 239-64; cf. Hamerton-Kelly, 'Some Techniques', 47-53.

[34] *Mekhilta, Nezikin* 8 (p. 277) on Exod 21:24.

slave must be freed for such an injury to any important, visible and irreplaceable member of his body.[35]

Daily sacrifice 'in its due season' is offered on the sabbath (Num 28:2, 10); by a *Gezera Shawa* analogy *(rule 2)* the Passover sacrifice (Num 9:2) should also be offered on the Sabbath since the same expression, 'due season', is used.[36] One might understand 'Honour your father and your mother' (Exod 20:12) to signify that the father should be given precedence since he is mentioned first; but in a similar passage 'mother' precedes 'father' (Lev 19:3) and, by analogy *(rule 6)*, shows that both are to be honoured equally.[37] The commandment, 'you shall not steal', refers to stealing a man and not money; for in the context *(rule 7)* the prohibitions against murder and adultery concern capital crimes and so must this one.[38]

The use of a number of these principles may be observed in the NT:[39]

Rule 1

The ravens neither sow nor reap, and God feeds them (Ps 147:9); of how much more value are you (Luke 12:24). If the scripture calls 'gods' those whom God addressed (Ps 82:6), how much more may he whom God sent into the world be called 'son of God' (John 10:34ff.). If the covenant at Sinai came with glory (Exod 34:30), how much more does the new covenant (Jer 31:31ff.) abound in glory (2 Cor 3:6-11). If in the old covenant the blood of animals could effect a cermonial, external cleansing (Lev 16; Num 19), how much more shall the blood of (the sacrificed) Messiah cleanse our conscience (Heb 9:13f.).[40]

Rule 2

David, who received the kingdom from God, was blameless when he and those with him violated the Law in eating the showbread (1 Sam 21:6; cf. 15:28); the Son of Man, who also received a kingdom from God (Dan 7:13f.), is equally blameless when those with him violate the sabbath law in similar circumstances (Luke 6:1-5).[41] The righteousness 'reckoned' to Abraham (Gen 15:6) may be explained in terms of forgiveness of sins in

---

[35] *Mekhilta, Nezikin* 9 (p. 279) on Exod 21:27. Or one might regard Exod 21:26f. as one passage and take this to be an application of rule three.

[36] *T. Pesahim* 4:1f.; *P.T. Pesahim* 6:1 (33a); *B.T. Pesahim* 66a.

[37] *Mekhilta, Pisha* 1 (p. 2) on Exod 12:1.

[38] *Mekhilta, Bahodesh* 8 (p. 232-33)on Exod 20:15; cf. *B.T. Sanh. 86a.* For other examples cf. Bacher, *Exegetische Terminologie*, 1, 9ff., 13-16, 75f., 80ff., 172ff.; Bonsirven, *Exégèse rabbinique*, 77-113; Doeve, *Jewish Hermeneutics*, 52-90; Ellis, *Paul's Use*, 41f.; Mielziner, *Introduction*, 130-87; Strack, *Introduction*, 93ff., 285-89.

[39] Doeve, *Jewish Hermeneutics*, 91-118; Gerhardsson, 'Hermeneutic Program'; Jeremias, 'Paulus als Hillelit', 92ff. For a critique of Hübner's ('Gal 3, 10', 222-29) view that Paul was, contra Jeremias, a Shammaite, see Sanders, *Palestinian Judaism*, 138n. Further cf. Cohn-Sherbok, 'Paul', 126-31.

[40] See further Luke 6:3-5; Rom 5:15, 17; 9:24; 11:12; 1 Cor 6:2f.; 9:9; Heb 2:2ff.; 10:28f.; 12:24f.

[41] The grounds on which this analogy can be drawn are considered by Doeve, *Jewish Hermeneutics*, 165.

Ps 32:1f. since the word 'reckoned' is also employed there (Rom 4:3, 7). Gen 14:17-20 may be interpreted in the light of Ps 110:4 where alone in the OT the name 'Melchizedek' again appears (Heb 7:1-28). Gen 15:5f. may be interpreted by Gen 22:9-19 and Isa 41:8 since the texts contain a common reference to Abraham's seed (Jas 2:21ff.).

Rule 3

God is not the God of the dead, and yet in Exod 3:14f. he affirmed a continuing covenant relationship with dead Abraham. Therefore, he must intend to raise Abraham out of death, and from this conclusion one may infer the resurrection of all the dead who had a similar covenantal relationship (Mark 12:26 parr). Cf. Jas 5:16ff.

Rule 4

The uncircumcised Abraham (Gen 15:6) and the circumcised David (Ps 32:1f.) establish the general principle that the righteousness of God is graciously given to the circumised Jew and to the uncircumcised Gentile apart from works (Rom 4:1-25). From the commands to unmuzzle the working ox (Deut 25:4) and to give the temple priests a share of the sacrifices (Deut 18:1-8) one may infer the general right of ministers of the gospel to a living (1 Cor 9:9, 13). The examples of Abraham (Gen 22:9-19) and Rahab (Josh 2:1-16) establish the general principle that genuine faith is manifested by works (Jas 2:22-26).

Rule 5

'The [particular] commandments, "you shall not commit adultery, . . . commit murder, . . . steal, . . . covet" (Exod 20:13-17; cf. Lev 18:20; 19:11) and any other commandment are summed up in this [general] sentence, "You shall love your neighbour as yourself" (Lev 19:18) . . Therefore, love is the fulfilling of the law' (Rom 13:9f.). That is, the particular commandments are apparently regarded as illustrative examples of the general.[42]

Rule 6

The prophecy in Gen 12:3 that all nations shall be blessed in Abraham may, in the light of the analogous passage in Gen 22:18, be understood of Abraham's offspring and thus of Messiah (Gal 3:8, 16). One might understand the 'rest' promised to God's people to have been fulfilled by Joshua (Num 14:21-30; Josh 1:13-15; 22:4), but the analogous and much later passage in Ps 95:7-11 shows that the prophecy is still outstanding (Heb 4:7-9). The covenant at Sinai (Exod 19:5f.; Lev 26:9-12) is shown to

---

[42] Cf. Daube, *New Testament*, 63-66.

be inadequate and temporary by a subsequent and similar passage (Jer 31:31-34) in which God speaks of a new covenant (Heb 8:7-13).

Rule 7

Indissoluble marriage was established at creation (Gen 1:27, 2:24), a context that takes priority over later (Deut 24:1) provisions for divorce (Matt 19:4-8). That righteousness was reckoned to Abraham (Gen 15:6) before he was circumcised (Gen 17:10f.) enables him to be the father of both Jewish and (uncircumcised) Gentile believers (Rom 4:10f.). Equally, because the covenant promise was established with Abraham (Gen 22:18) 430 years before the Mosaic Law (Exod 12:40), it has validity independent of that law (Gal 3:17). That God rested after the completion of the present creation, i.e. on the seventh or sabbath day (Gen 2:2), implies that those who enter God's future sabbath rest (Ps 95:7-11) will do so only when their and his present work is completed, i.e. at the resurrection (Heb 4:9f.; cf. 11:13-16, 35-40).

Some of the above NT passages are clearer than others, and since no 'rules' are mentioned, one cannot prove that the writer or the speaker cited by him had a specific exegetical rule consciously in mind. Nevertheless, a number of these texts almost certainly reflect the use of an exegetical principle or combination of principles. As a whole the examples show that the principles attributed to Hillel were also used by the messianic Judaism represented by Jesus and the NT writers. Certain of the principles, especially the association of biblical texts containing similar ideas (rule 6) or common words and phrases (rule 2), are important for the formation of larger commentary patterns in the NT. They are also evident in other techniques such as a string (חרז) of quotations[43] and merged or composite quotations[44] that often have appended to one text a snippet from another.[45] The latter practice appears to be infrequent in other Jewish literature.

MIDRASH

The Hebrew verb *darash* (דרש) and its substantive form *midrash* (מדרש) were used in pre-Christian Judaism for the interpretation of scripture[46] or for commentary on scripture.[47] For example, the 'house of midrash' in Ben Sira 51:23

---

[43] E.g. Rom 11:8-10; 15:9-12; 1 Cor 3:19f.; Heb 1:5-13; 1 Pet 2:7f. Some of these combine citations from the Law, the Prophets and the Writings. Cf. Bacher, *Proömien*, 9-14; Strack-Billerbeck, *Kommentar*, 3, 314; *B.T. Pesahim* 76-8a.

[44] Rom 3:10-18; 2 Cor 6:16ff.; 1 Cor 2:9. Cf. *Mekhilta, Pisha* 1 (p. 3) on Exod 12:1.

[45] Matt 21:5 (Isa 62:11 + Zech 9:9); Mark 1:2 (Mal 3:1 + Isa 40:3) etc. Cf. Ellis, *Paul's Use*, 186.

[46] Perhaps as early as Ezra 7:10 'Ezra had set his heart to interpret (דרש) the law of the Lord'.

[47] Perhaps as early as 2 Chron 13:22 ('Midrash of the prophet Iddo'); 24:27 ('Midrash on the Book of Kings').

refers to the place of instruction in the Law of God.[48] Similarly, at Qumran 'midrash' can mean the 'study' of Tora.[49] This study, i.e. interpretation of scripture, was an established practice in first-century Judaism in the synagogue service[50] as well as in the academic schools.[51]

As an *interpretive activity* the midrashic procedure (1) is oriented to scripture, (2) adapting it to the present (3) for the purpose of instructing or edifying the current reader or hearer.[52] It may take the form either of a simple clarification or of a specific application of the texts.

As a *literary expression* midrash has traditionally been identified with certain rabbinic commentaries on the OT. However, in accordance with its use in Ben Sira and at Qumran, the term is now employed more broadly to designate interpretive renderings of the biblical text (= implicit midrash) and of various kinds of 'text + exposition' patterns (= explicit midrash).[53]

(1) *Implicit midrash* first appears, as has been observed above, as a process of rewriting that occurs within the Hebrew OT itself. It may also involve the transposition of a biblical text to a different application. For example, the prophecy in Isa 19:19-22 transposes the words and motif of Israel's redemption from Egypt (Exod 1-12) to God's future redemption of Egypt.[54]

Implicit midrash is present also in biblical translations, that is, the Greek Septuagint and the Aramaic targums, where interpretive adaptation to a current understanding, interest, or application is interwoven into the translation process.[55] For example, in Lev 18:21 the prohibition of child-sacrifice 'to the god Molech' becomes in Targum Neofiti 'to an idol'. In the Septuagint it is a simple prohibition on idolatry, i.e. to serve or worship ($\lambda\alpha\tau\varrho\epsilon\acute{\upsilon}\epsilon\iota\nu$) a ruler. In Num 24:17 a 'star' and a 'scepter' become in Targum Neofiti a 'king' and a 'redeemer', in the Septuagint a 'star' and a 'man'. In Isa 9:11 (12) the Philistines become in the Septuagint 'the Greeks'. In Isa 52:13 'my servant' becomes in Targum Yonatan 'my servant the Messiah'.

Similarly, at Qumran rewritings of Genesis, the Genesis Apocryphon (*1QGenAp*) and Jubilees (*1Q17, 18*; etc.) may properly be designated implicit

---

[48] The 'house of midrash' *(beit ha-midrash)* may already here be a technical term and certainly becomes so in later rabbinic usage. Cf. Safrai, 'Education', 960ff.

[49] *1QS* 8:15, 26; *CD* 20:6.

[50] Cf. Luke 4:16-30; Acts 13:16-41. Philo, *De Spec. Leg.* 2, 60-64; *Hypothetica* 7, 11-13. Cf. *P.T. Megilla* 3:1 (73d): There were 480 synagogues in Jerusalem, each of which had a 'house of reading' and a 'house of learning' *(beit talmud)*.

[51] Paul's study 'at the feet of Gamaliel' (Acts 22:3) is one example. Cf. van Unnik, *Tarsus*; Neusner, *Rabbinic Traditions*, 3, 248-319.

[52] Bloch, 'Midrash' 1263-67; ET 29-34. Vermes, 'Bible and Midrash', *CHB* 1, 223ff.

[53] Cf. Ellis, *Prophecy*, 188-97.

[54] Isa 19:20 ('cry', 'send', 'oppressors', cf. Exod 3:9f.), 20ff. ('sign', 'know', 'sacrifice', 'smite', cf. Exod 7:27; 8:4, 18-25 = 8:2, 8, 22-29). Cf. Fishbane 'Torah and Tradition', 277.

[55] Le Déaut, 'Une phénomène spontané' 525, distinguishes midrash proper from 'targumism', in which the interpretive factor is spontaneous and unconditioned by hermeneutical rules and techniques.

midrash. The same may be said of interpretive alterations of OT texts, often based on word-play, in certain Qumran commentaries.[56]

These various forms of implicit midrash are also present in the NT. *Word-play* in Matt 2:23 connects Jesus' residence in Nazareth to an OT messianic text such as Isa 11:1 (נצר = 'branch') or Isa 49:6 (נצירי = 'preserved'?, 'branch'?, 'Nazorean'?). Luke 1-2 offers examples of the *transposition* of OT texts. The prophecy of Gabriel (Luke 1:30-35) is given literary expression via allusion to 2 Sam 7, Isa 7 and other passages. The song of Hannah (1 Sam 2:1-10), supplemented by other passages, is transposed to form the Magnificat (Luke 1:46-55). Other OT texts are used in the same way in the Benedictus (Luke 1:68-79) and in the Nunc Dimittis (Luke 2:29-32).

Events in Jesus' life that are described by the use of biblical allusions are also a form of implicit midrash. In this way the event can be clearly associated with or presented as a fulfilment of the OT. Thus, the angelic annunciation to Mary (Luke 1:26-38) is virtually a pastiche of biblical allusions (Isa 7:14, 13; Gen 16:11; Isa 9:6f.; 2 Sam 7:12-16; Dan 7:14). Somewhat differently, the visit of the wise men and the sequel (Matt 2:1-23) is structured upon both explicit quotations (Mic 5:1, 3[2, 4] + 2 Sam 5:2; Hos 11:1; Jer 31:15; ?Isa 11:1; Jer 23:5 or Judg 13:5) and implicit allusions to scripture (Num 24:17; Exod 2:15; 4:19). The feeding of the Five Thousand (Matt 14:13-21 parr) is described with clear allusions to the Exodus (Exod 16:12-15; 18:21; Deut 18:15; cf. *1QS* 2:21f.; *1QSa* 1:14f.; 2:1). The raising of the widow's son (Luke 7:11-17, 16) highlights the people's misunderstanding of who Jesus is by plain allusions to a similar miracle by Elijah (1 Kgs 17:10, 23). The Triumphal Entry (Mark 11:1-10) is a messianic act based upon Isa 62:11 and Zech 9:9, as the crowd recognizes and Matthew (21:4f.) and John (12:15) make explicit, and the Cleansing of the Temple (Matt 21:10-17; cf. John 2:17) and the Last Supper (Matt 26:20-29 parr) are presented in a similar manner.

This kind of narrative midrash is in several respects different from certain rabbinic midrashim that elaborate, usually via wordplay, a biblical word or verse into a fictional story:[57]

(1) While the rabbinic midrash seeks to discover some hidden element within the OT text itself, the NT midrash with its eschatological orientation applies the text theologically to some aspect of Jesus' life and ministry.

(2) While for the rabbis the text is primary, the NT writers give primacy to Jesus and to the surrounding messianic events, or tradition of events, and only then use OT texts to explain or illuminate them.

While they may describe the events in biblical language and may on occasion allude to a prior fictional midrash (e.g. 1 Cor 10:4), they never seem to reverse their priorities so as to make the OT text the locus for creating stories about

---

[56] E.g. *4QTest* 1:22 (Josh 6:26, omitting 'Jericho'); *1QpHab* 8:3 (Hab 2:5, changing 'wine' היין, to 'wealth', הון). Cf. Ellis, *Prophecy*, 175ff., 190, 201f.

[57] For examples, cf. Weingreen, *From Bible to Mishna*, 18; Ellis, *Prophecy*, 209-12.

Jesus. This holds true also for the Infancy Narratives where, even on the unlikely assumption of the writers' total loss of a salvation-history perspective, the wide-ranging mélange of citations and allusions could only have coalesced around preexisting traditions and, in any case, could not have produced the stories in the Gospels.[58] For example, only because Matthew (2:6, 23; 4:15) had a tradition that Jesus was born in Bethlehem and raised in Galilee does he use Mic 5:2 (1) of Jesus' birth and Jer 23:5; Isa 11:1; 9:2f. (8:23f.) of his youth and ministry and not vice versa. The texts themselves could be applied to either eventuality.

More subtly, certain of Jesus' parables are based upon OT passages; but this may be so because they are biblical expositions, exerpted from earlier explicit midrashim (see below). The Revelation of St. John represents a comprehensive adaptation of OT images and motifs, using midrashic techniques, to verbalize the eschatological visions of the Seer. In 1 Tim 1:9f. the fifth to the ninth commands of the Decalogue are transposed to accord with a current interpretation of the violation of these commandments:

Exodus 20:12-16	*1 Timothy 1:9f.*
Honour your father and your mother	Murderers of fathers and . . . mothers
You shall not commit murder	Manslayers
You shall not commit adultery	Immoral persons, sodomites
You shall not steal	Kidnappers
You shall not bear false witness	Liars, perjurers

Interpretive alterations within OT quotations are a third and more common form of implicit midrash. They are characteristic of certain classes of NT citations and, as will be seen below, are frequent in quotations used within explicit midrash patterns. Sometimes they simply contemporize the citation to the current audience. For example, 'Damascus' in Amos 5:27 becomes 'Babylon' in Acts 7:43. More generally, such alterations appear to serve the writer's purpose by accenting a particular interpretation or application of the citation. They may involve either elaborate alterations of the OT text[59] or the simple but significant change of one or two words, as in the following examples:

> Behold, I am sending my messenger *before your face*.
> Matt 11:10 (Mal 3:10)
> . . . you shall not steal, you shall not bear false witness, you shall not *defraud*.

---

[58] Otherwise: Gundry, *Matthew*, 26-41; Brodie, 'Unravelling' 263; Hanson, *Living Utterances*, 76, qualifying his better judgment in *Studies*, 207: 'We are never led to think that (the New Testament writers) are themselves inventing *Haggadah*, a narrative midrash'.

[59] These are often found in merged or composite citations of several OT texts, e.g. Rom 3:10-18; 1 Cor 2:9; 2 Cor 6:16ff. Cf. also the running summary of the Patriarchal and Exodus story in Acts 7.

Mark 10:19f. (Exod 20:12-16)

The stone set at naught by *you* builders . . .

Acts 4:11 (Ps 118:22)

Everyone who believes on him shall not be put to shame.

Rom 10:11 (Isa 28:16)

In burt offerings and sin offerings you did not *have pleasure*.

Heb 10:6 (Ps 40:6)

The textual alterations in the last two examples are designed to create verbal links within a larger exposition of scripture, i.e. a pattern of explicit midrash.[60] We may now turn to a closer examination of that phenomenon.

(2) *Explicit midrash* in the NT takes various forms. It may appear as a cluster of texts and commentary on a particular theme, similar to the *florilegia* found at Qumran[61] or as a special pattern.[62] More frequently, it occurs in literary forms found in rabbinic expositions, the 'proem' and *'yelammedenu rabbenu'* ('let our master teach us') midrashim. While in the rabbinic collections these forms date from several centuries after the NT,[63] they were hardly borrowed from the Christians. Also, similar patterns are present in the first-century Jewish writer, Philo.[64] One may infer then, with some confidence, that their presence in the NT reflects a common, rather widespread Jewish usage. The rabbinic proem midrash generally had the following form:[65]

> The (Pentateuchal) text for the day.
> A second text, the proem or 'opening' for the discourse.
> Exposition, including supplementary quotations, parables and other commentary with verbal links to the initial and final texts.
> A final text, usually repeating or alluding to the text for the day, and sometimes adding a concluding application.[66]

The *yelammedenu* midrash has the same general structure except for an interrogative opening in which there is posed a question or problem that the exposition serves to answer.

As might be expected, the NT exegetical patterns display a number of differences from those of the rabbis. They represent an earlier stage in the development of the art as well as a divergent theological orientation. In addition,

---

[60] Cf. Rom 10:12f, 16, 18; Heb 10:38.

[61] *4QFlor*. Cf. Heb 1:1-14; Jude 4-23; Ellis, *Prophecy*, 221-26.

[62] E.g. John 1:1-18; Matt 4:1-11; cf. Borgen, 'Observations'; Gerhardsson, *Testing*. Perhaps Heb 1:1-2:18, Luke 4:16-30 and Mark 13:5-29 appear to reflect expository patterns that have been partly dissipated in transmission.

[63] See Bowker, *Targums*, 74-77.

[64] E.g. Philo, *De Sacrif. Abel.* 76-87: Lev 2:14 + Commentary with verbal links and supplementary texts + Concluding allusion to the opening text + Final texts (Exod 6:7; Lev 26:12).

[65] E.g. *Pesikta Rabbati* 34:1: Zech 9:9 + Isa 61:9 + Commentary, with verbal links and illustrative stories + Isa 62:2 + Final reference to Isa 61:9.

[66] Cf. Stein, 'Homiletische Peroratio'.

they apparently have been frequently abbreviated and otherwise altered before their incorporation into the present NT context. Among the more notable differences, the NT midrashim (1) do not appear to be related to a (Penta-teuchal) lectionary cycle, (2) often lack a second, proem text and (3) use a final text that does not correspond or allude to the initial text. Occasionally, (4) they have lost their catchword connections.[67] More importantly, (5) they consistent-ly have an eschatological orientation. Nevertheless, the NT patterns show an unmistakable resemblance to rabbinic midrash that cannot be coincidental and that permits a qualified label of 'proem' and *'yelammedenu'*.

In the expositions attributed to Jesus by the Evangelists[68] the *yelammedenu* form is usually found in discussions about the halakha[69] or other questions[70] between Jesus and other Jewish theologians. Compare Matt 12:1-8 on what is permitted on the Sabbath:[71]

1-2	–	Theme and question raised by the initial texts (cf. Exod 20:10; 34:21)
3-5	–	Counter question and exposition via supplementary texts (1 Sam 21:7; Num 28:9; θυσία), verbally linked to the theme and the initial texts (ποιεῖν; ἐσθίειν).
6f.	–	Eschatological application via an *a fortiori* argument and a final text (Hos 6:6, θυσία).

In the teachings of Jesus given in the Gospels the proem form appears only infrequently. A striking example, dealing with God's judgement on the nation's leaders for their rejection of the Messiah occurs in Matt 21:33-46 and parallels:[72]

33	–	Initial text (Isa 5:1f.).
34-41	–	Exposition via a parable, verbally linked to the initial and/or

---

[67] E.g. Matt 11:7-15: Theme and initial text (7-10; Mal 3:1) + Exposition (11-13) + Final text (14; allusion to Mal 3:23 = 4:5).

[68] While they were somewhat altered in transmission, less so in Matthew than elsewhere apparently, these expositions belong to the bedrock of the Gospel traditions and originate in the preresurrection mission of Jesus. Cf. Ellis, *Prophecy*, 154-59, 247-53.

[69] Cf. further on ritual defilement, Matt 15:1-9: Question and initial texts (1-4; Exod 20:12; 21:17) + Exposition/application (5-6) + Concluding text (7-9; Isa 29:13). On divorce, Matt 19:3-8. On the meaning of a commandment, Luke 10:25-37. Cf. Ellis, *Prophecy*, 158f.

[70] On messianic themes e.g. Matt 21:15f.: Theme and initial text (Ps 118:25) + Objection + Counter question with concluding text (Ps 8:3). On resurrection, cf. Matt 22:23-33.

[71] It is similar to the *yelammedenu* pattern even though, like other midrashim of Jesus, it is an adversary rather than a teacher/disciple context. Daube, *New Testament*, 170-75 identifies the form as 'revolutionary action, protest, silencing of remonstrants'. However, the action usually involves a violation of an accepted halakha, and on that basis is objected to and the objection answered. It may be, then, that this represents a biblical dispute even when express biblical references are partial or absent, perhaps having disappeared in transmission (cf. Matt 9:9-13; 12:22-30; Luke 13:10-17).

[72] Cf. Ellis, *Prophecy*, 251f. Another proem-like pattern, somewhat reworked, appears in John 6:31-58: Initial texts (31; Exod 16:4) + Exposition with dialogue (32-44) + Supporting texts (45; Isa 54:13) + Exposition and concluding reference to the initial text (58). Cf. Borgen, *Bread From Heaven*, 37-43.

final texts (ἀμπελών, 33, 39; λίθος, 42, 44, cf. 35: Isa 5:2, סקל; cf. οἰκοδομεῖν, 33, 42).

42-44 – Concluding texts (Ps 118:22f.; Dan 2:34f., 44f.) and application.

In Acts and the Epistles the proem midrash is much more frequent, the *yelammedenu* relatively less so.[73] Gal 4:21-5:1 offers an instructive example:

21f. – Introduction and initial text (cf. Gen 21).

23-29 – A supplementary citation (27: Isa 54:1) and exposition, verbally linked to the initial and final text (ἐλευθέρα, 22f., 26, 30; παιδίσκη, 22f., 30f.; בן/υἱός = τέκνον, 22, 25, 27f., 30f.).

30ff. – Final texts and application, referring to the initial text (cf. Gen. 21:10).

It is noteworthy that the initial and final texts are, in fact, implicit midrash, the first a selective summary of Gen 21 and the last an interpolated citation shaped to underscore the key term ἐλευθέρα.[74] This kind of usage alerts one to recognize the presence of implicit (Rom 3:10-18) and explicit (Rom 4:1-25) midrashim as 'texts' in a more elaborate commentary pattern in Rom 1:17-4:25:[75]

1:17 – Initial texts (Hab 2:4, δίκαιος, πίστις).

1:18-3:3 – Exposition, verbally linked to the initial and/or subsequent texts (κρίνειν, 2:1, 3, 12, 16; δίκαιος, 2:13; πίστος, 3:3).

3:4 – Supplementary texts (Ps 51:6, δικαιοῦν, κρίνειν).

3:5-9 – Exposition (δικαιοσύνη, 5; κρίνειν, 6f.).

3:10-18 – Supplementary texts (Eccl 7:20; Ps 14:1-3; 5:10 (9); Isa 59:7f.; *etc.*; cf. δίκαιος, 10).

3:19-31 – Exposition (δικαιοῦν, 20, 24, 26, 28, 30; δικαιοσύνη 21f., 25.; δίκαιος, 26; πίστις 22, 25f., 27f., 30f.).

---

[73] But see Ellis, *Prophecy*, 137n, 218ff. and (for illustrations of proem-type expositions) 155ff. Cf. Rom 4:1-25; 9:6-29; 1 Cor 1:18-31; 2:6-16; Gal 3:6-14; Heb 10:5-39. It may be, as Bowker, 'Speeches in Acts' has suggested, that Acts 15:14-21 contains the remnant of a *yelammedenu* midrash on perhaps the last decisive halakhic question that engaged the Christian community as a whole: 'Must proselytes – and by inference any believer in Jesus as Messiah – be circumcised and keep the Mosaic regulations?'

[74] Cf. also 1 Cor 10:1-31: Initial 'texts' (1-5; Exod 13-17; Num 14:29) + Application (6) + Supplementary text (7; Exod 32:6) + Exposition/application (8-13) + Extended application (14-30) and concluding allusion to the initial 'texts' (31). Similar patterns are to be found in 2 Pet 3:5-13 and Heb 5:1-7:28. Cf. Ellis, *Prophecy*, 157.

[75] See Ellis, *Prophecy*, 217f. Cf. also 1 Cor 1:18-3:20: Initial 'text' (1:18-31) + Exposition (2:1-5) + Supplementary 'text' (2:6-16) + Exposition (3:1-17) + Final texts (3:18-20; Job 5:13; Ps 94:11).

4:1-25 – Final 'text'[76] (δικαιοῦν, 2, 5; δικαιοσύνη 3, 5f., 9, 11, 13, 22; πίστις, 5, 9, 11ff., 14, 16, 19f.).

The above examples indicate the way in which explicit midrash was employed, both by Jesus and by the early Christian prophets and teachers, to establish and justify their new understanding of the scriptures. There is some evidence that this usage represented only the first stage of a process that soon developed into an independent employment of the texts and of the expositions.

(3) *From midrash to testimonia*. Several scholars have argued that in rabbinic literature the mishna-form, that is, independent commentary that is topically arranged, developed in part from detaching the commentary from an earlier explicit midrash-form, that is, biblical texts + commentary.[77] Something similar seems to have occurred in the NT church. Explicit midrash was a means to establish a particular interpretation of scripture while isolated proof-texts did not, apparently, have that function or that effectiveness.[78] It is likely, then, that a midrash of a given text preceded its use as an isolated 'testimony' in which a Christian understanding of the text was assumed. The use of the same texts both in midrashim and as *testimonia* supports this supposition even if the particular NT midrash is not the direct antecedent of the 'testimony' text. For example, midrashim in Acts 2 and Heb 5-7 and (underlying) in Mark 13 establish, respectively, that Ps 110:1 and Dan 7:13 applied to Jesus; the independent use of the verses in Mark 14:62, summarizing Jesus' response at his trial, presupposes that understanding.[79]

On the same analogy certain clustered parables of Jesus, like those in Matt 13 or Luke 15, may have been excerpted from earlier commentary formats like those of Luke 10:25-37 or Matt 21:33-44. This is suggested especially for those parables that themselves echo OT passages[80] or utilize formulas customary in midrash.[81]

---

[76] Note the commentary pattern of Rom 4:1-25: Theme and initial text (1-3; Gen 15:6) + Exposition (4ff.) + Supplementary text (7f.; Ps 32:1f.) + Exposition (9-16) + Supplementary text with exposition (17; Gen 17:5) + ?Supplementary text (18; Gen 15:5) + Exposition (19-21) + Concluding allusion to the initial text and application (22-25). Cf. Borgen, *Bread From Heaven*, 47-52.

[77] Lauterbach, 'Midrash and Mishnah'; Halivni, *Midrash*; Otherwise, Safrai, 'Halakha', 148, 153-55. For a similar process in the targums cf. Kahle, *Cairo Geniza*, 202.

[78] Doeve, *Jewish Hermeneutics*, 116: 'Words lifted from their scriptural context can never be a testimonium to the Jewish mind. The word becomes a testimonium . . . after one has brought out its meaning with the aid of other parts of scripture'.

[79] Cf. Acts 2:14-36: Theme and initial text (14-21; Joel 2:28-32 = 3:1-5) + Exposition (22-24) + Supplementary text (25-28; Ps 16:8-11) + Exposition (29-34) + Final text and application (34ff.; Ps 110:1). See Ellis, *Prophecy*, 199-205. Cf. also Heb 2:6-9 with 1 Cor 15:27 and Eph 1:20, 22 (Ps 8); Acts 13:16-41 with Luke 3:22D, Heb 1:5 and 2 Cor 6:18 (2 Sam 7:6-16; Ps 2:7).

[80] E.g. cf. Luke 15:3-7 with Zech 10-11; 13:7; Ezek 34:11ff. Cf. France, *Jesus and the Old Testament*, 208f.

[81] E.g. οὗτός ἐστιν. Cf. Matt 13:20, 22f., 38.

Perspective and Presuppositions

It has been argued above that, in terms of method, the early Christian use of the OT was thoroughly Jewish and had much in common with other Jewish groups. Much more significant than method, however, was the interpretation of scripture offered by Jesus and his followers. In some respects this also agrees with previous Jewish interpretation, but in others it displays an innovative and unique departure. Sometimes the NT writers (to whom we shall limit this survey), and Jesus as he is represented by them, set forth their distinctive views in a biblical exegesis; sometimes they appear, at least to us, simply to presuppose a 'Christian' exegetical conclusion. They apparently derive their particular understanding of scripture both from Jesus' teaching and from implications drawn from his resurrection from the dead. Their perspective on the OT is especially shaped by presuppositions in at least four areas: (1) eschatology, (2) typology, (3) a corporate understanding of man and of Messiah, (4) a conception of scripture as a hidden Word of God. In the following survey their OT citations and commentary (i.e. midrash), illustrative of the early Christian perspective on these issues, will be indicated in the footnotes.

ESCHATOLOGY

The OT prophets predicted the coming of the 'last days' (אחרית הימים), and/or 'the day of the Lord' that would bring the 'kingdom of God', together with a final judgement and a redemption of God's people.[82] Apocalyptic Judaism, which was in important respects the midwife of first-century messianic Judaism, interpreted the coming kingdom in terms of a catastrophic and cosmic judgement of God followed by a renewed creation.[83] Two immediate antecedents of the Christian movement, the communities of Qumran and of John the Baptist, reflect this point of view and consider the kingdom of God to be 'at hand'. The Baptist points to Jesus as the one through whom God will accomplish the final redemption and judgement.[84] Jesus and the NT apostles and prophets are at one with apocalyptic Judaism in several respects.

(1) They conceive of history within the *framework of two ages*, this world or age and the age to come,[85] and they identify the kingdom of God with the

---

[82] Num 24:14; Isa 2:2-4; Dan 10:14; Hos 3:4f.; Amos 5:18-27 (cf. Acts 7:42f.); Mic 4:1ff.; Zech 14 (cf. Matt 25:31; Rev 21:6, 25; 22:1, 17). See von der Osten-Sacken, *Die Apokalyptik*, 39-43.

[83] Hanson, *The Dawn of Apocalyptic*, 150f. (in Isa 56-66), 371f. (Zech 14); Russell, *Method and Message*, 280-84; Ringgren, *Faith*, 155-66; Rowland, *Open Heaven*.

[84] Matt 3:2; cf. *1QpHab* 2:7; 7:2 where the Qumran writer identifies the community with 'the last generation' (הדור האחרון)'. Further, cf. Matt 3:1-12; 11:2-15; Mark 1:4-7; Luke 3:1-20; 7:18-28.

[85] I.e. αἰών (Matt 12:32; 2 Cor 4:4; Gal 1:4f.; Eph 1:21; Heb 6:5); κοσμος (John 16:11; 18:36; 1 Cor 7:29ff.; Eph 2:2; Jas 2:5; 2 Pet 3:6f.); οἰκουμένη (Acts 17:31; Heb 1:6; 2:5).

coming age.[86]

(2) They view themselves to be living in *the last* (ἔσχατος) days preceding the consummation.[87]

(3) They proclaim God's final redemption to be *a salvation in history*,[88] that is, a redemption of matter in time.[89]

Equally important, however, they modify apocalyptic ideas in significant ways.

(1) The two-fold consummation of redemption and judgement becomes *a two-stage consummation*. As 'redemption' the kingdom of God is regarded as already present in certain respects, that is, in the work of Jesus the Messiah,[90] and 'coming in power' within the lifetime of his hearers, that is, at the Transfiguration of Jesus and/or at the Christian Pentecost.[91] As 'judgement' and final redemption the kingdom will come only at the end of this age in the second and glorious appearing of the Messiah[92] which, as in the OT prophets, is represented to be just over the horizon, existentially 'near' but chronologically indefinite.[93]

(2) The two-age, horizontal perspective of apocalyptic Judaism is also modified by *a 'vertical', heaven/earth dimension*. A vertical perspective is already at hand, of course, in that the kingdom of God is 'the kingdom of the heavens' (ἡ βασιλεία τῶν οὐρανῶν).[94] Thus, the believers' 'treasure', 'reward'[95] and 'names' are 'in heaven', or 'in God', that is, where God's rule is now manifested

---

[86] Cf. Matt 13:40-43; Luke 21:31; Acts 1:6ff.; 1 Cor 15:50; Heb 12:26ff.; 2 Pet 1:10f.; Rev 11:15-18.

[87] E.g. Acts 2:17 in a commentary; Heb 1:2, introducing a *florilegium* of OT texts with commentary (?1:1-2:18); 2 Pet 3:3, introducing a commentary; Jude 18f. in an elaborate commentary on the theme of judgment (cf. Ellis, *Prophecy*, 221-36). Cf. also 2 Tim 3:1; 1 John 2:18.

[88] Cullmann, *Salvation*.

[89] This stands in contrast to conceptions dominant in current Platonic thought, which by the first century was also influential not only among the Stoics and Pythagoreans but also in some Jewish circles and which postulated a deliverance of the 'soul' from matter and out of time. See Perlan, 'Greek Philosophy' 126-29; Brehier, *History of Philosophy*, 137, 168-72. On body/soul dualism in rabbinic and intertestamental Jewish literature cf. Meyer, *Hellenistisches*; Russell, *Method and Message*, 353-90. See also Cullmann, *Immortality of the Soul*; id., *Christ and Time*, 139-43.

[90] E.g. Luke 10:9, 11:20; Col 1:12f.; John 11:24f. Kümmel, *Theology*, 36-39 Ellis, *Eschatology*, 11-14, 16f.

[91] Acts 2:16f. in a commentary. Cf. Mark 9:1f.; John 14:12; Acts 1:8; Rom 14:17; 15:18f. The eschatological power (δύναμις) of the Holy Spirit that was manifested in Jesus' ministry was, after Pentecost, experienced in the wider Christian community. Cf. Ellis, 'Present and Future Eschatology'. Otherwise: Kümmel, *Promise and Fulfilment*, 19-87.

[92] Luke 21:31, applying a re-worked commentary (21:8-28 = Mark 13:5-27 = Matt 24:4-31) on Daniel 7-12 (cf. Hartman, *Prophecy Interpreted*). Cf. Matt 25:31f.; Luke 22:18, 28ff.; John 5:25-29; 2 Thess 1:5-10; 2:8; Heb 9:27f.; 12:26ff. Note the omission of Isa 61:2b in Jesus' exposition of the passage at Luke 4:18-21. This accords with his conception elsewhere (e.g. Luke 9:54f.; Matt 11:4f.; 26:52ff.) of his present mission and is not to be regarded as a Lukan (or pre-Lukan) editorial even though it also serves a Lukan interest (cf. Luke 22:50f. with Mark 14:47).

[93] Mark 13:32, applying a re-worked commentary; 2 Thess 2:1-7, with allusions to Dan 11:36, Ezek 28:2 and Isa 11:4; Heb 10:37, concluding a commentary; 2 Pet 3:8-13 in a commentary. Cf. Isa 13:6; Joel 1:15; Luke 12:39f.; 1 Thess 5:10; Jas 5:7f.

[94] Matt 4:17 *et passim*. But see Strack-Billerbeck, *Kommentar* 1, 172-84.

[95] Matt 5:12; 6:19f.; 19:21; Luke 12:33f., which may have been extracted from a commentary on Zech 11 and 13; Bruce, 'Book of Zechariah', 342-49; France, *Jesus and the Old Testament*, 208.

and from which it shall be revealed.[96] This vertical element is given a specifically Christian understanding in terms of the Messiah who has been exalted into heaven.[97] For in the resurrected body of the Messiah the world to come has been brought into being and, pending its public revelation to earth on the last day,[98] is now manifested 'in heaven'.[99]

(3) Furthermore, the NT teachers regard this age and the age to come as standing in a *relationship of both discontinuity and continuity*, of *novum* and fulfilment. In contrast to some other Jewish views they consider resurrection life to be radically different from that of the present age.[100] They represent it, however, not as a 'non-material' life but rather as a modification of a strictly 'materialist' conception reflected in some sectors of Judaism.[101] In Paul's words the life of the age to come involves a 'Spirit-empowered body' (1 Cor 15:44), that is, the present body 'transformed' to be like Messiah's 'glorious body'.[102] One observes, here and elsewhere, that early Christianity defined the life of the age to come in terms of the testimony to Christ's resurrection in which the risen Messiah was seen to be both 'glory' and 'flesh', both a new creation and the physical body of the crucified Messiah redeemed from the tomb.[103] Thus, the age to come is regarded neither as a mere extension of the present age nor as isolated from it. The future age is considered to be rather a transformation and transfiguration of the present world that is brought about by a mighty act of God.

(4) Finally, unlike other Jewish groups, the first followers of Jesus teach that the age to come, the age of resurrection, would begin not at the end of the present age, as Judaism had usually believed, but in the midst of it. Already, in the resurrected Messiah, the first to rise from the dead and the firstfruits of those who have fallen asleep in death, the age to come has broken into the present age and now determines its ultimate course.[104] Again, they attribute

---

[96]   Cf. Luke 10:20; Rom 1:18 and 2:5f.; 1 Cor 3:13; 1 Pet 1:4f.; 4:13; Rev 20:15.

[97]   E.g. Acts 2:34 (cf. 3:21) in a commentary; Rom 10:6 in a commentary (? 10:4-11:12) on Deut 30:12f., etc.; Heb 1:13 in a *florilegium* (1:5-2:5) including Ps 110:1; Heb 8:1 in a commentary; cf. Acts 7:55; 1 Pet 3:22. Somewhat different is the commentary on Exod 16 in John 6:31-58 concerning the pre-existent Son, who has come down from heaven.

[98]   E.g. Matt 24:30 in a re-worked commentary; Heb 9:27f. and 10:37 in a commentary; 2 Pet 3:5-13 in a commentary. Cf. Acts 3:21; 1 Cor 15:22f.; Phil 3:21; 1 John 2:28.

[99]   E.g. Gal 4:26 in a commentary; Heb 2:9 (cf. 4:14) in a commentary (?1:1-2:18) on Ps 8 etc. Cf. Luke 24:25-27; Rev 21:1f.

[100]   Matt 22:30f. in a commentary; 1 Cor 15:44-49, commenting on Gen 2:7. Cf. Ellis, 'Life'.

[101]   E.g. in Matt 22:28 (presupposed); 2 Macc 7:7-29; 2 *Bar* 50:2-51:3; *Sib. Or.* 4:181-92.

[102]   1 Cor 15:44; Phil 3:21. Cf. 1 Cor 15:12-18.

[103]   Matt 28:8f.; Luke 24:26, 36-40; John 20:26f.; 1 Cor 15:4. The tendency to assign greater historical worth to traditions concerning the 'glory' than to those concerning the 'physical' character of the Messiah's resurrection does not appear to be justified. Cf. Alsup, *Post-Resurrection Appearance Stories*, 55-61, 266-74.

[104]   Cf. Acts 26:23; 1 Cor 15:20: Cullmann, *Salvation*, 166-85. For the thesis that Qumran also regarded the salvation of the age to come as already present cf. Kuhn, *Enderwartung*.

their convictions to their experience of the resurrected Jesus who becomes the model by which their views are shaped.[105]

TYPOLOGY

Typological interpretation had been employed earlier in Judaism[106] and became, in early Christianity, a basic key by which the scriptures were understood.[107] In NT usage it rested upon the conviction of a correspondence between God's acts in the present age and those in the person and work of Jesus that inaugurated the age to come. From past OT events and institutions it drew out the meaning of the present time of salvation and, in turn, interpreted present events as a typological prophecy of the future consummation.

(1) NT typological interpretation is to be distinguished from certain other approaches.[108] Unlike allegory, it regards the scriptures not as verbal metaphors hiding a deeper meaning (ὑπόνοια) but as historical accounts from whose literal sense the meaning of the text arises. Unlike the 'history of religions' hermeneutic, it seeks the meaning of current, NT events not from general religious history but from the salvation-history of Israel. Unlike the use of 'type' (τύπος) in pagan and some patristic literature, which assumes a cyclical-repetitive historical process, it relates the past to the present in terms of a historical correspondence and escalation in which the divinely ordered prefigurement finds a complement in the subsequent and greater event. Like rabbinic midrash, it applies the OT to contemporary situations, but it does so with historical distinctions different from those of the rabbis. Like Qumran exegesis, it gives to the OT a present-time, eschatological application, but it does so with an eschatological and messianic orientation different from that at Qumran.

(2) In the NT typology appears, broadly speaking, as *creation typology* and *covenant typology*. In the former case Adam 'is a type of the one to come', (Rom 5:14), that is, of Jesus the Messiah. A similar typological correspondence is implied in the designation of Adam, like Jesus, as 'son of God' and in the description of the age to come in terms of Paradise[109] or of a new creation.[110] Apparently, Jesus' teaching on divorce reflects the same perspective: the messianic age is to fulfil the intended order of creation in which both divorce

---

[105]   John 11:25f.; Acts 4:2; 1 Cor 15:12-22; Heb 2:10.

[106]   The Exodus provided the model or 'type' by which the OT prophets understood God's subsequent acts of redemption of Israel (Isa 40-66) and of Gentiles. Cf. Daube, *The Exodus Pattern*; Patte, *Early Jewish Hermeneutic*, 170ff.

[107]   Cf. Ellis, *Paul's Use*, 126-35; Kümmel, 'Schriftauslegung'; Goppelt, *TYPOS*; Luz, *Geschichtsverständnis*, 53-56.

[108]   Largely following Goppelt, *TYPOS*, 18f., 31-34, 235-48 (ET 17f., 29-32, 194-205). Cf. Luz, *Geschichtsverständnis*.

[109]   Luke 3:22, 38; cf. 23:43; 1 Cor 15:21f., 45-46; Rev 2:7; 22:2.

[110]   Rom 8:21ff.; 2 Cor 5:17; 1 Pet 3:20f.; 2 Pet 3:13 concluding a commentary.

and polygamy are excluded.[111] In a word the Messiah and his people stand at the head of a new creation in which, with a change of key, the original purposes of God are to be fulfilled.

In covenant typology various OT persons, events and institutions are viewed as prophetic prefigurements of NT realities. The Exodus events, Paul writes, were intended as 'types for us' and 'were written down for our admonition upon whom the ends of the ages have come'[112] or, more negatively, the ritual laws from Sinai were 'only a shadow (σκιά) of the good things to come.[113] In a typological correspondence oriented more specifically to Jesus, the royal and the servant psalms are applied to the Messiah who represents or incorporates in himself God's servant people and who is the heir to David's throne.[114] Similarly, Jesus can be described as the 'Passover Lamb'[115] who in his sacrificial death brings the covenant of Sinai to its proper goal and end[116] and establishes a new covenant.[117]

Since the new covenant associated with Jesus' death issues in the new creation associated with his resurrection, the two typologies may be closely intertwined. For example, the 'son of man' title given to Jesus is probably derived from typological interpretations of Dan 7:13 and of Ps 8:4-8 in which both covenant and Adamic motifs occur. The latter passage, apparently used in Israel's worship for the (messianic-ideal) king, also alludes to Adam.[118] In 1 Cor 15 and Heb 2 it is applied to Jesus, primarily as the resurrected head of a new

[111] Matt 19:8f. in a commentary. The phrase 'and marries another' (19:9) encompasses polygamy. The exception clause (19:9; contrast Mark 10:11) appears to be a postresurrection addition in which, if one accepts Matthew's prophetic credentials, the exalted Lord qualifies the principle in somewhat the same manner as God's command in Deut 24:1-4 qualifies Gen 1:27. A similar prohibition of polygamy and, probably, divorce with an appeal to Gen 1:27 is made also at Qumran (*CD* 4:20f.).

[112] 1 Cor 10:6, 11 in a commentary. Cf. Rom 15:4.

[113] Col 2:16f. (calendrical and food laws); Heb 8:5; 10:1 (Levitical system).

[114] E.g. Luke 4:18 (Isa 61:1f.; 58:6) in a synagogue exposition; Acts 13:33 (Ps 2:7) in a synagogue exposition, 13:16-41: Theme and initial texts (16-19; cf. Deut 4:34-38; 7:1) + Exposition (20ff.) + Supplementary text (22f. cf. 1 Sam 13:14; 2 Sam 7:6-16; Ps 89:21 (20)) + Exposition (23-33) + Supplementary texts (33-35; Ps 2:7; Isa 55:3; Ps 16:10) + Exposition (36-40) + Final text (41; Hab 1:5). Cf. Ellis, *Prophecy*, 199.

[115] 1 Cor 5:7; cf. John 1:29; Acts 8:32; 1 Pet 1:19; Rev 5:12.

[116] Rom 10:4. So, also, Heb 10:9f., which stands in a commentary covering Heb 10:5-39: Initial text (5-7; Ps 40:7-9) + Exposition with supplementary texts (16f., 30) and verbally linked to the initial text (8-36) + Final texts and application, verbally linked to the initial text (37-39; Isa 26:20; Hab 2:3f.). See Ellis, *Prophecy*, 155.

[117] Luke 22:20, 29. So, also, Heb 9:15, which stands in a commentary covering 8:1-10:39. Theme and initial text (8:1-13; Jer 31:31-34) + Exposition, incorporating allusions to various texts and verbally linked to the initial text (9:1-10:4) + Final 'text' (10:5-39), verbally linked to the initial text (διαθήκη, καινή, ἀληθινός).

[118] The terms 'glory' (כבוד) and 'honour' (הדר) elsewhere express the king's royal dignity (Ps 21:6[5]; 45:4f.[3f.]; Isa 22:18) and the affinities with Gen 1:26 are present in the references to dominion over the animal world. Cf. Bentzen, *King and Messiah*, 41-44; Wifall, 'Protevangelium?', 365 thinks that Gen 1-3 reflects a 'messianic' framework. But see also Kim, ' "Son of Man" ', 31-37: with the term, Son of Man (Dan 7:13), 'Jesus intended to reveal himself as the divine figure who was the inclusive representative (or the head) of the eschatological people of God' (36).

creation, but also as 'Messiah' and 'High Priest' and 'Seed of Abraham', terms with covenantal and national connotations.[119] Dan 7:13, in imagery similar to Ps 8, seems to identify 'one like a son of man' both with 'the people of the saints of the Most High' (7:27) and with the rightful ruler of creation, who is heir to the promises given to Adam.[120] In the synoptic apocalypse Jesus identifies his 'son of man' with his own future, glorious manifestation as Messiah.[121]

(3) An OT type may stand in a positive correspondence to the new-age reality or in contrast to it. This 'synthetic' and 'antithetic' typology[122] may be illustrated by two examples. Adam is like the 'eschatological Adam' in being the 'son of God' and the head of the race. But, in contrast, he brings mortality and sin while Jesus delivers man from these maladies.[123] Similarly, the law of Sinai in its ethical requirements reflects the character of God and is to be 'fulfilled' in the messianic age,[124] but in its ritual structures and obligations it served only as a 'custodian' (παιδαγωγός), to watch over us until the Messiah came, and contained only a 'shadow' of the new-age realities.[125]

(4) *A judgement typology*, in which God's earlier acts of destruction are understood as 'types' or 'examples' of eschatological judgements, also appears

---

[119] 1 Cor 15:20-28; Eph 1:20-22; Heb 2:6ff. in a commentary.

[120] Cf. Hooker, *Son of Man*, 11-32, 71f. For the view that identifies the 'son of man' in Dan 7 with a divine or an angelic figure cf. the discussion in Kim, *Origin*, 246-52.

[121] Mark 13:26f. concluding a commentary. Cf. also Mark 14:62; Rev. 1:7; 14:14ff. Betz, *Jesus*, 73-102.

[122] Cf. Luz, *Geschichtsverständnis*, 59f.; Hanson, *Studies*, 151ff. Abraham represents only a positive correspondence (i.e. his faith) and not an antithetic (e.g. his circumcision); Moses (Heb 3:2-6), Jerusalem (Gal 4:25; Rev 11:8; 21:2) and the Exodus (1 Cor 10:1-4; 2 Cor 3:7-11) may represent both.

[123] 1 Cor 15:21f., 45-49, commenting on Gen 2:7; 5:3; cf. Rom 5:12-21; Heb 2:6-9 in a commentary (1:1-2:18) with an unusual pattern.

[124] Specifically, 'love' (Deut 6:5; Lev 19:18) is the command on which the whole law depends (Matt 22:40) and by which it is to be 'fulfilled' (Rom 13:8; Gal 5:14) and without which it is transgressed. Cf. Matt 5:17-48, where the 'fulfillment' (17) of the law is related to being 'perfect as your heavenly father is perfect' (48). Cf. the commentary in Luke 10:25-37.

[125] In the NT the law is viewed from the perspective that 'Messiah is the end (τέλος) of the law' (Rom 10:4). However, as Cranfield, 'St. Paul', Davies, 'Law in the NT', 100 and Michel, *Brief*, 326f. have rightly observed, τέλος here does not mean simply 'termination' but carries connotations of 'completion', 'goal' and 'fulfilment'. Even legal observances that stand in contrast to the new-age realities, in spite of the dangers posed by them (cf. Heb 9:9f.; 10:1; 13:9) and the prohibition of them to Gentile Christians (e.g. Gal 5:2; Col 2:13, 16f.), were not forbidden to Jewish Christians when they were practiced in the right spirit (Matt 5:23f.; 6:2ff.; Acts 2:46; 3:1; 16:3; 18:18; 20:16; 21:20-26; Rom 14; 1 Cor 9:19-23). When not literally observed, they continued in their antitype, transposed into a new key: *Passover* continued in the removal of unethical leaven (1 Cor 5:7f.) and in the observance of Messiah's 'Passover' sacrifice of the new covenant (Luke 22:19f.; cf. 1 Cor 11:23-26); *circumcision* in the identification of the believer with Messiah's spilt covenant blood (Col 2:11; cf. Phil 3:3); *an altar* in the appropriation of Messiah's sacrificial offering (Heb 13:10; cf. John 6:53f.); *sacrifices* of praise and gifts (Phil 4:18; Heb 13:15; 1 Pet 2:5) and one's own life (Rom 12:1; 2 Tim 4:6) by which the afflictions of Messiah are 'completed' (ἀνταναπληροῦν, Col 1:24; cf. Rev 6:11). In the words of J.A. Sanders ('Torah and Paul', 137), the Tora was not eradicated in early Christianity but 'was caught up in Christ'.

in the NT. The flood and Sodom, for example, are used in this way.[126] Likewise, the faithless Israelite is a type of the faithless Christian;[127] the enemies of Israel a type of the (religious) enemies of the eschatological Israel, that is, the church.[128]

CORPORATE PERSONALITY

In the OT the individual person may be viewed as extending beyond himself to include those who 'belong' to him. Thus, the husband (at the family level) and the king (at the national level) both have an individual and a corporate existence encompassing, respectively, the household and the nation.[129] Corporate personality also characterizes the nature of God. It is not a metaphor, as modern Western man is tempted to perceive it, but an ontological affirmation from which the biblical writers' view of reality proceeds.

(1) For Jesus and the NT writers this perception of *man as a corporate being* is determinative for the proper understanding of scripture. It is exemplified, at its most basic level, in the interpretation of the sexual union in terms of Gen 2:24: 'The two shall be one (μίαν) flesh'.[130] At the national or covenant level it is reflected in such idioms as existence 'in Abraham' and as the nation's baptism 'into Moses'[131] or its existence as Moses' house or David's tabernacle.[132] More broadly, corporate personality of the whole of mankind appears as existence 'in Adam'.[133]

---

[126] 2 Pet 2:5f.; 3:5-7 in a commentary; Jude 7 in a commentary. The prospect of a final divine destruction of the wicked by fire (1 Cor 3:13ff.; 2 Thess 1:7-10; Heb 12:29; Rev 20:9-15; cf. 1 Pet 1:7) and even a cosmic conflagration (2 Pet 3:7, 10f.) has a part of its background in a 'Sodom' typology (Jude 7). Cf. Gen 19:24; Zeph 1:18; 3:8; Mal 4:1 = 3:19; *1 Enoch* 1:3-6; *Jubil.* 16:5f.; *1QH* 3:28-36; Thiede, 'Pagan Reader'.

[127] 1 Cor 10:6 in a commentary; Heb 4:11 in a commentary covering Heb 3:7-4:16: Initial text (3:7-11; Ps 95) + Exposition/application (3:12-15) + Supplementary text (3:16-18; allusion to Num 14:22f., 29) + Exposition (3:19-4:3) + Supplementary text (4:4; Gen 2:2) + Exposition with allusions to the initial and supplementary texts (4:5-10) + Concluding application and exhortation (4:11-16).

[128] Rev 11:8; Gal 4:28 in a commentary. Similarly, OT passages originally referring to Gentiles can be applied to Jews who persecute Christians (Rom 8:36 = Ps 44:22) or who indulge in sin (Rom 2:24 = Isa 52:5). Otherwise: Richardson, *Israel*; Jervell, *Luke*, 41-74. Cf. Ellis, *Paul's Use*, 136-39. Qumran similarly views its own community as Israel (Cross) or as the forerunner of eschatological Israel (Sanders) and the current Temple authorities as Gentiles. Cf. *1QpHab* 12:1-3 (on Hab 2:17); *CD* 3:18-4:4; 19:33f.; Cross, *Ancient Library*, 127ff. But see Sanders, *Palestinian Judaism*, 245-50.

[129] Johnson, *The One and the Many* 1-13; *Sacral Kingship*, 2f.; Pedersen, *Israel*, 62f., 263-71, 474-79; Robinson, *Corporate Personality*; Shedd, *Man in Community*, 29-41; Daube, *Studies*, 154-89.

[130] Matt 19:5 in a commentary; 1 Cor 6:16f.; Eph 5:31.

[131] 1 Cor 10:2 and Heb 7:9f. both within expository contexts.

[132] Heb 3:3-6, commenting on OT texts; Acts 15:16 in a commentary. Strictly speaking, in Heb 3 it is apparently God's house of the old covenant headed up by Moses in contrast to God's eschatological house headed up by the Messiah.

[133] 1 Cor 15:22; cf. Rom 5:12, 19.

Each level of corporeity is given a Christological application. As the two in sexual union become 'one flesh', so the believers in faith-union are 'one spirit' with Messiah or 'members of his body'.[134] In the 'new covenant' corporeity diverse images are used. At the Last Supper and, according to John, in a synagogue exposition at Capernaum Jesus identifies himself with the new-covenant Passover Lamb[135] and with the manna of the Exodus[136] that his followers are given to eat. In a similar typology Paul relates the Exodus baptism 'into Moses' and its manna and spring of water to the Lord's Supper understood as a participation (μετέχειν) in Messiah's death. This participation makes manifest that believers are 'one body', that is, the body of Christ.[137]

In imagery closely related to 'the body of Christ', the 'temple' (ναός) or 'house' (οἰκία, et al.) or 'tent' (σκῆνος, et al.) similarly reflects an interplay between the individual and corporate dimension of Messiah's person.[138] In the Gospels Jesus, that is, his individual body, is identified as God's (new) temple[139] or as the key-stone in that temple.[140] In Acts and the Epistles, as in the Qumran writings,[141] the community is God's temple or house.[142] But it is not the community abstracted from the Messiah but rather as the corporate dimension or extension of his person. Like the 'body' imagery, these expressions sometimes go beyond a covenant corporeity to express a contrast between two creations, 'in Adam' and 'in Christ'.[143] The conception of a corporate Adam and a corporate Christ underlie such Pauline expressions as 'the old (or outer) man' and 'the new (or inner) man',[144] 'the natural body' and 'the spiritual body'.[145]

This corporate view of man illumines the NT interpretation of a number of OT texts. For example, within this frame of reference the promise given to King Solomon can be understood to be fulfilled not only in the messianic king but also in his followers.[146] The 'seed of Abraham' has a similar individual and

---

[134] 1 Cor 6:16f.; Eph 5:30 referring to Gen 2:24.

[135] Matt 26:27f.; Luke 22:15, 19; cf. 1 Cor 5:7; 1 Pet 1:19.

[136] John 6:35, 49-56 in a commentary.

[137] 1 Cor 10:16f. in a commentary; cf. 1 Cor 12:12f.: here 'Christ' refers to the corporate body who 'unites the members and makes them an organic whole' (Robertson-Plummer, First Epistle, 271). Cf. Robinson, The Body; Moule, Origin, 47-96. 'The body of Christ' is a frequently used Pauline idiom for the church.

[138] Cf. John 2:19ff.; 2 Cor 5:1,6ff.; 1 Cor 6:15-20; McKelvey, The New Temple; Ellis, 'II Corinthians V.1-10'; Cole, The New Temple. See also Ellis, '1 Corinthians'.

[139] Mark 14:58; 15:29; John 2:19ff.

[140] Matt 21:42 (= Ps 118:22) in a commentary; cf. Acts 4:11; Rom 9:32f.; Eph 2:20ff.; 1 Pet 2:5, 6-8 (= Isa 8:14f.; 28:16; Ps 118:22).

[141] 1QS 8:4-10. For other passages indicating that the Qumran community regarded itself as the true Israel cf. Ringgren, Faith, 163, 188, 201-04; Fishbane, above, pp. 364-66.

[142] 1 Cor 3:9, 16; 2 Cor 5:1; Heb 3:6; 1 Pet 2:5; cf. Acts 7:49f.; 15:16.

[143] Heb 9:11 in a commentary; 2 Pet 1:13f.; 2 Cor 5:1; cf. Ellis, 'II Corinthians V.1-10'.

[144] Rom 6:6; 7:22; 2 Cor 4:16; Eph 3:16; 4:22, 24; Col 3:9f.

[145] 1 Cor 15:44; cf. Rom 6:6; 7:24; 2 Cor 5:6, 8, 10; Col 2:11.

[146] Heb 1:5 in a commentary; cf. 2 Cor 6:18 in a florilegium.

corporate reference.[147] Also, since Israel's Messiah-king incorporates the nation, those who belong to him – Jews and Gentiles – constitute the true Israel.[148]

(2) The NT writers' conception of corporate personality also extends to an understanding of *God himself as a corporate being*, a perspective which underlies their conviction that Jesus the Messiah has a unique unity with God and which later comes into definitive formulation in the doctrine of the Trinity. The origin of this conviction, which in some measure goes back to the earthly ministry of Jesus,[149] is complex, disputed and not easy to assess.[150] One can here only briefly survey the way in which the early Christian understanding and use of the OT may have reflected or contributed to this perspective on the relationship of the being of God to the person of the Messiah.

Already in the OT and pre-Christian Judaism the one God was understood to have 'plural' manifestations. In ancient Israel he was (in some sense) identified with and (in some sense) distinct from his Spirit or his Angel. Apparently, YHWH was believed to have 'an indefinable extension of the personality', by which he was present 'in person' in his agents.[151] Even the king as the Lord's anointed (= 'messiah') represented 'a potent extension of the divine personality'.[152]

In later strata of the OT and in intertestamental Judaism certain attributes of God – such as his Word (דבר/λόγος)[153] or his Wisdom (חכמה/σοφία)[154] – were viewed and used in a similar manner. In some instances the usage is only a

---

[147] Gal 3:16, 29 in a midrash covering Gal 3:6-29.

[148] Cf. Ellis, *Paul's Use*, 136-39; Goppelt, *TYPOS*, 140-51; Luke 19:9; Acts 3:22f.; 15:14-17; Rom 9:6f.; Gal 6:16; Phil 3:3; Heb 4:9; Rev 2:9, 3:9. Otherwise: Richardson, *Israel*; Jervell, *Luke*, 41-69.

[149] E.g. the impact of certain miracles in which Jesus by a word controlled nature (Mark 4:35-41 + Q; Matt 14:22-33 parr), created matter (Mark 6:32-44 + Q + John 6:1-15) and life (Mark 5:21-42 + Q). These miracles are in the earliest traditions and can hardly be regarded, *a la* classical form criticism, as 'mythological' accretions. Cf. Stuhlmacher, *Das Evangelium, passim*; Ellis, *Prophecy*, 43f., 239-47; Josephus, *Ant.* 18:63f. (παραδόξων ἔργων). However, they were attributed by Jesus' opponents (Mark 3:22 + Q) and later rabbinic tradition (*B.T. Sanhedrin* 43a, cf. 107b) to demonic power, by rationalists to misapprehensions or trickery (cf. Grant, *Miracle and Natural Law*; Smith, *Jesus the Magician*). Significant also were Jesus' sovereign 'I' sayings (Matt 5:22 etc.) and his claim to forgive sins (Mark 2:5 + Q), to have a unique and reciprocal knowledge of God (Matt 11:27 par; Mark 14:36) and (implicitly) to raise himself from the dead (Mark 14:58, ἀχειροποίητος cf. John 2:19f.) See Jeremias, *Abba*, 15-67 (= *Prayers*, 11-65); but see Harvey, *Jesus*, 168f.

[150] Dunn, *Christology*; Hengel, *Son of God*; Jeremias, *New Testament Theology*, 250-311; de Jonge, *Jesus*, 141-68; Kim, *Origin*; Marshall, *Origins*; Moule, *Origin*; Turner, *Jesus the Christ*, 7-28.

[151] Johnson, *The One and the Many*, 16; cf. Gen 18-19; Judg 6:11-23; Johnson, *Cultic Prophet*, 10f., 176f., 248ff., 318f.

[152] Johnson, *Sacral Kingship*, 14, 122f.; Bentzen, *King and Messiah*, 19.

[153] E.g. Isa 9:8; 55:10f.; cf. *Wis* 18:15; Schmidt 'Davar'. Quite different from the NT thought is the Greek (Stoic) philosophical conception of the Logos as the divine reason, which probably lies behind Philo's identification of the wisdom (σοφία) of God with the word (λόγος) of God and his designation of the latter as 'a second God' (*L.A.* 1:65; 2:86; *Q.G.* 2:62 on Gen 9:6). Cf. Bréhier, *Les idees philosophiques*, 83-86; Kleinknecht, 'Der Logos'. Otherwise: Wolfson, *Philo* 1, 289-94.

[154] Especially *Wis* 7:21-27, in which Wisdom is the omniscient and omnipotent creator and is identified with the Spirit of God; cf. Sir 24:3. Cf. Prov 8:22f.

poetic personification, a description of God's action under the name of the particular divine attribute that he employs. In others, however, it appears to represent a divine hypostasis, the essence of God's own being that is at the same time distinguished from God.

From this background, together with a messianic hope that included the expectation that YHWH himself would come to deliver Israel,[155] the followers of Jesus would have been prepared, wholly within a Jewish monotheistic and 'salvation history' perspective, to see in the Messiah a manifestation of God. In the event they were brought to this conclusion by their experience of Jesus' works and teachings, particularly as it came to a crescendo in his resurrection appearances and commands. Although during his earthly ministry they had, according to the Gospel accounts, occasionally been made aware of a strange otherness about Jesus,[156] only after his resurrection do they identify him as God. Paul, the first literary witness to do this,[157] probably expresses a conviction initially formed at his Damascus Christophany.[158] John the Evangelist, who wrote later but who either saw the risen Lord or was a bearer of early traditions about that event, also describes the confession of Jesus as God as a reaction to the resurrection appearances.[159] Yet, such direct assertions of Jesus' deity are exceptional in the NT[160] and could hardly have been sustained among Jewish believers apart from a perspective on the OT that affirmed and/or confirmed a manifestation of YHWH in and as Messiah.

---

[155] Mal 3:1; cf. Zech 4:10 with Zech 4:14; 6:5. On this expectation in first-century Judaism cf. *Ps Sol* 17:36; *Test Simeon* 6:5; *Test Levi* 2:11; 5:2; *Test Judah* 22:2; *Test Naph* 8:3; *Test Asher* 7:3. Similarly, Matt 11:3 = Luke 7:19 (John the Baptist's disciples); cf. Luke 1:16f. with 2:11 (σωτήρ . . . χριστὸς κύριος = משיח יהוה . . . מרשיע); Mark 1:2, a testimony which is probably an excerpt from an antecedent midrash (cf. Ellis, *Prophecy*, 150f., 161f.) expounding Mal 3:1 in terms of Isa 40:3 and applying the text to Jesus the Messiah.

[156] Cf. Mark 4:41 + Q; Mark 9:2f. + Q; Lk 5:8.

[157] Rom 9:5f.; cf. Cranfield, *The Epistle*, 2, 464-70; Tit 2:13. The argument of the 'history of religions' school that Jesus was perceived in the earliest Palestinian church solely as a human figure and was given the status of deity only later in the Diaspora is a somewhat artificial construct and is not supported by the sources. Cf. Hengel, *Son of God*, 3-6, 17ff., 77-83.

[158] 1 Cor 9:1; 15:8; Gal 1:12, 16; Acts 9:3ff., 20; 22:14; 26:19; cf. Ezek 1:26ff.; Kim, *Origin*, 193-268; Thrall, 'Origin' 311-15.

[159] John 20:28f.; cf. 1:1, 14, 18; 1 John 5:20.

[160] χριστὸς κύριος in Luke 2:11 may also represent 'Messiah YHWH' and refer to Jesus' birth as an epiphany of Yahweh. Cf. *Ps Sol* 17:36 (32); Sahlin, *Der Messias*, 217f., 383ff.

The NT writers usually set forth Messiah's unity with God by identifying him with God's Son[161] or Spirit[162] or image or wisdom[163] or by applying to him biblical passages that in their original context referred to YHWH.[164] They often do this within an implicit or explicit commentary (midrash) on the OT and thereby reveal their conviction that the 'supernatural' dimension of Jesus' person is not merely that of an angelic messenger[165] but is the being of God himself.

The use of the OT in first and second century Judaism, then, marked a watershed in the biblical doctrine of God. At that time the imprecise monotheism of the OT and early Judaism moved in two irreversible directions. On the one hand Jewish-Christian apostles and prophets, via 'corporate personality' conceptions and Christological exposition, set a course that led to the trinitarian monotheism of later Christianity. On the other hand the rabbinic writers, with their exegetical emphasis on God's unity, brought into final definition the unitarian monotheism of talmudic Judaism.[166]

CHARISMATIC EXEGESIS

Some NT writers, particularly the Evangelists and Paul, represent the OT as a hidden word of God, a divine mystery whose interpretation is itself a divine gift (χάρισμα) and act of revelation. For this viewpoint they appear to be dependent in the first instance on Jesus and, more generally, on prior Jewish apocalyptic conceptions. Jesus argues against the Sadducees that they 'do not know (εἰδέναι) the scriptures'[167] and against other religious opponents that by their

---

[161] Matt 11:27; Mark 1:2; Luke 1:35; Rom 8:3; Heb 1:2; Kim, *Origin*, 109-36; Cullmann, *Christology*, 270-305.

[162] 2 Cor 3:16 (= Exod 34:34) in a commentary (3:7-18) on Ezek 34. 'The Lord', who is the Spirit, refers to Jesus as (the messianic manifestation of) YHWH: Paul makes no distinction between the Spirit of God, the Spirit of Christ (Rom 8:9) and the Holy Spirit. See especially Kim, *Origin*, 11f., 231-39. Cf. Ellis, *Prophecy*, 63, 67f.; but see Moule, 'II Cor 3:18b'.

[163] On 'image': 2 Cor 4:4; Col 1:15 (εἰκών); Heb 1:3 (χαρακτήρ); cf. Kim, *Origin*, 137-41, 229-68; Wilckens, 'χαρακτήρ' 421f. On 'wisdom': 1 Cor 1:24; cf. Luke 11:49 with Matt 23:34. Cf. Burney, 'Christ as the APXH', 160-77 (on Col 1:15-18); Feuillet, *Le Christ Sagesse*. Otherwise: Aletti, *Colossiens* 1, 15-20, 148-76.

[164] E.g. Rom 10:13 (= Joel 3:5); 2 Cor 3:16ff. (= Exod 34:34); Eph 4:8 (= Ps 68:19); Heb 1:6 (= Ps 97:7); 1:10 (= Ps 102:25); probably 1 Cor 10:26 (= Ps 24:1).

[165] Cf. Johnston, *Spirit-Paraclete*, 119-22; Kobelski, *Melchizedek*, 99-141.

[166] For rabbinic references to disputes with heretics over the unity of God cf. Strack, *Jesus*, 70*-74*. More generally, Segal, *Two Powers*, 33-155. However, even into the second century some mystical Jewish writings apparently continued to identify YHWH in some sense with other beings. Cf. Odeberg, *3 Enoch*, 82 (Introduction), 32f. (Text): Metatron, the exalted Enoch, has divine glory, conferred on him and is called 'the lesser YHWH' (3 Enoch 12:5). See now Alexander, in Charlesworth, *OTP*, 1, 243, 265 n. Cf. also Strousma, 'Form(s) of God'; Hengel, *Judaism and Hellenism*, 1, 153-62; Oesterley-Box, *Religion and Worship*, 195-221. But see Klausner, *Messianic Idea*, 293, 466; Urbach, *Sages* 1, 19-36, 135-38, 207f.

[167] Mark 12:24, in a *yelammedenu*-type commentary (Mark 12:18-27 + Q); cf. Matt 12:7.

traditional interpretations they 'make void the word of God.'[168] Since he used methods of interpretation similar to theirs, his criticisms give rise to a question: How does one 'know' the true meaning of a biblical passage, that is, its 'word of God' import? Jesus gives no direct answer to this question, but he appears to connect it with his role as a prophet, a role that others ascribe to him[169] and that he himself affirms.[170] Unlike the professionally trained scripture-teachers of his day, the scribes (γραμματεῖς), Jesus is said to expound the OT with an authority (ἐξουσία)[171] that in the Gospels is related to his claim to possess the prophetic Spirit.[172] Likewise, he attributes the response to his 'kingdom of God' message and to his messianic signs, both of which are rooted in the interpretation of OT promises, to the fact that God revealed (ἀποκαλύπτειν) it to some and hid (ἀποκρύπτειν) it from others.[173] This is evident, for example, in his response to the Baptist as well as in his sermon at Nazareth.[174]

In similar imagery Jesus describes his parables as a veiling of his message from 'those outside' but an aid to understanding for his disciples because 'to you it is given [by God] to know the mysteries (γνῶναι τὰ μυστήρια) of the kingdom of God'.[175] As has been observed above, Jesus uses 'parable' in the sense of 'mystery' or 'dark saying', the meaning that the term carries in some other Jewish literature.[176] He also employs such veiled meanings in his exposition of scripture.[177]

There is then a paradox about Jesus' biblical exposition. He follows exegetical methods that were current in Judaism and regards them as a useful means to expound the biblical passages. Nevertheless, he recognizes that the meaning of scripture – even his exposition of it – remains hidden from many and, at least in the latter part of his ministry, he seems deliberately to veil the presentation of

[168] Matt 15:6, in a *yelammedenu*-type commentary (15:1-9 par). Perhaps the pericope extends to Matt 15:1-20; cf. Daube, *New Testament*, 143.

[169] Mark 6:15 par; 8:28 parrs; cf. 14:65 parr; 8:11 + Q; Luke 7:39.

[170] Mark 6:4 parr; Luke 13:33; John 4:44. His disclosure of visions in Luke 10:18; cf. Matt 4:2-11 (Q) falls into the same category. Cf. Hengel, *Charismatic Leader*, 63-71.

[171] Mark 1:22 par, in the context of synagogue teaching, i.e. biblical exposition. Cf. Matt 7:29. On the definition of γραμματεῖς and the distinction between the scribes and the Pharisees see Jeremias, *Jerusalem*, 233-45, 252-59; Neusner, *Early Rabbinic Judaism*, 66f.; Safrai, 'Halakha', 149-50.

[172] Cf. Luke 4:18, 21, 24, in a commentary.

[173] Matt 11:25, as a sequel to the identification of his message (11:5) and of the role of the Baptist (11:10-14) with the fulfilment of OT promises; similarly, in Luke 10:21f. the same saying is placed after the preaching of the seventy that the kingdom of God promised in the scriptures has come in Jesus (10:5f., 9). Cf. Matt 16:16f.; Luke 9:45; 19:42; 22:32, 45.

[174] Luke 7:22f. (Q); 7:35; 4:18f., 21, 25f.; cf. Isa 29:18f.; 61:1f.; cf. Ellis, *Gospel*, 120.

[175] Matt 13:11 (Q); cf. Mark 4:11. The passive form veils a reference to deity; cf. Blass-de Brunner-Funk, *A Greek Grammar*, 72, 164f., 176.

[176] Jeremias, *Parables*, 16. Cf. Ezek 17:2; Hab 2:6; Ps 49:5; 78:2; *1 Enoch* 68:1; Sir 47:17; *Barn* 6:10; 17:2.

[177] Cf. Matt 15:12, 15-20, explaining an exposition (15:1-9); Mark 12:1-12 + Q, in a commentary. Cf. Mark 12:12 with 12:36f.; John 7:38f. Certain assertions about his relationship to God, his messiahship and other matters also have this veiled character. Cf. Mark 4:33f. par.; 8:15-18 parrs; 14:58 with John 2:19f.; Luke 9:45; John 4:13f.; 12:32ff.; 16:25.

his message. The acceptance of his exposition, and of his teaching generally, depends in his view on a divine opening of the minds of the hearers:

> He who has ears to hear let him hear . . .
> Blessed are your ears because they hear.[178]

In the writings of Paul and of Peter[179] there is the same conception of the OT as a hidden wisdom that was long concealed but is now revealed. In Paul it often concerns the particular task of his ministry 'to make known the mystery (γνωρίσαι τὸ μυστήριον) of the gospel', namely, the inclusion of the Gentiles in eschatological Israel.[180] This purpose of God is a divine mystery or wisdom (σοφία) that was not made known (οὐκ γνωρισθῆναι) and indeed was hidden (σιγᾶν, ἀποκρύπτεσθαι) for ages but is now (νῦν) revealed (ἀποκαλύπτεσθαι), made known (γνωρισθῆναι) and manifest (φανερωθῆναι), especially in the writings of Paul and other pneumatics,[181] in his preaching 'by the Spirit'[182] and in his messianic/eschatological exposition of scripture.

In 1-2 Corinthians and in the Pastorals[183] Paul describes the broader gospel message in a similar way. In 2 Cor 3 he likens the hiddenness of the word of God to a veil on the mind of (Jewish) unbelievers that keeps them from understanding the meaning of the scriptures read in the synagogue, a veil that is taken away when they turn to the Lord, i.e. to the Messiah.[184] More often he represents the unveiling as a revelatory understanding of scripture gifted to the pneumatics (πνευματικοί) who, in turn, disclose its meaning by inspired exposition to the Christian community and to interested outsiders.

In 1 Cor 2:6-16, a proem-type midrash,[185] and in 1 Cor 12-14 he discloses his rationale for this view of God's revelation.[186] He argues that certain believers are given a gift of divine wisdom (12:8), a prophetic endowment that enables them to speak 'the wisdom that has been hidden in a mystery' (2:7) and, indeed, 'to know (εἰδέναι) all mysteries' (13:2; cf. 2:12) because 'God has revealed (ἀποκαλύψαι) them to us through the Spirit' (2:10). They are called pneumatics (2:13, 15; 12:1ff.), a term that is probably equivalent to 'man of the Spirit' in Hos 9:7, that is, a prophet (14:37). As recipients and transmitters of divine mysteries and of wisdom, they are the 'mature' (τέλειοι) believers who 'have the mind of Christ' (2:16) and who rightly interpret (συγκρίνειν) the things of

---

[178] Matt 13:9, 16; cf. Mark 4:9, 12 + Q; Matt 11:15; 13:43; Luke 24:32.
[179] 1 Pet 1:11f., 20.
[180] Rom 16:25f.; Eph 3:2f., 5f., 9f.; Col 1:25ff. The theme is present also in the cited (εἰδότες ὅτι) hymn in 1 Pet 1:18-21 if, as is probable, 1 Pet 1:18 identifies the audience as Gentiles, i.e. God-fearers. So, van Unnik, *Sparsa Collecta* 2, 3-82, 32f., 81.
[181] Rom 16:26.
[182] Eph 3:3, 5; cf. Col 1:28 ('in wisdom').
[183] 2 Tim 1:9f., 11, in a (preformed) hymn; Tit 1:2f. Cf. Ellis, 'Pastoral Epistles'.
[184] 2 Cor 3:14ff., in a commentary embracing 2 Cor 3:7-18; cf. 2 Cor 4:3.
[185] 1 Cor 2:6-16: Theme and initial texts (6-9; Isa 64:4; 65:16) + Exposition (10-15) + Concluding text and application (16; Isa 40:13). Cf. Eph 3:3ff. Ellis, *Prophecy*, 213ff.
[186] For the detailed argument cf. Ellis, *Prophecy*, 45-62.

the Spirit to others (2:6, 13), expounding the scripture and affirming or testing (διακρίνειν) the exposition of other prophets (14:29, 37).[187] Such a pneumatic interpreter of the word of God is best exemplified by Paul himself. What is the background of his perception of scripture as a hidden wisdom requiring a charismatic, revelatory exposition?

Various parts of the OT[188] as well as some rabbinic writings[189] speak of divine wisdom and knowledge as God's secret and his gift to selected individuals. However, it is the teaching of Jesus and conceptions current in the contemporary Qumran community which provide the more immediate and significant antecedents for Paul's thought. Traditions of Jesus' teaching were certainly known to Paul and to his churches,[190] and they may have included some on this theme. But the Dead Sea Scrolls, which have affinities with Pauline thought and hermeneutic in a number of areas,[191] display a greater number of parallels with the Apostle's writing on this subject.

The wise teachers or *maskilim* (משכילים) at Qumran, including the Teacher of righteousness, understand their role to be like 'the wise' in Dan 12:9f. Indeed, they may take as their paradigm Daniel himself, whose gifts of wisdom (שכל, חכמה/σοφία) and knowledge enable him to understand sacred writings and interpret (פשר/συγκρίνειν) them, i,e. to reveal the mystery (למגלא רזא/ἀποκαλύψαι τὸ μυστήριον).[192] The same gifts of wisdom enable him to understand and expound the prophecy of Jeremiah and, by implication, they will also give understanding to the 'wise teachers' (משכילים) at the time of the end.[193]

The *maskilim* at Qumran consider themselves to have this role. They confess to God that 'by your Holy Spirit' you opened knowledge 'in the mystery (רז) of your wisdom' (שכל).[194] They are 'to test' (לבחן; cf. LXX διακρίνειν) those in the community[195] and guide them with knowledge and wisdom (שכל) in the mysteries (רזי) . . . so that they may walk maturely (תמימה; cf. LXX τέλειοι) with one another in all that has been revealed (גלה) to them.[196] The *maskilim* probably regard the Teacher of righteousness, 'to whom God has revealed all the mysteries of his servants the prophets',[197] as the leading representative of

---

[187] 1 Cor 14:37 concludes a section concerned with *inter alia* the regulation of the conduct of wives (14:33b-36) that is partly based on an interpretation of Gen 3:16. Cf. Ellis, 'Silenced Wives'.

[188] E.g. Gen 41:38f. (Joseph); Num 24:15f. (Balaam); Deut 34:9 (Joshua); Dan 1:17; 2:21f. (Daniel); Von Rad, *Wisdom*, 55-68.

[189] Cf. Jeremias, *Jerusalem*, 235-42 re esoteric traditions. Cf. *M. Megilla* 4:10; *M. Hagiga* 2:1; *T. Hagiga* 2:1, 7; *B.T. Pesahim* 119a; *B.T. Sanhedrin* 21b. Further, *4 Ezra* 14:45f.

[190] 1 Cor 7:10; 9:14; 11:23; 15:3; 1 Tim 5:18; Dungan, *Sayings of Jesus*; Ellis, 'Gospels Criticism' 46; Ellis, '1 Corinthians'.

[191] E.g. Murphey-O'Connor, *Paul and Qumran*; Ellis, *Prophecy*, 33f., 173-81, 188-97; Brown, *Semitic Background*, 24-27.

[192] Dan 1:17; 5:12; 2:47. Cf. Bruce, 'Book of Daniel', 255ff.; Betz, *Offenbarung*, 73-98, 110-42.

[193] Dan 9:2, 22f.

[194] *1QH* 12:12f.

[195] *1QH* 2:13f.

[196] *1QS* 9:12, 17ff.

[197] *1QpHab* 7:4f.

723

their own ministry.[198] If so, they would also have emulated his exposition of scripture. Both in their gifts and in their ministry the *maskilim* bear a striking resemblance to the pneumatics in the Pauline churches, and they shed considerable light on the background of the charismatic exegesis of the early church.

Conclusion

Biblical interpretation in the NT church shows in a remarkable way the Jewishness of earliest Christianity. It followed exegetical methods common to Judaism and drew its perspective and presuppositions from Jewish backgrounds. However, in one fundamental respect it differed from other religious parties and theologies in Judaism, that is, in the christological exposition of the OT totally focused upon Jesus as the Messiah. This decisively influences both the perspective from which they expound the OT and the way in which their presuppositions are brought to bear upon the specific biblical texts. Their perspective and presuppositions provide, in turn, the theological framework for the development of their exegetical themes and for the whole of NT theology.

First-century Judaism was a highly diverse phenomenon, as becomes apparent from a comparison of the writings of Philo, Josephus, Qumran, the (traditions of the) rabbis and the NT. The NT, which as far as I can see was written altogether by Jews,[199] is a part of that diversity but also a part of that Judaism. Its writers were Jews, but Jews who differed from the majority of the nation and who in time found the greater number of their company of faith not among their own people but among the Gentiles. And still today, apart from a continuing Judeo-Christian minority, the church remains a community of Gentiles, but Gentiles with a difference. For as long as Gentile Christians give attention to their charter documents, they can never forget that as those who are joined to a Jewish Messiah they are in a manner of speaking 'adopted Jews' or, in Paul's imagery, branches engrafted into the ancient tree of Israel and a people who have their hope in the promise given to Abraham. The centrality of the OT in the message of Jesus and his apostles and prophets underscores that fact.

Bibliography

A convenient listing of OT quotations and allusions in the NT may be found in NESTLE-ALAND, *Novum Testamentum Graece*, (cf. pp. 739-75) and the texts of the quotations, together with the corresponding Septuagint and Hebrew OT passages, in ARCHER-CHIRICHIGNO, *Old Testament Quotations*, and DITTMAR, *The*

---

[198] This follows if the Teacher is the author of (some of) the Hymns, as is argued by Jeremias, *Lehrer der Gerechtigkeit*, 176f., 264. But see Mansoor, *Thanksgiving Hymns*, 45-49; Dimant, 'Qumran Sectarian Literature', 523 and n. 199.

[199] Luke is the only NT author whom many scholars identify as a Gentile. But see Ellis, *Gospel*, 51ff.; *ibid.*, 'St. Luke'.

Old Testament in the New. For the history of research into the NT quotations compare ELLIS, 'Quotations'.

On exegetical methods the following are particularly instructive: BONSIRVEN, *Exégèse rabbinique*; DAUBE, *New Testament* and DOEVE, *Jewish Hermeneutics*. More generally, compare also ELLIS, *Paul's Use*; *ibid.*, *Prophecy*; LONGEN-ECKER, *Biblical Exegesis*; MICHEL, *Paulus*.

The conceptual background and thematic emphases of NT biblical interpretation are treated by BETZ-GRIMM, *Jesus und das Danielbuch*; DODD, *According to the Scriptures*; Goppelt, TYPOS; GRIMM, *Die Verkündigung*; and, more popularly, by BRUCE, *New Testament Development*.

Chapter Twenty

Old Testament Interpretation in the Writings of the Church Fathers

William Horbury

I met with certain barbarian writings, older by comparison with the doctrines of the Greeks, more divine by comparison with their errors; and it came about that I was persuaded by these, because of the unpretending cast of the language, the unaffected character of the speakers, the readily comprehensible account of the making of all that is, the foreknowledge of things to come, the extraordinary quality of the precepts, and the doctrine of a single ruler of the universe.

TATIAN, *Ad Graecos* XXIX (circa A.D. 165),
on his conversion to Christianity.

Introduction

THE DEVELOPMENT OF THE JEWISH SCRIPTURES INTO THE CHRISTIAN OLD TESTAMENT

The biblical writings of the Jews formed the holy book of the early Christians ('the scriptures', 1 Cor 15:3f.). The Pentateuch, Prophets and Psalms constituted the core to which reference was most frequently made in the second century (and later), but the Wisdom literature was also valued.[1] This mainly fixed but partly variable corpus,[2] read normally in Greek rather than Hebrew, was indeed supplemented by some writings of Christian authorship. In the second century 'the memoirs of the apostles', as Justin Martyr calls gospels, were read

---

[1] Junod, 'Formation', p. 109, on the basis of citations and allusions noted by Allenbach et al., *Biblia Patristica*, 1-3; and p. 114, where the view that the Wisdom books first gain high significance in Clement of Alexandria should perhaps be complemented by reference to their earlier importance for Christology (Prov 8:21-5 quoted from 'Wisdom' as testimony to Christ's pre-existence by Justin, *Dial.* 139; cf. Col 1:15-18) and the tradition of the Exodus (Wis 17:2, 18:12 at Melito, *De Pascha* 140, 186) as well as morality (Prov 1:23-33 quoted at length from 'all-virtuous Wisdom', 1 Clement 57; cf. Rom 12:20 [Prov 25:21f.], Heb 12:5f. [Prov 3:11f.]). On Ecclesiasticus and the Wisdom of Solomon in early Christianity see Gilbert, 'Wisdom Literature', 300f., 312f.

[2] The number and order of the books, still the subject of discussion by Jews, were investigated by Melito and Origen (quoted by Eusebius, *Hist. Eccl.* 4:26, 6:25), Jerome and others; see Swete, *Introduction*, 197-230; de Lange, *Origen*, 49-55 and Junod, 'Formation' (variations of Jewish practice reflected in Christianity); contrast Beckwith, *Old Testament Canon*, 182-98 (Christians varied a substantially unified Jewish practice) and Barton, *Oracles*, 13-95. See also Beckwith, above, pp. 51ff.; Ellis, above, 655-79.

at the assemblies of the church just like 'the books of the prophets', and the same is probably true of epistles in the name of an apostle.[3] Nevertheless, it was only towards the end of the second century that the churches began to use, in theological work, a generally recognized body of authoritative writings of Christian origin as well as Moses and the prophets.[4] Until then the fundamental document, as emerges from the sentence of Tatian quoted at the head,[5] was the Greek bible of the Jews understood in a Christian sense – indeed attached, in the mental furniture of Christians, to the principal items of the baptismal creed.[6]

The scriptures inherited from the Jews continued to be of prime importance to Christians throughout the age of the church fathers – the ecclesiastical writers of approximately the first six centuries – as art as well as literature attests. Nevertheless, the growth of a 'New Testament' in the second and third centuries signals movement towards firmer definition of a Christian context for the law and the prophets. Pressures both to denigrate and to exalt the ancient scriptures were at work in the church of this period.

On the side of denigration, popular philosophy strongly contrasted the spiritual and the material orders, and dismissal of the materialist-sounding Jewish scriptures could form an aspect of this contrast. Thus Gnostic teaching developed parts of the Jewish biblical inheritance, but characteristically proceeded by criticism of Moses. Marcion (active c. 140-160) wholly rejected the Jewish scriptures, and cut out books and passages which he thought Judaistic from the scriptures of Christian authorship. The attraction exerted by censure of Moses and the prophets appears not only (by implication) from the full refutations of Marcion by Irenaeus and Tertullian, but also from the incorporation of a view of the scriptures like Marcion's in the influential teaching of Mani (216-277) (see below, on Augustine's Manichaean period).

The prestige of the law and the prophets, on the other hand, continued to commend the Jews and to draw pagans towards the synagogue. The second and third centuries thus also saw the making and dissemination of the Old Latin version, used by Jews and Christians in the western Roman provinces. Further,

---

[3] τὰ ἀπομνημονεύματα τῶν ἀποστόλων ἢ τὰ συγγράμματα τῶν προφητῶν ἀναγινώσκεται, Justin, 1 Apol. 67:3; epistles of contemporary churches and their past or present leaders were read out (1 Thess 5:27, Col 4:16 [first century]; Dionysius of Corinth [probably under Marcus Aurelius] in Eusebius, *Hist. Eccl.* 4:23), and at the beginning of the third century this is said of the Pauline epistles ('recitantur', Tertullian, *Praescr.* 36). See Westcott, *General Survey*, 109-116, 188f.; von Campenhausen, *Formation*, 143f., 167f.

[4] Carpenter, 'Popular Christianity', 301; von Campenhausen, *Formation*, 147-209.

[5] A closely similar account of conversion through contact with the scriptures is given by Theophilus, *Ad Autol.* 1:14; Justin Martyr, *Dial.* 8 portrays his conversion as preference for the prophets over the philosophers. The stylization of all three passages attests the *éclat* of the Greek Bible of the Jews for the gentile.

[6] Carpenter, 'Popular Christianity', 298f.

the Christians, less numerous and secure than the Jews,[7] urgently endeavoured to vindicate the church's title to the ancient scriptures, and thereby to gain credibility and respectability. Amid these conflicting impulses the law and the prophets acquired their classical Christian context as books of the 'Old Testament', too well loved, too closely linked with Christian tenets, and too much needed for teaching and apologetic to be dismissed on Marcionite lines, but complemented – here in divergence from Judaism – by books of a 'New Testament' within a single and recognizably Christian body of scriptures.

The unification of this body was possible because the Jewish scriptures inherited by the first Christians were already bound together by a developed traditional interpretation.[8] The Christians received an interpreted bible, and into its traditional but flexible interpretation they incorporated – by way of contrast as well as complement – their own affirmations and scriptural writings. These affirmations and writings had themselves already been influenced formatively by the interpreted Jewish bible, but in turn they considerably altered the sense attached to what was now the 'Old Testament'.

LANDMARKS IN PATRISTIC OLD TESTAMENT INTERPRETATION

Here attention is concentrated on this Old Testament of the Christian Bible, and its interpretation is surveyed below, through consideration of various settings of exegesis in literature and life. Thereby, it is hoped, the significance for the early church of the Jewish scriptures in particular will be more easily seen than would be the case in a single chronologically-ordered survey.

The early Christian writers considered here range from Clement of Rome, at the end of the first century, to Procopius of Gaza in the Greek east (beginning of sixth century) and Gregory the Great in the Latin west (end of sixth century). In time and space they are bounded for the most part by the Roman Empire, but Syriac writers in Mesopotamia lived on and beyond the frontier. The lion's share of attention is gained by the eastern Roman provinces, and by writers in the Greek language, which was current also to some extent in the west; but Latin Christian writing begins to be plentiful at the end of the second century, and Syriac at the end of the third. Correspondingly, although the Hebrew biblical text was known to be transmitted by the Jews, the versions of the OT familiar among Christians were, in Greek and above all others, the Septuagint (third-second centuries B.C.), and to a lesser extent the revised Greek versions; the Old Latin (second-third centuries A.D.), gradually superseded by Jerome's Vulgate (translated c. 390-406); and in Syriac the Peshitta, in which the Pentateuch and perhaps the Psalter are Jewish renderings, but Christian work ap-

---

[7] Blumenkranz, 'Kirche und Synagoge', 84-5, 89, on Jewish population and influence; envy of the Jews as well as scorn prompts Tertullian's epigram 'vectigalis libertas', 'their liberty of worship is paid for by tribute' (Tertullian, *Apol.* 18:8).

[8] See Vermes, *Scripture and Tradition* and 'Bible and Midrash'; Koenig, *L'Herméneutique analogique*; Fishbane, *Interpretation*.

pears elsewhere. As the shared Jewish and Christian use of most of these versions suggests, the Christians lived often in local as well as mental proximity to the large Jewish populations of the Roman Empire.

Second-century exegesis has to be gathered from works of apologetic, teaching and controversy. The Apostolic Fathers, especially in the Epistle of Barnabas (before 135), and the Apologists, especially Justin Martyr (c. 100-c. 165), Melito of Sardis (writing c. 160-180) and later Tertullian, use scripture freely to meet Jewish and gentile affirmations, notably by treating OT passages as 'testimonies' and 'types' of the gospel. Similar interpretation also abounds in catechesis and in internal debate with gnostic and Marcionite views, as can be seen in Irenaeus of Lyons (c. 130-200), who wrote in Greek, in the brilliant African Tertullian (c. 160-c. 220), whose Greek writings are lost but whose Latin works make him the father of western theology, and in his more sober literary follower Cyprian of Carthage, martyred in 258. In the surviving literature, interpretation of this kind is presented in directly exegetical work for the first time – probably at the beginning of the third century – in the OT commentaries ascribed to Hippolytus.

Meanwhile, however, a cultivated allegorical interpretation, in the manner of Philo, had been developed in the expositions of a Christian philosophy by Clement of Alexandria (c. 150-215). His great successor Origen (c. 185-254) influenced all future exegesis by his textual researches and commentary, but became a sign of contradiction for his daring allegorization. His biblical work was used and continued by Eusebius of Caesarea (c. 260-340).

The inception of a Christian empire after Constantine's acquisition of power (312) was accompanied within the church by the Arian controversy over the definition of the divine status of Christ, a great question at the councils of Nicaea (325) and Constantinople (381), and externally by the pagan reaction brought to a head by the emperor Julian (361-3). Exegesis in the fourth and fifth centuries was correspondingly marked by the doctrinal question, in which OT texts understood to refer to Christ (notably Prov 8:22) were central, and by endeavours to create a Christian literature which could compare with and incorporate the pagan classical inheritance. These concerns formed the background of exegetical debate between the allegorizing commentators of Alexandria, such as Didymus the Blind (c. 313-98), and the critics of allegorization from the Antiochene school of thought, notably Theodore of Mopsuestia (c. 350-429). Syriac commentators felt the influence of Antioch and western Syria; Aphrahat (writing 336-345) and Ephrem (c. 306-373) developed the imaginative typology of less philosophical exegesis, and were not inclined to the systematic cultivation of allegory, and the commentaries of Theodore of Mopsuestia were soon translated into Syriac. On the other hand, Greek literary aims and accomplishments are especially evident in the exegesis of the Cappadocian fathers, intellectual leaders of the revival of Nicene orthodoxy which gained strength in the reign of the anti-Arian emperor Theodosius I (379-395); Basil the Great (c. 330-379) and Gregory Nazianzen (c. 325-c. 392), who had been fellow students at Athens with the young Julian, collaborated in an anthology of Origen's work on interpretation, and Basil's younger brother Gregory of Nyssa (c. 335-c. 395) expounded the life of Moses, the psalm-titles and the Song of Songs.

Jerome (c. 342-420), who was proud to call Gregory Nazianzen his teacher, is best known for his translation of the Bible into Latin from the original tongues; but he transmitted such from Origen and from later Greek exegetes of varying outlook into western tradition through his Latin commentaries. His contemporary Ambrose of Milan (339-97) naturalized Philonic allegory in Latin homily, and under Ambrose's aegis Augustine of Hippo (354-430) embraced the orthodox Christian intellectual tradition. In the west as well as the east, therefore, the fourth and early fifth centuries were a golden age of exegesis.

The anticlimax of the following period can be attributed in some measure, as far as the east is concerned, to the escalation of the permanently divisive Monophysite controversy on the nature of Christ after the council of Chalcedon (451). The succession of great Alexandrian commentators ceased with Cyril (died 444), and the Antiochenes, including the prolific exegete Theodoret (died c. 458), were attacked in the doctrinal struggle. The most characteristic and valuable exegetical development – one traditionally ascribed to Procopius of Gaza (died c. 526) – was the formation of *Catenae*, compilations of extracts from earlier commentators with reference to particular books. In the west, the fifth and sixth centuries were the period of barbarian invasions, but they also saw the assimilation of Greek exegetical work both in hermeneutic treatises and in the psalter-commentary of Cassiodorus (after 550), and they culminated in the grand and fertile pastoral exegesis of Gregory the Great (c. 540-604).

Settings of Interpretation in Literature and Life

HOMILY

'In the beginning was the sermon', a dictum devised as satire on the NT form-critics, is not a wholly misleading comment on Christian literature. Christians will have adapted the custom of synagogue homily to their own use,[9] and Christian homily addressed to Jews and pagans as well as the church assembly is already presupposed in Acts (13:14-42, 17:16-34, 20:7-9).[10] The character of the internally-addressed homily can be inferred from epistles which in part or in

---

[9] Moule, *Worship*, 43-5, 65; Jewish homilies on Samson and Jonah, originally delivered in Greek, are preserved in the Armenian Philonic corpus (Duval, *Jonas*, 1, 77-82; Siegert, *Predigten*), and Palestinian synagogue homilies of the Christian period underly the 'homiletic midrashim' transmitted in Hebrew and Aramaic.

[10] For discussion see Wilckens, *Die Missionsreden*, 72-91 (content of preaching to pagans better attested than that of preaching to Jews); on the orientation of the imagined homilies towards the educated pagan, Downing, 'Ethical Pagan Theism', (Acts 13) and 'Common Ground with Paganism' (Acts 17).

whole resemble homilies (e.g. 1 Cor 10:1-13; Heb; 1 Clem). 2 Clement, in which the writer imagines that his addressees 'are being admonished by the presbyters' (2 Clem 17, cf. 19), exemplifies early second-century homily; instruction and exhortation customarily followed the reading of the apostles or prophets, according to Justin Martyr (1 *Apol.* 67).[11]

Externally-addressed homily continues to be envisaged in later writings such as the (pseudo-)Clementine Homilies, the apocryphal acts of the apostles, and the acts of the martyrs. Apologetic needs mean that the OT here characteristically supports assertion of monotheism and argument from prophecy, as in the Acts of Justin.[12]

Internally-addressed homily has left a far greater literary deposit, of first importance as a witness to OT interpretation, and of special interest because this literary genre permits a measure of contact with the worship and thought-world of the congregations. Collections of sermons as transmitted may be arranged with reference either (like those of Origen) to particular biblical books or (like those of Leo the Great) to the seasons of the Christian year. These arrangements are editorial, but in practice the seasonal sermon is attested from the second century onwards (notably by the Paschal homilies of Melito and others), and at least from Origen's time books were sometimes expounded in course.[13] The expository series verge on commentary when given literary guise. Important OT examples are offered by Origen's homilies on Numbers, Joshua and Jeremiah (among other books); Augustine's *Ennarrationes* on the Psalms; and the homilies of Chrysostom on Genesis, Basil the Great on the Hexaemeron, and Gregory the Great on Ezekiel. Great preachers who expounded the Song of Songs include Origen, Gregoryy of Nyssa, and Gregory the Great.

The OT is also pervasively significant, however, in homily on NT books and subjects. Correspondingly, early homilies may quote the NT relatively rarely, but deal extensively with the Old, still in order to make distinctively Christian points. These features recall the close links present from the first between the

---

[11] Moule, *Birth*, 41, 195; Lightfoot, *Clement of Rome*, 2, 194-7, 257 (on 2 Clem. 19, noting reference to sermons also in Origen, *Contra Celsum* 3:50 and *Apostolic Constitutions* 2:54, 'after the reading, the psalmody, and the teaching on the scriptures').

[12] On the pseudo-Clementine writings and the apocryphal acts of the apostles, see Hennecke-Schneemelcher and Wilson, *New Testament Apocrypha*, 2, 102-11, 167-88 (175 on the speeches), 487-9 (a specimen homily, Acts of Thomas 82-6), 532-5; Kohler, 'Clementina', on OT interpretation (the true teachings of Moses and Jesus are at one). For apologetic speeches in the acts of the martyrs, see Musurillo, *Christian Martyrs*, 53, 42-5, 90-103, 138-45, 150-59, 328-45 (Acts of Justin; Apollonius, 2-46; Pionius, 4-6 [externally addressed], 12-16 [internally addressed OT exempla and warnings against Jewish influence, cf. n. 7, above]; Phileas). Coneybeare, *Apology and Acts of Apollonius*, 29-48, comments on English translation of Armenian version. The *Acts of Justin* speak of 'the God of the Christians, whom alone we consider the craftsman of the making of the whole universe from the beginning, and the child of God, Jesus Christ, who was also proclaimed beforehand by the prophets' (Recension A, 2.4, in Musurillo, *Christian Martyrs*, 42f.).

[13] Wiles, 'Origen', 454f.; on the nature, setting and development of preaching, and the practice of using publicly circulated sermons written by others, see Cheetham, 'Homily and Homiliarium'; Barre-Grégoire, 'Homéliaires'; Eales, 'Preaching' and Lamb, 'The Bible in the Liturgy', 575-7.

new Christian tenets and the Jewish scriptures. Subject-matter may be controversial (against Judaism or heresy) as well as doctrinal, devotional and moral.

The widespread homiletic employment of the OT owes much to the 'spiritual' exegesis discussed below, which finds Christianity in the ancient scriptures by type, allegory or mystical interpretation. Thus, to take a famous instance, for Origen and other homilists on the Song of Songs the bridegroom was Christ, the bride the soul or the church.[14] A second mode of interpretation of abiding importance in the sermon is the treatment of the OT as a book of moral *exempla*. A sophisticated instance is Ambrose's *Apologia for David*, a sermon on Psalm 51 using David's example to inculcate penitence.[15] Both moral and mystical interpretations already appear in the homily-like 1 Corinthians 10, where the wilderness wanderings 'were written for our instruction' and 'the rock was the Christ' (verses 4 and 11). Here and in other early sources the Jewish derivation of these modes of interpretation can be sensed.

COMMENTARY

Continuous commentary on the Greek classics was an established and highly developed literary from in the first century of the Christian era, notably at Alexandria, and comparable treatment of Latin texts had begun.[16] Similarly, at least some Jews had commented on their own ancient writings. Hebrew commentaries on parts of the Pentateuch and the Prophets were made known, often fragmentarily, by the Judaean desert discoveries; and Philo, who can be called a commentator especially for his biblical Questions, may use lost commentaries.[17] Nevertheless, the earliest surviving Greek expositions of the Jewish scriptures in commentary form are Christian.[18]

---

[14] Rousseau, *Origène*, 7-57.

[15] Hadot-Cordier, *Ambroise de Milan: Apologie de David*, 7-43 (classifying the work as a rewritten exegetical homily). On exempla see also nn. 51, 56 and 59, below, and Daniélou, *Latin Christianity*, 322-8.

[16] Famous Alexandrian commentators were Aristarchus (2nd century B.C.), Didymus Chalcenteros (c. 80-10 B.C.), and Theon, who lived under Tiberius; in Latin, M. Valerius Probus (c. A.D. 20-105) commented on Virgil. See Pfeiffer, *Classical Scholarship* 1, 212-33, 276f.; Wilamowitz-Lloyd-Jones, *Classical Scholarship*, 12.

[17] Much of the Philonic corpus can be viewed as an allegorical commentary on the Pentateuch, modelled on the commentaries of the Greek poets (cf. Amir, above, pp. 450-52; Petit, *L'ancienne version latine* 1, 1-3; Dillon in Winston-Dillon, *Two Treatises of Philo*, 77-87 [specifying Stoic exegesis of Homer]); Philo's *Quaestiones* on Genesis and Exodus represent a form of exegesis later used by the church fathers (Bardy, *'Quaestiones'*), and such 'questions and answers' are viewed as the core of his exegesis in *De Gigantibus* and *Quod Deus Sit Immutabilis* by V. Nikiprowetsky in Winston-Dillon, *ibid.*, 5-75.

[18] The Platonists Celsus (2nd century A.D.) and Porphyry (c. 232-306) knew and criticized the OT, but probably relied on existing Christian and Jewish exegesis (Burke, 'Celsus and the Old Testament'; Casey, 'Porphyry and the Origin of the Book of Daniel'). On the origins and development of Christian commentary see Newlands, *Hilary*, 15-41.

At the beginning of the third century, Clement of Alexandria gives a commentary-like exegesis of Ps 19, perhaps from Pantaenus or some other predecessor; and from the OT commentaries of Hippolytus those on Daniel, the Song of Songs and the blessings of Isaac, Jacob and Moses survive.[19] The OT commentaries of Origen have been transmitted more fragmentarily than his homilies, but that on the Song of Songs is known in full. At the end of the century Eusebius of Caesarea, notable as biblical scholar as well as historian and apologist, commented on the Psalms and Isaiah.[20] Latin commentary was begun by his Pannonian contemporary Victorinus of Petau.[21]

From the beginning of the fourth century onwards commentators abound, but it is still the case that much of their work is lost, despite recoveries in modern times. Origen's pervasive influence was a cause of debate,[22] but his formulation of interpretative principles could not be ignored, and in this period the Cappadocian fathers – men of letters concerned with biblical exegesis both for its own sake and for its spiritual and doctrinal importance – composed their Philocalia of Origen, an anthology largely devoted to his biblical work.[23] The commentators of Alexandria and Antioch can roughly be classified as defenders and critics, respectively, of allegorical interpretation, but the Syrians can only be called an 'Antiochene school' in a loose sense.[24]

OT commentators of note include, in Alexandria, Didymus the Blind and Cyril of Alexandria , and in Syria Eusebius of Emesa,[25] Apollinaris of Laodicea,[26] Theodore of Mospsuestia and Theodoret of Cyrrhus. Among Latin commenta-

---

[19] Clement of Alexandria, *Eclogae Propheticae*, 51-62, with the comments by Bousset, *Schulbetrieb*, pp. 161-3, 190-2 and Nardi, *Clemente Alessandrino: Estratti Profetici*, pp. 15-18; Richard, 'Hippolyte de Rome' cols. 536-40; Simonetti, *Rufin d'Aquilée*.

[20] Barnes, *Constantine and Eusebius*, pp. 95-105; Rondeau, *Les commentaires patristiques du psautier* 1, 64-75.

[21] Commentaries by Victorinus (all now lost) on Genesis, Exodus, Leviticus, Isaiah, Ezekiel, Habakkuk 'and many others' are listed by Jerome, *De Viris Illustribus*, 74 (*PL* 23, 683).

[22] *ODCC* s. 'Origenism'; Kelly, *Jerome*, 227-63.

[23] Harl-de Lange, *Origène, Philocalie, 1-20 sur les Écritures, et la Lettre à Africanus*, 19-41.

[24] This traditional distinction is upheld by Duval, *Jonas*, p. 264, n. 114 (noting that Origen, influential on both groups, was less extreme as an allegorist than is sometimes maintained).

[25] Diestel, *Geschichte*, 127f.; Devréesse, *Octateuque*, 55-103; Lehmann, 'Eusebius of Emesa's Commentary' (on the Octateuch, preserved in Armenian).

[26] According to Jerome, who attended his lectures on the Bible at Antioch (Jerome, *Ep.* 84:3), he wrote 'innumerable volumes on the holy scriptures' (Jerome *De Viris Illustribus*, 104; Kelly, *Jerome*, 59f.); for his surviving OT work see Devréesse, *Octateuque*, 128-54 (edits fragments on Octateuch and Kings); Mühlenberg, *Psalmenkommentare*, 1, 1-118 (edits fragments on Psalms); fragments on Job, Proverbs, Song of Songs, Isaiah, Jeremiah, Lamentations, Ezekiel and Daniel edited as noted by Geerard, *CPG* 2, pp. 314f. Harl-Dorival, *La chaîne palestinienne* includes comment on catena texts of Apollinarius on Ps 119; Rondeau, *Les commentaires patristiques*, 1, 87-93 discusses Mühlenberg's view of the origens of the catena tradition of Apollinarius.

tors of the period Hilary of Poitiers on the Psalms reflects Origen's influence,[27] and the Ambrosiaster, famous for his Pauline commentary, is represented on the OT by *Quaestiones*.[28] Jerome, with his Greek biblical learning, Hebrew knowledge and Ciceronian eloquence, represents the mightiest achievement of Latin OT commentary; but Augustine's exposition of Genesis 1-3, *De Genesi ad litteram*, and Gregory the Great's *Moralia* and Job are monumental works, and lesser commentaries worth noting include Rufinus on the Blessings of the Patriarchs, Cassiodorus on the Psalms, and Verecundus of Iunca (sixth century) on the OT canticles used liturgically.[29]

The blossoming of commentary led by the middle of the fifth century to 'the sad necessity of Catenae',[30] commentaries formed by the combination of extracts from various authors on each section of the text.[31] The *Catenae* preserve in this way some portions of commentaries which are otherwise lost.[32]

The interpreter who chose the commentary as his literary form thereby accepted various conventions.[33] He had first to settle on his text, for Greek commentators almost always the Septuagint. Controversy as well as scholarship impelled recognition that the Greek was a translation, despite widespread belief in its inspired quality.[34] The currency of onomastica,[35] and the making and transmission of such vast works as Origen's Hexapla and Jerome's Vulgate, evince awareness of the significance of the Hebrew.[36] Commentators differ

---

[27] Zingerle, *Hilarii . . . Tractatus super Psalmos (CSEL)*; see especially E.W. Watson in *NPNF* 9, xl-xlv (on Hilary's transformation of Origen), 235-48 (ET of homilies on Pss 1, 54, 131), and Newlands, *Hilary*, 134-58; also Rondeau, *Les commentaires patristiques* 1, 145-9, and de Margerie, *Introduction*, 2, 88-91.

[28] Ambrosiaster, *Quaestiones Veteris et Novi Testamenti*, edited by A. Souter (*CSEL* 50 [1908]; Blumenkranz, *Judenpredigt*, 33-7 (on Quaestio 44 'adversus Iudaeos'); Duval, *Jonas* 1, 227-30 (literature); Rondeau, *Les commentaires patristiques* 1, 162f.; Kelly, *Jerome*, 89f., 149 (literature).

[29] *Verecundi Iuncensis Commentarii super Cantica Ecclesiastica . . .*, edited by R. Demeulenaere (*CCL* 93, 1976); the review by M. Winterbottom, *JTS* N.S. 29 (1978), 241-44 includes some characterization of the work and textual corrections, criticisms and conjectures; a more favourable estimate of Verecundus is given by Duval, *Jonas* 1, 550-56 (he draws on Jerome, but has his own originality).

[30] 'La triste necessité des Chaînes', Doutreleau, *Didyme l'Aveugle sur Zacharie* 1, 36f.

[31] Devréesse, 'Chaînes exégétiques grecques'; Wilson, *Scholars of Byzantium*, 32f. (urging that the traditional identification of Procopius of Gaza (c. 475-536) as the inventor of the catena should be taken seriously); a substantial sample of Psalter catenae is given by Harl-Dorival, *La chaîne palestinienne*; for discussion of Psalter catenae see Devréesse, *Les anciens commentateurs grecs des Psaumes*, with Harl-Dorival, Mühlenberg and Rondeau, as cited in n. 26, above; on editions of catena texts, Geerard, *CPG*, 3. 1.

[32] The commentaries of Apollinarius of Laodicea (n. 26, above) form a good example.

[33] The conventions imposed on an author by the commentary form are described by Doutreleau, *Didyme l'Aveugle sur Zacharie* 1, 27-30, 41-50 and Guinot, *Théodoret . . . sur Isaïe* 1, 37-42.

[34] De Lange, *Origen*, 50f.; Guinot, *Théodoret . . . sur Isaïe* 1, 54f.

[35] The onomasticon, or vocabulary interpreting names, was developed in ancient study of the Greek classics; on Eusebius's biblical onomasticon, and its predecessors by Origen and by a Jewish author, see Barnes, *Constantine and Eusebius*, 106-111, with nn. 32-3; De Lange, *Origen*, 16-17, 119-21.

[36] On the Hexapla see Tov above, pp. 181-87; on the Vulgate, Kedar, above, pp. 320-34.

considerably in their care for the text,[37] but reference to other Greek versions is widespread, and attempts to evaluate the evidence are made; scholarly Syrians, like Theodore of Mopsuestia and Theodoret, refer to Aquila, Symmachus and Theodotion, the Syriac bible and the Hebrew in their comments on the Septuagint.[38] Jerome is the most famous of a number of commentators who cite Jewish exegetical traditions.[39]

The commentary might receive an introductory prologue, and the text was then treated through division into a few long sections according to sense or convenience.[40] These sections were subdivided into brief passages, varying in length from about half a verse to about two verses of the division now standard; each such passage formed the *lemma*, or text upon which comment immediately followed.

A commentary could embrace all the interests and modes of exegesis already mentioned with regard to the homily, but of its nature it gave prominence to particular difficulties and points of detail rather than general discussion. Nevertheless, commentary and homily should not be too sharply distinguished. The commentator can envisage an auditory, his interests are likely to be spiritual and pastoral as well as exegetical, and preachers in turn draw upon commentaries.[41]

CATECHESIS

Catechesis, in its broad sense of education in belief and morals, was a prominent concern, inherited from the Jews, among the earliest Christians (e.g. Luke 1:4, Gal 6:6, Heb 6:1f.).[42] Such education inevitably overlapped with apologetic, to be considered in the following section. That the ot formed the basis of instruction from the first is suggested not only by later practice (see below), but also by nt emphasis on the pedagogic value of the Jewish scriptures (Rom 15:4, 1 Cor 10:11, 2 Tim 3:14-17).

---

[37] Thus, by contrast with Theodore of Mopsuestia and Theodoret (n. 38, below), Didymus the Blind appears to admit any received reading without criticism (Doutreleau, *Didyme l'Aveugle sur Zacharie* 1, 48-50).

[38] Wiles, 'Theodore of Mopsuestia', 496; Guinot, *Théodoret . . . sur Isaïe* 1, 43-56.

[39] Bardy, 'Saint Jérôme et ses maîtres hébreux'; De Lange, *Origen*, 123-35 (literature); Loewe, 'Midrashim and Patristic Exegesis'; Lamirande, 'Etude bibliographique'; Baskin, 'Rabbinic-Patristic Exegetical Contacts' (bibliography); Lattke, 'Halachah' and 'Haggadah'.

[40] In Didymus the Blind on Zechariah they appear to be dictated by length, and perhaps scribal convenience; in Theodoret on Isaiah they appear to correspond more closely to the sense of the text (Doutreleau, *Didyme l'Aveugle sur Zacharie* 1, 27-8; Guinot, *Théodoret . . . sur Isaïe* 1, 39-42).

[41] Duval, *Jonas* 1, 59f.

[42] Carrington, *Catechism*, Selwyn, *First Epistle*, 365-466; Davies, *Paul and Rabbinic Judaism*, 122-46; Davies, *Setting*, 406f.; C.F.D. Moule, *Birth*, 133, 177-200 (literature).

The OT formatively influenced Christian catechesis[43] not only through direct Christian resort to the scriptures, to be noticed shortly, but also through Jewish moral teaching, especially as expressed in summaries and expansions of the Law current among Greek-speaking Jews.[44] Thus, commandments, exhortations and maxims from the Pentateuch and the Wisdom literature appear in the second century in combinations sometimes inherited from Jewish moral teaching, now often in conjunction with sayings from the gospel tradition. The Decalogue stands out in this connection.[45] For example, an expanded adaptation of the Decalogue, with allusions to Proverbs, figures in *Didache* 2, *Barnabas* 19, and the Latin *Doctrina Apostolorum*, all probably indebted to originally Jewish exhortation on the 'Two Ways';[46] and in the *Didache* it is preceded by an exordium drawing on the sayings of Jesus. Similarly, the *Sentences of Sextus*, a second-century Christian collection of maxims which are largely of pagan origin, includes echoes not only of gospel sayings, but also of the Wisdom literature (155, cf. Prov 10:19; 419, cf. Wis 3:1).[47]

Such instruction will have been given during the second and third centuries not only in general preaching, and perhaps sometimes in teaching in Christian places of education,[48] but also and especially in connection with admission to baptism. Origen mentions 'beginners who are receiving elementary instruction (εἰσαγομένοι) and have not yet received the sign that they have been purified' (Origen, *Contra Celsum* 3:51). Catechesis in this more specialized sense included exposition of articles of belief – an element of instruction later to be

---

[43] Davies, *Paul and Rabbinic Judaism*, 129-36 (reviewing the work of G.Klein, P. Carrington and D. Daube); Selwyn and Daube in Selwyn, *First Epistle*, 460 (Selwyn), 484-8 (Daube); Daniélou, *Jewish Christianity*, 316-23 and *Gospel Message*, 192-4.

[44] Examples include Josephus, *Ag. Ap.* 2 (studied from this angle by Daube, *New Testament and Rabbinic Judaism*, 138-40; Kamlah, 'Frömmigkeit und Tugend'; and Vermes, 'Summary of the Law'), and the (probably first-century A.D.) Sentences of (Pseudo-)Phocylides (Gilbert, 'Wisdom Literature', 313-6), in which Leviticus 19, the Decalogue and the Wisdom books are important (van der Horst, 'Pseudo-Phocylides', 572). Greek translations of Hebrew Wisdom literature evince the importance of moral teaching; see McKane, *Proverbs*, 33-5 (on moralizing Septuagintal additions), and note that Ben Sira was translated for Jews 'who in the land of their sojourning are desirous to learn . . . so as to live according to the law' (Ecclesiasticus, Prologue).

[45] Grant, 'The Decalogue in Early Christianity'; Clement of Alexandria, *Strom.* 6:16 is a notable allegorical exposition of the Decalogue in a didactic setting.

[46] Latin text in Schlecht, *Doctrina*, 13f.; discussion of theories on the 'Two Ways' in Prigent-Kraft, *Barnabé*, 12-20, with commentary on *Barn.* 19, pp. 197-211 (noting a comparable expanded Decalogue in Clement of Alexandria, *Paed.* 2:89, 1; *Protr. 10:108, 5*).

[47] H. Chadwick, *Sextus*, 139, 180.

[48] Carpenter, 'Popular Christianity', 296 ('The constant need for moral instruction of converts exercised the ingenuity of Christian teachers. When Hermas or Second Clement spend a free half-hour in a little theological excursion it is sure to end abruptly in an earnest moral precept'). Christian schools of adult education are later attested at Alexandria and Nisibis (Eusebius, *Hist. Eccl.* 5:10, 1; Murray, *Symbols*, 23f.).

much elaborated[49] – and of the Lord's Prayer,[50] bu the OT retained its pride of place, although in Alexandria the books called 'uncanonized' by Athanasius (Wisdom, Ecclesiasticus and others) were used especially for beginners, perhaps following Jewish custom.[51] It was used in catechesis in two particularly notable ways.

First, and significantly for the fundamental position of the OT in the early church, the biblical narrative was re-told from creation onwards. This method, producing a shorter Christian counterpart of the book of Jubilees or Pseudo-Philo's *Biblical Antiquities*,[52] is followed in the first part of Irenaeus's *Demonstration of the Apostolic Preaching*; a consecutive account runs from creation to the building of Solomon's temple, whence Irenaeus passes to the prophets and the birth of Christ (Irenaeus, *Dem.* 9-30). This account is preceded by a brief exposition of the threefold Name of God, and followed (chapters 31-100) by an extensive demonstration from OT prophecies and proof texts of points already made.[53]

Such catechetical exposition by means of a narrative of biblical history was probably widespread; Irenaeus held that the true scope of Christian teaching was restricted to biblical themes (Irenaeus, *Haer.* 1:10).[54] The prevalence of this method may also help to explain the important place given to showing the dependence of Greek philosophy on the OT in the catechetically-oriented writings of Clement of Alexandria.[55] These inferences, like that already drawn

---

[49] For its fourth-century development see Cyril of Jerusalem, *Catecheses* (lectures to catechumens, introduced and translated by Telfer, *Cyril*); Gregory of Nyssa, *Catechetical Oration* (defence of the reasonableness of the incarnation, written as an aid for catechists; translated by W. Moore and H.A. Wilson, (*ANCL* 5), 472-509; Greek text edited with introduction and commentary by Srawley, *Catechetical Oration*); Theodore of Mopsuestia, *Homilies* on the creed, probably for catechumens (Syriac text with translation and introduction in Tonneau-Devréesse, *Les homélies catéchétiques* (see pp. xvi-xxviii, 2-281).

[50] Expounded by Tertullian, *On Prayer*, 1-10 (addressed to catechumens), followed by Cyprian, *On the Lord's Prayer*; Origen, *On Prayer*, especially chapters 22-30 (treatise translated with introduction and commentary by Oulton in Oulton-Chadwick, *Alexandrian Christianity*, 169-387; Origen's treatment compared with Tertullian's 224-30); and Theodore of Mopsuestia (Tonneau-Devréesse, *Les homélies catéchétiques*, 281-321).

[51] Carpenter, 'Popular Christianity', 298f.; Athanasius, *Festal Letter* 39, of 367, discussed by Harnack, *Bible Reading*, 73f. (the custom was known to Origen and may be Jewish), 121f., and Junod, 'Formation', 127f.

[52] On these Jewish works, and the comparable *Genesis Apocryphon* preserved in Aramaic, see Nickelsburg, 'Bible Rewritten', 97-110; the Syriac *Cave of Treasures* is a similar Christian compilation, perhaps fourth-century in its earliest form (Murray, *Symbols*, 37).

[53] Translation with introduction by Robinson, *Demonstration*, and J.P. Smith, *Proof*; translation and commentary by Froidevaux, *Démonstration*; Smith, *Proof*, 19-21, holds that the work does not really represent catechesis but see Carpenter 'Popular Christianity', 298, and compare Ireaneus and Augustine, discussed in the following paragraph.

[54] On Irenaeus as representative of catechesis, Carpenter, 'Popular Christianity', 298; on the biblical character of his teaching, Lawson, *Biblical Theology*.

[55] Clement of Alexandria, *Strom.* 1: 66ff., 5:86ff., discussed with other passages by H. Chadwick in Oulton-Chadwick, *Alexandrian Christianity*, 18-20 and Chadwick, *Early Christian Thought*, 43-5 and n. 52.

concerning the NT period, are supported by fourth-century evidence for the institution of the catechumenate.[56] Augustine assumes that an essential part of catechetical instruction is narration ('narratio') of the biblical history, to be carried on down to the present.[57] In the east, similarly, it was held that instruction before baptism should relate God's providential dealings from creation onwards; subjects noted include the flood, the destruction of Sodom and Gomorrah, and a list of OT saints from Seth to Phinehas (*Apostolic Constitutions* 7:39; fourth century, probably Syria).

In the Syriac *Acts of Philip* (perhaps fifth-century or later), correspondingly, a 'narration' betokens the miraculous conversion of Ananias the Jew; suspended by an angel head downwards above the sail of a ship at sea, he acknowledges to Philip the mighty acts of 'the Messiah thy God', in a long list running from creation through the events of the biblical history to the rescue of Susanna. In catechetical terms, this narration comes from the candidate rather than the instructor, and it may reflect a candidate's response more immediately than the narration itself; but, like the narration, it proceeds from confession of the Name, and after it Ananias is counted worthy of baptism.[58]

Narration in catechesis could be supported by biblical lessons and sermons in church services; Ambrose preached on Abraham to baptismal candidates, and he mentions that he gave daily discourses on right conduct, probably exemplified by the sermons on Abraham, 'at the time when the lives of the patriarchs or the precepts of the Proverbs were being read' (Ambrose, *De Abrahamo* 1:4, 25; 7, 59; *De Mysteriis* 1:50).[59] Further, a more summary but still comparable narration could find a place in liturgical prayer.

A second noteworthy catechetical use of the OT, to be viewed together with the narration, is the exposition of collected 'testimonies'. These are largely employed in apologetic, and are therefore considered in the following section, but their catechetical function has already been illustrated by the long final

---

[56] Information on the teaching of catechumens is summarized by Srawley in Thompson-Srawley, *St. Ambrose 'On the Mysteries'*, x-xiii.

[57] Augustine, *De Catechizandis Rudibus*, 1(1) (catechist unsure 'where to begin the narration, to what point it should be brought down, and whether at the close of the narration an exhortation should be added, or precepts only'); 3(5)-(6) ('The narration is complete when the beginner is first instructed from the text "In the beginning God created heaven and earth" down to the present period of Church history'); 6(10), 7(11); 17(28)-22(39) (first part of 'narratio' [from the creation to the birth of Christ; continuing to 24(45)], in a model catechetical discourse). See Christopher, *Augustinus de catechizandis rudibus* (text, translation, introductory and commentary), at pp. 3, 14f., 22-5, 34f., 74-97.

[58] Wright, *Apocryphal Acts*, 1, 78-80 (text), 2, 73-5 (translation); on the date, James, *Apocryphal New Testament*, 439 (451, summary of this passage) and Hennecke-Schneemelcher-Wilson, *New Testament Apocrypha*, 2, 577 (literature); a comparable list of mighty acts (ascribed to the Father rather than the Son) is incorporated in the oath exacted from Jews compelled to profess Christianity in the laws of the seventh-century Visigothic king Erwig (*Visigothic Laws* 12:3, 15, translated in Parkes, *Conflict*, 395-7). On lists of OT saints in Syriac writers and in early Christian prayer and art, see Murray, 'Rhetorical Patterns'.

[59] Thompson-Srawley, *St. Ambrose 'On the Mysteries'*, xi, 45.

section of Irenaeus's *Demonstration* (including developed Christian combinations of texts).[60] Illustrations of their use in catechesis, as more broadly defined, are offered by the third book of Cyprian's *Testimonies* (collection of texts with headings), and the Syriac *Demonstrations* of the fourth-century 'Persian sage', Aphrahat (imaginative concatenation and exposition of texts).[61]

The importance of OT interpretation in patristic exposition of Christianity is therefore heavily underlined by its centrality in catechesis. Advice to a catechist formed one context in which Augustine handed down his dictum that 'in the Old Testament the New is concealed, and in the New the Old is revealed'.[62]

APOLOGETIC

'Defence' or 'apologia' (Greek *apologiā*) 'on behalf of the gospel' (Phil 1:16, cf. 1:7) was viewed from the first as a duty of Christians; they should be 'ready always to offer explanation and defence' (*apologiā*, 1 Peter 3:15, 'to give answer').[63] Jews were similarly counselled 'Be alert to study the law, and know how to make answer to an unbeliever' (*M. Avot* 2:14, in the name of Elazar ben Arakh, end of first century C.E.). The link made in this rabbinic saying between biblical interpretation and apologetic[64] is normally also manifest in the Christian apologists. (Arnobius is the great exception who proves this rule.)

When addressing the gentile world Christians could develop existing Jewish apologiae, such as Philo's *Hypothetica* and Josephus, *Against Apion*; but a new and vital aspect of Christian apologetic was presented by argument against the Jews. A vast literature, in which OT interpretation is naturally central, continued the Christian side of the debates reflected in the NT.[65]

The earliest extant work of this kind is Justin Martyr's *Dialogue with Trypho the Jew* (about 162); many of its successors are also in dialogue form, as was its

---

[60] J.P. Smith, 'Hebrew Christian Midrash in Irenaeus (*Dem.* 43)'.

[61] Murray, *Symbols*, 42-4.

[62] Augustine, *De Catechizandis Rudibus* 4 (8) 'in veteri testamento est occultatio novi, in novo testamento est manifestatio veteris', in Christopher, *Augustinus de catechizandis rudibus*, 28f., 157f. (noting comparable formula in Augustine, *Quaestiones in Heptateuchum*, 2:73). With Christopher's translation, quoted in the text above and echoing the assonance of the Latin, compare H. Chadwick's explicative rendering 'The meaning of the New Testament lies hidden in the Old, the meaning of the Old Testament is revealed through the New' (Chadwick, *Augustine*, 36).

[63] This translation of 1 Peter is given with comment by Selwyn, *First Epistle*, 193; on the earliest Christian apologetic see Lindars, *New Testament Apologetic*.

[64] See the comment by Taylor, *Sayings of the Fathers*, in loc.

[65] For surveys see Stow, 'The Church and the Jews'; Williams, *Adversus Judaeos*; Parkes, *Conflict*, 276-91 (early eastern Christianity); Blumenkranz, *Judenpredigt*, 1-58 (Latin writings up to Augustine); Simon, *Verus Israel*, 135-78 (important discussion of setting and purpose); Blumenkranz, *Juifs et chrétiens*, 213-89 (discussion) and *Auteurs* (introduction and bibliography), both on the west in the period 430-1096; Blumenkranz, 'Kirche und Synagoge' (the west, 200-1200).

lost predecessor, Aristo of Pella's *Dialogue of Jason and Papiscus* (about 140).[66] Later authors of separate anti-Judaic treatises include Tertullian, Novatian *(On Jewish Floods)*, Hippolytus, Chrysostom and Augustine; but the theme is important far more widely, notably in apologetic to the gentiles (as in Tertullian's *Apology*, Origen's *Contra Celsum*, and Lactantius's *Divine Institutes*) and in catechesis, whether broadly or more strictly defined (in the former category, see the *Epistle of Barnabas* (before 135); in the latter, exposition of the Lord's Prayer).[67] The pervasiveness of anti-Judaic argument attests the church's need to vindicate its legitimacy, and notably its claim to the Jewish scriptures, in face of the seemingly prior claims of the synagogue (n. 7, above).[68]

The dialogues and other treatises 'against the Jews' correspondingly seek to show from the scriptures that Jesus of Nazareth is messiah, that the (ceremonial) law has been abrogated, and that the church of (the Jews and) the gentiles has been called into the place formerly held by Israel after the flesh.[69] Discussion of the law in particular invited symbolic and allegorical interpretation on the Christian side, as already in the *Epistle of Barnabas*, and approaches to the distinction between a moral and a ceremonial law.[70]

The most characteristic mode of OT interpretation in this setting, however, is the development of the biblical 'testimonies' mentioned above. Collections of such texts were current in various forms, for the most part recoverable only by conjecture. The earliest extant example is formed by Cyprian's *Testimonia*

---

[66] The book is criticized by Celsus, and defended by Origen, without mention of an author on either side (Origen, *Contra Celsum*, 4:52); Aristo is cited, without mention of the title of a book, by Eusebius, *Hist. Eccl.* 4:6, 3, but is named as author of the Dialogue by Maximus Confessor (seventh century), quoted and discussed by Harnack, *Chronologie*, 1, 268f.; see further H. Chadwick, *Origen contra Celsum*, 227, n. 1.

[67] See *Barn.* 2:9, 3:6, 4:6-8, 5:2, 9:4-5, and, in general, chapters 7-15, on circumcision, the dietary laws, the Day of Atonement, the Red Heifer, covenant, sabbath and temple (but Prigent-Kraft, *Barnabé*, 29 and n. 1, inclines to the view that the temptation to Judaize is past for the readership); in the Lord's Prayer, '*Our* Father' means Father of Christians rather than Jews, according to Tertullian, *Orat.*, 2, Cyprian, *Orat. Dom.*, 10, and Theodore of Mopsuestia, *Hom.* 11:7-8 (Tonneau-Devréesse, *Les homélies catechétiques*, 294-9).

[68] Simon, *Verus Israel*, 135-46; Blumenkranz, 'Kirche und Synagoge', 84f. (the west); Murray, *Symbols*, 19 (Mesopotamia).

[69] Simon, *Verus Israel* 156f.; emphasis in the ante-Nicene period, especially in the east, could fall entirely on the calling of the gentiles (see, for example, Murray, *Symbols*, 67); for later western emphasis on the calling of Jews also see, for example, Leo, *Serm. De Pass.* 19:2 (70, *PL* 54, 381), quoting Rom 11:32; Aponius, c. 405-15; and the mosaic of the church of S. Sabina in Rome (about 420), depicting 'the church of the circumcision' and 'the church of the gentiles' (illustrated and discussed by Huskinson, *Concordia Apostolorum*, 38-41, 120-2 who notes that its theme also supported the apostolic authority of the Roman bishop). Sgherri, *Chiesa e Sinagoga*, 284, finds that the idea of a church drawn from both Jews and gentiles is less central in Origen than in some Latin writing and in Roman iconography.

[70] Wiles, *Apostle*, 65-9.

(about 247), the first two books of which are anti-Judaic, but there is a good case for holding that such collections circulated from NT times.[71]

The scriptures claimed by the church in controversy with the Jews formed the great text of Christian apologetic to the gentiles. Three characteristic biblical arguments on this front were borrowed by the Christians from earlier Jewish apologetic. First, the venerable antiquity of the scriptures treasured by the church was stressed to the uttermost. They wee 'older by comparison with the opinions of the Greeks' (Tatian, quoted at the head of the chapter); 'supreme antiquity claims for these books the highest authority' (Tertullian, *Apology* 19:1).[72] The Jewish contention that the Greek philosophers were 'Moses's disciples' (Josephus *Ag. Ap.* 2:81) could therefore be perpetuated by Clement of Alexandria in the second century, by Eusebius, for whose presentation it was vital, at the end of the third century,[73] and again in the fifth century by Theodoret; Moses, 'older than all your poets, writers and philosophers' was 'the ocean of theology' whence Anaxagoras, Pythagoras, Socrates and Plato all derived their knowledge (Theodoret, *Graecarum Affectionum Cura*, 2:43-51).[74]

A distinctive Christian use of this claim for antiquity was to answer the pagan charge that Christians were innovators, comparatively recent rebels against Judaism (Celsus in Origen, *Contra Celsum* 3:5). On the contrary, it was replied, Christiantiy, 'which most people know to be rather modern', 'rests on the most ancient treatises of the Jews' (Tertullian, *Apology* 21:1). Under another aspect, this argument helped to justify the favourable attitude to the classics evinced by Justin and Clement of Alexandria,[75] and perpetuated by many of their successors.[76]

The argument from the antiquity of the Jewish scriptures, when advanced by Christians rather than Jews, needed the support of a second notable argument, that from prophecy. Jewish assertions of the accuracy of the prophets, even and especially when predicting national disasters (e.g. Josephus *Ant.* 10:79), were adapted to show that the prophets foretold the rejection of the Jews and the

[71] See Harris-Burch, *Testimonies*; Dodd, *According to the Scriptures*; Lindars, *New Testament Apologetic*; Prigent, *Testimonia* (on Barnabas) and *Justin*; Daniélou, *Études* (reviewed by Lindars, *JTS* N.S. 18 [1967] 481-3); H. Chadwick, 'Justin Martyr's Defence', 281 f. (reviews criticisms of Prigent, and holds it probable that Barnabas and Justin draw on testimony-collections), and 'Florilegium', cols. 1146-9. Hayman, *Sergius* (*CSCO* 339), 9*-32* (indications of a Greek fifth-century collection).

[72] The argument is popular, but not universal; Arnobius (fourth century) boldly advanced the contrary view that antiquity, as claimed by the Greeks, is no safeguard against error (Arnobius 1:57, cited with many other sources by Mayor, *Tertulliani Apologeticus*, 269f., on 19:1; cf. p. 281, on 21:1).

[73] Barnes, *Constantine and Eusebius*, 181 and n. 134, on book 10 of the *Preparation*.

[74] *PG* 83, cols. 840f.; Canivet, *Thérapeutique*, 1, 150-3.

[75] H. Chadwick, 'Philo and the Beginnings of Christian Thought', 162 (Justin), 170 (Clement).

[76] H. Chadwick, 'Philo and the Beginnings of Christian Thought', 185 (Origen), Sheldon-Williams, 'The Greek Christian Platonist Tradition', 440 (Gregory Nazianzen); Kelly, *Jerome*, 43f. (on Jerome's Letter 70); Wilson, *Scholars of Byzantium*, 8-12. Origen and Jerome both argue that the spoiling of the gentiles is justified, a contention complementing that considered in the text.

divine revelation through Christ to the gentiles (Justin, *1 Apol.* 31-53; Tertullian, *Apology* 20:1-21:6).[77] A particularly systematic and scholarly presentation of the two arguments in conjunction is found in Eusebius; his four books of *Prophetic Extracts* form part of a large-scale introduction to Christianity for sympathetic pagans, and quote the prophets from Origen's *Hexapla.*[78]

The Christian argument from prophecy was of course not merely a prop to the argument from the antiquity of scripture. It had independent value as 'the greatest and truest demonstration' (Justin, *1 Apol.* 37), for it appealed to the rooted Graeco-Roman respect for prophecies and oracles. This respect, strong in Plato and the Stoics, was never wholly counterbalanced in educated opinion by the scepticism of the Academics, Platonists of the Hellenistic age. When Cicero rejected belief in foreknowledge, following Academics like Carneades, in his dialogue *On Divination* (44 B.C.), he felt himself bound to rebut an array of arguments, especially from Stoics, on the other side.[79] It was a chink in the armour of the anti-Christian Platonist philosophers Celsus (second century) and Porphyry (third century) that they respected oracles.[80]

Accordingly, the scriptures were presented by Christian authors, in the steps of the Septuagint and Philo, as 'oracles' *(logia).*[81] An explicit contrast could be drawn, as by Origen and, on a larger scale, by Theodoret, between Hebrew prophecy and pagan oracles (a contrast already adumbrated in Deut 18:14f., as

---

[77] On Justin's presentation see H. Chadwick, 'Justin Martyr's Defence', 280-4 (noting its contemporary effectiveness); for further examples of the argument from prophecy, see Mayor, *Tertulliani Apologeticus* 279, on 20:3, noting that the only early apologist to neglect it is Arnobius (cf. H.C.G. Moule, 'Arnobius', 168f., on his appearance of not knowing the OT).

[78] Barnes, *Constantine and Eusebius*, 167-74; the argument is also advanced on the grand scale in Eusebius's *Preparation for the Gospel* and *Proof of the Gospel.*

[79] On the treatment of inspiration in Plato, neo-Platonism, Philo and the Fathers see Lampe, *God as Spirit*, 53-9 and H. Chadwick, 'Philo and the Beginnings of Christian Thought', 151f. Cicero, *On Divination* was attacked in the course of apologetic to pagans by Augustine, *City of God* 5:9, as seeking to subvert the lustre of true prophecy.

[80] See Origen, *Contra Celsum* 4:88-96, 7:2-7, 8:45f., translated with comments by H. Chadwick, *Origen contra Celsum*, 253-60, 395-401, 484-6; and Barnes, *Constantine and Eusebius*, 175f., 179, on Porphyry's *Philosophy from Oracles.*

[81] For *logia*, see the LXX especially at Num 24:4, 16 (Balaam's oracles); Deut 33:9 (Levi to keep the 'oracles', probably with allusion to the oracular priestly breastplate (*logeion* or *logion*, Exod 28:15, etc.); and in the Psalter, for example, Ps 11 (12):6, 118 (119):11 (and often elsewhere in this psalm); also Philo, *On the Decalogue* 16, Acts 7:38, Rom 3:2, and Clem. 53:1 (all referring to Jewish sacred texts); Origen, *Comm. in Ps 1 = Philocalia* 2:4, quoting Ps 11 (Hebrew 12):6 as suggesting the precision of the divine oracles, with the comments by Harl-de Lange, *Origène sur les Écritures*, 257f.; and the further instances in Lampe, *Lexicon*, pp. 805a-806a, s.v. (cf. p. 1528a, s.v. *chrèsmos*, and the following footnote).

Origen notes, perhaps following Philo).[82] Comparably but without insistence on the contrast, Lactantius dismisses oracles when attacking pagan error, and later defends Christianity at length from the prophets, together with whom he quotes Hermes Trismegistus and the Sibyl (*Divine Institutes*, 2:17, 4:5-8). The practical force of argument from prophecy and oracle is strikingly evinced, outside express apologetic, in the production of extensive Sibylline oracles by both Jews and Christians in the Roman empire.[83]

A third form of apologetic argument from the Jewish scriptures is a bold challenge of comparison not this time with the oracles, but with the philosophers. Just as Josephus could claim that the laws of Moses excel those of any Greek lawgiver (*Ag. Ap.* 2:163-286), Justin Martyr ascribes his conversion to the perception that the prophets excel the Greek philosophers (*Dial.* 3-8). In a lively development of this Christian commonplace Origen challenges Celsus to examine the writings of Linus, Musaeus, Orpheus and Pherecydes, the wise men of renown among the Greeks, side by side with the laws of Moses – to see which are more able to transform instantly those who hear them (Origen, *Contra Celsum* 1:18). The directness of the biblical precepts, presented without demonstrative argument (Justin, *Dial.* 7), will have appealed to the type of pagan reader who relished the pithy maxims in the *Sentences* of Sextus.

The importance of the Jewish scriptures in Christian apologetic, therefore, was by no means confined to the argument with the synagogue. On the contrary, as the examples just given suggest, the scriptures were at the heart of the presentation of Christianity to the gentile world. Gibbon, recognizing this point, thought that biblical demonstrations were singularly unfitted to convince pagans, 'who neither understand nor respect the Mosaic dispensation and the prophetic style'.[84] In fact, however, as has appeared, OT arguments appealed effectively to contemporary respect for antiquity, divination, and direct moral precept.

ECCLESIASTICAL LAW

Regulations occur in the earliest Christian literature, for example at Matt

---

[82] Jewish 'oracles' are as effective as the pagan ones, for they likewise inspire colonization (the exodus), according to Origen, *Contra Celsum* 8:45f.; the passage Deut 18:14f. is construed as a contrast between pagan divination and true prophecy by Philo, *Spec. Leg.* 1: 59-65 and Origen, *Contra Celsum* 4:95; a contrast is also drawn by Clement of Alexandria, who stresses the decay of pagan oracles (*chrēstēria*) and later advances the 'oracles' (*chrēsmoi*) of the Hebrew 'seers' (*chrēsmōdoi*) (*Protrepticus [Exhortation to the Greeks]*, [quoted by Eusebius, *Preparation for the Gospel*, 2:3] and 8); and by Theodoret, *Graecarum Affectionum Cura*, book 10 (pagan oracles contrasted with the true oracles found in the prophets, Moses, and the psalms; on the historical setting of this presentation, see Canivet, *Thérapeutique*, 1, 39-41).

[83] The Jewish and Christian Sibyllines are introduced by Collins, 'The Sibylline Oracles' and Kurfess, 'Christian Sibyllines'.

[84] Gibbon, *Decline and Fall*, book 1, chapter 15, end (London, 1895, vol. 1, 380); on the contemporary force of the argument from prophecy, cf. H. Chadwick, as cited in n. 77, above.

18:15-18, Acts 15:19-29 and 1 Cor 5:1-13 (all Pentateuchally based); and they were increasingly systematized in church orders and collections of canons.[85] Appeal was made to teaching viewed as apostolic as well as to Moses and the prophets, and spiritual interpretation of the OT naturally went hand in hand with questioning of its regulative force; but this force was never wholly abated.

The abiding prestige of OT law is illustrated when Tertullian, urging that Christians are bound to single marriages only, argues from 'the ancient documents of the legal scriptures' (in which he applies the priestly laws of Lev 20-21 to Christians) as well as from 'the law which is properly ours' (his significantly legal description of the gospel).[86] Two hundred years later the ascetic Ammonius relied on the same passages of Leviticus when, to escape ordination, he cut off his left ear – 'seeing that the law forbids a man with ear cut off to be raised to the priesthood' (cf. Lev. 21:17-23). The bishop responded, however, 'Let the Jews observe this law' – *he* would ordain a worthy man, even with his nose cut off; and Ammonius escaped only by threatening to cut off his tongue, his difficulty exemplifying the questions raised by the Pentateuch as well as its prestige (see Palladius, *Lausiac History*, 21:2f.).

OT influence appears in the church orders partly through existing summaries and rearrangements of biblical law, like the expanded decalogue in the 'Two Ways'. These early books of rules continue a Jewish genre examplified by the Qumran *Manual of Discipline*. Even when this channel of indirect influence is not perceptible, however, the OT has its effect on regulations. This is true not just of a collection like the *Apostolic Canons*, closely associated with the *Apostolic Constitutions*, but far more widely, as the foregoing paragraph would suggest (for examples see Leo, Basil, and the canons of Nicaea and Ancyra, cited in notes 92 and 94-6, below). Rules concerning the clergy were particularly strongly affected by this influence, given the tendency to compare the ecclesias-

---

[85] On the church orders (Didache, Didascalia Apostolorum, Apostolic Tradition, Apostolic Church Order, Apostolic Constitutions, Apostolic Canons) see *ODCC* under these headings (literature); Nautin, 'Canoni apostolici' and 'Canoni ecclesiastici degli apostoli'; and Gaudemet, *Les Sources du Droit*. For canons and canonical letters see the translations by Percival, *Ecumenical Councils*, with critical editions and literature noted in *ODCC*, s. 'Canon Law' and by Munier, 'Collezioni canoniche'; Bright, *Canons*; and Bickell, *Geschichte*, 13-18 (esp. 17f.) on OT laws considered to be binding on Christians; on Celtic canons, n. 99, below; on OT influence on early mediaeval canon law, Kottje, *Studien*; on the NT regulations cited in the text, Davies, *Setting*, 221-6 (Matthew 18 compared with Jewish sources); Simon, 'Apostolic Decree'; Bingham, *Antiquities*, book 16, chapter 2:15 (London, 1844, vol. 5, 495-502) and Lampe, 'Church Discipline' (on 1 Cor 5); the main Pentateuchal texts behind these regulations are Lev 19:7, Deut 19:15-19 (Matthew); Gen 9:4, Exod 34:15f., Lev 17:10-14, 18:6-26 (Acts); and Lev 18:8, Deut 17:7 (1 Cor.).

[86] Tertullian, *On Monogamy*, 7-8; cf. his *Exhortation to Chastity*, 7 (based on an interpretative paraphrase of Lev 21:14, discussed by Uglione, 'Seconde nozze', 172-4, 176-8); contrast Clement of Alexandria, *Strom.* 3:82 (second marriage not forbidden by the law); it was a common view that second marriage (digamy) is best avoided (so for example Justin Martyr, *1 Apol.* 15:5), and a series of canons forbid it to the clergy (cf. 1 Tim 3:2, 12; Titus 1:6; and Lev 21:7. 13f. [priest not to marry widow or divorcee]). See Ludlow, 'Digamy'; Bright, *Canons*, 32f., on Canon 8 of Nicaea; and H. Chadwick in Oulton-Chadwick, *Alexandrian Christianity*, 37f.

tical ministry with the levitical priesthood (for example in Cyprian, *Ep.* 66:1).[87] Thus the admonition to rise in the presence of a senior (Lev 19:32) warns one to rise at the coming of bishop and presbyter (Cyprian, *Testimonies* 3:85). A more 'spiritual' interpretation of the priestly laws can be found, for example in Origen, but their relevance to the church's ministry is still accepted.[88] The ancient law was similarly brought to bear, with greater or less acceptance, on the timing of infant baptism and the observance of Sunday and of two days for which Pentateuchal laws were especially well known, Saturday and Easter Day.[89]

Instinctive respect for the OT coexisted, however, as the story of Ammonius showed, with a potentially inconsistent instinct to differ from the synagogue; 'Let not your fasts be with the hypocrites' (*Didache* 8:1). The resultant tension contributed to the early elaboration of general views of the Mosaic code, notably in the *Epistle of Barnabas*, which shares a source with the *Didache* (the Jews do not know the true meaning of commandments like the dietary laws),[90] and in the *Didascalia Apostolorum*, where a distinction is drawn within the Pentateuch between the true and moral law, including at least the decalogue, and the (ceremonial) 'second legislation' *(deuterosis)*.[91]

Biblical quotations are rather more frequent in church orders and canonical letters than in collections of canons, but canonical rulings are often in fact bound up with an unstated biblical interpretation, as can occur with mishnaic rulings in rabbinic tradition. The OT gave guidance on some subjects which bulked large in legislation. Among these were digamy, and eligibility for marriage to the clergy (Lev 21:7, 13f. and Ezek 44:22 provide the rule, but are

---

[87] Cyprian applies this comparison thoroughly, but not without precedent or parallel; see Bernard, 'The Cyprianic Doctrine of the Ministry', at pp. 221-4 (on Tertullian), 226-8; von Campenhausen, *Ecclesiastical Authority*, 176f. (on the Apostolic Tradition of Hippolytus, 3:2-4), 241f. (on *Didascalia* 2:25f.).

[88] von Campenhausen, *Ecclesiastical Authority*, 255, citing Origen, *Hom. in Isa.* 17:2; for a more direct and literal application to the clergy, see *In Lev. Hom.* 5:4.

[89] For rejection of the view that baptism should be delayed until the child is eight days old, as suggested by the biblical law of circumcision, see Cyprian, *Ep.* 59(64); on Sunday, Saturday and Easter see Simon, *Verus Israel*, 310-38, with special reference to the Didascalia, and Hardinge, *Celtic Church*, 75-100; on the origin of 'quartodeciman' Easter observance (on 14th Nisan) see the review of discussion by Hall, *Melito*, xxiv-xxvi, and for its persistence in mainstream Christianity see Meredith, 'Answer', 293f. (arguing that Gregory of Nyssa and his Cappadocian flock still kept 14th Nisan in the late fourth century).

[90] Prigent in Prigent-Kraft, *Barnabé*, 158f., nn. 4 and 5 contrasts the moderation of this view with the scorn for the dietary laws expressed in the *Epistle to Diognetus* 4:1f. and by Tertullian, *Adv. Marc.* 5:5; 'that the Jews would not be able to understand the holy scriptures' (Cyprian, *Testimonies* 1:4) continued to be an important apologetic and exegetical commonplace (cf. 2 Cor 3:14f.); see further Simon, *Verus Israel*, 87f.

[91] Christ came 'that he might affirm the Law, and abolish the Second Legislation', and the bishop must be 'a good discriminator between the Law and the Second Legislation' (*Didascalia* 6:17; 2:5, respectively); see further Connolly, *Didascalia*, lvii-lxix, Simon, *Verus Israel*, 88-91. 'Deuterosis' is also used, somewhat comparably with Hebrew 'mishna', to denote rabbinic teaching (Bietenhard, 'Deuterosis'; de Lange, *Origen and the Jews*, 34f.).

not quoted);[92] the maintenance of the clergy, for which the levitical tithes and first-fruits formed an increasingly important precedent;[93] usury, on which Ps 15:5 was a standard text;[94] and divination, on which appeal was made to several Pentateuchal passages, including Deut 18:10-14.[95] A strikingly persistent example of the relatively rare transmission of proof-text together with ruling is the quotation of Nahum 1:9 (LXX) in *Apostolic Canon* 25 to show that a clerk deposed from holy orders for an offence should not also be deprived of communion, 'for the Lord does not avenge twice for the same thing'.[96]

The legislative importance of the OT in the post-Nicene period, exemplified by the development of tithing, appears plainly on the verges of the Roman Empire. The *Apostolic Tradition* of Hippolytus and the *Didascalia* were influential among Syriac-speaking Christians, whose ecclesiastical customs were also bound up with their own traditional OT exegesis.[97] In Spain the presence of a large Jewish population sharpened respect for the Mosaic code.[98] The Pentateuch shaped ecclesiastical laws above all among Celtic Christians, fervent biblical students who often upheld the literal sense and were possibly subject to

---

[92] *Apostolic Canons* 18 and 19, without proof-text (no-one who has married a widow, a divorcee, a harlot or a slave, two sisters or a brother's daughter to be a clerk in holy orders); cf. *Apostolic Constitutions* 6:17 ('as also the law says'); Leo, *Ep.* 4:2 (*PL* 54, 612) supports a comparable but more restricted prohibition by citing 'the rules of the canons' and quoting 1 Tim 3:2 and Lev 21:14.

[93] 1 Cor 9:13f.; *Didascalia* 2:25-7. 34f., and *Apostolic Constitutions, ibid.* quoting Num 18:1-32, 1 Sam 8:15-17 (the negative import of the latter passage is ignored) to show that the priestly offerings and the alsmgiving of the old law are still binding; Cyprian, *Ep.* 66:1 (the clergy taking their allowance *(sportulantes)* as if maintained by levitical tithes). Tithing in the strict sense, as contrasted with offering gifts, not necessarily tenths, on the general pattern of the biblical tithe, first becomes widespread in the fourth and fifth centuries (see John Cassian, *Conferences*, 21:1-5 [about 430], cited with other evidence by Sharpe, 'Tithes', 1964). On first-fruits, see *Apostolic Canon* 5, and canons 7-8 and synodical letter of Gangra, quoted with other evidence by Bingham, *Antiquities*, book 5, chapter 5.4 (London, 1844, vol. 2, 85-7); also n. 111, below.

[94] Cyprian, *Testimonies* 3:48, quoting Ps 15:5, Ezek 18:7f. and Deut 23:20; Canon 17 of Nicaea, quoting Ps 15:5, with Bright, *Canons*, 65-8.

[95] See Didache and *Doctrina Apostolorum* 2:2 (expanded decalogue runs 'thou shalt not commit adultery, [thou shalt not steal,] thou shalt not work magic, thou shalt not practise sorcery' [*ou pharmakeuseis*]; Exod 20:14f.; cf. Exod 22:17[18], LXX 'sorcerers' [*pharmakoi*], Lev 19:26, 31 and 20:27, and Deut 18:10f.); also *Didache* and *Doctrina Apostolorum* 3:4 (four forbidden magical professions, three of them banned in Deut 18:10f. LXX) and 5:1, the latter with parallels in Barn. 20:1, *Apostolic Constitutions* 7:18; in an enlargement of the two earlier Didache passages, in *Apostolic Constitutions* 7:3 and 6, reference is made to Exod 22:17(18), 1 Sam 15:23 and Num 23:23 (by quotation), and to Lev 19:26, 31 and Deut 18:10f. (by allusion). Tertullian, *On Idolatry*, 9 links astrologers with idolaters, like the source of *Didache* 3:4, 5:1, and also alludes to Gen 6:1-4, taken as in 1 Enoch 7:1 to mean that the fallen angels taught men magic (see n. 120, below). For literature on some of these passages see Thee, *Africanus*; see further Bingham, *Antiquities*, book 16, chapter 5 (London, 1844, vol. 6, 46-80), for patristic views and legislation on magic.

[96] Basil, *First Canonical Epistle* to Amphilochius, Canon 3; Turner, *Monumenta* 1, 33, on *Apostolic Canon* 25 (noting that Aquinas, *S.T.* 3:39.5, 2 still quotes Nahum 1:9 LXX [in Latin translation] for this ruling, important in western canon law and scripturally founded only in the LXX).

[97] Murray, *Symbols*, especially 6-24, 26, 334-7, 341.

[98] Simon, *Verus Israel*, 330f. (on canons of Elvira); Blumenkranz, *Auteurs*, 88-101 (on Isidore of Seville).

Spanish influence; a *Liber ex Lege Moisi* (before 800), transmitted with the Hibernian canons, comprises the decalogue with selections from Exodus, Leviticus, Numbers and Deuteronomy.[99]

LITURGY

The church service was pre-eminent as a medium and example of OT knowledge and interpretation, not only through lessons, sermons and psalmody, but also through the interconnection of prayers, rites and ceremonies with the Jewish scriptures.[100] In the first century it seems likely that the Christians held a solemn service of the word on the Jewish pattern, probably on Sunday, Wednesday and Friday mornings, and an evening assembly for a common meal (both agape and eucharist), at which there would also have been lessons, hymns and prayers.[101] However that may be, by the middle of the second century eucharist and agape were separated; the Sunday morning service of lessons and prayers now and henceforth ended with a eucharistic rite, and the evening assembly had become an agape, still with prayer and hymnody (Tertullian, *Apology*, 39). Weekday services of the word continued to be important.

Biblical lessons and exposition therefore played a great part. Thus in the second and third centuries the bible was studied informally in the agape, more formally in the solemn services of the word on Sunday (culminating in the eucharist), Wednesday and Friday, and also in daily assemblies for instruction, such as those at which Origen preached.[102] Such services continued in the fourth and fifth centuries, now in conjunction with daily morning and evening prayers; and biblical lessons also gained importance in the monastic office which grew up in the same period, and strongly influenced later common prayer.[103]

The OT was read in the Sunday morning assembly described by Justin, and in the fourth century the *Apostolic Constitutions* envisage four lessons on this occasion, two from the OT, one from the Acts or the Epistles, and the Gospel (2:57, cf. 8:5).[104] Three lessons (from the OT, one only) became customary both

---

[99] Hardinge, *Celtic Church*, 35, Plate facing p. 44, and pp. 48-50, 209-16 (summary of *Liber Ex Lege Moisi*), citing H. Bradshaw, *Hibernensis* and Fournier, 'Le Liber ex Lege Moysi'; N.K. Chadwick, *Age of the Saints*, 52-60 (influence from Spain); James, 'Ireland and Western Gaul' (attaching greater importance to Gallic influence).

[100] For surveys of worship see H. Chadwick, *Early Church*, 258-77; Lietzmann, *Constantine to Julian*, 288-328 (vivid reconstruction of fourth-century worship); Jones-Wainwright-Yarnold, *The Study of Liturgy*; P.F. Bradshaw, *Daily Prayer*. On the biblical aspect in particular see Lamb, 'The Place of the Bible' and Yarnold, 'Liturgia e Bibbia' (literature).

[101] This is the view of P.F. Bradshaw, *Daily Prayer*, 41-3, 66; cf. Lamb, 'The Place of the Bible', 566 and Yarnold, 'Liturgia e Bibbia', col. 2016 (Justin's First Apology is the first clear evidence of union between service of the word and eucharist).

[102] P.F. Bradshaw, *Daily Prayer*, 70f., 132f., 144-9, 152f.

[103] P.F. Bradshaw, *Daily Prayer*, 90-2, 98, 121.

[104] On Justin, *1 Apol.* 67 see Lamb, 'The Place of the Bible', 570f.; on the Apostolic Constitutions, see Lietzmann, *Constantine to Julian*, 298f. (interpreting the number of lessons as four) and Lamb, p. 571.

in east and west, but a tendency towards two only, already evident from Augustine's works, established itself in Roman usage and became general in the mediaeval west; either an OT lesson or an Epistle then preceded the Sunday morning Gospel, but neglect of the OT was considerably redressed by saint's-day and weekday lessons.[105] Discretion over lessons long rested with bishop or lector, but strong traces of fixed local lectionary customs appear in the fourth and fifth centuries, and proper lessons (including some from the OT) were associated with particular seasons from an earlier period, sometimes perhaps in continuation of synagogue usage. Thus Melito preaches his Paschal homily when 'the scripture of the Hebrew exodus has been read', giving a second-century attestation of a proper lesson (probably Exod 12) which was later widespread; Genesis was read in Lent (Chrysostom, *Hom. 7 Ad Pop. Ant.*), Job and Jonah in Passion week (Origen, *Comm. in Job*; Ambrose, *Ep. 20 Ad Marcellinam*).[106] Variety was nonetheless very considerable.[107] Not everyone attended to the lessons, but general awareness was such as to bring it about that the change of a single word in a well-loved passage of Jonah could cause disturbance.[108]

Another important OT element in worship was the singing of psalms and canticles, which had a considerable part in all the services just noted, and often separated the lessons on Sunday morning.[109]

Lastly, both ceremonies and prayers recalled the Jewish scriptures. The OT influenced worship not only directly, but also indirectly, through the synagogue inheritance and contemporary Jewish usage (compare the position in cate-

---

[105] Willis, *St. Augustine's lectionary*, 4f.; Frere, *Studies*, 3, pp. iv (on the Wisdom books as an important source of lessons; cf. n. 1, above), 1-25 (text of the book *Comes* [see *ODCC*, s.v.] representing the Roman epistolary of the eight century and later), 103-115 (schedule of lessons; OT, 103-8).

[106] Willis, *St. Augustine's Lectionary*, 5-9; Lamb, 'The Place of the Bible', 573-5; Hall, *Melito*, xxvi and 3, n. 2, with reference to *On Pascha*, 1; lessons for the whole year are found in an Armenian lectionary which probably represents fifth-century Jerusalem usage (Yarnold, 'Liturgia e Bibbia', col. 2016, citing Renoux, *Le Codex Arménien Jérusalem 121*).

[107] The point is stressed in a survey of the (mainly fourth- and fifth-century western) evidence for the public reading of Jonah by Duval, *Jonas*, 1, 39-51.

[108] Young ladies lie down as if they were in bed, to gossip during the lessons, according to Caesarius of Arles (*Serm.* 78:1, cited by Willis, *St. Augustine's Lectionary*, 1f.); but Augustine (*Ep.* 71:3, 5, cited by Duval, *Jonas*, 1, 41) tells Jerome that when the latter's new translation, in which Jonah's gourd became *hedera* rather than *cucurbita*, was read at Oea in Tripolitania, the congregation became so unruly that the bishop had to revert to the old translation.

[109] On psalmody see Niceta of Remesiana, *On the Value of Psalmody (De Psalmodiae Bono)*, discussed and edited by Burn, *Niceta*, lxxxiv-xcvii, 67-82; Lamb, 'The Place of the Bible', 568-70, 579, 581-3; P.F. Bradshaw, *Daily Prayer*, 43-5, 63f., 83-5, 89f., 94-110 (on the special character of monastic psalmody) and 111-54, passim (on morning and evening prayers, and the monastic office, in the west). Various uses of the psalms are vividly described by Augustine, *Confessions* 9:(4) 8-11 (reading by Alypius and himself as catechumens), 9:(12) 31 (Ps 101 sung at Monica's deathbed), 10:(33) 50 (he was moved to tears by the chanting of the psalms in church); see further H. Chadwick, *Augustine*, 44f. For canticles see n. 29, above; Burn, *Niceta*, xciv-xcvi, on *De Psalmodiae Bono*, 11 (list of canticles); and Jenny, 'Cantica'.

chesis, apologetic and law, discussed above). Baptism and the eucharist became focal points in the complex of typological interpretation. Thus the baptismal ceremonies of dipping, anointing and the gift of milk and honey recalled the flood, the Red Sea, the priestly unction and the entry into the promised land; and the eucharistic bread, water and wine similarly evoked Melchizedek, the manna, the banquet of Wisdom and the promised refreshment of the faithful.[110] It was common to speak of the service as a spiritual sacrifice, for which Malachi 1:11 becomes a favourite text (*Didache* 14:3; Justin, *Dial.* 41; Jerome, ad loc.), and sacrificial language was also extended to the offerings and 'first-fruits' given at the eucharist and to the bishop.[111]

The language of the prayers in the first three centuries varied according to the officiant's discretion, but themes were standard, and the eucharistic prayer might recall OT precedents, as in Ambrose (Abel, Abraham, Melchizedek) and, in an elaborate form, the *Apostolic Constitutions* (8:12).[112] Other prayers of praise and intercession, including striking parallels with synagogue prayer, are likewise permeated with OT language; an increasingly important example, which gained entry into many versions of the eucharistic prayer, is the seraphic hymn *Sanctus* (Isa 6:3).[113]

[110] For the ceremonies see H. Chadwick, *Early Church*, pp. 260-72; early interpretation is exemplified by 1 Peter 3:20-2, Justin, *Dial.* 138 (Noah); 1 Cor 10:3-4 (baptism into Moses); Tertullian, *On Baptism* 7-9 (Aaron's anointing, the flood, the Red Sea and the water from the rock); Barn. 6:8-17 (milk and honey signify possession of the land); Cyprian, *Ep.* 63:4 (Melchizedek); Ignatius, *Rom.* 7:3, alluding to John 6:33 (manna); Cyprian, *Testimonies* 2:2 (Prov 9: 2-5; Justin, *Dial.* 70 (bread and water promised in Isa 33:16; cf. H. Chadwick, 'Justin Martyr's Defence', 292, n. 10, on water eucharists). See in general Daniélou, *From Shadows*. Fifth-century Syrian comment on the baptismal and eucharistic liturgies includes developed OT allusion, for example the interpretation of the Sanctus as signifying the return of the gentiles from 'the whole earth' (Isa 6:3), as noted by Brock, 'An Early Syriac Commentary', 392f., 397; see also Brock, 'Some Early Syriac Baptismal Commentaries'.

[111] For the eucharist and its elements as sacrifice see Lampe, *Lexicon*, 659f., s.v. *thysiā*, 6 (very many examples analyzed); and Ambrose, On the *Sacraments*, 4:5-6 (paragraphs 21-8), with comments by Srawley in Thompson-Srawley, *St. Ambrose 'On the Mysteries'*, xxx-xxxiv, xxxixf., 113-6 and by H. Chadwick, *Early Church*, 268f. On first-fruits see n. 93, above; Dix-Chadwick, *Apostolic Tradition of Hippolytus*, 53-5 (on chapter 28); Cuming, 'ΚΑΡΠΟΦΟΡΙΑ' (review of evidence for offering in kind), with Scudamore, 'Fruits, Offering and Benediction of' (earlier review, also quoting seventh- to ninth-century prayers).

[112] On the prayer in the Apostolic Constitutions, which names fifteen OT saints from Adam to Joshua, see Lietzmann, *Constantine to Julian*, 292f.; a liturgical background is inferred for references to Abraham and Melchizedek, comparable with those of Ambrose, in the possibly slightly earlier Latin sermons of Zeno, by Jeanes, 'Early Latin Parallels'.

[113] See especially 1 *Clem.* 34:6 (quoting Dan 7:10, Isa 6:3) and 59:3-61 end, with Lightfoot, *Clement*, 1, pp. 382-96 (on OT background, and parallels in Christian liturgies and the Eighteen Benedictions); cf. Flusser, 'Sanktus und Gloria', Spinks, 'The Jewish Sources for the Sanctus' (literature), and Werner, *Bridge*, 2 108-26; see also the *Apostolic Constitutions*, especially 7:33-8, discussed with other passages by Fiensy, *Prayers Alleged to be Jewish* (bibliography).

750

POETRY

Christians continued a vigorous and varied Jewish poetic tradition. Its verse-forms ranged from Hebrew and Greek development of biblical poetry, as in Ecclesiasticus or the Psalms of Solomon, to work in the classical metres, like the hexameter Sibyllines or the iambic drama on the exodus by Ezekiel Tragicus.[114] Within this range there were striking confluences of Jewish and Greek style and thought, for example in the Wisdom of Solomon (perhaps first century B.C.) and the Hermetic hymns (perhaps second century A.D.).[115] As these examples suggest, Jewish poetry could share the strong didactic interest of much contemporary non-Jewish verse, it included some pieces which probably gained public use as hymns,[116] and it was charged with biblical expressions and reminiscences.

Much of this poetry was read and transmitted by Christians; but the history of distinctively Christian verse[117] begins with the NT, where the Lucan canticles (perhaps of Jewish origin) recall the Psalms of Solomon, and Revelation 15:3f. give a hymn in a mixed hebraic and rhetorical style recalling Wisdom.[118] Familiarity with the psalms and OT canticles helped to ensure the continuance of a biblically-related style in such later Christian compositions as Latin alphabetical psalms.[119]

Greek classical metres were also soon used by Christians, as in Sibylline hexameters; in some second-century iambic lines of OT based invective against

---

[114] On these texts see Gilbert, 'Wisdom Literature', Collins, 'The Sibylline Oracles' and Flusser, 'Psalms, Hymns and Prayers'.

[115] On the style of Wisdom, in which the forms of Hebrew poetry are sometimes dissolved by Greek rhetorical influence, see Larcher, *Sagesse*, 1, 89-91; on the Hermetic corpus, with its hymns in Septuagintal language and rhetorical form, see Dodd, *The Bible and the Greeks*, 99-248 (on the date, 201-9), Pearson, 'Jewish Sources', 474f., and Zuntz, 'On the Hymns in Corpus Hermeticum xiii'.

[116] Flusser, 'Psalms, Hymns, and Prayers', 551; cf. Philo, *On the Contemplative Life*, 80 (hymns new and old, in various metres, sung by the Therapeutae).

[117] Old but still useful are Lock, 'Verse-Writers', Baumstark, 'Hymns (Greek Christian)' and Maclean, 'Hymns (Syriac Christian)'; for more recent literature on ante-Nicene verse, see Jenny, 'Cantica' and Fontaine, *Naissance*, 291f. (on Greek as well as Latin sources); on Latin verse, Raby, *Christian-Latin Poetry* and Fontaine, *Naissance*, on Syriac, Landersdorfer, *Ausgewählte Schriften der syrischen Dichter* (Cyrillona, Balai, Isaac of Antioch and Jacob of Serug); Murray, *Symbols*, 29-33 (Ephrem and Cyrillona; literature); and Brock, *The Harp of the Spirit* (eighteen poems by Ephrem translated, with introduction and bibliography). Note the survey headed 'Early Church Music' (largely on hymns) by H. Chadwick, *Early Church*, 273-7.

[118] On the Lucan canticles see Flusser, 'Psalms, Hymns and Prayers', 551f., and Farris, *Hymns* (arguing that they were originally composed in Hebrew by Christians); on the sources of Rev 15:3f., Sweet, *Revelation*, ad loc., and on the phrase 'the song of Moses' here as possibly implying use of Deut 32 as a canticle see Jenny, 'Cantica', 625.

[119] On the probably third-century alphabetical psalm fragment published from a Barcelona papyrus as a hymn to the Virgin see Fontaine, *Naissance*, 31f., and n. 13 *bis* (literature); its subject was probably Christ (cf. n. 123, below) rather than the Virgin (Roberts, review of Roca-Puig, 493 [literature]). On Augustine's anti-Donatist psalm see Raby, *Christian-Latin Poetry*, 20f. and Fontaine, *Naissance*, 226f.

the gnostic Marcus, 'Thou idol-framer, Mark, and portent-gazer';[120] and in Clement of Alexandria, whose *Protrepticus* (1) had indeed presented the heavenly Word as 'the new, the levitical song' (cf. Pss 96:1, 98:1), yet more compelling than the songs of Orpheus. Clement is the likely author of the anapaestic hymn to Christ, 'Bridle of colts untamed, Wing of unwandering birds', preserved at the end of his *Paidagogos* (3:12); as in his prose, OT allusions are alluringly transformed by a new Hellenic and Christian context, so that the 'wing' of the second line, for example, recalls both Plato and the winged sun of righteousness (Mal 4:2 [3:20]).[121]

A comparable Christocentric and near-mystical atmosphere enfolds the stylistically very different second-century Odes of Solomon (preserved and perhaps written in Syriac), although it is not clear that they were sung; often recalling the OT, especially the Psalms, they regularly end with an Alleluia.[122] Other references to early hymnody bear out Pliny's famous phrase 'a song to Christ as to a god' as a characterization of the Christian hymn;[123] in the present context it should be noted that these distinctively Christian acclamations are often permeated with allusion to the Jewish scriptures.

From the third century onwards Christian poetry has a continuous history in Latin as well as Greek and Syriac. More literature now survives, and the OT can be seen to hold a prominent place in poetic subject-matter as well as language. Thus Commodian, the emergence of whose harshly impressive hexameters in the history of Latin verse (probably about 250-260) has been likened to the appearance of the star Wormwood in the Apocalypse, is steeped in the law, the prophets, and the Jewish and Christian apocalypses and Sibylline writings.[124] His didactic *Instructions* include Pentateuchally-based idol-satire, and ethical exhortation in the Wisdom tradition; and his apologetic *Carmen* deploys Old Testament texts, including many found in Cyprian's *Testimonies*, in argument

---

[120] Elder quoted by Irenaeus, *Haer.* 1:16, 6; see Keble, *Irenaeus*, 54 for John Keble's blank verse rendering, the first line of which was quoted; for 'portent-gazer' *(teratoskopos)* cf. Deut 18:11 LXX; Marcus is linked in the poem with fallen angels as well as idolatry, in the manner of Tertullian, *On Idolatry*, 9, cited with references to the biblical background in n. 95, above.

[121] See Stählin *et al.*, *Clemens Alexandrinus* 1, lxxvi, n. 2 (link with context, and choice of expressions, make Clementine authorship likely), and pp. 291f. (text); English verse rendering (by W.L. Alexander) and prose translation (by W. Wilson) in *ANCL* 4, 343-5; commentary by H.-I. Marrou in Mondésert-Matray-Marrou, *Clément d'Alexandrie: Le Pédagogue*, 3, 192-203.

[122] On the Odes of Solomon see Sparks, *The Apocryphal Old Testament*, 683-731 (introduction and bibliography, with translation by J.A. Emerton), and Murray, *Symbols*, 24f.; on Alleluia, H. Chadwick, *The Early Church*, 274 and Werner, *Bridge*, 2, 101-7.

[123] Pliny, *Ep.* 10:96; Eusebius, *Hist. Eccl.* 5:28, 5 (the Little Labyrinth [early third century] on the 'psalms and odes written from the beginning by faithful brethren, which hymn the word of God, the Christ, in divine praises') and 7:30, 10 (Paul of Samosata, later in the third century, charged with having prohibited some 'psalms' addressed to Christ; cf. Murray, *Symbols*, 159-72, on comparable Syriac and other material, including the Odes of Solomon.

[124] For Commodian, his hexameters (in which stress is becoming more important than quantity), and the comparison with Wormwood, see Fontaine, *Naissance*, 39-52.

against the Jews. Both poemes end with visions of the millennium, described in the second at considerable length.

A roughly contemporary Greek poem of not wholly dissimilar sentiments is the spirited Hymn of Thecla in Methodius, *Symposium* 11.[125] A marriage-hymn to Christ, it sets imagery from Ps 45 and the Song of Songs, and a series of OT exempla from Abel to Susanna, within the framework of the parable of the Ten Virgins; its subject is the union of the church with Christ in the millennium, which has been described in prose in *Symposium* 9 as the true feast of Tabernacles, in a remarkable exposition of Lev 23:39-43.[126] In the fourth century Gregory Nazianzen, a prolific poet in various metres, includes OT subjects not only in his short mnemonic verses (for example on the decalogue or the miracles of Elijah), but also as examples in his long moral poems; he expounds the relation of law and prophets in his ninth dogmatic poem 'On the Testaments and the Appearing of Christ'.[127] In the early fifth-century hymns of Synesius, which continue a series of Platonic hymns from the author's pre-Christian period, Christ is hailed as 'Jerusalemite' (*Solymēios*, Hymn 7:4), but Platonism is much less biblically coloured than it is in Clement of Alexandria.

During the period of these Greek literary hymns an elaborate popular hymnody had been growing up in Syria, classically expressed in Syriac by Ephrem Syrus (fourth century) and later in Greek by the *contakia* of Romanus (beginning of sixth century), who was probably born at Emesa, and perhaps of Jewish descent; the contemporary efflorescence of Hebrew *piyyutim* in synagogue poetry is a related phenomenon. This hymnody is popular, but scrupulously formed, richly allusive, and characterized by close intertwining of Old and New Testament imagery. Ephrem's work includes metrical homily, for example on Jonah,[128] as well as hymns building on the OT.[129] Romanus has a series of OT *contakia* on characters from Adam and Eve (in a poem on fasting) to the Three Children (traditionally remembered shortly before Christmas).[130]

The OT was comparably significant in the terser Latin hymnody of Ambrose and others which flourished from the fourth century onwards, for instance in the Christmas Eve hymn 'Intende, qui regis Israel', which turns on Pss 80 and

---

[125] On the date (260-300) see Barnes, 'Methodius, Maximus, and Valentinus'.

[126] Musurillo, *St. Methodius*, 20f., 35-7 (on his millenarianism); 151-7, 236-9 (translation of Thecla's hymn, with notes).

[127] A summary account of the poems is given by Watkins, 'Gregorius Nazianzenus', 756; more recent work is cited by Sykes, *'Poemata Arcana'* (on the group formed by numbers 1-4, 7-9 of the dogmatic poems).

[128] Duval, *Jonas*, 2, 546f. (noting its influence, through a Latin version, on Caesarius of Arles).

[129] Examples concerned with the paschal lamb and the breaking of the tables of the commandments are translated by Murray, *Symbols*, 53, 59f.; see also Brock, *The Harp of the Spirit*.

[130] On Romanus see Maas-Trypanis, *Romani Melodi Cantica*, 1, xi-xxxiv (bibliography); for the OT hymns, 312-94, 438-47 (text) and Grosdidier de Matons, *Romanos le Mélode-Hymnes*, 1 (text, French translation, introduction and comments).

19; among the canticles, a noble development of biblical style was attained in *Te Deum*, probably composed towards the end of the fourth century.[131]

In the abundant Christian-Latin verse of this period, however, distinguished by the lyrics of Prudentius and Paulinus of Nola, two less immediately attractive genres offer important instances of OT interpretation. First, didactic writing includes five hexameter books 'against Marcion', perhaps from the middle of the fourth century (compare Gregory Nazianzen's roughly contemporary poem on the law and the gospel); the Testaments are harmonized, and a united succession of old fathers and apostolic teachers is traced from righteous Abel to Anicetus of Rome.[132]

Secondly, biblical paraphrase in verse was popular. It had a long tradition in the Greek east; when the emperor Julian forbade Christians to teach the classics (361-3) Apollinaris of Laodicea and his father rewrote the historical books of the OT in iambics and the psalms in hexameters, but Jews had long ago produced such work, and paraphrase flourished independently of persecution.[133] On the following century the cultivated empress Eudocia rendered the Octateuch, Zechariah and Daniel into Homeric hexameters.[134] The first firmly-dated monument of Latin verse paraphrase is Juvencus on the gospels (early fourth century).[135] OT paraphrase figures in a Virgilian cento by the aristocratic poetess Faltonia Proba and, at the end of the fourth century, in versions of individual psalms by Paulinus of Nola; but more ambitious biblical epic was produced in the fifth century by Cyprianus Gallus (on the Heptateuch), Sedulius *(Paschal Poem)*, and Avitus of Vienne (subjects from the creation to the exodus).[136] Christian verse in this genre responded to the contemporary taste for centos

[131] On the hymns of Ambrose and his contemporaries see Raby, *Christian-Latin Poetry*, 32-6 and Fontaine, *Naissance*, 81-94 (Hilary of Poitiers), 127-41 (Ambrose); 'Intende, qui regis Israel' is printed and briefly annotated by Raby, *Medieval Latin Verse*, no. 12, and the contribution of Ps 19 is brought out in the English verse rendering by D.T. Morgan 'O come, redeemer of mankind, appear', printed in *Hymns Ancient and Modern*, Standard Edition (1922), no. 55 (the first stanza, based on Ps 80, is not translated); on *Te Deum* see Burn, *Niceta*, xcviii-cxxv (attributing it to Niceta of Remesiana).

[132] This poem, transmitted with Tertullian's works, is rendered into English blank verse by S. Thelwall in *ANCL* 18, (*Tertullian*, vol. 3), 318-83; on the date see Harnack, *Chronologie* 2, 442-9.

[133] Wilson, *Scholars of Byzantium*, 10; Thraede, 'Epos', cols. 999-1006 (Greek paraphrase), 1026-31 (Latin OT paraphrase); Nickelsburg, 'Bible Rewritten', 118-25. The authorship of the hexameter psalter extant under the name of Apollinaris is disputed; see Golega, *Der homerische Psalter*.

[134] Photius, *Bibliotheca*, nos. 183-4 describes these works; on Eudocia's background and writings see Hunt, *Pilgrimage*, 222f.

[135] On Juvencus see Fontaine, *Naissance*, 67-80. Some relatively short epic pieces are transmitted with the works of Tertullian and Cyprian; the fragments on Genesis, the Maccabees and the gospel can perhaps be attributed to Cyprianus Gallus, and those on Sodom and on Jonah to Avitus of Vienne. See Raby, *Christian-Latin Poetry*, 13f.; Fontaine, *Naissance*, 247 and 257; and the English blank verse renderings of the pieces on Jonah, Sodom and Genesis by S. Thelwall in *ANCL* 18 (*Tertullian*, vol. 3), 278-300.

[136] See Raby, *Christian-Latin Poetry*, 14 (Virgilian cento), 76-9 (Cyprianus Gallus and Avitus); Fontaine, *Naissance*, 95-8, 102-5 (Proba), 245-60 (Cyprianus Gallus, Sedulius and Avitus); Walsh, *Paulinus*, 16-20 (on his biblical paraphrase).

from Homer and Virgil, and is probably intended not only to give a classicized version of scripture, but also to show how Homer and Virgil harmonize with the bible.[137]

In poetry, then, the didactic and apologetic use of the OT continues, but light is also thrown on its importance as a fund of imagery of classical status for Christians. In hymns it can therefore play a part somewhat comparable with that of mythology in Graeco-Roman lyric, and spiritual interpretation deepens poetry as well as piety. In biblical paraphrase the OT so lends itself to epic treatment as to show its resemblance to Homer and Virgil, in that it forms a kind of national literature of the Christians and the story of their origins.

ART

The OT is more strongly attested than the New in the Christian art of the pre-Constantinian period, from about the year 200 onwards, and it continues to be represented often.[138] This prominence is consistent not only with the probably Jewish origins of Christian art,[139] but also with the centrality of the OT in preaching, catechesis, apologetic and worship. Various scenes and figures were valued as symbols of Christian truths, and their representation illuminates in more than one sense the literary deposit of OT interpretation.

Popular figures in the catacombs, probably taken to signify divine deliverance, include Noah, Abraham on mount Moriah, and Moses at the burning bush and striking the rock; the Three Children in the furnace, Daniel in the lions' den (also represented in brass in a fountain set up by Constantine), and Susanna and the elders; and, in a cycle, Jonah at the various stages of his story.[140]

From the fourth century onwards OT subjects were represented in series on church walls, as appears from poems by Prudentius and Paulinus of Nola; magnificent fifth-century mosaic series surmount the colonnades of the basilica

---

[137] Fontaine, *Naissance*, p. 105.

[138] For introduction and literature on Christian art see H. Chadwick, *Early Church*, 277-84; Grabar, *Iconography* (with illustrations and bibliography); Klauser, *Gesammelte Arbeiten* (with bibliography of his writings); on the interpretation of the Second Commandment with reference to art, H. Chadwick, *Early Church*, 277, 280f. (finding the tendency to condemn representations as graven images in vigour until the end of the fourth century) and C. Murray, 'Art and the Early Church' (arguing that this tendency has been over-rated), with the criticisms by J.D. Breckenridge, reviewing C. Murray, *Rebirth and Afterlife*; on biblical subjects in art, Milburn, *Early Christian Interpretations*, 96-116, and 'The "People's Bible" ', and Stevenson, *Catacombs*, 55-108.

[139] Leveen, *The Hebrew Bible in Art*, 59-62, 118-125; Klauser, *Gesammelte Arbeiten*, 346; H. Chadwick, *Early Church*, 279f.; Schubert, *Spätantikes Judentum und frühchristliche Kunst*; discussion with special reference to the Via Latina catacomb in Simon, *Verus Israel*, 389 (no need to posit direct Jewish influence); Kötzsche-Breitenbruch, *Die neue Katakombe*, 107; Stemberger, 'Patriarchenbilder'; and Fink, *Bildfrömmigkeit*.

[140] Stevenson, *Catacombs*, 66-81; fountains erected in Constantinople with figures of the Good Shepherd and of Daniel and the lions are described by Eusebius, *Life of Constantine*, 3:49; on Jonah in art, see also Duval, *Jonas*, 1, 19-39.

755

of S. Maria Maggiore in Rome.[141] Now, too, the illustration of biblical MSS seems to have become customary in various modes, as is suggested for the Septuagint by the Cotton Bible and the Vienna Genesis, both of the sixth century.[142] OT subjects are also attested on gems, gold-glass and sarcophagi; acceptable designs for signet-rings had already been discussed by Clement of Alexandria.[143]

Three types of representation distinguished by A. Grabar[144] can be seen broadly to correspond to types of OT interpretation. First, the single visual image can evoke a cluster of biblical passages, from the NT as well as the Old. An early example is the lyre, one of Clement's recommended devices for the Christian's signet, which could recall David and his psalmody (Ps 150:3, Aquila and Symmachus *Lyra*), but also the minstrelsy of Christ the Word (Clement of Alexandria, *Protrepticus* 1, mentioning David also). A second and thematically linked example is formed by the representations of the Good Shepherd in the catacombs (and elsewhere); depicted as a maker of music and charmer of wild beasts, like Orpheus, he evokes passages on God as shepherd of Israel (as in Pss 23 and 80), on David as shepherd and musician (1 Sam 16:23, Ps 78:70f.; Ps 151:1f., LXX), and on Christ the shepherd (John 10:11) and the Orpheus-like inventor of harmony (cf. Isa 11:6, on the wolf and the lamb, with other beasts).[145] In these cases the single image acts like the key-word which holds together a number of testimonies (n. 71, above), for example 'stone' in 1 Peter 2:4-8 or Cyprian, *Testimonies* 2:16-17.

Two further types of representation correspond to two different uses of juxtaposed images. Scenes or sequences from the OT, like those noted above, can be brought together visually with one or more NT scenes. This becomes common on sarcophagi, for example that of Junius Bassus (sixteen Old and New Testament scenes, A.D.359).[146] On a grander scale, the OT sequences on either side of the nave of S. Maria Maggiore lead to a NT composition, in which

---

[141] Lietzmann, *Constantine to Julian*, 313f.; Milburn, *Early Christian Interpretations*, 108. The S. Maria Maggiore OT mosaics (based on the Hexateuch) are described and illustrated by Cecchelli, *Mosaici*, 103-94.

[142] Grabar, *Iconography*, 88f., 155 (noting studies by K. Weitzmann); the MSS. are described by Swete, *Introduction*, pp. 132-4, 139.

[143] Clement of Alexandria, *Paidagogos* 3(2):59, 2; Stevenson, *Catacombs*, 55.

[144] Grabar, *Iconography*, P. 111.

[145] Stevenson, *Catacombs*, 98-104; on the lyre, note Paulinus of Nola, poem 20, lines 28-61 (Christ, the true David, restores the lyre of the body), translated by Walsh, *Paulinus*, 158f. Jewish depictions of a lyre-player with beasts may represent an Orphic David, and so form an antecedent of the Christian imagery; different views are noted by Sanders, *Psalms Scroll*, 61-3, to illustrate a Qumran Hebrew text corresponding in parts to the LXX Ps 151 (including verses 1-2, cited above). On the popularity of pastoral imagery in pagan art see Grabar, *Iconography*, 35f.

[146] Described by Milburn, 'The "People's Bible" ', 285 and Plate 7; cf. Grabar, *Iconography* 137f., on the scenes represented on the fourth-century Brescia ivory casket (lipsanotheca), and Stommel, *Ikonographie* (see the review by E. Wellesz), on the sarcophagus 'of the three Monograms' (about A.D. 325). A single OT scene is treated by Kaiser-Minn, *Die Erschaffung des Menschen*.

St. Peter and St. Paul are prominent, on the triumphal arch.[147] In cases like those just mentioned, however, although the OT scenes will have been interpreted symbolically in the usual Christian way, their figurative meaning is not drawn out, and there seems to be no special connection between the individual Old and New Testament scenes. The OT then appears, at least at S. Maria Maggiore, as the first part of a story leading up to the NT and church history, as in the catechetical narration, or as a 'preparation for the gospel' like that discerned by Eusebius.[148]

Thirdly, however, Old and New Testament scenes began to be linked as type and antitype, in the manner familiar from mediaeval stained glass. Some panels in the wooden doors of S. Sabina in Rome (about A.D. 430) appear to be arranged in this way, notably in a parallel between the miracles of Moses and of Christ.[149] In these instances the typology implicit in the single and juxtaposed visual images already considered is spelt out, but it is also inevitably restricted in range by comparison with the undefined field of association of the single image.

Art sometimes throws light on the presuppositions as well as the methods of written biblical interpretation. A striking instance is the scene of the handing-over of the law, 'traditio legis', in fourth-century art. 'The Lord gives the law', as painted inscriptions say, to Peter and Paul, but the model for this scene with Christ and the apostles seems to be Moses with the ancient law.[150] (Peter also acquired from Moses the popular miracle of striking the rock for water).[151] This elaboration of a new 'traditio legis' by Christ, not mentioned as such in the written NT, reflects not only the claims of the Roman see, but also the view that Christ's teaching was a law better than but comparable with the Law of Moses – a far-reaching exegetical principle already met in Tertullian.[152]

In art, as in poetry, the OT was prized as a 'garden of bright images', and the didactic and quasi-patriotic motives of the poets can also be detected in visual OT

---

[147] Grabar, *Iconography*, 46-9, 139-41; Huskinson, *Concordia Apostolorum*, 39 and 42.

[148] The preparatory character of the OT series is brought out by Milburn, 'The "People's Bible" ', 288f. and Grabar, *Iconography*, 139-41. A parallel relationship between the Testaments (cf. n. 152, below) might have been suggested by the two adjoining churches built by Paulinus of Nola, one with OT paintings, the other with New (Paulinus, poem 28, lines 167-79, discussed by Walsh, *Paulinus*, 410). Closer connections between individual Old and New Testament scenes are found by Stommel on the sarcophagus which he studies (n. 146, above).

[149] Grabar, *Iconography*, 142f., with photograph.

[150] Simon, *Verus Israel*, 76; Grabar, *Iconography*, 42, with photographs; Moses with the law appears often on sarcophagi, and Christ with a scroll in the catacombs; the two are back to back on the sarcophagus 'of the three Monograms' (Wellesz, review of Stommel, *Ikonographie*, 324), and either Moses or Christ may be the subject of a disputed Via Latina painting (Stevenson, *Catacombs* 71, 84, 104, 113); see Franke, 'Traditio Legis', on interpretation, Berger, 'Der traditionsgeschichtliche Ursprung', and literature cited by Huskinson, *Concordia Apostolorum*, 25f.

[151] Stevenson, *Catacombs*, 71-3; Huskinson, *Concordia Apostolorum*, 129-40.

[152] Cf. also Clement of Alexandria, *Paidagogos* 3:(12) 94, 1 'Both laws served the Word towards the education of humanity, both that given through Moses and that given through the apostles'; other similar patristic statements are discussed by Hanson, 'Biblical Exegesis', 425f.

representations;[153] but the few examples considered here are meant to illustrate the point of most note in the present connection, the importance of art as a guide to patristic OT interpretation.[154]

The eight settings for such interpretation now reviewed are from literature and the public life of the church, but the mention of gems and sarcophagi forms a reminder of the influence of the OT in private life. This was illustrated by Augustine's references to domestic psalmody, which themselves relate to the widespread private reading and memorization of the OT, especially in connection with catechesis.[155] It is with these varied literary, public and domestic settings in mind that the function and importance of OT interpretation can best be appreciated.

Old Testament and New

REJECTION AND CRITICISM OF THE OLD TESTAMENT

Marcion and his followers rejected the OT,[156] but were somewhat closer to other second-century Christians than that statement suggests. Less radical but similar views were widespread, and rabbinic texts show that Jews also felt the force of objections like those presented by Marcion.[157] His arguments have to be reconstructed from rebuttals.

The OT set forth, in Marcion's view, not the good God of Jesus Christ, but a second divinity, the inferior demiurge who made the world;

him he affirms not *good*, but owns him *just'*.[158]

The OT promises by this deity refer not to the Christians' Christ, but to a warlike messiah whom the Jews rightly expect.

Marcion therefore solved the problem of relating the Testaments by cutting the knot. He drew out the incompatibility of law and gospel in his *Antitheses*, and received as authoritative only the gospel of Luke and the Pauline corpus, both purged of Judaistic elements. Polemists naturally stress that he blas-

---

[153] Paulinus of Nola, poem 27, lines 542-95 (the paintings edify those unskilled in reading); in S. Maria Maggiore the OT mosaics lead up to the triumphal arch, the contemporary ecclesiastical significance of which is brought out by Huskinson, *Concordia Apostolorum*, 42.

[154] Compare the stress laid on this point by Murray, *Symbols*, 37.

[155] Harnack, *Bible Reading*, 55-68, 121-30.

[156] See in general Harnack, *Marcion*; Blackman, *Marcion*; Grant, *The Letter and the Spirit*, 62-6; Evans, *Tertullian Adversus Marcionem* (introduction, text and translation); Meijering, *Tertullian contra Marcion* (commentary on *Adv. Marc.* 1-2).

[157] Marmorstein, *Studies*, 1-47.

[158] Pseudo-Tertullian, *In Reply to Marcion* 1:97 (on this work, see n. 132, above); the proposal of two or more divine principles is also the first object of attack in Tertullian, *Adversus Marcionem* and the Dialogue of Adamantius (usually ascribed to the fourth century, but more probably of the third, as argued by Barnes, 'Methodius, Maximus and Valentinus').

phemes 'him who is declared God by the Law and the Prophets' (Irenaeus, *Haer.* 1:27, 2); but it is noteworthy that Marcion, eschewing symbolic interpretation, assessed the OT as no more than just, but true.[159] He and his followers characteristically noted weaknesses and inconsistencies in the OT, but their postion could be presented so as to set the Christian above the Jew, but the Jew still well above the gentile, with regard to divine illumination.[160]

The contrast between Marcion and those contemporaries of his who were won over by the excellence of the prophets was therefore less than total. The attraction of both positions appears in the apologist Tatian, who was accused (with regard to his ascetic teaching) of ascribing the law and the gospel to different divinities.[161] The classical patristic answer to Marcionite criticisms was to treat difficult passages as types and allegories, as already occurs in the anti-Jewish argument of the *Epistle of Barnabas*; but another set of responses evinced some kinship with Marcion by the appropriation of elements in his criticisms.

Thus the Valentinian Gnostic Ptolemy discerned in the law a mixture of legislation, proceeding from Moses, from the elders, and from God himself; this last division comprises the good and the unjust (completed and cancelled, respectively, in the gospel), and the exemplary and symbolic (changed from the literal to the spiritual in the gospel).[162]

A comparable discrimination of sources in the Pentateuch is found in the pseudo-Clementine *Homilies*, 2:38-40, 3:41-51, probably reproducing second-century teaching; here it is maintained that false paragraphs were interpolated into the law when it was handed down to the elders, and that Christ has taught uw how to discriminate between false and true.[163] In the third century the *Didascalia* likewise distinguishes the true law from the 'second legislation', and expects the bishop to be 'a good discriminator' between them.

The Clementine Homilist (2:39) makes Peter say that this doctrine of the corruption of the law should not be taught openly, for the undiscerning would then reject the law as a whole. For such reasons, doubtless, theories of interpolation did not enter the exegetical mainstream, except in the mild form of a

---

[159] Evans, *Tertullian adversus Marcionem*, 1, xiif.; cf. Quispel, *Ptolémée*, 13 (ancient polemists wrongly insinuate that Marcion viewed the OT deity as evil).

[160] The Marcionite speaker Megethius, in Adamantius, *Dialogue* 1 (Christians, Jews and gentiles are ruled by good, demiurgic and bad principles, respectively); but note that the second Marcionite speaker, Marcus, holds to two principles only. Marcionite variation on this point is also mocked by Rhodo (late second century) in Eusebius, *Hist. Eccl.* 5:13, 2-4.

[161] Clement of Alexandria, *Strom.* 3:(12) 82, discussed by H. Chadwick, *Alexandrian Christianity*, 22f.

[162] For Ptolemy's letter to Flora, quoted by Epiphanius, *Haer.* 33:3, 1-7, 10, see Quispel, *Ptolémée* (introduction, translation and commentary); Foerster, *Gnosis*, 1, 154-61 (introduction and translation).

[163] Quispel, *Ptolémée*, 25f.

distinction between the moral and the ceremonial law;[164] but similar views had been current in the pre-Christian period,[165] and Philo could domesticate them in a distinction between laws – all good – proceeding from God and from Moses.[166] Comparably but more drastically, among the Fathers, Irenaeus distinguished 'natural precepts', given by God himself, from 'bonds of servitude', laws given through Moses as punishment for sin.[167] In this negative assessment of parts of the Pentateuch he comes close to the *Didascalia*, and (like Peter disputing with Simon Magus in the Clementine Homilies) makes a striking concession to his Marcionite opponents.

The continuing appeal of Marcionite criticism is evoked by the enthusiastic adherence of the young Augustine to its Manichaean version (*Conf.* 3:[10] 18, 5:[14] 24), and his own later rebuttal (420) of a non-Manichaean adversary of the law and the prohets'.[168] In the east, likewise, it continued to be necessary to assert the harmony of law and gospel, as appeared from Gregory Nazianzen. Augustine was persuaded to discover this harmony (*Conf.* 5:[14] 24) not by a discrimination of sources, but by Ambrose's eloquent allegorization.

HARMONY OF THE TESTAMENTS

The unity of the Testaments was claimed in answer to Marcion, but abrogation of the law was also regularly stressed in order to explain why Christians did not keep the Mosaic observances. Thus 'law ordained against law has abrogated that which was before it' is represented as the first response of Justin to Trypho (*Dial.* 11).[169]

This widespread early formulation could be used to assert harmony, but its strong element of conflict then had to be reconciled with that assertion by gentler versions of the criticisms just noted. Thus Irenaeus, distinguishing the abiding moral law of the decalogue from the further but temporary 'precepts of bondage' given through Moses, appealed to Deut 4:13f.; here the Lord himself 'declared . . . the ten commandments', but also 'commanded *me* at that time to teach you statutes and judgements' (Vulgate 'caerimonias et iudicia', whence

---

[164] Wiles, *Apostle*, 69 (noting that solutions like those in Ptolemy and the Didascalia were not widely acceptable).

[165] Strabo, *Geog.* 16:2, 35-7, perhaps based on Poseidonius, ascribes the dietary laws and circumcision not to Moses, but to later tyrannical and superstitious priests; see Grant, *The Letter and the Spirit*, 20f. and Lebram, 'Idealstaat', 234-44 (arguing for a Jewish anti-Hasmonaean source).

[166] Philo, *Mos.* 2:187-91, discussed by Fallon, 'Philo and Ptolemy'.

[167] Irenaeus, *Haer.* 4:24-9 discussed by Connolly, *Didascalia*, lxiii-lxv.

[168] Augustine, *Contra Adversarium Legis et Prophetarum*, with the review of the edition of K.D. Daur (*CCL* 49; Turnhout, 1985) by H. Chadwick, *JTS* N.S. 37 (1986), 593-5.

[169] Treatments of the abrogation of the law are surveyed by Simon, *Verus Israel*, 76-91, 163-73; on the vocabulary of this topic in Tertullian, van der Geest, *Le Christ et l'Ancien Testament chez Tertullien*, 63-98.

the term 'ceremonial law').[170] Tertullian presented the same argument expressly 'against the Jews' (*Adv. Iud.* 2), without this appeal but with clearer allusion
to the underlying Gal 3:15-4:7, stressing that apart from the law of love summed
up in the decalogue, the law given through Moses was temporary. This distinction between the moral and the ceremonial law allowed all the ordinances to
be good in their time,[171] and deeply influenced patristic exegesis and later
Christian doctrine.[172] An alternative or additional approach, already noted in
the *Epistle of Barnabas*, was to claim that the true meaning of the ceremonial
law was spiritual; here pre-Christian Jewish allegorization was continued, with
the important difference that observance as understood by Jews was drop-
ped.[173] These two approaches broadly correspond to connection of the Testaments either within an historical framework or as timeless truth, and to typology or allegory, respectively.

Harmonization on these lines is presupposed in some of the art already
considered, but of course it goes back to a much earlier date and has antecedents, as seen above from Tertullian, in the NT (e.g. Matt 5:17, John 5:46f., Gal
3:24). The two Testaments were very soon brought into parallel by the interpretation of the new dispensation as a new law, exemplified above from
Justin and others. For Irenaeus, both laws are laws of love (*Haer.* 4:12,3); for
Clement of Alexandria, both are part of the education of humanity; and these
authors verge on the classical and timeless view developed by Origen, Ambrose, Cyril of Alexandria and others, whereby the Testaments reciprocally
acquire and impart their respective distinguishing features of law and grace.[174]
So Augustine teaches, setting aside the distinction between moral and ceremonial laws, that the one law of love is OT when approached in bondage and fear,
but NT when received in liberty.[175]

---

[170] Irenaeus, *Haer.* 4:16, 3-5 (the quotation in 5); cf. Justin, *Dial.* 45 (some laws naturally good,
others given because of hardness of heart); see Simon, pp. 163f.; Childs, *Exodus*, 431f., 488-92 (good
sketch of the history of exegesis, but underrates patristic attention to the ceremonial law).

[171] Van der Geest, *Le Christ et l'Ancien Testament chez Tertullien*, 75, 97.

[172] Wiles, *Apostle*, 67-9; Aquinas, *S.T.*, 1a, 2ae, 98:5 (the old law manifested the precepts of natural
law, and added certain special precepts), 99:3 (Deut 4:13-14 refer to the decalogue and then to the
ceremonial and judicial precepts, cf. n. 170, above). On Tertullian's use of *caerimonia(e)* for Jewish
rites, with stress on prophecies of their rejection, see van der Geest, *Le Christ et l'Ancien Testament
chez Tertullien*, 67, 97.

[173] Cf. 1 Cor 9:9; for pre-Christian allegorization see *Letter of Aristeas* 144-71, and contrast patristic
allegorization with Philo, *De Migratione* 89-93 (awareness of the symbolism of the laws should not be
a reason for neglect of their observance); see Pépin, *Mythe et Allégorie*, 221-44, on Jewish allegory.

[174] Tollinton, *Clement of Alexandria*, 2, 196-205; Mondésert, *Clément d'Alexandrie*, 98-104; Wiles,
Apostle, 65f. and 'Origen', 483; de Lubac, *Histoire et Esprit*, 166-78; Hahn, *Das wahre Gesetz* (on the
two Testaments in Ambrose); Wilken, *Cyril*, 80f.

[175] Augustine, *Expositio ad Galatas* (A.D. 394), 58, on 6:2; *On the Spirit and the Letter* (A.D. 412),
23-30, 42. In the latter book (translated with introduction by Burnaby, *Augustine: Later Works*,
182-250) the inclusion of moral as well as ceremonial laws within 'the letter that killeth' follows a vital
thread in Pauline thought (Rom 7:7), but is also of service as anti-Pelagian polemic.

COMMENTARY ON THE LAW OF MOSES

The concerns noted in the two preceding sections stimulated Pentateuchal exegesis, but it survives only fragmentarily from the second century. The *Epistle of Barnabas*, Justin, and Irenaeus reproduce traditional Christian interpretations, for the most part probably from testimony-collections on apologetically important topics like the messiah or circumcision (e.g. Gen 49:11, Lev 26:40f., Deut 10:16f., in Justin's *Dialogue*); but they also have interesting traces of more extended comment, as in Barnabas on the scapegoat and other matters, or in Melito on the slaying of the first-born, and of *quaestiones*, as in Irenaeus (e.g. *Haer.* 4:28, 3, on the exodus, perhaps from Marcion).[176]

Philo, a principal source of patristic Pentateuchal exegesis, first clearly appears in that capacity in Clement of Alexandria.[177] Also of about this time are the earliest of the many patristic treatments of two Philonic subjects from the Pentateuch, the Hexaemeron and the life of Moses.[178] A contemporary approach to a more comprehensive Pentateuchal commentary in Christian circles seems to have been the voluminous critical *Syllogisms* on the law of Moses by Marcion's pupil Apelles, towards the end of the second century; among other points answered by Origen and Ambrose he noted that Noah's ark, on its given dimensions, would have been too small to accomodate more than four elephants and their food.[179]

Origen and Ambrose, who stand close to the beginnings of Greek and Latin Pentateuchal commentary, respectively, both draw extensively on Philo.[180] Origen is the first Christian exegete from whom there has survived a full connected interpretation of the ceremonial law, for example in his homilies on Leviticus. From the fourth and fifth centuries in the east notable commentators on the laws are Eusebius of Emesa and Theodoret (using the form of *Quaes-*

---

[176] On early Pentateuchal comment see Daniélou, *Jewish Christianity* 97-115, and *Gospel Message and Hellenistic Culture*, 204-11, 224-8, 237-55 (on Justin, Irenaeus, and Clement of Alexandria).

[177] Petit, *Catena Sinaitica*, xvf., on Philo's importance; on Clement's debt to him, see Mondésert, *Clément d'Alexandrie*, 163-83; van Winden, 'Quotations'; H. Chadwick, *Early Christian Thought and the Classical Tradition*, 141f., n. 65; cf. his 'Justin Martyr's Defence', 296f., on the absence of anything approximating to Philonic allegory in the OT exegesis in Justin's *Dialogue*.

[178] Theophilus of Antioch, *Ad Autolycum*, 10-32 (notably literal, perhaps against gnostic views), about A.D.185, is the earliest surviving among the treatises on the Hexaemeron listed by Bouhot, 'Pentateuque chez les Pères', cols. 702-8; a great range of ancient Christian comment on this subject is analyzed by Petavius (Denis Pétau), *De Sex Primarum Mundi Dierum Opificio* (in his *De Theologicis Dogmatibus*, vol. 3 [1644]). On the life of Moses see Clement of Alexandria, *Strom.* 1:23-6, partly based on Philo, with Bouhot, *ibid.*, cols. 692f., on Gregory of Nyssa and others.

[179] H. Chadwick, *Origen contra Celsum*, 217, n. 3 (on 4:41) and de Lange, *Origen and the Jews*, 127 (both referring to Origen, *Hom. In Gen.* 2, 2); Eusebius, *Hist. Eccl.* 13, 9; Ambrose's references to Apelles (perhaps through Origen [Harnack] or Tertullian [Junod]) are collected with others by Harnack, *Marcion*; see Junod, 'Les attitudes d'Apelles'.

[180] See de Lange, *Origen and the Jews*, 16, 108-21; Lucchesi, *L'usage de Philon* and Savon, *Saint Ambroise*.

tiones), from the Antiochene school, and Cyril of Alexandria (*Glaphyra* on Genesis and Exodus, and *On Worship in Spirit*).[181] The makers of Pentateuchal catenae could later utilize a very wide range of Greek authors; for example, simply within the exegetical field, commentators on the Psalter and the Pauline corpus were bound to consider the Pentateuch.[182] Paraphrasès and anthologies of the Mosaic law have already been mentioned, and from the late fourth century Christians transmitted a Latin 'comparison of the Mosaic and Roman laws' demonstrating their agreement, *Collatio Legum Mosaicarum et Romanarum*.[183]

The richness of patristic Pentateuchal exegesis, which abounds for the ceremonial as well as the moral law, bespeaks the apologetic and pastoral needs of the congregations; but it remains an impressive demonstration of the effect of harmonization, and of the importance of 'Moses' in the Christian imagination.[184]

Modes of Exegesis

PATRISTIC VIEWS OF EXEGESIS

Patristic exegesis was shaped partly by distinctive features of the biblical text, partly by the logical principles classically but densely formulated by Aristotle, and partly by the typology and allegory already employed in pre-Christian biblical interpretation.[185] That proportion of content in which Christian exegesis differed from Jewish could therefore often be elicited from the text without overt reflection on method, other than a reference to the new light shed by the coming of the messiah.[186]

Development of Christian controversy and scholarship soon led, nevertheless, to discussion of exegetical rules, usually with special regard to the OT. These rules were naturally often also rules of belief;[187] a characteristically

---

[181] See in general n. 182, below, and Bouhot, 'Pentateuque chez les Pères'; on Cyril, Wilken, *Cyril*, 69-85.

[182] For Pentateuchal commentators se Devrèesse, *Les anciens commentateurs grecs*; on the sources of a single catena, Petit, *Catena Sinaitica*, xvi-xxi; for the law in comment on other books, Deissler, *Psalm 119*, 33-40, Harl-Dorival, *La chaîne palestinienne*, 1, 99-111, 121-59; and Wiles, *Apostle*, 49-72.

[183] Blumenkranz, *Judenpredigt*, 56f. (inclining to Jewish origin); Childs, *Exodus*, 492; Bammel, *Judaica*, 247-52 (on Deut 18:10f. in the *Collatio*).

[184] Comparing the Pentateuch with the Prophets, Clement of Alexandria's quotations or references stand in the proportion of 5 to 3 (Tollinton, *Clement of Alexandria* 2, 198, n. 3). The concentration of early typological exegesis on the Pentateuch and Joshua is noted by Simonetti, *Profilo*, 29.

[185] See n. 173 above, and Lampe, 'Exposition', 158-62.

[186] See Luke 24:45; Justin Martyr, *Dial.* 12; *Clementine Homilies* 3:49.

[187] Thus the five rules noted from Irenaeus by de Margerie, *Introduction*, 1, 65-71 are dominated by appeal to 'truth' and apostolic tradition; see *Haer.* 3, Preface-4.2, translated with comments by Wiles-Santer, *Documents*, 127-32, and cf. n. 54, above.

Christian norm was the harmonization of the Testaments. On the other hand, the second-century Marcionite titles cited above (Antitheses, Syllogisms) show awareness of the exegetical bearing of logic; and an adoptionist circle at the end of the second century in Rome, who produced many copies of the biblical books, provoked their opponents by their deference to Aristotelian logic and to their contemporary, Galen. 'If a text of divine scripture is adduced to them, they inquire whether it can be put in the form of a conjunctive or a disjunctive syllogism'.[188]

At about the same time a rationale of exegesis, with special reference to the Pentateuch, was sketched in various contexts by Clement of Alexandria.[189] He taught the need for logic in interpretation, and distinguished the literal sense – Moses at his burial – from the inward sense – Moses with the angels;[190] he expanded on the symbolic character of scripture;[191] and he divided 'Mosaic philosophy' into four parts made to correspond to ethics, physics and metaphysics, the three parts of philosophy.[192] In controversy he enunciated rules of attention to the whole of scripture, to context and to subject-matter, but also to the traditional faith.[193]

Origen developed this sketch magisterially in exegesis and in a hermeneutical treatise (*De Principiis* 4:1-23 = *Philocalia* 1:1-27). Here he argues that the authority of Moses is confirmed by Christ; that the scriptures have a threefold sense, corresponding to body, soul and spirit – historical (for the simple), moral, and mystical; and that the spiritual sense is the principal thing.[194]

---

[188] *The Little Labyrinth*, quoted by Eusebius, *Hist. Eccl.* 5:28, 13-19 (13); Barnes, *Constantine and Eusebius*, 134, and nn. 52-3 (literature); Kelly, *Doctrines*, 116f.; Walzer, *Galen*. Apocryphal 'Syllogisms' were ascribed to Daniel's companion, Mishael (Clement of Alexandria, *Strom*. 1:21).

[189] His hermeneutical remarks are gathered by Mondésert, *Clément d'Alexandrie*, 118-29; his practice did not always correspond (J.N. Sanders, review of Mondésert, p. 235). On his exegesis see Daniélou, *Gospel Message and Hellenistic Culture*, 237-55.

[190] *Strom*. 1:9, 43-5 (logic and the double meaning of scripture), 6:15, especially 124-32 (the parabolic style of scripture), discussed by Wolfson, *Church Fathers*, 1, 46-9; the reference in the latter passage to a double vision of the bodily and the spiritual Moses probably comes from a lost *Assumption of Moses* (Schürer, *History* [rev.ed.], 3.1, p. 286).

[191] *Strom*. 5:4-10, especially paragraphs 20-31, 41-50 (on symbolic teaching by the Egyptians, the Greeks, Moses and the apostles), discussed by Grant, *The Letter and the Spirit*, 86f. and Wolfson, *Church Fathers*, 1, 49-52; commentary by Le Boulluec, *Stromate V*.

[192] *Strom*. 1:28, 176-9, discussed by Wolfson, *Church Fathers*, 1, 52-7 (analyzing the debt to Philo) and de Lubac, *Exégèse médiévale*, 1.1., 171-7 (showing, against Wolfson and others, that adivision of subject-matter rather than a multiple sense of scripture is probably in view at the end of the passage); see also Méhat, 'Clément'. On the background in non-Christian exegesis see Whitman, *Allegory*, 60-3 and Harl, as cited in n. 194, below, 110-18.

[193] Mondésert, *Clément d'Alexandrie*, 127f., quoting *Strom*. 7:16, 96; Clement himself markedly favours some biblical books over others (Tollinton, *Clement of Alexandria*, 2, 208-10), but is assiduous in the 'connection of the Testaments' on which he insists (naming Marcion) in the sequel (nn. 161, 174, above).

[194] See Harl in Harl-de Lange, *Origène sur les Écritures*, 42-157 (on Origen's hermeneutics), 182-98 (analysis of this treatise). Origen can use a slightly different threefold scheme in which the moral sense is third (Kelly, *Doctrines*, 73; de Lubac, *Exégèse médiévale*, 1, 1, 198-207); the fundamental distinction is between letter and spirit (Harl-de Lange, ibid., 103; Wiles, 'Origen', 467-70).

Obscurity is a pointer to its discernment, and sometimes there is no literal sense.[195]

This section of *De Principiis* was influential in the east, and reached Latin-speakers through Rufinus's translation. In its Alexandrian love of allegory and concern for the individual educated reader it contrasts with some of the other hermeneutical work available in the west. Thus the church militant here in earth, with its corporate hopes for the tangible fulfilment of prophecy, has left a deep impress on the *Rules* of Tyconius the Donatist (about A.D. 380). He maps out 'the vast wood of prophecy' by dividing it, with attention to the ambiguities of biblical language, into references either to Christ and his church, or to the Devil and his followers. He is remembered for dating the millennium from the First rather than the Second Coming of Christ, but this was not without antecedent (Irenaeus, *Haer.* 5:20), and is far from spiritualization; 'what Daniel said is happening in Africa'. Augustine transferred these rules into a context closer to the Alexandrian spirit when he used them in his treatise 'on Christian culture' (*De Doctrina Christiana*, 3:30-37).[196]

In Italy Marius Victorinus (in fourth-century Rome) and Boethius (consul in 510) both advanced the western knowledge of Aristotelian logic, but applied it in theology rather than exegesis.[197] Allegory was part of a morally-oriented scheme of the biblical senses in Cassian's influential *Conferences* (fifth century), and it was advocated in an exegetical handbook by his pupil Eucherius; but a sixth-century Latin guide by Junilius Africanus, quaestor at Justinian's court in Byzantium, gives teaching of a more Antiochene tinge from Paul the Persian, of the school of Nisibis on the canonical books, the senses of scripture and the interpretation of prophecy.[198]

All these treatments, from the second century onwards, devote themselves in different ways to producing views of exegesis which will comprehend the phenomena of the OT. Tyconius, despite his date and sensitivity to logic, mainly continues second-century concern with schematizing the prophecies. More influential in the long term was the distinction drawn by Clement of Alexandria and Origen between a literal and a spiritual sense.

---

[195] Here he meets difficulties like those which gave rise to theories of interpolation; cf. Bigg, *Christian Platonists*, 84, 175-7, on this passage.

[196] Burkitt, *Tyconius*, xi-xviii, 56 (millennium of 'first resurrection' [Rev 20:5] dated from First Coming), 67 (Daniel in Matt 24:15); G.R. Evans, *Language and Logic*, 52; Bonner, 'Augustine as Biblical Scholar', 554.; on other hermeneutic statements in Augustine, including *de utilitate credendi* 5-8 (four senses in scripture), see Kelly, *Doctrines*, 75.

[197] Victorinus's Christian works include Pauline commentaries, but here as elsewhere his main interests were dogmatic; see H. Chadwick, *Boethius*, 115-8 (on Victorinus; literature), 24-9 (on Boethius's use of logic to interpret dogma). Simonetti, *Profilo*, 87 considers the significance of the limited extent of Victorinus's OT knowledge; see also n. 77, above, on Arnobius.

[198] See O. Chadwick, *John Cassian*, 101f. (on *Coll.* 14:8); Geffcken, 'Allegory' (Eucherius); and de Lubac, *Exégèse mediévale* 1. 1, 190-8 (Cassian and Eucherius); on Junilius, G. Salmon, 'Junilius'; Smalley, *The Study of the Bible in the Middle Ages*, 18f.; de Lubac, *Exégèse mediévale* 1. 2, 494f.

TYPOLOGY

The spiritual sense (Rev 11:8) was discerned especially by recognition of types and allegories (Rom 5:14, Gal 4:24). Typology can be said to differ from allegorical interpretation in that it takes seriously the historical setting of an OT law or event; type and antitype identify some correspondence between different stages in a sacred history, whereas allegory elicits timeless truth from beneath the veil of the biblical 'letter', which may be regarded as having no reference to history.[199]

This distinction is grounded in Antiochene criticism of Origen's allegories, but it has been developed in modern attempts to appropriate something of early Christian exegesis.[200] It is challenged in that context partly because types and allegories repeatedly mingle in the Fathers,[201] and partly because trends in theology and the interpretation of literature have led to questioning of the value of the stress on history associated with definitions of typology, and to a more favourable view of allegory.[202]

The distinction remains useful, however, so long as it is not over-pressed, in analysis of patristic interpretation. Typology, taking its name from *typos* in the sense of prefiguration (Rom 5:14, cf. 1 Peter 3:21 'antitype'),[203] is already found within the OT (as in passages on a new exodus)[204] and is obviously close to the scheme of prophecy or promise and fulfilment. This biblical association of typology and prophecy had analogies in classical literature, notably in the predictions and prefigurations of the Augustan age in the Aeneid.[205]

Patristic typology was important, as seen already, in catechesis, apologetic, worship and art; Moses typified Christ, and the exodus, baptism. Typological exegesis abounded in the second century, when Justin, Irenaeus and Tertullian appealed to such types in controversy with Jews and gnostics; but, despite the

---

[199] Lampe in Lampe-Woollcombe, *Essays in Typology*, 27-35; Kelly, *Doctrines*, 69-75; Pépin, *Mythe et Allégorie*, 506f.

[200] For Antiochene views see the commentators quoted to illustrate Theodore of Mopsuestia on Gal 4:24 by Swete, *Theodori Episcopi Mopsuesteni in Epistolas B. Pauli Commentarii* 1, 73f. (e.g. Chrysostom, Paul 'called the type an allegory by misuse of language'); modern advocacy of a 'spiritual' interpretation, without distinction of typology from allegory, is exemplified by Keble, *Mysticism* (discussed by Lock, *Keble*, 98-102) and de Lubac, *Histoire et esprit*; for approval of typology as opposed to allegory see Farrar, *History of Interpretation*, 217f. and Lampe-Woollcombe, *Essays in Typology*; see also writers discussed by Barr, *Old and New*, 103-48.

[201] De Lubac, *Histoire et esprit*; Barr, *Old and New*, 113-5; Tigcheler, *Didyme* 44-50 (summarizes debate between Daniélou and de Lubac).

[202] Barr, *Old and New*, 147f.; Barton, *Reading*, 104-27.

[203] The usage of *typos* is analyzed by Grant, *The Letter and the Spirit*, 137-9 and Lampe, *Lexicon*, 1418-20, s.v.; on Latin *typus* and *figura* in Tertullian see van der Geest, *Le Christ et l'Ancien Testament chez Tertullien*, 153-72.

[204] Charity, *Events*, 13-80 discusses examples including Isa 11:11f., 15f.; see also Lampe, as cited in n. 185, above, and Fishbane, *Biblical Interpretation*, 350-79.

[205] Griffin, *Virgil*, 65-8 (with special reference to *Aeneid* 8, on Aeneas at the site of Rome).

growing popularity of allegory from the third century onwards, it was typology in particular which gave unity to the continuing sacred history set forth in the catechetical narration, and, later on, in art and poetry.[206] The connection between narration and typology emerges in the last eight (largely narrative) books of Augustine's *City of God*, which can be compared with the detailed typological exegesis set out in the *Book of the Promises and Predictions of God* by Quodvultdeus; a characteristic heading in this fifth-century manual is 'promissio facta et figurata', 'promise made and typified'.[207]

ALLEGORY

Allegory likewise has roots both in the OT and the classical literature, where it was highly developed in philosophical exegesis of Homer, latterly by the Stoics; speculative thought was thereby brought under the aegis of the standard poet, and passages found morally offensive were made edifying.[208] Jews treated their scriptures similarly, as appears most extensively in Philo; Josephus anticipates a position often adopted by Christians when he criticizes the allegorization of Greek myths, but himself regards Moses as speaking in solemn allegories (Ant. 1:24).[209]

Allegorical interpretation was therefore widely familiar in simple form, but it was elaborately developed by Platonizing Jews and Christans to connect biblical law and narrative with their own concerns. Thus Joseph sold to Potiphar becomes in Philo the statesman sold over to the unprincipled multitude, and in Ambrose Christ sold over to sin on our behalf.[210] As these examples show, allegory was consonant with divergent convictions. Philo and his predecessors used it to enlarge the moral context of obedience to the Pentateuchal laws, but Origen, viewing both Moses and Christ as lawgivers, found regulations in both Testaments which, he held, were never meant to be observed; they had only a spiritual sense. The same applied to narrative (here he agreed with Philo); what careful reader could suppose that the Almighty 'planted a garden', or that

---

[206] Hanson, 'Biblical Exegesis', 416-8, 428; van der Geest, as cited in n. 203, above; for surveys of typology and allegory in the second and third centuries see Daniélou, *Gospel Message and Hellenistic Culture*, 197-300 and Simonetti, 'L'interpretazione patristica'.

[207] Bonner, 'Augustine as Biblical Scholar', 552-4; Braun, *Quodvultdeus* (1, 286, 294, 300 for examples of the heading); De Simone, 'Quodvultdeus' (noting Daniélou's view that the 'predictions' are types, but that the 'promises' are testimonies).

[208] Grant, *The Letter and the Spirit*, 1-30; Pépin, *Mythe et Allégorie*, 85-214. Porphyry (quoted by Eusebius, *Hist. Eccl.* 6:19,8) accused Origen of learning allegorization from Chaeremon the Stoic, and Cornutus, and importing it into biblical exegesis; see Rinaldi, 'L'Antico Testamento nella polemica anticristiana di Porfirio di Tiro', 108. On allegory in the OT and in Qumran interpretation see Lampe, as cited in n. 185, above, Hengel, *Judaism and Hellenism*, 1, 246 and n. 883 (literature), and writers cited by Brooke, *Exegesis at Qumran*, 39-42.

[209] Cf. n. 17; Pépin, *Mythe et Allégorie*, 221-44.

[210] Philo, *On Joseph*, 58-63; Ambrose, *On Joseph*, 4 (19) (where Joseph can be considered a *type* of Christ, but Potiphar represents Egypt, *allegorized* as sin (cf. Rev 11:8)).

Christ saw 'all the kingdoms of the world' with his bodily eye?[211] In practice Origen often defended the literal sense; when Africanus criticized the story of Susanna as historically improbable, and in part hardly worthy of a farce, Origen defended its historicity (but there his attachment to the Greek OT was at stake).[212] Philo, similarly, inculcated observance of the laws; but for systematic allegorizers such as these the non-literal significance was all-important, and it was herein especially that they provoked dissent.

If this shift of emphasis, implicit in the method itself, was sometimes criticized, the Christian applications of the method were very widely accepted; the interpreters' concerns were not felt inappropriate to the text interpreted. Thus, in the allegorizations of the Joseph story instanced above, Philo's politics and Ambrose's doctrine of redemption both stand in some genuine connection with the Pentateuchal narrative.[213] Pedagogically, allegory was a priceless boon to the imaginative preacher or teacher. Hence, although the methods was most heartily and characteristically embraced by Alexandrian commentators like Didymus and Cyril, it also contributed to moral teaching;[214] in the west it fitted Ambrose's preaching to move Augustine, Augustine himself sometimes used it in his own OT sermons,[215] and it enabled Gregory the Great to make Job and Ezekiel the staple of spiritual instruction.[216] In this homiletic and moralizing use of allegory the mainstream of patristic OT exegesis was close not only to Philo, but also to the rabbinic midrash.[217]

THE LITERAL SENSE

The importance of types and allegories in second and third-century OT exegesis did not overwhelm more literal interpretation. It appeared negatively in Apelles, but more positively when the laws were viewed as having been mandatory in their time or indeed as still in force; and literal interpretation of the promises was popular. Gen 1-3 were likewise commonly taken literally, perhaps in rebuttal of gnostic views of the cosmogony as well as in accord with the hope for the last things.[218] A *Refutation of the Allegorists* by the Egyptian bishop

---

[211] *De Principiis* 4:1, 14-20; see nn. 194-5, above. Philo, *de Plantatione* 32, also viewed the narrative of planting as one which could not be taken literally.

[212] Origen's defence of the literal sense is emphasized, for example, by Keble, *Mysticism*, 54-68 and de Lubac, *Histoire et esprit*; for the letters of Africanus and Origen see de Lange in Harl-de Lange, *Origène sur les Écritures*, 471-578, and 'Letter to Africanus'.

[213] Barr, *Old and New*, 108f., 116 notes the significance, in assessment of allegory, of the 'resultant system' of thought and practice to which the allegorization leads; Philo's system is perhaps less clearly heterogeneous from the OT than he assumes.

[214] O. Chadwick, *John Cassian*, 83f., 95f., shows the importance of Origen's Pentateuchal allegories for morality and the monastic life.

[215] Simonetti, 'Sulla tecnica esegetica'.

[216] Smalley, *Study of the Bible*, 32-5.

[217] De Lange, *Origen and the Jews*, 112-21.

[218] Hanson, 'Biblical Exegesis', 432; Simonetti, *Profilo*, 29, on Theophilus (n. 178, above) and the millenarians Justin, Irenaeus and Tertullian.

Nepos (about 240) rebutted spiritualization of the millennium (Dan 7:18-27, Rev 20:3-6), and Denys of Alexandria replied *On Promises* (Eusebius, *Hist. Eccl.* 7:24, 1-3).

At this time Africanus made historicity a criterion of worth in his letter to Origen on Susanna (n. 212, above), and Porphyry, whose *Against the Christians* has exegesis of Daniel resembling that later current in Syria, criticized OT allegorization in general and Origen in particular. Also perhaps of this period, and probably from Syria, is a passage of dialogue from the Clementine *Recognitions* (10:29-42), in which a rebuttal of allegorization of the Greek myths is significantly complemented by a warning, put in the mouth of Peter, against idiosyncratic interpretation of the law of God by learned ingenuity of this kind. Eusebius, Origen's disciple in biblical scholarship, nevertheless favoured historical rather than allegorical interpretation.[219]

Against this background it seems likely that Origen was among the exegetes attacked by Paul of Samosata (bishop of Antioch from about 260), who was himself denounced for inadequate Christology; and there may well be substance in the guess that the contemporary Antiochene biblical scholar Lucian, whose work is lost because he was viewed as an influence on Arius, had reservations concerning allegory.[220] However this may be, allegory was certainly opposed by the anti-Arian Eustathius, bishop of Antioch from about 324, and this opposition then characterized what may be called the Antiochene school of exegesis, led by Diodore, bishop of Tarsus from 378.[221] Diodore's book *On the difference between theoria* [spiritual interpretation] *and allegory* is lost, but this distinction is drawn, to the disadvantage of allegory, in the preface of the psalter commentary ascribed to him.[222] The Antiochene school is represented by Eusebius of Emesa and Apollinaris of Laodicea, two important commentators whose work is still being recovered, but its chief surviving literary monuments are the sermons of Chrysostom[223] and the commentaries of Theodore of Mopsuestia and Theodoret.

The differences in OT interpretation which arose from reservations on allegory may be illustrated by two examples. First, in the Wisdom literature, Ecclesiastes (Qohelet) was regarded by Theodore of Mopsuestia and the unidentified

---

[219] Pépin, *Mythe et Allégorie*, 393f., 443f., on the pseudo-Clementine passage; on Eusebius, Wallace-Hadrill, *Eusebius*, 82f., 96f. (he sometimes allegorizes) and Barnes, *Constantine and Eusebius*, 94-105 (his perspective is, nevertheless, basically historical).

[220] Eusebius, *Hist. Eccl.* 7:30,9 (Paul attacks exegetes); Barnes, *Constantine and Eusebius*, 144f. (Paul), 169 (OT exegesis by his followers), 194 (Lucian); Wiles, 'Theodore', 489f. (Lucian probably emphasized history); Duval, *Jonas* 1, 256 (lack of evidence for Lucian's exegesis).

[221] On Eustathius and Diodore see Duval, *Jonas* 1, 256-8 and nn. 80-83 (literature); the Antiochene view of *theoria* as a mean between literalism and fanciful allegory is illustrated by Lampe, *Lexicon*, 649, s.v., where Diodore's preface to his psalter commentary is quoted (see next footnote); on the Antiochene school, Simonetti, *Profilo*, 58-62, 65-73.

[222] Olivier, *Diodori Tarsensis Commentarii in Psalmos*, 1, 7f.; the debated ascription to Diodore is supported by Rondeau, *Les commentaires patristiques*, 102.

[223] The sermons are characterized by Lietzmann, *The Era of the Church Fathers*, 110-23.

Antiochene commentator Pseudo-Chrysostom as Solomon expounding common matters to the whole world, not as Christ mystically instructing the church; the latter was the view of Gregory of Nyssa, and Jerome combined the two interpretations.[224] Secondly, in the prophets and psalms, Theodore's comments strikingly limit the passages directly predictive of Christ, but they allow for typology and find much prophecy of later Israelite history, including the Maccabaean period.[225] The Antiochene approach to Wisdom continued earlier moral exegesis, and in the case of prophecy it allowed Theodore to distinguish firmly between two dispensations within a single divinely-guided historical development.[226] The Antiochene restoration of prophecies, psalms and proverbs to Israelite historical contexts is important as a development of elements in earlier interpretation which might otherwise have been obscured, as an anticipation, despite big differences, of much in modern historical exegesis, and as an attempt to integrate historical commentary with a theological understanding of the OT.

This scholarly exegesis probably gained strength from its convergence with a more popular approach, based on adherence to the plain sense of laws and promises (Nepos, Clementine *Recognitions*) and to the historicity of the biblical narratives (Irenaeus, Chrysostom), and therein close to much Jewish interpretation. As might be suggested by Basil the Great's jokes at the expense of allegory, and by the adoption of historical exegesis not only by Jerome, but also by Augustine (notably in *De Genesi ad litteram*) – in both cases side by side with spiritual exegesis, although Jerome was more rigorous in forming a scholarly basis – Antiochene commentary could appeal to the earnest believer as well as the rational critic. 'I know the laws of allegory', but 'for me, grass is grass' (Basil on the *Hexaemeron*, 9:1).

The Influence of the Hebrew Text and Jewish Interpretation

RECOGNITION OF THE IMPORTANCE OF HEBREW KNOWLEDGE

In 401 Jerome defended his zeal for the Hebrew biblical text and Jewish interpretation by an appeal to ecclesiastical precedent. 'Origen himself, and Clement [of Alexandria], and Eusebius, and many others are accustomed to write, in commendation of their statements on biblical questions, "A Hebrew reported it to me" and "I heard it from a Hebrew" and "That is the opinion of the Hebrews" ' (Jerome, *Apology against Rufinus* 1:13). This was a fair argu-

---

[224] Pseudo-Chrysostom on Eccl. 1:1, in Leanza, *Catena in Ecclesiasten necnon Pseudochrysostomi Commentarius*, 59-61, 67; Wiles, 'Theodore', 495; Jerome on Eccl. 1:1.

[225] Wiles, 'Theodore', 498-502; Duval, *Jonas*, 1, 264f., 311-24 suggests that Theodore allowed himself to draw on Origen for comment on Jonah, and urges that Origen's care for history (n. 212, above) as well as allegory should be remembered.

[226] Wiles, 'Theodore', 497-504, 507-10.

ment, for Christians inherited not only the Jewish reverence for the Septuagint (evident in Philo and Josephus as well as in Jerome's critics), but also something of the increasing Jewish recognition of its shortcomings. Some time-lag between the Christian sub-culture and its Jewish sources is indeed suggested by the indignation of Justin Martyr and Irenaeus at Jewish attempts to improve on the Septuagint, which cut the ground from Christian arguments (Justin, *Dial.* 71:1, cf. 68:7f. and Irenaeus, *Haer.* 3:21, 1-3, both in connection with Isa 7:14). Jewish Greek versions other than the Septuagint had probably circulated for some time, but Irenaeus in this passage is the first writer to mention by name those of Aquila and Theodotion. Christian authorship was claimed for only one such version, that of Symmachus, who is significantly described as an Ebionite (and therefore close to Jewish opinion) (Eusebius, *Hist. Eccl.* 17).[227] These three versions, however, with others, were soon synoptically incorporated into Origen's Hexapla (see below), and were regularly consulted by later Christian biblical students; Rufinus paid heavily for his copies, according to Jerome (*Apology against Rufinus* 2:34).

Other names, as he says, can be combined with the three he mentions to document Christian use of Jewish knowledge. Those which follow are mainly from the select number who can also be credited with some command of Hebrew (noted in each case),[228] but the ante-Nicene names include one or two who simply illustrate the patristic contacts with Jewish interpretation considered further in the following section. Such contacts were not greatly hindered by ignorance of Hebrew.[229]

In the second century Melito of Sardis inquired in the Holy Land about the biblical canon, and Pantaenus, who taught in Alexandria, commented on the meaning of the Hebrew tenses in the prophets. Clement of Alexandria, who mentions this (*Ecl. Proph.* 56, see n. 19, above), himself occasionally cites contemporary Jewish interpreters.[230] Origen, however, was peculiarly entitled, by his own textual labours, to remind Celsus that the bible is written in Hebrew (*Contra Celsum* 7:59). Origen's Hexapla set the various Greek versions side by

---

[227] Eusebius states that Origen received copies of interpretations of Matthew and other biblical books by Symmachus the Ebionite from Juliana, who had them from the author; but Epiphanius, *De Mens. et Pond.* 15, probably less well informed, says that Symmachus was a Samaritan who became a Jewish proselyte (Barnes, *Constantine and Eusebius*, 92). Some viewed Theodotion also as an Ebionite, according to Jerome, *Prologue to Commentary on Daniel* (*PL* 25.493); but Irenaeus, loc. cit., says that Aquila and Theodotion were both Jewish proselytes. Jewish features of Symmachus are considered by C. Taylor, 'The Hexapla', 19f. (with reference to A. Geiger's suggestion that he was a pupil of R. Meir) and J. Gonzáles Luis, 'Los "targumim" y la versión de Símaco'.

[228] For surveys see Elliott, 'Hebrew Learning among the Fathers'.

[229] De Lange, *Origen and the Jews*, 20-23 (Jewish interpretations available in Greek), 56-8 (public bible-reading and prayer by Jews in Greek).

[230] Krauss, 'Church Fathers', and De Lange, *Origen and the Jews*, 19f., quoting *Strom.* 1:23 'the Mystae say that Moses killed the Egyptian with a word', and comparing *Exod. Rabba* and Rashi on Exod 2:14; for Clement's use also of Philo (e.g. in the context of this passage) and of Jewish apocrypha see nn. 178, 188-90, above.

side with the Hebrew text (in Hebrew letters and in Greek transliteration), and he took much note of Jewish interpretation. On the whole, however, he gave pride of place in his exegesis to the Septuagint (as in his defence of Susanna), following ecclesiastical custom; and his writings show that he could not read Hebrew easily, despite his pains to acquire the Hebrew biblical texts for his library (Eusebius, *Hist. Eccl.* 6:16, 1).[231]

Origen's correspondent the chronicler Julius Africanus concerned himself with the Hebrew language and Jewish subjects (Africanus to Origen, 5, [*PG* 14:45], and to Aristides, in Eusebius, *Hist. Eccl.* 6:31). Later in the third century the presbyter Dorotheus of Antioch gave himself to the study of Hebrew, and is said by Eusebius, who knew him, to have read the Hebrew scriptures with understanding (*Hist. Eccl.* 7:32, 2). This attainment agrees with the indications of an historical emphasis in Syrian exegesis of the period already noted; Lucian of Antioch at the end of the century, corrected the Septuagint text, perhaps but not certainly by reference to the Hebrew.[232] A comparable revision, current in Alexandria and Egypt, was made by Hesychius.[233] These biblical studies form the background against which Eusebius of Caesarea built extensively on the basis of scholarship laid by Origen, once again with some knowledge of Hebrew and, as Jerome emphasized, of contemporary Jewish exposition.[234]

In the fourth century the heresiologist Epiphanius of Salamis in Cyprus, a labyrinth of information on Jewish life as on many other subjects, probably knew Hebrew.[235] At the beginning of the fifth century the Arian presbyter Timothy was noteworthy for the acquaintance with Hebrew evinced in his public biblical expositions (Socrates, *Hist. Eccl.* 7:6), and the Hebrew text was cited with some critical acumen in the commentaries of Theodoret.[236]

Jerome's Hebrew attainments were therefore more exceptional in degree than in kind.[237] He learned Hebrew more thoroughly than any other patristic commentator whose writings have survived, and taught it to Paula and Eu-

---

[231]   De Lange, *Origen and the Jews*, 21f., 50f., 58.

[232]   Barnes, *Constantine and Eusebius*, 194; Wallace-Hadrill, *Antioch*, 30f.; he was 'well versed in sacred learning' (Eusebius, *Hist. Eccl.* 9:6, 3), and a laudatory but dubious account included in Pseudo-Theodoret, *Methodos* (a late compilation, see Rondeau, *Psautier*, 137) claims that he consulted Hebrew copies (*PG* 84. 29-32).

[233]   The Hesuchius named in this connection by Jerome, *Prefaces to Chronicles* (*PL* 28. 1392-3) and to the Gospels (*PL* 29. 559), is perhaps identical with the Egyptian bishop Hesychius, martyred in 307, mentioned together with the learned Phileas of Thmuis by Eusebius, *Hist. Eccl.* 8:13, 17 (Barnes, *Constantine and Eusebius*, 194, n. 34).

[234]   So 'the teacher of the Jews said to us', Eusebius on Isaiah, 3:15, on 39:1-2; the limitations of Eusebius's Hebrew are stressed by Elliott, 'Hebrew Learning', pp. 859f., but he often referred to 'the Hebrew reading', probably through the Hexapla; see Ziegler, *Jesajakommentar*, xxxivf., xxxix, 245 (on 39:1-2), 444.

[235]   Elliott, 'Hebrew Learning', 863f.

[236]   Elliott, 'Hebrew Learning', 868f.; Guinot, *Théodoret . . . sur Isaïe* 1, 44f., 52 n. 1.

[237]   Sparks, 'Jerome as Biblical Scholar'; Barr, 'St Jerome's Appreciation of Hebrew'; Bardy, 'Saint Jérome et ses maîtres hébreux'; cf. Kedar, above, pp. 315-18.

stochium. His initial revision of the Old Latin versions of the Septuagint, exemplified by the 'Gallican Psalter',[238] was a Latin counterpart to the Septuagint recension of Origen, Lucian and others, but the Latin translation which he then made directly from the Hebrew was a rare and monumental achievement. His witness to Jewish interpretation, especially through his own Jewish instructors and informants, was also exceptionally full; but, as he insisted, it had ample precedent.

Recognition of the value of Jewish interpretation was therefore relatively widespread, and the point is underlined by the number of those who were prepared to learn at least some Hebrew. An impulse towards this recognition could arise in various ways. The ever-present need to purify the text led to revision of the Septuagint (Origen, Eusebius, Lucian, Hesychius) and thereby to renewed awareness of its character as a translation and of the importance, in principle, of the Hebrew text. (In practice, this awareness could be combined, as in Theodore of Mopsuestia, with neglect of the Hebrew language and adherence to the Septuagint).[239] Exceptionally, new Christian translations of the Hebrew appeared (Symmachus, Jerome). Jewish interpretation and Hebrew knowledge was of obvious value in exposition and commentary, particularly but not solely of an historical character (Clement of Alexandria, Origen, Eusebius and others), and including that given in public lectures or homilies (Dorotheus, Timothy, Jerome);[240] and they could strengthen apologetic, especially but not only with Jewish affirmations in view (Origen, Eusebius, Jerome, Theodoret).[241]

JEWISH INTERPRETATION IN CHRISTIAN SOURCES

The amplitude of the overlap between patristic and rabbinic interpretation can be quickly grasped from the twelve-page patristic index of Louis Ginzberg, *The Legends of the Jews* (Vol. 7 [Index by B. Cohen, 1938], pp. 586-98). His book summed up much earlier work on patristic-rabbinic exegetical contacts, which continue to be explored.

The examples abound in connection with standard procedures of the rabbinic aggada, or non-legal interpretation. Thus, narratives receive edifying development, as when Moses slays the Egyptian with a word (Exod 2:14 in Clement of Alexandria [a word] and *Exod. Rabba* 1:29 [the divine name]). Explanations are added where they seem necessary, as when Shebna, 'who is over the house', is described as high priest (Isa 22:15 in Eusebius, Jerome, and *Lev.*

---

[238] Kelly, *Jerome*, 158f.

[239] Wiles, 'Theodore of Mopsuestia', 496f.; examples in Sprenger, *Theodori Mopsuesteni Commentarius in xii Prophetas*, 72-8.

[240] Kelly, *Jerome*, 136f., on his homilies.

[241] See for example De Lange, *Origen and the Jews*, 69, 98-102 (Jewish knowledge in debate with Celsus and with Jews); Barnes, *Constantine and Eusebius*, 170, 178f.

Rabba 5:5, p. 114f., on 4:3).[242] Isolated and potentially problematic personages are more closely incorporated into the narrative, as when the fatherless and motherless Melchizedek is identified with the Hebrew ancestor Shem (Ephrem Syrus, Jerome, Epiphanius; Targums Pseudo-Yonatan and Neofiti on Gen 14:18; *B.T. Nedarim* 32b, R. Yishmael, *Midrash Tehillim* 171a on Ps 76:3); in this last case the interpretation won some Christian approval even though, as Epiphanius noted, it is allowed by the chronology of the Hebrew text, but not that of the Septuagint.[243]

There are also some contacts, however, in halakhic or legal interpretation. Thus the *Epistle of Barnabas* and Justin Martyr, followed by Tertullian, state (without express biblical warrant) that the two goats of the Day of Atonement must resemble one another, as recommended in the Mishna (*Yoma* 6:1, cf. *Barn.* 7:6, Justin, *Dial.* 40:4; Tertullian, *Adv. Iud.* 14:9f. = *Adv. Marc.* 3:7, 7f.).[244]

In these instances the Jewish and Christian interpretations coincide. Sometimes, however, interpretations thought to be Jewish were cited by Christians in order to be rejected. This was particularly the case with regard to disputed areas like messianic prophecy. 'The Jews, misguided by the names of towns and territories, hope for [the restoration of Judaea] exactly as described' (Tertullian, *Adv. Marc.* 3:24, 2). 'The Jews vainly dream that this prophecy is against the city of Rome and the Roman sovereignty; and they hold that in "the burden of Dumah" in Isaiah [21:11], by a tiny alteration in the crown of a latter, *Resh* can be read for *Dalet*, so that the word becomes "Roma"; for in their language the letter *Waw* is used for both u and o' (Jerome, *Commentary on Obadiah*, on verse 1 'to Edom').[245]

This large patristic-rabbinic overlap prompts the question by what media rabbinic interpretation reached the Christians. In this connection one should note that rabbinic tradition includes much from earlier Jewish interpretation.[246] Accordingly, an important medium was formed by pre-rabbinic Jewish literature known to Christians, most obviously the biblical versions of Jewish origin (Septuagint; Aquila and Theodotion; Peshitta Pentateuch) but also Jewish apocrypha, Philo and Josephus, and other Jewish works in Greek; instances already met include the use of a lost 'Two Ways' in the Apostolic Fathers, Enoch

---

[242]   Ginzberg, *Legends* 6, 364, notes 62-3; 'the Hebrew said that Somnas (Shebna) was high priest, a voluptuary and a man of unseemly life', Eusebius ad loc. (Ziegler, *Jesajakommentar*, 147), followed by Jerome at loc.

[243]   Ginzberg, *Legends* 5, 225f., n. 102; Gianotto, *Melchisedek*, 108-12, with discussion of the comment by Epiphanius, *Panarion* 55:6, 1; contrast Theodoret, *Qu. in Gen.* no. 64 (*PG* 80. 172), who thinks it probable that Melchizedek sprang from the pagan Palestinians (the ancestors of his own Syrians).

[244]   Daniélou, *Jewish Christianity*, 98f. ascribes the Barnabas passage to a Christian midrash on Leviticus.

[245]   On rabbinic interpretation of Edom as Rome see Ginzberg, *Legends*, 5, 272f., n. 19 and Maier, 'Zum rabbinischen Assoziationshorizont'.

[246]   Ginzberg, *Legends* 5, viiif.; De Lange, *Origen and the Jews*, 15f., 123f.

in Tertullian,[247] a lost Assumption of Moses in Clement of Alexandria, and Philo in Clement of Alexandria and Ambrose. Very many such works were transmitted, and often also translated and adapted, by Christians; influential examples are the Christianized Greek *Testaments of the Twelve Patriarchs* and Old Latin 4 Ezra (2 Esdras),[248] the Syriac *Cave of Treasures*, compiled from Jewish and Christian apocrypha, the probably fourth-century Latin version of Philo's *Questions on Genesis* and *Contemplative Life*,[249] and the fifth- and sixth-century Latin Josephus, sponsored for the *Antiquities* and *Against Apion* by Cassidorus.[250]

Among non-literary means of contact one should reckon biblical exposition in the synagogue, in cities often an impressive building and to some extent a public place; 'the Jews read the scriptures openly . . . there is common access every sabbath' (Tertullian, *Apol.* 18:8).[251] Further, the literary depiction of public and more private debates between Jewish and Christian teachers, in works like Justin Martyr's *Dialogue with Trypho*, found some measure of correspondence in life.[252] Personal contacts of a scholarly kind are documented in the writings of Origen, Eusebius, and especially Jerome, who mentions such teachers as Baraninas, who taught him Hebrew by night, and 'a certain Hebrew' who encouraged him when he despaired of mastering the Aramaic of Daniel.[253] Lastly, Christian Jews, such as the 'Hebrew by descent' mentioned in Clement

---

[247] On apocrypha, including 1 Enoch, in Tertullian see Daniélou, *Latin Christianity*, 161-76.

[248] Collins, 'Testaments' 342-4; Stone, 'Apocalyptic Literature', 412-4.

[249] Petit, *L'ancienne version latine* 1, 7-15.

[250] Schürer, *History*, (rev.ed.), 1, pp. 58f. (Cassiodorus probably knew the Christianized Latin paraphrase of the *War* current under the name of Hegesippus). Western Christian adoption of Josephus would be favoured by the quasi-patriotic view of the οτ found in contemporary Christian Latin verse and western ecclesiastical art. In Syriac the sixth book of the *War* was copied with the books of the Maccabees (Hayman, *Sergius* (*CSCO* 339), 32*-47*).

[251] De Lange, *Origen and the Jews*, 21 (Origen's statements that he heard Jewish interpreters [e.g. *In Ezech. Hom.* 4:8] give the impression that he had been present at Jewish lectures or sermons). The weekday Christian gatherings for prayer and biblical study perhaps had their Jewish counterparts.

[252] Simon, *Verus Israel*, 173-8; Neusner; *Aphrahat*, 123-9, 144-9; important evidence in Origen, *In Ps. Prol.* (discussion of 'certain oracles of God' with the Jewish patriarch Huillus) and *Contra Celsum* 1:45 (discussion of the authority of Moses and Jesus with Jewish 'wise men', before a large number of other people), 55 (discussion of Isa 53), is considered by De Lange, *Origen and the Jews*, 69, 72, 98, 101f.

[253] De Lange, *Origen and the Jews*, 20-8 (thus, 'the Hebrew' gave Origen the hermeneutical principle that the keys to the locked rooms of scripture are scattered throughout the whole 'house' of the Bible, *Philocalia* 2:3, on Psalm 1); Bardy, 'Saint Jérome et ses maîtres hébreux'; Sparks, 'Jerome as Biblical scholar', 515f.; for the examples cited see Jerome, *Ep.* 84, 3 and *Preface to Daniel*.

of Alexandria's list of his teachers (*Strom.* 1:11), were probably an important channel of information in the early period.[254]

Such contacts focussed a more general Christian awareness of Jewish claims to possess the authentic biblical interpretation. The bishop of Oea was forced to consult the Jews when his congregation rebelled against Jerome's translation of Jonah. Augustine's famous description of the Jews as 'our satchel-bearers' *(capsarii)* who 'carry the books for *us* who study them' (*Enarr. in Ps.* 40:14, cf. 56:9, on Pss 41:12, 57:3)[255] was rhetorical devaluation of the pastorally unsettling popular respect for the Jews as custodians and interpreters of the Hebrew scriptures.

Notable Authors and Expositions

The catalogue below offers some initial guidance to the patristic literature of OT interpretation, and also forms a schedule of many personages and primary sources of this chapter; but some hitherto unmentioned patristic writings are included. In the first part patristic authors of importance in the study of exegesis are listed selectively, with reference to texts, to translations into a modern language where possible, and usually also to the OT books mainly concerned. Selected further studies are noted. In the second part the books of the Hebrew bible are listed, followed by the books known to Jerome and in the Vulgate as Third and Fourth Ezra (1-2 Esdras), by the Septuagintal adjuncts to Jeremiah and Daniel, and by the other Septuagintal books which Jerome mentions as read in church.[256] For each book there is a note of patristic citation or interpretation, with reference usually to the foregoing list of authors, and sometimes to further secondary literature.

AUTHORS

ANTE-NICENE FATHERS.

1 Clement, to the Corinthians (c. 96), refers especially to the Pentateuch,

---

[254] The passage is quoted by Eusebius, *Hist. Eccl.* 5:11, 3-5; the 'Hebrew' is perhaps but not clearly identical with the unnamed teacher (probably Pantaenus) mentioned thereafter by Clement as the 'last' whom he found (De Lange, *Origen and the Jews*, 150, n. 39). Christian Jews are treated as an influential body in the church in Justin, *Dial.* 47:1-4, cf. 48:4, 55:1 (see Harnack, *Judentum und Judenchristentum in Justins Dialog mit Trypho*, 49f., 84-9); in the next century Origen, in whose eyes they are less important, often mentions them, and receives some of his Jewish interpretations from them (De Lange, *Origen and the Jews*, 25 and n. 87, 33 n. 38, 36 and n. 88, 116 and n. 86 (Ezekiel's *Tau* and the cross), 126f. and nn. 33-4 (Adam's burial at Golgotha, cf. Ginzberg *Legends*, 5, 126f., n. 137)).

[255] See Simon, *Verus Israel*, 71 and Blumenkranz, *Judenpredigt*, 162-4 for the context of this description in the polemical commonplace that the Jews cannot understand their own scriptures (2 Cor 3:15; n. 90, above).

[256] Jerome, *Preface to the Books of Solomon* (mentioning Ecclesiasticus, Wisdom, Judith, Tobit and the books of the Maccabees); see Weber, *Biblia Sacra* 2, 957; ET in *NPNF* 6, 492.

Isaiah, the Psalms and the Wisdom literature (n. 1, above). See J.B. Ligthfoot, *Clement of Rome* (text, ET and commentary); Jaubert (*SC* 167).

The Epistle of Barnabas before 135, includes an expanded decalogue (n. 46), anti-Judaic allegory of the laws (nn. 67, 90), midrash-like treatment of Leviticus (n. 244), testimonies (n. 71), and a veiled interpretation of Daniel (Horbury, 'Trajan and Hadrian', nn. 178-85). See Prigent-Kraft (*SC* 172).

Justin Martyr (c. 100-c. 165) freely used testimonies (n. 71) and types (nn. 110, 206) – especially from the Pentateuch, Isaiah and the Psalms – in his *Apologies* (ed. Blunt, with notes; ET in *ANCL* 2) and *Dialogue with Trypho* (tr. with introduction and notes by Lukyn Williams). See Otto, *Justini . . Opera* (Greek text with Latin tr. and notes); Prigent, *Justin et l'Ancien Testament*; Shotwell, *The Biblical Exegesis of Justin Martyr*; Osborn, *Justin Martyr*; Skarsaune, *The Proof from Prophecy*.

Melito of Sardis (writing c. 160-180) investigated the canon (n. 2) and preached on the exodus (n. 106). See Hall, *Melito (OECT)*; Daniélou, *Gospel Message*, 234-6.

Irenaeus (c. 130-200) supported his deliberately biblical theology (n. 54, n. 167; n. 227) especially from the Pentateuch, Prophets and Psalms. He criticized Gnostic views in *Against Heresies* (ed. and tr. A. Rousseau and Doutreleau, with Hemmerdinger and Mercier, in *SC*; ET by J. Keble (*LF* 42)); the catechetical basis of his teaching is prominent in his *Demonstration* (n. 53, above). His typological dexterity (n. 206), especially in showing the 'recapitulation' of the old order in Christ, is matched by a contrasting emphasis on the literal sense of Gen 1-3 and the prophetic promises (n. 218). See Lawson, *Biblical Theology of St. Irenaeus*; Daniélou, *Gospel Message*, 166-83, 221-34; Duval, *Jonas* 1, 131-47; n. 187.

Tertullian (c. 160-220) gave lively expression to esteem for the Jewish scriptures (with which he read some apocrypha) in his *Apology* (nn. 72, 77; ET by A. Souter in J.E.B. Mayor's commentary, and by T.R. Glover, *LCL*) and *Against Marcion* (E. Evans, *OECT*; n. 156, above). He closely resembles Irenaeus in the use of divergent exegetical approaches (n. 86, n. 152, nn. 169, 172). See Barnes, *Tertullian*; Van der Geest, *Le Christ et l'Ancien Testament chez Tertullien*; Daniélou, *Latin Christianity*, 161-76, 264-73, 297-338; Aziza, *Tertullien et le Judaisme*; Waszink, 'Tertullian's Principles and Methods of Exegesis'; Simonetti, *Profilo*, 27-30.

Cyprian (d. 258) attests regulative application of the Pentateuch (nn. 87, 93-4), and is notable for his *Testimonies* (ed. Weber, *CCL* 3, pp. liii-lx, 1-179 (important differences from *CSEL*; review by Greenslade); ET in *ANCL* 13, 78-198; n. 71). See Daniélou, *Latin Christianity*, 228-338.

Hippolytus (c. 170-c. 236) is credited in MS tradition with commentaries, all of currently debated authorship, but touching many themes of Irenaeus and Tertullian, on the Blessings of Isaac, Jacob and Moses (Greek, Armenian and Georgian ed. and tr. by Brière, Mariès and Mercier), on David and Goliath and the Song of Songs (Georgian ed. with Latin tr. by Garitte), and on Daniel

(Bardy, *SC* 14), with a related tract on Antichrist (ed. Achelis, *GCS*). See *ANCL* 6 and 9 (ET, mainly from fragmentary texts); *CPG* 1, nos. 1870-5, 1880-6; Bonwetsch, *Studien*; Richard, 'Hippolyte de Rome'; Rondeau, *Psautier* 1, 27-43; Simonetti, *Profilo*, 31-5.

Clement of Alexandria (c. 150-215) treated Genesis, Exodus and the Psalter in his lost exegetical *Hypotyposes* (Photius, *Bibliotheca*, no. 109; Westcott, 'Clement of Alexandria', 563ff.). The work is perhaps partly represented by *Prophetic Extracts* (n. 19; ed. and tr. Nardi; ET in *ANCL* 24, 117-35). Here and in Clement's other extant writings (ed. Stählin-Früchtel-Treu *(GCS)*; ET in *ANCL* 4 and 12) his exposition of Christianity (nn. 55, 75, 121) goes hand in hand with a philosophically envisaged and often allegorical exegesis, strikingly weighted in the OT towards the Pentateuch (n. 184), but also drawing on the Wisdom literature (n. 1), apocrypha (nn. 188, 190) and current Jewish interpretation (nn. 230, 254). See also Duckworth-Osborn, 'Clement of Alexandria's *Hypotyposeis*'; translations by G.W. Butterworth (*LCL*, *Protrepticus* and other works) and in Oulton-Chadwick, *Alexandrian Christianity* (*LCC*, selections with comment); commentaries cited in nn. 121, 191, above; on Clement's exegesis, n. 189, above, and Tollinton, *Clement of Alexandria* 2, 165-230; Ziegler, *Dulcedo Dei*; Wilde, *The Treatment of the Jews in the Greek Christian Writers*, 169-80.

Origen (c. 184-c. 254), the giant of ante-Nicene interpretation, moulded textual criticism by his Hexapla (nn. 227, 231, 234), hermeneutics by his allegorical method (nn. 22-3) and exposition by his voluminous exegetical works. Jerome classified these as Excerpta, corresponding to 'scholia' or short notes; Homilies; and Tomes, or fuller commentaries.[257] It is not always clear whether surviving exegetical pieces were originally scholia or extracts from other works.[258] Origen's OT exegesis includes fragments (some from scholia) on the Octateuch, printed in *PG* 12 before the Homilies on each book (see Devréesse, *Octateuque*, 26-52), and on Lamentations *(GCS)*; substantial remains of the Tomes on the Psalter (*PG* 12. 1050-1686, see n. 81, above, and Devréesse, *Psaumes*, 1-88) and the Song of Songs (*GCS*; ET by R.P. Lawson (1957), *ACW* 26); see Urbach, 'Rabbinic Exegesis'); Homilies, mostly transmitted in Latin versions, on the Octateuch (*GCS*; for Genesis and Exodus, see de Lubac, Doutreleau and Fortier *(SC)*; ET by Heine *(FC)*; for Leviticus, Numbers and Joshua, Borret, Méhat and Jaubert *(SC)*), on Jeremiah (Schadel; Nautin-Husson, *SC*), on the Psalms (Peri), and on the Song of Songs (*ACW* 26); and correspondence with Africanus on Susanna (nn. 95, 212). See Westcott, 'Origenes', at pp. 104-111 (descriptive catalogue of Origen's OT work), with *CPG* 1,

---

[257] Jerome, *Preface* to translation of *Origen's Homilies on Ezekiel* (*PL* 25. 585f.; *GCS* 33, p. 318); cf. *Preface to Commentary on Matthew* (*PL* 26. 20; Origen's tomes, homilies, and 'commatic' or concise comments on Matthew).

[258] Discussion is reviewed in connection with the psalms by Rondeau, *Psautier* 1, 44-51.

nos. 1410-44, *BP* vol. 3, Nautin, *Origène*, 227-41, and Rondeau, *Psautier* 1, 44-63, 158-61; On Origen's exegesis, works cited in n. 194, above, with Harnack, *Ertrag*; Tollinton, *Selections from the Commentaries and Homilies of Origen* (ET); de Lubac, *Histoire et esprit* (review by H. Chadwick); Hanson, *Allegory and Event*; de Lange, *Origen and the Jews*; Sgherri, *Chiesa e Sinagoga nelle opere di Origene*.

Eusebius of Caesarea (c. 260-340) attended both to literal and to spiritual interpretation in his commentaries (n. 20) on Isaiah (Ziegler, *Jesajakommentar*) and the Psalms (see Devréesse, *Psaumes*, 89-146 and Rondeau, *Psautier* 1, 64-75 on the editions in *PG* 23-4). See further nn. 35, 73, 78, 219; *BP*, vol. 4; Wallace-Hadrill, *Eusebius*; Barnes, *Constantine and Eusebius*; des Places, *Eusèbe de Césarée commentateur*.

ALEXANDRIANS.

Athanasius (c. 296-373) upheld a twenty-two book canon (n. 51) and outlined the modes of psalter-interpretation 'to Marcellinus', although the psalter-comments in his name are mainly inauthentic (Rondeau, *Psautier* 1, 79-87; Stead, 'St. Athanasius on the Psalms'). See also Sieben, 'Herméneutique'; de Margerie, *Introduction* 1, 137-64.

Didymus the Blind (c. 313-98), praised as a true 'seer' by Jerome (*PL* 23. 109), commented in Origen's manner on Genesis (Nautin-Doutreleau, *SC* 233, 244), Zechariah (Doutreleau, *SC* 83-5), Job (ed. Henrichs), and Ecclesiastes (ed. Binder et al.). These hitherto lost commentaries have been printed from Tura papyri (discovered 1941); on the Psalms, see Rondeau, *Psautier* 1, 116-121; fragments on Proverbs survive in Latin (*PG* 39. 1621-45). See *CPG* 2, nos. 2546-2556; Kelly, *Jerome*, 124-6; Tigcheler, *Didyme l'Aveugle et l'exégèse allégorique*.

Cyril (died 444; n. 181) commented, Christologically but with more interest in literal and moral interpretation than Didymus showed, on the Pentateuch (Cyril's *Glaphyra* on selected passages, *PG* 69. 9-678), Isaiah (*PG* 70. 9-1449), and the Minor Prophets (*PG* 71-2; ed. P.E. Pusey, 1868; see Simonetti, 'Note sul commento di Cirillo ai Profeti Minori'). On the recovery of Cyril's own work from the psalter-commentary in his name see Rondeau, *Psautier* 1, 131-4. See also *CPG* 3, nos. 5200-5; Kerrigan, *Cyril . . Interpreter of the Old Testament*; Wilken, *Judaism and the Early Christian Mind*; Simonetti, *Profilo*, 75-8; Duval, *Jonas*, 1, 397-416.

ANTIOCHENES.

(n. 24; Wallace-Hadrill, *Christian Antioch*).

Eusebius of Emesa (died c. 359), n. 25.

Apollinari(u)s of Laodicea (c. 310-390), nn. 26, 133.

Diodore of Tarsus (died c. 390), nn. 221-2. His pupil *John Chrysostom* (c. 347-407), as renowned for exegesis as for eloquence, gave continuous OT exposition (much more survives on the NT) in homilies on Genesis (Dumortier-Liefooghe,

SC 304) and the Psalms (*PG* 55, discussed by Rondeau, *Psautier* 1, 126-31). See also nn. 200, 223; *CPG* 2, nos. 4409-13; Duval, *Jonas* 1, 258-63; Meeks-Wilken, *Jews and Christians*.

Theodore of Mopsuestia (c. 350-429), also a pupil of Diodore and a homilist (nn. 49-50, 67), wrote bold historical commentary, surviving most fully on the Minor Prophets (ed. Sprenger) and the Psalms (ed. Devréesse; Syriac, ed. and tr. van Rompay); see nn. 38, 200, 224-26, 239. Fifth-century charges that he fostered Nestorianism and Pelagianism correspond to his influence among Syriac-speaking Nestorians and in the west, including Ireland (Rondeau, *Psautier* 1, 102-7, 175-88). See works cited in n. 225, above; *CPG* 2, nos. 3827-3838; Devréesse, *Essai*; Simonetti, 'Note sull' esegesi veterotestamentaria di Teodoro di Mopsuestia'; Wallace-Hadrill, *Christian Antioch*, 45-51.

Theodoret of Cyrrhus (c. 393-c. 458) was an outstandingly clear and learned commentator; see his Questions on the Octateuch, Kingdoms and Chronicles (*PG* 80. 77-858, re-edited by Fernandez Marcos with Saenz-Badillos [Octateuch] and Busto Saiz [Kingdoms and Chronicles]), and commentaries on the Major and Minor Prophets (*PG* 81. 215-1988; on Isaiah, Guinot, *SC*), the Psalms (*PG* 80. 857-2002; see Rondeau, *Psautier* 1), and the Song of Songs (*PG* 81. 27-214). See nn. 38, 74, 82, 243; *CPG* 3, nos. 6200-8; Ashby, *Theodoret . . as Exegete of the Old Testament*.

SYRIAC WRITERS.

Aphrahat (n. 61) wrote his twenty-three Demonstrations or homilies between 336 and 345 (Syriac text ed. Wright and [with Latin tr.] by Parisot; ET of eight by A.E. Johnston [*NPNF* 13], and of eight more by Neusner, *Aphrahat*). See Murray, *Symbols*, p. 29 and passim, on exegesis; Snaith, 'Aphrahat and the Jews'; Owens, *The Genesis and Exodus Citations of Aphrahat*.

Ephrem Syrus (c. 306-73) touched many OT texts and subjects in his poetry (nn. 117, 128-9; selections in ET in *LF* [J.B. Morris] and *NPNF* 13 [J. Gwynn, J.T.S. Stopford, A.E. Johnston]. His directly exegetical work includes commentaries on Genesis and Exodus (ed. with Latin tr. by Tonneau, *CSCO* 152-3). See Murray, *Symbols*, pp. 29-32 and passim, and de Margerie, *Introduction* 1, pp. 165-87, on exegesis; Brock, *The Harp of the Spirit*; Hidal, *Interpretatio Syriaca*; Deppe, *Kohelet*; Kronholm, *Motifs from Genesis I-XI in the genuine hymns of Ephrem Syrus*; Wallace-Hadrill, *Christian Antioch*, 39-43.

THE CAPPADOCIAN FATHERS.

Sheldon-Williams, 'Greek Christian Platonist Tradition', 432-56.

Basil of Caesarea in Cappadocia (c. 330-79) preached influential homilies on the literal sense of the Hexaemeron (Giet, *SC*, ET (B. Jackson) in *NPNF* 8, 51-107), and on the Psalms (*PG* 29, extracts in *NPNF* 8, pp. XLIV-XLIX; ET by Way, *FC* 46). See n. 96; Fedwick, ed., *Basil* (bibliography).

Gregory Nazianzen (c. 325-c. 392), orator and poet (n. 127), collaborated with Basil in the Philocalia of Origen (n. 23) and gave a canonical list close to that of

Athanasius (n. 257). See *CPG* 2, no. 3052 (catena fragments); Duval, *Jonas* 1, 248-50, 359-74.

Gregory of Nyssa (c. 335-c. 395), a gifted allegorist of mystical bent, expounded the life of Moses (n. 178; Daniélou, *SC*), the Psalm-titles (Rondeau, *Psautier* 1, 112-121), Ecclesiastes and the Song of Songs (*PG* 44; Cahill, 'The Date and Setting of Gregory of Nyssa's Commentary on the Song of Songs'). See n. 49 and 89; Spira-Klock, *Easter Sermons*; Harl, ed., *Écriture et culture philosophique*; Macleod, 'Allegory and Mysticism' and 'The Preface to Gregory of Nyssa's *Life of Moses*'; Heine, 'Gregory of Nyssa's Apology for Allegory'; Canévet, *Grégoire de Nysse et l'herméneutique biblique* (review by G.C. Stead).

WESTERN WRITERS.
Hilary of Poitiers (c. 315-67), n. 27.
The Ambrosiaster (?4th century), n. 28.
Jerome (c. 342-420), biblical translator (nn. 237-38) and champion of the Hebrew canon, studied under Apollinaris (n. 26), Gregory Nazianzen, Didymus the Blind, and Jewish instructors. The greatest Latin commentator, his exegetical work included translation from Origen, treatises on Hebrew Questions and Names (n. 35; Kelly, *Jerome*, 153-6), and learned commentaries using many sources, most notably on Ecclesiastes (*CCL* 72) and the Major and Minor Prophets (*CCL* 73-76A; on Jonah, Duval, *SC*). See Weber, *Biblia Sacra* (Jerome's prefaces to biblical translations); *NPNF* 6 (ET of selected prefaces to translations and commentaries); Krauss, 'Jerome'; Sparks, 'Jerome as Biblical Scholar'; and other works cited in n. 237, above; Kelly, *Jerome*; Duval, *Jonas* and *Jérôme et les prophètes*; Braverman, *Jerome's Commentary on Daniel* (review by N. de Lange); Nautin, 'Hieronymus'; Jay, *L'exégèse de Saint Jérôme*.

Ambrose (339-97) exploited OT exempla in his preaching (n. 15, n. 59), drawing freely from Philo's allegories on the Pentateuch (nn. 174, 179-80, 210, 213); see ET of much of his exegetical work in *FC* 42 (J. Savage) and 65 (M. McHugh). The OT was also important in his catechesis and hymnography (n. 111, n. 131). On his exposition of several Psalms (*CSEL* 62 and 64) see Rondeau, *Psautier* 1, 149-54 and (also on the Psalms elsewhere in Ambrose's writings) Auf der Maur, *Psalmenverständnis*. See, besides other works cited in the notes above, Hadot-Cordier on the *Apology for David (SC)*; Duval, *Jonas* 1, 230-6; de Margerie, *Introduction* 2, 99-143.

Augustine (354-430), alienated when young from the OT by its crudity, was later won back to it intellectually by Ambrose's allegories, and emotionally by psalmody (n. 109). He then asserted its harmony with the NT (nn. 62, 168, 175). His always pastorally-oriented exposition includes allegory (n. 215) as well as typology (nn. 196, 207), both exemplified in his *Enarrationes* on the Psalms (*CCL* 38-9; ET in *LF* [6 vols.]). Historical and literal exegesis was important in his catechetical teaching (nn. 57, 62) and his commentary on Genesis 1-3 *ad litteram* (ed. with French tr., introduction and notes by Zycha et al.); but he knew no Hebrew, shrank from the pastoral implications of Jerome's contention for the Hebrew verity, and threw his weight behind a Septuagintally-based canon. See Blumenkranz, *Judenpredigt*, 68-84; Willis, *Lectionary*; Knauer, *Psalmenzitate*; La Bonnardière, *Biblia Augustiniana, A.T.*; Strauss, *Schriftgebrauch*; Bonner, 'Augustine as Biblical Scholar'; de Margerie, *Introduction*, 3; H. Chadwick, *Augustine*, 11-13, 35-7.

THE FIFTH AND SIXTH CENTURIES.
(a) The East
Hesychius of Jerusalem (fl. 428) was admired as a preacher (Aubineau, *Hésychius* and *Homélies Festales*), and wrote commentaries in the Alexandrian manner on books including Leviticus (a spiritual interpretation preserved in Latin, *PG* 93), Isaiah (ed. Faulhaber) and the Psalter (triple commentary, discussed by Devréesse, *Psaumes*, 243-301, with a study of Hesychius as exegete, and by Rondeau, *Psautier* 1, 137-43; see *PG* 27. 849-1344). See also Duval, *Jonas* 2, 446-51, 629-45.

Procopius of Gaza (c. 475-c. 536), eminent in the Christian rhetorical school of his city (Glucker, *Gaza*, 51-7), wrote a commentary on the Octateuch surviving only in abbreviated form and edited in a Latin version (*PG* 87, 1); it consists mainly of extracts from other commentators, and has been taken to support the view that Procopius originated the biblical catena (n. 31). See also Leanza, *Procopii Gazaei Catena in Ecclesiasten*; Simonetti, *Profilo*, 105-6.

(b) The West
Cassiodorus (c. 485-c. 580), influential in passing on a unified classical and Christian literary tradition to the Middle Ages, considered biblical books (with discussion of their number) and commentators in his *Institutions* of sacred and profane letters (ed. R.A.B. Mynors, Oxford, 1937; ET by L.W. Jones, New York, 1946; see Wermelinger, 'Le canon des Latins', 195-6). His allegorizing Psalter-commentary (*CCL* 97-8) follows Augustine, but also uses Origen, Jerome and Cyril, and is marked by his own educational interest (Smalley, *Study of the Bible*, 30-2; Simonetti, *Profilo*, 109-110). See Schlieben, *Theologie und Philologie*; O'Donnell, *Cassiodorus*.

Gregory the Great (c. 540-604) preached allegorical expositions of Ezekiel (ed. and tr. Morel, *SC* 327) and Job (thirty-five books of *Moralia*, *CCL* 143 A, B, C, -; parts in *SC*; ET in *LF*); he commented on the Song of Songs (Bélanger, *SC*; review by C. Straw). See n. 216, and G.R. Evans, *The Thought of Gregory the Great*.

EXPOSITIONS

Relevant authors treated above are simply named. For further literature see the bibliographies of the history of the exegesis of each book in Childs, *Introduction*. Influential LXX renderings are listed by Swete, *Introduction*, 464-77.

PENTATEUCH.
(Bouhot, 'Pentateuque chez les Pères'; Harl et al., *La Bible d'Alexandrie*)
(a) Philo (nn. 17, 177-80).
(b) Early treatment of various passages (see n. 176): 1 Clement, Barnabas, Justin, Irenaeus, Tertullian, Cyprian, Hippolytus, Clement of Alexandria, Aphrahat.
(c) Comment on two or more books, including Genesis and Exodus: Origen, Cyril of Alexandria, Eusebius of Emesa, Apollinaris, Theodoret, Ephrem Syrus, the Ambrosiaster, Ambrose, Procopius; see also Petit, *Catenae Graecae*.
(d) Individual books.
Genesis (n. 178):L authors in (c), and Didymus; Chrysostom and Basil (Hexaemeron); Augustine (Gen 1-3). See Armstrong, *Die Genesis in der alten Kirche*; Harl, *La Genèse*; Levene, *The Early Syrian Fathers on Genesis* (review by W.D. McHardy); *In Principio*; Robbins, *The Hexaemeral Literature*; Wickham, 'The Sons of God and the Daughters of Men'; Daniélou, *Sacramentum Futuri* (Adam, Noah, Isaac); Stone, 'Apocalyptic Literature', 415-8, 420f. (Testament and Apocalypse of Abraham); Gianotto, *Melchisedek*; Norelli, 'La sabbia e le stelle'; Lerch, *Isaaks Opferung*; Brock, 'Genesis 22 in Syriac Tradition'; Posnanski, *Schiloh I*; Simonetti, *Rufin . . Les Benedictions* (Gen 49); Stemberger, 'Patriarchenbilder'; K. Schubert, 'Die Illustrationen der Wiener Genesis im Lichte der rabbinischen Tradition' (n. 142, above); n. 248, above (Testaments of the Twelve Patriarchs).
Exodus: authors in (c), and Melito, Clement of Alexandria, and Gregory of Nyssa (n. 178); n. 45 (the decalogue); Daniélou, 'Exodus'; Childs, *Exodus*.
Leviticus: Origen, Cyril of Alexandria, Eusebius of Emesa, Apollinaris, Theodoret, Hesychius, Procopius; nn. 85-86, 92, 95; Nickelsburg, 'Aaron'.
Numbers: Origen, Cyril of Alexandria, Eusebius of Emesa, Apollinaris, Theodoret, Procopius; Nordström, 'Rabbinica in frühchristlichen und byzantinischen Illustrationen zum 4. Buch Moses'.
Deuteronomy: Hippolytus; Cyril of Alexandria, Eusebius of Emesa, Apollinaris, Theodoret; n. 29 (Verecundus); n. 190 (Assumption of Moses); La Bonnardière, *Deutéronome*.

FORMER PROPHETS.
(La Bonnardière, *Livres historiques*).
Joshua-2 Kings: Eusebius of Emesa (fragments), Theodoret, Procopius.
Joshua-Judges: Origen; Daniélou, *Sacramentum Futuri*, book 5 (Joshua).
1-2 Samuel (LXX 1-2 Kingdoms): Origen (1 Samuel); Eustathius (the witch of En-dor; n. 221, and Wallace-Hadrill, *Christian Antioch*, 31f.); Ambrose (David; n. 15); nn. 141, 145; Daniélou, 'David'.

1-2 Kings (LXX 3-4 Kingdoms): Schürer, *History* (rev. ed.) 3.1, 372-9 (Schürer and P.S. Alexander on the Testament of Solomon and 'Solomon and Magic'); Sparks, *'Lebanon'*; Bardy, 'Elie'.

LATTER PROPHETS.
(Ps.-Epiphanius, *Lives of the Prophets* (D. Satran in *Compendia* II/2, 56-60)).
Isaiah: Origen, Eusebius of Caesarea, Cyril of Alexandria, Theodoret, Chrysostom, Jerome, Hesychius of Jerusalem; Ottley, *Isaiah according to the Septuagint* (commentary); Lupieri, *Il cielo e il mio trono*; Guinot, *Theodoret. . sur Isaie* 1, 19-24 (on patristic exegesis of the book); Sparks, *Apocryphal Old Testament*, 775-812 (on the Ascension of Isaiah, perhaps known to Origen, and mentioned by Didymus the Blind, Epiphanius and Jerome).
Jeremiah: Origen, Theodoret, Jerome; Kannengiesser, 'Jérémie'; La Bonnardière, *Jérémie*; see Baruch, below.
Ezekiel: Origen, Theodoret, Jerome, Gregory the Great; Daniélou, *Études*.
The Minor Prophets (The Twelve Prophets): Cyril of Alexandria, Theodore of Mopsuestia, Theodoret, Jerome; La Bonnardière, *Les douze*.
Hosea, Joel and Amos: Bouwman, *Des Julian von Aeclanum Kommentar*; Merx, *Die Prophetie des Joel und ihre Ausleger*; Dassmann, 'Amos'; Smythe, 'The Interpretation of Amos iv.13 in St. Athanasius and Didymus'.
Jonah: Duval, *Jonas*, cf. n. 140.
Habakkuk: Strobel, 'Habakuk'.
Zechariah: Didymus the Blind (ed. Doutreleau, pp. 30-41, on other patristic treatments).

THE WRITINGS.
(Hagiographa).
Psalms: Origen, Eusebius of Caesarea, Didymus the Blind, Athanasius, Apollinaris, Diodore, Chrysostom, Theodore of Mopsuestia, Theodoret, Basil, Gregory of Nyssa, Hilary of Poitiers, Ambrose, Augustine, Hesychius, Cassiodorus. See n. 109 (psalmody); Mühlenberg, *Psalmenkommentare*; Devréesse, *Psaumes*; Harl-Dorival, *La chaîne palestinienne*; Salmon, *Tituli Psalmorum*; Rondeau, *Psautier*; Neale-Littledale, *A Commentary on the Psalms from Primitive and Mediaeval Writers*.
Job: Origen (n. 106); Didymus the Blind, Apollinaris, Gregory the Great; see also D. Hagedorn, *Der Hiobkommentar des Arianers Julian* (fourth century), the Latin *Anonymus in Job* printed among Origen's spuria (*PG* 17. 371-522; Simonetti, *Profilo*, 85), Julian of Eclanum on Job (*PL* Suppl., 1), and U. and D. Hagedorn (*Olympiodor, Diakon von Alexandria, Kommentar zu Hiob* (sixth century); Dhorme, *Job*, pp. ccxxi-ccxxiii (on patristic exegesis); Sparks, *Apocryphal Old Testament*, 617-48 (on the Septuagintally-based Testament of Job); Kannengiesser, 'Job chez les Pères'.
Proverbs: nn. 1 (1 Clement, Justin), 110 (Cyprian); n. 59; Didymus the Blind, Apollinaris; Basil, *Hom.* 9, 'on the beginning of Proverbs' (*NPNF* 8, pp. lviii f.;

FC 46); La Bonnardière, *Proverbes*; Cottini, *La vita futura nel Libro dei Proverbi.*

Ruth: treated with Judges, notably by Theodoret, and in connection with Matt 1:5 (Chrysostom, *Hom. In Matt.* 3:5).

Song of Songs: Hippolytus, Origen, Apollinaris, Theodoret, Gregory of Nyssa, Gregory the Great; Philo of Carpasia (Ceresa-Gastaldo); Aponius (*PL* Suppl., 1), interpreting the bride as the church of the believing Jews (n. 69, above; Kampling, *Blut Christi*, 103-9; Witer, 'Aponius'). See Rowley, 'The Interpretation of the Song of Songs'; Ohly, *Hohelied-Studien*; McNeil, 'Avircius'; Littledale, *A Commentary on the Song of Songs from Ancient and Mediaeval Sources.*

Ecclesiastes: Didymus the Blind, Apollinaris, Ephrem Syrus, Gregory of Nyssa, Jerome, Procopius, n. 224 (Ps.-Chrysostom); Deppe, *Kohelet.*

Lamentations: Origen, Apollinaris (fragments); Theodoret; Daniélou, *Études,* 76-99.

Esther: Aphrahat, *Dem.* 21 (Neusner, pp. 109-11); Jerome, letter 53 (*NPNF* 6, p. 101).

Daniel: Hippolytus, Apollinaris, Theodoret, Jerome; n. 140; Berger, *Daniel-Diegese*; Casey, 'Porphyry' and *Son of Man*; Fraidl, *Die Exegese der siebzig Wochen.*

Ezra-Nehemiah (1-2 Ezra): Schneemelcher, 'Esra'.

Chronicles: Theodoret.

1 Esdras (3 Ezra): Schürer, *History* (rev.ed.), 3.2, 714f. (patristic references quoted).

2 Esdras (4 Ezra): Schürer, *History* (rev.ed.), 3.1, 301-3 (patristic references and allusions); Ryle, *Canon*, 253-8 (patristic passages dependent on ch. 14 quoted in translation); Daniélou, *Latin Christianity*, 17-31 (on chapters 1-2, sometimes designated '5 Ezra'); n. 248, above.

Wisdom: n. 1; La Bonnardière, *Sagesse*; seventh-century commentary (excerpted from Gregory the Great) by Taio of Saragossa (*PL* Suppl. 4).

Ecclesiasticus: nn. 44, 51; Schürer, *History* (rev.ed.), 3, 1. 207f. (patristic citation and use).

Judith: Jerome's Preface (Weber, *Biblia*, 691); Dubarle, *Judith*; Schürer, *History* (rev.ed.), 3.1, 220.

Tobit: Jerome's Preface (Weber, *Biblia*, 676); Kelly, *Jerome*, 285; Gamberoni, *Die Auslegung des Buches Tobias.*

Baruch: Theodoret; Schürer, *History* (rev.ed.), 3.2, 738-45 (patristic use of Baruch and the Epistle of Jeremy); on the Paralipomena of Jeremiah and the Apocalypse of Baruch see Nickelsburg and Stone, respectively, in *Compendia* II/2, 72-5, 408-12, and Wolff, *Jeremia im Frühjudentum und Urchristentum.*

Song of the Three, Susanna, and Bel and the Dragon: Hippolytus, Origen, Jerome (translating Origen's comments on Susanna and Bel); Song of the Three, also Theodoret, Verecundus (n. 29); Schürer, *History* (rev.ed.) 3.2, 725-9 (patristic use of the Song, Susanna and Bel).

1-2 Maccabees: Schürer, *History* (rev.ed.), 3.1, 182f., 534f.; for the use of the story told in 2 Macc. 7 in the cult of the Maccabees, see Gregory Nazianzen, Sermon 15, Augustine, Sermons 300-2, and Gilbert, 'Wisdom Literature', 316-9 (on 4 Maccabees).

Bibliography

PATRISTIC EXEGESIS IN GENERAL

General surveys: FARRAR, *History of Interpretaton* (1886), often antiquated, but vivid and helpful; GRANT-TRACY, *Short History*; CHADWICK, 'The Bible and the Greek Fathers'; KELLY, 'The Bible and the Latin Fathers'. More detail in *CHB*, 1-2 (LAMPE, 'Exposition and Exegesis' and HANSON, 'Exegesis in the Early Church', with WILES, 'Origen' and 'Theodore of Mopsuestia', SPARKS, 'Jerome' and BONNER, 'Augustine'). Collection: *La Bible et les Pères* (Biblical citations and testimonies, authority of text and versions, exegesis). Fuller introductions: DE MARGERIE, *Introduction* (3 vols.; modern ecclesiastical situation in view); SIMONETTI, *Profilo* (concise, lucid and informative). Use of the bible: HARNACK, *Bible Reading*; LAMB, 'The Place of the Bible'; YARNOLD, 'Liturgia e bibbia'. The later west: SMALLEY, *The Study of the Bible in the Middle Ages* (revised edition).

PATRISTIC OLD TESTAMENT INTERPRETATION

Historical survey: DIESTEL, *Geschichte* (outdated on editions and attributions). Typology: DANIELOU, *Sacramentum Futuri* and *History of Early Christian Doctrine*; CHARITY, *Events and their Afterlife*; MURRAY, *Symbols*. Patristic typology and modern hermeneutics: LAMPE-WOOLLCOMBE, *Essays on Typology*; BARR, *Old and New in Interpretation*. Allegory: GEFFCKEN, 'Allegory'; GRANT, *The Letter and the Spirit*; PÉPIN, *Mythe et allégorie*. Origen's allegories: DE LUBAC, *Histoire et esprit* (advocate); HANSON, *Allegory and Event* (critic). Allegory and mysticism: MACLEOD, *Essays*. Collection: *L'Antico Testamento nella Chiesa prenicena* (= *Augustinianum* 22.1-2 [1982]). Canon: RYLE, *Canon* (old, but generous in patristic quotation), with AMSLER et al., *Canon* (JUNOD and WERMELINGER on eastern and western views, respectively), BECKWITH, *The Old Testament Canon of the New Testament Church* (arguing for a fixed Jewish canon in the period of Christian origins), and BARTON, *Oracles of God* (arguing that a tripartite canon did not emerge until later). Catenae: HARL, *La chaîne palestinienne*. Comment on various biblical books: CHILDS, *Introduction* (bibliographies); HARL, *La Bible d'Alexandrie*. On individual patristic authors and biblical books: particularly useful are DE LANGE, *Origen and the Jews* and KELLY, *Jerome*; DUVAL, *Jonas* (a cross-section of exegesis) and RONDEAU, *Psautier*. For further literature on authors and biblical books see above.

BIBLIOGRAPHICAL WORKS

Books and articles on patristic OT exegesis are noted in the *Book List* of the Society for Old Testament Study (1946-; annual issues collected by ROWLEY, *Eleven Years of Bible Bibliography* [1957], ANDERSON, *A Decade of Bible Bibliography* [1967] and ACKROYD, *Bible Bibliography 1967-1973: Old Testament* [1975]) and in *Bibliographia Patristica*, edited by SCHNEEMELCHER (vols. 1-25) and SCHAEFERDIECK (vols. 26-7 and onwards); see also SIEBEN, *Exegesis Patrum*. Biblical citations and allusions in the Fathers are indexed by ALLENBACH et al., *Biblia Patristica*, 4 vols. (1, to Clement of Alexandria and Tertullian; 2, the third century, apart from Origen; 3, Origen; 4, Eusebius, Cyril of Jerusalem, Epiphanius).

PATRISTIC STUDY

For attributions, editions and translations see ALTANER, *Patrology*; QUASTEN, *Patrology*; DI BERARDINO, ed., *Patrologia*, 3; E. DEKKERS-A. GAAR, ed., *Clavis Patrum Latinorum* (Steenbrugge, 1951); M. GEERARD, *Clavis Patrum Graecorum*, Turnhout, 1 Patres Antenicaeni (1983), 2 Ab Athanasio ad Chrysostomum (1974), 3 A Cyrillo Alexandrino ad Iohannem Damascenum (1979), 4 Concilia, Catenae (1980). Word-study, especially of theological terms, is greatly aided by LAMPE, *A Patristic Greek Lexicon*.

Abbreviations

Names of biblical books, Apocrypha, Pseudepigrapha, early Christian writings and of the Nag Hammadi Treatises are abbreviated according to the usage of the Journal of Biblical Literature, Vol. 95 (1976) 335-38. For Qumran Writings see Fitzmyer, *Tools*, 3-53 and Dimant, 'Qumran Sectarian Literature'. For Philo, the abbreviations given in the Loeb ed., vol. 10, p. XXXVf. are used. Standard editions of rabbinic literature are mentioned in the source index below.

AASF	Annales academiae scientiarum Fennicae
AbrN	Abr-Nahrain
AC	Annual (Babylonian) Cycle
Actes	Actes du Premier Congrès Internationales de Linguistic Sémitique et Chamito-Sémitique
ACW	Ancient Christian Writers
AJSL	American Journal of Semitic Languages and Literatures
AJSR	Association for Jewish Studies Review
ALGHJ	Arbeiten zur Literatur und Geschichte des hellenistischen Judentums
Alttest.Abh.	Alttestamentliche Abhandlungen
ALUOS	Annual of the Leeds University Oriental Society
ANCL	Ante-Nicene Christian Library
ANET	Ancient Near Eastern Texts (Pritchard)
ANRW	Aufstieg und Niedergang der römischen Welt (Haase-Temporini)
AOAT	Alter Orient und Altes Testament
ASGW	Abhandlungen der kön. sächsischen Gesellschaft der Wissenschaft. Theol.-Hist. Klasse
ASTI	Annual of the Swedish Theological Institute in Jerusalem
AUSS	Andrews University Seminary Studies
BA	The Biblical Archaeologist
B.A.R.	British Archaeological Reports
BASOR	Bulletin of the American Schools of Oriental Research

BG	Berlin Gnostic Codex
BHH	Biblisch-historisches Handwörterbuch (Reicke-Rost)
BHK	Biblia Hebraica (Kittel)
BHS	Biblia Hebraica Stuttgartensia
BJRL	Bulletin of the John Rylands Library, Manchester
BP	Allenbach, *Biblia Patristica*
BSOAS	Bulletin of the School of Oriental and African Studies
B.T.	Babylonian Talmud
BWAT	Beiträge zur Wissenschaft vom Alten Testament
BZ	Biblische Zeitschrift
BZAW	Beihefte zur Zeitschrift für die alttestamentliche Wissenschaft
CBL	Collectanea Biblica Latina
CBQ	Catholic Biblical Quarterly
CCG	Corpus Christianorum, Series Graeca
CCL	Corpus Christianorum, Series Latina
CFC	Cuadernos de filologia clásica
CG	Cairo Geniza Fragments
CHB	The Cambridge History of the Bible
CHJ	The Cambridge History of Judaism
CHLGP	The Cambridge History of Later Greek and Early Medieval Philosophy
CII	Corpus Inscriptionum Iudaicarum (Frey)
Compendia	Compendia Rerum Iudaicarum ad Novum Testamentum
CPG	Clavis Patrum Graecorum (Geerard)
CPL	Clavis Patrum Latinorum (Dekkers-Gaar)
CSCO	Corpus Scriptorum Christianorum Orientalium
CSEL	Corpus Scriptorum Ecclesiasticorum Latinorum
DACL	Dictionnaire d'Archéologie Chrétienne et de Liturgie
DB	Dictionary of the Bible (Hastings)
DBS	Dictionnaire de la Bible, Suppléments
DCA	Dictionary of Christian Antiquities
DCB	Dictionary of Christian Biography
DJD	Discoveries in the Judaean Desert
DPAC	Dizionario patristico e di antichià christiana
DS	Dictionnaire de spiritualité
EB	Encyclopaedia Biblica (Hebr.)
EI	Encyclopaedia of Islam
EJ	Encyclopaedia Judaica
ERE	Encyclopaedia of Religion and Ethics (Hastings)
Eretz-Israel	Eretz-Israel. Archaeological, Historical and Geographical Studies
E.T.	English Translation

Evang. Theol.	Evangelische Theologie
ExpT	Expository Times
FC	The Fathers of the Church
FGH	Jacoby, *Fragmente der griechischen Historiker*
FRLANT	Forschungen zur Religion und Literatur des Alten und Neuen Testaments
FT	Fragmentary Targum
GCS	Die griechischen christlichen Schriftsteller der ersten drei Jahrhunderte
GLAJJ	Stern, *Greek and Latin Authors on Jews and Judaism*
GRBS	Greek, Roman and Byzantine Studies
G.T.	German Translation
HAT	Handbuch zum Alten Testament
Helikon	Helikon. Tradizione e Cultura Classica (Univ. Messina)
Hermes	Hermes. Klassische Philologie
HSM	Harvard Semitic Monographs
HTR	Harvard Theological Review
HUBP	Hebrew University Bible Project
HUCA	Hebrew Union College Annual
ICC	The International Critical Commentary of the Holy Scriptures
IDB(S)	The Interpreter's Dictionary of the Bible (Supplementary Volume)
IEJ	Israel Exploration Journal
IOMS	International Organization for Masoretic Studies
IOS	Israel Oriental Studies
IOSCS	International Organization for Septuagint and Cognate Studies
IOSOT	International Organization for the Study of the Old Testament
IPh	Mayer, *Index Philoneus*
ISBE	International Standard Bible Encyclopedia
JANES	Journal of Ancient Near Eastern Studies (Columbia University)
JAOS	Journal of the American Oriental Society
JBL	Journal of Biblical Literature
JBR	Journal of Bible and Religion
JE	The Jewish Encyclopedia
JEA	Journal of Egyptian Archaeology
JEOL	Jaarbericht van het Voorraziatisch-Egyptisch Genootschap Ex Oriente Lux
JJS	Journal of Jewish Studies
JNES	Journal of Near Eastern Studies

JQR	Jewish Quarterly Review
JSHRZ	Jüdische Schriften aus hellenistisch-römischer Zeit
JSJ	Journal for the Study of Judaism in the Persian, Hellenistic and Roman Period
JSNT	Journal for the Study of the New Testament
JSOS	Jewish Social Studies
JSOT	Journal for the Study of the Old Testament
JSOTSS	Journal for the Study of the Old Testament, Supplementary Series
JSS	Journal of Semitic Studies
JTS	Journal of Theological Studies
Kairos	Kairos. Zeitschrift für Religionswissenschaft und Theologie
Kasher, *Enc.*	Kasher, *Encyclopedia of Biblical Interpretation*
Kiryat Sefer	Kiryat Sefer, Bibliographical Quarterly of the Jewish National and University Library
KuD	Kerygma und Dogma
LCC	Library of Christian Classics
LCL	Loeb Classical Library
Leshonenu	Leshonenu. A Journal for the Study of the Hebrew Language and Cognate Subjects
LF	Library of the Fathers
LQR	Law Quarterly Review
LUÅ	Lunds Universitets Årsskrift (Acta Universitatis Lundensis)
M.	Mishna
MGWJ	Monatsschrift für Geschichte und Wissenschaft des Judenthums
Midr. Pss.	Midrash Psalms
Mm	Masora magna
Mp	Masora parva
MSU	Mitteilungen des Septuaginta-Unternehmens der Akademie der Wissenschaft in Göttingen
MT	Masoretic Text
Mus.	Museon
NAWG	Nachrichten von der kön. Gesellschaft der Wissenschaft zu Göttingen, Phil.-Hist. Klasse
Neof.	Targum Neofiti 1
NF	Neue Folge
NHC	Nag Hammadi Codices
NPNF	A Select Library of Nicene and Post-Nicene Fathers, Second Series
N.S.	New Series
NovT	Novum Testamentum.

NTS	New Testament Studies: An International Journal
NTT	Nederlands Theologisch Tijdschrift
Numen	Numen: International Review for the History of Religions
OBO	Orbis Biblicus et Orientalis
OCA	Orientalia Christiana Analecta
OCD	Oxford Classical Dictionary
OCP	Orientalia Christiana Periodica
ODCC	The Oxford Dictionary of the Christian Church
OECT	Oxford Early Christian Texts
OL	Old Latin (Version)
Onk.	Targum Onkelos
OrChr	Oriens Christianus
OTP	Charlesworth, *Old Testament Pseudepigrapha*
OTS	Oudtestamentische Studien
PAAJR	Proceedings of the American Academy for Jewish Research
Pal. Targ.	Palestinian Targum
Pap. Ryl. Gk. 458	Greek Papyrus 458 of John Rylands Library
PE	Eusebius, *Praeparatio Evangelica*
PETSE	Papers of the Estonian Theological Society in Exile
PG	Migne, *Patrologia Graeca*
PIASH	Proceedings of the Israel Academy of Sciences and Humanities
PIC	Peshitta Institute Communication
PL	Migne, *Patrologia Latina*
PO	Patrologia Orientalia
PRE	Realencyclopädie für Protestantische Theologie und Kirche
Ps-Y	Targum Pseudo-Yonatan
P.T.	Palestinian Talmud
PTA	Papyrologische Texte und Abhandlungen
PTL	A Journal for Descriptive Poetics and Theory of Literature
PTR	Princeton Theological Review
PW	Pauly-Wissowa, *Realencyclopädie der classischen Altertumswissenschaft*
RAC	Reallexicon für Antike und Christentum
RB	Revue biblique
RBen	Revue bénédictine
REJ	Revue des études juives
RGG	Die Religion in Geschichte und Gegenwart
RHPR	Revue d'histoire et de philosophie religieuse
RHR	Revue de l'histoire des religions

RQ	Revue de Qumran
RSR	Recherches de science religieuse
RSV	Revised Standard Version
SamPent	Samaritan Pentateuch
SBL	Society of Biblical Literature
SC	Sources chrétiennes
Scripta	Scripta Hierosolymitana
Sefarad	Sefarad, Revista del Instituto Arias Montano de Estudios Hebraicos, Sefardies y de Oriente Próximo
Semeia	Semeia: An Experimental Journal for Biblical Literature
Shnaton	Shnaton. An Annual for Biblical and Ancient Near Eastern Studies
Sidra	Sidra. A Journal for the Study of Rabbinic Literature
Sinai	Sinai. A monthly for Tora, science and literature
SJT	Scottish Journal of Theology
SNT	Supplements to Novum Testamentum
SP	Studia Patristica
ST	Studia Theologica
SuppRivBib	Supplements to Revista Biblica
SVT	Supplements to Vetus Testamentum
SVTG	Septuaginta Vetus Testamentum Graece
T.	Tosefta
TAPA	Transactions of the American Philological Association
TC	Triennial (Palestinian) Cycle
TDNT	Theological Dictionary of the New Testament
TDOT	Theological Dictionary of the Old Testament
Tel Aviv	Tel Aviv: Journal of the Tel Aviv University
Temenos	Temenos: Studies in Comparative Religion
Textus	Textus. Annual of the Hebrew University Bible Project
Tg.	Targum
Th	Theodotion
ThGl	Theologie und Glaube
ThWAT	Theologisches Wörterbuch zum Alten Testament (Botterweck-Ringgren)
ThWNT	Theologisches Wörterbuch zum Neuen Testament
TLZ	Theologische Literaturzeitung
TR	Theologische Rundschau
TRE	Theologische Realenzyklopädie
TRev	Theologische Revue
TS	Texts and Studies
TSK	Theologische Studien und Kritiken

TU	Texte und Untersuchungen zur Geschichte der altchristlichen Literatur
VC	Vgiliae Christianae
Vg	Vulgata
VT	Vetus Testamentum
WTJ	Westminster Theological Journal
WUNT	Wissenschaftliche Untersuchungen zum Neuen Testament
Yon	Targum Yonatan
ZAW	Zeitschrift für die alttestamentliche Wissenschaft
ZDMG	Zeitschrift des deutschen morgenländischen Gesellschaft
ZNW	Zeitschrift für die neutestamentliche Wissenschaft und die Kunde der älteren Kirche
ZRGG	Zeitschrift für Religions- und Geistesgeschichte
ZSS	Zeitschrift der Savigny-Stiftung für Rechtsgeschichte, Romanistische Abteilung
ZTK	Zeitschrift für Theologie und Kirche

Accumulative Bibliography

Not included here are (a) the 'Survey of Some Printed (Complete) Hebrew Bibles' appended to chapter 3, and (b) the list of scholarly editions of the Aramaic targumim in the selective bibliography of chapter 7.

ABEL, F.-M. *Les Livres des Maccabées*. Paris 1949

ABELESZ, A. *Die syrische Übersetzung der Klagelieder und Verhältniss zu Targum und LXX*. Privigye 1895

ABERBACH, M. *Jewish Education in the Mishnah and Talmud Periods*. Jerusalem 1983 (Hebr.)

ABU-ASSAF, A. - BORDREUIL, P. - MILLARD, A.R. *La Statue de Tell Fekherye et son inscription bilingue assyro-araméene*. Paris 1982

ACHELIS, H. - BONWETSCH, G. and others (eds.) *Hippolytus Werke*. *GCS* Berlin 1897

ACKROYD, P.R. *Bible Bibliography 1967-1973: Old Testament*. Oxford 1974

– 'The Chronicler as Exegete' *JSOT* 2 (1977) 2-32

ACKROYD, P.R. - EVANS, C.F. (eds.) *The Cambridge History of the Bible* 1. Cambridge 1970

ADLER, E.N. - SÉLIGSOHN, M. 'Une nouvelle chronique samaritaine' *REJ* 44 (1902) 188-222; 45 (1902) 70-98, 160, 223-54; 46 (1903) 123-46

AHARONY, Y. *The Arad Inscriptions*. Jerusalem 1975

ALBECK, H. (Ch.) *Das Buch der Jubiläen und die Halacha*. Berlin 1930

– 'Apocryphal Halakhah in the Targumim of Eretz-Israel and in the Aggadah' in *B.M. Lewin Jubilee Volume*, ed. J.L. Fishman, Jerusalem 1940, 93-104

– *Introduction to the Mishna*. Jerusalem-Tel Aviv 1959 (Hebr.; G.T. *Einführung in die Mischna*. Berlin-New York 1971)

– *Mavo la-Talmudim* (Introduction in the Talmud, Babli and Yerushalmi). Tel-Aviv 1969

ALBREKTSON, B. *Studies in the Text and Theology of the Book of Lamentations, with a Critical Edition of the Peshitta Text*. *Studia Theologica Lundensia* 21, Lund 1963

– 'Josephus, Rabbi Akiba och Qumran. Tre argument i discussionen om tidpunkten för den gemmaltestamentliga konsonanttextens standardisering' *Teologinen Aikakauskirja* 73 (1968) 201-15

ALBRIGHT, W.F. 'The Date and Personality of the Chronicler' *JBL* 40 (1921) 104-24

– The Gezer Calendar' *BASOR* 9 (1943) 16-26

– *Recent Discoveries in Bible Lands*. New York 1955

– 'New Light on Early Recensions of the Hebrew Bible' *BASOR* 140 (1955) 27-33 (also in LEIMAN, *Canon and Masorah* 327-33)

– *The Proto-Sinaitic Inscriptions and their Decipherment*. Cambridge, Mass. 1966.

– *Yahweh and the Gods of Canaan*. Garden City 1968

ALETTI, J.-N. *Colossiens 1, 15-20. Genre et exégèse du texte. Fonction de la thématique sapientielle*. Rome 1981

ALEXANDER, P.S. 'The Targumim and Early Exegesis of "Sons of God" in Genesis 6' *JJS* 23 (1972) 60-71

– *The Toponomy of the Targumim*. D.Phil. Dissertation. Oxford 1974

– 'The Rabbinic Lists of Forbidden Targumim' *JJS* 27 (1976) 177-91

– '3 Enoch' in Charlesworth, *OTP* 1, 223-315 (1983)

- 'Epistolary Literature' in *Compendia* II/2, 579-96
- 'The Targumim and the Rabbinic Rules for the Delivery of the Targum' *SVT* 36 (1985) 14-28
- 'The Textual Tradition of Targum Lamentations *AbrN* 24 (1986) 1-26
ALLENBACH, J. et al., *Biblia Patristica* 1-4. Paris 1975-82
ALON, G. *Studies in Jewish History in the Times of the Second Temple, the Mishna and the Talmud* 1-2. Tel Aviv 1958 (Hebr.)
- *Jews, Judaism and the Classical World*. Jerusalem 1977
ALONI, M. 'The Scroll of the Tora and the Codex in Public Reading among the Rabbinic and Karaite Congregations' *Bet-Mikra* 24 (1979) 321-34 (Hebr.)
- 'Books and the Production of Books in the Middle Ages in the Land of Israel' *Shalem* 4 (1984) 1-25 (Hebr.)
ALSUP, J.E. *The Post-Resurrection Appearance Stories of the Gospel Tradition*. Stuttgart and London 1975
ALTANER, B. *Patrology*. London 1960
ALTSHULER, D. *Descriptions in Josephus' Antiquities of the Mosaic Constitution*. (Diss. Hebrew Union College) Cincinnati 1976
- 'On the Classification of Judaic Laws in the *Antiquities* of Josephus and the Temple Scroll of Qumran *AJSR* 7-8 (1982-83) 1-14
AMELLI, A.M. *Liber Psalmorum iuxta antiquissimam Latinam versionem*. *CBL* 1, Rome, 1912
AMINOAH, N. *'Em la-Mikra* and *Em la-Masoret* as Normative Expressions' *Te'uda* 2 (1982) 43-56 (Hebr.)
AMIR, Y. 'The Figure of Death in the "Book of Wisdom" *JJS* 30 (1979) 154-78
- 'Wie verarbeitete das Judentum fremde einflüsse in hellenistischer Zeit?' *Judaica* 38 (1982) 150-63
- *Die hellenistische Gestalt des Judentums bei Philon von Alexandria*. Neukirchen 1983
- *Studien zum antiken Judentum*. Frankfurt a. M. 1985
AMIRAN, R. 'The Water Supply of Israelite Jerusalem' in Y. YADIN (ed.), *Jerusalem Revealed*. Jerusalem 1975, 75-78
AMSLER, S. et al. *Le Canon de l'Ancien Testament, sa formation et son histoire*. Geneva 1984
ANDERSON, G.W. 'Canonical and Non-Canonical' in *CHB* 1 (1970) 113-59
- *A Decade of Bible Bibliography*. Oxford 1967
ANDERSON, H. '4 Maccabees' in Charlesworth, *OTP* 2, 531-43
ANTIN, P. *Jérôme, Sur Jonas*. SC 43 Paris 1956
APTOWITZER, V. *Das Schriftwort in der rabbinischen Literatur* 1-5. (1906-1915) repr. with *Prolegomenon* by S. Loewinger, New York 1970.
ARARAT, N. *Ezra and His Deeds in the Sources*. (Diss. Yeshiva University), New York 1971
ARCHER, G.L. (transl. and ed.) *Jerome, Commentary on Daniel*. Grand Rapids 1958
- 'The Hebrew of Daniel Compared with Qumran' in J.H. Skilton, ed. *The Law and the Prophets*. Nutley NJ 1974, 470-81
ARCHER, G.L. - CHIRICHIGNO, G. *Old Testament Quotations in the New Testament*. Chicago 1983
ARMSTRONG, G.T. *Die Genesis in der alten Kirche*. Tübingen 1962
ARNALDEZ, R. - MONDÉSERT C. - POUILLOUX J. (eds.) *Philon d'Alexandrie*. Paris 1967
ASHBY, G.W. *Theodoret of Cyrrhus as Exegete of the Old Testament*. Grahamstown 1972
ASHKENAZI, S. 'Scribes' Errors' *Jerusalem* 2 (1967) 379-95 (Hebr.)
ATTRIDGE, H.W. *The Interpretation of Biblical History in the Antiquitates Judaicae of Flavius Josephus*. Missoula, Montana 1976
- 'Historiography' in *Compendia* II/2, 157-84
- 'Josephus and His Works' in *Compendia* II/2, 185-232
- *Nag Hammadi Codex I (The Jung Codex)* 1-2, Leiden 1985
AUBINEAU, M. *Hésychius de Jérusalem, Basile de Séleucie, Jean de Béryte, Pseudo-Chrysostome, Léonce de Jérusalem, Homélies Pascales*. SC 187, Paris 1972
- *Les Homélies Festales d'Hésychius de Jérusalem* 1. Brussels 1978
AUDET, J.-P. 'A Hebrew-Aramaic List of Books of the Old Testament in Greek Transcription' *JTS* 1 (1950) 135-54 (also in Leiman, *Canon and Masorah*, 52-71)

AUF DER MAUR, H.J. *Das Psalmenverständnis des Ambrosius von Mailand: Ein Beitrag zum Deutungs hintergrund der Psalmenverwendung im Gottesdienst der alten Kirche.* Leiden 1977

AVENARIUS, G. *Lukians Schrift zur Geschichtsschreibung.* Meisenheim/Glan 1956

AVIGAD, N. *The Palaeography of the Dead Sea Scrolls and Related Documents' Scripta* 4 (1958) 56-87
- 'Seal, Seals, – In the Ancient Period' *EJ* 14 (1972) 1072-74
- 'The Priest of Dor' *IEJ* 25 (101-05
- 'A Hebrew Seal Depicting a Sailing Ship' *BASOR* 246 (1982) 59-61

AVIGAD, N. - YADIN, Y. *A Genesis Apocryphon.* Jerusalem 1956

AVI-YONAH, M. *Oriental Art in Roman Palestine.* Rome 1961
- *Geschichte der Juden im Zeitalter des Talmud in den Tagen von Rom und Byzanz.* Berlin 1962

AYUSO MARAZUELA, T. *La Vetus Latina Hispana I. Prolegómenos.* Madrid 1953 *II. El Octateucho.* Madrid 1967 *V. El Salterio.* Madrid 1962

AZIZA, C. *Tertullien et le judaïsme.* Nice 1977

BACHER, W. *Die Agada der Tannaiten* 1-2. Strassburg 1884-1890; repr. Berlin 1965-66
- *Die hebräische Sprachwissenschaft vom X. bis zum XVI. Jahrhundert. Mit einem einleitenden Abschnitte über die Massora.* Trier 1892 (also in Winter-Wünsche), *Die jüdische Litteratur* 2, 121-235; repr. Amsterdam 1974
- *Die älteste Terminologie der jüdischen Schriftauslegung.* Leipzig 1899
- *Die exegetische Terminologie der jüdischen Traditionsliteratur* 1-2. Leipzig 1899-1905; repr. Darmstadt 1965
- 'Synagogue, The Great' *JE* 11, 640-43
- *Die Proömien der alten jüdischen Homilie.* Leipzig 1913; repr. Farnborough 1970

BAER, S. 'Die Metheg-Setzung nach ihren überlieferten Gesetzen dargestellt' *Archiv für wissenschaftliche Erforschung des Alten Testaments* (ed. A. Merx) 1 (1869) 55-67; 194-207

BAILLET, M. 'La récitation de la Loi chez les Samaritaines d'après Z. Ben-Hayyim' *RB* 79 (1962) 570-87
- 'Le calendrier samaritain' *RB* 85 (1978) 481-99
- *Qumrân Grotte 4-III. DJD* 7, Oxford 1982

BAINES, J. 'Literacy and Ancient Egyptian Society' *Man* (N.S.) 18 (1983) 572-99

BAINES, J. - EYRE, C.J. 'Four Notes on Literacy' *Goettinger Miszellen* 61 (1983) 65-96

BALDWIN, J.G. *Daniel. (Tyndale Old Testament Commentary)* Leicester (UK)/Downers Grove (IL) 1978

BAMMEL, E. *Judaica. (WUNT* 37) Tübingen 1986

BARC, B. *L'Hypostase des Archontes. Traité gnostique sur l'origine de l'homme, du monde et des archontes (NH II,4).* Québec/Louvain 1980
- 'Samaèl-Saklas-Yaldabaôth: Recherche sur la genèse d'un mythe gnostique' in Barc, *Colloque International* 123-50

BARC, B. (ed.) *Colloque International sur les textes de Nag Hammadi (Québec, 22-25 août 1978).* Québec/Louvain 1981

BARDENHEWER, O. *Geschichte der altchristlichen Literatur* 3. Freiburg 1912

BARDOWICZ, L. *Die Abfassungszeit der Baraita der 32 Normen für die Auslegung der heiligen Schrift. Eine Untersuchung.* Berlin 1913

BARDY, G. 'La littérature patristique des "Quaestiones et responsiones" sur l'Écriture sainte' *RB* 41 (1932) 210-34, 341-96, 515-37; 42 (1933) 14-30, 211-29, 328-52
- 'Saint Jérôme et ses maîtres hébreux' *RBen* 46 (1934) 145-64
- 'Le souvenir d'Élie chez les Pères Grecs' in *Élie le Prophète* 1 *Etudes Carmélitaines* 1956, 131-58

BARDY, G. - LEFEVRE, M. (tr.) *Hippolyte de Rome, Commentaire sur Daniel. (SC* 14) Paris 1947

BAR-ILAN, M. *The Polemics between Sages and Priests towards the end of the days of the Second Temple.* Ph.D. Thesis, Bar-Ilan University, Ramat-Gan 1982 (Hebr.)
- 'Writing Torah Scrolls, Tefillin, Mezuzoth and Amulets on Deer Leather' *Bet-Mikra* 52 (1985) 375-81 (Hebr.)
- 'A Rock, a Stone and a Seat that Moses sat on' *Sidra* 2 (1986) 15-23 (Hebr.)
- 'The Significance and the Source of Megilat-Ta'anit' *Sinai* 98 (1986) 114-37 (Hebr.)

799

– Magic Seals on the Body among Jews in the First Centuries C.E.' *Tarbiz* (forthcoming; Hebr.)
BARKAI, G. *Ketef Hinnom – A Treasure Facing Jerusalem's Walls.* Jerusalem 1986
BARNES, T.D. *Tertullian.* Oxford 1971
– 'Methodius, Maximis, and Valentinus' *JTS* (N.S.) 30 (1979) 47-55
– *Constantine and Eusebius.* Cambridge, Mass./London 1981
BARNES, W.E. *An Apparatus Criticus to Chronicles in the Peshitta Version with a Discussion of the Value of the Codex Ambrosianus.* Cambridge 1897
– *The Peshitta Psalter according to the West Syrian Text Edited with an Apparatus Criticus.* Cambridge 1904
BARR, J. *The Semantics of Biblical Language.* London 1961
– 'St. Jerome's Appreciation of Hebrew' *BJRL* 49 (1966-67) 281-302
– 'St. Jerome and the Sounds of Hebrew' *JSS* 12 (1967) 1-36
– 'The Typology of Literalism in Ancient Bible Translations' *NAWG* 11 (Göttingen 1979) 279-35
– *Old and New in Interpretation.* 2nd ed. London 1982
– *Holy Scripture: Canon, Authority, Criticism.* Philadelphia 1983
BARRE, H. - GRÉGOIRE, R. 'Homéliaires' *DS* 7 (1969) 597-617)
BARROIS, G.A. 'Moriah' *IDB* 3 (1962) 438-39
BARTH, L.M. 'The "Three of Rebuke and Seven of Consolation" Sermons in the Pesikta de Rav Kahana' *JJS* 33 (1982) 503-15
BARTHÉLEMY, D. *Les devanciers d'Aquila.* (*SVT* 10) Leiden 1963
– 'Les Tiqquné Sopherim et la Critique Textuelle de l'Ancien Testament' *SVT* 9 (1963) 285-304; repr. in Barthélemy, *Études*, 91-110.
– 'Origène et le texte de l'Ancien Testament' in *Epektasis, Mélanges J. Danièlou.* 1972, 247-61
– 'Qui est Symmaque?" *CBQ* 36 (1974) 451-65
– 'Text, Hebrew, History of' *IDBS* (Nashville 1976) 878-84
– *Études d'Histoire du Texte de l'Ancien Testament.* Fribourg/Göttingen 1978
– *Critique textuelle de l'Ancien Testament.* Fribourg/Göttingen 1982
BARTLETT, J.R. *Jews in the Hellenistic World.* Cambridge 1985
BARTON, J. *Reading the Old Testament.* London 1984
– *Oracles of God: Perceptions of Ancient Prophecy in Israel after the Exile.* London 1986
BASKIN, J.R. 'Rabbinic-Patristic Exegetical Contacts in Late Antiquity: a Bibliographical Reappraisal' in Green, W.S. (ed.) *Approaches to Ancient Judaism* 5. Atlanta 1985, 53-80
BATE, H.N. *The Sibylline Oracles: Books III-V.* London 1918
BATEY, R. 'Jewish Gnosticism and the *hieros gamos* of Eph. V, 21-33' *NTS* 10 (1963/64) 121-27
BAUER, W. *Orthodoxy and Heresy in Earliest Christianity.* (ET edited by R. Kraft and G. Krodel) Philadelphia 1971
BAUER, H. - LEANDER, P. *Historische Grammatik der hebräischen Sprache des Alten Testaments.* Halle 1922; repr. Hildesheim 1965
BAUMGARTEN, J.M. *Studies in Qumran Law.* Leiden 1977
BAUMSTARK, A. 'Hymns (Greek Christian)' *ERE* 7 (1914) 5-12
– *Geschichte der syrischen Literatur.* Bonn 1922; repr. Berlin 1968
– 'Wege zum Judentum des neutestamentlichen Zeitalters' *Bonner Zeitschrift für Theologie und Seelsorge* 4 (1927) 24-34
– 'Pešiṭta und palästinensisches Targum' *BZ* 19 (1931) 257-70
– 'Das Problem der Bibelzitate in der syrischen Übersetzungsliteratur' *OrChr* 8 (1933) 208-25
– 'Neue orientalistische Probleme biblischer Textgeschichte' *ZDMG* 89 (1935) 89-118
– 'Ps.-Jonathan zu Dtn 34:6 und die Pentateuchzitate Afrahats' *ZAW* 59 (1942/43) 99-111
BECKWITH, R.T. 'The Significance of the Calender for Interpreting Essene Chronology and Eschatology' *RQ* 10 (1980) 167-202
– 'The Earliest Enoch Literature and its Calender: Marks of their Origin, Date and Motivation' *RQ* 10 (1981) 365-403
– *The Old Testament Canon of the New Testament Church and its Background in Early Judaism.* London 1985

BEECHER, J.W. 'The Alleged Triple Canon of the Old Testament' *JBL* 15 (1896) 118-28

BEER, G. 'Das Buch Henoch' in Kautzsch, G. (ed.) *Die Apokryphen und Pseudepigraphen des Alten Testaments*. Tübingen 1900, 2, 217-310

BÉLANGER, R. (ed.) *Grégoire le Grand. Commentaire sur le Cantique des Cantiques*. (*SC* 314) Paris 1984

BELKIN, S. *Philo and the Oral Law: The Philonic Interpretation of Biblical Law in Relation to the Palestinian Halakha*. Cambridge, Mass. 1940

BELSHEIM, J. *Palimpsestus Vindobonensis*. Christiana 1885

BELTZ, W. 'Gnosis und Altes Testament – Überlegungen zur Frage nach dem jüdischen Ursprung der Gnosis' *ZRGG* 28 (1976) 353-57

– 'Elia redivivus: Ein Beitrag zum Problem der Verbindung von Gnosis und Altem Testament' in Tröger, *Altes Testament*, 137-41.

BEN-DOV, M. 'Hebrew Inscription carved on stone from the Temple Mount and its surroundings' *Cathedra* 40 (1986) 3-30 (Hebr.)

BEN-HAYYIM, Z. 'Samaritan Liturgical Poems for Joyous Occasions' *Tarbiz* 10 (1939) 190-200, 333-74 (Hebr.)

– 'The Book of Asatir' *Tarbiz* 14 (1942-43) 104-25, 174-90; 15 (1943-44) 71-87, 128 (Hebr.)

– 'On the Pronunciation of the Tetragrammaton by the Samaritans' *Eretz-Israel* 3 (1954) 147-154 (Hebr.)

– 'Masora and Masoret' *Leshonenu* 21 (1957-58) 283-92 (Hebr.)

– *The Literary and Oral Tradition of Hebrew and Aramaic amongst the Samaritans 1-5*. Jerusalem 1957-77 (Hebr.)

– 'Memar Marqah, The Teaching of Marqah, edited by J. Macdonald' (review) *BiOr* 23 (1966) 185-91

BENOIT, P. 'L'Inspiration des LXX d'après les pères' in *Mélanges H. de Lubac*. Paris 1963, 169-87

BENOIT, P. - MILIK, J.T. - DE VAUX, R. *Les Grottes de Murabaat*. (*DJD* 2) Oxford 1961

BEN-PORAT, Z. 'The Poetics of Literary Allusion' *PTL* 1 (1976) 105-07

BENTZEN, A. *King and Messiah*. London 1955

BEN-ZVI, I. 'The Codex of Ben Asher' *Textus* 1 (1960) 1-16

– *The Book of the Samaritans*. 3d ed. Jerusalem 1976 (Hebr.)

BERGER, K. 'Hartherzigkeit und Gottes Gesetz. Die Vorgeschichte des antijüdischen Vorwurfs in Mc 10:5' *ZNW* 61 (1970) 1-47

– 'Der traditionsgeschichtliche Ursprung der "Traditio Legis" ' *VC* 29 (1973) 104-22

– *Die griechische Daniel-Diegese*. Leiden 1976

– 'Hellenistische Gattungen im Neuen Testament' *ANRW* II.25.2 Berlin 1984, 1031-1432

BERGER, S. *Histoire de la Vulgate pendant les premiers siècles du moyen âge*. Paris 1893

BERGSTRÄSSER, G. *Hebräische Grammatik 1*. Leipzig 1918

BERLINER, A. *Beiträge zur hebräischen Grammatik im Talmud und Midrasch*. Berlin 1879

BERLINGER, J. *Die Peschitta zum 1. (3.) Buch der Könige und ihr Verhältnis zu MT, LXX und Trg.*. Berlin 1897

BERNARD, J.H. 'The Cyprianic Doctrine of the Ministry' in Swete, H.B. (ed.) *Essays on the Early History of the Church and the Ministry*. London 1918, 215-62

BERTHOLDT, L. *Historischkritische Einleitung in sämmtliche kanonische und apokryphische Schriften des alten und neuen Testaments*. Vol. I (Teil 1,2) Erlangen 1813

BETHGE, H.-G. 'Die Ambivalenz alttestamentlicher Geschichttraditionen in der Gnosis' in Tröger, *Altes Testament*, 89-109

BETZ, O. *Offenbarung und Schriftforschung in der Qumransekte*. (*WUNT* 6) Tübingen 1960

– 'Was am Anfang geschah: Das jüdische Erbe in den neugefundenen koptisch-gnostischen Schriften' in O. Betz - M. Hengel - P. Schmidt (eds.) *Abraham Unser Vater: Juden und Christen im Gespräch über die Bibel. Festschrift für Otto Michel*. Leiden/Köln 1963, 24-43

BETZ, O. et al. *Josephus-Studien*. Göttingen 1974

BETZ, O - GRIMM, W. *Jesus und das Danielbuch 1-2*. Frankfurt 1985

BIBLIA SACRA *iuxta Latinam Vulgatam versionem ad codicum fidem. . . cura et studio monachorum abbatiae pontificiae S. Hieronymi in urbe ordinis S. Benedicti edita 1-16*. Rome 1926-81

BIBLIA SACRA *iuxta Vulgatam versionem* 1-2. (ed. R. Weber assisted by B. Fischer, J. Gribomont, H.F.D. Sparks, W. Thiele) Stuttgart 1969

BICKELL, J.W. *Geschichte des Kirchenrechts* 1. Giessen 1843

BICKERMAN, E.J. 'The Colophon of the Greek Book of Esther' *JBL* 63 (1944) 339-62; repr. in *Studies* 1, 225-45

- 'Some Notes on the Transmission of the Septuagint' in *A. Marx Jubilee Volume*. New York 1950, 149-78

- 'Notes on the Greek Book of Esther' *PAAJR* 20 (1951) 101-33

- 'The Septuagint as a Translation' *PAAJR* 28 (1959) 1-39

- 'The Jewish Historian Demetrios' in *Judaism, Christianity and Other Greco-Roman Cults. Studies for Morton Smith at Sixty*. Leiden, 1975, 3, 72-84; repr. in *Studies* 2, 347-58

- *Studies in Jewish and Christian History* 1-2. Leiden 1976-80

BIETENHARD, H. 'Deuterosis' *RAC* 3 (1975) cols 842-49

BIGG, C. *The Christian Platonists of Alexandria*. Repr. with additions, Oxford 1913

BILLEN, A.V. *The Old Latin Text of the Heptateuch*. London 1927

BILLERBECK, P. 'Ein Synagogengottesdienst in Jesu Tagen' *ZNW* 55 (1964) 143-61

BILLERBECK, P. - STRACK, H.L. *Kommentar zum Neuen Testament aus Talmud und Midrasch* 1-4. München 1922-28

BINDER, G. - GRONEWALD, M. - KRAMER, J. - KREBBER, B. - LIESENBORGHS, L. *Dydimus der Blinde: Kommentar zum Ekklesiastes* 1-6. (*PTA* 7, 9, 13, 16, 22, 24-26) Bonn 1969-83

BINGHAM, J. *The Antiquities of the Christian Church*. (1708-22) Repr. in J. Bingham, *Origines Ecclesiasticae; or, The Antiquities of the Christian Church and Other Works* 1-9. London 1843-45

BIRDSALL, J.N. 'The New Testament Text' *CHB* 1 (1970) 308-77

- 'The Latin Versions' *CHB* 1 (1970) 370-74

BIRT, T. *Das Antike Buchwesen*. Aalen 1959 (1882)

BIZETTI, P. *Il Libro della Sapienza*. (*SuppRivBib* 11) Brescia 1984

BLACK, M. *Apocalypsis Henochi Graece*. Leiden 1970

- *The Book of Enoch or I Enoch*. Leiden 1985

BLACKMAN, E.C. *Marcion and his Influence*. London 1948

BLAISE, A. *Manuel du Latin chrétien*. Strasbourg 1955

BLASS, F. - DEBRUNNER, A. *A Greek Grammar of the New Testament*. (transl. and revised by R.W. Funk) Cambridge 1961

BLAU, L. *Zur Einleitung in die Heilige Schrift*. Budapest 1894

- 'Massoretic Studies' *JQR* 9 (1897) 139

- *Studien zum althebräischen Buchwesen und zur biblischen Literatur und Textgeschichte*. Strassburg 1902

- 'Bible Canon' *JE*, 3, 140-50

BLENKINSOPP, J. *Prophecy and Canon*. Notre Dame IN, 1977

BLIDSTEIN, G.J. 'A Note on the History of the Term *Tora She-Be-'al Peh*' *Tarbiz* 42 (1972-73) 496-98 (Hebr.)

BLOCH, H. *Die Quellen des Flavius Josephus in seiner Archäologie*. Leipzig 1879

BLOCH, J. 'The Printed Texts of the Peshitta Old Testament' *AJSL* 37 (1920/21) 136-44

BLOCH, R. 'Note méthodologique pour l'étude de la littérature rabbinique' *RSR* 43 (1955) 194-227

- 'Midrash' *DBS* 5 (1957) 1263-81; ET in W.S. Green (ed.) *Approaches to Ancient Judaism*. Missoula 1978.

BLONDHEIM, D.S. *Les parlers judéo-romains et la Vetus Latina. Étude sur le rapport entre les traductions bibliques en langue romaine des Juifs au Moyen Age et les anciennes versions*. Paris 1925

BLUMENKRANZ, B. *Die Judenpredigt Augustins*. Basle 1946

- *Juifs et chrétiens dans le mond occidental, 430-1096*. Paris 1960

- *Juifs et chrétiens. Patristique et Moyen Age*. Variorum Reprints, London 1977

- 'Kirche und Synagoge: Die Entwicklung im Westen zwischen 200 und 1200' repr. in *Patristique et Moyen Age*.

– *Les auteurs chrétiens latins du moyen âge sur les juifs et le judaïsme.* Paris 1963

BLUNT, A.W.F. (ed.) *The Apologies of Justin Martyr.* Cambridge 1911

BODINE, W.R. *The Greek Text of Judges – Recensional Developments. (HSM)* Chico, CA 1980

BÖHL, F. *Aufbau und literarische Formen des aggadischen Teils im Jelammedenu-Midrash.* Wiesbaden 1977

BÖHLIG, A. - LABIB, P. *Die Koptisch-Gnostische Schrift ohne Titel aus Codex II von Nag Hammadi.* Berlin 1962

BOER, P.A.H. DE *Research into the Text of 1 Sam. I-XVI.* Amsterdam 1938

– '1 Sam. XVII, Notes on the text and the ancient versions' *OTS* 1, Leiden 1942, 79-103

– 'Research into the text of 1 Samuel XVIII-XXXI' *OTS* 6, Leiden 1949, 1-100

BOGAERT, P.M. 'Le personnage de Baruch et l'histoire du livre de Jérémie' *Studia Evangelica* 7 (ed. E.A. Livingstone) Berlin 1982, 73-81

BÓID, I.R.M. (M.N. SARAF) *Principles of Samaritan Halachah.* Leiden 1988

– 'Halakha' (forthcoming)

BOMSTAD, R.G. *Governing Ideas of the Jewish War of Flavius Josephus.* (Diss. Yale Univ.) New Haven 1979

BONNER, G. 'Augustine as Biblical Scholar' *CHB* 541-63

BONSIRVEN, J. *Exégèse rabbinique et exégèse paulinienne.* Paris 1939

BONWETSCH, N. *Studien zu den Kommentaren Hippolyts zum Buche Daniel und Hohenliede. (TU* 16.2) Leipzig 1897

BORGEN, P. *Bread from Heaven. An Exegetical Study of the Concept of Manna in the Gospel of John and the Writings of Philo.* Leiden 1960; repr. 1981

– 'Observations on the Targumic Character of the Prologue of John' *NTS* 16 (1969-70) 288-95 (also in *Logos was the True Light.* Trondheim 1983, 13-20)

– 'Philo of Alexandria' in *Compendia* II/2, 233-82

BORRET, M. (ed. and tr.) *Origène, Homélies sur le Lévitique. (SC* 286-87) Paris 1981

BOTTE, B. 'Latines (Versions) Antérieures A S. Jérome' *DBS* 5, 334-47 (1957)

BOUHOT, J.-P. 'Pentateuque chez les Pères' *DBS* 7, 687-708

BOUSSET, W. *Jüdisch-Christlicher Schulbetrieb in Alexandria und Rom.* Göttingen 1915

BOUWMAN, G. *Des Julian von Aeclanum Kommentar zu den Propheten Osee, Joel und Amos: Ein Beitrag zur Geschichte der Exegese.* Rome 1958

BOWKER, J.W. 'Speeches in Acts: A Study in Proem and Yelammedenu Form' *NTS* 14 (1967) 96-111

– 'Haggadah in the Targum Onkelos' *JSS* 12 (1967) 51-65

– *The Targums and Rabbinic Literature.* Cambridge 1969

– *Jesus and the Pharisees.* Cambridge 1973

BOWMAN, J. 'The Importance of Samaritan Researches' *ALUOS* 2 (1960) 43-54

– 'Pilgrimage to Mount Gerizim' *EI* 7 (1963) 17-28

– *Samaritanische Probleme.* Stuttgart 1967

– *Samaritan Documents Relating to their History, Religion and Life.* Pittsburgh 1977

BOYARIN, D. 'From the Hidden Light of the *Geniza*: towards the original text of the *Mekhilta d'Rabbi Ishmael' Sidra* 2 (1986) 5-13 (Hebr.)

BRADSHAW, H. *The Early Collection of Canons Known as the Hibernensis, Two Unfinished Papers.* Cambridge 1893

BRADSHAW, P.F. *Daily Prayer in the Early Church.* London 1981

BRAUN, M. *History and Romance in Graeco-Oriental Literature.* Oxford 1938

BRAUN, R. *Deus Christianorum.* Paris 1962

– *Quodvultdeus: Livre des Promesses et des Prédictions de Dieu* 1-2. *(SC* 101-02) Paris 1964

BRAVERMAN, J. *Jerome's Commentary on Daniel: A Study of Comparative Jewish and Christian Interpretations of the Hebrew Bible. (CBQ Monograph Series* 7) Washington 1978

BRECKENRIDGE, J.D. Review of C. Murray, *Rebirth and Afterlife,* in *JTS* N.S. 34 (1983) 630

BREGMAN, M. 'The Triennial Haftarot and the Perorations of the Midrashic Homilies' *JJS* 32 (1981) 74-84

– 'An Early Fragment of Avot de-Rabbi Natan from a Scroll' *Tarbiz* 52 (1983) 201-22 (Hebr.)

BRÉHIER, E. *Les idées philosophiques et religieuses de Philon d'Alexandrie*. Paris 2nd ed. 1925 (1908)
- *History of Philosophy: The Hellenistic and Roman Age*. Chicago 1965
BREITENSTEIN, U. *Beobachtungen zu Sprache, Stil und Gedankengut des Vierten Makkabäerbuches*. Basel-Stuttgart 1978
BRIÈRE, M. - MARIÈS L. - MERCIER, B. (ed. and tr.) *Hippolyte, Sur les Bénédictions d'Isaac, de Jacob et de Moïse* 1-2. (*PO* 27) Paris 1954
BRIGHT, W. *The Canons of the First Four Councils and Nicaea, Constantinople, Ephesus and Chalcedon, with Notes*. 2nd ed. Oxford 1892
BRIN, G. 'The Bible in the Temple Scroll' *Shnaton* 4 (1980) 182-225 (Hebr.)
BROADIE, A. *A Samaritan Philosophy*. Leiden 1981
BROCK, S.P. *The Recensions of the Septuagint Version of I Samuel*. Oxford 1966
- 'The Phenomenon of the Septuagint' *OTS* 17 (1972) 11-36
- 'Aspects of Translation Technique in Antiquity' *GRBS* 20 (1979) 69-87
- 'Bibelhandschriften I Altes Testament' *TRE* 6, Berlin 1980, 109-14
- 'Bibelübersetzungen, 4. Die Übersetzungen ins Syrische' *TRE* 6, Berlin, New York 1980, 181-87
- 'Vetus Latina (Old Testament)' *TRE* 6, Berlin 1980, 177-78
- 'Some Early Syriac Baptismal Commentaries' *OCP* 46 (1980) 20-61
- Genesis 22 in Syriac Tradition' in P. Casetti, O. Keel, A. Schenker (eds.) *Mélanges Dominique Barthélémy*. Fribourg/Göttingen 1981, 2-30
- *The Harp of the Spirit: Eighteen Poems of Saint Ephrem*. 2nd enlarged ed. London 1983
- 'An Early Syriac Commentary on the Liturgy' *JTS* N.S. 37 (1986) 387-403
BROCK, S.P. - FRITSCH, C.T. - JELLICOE, S. *A Classified Bibliography of the Septuagint*. Leiden 1973 (*ALGHJ* 6)
BROCKELMANN, C. *Lexicon Syriacum*. Halle 1928 (2nd ed.)
BRODIE, T.L. 'Towards Unravelling Luke's Use of the Old Testament: Luke 7.11-17 as an *Imitatio* of I Kings 17.17-24' *NTS* 32 (1986) 247-67
BROEK, R. VAN DEN, *The Myth of the Phoenix according to Classical and Early Christian Traditions*. Leiden 1972
- 'The Creation of Adam's Psychic Body in the Apocryphon of John' in Van den Broek-Vermaseren, *Studies in Gnosticism*, 38-57
- 'The Present State of Gnostic Studies' *VC* 37 (1983) 41-71
BROEK, R. VAN DEN, - VERMASEREN, M.J. (eds.) *Studies in Gnosticism and Hellenistic Religions presented to Gilles Quispel*. Leiden 1981
BROOKE, A.E. - MCLEAN, N. - THACKERAY, H.ST.J. *The Old Testament in Greek*. Cambridge 1906-40
BROOKE, G.J. *Exegesis at Qumran: 4QFlorilegium in its Jewish Context*. (*JSOTSS* 29) Sheffield 1985
BROWN, R.E. *The Semitic Background of the Term 'Mystery' in the New Testament*. Philadelphia 1968
BROWNLEE, W.H. 'Biblical Interpretation Among the Sectaries of the Dead Sea Scrolls' *BA* 14 (1951) 54-76
- 'The Habakkuk Midrash and the Targum of Jonathan' *JSJ* 7 (1956) 169-86
- *The Meaning of the Dead Sea Scrolls for the Bible with Special Attention to the Book of Isaiah*. New York 1964
- 'The Background of Biblical Interpretation at Qumran' in M. Delcor (ed.) *Qumrân. Sa piété, sa théologie et son milieu*. Paris/Leuven 1978, 183-93
- *The Midrash Pesher of Habakkuk*. Missoula 1979
BRUCE, F.F. *Biblical Exegesis in the Qumran Texts*. Den Haag 1959
- 'The Book of Zechariah and the Passion Narrative' *BJRL* 43 (1960-61) 336-53
- 'The Book of Daniel and the Qumran Community' in E. Ellis and M. Wilcox (eds.) *Neotestamentica et Semitica in Honour of M. Black*. Edinburgh 1969, 221-35
- *New Testament Development of Old Testament Themes*. Exeter and Grand Rapids 1969
BRÜLL, A. *Das samaritanische Targum zum Pentateuch*. Frankfurt a. M. 1873-75
BRÜNE, B. *Flavius Josephus und seine Schriften in ihrem Verhältnis zum Judentume, zur griechisch-römischen welt und zum Christentume mit griechischer Wortkonkordanz zum Neuen Testament und I. Clemensbrief nebst Sach- und Namen-Verzeichnis. Anhang: Inhalt nebst Sachregister zu "Josephus der Geschichtsschreiber"*. Gütersloh 1913

BÜCHLER, A. 'The Reading of the Law and the Prophets in a Triennial Cycle' *JQR* 5 (1893) 420-86; 6 (1894) 1-73
- *Die Priester und der Cultus im letzten Jahrzehnt des jerusalemischen Tempels.* Vienna 1895
BUFFIÈRE, F. *Les mythes d'Homère et la pensée grecque.* Paris 1956
BUHL, F. *Canon and Text of the Old Testament.* Edinburgh 1892
- 'Bibeltext des AT.; Geschichte desselben' *PRE* (3rd ed.) 2, 713-28
BULTMANN, R. *Der Stil der Paulinischen Predigt und die kynisch-stoische Diatribe.* Göttingen 1910; repr. 1984
BURCHARD, C. *Bibliographie zu den Handschriften vom Toten Meer.* (*BZAW* 76 and 89) Berlin 1957-1965
BURKE, G.T. 'Celsus and the Old Testament' *VT* 36 (1986) 241-45
BURKITT, F.C. *The Rules of Tyconius.* (*TS* 3.1) Cambridge 1894
- *The Old Latin and the Itala.* (*TS* 4.3) Cambridge 1896
- 'The Debt of Christianity to Judaism' in E.R. Bevan and Ch. Singer (eds.) *The Legacy of Israel.* Oxford 1927, 69-96
BURN, A.E. *Niceta of Remesiana.* Cambridge 1905
BURNABY, J. (tr.) *Augustine: Later Works.* (*LCC* 8) London 1958
BURNEY, C.F. 'Christ as the ARXH of Creation' *JTS* 27 (1926) 160-77
BUSTO SAÍZ. J.R. *La Traducción de Símaco en el libro de los Salmos.* Madrid 1978
BUTIN, R. *The Ten Nequdoth of the Torah.* Baltimore 1906; New York 1969
CAHILL, J.B. 'The Date and Setting of Gregory of Nyssa's Commentary on the Song of Songs' *JTS* N.S. 32 (1981) 447-60
CAMPENHAUSEN, H. VON, *Men who shaped the Western Chruch.* E.T. by M. Hoffman. New York 1964
- *Ecclesiastical Authority and Spiritual Power in the Church of the First Three Centuries.* E.T. London 1969
- *The Formation of the Christian Bible.* E.T. by J. Baker, Philadelphia, London 1972
CANÉVET, M. *Grégoire de Nysse et l'Herméneutique Biblique.* Paris 1983
CANIVET, P. *Théodoret de Cyr: Thérapeutique des maladies helléniques* 1-2 *SC* 57, Paris 1958
CANNON, W.W. 'Jerome und Symmachus' *ZAW* 45 (1927) 191-99
CANTERA, J. Ortiz de Urbina, 'Puntos de contacto de la Vetus Latina con el Targum arameo y con la Pešitta. Hipótesis de un origen targúmico de la Vetus Latina' *Seferad* 25 (1965) 223-40
CAPELLE, W. - MARROU, H. 'Diatribe' *RAC* 3 (1957) 990-1009
CAQUOT, A. 'Jubiles' *La Bible, Écrits Intertestamentaires.* Paris 1987, 635-810
CARDAUNS, B. 'Juden und Spartaner. Zur hellenistisch-jüdischen Literatur' *Hermes* 95 (1967) 317-24
CARMIGNAC, J. 'Les citations de l'Ancien Testament dans la "Guerre des fils de lumière contre les fils de ténèbres" ' *RB* 63 (1956) 234-60, 375-90
- 'Les citations de l'Ancien Testament, et spécialement des Poèmes du Serviteur, dans les *Hymnes* de Qumrân' *RQ* 2 (1959-1960) 357-94
CARPENTER, H.J. 'Popular Christianity and the Theologians in the Early Centuries' *JTS* N.S. 14 (1963) 294-310
CARRINGTON, P. *The Primitive Christian Catechism.* Cambridge 1940
CARROLL, R.P. 'Canonical Criticism' *ExpT* 92 (1980) 73-8
CARVALHO, D.N. *Forty Centuries of Ink.* repr. New York 1971
CASEY, P.M. 'Porphyry and the Origin of the Book of Daniel' *JTS* N.S. 27 (1976) 15-33
- *Son of Man.* London 1979
CASTELLUS E. *Lexicon Heptaglotton.* Londini 1669
CASSUTO, U. 'Hattargûm hayyehûdî šel hammiqrâ' lelāṭînît' (Hebr.) *Biblical and Canaanite Literatures.* Jerusalem 1972, 205-16
CASSUTO-SALZMAN, M. 'Hebrew Inscriptions of the End of the Second Temple Period' in A.M. Rabello (ed.) *Studies in Judaism. Jubilee Volume presented to David Kotlar.* Tel Aviv 1976, 123-44 (Hebr.)
CAVALLERA, F. *St. Jérôme - sa vie et son oeuvre.* Louvain-Paris 1922
CAZEAUX, J. *La Trame et la Chaîne.* Leiden 1983
CECCHELLI, C. *I mosaici della Basilica di S. Maria Maggiore.* Turin 1956

CERESA-GASTALDO, A. *Il Latino dell Antiche versioni Bibliche.* Rome 1975
- (ed. and tr.) *Philonis Carpasii Commentarium in Canticum Canticorum ex antiqua versione latina Epiphanii Scholastici.* Turin 1979
CERFAUX, L. 'La connaisance des secrets du Royaume d'après Matt XIII.11 et parr.' *NTS* 2 (1955-1956) 238-49
CERIANI, A.M. *Translatio Syra Pescitto Veteris Testamenti ex codice Ambrosiano sec. fere VI photo-lithographice edita.* Milan 1876-1883
CHADWICK, H. Review of De Lubac *Histoire et esprit, JTS* N.S. 2 (1951) 102-4
- (ed.) *The Sentences of Sextus.* Cambridge 1959
- 'Justin Martyr's Defence of Christianity' *BJRL* 47 (1965) 275-97
- (tr. with introduction and notes) *Origin: Contra Celsum.* (corrected repr.) Cambridge 1965
- *Early Christian Thought and the Classical Tradition: Studies in Justin, Clement and Origen.* Oxford 1966
- *The Early Church.* Harmondsworth 1967
- 'Florilegium' *RAC* 7 (1969) 1131-60
- *Boethius.* Oxford 1981
- *Augustine.* Oxford 1986
- 'The Bible and the Greek Fathers' in Nineham, *The Church's Use*, 25-39
- 'Philo and the Beginnings of Christian Thought' *CHLGP* (Cambridge 1967) 133-92
CHADWICK, N.K. *The Age of the Saints in the Early Celtic Church.* London 1961; corrected repr. 1963
CHADWICK, O. *John Cassian.* 2nd ed. Cambridge 1968
CHARITY, A.C. *Events and their Afterlife.* Cambridge 1966
CHARLES, R.H. *The Ethiopic Version of the Hebrew Book of Jubilees.* Oxford 1895
- *The Book of Jubilees.* London 1902
- *The Book of Enoch.* Oxford 1912
- *The Apocrypha and Pseudepigrapha of the Old Testament in English* 1-2. Oxford 1913
CHARLESWORTH, J.H. 'Jewish Astrology in the Talmud, the Pseudepigrapha, the Dead Sea Scrolls, and Early Palestinian Synagogues' *HTR* 70 (1977) 183-200
- *The Pseudepigrapha and Modern Research*, Missoula 1976 (2nd ed. 1981)
- (ed.) *The Old Testament Pseudepigrapha* 1-2. London 1983-1985
- 'Odes of Solomon' in ibid. *OTP* 2, 725-71
CHEETHAM, S. 'Homily and Homiliarium' *DCA* 781-3
CHERIX, P. *Le Concept de Notre Grande Puissance, CG* VI, 4 Fribourg, Göttingen 1982
CHERNICK, M.L. *Kelal u'ferat u'kelal and ribbui u'mi'ut we-ribbui in the Talmuds and Halakhic Midrashim.* Unpubl. Diss. Yeshiva University, New York 1978
- 'The Use of *Ribbuyim* and *Mi'utim* in the Halakic Midrash of R. Ishmael' *JQR* 70 (1979-1980) 96-116
- 'Development, Form and Structure in *Derasjot* of *Ribbuyim* and *Mi'utim*' *PAAJR* 49 (1982) 105-22 (Hebr. section)
- 'The Formal Development of *Kelal u'ferat u'kelal*' *Tarbiz* 52 (1983) 393-410 (Hebr.)
CHIESA, B. *L'Antico Testamento Ebraico secondo la tradizione palestinense.* Torino 1978
CHILDS, B.S. 'Midrash and the Old Testament' in *Understanding the Sacred Text.* (ed.), Reumann, J. Valley Forge PA 1972, 45-59
- *Exodus.* London 1974
- *Introduction to the Old Testament as Scripture.* Philadelphia 1979, 3rd ed. 1982
CHRIST, W. VON - SCHMID W. - STÄHLIN, O. *Geschichte der griechischen Litteratur.* 2/1, München 1920[6]
CHRISTIANSEN, I. *Die Technik der allegorischen Auslegungswissenschaft Philons von Alexandria.* Tübingen 1969
CHRISTOPHER, J.P. *S. Aureli Augustini Hipponiensis Episcopi De catechezandis rudibus liber unus, Translated with an Introduction and Commentary.* Washington DC, 1926
CHURGIN, P. *Targum Jonathan to the Prophets.* New Haven 1927
- *The Targum to the Hagiographa.* New York 1945 (Hebr.)
CLARKE, E.G. 'The Neofiti I Marginal Glosses and the Fragmentary Targum Witnesses to Gen. VI-IX' *VT* 22 (1972) 257-65

CLARKE, M.L. *Rhetoric at Rome*. New York 1963

COGGINGS, R.J. *Samaritans and Jews*. Oxford 1975

COHEN, A. (ed.) *The Minor Tractates of the Talmud* 1-2. 2nd ed. London 1971 (1965)

COHEN, B. 'Civil Bondage in Jewish and Roman Law' in *Louis Ginzberg Jubilee Volume on the Occasion of His Seventieth Birthday*. New York 1945, 113-32

COHEN, J.M. *A Samaritan Chronicle*. Leiden 1981

COHEN, N.G. 'Josephus and Scripture: Is Josephus' Treatment of the Scriptural Narrative similar throughout the Antiquities I-XI?' *JQR* 54 (1963-1964) 311-32

– *Jewish Names and Their Significance in the Hellenistic and Roman Periods in Asia Minor* 1-2. Jerusalem 1969 (Hebr.)

COHEN, N.J. 'Leviticus Rabbah. Parashah 3. An Example of a Classic Rabbinic Homily' *JQR* 72 (1981) 18-31

COHEN, S.J.D. *Josephus in Galilee and Rome: His Vita and Development as a Historian*. Leiden 1979

– 'Sosates, the Jewish Homer' *HTR* 74 (1981) 391-6

COHEN, H. 'Flavius Josephus as Historian of the Laws of Punishment' (Hebr.) Unpublished lecture, Hebrew University, Jerusalem 27 March 1972

COHN-SHERBOK, D. 'Paul and Rabbinic Exegesis' *SJT* 35 (1982) 117-32

COLE, A. *The New Temple*. London 1950

COLLINS, J.J. 'The Jewish Apocalypses' *Semeia* 14 (1979) 21-60

– (ed.) *Apocalypse. The Morphology of a Genre*. Missoula 1979

– 'The epic of Theodotus and the Hellenism of the Hasmoneans' *HTR* 73 (1980) 91-104

– *Between Athens and Jerusalem. Jewish Identity in the Hellenistic Diaspora*.

– 'Testaments' *Compendia* II/2, 325-55

– The Sibylline Oracles' *Compendia* II/2, 357-81

COLSON, F.M. - WHITAKER, G.H. - MARCUS, R. *Philo Works, Greek Text and English Translation* 1-10 and Suppl. 1-2. (LCL) London 1929-1953

CONNOLLY, R.H. *Didascalia Apostolorum*. Oxford 1929

CONYBEARE, F.C. *The Apology and Acts of Apollonius*. London 1894

– *Philo about the Contemplative Life*. Oxford 1895

COOK, J. *'n Onderzoek na die Komposisie van die Peshitta (Pentateug)*; Navorsingsverslag vir die Raad vir geesteswetenskaplige Navorsing, Universiteit van Stellenbosch 1985 (unpubl.)

CORNILL, C.H. *Das Buch des Propheten Ezechiel*, Leipzig 1886

COSIN, J. *A Scholastic History of the Canon of the Holy Scripture*. London 1657 also in *The Works of John Cosin* 1-5. Oxford 1843-1855, 3 (1849)

COTTINI, V. *La vita futura nel Libro dei Proverbi: Contributo alla storia dell'esegesi*. Jerusalem 1984

COWLEY, A.E. 'The Samaritan Liturgy and Reading of the Law' *JQR* 8 (1894) 121-40

– (ed.) *The Samaritan Liturgy* 1-2. Oxford 1909

– *Aramaic Papyri of the Fifth Century B.C.* Oxford 1923

CRANE, O.T. *The Samaritan Chronicle: or the Book of Joshua, the Son of Nun: translated from the Arabic*. New York 1890

CRANFIELD, C.E.B. 'St. Paul and the Law' *SJT* 17 (1964) 43-68

– *The Epistle to the Romans* 1-2. Edinburgh 1979

CRAVEN, T. *Artistery and Faith in the Book of Judith*. Chico 1983

CREDNER, C.A. *De Prophetarum Minorum Versionis Syriacae Quam Peschito Dicunt Indole*. Göttingen 1827

CROCKETT, L. 'Luke 4:16-30 and the Jewish Lectionary Cycle' *JJS* 17 (1966) 13-48

CRONE, P. - COOK, M. *Hagarism: The Making of the Islamic World*. Cambridge 1977

CROSS, F.M. *The Ancient Library of Qumran and Modern Biblical Studies* (The Haskell Lectures 1956-1957) New York 1958

– 'Epigraphic Notes on Hebrew Documents of the Eight - Sixth Centuries: II The Murabba'at Papyrus and the Letter Found near Yabneh-Yam' *BASOR* 165 (1962) 34-46

– 'Epigraphic Notes III: The Inscribed Jar Handles from Gibeon' *BASOR* 168 (1962) 18-23

- 'The History of the Biblical Text in the Light of Discoveries in the Judaean Desert' *HTR* 57 (1964) 281-99) (= Cross/Talmon, 177-95)
- 'The Development of the Jewish Scripts' in G.E. Wright (ed.) *The Bible and the Ancient Near East*. Garden City 1965, 170-264
- 'The Contribution of the Qumran Discoveries to the Study of the Biblical Text' *IEJ* 16 (1966) 81-95 (= Leiman, *Canon and Masorah*, 334-48; Cross/Talmon, 278-92)
- 'The Origin and Early Evolution of the Alphabet' *Eretz Israel* 8 (1967) 8-24 (English section)
- 'The Evolution of a Theory of Local Texts' *1972 Proceedings of the IOSCS: Pseudepigrapha.* 108-26 (= Cross/Talmon, 306-20)
- 'Two Offering Dishes with Phoenician Inscriptions from the Sanctuary of 'Arad' *BASOR* 235 (1979) 75-8
- 'Early Alphabetic Scripts' in Cross (ed.) *Symposia Celebrating the Seventy-fifth Anniversary of the American Schools of Oriental Research*. Cambridge, Mass. 1979, 97-123
- 'Newly Found Inscriptions in Old Canaanite and Early Phoenician Scripts' *BASOR* 238 (1980) 1-20
CROSS, F.M. - LAMBDIN, T.O. 'A Ugaritic Abecedary and the Origins of the Proto-Caanite Alphabet' *BASOR* 160 (1960) 21-6
CROSS, F.M. - TALMON, S. *Qumran and the History of the Biblical Text*. Cambridge, MA-London 1975
CROWN, A.D. *A Critical Re-evaluation of the Samaritan Sepher Yehoshua*. Doctoral thesis, Sydney University, 1966
- 'New Light on the Inter-Relationships of Samaritan Chronicles from some Manuscripts in the John Rylands Library' *BJRL* 54 (1971-72) 282-313; 55 (1972-73) 86-111
- 'Studies in Samaritan Scribal Practices and Manuscript History – The Rate of Writing Samaritan Mss. and Scribal Output' *BJRL* 66 (1984) 97-123
- *A Bibliography of the Samaritans*. Metuchen (U.S.A.), London 1984
- 'The Samaritans in the Byzantine Orbit' (forthcoming)
CULIANU, I. 'The Angels of the Nations and the Origins of Gnostic Dualism' in Van den Broek - Vermaseren, *Studies in Gnosticism*, 78-91
CULLMANN, O. *Christ and Time*. London 1953
- *Immortality of the Soul or Resurrection of the Dead?* London 1958
- *Christology of the New Testament*. London 1959
- *Salvation in History*. London 1967
CUMING, G.J. 'Η ΚΑΡΠΟΦΟΡΙΑ' *Ephemerides Liturgicae* 95 (1981) 556-8
DAHL, N.A. *Studies in Paul*. Minneapolis 1977 (*ST* 25, 1971, 1-19)
- 'The Arrogant Archon and the Lewd Sophia: Jewish Traditions in Gnostic Revolt' in Layton, *Rediscovery* 2, 689-712
DALBERT, P. *Die Theologie der hellenistisch-jüdischen Missionsliteratur*. Hamburg 1954
DANBY, H. *Tractate Sanhedrin: Mishna and Tosephta*. London 1919
DANIÉLOU, J. *Sacramentum Futuri*. Paris 1950; *From Shadows to Reality*. London 1960
- *A History of Early Christian Doctrine before the Council of Nicea*, 1, *The Theology of Jewish Christianity*; 2 *Gospel Message and Hellenistic Culture*; 3, *The Origins of Latin Christianity*. E.T. With Postscripts to 2 and 3 by J.A. Baker, London, Philadelphia 1964, 1973 and 1977
- 'David' *RAC* 3, 594-603
- Études d'exégèse judéo-chrétienne. Paris 1966
- (ed.) *Grégoire de Nysse. Vie de Moise*. SC 1, 3rd ed. Paris 1968
- 'Exodus' *RAC* 7 (1969) 22-44
DASSMANN, E. 'Amos' *RAC* Supp. 3 (1985), 333-50
DAUBE, D. 'Zur frühtalmudischen Rechtspraxis' *ZAW* 59 (1932) 148-59
- *Studies in Biblical Law*. Cambridge 1947
- 'Rabbinic Methods of Interpretation and Hellenistic Rhetoric' *HUCA* 22 (1949) 236-64
- 'Alexandrian Methods of Interpretation and the Rabbis' *Festschrift H. Lewald*. M. Gerwig et al. (ed.) Basel 1953, 27-44 (Vaduz 1978)
- *The New Testament and Rabbinic Judaism*. London 1956

- *The Exodus Pattern in the Bible.* London 1963
- 'Three Legal Notes on Josephus after His Surrender' *LQR* 93 (1977) 191-4
- 'Typology in Josephus' *JJS* 31 (1980) 18-36
DAVIES, W.D. 'Law in the New Testament' *IDB* 3, 95-102
- *The Setting of the Sermon on the Mount.* Cambridge 1964
- *Paul and Rabbinic Judaism.* 3rd ed. London 1970
DEBRUNNER, A. - SCHERER, A. *Geschichte der griechischen Sprache* 2. Berlin 1969
DEISSLER, A. *Psalm 119 (118) und seine Theologie.* Munich 1955
DEISSMANN, A. *Bibelstudien. Beiträge zumeist aus den Papyri und Inschriften, zur Geschichte der Sprache, des Schrifttums und der Religion des hellenistischen Judenthums und des Urchristenthums.* Marburg 1895
- *Neue Bibelstudien. Sprachgeschichtliche Beiträge zumeist aus den Papyri und Inschriften, zur Erklärung des Neuen Testaments.* Marburg 1897
DEIST, F.E. *Towards the Text of the Old Testament.* Pretoria 1978
DEL AGUA PÉREZ, A. 'La sinagoga: origines, ciclos de lectura y oración' *Estudios bíblicos* 41 (1983) 341-66
DE LANGE, N. *Origen and the Jews.* Cambridge 1976
- Review of Braverman, *Jerome's Commentary on Daniel.* JTS N.S. 31 (1980) 211-5
- 'The Letter to Africanus: Origen's recantation' in E.A. Livingstone (ed.) *Studia Pastristica* 16, 2 (*TU* 129) Berlin 1985, 242-47
DELCOR, M. (ed.) *Qumrân. Sa piété, sa théologie, et son milieu.* Paris, Leuven 1978
DELEKAT, L. 'Die Peschitta zu Jesaja zwischen Targum und Septuaginta' *Biblica* 38 (1957) 185-99; 321-35
DELLING, G. 'Josephus und das Wunderbare' *NovT* 2 (1957-8) 291-309
- 'Die Kunst des Gestaltens in "Joseph und Aseneth" ' *NovT* 26 (1984) 1-42
DE LUBAC, H. *Histoire et Esprit.* Paris 1950
- *Exégèse médiévale: les quatre sens del' écriture.* 1-3 (in 4 vols), Paris 1959-1964
DE LUBAC, H. - DOUTRELEAU, L. (eds.) *Origène, Homélies sur la Genèse.* SC 7, Paris 1976
DE LUBAC, H. - FORTIER, J. (eds.) *Origène, Homélies sur l'Exode.* SC 16 (in preparation)
DE MARGERIE, B. *Introduction à l'histoire de l'exégèse*, 1, *Les Pères grecs et orientaux*; 2, *Les premiers grands exégètes latins*; 3, *Saint Augustin.* Paris 1980 (1); 1982 (2-3)
DEMSKY, A. 'Education in the Biblical Period' *EJ* 6 (1971) 382-98
- 'Writing and Writing Materials' *EJ* 16 (1971) 654-65
- 'The Genealogy of Gibeon: Biblical and Epigraphic Considerations' *BASOR* 202 (1971) 16-23
- ' "Dark Wine" from Judah' *IEJ* 22 (1972) 233-34
- 'A Proto-Canaanite Abecedary Dating from the Period of the Judges and its Implications for the History of the Alphabet' *Tel Aviv* 7 (1977) 14-27
- 'Sheshakh' *EB* 8 (1982) 267-68 (Hebr.)
- 'Ezra and Nehemiah' in H. Tadmor (ed.) *The Restoration - The Persian Period.* Jerusalem 1983, 40-65
- 'On the Extent of Literacy in Ancient Israel' *Biblical Archaeology Today, Proceedings of the International Congress on Biblical Archaeology.* Jerusalem 1985, 349-53
- 'The 'Izbet Sartah Ostracon Ten Years Later' in I. Finkelstein (ed.) *'Izbet Sartah - An Early Iron Age Site near Rosh Ha'ayin, Israel.* Oxford 1986, 186-97
DENIS, A.M. *Introduction aux pseudépigraphes grecs d'Ancien Testament.* Leiden 1970
- *Fragmenta pseudepigraphorum quae supersunt graeca una cum historicorum et auctorum judaeorum hellenistarum fragmentis.* Leiden 1970
DEPPE, K. *Kohelet in der syrischen Dichtung: drei Gedichte über das Kohelet-Buch von Afrem, Jacob von Serug und Johannes von Mossul.* Wiesbaden 1975
DESELAERS, P. *Das Buch Tobit.* Göttingen 1982
DE SIMONE, R. 'The Baptismal and Christological Catechesis of Quodvultdeus' *Augustinianum* 25 (1985) 265-82
DES PLACES, E. *Eusèbe de Césarée commentateur: platonisme et écriture sainte.* Paris 1982

DEVRÉESSE, R. *Le commentaire de Théodore de Mopsueste sur les Psaumes (I-LXXX). Studi e Testi* 93, Vatican 1939
- *Essai sur Théodore de Mopsueste.* Vatican 1948
- 'Chaines exégétiques grecques' *DBS* 1, 1083-1234
- *Les anciens commentateurs grecs de l'Octateuque et des Rois (fragments tirés des chaînes). Studi e Testi* 201, Vatican 1959
- *Les anciens commenteurs grecs des Psaumes. Studi e Testi* 264, Vatican 1970
DHORME, E. *A Commentary on the Book of Job.* E.T. London 1967
DIAZ ESTEBAN, F. *Sefer 'oklah we-'oklah. Coleccion de listas de palabras destinados a conservar la interidad del texto hebreo de la Biblia entre los Judios de la Edad Media.* Madrid 1975
DI BARARDINO, A. ed. *Patrologia,* 3 Turin 1978
- ed. *Dizionario patristico e di antichitá christiane* 1-2. Casale Monferrato 1983, 1984
DIESTEL, L. *Geschichte des Alten Testaments in der christlichen Kirche.* Jena 1869
DIETTRICH, G. *Ein Apparatus criticus zur pešitto zum Propheten Jesaia. BZAW* 8 Giessen 1905
DÍEZ MACHO, A. 'The Recently Discovered Palestinian Targum: its Antiquity and Relationship with the Other Targums' *SVT* 7 (1959) 222-45
- *Ms. Neophyti 1, Targum Palestinense* 1-6. Madrid 1968-1979
- *El Targum: Introducción a las Traducciones Aramaicas de la Biblia.* Barcelona 1972
DILELLA, A.A. - HARTMAN, L.F. *The Book of Daniel.* (*Anchor Bible* 23) 1978
DILLON, J.M. *The Middle Platonists.* London 1977
DIMANT, D. 'The Fallen Angels' in the Dead Sea Scrolls and in the Apocryphal and Pseudepigraphic Books related to them.* Jerusalem 1974 (Hebr.)
- '1 Enoch 6-11: A Methodological Perspective' *SBL 1978 Seminar Papers,* P.J. Achtemeier (ed.), Missoula 1978, 323-39
- 'The "Pesher on the Periods" (4Q180) and 4Q181' *IOS* 9 (1979) 77-102
- 'The Biography of Enoch and the Books of Enoch' *VT* (1983) 14-29
- 'Qumran Sectarian Literature' *Compendia* II/2 (1984) 483-550
- 'Pseudonimity in the Wisdom of Solomon' in *La Septuaginta en La Investigacion Contemporanea.* Madrid 1985, 243-55
- '4QFlorilegium and the Idea of the Community as Temple' in A. Caquot, M. Hadas-Lebel, J. Riaud (eds.) *Hellenica et Judaica. Hommage à Valentin Nikiprowetzky.* Paris 1986, 165-89
- 'The Problem of a Non-Translated Biblical Greek' in C.E. Cox (ed.) *Proceedings of the VI Congress of the IOSCS,* Jerusalem 1986, Decatur 1987
- Review of Nitzan, *Pesher Habakkuk. RQ* 48 (1987) 599-600
DIRINGER, D. 'Early Hebrew Script versus Square Hebrew Script' *Essays and Studies Presented to S.A. Cook.* London 1950, 46-9
DIRKSEN, P.B. 'East and west, old and young in the text tradition of the Old Testament Peshiṭta' *PIC* 19, *VT* 35 (1985) 468-84
DITTMAR, W. *The Old Testament in the New.* Grand Rapids 1987 (1903)
DIX, G. - CHADWICK, H. *The Treatise on the Apostolic Tradition of St. Hippolytus of Rome.* London 1968
DOBSCHÜTZ, E. VON (ed.) *Das Decretum Gelasianum De Libris Recipiendis et Non Recipiendis.* Leipzig 1912 (*TU* 38. 4/1912)
DOBSCHUETZ, L. *Die Einfache Bibelexegese der Tannaim.* Breslau 1893
DODD, C.H. *The Bible and the Greeks.* London 1935
- *According to the Scriptures: The Sub-Structure of New Testament Theology.* London 1952
DÖRRIE, H. - DÖRRIES, H. 'Erotapokriseis' *RAC* 6 (1966) 342-70
DOEVE, J.W. *Jewish Hermeneutics in the Synoptic Gospels and Acts.* Assen 1954
DOLD, A. *Konstanzer altlateinische Propheten- und Evangelienbruchstücke mit Glossen.* Beuron 1923
- *Neue St. Galler vorhieronymianische Propheten-Fragmente.* Beuron 1940
DOTAN, A. *The Diqduqé Haṭṭe'amim of Aharon ben Moše ben Ašēr.* Jerusalem 1967
- 'Masorah' *EJ* 16, 1401-82
DOUTRELEAU, L. (ed.) *Didyme l'Aveugle, Sur Zacharie* 1-3. *SC* 83-5, Paris 1962

DOWNING, F.G. 'Redaction Criticism: Josephus' *Antiquities* and the Synoptic Gospels' *JSNT* 8 (1980) 46-65; 9 (1980) 29-48

– 'Ethical Pagan Theism and the Speeches in Acts' *NTS* 27 (1981) 544-63

– 'Common Ground with Paganism in Luke and in Josephus' *NTS* 28 (1982) 546-59

DRIJVERS, H.J.W. 'Edessa und das jüdische Christentum' *VC* 24 (1970) 4-33

DRIVER, G.R. 'Glosses in the Hebrew Text of the Old Testament' *L'Ancien Testament et l'Orient* (Études présentées aux VI⁰ˢ Journées Bibliques de Louvain 11-13 septembre 1954) Louvain 1957, 123-61

– 'Once Again Abbrevations' *Textus* 4 (1964) 76-94

– *Semitic Writing from Pictograph to Alphabet.* 3rd ed. London 1976

DRIVER, S.R. *Notes on the Hebrew Text of the Books of Samuel.* Oxford 1890, 2nd ed. 1913

– *Deuteronomy. (ICC)* Edinburgh 1895

DROGE, A.J. 'The Interpretation of the History of Culture in Hellenistic-Jewish Historiography' *SBL Seminar Papers 1984.* Chico 1984, 135-59

DUBARLE, A.M. *Judith: Formes et sens des diverses traditions* 1-2. Rome 1966

DUCKWORTH, C. - OSBORN, E. 'Clement of Alexandria's *Hypotyposeis:* A French Eighteenth-Century Sighting' *JTS* N.S. 36 (1985) 67-83

DUMAIS, M. *Le langage de l'évangélisation.* Montréal 1976

DUMORTIER, J. - LIEFOOGHE, A. (eds.) *Jean Chrysostome, Commentaire sur Isaïe.* SC 304 Paris 1983

DUNGAN, D. *The Sayings of Jesus in the Churches of Paul.* Oxford 1971

DUNN, J.D.G. *Christology in the Making.* London 1980

DUPONT-SOMMER, A. *Le Quatrieme Livre des Maccabees.* Paris 1939

– *Les Ecrits esséniens découvertes près de la mer Morte* 3. Paris 1964

– (ed.) *La Bible, Écrits Intertestamentaires.* Paris 1987

DUVAL, R. *La littérature Syriaque.* Paris 1907 (repr. Amsterdam 1970)

DUVAL, Y.-M. *Le livre de Jonas dans la littérature chrétienne grecque et latine: Sources et influence du Commentaire sur Jonas de Saint Jérôme* 1-2. Paris 1973

– (ed.) *Jérôme, Commentaire sur Jonas.* SC 323 Paris 1985

– 'Jérôme et les prophètes' in J.A. Emerton (ed.) *Congress Volume: Salamanca 1983, SVT* 36, Leiden 1985, 108-31

EALES, S.J. 'Preaching' *DCA* 2, 1684-9

EBNER, E. *Elementary Education in Ancient Israel: During the Tannaitic Period (10-220 C.E.).* New York 1956

EHRHARDT, A. 'Parakatatheke' *ZSS* 75 (1958) 32-90

EISSFELDT, O. *The Old Testament: An Introduction.* (E.T. P.R. Ackroyd) Oxford 1966

ELBAUM, J. 'R. Eleazar Hamodai and R. Joshua on the Amalek Pericope' in I. Ben-Amni, J. Dan (eds.) *Studies in Aggadah and Jewish Folklore.* Jerusalem 1983, 99-116 (Hebr. section)

ELBOGEN, I. *Der jüdische Gottesdienst in seiner geschichtlichen Entwicklung.* Frankfurt 1931 (repr. Hildesheim 1967)

ELINER, A. 'Ambiguous Scriptural Readings in Isaiah in Light of the Qumran Scrolls' *S. Dim Volume.* Jerusalem 1958, 280-83 (Hebr.)

ELIYAHU NIKOMODEO, *Sefer Keter Torah.* Gozolva (Eupatoria) 1867, Ramleh 1972

ELLIGER, K. *Studien zum Habakkuk-Kommentar.* Tübingen 1953

ELLIOTT, C.J. 'Hebrew Learning among the Fathers' *DCB* 2 (1880) 851-72

ELLIS, E.E. *Paul's Use of the Old Testament.* Edinburgh 1957 (3rd ed. Grands Rapids 1985)

– II Corinthians V.1-10 in Pauline Eschatology' *NTS* 6 (1959-1960) 211-24

– 'Present and Future Eschatology in Luke' *NTS* 12 (1965-1966) 27-41

– ' "Those of the Circumcision" and the Early Christian Mission' *TU* 102 (1968) 390-99 (= *Proph. and Herm.* cap. 7)

– *Eschatology in Luke.* Philadelphia 1972

– 'St. Luke' *Encyclopaedia Britannica* 11, 177-78, Chicago 1974 (15th ed.)

– ' "Weisheit" und "Erkentnis" im 1 Korintherbrief' in E.E. Ellis, E. Grässer (eds.) *Jesus und Paulus. Festschrift für W.G. Kümmel zum 70. Geburtstag,* Göttingen 1975, 109-28 (= *Proph. and Herm.* cap. 3)

– *Prophecy and Hermeneutic* (*WUNT* 18) Tübingen, Grand Rapids 1978
– 'Life' *The New Bible Dictionary* (Revised Ed.) J.D. Douglas and N. Hillyer (eds.) Leicester 1979, 735-39 (revised in *The Illustrated Bible Dictionary 1-3*, N. Hillyer [ed.] Leicester and Wherton IL 1980, 2, 901-04
– 'Quotations' *ISBE* (2nd ed.), 4 (1987) ed. G.W. Bromiley, Grand Rapids 1979-1987
– 'The Silenced Wives of Corinth (1 Cor. 14:34-35)' *New Testament Criticism. Essays in Honour of B.M. Metzger*. eds. E.J. Epp and G.D. Fee, Oxford 1981, 213-20
– 'Gospels Criticism: A Perspective on the State of Art' in P. Stuhlmacher (ed.) *Das Evangelium und die Evangelien*. Tübingen 1983, 27-54
– *The Gospel of Luke*. London and Grand Rapids 1983 (4th ed.)
– 'Traditions in 1 Corinthians' *NTS* 32 (1986) 481-502
– 'Traditions in the Pastoral Epistles' in C.A. Evans, W.F. Stinespring, (eds.) *Early Jewish and Christian Exegesis*. Decatur GA, 1987
ELON, M. *Jewish Law, History, Sources, Principles* 1-2. 2nd ed. Jerusalem 1978 (1973) (Hebr.)
EL-SAKKA, A.H. (ed.) *At-Tôrâh as Sâmiriyah ... tarjamuh al Kâhin as-Sâmiri Abu 'l-Ḥaṣan aṣ-Ṣûri*. Cairo 1978
ELZE, M. 'Häresie und Einheit der Kirche im 2. Jahrhundert' *ZTK* 71 (1974) 389-409
EMERTON, J.A. 'The Purpose of the Second Column of the Hexapla' *JQR* N.S. 7 (1956) 79-87
– 'The Origin of the Son of Man Imagery' *JTS* 9 (1958) 225-42
– 'Unclean Birds and the Origin of the Peshitta' *JSS* 7 (1962) 204-11
– 'The printed editions of the Song of Songs in the Peshiṭta Version' *VT* 17 (1967) 416-29
ENDRES, J.C. *Biblical Interpretation in the Book of Jubilees*. Washington 1987
ENELOW, H.G. *The Mishnah of Rabbi Eliezer*. New York 1933
ENGNELL, I. *A Rigid Scrutiny*. (tr. J.T. Willis) Nashville 1969
– *Critical Essays on the Old Testament*. London 1970
ENSLIN, M.S. *The Book of Judith*. Leiden 1972
EPSTEIN, A. 'Les Chamites de la table ethnographique selon le Pseudo-Jonathan comparé avec Josèphe et le livre Jubilés' *REJ* 24 (1892) 82-98
EPSTEIN, J.N. *Introduction to Tannaitic Literature. Mishnah, Tosephta and Halakhic Midrashim*. (ed. E.Z. Melamed) Jerusalem, Tel-Aviv 1957
– *Mavo le-nosah ha-Mishna* 1-2. 2nd ed. Jerusalem 1964
EVANS, E. (ed. and tr.) *Tertullian, Adversus Marcionem*. *OECT* 1-2, Oxford 1972
EVANS, G.R. *The Language and Logic of the Bible: The Earlier Middle Ages*. Cambridge 1984
– *The Tought of Gregory the Great*. Cambridge 1986
EYBERS, I.H. 'Some Light on the Canon of the Qumran Sect' in Leiman, *Canon and Masorah*, 23-36
FABER VAN DER MEULEN, H.E. *Das Salomobild im hellenistisch-jüdischen Schrifttum*. Kampen 1978
FALLON, F.T. 'The law in Philo and Ptolemy: A Note on the Letter to Flora' *VC* 30 (1976) 45-51
– *The Enthronement of Sabaoth. Jewish Elements in Gnostic Creation Myths*. Leiden 1978
– 'The Prophets of the Old Testament and the Gnostics: A Note on Irenaeus, Adversus Haereses, I.30.10-11' *VC* 32 (1978) 191-94
– 'The Gnostic Apocalypses' in Collins *Apocalypse*, 123-58
– 'Theodotus' in Charlesworth *OTP* 2 (1985) 785-93
FARRAR, F.W. *History of Interpretation*. London 1886
FARRIS, S. *The Hymns of Luke's Infancy Narratives*. Sheffield 1985
FASCHER, E. *ΠΡΟΦΗΤΗΣ*. Giessen 1927
FAULHABER, M. (ed.) *Hesychii Hierosolymitani Interpretatio Isaiae Prophetae*. Freiburg 1900
FAUR, J. 'The Targumim and Halakha' *JQR* 66 (1975) 19-26
FEDWICK, P.J. (ed.) *Basil of Caesarea: Christian, Humanist, Ascetic: A Sixteen-Hundredth Anniversary Symposium* 1-2. Toronto 1981
FELDMAN, L.H. *Cicero's Conception of Historiography*. Cambridge 1951
– 'The Orthodoxy of the Jews in Hellenistic Egypt' *JSOS* 22 (1960) 215-37
– 'Abraham the Greek Philosopher in Josephus' *TAPA* 99 (1968) 143-56
– 'Hellenizations in Josephus' Portrayal of Man's Decline' in *Religions in Antiquity: Essays in Memory of Erwin Ramsdell Goodenough*. Leiden 1968, 336-53

- 'Hellenizations in Josephus' Version of Esther' *TAPA* 101 (1970) 143-70
- 'Prolegomenon' in *The Biblical Antiquities of Philo* by M.R. James, New York 1971, vii-clxix
- 'Epilegomenon to Pseudo-Philo's *Liber Antiquitatum Biblicarum (LAB)*' *JSS* 25 (1974) 305-12
- 'Josephus as an Apologist to the Greco-Roman World: His Portrait of Solomon' in *Aspects of Religious Propaganda in Judaism and Early Christianity.* ed. by E.S. Fiorenza, Notre Dame 1976, 69-98
- 'Josephus' Commentary on Genesis' *JQR* 72 (1981-1982) 121-31
- 'Josephus' Portrait of Saul' *HUCA* 53 (1982) 45-99
- *Josephus and Modern Scholarship (1937-1980).* Berlin 1984
- 'Josephus as a Biblical Interpreter: The *'Aqeda' JQR* 75 (1984-1985) 212-52

FELIKS, Y. 'The Oak and its Products in our Ancient Literature' *Sinai* 38 (1956) 85-102 (Hebr.)

FERNÁNDEZ MARCOS, N. 'Los estudios de "Septuaginta". Visión retrospectiva y problemática más reciente' *CFC* 11 (1976) 413-68
- *Introduction a las versiones griegas de la Biblia.* Madrid 1979

FERNANDEZ MARCOS, N. - BUSTO SAIZ, R. (eds.) *Theodoreti Quaestiones in Reges et Paralipomena.* Madrid 1984

FERNANDEZ MARCOS, N. - SAENZ-BADILLOS, A. (eds.) *Theodoreti Quaestiones in Ocateuchum.* Madrid 1979

FEUILLET, A. *Le Christ Sagesse de Dieu d'après les epîtres pauliniennes.* Paris 1966

FICHTNER, J. 'Der AT-Text der Sapientia Salomonis' *ZAW* 57 (1939) 155-92

FIELD, F. *Origenis Hexaplorum quae supersunt; sive veterum interpretum graecorum in totum Vetus Testamentum fragmenta.* Oxford 1867, 1874 (1-2) Repr. Hildesheim 1964

FIENSY, D.A. *Prayers Alleged to be Jewish: An Examination of the Constitutiones Apostolorum.* Chico 1985

FILORAMO, G. - GIANOTTO, C. 'L'interpretazione gnostica dell' Antico Testamento: Posizioni ermeneutiche e techniche esegetiche' *Augustinianum* 22 (1982) 53-74
- *L'attesa della fine: Storia delle gnosi.* Roma 1983

FINK, J. *Bildfrömmigkeit und Bekenntnis: Das Alte Testament. Herakles und die Herrlichkeit Christi an der Via Latina in Rom.* Cologne 1978

FINKEL, A. *The Pharisees and the Teacher of Nazareth.* Leiden 1964

FINKELSTEIN, L. 'The Prophetic Readings According to the Palestinian, Byzantine and Karaite Rites' *HUCA* 17 (1942-1943) 423-26
- (ed.) *Sifre on Deuteronomy.* New York 1969

FISCHER, B. *Vetus Latina. Die Reste der altlateinischen Bibel nach Petrus Sabatier neu gesammelt und herausgegeben von der erzabtei Beuron.* 1. *Verzeichnis der Sigel für Handschriften und Krichenschriftsteller.* Freiburg 1949 (Supplements 1963, 1964-1970); 2. *Genesis.* Freiburg 1951
- 'Lukian-Lesarten in der Vetus Latina der vier Königsbücher' *Studia Anselmiana* 27/8 (Rome 1951) 169-77
- (ed.) *Biblica Sacra iuxta Vulgatam Versionem* 1-2. Stuttgart 1969

FISHBANE, M. 'The Qumran Pesher and Traits of Ancient Hermeneutics' *Proceedings of the Sixth World Congress of Jewish Studies* 1. Jerusalem 1977, 97-114
- 'Torah and Tradition' in *Tradition and Theology in the Old Testament.* D.A. Knight (ed.) Philadelphia 1977, 275-300
- *Biblical Interpretation in Ancient Israel.* Oxford 1985

FISHBANE, M. - TALMON, S. 'The Structuring of Biblical Books, Studies in the Book of Ezekiel' *ASTI* 10 (1976) 129-53

FITZMYER, J.A. 'The Use of Explicit Old Testament Quotations in Qumran Literature and in the New Testament' *NTS* 7 (1960-1961) 297-333
- 'The Languages of Palestine in the First Century A.D.' *CBQ* 32 (1970) 501-31
- *The Genesis Apocryphon from Qumran Cave I. A Commentary.* Rome 1971, 2nd ed.
- *The Dead Sea Scrolls.* Missoula Mont. 2nd ed.1977
- *A Wandering Aramean.* Ann Arbor 1979

FLASHAR, M. 'Exegetische Studien zum Septuagintapsalter I' *ZAW* 32 (1912) 81-116

813

FLUSSER, D. 'Sanktus und Gloria' in O. Betz, (ed.), *Abraham unser Vater: Festschrift für Otto Michel*. Leiden 1963, 129-52
- 'Pharisees, Sadducees, and Essenes in Pesher Nahum' in *Mehqarim be-Toledot Yisrael ube-Lashon ha-Ivrit*. M. Dormann, S. Safrai, and M. Stern (eds.) Tel Aviv 1970, 133-68 (Hebr.)
- 'Psalms, Hymns and Prayers' in *Compendia* II/2, 551-77
FOERSTER, W. (ed.) *Gnosis: A Selection of Gnostic Texts* 1-2. E.T. by R.M. Wilson, Oxford 1972-1974
FOHRER, G. 'Morija' *BHH* 2 (1964) 1239
FONTAINE, J. *Naissance de la Poésie dans l'Occident Chrétien*. Paris 1981
FORNARO, P. *La voce fuori scena. Saggio sull'Exagogê di Ezechiele con testo greco, note e traduzione*. Torino 1982
FOSSUM, J.E. *The Name of God and the Angel of the Lord. The origins of the Idea of Intermediation in Gnosticism*. Tübingen 1985 (diss. Utrecht 1982)
FOUL, S. 'The Canonical Approach of Brevard Childs' *ExpT* 96 (1984-1985) 173-76
FOURNIER, P. 'Le Liber ex Lege Moysi et les tendances bibliques du droit canonique irlandais' *Revue Celtique* 30 (1909) 221-34
FRÄNKEL, S. 'Die syrische Übersetzung zu den Büchern der Chronik' *Jahrb. f. Prot. Theol.* 5. Leipzig 1879, 508-36; 720-58
FRAIDL, F. *Die Exegese der siebzig Wochen Daniels in der alten und mittleren Zeit*. Graz 1883
FRANCE, R.T. *Jesus and the Old Testament*. London 1971
FRANKE, P. 'Traditio Leges und Petrusprimat' *VC* 26 (1972) 263-71
FRANKEL, I. *Peshat in Talmudic and Midrashic Literature*. Toronto 1956
FRANKEL, Z. *Über den Einfluss der palästinischen Exegese auf die alexandrinische Hermeneutik*. Leipzig 1851
FRANXMAN, T.W. *Genesis and the 'Jewish Antiquities' of Flavius Josephus*. Rome 1979
FRASER, P.M. *Ptolemaio Alexandria* 1-2. Oxford 1972
FREED, E.D. *Old Testament Quotations in the Gospel of John*. Leiden 1965
FREEDMAN, D.N. 'The Law and the Prophets' *SVT* 9 (1962) 250-65 (= Leiman, Canon, 5-20)
FRENSDORFF, S. *Das Buch Ochlah W'ochlah*. Hannover 5624 (1864)
- *Massorah Magna, Massoretisches Wörterbuch*. Hannover, Leipzig 1876
FRERE, W.H. *Studies in Early Roman Liturgy* 3, *The Roman Epistle-Lectionary*. Oxford 1935
FREUDENTHAL, J. *Hellenistische Studien. Alexander Polyhistor und die ihm erhaltenen Reste jüdäischer und samaritanischer Geschichtswerke* 1-2. Breslau 1874-75
FRICKEL, J. *Hellenistische Erlösung in christlicher Deutung: Die gnostische Naassenerschrift*. Leiden 1984
FRIED, N. 'Haftara' *Talmudic Encyclopedia* 10 (1961) 1-32 (Cf. Appendix 702-24)
- 'List of the Sedarim for Numbers' *Textus* 7 (1969) 103-13
- 'Triennial Cycle' *EJ* 15, 1386-89
- 'A new Hebrew version of Megilat Antiochus' *Sinai* 64 (1969) 97-140 (Hebr.)
FRIEDMAN, M. *Onkelos und Akylas*. Vienna 1896
FRIEDMAN, M.A. 'Wekhatav lo - 'Osse lo ketav' *Sinai* 84 (1979) 177-9
FRITSCH, CH. *The Anti-anthropomorphisms of the Greek Pentateuch*. Princeton 1943
FROIDEVAUX, L. (tr.) *Irénée de Lyon: Démonstration de la prédication apostolique*. SC 62, Paris 1959
FUCHS, H. *Pesîq, ein Glossenzeichen*. Breslau 1907
GABRION, H. 'L'Interprétation de l'Écriture dans la littérature de Qumrân' *ANRW* II.19.1 (Berlin 1979) 749-848
GAFNI, I.M. 'The Historical Background' in *Compendia* II/3a, 1-34
- 'On the Use of I Maccabees by Josephus Flavius' *Zion* 45 (1980) 81-95 (Hebr.)
GAGER, J.G. *Moses in Greco-Roman Paganism*. Nashville, New York 1972
- *The Origins of Anti-Semitism. Attitudes Towards Judaism in Pagan and Christian Antiquity*. New York, Oxford 1983
GALL, A. VON, *Der hebräische Pentateuch der Samaritaner* 1-4. Giessen [1913-]1918 (repr. Berlin 1966)
GAMBERONI, J. *Die Auslegung des Buches Tobias in der griechisch-lateinischen Kirche der Antike und der Christenheit des Westens bis um 1600*. Munich 1969

GARDINER, A.H. 'The Egyptian Origin of the Semitic Alphabet' *JEA* 3 (1916) 1-16
GARITTE, G. (ed. and tr.) *Traités d'Hippolyte sur David et Goliath, le Cantique des Cantiques et sur l'Antéchrist. CSCO* 263-264, Louvain 1965
GASQUET, F.A. 'Vulgate, Revision of' *Catholic Encyclopedia* 15. London 1912, 515-20
GASTER, M. *The Samaritans: Their History, Doctrine, and Literature.* London 1925
– *The Sword of Moses.* London 1896 (= *Studies and Texts* 3, New York 1971, 70-108)
– *The Asatir: The Samaritan Book of the 'Secrets of Moses' together with the Pitron or Samaritan Commentary and the Samaritan Story of the Death of Moses.* London 1927
– 'Demetrius and Seder Olam' *Studies and Texts* 2. New York 1928 (repr. 1971), 650-59
– *The Samaritan Oral Law and Ancient Traditions.* 1, *Samaritan Eschatology.* London 1932
– 'The Samaritan Literature' in *EI* 4, 1934, end (separately paginated, 1-15)
GASTER, T.H. 'A Samaritan Poem about Moses' in *The Joshua Bloch Memorial Volume.* New York 1960, 115-39
GAUDEMET, J. *Les Sources du Droit de l'Église en Occident du IIe au IIIe Siècle.* Paris 1985
GEDEN, A.S. *Outlines of Introduction of the Hebrew Bible.* Edinburgh 1909
GEDEN, A.S. - KILGOUR, R. *Introduction to the Ginsburg Edition of the Hebrew Old Testament.* London 1928
GEEST, J.E.L. VAN DER, *Le Christ et l'Ancien Testament chez Tertullien.* (*Latinitas Christianorum Primaeva* 22) Nijmegen 1972
GEFFCKEN, J. 'Allegory, Allegorical Interpretation' *ERE* 1 (1908) 327-31
GEIGER, A. 'Einiges über Plan und Anordnung der Mischnah' *Wissenschaftliche Zeitschrift für jüdische Theologie* 2 (1836) 472-92
– 'Zur Theologie und Schrifterklärung der Samaritaner' in *Nachgelassene Schriften* 3, 255-66 (= *ZDMG* 12 [1858] 132-42)
– 'Neuere Mittheilungen über die Samaritaner' *ZDMG* 16 (1862) 714-28; 18 (1864) 590-97, 813-24; 19 (1865) 601-15; 20 (1866) 143-70; 21 (1867) 169-82; 22 (1868) 523-38
– 'Die gesetzlichen Differenzen zwischen Samaritanern und Juden' in *Nachgelassene Schriften* 3, 283-321 (= ZDMG 20 [1866] 527-75)
– *Nachgelassene Schriften* 1-5. Berlin 1875-1878; New York 1980 (3 parts)
– *Urschrift und Übersetzungen der Bibel in ihrer Abhängigkeit von den innern Entwicklung des Judentums.* 2nd ed. Frankfurt a/M 1928 (1857)
– *Ha-Mikra ve-Targumav be-Zikatam le-Hitpaṭḥutah ha-Penimit shel ha-Yahadut.* Jerusalem 1949
GELB, I.J. *A Study of Writing.* Chicago 1963
GELSTON, A. *The Peshitta of the Twelve Prophets.* Oxford 1987
GENEBRARD, G. *Chronographia* 1-2. Lugdensi 1572
GEORGI, D. *Die Gegner des Paulus im 2. Korintherbrief.* Neukirchen 1964
– *Weisheit Salomos.* (*JSHRZ* III/4) Gütersloh 1980
GERHARDSSON, B. 'The Hermeneutic Program in Matthew 22:37-40; in Hamerton-Kelly, Scroggs, *Jews, Greeks and Christians*, 129-50
– *The Testing of God's Son.* Lund 1966
GERLEMAN, G. *Synoptic Studies in the Old Testament. LUÅ* N.F. I, xliv, 5 (1948)
– *Studies in the Septuagint. III, Proverbs. LUÅ* 52,3 Lund 1956
GERTNER, M. 'Midrashim in the New Testament' *JSS* 7 (1962) 267-92
– 'Terms of Scriptural Interpretation: A Study in Hebrew Semantics' *BSOAS* 25 (1962) 1-27
GESENIUS, W. *Philologisch-kritisches und historisches Commentar über den Jesaia* 1. Leipzig 1821
– *Carmina Samaritana.* Lipsiae 1824
GIANOTTO, C. *Melchisedek e la sua Tipologia.* Brescia 1984
GIBBON, E. *The Decline and Fall of the Roman Empire.* 1776-1788 (repr. in 4 vols. London 1895)
GIET, S. (ed.) *Basile de Césarée sur l'Hexaémeron. SC* 26, Paris 1968
GILAT, Y.D. *R. Eliezer Ben Hyrcanus. A Scholar Outcast.* Ramat-Gan 1984
GILBERT, M. 'La structure de la prière de Salomon (Sg 9)' *Biblica* 51 (1970) 301-31
– *La critique des dieux dans le Livre de la Sagesse (Sg 13-15).* Rome 1973
– 'Wisdom Literature' *Compendia* II/2, 283-324

GINSBURG, C.D. *Introduction to the Massoretico-Critical Edition of the Hebrew Bible.* London 1897 (repr. New York 1966) (Prolegomen by H.M. Orlinsky)

GINSBURGER, M. *Das Fragmenthargum.* Berlin 1899

– *Pseudo-Jonathan.* Berlin 1903

GINZBERG, L. *The Legends of the Jews* 1-7. Philadelphia 1909-1938

– 'The Significance of the Halachah for Jewish History' in *On Jewish Law and Lore.* New York 1970, 77-124

– 'The Codification of Jewish Law' in *On Jewish Law and Lore.* New York 1970, 151-84

– *An Unknown Jewish Sect.* New York 1976

– 'Allegorical Interpretation' *JE* 1, 403-11

GIVERSEN, S. *Apocryphon Johannis.* Copenhagen 1963

– 'The Apocryphon of John and Genesis' *ST* 17 (1963) 60-76

GLASSON, T.F. 'The Son of Man Imagery: Enoch XIV and Daniel VII' *NTS* 23 (1976-1977) 82-90

GLAUE, P. - RAHLFS, A. 'Fragmente einer griechischen Übersetzung des samaritanischen Pentateuchs' *Nachrichten* 2 (1911) 167-200

GLUCKER, C.A.M. *The city of Gaza in the Romand and Byzantine Periods.* (*B.A.R.* International Series 325) Oxford 1987

GOELZER, H. *Latinité de Saint Jérôme.* Paris 1884

GOLDBERG, A. 'The Mishnah – A Study Book of Halakha' *Compendia* II/3a, 211-62

GOLDBERG, L. *Das samaritanische Pentateuchtargum. Eine Untersuchung seiner handschriftlichen Quellen.* Stuttgart 1935

GOLDENBERG, D. *The Halakhah in Josephus and in Tannaitic Literature: A Comparative Study.* Philadelphia 1978

GOLDENBERG, R. *The Sabbath-Law of Rabbi Meir.* Missoula 1978

GOLDSTEIN, J.A. *I Maccabees.* (*The Anchor Bible*) New York 1984

GOLEGA, J. *Der homerische Psalter.* Ettal 1960

GONZÁLEZ LUIS, J. 'Los "targumim" y la version de Símaco' in N. Fernandez Marcos, J. Trebolle Barrera and J. Fernandez Vallina (eds.) *Simposio Biblico Español.* Madrid 1984, 255-68

GOODENOUGH, E.R. *By Light, Light. The Mystic Gospel of Hellenistic Judaism.* New Haven 1935

– *The Politics of Philo Judaeus.* New Haven 1938

– *Jewish Symbols in the Greco-Roman Period* 1-13. New York 1953-1968

GOODING, D.W. *Recensions of the Septuagint Pentateuch.* London 1955

– 'The Account of the Tabernacle' *TS* N.S. 6 (1959) 8-13

– 'Aristeas and Septuagint Origins: a Review of Recent Studies' *VT* 13 (1963) 357-79

– 'Problems of Text and Midrash in the Third Book of Reigns' *Textus'* 7 *(1969) 1-29*

– 'Text-sequence and translation-revision in 3 Reigns IX 10 – X 33' *VT* 19 (1969) 448-63

– 'A Recent Popularization of Professor F.M. Cross' Theories on the Text of the Old Testament' *Tyndale Bulletin* 26 (1975) 113-32

– *Relics of Ancient Exegesis. A Study of the Miscelleanies in 3 Reigns 2.* Cambridge 1976

GOPPELT, L. 'τυπος etc.' *ThWNT* 8, 246-60

– TYPOS: Die typologische Deuting des Alten Testaments im Neuen. 2nd ed. Darmstadt 1964 (ET Grand Rapids 1982)

GORDIS, R. *The Biblical Text in the Making. A Study of the Kethib-Qere.* 2nd ed., New York 1971 (1937)

GORDON, R.P. 'The second Septuagint account of Jeroboam: history or midrash?' *VT* 25 (1975) 368-93

GOSHEN-GOTTSTEIN, M.H., 'Die Jesaia-Rolle im Lichte von Peschitta und Targum' *Biblica* 35 (1954) 51-71 (= M.H. Goshen-Gottstein, *Text and Language in Bible and Qumran.* Jerusalem, Tel Aviv 1960, 65-71)

– review of A. Vööbus, *Peschitta und Targumim. JSS* 6 (1961) 266-70

– 'The Authenticity of the Aleppo Codex' *Textus* 1 (1960) 17-58

– *The Book of Isaiah. Sample Edition with Introduction.* Jerusalem 1965

– 'Hebrew Biblical Manuscripts' *Biblica* 48 (1967) 243-90

816

- 'The "Third Targum" on Esther and MS Neofiti 1' *Biblica* 56 (1975) 301-29
GOTTLIEB, I.B. 'Formula Comparison in Midrash Research' *JQR* 70 (1979-1980) 28-40
GOULDER, M.D.*Midrash and Lection in Matthew*. London 1974
GRABAR, A. *Christian Iconography: A Study of its Origins*. Princeton 1968
GRABE, J.E. *Vetus Testamentum juxta LXX Interpretes*. Oxford 1707-1720
GRAETZ, H. *Kohelet oder der Salomonische Prediger*. Leipzig 1871
GRAF, M.R. *The Hellenization of Moses*. Cincinnati 1976
GRANT, R.M. 'The Decalogue in Early Christianity' *HTR* 40 (1947) 1-17
- *Miracle and Natural Law in Greco-Roman and Early Christian Thought*. Amsterdam 1952
- *The Letter and the Spirit*. London 1957
- 'Tatian and the Bible' in K. Aland and F.L. Cross (eds.) *SP* 1-2 (*TU* 63-4 Berlin 1957) 1, 297-306
GRANT, R.M. - TRACY, D. *A Short History of the Interpretation of the Bible*. 3rd ed. London 1984
GREEN, W.H. *General Introduction to the Old Testament: the Canon*. New York 1898, London 1899
GREENBAUM, A. *The Biblical Commentary of Rav Samuel ben Hofni Gaon*. Jerusalem 1979 (Hebr.)
GREENBERG, M. 'Nash Papyrus' *EJ* 12, 833
- 'The Rabbinic Exegesis' in *Jewish Bible Exegesis. An Introduction.* (*The Biblical Encyclopaedia Library* 1) Jerusalem 1983, 3-9
- Review of Fishbane, *Biblical Interpretation*. *Numen* 34 (1987) 128-30
GREENFIELD, J.C. '*Standard Literary Aramaic*' in A. Caquot and D. Cohen, *Actes du Premier Congrès International de Linguistique Sémitique et Chamito-Sémitique* 1969, The Hague, Paris 1974, 280-89
GREENSLADE, S.L. Review of Weber and Bévenot, *Sancti Cypriani Episcopi Opera (CCL* 3) *JTS* N.S. 24 (1973) 583-5
GREENSPOON, L. *Textual Studies in the Book of Joshua*. Chico, CA 1983
GRELOT, P. 'Les Targums du Pentateuque, Étude comparative d'après Genèse, IV, 3-16' *Semitica* 9 (1959) 59-88
GRIBOMONT, J. 'Vetus Latina' *Enciclopedia de la Biblia* 6, 1177-83, Barcelona 1963
- 'Vulgata' ibid. 6, 1253-60
GRIFFIN, J. *Virgil*. Oxford 1986
GRIMM, W. *Die Verkündigung Jesu und Deuterojesaja*. Frankfurt 1981
GRINTZ, Y.M. *The Book of Judith*. Jerusalem 1957 (Hebr.)
GRÖZINGER, K.E. e.a. *Qumran* (*Wege der Forschung* 410) Darmstadt 1981
GROSDIDIER DE MATONS, J. *Romanos le Mélode, Hymnes*. SC 99, 110, 114, 128; Paris 1964-1967
GRUBER, M.I. 'The Mishnah as Oral Torah. A Reconsideration' *JSJ* 15 (1984) 112-22
GRUENWALD, I. *Apocalyptic and Merkavah Mysticism*. Leiden 1980
GRÜTZMACHER, G. *Hieronymus. Eine biographische Studie zur alten Kirchengeschichte* 1-3. Leipzig, Berlin 1901-1908
GUILDING, A. *The Fourth Gospel and Jewish Worship*. Oxford 1960
GUILLAUMONT, A. 'Une citation de l'Apocryphe d'Ezéchiel dans l'Exégèse au sujet de l'âme: Nag Hammadi II, 6' in Krause, *Essays*, 35-39
GUINOT, J.-N. (ed.) *Théodoret de Cyr, Commentaire sur Isaïe* 1-3. SC 276, 295, 315, Paris 1980, 1982, 1984
GUNDRY, R.H. *The Use of the Old Testament in St. Matthew's Gospel*. Leiden 1967
- *Matthew*. Grand Rapids 1982
GUTMAN, Y. 'Philo the Epic Poet' *Scripta* 1 (1954) 36-63
- *The Beginnings of Jewish-Hellenistic Literature* 1-2. Jerusalem 1958-1963 (Hebr.)
GUTTMANN, M. *Clavis Talmudis* 3a. Breslau 1924, Supplement *Asmakhta*, 1-41
HAAG, E. *Studien zum Buche Judith*. Trier 1963
HAARDT, R. 'Schöpfer und Schöpfung in der Gnosis' in Tröger, *Altes Testament*, 37-48
HABERMAN, A.M. *The Hebrew Book in its Development*. Jerusalem 1938 (Hebr.)
HADAS, M. *The Third and Fourth Books of Maccabees*. New York 1953
HADOT, P. - CORDIER, M. (eds.) *Ambroise de Milan, Apologie de David*. SC 239, Paris 1977
HAEFELI, L. *Die Peschitta des Alten Testaments mit Rücksicht auf ihre textkritische Bearbeitung und Herausgabe*. Alttest. Abh. 11,1, Münster i. W. 1927

HAGEDORN, D. *Der Hiobkommentar des Arianers Julian.* Berlin 1973
HAGEDORN, U. and D. *Olympiodor, Diakon von Alexandria – Kommentar zu Hiob.* Berlin 1984
HAHN, V. *Das wahre Gesetz: Eine Untersuchung der Auffassung des Ambrosius von Mailand vom Verhältnis der beiden Testamente.* Münster 1969
HALEVI, Y.A. *Dorot ha-Rishonim.* Frankfurt 1906, Jerusalem 1967
HALIVNI, D.W. 'A Note on אשר לא ארשה' *JBL* 81 (1962) 67-9
– *Midrash, Mishnah and Gemara.* Cambridge MA. 1986
HALKIN, A.S. 'Samaritan Polemics against the Jews' *PAAJR* 7 (1936) 13-59
– 'The Relation of the Samaritans to Saadia Gaon' in *Saadia Anniversary Volume (The American Academy for Jewish Research, Text and Studies* 2) New York 1943
– 'The Jewish Arabic Exegesis' in *Jewish Bible Exegesis. An Introduction.* Jerusalem 1983, 15-22
HALL, B. 'Biblical Scholarship: Editions and Commentaries' in *CHB* 3 *(The West from the Reformation to the Present Day)* Cambridge 1963, 38-93
HALL, B.W. *Samaritan Religion from Hyrcanus to Baba Rabba.* Sydney 1987
HALL, S.G. (ed.) *Melito of Sardis, on Pascha and Fragments.* Oxford 1979
HALLEWY, E.E. 'Biblical Midrash and Homeric Exegesis' *Tarbiz* 31 (1961-1962) 157-69; 264-80 (Hebr.)
– *Sharei Ha-Aggadah.* Tel Aviv 1963 (Hebr.)
– *Erkhei Ha-Aggadah Veha-Halakhah.* Tel-Aviv 1979 (Hebr.)
HALLO, W.W. 'Isaiah 28:9-13 and the Ugaritic Abecedaries' *JBL* 77 (1958) 324-38
HAMERTON-KELLY, R.G. 'Some Techniques of Composition in Philo's Allegorical Commentary with special Reference to *De Agricultura* – A Study in the Hellenistic Midrash' in *Jews, Greek and Christians*, 45-56
HAMERTON-KELLY, R.G. - SCROGGS, R. *Jews, Greeks and Christians. Religious Cultures in Late Antiquity. Essays in honour of W.D. Davies.* Leiden 1976
HANHART, R. (ed.) *Maccabaeorum Liber III. SVTG* IX/3, Göttingen 1960
– *Iudith. SVTG* VIII/4, Göttingen 1979
– *Text und Textgeschichte des Buches Judith.* Göttingen 1979
– *Tobit. SVTG* VIII/5, Göttingen 1983
– *Text und Textgeschichte des Buches Tobit.* Göttingen 1984
ḤANSON, A.T. *Studies in Paul's Technique and Theology.* London 1974
– *The Living Utterances of God.* London 1983
HANSON, P.D. *The Dawn of Apocalpytic.* Philadelphia 1975
– 'Rebellion in Heaven, Azazel, and Euhemeristic Heroes in 1 Enoch 6-11' *JBL* 96 (1977) 195-233
HANSON, R.P.C. *Allegory and Event.* London 1959
– 'Biblical Exegesis in the Early Church' *CHB* 1, 412-53
HARAN, M. 'Problems of the Canonization of Scripture' *Tarbiz* 25(1955-1956) 245-71 (Hebr.) (= Leiman, Canon, 227-53)
– *The Song of the Precepts of Aaron ben Manir.* Jerusalem 1974 (= *PIASH* 5:7)
– *Temples and Temple-Service in Ancient Israel.* Oxford 1978; Winona Lake, Ind. 1985
– 'Scribal Workmanship in Biblical Times – The Scroll and the Writings Implements' *Tarbiz* 50 (1980-1981) 65-87 (Hebr.) (partly transl. in *JJS* 33 [1982] 161-73)
– 'Book-Scrolls at the Beginning of the Second Temple Period: The Transition from Papyrus to Skins' *HUCA* 54 (1983) 111-22
– 'Bible Scrolls in Eastern and Western Lands from Qumran to the High Middle Ages' *HUCA* 56 (1985) 21-62)
HARDINGE, L. *The Celtic Church in Britain.* London 1972
HARL, M. (ed.) *Écriture et culture philosophique dans la pensée de Grégoire de Nysse.* Leiden 1971
– *La Bible d'Alexandrie. 1. La Genèse.* Paris 1986
HARL, M. - DE LANGE, N. *Origène, Philocalie 1-20, sur les Écritures, et la Lettre à Africanus sur l'Histoire de Suzanne. SC* 302, Paris 1983
HARL, M. - DORIVAL, G. *La chaine palestinienne sur le psaume 118. SC* 189-90, Paris 1972
HARNACK, A. VON, *Geschichte der altchristlichen Litteratur bis Eusebius. 1 Überlieferung und Bestand, 2 Die Chronologie der altchristlichen Litteratur bis Eusebius* (2 Vols.) Leipzig 1893, 1897, 1904

- *History of Dogma* 1-7. E.T. by N. Buchanan, London 1900 (repr. New York 1961)
- *Bible Reading in the Early Church.* E.T. London 1912
- *Judentum und Judenchristentum in Justins Dialog mit Trypho. TU* 39.1, 2, Leipzig 1913
- *Der kirchengeschichtliche Ertrag der exegetischen Arbeiten des Origenes. TU* 41, 3 und 4, Leipzig 1918-1919
- *Marcion: Das Evangelium vom Fremden Gott.* Leipzig 1924
- 'Das Alte Testament in den paulinischen Briefe' *Sitzungsberichte der Preussischen Akademie der Wissenschaften.* Berlin 1928, 121-41
HARRIS, R. - BURCH, V. *Testimonies* 1-2. Cambridge 1916-1920
HARRIS, R.L. *Inspiration and Canonicity of the Bible.* Grand Rapids 1957
HARRINGTON, D.J. 'The Biblical Text of Pseudo-Philo's *Liber Antiquitatum Biblicarum*' *CBQ* 33 (1971) 1-17
- 'Interpretation of Israel's History: The Testament of Moses as Rewriting of Deut 31-34' *Studies of the Testament of Moses.* G.W.E. Nickelsburg (ed.) Cambridge 1973, 59-68
- 'Palestinian Adaptations of Biblical Narratives and Prophecies' in R.A. Kraft - G.W.E. Nickelsburg, *Early Judaism and its Modern Interpreters* 2, 239-40
- 'The Wisdom of the Scribe According to Ben Sira' in G.W.E. Nickelsburg and J.J. Collins (eds.) *Ideal Figures in Ancient Judaism – Profiles and Paradigms.* Ann Arbor, Michigan 1980
HARRINGTON, D.J. - CAZEAUX, J. *Pseudo-Philon, Les Antiquités Bibliques.* Vol. 1 *SC* 229-30, Paris 1976
HARTMAN, L. *Prophecy Interpreted.* Lund 1966
- *Asking for a Meaning.* Lund 1979
- 'Survey of the Problem of Apocalyptic Genre' in D. Hellholm (ed.) *Apocalypticism in the Mediterrenean World and the Near East.* Tübingen 1983, 333-34
HARVEY, A.E. *Jesus and the Constraints of History.* London 1982
HATCH, E. *Essays in Biblical Greek.* Oxford 1899
HATCH, E. - REDPATH, H.A. *A Concordance to the Septuagint and the Other Greek Versions of the OT (Including the Apocryphal Books).* Oxford 1897 (repr. Graz 1954)
HAWKINS, J.D. 'The Origin and Dissemination of Writing in Western Asia' in P.R.S. Moorey (ed.) *The Origins of Civilization.* Oxford 1979, 128-66
- 'Writing in Anatolia: Imported and Indigenous Systems' *World Archaeology* 17 (1986) 363-75
HAY, D.M. 'Philo's References to Other Allegorists' *Studia Philonica* 6 (1979-1980) 41-76
HAYMAN, A.P. (ed. and tr.) *The Disputation of Sergius the Stylite against a Jew. CSCO* 338-9, Louvain 1973
HAYWARD, R. *Divine Name and Presence: The Memra.* Totowa, New Jersey 1981
HEGERMANN, H. *Jesaja 53 in Hexapla, Targum und Peschitta.* Beitr. zur Förderung chr. Theol. 2. Reihe, 56 Band, Gütersloh 1954
HEIDENHEIM, W. *Bibliotheca Samaritana* 1-3. Leipzig und Weimar 1884-1896, Amsterdam 1971 (in one vol.)
HEINE, R.E. (tr.) *Origen, Homilies on Genesis and Exodus. FC* 71, Washington 1982
- 'Gregory of Nyssa's Apology for Allegory' *VC* 38 (1984) 360-70
HEINEMANN, I. *Philons griechische und jüdische Bildung.* Breslau 1932
- 'Therapeutai' *PW* 2. V. 2 (1934) 2331-46
- 'Josephus' Method in the Presentation of Jewish Antiquities' *Zion* 5 (1940) 180-203 (Hebr.)
- 'The Development of Technical Terms for the Explanation of Scripture' *Leshonenu* 14 (1946) 182-9; 15 (1947) 108-15; 16 (1948) 20-8
- *Darkhei ha-Aggada.* Jerusalem 1942
HEINEMANN, J. 'The Triennial Cycle and the Calender' *Tarbiz* 38 (1963-1964) 362-68
- 'The Triennial Lectionary Cycle' *JJS* 19 (1968) 41-8
- 'Targum Exodus 22:4 and Early Halakhah' *Tarbiz* 38 (1968-1969) 294-6 (Hebr.)
- *Public Sermons in the Talmudic Period.* Jerusalem 1971 (Hebr.)
- '210 Years of Egyptian Exile' *JJS* 22 (1971) 19-30
- 'The Proem in the Aggadic Midrashim: A Form-Critical Study' *Scripta* 22 (Jerusalem 1971) 100-22
- 'Early Halakhah in the Palestinian Targumim' *JJS* 25 (1974) 114-22

- *Aggadah and its Development*. Jerusalem 1974
- *Prayer in the Talmud: Forms and Patterns*. Berlin – New York 1977
- 'On the Attitude of the Sages to Biblical Chronology' in *Studies in Bible and the Ancient Near East Presented to S.E. Loewenstamm*. Jerusalem 1978, 145-52 (Hebr. section)
HEINISCH, P. *Der Einfluss Philos auf die älteste christliche Exegese*. Münster 1908
HELLER, B. 'Grundzüge der Aggada des Flavius Josephus' *MGWJ* 80 (1936) 237-46, 363
- 'Die Scheu vor Unbekanntem, Unbenanntem in Agada und Apokryphen' *MGWJ* 83 (1939) 170-84
HELLER, CH. *Untersuchung über die Peshitta zur gesamten hebräischen Bibel*. Berlin 1911
HELLER, J. 'Grenzen sprachlicher Entsprechung der LXX. Ein Beitrag zur Übersetzungstechnik der LXX auf dem Gebiet der Flexionskategorien' *Mitteilungen des Instituts für Orientforschung* 15 (1969) 234-48
HENGEL, M. 'Anonymität, Pseudepigraphie und "literarische Fälschung" in der Jüdisch-hellenistischen Literatur' in *Pseudepigrapha* 1. Vandoeuvres, Geneva 1972, 234-44
- *Judentum und Hellenismus, Studien zu ihrer Begegnung unter besonderer Berücksichtigung Palästinas bis zur Mitte des 2.Jh. vor Chr*. Tübingen 2nd ed. 1973
- *Judaism and Hellenism: Studies in their Encounter in Palestine During the Early Hellenistic Period* 1-2. Philadelphia 1974
- *Die Zeloten*. Leiden 1976
- *The Son of God*. London 1976
- *The Charismatic Leader and His Followers*. New York 1981
HENNECKE, E. - SCHNEEMELCHER, W. - WILSON, R.MCL. (eds.) *New Testament Apocrypha*. E.T. 1-2, London 1963, 1965
HENRICHS, A. (ed.) *Didymus der Blinde: Kommentar zu Hiob*. PTA 1-2, Bonn 1968
HERCHBERG, A.S. 'Tanning of Leather in the Mishnaic and Talmudic Periods' *Hakedem* 3 (1912) 93-106 (Hebr.)
- *Cultural Life in the Land of Israel in the Mishnaic and Talmudic Periods*. Warsaw 1924
HERR, M.D. 'Continuum in the Chain of Transmission' *Zion* 44 (1979) 43-56 (Hebr.)
- 'The Conception of History among the Sages' *Proceedings of the Sixth World Congress of Jewish Studies* 3 (1977) 129-42 (Hebr.)
ḤESCHEL, A.J. *Theology of Ancient Judaism* 1-2. London – New York 1962-1965
HEYSE, TH. - TISCHENDORF, C. VON, *Biblia Sacra Latina V.T. Hieronymo interprete*. Leipzig 1873
HIDAL, S. *Interpretatio Syriaca: Die Kommentare des heiligen Ephräms des Syrers zu Genesis u. Exodus, mit besonderer Berücksichtung ihrer auslegungsgeschichtlichen Stellung*. Coniectanea Biblica OT, 6, Lund 1974
HIGGER, M. *Massekhet Soferim*. New York 1937
HILDESHEIMER, E. (ed.) *Halakhot Gedolot* 1-2. Jerusalem 1971-80
HIRZEL, L. *De Pentateuchi Versionis Syriacae Quam Peschito Vocant Indole Commentatio Critico-Exegetica*. Leipzig 1825
HIRZEL, R. 'Agraphos Nomos' *ASGW* 20 (1900) 1-18
HÖLSCHER, G. *Die Quellen des Josephus für die Zeit vom Exil bis zum jüdischen Kriege*. Leipzig 1904
- *Kanonisch und Apokryph*. Leipzig 1905
- 'Josephus' *PW* (1916) 1934-2000
HOFFMANN, R. *Marcion: On the Restitution of Christianity*. Chico, CA 1984
HOLLADAY, C.R. 'Theios Aner in Hellenistic Judaism: A Critique of the Use of This Category in New Testament Christology. Missoula, Montana 1977
- *The Fragments from Hellenistic-Jewish Authors, 1: The Historians*. Chico 1983
HOLLANDER, H.W. *Joseph as an Ethical Model in the Testaments of the Twelve Patriarchs*. Leiden 1981
HOLLANDER, H.W. - DE JONGE, M. *The Testaments of the Twelve Patriarchs*. Leiden 1985
HOLZ, T. *Untersuchungen über die alttestamentliche Zitate bei Lukas*. Berlin 1968
HOOKER, M. *The Son of Man in Mark*. London 1967
HORBURY, W. 'The Jewish Revolts under Trajan and Hadrian' forthcoming in *CHJ* 4
HORGAN, M.P. *Pesharim: Qumran Interpretations of Biblical Books*. Washington 1979

HORNEMANN, C.F. *Observationes ad illustrationem doctrinae de Canone Veteris Testamenti ex Philone* (prefixed to his *Specimen Secundum) Copenhagen 1776*

HORST, P.W. VAN DER, 'De Joodse toneelschrijver Ezechiël' *NTT* 36 (1982) 97-112
- 'Moses' Throne Vision in Ezekiel the Dramatist' *JJS* 34 (1983) 21-9
- 'Some Notes on the *Exagoge* of Ezekiel' *Mnemosyne* (ser. IV) 37 (1984) 354-75
- *Chaeremon, Egyptian Priest and Stoic Philosopher. The Fragments collected and translated with explanatory notes.* Leiden 1984
- 'Korte notities over vroeg-joodse epiek' *NTT* 39 (1985) 102-9
- 'Schriftgebruik bij drie vroege joods-hellenistische historici: Demetrius, Artapanus, Eupolemus' *Amsterdamse cahiers voor exegese en bijbelse theologie* 6 (1985) 144-61
- 'Pseudo-Phocylides' in Charlesworth, *OTP* 2, 565-82

HORTON, F.L. Jr. 'Formulas of Introduction in the Qumran Literature' *RQ* 7 (1971) 505-14

HOSPERS, J.H. 'The Present-Day State of Research on the Pešiṭta (since 1948)' in *Verbum, dedicated to H.W. Obbink, Studia Theol. Rheno-Traiectina* 6. ed. by H.W. Obbink and others, Utrecht 1964, 148-57
- 'Some Remarks with regard to the Text and Language of the Old Testament Peshiṭta' in *Von Kanaan bis Kerala. Festschrift J.P.M. van der Ploeg*, ed. by W.C. Delsman and others, Neukirchen-Vluyn 1982, 443-55

HOWARD, G.E. 'The Septuagint: A Review of Recent Studies' *Restoration Quarterly* 13 (1970) 154-64
- 'Kaige Readings in Josephus' *Textus* 8 (1973) 45-54

HOWORTH, H.H. 'The Influence of St. Jerome on the Canon of the Western Church' *JTS* 10 (1909) 481-96; 11 (1909-1910) 321-47; 13 (1911-1912) 1-18

HRUBY, K. 'Le sabbat et sa célébration d'après les sources juives anciennes' *L'Orient Syrien* 8 (1963) 55-86
- 'La Synagogue dans la littérature rabbinique' *L'Orient Syrien* 9 (1964) 473-514
- 'La place des lectures bibliques et la prédication dans la liturgie synagogale ancienne' *La Parole dans la liturgie (Lex Orandi* 48) Paris 1960

HÜBNER, H. 'Gal. 3, 10 und die Herkunft des Paulus' *KuD* 19 (1973) 215-31

HUNT, E.D. *Holy Land Pilgrimage in the Later Roman Empire, A.D. 312-460.* Oxford 1982

HUSKINSON, J.M. *Concordia Apostolorum: Christian Propaganda at Rome in the Fourth and Fifth Centuries. (B.A.R. International Series* 148) Oxford 1982

HYVÄRINEN, K. *Die Übersetzung von Aquila. Coniectanea Biblica* 10 (1977) Lund 1977

IN PRINCIPIO, *Interprétations des premiers versets de la Genèse. Études Augustiniennes*, Paris 1973

ISENBERG, S.R. *Studies in the Jewish Aramaic Translations of the Pentateuch.* Cambridge MA. 1968 (unpubl.)
- 'An Anti-Sadducee Polemic in the Palestinian Targum Tradition' *HTR* 63 (1970) 433-44
- 'On the Jewish-Palestinian Origins of the Peshitta to the Pentateuch' *JBL* 90 (1971) 69-81

ISHOᶜDAD OF MERW, *Commentaire d'Ishoᶜdad de Merw sur l'Ancien Testament.* 1, *Genèse*, ed. by J.M. Vosté and C. van den Eynde, *CSCO* 126, Scriptores Syri, tome 67, Louvain 1950

ISSER, S.J. *The Dositheans: A Samaritan Sect in Late Antiquity.* Leiden 1976

ITALA. ed. by A. Jülicher, W. Matzkov, K. Aland, Berlin 1938-1963; 2nd ed. 1970-1976

ITZCHAKY, E. *The Halacha in Targum Jerushalmi I (Pseudo-Jonathan Ben Uziel) and its Exegetic Methods.* Ramat-Gan 1982 (Ph.D. Diss.; Hebr.)

JACKSON, B.S. 'The Fence-Breaker in Early Jewish Law' *JJS* 25 (1974) 127-29
- *Essays in Jewish and Comparative Legal History.* Leiden 1975

JACOBS, L. *Studies in Talmudic Logic and Methodology.* London 1961
- *Principles of the Jewish Faith.* London 1964
- *The Talmudic Argument. A Study in Talmudic Reasoning and Methodology.* Cambridge 1984

JACOBSON, H. 'Two Studies on Ezekiel the Tragedian' *GRBS* 22 (1981) 167-78
- 'Mysticism and Apocalyptic in Ezekiel the Tragedian' *Illinois Classical Studies* 6 (1981) 272-93
- *The Exagoge of Ezekiel.* Cambridge 1983

JACOBY, F. (ed.) *Die Fragmente der griechischen Historiker* 3A, 1-2. Leiden 1964

JAHN, JOH. *Einleitung in die Göttlichen Bücher des Altes Bundes* 1. 2nd ed. Wien 1802

JAMES, E. 'Ireland and Western Gaul in the Merovingian Period' in D. Whitelock, R. McKitterick and D. Dumville (eds.) *Ireland in Early Medieval Europe: Studies in Memory of Kathleen Hughes*. Cambridge 1982, 362-86

JAMES, M.R. *The Apocryphal New Testament*. Oxford 1924 (repr. with additions 1953)

JANSEN, H. *Kultur und Sprache. Zur Geschichte der alten Kirche im Spiegel der Sprachenentwicklung von Tertullian bis Cyrian*. Nijmegen 1938

JANSMA, T. 'Vijf teksten in de Tora met een dubieuze constructie' *NTT* 12 (1957-1958) 161-79

JASTROW, M. *A Dictionary of the Targumim, the Talmud Babli and Yerushalmi, and the Midrashic Literature*. New York 1903

JAUBERT, A. *Origène, Homélies sur Josué. SC* 71, Paris 1960

– *Clément de Rome, Épitre aux Corinthiens. SC* 167, Paris 1971

JAY, P. *L'exégèse de Saint Jérôme d'après son 'Commentaire sur Isaïe'*. Paris 1985

JEANES, G. 'Early Latin Parallels to the Roman Canon? Possible References to a Eucharistic Prayer in Zeno of Verona' *JTS* N.S. 37 (1986) 427-31

JELLICOE, S. 'The Hesychian Recension Reconsidered' *JBL* 82 (1963) 409-18

– 'The Occasion and Purpose of the Letter of Aristeas: A Re-examination' NTS 12 (1965-1966) 144-50

– *The Septuagint and Modern Study*. Oxford 1968

– *Studies in the Septuagint: Origins, Recensions and Interpretations*. New York 1974

JELLINEK, A. *Bet ha-Midrasch. Sammlung kleiner Midraschim und vermischter Abhandlungen aus der ältern jüdischen Literatur. 1-6 in 2 vols; 3rd ed.* Jerusalem 1967

JENNY, M. 'Cantica' *TRE* 7 (1981) 624-28

JEPSEN, A. 'Bemerkungen zum Danielbuch' *VT* 11 (1961) 386-91

JEREMIAS, G. *Der Lehrer der Gerechtigkeit. (SNT* 2) Göttingen 1963

JEREMIAS, J. *The Parables of Jesus*. New York[6] 1963

– *Abba*. Göttingen 1966 (15-67 = *The Prayers of Jesus*. London 1976, 11-65)

– *The Rediscovery of Bethesda*. Louisville 1966

– 'Paulus als Hillelit' in E.E. Ellis and M. Wilcox (eds.) *Neotestamentica et Semitica. Studies in Honour of Matthew Black*. Edinburgh 1969, 88-94

– *Jerusalem in the Time of Jesus*. London 1969

– *New Testament Theology* I. London 1971

JERVELL, J. *Luke and the People of God*. Minneapolis 1972

JOHANNESSOHN, M. 'Zur Entstehung der Ausdrucksweise der lateinischen Vulgata aus den jüngeren griechischen alttestamentlichen Übersetzungen' *ZNW* 44 (1952-1953) 90-102

JOHNSON, A.R. *Sacral Kingship in Ancient Israel*. Cardiff 1956

– *The One and the Many in the Israelite Conception of God*. Cardiff 1961

– *The Cultic Prophet and Israel's Psalmody*. Cardif 1979

JOHNSON, F. *The Quotations of the New Testament*. London 1896

JOHNSTON, G. *The Spirit-Paraclete in the Gospel of John*. Cambridge 1970

JONAS, H. *The Gnostic Religion: The Message of the Alien God and the Beginnings of Christianity*. 2nd ed. Boston 1963

– 'The Gnostic Syndrome: Typology of its Thought, Imagination, and Mood' in *Philosophical Essays: From Ancient Creed to Technological Man*. Englewood Cliffs, NJ 1974, 263-76

JONES, C. - WAINWRIGHT, G. - YARNOLD, E. (eds.) *The Study of Liturgy*. London 1978

JONGE, M. DE, *Jesus: Stranger from Heaven and Son of God*. Missoula MT 1977

– (ed.) *The Testaments of the Twelve Patriarchs. A critical edition of the Greek text*. Leiden 1978

– Review of E. von Nordheim, *Die Lehre der Alten* 1. *JSJ* 12 (1981) 112-17

JONGELING, B. *A Classified Bibliography of the Finds in the Desert of Judah 1958-1969*. Leiden 1971

JUNOD, E. 'Les attitudes d'Apelles, disciple de Marcion, à l'égard de l'Ancien Testament' *Augustinianum* 22 (1982) 113-33

– 'La formation et la composition de l'Ancien Testament dans l'Église grecque des quatres premiers siècles' in Amsler et al, *Canon*, 105-51

JUYNBOLL, T.G.J. *Chronicon Samaritanum, cui titulus est Liber Josuae*. Leiden 1848

822

KADUSHIN, M. *The Rabbinic Mind*. New York 1952; 2nd ed. New York, Toronto, London 1965

KAESTLI, J.-D. 'L'interpretation du serpent de Genèse 3 dans quelques textes gnostiques et la question de la gnose "ophite"' in J. Ries (ed.) *Gnosticisme et Monde Hellénistique: Actes du Colloque de Louvain-la-Neuve (11-14 mars 1980)*. Louvain 1982, 116-30

KAHANA, A. *The Apocrypha and Pseudepigrapha*. Tel Aviv 1937

KAHLE, P.E. *Textkritische und lexikalische Bemerkungen zum samaritanischen Pentateuchtargum*. Halle a/S 1898

– *Der masoretische Text des Alten Testaments nach der überlieferung der babylonischen Juden*. Leipzig 1902

– *Masoreten des Osten. Die ältesten punktierten Handschriften des Alten Testaments und der Targume*. Leipzig 1913

– 'Untersuchungen zur Geschichte des Pentateuchtextes' *TSK* (1915) 399-439 (= *Opera Minora*. Leiden 1956, 3-37)

– 'Die masoretische Überlieferung des hebräischen Bibeltextes' etc. in: Bauer - Leander, *Historische Grammatik der hebräischen Sprache des Alten Testaments*. Halle 1922, 71-162

– *Masoreten des Westens* 1-2. Stuttgart 1927-1930 (repr. Hildesheim 1967)

– 'Die Septuaginta, Prinzipielle Erwägungen' *Festschrift O. Eissfeldt*. Halle 1947, 161-80

– *The Cairo Genizah*. London 1947 (2nd ed. Oxford 1959)

– 'The new Hebrew Bible, Jerusalem 1953' *VT* 3 (1953) 416-20

– *Opera Minora*. Leiden 1956

– *Der hebräische Bibeltext seit Franz Delitzsch*. Stuttgart 1961

KAISER, O. *Introduction to the Old Testament*. Oxford 1975

KAISER, W.C. *The Use of the Old Testament in the New*. Chicago 1985

KAISER-MINN, H. *Die Erschaffung des Menschen auf den spätantiken Monumenten des 3. und 4. Jahrhunderts*. Munster 1981

KAMLAH, E. 'Frömmigkeit und Tugend: Die Gesetzestypologie des Josephus in cAp 2, 145-295' in O. Betz, K. Haacker and M. Hengel (eds.) *Josephus-Studien*. Göttingen 1974, 220-32

KAMPLING, R. *Das Blut Christi und die Juden: Mt 27, 25 bei den lateinsprachigen christlichen Autoren bis zu Leo dem Grossen*. Münster 1984

KANNENGIESSER, C. 'Jérémie ches les Pères de l'Église' *DS* 8.1 (1974) 889-90

– 'Job chez les Pères *DS* 8.1 (1974) 1218-25

KAPLAN, A. *A Handbook of Jewish Tought*. New York 1983

KAPPELMACHER, A. 'Zur Tragoedie der hellenistischen Zeit' *Wiener Studien* 44 (1924-1925) 69-86

KAPPLER, W. *Maccabaeorum Liber I*. SVTG IX/1, Göttingen 1967

KARMELI-WEINBERGER, M. *Sefer Wesayif*. Jerusalem, New York 1967

KASHER, M.M. *Encyclopedia of Biblical Interpretation* 1. New York 1953

– *Torah Shelemah. Talmudic-Midrashic Encyclopedia of the Pentateuch* 1-34. Jerusalem 1961-1981 (hebr.)

KASSER, R. 'Citations des grands prophètes bibliques dans les textes gnostiques coptes' in M. Krause, *Essays*, 56-64

KASSER, R. (et al.) *Tractatus Tripartitus*. Bern 1973

KATZ, P. *Philo's Bible*. Cambridge 1950

– 'The Old Testament Canon in Palestine and Alexandria' *ZNW* 47 (1956) 191-217; 49 (1958) 233 (= Leiman, 72-98)

– 'Septuagint Studies in the Mid-Century. Their Links with the Past and their Present Tendencies' in W.D. Davies and D. Daube (eds.) *The Background to the NT and Its Eschatology*. Cambridge 1956, 176-208

KATZ, S.T. 'Issues in the Separation of Judaism and Christianity After 70 C.E.: A Reconsideration' *JBL* 103 (1984) 43-76

KAUFMAN, S.A. 'The Temple Scroll and Higher Criticism' *HUCA* 53 (1982) 29-43

KAUFMANN, Y. *The Religion of Israel*. Chicago 1960 (E.T. by M. Greenberg)

– *History of the Religion of Israel* 1-4. Tel-Aviv 1937-56

KAULEN, F. *Geschichte der Vulgata*. Mainz 1868

823

- *Handbuch zur Vulgata. Eine systematische Darstellung ihres lateinischen Sprachcharakters.* Mainz 1870
KEBLE, J. *On the Mysticism Attributed to the Early Fathers of the Church.* Oxford 1839 (repr. 1868)
- (tr.) *Five Books of S. Irenaeus, Bishop of Lyons, Against Heresies.* Library of the Fathers 42, Oxford 1872
KEDAR, B. 'Divergent Hebrew Readings in Jerome's Isaiah' *Textus* 4 (1964) 176-210
- *The Vulgate as a Translation. Some Semantic And Syntactical Aspects of Jerome's Version of the Hebrew Bible.* Jerusalem 1968 (Diss. Hebrew Univ.)
- 'Die Wiedergabe des hebräischen Kausativs in der Vulgata' *ZAW* 85 (1973) 196-219
KEIL, C.F. *Lehrbuch der historisch-kritischen Einleitung in die kanonischen und apokryphischen Schriften des Alten Testamentes³.* Frankfurt a/M 1873
KELLY, J.N.D. (ed.) *Rufinus' Commentary on the Apostles Creed.* (Ancient Christian Writers 20) Westminster (Md) 1955
- 'The Bible and the Latin Fathers' in D.E. Nineham (ed.) *The Church's Use of the Bible*, 41-56
- *Jerome.* London 1975
- *Early Christian Doctrines.* 5th ed. London 1977
KENNEDY, H.A.A. *Sources of New Testament Greek or the Influence of the Septuagint on the Vocabulary of the New Testament.* Edinburgh 1895
- 'Latin Versions, the Old' *DB* 3, 47-62
KENNEDY, J. *The Note-line in the Hebrew Scriptures commonly called Pāsēq or Pesiq.* Edinburgh 1903
KENNICOTT, B. *Vetus Testamentum Hebraicum cum variis lectionibus* 1-2. Oxonii (Oxford) 1776-1780. Appended to the second volume is *Dissertatio generalis in Vetus Testamentum Hebraicum; cum variis lectionibus ex codicibus manuscriptis et impressis.* Oxonii 1780
KENYON, F.G. *The Text of the Greek Bible.* 2nd ed. London 1949
- *Books and Readers in Ancient Greece and Rome.* 2nd ed. Oxford 1951
KERN, O. (ed.) *Orphicorum fragments.* Berlin 1963 (= 1922)
KERRIGAN, A. *St. Cyril of Alexandria, Interpreter of the Old Testament.* Rome 1952
KIM, S. *The 'Son of Man' as the Son of God.* Tübingen 1983
- *The Origin of Paul's Gospel.* Tübingen 2nd ed. 1984
KIPPENBERG, H.G. *Garizim und Synagoge. Traditionsgeschichtliche Untersuchungen zur samaritanischen Religion der aramäischen Periode.* Berlin, New York 1971
KIRCHEIM, R. *Karmei Shomron: Petiḥah le Maschet Kutim.* Frankfurt a/M 1851, Jerusalem 1970 (includes a translation of the Samaritan Arabic *Book of Joshua*)
KITCHEN, K.A. 'The Aaramaic of Daniel' in D.J. Wiseman (ed.) *Notes on some Problems in the Book of Daniel.* London 1965, 31-79
KITTEL, G. - FRIEDRICH, G. *Theologisches Wörterbuch zum Neuen Testament.* Stuttgart 1933-1979 (E.T. Grand Rapids 1964-1974)
KITTEL, R. *Über die Notwendigkeit und Möglichkeit einer neuen Ausgabe der hebräischen Bibel. Studien und Erwägungen.* Leipzig 1902
KLAUSER, T. *Gesammelte Arbeiten zur Liturgiegeschichte, Kirchengeschichte und christlichen Archäologie.* Münster 1974
KLAUSNER, J. *The Messianic Idea in Israel.* London 1956
KLEIN, M.L. 'The Extant Sources of the Fragmentary Targum to the Pentateuch' *HUCA* 46 (1975) 115-37
- 'Converse Translation: A Targumic Technique' *Biblica* 57 (1976) 515-37
- 'The Preposition QDM ("Before"): A Pseudo-Anti-Anthropomorphism in the Targums' *JTS* N.S. 30 (1979) 502-7
- *The Fragment-Targums of the Pentateuch* 1-2. Roma 1980
- 'The Translation of Anthropomorphisms and Anthropopathisms in the Targumim' *SVT* 32 (1981) 162-77
- 'Four Notes on the Triennial Lectionary Cycle' *JJS* 32 (1981) 65-73
- 'Associative and Complementary Translation in the Targumim' *Eretz-Israel* 16 (1982) 134-40
- *Anthropomorphisms and Anthropopathisms in the Targumim of the Pentateuch.* Jerusalem 1982 (Hebr.)

824

KLEIN, R.W. 'Ezra and Nehemiah in Recent Studies' in F.M. Cross (ed.) *Magnalia Dei. In Memoriam G.E. Wright.* Garden City, N.Y. 1976, 361-76

KLEIN, S. 'R. Shim'on the Scribe of Tarbant' in *Mincha LeDavid – Collected Essays in Jewish Wissenschaft presented to R. David Yellin on his Seventieth Birthday.* Jerusalem 1935, 96-9 (Hebr.)

KLEINKNECHT H. 'Der Logos in Griechentum und Hellenismus' *ThWZN* 4, 76-89

KLUMEL, M. *Mischpâtîm. Ein samaritanisch-arabischer Commentar zu Ex. 21-22,15.* Berlin 1902

KNAUER, G.N. *Die Psalmenzitate in Augustins Konfessionen.* Göttingen 1955

KNIBB, M.A. *The Ethiopic Book of Enoch 1-2.* Oxford 1978

– (ed.) *The Qumran Community.* Cambridge 1987

KNIGHT, D.A. *Rediscovering the Traditions of Israel. The Development of the Traditio – Historical Research of the Old Testament, with Special Consideration of Scandinavian Contributions.* Missoula, Montana, 1975

KNIGHT, G.W. *The Faithful Sayings in the Pastoral Epistles.* Kampen 1968

KNOX, W.L. 'Abraham and the Quest for God' *HTR* 28 (1935) 55-60

KOBELSKI, P.J. *Melchisedek and Melchireša.* Washington, DC 1981

KOCH, K. *The Rediscovery of Apocalyptic.* London 1981

KOEHLER, L. - BAUMGARTNER, W. *Hebräisches und Aramäisches Lexikon zum Alten Testament* 2. Leiden 1974

KÖNIG, F.E. *Historisch-kritisches Lehrgebäude der hebräischen Sprache* 1. Leipzig 1881

KOENIG, J. *L'Herméneutique analogique du Judaïsme antique d'après les témoins textuels d'Isaïe.* SVT 33, Leiden 1982

KOETZSCHE-BREITENBRUCH, L. *Die neue Katakombe an der Via Latina in Rom. (Jahrbuch für Antike und Christentum,* Ergänzungsband 4) Münster 1976

KOHLER, K. 'The Halakhik Portions in Josephus' Antiquities (IV, 8, 5-43)' in Kohler, *Studies, Addresses, and Personel Papers.* New York 1931, 69-85

– 'Clementina' *JE* 4, 114-6

KOHN, S. *Samaritanische Studien.* Breslau 1868

– *Zur Sprache, Literatur und Dogmatik der Samaritaner.* Leipzig 1876

– 'Die Samaritanische Pentateuchübersetzung nach der Ausgabe von Petermann und Vollers' *ZDMG* 47 (1893) 626-97

KOHUT, A. (ed.) *Aruch Completum.* New York 1926

KOMLOSH, Y. *The Bible in the Light of the Aramaic Translations.* Jerusalem 1973 (Hebr.)

KOOIJ, A. VAN DER, *Die alten Textzeugen des Jesajabuches.* OBO 35, Freiburg, Göttingen 1981

– 'De Tekst van Samuel en het tekstkritisch Onderzoek' *NT* 36 (1982) 177-204

– 'On the Place of Origin of the Old Greek of Psalms' *VT* 33 (1983) 67-74

KOSCHORKE, K. *Die Polemik der Gnostiker gegen das kirchliche Christentum.* Leiden 1978

KOSMALA, H. 'Jerusalem' *BHH* 2 (1964) 820-50

KOSTER, M.D. *The Peshitta of Exodus. The Development of its Text in the Course of Fifteen Centuries. Studia Semitica Neerlandica* 19, Assen, Amsterdam 1977

KOTTJE, R. *Studien zum Einfluss des Alten Testaments auf Recht und Liturgie des frühen Mittelalters.* Bonn 1964

KRAGERUD, A. *Die Hymnen der Pistis Sophia.* Oslo 1967

KRAUS, H.J. *Geschichte der historisch-kritischen Erforschung des Alten Testaments²*. Neukirchen-Vluyn 1969

KRAUSE, M. 'Das literarische Verhältnis des Eugnostosbriefes zur Sophia Jesu Christi' in Mulles, *Festschrift für Theodor Klausner.* Münster 1964, 215-23

– 'Aussagen über das Alten Testament in z.T. bisher unveröffentlichten gnostischen Texten aus Nag Hammadi' in *Ex Orbe Religionum: Studia G. Widengren* 1. Leiden 1972, 449-56

– (ed.) *Essays on the Nag Hammadi Texts in Honour of Pahor Labib.* Leiden 1975

KRAUSE, M. - LABIB, P. *Die Drei Versionen des Apokryphon des Johannes im koptischen Museum zu Alt-Kairo.* Wiesbaden 1962.

– *Gnostische und hermetische Schriften aus Codex II und Codex VI.* Glückstadt 1971

825

KRAUSS, S. 'Moses the Great Scribe of Israel' *Hagoren* 7 (1908) 29-34 (Hebr.)
- *Talmudische Archaeologie* 3. Leipzig 1912, 131-98; 300-36
- 'Church Fathers' *JE* 4, 80-6
- 'Jerome' *JE* 7, 115-8
KRONHOLM, T. *Motifs from Genesis I – XI in the Genuine Hymns of Ephrem the Syrian with Particular Reference to the Influence of Jewish Exegetical Tradition. Coniectanea Biblica* OT 11, Lund 1978
KRUSE-BLINKENBERG, L. The Pešiṭta of the Book of Malachi' *Studia Theol.* 20 (1966) 95-119
KUECHLER, M. *Frühjüdische Weisheitstraditionen.* Göttingen 1979
KUENEN, A. (ed.) *Libri Exodi et Levitici secundum Arabicam Pentateuchi Samaritani Versionem ab Abŭ-Sa'ido conscriptam.* Leiden 1854
- 'De stamboom van den masoretischen tekst des O. Testaments' in *Verslagen en Mededeelingen der Kon. Akademie van Wetenschappen, Afd. Letterkunde,* 2nd series, 3. Amsterdam 1873, 289-339 (German Translation in: *Gesammelte Abhandlungen zur biblischen Wissenschaft;* Freiburg i.Br., Leipzig 1894, 82-124)
- 'Über die Männer der grossen Synagoge' (1876) in *Gesammelte Abhandlungen zur biblischen Wissenschaft,* 125-69
KUHN, H.G.*Enderwartung und Gegenwärtiges Heil.* Göttingen 1966
KUIPER, G.J. *The Pseudo-Jonathan Targum and its Relation to Targum Onkelos.* Rome 1972
KÜMMEL, W.G. *Promise and Fulfillment.* London 1957
- 'Schriftauslegung' *RGG*³ 5 (1961) 1519
- *The Theology of the New Testament.* Nashville, New York, Londen 1974
KURFESS, A. 'Christian Sibyllines' in Hennecke, Schneemelcher and Wilson, *New Testament Apocrypha 2,* 703-45
- *La Bible et les Pères, Colloque de Strasbourg.* Paris 1971
KUTSCHER, E.Y. 'The Language of the Genesis Apocryphon' *Scripta* 4 (1958) 1-35
- 'Current Trends in Linguistics' in T.A. Sebock (ed.) *Linguistics in South-West Asia and North-Africa.* (6) 1970, 347-412
KVANVIG, S.H. 'Henoch und der Menschensohn: Das Verhältnis von Hen 14 zu Dan 7' *ST* 38 (1984) 101-33
KVIDELAND, K. 'Elohims Himmelfahrt' *Temenos* 10 (1974) 68-78
LA BONNARDIERE, A. *Biblia Augustiniana, A.T.* Paris 1960– (*Le Deutéronome* 1967; *Livres historiques* 1960; *Les douze Petits Prophètes* 1964; *Le Livre de la Sagesse* 1970; *Le Livre de Jérémie* 1972; *Le Livre des Proverbes* 1975)
LABUSCHAGNE, C.J. 'The Pattern of the Divine Speech Formulas in the Pentateuch' *VT* 32 (1982) 268-96
- 'De literairkritische methode' in *Inleiding tot de studie van het Oude Testament.* A.S. van der Woude (ed.) Kampen 1986, 102-27
LADOUCEUR, D.J. 'Masada: A Consideration of the Literary Evidence' *GRBS* 21 (1980) 245-60
LAGARDE, P. *Anmerkungen zur griechischen übersetzung der Proverbien.* Leipzig 1863
- *Librorum Veteris Testamenti canonicorum pars prior graece.* Göttingen 1883
- *Mittheilungen I.* Göttingen 1884
LAKE, K. (ed.) *Eusebius, the Ecclesiastical History* 1-2. London 1953
LAMB, J.A. 'The Place of the Bible in the Liturgy' *CHB* 1, 563-86
LAMIRANDE, E. 'Étude bibliographique sur les Pères de l'église et l'aggadah' *VC* 21 (1967) 1-11
LAMPE, A. 'Exemplum' *RAC* 6 (1966) 1229-57
LAMPE, G.W.H. *A Patristic Greek Lexicon.* Oxford 1961
- 'Church Discipline and the Interpretation of the Epistles to the Corinthians' in W.H. Farmer, C.F.D. Moule, R.R. Niebuhr (eds.) *Christian History and Interpretation: Studies Presented to John Knox.* Cambridge 1967, 337-61
- (ed.) *The Cambridge History of the Bible.* 2. Cambridge 1969
- 'The Exposition and Exegesis of Scripture to Gregory the Great' *CHB* 2, 155-83
- *God as Spirit.* Oxford 1977

LAMPE, G.W.H. - WOOLLCOMBE, K.J. *Essays on Typology*. London 1957
LANDERSDORFER, S. *Ausgewählte Schriften syrischer Dichter*. Kempten, Münich 1912
LANGLAMET, F. 'Le Seigneur dit à Moïse. Une clé de lecture des divisions massorétiques' *Mélanges M. Delcor (AOAT)* Neukirch 1985
LARCHER, C. *Le Livre de la Sagesse ou La Sagesse de Salomon* 1-2. Paris 1983–
LATTKE, M. 'Haggadah' *RAC* 13 (1986) 328-60
– 'Halachah' *RAC* 13 (1986) 372-402
LAUTERBACH, J.Z. 'The Ancient Jewish Allegorists in Talmud and Midrash' *JQR* N.S. 1 (1910-1911) 291-333; 503-31
– 'Midrash and Mishna' *JQR* 5 (1914-1915) 503-27; 6 (1915-1916) 23-95, 303-23 (= *Rabbinic Essays*. Cincinatti 1951, 163-256)
LAWSON, J. *The Biblical Theology of Saint Irenaeus*. London 1948
LAYTON, B. 'The Hypostasis of the Archons, or The Reality of the Rulers' *HTR* 67 (1974) 351-425; 69 (1976) 31-101
– (ed.) *The Rediscovery of Gnosticism: Proceedings of the International Conference on Gnosticism at Yale 1978* 1-2. Leiden 1981-1982
LEANZA, S. (ed.) *Procopii Gazaei Catena in Ecclesiasten necnon Pseudochrysostomi Commentarius in eundem Ecclesiasten*. CCG 4, Turnhout 1978
LE BOULLUEC, A. *Clément d'Alexandrie, Stromate V, 2, Commentaire*. SC 279, Paris 1981
LEBRAM, J.C.H. 'Der Idealstaat der Juden' in Betz-Haacker – Hengel, *Josephus-Studien*, 233-53
– 'Die literarische Form des Vierten Makkabäerbuches' *VC* 28 (1974) 81-96
LECLERQ, H. 'Hymnes' *DACL* (1925) 2826-2928
LE DÉAUT, R. 'Traditions targumiques dans le corpus paulinien?' *Biblica* 42 (1961) 28-48
– *La nuit pascale. Essai sur la signification de la Pâque juive à partir du Targum d'Exode XII 42.* Rome 1963 (*Analecta Biblica* 22, 2nd ed. Rome 1975)
– *Introduction à la littérature targumique*.
– 'Lévitique XXII 26 - XXIII 44 dans le Targum Palestinien' *VT* 18 (1968) 458-71
– 'A propos d'une définition du midrash' *Biblica* 50 (1969) 395-413
– 'Une phénomène spontané de l'herméneutique juive ancienne: le "targumisme" ' *Biblica* 52 (1971) 505-25
– 'La tradition juive ancienne et l'exégèse chrétienne primitive' *RHPR* 51 (1971) 31-50
– *Targum du Pentateuque* 1-5. Paris 1978-1981 (*SC* 245, 256, 261, 271, 282)
– 'A propos du Targum d'Exode 13, 18: La Tôrah, arme secrète d'Israel' in N. Carrez et alli (eds.) *De la Tôrah au Messie. Mélanges H. Cazelles*. Paris 1981, 525-33
LEE, F. 'Prolegomena' in Grabe, *Vetus Testamentum juxta LXX Interpretes* 1-2. Oxford 1707-20
LEE, J.A.L. 'A Lexical Study of the Septuagint Version of the Pentateuch' *Septuagint and Cognate Studies* 14 (1983) 85-117
LEE, TH.R. *Studies in the Form of Sirach 44-50*. Atlanta 1986
LEHMANN, H.J. 'An Important Text Preserved in MS. Ven. Mekh. No.873, dated A.D. 1299 (Eusebius of Emesa's Commentary on Historical Writings of the Old Testament)' in T.J. Samuelian - M.E. Stone (eds.) *Medieval Armenian Culture*. Chico 1984, 142-60
LEIMAN, S.Z. *The Canon and Masorah of the Hebrew Bible: an Introductory Reader*. New York 1974
– *The Canonization of Hebrew Scripture: The Talmudic and Midrashic Evidence*. Hamden, CT 1976
– 'Inspiration and Canonicity (Reflections on the Formation of the Biblical Canon)' in E.P. Sanders (ed.), *Jewish and Christian Self-Definition* 2, 56-63
LEISEGANG, H. *Der heilige Geist*. Leipzig 1919
– 'Sophia' *PW* 3, 1 pp. 1019-39
LEKSIKON MIKRA'I 1-2. Tel Aviv 1965
LEMAIRE, A. *Les Ecoles et la Formation de la Bible dans l'ancien Israël*. Fribourg 1981
– 'Une inscription paleo-hébraique sur grenade en ivoire' *RB* 88 (1981) 236-9
LE MOYNE, J. *Les Sadducéens*. (*Études Bibliques*) Paris 1972
LERCH, D. *Isaaks Opferung christlich gedeutet*. Tübingen 1950
LESHEM, H. *Shabbat and Jewish Festivals* 1-3. Tel Aviv 1962-1969 (Hebr.)

LESKY, A. *Geschichte der griechischen Literatur*. Bern 1971[3]
LEVEEN, J. *The Hebrew Bible in Art*. London 1944
LEVENE, A. *The Early Syrian Fathers on Genesis*. London 1951
LEVIAS, C. 'Masorah' *JE* 8 (New York, London 1904) 365
LEVIN, B.M. *Trésor des Divergences de Coutume*. Jerusalem 1942
LEVINE, B.A. 'Damascus Document IX, 17-22: A New Translations and Comments' *RQ* 8 (1973) 195-6
- 'The Temple Scroll: Aspects of its Historical Provenance and Literary Character' *BASOR* 232 (1978) 5-23
- 'From the Aramaic Enoch Fragments: The Semantics of Cosmography' *JJS* 33 (1982) 316-26
- 'The Balaam Inscription from Deir 'Alla: Historical Aspects' *Biblical Archaeology Today*. Jerusalem 1985, 326-39
LEVINE, E. 'The Syriac version of Genesis IV 1-16' *VT* 26 (1976) 71-8
LEVY, B.B. *Targum Neophyti 1, A Textual Study* 1. New York, London 1986
LÉVY, I. 'Moïse en Éthiopie' *REJ* 53 (1907) 201-11
- *La Légende de Pythagore de Grèce en Palestine*. Paris 1927
LEVY, J. *Neuhebräisches und chaldäisches Wörterbuch über die Talmudim und Midrashim* 3. Leipzig 1883
LEWIS, J.P. 'What do we mean by Jabneh' *JBR* 32 (1964) 125-32 (= Leiman, *Canon and Masorah*, 254-61)
LIDDELL, H.G. - SCOTT, R. *Greek-English Lexicon*. Oxford 1968
LIEBERMAN, S. *About the Palestinian Talmud*. Jerusalem 1929 (Hebr.)
- 'Ktoveth Uzziahu vetoratan shel rishonim' *Tarbiz* 4 (1933) 292-3 (Hebr.)
- *Greek in Jewish Palestine*. New York 1942
- *Hellenism in Jewish Palestine*. New York 1950 (2nd ed. New York 1962)
LIETZMANN, H. 'Hieronymus' *PW* 16 (1913) 1565-81
- *A History of the Early Church*, 3, *From Constantine to Julian*. E.T. London 1950; 4, *The Ezra of the Church Fathers*. E.T. London 1950
LIGHTFOOT, J.B. (ed.) *The Apostolic Fathers*. *1, S. Clement of Rome* 1-2, 2nd ed. London 1890; 2. *S. Ignatius, S Polycarp* 1-3, 2nd ed. London 1889
LINDARS, B. *New Testament Apologetic*. London 1961
LINDENBERGER, J.M. 'Ahiqar' in Charlesworth, *OTP* 2, 498-507
LIPSCHÜTZ, L. *Der Bibeltext der tiberischen Masoretenschulen: Ben Ascher - Ben Naftali*. Bonn 1935
- 'Mishael ben Uzziel's Treatise on the Differences between Ben Asher and Ben Naphtali' *Textus* 2 (1962) 1-58 (Hebr.)
- 'Kitāb al Khilaf. The Book of the Hillufim. Mishael ben Uzziel's Treatise on the Differences between Ben Asher and Ben Naphtali' *Textus* 4 (1964) 1-29
LITTLEDALE, R.F. *A Commentary on the Song of Songs from Ancient and Mediaeval Sources*. London 1869
LOCK, W. 'Verse-Writers' *DCB* 4, 1108-16
- *John Keble*. London 1892
LOEWE, R. 'The Jewish Midrashim and Patristic and Scholastic Exegesis of the Bible' *SP* 1 (1957) 492-514
- 'The "Plain" Meaning of Scripture in Early Jewish Exegesis' *Papers of the Institute of Jewish Studies*. London (1964) 140-85
LOGAN, A. 'The Jealousy of God: Exodus 20:5 in Gnostic and Rabbinic Theology' in *Studia Biblica* 1978, 1, *Papers on Old Testament and Related Themes*. Sheffield 1979, 197-203
LONGENECKER, R. *Biblical Exegesis in the Apostolic Period*. Grand Rapids 1975
LOWY, S. *The Principles of Samaritan Bible Exegesis*. Leiden 1977
LUCCHESI, E. *L'usage de Philon dans l'oeuvre exégétique de Saint Ambroise*. Leiden 1977
LUDLOW, J.M. 'Digamy' *DCA* 551-7
LUPIERI, E. *Il cielo e il mio trono: Isaia 40,12 e 66,1 nella tradizione testimonaria*. Rome 1980
LURIA, B.Z. *From Yanai to Herod - Studies in the History of the Second Temple Period*. Jerusalem 1974 (Hebr.)

LUZ, U. *Das Geschichtsverständnis des Paulus.* München 1980 (1968)
- 'Jesus und die Pharisäer' *Judaica* 38 (1982) 229-46
MAAS, P. - TRYPANIS, C.A. (ed.) *Sancti Romani Melodi Cantica*, 1, *Cantica Genuina.* Oxford 1963; 2, *Cantica Dubia.* Berlin 1970
MACDERMOT, V. *Pistis Sophia.* Leiden 1978
MACDONALD, J. 'Comprehensive and Thematic Reading of the Law by the Samaritans' *JJS* 10 (1959) 65-74
- *Memar Marqah. The Teaching of Marqah.* Berlin 1963
- *The Theology of the Samaritans.* London 1964
- *The Samaritans Chronicle No. II (or: Sepher ha-Yamim) From Joshua to Nebuchadnezzar.* Berlin 1969
MACK, B.L. 'Under the shadow of Moses. Authorship and Authority in Hellenistic Judaism' *SBL Seminar Papers 1982.* Chico 1982, 299-318
MACLEAN, A.J. 'Hymns (Syriac Christian)' *ERE* 7 (1914) 12-15
MACLEOD, C.W. 'Allegory and Mysticism in Origen and Gregory of Nyssa' and 'The Preface to Gregory of Nyssa's *Life of Moses*' reprinted (with addenda) from *JTS* N.S. 22 (1971) 362-79; 33 (1982) 183-91, in C.W. Macleod, *Collected Essays.* Oxford 1983, 309-26, 329-37
MACRAE, G.W. 'Miracle in *The Antiquities* of Josephus' in *Miracles: Cambridge Studies in Their Philosophy and History*, ed. by C.F.d. Moule, London 1965, 127-47
- 'Apocalypse of Adam' in Charlesworth, *OTP* 1, 707-19
MACUCH, R. *Grammatik des samaritanischen Aramäisch.* Berlin, New York 1982
MAGER, H. *Die Peschittho zum Buche Josua. Freiburger Theologische Studien* 19. Freiburg i/Br 1916
MAIER, J. 'Jüdische Faktoren bei der Entstehung der Gnosis?' in Tröger, *Altes Testament*, 239-58
- ' "Siehe, ich mach(t)e dich klein unter den Völkern": Zum rabbinischen Assoziationshorizont von Obadja 2' in *Künder des Wortes: Beiträge zur Theologie der Propheten. Joseph Schreiner zum 60. Geburtstag.* Würzburg 1982, 203-15
MALINA, B.J. *The Palestinian Manna Tradition: The Manna Tradition in the Palestinian Targums and Its Relationship to the New Testament Writings.* Leiden 1968
MANDELBAUM, B. *Pesikta de Rav Kahana.* New York 1962
MANDL, A. *Die Peshittha zu Hiob nebst einem Anhang über ihr Verhältnis zu LXX und Targum.* Budapest 1892
MANGENOT, E. 'Vulgate' *Dictionnaire de la Bible* 5, 2456-99
MANN, J. 'Anan's Liturgy and his Half Reading of the Law' *Journal of Jewish Lore and Philosophy* 1 (1919) 329-53
- *The Bible as Read and Preached in the Old Synagogue* 1. Cincinatti 1940 (New York 1971 with foreword by B.Z. Wacholder) 2 (ed. by I. Sonne) Cincinatti 1966
MANSOOR, M. *The Thanksgiving Hymns.* Leiden 1961
MANTEL, H.D. 'The Soferim' in M. Avi-Yona and Z. Baras (eds.) *The World History of the Jewish People – Society and Religion in the Second Temple Period.* Jerusalem 1977, 52-7
MAORI, Y. 'Biblical citations in Talmudic literature' *Machanaim* 70 (1962) 90-99 (Hebr.)
- 'On the Relationship of Pseudo-Jonathan to Halakhic Sources' *Te'udah* 3 (1973) 235-50 (Hebr.)
- *The Peshitta Version of the Pentateuch in its Relation to the Sources of Jewish Exegesis.* Jerusalem 1975, 69f (unpubl.)
MARCOVICH, M. 'The Naassene Psalm in Hyppolytus (*Haer.* 5.10.2)' in Layton, *Rediscovery* 2, 770-8
MARGALIOTH, M. *Ha-hilukim she-bein anshei ha-mizrah u-benei Erets Yisrael.* Jerusalem 1938
- (ed.) *Entsiklopedya le-Hakhmei ha-Talmud we-ha-Ge'onim* 1-2. Tel Aviv 1960
- (ed.) *Sepher HaRazim.* Jerusalem 1966 (Hebr.)
MARGALIOTH, R. 'Abbreviations and Shortenings' *Sinai* 50 (1962) 397-404 (Hebr.)
MARGOLIOTH, E. 'The Term "DRŠ" in the Talmud and Midrashim' *Leshonenu* 20 (1956) 50-61 (Hebr.)
MARGOLIS, M.L. *The Hebrew Scriptures in the Making.* Philadelphia 1922
- *The Book of Joshua in Greek* 1-4. Paris 1931-1938
MARKS, J.H. *Der textkritische Wert des Psalt. Hieronymi iuxta Hebraeos.* Winterthur 1956

829

MARMORSTEIN, A. 'Agada u. Kirchenväter' *Encylopaedia Judaica* 1 (Berlin 1928) 972-9
- *Studies in Jewish Theology.* London 1950
MARQUART, J. *Osteuropäische und ostasiatische Streifzüge.* Leipzig 1903
MARROU, H.I. *A History of Education in Antiquity.* E.T. by G. Lamb. New York 1956
MARSHALL, I.H. *The Origins of New Testament Christology.* Leicester 1976
MARTIN, L.H. 'Josephus' Use of *Heimarmene* in the *Jewish Antiquities* XIII, 171-3' *Numen* 28 (1981) 127-37
MARTIN, M. *The Scribal Character of the Dead Sea Scrolls.* Louvain 1958
MARTOLA, N. *Capture and Liberation.* Abo 1984
MAYBAUM, S. 'Über die Sprache des Targum zu den Sprüchen und dessen Verhältniss zum Syrer' in *Archiv. f. Wiss. Erf. des AT.* ed. by A. Merx, Bd II,1 (1871) 66-93
MAYER, G. 'Aspekte des Abrahambildes in der hellenistisch-jüdischen Literatur' *Evang. Theol.* 32 (1972) 118-27
- *Index Philoneus.* Berlin, New York 1974
MAYER, L.A. *Bibliography of the Samaritans.* London 1964
MAYOR, J.E.B. *Q. Septimi Florentis Tertulliani Apologeticus.* Cambridge 1917
MAZAR, A. 'The Aquaducts of Jerusalem' in Y. Yadin (ed.) *Jerusalem Revealed.* Jerusalem 1975, 79-84
MAZAR, B. 'The Philistines and the Rise of the Israelite and Tyrian Kingdoms' *Canaan and Israel - Historical Essays.* Jerusalem 1974, 152-73 (Hebr.)
- 'The Aramean Kingdom and Its Relation with Israel' *ibid.* 245-69 (Hebr.)
MCCARTHY, C. *The Tiqqune Sopherim and Other Theological Corrections in the Massoretic Text of the Old Testament.* Freiburg, Göttingen 1981
- 'Emendations of the Scribes' *IDBS*, 263f
MCHARDY, W.D. Review of Levene, *Syrian Fathers. JTS* N.S. 3 (1952) 262-4
MCKANE, W. *Proverbs: A New Approach.* London 1970
- 'Observations on the Tiķķûnê – Sôp̄e rîm' in *On Language, Culture and Religion: in Honor Of E.A. Nida.* The Hague, Paris 1974, 53-77
MCKELVEY, R.J. *The New Temple.* Oxford 1969
MCNAMARA, M. *Targum and Testament.* Shannon, Grand Rapids 1972
-, *The New Testament and the Palestinian Targums to the Pentateuch.* (*Analecta Biblica* 27a) Rome 1978
MCNEIL, B. 'Avircius and the Song of Songs' *VC* 31 (1977) 23-34
MEADE, D.G. *Pseudonimity and Canon.* Tübingen 1986
MECHINEAU, L. 'Latines (Versions)' *Dictionnaire de la Bible* 4, 96-123
MEEKS, W.A. *The Prophet-King. Moses Traditions and the Johannine Christology.* Leiden 1967
- 'Moses as God and King' in J. Neusner (ed.) *Religions in Antiquity. Essays in Memory of E.R. Goodenough.* Leiden 1968, 354-71
MEEKS, W.A. - WILKEN, R.L. (eds.) *Jews and Christians in the First Four Centuries of the Common Era.* Missoula 1978
MÉHAT, A. 'Clément d'Alexandrie et les sens de l'écriture, I er Stromate, 176,1 et 179,3' in *Epektasis, Mélanges Daniélou.* Paris 1972, 355-66
- *Origène, Homélies sur les Nombres.* (to form *SC* 29)
MEIJERING, E.P. *Tertullian Contra Marcion: Gotteslehre in der Polemik. Adversus Marcionem 1-2.* Leiden 1977
MELAMED, E.Z. 'Josephus and Maccabees I: A Comparison' *Eretz Israel* 1 (1951) 122-30 (Hebr.)
- *Pirkei Mavo le-Sifrut ha-Talmud.* Jerusalem 1973
- *Bible Commentators 1-2.* 2nd enlarged ed. Jerusalem 1978 (Hebr.)
MENDELSON, A. *Secular Education in Philo of Alexandria.* Cincinatti 1982
MERCATI, G. *Psalterii Hexapli Reliquiae.* Cittá del Vaticano 1958
MEREDITH, A. 'The Answer to Jewish Objections (*De Tridui Spatio* p. 294.14-298.18)' in Spira - Klock (eds.) *The Easter Sermons of Gregory of Nyssa*, 293-303
MERENTITIS, K.L. *Ὁ Ἰουδαῖος λογιος Ἀρτάπανος καὶ τὸ Ἔργον αὐτου.* Athens 1961

MERLAN, P. 'Greek Philosophy from Plato to Plotinus' in *Later Greek and Early Medieval Philosophy*. A.H. Armstrong (ed.) Cambridge 1967, 14-132

MERX, A. *Die Prophetie des Joel und ihre Ausleger*. Halle 1879

MESHEL, Z. *Kuntilat 'Agrud*. Israel Museum (cat. 175) Jerusalem 1978

METZGER, B.M. 'The Formulas Introducing Quotations of Scripture in the NT and the Mishna' *JBL* 70 (1951) 297-307

– 'Seventy or Seventy-two disciples?' *NTS* 5 (1958) 65-74

– *The Text of the New Testament²*. Oxford 1968

– 'Names for the Nameless in the New Testament' *New Testament Studies, Philological, Versional and Patristic*. Leiden 1980, 23-45

MEYER, R. *Hellenistisches in der rabbinischen Anthropologie*. Stuttgart 1937

– 'Kanonisch and apokryph' *ThWNT* 3, 979-87

– 'Bemerkungen zum literargeschichtlichen Hintergrund der Kanontheorie des Josephus' in O. Betz, K. Haacker, M. Hengel (eds.) *Josephus Studien. Untersuchungen zu Josephus, dem antiken Judentum und dem Neuen Testament. Otto Michel zum 70. Geburtstag gewidmet*. Göttingen 1974, 285-99

MEZ, A. *Die Bibel des Josephus untersucht für Buch V-VII der Archäologie*. Basel 1895

MICHAELIS, J.D. 'Von critischen Uhrkunden und Hülfsmitteln zu Berichtigung der wahren Lesearten der Bibel' *Orientalische und Exegetische Bibliothek* 1. (1771) 207-22

MICHEL, O. *Der Brief an die Römer*. Göttingen 1955

– *Paulus und seine Bibel*. Darmstadt 1972 (1929)

MIELZINER, M. *Introduction to the Talmud*. 4th ed. New York 1968 with new bibliography by A. Guttmann

MILBURN, R.L.P. *Early Christian Interpretations of History*. London 1954

– 'The "People's Bible": Artists and Commentators' *CHB* 2 (Cambridge 1969) 280-308

MILIK, J.T. *'Ten Years of Discovery in the Wilderness of Judea*. London 1963

– *The Books of Enoch*. Oxford 1976

– *Qumran Grotte 4, II: Tefillin, Mezuzot et Targum (4Q128-4Q157)*. *DJD* 6, Oxford 1977

– '«Prière de Nabonide» et autres écrits d'un cycle de Daniel. Fragments araméens de Qumrân 4 (Pl. I)' *RB* 63 (1956) 407-15

MILLARD, A.R. 'The Practice of Writing in Ancient Israel' *BA* 35 (1972) 98-111

– 'In Praise of Ancient Scribes' *BA* (1982) 143-53

– 'An Assessment of the Evidence for Writing in Ancient Israel' *Biblical Archaeology Today*. Jerusalem 1985, 301-12

– 'The Infancy of the Alphabet' *World Archaeology* 17 (1986) 390-8

MILLER, A. 'Aufenthalt und Reisen des hl. Hieronymus in Land der Bibel' in *Hieronymi Festschrift* 40.54 Beuron 1920

MILLER, M.P. 'Targum, Midrash and the Use of the Old Testament in the New Testament' *JSJ* 2 (1971) 29-82

– 'Midrash' *IDBS* (Nashville 1976) 593-97

MOHRMANN, CH. 'Linguistic Problems in the Early Christian Church' *VC* 11 (1957) 22-9

– *Études sur le latin des chrétiens* 1-3. Rome 1961-1965

MONDÉSERT, C. *Clément d'Alexandrie*. Paris 1944

MONDÉSERT, C. - MARROU, H.I. with HARL, M. and MATRAY, C. *Clément d'Alexandrie: Le Pédagogue*. *SC* 70, 108, 158 Paris 1960, 1965, 1970

MONTGOMERY, J.A. *The Samaritans, the earliest Jewish sect. Their History, Theology and Literature*. Philadelphia 1907, New York 1968

MOODY SMITH, D. 'The Use of the Old Testament in the New' in J.M. Efird (ed.) *The Use of the Old Testament in the New and Other Essays: Studies in Honor of W.F. Stinespring*. Durham 1972, 3-65

MOORE, C.A. *Judith. (The Anchor Bible)* New York 1985

MOORE, G.F. 'The Definition of the Jewish Canon and the Repudiation of Christian Scriptures' in G.F. Moore et al, *Essays in Modern Theology and Related Subjects as a Testimonial to C.A. Briggs*.

New York 1911, 99-125
- 'The Antiochian Recension of the Septuagint' *AJSL* 29 (1912-1913) 37-62
- *Judaism in the First Centuries of the Christian Era: the Age of the Tannaim* 1-3. Cambridge MA 1927-1930
MOR, M. 'More Bibliography on the Samaritans' *Henoch* 1 (1979) 99-122
MORAG, S. 'The Vocalization of Codex Reuchlinianus: Is the "Pre-Masoretic" Bible Pre-Masoretic?' *JSS* 4 (1959) 216-37
- 'Some aspects of the Methodology and Terminology of the Early Massoretes' *Leshonenu* 38 (1973-1974) 49-77 (Hebr.)
MOREL, C. (ed.) *Grégoire le Grand, Homélies sur Ezéchiel* 1 (to form *SC* 327)
MORINUS, J. *Biblia Polyglotta*. Paris 1645
MORRIS, L. *The New Testament and the Jewish Lectionaries*. London 1964
MOTZO, B.R. 'Il testo di Ester in Giuseppe' *Studi e Materiali di Storia delle Religioni* 4 (1928) 84-105
MOULE, C.F.D. *Worship in the New Testament*. London 1961
- 'II Cor 3: 18b' in *Neues Testament und Geschichte*. H. Baltensweiler (ed.) Zürich 1972, 231-7
- *The Origin of Christology*. Cambridge 1977
- *The Birth of the New Testament*. 3rd revised ed. London 1981
MOULE, H.C.G. 'Arnobius' *DCB* 1, 167-9
MOULTON, J.H. - MILLIGAN, G. *The Vocabulary of the Greek Testament. Illustrated from the Papyri and Other Non-literary Sources*. London 1952 (1914-1929)
MOVERS, F.C. *Loci Quidam Historiae Canonis Veteris Testamenti Illustrati*. Breslau 1842
MRAS, K. (ED.) *Eusebius' Werke 8,1* (Die Griechischen christlichen Schriftsteller der ersten Jahrhunderte 43) 1-2. Berlin 1954-1956
MÜHLENBERG, E. *Psalmenkommentare aus der Katenenüberlieferung* 1-3. Berlin, New York 1975, 1977, 1978
MÜLLER, K. 'Die Rabbinischen Nachrichten über die Anfänge der Septuaginta' *Forschungen zur Bibel* 1. Festschrift für J. Ziegler. Würzburg 1972, 73-93
MULDER, M.J. 'Un euphémisme dans 2 Sam. XII 14?' *VT* 18 (1968) 108-14
- 'The Use of the Peshiṭta in Textual Criticism' in *La Septuaginta en la Investigación Contemporánea (V Congreso de la IOSCS)* ed. by N. Fernández Marcos, Madrid 1985, 37-53
MULLEN, T. *The Canon of the Old Testament*. New York 1892
MUNIER, CH. 'Collezioni canoniche' *DPAC* 1, 729-34
MUÑOZ LEÓN, D. *Dios Palabra: Memra en los Targumim del Pentateuco*. Granada 1974
- *Gloria de la Shekina en los Targumim del Pentateuco*. Madrid 1977
MURAOKA, T. 'The Greek Text of 2 Samuel 11 in the Lucianic Manuscripts' *AbrN* 20 (1981-1982) 37-59
- 'The Greek Texts of Samuel-Kings: Incomplete Translations or Recensional Activity? *AbrN* 21 (1982-1983) 28-49
MURPHY-O'CONNOR, J. (ed.) *Paul and Qumran*. London 1968
MURRAY, C. 'Art and the Early Church' *JTS* N.S. 28 (1977) 303-45
MURRAY, R. *Symbols of Church and Kingdom: A Study in Early Syriac Tradition*. Cambridge 1975 (repr. with corrections 1977)
- 'Some Rhetorical Patterns in Early Syriac Literature' in R.H. Fischer (ed.) *A Tribute to Arthur Vööbus*. Chicago 1977, 109-25
MUSSIES, G. 'The interpretatio judaica of Sarapis' in M.J. Vermaseren (ed.) *Studies in Hellenistic Religions*. Leiden 1979, 189-214
- 'The interpretatio judaica of Thot-Hermes' in M. Heerma van Voss et al (eds.) *Studies in Egyptian Religion dedicated to Prof. Jan Zandee*. Leiden 1982, 89-120
MUSURILLO, H. (ed.) *The Acts of the Christian Martyrs*. *OECT*, Oxford 1972
MYNORS, R.A.B. (ed.) *Cassiodori Senatoris Institutiones*. Oxford 1937 (repr. Oxford 1961)
NAGEL, P. 'Die Septuaginta-Zitate in der koptisch-gnostischen "Exegese über die Seele" (Nag Hammadi Codex II)' *Archiv für Papyrusforschung* 22/23 (1974) 249-69
- 'Die Auslegung der Paradieserzählung in der Gnosis' in Tröger, *Altes Testament*, 49-70
NARDI, C. (ed. and tr.) *Clemente Alessandrino. Estratti Profetici*. Florence 1985

832

NAUTIN, P. 'Canoni apostolici' *DPAC* 1, 576f
- 'Canoni ecclesiastici degli apostoli' *DPAC* 1, 577f
- *Origène. Sa vie et son oeuvre.* Paris 1977
- 'Hieronymus' *TRE* 15 (1986) 304-15
NAUTIN, P. - DOUTRELEAU, L. *Didyme l'Aveugle Sur la Genèse. SC* 233, 244, Paris, 1976, 1978
NAUTIN, P. - HUSSON, P. *Origène, Homélies sur Jérémie. SC* 232, 238, Paris 1976, 1977
NAVEH, J. 'A Palaeographic Note on the Distribution of the Hebrew Script' *HTR* 61 (1968) 68-74
- The Development of the Aramaic Script. *PIASH* 5/1, Jerusalem 1970
- *On Stone and Mosaic.* Jerusalem 1978 (Hebr.)
- 'The Date of the Tell Fekheryeh Inscription' *Shnaton* 5-6. Jerusalem 1978-1979, 131-40 (Hebr.)
- *Early History of the Alphabet.* Jerusalem 1982
- ' "A Good Subdoing, there is none like it"; an ancient amulet from Horvat Marish in the Galilee' *Tarbiz* 54 (1985) 367-82 (Hebr.)
NEALE, J.M. - LITTLEDALE, R.F. *A Commentary on the Psalms from Primitive and Mediaeval Writers* 1-4. London 1860-1874
NESTLE, EB. 'Polyglottenbibeln' *PRE*³ 528-35
- review of I. Prager, *De Veteris Testamenti. . . TLZ* 1 (1876) 281-4
- 'Zum Namen der syrischen Bibelübersetzung Peschiṭṭâ' *ZDMG* 47 (1893) 157-9
- 'Syrische Bibelübersetzungen' *RE* 3, Leipzig 1897, 167-72
NESTLE, EB. - ALAND, K. *Novum Testamentum Graece.* Stuttgart 1979 (26th ed.)
NEUBAUER, A. *Chronique samaritaine.* Paris 1873
NEUHAUS, G.O. *Studien zu den poetischen Stucken im 1. Makkabäerbuch.* Wurzburg 1974
NEUSNER, J. *Development of a Legend.* Leiden 1970
- *The Rabbinic Traditions about the Pharisees Before 70* 1-3. Leiden 1971
- *Aphrahat and Judaism.* Leiden 1971
- *Early Rabbinic Judaism.* Leiden 1975
- (ed.) *The Tosefta* 1-6. New York 1977-1986
NEWLANDS, G.M. *Hilary of Poitiers: A Study in Theological Method.* Berne 1978
NEWMAN, R.C. 'The Council of Jamnia and the Old Testament Canon' *WTJ* 38 (1976) 319-49
NEWSOM, C.A. 'The Development of 1 Enoch 6-19: Cosmology and Judgment' *CBQ* 42 (1980) 310-29
NICKELSBURG, G.W.E. *Resurrection, Immortality, and Eternal Life in Intertestamental Judaism.* Cambridge, MA 1972
- 'Stories of Biblical and Early Post-Biblical Times' *Compendia* II/2, 33-87
- 'The Bible Rewritten and Expanded' *Compendia* II/2, 89-156
- 'Aaron' *RAC* Suppl.-Lieferung 1/2 (1985) 1-11
NIEHR, H. 'Sofēr' *ThWAT* 5, Stuttgart 1986, 921-9
NIELSEN, E. *Oral Tradition.* London 1954
NIKIPROWETZKY, V. *Le commentaire de l'écriture chez Philon d'Alexandrie.* Leiden 1977
- 'L'exégèse de Philon d'Alexandrie dans le *De Gigantibus* et le *Quod Deus*' in Winston and Dillon, *Two Treatises,* 5-75
NINEHAM, D.E. (ed.) *The Church's Use of the Bible.* London 1963
NISSEN, H.J. 'The Archaic Texts from Uruk' *World Archaeology* 17 (1986) 317-34
NITZAN, B. *Pesher Habakkuk.* Jerusalem 1986 (Hebr.)
NOCK, A.D. 'The Apocryphal Gospels' *JTS* 11 (1960) 63-70
NÖLDEKE, TH. *Die Alttestamentliche Litteratur.* Leipzig 1868
- review of J.M. Schönfelder, *Onkelos und Peschittho. Lit. Centralblatt* 1869, 1293f
- 'Das Targum zu den Sprüchen von der Peschita abhängig' in: *Archiv f. Wiss. Erf. des AT.* ed. by A. Merx, Bd. II,2 (1872) 246-9
- review of (F. Bleek -) J. Wellhausen, *Einleitung. ZDMG* 32 (1878) 586-95 (remarks concerning the Peshitta on 589f)
- review of A. Mandl, *Die Peshittha zu Hiob. Lit. Centralblatt* 1893, 34-6
NOJA, S. *Il-Kitāb al-Kāfi dei Samaritani.* Napels 1970
NORDHEIM, E. VON, *Die Lehre der Alten I. Das Testament als Literaturgattung im Judentum der hellenistisch-römischen Zeit. ALGHJ* 13, Leiden 1980

833

– *Die Lehre der Alten II. Das Testament als Literaturgattung im Alten Testament und im Altem vorderen Orient.* ALGHJ 18, Leiden 1985

NORDSTRÖM, C.O. 'Rabbinica in frühchristlichen und byzantinischen Illustrationen zum 4. Buch Moses' *Figura* N.S. 1 (1959) 24-47

NORELLI, E. 'La sabbia e le stelle: Gen 13,16; 15,5; 22,17 nell'esegesi cristiana dei primi tre secoli' *Augustinianum* 22 (1982) 285-312

NOTH, M. *Die Welt des Alten Testaments.* 3rd ed. Berlin 1957

– *Gesammelte Studien.* München 1969

NOVUM TESTAMENTUM DOMINI NOSTRI IESU CHRISTI LATINE SECUNDUM EDITIONEM SANCTI HIERONYMI *Latine recensuerunt J.* Wordsworth, H.J. White *et alii* 1-3. Oxford 1889-1954

NOWACK, W. *Die Bedeutung des Hieronymus für die alttestamentliche Textkritik.* Göttingen 1875

NUTT, J.W. *Fragments of a Samaritan Targum.* London 1874 (repr. Hildesheim, New York 1980

NYBERG, H.S. *Studien zum Hoseabuche. Zugleich ein Beitrag zur Klärung des Problems der alttestamentliche Textkritik.* Uppsala 1935

O'CONNELL, K.G. *The Theodotionic Revision of the Book of Exodus.* Harvard Semitic Monographs 1. Cambridge MA 1968

ODEBERG, H. *3 Enoch.* Cambridge 1928

O'DONNELL, J.J. *Cassiodorus.* Berkeley 1979

OEPKE, A. 'ϰρυπτω' *TDNT* 3 (1965) 987-92

OESCH, J.M. *Petucha und Setuma. Untersuchungen zu einer überlieferten Gliederung im hebräischen Text des Alten Testaments.* (*Orbis Biblicus et Orientalis* 27) Freiburg, Göttingen 1979

ÖSTBORN, G. *Cult and Canon: A Study in the Canonization of the Old Testament.* Uppsala 1950

OESTERLEY, W.O.E. - BOX, G.H. *The Religion and Worship of the Synagoge.* London 1911[2]

OHLY, F. *Hohelied-Studien.* Wiesbaden 1958

OLITZKI, M. *Flavius Josephus und die Halacha I. Einleitung, die Opfer,* Berlin 1885

OLIVIER, J.-M. (ed.) *Diodori Tarsensis Commentarii in Psalmos 1.* CCG 6, Turnhout, Leuven 1980

OLSHAUSEN, J. *Lehrbuch der hebräischen Sprache.* Braunschweig 1861

OPPENHEIM, A.L. *Ancient Mesopotamia – Portrait of a Dead Civilization.* Chicago 1964

OPPENHEIM, B. *Die syrische Übersetzung des Fünften Buches der Psalmen (Psalm 107-150) und ihr Verhältnis zu dem Massoretischen Texte und den älteren Übersetzungen, namentlich den LXX,* Targ. Leipzig 1891

ORLINSKY, H.M. 'Some Corruptions in the Greek Text of Job' *JQR* 26 (1935-1936) 133-45

– 'Current Progress and Problems in LXX Research' in H.R. Willoughby (ed.) *The Study of the Bible To-Day and Tomorrow.* Chigago 1947, 144-61

– 'Prolegomenon: The Masoretic Text: A Critical Evaluation' in Ginsburg, *Introduction.* 2nd ed. New York 1966, I-XXXVII (= Leiman, *Canon and Masorah,* 833-69)

– 'The Septuagint as Holy Writ and the Philosophy of the Translators' *HUCA* 46 (1975) 89-114

OSBORN, E.F. *Justin Martyr.* Tübingen 1973

OSSWALD, E. 'Zur Hermeneutik des Habakuk-Kommentars' *ZAW* 68 (1956) 243-56

OSTEN-SACKEN, P. VON DER, *Die Apokalyptik in ihrem Verhältnis zu Prophetie und Weisheit.* München 1969

OSTROWSKY, M. *Ha-Middot she-ha-Tora Nidreshet ba-Hem.* Jerusalem 1924

OTTE, K. *Das Sprachverständnis bei Philon von Alexandria.* Tübingen 1968

OTTLEY, R.R. (ed. and tr.) *The Book of Isaiah according to the Septuagint (Codex Alexandrinus)* 1-2. Cambridge 1906

OTTO, J.C.T. (ed.) *S. Justini Philosophi et Martyris Opera.* (introductory study and 2 futher vols.) Jena 1841, 1842, 1843

OULTON, J.E.L. - CHADWICK, H. *Alexandrian Christianity.* LCC 2, London 1954

OWENS, R.J. *The Genesis and Exodus Citations of Aphrahat the Persian Sage.* Leiden 1983

PAINCHAUD, L. *Le Deuxième Traité du Grand Seth (NH VII,2).* Québec 1982

PALMER, L.K. *The Latin Language.* London 1954

PANITZ, R.I. *Textual Exegesis and Other Kinds of Interpretation in the Scripture.* Unpubl. Diss. University of Pennsylvania 1983

PAOLI, U.E. *Rome, its People, Life and Customs*. London 1983 (1940)

PARDEE, D. et al. *Handbook of Ancient Hebrew Letters*. Chico, Calif. 1982

PARISOT, J. (ed.) *Aphraatis Sapientis Persae Demonstrationes* 1-2. Paris 1894, 1907

PARKES, J.W. *The Conflict of the Church and the Synagogue*. London 1934

PARROTT, D. 'Evidence of Religious Syncretism in Gnostic Texts from Nag Hammadi' in B. Pearson (ed.) *Religious Syncretism in Antiquity*. Missoula 1975, 173-83

– (ed.) *Nag Hammadi Codices V, 2-5 and VI, with Papyrus Berolonensis 8502,1 and 4*. Leiden 1979

PATTE, D. *Early Jewish Hermeneutic in Palestine*. (*SBL Monograph Series* 22) Missoula, Montana 1975

PAUL, S.M. 'Heavenly Tablets and the Book of Life' *JANES* 5 (1973) 345-53

PEARSON, B.A. 'Jewish Haggadic Traditions in The Testimony of Truth from Nag Hammadi (CG IX 3)' in *Ex Orbe Religionum: Studia G. Widengren* 1. Leiden 1972, 456-70

– 'Anti-Heritical Warnings in Codex IX from Nag Hammadi' in Krause, *Essays*, 145-54

– 'Biblical Exegesis in Gnostic Literature' in M. Stone (ed.) *Armenian and Biblical Studies*. Jerusalem 1976, 70-80

– 'Gnostic Interpretation of the Old Testament in the *Testimony of Truth* (NHC IX,3)' *HTR* 73 (1980) 311-9

– The Figure of Seth in Gnostic Literature' in Layton, *Rediscovery* 2, 472-504

– (ed.) *Nag Hammadi Codices IX and X*. Leiden 1981

– 'Jewish Sources in Gnostic Literature' *Compendia* II/2, 443-81

– 'The Problem of "Jewish Gnostic" Literature' in C. Hedrick and R. Hodgson (eds.) *Nag Hammadi, Gnosticism, and Early Christianity*. Peabody MA 1986 15-36

PEDERSEN, J. *Israel*. London 1959 (1926) (4 Vols. in 2)

PELLETIER, A. *Flavius Josèphe, Adaptateur de La Lettre d'Aristée. Une réaction atticisante contre la koinè*. Paris 1962

PENKOWER, J.S. 'Maimonides and the Aleppo Codex' *Textus* 9 (1981) 39-128

PÉPIN, M.J. *Mythe et allégorie: Les origines grecques et les contestations judéo-chrétiennes*. Aubier 1958 (revised ed. Paris 1976)

– 'Remarques sur la théorie de l'exégèse allégorique chez Philon' in *Philon d'Alexandrie*. Colloques nationaux Lyon 1966, Paris 1967, 131-67

PERCIVAL, H.R. (tr.) *The Seven Ecumenical Councils*. *NPNF* 14, New York, Oxford and London 1900

PERELMAN, CH. - OLBRECHTS-TYTECA, L. *Traité de L'Argumentation: La Nouvelle Rhétorique*. Bruxelles 1970

PERI, V. *Omelie origeniane sui Salmi: Contributo all'identificazione del testo latino. Studi e Testi* 289, Vatican 1980

PERKINS, P. 'Ireneus and the Gnostics: Rhetoric and Composition in Adversus Haereses Book One' *VC* 30 (1976) 193-200

– *The Gnostic dialogue. The Early Church and the Crises of Gnosticism*. New York 1980

PERLES, J. *Meletemata Peschitthoniana*. Breslau 1859

PERRENCHIO, F. 'Struttura e analisi letteraria di Sapienza 1,1-15, nel quadro del suo contesto letteraria immediato' *Salesianum* 37 (1975) 289-325

– 'Struttura e analisi letteraria di Sapienze 1,16-2,24 e 5,1-23' *Salesianum* 43 (1981) 3-43

PERROT, C. 'La lecture synagogale d'Ex 21,1-22,23 et son influence sur la littérature néotestamentaire' in *A la rencontre de Dieu. Mémorial A. Gelin*. Le Puy 1963, 223-39

– 'Petuhot et Setumot. Études sur les alinéas du Pentateuque' *RB* 76 (1969) 50-91

– *La Lecture de la Bible dans la synagogue. Les anciennes lectures palestiniennes du shabbat et des fêtes*. Hildesheim 1973

– 'Luc 4:16-30 et la lecture biblique dans l'ancienne synagogue' *Exégèse bibliques et Judaisme*. ed. by J.E. Menard, Strasbourg 1973, 170-86

– 'La lecture de la Bible dans la Diaspora hellénistique' *Études sur le Judaïsme hellénistique*. Paris 1984, 109-34

PERROT, C. - BOGAERT, P.M. *Pseudo-Philon Les Antiquités Bibliques* 2. SC 230, Paris 1976

PETERMANN, H. - VOLLERS, C. *Pentateuchus Samaritanus*. Berlin 1872-1891

PETERS, C. 'Peschittha und Targumim des Pentateuchs. Ihre Beziehungen untersucht in Rahmen ihrer Abweichungen vom Masoretischen Text' *Mus*. 48 (1935) 1-54
- 'Pešiṭṭa-Psalter und Psalmentargum' *Mus*. 52 (1939) 275-96
- 'Zur Herkunft der Pešiṭṭa des ersten Samuel-Buches' *Biblica* 22 (1941) 25-34
PETIT, F. (ed.) *L'ancienne version latine des Questions sur la Genèse de Philon d'Alexandrie. TU* 113-114, 1-2, Berlin 1973
- (ed.) *Catenae Craecae in Genesim et in Exodum* 1, *Catena Sinaitica. CCG* 2 Turnhout 1977
PFEIFFER, R.H. *Introduction to the Old Testament*. New York, London 1941
- *History of Classical Scholarship* 1-2. Oxford 1968-1976
PFISTER, F. 'Die Prooimia der platonischen Gesetze' *Mélange Boisacq* 1-2, 1938, 173-79
PINKUSS, H. 'Die syrische Übersetzung der Proverbien, textkritisch und in ihrem Verhältnisse zu dem masoretischen Text, den LXX und dem Targum untersucht' *ZAW* 14 (1894) 65-222
PLATER, W.E. - WHITE, H. *A Grammar of the Vulgate*. Oxford 1926
PLOEG, J.P.M. VAN DER, 'Recente Pešiṭṭa-Studies (sinds 1927)' *Jaarbericht Ex Oriente Lux* 10, dl. III, 1944-1948, Leiden 1952, 392-9
- 'The Peshitta of the Old Testament' in J. Vellian (ed.) *The Malabar Church. Or. Chr. An*. 186, Roma 1970, 23-32
PORTER, J.R. 'The Pentateuch and the Triennial Cycle' in *Promise and Fulfilment*. ed. by F. Bruce, Edinburgh 1963
PORTON, G. *The Legal Traditions of Rabbi Ishmael: A Form-Critical and Literary-Critical Approach*. Unpubl. Diss. Brown Univ. 1973
- *The Traditions of Rabbi Ishmael* 1-4. Leiden 1976-82
- 'Midrash: Palestinian Jews and the Hebrew Bible in the Greco-Roman Period' *ANRW* 19.2 (1979) 103-38
POSNANSKI, A. *Schiloh* 1. Leipzig 1904
PRAGER, I. *De Veteris Testamenti Versione Syriaca Quam Peschittho Vocant Quaestiones Criticae*. Göttingen 1875
PRATO, G.L. 'Babilonia fondata dai giganti: il significato cosmico di Gen. 11,1-9 nella storiografia dello Pseudo-Eupolemo' in V. Collado and E. Zurro (eds.) *El Misterio de la Palabra. Homenaje a Luis Alonso Schökel*. Madrid 1983, 121-46
PRIGENT, P. *Les testimonia dans le christianisme primitif: l'Epître de Barnabé I-XVI et ses sources*. Paris 1961
- *Justin et l'Ancien Testament*. Paris 1964
PRIGENT, P. - KRAFT, R.A. *L'Epître de Barnabé. SC* 172 Paris 1971
PRIJS, L. *Jüdische Tradition in der Septuaginta*. Leiden 1948
PUECH, E. 'Abécédaire et Liste Alphabétique de noms Hébreux du début du IIᵉ s. A.D.' *RB* 83 (1980) 118-26
- 'Origine de l'alphabet. Documents en alphabet linéaire et cunéiforme du IIᵉ millénaire' *RB* 93 (1986) 161-213
PUMMER, R. 'Genesis 34 in Jewish Writings of the Hellenistic and Roman Periods' *HTR* 75 (1982) 177-88
PURVIS, J.D. *The Samaritan Pentateuch and the Origin of the Samaritan Sect*. Cambridge MA 1968
PUSEY, P.E. (ed.) *Sancti Patris Cyrilli archiepiscopi Alexandrini in XII Prophetas* 1-2. Oxford 1868
PUYVELDE, CL. VAN, 'Versions Syriaques' *DBS* tome 6, Paris 1960, 834-84
QUASTEN, J. *Patrology* 1-3. Utrecht, Antwerpen and Westminister Maryland 1960
QUENTIN, H. *Mémoire sur l'établissement du texte de la Vulgate. CBL* VI, Rome 1922
QUISPEL, G. *Ptolémée: Lettre à Flora. SC* 24, Paris 1966 (2nd ed.)
- 'Valentinian Gnosis and the Apocryphon of John' in Layton, *Rediscovery* 1, 118-27
RABIN, C. *Qumran Scrolls. London* 1957
- *The Zadokite Documents*. Oxford 1958
- 'The Translation Process and the Character of the Septuagint' *Textus* 6 (1968) 1-26
- 'Hebrew and Aramaic in the First Century' *Compendia* I/2, 1007-39
- 'Jubilees' Revision of R.H. Charles translation in H.F.D. Sparks, *The Apocryphal Old Testament*. Oxford 1984

RABINOWITZ, I. 'The Authorship, Audience and Date of the De Vaux Fragment of an Unknown Work' *JBL* 71 (1952) 19-32

RABY, F.J.E. *Christian Latin Poetry.* 2nd ed. Oxford 1953

– *The Oxford Book of Mediaeval Latin Verse.* Oxford 1959

RAD, G. VON 'Hiob XXXVIII und die altägyptische Weisheit' *SVT* 3 (1955) 293-301

– *Old Testament Theology* 1-2. London 1975 (1957)

– *Wisdom in Israel.* London 1972

RAHLFS, A. 'Beiträge zur Textkritik der Peschita' *ZAW* 9 (1889) 161-210

– *Lucians Rezension der Königsbücher. Septuaginta Studien* 3, Göttingen 1911

– *Septuaginta, id est Vetus Testamentum graece iuxta LXX interpretes* 1-2. Stuttgart 1935

RAHMER, M. *Die hebräische Traditionen in den Werken des Hieronymus* 1-2. Breslau 1861, Berlin 1902

RAINEY, A.F. 'The Scribe at Ugarit, His Position and Influence' *PIASH* 3. Jerusalem 1968, 1-22

RAJAK, T. *Flavius Josephus: Jewish History and the Greek World* 1-2. Oxford 1974

– 'Moses in Ethiopia: Legend and Literature' *JJS* 29 (1978) 111-22

RANKE, E. *Par palimpsestorum Wirceburgensium Antiquissimae Veteris Testamenti Versionis Latinae Fragmenta.* Vienna 1871

RAPALLO, U. *Calchi ebraici nelle antiche versioni del 'Levitico'. Studi Semitici* 39, Roma 1971

RAPPAPORT, S. *Agada und Exegese bei Flavius Josephus.* Vienna 1930

REDDITT, P.L. 'The Concept of *Nomos* in Fourth Maccabees' *CBQ* 45 (1983) 249-70

REESE, J.M. *Hellenistic Influence on the Book of Wisdom and its Consequences.* Rome 1970

REHM, M. 'Die Bedeutung hebräischer Wörter bei Hieronymus' *Biblica* 35 (1954) 174-97

REICHMANN, V. 'Vetus Latina' (NT) *TRE* 6, 172-6

– 'Vulgata' *TRE* 6, 178-81

REIDER, J. *Prolegomena to a Greek-Hebrew and Hebrew-Greek Index to Aquila.* Philadelphia 1916

REIM, G. 'Studien zum alttestamentlichen Hintergrund des Johannesevangeliums. Cambridge 1974

REINER, F.N. 'Masoretes, Rabbis, and Karaites: A Comparison of Biblical Interpretations' *Masoretic Studies* 1 (1974) 137-45

RENOUX, C. *Le Codex Arménien Jérusalem 121.* PO 35, 1-215; 36, 139-388, Turnhout 1969-1971

REUSCHENBACH, D.F. *Hieronymus als Übersetzer der Genesis.* Freiburg 1942

REVEL, B. 'Some Anti-Traditional Laws of Josephus' *JQR* 14 (1923-1924) 293-301

– 'The Karaite Halakah' in P. Birnbaum (ed.) *Karaite Studies.* New York 1971, 1-88

REVELL, E.J. 'The Oldest Accent List in the Diqduqe Haṭeᶜamim' *Textus* 8 (1973) 138-59

– *Biblical Texts with Palestinian Pointing and their Accents. Masoretic Studies* 4, Missoula Mont. 1977

REYNOLDS, L.D. - WILSON, N.G. *Scribes and Scholars.* 2nd ed. Oxford 1974

RICHARD, M. 'Hippolyte de Rome' *DS* 8 (1967) 531-71 (bibliography)

RICHARDSON, P. *Israel in the Apostolic Church.* Cambridge 1969

RICOEUR, P. 'The Narrative Function' *Semeia* 13 (1978) 178-86

RINALDI, F. 'L'Antico Testamento nella polemica anticristiana di Porfirio di Tiro' *Augustinianum* 22 (1982) 97-111

RINGGREN, H. 'Oral and Written Transmission in the Old Testament. Some Observations' *ST* 3 (1949) 34-59

– *The Faith of Qumran.* Philadelphia 1963

RISKIN, S. *The Halakhah in Josephus as Reflected in Against Apion and The Life.* New York 1970

ROBBINS, F.E. *The Hexaemeral Literature.* Chicago 1912

ROBERGE, M. 'Le rôle du *Noûs* dans la *Paraphrase de Sem*' in Barc, *Colloque Inᵗᵉrnational*, 328-39

ROBERT, A. 'Littéraires (Genres)' *DBS* 5 (1975) 411-3

ROBERT, U. *Pentateuchi versio latina antiquissima.* Paris 1881

– *Heptateuchi partis posterioris versio latina antiquissima.* Lyon 1900

ROBERTS, A. - DONALDSON, J. (eds.) *The Ante-Nicene Fathers* 1-10. Grand Rapids 1956 (1885)

ROBERTS, B.J. *The Old Testament Text and Versions. The Hebrew Text in Transmission and the History of the Ancient Versions.* Cardiff 1951

– 'The Hebrew Bible since 1937' *JTS* N.S. 15 (1964) 253-264

– 'Text OT' *IDB* 4, 580-94

ROBERTS, C.H. 'The Codex' *Proceedings of the British Academy* 40 (1954) 169-204
- Review of R. Roca-Puig, *Himne a la Verge Maria 'Psalmus Responsorius'* (2nd ed. Barcelona 1965) in *JTS* N.S. 18 (1967) 492-4
ROBERTS, C.H. - SKEAT, T.C. *The Birth of the Codex*. London 1983
ROBERTSON, A. - PLUMMER, A. *First Epistle of St. Paul to the Corinthians*. Edinburgh 1953 (repr. of the second ed. 1914)
ROBERTSON, E. *Catalogue of the Samaritan Manuscripts in the John Rylands Library* 1-2. Manchester 1938, 1962
ROBINSON, H.W. *Corporate Personality in Ancient Israel*. Philadelphia 1964 (1935)
ROBINSON, J.A. (tr.) *St. Irenaeus, The Demonstration of the Apostolic Preaching*. London 1920
ROBINSON, J.A.T. *The Body*. London 1952
ROBINSON, J.M. (ed.) *The Facsimile Edition of the Nag Hammadi Codices. Codices I-XIII*, Leiden 1972-1979
ROBINSON, J.M. - MEYER, M. (eds.) *The Nag Hammadi Library in English*. Leiden, San Francisco 1977
ROBINSON, W. 'The Exegesis on the Soul' *NovT* 12 (1970) 102-17
RÖNSCH, H. *Itala und Vulgata*. 2nd ed. Marburg 1875
ROKEAH, D. 'A New Onomasticon Fragment from Oxyrhynchus and Philo's Etymologies' *JTS* 19 (1968) 70-82
ROMPAY, L. VAN, (ed. and tr.) *Fragments syriaques du commentaire des Psaumes de Théodore de Mopsueste*. *CSCO* 435-6, Louvain 1982
RONDEAU, M.-J. *Les commentaires patristiques du psautier (IIIe - Ve siècles)*. 1 *Les travaux des pères grecs et latins sur le psautier, Recherches et bilan*. *OCA* 219, Rome 1982
ROS, J. *De Studie van het Bijbelgrieksch van Hugo Grotius tot Adolf Deissmann*. Nijmegen 1940
ROSENBLATT, S. *The Interpretation of the Bible in the Mishnah*. Baltimore 1935
ROSENMÜLLER, E.F.K. *Handbuch für die Literatur der biblischen Kritik und Exegese* 1-2. Göttingen 1797-1798
ROSENTHAL, D. 'The Torah Reading in the Annual Cycle in the Land of Israel' *Tarbiz* 51 (1981-1982) 187-220; 52 (1983-1984) 144-8
- 'The Sages' Methodical Approach to Textual Variants within the Hebrew Bible' in *I.L. Seeligmann Volume* 2. Jerusalem 1983, 395-417 (Hebr. section)
ROSENTHAL, F. *Die Aramaistische Forschung seit Th. Nöldeke's Veröffentlichungen*. Leiden 1939 (repr. 1964)
ROSENZWEIG, F. *Kleinere Schriften*. Berlin 1937
ROSSI, J.B. DE, *Variae lectiones Veteris Testamenti ex immensa MSS. Editorumq. Codicum congerie haustae . . .*, etc. 1-5. Parma 1784-1788 (repr. Amsterdam 1969)
ROUSSEAU, A. - DOUTRELEAU, L. (eds.) *Irénée de Lyon, Contre les Hérésies*, 1 (*SC* 263-4, Paris 1979) 2 (*SC* 293-4, Paris 1982) 3 (*SC* 210-1, Paris 1974) 4 (with B. Hemmerdinger and C. Mercier, *SC* 100, 1-2, Paris 1965) 5 (with C. Mercier, *SC* 152-3, Paris 1969)
ROUSSEAU, O. Origène, Homélies sur le Cantique. SC 37, Paris 1966
ROUX, J.H. LE 'The Use of Scripture in 1 Enoch 6-11' *Neotestamentica* 17 (1983) 40-8
ROWLAND, C. *The Open Heaven: A Study of Apocalyptic in Judaism and Early Christianity*. London, New York 1982
- *Christian Origins. An Account of the Setting and Character of the Most Important Messianic Sect of Judaism*. London 1985
ROWLANDS, E.R. 'The Targum and the Peshitta Version of the Book of Isaiah' *VT* 9 (1959) 178-91
ROWLEY, H.H. 'The Interpretation of the Song of Songs' in *The Servant of the Lord*. London 1952, 187-234
- *Eleven Years of Bible Bibliography*. Indian Hills Colorado 1957
RUBINKIEWICZ, R. *Die Eschatologie von Henoch 9-11 und das Neue Testament*. Lublin 1980
RUDOLF, W. *Esra und Nehemia: samt 3. Esra* (*HAT* 20). Tübingen 1949
RUDOLPH, K. 'Ein Grundtyp gnostischer Urmensch-Adam-Spekulation' *ZRGG* 9 (1957) 1-20
- 'Coptica-Mandaica. Zu einigen Übereinstimmungen zwischen koptischen-gnostischen und mandäischen Texten' in Krause, *Essays*, 191-216

– *Gnosis: The Nature and History of Gnosticism.* (E.T. ed. by R.M. Wilson) Edinburgh, San Francisco 1983

RUNNALLS, D. 'Moses' Ethiopian Campaign' *JSJ* 14 (1983) 135-56

RUNNING, L.G. *An Investigation of the Syriac Version of Isaiah.* unpubl. Baltimore, Maryland 1964

– 'An Investigation of the Syriac Version of Isaiah' *AUSS* part I: 3 (1965) 138-57; part II: 4 (1966) 37-64; part III: 4 (1966) 135-48

RUSSELL, D.S. *The Method and Message of Jewish Apocalyptic.* London 1964

RYLE, H.E. *The Canon of the Old Testament.* London 1892, 2nd ed. 1909

– *Philo and Holy Scripture.* London 1895

RYLE, J.C. *The Canon of the Old Testament.* 2nd ed. London 1904

SABATIER, P. *Bibliorum Sacrorum Latinae Versiones Antiquae sue Vetus Italica.* Rheims 1739-1743, Paris 1751

SAFRAI, S. 'The Synagogue' *Compendia* I/2, 927-33

– 'Education and the Study of the Torah' *Compendia* I/2, 945-70

– 'Oral Tora' *Compendia* II/3a, 35-119

– 'Halakha' *Compendia* II/3a, 121-209

SAHLIN, H. *Der Messias und das Gottesvolk.* Uppsala 1945

SAINT-MARIE, H. DE, *Richesses et Déficiences des Anciens Psautiers Latins.* CBL 13, Rome 1959

SALKIND, J.M. *Die Peschitta zu Schir-haschirim textkritisch und in ihrem Verhältnisse zu MT. und LXX untersucht.* Leiden 1905

SALMON, G. 'Junilius' *DCB* 3 (1882) 534f

SALMON, P. *Les 'Tituli Psalmorum' des manuscripts latins.* CBL 12, Rome 1959

SANDAY, W. 'The Cheltenham List of the Canonical Books of the Old and New Testament and of the Writings of Cyprian' in S.R. Driver (ed.) *Studia Biblica* 3, Oxford 1891, 217-325

SANDERS, E.P. *Paul and Palestinian Judaism. A Comparison of Patterns of Religion.* Philadelphia 1977, 2nd ed. London 1981

– (et al) *Jewish and Christian Self-Definition* 2. London 1981

SANDERS, J.A. *The Psalms Scroll of Qumran Cave 11.* DJD 4, Oxford 1965

– *Torah and Canon.* Philadelphia 1972

– 'Adaptable for Life. The Nature and Function of Canon' in F.M. Cross (ed.) *Magnalia Dei. Essays on the Bible and Archaeology in Memory of G. Ernest Wright.* Garden City, NY 1976, 531-60

– 'Torah and Paul' in J. Jervell, W.A. Meeks (eds.) *God's Christ and His People.* Oslo-Bergen-Tromsö 1977, 132-40

– *Canon and Community.* Philadelphia 1984

SANDERS, J.N. Review of Mondésert, *Clément d'Alexandrie. JTS* 47 (1947) 233-6

SANDMEL, S. *Philo's Place in Judaism. A Study of Conceptions of Abraham in Jewish Literature.* Cincinatti 1956, New Edition New York 1971

– 'Philo's Knowledge of Hebrew' *Studia Philonica* 5 (1978) 107-12

SARASON, R.S. 'The Petiḥtot in Leviticus Rabba: "Oral Homilies" or Redactional Constructions?' *JJS* 33 (1982), 557-65

SARNA, N.M. 'The Order of the Books' in Ch. Berlin (ed.) *Studies in Jewish Bibliography, History and Literature in Honor of I. Edward Kiew.* New York 1971, 407-13

SASS, B. *The Genesis of the Alphabet and Its Development in the Second Millennium B.C.* Tel Aviv 1985 (Ph.D. Dissertation; Hebr.)

SATRAN, D. 'Daniel, Seer, Philosopher, Holy Man' in J.J. Collins and G.W.E. Nickelsburg (eds.) *Ideal Figures in Ancient Judaism: Profiles and Paradigms.* Chico 1980, 33-48

SAVON, H. *Saint Ambroise devant l'exégèse de Philon le Juif* 1-2. Paris 1977

SCANLON, L. 'Translations from the history of Abu 'l-Fath' in S.J. Isser, *The Dositheans.* Leiden 1976, 75-82

SCHABERG, J. 'Major Midrashic Traditions in Wisdom 1,1-6,25' *JSJ* 13 (1982) 75-101

SCHADEL, E. *Die griechisch erhaltenen Jeremiahomilien Origenes.* (intr., tr. and notes) Stuttgart 1980

SCHÄFER, K.TH. *Die altlateinische Bibel.* Bonn 1957

SCHÄFER, P. 'Die sogenannte Synode von Jabne' *Judaica* 31 (1975) 54-64, 116-24 (= *Studien zur Geschichte und Theologie des rabbinischen Judenthums.* Leiden 1978, 45-64)

839

– (ed.) *Synopse zur Hekhalot-Literature*. Tübingen 1981

SCHAFF, P. - WACE, M. (eds.) *Nicene and Post-Nicene Fathers, Second Series* 1-4, Grand Rapids 1955 (1890-99)

SCHALIT, A. *Introduction to translation into Hebrew of Josephus, Antiquitates Judaicae* 1. Jerusalem 1944

– Namenwörterbuch zu Flavius Josephus. in K.H. Rengstorf (ed.) *A Complete Concordance to Flavius Josephus* Suppl. 1. Leiden 1968

– 'Artapanus' *EJ* 2, 646-7

SCHEDL, C. *Baupläne des Wortes. Einführung in die biblische Logotechnik*. Wien 1974

SCHELBERT, G. 'Exodus XXII 4 im Palästinischen Targum' *VT* 8 (1958) 253-63

SCHENK, W. 'Textverarbeitung in Frühjudentum, Frühkirche und Gnosis' in Tröger, *Altes Testament*, 299-313

SCHENKE, H.-M. *Der Gott 'Mensch' in der Gnosis*. Göttingen 1962

– 'The Phenomenon and Significance of Gnostic Sethianism' in Layton, *Rediscovery* 2, 588-616

SCHENKER, A. 'Wo steht die heutige Textkritik am Alten Testament' *Neue Zürcher Zeitung* 31 Okt. 1986

SCHIFFMAN, L.H. *The Halakha at Qumran*. Leiden 1975

– 'The *Temple Scroll* in Literary and Historical Perspective' in W. Green (ed.) *Approaches to Ancient Judaism* 2. Chico 1980, 143-58

– *Sectarian Law in the Dead Sea Scrolls*. Chico 1983

SCHILDENBERGER, J. *Die altlateinische Texte des Proverbien-Buches I*. Beuron 1941

SCHLECHT, J. (ed.) *Doctrina XII Apostolorum una cum antiqua versione latina prioris partis De Duabus Viis*. Frieburg i.B. 1900

SCHLEUSNER, J.F. *Novus thesaurus philologico-criticus, sive lexicon in LXX*. Leipzig 1820-1821

SCHLIEBEN, R. *Christliche Theologie und Philologie in der Spätantike; die schulwissenschaftlichen Methoden der Psalmenexegese Cassiodors. Arbeiten z. Kircheng*. 46, Berlin 1974

SCHMIDT, W.H. 'Davar' *TDOT* 3 (1978) 120-5; *ThWAT* 2, 101-33

SCHMITHALS, W. *Paul and James*. London 1965

SCHMITT, A. 'Stammt der sogenannte ,,ϑ''-Text bei Daniel wirklich von Theodotion?' *MSU* 9 (1966) 11-16

– 'Struktur, Herkunft und Bedeutung der Beispielreihe in Weish 10' *BZ* 21 (1977) 1-22

SCHNABEL, E.J. *Law and Wisdom from Ben Sira to Paul*. Tübingen 1985

SCHNEEMELCHER, W. 'Esra' *RAC* (1965) 595-612

SCHNEEMELCHER, W. - SCHÄFERDIECK, K. (eds.) *Bibliographia Patristica* 1-27. Berlin, New York 1959 - ...

SCHÖNFELDER, J.M. *Onkelos und Peschitto. Studien über das Alter des Onkelos'schen Targums*. München 1869

SCHOEPS, H.J. 'Ebionitisches bei Symmachus' *Coniectanea Neotestamentica* 6 (1942) 62-93

– 'Mythologisches bei Symmachus' *Biblica* 26 (1945) 100-11

– 'Symmachusstudien III: Symmachus und der Midrasch' *Biblica* 29 (1948) 31-51

SCHOFIELD, R.S. 'The Measurement of Literacy in Pre-Industrial England' in J. Goody (ed.) *Literacy in Traditional Societies*. Cambridge 1968, 311-25

SCHOLAR, D. *Nag Hammadi Bibliography 1948-1969*. Leiden 1971

– 'Bibliographia Gnostica, Supplement (a)' *NT* 13 (1971) 322-36; 14 (1972) 312-31; 15 (1973) 327-45; 16 (1974) 316-36; 17 (1975) 305-36; 19 (1977) 294-336; 20 (1978) 300-31; 21 (1979) 358-82; 22 (1980) 352-84; 23 (1981) 361-80; 24 (1982) 340-68; 25 (1983) 356-81; 26 (1984) 341-73; 27 (1985) 349-78

SCHREINER, J. 'Hermeneutische Leitlinien in der LXX' in O. Lorentz and W. Strolz (eds.) *Die hermeneutische Frage in der Theologie. Schriften zum Weltgespräch* 3. Freiburg 1968, 356-94

SCHUBERT, K. 'Die Illustrationen in der Wiener Genesis im Lichte der rabbinischen Tradition' *Kairos* NF 25 (1983) 1-17

SCHUBERT, U. *Spätantikes Judentum und frühchristliche Kunst*. Vienna 1974

840

SCHÜRER, E. *Geschichte des jüdischen Volkes im Zeitalter Jesu Christi* 1-3. 4th ed. Leipzig 1901-1909
- *The History of the Jewish People in the Age of Jesus Christ* (175 B.C. - A.D. 135) 1-3 (4 vols) Revised edition by G. Vermes, F. Millar, M. Black, M. Goodman. Edinburgh 1973-1987
SCHULLER, E.M. *Non-Canonical Psalms from Qumran.* Atlanta 1986
SCHWARTZ, E. *Die syrische Übersetzung des ersten Buches Samuelis und ihr Verhältniss zu MT., LXX und Trg.* Berlin 1897
- 'Aporien im vierten Evangelium' *NAWG* (1907) 342-72; (1908) 115-48, 149-88; 497-560
- 'Zum Decretum Gelansianum' *ZNW* 29 (1930) 161-8
SCHWARZ, A. *Die hermeneutische Analogie in der talmudischen Litteratur.* Wien 1897
- *Der hermeneutische Syllogismus in der talmudischen Litteratur.* Karlsruhe 1901
- *Die hermeneutische Induktion in der talmudischen Litteratur.* Wien, Leipzig 1909
- *Die hermeneutische Antinomie in der talmudischen Litteratur.* Wien, Leipzig 1913
- *Die hermeneutische Quantitätsrelation in der talmudischen Litteratur.* Wien 1916
- *Die hermeneutische Kontext in der talmudischen Litteratur.* Wien 1921
SCHWARZ, W. *Principles and Problems of Biblical Translation.* Cambridge 1955
SCHWEIZER, E. *Das Evangelium nach Markus.* Göttingen 1967
SCOPELLO, M. *L'Exégèse de l'âme: Nag Hammadi Codex II,6.* Leiden 1985
SCUDAMORE, W.E. 'Fruits, Offering and Benediction of' *DCA* 1, 702f
SEBÖK, M. (Schönberger) *Die syrische Übersetzung der zwölf kleinen Propheten und ihr Verhältniss zu dem massoretischen Text und zu den älteren Übersetzungen namentlich den LXX und dem Targum.* Breslau 1887
SED, N. 'Le Mēmar samaritain, Le Sefer Yeşira et les trente-deux sentiers de la Sagesse' *RHR* 170 (1966) 159-84
SEELIGMANN, I.L. 'Problemen en perspectieven in het moderne LXX-onderzoek' *JEOL* II,7 (1940) 359-90, 763-6
- *The Septuagint Version of Isaiah. A Discussion of Its Problems.* Leiden 1948
SEGAL, A.F. *Two Powers in Heaven: Early Rabbinic Reports about Christianity and Gnosticism.* Leiden 1977
- 'Ruler of this World. Attitudes about Mediator Figures and the Importance of Sociology for Self-Definition' in E.P. Sanders (ed.) *Jewish and Christian Self-Definition* 2. London 1981, 245-68
SEGAL, J.B. Review of A. Vööbus, *Peschitta und Targumim. BSOAS* 26 (1963) 179
SEGAL, M.H. *The Bible Exegesis.* 2nd ed. Jerusalem 1952 (Hebr.)
- 'The Promulgation of the Authoritative Text of the Hebrew Bible' *JBL* 72 (1953) 35-47 (= Leiman, *Canon and Masorah,* 283-97)
SEGER, J.D. 'The Gezer Jar Signs: New Evidence of the Earliest Alphabet' in C.L. Meyers, M. O'Conner, *The Word of the Lord Shall Go Forth.* Philadelphia 1983, 477-95
SELIGSOHN, M. 'Peshitta' *JE* 9, New York 1905, 654
SELWYN, E.G. *The First Epistle of Peter.* 2nd ed. London 1958
SEVENSTER, J.N. *The Roots of Pagan Anti-Semitism in the Ancient World.* Leiden 1975
SEVRIN, J.-M. *L'Exégèse de l'âme. (NHC II, 6).* Québec 1983
SEYBERLICH, R.-M. 'Esther in der Septuaginta und bei Flavius Josephus' in *Neue Beiträge zur Geschichte der Alten Welt.* Bd. 1: *Alter Orient und Griechenland.* ed. by C. Welskopf, Berlin 1964, 363-6
SGHERRI, G. *Chiesa e Sinagoga nella opere di Origene.* Milan 1982
SHANKS, H. *Judaism in Stone.* Tell Aviv 1979
SHARPE, J. 'Tithes' *DCA* 2, 1963-6
SHEDD, R.P. *Man n Community.* London, Grand Rapids 1958
SHEHADE, H. *The Arabic Translation of the Samaritan Pentateuch. Prolegomena to a Critical Edition.* (Diss.) Jerusalem 1977 (Hebr.)
SHELDON-WILLIAMS, I.P. 'The Greek Christian Platonist Tradition from the Cappadocians to Maximus and Eriugena' *CHLGP*, 425-533
SHENKEL, J.D. *Chronology and Recensional Development in the Greek Text of Kings. HSM* 1. Cambridge MA 1968

SHEPPARD, G.T. 'Wisdom and Torah: The Interpretation of Deuteronomy Underlying Sirach 24,23' in G.A. Tuttle (ed.) *Biblical and Near Eastern Studies, Festschrift W.S. Lasor*. Grand Rapids 1978, 166-76
– *Wisdom as Hermeneutical Construct*. Berlin 1980
SHINAN, A. 'The Sins of Nadab and Abihu in Rabbinic Literature' *Tarbiz* 48 (1978-1979) 201-14 (Hebr.)
– *The Aggadah in the Aramaic Targums to the Pentateuch*. Jerusalem 1979
– 'The "Palestinian" Targums – Repetitions, Internal Unity, Contradictions' *JJS* 36 (1985) 72-87
SHINAN, A. - ZAKOVITCH, Y. 'Midrash on Scripture and Midrash within Scripture' *Scripta* 31 (1986) 257-77
SHOTTWELL, W.A. *The Biblical Exegesis of Justin Martyr*. London 1965
SHROYER, J.M. 'Alexandrian Jewish Literalists' *JBL* 55 (1936) 261-84
SHUTT, R.J.H. 'Biblical Names and Their Meanings in Josephus, Jewish Antiquities, Books I and II, 1-200' *JSJ* 2 (1971) 167-82
SIEBEN, H.J. 'Herméneutique de l'exégèse dogmatique d'Athanase' in C. Kannengiesser (ed.) *Politique et Théologie chez Athanase d'Alexandrie*. Paris 1974, 195-214
– *Exegesis Patrum, Saggio Bibliografico sull'esegesi biblica dei Padri della Chiesa*. Rome 1983
SIEGEL, J.P. 'The Employment of Palaeo-Hebrew Characters for the Divine Names at Qumran in the Light of Tannaitic Sources' *HUCA* 42 (1971) 159-72
– 'The Alexandrians in Jerusalem and their Torah Scroll with Gold Tetragrammata' *IEJ* 22 (1972) 39-43
– 'The Severus Scroll and 1QIs[a]' in *1972 and 1973 Proceedings IOMS (Masoretic Studies* 1) Missoula, Mont. 1974, 159-65
– *The Severus Scroll and 1QIs[a]*. New York 1975
– *The Scribes of Qumran*. Leiden 1975
SIEGERT, F. *Drie hellenistisch-jüdische Predigten*. Tübingen 1980
SIEGFRIED, C. *Philo von Alexandria als Ausleger des Alten Testaments*. Jena 1875
– 'Die Hebräischen Worterklärungen des Josephus' *ZAW* 3 (1883) 32-52
– 'Die Aussprache des Hebräischen bei Hieronymus' *ZAW* 4 (1884) 34-83
SIGAL, PH. 'Manifestations of Hellenistic Historiography in select Judaic Literature' *SBL Seminar Papers 1984*. Chico 1984
– *The Halakah of Jesus according to the Gospel of Matthew*. Lanham MD 1986
SILBERMAN, L.H. 'Unriddling the Riddle. A Study in the Structure and Language of the Habakkuk Pesher (1QpHab)' *RQ* 3 (1961) 323-64
SILVERSTONE, A.E. *Aquila and Onkelos*. Manchester 1931
SIMON, L. 'The Jerusalem Bible' *VT* 4 (1954) 109f
SIMON, M. *Verus Israel*. Paris 1964 (ET London 1986)
– 'The Apostolic Decree and its Setting in the Ancient Church' *BJRL* 52 (1970) 437-60
SIMONETTI, M. (ed.) *Rufin d'Aquilée, Les Bénédictions des Patriarches*. SC 140, Paris 1968
– 'Note sull' interpretazione gnostica dell' Antico Testamento' *Vetera Christianorum* 9 (1972) 331-59; 10 (1973) 103-26
– 'Note sull'esegesi veterotestamentaria di Teodoro di Mopsuestia' *Vetera Christianorum* 14 (1977) 69-102
– 'Note sul commento di Cirillo ai Profeti Minori' *Vetera Christianorum* 14 (1977) 301-30
– *Profilo storico dell'esegesi patristica*. Rome 1981
– 'L'interpretazione patristica del Vecchio Testamento fra II e III secolo' *Augustinianum* 22 (1982) 7-33
– 'Sulla tecnica esegetica di alcuni sermones veterotestamentari di Agostino' *Augustinianum* 25 (1985) 185-203
SKARSAUNE, O. *The Proof from Prophecy: A Study in Justin Martyr's Proof-Text Tradition*. SNT 56. Leiden 1987
SKEHAN, P.W. 'Exodus in the Samartian Recension from Qumran' *JBL* 74 (1955) 182-7
– 'The Qumran Manuscripts and Textual Criticism' *SVT* 4 (1957) 148-60 (= Cross-Talmon, 212-25)

- 'The Biblical Scrolls from Qumran and the Text of the Old Testament' *BA* 28 (1965) 87-100
- *Studies in Israelite Poetry and Wisdom.* Washington 1971
- '4QLXX^Num: A Pre-Christian Reworking of the Septuagint' *HTR* 70 (1977) 39-50
SLOMOVIC, E. 'Toward an Understanding of the Exegesis in the Dead Sea Scrolls' *RQ* 7 (1969) 3-15
SLOTKI, I.W. *Masseketh Soferim, The Minor Tractates of the Talmud. Massektoth Ketannoth* 1. London 1965, 211-324
SMALLEY, B. *The Study of the Bible in the Middle Ages.* 3rd ed. Oxford 1982
SMITH, H.P. 'The Value of the Vulgate Old Testament for Textual Criticism' *Presbyterian and Reformed Review* 1891
SMITH, J.P. (tr.) *St. Irenaeus, Proof of the Apostolic Preaching. ACW* 16 Westminister, Maryland and London 1952
- 'Hebrew Christian Midrash in Irenaeus (*Dem.* 43)' *Biblica* 38 (1957) 24-34
SMITH, M. *Palestinian Parties and Politics that Shaped the Old Testament.* London, New York 1971
- *Jesus the Magician.* London 1978
SMITH, W. - CHEETHAM, S. (ed.) *A Dictionary of Christian Antiquities* 1-2. London 1875-1880 (repr. 1908)
SMITH, W.R. *The Old Testament in the Jewish Church.* 2nd ed. London 1892
SMITH-LEWIS, A. - DUNLOP-GIBSON, M. *The Palestinian Syriac Lectionary of the Gospels.* London 1899
SMYTHE, H.R. 'The Interpretation of Amos iv 13 in St. Athanasius and Didymus' *JTS* NS 1 (1950) 158-68
SNAITH, J.G. 'Aphrahat and the Jews' in J.A. Emerton - S.C. Reif (eds.) *Interpreting the Hebrew Bible: Essays in Honour of E.I.J. Rosenthal.* Cambridge 1982, 235-50
SNAITH, N.H. 'New Edition of the Hebrew Bible' *VT* (1957) 207f
- Review of *Hebrew Bible: Jerusalem edition* in Rowley, *Eleven Years of Bible Bibliography.* Indian Hills, Colorado 1957, 564-65
- 'The Ben Asher Text' *Textus* 2 (1962) 8-13
SNELL, B. (ed.) *Tragicorum graecorum fragmenta* 1. Göttingen 1971
- *Szenen aus griechischen Dramen.* Berlin 1971
SOISALINEN-SOININEN, I. *Der Character der asterisierten Zusätze in der Septuaginta. AASF* B 114, Helsinki 1959
SOUTER, A. 'A Glossary of Later Latin. Oxford 1949
SOWERS, S.G. *The Hermeneutics of Philo and Hebrews.* Richmond, Zürich 1965
SPARKS, H.F.D. 'The Latin Bible' in H.W. Robinson (ed.) *The Bible in its Ancient and English Versions.* 2nd ed. London 1954 (Oxford 1940) 100-27
- 'The Symbolical Interpretation of *Lebanon* in the Fathers' *JTS* NS 10 (1960) 264-79
- 'Jerome as Biblical Scholar' in *CHB* 1 (1970) 510-41
- *The Apocryphal Old Testament.* Oxford 1984
SPEIER, S. 'The Relationship between the 'Arukh and Targum Neofiti I' *Leshonenu* 31 (1966-1967) 23-32, 189-98; 34 (1969-1970) 1972-9 (Hebr.)
SPERBER, A. *Septuaginta-Probleme. BWAT* III, 13, Stuttgart 1929
- 'Peschitta und Onkelos' in S.W. Baron - A. Marx (eds.) *Jewish Studies in Memory of G.A. Kohut.* New York 1935, 554-64
- 'Hebrew Based upon Greek and Latin Transliterations' *HUCA* 12/13 (1937-1938) 103-274
- 'New Testament and Septuagint' *JBL* 59 (1940) 193-293
- *A Historical Grammar of Biblical Hebrew.* Leiden 1966
- *The Bible in Aramaic* 1-4b (5 vols.) Leiden 1959-1973
SPERBER, D. (ed.) *Masechet Derech Eretz Zutta.* 2nd ed. Jerusalem 1982 (Hebr.)
SPINKS, B.D. 'The Jewish Sources for the Sanctus' *Heythrop Journal* 21 (1980) 168-79
SPIRA, A. - KLOCK, C. (ed.) *The Easter Sermons of Gregory of Nyssa. Patristic Monograph Series* 9, Cambridge MA 1981
SPRENGER, H.N. (ed.) *Theodori Mopsuesteni Commentarius in XII Prophetas.* Wiesbaden 1977.
SPRÖDOWSKY, H. *Die Hellenisierung der Geschichte von Joseph in Aegypten bei Flavius Josephus.* Greifswald 1937

843

SRAWLEY, J.H. (ed.) *The Catechetical Oration of Gregory of Nyssa*. Cambridge 1903

STADELMANN, H. *Ben Sira als Schriftgelehrter*. Tübingen 1980

STÄHLIN, O. - FRÜCHTEL, L. - TREU, U. (eds.) *Clemens Alexandrinus. GCS* 1-4. 2nd revised edition, Berlin 1960, 1970, 1972, 1980

STAROBINSKI-SAFRAN, E. 'Un poète judéo-hellénistique: Ézéchiel le tragique' *Museum Helveticum* 31 (1974) 216-24

STEAD, G.C. 'St. Athanasius on the Psalms' *VC* 39 (1985) 65-78

– Review of Canévet. *JTS* NS 37 (1986) 223-6

STEIN, E. *Die allegorische Exegese des Philo aus Alexandria (BZAW* 51) Giessen 1929

– *Philo und der Midrash (BZAW* 57) Giessen 1931

– 'Die Homiletische Peroratio im Midrash' *HUCA* 8-9 (1931-1932) 353-71

STEINSCHNEIDER, M. *Vorlesungen über die Kunde hebräischer Handschriften deren Sammlungen und Verzeichniss*. Leipzig 1897

STEMBERGER, G. 'Die Patriarchenbilder der Katakombe in der Via Latina im Lichte der jüdischen Tradition' *Kairos* NF 16 (1974) 19-78

STENDAHL, K. *The School of St. Matthew and its Use of the Old Testament*. Lund 1954

STENHOUSE, P. *The Kitāb Al-Tarīkh of Abú 'l-Fath*. Sydney 1985

STENZEL, M. 'Zur Frühgeschichte der Lateinischen Bibel' *TRev* 49 (1953) 97-103

STERN, M. 'The Jewish Diaspora' in *Compendia* I/1, 117-83

– *Greek and Latin Authors on Jews and Judaism* 1-2. Jerusalem 1974-1980

STEVENSON, J. *The Catacombs*. London 1978

STOMMEL, E. *Beiträge zur Ikonographie der Konstantinischen Sarkophagplastik*. Bonn 1954

STONE, M.E. 'The Book of Enoch and Judaism in the Third Century B.C.E.' *CBQ* 40 (1978) 479-92

– 'Apocalyptic Literature' *Compendia* II/2, 383-441

STOW, K.R. 'The Church and the Jews from St. Paul to Paul IV' in L.V. Berman and others. *Bibliographical Essays in Mediaeval Jewish Studies: The Study of Judaism* 2. New York 1976, 109-65

STOWERS, S.K. *The Diatribe and Paul's letter to the Romans*. Chico 1981

STRACK, H.L. *Prolegomena critica in Vetus Testamentum Hebraicum*. Lipsiae 1873

– 'Masora' *PRE³* 12, 393-9

– *Einleitung in das Alten Testament*. 6th ed. München 1906

– *Jesus, die Häretiker und die Christen nach den ältesten jüdischen Angaben*. Leipzig 1940

– *Introduction to the Talmud and Midrash*. New York 1969

STRACK, H.L. - BILLERBECK, P. *Kommentar zum Neuen Testament aus Talmud und Midrasch* 1-6 Münich 1926-1956

STRACK, H.L. - STEMBERGER, G. *Einleitung in Talmud und Midrasch*. München 1982

STRAUSS, G. *Schriftgebrauch, Schriftauslegung und Schriftbeweis bei Augustin*. Tübingen 1959

STRAW, C. Review of Bélanger, Grégoire . . . sur le Cantique. *JTS* NS 37 (1986) 600-3

STROBEL, A. 'Habakuk' *RAC* 13 (1986) 203-26

STROUSMA, G.G. 'Form(s) of God: Some Notes on Metatron and Christ' *HTR* 76 (1983) 269-88

– *Another Seed: Studies in Gnostic Mythology*. Leiden 1984

STUART, M. *Critical History and Defence of the Old Testament Canon*. London 1849

STUMMER, F. 'Die lateinische Bibel vor Hieronymus und das Judentum' *ThGl* 19 (1927) 184-99

– *Einführung in die lateinische Bibel*. Paderborn 1928

– 'Spuren jüdischer und christlicher Einflüsse auf die Übersetzung der Grossen Propheten durch Hieronymus' *JAOS* 8 (1928) 35-48

– 'Einige Beobachtungen über die Arbeitsweise des Hieronymus bei der Übersetzung des Alten Testament aus der hebraica veritas' *Biblica* 10 (1929) 3-30

– 'Beiträge zur Exegese der Vulgata' *ZAW* (1950) 152-67

STUHLMACHER, P. (ed.) *Das Evangelium and die Evangelien*. Tübingen 1983

STURDY, J.V.M. 'The Authorship of the "Prose Sermons" of Jeremiah' in J.A. Emerton (ed.) *Prophecy*. Berlin 1980, 143-50

SUNDBERG, A.C. *The Old Testament of the Early Church*. Cambridge MA 1964

SUSEMIHL, F. *Geschichte der griechischen Litteratur der Alexandrinerzeit* 1-2. Leipzig 1891-1892

SUTCLIFFE, E.F. 'St. Jerome's Pronunciation of Hebrew' *Biblica* 29 (1948) 112-25

– 'The Name "Vulgate" ' *Biblica* 29 (1948) 345-52

SWEET, J.P.M. *Revelation*. London 1979

SWETE, H.B. (ed.) *Theodori Episcopi Mopsuesteni in Epistolas B. Pauli Commentarii* 1-2. Cambridge 1880-1882

– *An Introduction to the Old Testament in Greek*. Cambridge 1902; 2nd ed. 1914 (repr. New York 1968)

SYKES, D.A. 'The *Poemata Arcana* of St. Gregory Nazianzen' *JTS* NS 11 (1970) 32-42

SZABÓ, A. 'Die Engelvorstellung vom Alten Testament bis zur Gnosi' in Tröger, *Altes Testament*, 143-52

TACHAUER, G. *Das Verhältniss von Flavius Josephus zur Bibel und Tradition*. Erlangen 1871

TAL, A. (ed.) *The Language of the Targum of the Former Prophets and its Position within the Aramaic Dialects*. Tel Aviv 1975 (Hebr.)

– 'The Stratigraphy of the Palestinian Jewish Aramaic.' *Leshonenu* 43 (1978-1979) 165-84 (Hebr.)

– 'The Demonstrative Pronoun in Palestinian Aramaic' *Leshonenu* 44 (1979-1980) 43-65 (Hebr.)

– *The Samaritan Targum of the Pentateuch. A Critical Edition* 1-3. Tel Aviv 1980-1983 (Hebr.)

– *The Infinitive in Palestinian Aramaic'* in *Hebrew Language Studies presented to Professor Zeev Ben-Hayyim*. Jerusalem 1983, 201-18

TALMON, S. 'Aspects of the Textual Transmission of The Bible in the Light of the Qumran Manuscripts' *Textus* 4 (1964) 95-132 (= Cross-Talmon, 226-63)

– 'The Old Testament Text' in *CHB* 1 (Cambridge 1970) 159-99

– 'The Textual Study of the Bible – A New Outlook' in Cross - Talmon (eds.) *Qumran and the History of the Biblical Text*. Cambridge MA, London 1975, 321-400

– 'Ezra and Nehemiah, Books and Message' *IDBS*. K. Crim ed., Nashville 1976, 317-28

– 'The Structuring of Biblical Books; Studies in the Book of Ezekiel' *ASTI* 10 (1976) 131-6

– 'Tenakh, Nosah' *EB* 8, Jerusalem 1982, 621-41

TARN, W.W. - GRIFFITH, G.T. *Hellenistic Civilisation*. 3rd ed. London 1952

TATE, J. 'On the History of Allegorism' *Classical Quarterly* 28 (1934) 105-14

TAYLOR, C. 'The Hexapla' *DCB* 3 (1882) 14-23

– *Sayings of the Jewish Fathers. Comprising Pirqe Aboth in Hebrew and English with Notes and Excursuses*. 2nd ed. Cambridge 1897

TCHERIKOVER, V.A. *Hellenistic Civilization and the Jews*. New York 1975

TELFER, W. *Cyril of Jerusalem and Nemesius of Emesa*. *LCC* 4, London 1955

THACKERAY, H.ST.J. 'Josephus' *DB*, extra volume, Edinburgh 1904, 461-73

– *A Grammar of the Old Testament in Greek according to the Septuagint*. I *Introduction, Orthography and Accidence*. Cambridge 1909 (repr. 1970)

– 'New Light on the Book of Jashar (A Study of 3 Regn. VIII 53^{b}LXX)' *JTS* 11 (1910) 518-32

– 'Primitive Lectionary Notes in the Psalms of Habakkuk' *JTS* 12 (1911) 191-213

– *The Septuagint and Jewish Worship. A Study in Origins*. London 1923^2 (1921)

– 'Note on the Evidence of Josephus' in *The Old Testament in Greek* 2/1: *1 and 2 Samuel*. ed. by A.E. Brooke, N. McLean and H.St.J. Thackeray. Cambridge 1927, ix

– *Josephus, the Man and the Historian*. New York 1929 (repr. with introd. by S. Sandmel, New York 1967)

– et al. *Josephus. With an English Translation (LCL)* 1-10. Cambridge MA, London 1926-1965

THEE, F.C.R. *Julius Africanus and the Early Christian View of Magic*. Tübingen 1984

THEODOR, J. 'Die Midraschim zum Pentateuch und der dreijährige palästinensische Cyclus' *MGWJ* 34 (1885) 351-66; 35 (1886) 212-8, 252-65, 299-313, 406-15, 443-59, 558-64; 36 (1878) 35-48, 357-61

THÉROND, B. *Le discours de l'histoire dans 'La guerre des Juifs' de Flavius Josèphe*. Paris 1979

THIEDE, C.P. 'A Pagan Reader of 2 Peter' *JSNT* 26 (1986) 79-96

THOMPSON, T. - SRAWLEY, J.H. *St. Ambrose 'On the Mysteries' and the Treatise 'On the Sacraments'*. London 1919

THRAEDE, K. 'Epos' *RAC* 5 (1962) 983-1042

- 'Erfinder (geistesgeschichtlich)' *RAC* 5 (1962) 1191-1278
THRALL, M. 'The Origin of Pauline Christology' in W.W. Gasque - R.P. Martin, *Apostolic History and the Gospel.* Grand Rapids 1970, 304-16
THYEN, H. *Der Styl der Jüdisch-Hellenistischen Homilie.* Göttingen 1935
TIEDE, D.L. *The Charismatic figure as a Miracle Worker.* Missoula 1972
TIGAY, J.H. 'An Emperical Basis for the Documentary Hypothesis' *JBL* 94 (1975) 329-42
- 'An Early Technique of Aggadic Exegesis' in H. Tadmor - M. Weinfeld (eds.) *History, Historiography and Interpretation.* Jerusalem 1983, 169-89
TIGCHELER, J. *Didyme l'Aveugle et l'exégèse allégorique (Graecitas Christianorum Primaeva* 6. Nijmegen 1977
TILL, W.C. - SCHENKE, H.M. (eds.) *Die gnostischen Schriften des koptischen Papyrus Berolinensis 8502.* 2nd ed. Berlin 1972
TÖTTERMAN, C.A.R. Pelguta qadmayta dᵉbaryamin cum hebraeis collata. Helsinforsiae 1870
TOLLINTON, R.B. *Clement of Alexandria: A Study in Christian Liberalism* 1-2. London 1914
- (tr.) *Selections from the Commentaries and Homilies of Origen.* London 1929
TONNEAU, R. - DEVRÉESSE, R. (ed. and tr.) *Les homélies catéchétiques de Théodore de Mospsueste. Studie e Testi* 145. Vatican 1949
- (ed.) *S. Ephraem Syri In Genesim et in Exodum Commentarii.* (*CSCO* 152-153) Louvain 1955
TORCZYNER, H. 'Al Tikre' *JE* 2, 74-87
TORREY, C.C. 'The Older Book of Esther' *HTR* 37 (1944) 1-40
TOURNAY, R. 'Quelques relectures bibliques anti-samaritaines' *RB* 71 (1964) 504-36
TOV, E. 'Lucian and proto-Lucian. Toward a New Solution of the Problem' *RB* 79 (1972) 101-13 (= Cross-Talmon, 293-305)
- 'Transliterations of Hebrew Words in the Greek Versions of the Old Testament' *Textus* 8 (1973) 78-92
- *The Septuagint Translation of Jeremiah and Baruch: A Discussion of the LXX of Jeremiah 29-52 and Baruch 1:1-3:8.* Missoula 1976
- 'Three Dimensions of LXX Words' *RB* 83 (1976) 529-44
- 'Septuagint, The Contribution of the Septuagint to OT Scholarship' *IDBS* 1976, 807-11
- 'Midrash-Type Exegesis in the LXX of Joshua' *RB* 85 (1978) 50-61
- 'The Textual Affiliations of 4QSamᵃ' *JSOT* 14 (1979) 37-53
- (ed.) *The Hebrew and Greek Texts of Samuel.* Jerusalem 1980
- 'The Impact of the LXX Translation of the Pentateuch on the Translation of the Other Books' *Mélanges Dominique Barthélemy. OBO* 38 (1981) 577-92
- *The Text-Critical Use of the Septuagint in Biblical Research.* Jerusalem 1981 (*Jerusalem Biblical Studies* 3)
- *A Classified Bibliography of Lexical and Grammatical Studies on the Language of the Septuagint and Its Revisions.* Jerusalem 1982
- 'A Modern Textual Outlook Based on the Qumran Scrolls' *HUCA* 53 (1982) 11-27
- 'The Rabbinic Tradition Concerning the "Alterations" Inserted into the Greek Pentateuch and their Relation to the Original Text of the LXX' *JSJ* 15 (1984) 65-89
- 'The Fifth Fascicle of Margolis' The Book of Joshua in Greek' *JQR* 74 (1984) 397-407
- 'Did the Septuagint Translators Always Understand Their Hebrew Text?' in *De Septuaginta, Festschrift J.W. Wevers.* Mississauga, Ont. 1984, 53-70
- 'The Nature and Background of Harmonizations in Biblical Manuscripts' *JSOT* 31 (1985) 3-29
- 'The Text of the Old Testament' in *The World of the Bible.* A.S. van der Woude, M.J. Mulder, etc. (eds.) 1 Grand Rapids Mich. 1986, 156-90
- 'Die Septuaginta in ihrem theologischen und traditionsgeschichtlichen Verhältnis zur hebräischen Bibel' (forthcoming)
TOV, E. - WRIGHT, B.G. 'Computer Assisted Study of the Criteria for Assessing the Literalness of Translation Units in the LXX' *Textus* 12 (1985) 149-87
TOWNER, W.S. 'Hermeneutical Systems of Hillel and the Tannaim: A Fresh Look' *HUCA* 53 (1982) 101-35

TRAUTMANN, C. 'La citation du Psaume 85 (84) 11-12 et ses commentaires dans la Pistis Sophia' *RHPR* 59 (1979) 551-7

TRÖGER, K.-W. *Altes Testament – Frühjudentum – Gnosis: Neue Studien zu 'Gnosis und Bibel'.* Gütersloh, Berlin 1980

TSEDAKAH, A. and R. (eds.) *Ḥamishah Ḥumshei Torah, Nusaḥ Yehudi Nusaḥ Shomroni.* Tel-Aviv 1966

TSEVAT, M. 'Betula' *TDOT* 2, 338-43

TURNER, C.H. (ed.) *Ecclesiae Occidentalis Monumenta Iuris Antiquissima*, 1.1 *Canones qui dicunter Apostolorum: Nicaenorum Patrum Subscriptiones.* Oxford 1899

– 'Latin Lists of the Canonical Books' *JTS* 1 (1900) 554-60

TURNER, H.E.W. *Jesus the Christ.* London 1976

TUR-SINAI, N.H. *Halashon Wehasefer: Halashon.* 2nd ed. Jerusalem 1954 (Hebr.)

UGLIONE, R. 'L'Antico Testamento negli scritti Tertullianei sulle seconde nozze' *Augustinianum* 22 (1982) 165-78

UHLIG, S. *Das Äthiopische Henochbuch. JSHRZ* V/6. Gütersloh 1984

ULRICH, E.C. *The Qumran Text of Samuel and Josephus.* Missoula, Montana 1978

UNGER, G.F. 'Wenn schrieb Alexander Polyhistor?' *Philologus* 43 (1884) 528-31

– 'Die Blüthezeit des Alexander Polyhistor' *Philologus* 47 (1889) 177-83

UNNIK, W.C. VAN, *Tarsus or Jerusalem.* London 1962

– *Sparsa Collecta* 1-2. Leiden 1973, 1980

– 'Josephus' Account of the Story of Israel's Sin with Alien Women in the Country of Midian (Num. 25.1ff)' in M.S.H.G. Heerma van Voss (ed.) *Travels in the World of the Old Testament: Studies Presented to Professor M.A. Beek.* Assen 1974, 241-61

URBACH, E.E. 'Law and Prophecy' *Tarbiz* 18 (1947) 1-27 (Hebr.)

– 'The Derasha as a Basis of the Halakha and the Problem of the Soferim' *Tarbiz* 27 (1957-1958) 166-82 (Hebr.)

– 'Rabbinic Exegesis and Origenes' Commentaries on the Song of Songs and Jewish-Christian Polemics' *Tarbiz* 30 (1960-1961) 148-70 (Hebr.)

– 'The Homiletical Interpretation of the Sages and the Expositions of Origen on Canticles, and Jewish-Christian Disputation' *Scripta* 22 (1971) 247-75

– *The Sages. Their Concepts and Beliefs* 1-2. Jerusalem 1975

– *Ha-Halakha. Mekoroteha we-hitpathuta.* Givataim 1984

VALLARSI, D. *Sancti Eusebii Hieronymi Stridonensis Presbyteri opera.* 1-11. Verona 1734-1742, editio altera Venetiis 1766-1772

VANDERKAM, J.C. *Enoch and the Growth of an Apocalyptic Tradition.* Washington 1984

VERCELLONE, C. *Variae Lectiones Vulgatae Latinae Bibliorum editionis* 1-2. Rome 1860-1864

– *Biblia Sacra Vulgatae Editionis Sixti V. et Clementis VIII. Pontt. Maxx. iussu recognita atque edita.* Rome 1861

VERGOTE, J. 'Grec, Biblique' *DBS* 3 (1938) 1320-69

VERMES, G. 'A Propos des commentaires bibliques découvertes à Qumrân' in *La Bible et l'Orient. RHPR* 35 (1955) 95-103

– 'La figure de Moïse au tournant des deux testaments' in H. Cazelles (ed.) *Moïse, l'homme de l'alliance.* Paris-Tournai 1955

– *Scripture and Tradition in Judaism. Haggadic Studies.* Leiden 1961, 2nd ed. 1973

– 'The life of Abraham' *Scripture and Tradition*, 67-126

– 'Bible and Midrash: Early Old Testament Exegesis' in *CHB* 1 (1970) 199-231, also in *Post-Biblical Jewish Studies*, 59-91

– 'The Qumran Interpretation of Scripture in its Historical Setting' in *Post-Biblical Jewish Studies*, 37-49

– 'The Targumic Versions of Genesis 4: 3-16' in *Post-Biblical Jewish Studies*, 92-126

– 'Haggadah in the Onkelos Targum' in *Post-Biblical Jewish Studies*, 127-38

– *Post-Biblical Jewish Studies (Studies in Judaism in Late Antiquity* 8) Leiden 1975

– 'The Archangel Sariel' in J. Neusner (ed.) *Judaism, Christianity and Other Greco-Roman Cults. Studies for Morton Smith at Sixty.* Leiden 1975, 3, 159-66

- *The Dead Sea Scrolls: Qumran in Perspective.* Philadelphia-London 1977
- 'Leviticus 18:21 in Ancient Jewish Bible Exegesis' in J.J. Petuchowsky and E. Fleischer, *Studies in Aggadah, Targum and Jewish Liturgy in Memory of J. Heinemann.* Jerusalem 1981, 108-24
- 'A Summary of the Law by Flavius Josephus' *NovT 24* (1982) 289-303
VETUS LATINA, *Die Reste der altlateinischen Bibel nach Petrus Sabatier neu gesammelt und herausgegeben von der Erzabtei Beuron.* (ed. by B. Fischer et al.) Beuron 1949–
VETUS LATINA HISPANA (ed. by T. Ayuso Marazucla) Madrid 1953–
VILMAR, E. *Abulfathi Annales Samaritani.* Gotha 1865
VÖLKER, W. *Fortschritt und Vollendung bei Philo von Alexandria.* Leipzig 1938
VÖÖBUS, A. *Peschitta und Targumim des Pentateuchs. Neues Licht zur Frage der Herkunft der Peschitta aus dem altpalästinischen Targum. PETSE* 9. Stockholm 1958
VON SODEN, W. *Akkadisches Handwörterbuch.* Wiesbaden 1959-1978
VOSTÉ, J.-M. - EYNDE C. VAN DEN (eds.) *Commentaire d'Išoʻdad de Merv sur l'Ancien Testament I. Genèse. CSCO* 126, Scriptores Syri, tome 67, Louvain 1950
VRIES, B. DE, 'Baraita, Beraitot' *EJ* 4, 189-93
WACHOLDER, B.Z. 'A Qumran Attack on the Oral Exegesis? The Phrase *'šr btlmwd šgrm* in 4Q Pesher Nahum' *RQ* 5 (1966) 575-8
- 'Pseudo-Eupolemus' Two Greek Fragments on the Life of Abraham' *HUCA* 34 (1963) 83-113
- 'How long did Abraham stay in Egypt?' *HUCA* 35 (1964) 43-65
- 'Philo (the Elder)' *EJ* 13 (1972) 407-8
- *Eupolemus: A Study of Judaeo-Greek Literature.* Cincinnati 1974
- *Messianism and Mishnah. Time and Place in Early Halakhah.* Cincinnati 1979
- *The Dawn of Qumran.* Cincinnati 1983
WÄCHTER, L. 'Astrologie und Schicksalsglaube im rabbinischen Judentum' *Kairos* 11 (1969) 181-200
WALKER, N. 'The Peshiṭa puzzle and its implications' *VT* 18 (1968) 268-70
WALLACHE-HADRILL, D.S. *Eusebius of Caesarea.* London 1960
- *Christian Antioch.* Cambridge 1982
WALLENSTEIN, M. 'A Hymn from the Scrolls' *VT* 5 (1955) 277-83
WALLIS-BUDGE, E.A. (ed.) *The Chronography of Gregory Abû'l Faraj . . . commenly known as Bar Hebraeus . . .* 1-2. London 1932
WALSH, P.G. *Paulinus of Nola. ACW,* New York, Paramus 1975
WALTER, H. *Lateinische Sprichwörter aus dem Mittelalter.* Göttingen 1967
WALTER, N. 'Zu Pseudo-Eupolemos' *Klio* 43-45 (1965) 282-90
- 'Demetrios' *JSHRZ* III/2 (1975) 280-92
- 'Aristeas' *JSHRZ* III/2 (1975) 293-96
- 'Eupolemos' *JSHRZ* I/2 (1976) 93-108
- 'Kleodemos-Malchas' *JSHRZ* I/2 (1976) 115-20
- 'Artapanos' *JSHRZ* I/2 (1976) 121-36
- 'Pseudo-Eupolemos' *JSHRZ* I/2 (1976) 137-43
- 'Philon der Epiker' *JSHRZ* IV/3 (1983) 139-53
- 'Theodotus der Epiker' *JSHRZ* IV/3 (1983) 154-71
- 'Pseudo-Orpheus' *JSHRZ* IV/3 (1983) 217-34
- *Poetische Schriften. JSHRZ* IV/3 Gütersloh, 1983
- Review of C.R. Holladay, *Fragments* in *Helikon* 3 (1963) 789-92
WALTERS, P. *The Text of the Septuagint. Its Corruptions and their Emendation.* Cambridge 1973
WALTON, B. *Biblia Sacra Polyglotta.* London 1657
WALZER, R. *Galen on Jews and Christians.* London 1949
WARFIELD, B.B. 'Scripture' *DB* 2, 584-87
- *The Inspiriation and Authority of the Bible.* Philadelphia 1948
WARSZAWSKI, L. *Die Peschitta zu Jesaja (Kap. 1-39), ihr Verhältnis zum massoretischen Texte, zur Septuaginta und zum Targum.* Berlin 1897
WASZINK, J.H. 'Tertullian's Principles and Methods of Exegesis' in W.R. Schoedel (ed.) *Early Christian Literature and the Classical Intellectual Tradition* (Festschrift for R.M. Grant) Paris 1979, 17-31

WATKINS, H.W. 'Gregorius Nazianzenus' *DCB* 2 (1880) 741-61

WATSON, E.W. 'The Style and Language of St. Cyprian' *Studia Biblica et Ecclesiastica* 4 (Oxford 1896) 193-245

WEBER, R. *Les anciennes versions latines du deuxièmes livre des Paralipomènes. CBL* 8, Rome 1945

– *Le Psautier romain et les autres anciens Psautiers latins. CBL* 10, Rome 1953

– (ed.) *Biblica Sacra iuxta Vulgatam Versionem* 1-2. Stuttgart 2nd ed. 1975

WEBER, R. - BÉVENOT, M. (eds.) *Sancti Cypriani Episcopi Opera. CCL* 3, Turnhout 1972

WEIL, G.E. *Initiation à la Massorah.* Leiden 1964

– *Massorah Gedolah iuxta codicem Leningradensem B 19a, I* (Catalogi) Rome 1971

– 'La Massorah' *REJ* 131 (1972) 11

WEINBERG, R. 'Letteris, Meir' *EJ* 11, 54-5

WEINFELD, M. 'Covenant' *EJ* 5, 1012-22

– 'The Secret of the En-Gedi Community' *Tarbiz* 51 (1981) 125-9 (Hebr.)

WEINGREEN, J. *From Bible to Mishna.* Manchester 1976

WEINREICH, O. 'Türöffnung im Wunder-, Prodigien- und Zauberglauben der Antike, des Judentums und Christentums' *Religionsgeschichtliche Studien.* Darmstadt 1968, 38-290

WEISS, H. *Die Peschitta zu Deuterojesaia und ihr Verhältniss zu MT, LXX, u. Trg.* Halle 1893

WEISS, H.F. 'Das Gesetz in der Gnosis' in Tröger, *Altes Testament,* 71-88

WEISS, R. *Mishut BaMikra.* Jerusalem 1976 (Hebr.)

– *The Aramaic Targum of Job.* Tel-Aviv 1979 (Hebr.)

WEITZMAN, M.P. 'The Origin of the Peshitta Psalter' in J.A. Emerton, S.C. Reif (eds.) *Interpreting the Hebrew Bible, Festschrift E.I.J. Rosenthal.* Cambridge 1982, 277-98

– 'The Peshiṭta Psalter and its Hebrew *Vorlage*' *VT* 35 (1985) 341-54

WELLESZ, E. Review of Stommel, *Ikonographie* in *JTS* NS 7 (1956) 323-5

WELLHAUSEN, J. (bearb.) in F. Bleek, *Einleitung in das Alte Testament.* Berlin 1878[4]

WENDLAND, P. *Aristeae ad Philocratem Epistula cum ceteris de origine versionis LXX interpretum testimoniis.* Leipzig 1900

WERMELINGER, O. 'Le canon des Latins au temps de Jérôme et d'Augustin' in Amsler et al, *Canon,* 153-210

WERNBERG-MØLLER, P. 'Some Reflections on the Biblical Materials in the Manual of Discipline' *ST* 9 (1955) 40-66

– 'Prolegomena to a Re-examination of the Palestinian Targum Fragments of the Book of Genesis Published by P. Kahle, and their Relationship to the Peshitta' *JSS* 7 (1962) 253-66

– 'Some Observations on the Relationship of the Peshitta Version of the Book Genesis to the Palestinian Targum Fragments, Published by Professor Kahle, and to Targum Onkelos' *ST* 15 (1962) 128-80

WERNER, E. The Sacred Bridge 1-2. New York 1959, 1984

WEST, M.L. The Orphic Poems. Oxford 1983

WESTCOTT, B.F. 'Clement of Alexandria' *DCB* 1 (1877) 559-67

– *A General Survey of the History of the Canon of the New Testament.* 5th ed. Cambridge, London 1881

– 'Origenes' (completed 1882) DCB 4 (1887) 96-142

– *The Bible in the Church.* Grand Rapids 1979 (1864)

WEVERS, J.W. 'Septuaginta Forschungen' *TR* NF 22 (1954) 85-137, 171-90

– 'Septuaginta Forschungen seit 1954' *TR* NF 33 (1968) 18-76

– *Text History of the Greek Genesis.* Göttingen 1974

– 'The Earliest Witness to the LXX Deuteronomy' *CBQ* 39 (1977) 240-4

– 'An Early Revision of the Septuagint of Numbers' *Eretz-Israel* 16 (1982) 235-9

WEYL, H. Die jüdischen Strafgesetze bei Flavius Josephus in ihrem Verhältnis zu Schrift und Halacha (Mit einer Einleitung: Flavius Josephus über die jüdischen Gerichtshöfe und Richter). Berlin 1900

WHITE, H. 'Vulgate' *DB* 5, 873-90

WHITE, R.T. *A Linguistic Analysis of the Targum to Chronicles, with Specific Reference to its Relationship with Other Forms of Aramaic.* Oxford 1981 (Diss.)

WHITMAN, J. *Allegory*. Oxford 1987

WHYBRAY, R.N. *The Intellectual Tradition in the Old Testament*. BZAW 135 (1974)

WICHELHAUS, J. *De Novi Testamenti Versione Syriaca Antiqua*. Halle 1850

WICKHAM, L.R. 'The Sons of God and the Daughters of Men: Genesis VI,2 in Early Christian Exegesis' OTS 19 (Leiden 1974) 134-47

WIDENGREN, G. Literary and Psychological Aspects of the Hebrew Prophets. Uppsala 1948

- 'Die Hymnen der Pistis Sophia und die gnostische Schriftauslegung' in *Liber Amiocorum: Studies in Honour of J. Bleeker*. Leiden 1969, 269-81

WIEDER, N. 'The Habakkuk Scroll and the Targum' *JJS* 4 (1953) 14-18

- *The Judean Scrolls and Karaism*. London 1962

WIENEKE, J. *Ezechielis Iudaei poetae Alexandrini fabulae qua inscribitur ΕΞΑΓΩΓΗ fragmenta*. Münster 1931

WIFALL, W. 'Gen 3:15 – A Protevangelium?' *CBQ* 36 (1974) 361-5

WILAMOWITZ-MOELLENDORFF, U. VON - LLOYD-JONES, H. *History of Classical Scholarship*. ET London 1982

WILCKENS, U. 'χαρακτήρ' *TDNT* 9 (1974) 421f

- *Die Missionsreden der Apostelgeschichte*. Neukirchen 3rd ed. 1974

WILDE, R. *The Treatment of the Jews in the Greek Christian Writers of the First Three Centuries*. Washington 1949

WILDEBOER, G. *The Canon of the Old Testament*. London 1895

WILES, M.F. *The Divine Apostle*. Cambridge 1967

- 'Origen as Biblical Scholar' *CHB* 1, 454-89

- 'Theodore of Mopsuestia as Representative of the Antiochene School' *CHB* 1, 489-510

WILES, M.F. - SANTER, M. (ed.) *Documents in Early Christian Thought*. Cambridge 1975

WILKEN, R.L. *Judaism and the Early Christian Mind: A Study of Cyril of Alexandria's Exegesis and Theology*. New Haven, London 1971

WILLI, T. *Die Chronik als Auslegung*. FRLANT 106, Göttingen 1972

WILLIAMS, A.L. *Adversus Judaeos*. Cambridge 1935

- *Justin Martyr. The Dialogue with Trypho: Translation, Introduction and Notes*. London 1930

WILLIAMS, R.J. 'Scribal Training in Ancient Egypt' *JAOS* 92 (1972) 214-21

WILLIAMSON, H.G.M. *Israel in the Book of Chronicles*. Cambridge 1977

- *1 and 2 Chronicles*. London 1982

WILLIS, G.G. *St. Augustine's Lectionary*. London 1962

WILSON, N.G. *Scholars of Byzantium*. London 1983

WILSON, R.D. 'The Book of Daniel and the Canon' *PTR* 13 (1915) 352-408 (repr. in *Studies*, 9-64)

- *Studies in the Book of Daniel. Second Series*. New York 1938

WILSON, R.M. 'The Gnostics and the Old Testament' in *Proceedings of the International Colloquium on Gnosticism, Stockholm August 20-25 1973*. Stockholm 1977, 164-8

- 'Old Testament Exegesis in the Gnostic Exegesis on the Soul' in Krause, *Essays*, 217-24

WINDEN, J.C.M. VAN, 'Quotations from Philo in Clement of Alexandria's *Protrepticus*' *VC* 32 (1978) 208-13

WINSTON, D. *The Wisdom of Solomon (The Anchor Bible)* New York 1979

WINSTON, D. - DILLON, J. *Two Treatises of Philo of Alexandria*. Chico 1983

WINTERMUTE, O.S. 'Apocalypse of Zephaniah' in Charlesworth, *OTP* 1, 497-515

- 'A Study of Gnostic Exegesis of the Old Testament' in *The Use of the Old Testament in the New and Other Essays: Studies in Honour of William Franklin Stinespring*. Durham, NC 1972, 241-70

WISEMAN, N. *Horae Syriacae* 1. Roma 1828

WITER, F. 'Aponius' RAC Suppl. 4 (1986) 506-14

WOHL, S. *Das Palästinische Pentateuch-Targum. Untersuchungen zu den Geniza-Fragmenten und ihrem Verhältnis zu den übrigen Targumen und der Peschitta*. Zwickau i.Sa. 1935

WOLDBERG, S. *Sefer Darkhei Hashinuim*. Lemberg 1870

WOLFF, C. Jeremia im Frühjudentum und Urchristentum. TU 118, Berlin 1976

WOLFSON, H.A. *Philo. Foundations of Religious Philosophy in Judaism, Christianity, and Islam* 1-2. Cambridge MA, 1947

850

- *The Philosophy of the Church Fathers* 1. 3rd ed. Cambridge MA 1970
WONNEBERGER, R. *Leitfaden zur Biblia Hebraica Stuttgartensia.* 2nd ed. Göttingen 1986
WRIGHT, A.G. *The Literary Genre Midrash.* New York 1967
- 'The Structure of the Book of Wisdom' *Biblica* 48 (1967) 165-84
WRIGHT, C.H.H. *Daniel and his Prophecies.* London 1906
WRIGHT, J.S. *The Date of Ezra's Coming to Jerusalem.* 2nd ed. London 1958
WRIGHT, W. (ed.) *The Homilies of Aphraates, the Persian Sage.* London 1869
- (ed. and tr.) *Apocryphal Acts of the Apostles* 1-2. London, Edinburgh 1871
WÜRTHWEIN, E. Review of A. Vööbus, *Peschitta und Targum.* TLZ 87 (1962) 677-9
- *Der Text der Alten Testaments.* 4th ed. Stuttgart 1973
WUTZ, F.X. Die Transkriptionen von der Septuaginta bis zur Hieronymus. *BWAT* II.9 Stuttgart 1925
YADIN, Y. *Tefillin from Qumran (XQ Phyl 1-4).* Jerusalem 1969
- (ed.) *The Temple Scroll* 1-3 and Suppl. Jerusalem 1977 (Hebr.; E.T. Jerusalem 1983)
YAHALOM, J.A. *A Collection of Geniza Fragments of Piyyute Yannaï.* Leiden 1978
YAMAUCHI, E. 'Jewish Gnosticism? The Prologue of John, Mandaean Parallels, and the Trimorphic
   Protennoia' in Van den Broek - Vermaseren, *Studies in Gnosticism,* 467-97
- *Pre-Christian Gnosticism: A Survey of the Proposed Evidences.* Grand Rapids 1973 (2nd ed. 1983)
YARNOLD, E. 'Liturgia e Bibbia' DPAC 2, 2013-9
YEIVIN, I. 'Masora' EB 5, Jerusalem 1968, 130-59
- *Geniza Bible Fragments with Babylonian Massorah and Vocalization* 1-5. Jerusalem 1973
- *Introduction to the Tiberian Masorah (Masoretic Studies* 5) Chico 1980
YOEL, J. 'A Bible Manuscript Written in 1260' *Kiryat Sepher* 32 (1962) 122-32
YORK, A.D. 'The Dating of Targumic Literature' JSJ 5 (1974) 49-62
- 'The Targum in the Synagogue and in the School' JSJ 10 (1979) 74-86
ZAHN, T. *Geschichte des Neutestamentlichen Kanons* 1-2. Erlangen 1888-1892
- *Grundriss der Geschichte des Neutestamentlichen Kanons.* 2nd ed. Leipzig 1904
ZANDEE, J. 'Das Alte Testament im Urteil des Gnostizismus' in *Symbolae Biblicae et Mesopotamicae:
   Francisco Mario Theodoro de Liagra Böhl dedicatae.* Leiden 1973, 403-11
ZANGARA, V. 'Interpretazioni origeniane di Gen 6,2' *Augustinianum* 22 (1982) 239-49
ZARB, S.M. *De Historia Canonis Utriusque Testamenti.* Rome 1934
ZEITLIN, S. 'A Historical Study of the Canonization of the Hebrew Scriptures *PAAJR* 3 (1931-1932)
   121-58 (= Leiman, *Canon and Masorah,* 164-99)
ZENGER, E. *Das Buch Judith.* JSHRZ I/6, Gütersloh 1981
ZERON, A. 'Erwägungen zu Pseudo-Philos Quellen und Zeit' *JSJ* 11 (1980) 38-52
ZIEGLER, J. *Dulcedo Dei: Ein Beitrag zur Theologie der griechischen und lateinischen Bibel. (Álttest.
   Abh.* 13.2) Münster 1937
- *Die jüngere griechische Übersetzungen als Vorlage der Vulgata in den prophetischen Schriften.*
   Braunsberg 1943-1944
- 'Zur Septuaginta-Vorlage im Deuteronomium' *ZAW* 31 (1960) 237-62
- (ed.) *Sapientia Salomonis.* SVTG XII,1, Göttingen 1962
- (ed.) *Eusebius Werke,* 9 *Der Jesajakommentar.* GCS, Berlin 1975
ZIEGLER, K. *Das hellenistische Epos. Ein vergessenes Kapitel griechischer Dichtung.* Leipzig 1966[2]
ZIEGLER, L. *Die lateinischen Bibelübersetzungen von Hieronymus.* Münich 1879
ZIMMERMANN, F. *The Book of Tobit.* New York 1958
ZINGERLE, A. (ed.) *S. Hilarii Episcopi Pictaviensis Tractatus super Psalmos.* CSEL 22, Vienna 1891
ZINK, J.K. *The Use of the Old Testament in the Apocrypha.* Ann Arbor 1963 (Diss.)
ZOHARY, M. *The Plants of the Bible.* Cambridge 1982
ZUCKER, M. 'Lefitron Bayat Lamed-Bet Middot u "Mishnat Rabbi Eliezer" ' *PAAJR* 23 (1954) 1-19
   (Hebr. section)
- *Rav Saadya Gaon's Translation of the Torah. (The Michel Higger Memorial Publications* 3), New
   York 1959 (Hebr.)
ZUNTZ, G. 'On the hymns in Corpus Hermeticum xiii' in G. Zuntz, *Opuscula Selecta.* Manchester
   1972, 150-77 (repr. from *Hermes* 83 [1955] 68-92)

ZUNZ, L. *Die gottesdienstlichen Vorträge der Juden historisch entwickelt.* 2nd ed. Frankfurt 1892 (Berlin 1832)

ZUSSMAN, V. *Ornamental Clay-Candles from the Destruction of the Second Temple until after the Bar-Kokhba Revolt.* Jerusalem 1972 (Hebr.)

ZYCHA, J. - AGAESSE, P. - SOLIGNAC, A. (eds. and tr.) *Augustin, La Genèse au sens littéral* 1-2. Paris 1978

Index of Sources

1. HEBREW BIBLE

Genesis

1-Exod.14	649	2:43	48
1-11	636	3	695
1-7	647, 649	3:3	451n.
1-3	714n., 735, 768, 777, 781	3:5	202, 226, 276
1:1-2:4	150	3:16	648n.
1	650	3:17-18	233
1:1	184, 141, 325, 461n., 569, 650	3:22	141, 387n., 583
		3:23-24	648n.
1:2	174, 459, 477, 647, 648n., 650	3:23	648n.
		3:24	325
1:3	467	4:1-16	284
1:4	304, 650	4:1	569
1:5	426n.	4:2	228, 433
1:6	478	4:3-16	229
1:9	467	4:3-15	54
1:10	467, 650	4:4	227
1:12	650	4:7	91n., 232
1:17	426n.	4:8	229, 231
1:18	650	4:10	234
1:20f.	280	4:12	233
1:21	650	4:13	227, 233, 459
1:25	650	4:14	228
1:26f.	650	4:15	232, 233
1:26	477, 648n., 687n., 714n.	4:16	233, 447n.
1:27	388n., 702, 714	4:24	233
2-3	637n.	4:25	648n.
2:2	702, 716n., 762n.	5:1	141, 199, 203
2:4	141	5:3	715n.
2:7	413n., 478, 648n., 712n., 715n.	5:24	203, 523, 541n.
		5:26	196
2:8	233n., 278, 446n.	6:1-4	404, 404n., 541n., 648n., 747n.
2:9	648n.	6:1-2a	404
2:13	531n.	6:2	203
2:15-16	648n.	6:3	245, 403n.
2:17	477, 648n.	6:4	203, 245, 314, 405, 483, 526
2:18	385, 387, 388		
2:21-22	648n.	6:5f.	141
2:21	648n.	6:5	141, 500
2:22	388n.	6:6	648n.
2:24	648n., 702, 716, 717n.	6:9f.	141
2:26	48	6:9	141

867

876

4. APOCRYPHA AND PSEUDEPIGRAPHA

5. NEW TESTAMENT

8. TOSEFTA

10. BABYLONIAN TALMUD

11. MIDRASH AND RELATED WORKS

7 p.24	562n.
9 p.30	698
9 p.33	573n.
10 p.34	565n.
11 p.38-39	562n.
14 p.48	555n.
14 p.50	531
16 p.61-62	572n.
17 p.66	565n.
17 p.67	566n.
18 p.73	556n.

Shirta

1 p.116	556n., 573n.
6 p.135ff.	92, 563n.
7 p.139	559n., 590n.

Wayassa

1 p.152	592n.
1 p.154	148n.
1 p.156-57	556n.
3 p.166	583
4 p.167	558
4 p.168-69	570

Wayehi

4 p.101	577n.

Yitro

4 p.218	369n.

Mekhilta de R.Shimon b. Yohai
(Ed. J.N. Epstein-E.Z. Melammed, 1955)

Beshallah

13:21 p.47	567n.
15: p.101	592n.
15: p.105	202n.
15:9 p.88	559n.
15:11 p.92	568

Bo

12:13 p.16	567n.
12:27 p.27	567

Pisha

14: p.48	592n.

On Exodus

12:6 p.20	557n.
12:12 p.14	562n.
12:37 p.33	555n.
19:18 p.144	562n.

On Numeri

4:22 p.104-05	556n.

Sifra
(Ed. I.H. Weiss, 1862)

Aharei Mot

1:79c	586n.

Behukotai

2:112c	550n.
5:115d	552n.
13:115d	552n.

Emor (on Lev.22:3)

p. 96a	514

Kedoshim

9:92b	572n.
10:91b	589

Shemini

8:1-3 p.54d	310n.

Tazri'a

p.58d	592n.

Wayikra

1:3a	586n.
1:3b	65

Sifrei Num.
(Ed. H.S. Horovitz 1917)

2, p.4-5	591n.
2, p.5	591n.
5, p.5-6	591
20, p.24	557n.
23, p.27	556
32, p.38-39	563n.
38, p.41	557n.
42, p.45-48	575
42, p.45	65

12. SAMARITAN WRITINGS

13. EARLY CHRISTIAN AND MEDIEVAL WRITINGS

14. GREEK AND LATIN AUTHORS

924

16. GNOSTIC WRITINGS

17. VARIA